Operations Research

Operations Research

An Introduction

Fifth Edition

Hamdy A. Taha

Department of Industrial Engineering
University of Arkansas, Fayetteville

MACMILLAN PUBLISHING COMPANY
New York

MAXWELL MACMILLAN CANADA
Toronto

MAXWELL MACMILLAN INTERNATIONAL
New York   Oxford   Singapore   Sydney

Editor: C. E. Stewart, Jr.
Production Supervisor: Elaine W. Wetterau
Production Manager: Valerie Sawyer
Cover Designer: Blake Logan
Illustrations: Precision Graphics
This book was set in Times Roman by Santype International Limited, printed and bound by Hamilton Printing Company.
The cover was printed by Hamilton Printing Company.

Printed in the United States of America

Macmillan Publishing Company
866 Third Avenue, New York, New York 10022

Macmillan Publishing Company is part of the Maxwell Communication Group of Companies.

Maxwell Macmillan Canada
1200 Eglinton Avenue, E.
Suite 200
Don Mills, Ontario M3C 3N1

Library of Congress Cataloging in Publication Data

Taha, Hamdy A.
Operations research : an introduction / Hamdy A. Taha.—5th ed.
p. cm.
Includes index.
ISBN 0-02-418975-8
1. Operations research. 2. Programming (Mathematics) I. Title.
T57.6.T3 1992
658.4′034—dc20 91-10753
CIP

Printing: 2 3 4 5 6 7 8 Year: 3 4 5 6 7 8 9 0 1

To Karen

Los ríos no llevan agua,
el sol las fuentes secó ...

¡Yo sé donde hay una fuente
que no ha de secar el sol!

La fuente que no se agota
es mi propio corazón ...

V. Ruiz Aguilera (1862)

Preface

This fifth edition is a major revision of *Operations Research: An Introduction.* Old topics have been thoroughly revamped and updated, new topics have been added, and software tailored to the needs of the book has been developed. The result is a volume that provides balanced coverage of the theory, applications, and computations of operations research.

The book includes three parts and two appendixes. Part I on mathematical programming (Chapters 2 through 10) covers linear, integer, and dynamic programming, as well as networks. Part II (Chapters 11 through 18) deals with probabilistic models that include data representation and analysis, PERT–CPM, inventory, queueing, simulation, and Markov decisions. Part III (Chapters 19 and 20) covers classical and nonlinear optimization models. Appendix A reviews matrix algebra and Appendix B documents the TORA and SIMNET II software.

The material on linear programming has been revamped and consolidated. Starting with the first chapter, the two-dimensional graphical solution method is used effectively to explain the importance of dual values and reduced costs. These concepts, which form part of the TORA output, are used to interpret the results of interesting linear programming models. The succeeding chapters then introduce the necessary mathematical background that explains why the technique works. The traditional topics of the primal/dual (regular and revised) simplex, transportation, upper bounding, and decomposition are all presented under the unifying theory of extreme point solution. Duality theory is used to explain the basics of sensitivity analysis and parametric programming. The material concludes with a presentation of the Karmarkar interior-point algorithm.

The presentation of networks has been revised and reinforced with new examples. Emphasis is also placed on the relationship between networks and linear programming. New material includes the simplex-like algorithm for solving capacitated networks.

The new presentation of integer programming recognizes the importance of branch-and-bound as the most effective tool for solving discrete problems.

Part II (Probabilistic Models) starts with a new chapter that explains the mathematical and statistical techniques for converting raw data into a format suitable for formulating and solving probabilistic models. The chapter includes techniques for testing the goodness of fit of distributions and for forecasting future trends.

The chapter on inventory now integrates both MRP and JIT into the inventory control systems.

The chapter on queueing models has been revised to make use of transition-rate diagrams. Also, with the availability of TORA, the need for computing the (usually tedious) queueing formulas is no longer necessary. Instead, the software can be used effectively to carry out desired queueing comparisons.

In the first four editions, the subject of simulation was presented in a generic manner. With the recent surge in the use of simulation, I feel that it is necessary to provide a concrete appreciation of how simulation models are developed and executed in practice. The SIMNET II software and the new simulation chapter will prove effective in fulfilling this need.

The software accompanying the book includes TORA and SIMNET II. Both systems were developed by the author. TORA covers linear programming, transportation, networks, PERT–CPM, integer programming, inventory, data representation, and queueing. The second system is a limited student version of the general-purpose SIMNET II simulation language. Because of cost considerations to students, an editorial decision was made to include only the TORA software with the book. The SIMNET II software is distributed by the publisher free of charge with the Instructor's Manual.

TORA is totally menu-driven and may be used both as a tutorial tool and a production code. The user-guided option will allow you to step through the iterative computations of the different techniques. The development conforms with the format and style of presentation used throughout the book, including nomenclature and notation. Computer drills based on TORA are used to reinforce your understanding of many theoretical and computational concepts. By relieving you of the burden of doing computations by hand, you will be able to concentrate on understanding the basic concepts of the various operations research techniques.

SIMNET II is a totally interactive general-purpose discrete simulation language available for mainframe, mini-, and microcomputers. The version provided with this book is limited to small textbook problems. It also excludes a number of capabilities (e.g., interactive environment, external file READ/WRITE options, and PROCs) mainly because of space limitation. However, even with this limited version, you will be able to write meaningful simulation models and gain a fundamental understanding of how simulation is used in practice. SIMNET II is easy to learn, yet it possesses exceptional modeling capabilities that are not available in other languages. As my students tell me, SIMNET II makes simulation "great fun."

Further details about the complete SIMNET II system, including the expanded student version, and the full mainframe, mini-, and microcomputer versions, may be obtained by contacting SimTec, Inc., P.O. Box 3492, Fayetteville, AR 72702.

ACKNOWLEDGMENTS

I am grateful to the hundreds of colleagues worldwide who over the past 20 years have written to me with their comments and criticisms. Your feedback has certainly influenced my thinking on how operations research topics should be presented, and I look forward to receiving your comments in the future.

I especially should like to acknowledge the contributions of Professors Gilles Cormier (Université de Moncton, Canada), Guy L. Curry (Texas A & M University), Kiseog Kim (Pusan National University, Republic of Korea), V. N. Murty (Penn State University, Harrisburg), and Chris Palmer (University of Reading, United Kingdom).

Thousands of students in the United States and abroad have been introduced to operations research through the English edition and its foreign translations, and many of them have written to me with suggestions and comments. It gives me pleasure to acknowledge their contributions; I appreciate their confidence and interest in the book.

Mrs. Elaine Wetterau, who superbly supervised the production of the third and fourth editions, was once more put in charge of the production of the fifth edition. I truly appreciate Mrs. Wetterau's help and feel fortunate to have had the opportunity to benefit from her editorial experience.

The timely completion of the fifth edition would have been impossible without the superior talent of Nancy Sloan, who undertook the editing, typing, and proofreading of the manuscript. I am grateful to Nancy for her help and support.

H. A. T.

Contents

Chapter 14 Inventory Models 479

Chapter 15 Queueing Models 544

Chapter 16 Queueing Theory in Practice 598

Chapter 17 Simulation Modeling with SIMNET II 612

APPENDIXES

Operations Research

Chapter 1

Decision Making in Operations Research

1.1 THE ART AND SCIENCE OF OPERATIONS RESEARCH

Operations research (OR) seeks the determination of the best (optimum) course of action of a decision problem under the restriction of limited resources. The term **operations research** quite often is associated almost exclusively with the use of **mathematical techniques** to model and analyze decision problems. Although mathematics and mathematical models represent a cornerstone of OR, there is more to problem solving than the construction and solution of mathematical models. Specifically, decision problems usually include important intangible factors that cannot be translated directly in terms of the mathematical model. Foremost among these factors is the presence of the human element in almost every decision environment. Indeed, decision situations have been reported where the effect of human behavior has so influenced the decision problem that the solution obtained from the mathematical model is deemed impractical. A good illustration of these cases is a version of the widely circulated **elevator problem**. In response to tenants' complaints about the slow elevator service in a large office building, a solution based on analysis by waiting line theory was found unsatisfactory. After studying the system further, it was discovered that the tenants' complaints were more a case of boredom, since in reality the actual waiting time was quite small. A solution was proposed whereby full-length mirrors were installed at the entrances of the elevators. The complaints disappeared because the elevator users were kept occupied watching themselves and others while waiting for the elevator service.

The elevator illustration underscores the importance of viewing the mathematical aspect of operations research in the wider context of a decision-making process whose elements cannot be represented totally by a mathematical model. Indeed, this point was recognized by the British scientists who pioneered the first OR activities during World War II. Although their work was concerned primarily with the optimum allocation of the limited resources of war materiel, the team included scientists from such fields as sociology, psychology, and behavioral science in recognition of the importance of their contribution in considering the intangible factors of the decision process.

As a problem-solving technique, OR must be viewed as both a science and an art. The science aspect lies in providing mathematical techniques and algorithms for solving appropriate decision problems. Operations research is an art because success in all the phases that precede and succeed the solution of a mathematical model depends largely on the creativity and personal abilities of the decision-making analysts. Thus gathering of the data for model construction, validation of the model, and implementation of the obtained solution will depend on the ability of the OR team to establish good lines of communication with the sources of information as well as with the individuals responsible for implementing recommended solutions.

It must be emphasized that a successful OR team is expected to exhibit adequate ability in the science and art aspects of OR. Emphasis on one aspect and not the other is apt to impede the effective utilization of OR in practice.

1.2 ELEMENTS OF A DECISION MODEL

A decision model is merely a vehicle for "summarizing" a decision problem in a manner that allows systematic identification and evaluation of all decision alternatives of the problem. A decision is then reached by selecting the alternative that is judged to be the "best" among all available options.

We illustrate the basic elements of a decision model by the following simple, but instructive, example. During the summer months, a professor who lives in Fayetteville (FYV), Arkansas, has a 5-week consulting commitment in Denver (DEN), Colorado. The professor flies there on Monday and returns on Wednesday of the same week. A round-trip ticket that is bought on Monday for return on Wednesday of the same week will cost 20% more than a ticket that spans a weekend. One-way tickets in either direction will cost 75% of the price of a regular (no-discount) round-trip ticket. The price of a regular round-trip ticket is $900. How should the professor buy the tickets during the 5-week consulting period?

We use this example to introduce the three basic components of the decision-making process: **decision alternatives, problem constraints**, and **objective criterion**.

What are the possible alternatives for buying the tickets for the 5-week period? The first and most obvious alternative is simply to buy five round-trip tickets

(FYV–DEN–FYV) on each Monday for return on Wednesday of the same week. This alternative offers no discount. A second alternative calls for buying a one-way ticket (FYV–DEN) on Monday of the first week and another one-way return ticket (DEN–FYV) on Wednesday of the fifth week. The remaining trips are covered by buying round-trip tickets (DEN–FYV–DEN) on each Wednesday of the first 4 weeks. The third alternative extends the idea of the second alternative by buying one round-trip ticket (FYV–DEN–FYV) to cover Monday of the first week and Wednesday of the fifth week. The remaining four round-trip tickets are the same as in the second alternative.

The decision alternatives of the problem are thus summarized as:

1. Buy five (FYV–DEN–FYV) on Monday of each week.
2. Buy one (FYV–DEN) on Monday of the first week, four (DEN–FYV–DEN) on Wednesday of the first 4 weeks, and one (DEN–FYV) on Wednesday of the fifth week.
3. Buy one (FYV–DEN–FYV) to cover Monday of the first week and Wednesday of the fifth week, and four (DEN–FYV–DEN) on each Wednesday of the first 4 weeks.

Each of the three alternatives satisfy the problem restrictions: making five round-trips that start in FYV on Mondays and terminate again in FYV on Wednesdays. In this regard we say that the listed alternatives are **feasible solutions**, as opposed to infeasible solutions that would not allow the professor to make the five round-trips. Obviously, insofar as the decision problem is concerned, only feasible solutions are of interest to us.

To determine the best solution of the problem, we need to devise an appropriate criterion that can be used to compare the given feasible alternatives. In the present example, the minimization of the total price of the tickets during the 5-week period is the obvious objective of the problem. Applying this criterion to the three alternatives, we get:

$$\text{alternative 1 cost} = 5 \times 900 = \$4500$$

$$\text{alternative 2 cost} = .75 \times 900 + 4 \times (.8 \times 900) + .75 \times 900 = \$4230$$

$$\text{alternative 3 cost} = 5 \times (.8 \times 900) = \$3600$$

Based on this evaluation, alternative 3 is the least costly and hence gives the **optimum solution**.

From the author's experience in the classroom, most students usually identify the first two alternatives only. A decision based on the first two alternatives only would yield what is referred to as a **suboptimal solution**. This remark points to the importance of being able to recognize *all* the feasible alternatives of the decision problem if one is interested in obtaining the *best* solution to the decision problem. In effect, the "quality" of the optimal solution is a function of the set of the feasible alternatives that we define for the problem. In some situations, the identification of *all* feasible solutions is either too costly or impossible, in which case one would have no choice but to "live with" the suboptimal solution.

1.3 ART OF MODELING

In Section 1.2, the decision-making process in OR is shown to consist of constructing a decision model and then solving it to determine the optimum decision. The

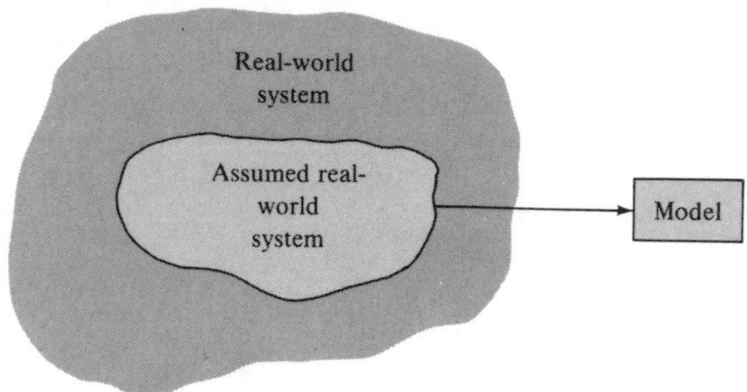

Figure 1-1

model is defined as an objective function and restrictions expressed in terms of the decision variables (alternatives) of the problem.

Although a real situation may involve a substantial number of variables and constraints, usually only a fraction of these variables and constraints truly dominates the behavior of the real system. Thus the simplification of the real system for the purpose of constructing a model should concentrate primarily on identifying the dominant variables and constraints as well as other data pertinent to decision making.

Figure 1-1 depicts the levels of abstraction of a real-life situation that lead to the construction of a model. The **assumed real system** is abstracted from the real situation by concentrating on identifying the dominant factors (variables, constraints, and parameters) that control the behavior of the real system. The model, being an abstraction of the *assumed* real system, then identifies the pertinent relationships of the system in the form of an objective and a set of constraints.

The following example is introduced to gain an appreciation of the significance of the different levels of abstraction.

Example 1.3-1. A manufactured product typically undergoes a number of operations from the time it is conceived by the designer until it reaches the consumer. After the design is approved, a production order is issued to the production department, which in turn requests the necessary materials from the materials department. The materials department either satisfies the request from its stocks or contacts the purchasing department to initiate a purchase order. After the final product is completed, the sales department, in conjunction with the marketing department, assumes the responsibility for distributing it to the consumer.

Suppose that it is desired to determine the "best" level of production in the plant manufacturing the product. Looking at the overall system, we can see that a large number of factors can influence the production level. The following are some examples:

1. *Production department.* Available machine hours, specific sequencing of operations on machines, in-process inventory, number of defective items produced, and inspection rate.
2. *Materials department.* Available stock of material, rate of delivery of purchased material, and storage limitations.
3. *Marketing department.* Sales forecast, intensity of advertising campaign, capacity of distribution facilities, and effect of competition.

If each of these factors is to be considered explicitly in a model that determines the level of production, we would be faced with a staggering task indeed. For example, we can consider explicitly such variables as the assignment of machine hours, the assignment of labor hours, and the inspection rate. As for the constraints, we can include capacities of the machines, limit on labor hours, limit on in-process inventory, limit on demand, and storage limitation. Already you can see the complexity of the relationships that express the level of production in terms of such detailed variables as those exemplified here.

The definition of the "assumed real" system for the foregoing situation entails looking at the system as an entity rather than initially concerning ourselves with the finer details of the problem. In essence, we can look at the entire system in a general sense from the standpoint of the producer and the consumer. With some reflection, we can see that the producer's side can be expressed in terms of the **production rate**, whereas the consumer's side can be represented by a **consumption rate**.

Naturally, the production rate is a function of such factors as the availability of machine and labor hours, sequencing of operations, and availability of raw material. Similarly, the consumption rate is based on the limitation of the distribution system and the sales forecast. In essence, the simplification from the "real" to the "assumed real" system is effected by "lumping" several factors in the assumed system.

It is easier now to think in terms of the assumed real system. The desired model would now seek the determination of the stock level in terms of the production and consumption rates. A proper objective could be to select the stock level that balances the cost of carrying excess inventory against the cost of running out of stock when the product is needed.

We must keep in mind, however, that the degree of complexity of the model is always an inverse function of the degree of simplification of the assumed real system as abstracted from the real system. For example, we can assume that the production and consumption rates are constant or change as functions of time. The latter case should lead to a more complex model, naturally. ◀

In general, there are no fixed rules for effecting the levels of abstraction cited in Figure 1-1. The reduction of the factors controlling the system to a relatively small number of dominant factors and the abstraction of a model from the assumed real system is more an art than a science. The validity of the model in representing the real system depends primarily on the creativity, insight, and imagination of the OR team. Such personal qualities cannot be regulated by the establishment of fixed rules for constructing models.

Although it is not possible to present fixed rules about *how* a model is constructed, it may be helpful to present ideas about possible types of models, their general structures, and their characteristics. This is the subject of the next section.

1.4 TYPES OF OR MODELS

The discussions in Sections 1.2 and 1.3 stress the fact that the model construction phase comes first, followed by solving the model to secure a desired solution. The solution methods are usually devised to take advantage of the special structures of the resulting models. As such, the wide variety of models associated with existing real systems gives rise to a corresponding number of solution techniques. Hence are the familiar names of linear, integer, dynamic, and nonlinear programming that represent algorithms for solving special classes of OR models.

In most OR applications, it is assumed that the objective and constraints of the model can be expressed quantitatively or mathematically as functions of the decision variables. In such a case, we say that we are dealing with a **mathematical model**.

Unfortunately, despite the impressive advances in mathematical modeling, a considerable number of real situations still lies well beyond the capabilities of presently available mathematical techniques. For one thing, the real system may be too involved to allow an "adequate" mathematical representation. Alternatively, even when a mathematical model can be formulated, it may prove to be too complex to be solved by available solution methods.

A different approach to modeling (complex) systems is to use **simulation**. Simulation models differ from mathematical models in that the relationships between input and output are not explicitly stated. Instead, a simulation model breaks down the modeled system into basic or elemental modules that are then linked to one another by well-defined logical relationships (in the form of IF/THEN). Thus starting from the input module, the computations will move from one module to another until an output result is realized.

Simulation models, when compared with mathematical models, do offer greater flexibility in representing complex systems. The main reason for this flexibility is that simulation views the system from a basic elemental level. Mathematical modeling, on the other hand, tends to consider the system from a less detailed level of representation.

The flexibility of simulation is not without drawbacks. The development of a simulation model is usually quite costly both in time and resources. Additionally, the execution of a simulation model, even on the fastest computer, could incur considerable cost. On the other hand, successful mathematical models are usually manageable computationally.

1.5 EFFECT OF DATA AVAILABILITY ON MODELING

Models of any kind, regardless of sophistication and accuracy, may prove of little practical value if they are not supported by reliable data. Although a model may be well defined, the quality of the solution is obviously dependent on how well we can estimate the data. If the estimates are distorted, the obtained solution, though optimum in a mathematical sense, may actually be of inferior quality from the standpoint of the real system.

In some situations, data may not be known with certainty. Rather, they are estimated by probability distributions. In such situations, it may be necessary to change the structure of the model to accommodate the probabilistic nature of the demand. This gives rise to the so-called **probabilistic** or **stochastic models** as opposed to **deterministic models**.

Sometimes a model is constructed under the assumption that certain data can be secured, but later search may prove that such information is difficult to obtain. In this case, it may be necessary to reconstruct the model to reflect the lack of data. Thus the degree of data availability may also affect the accuracy of the model. As an illustration, consider an inventory model in which the stock level of a certain item is determined such that the total cost of holding excess inventory and not satisfying all demand is minimized. This requires estimating a holding cost per excess unit held in stock and a shortage cost per unsatisfied unit of demand. The holding cost, which depends on storage expenses and cost of capital, may be relatively simple to estimate. But if the shortage cost accounts for the loss in customer's goodwill, it may be difficult to quantify such an intangible factor. Under such conditions, the model may have to be changed so that the shortage cost is not spelled out explicitly. For example, one may have to specify an acceptable upper limit on the shortage quantity at any time. In essence the specified upper limit implies a certain estimate of shortage cost. But it appears much simpler to determine such a limit than to estimate a shortage cost.

The gathering of data may actually be the most difficult part of completing a model. Unfortunately, no rules can be suggested for this procedure. While accumulating experience in modeling in an organization, the OR analyst should also develop means for gathering and documenting data in a manner useful for both present and future projects.

1.6 COMPUTATIONS IN OR

In OR there are two distinct types of computations: those involving simulation and those dealing with mathematical models. In simulation models, computations are typically voluminous and mostly time consuming. Yet, in simulation one is always assured that the desired results will definitely be secured. It is simply a matter of providing sufficient computer time!

Computations in OR mathematical models, on the other hand, are typically **iterative** in nature. By this we mean that the optimum solution of a mathematical model usually is not available in a closed form. Instead, the final answer is reached in steps or **iterations**, with each new iteration bringing the solution closer to the optimum. In this respect, we say that the solution *converges* iteratively to the optimum.

Unfortunately, not all OR mathematical models possess solution algorithms (methods) that always converge to the optimum. There are two reasons for this difficulty:

1. The solution algorithm may be proven to converge to the optimum, but only in a theoretical sense. Theoretical convergence says that there is a finite upper ceiling on the number of iterations, but it does not say how high this ceiling may be. Thus one can consume hours of computer time without reaching the final iteration. Worse still, if the iterations are stopped prematurely before reaching the optimum, one is usually unable to measure the quality of the obtained solution relative to the true optimum. (Notice the difference between this situation and that of simulation. In simulation, one has control over the computational time simply by reducing the observation period of the model. In mathematical models, the number of iterations is a function of the efficiency of the solution algorithm and the specific structure of the model, both of which may not be controllable by the user.)
2. The complexity of the mathematical model may make it impossible to devise a solution algorithm. In this case, the model may remain computationally unsolvable.

The apparent difficulties in mathematical model computations have forced practitioners to seek alternative computational methods. These methods are also iterative

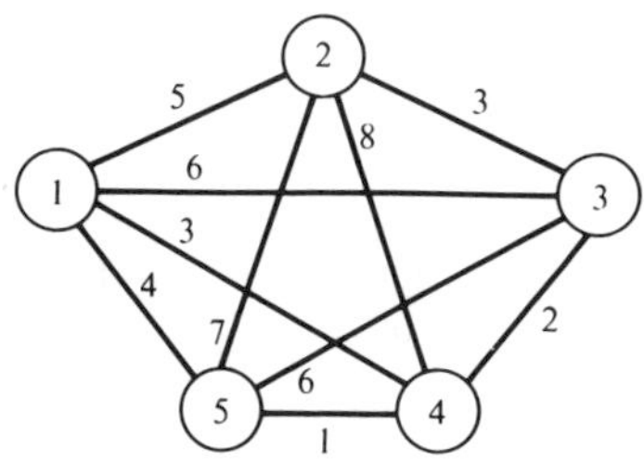

Figure 1-2

in nature, but they do not guarantee optimality. Instead, they simply seek a *good* solution to the problem. Such methods are usually known as **heuristics** because their logic is based on rules of thumb that are conducive to obtaining a good solution. The advantage of heuristics is that they normally involve less computations when compared with exact algorithms. Also, because they are based on rules of thumb, they normally are easier to explain to users who are not mathematically oriented.

In OR, heuristics are generally employed for two different purposes:

1. They can be used within the context of an exact optimization algorithm to speed up the process of reaching the optimum. The need for "beefing up" the optimization algorithm becomes more evident with large-scale models.
2. They are simply used to find a "good" solution to the problem. The resulting solution is not guaranteed to be optimum, and, in fact, its quality relative to the true optimum may be difficult to measure.

To illustrate the second type of heuristics, consider the problem of a traveling salesperson who must travel to five cities, with *each city visited exactly once* before returning back to his or her hometown. Figure 1-2 summarizes the distance (in miles) between all cities. The objective of the salesperson is to minimize the total travel distance.

This problem can be formulated as an exact mathematical model. However, obtaining the exact optimum solution to this problem has proven to be formidable. However, a "good" solution can be obtained by using a heuristic that calls for traveling from the present city to the closest unvisited city. Thus, starting from city 1, the salesperson will travel to 4 (distance = 3 miles), then from 4 to 5, followed by 5 to 3, and then 3 to 2, from which the trip is completed by returning back to 1. The total traveled distance of the tour is 18 miles, which is not optimal since the route 1–2–3–4–5–1 is shorter by 3 miles.

Exercise 1.6-1

Devise rules of thumb that may improve on the solution obtained by the foregoing heuristic.

1.7 PHASES OF OR STUDY

An OR study cannot be conducted and controlled by the OR analyst alone. Although he or she may be the expert on modeling and model solution techniques, the analyst cannot possibly be an expert in all the areas where OR problems arise. Consequently, an OR team should include members of the organization directly responsible for the functions in which the problem exists as well as for the execution and implementation of the recommended solution. In other words, an OR analyst commits a grave mistake by not seeking the cooperation of those who will implement recommended solutions.

The major phases through which the OR team would proceed to effect an OR study include

1. Definition of the problem.
2. Construction of the model.
3. Solution of the model.
4. Validation of the model.
5. Implementation of the final results.

Although this sequence is by no means standard, it seems generally acceptable. Except for the "model solution" phase, which is based generally on well-developed techniques, the remaining phases do not seem to follow fixed rules. This stems from the fact that the procedures for these phases depend on the type of problem under investigation and the operating environment in which it exists. In this respect, an operations research team would be guided in the study principally by the professional experiences of its members rather than by fixed rules.

Despite the apparent difficulties in setting fixed rules for the execution of these phases, it seems desirable to establish general guidelines. The remainder of this section is thus devoted to providing an orientation of the main points involved in an operations research study.

The first phase of the study deals with the **problem definition**. From the viewpoint of operations research, this indicates three major aspects: (1) a description of the goal or the objective of the study, (2) an identification of the decision alternatives of the system, and (3) a recognition of the limitations, restrictions, and requirements of the system.

The second phase of the study deals with the **model construction**. Depending on the definition of the problem, the operations research team should decide on the most suitable model for representing the system. Such a model should specify quantitative expressions for the objective and the constraints of the problem in terms of its decision variables. If the resulting model fits into one of the common mathematical models (e.g., linear programming), a convenient solution may be obtained by using mathematical techniques. If the mathematical relationships of the model are too complex to allow analytic solutions, a simulation model may be more appropriate. Some cases may require the use of a combination of mathematical, simulation, and heuristic models. This, of course, is largely dependent on the nature and the complexity of the system under investigation.

The third phase of the study deals with the **model solution**. In mathematical models, this is achieved by using well-defined optimization techniques and the model is said to yield an optimum solution. If simulation or heuristic models are used, the concept of optimality is not as well defined, and the solution in these cases is used to obtain approximate evaluations of the measures of the system.

In addition to the (optimum) solution of the model, one must also secure, whenever possible, additional information concerning the behavior of the solution due to changes in the system's parameters. This is usually referred to as **sensitivity analysis**. In particular, such an analysis is needed when the parameters of the system cannot be estimated accurately. In this case, it is important to study the behavior of the optimal solution in the neighborhood of these estimates.

The fourth phase calls for checking the **model validity**. A model is valid if, despite its inexactness in representing the system, it can give a reasonable prediction of the system's performance. A common method for testing the validity of a model is to compare its performance with some past data available for the actual system. The model will be valid if under similar conditions of inputs, it can reproduce the past performance of the system. The problem here is that there is no assurance that future performance will continue to duplicate past behavior. Also, since the model is based on careful examination of past data, the comparison should always reveal favorable results. In some instances this problem may be overcome by using data from trial runs of the system.

It must be noted that such a validation method is not appropriate for nonexisting systems, since data will not be available for comparison. In some cases, if the original system is investigated by a mathematical model, it may be feasible to construct a simulation model from which data are obtained to carry out the comparison.

The final phase of the study deals with the **implementation** of the tested results of the model. The burden of executing these results lies primarily with the operations researchers. It involves the translation of these results into detailed operating instructions issued in an understandable form to the individuals who will administer and operate the recommended system. The interaction between the operations research team and the operating personnel will reach its peak in this phase. Communication between the two groups can be improved by seeking the participation of the operating personnel in developing the implementation plan. In fact, this participation should be sought throughout all phases of the study. In this way no practical consideration that might lead to system failure will be overlooked. Meanwhile, possible modifications or adjustments in the system may be checked for feasibility by the operating personnel. In other words, it is imperative that the implementation phase be executed through the cooperation of both the operations research team and those who will be responsible for managing and operating the system.

1.8 ABOUT THIS BOOK

This chapter opened with the strong statement that operations research is both an *art* and a *science*. As you advance through the remaining chapters, you will get the impression that the book puts more emphasis on the scientific aspect of OR. In essence, the topics of the book are classified according to the well-known mathematical models of OR (e.g., linear programming, integer programming, inventory, and queueing theory). There are two reasons for this. First, as may be expected, there are no definite rules that can be prescribed for the art aspect of OR. The diversity of the situations where OR can be applied makes attempts in this direction almost futile. Second, we believe that it is essential that the OR practitioner acquire an adequate understanding of the capabilities and limitations of the mathematical techniques of OR. The viewpoint that an OR user need not learn about the mathematics of OR because the computer can "take care" of solving the problem is dangerous. We must keep in mind that the computer solves the model as presented by the user. If the user is unaware of the limitations of the model being used, the quality of the solution will reflect this deficiency.

We must point out that the book does not neglect the art aspect of OR. The numerous examples presented throughout the book should provide insight into the art of OR modeling. We have also stressed topics that are most useful in the analysis of practical problems. One example is the topic of sensitivity analysis, which plays important roles in the study of OR problems.

We believe that a first course in OR should give students a good foundation in the mathematics of OR, coupled with meaningful application examples and mini-cases. This plan will provide OR users with the kind of *confidence* that normally would be missing if they direct their principal training toward the philosophical and artistic aspects of decision making. Once a fundamental knowledge of the mathematical foundation of OR is acquired, students can increase their capacity as decision makers by studying reported case studies and actually working on real-life problems.

SELECTED REFERENCES

ACKOFF, R. L., *The Art of Problem Solving*, Wiley, New York, 1978.
OSBORN, A. F., *Applied Imagination*, 3rd rev. ed., Scribner, New York, 1963.
SALE, K., *Human Scale*, Coward, New York, 1980.

PART I

MATHEMATICAL PROGRAMMING

CHAPTERS 2 THROUGH 7 COVER LINEAR PROGRAMMING. Network algorithms and their relationship to linear programming are presented in Chapter 8. Chapter 9 covers integer linear programming. The last topic in this part is dynamic programming (Chapter 10).

The material in Chapters 2 through 7 is sufficient to support a serious course in the theory, applications, and computations of linear programming. Additional related material is available in Chapter 8 (networks), Chapter 9 (integer linear programming), and Section 12.4 (game theory).

Chapter 2 is designed to introduce the practical essence of sensitivity analysis in linear programming. Through the use of simple graphical models, you will develop an early appreciation of such important concepts as dual values and reduced costs which nowadays are part of the standard vocabulary used among managers. With the use of the TORA software, numerous large-scale models are presented and their solutions are analyzed from the standpoint of these concepts. With such an early introduction of these valuable tools, you can then embark on studying the mathematical foundation of linear programming (Chapters 3 through 7) with better awareness of the important role they play in the decision-making process.

With the exception of dynamic programming (Chapter 10), which can be studied independently, the sequence of the other chapters as presented in this book provides a logical order for the study of linear programming.

Chapter 2

Linear Programming: Formulations and Graphical Solution

The success of an OR technique is ultimately measured by the spread of its use as a decision-making tool. Ever since its introduction in the late 1940s, linear programming (LP) has proven to be one of the most effective operations research tools. Its success stems from its flexibility in describing multitudes of real-life situations in the following areas: military, industry, agriculture, transportation, economics, health systems, and even behavioral and social sciences. Additionally, the availability of very efficient computer codes for solving very large LP problems is an important factor in the widespread use of the technique.

The usefulness of LP extends beyond its immediate applications. Indeed, LP should be regarded as an important foundation for the development of other OR techniques, including integer, stochastic, network flow, and quadratic programming. In this regard, an understanding of LP is essential for the implementation of these additional techniques.

The material in this chapter is designed to provide an understanding of the essence of linear programming as a decision-making tool, from both the formulation and solution standpoints. Additionally, since the use of computers is a necessity for solving problems of any practical size, certain conventions must be observed in setting up the LP problem with the objective of reducing the adverse effect of computer round-off errors. These conventions are discussed throughout the chapter.

Linear programming is a deterministic tool, meaning that all the model parameters are assumed to be known with certainty. In real life, however, it is rare that one encounters a problem in which true certainty prevails. The LP technique compensates for this "deficiency" by providing systematic postoptimal and parametric analyses that allow the decision maker to test the sensitivity of the "static" optimum solution to discrete or continuous changes in the parameters of the model. In essence, these additional techniques add a dynamic dimension to the property of optimum LP solution. In this chapter we introduce the basics of sensitivity analysis and demonstrate its application via realistic examples.

2.1 A TWO-VARIABLE MODEL AND ITS GRAPHICAL SOLUTION

In this section we introduce a simple LP model with two decision variables and show how it can be solved graphically. Although a two-dimensional graphical solution is hardly useful in real-life situations (which normally encompass hundreds or thousands of variables and constraints), the procedure does offer an unusual opportunity to understand how the LP optimization process works. It also allows us to introduce the concept of sensitivity analysis in a logical and understandable manner. In fact, the example below is used in Chapter 3 to explain the algebraic simplex method for solving general linear programs.

Example 2.1-1 (The Reddy Mikks Company). The Reddy Mikks Company owns a small paint factory that produces both interior and exterior house paints for wholesale distribution. Two basic raw materials, A and B, are used to manufacture the paints. The maximum availability of A is 6 tons a day; that of B is 8 tons a day. The daily requirements of the raw materials *per ton* of interior and exterior paints are summarized in the following table.

	Tons of Raw Material per Ton of Paint		Maximum Availability (tons)
	Exterior	Interior	
Raw material A	1	2	6
Raw material B	2	1	8

A market survey has established that the daily demand for interior paint cannot exceed that of exterior paint by more than 1 ton. The survey also shows that the maximum demand for interior paint is limited to 2 tons daily. The wholesale price per ton is \$3000 for exterior paint and \$2000 for interior paint. How much interior and exterior paints should the company produce daily to maximize gross income?

Construction of the Mathematical Model

The construction of a mathematical model can be initiated by answering the following three questions:

1. What does the model seek to determine? In other words, what are the **variables** (unknowns) of the problem?
2. What **constraints** must be imposed on the variables to satisfy the limitations of the modeled system?
3. What is the **objective** (goal) that needs to be achieved to determine the optimum (best) solution from among all the *feasible* values of the variables?

An effective way to answer these questions is to give a verbal summary of the problem. In terms of the Reddy Mikks example, the situation is described as follows: The company seeks to determine the *amounts* (in tons) of interior and exterior paints to be produced to *maximize* (increase as much as is feasible) the total gross income (in thousands of dollars) while satisfying the *constraints* of demand and raw materials usage.

The crux of the mathematical model is first to identify the variables and then to express the objective and constraints as mathematical functions of the variables. Thus, for the Reddy Mikks problem, we have the following:

Variables. Since we desire to determine the amounts of interior and exterior paints to be produced, the variables of the model can be defined as

x_E = tons produced daily of exterior paint
x_I = tons produced daily of interior paint

Objective Function. Since each ton of exterior paint sells for \$3000, the gross income from selling x_E tons is $3x_E$ thousand dollars. Similarly, the gross income from x_I tons of interior paints is $2x_I$ thousand dollars. Under the assumption that the sales of interior and exterior paints are independent, the total gross income becomes the sum of the two revenues.

If we let z represent the total gross revenue (in thousands of dollars), the objective function may be written mathematically as $z = 3x_E + 2x_I$. The goal is to determine the (feasible) values of x_E and x_I that will maximize this criterion.

Constraints. The Reddy Mikks problem imposes restrictions on the usage of raw materials and on demand. The usage restriction may be expressed verbally as

$$\begin{pmatrix}\text{usage of raw material}\\ \text{by both paints}\end{pmatrix} \leq \begin{pmatrix}\text{maximum raw material}\\ \text{availability}\end{pmatrix}$$

This leads to the following restrictions (see the data for the problem):

$$x_E + 2x_I \leq 6 \qquad \text{(raw material A)}$$
$$2x_E + x_I \leq 8 \qquad \text{(raw material B)}$$

The demand restrictions are expressed verbally as

$$\begin{pmatrix}\text{excess amount of interior}\\ \text{over exterior paint}\end{pmatrix} \leq 1 \text{ ton per day}$$

$$(\text{demand for interior paint}) \leq 2 \text{ tons per day}$$

Mathematically, these are expressed, respectively, as

$$x_I - x_E \leq 1 \quad \text{(excess of interior over exterior paint)}$$
$$x_I \leq 2 \quad \text{(maximum demand for interior paint)}$$

An implicit (or "understood-to-be") constraint is that the amount produced of each paint cannot be negative (less than zero). To avoid obtaining such a solution, we impose the **nonnegativity restrictions**, which are normally written as

$$x_I \geq 0 \quad \text{(interior paint)}$$
$$x_E \geq 0 \quad \text{(exterior paint)}$$

The values of the variables x_E and x_I are said to constitute a **feasible solution** if they satisfy *all* the constraints of the model, including the nonnegativity restrictions.

The complete mathematical model for the Reddy Mikks problem may now be summarized as follows:

Determine the tons of interior and exterior paints, x_I and x_E, to be produced to

$$\text{maximize } z = 3x_E + 2x_I \quad \text{(objective function)}$$

subject to

$$\begin{aligned} x_E + 2x_I &\leq 6 \\ 2x_E + x_I &\leq 8 \\ -x_E + x_I &\leq 1 \quad \text{(constraints)} \\ x_I &\leq 2 \\ x_E \geq 0, \quad x_I &\geq 0 \end{aligned}$$

◀

What makes this model a linear program? Technically, it is a linear program because all its functions (constraints and objective) are *linear*. Linearity implies that both the **proportionality** and **additivity** properties are satisfied.

1. *Proportionality* requires that the contribution of each variable (i.e., x_E and x_I) in the objective function or its usage of the resources be *directly proportional* to the level (value) of the variable. For example, if the Reddy Mikks Company grants quantity discounts by selling a ton of exterior paint for $2500 when the sales exceed 2 tons, it will no longer be true that each ton produced will bring a revenue of $3000. Rather, it will bring $3000 per ton for $x_E \leq 2$ tons and $2500 per ton for $x_E > 2$ tons. This situation does not satisfy the condition of *direct* proportionality with x_E.

2. *Additivity* requires that the objective function be the *direct sum* of the individual contributions of the different variables. Similarly, the left side of each constraint

must be the sum of the individual usages of each variable from the corresponding resource. For example, in the case of two *competing* products, where an increase in the sales level of one product adversely affects that of the other, the two products do not satisfy the additivity property.

Exercise 2.1-1

The following questions apply to the model just described.

(a) Rewrite each of the constraints below under the stipulated conditions.

(1) The daily demand for interior paint exceeds that of exterior paint by *at least* 1 ton.
[*Ans.* $x_I - x_E \geq 1$.]

(2) The daily usage of raw material A is *at most* 6 tons and *at least* 3 tons.
[*Ans.* $x_E + 2x_I \leq 6$ and $x_E + 2x_I \geq 3$.]

(3) The demand for interior paint cannot be less than the demand for exterior paint.
[*Ans.* $x_I - x_E \geq 0$.]

(b) Check whether the following solutions are feasible.

(1) $x_E = 1$, $x_I = 4$; (2) $x_E = 2$, $x_I = 2$; (3) $x_E = 3\frac{1}{3}$, $x_I = 1\frac{1}{3}$; (4) $x_E = 2$, $x_I = 1$; (5) $x_E = 2$, $x_I = -1$.
[*Ans.* All solutions are feasible except (1) and (5).]

(c) Consider the feasible solution $x_E = 2$, $x_I = 2$. Determine

(1) Slack (unused) amount of raw material A.
[*Ans.* Zero.]

(2) Slack amount of raw material B.
[*Ans.* 2 tons.]

(d) Determine the best solution among all the feasible solutions in part (b).
[*Ans.* (2) $z = 10$; (3) $z = 12\frac{2}{3}$; (4) $z = 8$. Solution (3) is the best.]

(e) Can you guess the number of *feasible* solutions the Reddy Mikks problem may have?
[*Ans.* Infinity of solutions, which makes it futile to use an enumeration procedure and points to the need for a more "selective" technique, as we show in the following section.]

2.1.1 GRAPHICAL SOLUTION OF LP MODELS

In this section we consider the solution of the Reddy Mikks LP model. The model can be solved graphically because it has only two variables. For models with three or more variables, the graphical method is impractical. Nevertheless, we shall be able to draw general conclusions from the graphical method that will serve as the basis for the development of the general solution method in Chapter 3.

The first step in the graphical method is to plot the feasible **solution space** that satisfies all the constraints *simultaneously*. Figure 2-1 depicts the required solution space. The nonnegativity restrictions $x_E \geq 0$ and $x_I \geq 0$ confine all the feasible values to the first quadrant (which is defined by the space above or on the x_E-axis and to the right or on the x_I-axis). The space enclosed by the remaining constraints is determined by first replacing ($\leq$) by ($=$) for each constraint, thus yielding a straight-line equation. Each straight line is then plotted on the (x_E, x_I) plane, and the region in which each constraint holds when the inequality is activated is indicated by the direction of the arrow on the associated straight line. An easy way to determine the direction of the arrow is to use the origin $(0, 0)$ as a reference point. If $(0, 0)$ satisfies the inequality, the feasible direction should include the origin; otherwise, it should be on the opposite side. For example, $(0, 0)$ satisfies the inequality $-x_E + x_I \leq 1$, meaning that inequality is feasible in the (half) space that includes the origin. If the constraint happens to pass through the origin, a reference point that

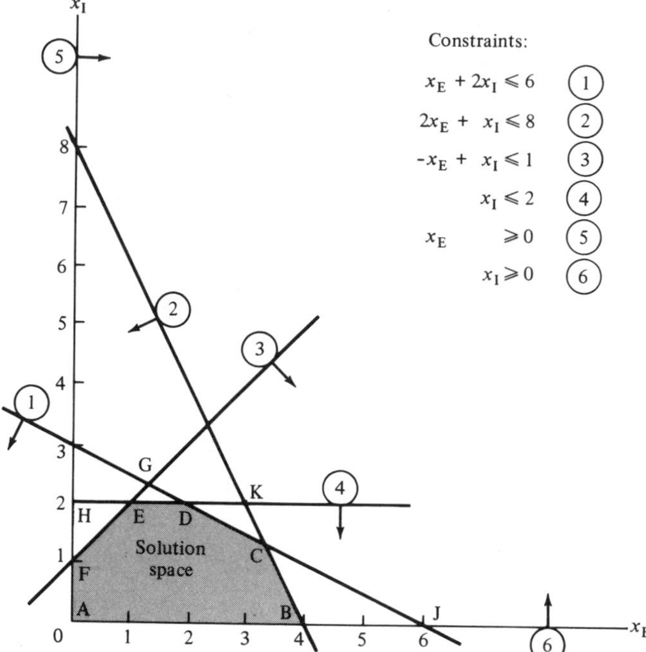

Figure 2-1

does not lie on the associated straight line must be selected. Applying this procedure to our example, we obtain the solution space *ABCDEF* shown in Figure 2-1.

To find the optimum (maximum) solution, we move the revenue line "uphill" to the point where any further increase in revenue would render an infeasible solution. Figure 2-2 shows that the optimum solution occurs at point *C*. Since *C* is the intersection of lines ① and ② (see Figure 2-1), the values of x_E and x_I are determined by solving the following two equations simultaneously:

$$x_E + 2x_I = 6$$
$$2x_E + x_I = 8$$

Each point within or on the boundary of the solution space *ABCDEF* satisfies all the constraints and hence represents a *feasible* point. Although there is an *infinity* of feasible points in the solution space, the **optimum solution** can be determined by observing the direction in which the objective function $z = 3x_E + 2x_I$ increases.

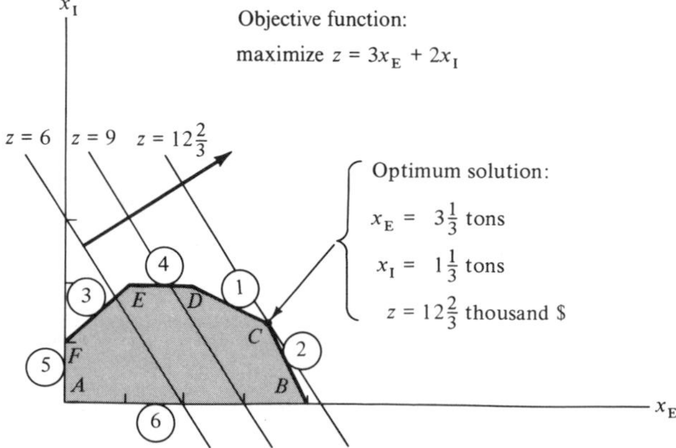

Figure 2-2

```
*** OPTIMUM SOLUTION SUMMARY ***

Title: Reddy Mikks model
Final iteration No: 3
Objective value (max) =    12.6667

Variable      Value      Obj Coeff    Obj Val Contrib    Reduced Cost

x1 xE         3.3333     3.0000       10.0000            0.0000
x2 xI         1.3333     2.0000        2.6667            0.0000

Constraint  RHS     Slack(-)/Surplus(+)          Dual Price

1(<)        6.0000       0.0000-                  0.3333
2(<)        8.0000       0.0000-                  1.3333
3(<)        1.0000       3.0000-                  0.0000
4(<)        2.0000       0.6667-                  0.0000
```

Figure 2-3

Figure 2-2 illustrates this result. The parallel lines representing the objective function are plotted by assigning (arbitrary) increasing values to $z = 3x_E + 2x_I$ to determine both the slope and the direction in which total revenue (objective function) increases. In Figure 2-2 we used $z = 6$ and $z = 9$. (Verify!)

The two equations yield $x_E = 3\frac{1}{3}$ and $x_I = 1\frac{1}{3}$. The solution thus says that the daily production should be $3\frac{1}{3}$ tons of exterior paint and $1\frac{1}{3}$ tons of interior paint. The associated revenue is

$$z = 3(3\tfrac{1}{3}) + 2(1\tfrac{1}{3}) = 12\tfrac{2}{3} \text{ thousand dollars}$$

The output of the Reddy Mikks model using the TORA software is given in Figure 2-3. The output provides a summary of the solution ($x_E = 3.3333$, $x_I = 1.3333$, and $z = 12.6667$). It also provides the contribution of each individual variable to the objective function. The second portion of the output in Figure 2-3 lists the constraints and their type together with the associated values of their slack or surplus variables. A **slack** variable is associated with the ($\leq$) constraint and represents the amount by which the right-hand side of the constraint exceeds its left-hand side. A **surplus** variable is identified with a ($\geq$) constraint and represents the excess of the left-hand side over the right-hand side. For constraints of the type ($\leq$), the right-hand side normally represents the limit on the availability of a resource, whereas its left-hand side represents the usage of this limited resource by the different activities (variables) of the model. In this regard, the slack variable represents the unused amount of the resource. Constraints of the type ($\geq$) normally set minimum specification requirements, in which case the surplus variable would represent the excess amount by which the minimum specification is satisfied. In the Reddy Mikks model, the first two constraints represent the availability of raw materials A and B. Both constraints show zero slacks, meaning that they have been used completely. Demand constraints 3 and 4 have positive slacks, which means that their limits are higher than needed by the optimum solution.

Figure 2-3 includes two additional columns, "reduced cost" and "dual price." The significance of this information will be explained in the next section after we introduce the subject of sensitivity analysis.

Exercise 2.1-2

(a) Identify the solution space and the optimum solution (including slack/surplus variables corresponding to constraints 1, 2, 3, and 4) for the Reddy Mikks model if each of the following changes is effected separately. Assume that each change replaces, rather than augments, an existing condition in the model and that the remaining information of the model remains unchanged. (Refer to Figure 2-1 for identifying and checking the answer.)

(1) The maximum demand for interior paint is 3 tons daily.
[*Ans.* Solution space = *ABCGF*. Optimum remains at *C* with slack $s_4 = 1.6667$ and all the other slacks remain unchanged.]

(2) Demand for interior paint is at least 2 tons daily.
[*Ans.* Solution space = *EDG*. Optimum at *D*, $z = 10$, $x_E = x_I = 2$, slacks $s_1 = 0$, $s_2 = 2$, $s_3 = 1$, and surplus $s_4 = 0$.]

(3) Demand for interior paint is exactly 1 ton higher than for exterior paint.
[*Ans.* Solution space = *EF*. Optimum at *E*, $z = 7$, $x_E = 1$, $x_I = 2$, slacks $s_1 = 1$, $s_2 = 4$, $s_3 = 0$. Equality constraint 4 has neither slack nor surplus.]

(4) Daily availability of raw material B is at least 8 tons.
[*Ans.* Solution space = *BCJ*. Optimum at *J*, $z = 18$, $x_E = 6$, $x_I = 0$, slack $s_1 = 0$, surplus $S_2 = 4$, slacks $s_3 = 7$, $s_4 = 2$.]

(5) Availability of raw material B is at least 8 tons and the demand for interior paint exceeds that of exterior paint by at least 1 ton.
[*Ans.* No feasible space exists.]

(b) Identify the optimum solution in Figure 2-2 if the objective function is changed as shown:

(1) $z = 3x_E + x_I$
[*Ans.* $x_E = 4$, $x_I = 0$ at *B*.]

(2) $z = 3x_E + 1.5x_I$
[*Ans.* Any point on the line segment joining points *B* and *C*.]

(3) $z = x_E + 3x_I$
[*Ans.* $x_E = 2$, $x_I = 2$ at *D*.]

(4) In case (2) the problem has more than one optimum solution. What is the value of the objective function at all these optima?
[*Ans.* The value of the objective function remains *the same* and equal to 12. We refer to such solutions as **alternative optima** because they yield the *same* optimum objective value.]

Exercise 2.1-2(b) reveals the interesting observation that the optimum solution can always be identified with one of the feasible **corner** (or **extreme**) **points** of the solution space: *A*, *B*, *C*, *D*, *E*, and *F* in Figure 2-2. The choice of the specific corner point depends in the first place on the slope (coefficients) of the objective function. Notice that even in case (2), where the optimum solution need not occur at a corner point, all the alternative optima are known once the corner points *B* and *C* are determined.

We shall show in Chapter 3 that the observation just discussed is the key idea to solving linear programs in general. Indeed, we can see that we no longer have to concern ourselves with the fact that the solution space has an infinity of solutions because we can now concentrate on a *finite* number of *corner* points.

2.1.2 SENSITIVITY ANALYSIS: AN ELEMENTARY PRESENTATION

Sensitivity analysis is designed to study the effect of changes in the parameters of the LP model on the optimal solution. Such analysis is regarded as an integral part of the (extended) solution of any LP problem. It gives the model a dynamic characteristic that allows the analyst to study the behavior of the optimal solution as a result of making changes in the model's parameters. The ultimate objective of the analysis is to obtain information about possible new optimum solutions (corresponding to changes in the parameters) with minimal additional computations.

Sensitivity analysis is particularly well suited for studying the effect on the optimum solution of variations in the cost/profit coefficients and in the amounts of available resources. Although sensitivity analysis computations have been automated in most OR software (including TORA), a fundamental understanding of how the procedure works is essential for a successful implementation of the results. In this section we utilize a graphical procedure to explain the basic elements of the analysis. Later, in Chapters 3 and 5, a more rigorous treatment of the technique will be presented.

Sensitivity Problem 1. How much change is allowed in the objective function coefficients?

A change in the objective function coefficients can affect only the slope of the straight line representing it. We have demonstrated in Section 2.1.1 [Exercise 2.1-2(b)] that the determination of the optimum corner point of a given solution space depends totally on the slope of the objective function. Our goal from the standpoint of sensitivity analysis is to determine the range of variation in each of the objective function coefficients that will keep a current optimum corner point unchanged. The details of the procedure are demonstrated by using the Reddy Mikks model.

Let c_E and c_I represent general revenues per ton of the exterior and interior paints. Thus the objective may be written as

$$z = c_E x_E + c_I x_I$$

Figure 2-4 shows that the effect of the increase/decrease in c_E and c_I is to rotate the line representing z in a clockwise or counterclockwise direction about the current optimum point C. The idea is to determine the ranges of variation for c_E and c_I that

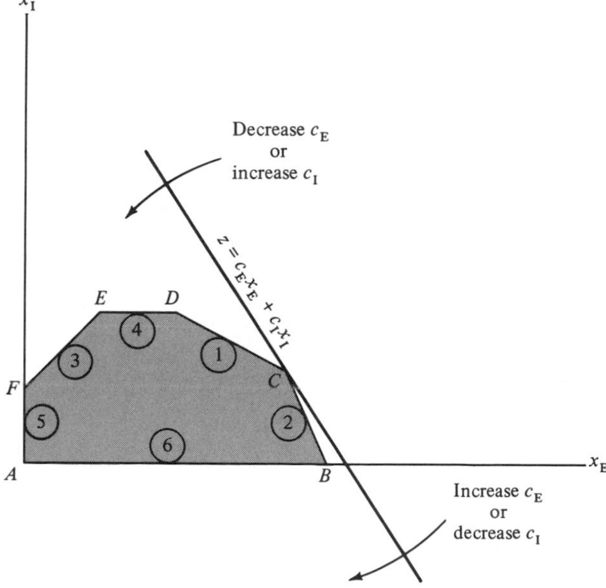

Figure 2-4

will keep the optimum at point C. An investigation of Figure 2-4 reveals that as long as the slope of z remains inclusively between those of lines CB and CD, the optimum will always be at C. (When the slope of z coincides with either that of CB or CD, an alternative optimum will result.) We can express this condition algebraically as

$$\frac{1}{2} \leq \frac{c_E}{c_I} \leq \frac{2}{1}$$

The relationship above is correct only if $c_I \neq 0$; that is, the range of admissible slopes excludes vertical objective function. If $c_I = 0$ is a possibility, we can use the ratio c_I/c_E, again provided $c_E \neq 0$. If both $c_I = 0$ and $c_E = 0$ are possible, the range must be partitioned into two (overlapping) ranges.

The bounding fractions directly equal the respective (algebraic) ratios of the coefficients of x_E and x_I for lines CB and CD. The direction of the inequality is automatically decided then by the relative values of the bounding fractions 1/2 and 2/1.

The inequality above says that any changes in c_E or c_I that keep c_E/c_I *within* the range $[1/2, 2]$ will always maintain C as the optimum point. Changes outside this range will move the optimum to B or D. We can obtain more specific information about the objective coefficient if we consider changing them one at a time while keeping all other coefficients fixed at their present values. In the Reddy Mikks model, if we fix c_I at its present value ($= 2$), the inequality above will yield the following range:

$$\frac{1}{2} \leq \frac{c_E}{2} \leq 2$$

or

$$1 \leq c_E \leq 4$$

This means that for $c_I = 2$, point C will remain optimal as long as c_E lies in the range $[1, 4]$. A similar range can be determined for c_I given that c_E is fixed at 3. Notice that it is easier in this case to rewrite the inequality with c_I in the numerator; that is,

$$\frac{1}{2} \leq \frac{c_I}{c_E} \leq \frac{2}{1}$$

Putting $c_E = 3$, we obtain the range $\frac{3}{2} \leq c_I \leq 6$.

Figure 2-5 gives TORA output for the sensitivity analysis of the objective coefficient. The results appear in two parts: single changes and simultaneous changes. The ranges associated with single changes agree with the results above. As for the case of simultaneous changes, we need to point out that d_1 and d_2 are defined as $d_1 = c_E - 3$ and $d_2 = c_I - 2$; that is, they represent the amount of change relative to the current value of the coefficient. Given these substitutions, the simultaneous changes condition

$$\frac{1}{2} \leq \frac{c_E}{c_I} \leq 2$$

directly yields the simultaneous conditions shown in Figure 2-5. Specifically, $c_E/c_I \leq 2$ yields $-d_1 + 2d_2 + 1 \geq 0$ (verify), which is the same as the first condition. In a similar manner, $c_E/c_I \geq 1/2$ will yield the second condition.

```
                *** SENSITIVITY ANALYSIS ***
Objective coefficients -- Single Changes:
-----------------------------------------------------------------------------
Variable  Current Coeff    Min Coeff        Max Coeff        Reduced Cost
-----------------------------------------------------------------------------
x1 xE         3.0000         1.0000           4.0000           0.0000
x2 xI         2.0000         1.5000           6.0000           0.0000

Objective Coefficients -- Simultaneous Changes d:
-----------------------------------------------------------------------------
Nonbasic Var    Optimality Condition
-----------------------------------------------------------------------------
sx3              0.3333 +      0.6667 d2 +     -0.3333 d1 >= 0
sx4              1.3333 +     -0.3333 d2 +      0.6667 d1 >= 0
```

Figure 2-5

We have accounted for all the entries in Figure 2-5 except for the "reduced cost" column. Associated with each decision variable in the optimum solution is a parameter that measures its potential profitability. If the decision variable is already positive in the solution, its measure of potential profitability is always zero because the optimization process has already "exploited" the associated activity economically. On the other hand, if the decision variable is at zero level in the optimum solution, its measure of potential profitability will assume a nonzero value. This measure, referred to in the literature as the **reduced cost**, provides the amount by which the associated objective function coefficient must be adjusted in order for the variable to be just profitable. Actually, the reduced cost is a function of both the objective function and the constraint coefficients of the variable under consideration. However, we are not in a position to introduce this detail at this point and will thus postpone its discussion until Chapter 3. In Figure 2-5 both x_E and x_I are positive in the optimum solution, thus resulting in zero reduced cost for both variables.

Exercise 2.1-3

(a) Verify that the conditions representing the simultaneous changes d_1 and d_2 in Figure 2-5 are exactly equivalent to $1/2 \leq c_E/c_I \leq 2$.

(b) For the ranges specified for single changes in c_E and c_I, show on Figure 2-4 the optimum solution in each of the following cases:

  (1) c_E is increased just above its upper bound ($= 4$).
  [*Ans.* Point *B*.]

  (2) c_I is increased just above its upper bound ($= 6$).
  [*Ans.* Point *D*.]

  (3) c_I is decreased just below its lower bound ($= 1.5$).
  [*Ans.* Point *B*.]

(c) Suppose that the objective function is originally given as $z = 3x_E + x_I$ (instead of $z = 3x_E + 2x_I$). The associated optimum solution will then occur at B ($x_E = 4$, $x_I = 0$). This means that no interior paint will be produced. By how much should the profit per ton of interior paint be adjusted just to start producing positive quantities of interior paint?
[*Ans.* Increase c_I by at least .5 (from 1 to at least 1.5).]

(d) Use TORA to solve part (c) to show that the result is given directly by the reduced cost of x_I.

Sensitivity Problem 2. How much is the worth of a resource unit?

This problem deals with the study of the sensitivity of the optimum solution to changes in the right-hand side of the constraints. If the constraint represents a limited resource, the problem reduces to studying the effect of changing the availability of the resource. The specific goal of this sensitivity problem is to determine the effect of changes in the right-hand side of constraints on the optimum objective value. In essence, the results are given as predetermined ranges of the right-hand side within which the objective optimum value will change (increase or decrease) at a given *constant rate*. Let us discuss the situation in terms of the Reddy Mikks example.

Consider the first constraint dealing with raw material A. Any changes in the amount of raw material A will cause the associated constraint line to move parallel to itself as shown in Figure 2-6. A corresponding change in the optimum objective value will occur at a constant rate as long as the optimum solution is determined by the intersection of constraints (1) and (2). An investigation of Figure 2-6 shows that such requirement is satisfied as long as the changes are confined to the range represented by the line segment *KB*. If raw material A is increased past the amount associated with point *K*, the constraint will be redundant and hence will have no effect on the solution space. If the amount of raw material A is decreased below the value associated with point *B*, the optimum solution will no longer be determined by the intersection lines (1) and (2). This condition will destroy the linear relationship between the optimum objective value and the change in the amount of raw material A.

We can thus obtain the range of variation for raw material A as follows. The lower bound corresponds to point *B* ($x_E = 4$, $x_I = 0$), and is obtained by direct substitution in the left-hand side of constraint (1), that is, $1(4) + 2(0) = 4$ tons. Similarly, the upper bound is computed by substituting point *K* ($x_E = 3$, $x_I = 2$) in the left-hand side of constraint (1), that is, $1(3) + 2(2) = 7$ tons. In effect, the range of variation in the amount of raw material A that will render a linear relationship between the change in A and the corresponding optimum value of z is given as

$$4 \leq \text{amount of raw material A} \leq 7$$

The constant of proportionality between the amount of A and the optimum value of z is determined in a straightforward manner. Specifically, the values of z corre-

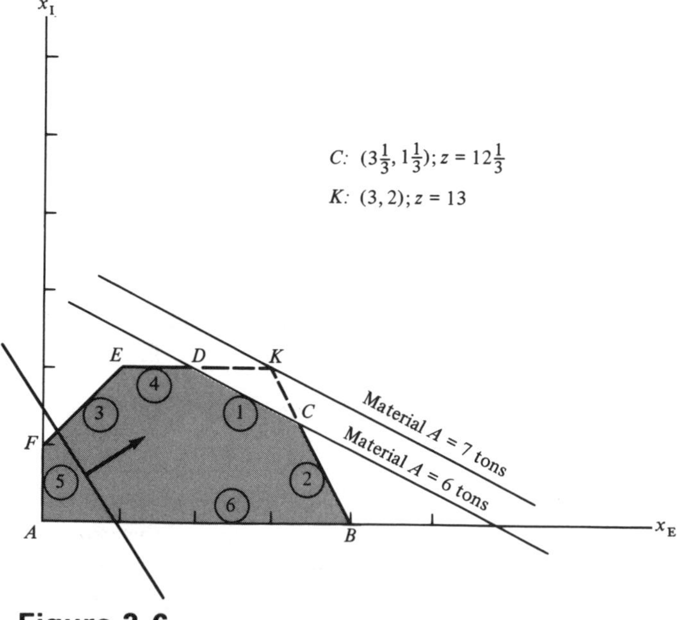

Figure 2-6

sponding to points B and K are obtained by direct substitution in the objective value to yield

$$z = 3(4) + 2(0) = 12 \qquad \text{at point } B$$
$$z = 3(3) + 2(2) = 13 \qquad \text{at point } K$$

Thus the constant of proportionality between z and the amount of A is computed as

$$y_1 = \frac{13 - 12}{7 - 4} = \frac{1}{3} \text{ thousand dollars per ton of A}$$

The constant y_1 actually represents the worth per unit of raw material A. Thus an increase (decrease) in the amount of A will increase (decrease) the value of z by 1/3. This proportionality is valid only as long as the amount of raw material A is within the inclusive range [4, 7].

Considering raw material B, Figure 2-7 shows that the limiting points that will maintain the linearity assumption between the amount of raw material B and the optimum value of z are given by D and J. The corresponding ranges of raw material B and z are determined in a manner similar to that used with raw material A. This yields the range [6, 12] for the raw material and [10, 18] for z (verify!). The worth per unit of raw material B is thus computed as

$$y_2 = \frac{18 - 10}{12 - 6} = \frac{4}{3} \text{ thousand dollars per ton of B}$$

We now turn attention to a different type of constraint. You will notice that the constraints associated with raw materials A and B have zero slacks because their associated straight lines pass through the current optimum solution at C. What about those (nonzero slack) constraints that do not pass through the optimum point C: namely, constraints (3) and (4)? An investigation of Figure 2-1 shows that the right-hand side of constraint (3) can be increased indefinitely without having any effect on the optimum solution or the objective value. In fact, the right-hand side can be decreased until the constraint passes through point C again without affecting

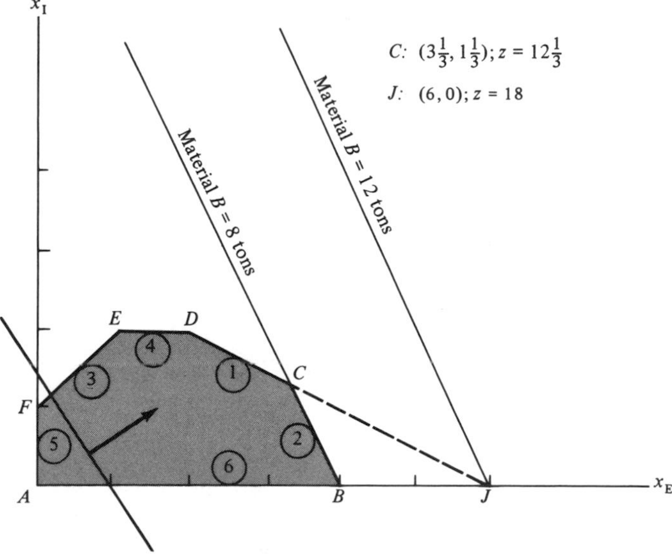

Figure 2-7

*** SENSITIVITY ANALYSIS ***

Right-hand Side -- Single Changes:

Constraint	Current RHS	Min RHS	Max RHS	Dual Price
1(<)	6.0000	4.0000	7.0000	0.3333
2(<)	8.0000	6.0000	12.0000	1.3333
3(<)	1.0000	-2.0000	infinity	0.0000
4(<)	2.0000	1.3333	infinity	0.0000

Right-hand Side Ranging -- Simultaneous Changes D:

Basic Var	Value/Feasibilty Condition			
x2 xI	1.3333 +	0.6667 D1 +	-0.3333 D2 >= 0	
x1 xE	3.3333 +	-0.3333 D1 +	0.6667 D2 >= 0	
sx5	3.0000 +	-1.0000 D1 +	1.0000 D2 +	1.0000 D3 >= 0
sx6	0.6667 +	-0.6667 D1 +	0.3333 D2 +	1.0000 D4 >= 0

Figure 2-8

the optimum value of z. Thus the corresponding range for the right-hand side of constraint (3) is $[-2, \infty]$ (verify!). Since the value of z remains unchanged, the corresponding worth per unit is zero. In a similar fashion, constraint (4) may change in the range $[4/3, \infty]$ (verify!) without affecting the optimum solution or the optimum value of z.

Figure 2-8 shows the TORA output for the right-hand side ranging. The results agree with the computations given above. For historical reasons, the worth per unit values (e.g., y_1 and y_2) are referred to in the literature by the standard, though nonsuggestive, name **dual prices**. The name arises from the mathematical definition of the dual problem in linear programming (see Chapter 5). Dual prices also are sometimes referred to by the equally nonsuggestive name **shadow prices**. Although we will continue to use the (now standard) name *dual price* throughout the book, the reader should think of these parameters more descriptively as the *worth per unit* of resources.

The second part of Figure 2-8 provides the conditions necessary for effecting simultaneous changes in the right-hand sides of all four constraints. These changes are represented by D_1, D_2, D_3, and D_4 for the four respective constraints. These conditions actually give the corresponding new values of the variables x_E and x_I, and the slacks sx_5 and sx_6 associated with the last two constraints (the slacks sx_3 and sx_4 associated with constraints 1 and 2 are zero). Thus any combination of D_1, D_2, D_3, and D_4 that results in nonnegative values of these four variables automatically yields the new optimum solution. For example, suppose that both raw materials A and B are increased from their present levels of 6 and 8 to 9 and 13 whereas the right-hand sides of the other two constraints remain unchanged. This means that $D_1 = 9 - 6 = 3$, $D_2 = 13 - 8 = 5$, $D_3 = 0$, and $D_4 = 0$. Substituting these values in the expressions in Figure 2-8 we get the solution $x_E = 17/3$, $x_I = 5/3$, $sx_5 = 5$, and $sx_6 = 1/3$ (verify!). Since all the values are nonnegative, the new solution provides the new optimum directly.

Exercise 2.1-4

(a) In the Reddy Mikks model, suppose that the constraint of raw material A is changed from $x_E + 2x_I \leq 6$ to $2x_E + 3x_I \leq 10$, with all the remaining information unchanged. Compute the resulting dual prices and ranges for all the constraints manually; then verify the results using TORA.

[*Ans.* Ranges = (8, 12), (6, 10), (−2.5, ∞), (1, ∞).
Dual prices = .25, 1.25, 0, 0.]

(b) In the results in Figure 2-8, suppose that we change the availabilities of raw materials A and B to 10 and 11, respectively. Can we determine the optimum solution directly?
[*Ans.* No, because $D_1 = 4$ and $D_2 = 3$ will result in a negative value of slack sx6 (= −1).]

2.2 LP FORMULATIONS

In this section we present two LP models. You will notice that the decision variables in the two examples are easy to define. In the next section we present other formulations in which the identification and/or use of the decision variables are more subtle.

The availability of the software TORA, together with the sensitivity analysis discussion that we presented in Section 2.1.2, will allow us to investigate the optimum solution of each model. The investigation will reveal intriguing interpretations of the output results, which should lead to a better understanding and appreciation of LP as a decision-making tool.

Example 2.2-1 (Bank Loan Policy). A financial institution, the Thriftem Bank, is in the process of formulating a loan policy involving a total of $12 million. Being a full-service facility, the bank is obligated to grant loans to different clientele. The following table provides the types of loans, the interest rate charged by the bank, and the probability of bad debt as estimated from past experience:

Type of Loan	Interest Rate	Probability of Bad Debt
Personal	.140	.10
Car	.130	.07
Home	.120	.03
Farm	.125	.05
Commercial	.100	.02

Bad debts are assumed unrecoverable and hence produce no interest revenue.

Competition with other financial institutions in the area requires that the bank allocate at least 40% of the total funds to farm and commercial loans. To assist the housing industry in the region, home loans must equal at least 50% of the personal, car, and home loans. The bank also has a stated policy specifying that the overall ratio for bad debts on all loans may not exceed .04.

Mathematical Model

The variables of the model can be defined as follows:

x_1 = personal loans (in millions of dollars)
x_2 = car loans
x_3 = home loans
x_4 = farm loans
x_5 = commercial loans

The objective of the Thriftem Bank is to maximize its net return comprised of the difference between the revenue from interest and lost funds due to bad debts. Since bad debts are not recoverable, both as principal and interest, the objective function may be written as

$$\text{maximize } z = .14(.9x_1) + .13(.93x_2) + .12(.97x_3) + .125(.95x_4) + .1(.98x_5) - .1x_1 - .07x_2 - .03x_3 - .05x_4 - .02x_5$$

This function simplifies to

$$\text{maximize } z = .026x_1 + .0509x_2 + .0864x_3 + .06875x_4 + .078x_5$$

The problem has five constraints:

1. *Total funds*

$$x_1 + x_2 + x_3 + x_4 + x_5 \leq 12$$

2. *Farm and commercial loans*

$$x_4 + x_5 \geq .4 \times 12$$

or

$$x_4 + x_5 \geq 4.8$$

3. *Home loans*

$$x_3 \geq .5(x_1 + x_2 + x_3)$$

4. *Limit on bad debts*

$$\frac{.1x_1 + .07x_2 + .03x_3 + .05x_4 + .02x_5}{x_1 + x_2 + x_3 + x_4 + x_5} \leq .04$$

or

$$.06x_1 + .03x_2 - .01x_3 + .01x_4 - .02x_5 \leq 0$$

5. *Nonnegativity*

$$x_1 \geq 0,\ x_2 \geq 0,\ x_3 \geq 0,\ x_4 \geq 0,\ x_5 \geq 0$$

A subtle assumption in the formulation above is that all loans are issued at approximately the same time. This assumption allows us to ignore differences in the time values of the funds allocated to the different loans.

The output of the Bank Policy model is shown in Figure 2-9. It shows that only home and commercial loans are recommended. Of the remaining types, personal loans are the least attractive, not only because they have the smallest objective coefficient (= .026) but also because their reduced cost is the highest among all the variables (= .0604). The reduced cost means that the "profitability" of the personal loan variable must be increased by .0604 in order for the variable to be just profitable. Looking at the dual prices, the first constraint shows that an increase of 1 (million) dollars in allocated funds will increase the net return from all loans by .0864 (million) dollars. This is equivalent to an annual return of 8.64% on investment. Since the associated range is $(4.8, \infty)$, this return is guaranteed for any increase in allocated funds above the present 12 (million) dollars. A return of 8.64% appears to be low, however, especially since the lowest interest rate that the bank charges is 10%. The difference can be attributed to bad debts, which are not recoverable both as principal and interest. Indeed, the highest objective coefficient in the model is .0864 (home loans). Interestingly, this coefficient happens to equal the dual price of constraint 1 (allocated funds). The conclusion from this observation is that any new additional funds will necessarily be allocated by the optimum solution to home loans.

*** OPTIMUM SOLUTION SUMMARY ***

Title: Bank model
Final iteration No: 6
Objective value (max) = 0.9965

Variable	Value	Obj Coeff	Obj Val Contrib	Reduced Cost
x1 pers'nl	0.0000	0.0260	0.0000	0.0604
x2 car	0.0000	0.0509	0.0000	0.0355
x3 home	7.2000	0.0864	0.6221	0.0000
x4 farm	0.0000	0.0688	0.0000	0.0092
x5 comm'l	4.8000	0.0780	0.3744	0.0000

Constraint	RHS	Slack(-)/Surplus(+)	Dual Price
1(<)	12.0000	0.0000-	0.0864
2(>)	4.8000	0.0000+	-0.0084
3(>)	0.0000	3.6000+	0.0000
4(<)	0.0000	0.1680-	0.0000

*** SENSITIVITY ANALYSIS ***

Objective coefficients -- Single Changes:

Variable	Current Coeff	Min Coeff	Max Coeff	Reduced Cost
x1 personl	0.0260	-infinity	0.0864	0.0604
x2 car	0.0509	-infinity	0.0864	0.0355
x3 home	0.0864	0.0780	infinity	0.0000
x4 farm	0.0688	-infinity	0.0780	0.0092
x5 comm'l	0.0780	0.0688	0.0864	0.0000

Right-hand Side -- Single Changes:

Constraint	Current RHS	Min RHS	Max RHS	Dual Price
1(<)	12.0000	4.8000	infinity	0.0864
2(>)	4.8000	0.0000	12.0000	-0.0084
3(>)	0.0000	-infinity	3.6000	0.0000
4(<)	0.0000	-0.1680	infinity	0.0000

Figure 2-9

You will also notice that the dual price associated with constraint 2 is negative (= −.0084). The constraint is associated with the minimum limit set for farm and commercial loans. Since its dual price is negative, an increase in that limit will have an adverse effect on the net return. In other words, there is no economic advantage in setting a minimum limit on the amount of farm and commercial loans. This observation is consistent with the interpretation of the first constraint which stipulates that any new additional funds will be allocated to home loans rather than to farm and commercial loans. As a matter of fact, if we were to remove the minimum limit requirement on farm and commercial loans, all the funds would be allocated to home loans (verify this conclusion by "yanking" constraint 2 using TORA's MODIFY option). ◀

Example 2.2-2 (Land Use and Development). The Birdeyes Real Estate Co. owns 800 acres of prime, but undeveloped, land on a scenic lake in the heart of the Ozark Mountains. In the past, little or no regulation was applied to new developments around the lake. The lake shores are now lined with clustered vacation homes. Because of the lack of sewage service, septic tanks, mostly improperly installed, are in extensive use. Over the years, seepage from the septic tanks has resulted in a severe water pollution problem.

To curb further degradation in the quality of water, county officials introduced and approved some stringent ordinances applicable to all future developments.

1. Only single-, double-, and triple-family homes can be constructed, with the single-family homes accounting for at least 50% of the total.
2. To limit the number of septic tanks, minimum lot sizes of 2, 3, and 4 acres are required for single-, double-, and triple-family homes.
3. Recreation areas of 1 acre each must be established at the rate of one area per 200 families.
4. To preserve the ecology of the lake, underground water may not be pumped for house or garden use.

The president of Birdeyes Real Estate is studying the possibility of developing the company's 800 acres on the lake. The new development will include single-, double-, and triple-family homes. He estimates that 15% of the acreage will be consumed in the opening of streets and easements for utilities. He also estimates his returns from the different housing units:

Housing Units	Single	Double	Triple
Net Return per Unit ($)	10,000	12,000	15,000

The cost of connecting water service to the area is proportionate to the number of units constructed. However, the county stipulates that a minimum of $100,000 must be collected for the project to be economically feasible. Additionally, the expansion of the water system beyond its present capacity is limited to 200,000 gallons per day during peak periods. The following data summarize the cost of connecting water service as well as the water consumption assuming an average size family:

Housing Unit	Single	Double	Triple	Recreation
Water service cost per unit ($)	1000	1200	1400	800
Water consumption per unit (gal/day)	400	600	840	450

Mathematical Model

The company must decide on the number of units to be constructed of each housing type together with the number of recreation areas satisfying county ordinances. Define

x_1 = number of units of single-family homes
x_2 = number of units of double-family homes
x_3 = number of units of triple-family homes
x_4 = number of recreation areas

An apparent objective of the company is to maximize total return. The objective function is thus given as

$$\text{maximize } z = 10{,}000x_1 + 12{,}000x_2 + 15{,}000x_3$$

The constraints of the problem include

1. Limit on land use.
2. Limit on the requirements for single-family homes relative to other styles.
3. Limit on the requirements for recreation areas.
4. Capital requirement for connecting water service.
5. Limit on peak-period daily water consumption.

These constraints are expressed mathematically as follows:

1. *Land use*

$$2x_1 + 3x_2 + 4x_3 + 1x_4 \leq 680$$

2. *Single-family homes*

$$\frac{x_1}{x_1 + x_2 + x_3} \geq .5$$

or

$$.5x_1 - .5x_2 - .5x_3 \geq 0$$

3. *Recreation areas*

$$x_4 \geq \frac{x_1 + 2x_2 + 3x_3}{200}$$

or

$$200x_4 - x_1 - 2x_2 - 3x_3 \geq 0$$

4. *Capital*

$$1000x_1 + 1200x_2 + 1400x_3 + 800x_4 \geq 100{,}000$$

5. *Water consumption*

$$400x_1 + 600x_2 + 840x_3 + 450x_4 \leq 200{,}000$$

6. *Nonnegativity*

$$x_1 \geq 0,\ x_2 \geq 0,\ x_3 \geq 0,\ x_4 \geq 0$$

It is a good practice in model formulation to pay attention to the impact of computational roundoff error. In the model above, you will notice that the coefficients in constraints 4 and 5 (capital and water consumption) are relatively larger than most of the coefficients in the remaining constraints. This inconsistency could, in general, lead to undesirable machine round-off error resulting from the mixed manipulation of relatively large and relatively small coefficients in the same problem. In our present example, we can rectify this potential problem by scaling down all the coefficients of each constraint by the constant 1000. This reduces the constraints to

$$x_1 + 1.2x_2 + 1.4x_3 + .8x_4 \geq 100$$
$$.4x_1 + .6x_2 + .84x_3 + .45x_4 \leq 200$$

It is equally damaging computationally to deal with very small constraint coefficients. In such situations it may be advisabie to scale up all the small coefficients to produce some consistency in the formulation of the model. Most software (TORA included) will attempt to achieve this consistency prior to solving the problem. However, it is a good modeling practice to implement this step during the formulation of the model.

Figure 2-10 provides the optimal solution of the model. We notice that linear programming does not provide integer solutions in general. The present solution yields SINGLE = 339.152 and RECR'N = 1.696 with DOUBLE = TRIPLE = 0. For practical purposes, we can round this solution to SINGLE = 339 and RECR'N = 2 (which, incidentally, happens to be the optimum integer solution).

It is interesting that the optimum solution does not recommend the construction of double and triple homes, despite the fact that their returns per unit ($12,000 and $15,000) are higher in absolute sense than that for a single home. This result shows that the marginal returns as expressed in the objective function are not sufficient to judge the profitability of an activity. We must additionally consider the cost of the

*** OPTIMUM SOLUTION SUMMARY ***

Title: Land development
Final iteration No: 6
Objective value (max) =3391521.2500

Variable	Value	Obj Coeff	Obj Val Contrib	Reduced Cost
x1 SINGLE	339.1521	10000.0000	3391521.2500	0.0000
x2 DOUBLE	0.0000	12000.0000	0.0000	3012.4688
x3 TRIPLE	0.0000	15000.0000	0.0000	5024.9351
x4 RECR'N	1.6958	0.0000	0.0000	0.0000

Constraint	RHS	Slack(-)/Surplus(+)	Dual Price
1(<)	680.0000	0.0000-	4987.5308
2(>)	0.0000	169.5760+	0.0000
3(>)	0.0000	0.0864+	-24.9377
4(>)	100.0000	240.5087+	0.0000
5(<)	200.0000	63.5761-	0.0000

*** SENSITIVITY ANALYSIS ***

Objective coefficients -- Single Changes:

Variable	Current Coeff	Min Coeff	Max Coeff	Reduced Cost
x1 SINGLE	10000.0000	7993.3557	infinity	16.4f
x2 DOUBLE	12000.0000	-infinity	15012.4688	3012.4688
x3 TRIPLE	15000.0000	-infinity	20024.9351	5024.9351
x4 RECR'N	0.0000	-2000000.1250	5000.0000	0.0000

Right-hand Side -- Single Changes:

Constraint	Current RHS	Min RHS	Max RHS	Dual Price
1(<)	680.0000	199.7012	996.8926	4987.5308
2(>)	0.0000	-infinity	169.5760	0.0000
3(>)	0.0000	-340.0000	50988.0195	-24.9377
4(>)	100.0000	-infinity	340.5087	0.0000
5(<)	200.0000	136.4239	infinity	0.0000

Figure 2-10

resources used by the activity. Indeed, this is what the **reduced cost** accomplishes. The present reduced costs of \$3012.45 and \$5024.94 for DOUBLE and TRIPLE provide the excess of the per unit cost of resources over the marginal return. Thus, in order for either activity to be *just* profitable, we must either reduce the per unit cost of the resources or increase the marginal return by an amount equal to its reduced cost.

Constraints 2, 4, and 5 have positive slack/surplus values, which indicates that their resources are "abundant." As a result, their **dual prices** (worth per unit) are zero. Constraint 1 representing available land has a dual value of \$4987.53, indicating that a 1-acre increase in available land is worth \$4987.53 in *net* revenue. This information could be valuable in deciding on the purchase price of new land.

Constraint 4 has a dual price of −\$24.937, and because it is negative, it immediately tells us that any increase in its "resource" will have an adverse effect on the total revenue. But why is it so? We can answer this question only if we know what the units of the "resource" of that constraint are. Let us look at the constraint once again:

$$200\ \text{RECR'N} - \text{SINGLE} - 2\ \text{DOUBLE} - 3\ \text{TRIPLE} \geq 0$$

The constraint specifies the minimum number of recreation areas (RECR'N) in relationship to the number of homes. As the constraint now stands, the units of its left-hand side are convoluted. However, if we divide the entire constraint by 200, we then obtain

$$\text{RECR'N} - (.005\ \text{SINGLE} + .01\ \text{DOUBLE} + .015\ \text{TRIPLE}) \geq 0$$

Now, the variable RECR'N represents the number of recreation areas. Since each recreation area occupies 1 acre, the units of RECR'N and those of the expression in parentheses must also be in acres. Thus an increase of 1 unit in the right side (i.e., an increase from zero to 1) can be interpreted as a 1-acre increase in RECR'N. With the new presentation of the constraint, we can now say that the dual price represents the worth per acre increase in the recreation area. However, with the new constraint, the dual price must be 200 × −\$24.937 = −\$4987.53. (Actually, if you modify the constraint as shown and rerun the model, the TORA output will yield the new dual value directly—try it!)

The new dual price now tells us that an acre increase in recreation area will reduce the revenue by \$4987.53. Interestingly, this exactly equals the dual price of the land use resource (constraint 2) but with opposite sign. The result makes economic sense, because an acre allocated to the recreation area is, by definition, an acre taken away from constructing homes. It is thus no coincidence that the dual prices match. ◀

2.3 ADDITIONAL LP FORMULATIONS

In Section 2.2 we presented two LP formulations in which the definitions of the decision variables as well as the construction of the objective and constraint functions are almost straightforward. In this section we present three additional formulations that are characterized by a degree of subtlety in the way the variables are

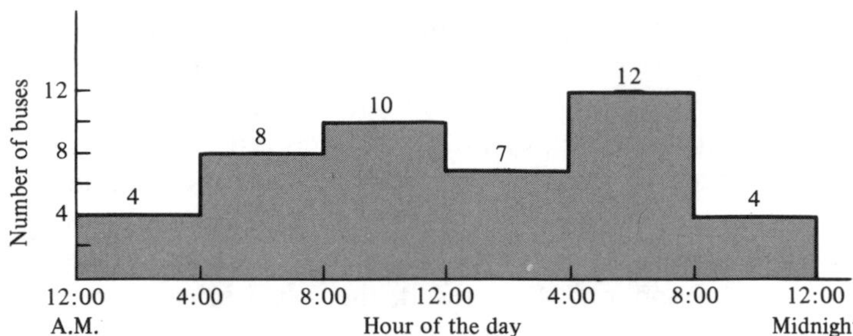

Figure 2-11

defined and used in the model. The objective, of course, is to expose you to new ideas in model development.

Example 2.3-1 (Bus Scheduling Problem). Progress City is studying the feasibility of introducing a mass transit bus system that will alleviate the smog problem by reducing in-city driving. The initial study seeks the determination of the minimum number of buses that can handle the transportation needs. After gathering necessary information, the city engineer noticed that the minimum number of buses needed to meet demand fluctuates with the time of the day. Studying the data further, it became evident that the required number of buses can be assumed constant over successive intervals of 4 hours each. Figure 2-11 summarizes the engineer's findings. It was decided that to carry out the required daily maintenance, each bus could operate only 8 successive hours a day.

Mathematical Representation

It is required to determine the *number of buses to operate during different shifts* (variables) that will *meet the minimum demand* (constraints) while *minimizing the total number of daily buses in operation* (objective).

You may already have noticed that the definition of the variables is ambiguous. We know that each bus will run 8-hour shifts, but we do not know when a shift should start. If we follow a normal three-shift schedule (8:01 A.M.–4:00 P.M., 4:01 P.M.–12:00 midnight, and 12:01 A.M.–8:00 A.M.) and assume that x_1, x_2, and x_3 are the number of buses starting in the first, second, and third shifts, we can see from Figure 2-11 that $x_1 \geq 10$, $x_2 \geq 12$, and $x_3 \geq 8$, with the corresponding minimum number equal to $x_1 + x_2 + x_3 = 10 + 12 + 8 = 30$ buses daily.

This solution is acceptable only if the shifts *must* coincide with the normal three-shift schedule. It may be advantageous, however, to allow the optimization process to choose the "best" starting time for a shift. A reasonable way to accomplish this is to allow a shift to start every 4 hours. Figure 2-12 illustrates this concept where (overlapping) shifts may start at 12:01 A.M., 4:01 A.M., 8:01 A.M., 12:01 P.M., 4:01 P.M., and 8:01 P.M., with each shift continuing for 8 consecutive hours. We are now ready to define the variables:

x_1 = number of buses starting at 12:01 A.M.
x_2 = number of buses starting at 4:01 A.M.
x_3 = number of buses starting at 8:01 A.M.
x_4 = number of buses starting at 12:01 P.M.
x_5 = number of buses starting at 4:01 P.M.
x_6 = number of buses starting at 8:01 P.M.

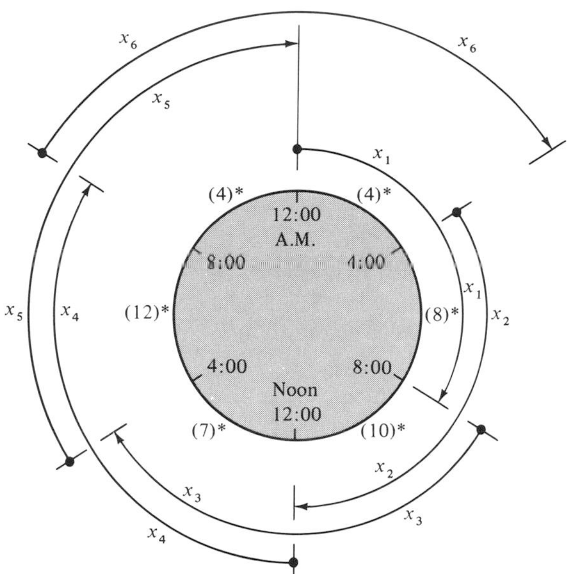

*Represents the minimum requirement in the 4-hour period.

Figure 2-12

The mathematical model (see Figure 2-12) is thus written as

$$\text{minimize } z = x_1 + x_2 + x_3 + x_4 + x_5 + x_6$$

subject to

$$\begin{aligned}
x_1 \qquad\qquad\qquad\qquad\qquad + x_6 &\geq 4 \quad \text{(12:01 A.M.–4:00 A.M.)} \\
x_1 + x_2 \qquad\qquad\qquad\qquad &\geq 8 \quad \text{(4:01 A.M.–8:00 A.M.)} \\
x_2 + x_3 \qquad\qquad\qquad &\geq 10 \quad \text{(8:01 A.M.–12:00 noon)} \\
x_3 + x_4 \qquad\qquad &\geq 7 \quad \text{(12:01 P.M.–4:00 P.M.)} \\
x_4 + x_5 \qquad &\geq 12 \quad \text{(4:01 P.M.–8:00 P.M.)} \\
x_5 + x_6 &\geq 4 \quad \text{(8:01 P.M.–12:00 A.M.)} \\
x_j \geq 0, \quad j = 1, 2, \ldots, 6
\end{aligned}$$

The output of the model in Figure 2-13 shows that a total of 26 buses is needed to satisfy the demand. The optimum schedule calls for $x_1 = 4$ buses to start at 12:01 A.M., $x_2 = 10$ at 4:01 A.M., $x_4 = 8$ at 12:01 P.M., and $x_5 = 4$ at 4:01 P.M. The reduced costs are all zero, which indicates that the problem has alternative optimum solutions. The dual prices yield interesting information. A dual price of 1 indicates that a unit increase in the minimum number of buses required for the corresponding period is coupled with an equal increase in the total number of buses in operation. On the other hand, a dual price of zero indicates that an increase in the minimum requirements will not result in an increase of the total number of buses in operation. These increases, however, are limited by the ranges specified in Figure 2-13. For example, the minimum requirement for period 2 (constraint 2) can be increased from 8 to 14 without requiring a net increase in the total number of buses in operation. Similarly, each unit increase in the minimum requirement of period 3 beyond 10 will increase the total number of operations by an equal amount. This type of information is significant in shedding light on the behavior of the optimum solution.

```
                 *** OPTIMUM SOLUTION SUMMARY ***
---------------------------------------------------------------------------
Title: Bus scheduling
Final iteration No: 5
Objective value (min) =    26.0000
==>ALTERNATIVE solution detected at x3
---------------------------------------------------------------------------
Variable     Value        Obj  Coeff     Obj Val Contrib    Reduced Cost
---------------------------------------------------------------------------
x1            4.0000        1.0000           4.0000           0.0000
x2           10.0000        1.0000          10.0000           0.0000
x3            0.0000        1.0000           0.0000           0.0000
x4            8.0000        1.0000           8.0000           0.0000
x5            4.0000        1.0000           4.0000           0.0000
x6            0.0000        1.0000           0.0000           0.0000

---------------------------------------------------------------------------
Constraint   RHS          Slack(-)/Surplus(+)        Dual Price
---------------------------------------------------------------------------
1(>)         4.0000           0.0000+                   1.0000
2(>)         8.0000           6.0000+                   0.0000
3(>)        10.0000           0.0000+                   1.0000
4(>)         7.0000           1.0000+                   0.0000
5(>)        12.0000           0.0000+                   1.0000
6(>)         4.0000           0.0000+                   0.0000

                  *** SENSITIVITY ANALYSIS ***
Objective coefficients -- Single Changes:
==>DEGENERATE or ALTERNATE optimum. Dual prices may not be unique
---------------------------------------------------------------------------
Variable    Current  Coeff   Min Coeff       Max Coeff       Reduced Cost
---------------------------------------------------------------------------
x1           1.0000          0.0000          1.0000           0.0000
x2           1.0000          0.0000          1.0000           0.0000
x3           1.0000          1.0000          infinity         0.0000
x4           1.0000          1.0000          1.0000           0.0000
x5           1.0000          1.0000          1.0000           0.0000
x6           1.0000          1.0000          infinity         0.0000

Right-hand Side -- Single Changes:
==>DEGENERATE or ALTERNATE optimum. Dual prices may not be unique
---------------------------------------------------------------------------
Constraint  Current RHS     Min RHS        Max RHS          Dual Price
---------------------------------------------------------------------------
1(>)           4.0000       0.0000        infinity           1.0000
2(>)           8.0000      -infinity      14.0000            0.0000
3(>)          10.0000       4.0000        infinity           1.0000
4(>)           7.0000      -infinity       8.0000            0.0000
5(>)          12.0000      11.0000        infinity           1.0000
6(>)           4.0000       0.0000         5.0000            0.0000
```

Figure 2-13

It is important to point out that a sensitivity analysis of the objective coefficients may not be meaningful in the present example because the nature of the model requires these coefficients to equal 1 always. If, however, the objective function is restructured to reflect other measures (e.g., minimization of the operating cost of the buses), the situation will be different and a sensitivity analysis of these coefficients would be meaningful. ◀

Exercise 2.3-1

(a) Study the application of the model to the following situations:

(1) Number of nurses in a hospital.

(2) Number of police officers in a city.
(3) Number of waiters and waitresses in a 24-hour cafeteria.
(4) Number of operators in a telephone exchange center.

(b) If the operating cost for buses that *start* between 8:01 A.M. and 8:00 P.M. is about 80% that of buses that *start* between 8:01 P.M. and 8:00 A.M., how can this information be incorporated in the model?
[*Ans.* Change the objective function to minimize $z = .8(x_3 + x_4 + x_5) + (x_1 + x_2 + x_6)$.]

Example 2.3-2 (Trim-Loss or Stock-Slitting Problem). The Pacific Paper Company produces paper rolls with a standard width of 20 feet each. Special customer orders with different widths are produced by slitting the standard rolls. Typical orders (which may vary from day to day) are summarized in the following table:

Order	Desired Width (ft)	Desired Number of Rolls
1	5	150
2	7	200
3	9	300

In practice, an order is filled by setting the slitting knives to the desired widths. Usually, there are a number of ways in which a standard roll can be slit to fill a given order. Figure 2-14 shows three possible knife settings for the 20-foot roll. Although there are other feasible settings, we limit the discussion for the moment to considering settings *A*, *B*, and *C* in Figure 2-14. We can combine the given settings in a number of ways to fill orders for widths 5, 7, and 9 feet. The following are two examples of feasible combinations:

1. Slit 300 (standard) rolls using setting *A* and 75 rolls using *B*.
2. Slit 200 rolls using setting *A* and 100 rolls using setting *C*.

Which combination is better? We can answer this question by considering the "waste" that each combination will produce. In Figure 2-14 the shaded portion represents surplus rolls not wide enough to fill the required orders. These surplus

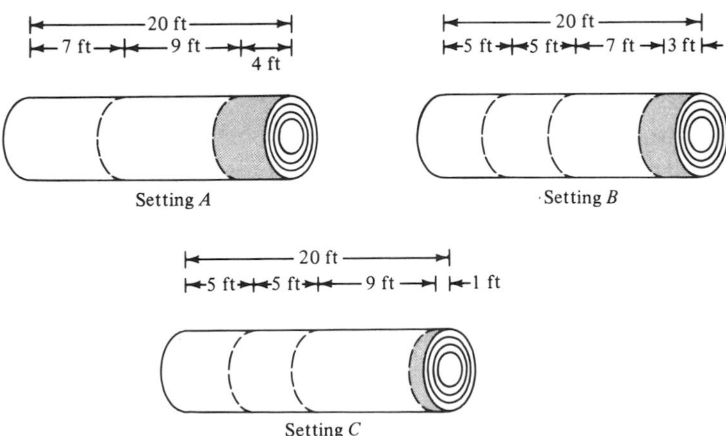

Figure 2-14

rolls are referred to as *trim loss.* We can thus evaluate the "goodness" of each combination by computing its trim loss. However, since the surplus rolls may have different widths, we should base the evaluation on the *area* of trim loss rather than the number of surplus rolls. Thus, assuming that the standard roll has a length L feet, we can compute the trim-loss area as follows (see Figure 2-14):

combination 1: $300(4 \times L) + 75(3 \times L) = 1425L \text{ ft}^2$

combination 2: $200(4 \times L) + 100(1 \times L) = 900L \text{ ft}^2$

These areas account only for the shaded portions in Figure 2-14. Note, however, that any surplus production of the 5-, 7-, and 9-foot rolls must be considered in the computation of the trim-loss area. Thus, in combination 1, setting A will produce a surplus of $300 - 200 = 100$ extra 7-foot rolls while setting B will produce 75 extra 7-foot rolls. Thus the additional "waste" area is $175\ (7 \times L) = 1225L \text{ ft}^2$. Combination 2 does not produce surplus rolls of the 7- and 9-foot rolls. Setting C, however, does produce $200 - 150 = 50$ extra 5-foot rolls, with an added waste area of $50\ (5 \times L) = 250L \text{ ft}^2$. As a result we have

$$\begin{pmatrix}\text{total trim loss area}\\ \text{for combination 1}\end{pmatrix} = 1425L + 1225L = 1650L \text{ ft}^2$$

$$\begin{pmatrix}\text{total trim loss area}\\ \text{for combination 2}\end{pmatrix} = 900L + 250L = 1150L \text{ ft}^2$$

Combination 2 is thus better because it yields a smaller trim-loss area.

To obtain the optimum solution to the problem, it would be necessary first to determine all possible knife settings and then generate *all* the feasible combinations. Although the determination of all the settings may not be too difficult, generating all feasible combinations may be a formidable task. The need for a systematic approach is thus evident. This is what the LP model will accomplish.

Mathematical Representation

We seek to determine the *knife setting combinations* (variables) that will *fill the required orders* (constraints) with the *least trim-loss area* (objective).

The definition of the variables as given must be translated in a way that the mill operator can use. By studying the way we constructed the two combinations, we note that the variables should be defined as *the number of standard rolls to be slit according to a given knife setting.* This definition obviously requires identifying all possible knife settings as summarized in the following table. Settings 1, 2, and 3 are given in Figure 2-14. You should convince yourself of the validity of the remaining settings and that no "promising" settings have been forgotten. Keep in mind that a promising setting cannot yield a trim-loss roll of width 5 feet or higher.

Required Width (ft)	Knife Settings						Minimum Number of Rolls
	1	2	3	4	5	6	
5	0	2	2	4	1	0	150
7	1	1	0	0	2	0	200
9	1	0	1	0	0	2	300
Trim loss per foot of length	4	3	1	0	1	2	

To express the model mathematically, we define the variables as

x_j = number of standard rolls to be slit according to setting j
$j = 1, 2, \ldots, 6$

The constraints of the model deal directly with satisfying the minimum number of rolls ordered. Thus, if all the settings exhibited in the table are used, we get

$$\text{number of 5-ft rolls produced} = 2x_2 + 2x_3 + 4x_4 + x_5$$
$$\text{number of 7-ft rolls produced} = x_1 + x_2 + 2x_5$$
$$\text{number of 9-ft rolls produced} = x_1 + x_3 + 2x_6$$

These expressions represent the actual number of rolls produced with widths of 5, 7, and 9 feet, and thus must equal at least 150, 200, and 300 rolls, respectively. These are all the constraints of the model.

To construct the objective function, we observe the following: The total trim loss area is the difference between the total area of the standard rolls used and the total area representing all the orders. Thus

$$\text{total area of standard rolls} = 20L(x_1 + x_2 + x_3 + x_4 + x_5 + x_6)$$
$$\text{total area of orders} = L(150x_5 + 200x_7 + 300x_9) = 4850L$$

Given that the length L of the standard roll is a constant, the objective function effectively reduces to

$$\text{minimize } z = x_1 + x_2 + x_3 + x_4 + x_5 + x_6$$

The general model may thus be written as

$$\text{minimize } z = x_1 + x_2 + x_3 + x_4 + x_5 + x_6$$

subject to

$$\begin{aligned} 2x_2 + 2x_3 + 4x_4 + x_5 &\geq 150 \quad \text{(5-ft rolls)} \\ x_1 + x_2 + 2x_5 &\geq 200 \quad \text{(7-ft rolls)} \\ x_1 + x_3 + 2x_6 &\geq 300 \quad \text{(9-ft rolls)} \\ x_j \geq 0, \quad j &= 1, 2, \ldots, 6 \end{aligned}$$

◀

Exercise 2.3-2

(a) Using the table of knife settings given in Example 2.3-2, express each of the following feasible solutions in terms of the variables x_j and compute the trim-loss area in each case.
  (1) 200 rolls using setting 1 and 100 rolls using setting 3.
  [*Ans.* $x_1 = 200$, $x_3 = 100$, trim-loss area $= 1150L$ ft^2.]
  (2) 50 rolls using setting 2, 75 rolls using setting 5, and 150 rolls using setting 6.
  [*Ans.* $x_2 = 50$, $x_5 = 75$, $x_6 = 150$, trim-loss area $= 650L$ ft^2.]

(b) Suppose that the only available standard roll is 15 feet wide. Generate all possible knife settings for producing 5-, 7-, and 9-foot rolls and compute the associated trim loss per foot length.
[*Ans.* Settings: (3, 0, 0), (0, 2, 0), (1, 1, 0), and (1, 0, 1). Trim loss per foot for the four settings: (0, 1, 3, 1).]

The optimum solution of the model in Figure 2-15 indicates that the problem has more than one alternative optimum, which means that for the same number of standard rolls different settings may be used to satisfy the order on hand. Notice,

```
*** OPTIMUM SOLUTION SUMMARY ***

Title: Trim loss problem
Final iteration No: 5
Objective value (min) =  262.5000
==>ALTERNATIVE solution detected at x4
```

Variable	Value	Obj Coeff	Obj Val Contrib	Reduced Cost
x1 stng 1	0.0000	1.0000	0.0000	-0.1250
x2 stng 2	0.0000	1.0000	0.0000	-0.1250
x3 stng 3	25.0000	1.0000	25.0000	0.0000
x4 stng 4	0.0000	1.0000	0.0000	0.0000
x5 stng 5	100.0000	1.0000	100.0000	0.0000
x6 stng 6	137.5000	1.0000	137.5000	0.0000

Constraint	RHS	Slack(-)/Surplus(+)	Dual Price
1(>)	150.0000	0.0000+	0.2500
2(>)	200.0000	0.0000+	0.3750
3(>)	300.0000	0.0000+	0.5000

```
*** SENSITIVITY ANALYSIS ***
Objective coefficients -- Single Changes:
==>DEGENERATE or ALTERNATE optimum. Dual prices may not be unique
```

Variable	Current Coeff	Min Coeff	Max Coeff	Reduced Cost
x1 stng 1	1.0000	0.8750	infinity	-0.1250
x2 stng 2	1.0000	0.8750	infinity	-0.1250
x3 stng 3	1.0000	0.5000	1.0000	0.0000
x4 stng 4	1.0000	1.0000	infinity	0.0000
x5 stng 5	1.0000	0.2500	1.2500	0.0000
x6 stng 6	1.0000	1.0000	1.2000	0.0000

```
Right-hand Side -- Single Changes:
==>DEGENERATE or ALTERNATE optimum. Dual prices may not be unique
```

Constraint	Current RHS	Min RHS	Max RHS	Dual Price
1(>)	150.0000	100.0000	700.0000	0.2500
2(>)	200.0000	0.0000	300.0000	0.3750
3(>)	300.0000	25.0000	infinity	0.5000

Figure 2-15

however, that the given solution calls for cutting 25 standard rolls according to setting 3, 100 according to setting 5, and 137.5 according to setting 6. The solution is not implementable because x_6 is noninteger. We can either use an integer algorithm to solve the problem (see Chapter 9), or round the LP solution so that x_6 will assume the conservative value of 138 instead.

In view of the nature of the trim-loss model, particularly regarding the integer requirement, the solution results may have to be interpreted in a slightly different manner. For example, the dual price of .25 corresponding to constraint 1 signifies that an increase of 1 roll in the demand for the 5-foot rolls will require cutting an additional one-fourth of a standard 20-foot roll. This recommendation is obviously impractical. However, we can instead recommend that for every four additional 5-foot rolls, it will be necessary to cut an extra standard 20-foot roll. This recommendation is valid so long as we are within the range [100, 700] specified by the right-hand-side ranging. A similar analysis applies to the remaining dual prices.

Example 2.3-3 (Goal Programming). In the previous examples, the constraints represent permanent relationships; that is, the left and right sides of each constraint are related by one of three relationships: $\leq$, $\geq$, or $=$. Practical situations exist, however, where it may be advantageous to violate a constraint, possibly at the expense of incurring a penalty. For example, a company entertaining a number of business ventures usually operates under limited capital restrictions, but may elect to exceed that limit by borrowing additional money. The penalty incurred in this case is the cost of borrowed money (interest). Naturally, a loan can be justified on an economic basis only if the new business ventures are profitable. This type of modeling is sometimes referred to as **goal programming**, since the model automatically adjusts the level of certain resources to satisfy the goal of the decision maker.

We illustrate the goal programming model by a simple example. Two products are manufactured by passing sequentially through two different machines. The time available for the two products on each machine is limited to 8 hours daily but may be exceeded by up to 4 hours on an overtime basis. Each overtime hour will cost an additional \$5. The production rates for the two products together with their profits per unit are summarized in the table that follows. It is required to determine the production level for each product that will maximize the net profit.

	Production Rate (units/hr)	
Machine	Product 1	Product 2
1	5	6
2	4	8
Profit per unit	\$6	\$4

Mathematical Representation

It is required to determine the *number of units of each product* (variables) that *maximizes net profit* (objective) provided that the *maximum allowable machine hours are exceeded only on an overtime basis* (constraints).

Let

$$x_j = \text{number of units of product } j, \qquad j = 1, 2$$

In the absence of the overtime option, the constraints of the model are written as

$$x_1/5 + x_2/6 \leq 8 \qquad \text{(machine 1)}$$
$$x_1/4 + x_2/8 \leq 8 \qquad \text{(machine 2)}$$

To include the overtime option, we can rewrite the constraints as

$$x_1/5 + x_2/6 - y_1 \qquad = 8$$
$$x_1/4 + x_2/8 \qquad - y_2 = 8$$

where the variables y_1 and y_2 are unrestricted in sign for the following reason. If y_i is *negative*, the 8-hour limit on the capacity of the machine is not exceeded and no overtime is used. If it is *positive*, the used machine hours will exceed the daily limit and y_i will thus represent the overtime hours.

We have accounted for the overtime option by letting y_i assume unrestricted values. Next, we need to limit the daily use of overtime to 4 hours and also to include the cost of overtime in the objective function. Since y_i is positive only when overtime is used, the constraints

$$y_i \leq 4, \qquad i = 1, 2$$

will provide the desired restriction on the use of overtime. Note that the constraint becomes redundant when $y_i < 0$ (no overtime).

We now consider the objective function. Our goal is to maximize the net profit that equals the total profit from the two products *less* the additional cost of overtime. The expression for the total profit is given directly by $6x_1 + 4x_2$. To include the overtime cost, we note that it is incurred only when $y_i > 0$. Thus a suitable way for expressing the overtime cost is

$$\begin{aligned}\text{overtime cost} &= \text{cost per hour} \times \text{overtime hours}\\ &= 5(\max\{0, y_i\})\end{aligned}$$

Note that $\max\{0, y_i\} = 0$ when $y_i < 0$, which yields zero overtime cost, as desired.

The complete model can thus be written as

$$\text{maximize } z = 6x_1 + 4x_2 - 5(\max\{0, y_1\} + \max\{0, y_2\})$$

subject to

$$\begin{aligned}
x_1/5 + x_2/6 - y_1 \qquad &= 8\\
x_1/4 + x_2/8 \qquad - y_2 &= 8\\
y_1 \qquad &\leq 4\\
y_2 &\leq 4\\
x_1, x_2 &\geq 0\\
y_1, y_2 &\text{ unrestricted in sign}
\end{aligned}$$

To convert the model to a linear program, we use the substitution

$$w_i = \max\{0, y_i\}$$

which is equivalent to

$$w_i \geq y_i \qquad \text{and} \qquad w_i \geq 0$$

because the *negative* coefficient of w_i in the objective function will force it to assume the smallest possible *nonnegative* value: zero or y_i. Thus the LP model can be written as

$$\text{maximize } z = 6x_1 + 4x_2 - 5(w_1 + w_2)$$

subject to

$$\begin{aligned}
x_1/5 + x_2/6 - y_1 \qquad\qquad &= 8\\
x_1/4 + x_2/8 \qquad - y_2 \qquad\qquad &= 8\\
y_1 \qquad - w_1 \qquad &\leq 0\\
y_2 \qquad - w_2 &\leq 0\\
y_1 \qquad\qquad &\leq 4\\
y_2 \qquad\qquad &\leq 4\\
x_1, x_2, w_1, w_2 &\geq 0\\
y_1, y_2 &\text{ unrestricted in sign}
\end{aligned}$$

◀

Exercise 2.3-3

(a) Suppose that a feasible solution to the model of Example 2.3-3 yields $y_1 = 2$ and $y_2 = -1$, what does this mean in terms of the use of regular time and overtime?

[*Ans.* Machine 1 will use 2 hours of overtime and machine 2 will have 1 hour of unused regular time.]

(b) In part (a), compute the additional cost due to overtime using the objective function as defined in terms of w_i.
[*Ans.* $y_1 = 2$ will make $w_1 \geq 2$. By the optimization process $w_1 = 2$ and the associated term in the objective function is $-5 \times 2 = -\$10$. For $y_2 = -1$, $w_2 \geq -1$, but since $w_2 \geq 0$ by definition, the optimization process will force w_2 to equal zero. Hence its term in the objective function will be $-5 \times 0 = 0$.]

The dual prices in Figure 2-16 show that within the ranges [5.6, 12] and [5, 11], an increase of 1 hour of regular time for machines 1 and 2 results in a corresponding

*** OPTIMUM SOLUTION SUMMARY ***

Title:Goal Programming
Final iteration No: 9
Objective value (max) = 283.9998

Variable	Value	Obj Coeff	Obj Val Contrib	Reduced Cost
x1 x1	30.0001	6.0000	180.0005	0.0000
x2 x2	35.9998	4.0000	143.9993	0.0000
x3 y1	4.0000	0.0000	0.0000	0.0000
x4 y2	4.0000	0.0000	0.0000	0.0000
x5 w1	4.0000	-5.0000	-20.0000	0.0000
x6 w2	4.0000	-5.0000	-20.0000	0.0000

Constraint	RHS	Slack(-)/Surplus(+)	Dual Price
1(=)	8.0000	0.0000	14.9999
2(=)	8.0000	0.0000	12.0001
3(<)	0.0000	0.0000-	5.0000
4(<)	0.0000	0.0000-	5.0000
5(<)	4.0000	0.0000-	9.9999
6(<)	4.0000	0.0000-	7.0001

*** SENSITIVITY ANALYSIS ***

Objective coefficients -- Single Changes:

Variable	Current Coeff	Min Coeff	Max Coeff	Reduced Cost
x1 x1	6.0000	5.3000	7.3333	0.0000
x2 x2	4.0000	3.3333	4.5833	0.0000
x3 y1	0.0000	-9.9999	infinity	0.0000
x4 y2	0.0000	-7.0001	infinity	0.0000
x5 w1	-5.0000	-14.9999	0.0000	0.0000
x6 w2	-5.0000	-12.0001	0.0000	0.0000

Right-hand Side -- Single Changes:

Constraint	Current RHS	Min RHS	Max RHS	Dual Price
1(=)	8.0000	5.6000	12.0000	14.9999
2(=)	8.0000	5.0000	11.0000	12.0001
3(<)	0.0000	-infinity	4.0000	5.0000
4(<)	0.0000	-infinity	4.0000	5.0000
5(<)	4.0000	1.6000	8.0000	9.9999
6(<)	4.0000	1.0000	7.0000	7.0001

Figure 2-16

revenue increase of \$14.9999 and \$12.0001, respectively. On the other hand, within the ranges [1.6, 7] and [1, 7] an increase of 1 hour of overtime for machines 1 and 2 will increase the revenue by \$9.9999 and \$7.0001, respectively. The difference between the two cases is \$5.00, which actually represents the (additional) cost per hour of overtime.

2.4 SUMMARY

The graphical LP formulation is used in this chapter to draw general conclusions about the LP problem, its method of solution, and the sensitivity of the optimum to changes in the parameters of the LP model. From the standpoint of devising a general solution method for the LP problem, the graphical solution reveals the important observation that the optimum LP solution will always be associated with a corner (or extreme) point of the solution space. This result is the key idea for the development of the general procedure, called the simplex method, for solving linear programs algebraically.

The LP problem can be viewed in a unified framework as a resource allocation model in which limited resources (represented by the constraints) are allocated to economic activities (the variables). Assuming a maximization LP problem, the profitability of an economic activity is measured in terms of its usage of the resources and its contribution to the objective function. The net effect of these two factors is measured by the *reduced* cost of the economic activity. *Dual prices*, on the other hand, provide a measure of the impact of changes in the availability of the resources on the optimum objective value. This information, coupled with objective coefficient and right-hand-side ranging, form an important basis for the analysis of the behavior of the optimum solution.

SELECTED REFERENCES

BAZARAA, M., J. JARVIS, and H. SHERALI, *Linear Programming and Network Flows*, Wiley, New York, 1990.

BRADLEY, S., A. HAX, and T. MAGNANTI, *Applied Mathematical Programming*, Addison-Wesley, Reading, Mass., 1977.

SCHRAGE, L., *Linear, Integer, and Quadratic Programming with LINDO*, 3rd ed., Scientific Press, Palo Alto, Calif., 1986.

WILLIAM, H., *Model Building in Mathematical Programming*, 2nd ed., Wiley, New York, 1985.

PROBLEMS

Section	Assigned Problems
2.1.1	2–1 to 2–20
2.1.2	2–21 to 2–27
2.2, 2.3	2–28 to 2–38

□ **2–1** Using the rule given at the start of Section 2.1.1, identify the feasible space for each of the following constraints independently. Assume that all variables are nonnegative.

(a) $-3x_1 + x_2 \le 7$. (b) $x_1 - 2x_2 \ge 5$. (c) $2x_1 - 3x_2 \le 8$.
(d) $x_1 - x_2 \le 0$. (e) $-x_1 + x_2 \ge 0$.

□ **2–2** Identify the direction of increase or decrease in z for each of the following cases:

(a) Maximize $z = x_1 - x_2$. (b) Minimize $z = -3x_1 + x_2$.
(c) Minimize $z = -x_1 - 2x_2$. (d) Maximize $z = -5x_1 - 6x_2$.

□ **2–3** A small furniture factory manufactures tables and chairs. It takes 2 hours to assemble a table and 30 minutes to assemble a chair. Assembly is carried out by four workers on the basis of a single 8-hour shift per day. Customers usually buy at most four chairs with each table, meaning that the factory must produce at most four times as many chairs as tables. The sale price is \$135 per table and \$50 per chair. Determine the daily production mix of chairs and tables that would maximize the total daily revenue to the factory and comment on the significance of the obtained solution.

□ **2–4** A farmer owns 200 pigs that consume 90 lb of special feed daily. The feed is prepared as a mixture of corn and soybean meal with the following compositions:

Feedstuff	Pounds per Pound of Feedstuff			Cost (dollars/lb)
	Calcium	Protein	Fiber	
Corn	.001	.09	.02	.20
Soybean meal	.002	.60	.06	.60

The dietary requirements of the pigs are

1. At most 1% calcium.
2. At least 30% protein.
3. At most 5% fiber.

Determine the daily minimum-cost feed mix.

□ **2–5** A small bank is allocating a maximum of \$20,000 for personal and car loans during the next month. The bank charges an annual interest rate of 14% for personal loans and 12% for car loans. Both types of loans are repaid at the end of a one-year period. The amount of car loans should be at least twice as much as that of personal loans. Past experience has shown that bad debts amount to 1% of all personal loans. How should the funds be allocated?

□ **2–6** The Popeye Canning Company is contracted to receive 60,000 lb of ripe tomatoes at 7 cents/lb from which it produces both canned tomato juice and tomato paste. The canned products are packaged in cases of 24 cans each. A single can of juice requires 1 lb of fresh tomatoes whereas that of paste requires 1/3 lb only. The company's share of the market is limited to 2000 cases of juice and 6000 cases of paste. The wholesale prices per case of juice and paste stand at \$18 and \$9, respectively. Devise a production schedule for Popeye.

□ **2–7** A radio assembly plant produces two models, HiFi-1 and HiFi-2, on the same assembly line. The assembly line consists of three stations. The assembly times in the workstations are

	Minutes per Unit of:	
Workstation	HiFi-1	HiFi-2
1	6	4
2	5	5
3	4	6

Each workstation has a maximum availability of 480 minutes per day. However, the workstations require daily maintenance, which amounts to 10%, 14%, and 12% of the 480 minutes daily availability for stations 1, 2, and 3, respectively. The company wishes to determine the daily units to be assembled of HiFi-1 and HiFi-2 to minimize the sum of unused (idle) times at all three workstations.

□ **2–8** An electronic company manufactures two radio models, each on a separate production line. The daily capacity of the first line is 60 radios and that of the second is 75 radios. Each unit of the first model uses 10 pieces of a certain electronic component, whereas each unit of the second model requires 8 pieces of the same component. The maximum daily availability of the special component is 800 pieces. The profit per unit of models 1 and 2 is \$30 and \$20, respectively. Determine the optimum daily production of each model.

□ **2–9** Two products are manufactured by passing sequentially through three machines. Time per machine allocated to the two products is limited to 10 hours per day. The production time and profit per unit of each product are

	Minutes per Unit			
Product	Machine 1	Machine 2	Machine 3	Profit
1	10	6	8	\$2
2	5	20	15	\$3

Find the optimal mix of the two products.

□ **2–10** A company can advertise its product by using local radio and TV stations. Its budget limits the advertisement expenditures to \$1000 a month. Each minute of radio advertisement costs \$5, and each minute of TV advertisement costs \$100. The company would like to use the radio at least twice as much as the TV. Past experience shows that each minute of TV advertisement will usually generate 25 times as many sales as each minute of radio advertisement. Determine the optimum allocation of the monthly budget to radio and TV advertisements.

□ **2–11** A company produces two products, A and B. The sales volume for product A is at least 60% of the total sales of the two products. Both products use the same raw material, of which the daily availability is limited to 100 lb. Products A and B use this raw material at the rates of 2 lb/unit and 4 lb/unit, respectively. The sales price for the two products are \$20 and \$40 per unit. Determine the optimal allocation of the raw material to the two products.

☐ **2–12** A company produces two types of cowboy hats. Each hat of the first type requires twice as much labor time as does each hat of the second type. If all hats are of the second type only, the company can produce a total of 500 hats a day. The market limits daily sales of the first and second types to 150 and 200 hats. Assume that the profit per hat is \$8 for type 1 and \$5 for type 2. Determine the number of hats of each type to produce to maximize profit.

☐ **2–13** Determine the solution space graphically for the following inequalities.

$$x_1 + x_2 \leq 4$$
$$4x_1 + 3x_2 \leq 12$$
$$-x_1 + x_2 \geq 1$$
$$x_1 + x_2 \leq 6$$
$$x_1, x_2 \geq 0$$

Which constraints are redundant? Reduce the system to the smallest number of constraints that will define the same solution space.

☐ **2–14** Write the constraints associated with the solution space shown in Figure 2-17 and identify all redundant constraints.

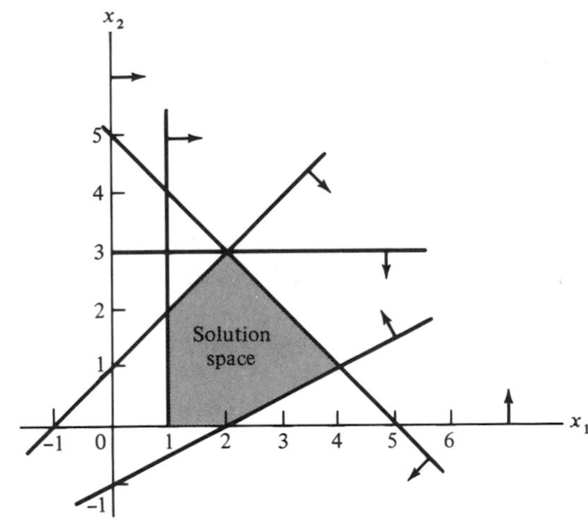

Figure 2-17

☐ **2–15** Consider the following problem:

$$\text{maximize } z = 6x_1 - 2x_2$$

subject to

$$x_1 - x_2 \leq 1$$
$$3x_1 - x_2 \leq 6$$
$$x_1, x_2 \geq 0$$

Show graphically that at the optimal solution the variables x_1 and x_2 can be increased indefinitely while the value of the objective function remains constant.

☐ **2–16** Solve the following problem graphically:

$$\text{maximize } z = 5x_1 + 6x_2$$

subject to

$$\begin{aligned} x_1 - 2x_2 &\geq 2 \\ -2x_1 + 3x_2 &\geq 2 \\ x_1, x_2 &\text{ unrestricted in sign} \end{aligned}$$

☐ **2–17** Consider the following problem:

$$\text{maximize } z = 3x_1 + 2x_2$$

subject to

$$\begin{aligned} 2x_1 + x_2 &\leq 2 \\ 3x_1 + 4x_2 &\geq 12 \\ x_1, x_2 &\geq 0 \end{aligned}$$

Show graphically that the problem has no *feasible* extreme points. What can one conclude concerning the solution to the problem?

☐ **2–18** Solve the following problem graphically:

$$\text{maximize } z = 5x_1 + 2x_2$$

subject to

$$\begin{aligned} x_1 + x_2 &\leq 10 \\ x_1 &= 5 \\ x_1, x_2 &\geq 0 \end{aligned}$$

☐ **2–19** In Problem 2–18, identify numerically the extreme points of the solution space. If the constraint $x_1 = 5$ is changed to $x_1 \leq 5$, determine all the *feasible* extreme points and find the optimum by evaluating the objective function numerically at each point. Show that the answer agrees with the graphical solution. Repeat the procedure with $x_1 = 5$ replaced by $x_1 \geq 5$.

☐ **2–20** Consider the solution space in Figure 2–17 (Problem 2–14). Determine the optimum solution assuming that the objective function is as given:

(a) Minimize $z = 2x_1 + 6x_2$. (b) Maximize $z = -3x_1 + 4x_2$.
(c) Minimize $z = 3x_1 + 4x_2$. (d) Minimize $z = x_1 - 2x_2$.
(e) Minimize $z = x_1$. (f) Maximize $z = x_1$.

☐ **2–21** In Problem 2–3, determine the following:

(a) The dual price (worth per unit) of an extra hour of labor and the range for which the price applies.
(b) The dual price for the constraint limiting the number of chairs relative to the number of tables. What is the economic meaning of the dual price of this constraint?

(c) The conditions on the sale prices of chairs and tables that will keep the current optimum unchanged.

□ **2–22** Consider the model in Problem 2–4. Determine the cost per additional pound of feed. What is the maximum amount of daily feed that can be acquired at this cost? Provide an interpretation of the constraints associated with the dietary requirements.

□ **2–23** Consider the model of Problem 2–5. What is the effective annual rate of return for each additional $1000 invested in loans? What is the maximum investment that can be gained at this rate?

□ **2–24** Consider the model in Problem 2–7.

(a) Determine all the dual prices and their associated applicability ranges.
(b) Which machines should be increased in capacity and what effect will this have on the optimum idle time?

□ **2–25** Consider the model in Problem 2–8.

(a) Determine the worth per unit of supplying additional electronic components and the range in which this price prevails.
(b) Determine the conditions relating the profit per unit for the two models that will keep the current solution optimal.
(c) Study the impact of increasing the capacities of the two lines on the optimum solution.

□ **2–26** Consider Problem 2–9, where three machines are used to manufacture two products.

(a) Determine the worth per unit increase in the capacity of each machine and their associated applicability ranges.
(b) Determine the ranges for the profit per unit of each product that will keep the current solution optimum.

□ **2–27** Consider the model in Problem 2–10.

(a) Determine the dual prices for the model.
(b) Is it economically attractive to recommend an increase in radio advertisement over the limits imposed by the model? Explain.
(c) Determine the increase in sales per minute of radio advertisement that will make it more attractive economically to assign the entire monthly budget to radio advertisement only.

□ **2–28** Four products are processed successively on two machines. The manufacturing times in hours per unit of each product are tabulated for the two machines:

	Time per Unit (hr)			
Machine	Product 1	Product 2	Product 3	Product 4
1	2	3	4	2
2	3	2	1	2

The total cost of producing 1 unit of each product is based directly on the machine time. Assume that the cost per hour for machines 1 and 2 is \$10 and \$5, respectively. The total hours budgeted for all the products on machines 1 and 2 are 500 and 380. If the sales price per unit for products 1, 2, 3, and 4 are \$65, \$70, \$55, and \$45, formulate the problem as a linear programming model to maximize total net profit. Analyze the optimum solution.

☐ **2–29** A manufacturer produces three models (I, II, and III) of a certain product. He uses two types of raw material (A and B), of which 4000 and 6000 units are available, respectively. The raw material requirements per unit of the three models are

Raw Material	Requirements per Unit of Given Model		
	I	II	III
A	2	3	5
B	4	2	7

The labor time for each unit of model I is twice that of model II and three times that of model III. The entire labor force of the factory can produce the equivalent of 1500 units of model I. A market survey indicates that the minimum demand for the three models is 200, 200, and 150 units, respectively. However, the ratios of the number of units produced must be equal to 3 : 2 : 5. Assume that the profit per unit of models I, II, and III is \$30, \$20, and \$50, respectively. Formulate the problem as a linear programming model to determine the number of units of each product that will maximize profit. Analyze the optimum solution.

☐ **2–30**† A construction company can participate over the next year in two upcoming projects. The quarterly cash flow for the two projects (the upward arrows represent expenses) is summarized in Figure 2-18. All funds are in millions of dollars. The company has cash funds of \$1,000,000 per quarter and may borrow an equal amount at the start of each quarter at the nominal rate of 10% annually. Any borrowed amount must be repaid at the beginning of the following quarter. Surplus funds may be invested at 8% per year.

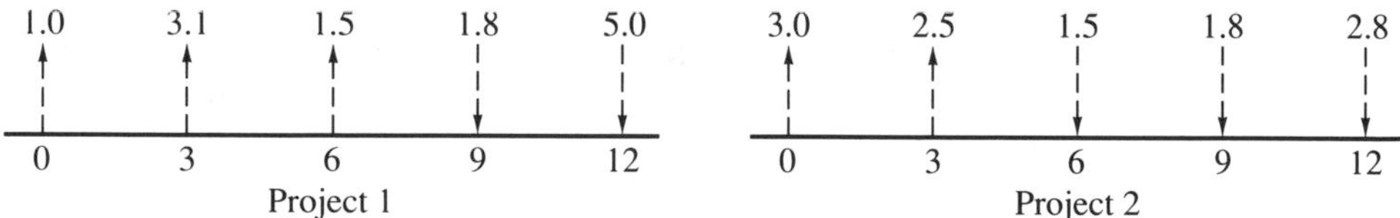

Figure 2-18

The construction company wishes to determine the net result (profit or loss) if the projects are undertaken. We shall assume that the company may participate in the projects either partially or fully. Partial participation will scale the cash flow funds proportionately.

† This problem is motivated by a similar model in Schrage (1986, pp. 104–105) (see Selected References).

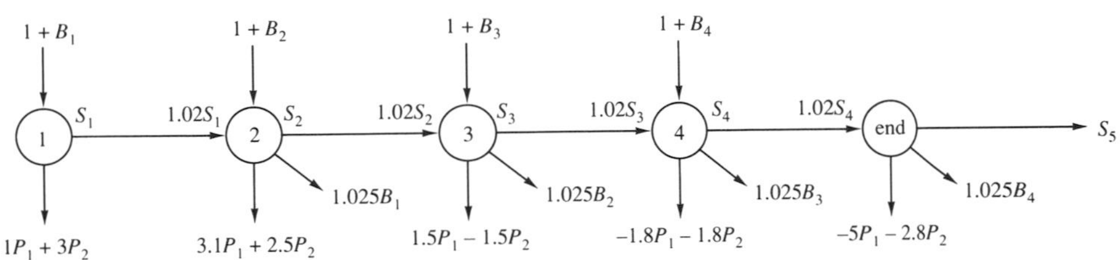

Figure 2-19

The cash flow of the model can be depicted as shown in Figure 2-19. The constraints can be written directly as balance equations for each of the five nodes. Notice that node 5 represents the end of the fourth quarter. The objective is to maximize the accumulated funds at the end of the year. The model is given as

$$\text{maximize } z = S_5$$

subject to

$$\begin{aligned}
P_1 + 3P_2 + S_1 - B_1 &= 1 \\
3.1P_1 + 2.5P_2 - 1.02S_1 + S_2 + 1.025B_1 - B_2 &= 1 \\
1.5P_1 - 1.5P_2 - 1.02S_2 + S_3 + 1.025B_2 - B_3 &= 1 \\
-1.8P_1 - 1.8P_2 - 1.02S_3 + S_4 + 1.025B_3 - B_4 &= 1 \\
-5P_1 - 2.8P_2 - 1.02S_4 + S_5 + 1.025B_4 &= 1 \\
0 \le P_i \le 1, \quad & i = 1, 2 \\
0 \le B_j \le 1, \quad & j = 1, 2, 3, 4
\end{aligned}$$

where

P_i = fraction of project i to be undertaken ($0 \le P_i \le 1$), $i = 1, 2$
B_j = amount borrowed (millions of dollars) in quarter j, $j = 1, 2, 3, 4$
S_j = surplus amount (millions of dollars) at the start of quarter j, $j = 1, 2, 3, 4$

The optimum solution of the model is shown in Figure 2-20.

(a) What is the solution recommended for the problem?
(b) Is it possible in any period to borrow money and simultaneously end up with surplus funds? Explain.
(c) Give an economic interpretation of the dual prices associated with the first five constraints of the model.
(d) Show how the dual price associated with the upper bound on B_3 (= .149) can be computed directly from the dual prices of the first five constraints.

□ **2–31** In anticipation of the immense college expenses of their child, a couple has started an annual investment program on the child's eighth birthday that will last until the eighteenth birthday. Judging from their expected financial position over the next 10 years, the couple estimates that they will be able to invest the following amounts at the beginning of each year:

Year	1	2	3	4	5	6	7	8	9	10
Amount	$2000	2000	2500	2500	3000	3500	3500	4000	4000	5000

*** OPTIMUM SOLUTION SUMMARY ***

Title: investment
Final iteration No: 9
Objective value (max) = 5.8366

Variable	Value	Obj Coeff	Obj Val Contrib	Reduced Cost
x1 P1	0.7113	0.0000	0.0000	0.0000
x2 P2	0.0000	0.0000	0.0000	0.3796
x3 S1	0.2887	0.0000	0.0000	0.0000
x4 S2	0.0000	0.0000	0.0000	0.0060
x5 S3	0.0000	0.0000	0.0000	0.1541
x6 S4	1.2553	0.0000	0.0000	0.0000
x7 S5	5.8366	1.0000	5.8366	0.0000
x8 B1	0.0000	0.0000	0.0000	0.0061
x9 B2	0.9104	0.0000	0.0000	0.0000
x10 B3	1.0000	0.0000	0.0000	0.0000
x11 B4	0.0000	0.0000	0.0000	0.0050

Constraint	RHS	Slack(-)/Surplus(+)	Dual Price
1(=)	1.0000	0.0000	1.2488
2(=)	1.0000	0.0000	1.2243
3(=)	1.0000	0.0000	1.1945
4(=)	1.0000	0.0000	1.0200
5(=)	1.0000	0.0000	1.0000
UB-x1 P1	1.0000	0.2887-	0.0000
UB-x2 P2	1.0000	1.0000-	0.0000
UB-x8 B1	1.0000	1.0000-	0.0000
UB-x9 B2	1.0000	0.0896-	0.0000
UB-x10 B3	1.0000	0.0000-	0.1490
UB-x11 B4	1.0000	1.0000-	0.0000

Figure 2-20

To avoid unpleasant surprises, the couple opts to invest the money very safely. The following options are open to them:

1. Insured savings with 7.5% annual yield.
2. Six-year government bonds that yield 7.9% and have a current market price equal to .98 face value.
3. Nine-year municipal bonds yielding 8.5% and having a current market price equal to 1.02 face value.

How should the couple invest the money over the next 10 years?

☐ **2–32** A business executive has the option of investing money in two plans. Plan A guarantees that each dollar invested will earn 70 cents a year hence, and plan B guarantees that each dollar invested will earn $2.00 two years hence. In plan B, only investments for periods that are multiples of 2 years are allowed. How should the executive invest $100,000 to maximize the earnings at the end of 3 years? Formulate the problem as a linear programming model and analyze the optimum solution.

☐ **2–33** Suppose that the *minimum* number of buses required at the ith hour of the day is b_i, $i = 1, 2, \ldots, 24$. Each bus runs 6 consecutive hours. If the number of buses in period i exceeds the minimum required b_i, an excess cost c_i per bus hour is incurred. Formulate the problem as a linear programming model so as to minimize the total excess cost incurred.

□ **2–34** Consider the problem of assigning three types of aircraft to four routes. The table gives the pertinent data:

Aircraft Type	Capacity (passengers)	Number of Aircraft	Number of Daily Trips on Route			
			1	2	3	4
1	50	5	3	2	2	1
2	30	8	4	3	3	2
3	20	10	5	5	4	2
	Daily number of customers		1000	2000	900	1200

The associated costs are

Aircraft Type	Operating Cost per Trip on Given Route ($)			
	1	2	3	4
1	1000	1100	1200	1500
2	800	900	1000	1000
3	600	800	800	900
Penalty per lost customer	40	50	45	70

Formulate the problem as a linear programming model and analyze the optimum solution.

□ **2–35** Two alloys, A and B, are made from four different metals, I, II, III, and IV, according to the following specifications.

Alloy	Specifications
A	At most 80% of I At most 30% of II At least 50% of IV
B	Between 40 and 60% of II At least 30% of III At most 70% of IV

The four metals are extracted from three different ores:

Ore	Maximum Quantity (tons)	Constituents (%)					($/ton)
		I	II	III	IV	Others	
1	1000	20	10	30	30	10	30
2	2000	10	20	30	30	10	40
3	3000	5	5	70	20	0	50

Assuming that the selling prices of alloys A and B are $200 and $300 per ton, formulate the problem as a linear programming model and analyze the results.

[*Hint:* Let X_{ij} be tons of ore i allocated to alloy k and, w_k tons of alloy k produced.]

☐ **2–36** A gambler plays a game that requires dividing bet money among four different choices. The game has three outcomes. The following table gives the corresponding gain (or loss) per dollar deposited in each of the four choices for the three outcomes.

	Gain (or Loss) per Dollar Deposited in Given Choice			
Outcome	1	2	3	4
1	−3	4	−7	15
2	5	−3	9	4
3	3	−9	10	−8

Assume that the gambler has a total of $500, which may be played only once. The exact outcome of the game is not known a priori, and in face of this uncertainty the gambler decided to make the allocation that would maximize the *minimum* return. Formulate the problem as a linear programming model and analyze the results.

[*Hint:* The gambler's return may be negative, zero, or positive.]

☐ **2–37** A manufacturing company produces a final product that is assembled from three different parts. The parts are manufactured within the company by two different departments. Because of the specific setup of the machines, each department produces the three parts at different rates. The following table provides the production rates together with the maximum number of hours the two departments can allocate weekly to manufacturing the three parts.

	Maximum Weekly	Production Rate (units/hr)		
Department	Capacity (hr)	Part 1	Part 2	Part 3
1	100	8	5	10
2	80	6	12	4

It would be ideal if the two departments could adjust their production facilities to produce equal quantities of the three parts, as this would result in perfect matches in terms of the final assembly. This objective may be difficult to accomplish because of the variations in production rates. A more realistic goal would be to maximize the number of final assembly units, which in essence is equivalent to minimizing the mismatches resulting from shortages in one or more parts.

Formulate the problem as an LP model and analyze the results.

☐ **2–38** In Example 2.3-3, we can use the following substitution for the unrestricted variable y_i.

$$y_i = -(y_i' - y_i'')$$

where y_i' and y_i'' are *nonnegative* variables. This substitution has the property that when $y_i' > 0$, $y_i'' = 0$ and when $y_i'' > 0$, $y_i' = 0$. We can thus think of y_i' as the amount of unused resource. In this case, y_i'' will represent the amount by which the available resource is exceeded. Show how this substitution can be implemented in Example 2.3-3 and analyze the results.

Chapter 3

Linear Programming: The Simplex Method

In this chapter we present the details of the simplex algorithm, an algebraic method that can solve any linear programming problem. The information that can be secured from the simplex method goes beyond determining the optimum values of the variables and the objective function. Indeed, the simplex solution provides economic interpretations and sensitivity analysis results similar to those presented in Chapter 2.

3.1 OVERALL IDEA OF THE SIMPLEX METHOD

The graphical method presented in Chapter 2 demonstrates that the optimum LP is always associated with an extreme or corner point of the solution space. This idea precisely governs the development of the simplex method. In essence, what the simplex method does is to translate the geometric definition of the extreme point into an algebraic definition. This point should be kept in mind throughout the presentation of the simplex method.

How does the simplex method identify the extreme (or corner) points algebraically? As an initial step, the simplex method requires that each of the constraints be put in a special standard form (see Section 3.2.1) in which all the constraints are expressed as equations by augmenting slack or surplus variables as necessary. This type of conversion normally results in a set of simultaneous equations in which the number of variables exceeds the number of equations, which generally means that the equations yield an infinite number of solution points (compare with the graphical solution space). The extreme points of this space can be identified algebraically by the **basic solutions** of the system of simultaneous equations. From the theory of linear algebra, a basic solution is obtained by setting to zero as many variables as the difference between the total number of variables and the total number of equations and then solving for the remaining variables, provided that the condition results in a unique solution. In essence, the transition from the graphical to the algebraic procedure rests squarely on the validity of the following important relationship:

$$\text{extreme points} \Leftrightarrow \text{basic solutions}$$

In the absence of a graphical solution space to guide us toward the optimum point, we need a procedure that identifies promising basic solutions intelligently. What the simplex method does is to identify a starting basic solution and then move systematically to other basic solutions that have the potential to improve the value of the objective function. Eventually, the basic solution corresponding to the optimum will be identified and the computational process will end. In effect, the simplex method is an iterative computational procedure in which each iteration is associated with a basic solution.

The determination of a basic solution in the simplex method typically involves tedious computational details. Such details should not distract you from concentrating on the fundamental idea of the method: to generate successive basic solutions in a manner that will lead you to the optimum extreme point. All the computational details are thus secondary to this basic idea and you should treat them as such.

3.2 DEVELOPMENT OF THE SIMPLEX METHOD

In this section we present the details of the simplex method. It starts with the construction of the standard form needed to represent the LP solution space by a system of simultaneous equations. The remainder of the presentation shows how the successive basic solutions are determined selectively for the purpose of reaching the optimum solution point in a finite number of iterations.

As you study the remainder of this chapter, you will be introduced to two variants of the simplex method: the primal simplex and the dual simplex algorithms. On the surface, the two methods appear to be different. This is not the case, and indeed the essence of the two algorithms is still based on the idea that the extreme points of the solution space are completely identified by the basic solutions of the LP model. Basically, the two algorithms appear to be different because they are designed to take advantage of the special initial setup of the LP model. This point will be stressed as we present the details of the two procedures.

3.2.1 STANDARD LP FORM

We have seen in Chapter 2 that an LP model may include constraints of all types ($\leq$, $\geq$, $=$). Moreover, the variables may be nonnegative or unrestricted in sign. To develop a general solution method, the LP problem must be put in a common format, which we will call the standard form. The properties of this form are as follows:

1. All the constraints are equations (with nonnegative right-hand side if the model is solved by the primal simplex method—see Section 3.3).
2. All the variables are nonnegative.
3. The objective function may be maximization or minimization.

As explained later, the second property requiring all the variables to be nonnegative is crucial in the development of the (primal and dual) simplex methods.

We now show how any LP model can be put in the standard form.

A. Constraints

1. A constraint of the type $\leq$ ($\geq$) can be converted to an equation by adding a **slack** variable to (subtracting a **surplus** variable from) the left side of the constraint. For example, in the constraint

$$x_1 + 2x_2 \leq 6$$

we add a *slack* $s_1 \geq 0$ to the left side to obtain the equation

$$x_1 + 2x_2 + s_1 = 6, \qquad s_1 \geq 0$$

Next, consider the constraint

$$3x_1 + 2x_1 - 3x_3 \geq 5$$

Since the left side is not smaller than the right side, we subtract a *surplus* variable $s_2 \geq 0$ from the left side to obtain the equation

$$3x_1 + 2x_1 - 3x_3 - s_2 = 5, \qquad s_2 \geq 0$$

2. The right side of an equation can always be made nonnegative by multiplying both sides by -1. For example, $2x_1 + 3x_2 - 7x_3 = -5$ is mathematically equivalent to $-2x_1 - 3x_2 + 7x_3 = +5$.

3. The direction of an inequality is reversed when both sides are multiplied by -1. For example, whereas $2 < 4$, $-2 > -4$. Thus the inequality $2x_1 - x_2 \leq -5$ can be replaced by $-2x_1 + x_2 \geq 5$.

Exercise 3.2-1

Convert the following inequalities to equations with nonnegative right-hand sides by using two procedures: (1) Multiply both sides by -1 and then augment the slack or surplus variable. (2) Convert the inequalities to equations first and then multiply both sides by -1. Does it make a difference which procedure is followed?

(a) $x_1 - 2x_2 \geq -2$.

(b) $-2x_1 + 7x_2 \leq -1$.

[*Ans.* (a) $-x_1 + 2x_2 + s_1 = 2$, $s_1 \geq 0$. (b) $2x_1 - 7x_2 - s_1 = 1$, $s_1 \geq 0$. The two procedures are exactly equivalent.]

B. Variables

An **unrestricted** variable y_i can be expressed in terms of two *nonnegative* variables by using the substitution

$$y_i = y_i' - y_i'' \qquad y_i', y_i'' \geq 0$$

The substitution must be effected throughout *all* the constraints and in the objective function.

The LP problem is normally solved in terms of y_i' and y_i'', from which y_i is determined by reverse substitution. An interesting property of y_i' and y_i'' is that in the optimal (simplex) LP solution only *one* of the two variables can assume a positive value, but never both. Thus, when $y_i' > 0$, $y_i'' = 0$, and vice versa. In the case where (unrestricted) y_i represents both slack and surplus, we can think of y_i' as a *slack* variable and of y_i'' as a *surplus* variable since only one of the two can assume a positive value at a time. This observation is used extensively in *goal programming* (see Example 2.3-3) and, indeed, is the basis for the conversion idea introduced in Problem 2–38.

Exercise 3.2-2

The substitution $y = y' - y''$ is used in an LP model to replace unrestricted y by the two nonnegative variables y' and y''. If y assumes the respective values -6, 10, and 0, determine the associated optimal values of y' and y'' in each case.

[*Ans.* (1) $y' = 0$, $y'' = 6$; (2) $y' = 10$, $y'' = 0$; (3) $y' = y'' = 0$.]

C. Objective Function

Although the standard LP model can be of either the maximization or the minimization type, it is sometimes useful to convert one form to the other. The maximization of a function is equivalent to the minimization of the *negative* of the same function, and vice versa. For example,

$$\text{maximize } z = 5x_1 + 2x_2 + 3x_3$$

is mathematically equivalent to

$$\text{minimize } (-z) = -5x_1 - 2x_2 - 3x_3$$

Equivalence means that for the same set of constraints the *optimum* values of x_1, x_2, and x_3 are the same in both cases. The only difference is that the values of the objective functions, although equal numerically, will appear with opposite signs.

Example 3.2-1. Write the following LP model in the standard form

$$\text{minimize } z = 2x_1 + 3x_2$$

subject to

$$\begin{aligned} x_1 + x_2 &= 10 \\ -2x_1 + 3x_2 &\leq -5 \\ 7x_1 - 4x_2 &\leq 6 \\ x_1 &\text{ unrestricted} \\ x_2 &\geq 0 \end{aligned}$$

The following changes must be effected.

1. Add the slack $s_2 \geq 0$ to the left side of the second constraint.
2. Add a slack variable $s_3 \geq 0$ to the left side of the third constraint.
3. Substitute $x_1 = x_1' - x_1''$, where $x_1', x_1'' \geq 0$, in the objective function and all the constraints.

Thus we get the standard form as

$$\text{minimize } z = 2x_1' - 2x_1'' + 3x_2$$

subject to

$$\begin{aligned} x_1' - x_1'' + x_2 \qquad\qquad &= 10 \\ -2x_1' + 2x_1'' + 3x_2 + s_2 \qquad &= -5 \\ 7x_1' - 7x_1'' - 4x_2 \qquad + s_3 &= 6 \\ x_1', x_1'', x_2, s_2, s_3, &\geq 0 \end{aligned}$$

If it is desired to make all the right-hand sides of the equations positive, we simply multiply both sides of the second equation by -1. ◀

3.2.2 BASIC SOLUTIONS

Consider the standard LP model defined in Section 3.2.1 with m equations and n unknowns. An associated basic solution is determined by setting $n - m$ variables equal to zero and then solving the m equations in the remaining m variables, provided that the resulting solution exists and is unique. To illustrate this point, consider the following system of equations:

$$\begin{aligned} 2x_1 + x_2 + 4x_3 + x_4 &= 2 \\ x_1 + 2x_2 + 2x_3 + x_4 &= 3 \end{aligned}$$

In this example we have $m = 2$ and $n = 4$. A basic solution is thus associated with $n - m = 4 - 2 = 2$ *zero* variables. This means that the given set of equations can have $n!/m!(n - m)! = 4!/2!2! = 6$ possible basic solutions. We say "possible" basic solutions because some combinations may not yield basic solutions at all. For example, take the combination in which x_2 and x_4 are set equal to zero. In this case the system reduces to

$$2x_1 + 4x_3 = 2$$
$$x_1 + 2x_3 = 3$$

The two equations are inconsistent, and hence no solution exists. The conclusion is that x_1 and x_3 cannot form a basic solution and hence do not correspond to an extreme point.

Alternatively, consider the case where x_3 and x_4 are set equal to zero. This yields the equations

$$2x_1 + x_2 = 2$$
$$x_1 + 2x_2 = 3$$

The corresponding unique solution ($x_1 = 1/3$, $x_2 = 4/3$), together with $x_3 = 0$ and $x_4 = 0$, define a basic solution and hence an extreme point of the LP solution space.

In LP, we refer to the $n - m$ variables that are set equal to zero as **nonbasic variables**, in which case the remaining m variables are referred to as **basic variables** (provided, of course, that a unique solution exists). A basic solution is said to be **feasible** if all its solution values are nonnegative. An example of this case is the basic feasible solution ($x_1 = 1/3$, $x_2 = 4/3$, $x_3 = 0$, $x_4 = 0$). To illustrate the case of an **infeasible** basic solution, consider the combination in which the nonbasic variables are $x_1 = 0$ and $x_2 = 0$. The equations above thus yield

$$4x_3 + x_4 = 2$$
$$2x_3 + x_4 = 3$$

The corresponding basic solution is ($x_3 = -1/2$, $x_4 = 4$), which is infeasible because x_3 is negative.

In solving the LP problem, we will be interested in both feasible and infeasible basic solutions. Specifically, we will see that all the iterations of the primal simplex method are always associated with basic *feasible* solutions only. The dual simplex method, on the other hand, deals with *infeasible* basic solutions until the last iteration where the associated basic solution must be feasible. In essence, the primal simplex method deals with feasible extreme points only, whereas in the dual simplex method all but the last iteration are associated with infeasible extreme points. At the end, both methods yield feasible basic solutions as stipulated by the nonnegativity conditions of the LP model.

3.3 PRIMAL SIMPLEX METHOD

The primal simplex method starts from a *feasible basic* solution (extreme point) and continues to iterate through successive *feasible basic* solutions until the optimum is reached. Figure 3-1 illustrates the application of this process to the Reddy Mikks model. The process starts at the origin extreme (point A) and moves along the **edge** AB of the solution space to the **adjacent** extreme point B (iteration 1). From B it moves along the edge BC to the adjacent extreme point C (iteration 2), which is the

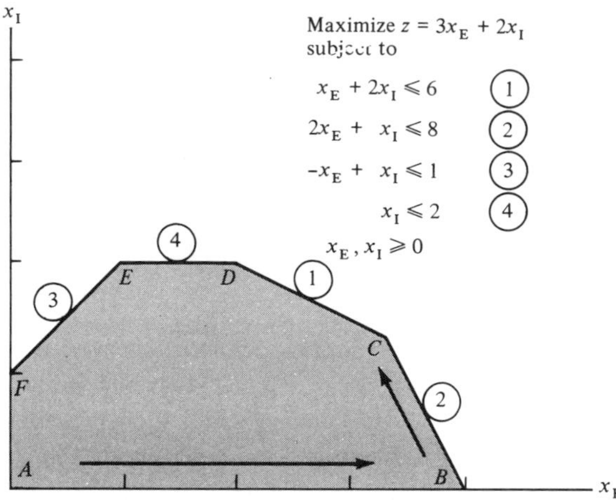

Figure 3-1

optimum. Notice that the procedure is not capable of cutting across the solution space (e.g., from A to C) but must always move along the edges among *adjacent* extreme points.

How does the iterative procedure given above translate algebraically? All we have to do is show how extreme points such as A, B, and C are identified without the benefit of the graphical solution space. Consider the Reddy Mikks model in standard form given below:

$$\text{maximize } z = 3x_E + 2x_I + 0s_1 + 0s_2 + 0s_3 + 0s_4$$

subject to

$$\begin{aligned}
x_E + 2x_I + s_1 \qquad\qquad\qquad &= 6\\
2x_E + x_I \qquad + s_2 \qquad\qquad &= 8\\
-x_E + x_I \qquad\qquad + s_3 \qquad &= 1\\
x_I \qquad\qquad\qquad + s_4 &= 2\\
x_E, x_I, s_1, s_2, s_3, s_4 &\geq 0
\end{aligned}$$

The model has $m = 4$ equations and $n = 6$ variables. Thus the number of nonbasic (zero) variables must equal $6 - 4 = 2$. If we choose $x_1 = 0$ and $x_2 = 0$ as the nonbasic variables, immediately, and without any computations, we obtain the basic feasible solution $s_1 = 6$, $s_2 = 8$, $s_3 = 1$, and $s_4 = 2$ (the origin point A in Figure 3-1). This basic solution represents the **starting solution** (or iteration) of the simplex method. The corresponding objective value is determined by expressing the objective function in the following form (which we will refer to as the z-equation):

$$z - 3x_E - 2x_I = 0$$

Since x_E and x_I at A are zero, the associated value of z is automatically given by the right-hand side of the equation above (= 0).

The easy algebraic determination of the starting basic solution in the Reddy Mikks model is attributed to:

1. Each equation has a slack variable.
2. The right-hand sides of all the constraints are nonnegative.

The first property guarantees that the number of slacks is equal to the number of equations. Thus all the remaining variables can be used as nonbasic (zero) variables.

Since by property 2 all the right-hand sides of the equations are nonnegative, the resulting basic solution is automatically feasible, as required by the primal simplex method.

The next logical point following the identification of the starting solution is to investigate moving to a new basic solution. From the standpoint of optimization, we would be interested in moving to another basic solution only if we can realize improvements in the value of the objective function. First keep in mind that a new basic solution is secured only by making at least one of the current nonbasic (zero) variables basic. In the simplex method, we make the change by bringing in one nonbasic variable at a time. Intuitively, such a nonbasic variable can be brought into the solution only if it improves the value of the objective function. In terms of the Reddy Mikks model, x_E and x_I are nonbasic ($= 0$) at A. Looking at the objective z-equation

$$z - 3x_E - 2x_I = 0$$

we see that a unit increase in x_E will increase z by 3 and a unit increase in x_I will increase z by 2. Since we are maximizing, either one of the two variables can improve the objective value. However, to devise an unambiguous computational rule, the simplex method uses a heuristic; namely, in the case of maximization, the selected nonbasic variable is the one having the most negative coefficient in the objective z-equation. By using such a heuristic, it is hoped (but not guaranteed) that the simplex method will make the largest "jumps" in the objective value as it moves from one iteration to the next, thus reaching the optimum in the smallest number of iterations. The application of this condition to the Reddy Mikks model will result in x_E being the **entering variable.**

The new basic solution obtained by admitting the entering variable must include exactly m basic variables. This means that one of the current basic variables must leave the solution. In the Reddy Mikks example, the **leaving variable** must be one of the variables s_1, s_2, s_3, or s_4. Looking at Figure 3-2, we notice that the value of the entering variable in the *new* solution corresponds to point B. Any increase beyond this point will put us outside the feasible space. From the definition of the constraints, this means that s_2 (associated with constraint 2) will be zero, which means that s_2 is the leaving variable.

We can select the leaving variable directly from the constraint equations simply by computing the *nonnegative* intercepts of all the constraints with the x_E axis. The smallest such intercept will identify the leaving variable. In the Reddy Mikks model, only constraints 1 and 2 intersect the x_E axis in the positive direction, with the respective intercepts being equal to $6/1 = 6$ and $8/2 = 4$, respectively. Since the smaller intercept ($= 4$) is associated with the second constraint, the basic variable s_2 must leave the solution.

How can we automate the process of selecting the leaving variable without the benefit of the graphic solution space? All we have to do is to compute all the intercepts of the constraints with the x_E axis as the *ratio* of the right-hand side to the corresponding constraint coefficient of x_E; namely,

$$\begin{aligned}
&\text{constraint 1 intercept} = 6/1 = 6\\
&\text{constraint 2 intercept} = 8/2 = 4\\
&\text{constraint 3 intercept} = 1/-1 = -1\\
&\text{constraint 4 intercept} = 2/0 = \text{infinity}
\end{aligned}$$

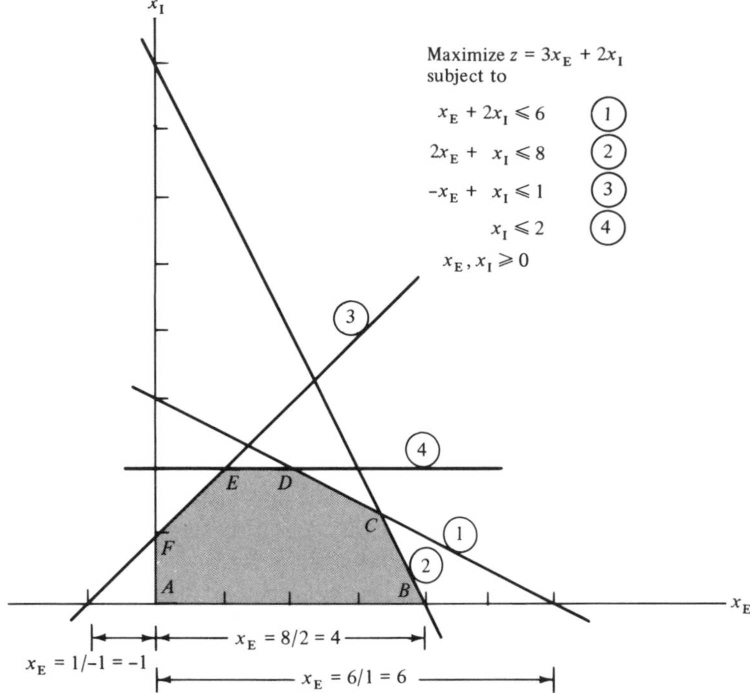

Figure 3-2

The first three intercepts are depicted in Figure 3-2. The fourth intercept cannot be shown because constraint 4 is parallel to the x_E axis. We are not interested in the third intercept because it is negative, meaning that the third constraint does not limit x_E in the positive direction. Neither are we interested in constraint 4, since it does not intersect x_E at all. That leaves only intercepts 1 and 2, with the conclusion that s_2 must be the leaving variable. In a mechanical sense, we can automate the process above by considering only those constraints that have *strictly positive* constraint coefficients for the entering variable.

The procedures given above for selecting the entering and the leaving variables are referred to as the **optimality** and **feasibility conditions**. We note that the feasibility (minimum intercept) condition is equally applicable to both the maximization and the minimization problems. On the other hand, the optimality condition for the minimization problem differs in that the entering variable is associated with the most positive nonbasic coefficient (as compared with the most negative in the case of maximization).

The following is a formal summary of the two simplex conditions:

Optimality Condition: The entering variable in maximization (minimization) is the nonbasic variable with the most negative (positive) coefficient in the objective z-equation. A tie may be broken arbitrarily. The optimum is reached when *all* the nonbasic coefficients in the z-equation are nonnegative (nonpositive).

Feasibility Condition: For both maximization and minimization problems, the leaving variable is the current basic variable having the smallest intercept (minimum ratio with strictly positive denominator) in the direction of the entering variable. A tie is broken arbitrarily.

We are now ready to present the formal iterative steps of the primal simplex method:

Step 0: Using the standard form (with all nonnegative right-hand sides), determine a starting basic feasible solution.

Step 1: Select an *entering variable* from among the current *nonbasic* variables using the optimality condition.

Step 2: Select the *leaving variable* from the current *basic* variables by using the feasibility condition.

Step 3: Determine the values of the new basic variables by making the entering variable basic and the leaving variable nonbasic. Go to step 1.

With some reflection, you will realize that the primal simplex method is based on rather plausible arguments. Specifically, at a given basic solution (extreme point) we seek a new basic solution only if an increase in the values of any of the current nonbasic variables can improve the objective value (optimality condition). If we find such a nonbasic variable, one of the current basic variables must leave the solution to satisfy the requirement that the number of basic variables must exactly equal m. The selection of the leaving variable is achieved by using the feasibility condition. The process of "swapping" a basic variable with a nonbasic variable is exactly equivalent to moving between adjacent extreme points along the edges of the solution space (compare with Figure 3-1). This is really all there is in the primal simplex method. However, you need to heed the following advice. When we start explaining how the so-called Gauss–Jordan method is used to effect the "swapping" of the entering and the leaving variables, you will encounter computational details that are both monotonous and tedious. Our long teaching experience indicates that most beginners are "consumed" by these details, thus losing track of what the simplex method actually accomplishes. To avoid falling in this trap, remember that the main goal of the Gauss–Jordan computational procedure is to transform the equations in a manner that enables us to obtain the new basic solution by assigning zero values to the current nonbasic variables. Other than that, the Gauss–Jordan procedure has no special significance as far as the theory of the simplex method is concerned. Better yet, remember that you need to go through these tedious computations only a few times, after which you can use TORA (or any other software) to handle this chore. What you should concentrate on throughout the chapter is the interpretation of the solutions obtained by the Gauss–Jordan computations. This will be the essence of our presentation.

Example 3.3-1. We use the Reddy Mikks model to explain the computational details of the primal simplex method. This will require expressing the problem in the standard form. A convenient way for summarizing these equations is to use the following tableau form:

Basic	z	x_E	x_I	s_1	s_2	s_3	s_4	Solution	
z	1	−3	−2	0	0	0	0	0	z-equation
s_1	0	1	2	1	0	0	0	6	s_1-equation
s_2	0	2	1	0	1	0	0	8	s_2-equation
s_3	0	−1	1	0	0	1	0	1	s_3-equation
s_4	0	0	1	0	0	0	1	2	s_4-equation

The tableau above corresponds to the starting basic solution of the model. The information in the tableau reads as follows. The "basic" column identifies the current basic variables s_1, s_2, s_3, and s_4, whose values are given in the "solution" column. This implicitly assumes that the nonbasic variables x_E and x_I (those not present in the "basic" column) are at zero value. The corresponding value of the objective function is $z = 3 \times 0 + 2 \times 0 + 0 \times 6 + 0 \times 8 + 0 \times 1 + 0 \times 2 = 0$, as shown in the solution column.

Upon applying the optimality condition, x_E has the most negative coefficient in the z-equation and hence is selected as the entering variable. The feasibility condition shows that s_2 corresponds to the smallest intercept and hence must leave the solution.

Having identified the entering and the leaving variables, we need to determine the new basic solution that now must include s_1, x_E, s_3, and s_4. This is achieved by applying the **Gauss–Jordan elimination** method. The method starts by identifying the column under the entering variable x_E as the **entering column.** The row associated with the leaving variable will be called the **pivot equation** and the element at the intersection of the entering column and the pivot equation will be referred to as the **pivot element.** The following tableau summarizes these definitions:

Entering column ↓ (x_E)

	Basic	z	x_E	x_I	s_1	s_2	s_3	s_4	Solution	x_E intercepts (ratios)
	z	1	-3	-2	0	0	0	0	0	
	s_1	0	1	2	1	0	0	0	6	$6/1 = 6$
Pivot ← equation	s_2	0	2 ← Pivot element	1	0	1	0	0	8	$8/2 = ④$
	s_3	0	-1 (crossed out)	1	0	0	1	0	1	—
	s_4	0	0 (crossed out)	1	0	0	0	1	2	—

The Gauss–Jordan method effects a change of basis by using two types of computations:

1. Pivot equation:

$$\text{new pivot equation} = \text{old pivot equation} \div \text{pivot element}$$

2. All other equations, including z:

$$\text{new equation} = (\text{old equation}) - (\text{its } \textbf{entering column} \text{ coefficient}) \times (\text{new pivot equation})$$

These two types of computation essentially solve for the new basic solution by substituting out the entering variable in all but the pivot equation.

Applying type 1 computations to the tableau above, we divide the s_2-equation by the pivot element 2. Since x_E takes the place of s_2 in the basic column, type 1 computations will change the starting tableau as shown below.

Basic	z	x_E	x_I	s_1	s_2	s_3	s_4	Solution
z								
s_1								
x_E	0	1	1/2	0	1/2	0	0	$8/2 = 4$
s_3								
s_4								

Notice that the "solution" column yields the new value of x_E (= 4), which equals the minimum ratio of the feasibility condition.

To complete the tableau, we carry out the following type 2 computations.

1. z-equation:

old z-equation:	(1	-3	-2	0	0	0	0	0)
$-(-3) \times$ new pivot equation:	(0	3	3/2	0	3/2	0	0	12)
= new z-equation:	(1	0	$-1/2$	0	3/2	0	0	12)

2. s_1-equation:

old s_1-equation:	(0	1	2	1	0	0	0	6)
$-(1) \times$ new pivot equation:	(0	-1	$-1/2$	0	$-1/2$	0	0	-4)
= new s_1-equation:	(0	0	3/2	1	$-1/2$	0	0	2)

3. s_3-equation:

old s_3-equation:	(0	-1	1	0	0	1	0	1)
$-(-1) \times$ new pivot equation:	(0	1	1/2	0	1/2	0	0	4)
= new s_3-equation:	(0	0	3/2	0	1/2	1	0	5)

4. s_4-equation. The new s_4-equation is the same as the old s_4-equation because its *entering column* coefficient is zero.

The complete new tableau thus looks as follows:

Basic	z	x_E	x_I	s_1	s_2	s_3	s_4	Solution	x_I intercepts (ratios)
z	1	0	$-1/2$	0	3/2	0	0	12	
s_1	0	0	3/2	1	$-1/2$	0	0	2	$\frac{2}{3/2} = \frac{4}{3}$ (circled)
x_E	0	1	1/2	0	1/2	0	0	4	$\frac{4}{1/2} = 8$
s_3	0	0	3/2	0	1/2	1	0	5	$\frac{5}{3/2} = \frac{10}{3}$
s_4	0	0	1	0	0	0	1	2	$2/1 = 2$

The new solution gives $x_E = 4$ and $x_I = 0$ (point B in Figure 3-2). The value of z has increased from 0 to 12. The increase follows because each unit increase in x_E contributes 3 to the value of z; thus the total increase in z is $3 \times 4 = 12$.

Notice that the new tableau has the same properties as the preceding one; namely, once the nonbasic variables x_I and s_2 are set equal to zero, the values of the basic variables are immediately given in the solution column. This is precisely what the Gauss–Jordan method accomplishes.

Examining the last tableau, we find that the optimality condition selects x_I as the entering variable because its z-coefficient is $-1/2$. The feasibility condition then shows that s_1 is the leaving variable. The ratios shown in the last tableau indicate that x_I enters the basic solution at the value 4/3 (= minimum ratio), thus improving the value of the objective function by $(4/3) \times (1/2) = 2/3$.

The following Gauss–Jordan operations will produce the new tableau:

(i) New pivot (s_1) equation = old s_1-equation $\div$ (3/2).
(ii) New z-equation = old z-equation $-$ $(-1/2) \times$ new pivot equation.
(iii) New x_E-equation = old x_E-equation $-$ $(1/2) \times$ new pivot equation.
(iv) New s_3-equation = old s_3-equation $-$ $(3/2) \times$ new pivot equation.
(v) New s_4-equation = old s_4-equation $-$ $(1) \times$ new pivot equation.

These computations lead to the following tableau.

Basic	z	x_E	x_I	s_1	s_2	s_3	s_4	Solution
z	1	0	0	1/3	4/3	0	0	$12\frac{2}{3}$
x_I	0	0	1	2/3	$-1/3$	0	0	4/3
x_E	0	1	0	$-1/3$	2/3	0	0	10/3
s_3	0	0	0	-1	1	1	0	3
s_4	0	0	0	$-2/3$	1/3	0	1	2/3

The solution yields $x_E = 3\frac{1}{3}$ and $x_I = 1\frac{1}{3}$ (point C in Figure 3-2). The value of z has increased from 12 in the preceding tableau to $12\frac{2}{3}$. The increase $(12\frac{2}{3} - 12) = 2/3$ is the result of x_I increasing from 0 to 4/3, with each unit increase accounting for 1/2 in the objective function. The total increase in z thus equals $(4/3) \times (1/2) = 2/3$.

The last tableau is optimal because *none* of the *non*basic variables have a negative coefficient in the z-equation. This completes the simplex method computations. ◀

Computer Drill

Use TORA's ("user-guided") option to force s_1 (= sx3 in the TORA output) to leave the basic solution even though it is not associated with the minimum ratio. Now view the resulting tableau and note how the value of s_2 (= sx4) becomes negative, indicating that the resulting solution is infeasible. The exercise demonstrates why the leaving variable must correspond to the smallest ratio. (To reinforce your understanding of infeasibility, mark TORA's solution on the solution space in Figure 3-2.)

Computer Drill

The optimality condition stipulates that the entering variable in the maximization problem is associated with the most negative objective coefficient. Actually, the condition is only a *rule of thumb* that is *likely* to lead to the optimum solution more rapidly. In fact, *any* nonbasic variable having a negative objective coefficient can be a candidate for entering the solution. You can experiment with this point by applying TORA's interactive option to the Reddy Mikks model, always selecting the entering variable as the one with the *least* negative objective coefficient. The number of iterations will be larger, but the final optimal solution will remain the same. Experience has shown that this result is true in most (but not necessarily all) cases.

Exercise 3.3-1

(a) In the application of the simplex method to a *maximization* model, suppose that the entering variable is selected to be *any* of the nonbasic variables with a negative coefficient in the z-equation. Will the simplex method eventually reach the optimum solution?
[*Ans.* Yes, because a negative z-coefficient of a nonbasic variable indicates that the value of z can increase when this variable is increased above zero. The only advantage of selecting the nonbasic variable with the most negative coefficient is that it has the potential to reach the optimum in the smallest number of iterations.]

(b) Consider the graphical solution of the Reddy Mikks model given in Figure 3-2. Starting at the origin (point A), suppose that x_I is selected as the entering variable. Determine the ratios of the feasibility condition directly from the graphical space; then compare them with those obtained from the starting simplex tableau. Which current basic variable should leave the basic solution?
[*Ans.* The ratios (intercepts) are 3, 8, 1, and 2. Also, s_3 leaves the solution.]

(c) In part (b) determine the increase in the value of z when x_I enters the solution without carrying out the Gauss–Jordan computations.
[*Ans.* Increase in $z = 2 \times 1 = 2$.]

(d) Examine Figure 3-2 and determine how many iterations will be needed to reach the optimum at C if x_I is selected as the entering variable in the starting tableau.
[*Ans.* Five iterations, corresponding to extreme points A, F, E, D, and C.]

(e) In the optimum tableau of the Reddy Mikks model, determine the leaving variable and the corresponding change (increase or decrease) in the value of z if the entering variable is given by
(1) s_1. [*Ans.* x_I leaves and z *decreases* by $2 \times 1/3 = 2/3$.]
(2) s_2. [*Ans.* s_4 leaves and z *decreases* by $2 \times 4/3 = 8/3$.]

(f) What conclusion can be drawn from the computations in part (e)?
[*Ans.* Any attempt to make a nonbasic variable with a positive coefficient in the z-equation enter the basic solution can never increase the value of z. This is why we say that the *maximum* value of z has been attained when all the nonbasic coefficients of the z-equation have become nonnegative.]

3.3.1 ARTIFICIAL STARTING SOLUTION FOR THE PRIMAL SIMPLEX METHOD

In the Reddy Mikks model, all the constraints are of the type $\leq$. This property, together with the fact that the right-hand side of all the constraints is nonnegative, provides us with a ready starting basic feasible solution that is comprised of all slack variables. Such conditions are not satisfied in all LP models, giving rise to the need for devising an automatic computational procedure for starting the simplex iterations. We accomplish this task by adding **artificial** (or extraneous) **variables** where needed to play the role of the slack variables. However, since such artificial variables have no physical meaning in the original model (hence the name "artificial"), provisions must be made to drive them to zero level at the optimum iteration. In other words, we use them to start the solution, and then abandon them once their mission has been accomplished!

We accomplish this task by using information feedback, which will make these variables unattractive from the optimization standpoint. A logical way to achieve this objective is to *penalize* the artificial variables in the objective function. Two (closely related) methods based on the use of penalties are available for this purpose:

(1) the M-method or method of penalty and (2) the two-phase method. The details of the two procedures are given below.

A. The *M*-Technique (Method of Penalty)

We describe the method by using the following numerical example:

$$\text{minimize } z = 4x_1 + x_2$$

subject to

$$\begin{aligned} 3x_1 + x_2 &= 3 \\ 4x_1 + 3x_2 &\geq 6 \\ x_1 + 2x_2 &\leq 4 \\ x_1, x_2 &\geq 0 \end{aligned}$$

The standard form of this model thus becomes

$$\text{minimize } z = 4x_1 + x_2$$

subject to

$$\begin{aligned} 3x_1 + x_2 \qquad\qquad &= 3 \\ 4x_1 + 3x_2 - x_3 \qquad &= 6 \\ x_1 + 2x_2 \qquad + x_4 &= 4 \\ x_1, x_2, x_3, x_4 &\geq 0 \end{aligned}$$

The first and second equations do not have variables that play the role of a slack. Hence we augment the two artificial variables R_1 and R_2 in these two equations as follows:

$$\begin{aligned} 3x_1 + x_2 \qquad + R_1 \qquad &= 3 \\ 4x_1 + 3x_2 - x_3 \qquad + R_2 &= 6 \end{aligned}$$

We can *penalize* R_1 and R_2 in the objective function by assigning them very large positive coefficients in the objective function. Let $M > 0$ be a very large constant; then the LP with its artificial variables becomes

$$\text{minimize } z = 4x_1 + x_2 + MR_1 + MR_2$$

subject to

$$\begin{aligned} 3x_1 + x_2 \qquad + R_1 \qquad\qquad &= 3 \\ 4x_1 + 3x_2 - x_3 \qquad + R_2 \qquad &= 6 \\ x_1 + 2x_2 \qquad\qquad\qquad + x_4 &= 4 \\ x_1, x_2, x_3, R_1, R_2, x_4 &\geq 0 \end{aligned}$$

Notice the reason behind the use of the artificial variables. We have three equations and six unknowns. Hence the starting basic solution must include $6 - 3 = 3$ zero variables. If we put x_1, x_2, and x_3 at zero level, we immediately obtain the solution $R_1 = 3$, $R_2 = 6$, and $x_4 = 4$, which is the required starting *feasible* solution.

Now, observe how the "new" model automatically forces R_1 and R_2 to be zero. Since we are minimizing, by assigning M to R_1 and R_2 in the objective function, the optimization process that is seeking the *minimum* value of z will eventually assign zero values to R_1 and R_2 in the *optimum* solution. Notice that the intermediate iterations preceding the optimum iteration are of no importance to us. Consequently, it is immaterial whether or not they include artificial variables at positive level.

How does the M-technique change if we are maximizing instead of minimizing? Using the same logic of penalizing the artificial variable, we must assign them the coefficient $-M$ in the objective function ($M > 0$), thus making it unattractive to maintain the artificial variable at a positive level in the optimum solution.

Exercise 3.3-2

In the foregoing example, suppose that the problem is of the maximization type. Write the objective function after augmenting the artificial variables.
[*Ans.* Maximize $z = 4x_1 + x_2 - MR_1 - MR_2$.]

Having constructed a starting feasible solution, we must "condition" the problem so that when we put it in tabular form, the right-side column will render the starting solution directly. This is done by using the constraint equations to substitute out R_1 and R_2 in the objective function. Thus

$$R_1 = 3 - 3x_1 - x_2$$
$$R_2 = 6 - 4x_1 - 3x_2 + x_3$$

The objective function thus becomes

$$\begin{aligned} z &= 4x_1 + x_2 + M(3 - 3x_1 - x_2) + M(6 - 4x_1 - 3x_2 + x_3) \\ &= (4 - 7M)x_1 + (1 - 4M)x_2 + Mx_3 + 9M \end{aligned}$$

and the z-equation now appears in the tableau as

$$z - (4 - 7M)x_1 - (1 - 4M)x_2 - Mx_3 = 9M$$

Now you can see that at the starting solution, given $x_1 = x_2 = x_3 = 0$, the value of z is $9M$, as it should be when $R_1 = 3$ and $R_2 = 6$.

The sequence of tableaus leading to the optimum solution is shown in Table 3-1. Observe that this is a *minimization* problem so that the entering variable must have the most *positive* coefficient in the z-equation. The optimum is reached when *all* the nonbasic variables have *non*positive z-coefficients. (Remember that M is a very large positive constant.)

The optimum solution is $x_1 = 2/5$, $x_2 = 9/5$, and $z = 17/5$. Since it contains no artificial variables *at positive level*, the solution is feasible with respect to the original problem before the artificials are added. (If the problem has no feasible solution, at least one artificial variable will be positive in the optimum solution. This case is treated in the next section.)

Exercise 3.3-3

(a) Write the z-equation for the preceding example as it appears in the starting tableau when each of the following changes occurs independently.
  (1) The third constraint is originally of the type $\geq$.
  [*Ans.* $z + (-4 + 8M)x_1 + (-1 + 6M)x_2 - Mx_3 - Mx_4 = 13M$. Use artificial variables in all three equations.]
  (2) The second constraint is originally of the type $\leq$.
  [*Ans.* $z + (-4 + 3M)x_1 + (-1 + M)x_2 = 3M$. Use an artificial variable in the first equation only.]
  (3) The objective function is to maximize $z = 4x_1 + x_2$.

Table 3-1[a]

Iteration	Basic	x_1	x_2	x_3	R_1	R_2	x_4	Solution
0 (starting)	z	$-4+7M$	$-1+4M$	$-M$	0	0	0	$9M$
x_1 enters	R_1	3	1	0	1	0	0	3
R_1 leaves	R_2	4	3	-1	0	1	0	6
	x_4	1	2	0	0	0	1	4
1	z	0	$\frac{1+5M}{3}$	$-M$	$\frac{4-7M}{3}$	0	0	$4+2M$
x_2 enters	x_1	1	1/3	0	1/3	0	0	1
R_2 leaves	R_2	0	5/3	-1	$-4/3$	1	0	2
	x_4	0	5/3	0	$-1/3$	0	1	3
2	z	0	0	1/5	$8/5-M$	$-1/5-M$	0	18/5
x_3 enters	x_1	1	0	1/5	3/5	$-1/5$	0	3/5
x_4 leaves	x_2	0	1	$-3/5$	$-4/5$	3/5	0	6/5
	x_4	0	0	1	1	-1	1	1
3	z	0	0	0	$7/5-M$	$-M$	$-1/5$	17/5
(optimum)	x_1	1	0	0	2/5	0	$-1/5$	2/5
	x_2	0	1	0	$-1/5$	0	3/5	9/5
	x_3	0	0	1	1	-1	1	1

[a] We have eliminated the z column for convenience, since it never changes. We shall follow this convention throughout the book.

[*Ans.* $z+(-4-7M)x_1+(-1-4M)x_2+Mx_3=-9M$. Use artificial variables in the first and second equations.]

(b) In each of the following cases, indicate whether it is *absolutely necessary* to use artificial variables to secure a starting solution. Assume that all variables are nonnegative.

(1) Maximize $z = x_1 + x_2$
subject to

$$2x_1 + 3x_2 = 5$$
$$7x_1 + 2x_2 \leq 6$$

[*Ans.* Yes, use R_1 in the first equation and a slack in the second.]

(2) Minimize $z = x_1 + x_2 + x_3 + x_4$
subject to

$$2x_1 + x_2 + x_3 = 7$$
$$4x_1 + 3x_2 + x_4 = 8$$

[*Ans.* No, use x_3 and x_4; however, first substitute them out in the z-function using $x_3 = 7 - 2x_1 - x_2$ and $x_4 = 8 - 4x_1 - 3x_2$.]

Computer Drill

The design of the M-method is based on the requirement that the value of M be sufficiently large. Theoretically, M should tend to infinity. However, from the computational standpoint, the specific choice of M may have a dramatic effect on the results because of machine round-off error. To illustrate this point, consider the following problem:

$$\text{maximize } z = .2x_1 + .5x_2$$

subject to

$$\begin{aligned} 3x_1 + 2x_2 &\geq 6 \\ x_1 + 2x_2 &\leq 4 \\ x_1, x_2 &\geq 0 \end{aligned}$$

Using TORA's user-guided procedure, apply the primal simplex method using $M = 10$ and then repeat it using $M = 999{,}999$. The first M yields the correct solution $z = .95$, $x_1 = 1$, $x_2 = 1.5$, whereas the second gives the incorrect solution $z = 1.18$, $x_1 = 4$, $x_2 = 0$ (notice the inconsistency in the resulting value of z). Now, multiply the coefficients of the objective function by 1000 to read $z = 200x_1 + 500x_2$ and solve the problem using $M = 10$ and $M = 999{,}999$ and observe that the second value is the one that yields the correct solution. The exercise shows that the value M should be chosen relative to the values of the objective coefficients.

B. The Two-Phase Technique

As illustrated by the last computer drill above, a drawback of the M-technique is the possible computational error that could result from assigning a very large value to the constant M. The two-phase method is designed to alleviate this difficulty. Although the artificial variables are added in the same manner employed in the M-technique, the use of the constant M is eliminated by solving the problem in two phases (hence the name "two-phase" method). These two phases are outlined as follows:

Phase I. Augment the artificial variables as necessary to secure a starting solution. Form a new objective function that seeks the *minimization* of the *sum* of the artificial variables subject to the constraints of the original problem modified by the artificial variables. If the *minimum* value of the new objective function is zero (meaning that all artificials are zero), the problem has a feasible solution space. Go to phase II. Otherwise, if the minimum is positive, the problem has no feasible solution. Stop.

Phase II. Use the optimum basic solution of phase I as a starting solution for the original problem.

We illustrate the procedure using the M-technique example in Section 3.3.1A.

Phase I. Since we need artificials R_1 and R_2 in the first and second equations, the phase I problem reads as

$$\text{minimize } r = R_1 + R_2$$

subject to

$$\begin{aligned} 3x_1 + x_2 \qquad + R_1 \qquad\qquad &= 3 \\ 4x_1 + 3x_2 - x_3 \qquad + R_2 \qquad &= 6 \\ x_1 + 2x_2 \qquad\qquad\qquad + x_4 &= 4 \\ x_1, x_2, x_3, R_1, R_2, R_2, x_4 &\geq 0 \end{aligned}$$

Because R_1 and R_2 are in the starting solution, they must be substituted out in the objective function (compare with the M-technique) as follows:

$$\begin{aligned} r &= R_1 + R_2 \\ &= (3 - 3x_1 - x_2) + (6 - 4x_1 - 3x_2 + x_3) \\ &= -7x_1 - 4x_2 + x_3 + 9 \end{aligned}$$

The *starting* tableau thus becomes

Basic	x_1	x_2	x_3	R_1	R_2	x_4	Solution
r	7	4	−1	0	0	0	9
R_1	3	1	0	1	0	0	3
R_2	4	3	−1	0	1	0	6
x_4	1	2	0	0	0	1	4

The *optimum* tableau is obtained in *two* iterations and is given by (verify)

Basic	x_1	x_2	x_3	R_1	R_2	x_4	Solution
r	0	0	0	−1	−1	0	0
x_1	1	0	1/5	3/5	−1/5	0	3/5
x_2	0	1	−3/5	−4/5	3/5	0	6/5
x_4	0	0	1	1	−1	1	1

Since the minimum $r = 0$, the problem has a feasible solution; therefore we move to phase II.

Phase II. The artificial variables have now served their purpose and must be dispensed with in all subsequent computations. This means that the equations of the optimum tableau in phase I can be written as

$$\begin{aligned} x_1 \quad + \frac{1}{5}x_3 \quad &= 3/5 \\ x_2 - \frac{3}{5}x_3 \quad &= 6/5 \\ x_3 + x_4 &= 1 \end{aligned}$$

These equations are *exactly equivalent* to those in the standard form of the original problem (before artificials are added). Thus the original problem can be written as

$$\text{minimize } z = 4x_1 + x_2$$

subject to

$$\begin{aligned} x_1 \quad + \frac{1}{5}x_3 \quad &= 3/5 \\ x_2 - \frac{3}{5}x_3 \quad &= 6/5 \\ x_3 + x_4 &= 1 \\ x_1, x_2, x_3, x_4 &\geq 0 \end{aligned}$$

As you can see, the principal contribution of the phase I computations is to provide a ready starting solution to the original problem. Since the problem has three equations and four variables, by putting $4 - 3 = 1$ variable, namely, x_3, equal to zero, we immediately obtain the starting basic feasible solution $x_1 = 3/5$, $x_2 = 6/5$, and $x_4 = 1$.

To solve the problem, we need to substitute out the basic variables x_1 and x_2 in the objective function as we did in the M-technique. This is accomplished by using the constraint equations as follows:

$$\begin{aligned} z &= 4x_1 + x_2 \\ &= 4\left(3/5 - \frac{1}{5}x_3\right) + \left(6/5 + \frac{3}{5}x_3\right) \\ &= -\frac{1}{5}x_3 + 18/5 \end{aligned}$$

Thus the starting tableau for phase II becomes

Basic	x_1	x_2	x_3	x_4	Solution
z	0	0	1/5	0	18/5
x_1	1	0	1/5	0	3/5
x_2	0	1	$-3/5$	0	6/5
x_4	0	0	1	1	1

The tableau is not optimal, since x_3 must enter the solution. If we carry out the simplex computations, we shall obtain the optimum solution in one iteration (verify).

The removal of the artificial variables at the end of phase I is effected only when they are all *nonbasic* (as the example above illustrates). It is possible, however, that one or more artificial variables remain *basic* but at *zero* level at the end of phase I. In this case, such a variable, by necessity, must be part of the phase II starting solution. As such, the computations in phase II must be modified to prevent an artificial variable from ever assuming a positive value during the iterations of phase II.

The rule for guaranteeing that a *zero* artificial variable never becomes positive in phase II is simple. Observe that in the entering column, the constraint coefficient associated with the artificial variable row can be either positive, zero, or negative. If it is positive, it will define the pivot element automatically (because it will correspond to the minimum ratio of zero) and the artificial variable will necessarily leave the basic solution to become nonbasic in the next iteration (good riddance!). If the coefficient is zero, then, although the pivot element will be elsewhere in the entering column, the nature of row operations guarantees that the artificial row remain unchanged, which leaves the artificial variable basic at zero level as desired. The only remaining case is that of a negative coefficient. In this case, the pivot element will necessarily be elsewhere in the entering column and if the resulting minimum ratio happens to be positive, then the artificial variable will assume a positive value in the next iteration (can you see why?). To prevent this from happening, all we have to do is to *force* the artificial variable to leave anyway, simply by selecting the negative coefficient as the iteration pivot element. Although we are violating the minimum ratio rule, we will not be violating the feasibility of the problem (which is the essence of the minimum ratio rule) because the artificial variable has a zero value. Thus, when you carry out the row operations, the right-hand side of the tableau will remain unchanged, and hence feasible.

To summarize, the "new" rule for phase II calls for selecting the artificial variable to leave the basic solution any time its constraint coefficient in the entering column assumes a *nonzero* (positive or negative) value. (As a matter of fact, this rule can be applied to any *zero* basic variable in any simplex tableau without fear of violating the feasibility condition.) The next Computer Drill provides an illustration of this rule using TORA's user-guided mode.

Computer Drill

Consider Problem 3–38. Use TORA's user-guided procedure to select the primal simplex with the two-phase starting solution. You will notice that phase II starts at iteration 2 with the artificial variable Rx6 basic at zero level. At iteration 3, you will notice that x3 is the entering variable. Normally, the minimum ratio would correspond to x2 because it has the only positive coefficient under x3. However, since the constraint coefficient of artificial Rx6 is nonzero, the simplex method will instead remove Rx6 from the basic set to prevent it from assuming a positive value (iteration 4). If you force x_2 to leave the solution, you will discover that the solution in iteration 4 will become infeasible (try it!).

Exercise 3.3-4

(a) In phase I, what do the artificial variables signify? Specifically, why is the sum of the artificial variables minimized?
[*Ans.* Artificials may be regarded as a "measure of infeasibility" in the constraints. When the minimum sum of the (nonnegative) artificial variables is zero, each of these variables must be zero. Thus the resulting basic solution must be feasible for the original problem.]

(b) If the original linear program is of the maximization type, do we maximize the sum of the artificial variables in phase I?
[*Ans.* No, we should always minimize in phase I, since this is equivalent to penalizing the artificial variables.]

3.4 DUAL SIMPLEX METHOD

In Section 3.3.1 we used artificial variables to solve LP problems that do not have an all-slack starting basic feasible solution. There is a class of LP problems that do not have an all-slack starting basic feasible solution, yet can be solved without the use of the artificial variables. The procedure for solving this class of problems is called the **dual simplex method**. In this method, the solution starts infeasible and optimal (as compared with primal simplex which starts feasible but nonoptimal). We first demonstrate the idea of the dual simplex method graphically and then present the algebraic steps.

Consider the following LP problem:

$$\text{minimize } z = 3x_1 + 2x_2$$

subject to

$$\begin{aligned} 3x_1 + x_2 &\geq 3 \\ 4x_1 + 3x_2 &\geq 6 \\ x_1 + x_2 &\leq 3 \\ x_1, x_2 &\geq 0 \end{aligned}$$

If we convert the constraints into equation form by augmenting surplus or slack variable, the problem may be written as

$$\text{minimize } z = 3x_1 + 2x_2$$

subject to

$$\begin{aligned} -3x_1 - x_2 + x_3 \qquad\qquad &= -3 \\ -4x_1 - 3x_2 \qquad + x_4 \qquad &= -6 \\ x_1 + x_2 \qquad\qquad + x_5 &= 3 \\ x_1, x_2, x_3, x_4, x_5 &\geq 0 \end{aligned}$$

The form above may be regarded as the *standard form* of the dual simplex method. The conversion is made such that all the surplus variables in the constraints will have a coefficient of $+1$ simply by multiplying their equations by -1. In this case the right-hand side of the constraint becomes negative. We can immediately see that the starting basic solution

$$x_3 = -3, \qquad x_4 = -6, \qquad x_5 = 3$$

is infeasible. It is also optimal (actually, better than optimal) because the associated value of z is zero ($x_1 = x_2 = 0$), which cannot be any smaller for $x_1 \geq 0$ and $x_2 \geq 0$ because all their coefficients are positive (namely, 3 and 2). These starting conditions are typical of those required for the application of the dual simplex method.

The general idea of the dual simplex procedure is that whereas the first iteration starts infeasible and (better than) optimal, succeeding iterations move toward the feasible space without ever losing the optimality property (recall that the regular simplex maintains feasibility while moving toward optimality). At the iteration where the solution becomes feasible for the first time, the process ends. Figure 3-3 illustrates the idea graphically. The solution starts at point A ($x_1 = x_2 = 0$ and $x_3 = -3$, $x_4 = -6$, $x_5 = 3$) with $z = 0$, which is infeasible with respect to the solution space. The next iteration is secured by moving to point B ($x_1 = 0$, $x_2 = 2$) with $z = 4$, which is still infeasible. Finally, we reach point C ($x_1 = 3/5$, $x_2 = 6/5$), at which $z = 21/5$. This is the first time we encounter a feasible solution, thus signifying the end of the iterative process. Notice that the iterations could as well have proceeded in the order $A \rightarrow D \rightarrow C$ instead of $A \rightarrow B \rightarrow C$, with the same conclusion. We will show below how the dual simplex selects a specific path. Notice also that the values of z associated with A, B, and C are 0, 4, and $4\frac{1}{5}$, respectively, which explains why the solution starts at A better than optimal.

You will notice that the dual simplex iterations continue to be associated with corner (or extreme) points, just as in the primal simplex method. Hence the successive iterations are obtained by applying the regular Gauss–Jordan row operations. The main difference between the two procedures occurs in the manner in which the entering and leaving variables are selected, as we explain below.

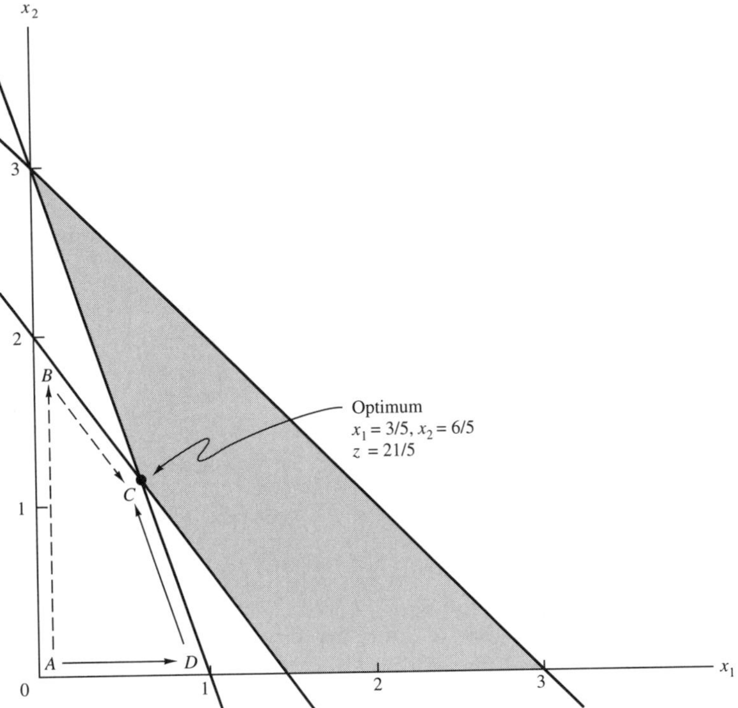

Figure 3-3

The starting tableau for the dual simplex iteration for the given example is as follows:

Entering variable ↓

	Basic	x_1	x_2	x_3	x_4	x_5	Solution
	z	-3	-2	0	0	0	0
	x_3	-3	-1	1	0	0	-3
Leaving variable →	x_4	-4	-3	0	1	0	-6
	x_5	1	1	0	0	1	3

This tableau corresponds to point A in Figure 3-3. Notice that the objective row satisfies the (minimization) optimality condition. It is also infeasible because x_3 and x_4 assume negative values. These are the conditions (optimal and infeasible) required for the starting iteration of the dual simplex method.

Since our goal is to remove infeasibility, we do so by attempting to force the *negative* basic variables out of the solution. Although either x_3 $(= -3)$ or x_4 $(= -6)$ will qualify for this purpose, a rule of thumb calls for removing the most infeasible (most negative) among all candidates in the hope that it will lead to the feasible solution more rapidly. Thus, in our example, we select x_4 as the leaving variable.

The entering variable must now be selected from among the current nonbasic variables provided that the optimality is not lost. Such is achieved by taking the ratios of the left-hand coefficients of the z-equation to the corresponding coefficients in the equation of the leaving variable. To maintain optimality, those ratios with positive or zero denominators are discarded. The entering variable is the one associated with the ratio having the *smallest* value.

In our starting tableau, the ratios are computed as follows:

Variable	x_1	x_2	x_3	x_4	x_5
z-equation	-3	-2	0	0	0
x_4-equation	-4	-3	0	1	0
Ratio	3/4	**2/3**	—	—	—

The ratios show that x_2 will enter the solution. The next tableau is thus obtained using the regular row operations, thus leading to the following tableau:

Basic	x_1	x_2	x_3	x_4	x_5	Solution
z	−1/3	0	0	−2/3	0	4
x_3	−5/3	0	1	−1/3	0	−1
x_2	4/3	1	0	−1/3	0	2
x_5	−1/3	0	0	1/3	1	1
Ratio	**1/5**	—	—	2	—	

Next x_3 leaves the basic solution and x_1 enters, which yields the following tableau:

Basic	x_1	x_2	x_3	x_4	x_5	Solution
z	0	0	$-1/5$	$-3/5$	0	21/5
x_1	1	0	$-3/5$	1/5	0	3/5
x_2	0	1	4/5	$-3/5$	0	6/5
x_5	0	0	$-1/5$	2/5	1	6/5

The tableau now is feasible and optimal. The corresponding solution is $x_1 = 3/5$, $x_2 = 6/5$, and $z = 21/5$.

The dual simplex applies equally to maximization problems provided that the starting solution is again optimal but infeasible. The only difference, as you would expect, occurs in the condition for selecting the entering variable, as explained below.

Feasibility Condition: The **leaving variable** is the basic variable having the most negative value (break ties arbitrarily). If all basic variables are nonnegative, the process ends.

Optimality Condition: The **entering variable** is the nonbasic variable associated with the smallest ratio if minimizing or the smallest *absolute* value of the ratios if maximizing (break ties arbitrarily). The ratios are determined by dividing the left-hand-side coefficients of the z-equation by the corresponding *negative* coefficients in the equation by the corresponding *negative* coefficients in the equation associated with the leaving variable. If all the denominators are zero or positive, no feasible solution exists.

The dual simplex method, aside from its use to solve a special class of LP problems, is useful in carrying out postoptimization in sensitivity analysis and parametric programming. These techniques are discussed in Chapter 5.

Computer Drill

Consider the example at the start of Section 3.3. This problem can be put in the dual simplex format by converting the constraint equation $3x_1 + x_2 = 3$ into two inequalities: $3x_1 + x_2 \geq 3$ and $3x_1 + x_2 \leq 3$. Make this conversion and then solve the problem using TORA (user-guided option).

Computer Drill (Generalized Simplex Procedure)

After studying the primal and dual simplex methods and their variants, one may lose sight of what the simplex method truly entails. What we are going to demonstrate in this drill is that you can actually "tailor" your own simplex procedure. In fact, we will do so by starting with a tableau that is neither optimal nor feasible, conditions that violate the starting solutions of both the primal and the dual simplex methods.

Consider the following linear program:

$$\text{maximize } z = 3x_1 + 2x_2 + 5x_3$$

subject to

$$\begin{aligned} x_1 + 2x_2 + x_3 &\leq 430 \\ 3x_1 \qquad + 2x_3 &\leq 460 \\ x_1 + 4x_2 \qquad &\leq 420 \\ x_1, x_2, x_3 &\geq 0 \end{aligned}$$

This model is ideal for the application of the primal simplex method. However, we will use TORA's user-guided option to force x_1 to enter the basic solution as a replacement to x_4, the starting basic variable in constraint 1. Now, view the resulting tableau and you will notice that it is both nonoptimal and infeasable. We will regard this tableau as our "starting" tableau.

The next step is to try to make the z-equation satisfy the optimality condition without regard to the feasibility problem. So we let x_3 enter and force x_6 to leave (even though x_6 would not be the simplex default choice). Since x_6 shows nonoptimality, we choose it to enter and let x_1 leave the solution. Now view the resulting tableau. The z-row is optimal but the solution is infeasible. We thus apply the dual simplex conditions recognizing that x_2 must enter and x_5 must leave. By forcing x_2 to enter and x_5 to leave, we then obtain a tableau that is both optimal and feasible.

The procedure given above is not haphazard. It is based on the valid theory that says that so long as we are dealing with *corner* (or *extreme*) *points* of the solution space (basic solutions), we are actually considerng a candidate for the optimal solution. Thus, by working on the optimality condition first and then following it by the feasibility condition, we eventually will reach the optimum feasible solution (if one exists).

The essence of this drill is to show that the simplex method is not rigid. The literature abounds with variations of the simplex method (the *primal–dual* method, the *crisscross* method, the *symmetric* method, and the *multiplex* method) that give the impression that each procedure is a totally "different animal," when in effect they all seek an extreme point solution perhaps with a slant toward computational efficiency.

3.5 SPECIAL CASES IN SIMPLEX METHOD APPLICATION

In this section we consider special cases that can arise in the application of the simplex method, which include

1. Degeneracy.
2. Alternative optima.
3. Unbounded solutions.
4. Nonexisting (or infeasible) solutions.

Our interest in studying these special cases is twofold: (1) to present a *theoretical* explanation for the reason these situations arise and (2) to provide a *practical* interpretation of what these special results could mean in a real-life problem.

3.5.1 DEGENERACY

In Section 3.3 we indicated that in the application of the feasibility condition of the primal simplex, a tie for the minimum ratio may be broken arbitrarily for the purpose of determining the leaving variable. When this happens, however, one or more of the *basic* variables will necessarily equal zero in the next iteration. In this case, we say that the new solution is **degenerate**. (In all the LP examples we have solved so far, the basic variables always assumed strictly positive values.)

There is nothing alarming about dealing with a degenerate solution, with the exception of a small theoretical inconvenience, which we shall discuss shortly. From the practical standpoint, the condition reveals that the model has at least one *redundant* constraint. To be able to provide more insight into the practical and theoretical impacts of degeneracy, we consider a numeric example. The graphical illustration should enhance the understanding of ideas underlying this special situation.

Example 3.5-1 (Degenerate Optimal Solution)

$$\text{Maximize } z = 3x_1 + 9x_2$$

subject to

$$x_1 + 4x_2 \leq 8$$
$$x_1 + 2x_2 \leq 4$$
$$x_1, x_2 \geq 0$$

Using x_3 and x_4 as slack variables, we list the simplex iterations for the example in Table 3-2. In the starting iteration, a tie for the leaving variable exists between x_3 and x_4. This is the reason the basic variable x_4 has a zero value in iteration 1, thus resulting in a degenerate basic solution. The optimum is reached after an additional iteration is carried out.

Table 3-2

Iteration	Basic	x_1	x_2	x_3	x_4	Solution
0 (starting)	z	-3	-9	0	0	0
x_2 enters	x_3	1	4	1	0	8
x_3 leaves	x_4	1	2	0	1	4
1	z	$-3/4$	0	9/4	0	18
x_1 enters	x_2	1/4	1	1/4	0	2
x_4 leaves	x_4	1/2	0	$-1/2$	1	0
2 (optimum)	z	0	0	3/2	3/2	18
	x_2	0	1	1/2	$-1/2$	2
	x_1	1	0	-1	2	0

What is the practical implication of degeneracy? Look at Figure 3-4, which provides the graphical solution to the model. Three lines pass through the optimum ($x_1 = 0$, $x_2 = 2$). Since this is a two-dimensional problem, the point is said to be *overdetermined*, since we only need two lines to identify it. For this reason, we conclude that one of the constraints is redundant. In practice, the mere knowledge that some resources are superfluous can prove valuable during the implementation of the solution. Such information may also lead to discovering irregularities in the construction of the model. Unfortunately, there are no reliable techniques for identifying redundant constraints directly from the tableau. In the absence of graphical representation, we may have to rely on other means to identify redundancy in the model.

From the theoretical standpoint, degeneracy has two implications. The first deals with the phenomenon of **cycling** or **circling**. If you look at iterations 1 and 2 in Table 3-2, you will find that the objective value has not improved ($z = 18$). It is thus conceivable, in general, that the simplex procedure would repeat the *same sequence* of iterations, never improving the objective value and never terminating the computations. Although there are methods for avoiding the occurrence of cycling, these methods could lead to a drastic slowdown in computations. For this reason, most LP codes do not include provisions for cycling, relying on the fact that the percentage of LP problems having this complication is usually too small to warrant a routine implementation of the cycling procedures.

The second theoretical point arises in the examination of iterations 1 and 2. Both iterations, although differing in classifying the variables as basic and nonbasic, yield

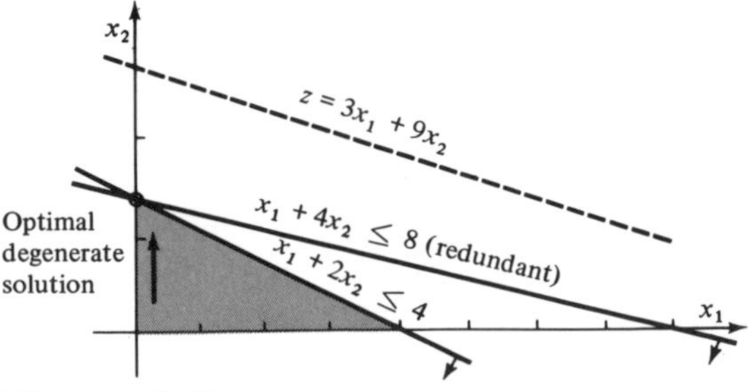

Figure 3-4

identical values of all the variables and objective value, namely,

$$x_1 = 0, \quad x_2 = 2, \quad x_3 = 0, \quad x_4 = 0, \quad z = 18$$

An argument thus arises as to the possibility of stopping the computations at iteration 1 (when degeneracy first appears), even though it is not optimum. This argument is not valid because, in general, a solution may be *temporarily* degenerate (see Problem 3–33). ◀

Exercise 3.5-1

(a) If, in a two-dimensional problem such as Example 3.5-1, we have three zero basic variables at a simplex iteration, how many redundant constraints exist at this corner point?
[*Ans.* 3.]

(b) In an n-dimensional problem, how many planes (constraints) must pass through a corner point to produce a degenerate situation?
[*Ans.* At least $n + 1$ planes.]

(c) Judging from the foregoing discussion, is the number of basic solutions larger than the number of corner points under degenerate conditions?
[*Ans.* Yes, definitely.]

(d) Assuming that cycling will not occur, what is the ultimate effect of degeneracy on computations as compared to the case where redundant constraints are removed, that is, degeneracy is removed?
[*Ans.* The number of iterations until the optimum is reached may be larger under degeneracy, since a corner point may be represented by more than one basic solution.]

Computer Drill

Use TORA's interactive option to "thumb" through the successive (primal) simplex iterations of the example below (due to E. M. Beale). The starting tableau with all slack basic solutions (sx5, sx6, sx7) will reappear identically in iteration 7. The example illustrates the occurrence of *cycling* in simplex iterations and the possibility of the simplex method never converging to the optimal solution.

$$\text{Maximize } z = \frac{3}{4}x_1 - 20x_2 + \frac{1}{2}x_3 - 6x_4$$

subject to

$$\frac{1}{4}x_1 - 8x_2 - x_3 + 9x_4 \le 0$$

$$\frac{1}{2}x_1 - 12x_2 - \frac{1}{2}x_3 + 3x_4 \le 0$$

$$x_3 \le 1$$

$$x_1, x_2, x_3, x_4 \ge 0$$

It is interesting that if all the coefficients in the problem above are converted to integer values, the simplex method will reach the optimum in a finite number of iterations.

(*Warning*: Do not use TORA's "automated" solution option; otherwise, the iterations will cycle indefinitely.)

3.5.2 ALTERNATIVE OPTIMA

When the objective function is parallel to a *binding* constraint (i.e., a constraint that is satisfied in the equality sense by the optimal solution), the objective function will assume the *same optimal value* at more than one solution point. For this reason they are called **alternative optima**. The next example shows that normally there is an *infinity* of such solutions. The example also demonstrates the practical significance of encountering alternative optima.

Example 3.5-2 (Infinity of Solutions)

$$\text{Maximize } z = 2x_1 + 4x_2$$

subject to

$$\begin{aligned} x_1 + 2x_2 &\leq 5 \\ x_1 + x_2 &\leq 4 \\ x_1, x_2 &\geq 0 \end{aligned}$$

Figure 3-5 demonstrates how alternative optima can arise in LP model when the objective function is parallel to a binding constraint. Any point on the *line segment BC* represents an alternative optimum with the same objective value $z = 10$.

Algebraically, we know that the simplex method is capable of encountering corner-point solutions only. Table 3-3 shows that the optimum ($x_1 = 0$, $x_2 = 5/2$, $z = 10$) is encountered in iteration 1 at point B. How do we know from this tableau that alternative optima exist? Look at the coefficients of the *non*basic variables in the z-equation of iteration 1. The coefficient of (nonbasic) x_1 is zero, indicating that x_1 can enter the basic solution without changing the value of z, but causing a change in the values of the variables. Iteration 2 does just that—letting x_1 enter the basic solution, which will force x_4 to leave. This results in the new solution point at C ($x_1 = 3$, $x_2 = 1$, $z = 10$).

As expected, the simplex method determines only the two corner points B and C. Mathematically, we can determine all the points $(\hat{x}_1, \hat{x}_2)$ on the line segment BC as a nonnegative weighted average of the points B and C. That is, given $0 \leq \alpha \leq 1$ and

$$\begin{aligned} B&: \quad x_1 = 0, \quad x_2 = 5/2 \\ C&: \quad x_1 = 3, \quad x_2 = 1 \end{aligned}$$

then all the points on the line segment BC are given by

$$\begin{aligned} \hat{x}_1 &= \alpha(0) + (1 - \alpha)(3) = 3 - 3\alpha \\ \hat{x}_2 &= \alpha(5/2) + (1 - \alpha)(1) = 1 + 3\alpha/2 \end{aligned}$$

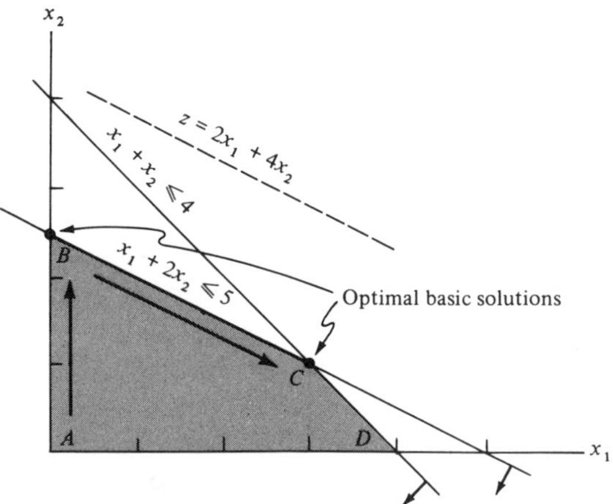

Figure 3-5

Table 3-3

Iteration	Basic	x_1	x_2	x_3	x_4	Solution
0	z	-2	-4	0	0	0
(starting)						
x_2 enters	x_3	1	2	1	0	5
x_3 leaves	x_4	1	1	0	1	4
1	z	0	0	2	0	10
(optimum)						
x_1 enters	x_2	1/2	1	1/2	0	5/2
x_4 leaves	x_4	1/2	0	$-1/2$	1	3/2
2	z	0	0	2	0	10
(alternate						
optimum)	x_2	0	1	1	-1	1
	x_1	1	0	-1	2	3

Observe that when $\alpha = 0$, $(\hat{x}_1, \hat{x}_2) = (3, 1)$, which is point C. When $\alpha = 1$, $(\hat{x}_1, \hat{x}_2) = (0, 5/2)$, which is point B. For values of α between 0 and 1, $(\hat{x}_1, \hat{x}_2)$ lies between B and C. ◀

In practice, knowledge of alternative optima is useful because it gives management the opportunity to choose the solution that best suits their situation without experiencing any deterioration in the objective value. In the example, for instance, the solution at B shows that only activity 2 is at a positive level, whereas at C both activities are positive. If the example represents a product-mix situation, it may be advantageous from the standpoint of sales competition to produce two products rather than one. In this case the solution at C would be recommended.

Exercise 3.5-2

(a) What is the value of α that will locate $(\hat{x}_1, \hat{x}_2)$ halfway on the line segment BC? one-third of the way from B? Compute $(\hat{x}_1, \hat{x}_2)$ in each case.
[*Ans.* $\alpha = 1/2$ gives (3/2, 7/4); $\alpha = 2/3$ gives (1, 2).]

(b) Show that for $(\hat{x}_1, \hat{x}_2) = (3 - 3\alpha, 1 + 3\alpha/2)$, the value of $z\,(= 2\hat{x}_1 + 4\hat{x}_2)$ equals 10 for all α such that $0 \leq \alpha \leq 1$.

3.5.3 UNBOUNDED SOLUTION

In some LP models, the values of the variables may be increased indefinitely without violating any of the constraints, meaning that the solution space is **unbounded** in at least one direction. As a result, the objective value may increase (maximization case) or decrease (minimization case) indefinitely. In this case we say that both the solution space and the "optimum" objective value are unbounded.

Unboundedness in a model can point to one thing only: the model is poorly constructed. Having a model that produces an "infinite" profit is obviously nonsensical. The most likely irregularities in such models are: one or more nonredundant constraints are not accounted for, and the parameters (constants) of some constraints are not estimated correctly.

The following examples show how unboundedness, both in the solution space and the objective value, can be recognized in the simplex tableau.

Example 3.5-3 (Unbounded Objective Value)

$$\text{Maximize } z = 2x_1 + x_2$$

subject to

$$\begin{aligned} x_1 - x_2 &\leq 10 \\ 2x_1 \qquad &\leq 40 \\ x_1, x_2 &\geq 0 \end{aligned}$$

Starting Iteration

Basic	x_1	x_2	x_3	x_4	Solution
z	−2	−1	0	0	0
x_3	1	−1	1	0	10
x_4	2	0	0	1	40

In the starting tableau, both x_1 and x_2 are candidates for entering the solution. Since x_1 has the most negative coefficient, it is normally selected as the entering variable. Notice, however, that *all* the *constraint* coefficients under x_2 are *negative* or *zero*, meaning that x_2 can be increased indefinitely without violating any of the constraints. Since each unit increase in x_2 will increase z by 1, an infinite increase in x_2 will also result in an infinite increase in z. Thus we conclude without further computations that the problem has no bounded solution. This result can be seen in Figure 3-6. The solution space is unbounded in the direction of x_2 and the value of z can be increased indefinitely. ◀

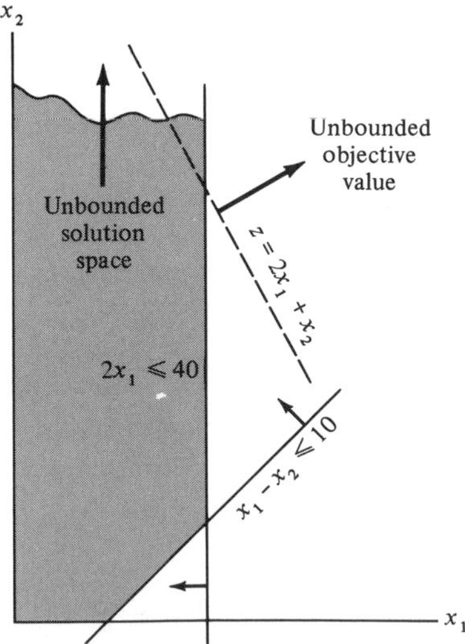

Figure 3-6

The general rule for recognizing unboundedness is as follows. If at any iteration the constraint coefficients of any *nonbasic* variable are nonpositive, then the *solution space* is unbounded in that direction. If, in addition, the objective coefficient of that variable is negative in the case of maximization or positive in the case of minimization, then the *objective value* also is unbounded.

Computer Drill

In Example 3.5-3, use TORA's interactive procedure to show that starting with x_1 as the first entering variable, the simplex iterations will eventually lead to an unbounded solution.

Exercise 3.5-3

(a) In Example 3.5-3, explain why negative or zero constraint coefficients of a nonbasic variable indicate that the variable can be increased indefinitely without violating feasibility.
[*Ans.* Negative or zero constraint coefficients indicate that *no* constraints intersect the *positive* direction of the axis representing the entering variable; see Figure 3-2.]

(b) Can the condition of unboundedness *always* be detected from the *starting* simplex iteration?
[*Ans.* No, it may become evident for the first time at a later iteration.]

3.5.4 INFEASIBLE SOLUTION

If the constraints cannot be satisfied simultaneously, the model is said to have no feasible solution. This situation can never occur if *all* the constraints are of the type $\leq$ (assuming nonnegative right-side constants), since the slack variable always provides a *feasible* solution. However, when we employ the other types of constraints, we resort to the use of artificial variables which, by their very design, do not provide a feasible solution to the *original* model. Although provisions are made (through the use of penalty) to force the artificial variables to zero at the optimum, this can occur only if the model has a feasible space. If it does not, at least one artificial variable will be *positive* in the optimum iteration. This is our indication that the problem has no feasible solution.

From the practical standpoint, an infeasible space points to the possibility that the model is not formulated correctly, since the constraints are in conflict. It is also possible that the constraints are not meant to be satisfied simultaneously. In this case, a completely different model structure that does not admit all constraints simultaneously may be needed. Examples of such models using the so-called **either–or constraints** are presented in Chapter 9 as applications of integer programming.

The following example illustrates the case of infeasible solution space.

Example 3.5-4 (Infeasible Solution Space)

$$\text{Maximize } z = 3x_1 + 2x_2$$

subject to

$$\begin{aligned} 2x_1 + x_2 &\leq 2 \\ 3x_1 + 4x_2 &\geq 12 \\ x_1, x_2 &\geq 0 \end{aligned}$$

Table 3-4

Iteration	Basic	x_1	x_2	x_4	x_3	R	Solution
0 (starting)	z	$-3-3M$	$-2-4M$	M	0	0	$-12M$
x_2 enters	x_3	2	1	0	1	0	2
x_3 leaves	R	3	4	-1	0	1	12
1 (pseudo-	z	$1+5M$	0	M	$2+4M$	0	$4-4M$
optimum)	x_2	2	1	0	1	0	2
	R	-5	0	-1	-4	1	4

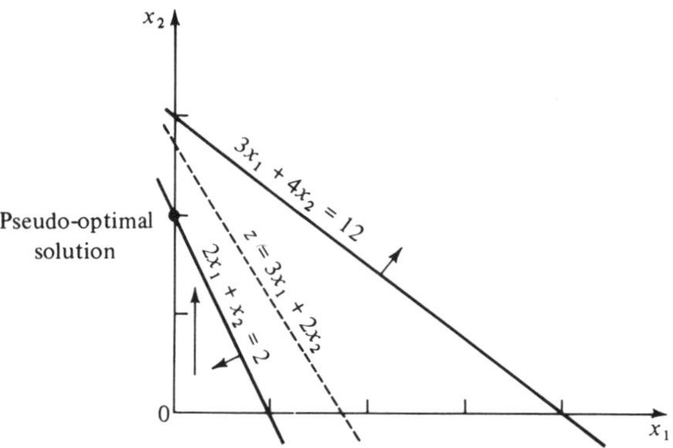

Figure 3-7

The simplex iterations in Table 3-4 show that the artificial variable R is *positive* ($= 4$) in the optimal solution. This is an indication that the solution space is infeasible. Figure 3-7 demonstrates the infeasible solution space. The simplex method, by allowing the artificial variable to be positive, in essence has reversed the direction of the inequality from $3x_1 + 4x_2 \geq 12$ to $3x_1 + 4x_2 \leq 12$. (Can you explain how?) The result is what we may call the **pseudo-optimal solution**, as shown in Figure 3-7.

Computer Drill

Use TORA's two-phase method to show how the procedure will conclude that the problem of Example 3.5-4 has no feasible solution space by showing that the optimum objective value at the end of phase I is positive ($= 4$).

3.6 INTERPRETING THE SIMPLEX TABLEAU: SENSITIVITY ANALYSIS

In the preceding sections we have introduced the basic details of the simplex method. We now pay attention to interpreting the output of the simplex method computations. The following list summarizes the information that can be obtained from the simplex tableau:

1. The optimum solution.
2. The status of the resources.
3. The dual prices (unit worth of resources) and reduced costs.
4. The sensitivity of the optimum solution to changes in availability of resources, marginal profit/cost (objective function coefficients), and the usage of the resources by the model activities.

All the items listed above have been discussed and explained in Chapter 2, mostly through the use of the TORA software. Our goal in this section is to give insight into how the results given in Chapter 2 are obtained from the simplex method computations.

We will use the Reddy Mikks model (Example 2.1-1) as a vehicle of explanation. The model is repeated here for convenience:

$$\text{maximize } z = 3x_E + 2x_I \qquad \text{(profit)}$$

subject to

$$\begin{aligned}
x_E + 2x_I + s_1 \qquad\qquad &= 6 \qquad \text{(raw material A)} \\
2x_E + x_I \quad + s_2 \qquad\quad &= 8 \qquad \text{(raw material B)} \\
-x_E + x_I \qquad + s_3 \quad &= 1 \qquad \text{(demand)} \\
x_I \qquad\qquad + s_4 &= 2 \qquad \text{(demand)} \\
x_E, x_I, s_1, s_2, s_3, s_4 &\geq 0
\end{aligned}$$

The optimum tableau is given as

Basic	x_E	x_I	s_1	s_2	s_3	s_4	Solution
z	0	0	1/3	4/3	0	0	$12\frac{2}{3}$
x_I	0	1	2/3	−1/3	0	0	$1\frac{1}{3}$
x_E	1	0	−1/3	2/3	0	0	$3\frac{1}{3}$
s_3	0	0	−1	1	1	0	3
s_4	0	0	−2/3	1/3	0	1	2/3

3.6.1 OPTIMUM SOLUTION

From the standpoint of *implementing* the LP solution, the mathematical classification of the variables as basic and nonbasic is of no importance and should be totally ignored in reading the optimum solution. The variables *not* listed in the "basic" column necessarily have zero values. The rest have their values in the solution column. In terms of the optimum solution of the Reddy Mikks model, we are interested primarily in the product mix of exterior and interior paint, that is, the decision variables x_E and x_I. From the optimum tableau we have the following summary.

Decision Variable	Optimum Value	Decision
x_E	$3\frac{1}{3}$	Produce $3\frac{1}{3}$ tons of exterior paint
x_I	$1\frac{1}{3}$	Produce $1\frac{1}{3}$ tons of interior paint daily
z	$12\frac{2}{3}$	Resulting profit is $12\frac{2}{3}$ thousand dollars

Notice that $z = 3x_E + 2x_I = 3x(3\frac{1}{3}) + 2(1\frac{1}{3}) = 12\frac{2}{3}$, as given in the optimum tableau.

3.6.2 STATUS OF RESOURCES

A constraint is classified as *scarce* or *abundant* depending, respectively, on whether or not the optimum solution "consumes" the entire available amount of the associated resource. Our objective is to secure this information from the optimum tableau.

In the Reddy Mikks model we have four constraints of the type $\leq$. The first two (representing raw materials usage) are "authentic" resources restrictions. The third and fourth constraints deal with demand limitations imposed by the market conditions. We can think of these constraints as limited "resources," since increasing demand limits is equivalent to expanding the company's share in the market. Monetarily, this has the same effect as increasing availability of physical resources (such as raw materials) through allocation of additional funds.

The status of the resources (abundant or scarce) in any LP model can be secured directly from the optimum tableau by observing the values of the *slack* variables. A positive slack means that the resource is not used completely, thus is abundant, whereas a zero slack indicates that the entire amount of the resource is consumed by the activities of the model. In the Reddy Mikks model we thus have the following summary:

Resource	Slack	Status of Resource
Raw material A	$s_1 = 0$	Scarce
Raw material B	$s_2 = 0$	Scarce
Limit on excess of interior over exterior paint	$s_3 = 3$	Abundant
Limit on demand for interior paint	$s_4 = 2/3$	Abundant

The resources that can be increased for the purpose of improving the solution (increasing profit) are raw materials A and B, since the optimum tableau shows they are scarce. A logical question would naturally arise: Which of the scarce resources should be given priority in the allocation of additional funds to improve profit most advantageously? We answer this question when we consider the dual prices of the different resources.

3.6.3 DUAL PRICE (UNIT WORTH OF A RESOURCE)

In Section 2.1.2 we applied a graphical procedure to the Reddy Mikks example to show how the dual price (unit worth of a resource) is computed. Specifically, given that y_1, y_2, y_3, and y_4 are the dual prices of resources 1, 2, 3, and 4 in the Reddy Mikks model, we obtained the following results:

$y_1 = 1/3$ thousand dollars per ton of material A
$y_2 = 4/3$ thousand dollars per ton of material B
$y_3 = 0$
$y_4 = 0$

This information is readily available in the optimum simplex tableau. Look at the coefficients in the z-equation under the starting basic variables s_1, s_2, s_3, and s_4, which we reproduce here for convenience:

Basic	x_E	x_I	s_1	s_2	s_3	s_4	Solution
z	0	0	1/3	4/3	0	0	$12\frac{2}{3}$

These coefficients (1/3, 4/3, 0, 0) exactly equal the dual prices listed above. The theory of linear programming tells us that it is always possible to secure the dual price of a resource from optimum objective coefficients of the starting basic variables. There should be no confusion as to which coefficient applies to which resource, since s_i is uniquely associated with resource i.

Although Section 2.1.2 has provided a rationale behind the definition of dual prices, we can deduce the same result directly from the optimum z-equation of the Reddy Mikks model, that is,

$$z = 12\frac{2}{3} - \left(\frac{1}{3}s_1 + \frac{4}{3}s_2 + 0s_3 + 0s_4\right)$$

If we change s_1 from its current zero level, the value of z will change at the rate of 1/3 thousand dollars per ton. But a change in s_1 actually is equivalent to changing resource 1 (raw material A) by an equal amount, as can be seen from the associated constraint equation:

$$x_E + 2x_I + s_1 = 6$$

This means that the dual price of raw material A is 1/3. A similar argument applies to resource 2.

Turning to resources 3 and 4, we find that their dual prices are zero ($y_3 = y_4 = 0$). This should be expected, since the two resources are already abundant as evidenced by the fact that their associated slack values are positive.

Exercise 3.6-1

In the Reddy Mikks model, if the objective function is changed from $z = 3x_E + 2x_I$ to $z = 2x_E + 5x_I$ while maintaining the same constraints, the simplex computations will yield the following optimum z-equation:

$$z + 2s_1 + s_4 = 14$$

The associated optimal values of the variables are $x_E = x_I = 2$, $s_2 = 2$, $s_3 = 1$. All others are zero.

(a) Classify the status of the four resources of the model.
[*Ans.* 1 and 4: scarce; 2 and 3: abundant.]

(b) Find the dual prices for the four resources.
[*Ans.* $y_1 = 2$, $y_2 = y_3 = 0$, $y_4 = 1$.]

(c) Can the optimum value of z improve by increasing the availability of raw material B?
[*Ans.* No, because $y_2 = 0$, which implies that the resource is abundant.]

(d) Since $y_4 = 1$, an increase in the fourth resource will improve the optimum value of z. Give a physical interpretation of what it means to increase the fourth resource.
[*Ans.* The fourth constraint represents the maximum limit on demand. The fourth resource can be increased by expanding the company's share in the market.]

(e) Which of the four resources should be given priority in the allocation of new funds?
[*Ans.* Raw material A, because it has the largest dual price, $y_1 = 2$.]

Observe that the definition of dual prices (unit worth of a resource) gives us the *rate* of improvement in optimum z. It does not specify the *amount* by which a resource can be changed while maintaining the same rate of improvement. The following presentation addresses the point of determining the maximum change in the availability of a resource.

3.6.4 MAXIMUM CHANGE IN RESOURCE AVAILABILITY

In this section, we seek to determine the range of variation in the availability of a resource for which the dual prices remain applicable. To achieve this, we need to perform additional computations. We shall first demonstrate how the procedure works and then show how the same information can be secured from the optimum tableau.

Suppose that we consider changing the first resource in the Reddy Mikks model by the amount D_1, meaning that available raw material A is $6 + D_1$ tons. If D_1 is positive, the resource increases; if it is negative, the resource decreases.

How is the simplex tableau changed when the change D_1 is effected? The simplest way to answer the question is to augment D_1 to the right side of the first constraint in the starting tableau and then apply the same arithmetic operations that were used to develop the successive iterations. If we keep in mind that the right-side constants are never used as *pivot elements*, it is evident that the change D_1 will affect only the right side of each iteration. You should verify that the successive iterations of the model will change as shown in Table 3-5.

Actually, the changes in the right sides resulting from D_1 can be obtained *directly* from the successive tableaus. First, notice that in each iteration the elements of the new right side consist of a constant and a linear term in D_1. The constant components exactly equal the right side of the iteration *before* D_1 is added. The coefficients of the linear term in D_1 are essentially those under s_1 in the same iteration. For example, in the optimum iteration the constants ($12\frac{2}{3}$, 4/3, 10/3, 3, 2/3) represent the right side of the optimum tableau before D_1 is effected, and (1/3, 2/3, $-1/3$, -1, $-2/3$) are the coefficients under s_1 in the same tableau. Why s_1? Because it is uniquely associated with the first constraint. In other words, for right-side changes in the second, third, and fourth constraints, we should use the coefficients under s_2, s_3, and s_4, respectively.

What does this information mean? Since we have concluded that the change D_1 will affect only the right side of the tableau, it means that such a change can affect only the *feasibility* of the solution. Thus D_1 should not be changed in a manner that will make any of the (basic) *variables* negative. This means that D_1 must be

Table 3-5

	Right-Side Elements in Iteration		
Equation	0 (starting)	1	2 (optimum)
z	0	12	$12\frac{2}{3} + \frac{1}{3} D_1$
1	$6 + D_1$	$2 + D_1$	$\frac{4}{3} + \frac{2}{3} D_1$
2	8	4	$\frac{10}{3} - \frac{1}{3} D_1$
3	1	5	$3 - 1\, D_1$
4	2	2	$\frac{2}{3} - \frac{2}{3} D_1$

restricted to the range that will maintain the *nonnegativity* of the right side of the constraint equations in the optimum tableau. That is,

$$x_I = \frac{4}{3} + \frac{2}{3} D_1 \geq 0 \tag{1}$$

$$x_E = \frac{10}{3} - \frac{1}{3} D_1 \geq 0 \tag{2}$$

$$s_3 = 3 - D_1 \geq 0 \tag{3}$$

$$s_4 = \frac{2}{3} - \frac{2}{3} D_1 \geq 0 \tag{4}$$

To determine the admissible range for D_1, we consider two cases.

Case 1: $D_1 > 0$. Relation (1) is always satisfied for $D_1 > 0$. Relations (2), (3), and (4), on the other hand, produce the following respective limits: $D_1 \leq 10$, $D_1 \leq 3$, and $D_1 \leq 1$. Thus all four relations are satisfied for $D_1 \leq 1$.

Case 2: $D_1 < 0$. Relations (2), (3), and (4) are always satisfied for $D_1 < 0$, whereas relation (1) yields the limit $D_1 \geq -2$.

By combining cases 1 and 2, we see that

$$-2 \leq D_1 \leq 1$$

will always result in a feasible solution. Any change outside this range (i.e., *decreasing* raw material A by more than 2 tons or *increasing* it by more than 1 ton) will lead to infeasibility and a new set of basic variables (see Chapter 5). This means that the maximum and minimum amounts of raw material A for which the dual price $y_1 = 1/3$ remains applicable $6 + 1 = 7$ and $6 - 2 = 4$, respectively.

Exercise 3.6-2

Consider the Reddy Mikks model.

(a) Given $D_1 = 1/2$ ton, find the new optimum solution.
[*Ans.* $z = 12\frac{5}{6}$, $x_E = 3\frac{1}{6}$, $x_I = 1\frac{2}{3}$, $s_1 = s_2 = 0$, $s_3 = 2\frac{1}{2}$, $s_4 = 1/3$.]

(b) Determine the optimum right side of the constraint equations resulting from *independently* changing resources 2, 3, and 4 by D_2, D_3, and D_4.
[*Ans.* D_2: $4/3 - D_2/3$, $10/3 + 2D_2/3$, $3 + D_2$, $2/3 + D_2/3$
D_3: $4/3$, $10/3$, $3 + D_3$, $2/3$
D_4: $4/3$, $10/3$, 3, $2/3 + D_4$.]
(c) Determine the feasible ranges for D_2, D_3, D_4 in part (b).
[*Ans.* $-2 \leq D_2 \leq 4$, $-3 \leq D_3 < \infty$, $-2/3 \leq D_4 < \infty$.]
(d) Determine the ranges in optimal z resulting from the changes in part (c).
[*Ans.* D_2: $10 \leq z \leq 18$. D_3 and D_4: $z = 12\frac{2}{3}$ regardless of the values of D_3 and D_4. The answer agrees with earlier analysis on unit worth of resources.]
(e) Are the ranges in part (d) correct if the changes D_2, D_3, and D_4 are effected *simultaneously*?
[*Ans.* No, because *simultaneous* changes will make the right-side elements functions of D_2, D_3, and D_4. The analysis above is correct only when we consider one resource at a time.]

3.6.5 MAXIMUM CHANGE IN MARGINAL PROFIT/COST

Just as we did in studying the permissible ranges for changes in resources, we are also interested in studying the permissible ranges for changes in marginal profits (or costs). We have shown graphically in Section 2.1.2 (Sensitivity Problem 1) that the objective function coefficients can change within limits without affecting the optimum values of the variables (the optimum value of z will change, though). In this presentation, we show how this information can be obtained from the optimum tableau.

In the present situation, as in the case of resource changes, the objective equation is never used as a pivot equation. Thus any changes in the coefficients of the objective function will affect only the objective equation in the optimum tableau. This means that such changes can have the effect of making the solution nonoptimal. Our goal is to determine the range of variation for the object coefficients (one at a time) for which the current optimum remains unchanged.

Two distinct cases arise depending on whether or not the variable is basic or nonbasic in the optimal tableau.

Case 1: Basic Variables. The nature of row operations in the simplex tableau reveals that any changes in the original coefficients of the optimal basic variables will affect *all* the *nonbasic* coefficients in the objective row of the optimum tableau. Such a change may thus affect the current optimum because one or more of its nonbasic variables may become eligible to enter the basic solution. Our interest is to find the range of variation for the original objective coefficient that will keep the current optimum unchanged.

We illustrate the associated computations by changing the marginal profit of x_E in the Reddy Mikks model form 3 to $3 + d_1$, where d_1 may be either positive or negative. Thus the objective function reads as

$$z = (3 + d_1)x_E + 2x_I$$

If we were to use this function in the starting tableau and carry out the *same* sequence of computations used to produce the original optimum tableau, we would obtain the following (verify!):

Basic	x_E	x_I	s_1	s_2	s_3	s_4	Solution
z	0	0	$\frac{1}{3}-\frac{1}{3}d_1$	$\frac{4}{3}+\frac{2}{3}d_1$	0	0	$12\frac{2}{3}+\frac{10}{3}d_1$
x_I	0	1	2/3	−1/3	0	0	4/3
x_E	1	0	−1/3	2/3	0	0	10/3
s_3	0	0	−1	1	1	0	3
s_4	0	0	−2/3	−1/3	0	1	2/3

The only changes in the tableau occur in the nonbasic coefficients (of s_1 and s_2) in the z-row. Moreover, the changes can be obtained from the original tableau by multiplying the nonbasic coefficients and the right-hand side in the x_E-row by d_1 and then adding it to the original optimum z-row (see the tableau above).

Now the original optimal solution remains unchanged as long as the z-equation coefficients of s_1 and s_2 remain nonnegative (maximization case); that is,

$$\frac{1}{3}-\frac{d_1}{3}\geq 0 \quad \text{and} \quad \frac{4}{3}+\frac{2d_1}{3}\geq 0$$

The first inequality is satisfied for $d_1 \leq 1$ and the second for $d_1 \geq -2$, thus yielding the limits $-2 \leq d_1 \leq 1$. In terms of the coefficient c_E of x_E, this yields $3-2 \leq c_E \leq 3+1$, or $1 \leq c_E \leq 4$, signifying that the current optimum remains unchanged for the range [1, 4] (compare with Sensitivity Problem 1, Section 2.1.2). The value of z will change, however, according to the expression $12\frac{2}{3}+\frac{10}{3}d_1$, $-2 \leq d_1 \leq 1$.

Exercise 3.6-3

Find the range of variation for the objective coefficient of x_I.
[*Ans.* $3/2 \leq c_I \leq 6$.]

Case 2: Nonbasic Variables. The nonbasic variables case is simpler, since changes in their original objective coefficients can affect only their z-equation coefficient and nothing else. This follows because the corresponding column is not pivoted as in a basic column.

The current Reddy Mikks example does not serve to illustrate the nonbasic case because both x_E and x_I happen to be basic in the current optimum tableau. For this reason, we will consider the same example with the following objective function that is designed to render x_I nonbasic:

$$\text{maximize } z = 5x_E + 2x_I$$

The associated optimum tableau is given below.

Basic	x_E	x_I	s_1	s_2	s_3	s_4	Solution
z	0	1/2	0	5/2	0	0	20
s_3	0	3/2	1	−1/2	0	0	2
x_E	1	1/2	0	1/2	0	0	4
s_3	0	3/2	0	1/2	1	0	5
s_4	0	1	0	0	0	1	2

The variable x_I is now nonbasic. Our objective is to change its original z-coefficient (revenue per unit) from $c_I = 2$ to $c_I = 2 + d_2$, and then find the range of

d_2 for which the given solution remains unchanged. We mentioned above that any change in c_I can only affect its z-equation coefficient. In fact, if you reproduce the above tableau starting with $c_\text{I} = 2 + d_2$ instead of $c_\text{I} = 2$, you will discover that the objective equation coefficient will change from $\frac{1}{2}$ to $\frac{1}{2} - d_2$. In general, the change d of the original objective coefficient of a *nonbasic* variable *always* results in decreasing the objective coefficient in the current optimum tableau by the same amount.

We can see then that the given tableau will remain optimal as long as $1/2 - d_2 \geq 0$ is satisfied. This yields $d_2 \leq 1/2$, indicating that the range of variation for c_I is $c_\text{I} \leq 1/2 + 2$ or $c_\text{I} \leq 5/2$.

From the discussion above we conclude that if d_2 is increased beyond 1/2, then x_I will become profitable because its objective coefficient will become negative (maximization case). Right now, if we attempt to force x_I into the basic solution without changing its objective coefficient (i.e., $c_\text{I} = 2$), the value of z will deteriorate at the rate of 1/2 dollar per unit increase in x_I. This can be seen directly because the objective equation in the optimum tableau reads as

$$z = 20 - \frac{1}{2}x_\text{I} - \frac{5}{2}s_2$$

For this reason, the optimal objective coefficients of the nonbasic variables are usually referred to as the **reduced costs** as they represent the net *rate* of decrease in the optimum objective value resulting from increasing the associated nonbasic variable. Actually, the *reduced cost* represents the net difference between the cost of the resources used to produce *one unit* of x_I (input) and its per unit revenue (output). Thus, if the per unit cost of the resources exceeds that of the revenue, the *reduced cost* is positive and there will be no economic advantage in producing that item. This is the main reason a nonbasic variable with a negative *reduced cost* is always a candidate for becoming positive in the optimum solution.

You can now see that an unused economic activity (i.e., a nonbasic variable) can become economically viable in one of two ways: by decreasing its per unit use of the resources, or by increasing its per unit revenue (through price increase). (Of course, a combination of the two ways is also permissible.) In an economic sense, it is logical to think of the first option as being more viable an option because it implies that any improvement is being realized through a more efficient use of the resources. Raising prices, on the other hand, may not be as viable because the market may be controlled by other factors, including competition.

Exercise 3.6-4

Obtain a TORA solution of the Reddy Mikks model using the objective function

$$\text{maximize } z = 4x_1 + 2x_2$$

The optimum tableau indicates that x_I remains at zero level. Yet its reduced cost is zero. What is the economic interpretation of this result?

[*Ans.* The per unit cost of resources for x_I equals its per unit profit, just as in any other positive (basic) activity. This means that x_I can be made positive without penalty in terms of the objective value (technically, we say that the problem has an *alternative* optimum).]

3.7 SUMMARY

In this chapter we have presented two variants of the simplex method: the primal and the dual. Both variants are based on the fundamental theory that states that the optimum solution is associated with an extreme (or corner) point of the solution space and that extreme points are completely identified by the basic solutions of the standard form of the linear program. The primal simplex starts feasible but nonoptimal and continues to be nonoptimal until the final iteration is reached, whereas the dual simplex starts (better than) optimal but infeasible and continues to be infeasible until the end of the iterative process. The chapter also demonstrates that a generalized simplex procedure based on a combination of the optimality and feasibility conditions of both the primal and the dual methods can also be devised to solve problems that start both nonoptimal and infeasible.

We have discussed the special cases of degeneracy, cycling, alternative optima, unboundness, and infeasibility. Both the theoretical and practical implications of each of these cases were discussed.

The optimum tableau offers more than just the optimum values of the variables and the objective function. It gives the worth of the resources (dual prices) and provides insight into sensitivity analysis in linear programming.

SELECTED REFERENCES

BAZARAA, M., J. JARVIS, and H. SHERALI, *Linear Programming and Network Flows*, Wiley, New York, 1990.

DANTZIG, G., *Linear Programming and Extensions*, Princeton University Press, Princeton, N.J., 1963.

HADLEY, G., *Linear Programming*, Addison-Wesley, Reading, Mass., 1962.

PROBLEMS

Section	Assigned Problems
3.1	3–1, 3–2
3.2.1	3–3, 3–4
3.2.2	3–5 to 3–7
3.3	3–8 to 320
3.3.1	3–21 to 3–27
3.4	3–28 to 3–31
3.5	3–32 to 3–38
3.6	3–39 to 3–47

□ **3–1** Consider the following linear program:

$$\text{maximize } z = 2x_1 + 3x_2$$

subject to

$$x_1 + 3x_2 \leq 6$$
$$3x_1 + 2x_2 \leq 6$$
$$x_1, x_2 \geq 0$$

(a) Determine the solution space graphically.
(b) Identify all the feasible and infeasible extreme points of the solution space.
(c) Determine the optimum solution point by direct substitution of the feasible extreme points in part (b) in the objective function.

☐ **3–2** Repeat Problem 3–1 for the following objective functions:

(a) Maximize $z = 6x_1 + x_2$.

(b) Minimize $z = 2x_1 - x_2$.

Observe that for the same solution space, a change in the objective function leads to a selection of a different extreme point solution.

☐ **3–3** Convert the following LP to the standard form with and without non-negative right-hand side of the constraints:

$$\text{maximize } z = 2x_1 + 3x_2 + 5x_3$$

subject to

$$\begin{aligned} x_1 + x_2 - x_3 &\geq -5 \\ -6x_1 + 7x_2 - 9x_3 &\leq 4 \\ x_1 + x_2 + 4x_3 &= 10 \\ x_1, x_2 &\geq 0 \\ x_3 &\text{ unrestricted} \end{aligned}$$

☐ **3–4** Repeat Problem 3–3 for each of the following independent changes.

(a) The first constraint is $x_1 + x_2 - x_3 \leq -5$.

(b) The second constraint is $-6x_1 + 7x_2 - 9x_3 \geq 4$.

(c) The third constraint is $x_1 + x_2 + 4x_3 \geq 10$.

(d) $x_3 \geq 0$.

(e) x_1 unrestricted.

(f) The objective function is minimize $z = 2x_1 + 3x_2 + 5x_3$.

(g) Changes (a), (b), and (c) are effected simultaneously.

(h) Changes (c), (d), (e), and (f) are effected simultaneously.

☐ **3–5** Consider the following problem:

$$\text{maximize } z = 2x_1 - 4x_2 + 5x_3 - 6x_4$$

subject to

$$\begin{aligned} x_1 + 4x_2 - 2x_3 + 8x_4 &\leq 2 \\ -x_1 + 2x_2 + 3x_3 + 4x_4 &\leq 1 \\ x_1, x_2, x_3, x_4 &\geq 0 \end{aligned}$$

Determine:

(a) The maximum number of possible basic solutions.

(b) The feasible extreme points.

(c) The optimal basic feasible solution.

☐ **3–6** Repeat Problem 3–5 for the following LP:

$$\text{maximize } z = x_1 + 2x_2 - x_3 + 4x_4$$

subject to

$$\begin{aligned} x_1 + 2x_2 - 3x_3 + x_4 &= 4 \\ x_1 + 2x_2 + x_3 + 2x_4 &= 4 \\ x_1, x_2, x_3, x_4 &\geq 0 \end{aligned}$$

□ **3–7** Consider the following LP:

$$\text{maximize } z = x_1 + x_2$$

subject to

$$x_1 + 2x_2 \leq 6$$
$$2x_1 + x_2 \geq 9$$
$$x_1, x_2 \geq 0$$

(a) Without investigating the graphical solution space, determine the basic solutions of the system and their associated extreme points.
(b) What can we conclude regarding the optimum solution?

□ **3–8** Consider the three-dimensional LP solution space shown in Figure 3-8 with its feasible extreme points identified by *A*, *B*, *C*, ..., *J*. The coordinates of each point are shown in the figure.

(a) Indicate whether or not the following pairs of extreme points are adjacent: (1) *A*, *B*; (2) *B*, *D*; (3) *E*, *H*; (4) *A*, *I*.
(b) From the standpoint of the simplex method, suppose that the solution starts at *A* and that the optimum occurs at *H*. Indicate whether or not the simplex iterations from *A* to *H* can be identified by the following sequences of extreme points, and state the reason.
(1) $A \rightarrow B \rightarrow G \rightarrow H$.
(2) $A \rightarrow C \rightarrow F \rightarrow J \rightarrow H$.
(3) $A \rightarrow C \rightarrow I \rightarrow H$.
(4) $A \rightarrow I \rightarrow H$.
(5) $A \rightarrow D \rightarrow G \rightarrow H$.
(6) $A \rightarrow D \rightarrow A \rightarrow B \rightarrow G \rightarrow H$.
(7) $A \rightarrow C \rightarrow F \rightarrow D \rightarrow A \rightarrow B \rightarrow G \rightarrow H$.

□ **3–9** In Figure 3-8, all the constraints associated with the solution space are of the type $\leq$. Let s_1, s_2, s_3, and s_4 represent the slack variables associated with the constraints represented by the planes *CEIJF*, *BEIHG*, *DFJHG*, and *HIJ*, respectively. Identify the basic and nonbasic variables associated with each feasible extreme point. (Note that the problem implicitly assumes that $x_1, x_2, x_3 \geq 0$.)

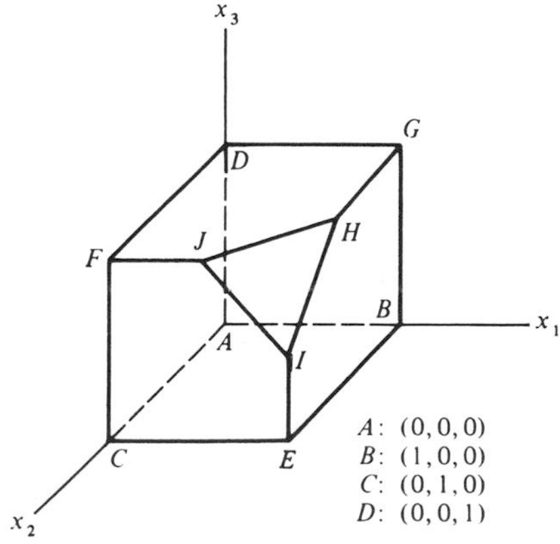

Figure 3-8

☐ **3–10** In Problem 3–9, identify the entering and leaving variables when the solution moves between the following pairs of extreme points: (a) $A \to B$, (b) $E \to I$, (c) $F \to J$, (d) $D \to G$.

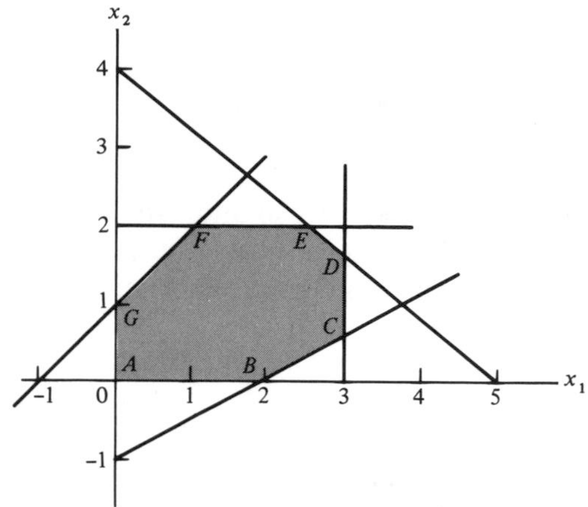

Figure 3-9

☐ **3–11** In Figure 3-8, suppose that the simplex method starts at A. Determine the entering variable in the *first* iteration together with its value and the improvement in the objective value given that the objective function is defined as follows.

(a) Maximize $z = x_1 - 2x_2 + 3x_3$.
(b) Maximize $z = 5x_1 + 2x_2 + 4x_3$.
(c) Maximize $z = -2x_1 + 7x_2 + 2x_3$.
(d) Maximize $z = x_1 + x_2 + x_3$.

☐ **3–12** Consider the two-dimensional solution space in Figure 3-9. Suppose that the objective function is given by

$$\text{maximize } z = 3x_1 + 6x_2$$

(a) Determine the optimum extreme point graphically.
(b) Suppose that the simplex method starts at A, identify the successive extreme points that will lead to the optimum obtained in part (a).
(c) Determine the entering variable and the ratios of the feasibility condition assuming that the simplex solution is at A and the objective function is given by

$$\text{maximize } z = 4x_1 + x_2$$

(d) Repeat part (c) when the objective function is replaced by

$$\text{maximize } z = x_1 + 2x_2$$

(e) In parts (c) and (d), determine the resulting improvements in the value of z.

☐ **3–13** Consider the following system of equations:

$$\begin{aligned}
x_1 + 2x_2 - 3x_3 + 5x_4 + x_5 \qquad\qquad\qquad &= 4\\
5x_1 - 2x_2 \qquad + 6x_4 \qquad + x_6 \qquad\quad &= 8\\
2x_1 + 3x_2 - 2x_3 + 3x_4 \qquad\qquad + x_7 \quad &= 3\\
-x_1 \qquad + x_3 + 2x_4 \qquad\qquad\qquad + x_8 &= 0\\
x_1, x_2, \ldots, x_8 \geq 0 &
\end{aligned}$$

Let $(x_5, \ldots, x_8)$ be a given initial basic solution. If x_1 becomes basic, which of the current basic variables must become nonbasic at zero level in order for all the variables to remain nonnegative, and what would be the value of x_1 in the new basic solution? Repeat this procedure for x_2, x_3, and x_4.

☐ **3–14** The following tableau represents a specific simplex iteration.

Basic	x_1	x_2	x_3	x_4	x_5	x_6	x_7	x_8	Solution
z	0	−5	0	4	−1	−10	0	0	620
x_8	0	3	0	−2	−3	−1	5	1	12
x_3	0	2	1	3	1	0	3	0	6
x_1	1	−1	0	0	6	−4	0	0	0

(a) Determine the leaving variable if the entering variable is (1) x_2, (2) x_4, (3) x_5, (4) x_6, (5) x_7.

(b) For each of the cases in part (a), determine the resulting increase *or* decrease in z.

☐ **3–15** Solve the following sets of simultaneous linear equations by using the row operations (Gauss–Jordan) method introduced with the simplex method (Section 3.2.2).

(a)
$$\begin{aligned} -3x_1 + 2x_2 + 5x_3 &= 5 \\ 4x_1 + 3x_2 + 2x_3 &= 8 \\ x_1 - x_2 + 3x_3 &= 10 \end{aligned}$$

(b)
$$\begin{aligned} x_2 + x_3 &= 5 \\ 2x_1 + x_2 - x_3 &= 12 \\ x_1 + 3x_2 + 4x_3 &= 10 \end{aligned}$$

☐ **3–16** Consider the following set of constraints:

$$\begin{aligned} x_1 + 7x_2 + 3x_3 + 7x_4 &\le 46 \\ 3x_1 - x_2 + x_3 + 2x_4 &\le 8 \\ 2x_1 + 3x_2 - x_3 + x_4 &\le 10 \end{aligned}$$

Solve the problem by the simplex method assuming that the objective function is given as follows:

(a) Maximize $z = 2x_1 + x_2 - 3x_3 + 5x_4$.
(b) Maximize $z = -2x_1 + 6x_2 + 3x_3 - 2x_4$.
(c) Maximize $z = 3x_1 - x_2 + 3x_3 + 4x_4$.
(d) Minimize $z = 5x_1 - 4x_2 + 6x_3 + 8x_4$.
(e) Minimize $z = 3x_1 + 6x_2 - 2x_3 + 4x_4$.

☐ **3–17** Solve the following problem by inspection and justify the method of solution in terms of the simplex method.

$$\text{maximize } z = 5x_1 - 6x_2 + 3x_3 - 5x_4 + 12x_5$$

subject to

$$x_1 + 3x_2 + 5x_3 + 6x_4 + 3x_5 \le 90$$
$$x_1, x_2, x_3, x_4, x_5 \ge 0$$

[*Hint*: A basic solution consists only of one variable.]

☐ **3–18** Consider the following LP:

$$\text{maximize } z = 16x_1 + 15x_2$$

subject to

$$\begin{aligned} 40x_1 + 31x_2 &\leq 124 \\ -x_1 + \quad x_2 &\leq \quad 1 \\ x_1 \qquad\quad &\leq \quad 3 \\ x_1, x_2 &\geq 0 \end{aligned}$$

Use TORA where appropriate to answer the following:

(a) Solve the problem by the simplex method, where the entering variable is the nonbasic variable with the *most* negative objective coefficient.

(b) Resolve the problem by the simplex method, always selecting the entering variable as the nonbasic variable with the *least* negative coefficient.

(c) Compare the number of iterations in parts (a) and (b) and draw a general conclusion.

(d) Suppose that the sense of optimization is changed to minimization by multiplying the maximization objective function by -1, in which case we must use the minimization optimality condition. How would this change affect the simplex computations?

☐ **3–19** Solve the following problem by using x_4, x_5, and x_6 for the starting basic (feasible) solution:

$$\text{maximize } z = 3x_1 + x_2 + 2x_3$$

subject to

$$\begin{aligned} 12x_1 + 3x_2 + 6x_3 + 3x_4 \qquad\qquad &= 9 \\ 8x_1 + x_2 - 4x_3 \qquad + 2x_5 \qquad &= 10 \\ 3x_1 \qquad\qquad\qquad\qquad\qquad - x_6 &= 0 \\ x_1, x_2, \ldots, x_6 &\geq 0 \end{aligned}$$

☐ **3–20** Consider the following linear program:

$$\text{maximize } z = c_1x_1 + c_2x_2$$

subject to

$$\begin{aligned} a_{11}x_1 + a_{12}x_2 &\leq b_1 \\ a_{21}x_1 + a_{22}x_2 &\leq b_2 \\ x_1, x_2 &\geq 0 \end{aligned}$$

where $1 \leq c_1 \leq 3$, $4 \leq c_2 \leq 6$, $-1 \leq a_{11} \leq 3$, $2 \leq a_{12} \leq 5$, $8 \leq b_1 \leq 12$, $2 \leq a_{21} \leq 5$, $4 \leq a_{22} \leq 6$, and $10 \leq b_2 \leq 14$. Find the upper and lower bounds on the optimum value of z.

[*Hint*: A more restrictive solution space yields a smaller value of z.]

☐ **3–21** Consider the following set of constraints:

$$-2x_1 + 3x_2 = 3 \quad (1)$$
$$4x_1 + 5x_2 \geq 10 \quad (2)$$
$$x_1 + 2x_2 \leq 5 \quad (3)$$
$$6x_1 + 7x_2 \leq 3 \quad (4)$$
$$4x_1 + 8x_2 \geq 5 \quad (5)$$

Assuming that x_1, $x_2 \geq 0$, determine the starting objective equation in each of the following cases after the artificial variables are substituted out in the M-technique.

(a) Maximize $z = 5x_1 + 6x_2$ subject to constraints (1), (3), and (4).
(b) Maximize $z = 2x_1 - 7x_2$ subject to constraints (1), (2), (4), and (5).
(c) Minimize $z = 3x_1 + 6x_2$ subject to constraints (3), (4), and (5).
(d) Minimize $z = 4x_1 + 6x_2$ subject to constraints (1), (2), and (5).
(e) Minimize $z = 3x_1 + 2x_2$ subject to constraints (1) and (5).

☐ **3–22** Consider the following set of constraints:

$$x_1 + x_2 + x_3 = 7$$
$$2x_1 - 5x_2 + x_3 \geq 10$$
$$x_1, x_2, x_3 \geq 0$$

Solve by using the M-technique, assuming that the objective function is given as follows:

(a) Maximize $z = 2x_1 + 3x_2 - 5x_3$.
(b) Minimize $z = 2x_1 + 3x_2 - 5x_3$.
(c) Maximize $z = x_1 + 2x_2 + x_3$.
(d) Minimize $z = 4x_1 - 8x_2 + 3x_3$.

☐ **3–23** Consider the problem

$$\text{maximize } z = x_1 + 5x_2 + 3x_3$$

subject to

$$x_1 + 2x_2 + x_3 = 3$$
$$2x_1 - x_2 = 4$$
$$x_1, x_2, x_3 \geq 0$$

Let R be an artificial variable in the second constraint equation. Solve the problem by using x_3 and R for a starting basic solution.

☐ **3–24** Consider the problem

$$\text{maximize } z = 2x_1 + 4x_2 + 4x_3 - 3x_4$$

subject to

$$x_1 + x_2 + x_3 = 4$$
$$x_1 + 4x_2 + x_4 = 8$$
$$x_1, x_2, x_3, x_4 \geq 0$$

Find the optimum solution by using (x_3, x_4) as the starting basic solution.

□ **3–25** Solve the following problem by using x_3 and x_4 as a starting basic feasible solution:

$$\text{minimize } z = 3x_1 + 2x_2 + 3x_3$$

subject to

$$\begin{aligned} x_1 + 4x_2 + x_3 \quad\quad &\geq 7 \\ 2x_1 + x_2 \quad\quad + x_4 &\geq 10 \\ x_1, x_2, x_3, x_4 &\geq 0 \end{aligned}$$

□ **3–26** In Problem 3–21, write the objective function for phase I in each case.

□ **3–27** Solve Problem 3–22 by the two-phase method and compare the resulting number of iterations with those in the M-technique.

□ **3–28** Solve the following problems by the dual simplex method.

(a) Minimize $z = 2x_1 + 3x_2$
subject to

$$\begin{aligned} 2x_1 + 2x_2 &\leq 30 \\ x_1 + 2x_2 &\geq 10 \\ x_1, x_2 &\geq 0 \end{aligned}$$

(b) Minimize $z = 5x_1 + 6x_2$
subject to

$$\begin{aligned} x_1 + x_2 &\geq 2 \\ 4x_1 + x_2 &\geq 4 \\ x_1, x_2 &\geq 0 \end{aligned}$$

(c) The bus scheduling problem of Example 2.3-1.

□ **3–29** Solve the following problems by the dual simplex method:

(a) Minimize $z = 4x_1 + 2x_2$
subject to

$$\begin{aligned} x_1 + x_2 &= 1 \\ 3x_1 - x_2 &\geq 2 \\ x_1, x_2 &\geq 0 \end{aligned}$$

(b) Minimize $z = 2x_1 + 3x_2$
subject to

$$\begin{aligned} 2x_1 + 3x_2 &\leq 1 \\ x_1 + x_2 &= 2 \\ x_1, x_2 &\geq 0 \end{aligned}$$

[*Hint*: Replace the equality constraint with two inequalities.]

□ **3–30 (Dual Simplex Method with Artificial Constraint).** Consider the following problem:

$$\text{maximize } z = 2x_1 - x_2 + x_3$$

subject to

$$\begin{aligned} 2x_1 + 3x_2 - 5x_3 &\geq 4 \\ -x_1 + 9x_2 - x_3 &\geq 3 \\ 4x_1 + 6x_2 + 3x_3 &\leq 8 \\ x_1, x_2, x_3 &\geq 0 \end{aligned}$$

The starting basic solution for this problem consisting of all slacks is infeasible; that is, $s_1 = -4$, $s_2 = -3$, and $s_3 = 8$. However, the dual simplex method cannot be applied directly, since neither x_1 nor x_3 satisfies the optimality condition for a maximization problem. Show that by augmenting the *artificial constraints* $x_1 + x_3 \leq M$ (where $M > 0$ is sufficiently large that it is not restrictive with respect to the original constraints) and then using the augmented constraint as a pivot row, the selection of x_1 as the entering variable will render an objective row that is all optimal. Hence it is possible to carry out the regular dual simplex calculations. (Notice that generally, in a maximization problem, the entering variable is the one having the largest objective coefficient among the variables that do not satisfy the optimality condition.)

□ **3–31** Using the artificial constraint procedure of Problem 3–30, solve the following problems by the dual simplex method. In each case, indicate whether the solution is feasible, infeasible, and/or unbounded.

(a) Minimize $z = -x_1 + x_2$
subject to

$$\begin{aligned} x_1 - 4x_2 &\geq 5 \\ x_1 - 3x_2 &\leq 1 \\ 2x_1 - 5x_2 &\geq 1 \\ x_1, x_2 &\geq 0 \end{aligned}$$

(b) Maximize $z = x_1 - 3x_2$
subject to

$$\begin{aligned} x_1 - x_2 &\leq 2 \\ x_1 + x_2 &\geq 4 \\ 2x_1 - 2x_2 &\geq 3 \\ x_1, x_2 &\geq 0 \end{aligned}$$

(c) Maximize $z = 2x_3$
subject to

$$\begin{aligned} -x_1 + 3x_2 - 7x_3 &\geq 5 \\ -x_1 + x_2 - x_3 &\leq 1 \\ 3x_1 + x_2 - 10x_3 &\leq 8 \\ x_1, x_2, x_3 &\geq 0 \end{aligned}$$

□ **3–32** Consider the graphical solution space shown in Figure 3-10. Suppose that the simplex iterations start at A and that the optimum solution occurs at D. Further, assume that the objective function is defined such that x_1 enters the solution first.

(a) Identify (on the graph) the extreme (corner) points that define the simplex method path to the optimum point.

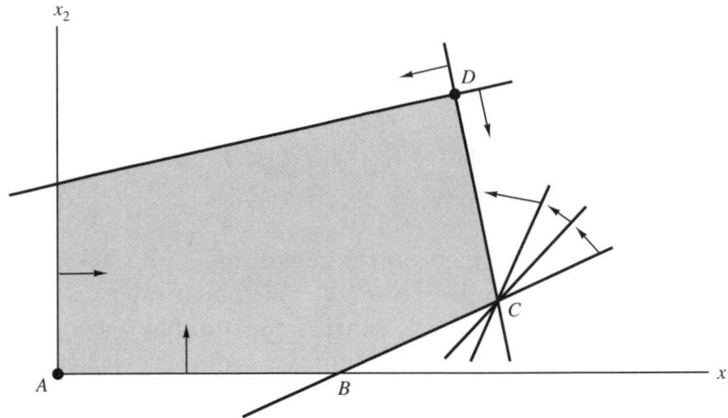

Figure 3-10

(b) Determine the maximum possible number of simplex iterations needed to reach the optimum solution. Explain.

□ **3–33** Show that the following LP problem is *temporarily* degenerate:

$$\text{maximize } z = 3x_1 + 2x_2$$

subject to

$$\begin{aligned} 4x_1 + 3x_2 &\le 12 \\ 4x_1 + x_2 &\le 8 \\ 4x_1 - x_2 &\le 8 \\ x_1, x_2 &\ge 0 \end{aligned}$$

□ **3–34** Consider the problem

$$\text{maximize } z = x_1 + 2x_2 + 3x_3$$

subject to

$$\begin{aligned} x_1 + 2x_2 + 3x_3 &\le 10 \\ x_1 + x_2 \qquad &\le 5 \\ x_1 \qquad\qquad &\le 1 \\ x_1, x_2, x_3 &\ge 0 \end{aligned}$$

Find at least three alternative optimal basic solutions and then write a general expression for all the *non*-basic optimal solutions comprised by the basic optima obtained.

□ **3–35** Consider the following linear programming problem:

$$\text{maximize } z = 2x_1 - x_2 + 3x_3$$

subject to

$$\begin{aligned} x_1 - x_2 + 5x_3 &\le 10 \\ 2x_1 - x_2 + 3x_3 &\le 40 \\ x_1, x_2, x_3 &\ge 0 \end{aligned}$$

Show that the problem has alternative solutions that are all *non*basic. What could one conclude concerning the solution space and the objective function? Show that the values of the optimal basic variables can be increased indefinitely while the value of z remains constant.

☐ **3–36** Consider the problem

$$\text{maximize } z = 3x_1 + x_2$$

subject to

$$\begin{aligned} x_1 + 2x_2 \qquad &\leq 5 \\ x_1 + x_2 - x_3 &\leq 2 \\ 7x_1 + 3x_2 - 5x_3 &\leq 20 \\ x_1, x_2, x_3 &\geq 0 \end{aligned}$$

Show that the optimal solution is degenerate and that there exist alternative solutions that are all nonbasic.

☐ **3–37** In the problem

$$\text{maximize } z = 20x_1 + 10x_2 + x_3$$

subject to

$$\begin{aligned} 3x_1 - 3x_2 + 5x_3 &\leq 50 \\ x_1 \qquad + x_3 &\leq 10 \\ x_1 - x_2 + 4x_3 &\leq 20 \\ x_1, x_2, x_3 &\geq 0 \end{aligned}$$

in which direction is the solution space unbounded? Without further computations, what could one conclude concerning the optimal solution to the problem?

☐ **3–38** Consider the problem

$$\text{maximize } z = 3x_1 + 2x_2 + 3x_3$$

subject to

$$\begin{aligned} 2x_1 + x_2 + x_3 &\leq 2 \\ 3x_1 + 4x_2 + 2x_3 &\geq 8 \\ x_1, x_2, x_3 &\geq 0 \end{aligned}$$

By using the M-technique, show that the optimal solution can include an artificial basic variable at the *zero* level. Hence conclude that a feasible optimal solution exists.

☐ **3–39** Consider the following LP allocation model:

$$\text{maximize } z = 3x_1 + 2x_2 \qquad \text{(profit)}$$

subject to

$$\begin{aligned} 4x_1 + 3x_2 &\leq 12 \qquad \text{(resource 1)} \\ 4x_1 + x_2 &\leq 8 \qquad \text{(resource 2)} \\ 4x_1 - x_2 &\leq 8 \qquad \text{(resource 3)} \\ x_1, x_2 &\geq 0 \end{aligned}$$

The optimum tableau of the model is given by

Basic	x_1	x_2	x_3	x_4	x_5	Solution
z	0	0	5/8	1/8	0	17/2
x_2	0	1	1/2	−1/2	0	2
x_1	1	0	−1/8	3/8	0	3/2
x_5	0	0	1	−2	1	4

(a) Determine the status of each resource.
(b) Determine the unit worth of each resource.
(c) Based on the unit worth of each resource, which resource should be given priority for an increase in level?
(d) Determine the maximum range of change in the availability of the first resource that will keep the current solution feasible.
(e) Repeat part (d) for resource 2.
(f) In parts (d) and (e), determine the associated change in the optimal value of z.
(g) Determine the maximum change in the profit coefficient of x_1 that will keep the solution optimal.
(h) Repeat part (g) for x_2.

☐ **3–40** Consider the following LP allocation model:

$$\text{maximize } z = 2x_1 + 4x_2 \qquad \text{(profit)}$$

subject to

$$x_1 + 2x_2 \leq 5 \qquad \text{(resource 1)}$$
$$x_1 + x_2 \leq 4 \qquad \text{(resource 2)}$$
$$x_1, x_2 \geq 0$$

The optimal tableau is given by

Basic	x_1	x_2	x_3	x_4	Solution
z	0	0	2	0	10
x_2	1/2	1	1/2	0	5/2
x_4	1/2	0	−1/2	1	3/2

(a) Classify the two resources as scarce or abundant.
(b) Determine the maximum range of change in the availability of each resource that will keep the solution optimal.
(c) Compute the range of optimal z associated with the results in part (b).
(d) Compute the maximum change in the unit profit of x_1 that will keep the solution optimal.
(e) Repeat part (d) for x_2.

□ **3–41** Consider the following LP allocation model:

$$\text{maximize } z = 3x_1 + 2x_2 + 5x_3 \qquad \text{(profit)}$$

subject to

$$\begin{aligned} x_1 + 2x_2 + x_3 &\leq 430 \qquad \text{(resource 1)} \\ 3x_1 + \quad + 2x_3 &\leq 460 \qquad \text{(resource 2)} \\ x_1 + 4x_2 \qquad &\leq 420 \qquad \text{(resource 3)} \\ x_1, x_2, x_3 &\geq 0 \end{aligned}$$

The optimal tableau of the model is given by

Basic	x_1	x_2	x_3	x_4	x_5	x_6	Solution
z	4	0	0	1	2	0	1350
x_2	−1/4	1	0	1/2	−1/4	0	100
x_3	3/2	0	1	0	1/2	0	230
x_6	2	0	0	−2	1	1	20

(a) In each of the following cases, indicate whether the given solution remains feasible. If feasible, compute the associated values of x_1, x_2, x_3, and z.
  (1) Resource 1 availability is increased to 500 units.
  (2) Resource 1 availability is decreased to 400 units.
  (3) Resource 2 availability is decreased to 450 units.
  (4) Resource 3 availability is increased to 440 units.
  (5) Resource 3 availability is decreased to 380 units.

(b) In each if the following cases, indicate whether the given solution remains optimal.
  (1) The profit coefficient of x_1 is decreased to 2.
  (2) The profit coefficient of x_1 is increased to 9.
  (3) The profit coefficient of x_2 is increased to 5.
  (4) The profit coefficient of x_3 is reduced to 1.

□ **3–42** In Problem 3–39, determine the optimal values of x_1 and x_2 when resource 1 is increased by 2 units and, simultaneously, resource 2 is decreased by 1 unit.

□ **3–43** In Problem 3–40, suppose that resource 1 and resource 2 are changed simultaneously by the quantities D_1 and D_2. Determine the relationship between D_1 and D_2 that will always keep the solution optimal.

□ **3–44** Show that the *m equalities*

$$\sum_{j=1}^{n} a_{ij} x_j = b_i, \qquad i = 1, 2, \ldots, m$$

are equivalent to the $m + 1$ *inequalities*

$$\sum_{j=1}^{n} a_{ij} x_j \leq b_i, \qquad i = 1, 2, \ldots, m$$

$$\sum_{j=1}^{n} \left(\sum_{i=1}^{m} a_{ij} \right) x_j \geq \sum_{i=1}^{m} b_i$$

☐ **3–45** In linear programming problems in which there are several unrestricted variables, a transformation of the type $x_j = x'_j - x''_j$ will double the corresponding number of nonnegative variables. Show that it is possible, in general, to replace k unrestricted variables with exactly $k + 1$ nonnegative variables and develop the details of the substitution method.

[*Hint*: Let $x_j = x'_j - w$, where $x'_j, w \geq 0$.]

☐ **3–46** Show how the following inequality in absolute form can be replaced by two regular inequalities.

$$\left| \sum_{j=1}^{n} a_{ij} x_j \right| \leq b_i, \qquad b_i > 0$$

☐ **3–47** Show how the following objective function can be linearized:

$$\text{minimize } z = \max \left\{ \left| \sum_{j=1}^{n} c_{1j} x_j \right|, \ldots, \left| \sum_{j=1}^{n} c_{mj} x_j \right| \right\}$$

Chapter 4

Linear Programming: Revised Simplex Method

In Chapter 3 we presented the primal and dual simplex methods for solving linear programs. In this chapter we introduce the **revised simplex** method, an algorithm that offers opportunities for improving computational efficiency and accuracy. We wish to emphasize, however, that the revised algorithm uses *exactly the same* steps as those presented in Chapter 3. The only difference occurs in the details of computing the entering and the leaving variables. The presentation requires a background in linear algebra. A review of the material in Appendix A should suffice for this purpose.

4.1 MATHEMATICAL FOUNDATIONS

In this section we define the LP problem in matrix form. Based on this definition, we show how the basic solutions are determined. We then use this information to develop the general simplex tableau in matrix form. This development forms the foundation for presenting the details of the revised simplex method.

4.1.1 STANDARD LP MODEL IN MATRIX FORM

The linear programming problem in standard form (all equality constraints with all nonnegative variables; see Section 3.2.1) can be expressed in matrix form as follows:

$$\text{maximize or minimize } z = \mathbf{CX}$$

subject to

$$(\mathbf{A}, \mathbf{I})\mathbf{X} = \mathbf{b}$$
$$\mathbf{X} \geq \mathbf{0}$$

where $\mathbf{I}$ is the m-identity matrix and

$$\mathbf{X} = (x_1, x_2, \ldots, x_n)^T, \qquad \mathbf{C} = (c_1, c_2, \ldots, c_n)$$

$$\mathbf{A} = \begin{bmatrix} a_{11} & a_{12} & \cdots & a_{1,n-m} \\ a_{21} & a_{22} & \cdots & a_{2,n-m} \\ \vdots & \vdots & & \vdots \\ a_{m1} & a_{m2} & \cdots & a_{m,n-m} \end{bmatrix}, \qquad \mathbf{b} = \begin{bmatrix} b_1 \\ b_2 \\ \vdots \\ b_m \end{bmatrix}$$

The right-hand side is expected to be nonnegative in the case of the primal simplex method.

The identity matrix $\mathbf{I}$ can always be made to appear as shown in the constraint equations by augmenting and arranging the slack, surplus, and/or artificial variables as necessary (see Chapter 3). This means that the n elements of the vector $\mathbf{X}$ include any augmented slack, surplus, and artificial variables, with the rightmost m elements representing the starting solution variables.

To clarify the foregoing definition, we introduce a numerical example.

Example 4.1-1. The linear program

$$\text{maximize } z = 2x_1 + 3x_2 + 4x_3$$

subject to

$$\begin{aligned} x_1 + x_2 + x_3 &\geq 5 \\ x_1 + 2x_2 \quad &= 7 \\ 5x_1 - 2x_2 + 3x_3 &\leq 9 \\ x_1, x_2, x_3 &\geq 0 \end{aligned}$$

is expressed in the standard matrix form as

$$\text{maximize } z = (2, 3, 4, 0, -M, -M, 0) \begin{bmatrix} x_1 \\ x_2 \\ x_3 \\ x_4 \\ x_5 \\ x_6 \\ x_7 \end{bmatrix}$$

subject to

$$\begin{bmatrix} 1 & 1 & 1 & -1 & 1 & 0 & 0 \\ 1 & 2 & 0 & 0 & 0 & 1 & 0 \\ 5 & -2 & 3 & 0 & 0 & 0 & 1 \end{bmatrix} \begin{bmatrix} x_1 \\ x_2 \\ x_3 \\ x_4 \\ x_5 \\ x_6 \\ x_7 \end{bmatrix} = \begin{bmatrix} 5 \\ 7 \\ 9 \end{bmatrix}$$

$$x_j \geq 0, \qquad j = 1, 2, \ldots, 7$$

Notice that x_4 is a surplus variable whereas x_7 is a slack. The variables x_5 and x_6 are artificial.

In terms of the matrix definition, we have

$$\mathbf{X} = (x_1, x_2, \ldots, x_7)^T$$

$$\mathbf{C} = (2, 3, 4, 0, -M, -M, 0)$$

$$\mathbf{b} = (5, 7, 9)^T$$

$$\mathbf{A} = \begin{bmatrix} 1 & 1 & 1 & -1 \\ 1 & 2 & 0 & 0 \\ 5 & -2 & 3 & 0 \end{bmatrix}, \qquad \mathbf{I} = \begin{bmatrix} 1 & 0 & 0 \\ 0 & 1 & 0 \\ 0 & 0 & 1 \end{bmatrix}$$

◀

4.1.2 BASIC SOLUTIONS AND BASES

In Chapter 3 we stressed that the fundamental idea underlying the primal and dual simplex methods is that the optimum solution, when finite, must be associated with an **extreme** or **corner** point of the solution space. Algebraically, an extreme point is associated with a **basic solution** of the constraint equations $(\mathbf{A}, \mathbf{I})\mathbf{X} = \mathbf{b}$.

Given that $(\mathbf{A}, \mathbf{I})\mathbf{X} = \mathbf{b}$ has m equations and n unknowns $[\mathbf{X} = (x_1, x_2, \ldots, x_n)^T]$, a basic solution is obtained by setting $n - m$ variables equal to zero and then solving the m equations in the remaining m unknowns, *provided that a unique solution exists.* Mathematically, let

$$(\mathbf{A}, \mathbf{I})\mathbf{X} = \sum_{j=1}^{n} \mathbf{P}_j x_j$$

where $\mathbf{P}_j$ is the jth column vector of $(\mathbf{A}, \mathbf{I})$. Any m **linearly independent** vectors among $\mathbf{P}_1, \mathbf{P}_2, \ldots, \mathbf{P}_n$ will correspond to a basic solution of $(\mathbf{A}, \mathbf{I})\mathbf{X} = \mathbf{b}$ and hence to an extreme point of the solution space. In this case, the selected m vectors comprise a **basis** for which the associated square matrix must be **nonsingular**.

To illustrate the definition of a basis, in Example 4.1-1 we have $m = 3$ and $n = 7$. This means that a basis must comprise m $(= 3)$ vectors with the $n - m$ $(= 7 - 3 = 4)$ variables associated with the remaining vectors necessarily set equal to zero. Letting $x_4 = x_5 = x_6 = x_7 = 0$, we find that the vectors

$$\mathbf{P}_1 = \begin{pmatrix} 1 \\ 1 \\ 5 \end{pmatrix}, \quad \mathbf{P}_2 = \begin{pmatrix} 1 \\ 2 \\ -2 \end{pmatrix}, \quad \mathbf{P}_3 = \begin{pmatrix} 1 \\ 0 \\ 3 \end{pmatrix}$$

associated with x_1, x_2, and x_3 will form a basis if, and only if, the square matrix

$$\mathbf{B} = (\mathbf{P}_1, \mathbf{P}_2, \mathbf{P}_3) = \begin{pmatrix} 1 & 1 & 1 \\ 1 & 2 & 0 \\ 5 & -2 & 3 \end{pmatrix}$$

is nonsingular. Since the determinant of $\mathbf{B}$ is not zero ($= -9$), the condition is satisfied and the solution of the equations

$$\begin{pmatrix} 1 & 1 & 1 \\ 1 & 2 & 0 \\ 5 & -2 & 3 \end{pmatrix} \begin{pmatrix} x_1 \\ x_2 \\ x_3 \end{pmatrix} = \begin{pmatrix} 5 \\ 7 \\ 9 \end{pmatrix}$$

must be unique ($x_1 = 23/9$, $x_2 = 20/9$, $x_3 = 2/9$). As a result, the point (23/9, 20/9, 2/9, 0, 0, 0, 0) is an extreme point of the solution space $(\mathbf{A}, \mathbf{I})\mathbf{X} = \mathbf{b}$. On the other hand, the two vectors

$$\mathbf{P}_4 = \begin{pmatrix} -1 \\ 0 \\ 0 \end{pmatrix}, \quad \mathbf{P}_5 = \begin{pmatrix} 1 \\ 0 \\ 0 \end{pmatrix}$$

cannot be included *simultaneously* in *any* basis because they are dependent ($\mathbf{P}_4 = -\mathbf{P}_5$).

We can demonstrate graphically the relationship between vectors and bases by considering the following set of equations in vector form:

$$\begin{bmatrix} 2 \\ 1 \end{bmatrix} x_1 + \begin{bmatrix} 1 \\ 2 \end{bmatrix} x_2 + \begin{bmatrix} 1 \\ 1 \end{bmatrix} x_3 + \begin{bmatrix} 2 \\ -1 \end{bmatrix} x_4 + \begin{bmatrix} 4 \\ 2 \end{bmatrix} x_5 = \begin{bmatrix} 2 \\ 2 \end{bmatrix}$$

or

$$\mathbf{P}_1 x_1 + \mathbf{P}_2 x_2 + \mathbf{P}_3 x_3 + \mathbf{P}_4 x_4 + \mathbf{P}_5 x_5 = \mathbf{b}$$

Figure 4-1 plots the two-dimensional vectors $\mathbf{P}_1$, $\mathbf{P}_2$, $\mathbf{P}_3$, $\mathbf{P}_4$, and $\mathbf{P}_5$. Since we have two equations and five variables, a basis must include exactly $5 - 3 = 2$ independent vectors. We can see in Figure 4-1 that all combinations of two vectors will yield a basis except the combination $(\mathbf{P}_1, \mathbf{P}_5)$ because $\mathbf{P}_1$ and $\mathbf{P}_5$ are *dependent*.

In the primal simplex method, we deal only with *feasible* basic solutions. A basic solution of the system $(\mathbf{A}, \mathbf{I})\mathbf{X} = \mathbf{b}$ is feasible for the linear program if it also satisfies the nonnegativity restriction $\mathbf{X} \geq \mathbf{0}$.

Exercise 4.1-1

(a) In Figure 4-1, can the combination $(\mathbf{P}_1, \mathbf{P}_4)$ be used as a basis in any of the primal simplex iterations?

[*Ans.* No, because this basis will result in a *negative* value of x_4, which is not admissible, since the primal simplex method deals with *feasible* basic solutions only.]

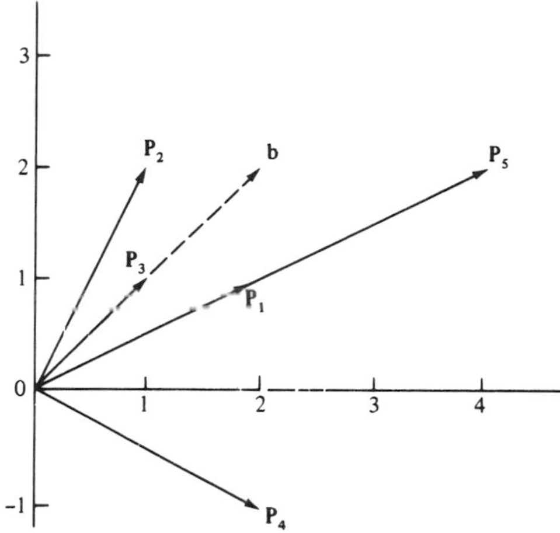

Figure 4-1

(b) In the following sets of equations, the first two have unique solutions, the third set has infinity of solutions, and the fourth set has no solution. Use graphical vector representation to show that in each of the first two cases (unique solutions), the left-side vectors are independent and hence form a basis, whereas in the last two cases the left-side vectors are necessarily dependent. In particular, you must get a clear understanding of the meaning of "dependence" and "independence" among vectors.

$$\begin{array}{ll} (1)\ \ x_1 + 3x_2 = 2 & (2)\ \ 2x_1 + 3x_2 = 1 \\ \quad\ \ 3x_1 + x_2 = 3 & \quad\ \ 2x_1 - x_2 = 2 \\ (3)\ \ 2x_1 + 6x_2 = 4 & (4)\ \ 2x_1 - 4x_2 = 2 \\ \quad\ \ x_1 + 3x_2 = 2 & \quad\ \ -x_1 + 2x_2 = 1 \end{array}$$

[*Ans.* See Figure 4-2.]

(c) In Figure 4-1, how many distinct extreme points are associated with the bases $(\mathbf{P}_1, \mathbf{P}_3)$, $(\mathbf{P}_2, \mathbf{P}_3)$, $(\mathbf{P}_3, \mathbf{P}_4)$, and $(\mathbf{P}_3, \mathbf{P}_5)$?
[*Ans.* Exactly one, because $\mathbf{P}_3$ and $\mathbf{b}$ are dependent. Thus any of these bases will yield $x_3 = 2$ and zero for *all* the remaining variables. The basic solutions are thus *degenerate.* The answer demonstrates that in case of degeneracy, an extreme point may be represented by more than one basic solution. A *nondegenerate* extreme point, however, has exactly one basic solution associated with it.]

4.1.3 THE SIMPLEX TABLEAU IN MATRIX FORM

The general idea of the simplex method (primal or dual) is to start from an extreme point and then proceed to an *adjacent* extreme point with the objective of improving optimality while maintaining feasibility (primal method) or moving toward feasibility without destroying optimality (dual method). The simplest way to select a starting extreme point is to use the basis $\mathbf{B}$ comprised of slack and/or artificial variables as we have done in Chapter 3. In this manner the starting $\mathbf{B}$ is an identity matrix $\mathbf{I}$ that clearly is a basis. Adjacent extreme points are then determined by

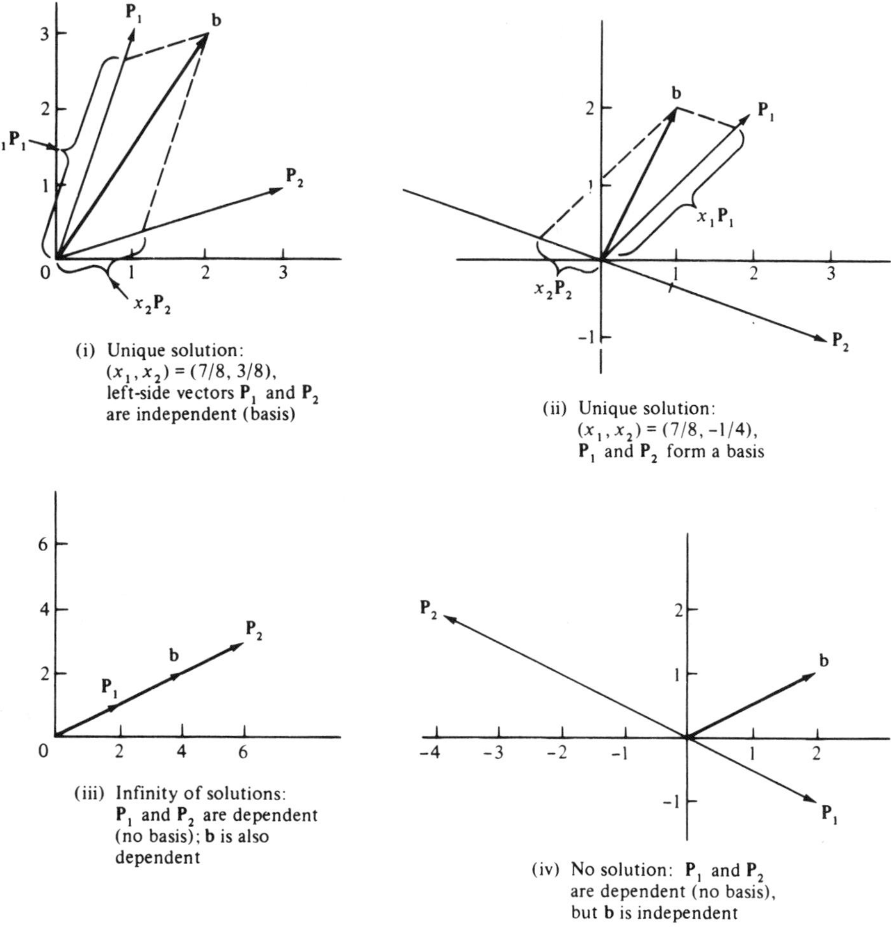

(i) Unique solution: $(x_1, x_2) = (7/8, 3/8)$, left-side vectors $\mathbf{P}_1$ and $\mathbf{P}_2$ are independent (basis)

(ii) Unique solution: $(x_1, x_2) = (7/8, -1/4)$, $\mathbf{P}_1$ and $\mathbf{P}_2$ form a basis

(iii) Infinity of solutions: $\mathbf{P}_1$ and $\mathbf{P}_2$ are dependent (no basis); $\mathbf{b}$ is also dependent

(iv) No solution: $\mathbf{P}_1$ and $\mathbf{P}_2$ are dependent (no basis), but $\mathbf{b}$ is independent

Figure 4-2

exchanging one vector in $\mathbf{B}$ with a current nonbasic vector that will move the solution toward optimality (primal method) or feasibility (dual method).

We now show how the general simplex tableau is represented for the following problem:

$$\text{maximize } z = \mathbf{CX} \quad \text{subject to} \quad (\mathbf{A}\ \mathbf{I})\mathbf{X} = \mathbf{b},\ \mathbf{X} \geq \mathbf{0}$$

We partition the vector $\mathbf{X}$ into $\mathbf{X}_\mathrm{I}$ and $\mathbf{X}_\mathrm{II}$, where $\mathbf{X}_\mathrm{II}$ corresponds to the elements of $\mathbf{X}$ associated with the starting basis $\mathbf{B} = \mathbf{I}$. We further partition $\mathbf{C}$ into $\mathbf{C}_\mathrm{I}$ and $\mathbf{C}_\mathrm{II}$ to correspond to $\mathbf{X}_\mathrm{I}$ and $\mathbf{X}_\mathrm{II}$. The given standard LP problem may thus be written as

$$\begin{pmatrix} 1 & -\mathbf{C}_\mathrm{I} & -\mathbf{C}_\mathrm{II} \\ \mathbf{0} & \mathbf{A} & \mathbf{I} \end{pmatrix} \begin{pmatrix} z \\ \mathbf{X}_\mathrm{I} \\ \mathbf{X}_\mathrm{II} \end{pmatrix} = \begin{pmatrix} 0 \\ \mathbf{b} \end{pmatrix}$$

Now, at any iteration, let $\mathbf{X}_B$ represent the current basic variables with $\mathbf{B}$ being its associated basis. This means that $\mathbf{X}_B$ represents m elements of $\mathbf{X}$ with $\mathbf{B}$ representing the vectors of $(\mathbf{A}, \mathbf{I})$ associated with $\mathbf{X}_B$. Correspondingly, let $\mathbf{C}_B$ be the elements of

$\mathbf{C}$ associated with $\mathbf{X}_B$. We thus obtain

$$\mathbf{B}\mathbf{X}_B = \mathbf{b} \quad \text{and} \quad z = \mathbf{C}_B\mathbf{X}_B$$

Equivalently, we have

$$\begin{pmatrix} 1 & -\mathbf{C}_B \\ \mathbf{0} & \mathbf{B} \end{pmatrix}\begin{pmatrix} z \\ \mathbf{X}_B \end{pmatrix} = \begin{pmatrix} 0 \\ \mathbf{b} \end{pmatrix}$$

We can thus solve for the current value of z and $\mathbf{X}_B$ by inverting the partitional matrix (see Section A.2.7), which yields

$$\begin{pmatrix} z \\ \mathbf{X}_B \end{pmatrix} = \begin{pmatrix} 1 & \mathbf{C}_B\mathbf{B}^{-1} \\ \mathbf{0} & \mathbf{B}^{-1} \end{pmatrix}\begin{pmatrix} 0 \\ \mathbf{b} \end{pmatrix} = \begin{pmatrix} \mathbf{C}_B\mathbf{B}^{-1}\mathbf{b} \\ \mathbf{B}^{-1}\mathbf{b} \end{pmatrix}$$

The general simplex tableau corresponding to $\mathbf{X}_B$ is then obtained by considering

$$\begin{pmatrix} 1 & \mathbf{C}_B\mathbf{B}^{-1} \\ \mathbf{0} & \mathbf{B}^{-1} \end{pmatrix}\begin{pmatrix} 1 & -\mathbf{C}_{\mathrm{I}} & -\mathbf{C}_{\mathrm{II}} \\ \mathbf{0} & \mathbf{A} & \mathbf{I} \end{pmatrix}\begin{pmatrix} z \\ \mathbf{X}_{\mathrm{I}} \\ \mathbf{X}_{\mathrm{II}} \end{pmatrix} = \begin{pmatrix} 1 & \mathbf{C}_B\mathbf{B}^{-1} \\ \mathbf{0} & \mathbf{B}^{-1} \end{pmatrix}\begin{pmatrix} 0 \\ \mathbf{b} \end{pmatrix}$$

Carrying out the matrix manipulations, we obtain the following general simplex iteration expressed in matrix form:

Basic	$\mathbf{X}_{\mathrm{I}}$	$\mathbf{X}_{\mathrm{II}}$	
z	$\mathbf{C}_B\mathbf{B}^{-1}\mathbf{A} - \mathbf{C}_{\mathrm{I}}$	$\mathbf{C}_B\mathbf{B}^{-1} - \mathbf{C}_{\mathrm{II}}$	$\mathbf{C}_B\mathbf{B}^{-1}\mathbf{b}$
$\mathbf{X}_B$	$\mathbf{B}^{-1}\mathbf{A}$	$\mathbf{B}^{-1}$	$\mathbf{B}^{-1}\mathbf{b}$

You should carefully study the tableau above. It literally includes all the computational details of any of the simplex method variations. You will notice that the entire tableau at any iteration can be computed once the basis $\mathbf{B}$ associated with $\mathbf{X}_B$ (and hence its inverse $\mathbf{B}^{-1}$) is known. Every other element in the tableau is a function of $\mathbf{B}^{-1}$ and *the original data of the problem.*

As an illustration, consider the starting tableau of the all-slack primal simplex method. In this case, we have $\mathbf{C}_{\mathrm{II}} = \mathbf{0}$. The starting basic solution is identified as

$$\mathbf{X}_B = \mathbf{X}_{\mathrm{II}}, \qquad \mathbf{C}_B = \mathbf{C}_{\mathrm{II}} = \mathbf{0}, \qquad \mathbf{B} = \mathbf{I}$$

Since $\mathbf{B} = \mathbf{I}$, $\mathbf{B}^{-1} = \mathbf{I}$ and the all-slack starting tableau is obtained from the general tableau by direct substitution as:

Basic	$\mathbf{X}_{\mathrm{I}}$	$\mathbf{X}_{\mathrm{II}}$	Solution
z	$-\mathbf{C}_{\mathrm{I}}$	$\mathbf{0}$	0
$\mathbf{X}_{\mathrm{II}}$	$\mathbf{A}$	$\mathbf{I}$	$\mathbf{b}$

Compare this tableau with the one used in Chapter 3 and carefully observe the significance of the notation. You will then see that the "mechanical" procedure we followed in Chapter 3 to construct the starting tableau exactly gives the tableau above.

Another illustration deals with the use of the artificial variables in Section 3.3.1. For the M-method, $\mathbf{C}_{\mathrm{II}} = (-M, -M, \ldots, -M)$ (maximization) and for the two-phase method $\mathbf{C}_{II} = (1, 1, \ldots, 1)$. The starting basic solution is then identified as

$$\mathbf{X}_B = \mathbf{X}_{II}, \quad \mathbf{C}_B = \mathbf{C}_{II}, \quad \mathbf{B} = \mathbf{I}, \quad \mathbf{B}^{-1} = \mathbf{I}$$

The corresponding starting tableau thus reduces to

Basic	$\mathbf{X}_I$	$\mathbf{X}_{II}$	Solution
z	$\mathbf{C}_{II}\mathbf{A} - \mathbf{C}_I$	$\mathbf{0}$	$\mathbf{C}_{II}\mathbf{b}$
$\mathbf{X}_{II}$	$\mathbf{A}$	$\mathbf{I}$	$\mathbf{b}$

The tableau above shows why it was necessary in both the M-method and the two-phase method (Section 3.3.1) to carry out the initial step of substituting out the objective coefficients of the artificial variables under $\mathbf{X}_{II}$. Convince yourself that what we have done in Section 3.3.1 is precisely what the tableau above says. You will find it instructive to reconstruct the numerical examples in Section 3.3.1 using the matrix notation.

Exercise 4.1-2

Consider the following linear program:

$$\text{maximize } z = 2x_1 + 3x_2 + 7x_3$$

subject to

$$2x_1 + x_2 + 2x_3 = 4$$
$$3x_1 - x_2 - 2x_3 = 1$$
$$x_1, x_2, x_3 \geq 0$$

Let $\mathbf{P}_1$, $\mathbf{P}_2$, $\mathbf{P}_3$ be the constraint vectors associated with x_1, x_2, and x_3 and observe that all the constraints are equations so that the problem does not have an all-slack starting solution.

(a) How many vectors are needed to form a basis?
[*Ans.* Two.]

(b) Can $\mathbf{P}_2$ and $\mathbf{P}_3$ form a basis?
[*Ans.* No, because they are dependent.]

(c) Verify that $\mathbf{P}_1$ and $\mathbf{P}_2$ form a basis and find its inverse.

$$\left[\textit{Ans. } \mathbf{B} = \begin{pmatrix} 2 & 1 \\ 3 & -1 \end{pmatrix}, \mathbf{B}^{-1} = \begin{pmatrix} \frac{1}{5} & \frac{1}{5} \\ \frac{3}{5} & -\frac{2}{5} \end{pmatrix}\right]$$

(d) Identify $\mathbf{X}_B$, $\mathbf{C}_B$ associated with the basis $\mathbf{B}$. Also, identify $\mathbf{b}$.
[*Ans.* $\mathbf{X}_B = (x_1, x_2)^T$, $\mathbf{C}_B = (2, 3)$, $\mathbf{b} = (4, 1)^T$.]

(e) Is $\mathbf{X}_B$ feasible?
[*Ans.* Yes, $(x_1, x_2)^T = \mathbf{B}^{-1}\mathbf{b} = (1, 2)$ and $x_3 = 0$ satisfies all the constraints, including non-negativity.]

(f) Is $\mathbf{X}_B$ optimal?
[*Ans.* No, $(\mathbf{C}_B\mathbf{B}^{-1}\mathbf{A} - \mathbf{C}_I, \mathbf{C}_B\mathbf{B}^{-1} - \mathbf{C}_{II}) = (0, 0, -1)$ shows that $\mathbf{P}_3$ must enter the basis.]

(g) If $\mathbf{P}_3$ enters the basis, which of the two vectors $\mathbf{P}_1$ and $\mathbf{P}_2$ must leave?
[*Ans.* $\mathbf{B}^{-1}\mathbf{P}_3 = (0, 2)^T$ and $\mathbf{B}^{-1}\mathbf{b} = (1, 2)^T$, hence by the feasibility condition $\mathbf{P}_2$ must leave.]

(h) Identify the new basis.

$$\left[\textit{Ans. } \mathbf{X}_B = (x_1, x_3)^T, \mathbf{C}_B = (2, 7), \mathbf{B} = \begin{pmatrix} 2 & 2 \\ 3 & -2 \end{pmatrix}.\right]$$

In Exercise 4.1-2 we have gone through a complete iteration of the primal simplex method using matrix manipulation (in place of the Gauss–Jordan row operations). Again observe carefully that once **B**, and hence $\mathbf{B}^{-1}$, is identified, every element of the simplex tableau can immediately be computed, thus allowing us to check the optimality and feasibility of the iteration. In essence, the successive simplex iterations differ only in the basis **B**. This observation is the principal idea underlying the development of the **revised simplex method** as presented in the next section.

4.2 REVISED (PRIMAL) SIMPLEX METHOD

The tableau in Section 4.1-3 applies equally to both the primal and dual simplex methods; namely, once the basic variables are defined, the basis **B** is automatically known and the entire tableau can be generated from the original data in the standard form and the inverse $\mathbf{B}^{-1}$. The specific rules of the primal or the dual simplex method can then be implemented using the information in the tableau. This essentially means that the primal and dual simplex methods in matrix form differ only in the selection of the entering and leaving vectors. Other than that, all other computations are the same. For the sake of brevity, we will be dealing with the primal revised simplex method only.

In the revised simplex method (primal or dual), the fact that the simplex iterations differ only in the definition of the basis **B** points to potential computational advantages:

1. In large LP problems, the use of the regular Gauss–Jordan row operations normally leads to uncontrollable cumulative machine round-off error with adverse effects on the final results. In the revised method we use $\mathbf{B}^{-1}$ and the *original* data of the problem. We can thus control the accuracy of the computations by controlling the round-off error in computing $\mathbf{B}^{-1}$ alone.
2. The nature of matrix manipulations indicates that it is not necessary to compute all the entries of the simplex tableau, which for certain sizes of the LP problem may require fewer computations.

The revised simplex method thus offers a procedure that is advantageous from the standpoint of computational accuracy (and possibly the amount of computations) because of the way it computes the inverse $\mathbf{B}^{-1}$. It is emphasized, however, that the revised method utilizes the *exact* steps used in Chapter 3.

In this section we first show how the successive $\mathbf{B}^{-1}$ matrices are computed in a manner that is amenable to controlling machine round-off error. We conclude the section with the computational details of the revised simplex method.

4.2.1 PRODUCT FORM OF THE INVERSE

The product-form method is a matrix algebra procedure that computes the inverse of a new basis from the inverse of another basis provided that the two bases differ in exactly one column vector. The procedure is suited particularly for the simplex method computations, since the successive bases differ in exactly one column (vector) as a result of interchanging the entering and leaving vectors. In other words, given the current basis $\mathbf{B}$, the next basis $\mathbf{B}_{\text{next}}$ in the immediately succeeding iteration will differ from $\mathbf{B}$ in one column only. The product-form procedure then computes the next inverse $\mathbf{B}_{\text{next}}^{-1}$ by premultiplying the current inverse $\mathbf{B}^{-1}$ by a specially constructed matrix $\mathbf{E}$.

Define the identity matrix $\mathbf{I}_m$ as

$$\mathbf{I}_m = (\mathbf{e}_1, \mathbf{e}_2, \ldots, \mathbf{e}_m)$$

where $\mathbf{e}_i$ is a unit column vector with a one-element in the ith place and zero elsewhere. Suppose that we are given $\mathbf{B}$ and $\mathbf{B}^{-1}$ and assume that the vector $\mathbf{P}_r$ in $\mathbf{B}$ is replaced by a new vector $\mathbf{P}_j$ (in terms of the simplex method, $\mathbf{P}_j$ and $\mathbf{P}_r$ are the entering and leaving vectors). For simplicity, define

$$\boldsymbol{\alpha}^j = \mathbf{B}^{-1}\mathbf{P}_j$$

so that α_k^j is the kth element of $\boldsymbol{\alpha}^j$. Then the new inverse $\mathbf{B}_{\text{next}}^{-1}$ can be computed as follows:

$$\mathbf{B}_{\text{next}}^{-1} = \mathbf{E}\mathbf{B}^{-1}$$

where

$$\mathbf{E} = (\mathbf{e}_1, \ldots, \mathbf{e}_{r-1}, \boldsymbol{\xi}, \mathbf{e}_{r+1}, \ldots, \mathbf{e}_m)$$

and

$$\boldsymbol{\xi} = \begin{pmatrix} -\alpha_1^j/\alpha_r^j \\ -\alpha_2^j/\alpha_r^j \\ \vdots \\ +1/\alpha_r^j \\ \vdots \\ -\alpha_m^j/\alpha_r^j \end{pmatrix} \leftarrow r\text{th place}$$

provided that $\alpha_r^j \neq 0$. If $\alpha_r^j = 0$, $\mathbf{B}_{\text{next}}^{-1}$ does not exist.† Note that $\mathbf{E}$ is obtained from $\mathbf{I}_m$ by replacing its rth column $\mathbf{e}_r$ by $\boldsymbol{\xi}$.

To illustrate the procedure, consider the following information:

$$\mathbf{B} = \begin{pmatrix} 2 & 1 & 0 \\ 0 & 2 & 0 \\ 4 & 0 & 1 \end{pmatrix}, \quad \mathbf{B}^{-1} = \begin{pmatrix} 1/2 & -1/4 & 0 \\ 0 & 1/2 & 0 \\ -2 & 1 & 1 \end{pmatrix}$$

† The formula $\mathbf{B}_{\text{next}}^{-1} = \mathbf{E}\mathbf{B}^{-1}$ can be justified as follows. Define $\mathbf{F} = (\mathbf{e}_1, \ldots, \mathbf{e}_{r-1}, \boldsymbol{\alpha}^j, \mathbf{e}_{r+1}, \ldots, \mathbf{e}_m)$, where $\boldsymbol{\alpha}^j = \mathbf{B}^{-1}\mathbf{P}_j$. When the current basis $\mathbf{B}$ is postmultiplied by $\mathbf{F}$, the result will be the next basis $\mathbf{B}_{\text{next}}$; that is, $\mathbf{B}_{\text{next}} = \mathbf{BF}$. $\mathbf{B}_{\text{next}}$ is identical to $\mathbf{B}$ except that the rth column of $\mathbf{B}$ is replaced by $\mathbf{P}_j$. Thus

$$\mathbf{B}_{\text{next}}^{-1} = (\mathbf{BF})^{-1} = \mathbf{F}^{-1}\mathbf{B}^{-1}$$

However, $\mathbf{E}$ as defined is nothing but the inverse of $\mathbf{F}$ ($\mathbf{EF} = \mathbf{I}$). The formula follows directly.

If, for example, the third column vector $\mathbf{P}_3 = (0, 0, 1)^T$ of $\mathbf{B}$ is changed to $\mathbf{P}_3^* = (2, 1, 5)^T$, we can find the new inverse as follows:

$$\boldsymbol{\alpha}^3 = \mathbf{B}^{-1}\mathbf{P}_3^* = \begin{pmatrix} 1/2 & -1/4 & 0 \\ 0 & 1/2 & 0 \\ -2 & 1 & 1 \end{pmatrix}\begin{pmatrix} 2 \\ 1 \\ 5 \end{pmatrix} = \begin{pmatrix} 3/4 \\ 1/2 \\ \mathbf{2} \end{pmatrix} = \begin{pmatrix} \alpha_1^3 \\ \alpha_2^3 \\ \alpha_3^3 \end{pmatrix}$$

$$\xi = \begin{pmatrix} -(3/4)/\mathbf{2} \\ -(1/2)/\mathbf{2} \\ +1/\mathbf{2} \end{pmatrix} = \begin{pmatrix} -3/8 \\ -1/4 \\ 1/2 \end{pmatrix} \leftarrow r = 3$$

$$\mathbf{B}_{\text{next}}^{-1} = \begin{pmatrix} 1 & 0 & -3/8 \\ 0 & 1 & -1/4 \\ 0 & 0 & 1/2 \end{pmatrix}\begin{pmatrix} 1/2 & -1/4 & 0 \\ 0 & 1/2 & 0 \\ -2 & 1 & 1 \end{pmatrix}$$

$$= \begin{pmatrix} 5/4 & -5/8 & -3/8 \\ 1/2 & 1/4 & -1/4 \\ -1 & 1/2 & 1/2 \end{pmatrix}$$

Exercise 4.2-1

(a) Find $\mathbf{B}^{-1}$ for each of the following matrices using the product-form procedure.

$$\mathbf{B}_1 = \begin{pmatrix} 1 & 2 \\ 0 & 4 \end{pmatrix}, \quad \mathbf{B}_2 = \begin{pmatrix} 1 & 2 \\ 1 & 4 \end{pmatrix}$$

Notice that $\mathbf{B}_1$ differs from $\mathbf{I}$ in only one column and that $\mathbf{B}_2$ differs from $\mathbf{B}_1$ in one column also.

$\left[\textit{Ans. } \mathbf{B}_1^{-1} = \mathbf{E}_1\mathbf{I} = \begin{pmatrix} 1 & -1/2 \\ 0 & 1/4 \end{pmatrix}, \mathbf{B}_2^{-1} = \mathbf{E}_2\mathbf{B}_1^{-1} = \begin{pmatrix} 2 & -1 \\ -1/2 & 1/2 \end{pmatrix}.\right]$

(b) If the first column of $\mathbf{B}_2$ is $(-1/2, -1)^T$ instead, find $\mathbf{B}_2^{-1}$.

[*Ans.* $\mathbf{B}_2^{-1}$ does not exist because $\alpha_1^1 = 0$. Note the vectors' dependence in the new $\mathbf{B}_2$.]

4.2.2 STEPS OF THE PRIMAL REVISED SIMPLEX METHOD

The main idea of the revised method is to use the current basis inverse $\mathbf{B}^{-1}$ (and the original data of the problem) to carry out the necessary computations for determining the entering and leaving variables. The use of the *product form* makes it convenient to compute the successive inverses without having to invert any bases directly from raw data. Specifically, as in the simplex method, the starting basis in the revised method is always an identity matrix $\mathbf{I}$ whose inverse is itself. Thus, if $\mathbf{B}_1^{-1}$, $\mathbf{B}_2^{-1}, \ldots,$ and $\mathbf{B}_i^{-1}$ represent the successive inverses up to iteration i and if $\mathbf{E}_1$, $\mathbf{E}_2$, $\ldots$, $\mathbf{E}_i$ are their associated matrices as defined in Section 4.2.1, then

$$\mathbf{B}_1^{-1} = \mathbf{E}_1\mathbf{I}, \quad \mathbf{B}_2^{-1} = \mathbf{E}_2\mathbf{B}_1^{-1}, \ldots, \quad \mathbf{B}_i^{-1} = \mathbf{E}_i\mathbf{B}_{i-1}^{-1}$$

Successive substitution then yields

$$\mathbf{B}_i^{-1} = \mathbf{E}_i\mathbf{E}_{i-1} \cdots \mathbf{E}_1$$

We emphasize that the use of the *product form* is not an essential part of the revised method and that any inversion process can be employed at each iteration.

What is important from the standpoint of the revised method is that the inverse be computed in a manner that reduces the adverse effect of machine round-off error.

The steps of the primal revised method are essentially those of the primal simplex method of Chapter 3. Given the starting basis $\mathbf{I}$, we determine its associated objective coefficients vector $\mathbf{C}_B$ depending on whether the starting basic variables are slack (surplus) and/or artificial.

Step 1: Determination of the Entering Vector $\mathbf{P}_j$. Compute $\mathbf{Y} = \mathbf{C}_B\mathbf{B}^{-1}$. For every nonbasic vector $\mathbf{P}_j$, compute

$$z_j - c_j = \mathbf{YP}_j - c_j$$

For maximization (minimization) programs, the entering vector $\mathbf{P}_j$ is selected to have the most negative (positive) $z_j - c_j$ (break ties arbitrarily). Then if *all* $z_j - c_j \geq 0$ (≤ 0), the optimal solution is reached and is given by

$$\mathbf{X}_B = \mathbf{B}^{-1}\mathbf{b} \qquad \text{and} \qquad z = \mathbf{C}_B\mathbf{X}_B$$

Otherwise,

Step 2: Determination of the Leaving Vector $\mathbf{P}_r$. Given the entering vector $\mathbf{P}_j$, compute:

1. The values of the current basic variables, that is,

$$\mathbf{X}_B = \mathbf{B}^{-1}\mathbf{b}$$

2. The constraint coefficients of the entering variables, that is,

$$\boldsymbol{\alpha}^j = \mathbf{B}^{-1}\mathbf{P}_j$$

The leaving vector $\mathbf{P}_r$ (for *both* maximization and minimization) must be associated with

$$\theta = \min_k \left\{\frac{(\mathbf{B}^{-1}\mathbf{b})_k}{\alpha_k^j}, \ \alpha_k^j > 0\right\}$$

where $(\mathbf{B}^{-1}\mathbf{b})_k$ are α_k^j are the kth elements of $\mathbf{B}^{-1}\mathbf{b}$ and $\boldsymbol{\alpha}^j$. If all $\alpha_k^j \leq 0$, the problem has no bounded solution.

Step 3: Determination of the Next Basis. Given the current inverse basis $\mathbf{B}^{-1}$, we find that the next inverse basis $\mathbf{B}_{\text{next}}^{-1}$ is given by

$$\mathbf{B}_{\text{next}}^{-1} = \mathbf{EB}^{-1}$$

Now set $\mathbf{B}^{-1} = \mathbf{B}_{\text{next}}^{-1}$ and go to step 1.

Steps 1 and 2 are exactly equivalent to those of the simplex tableau in Chapter 3, as the following tableau shows:

Basic	x_1	x_2	$\cdots$	x_j	$\cdots$	x_n	Solution
z	$z_1 - c_1$	$z_2 - c_2$	$\cdots$	$z_j - c_j$	$\cdots$	$z_n - c_n$	
$\mathbf{X}_B$				$\mathbf{B}^{-1}\mathbf{P}_j$			$\mathbf{B}^{-1}\mathbf{b}$

Step 1 computes the z-row coefficients and determines the entering variable x_j. Step 2 then determines the leaving variable by computing the right-side elements $(= \mathbf{B}^{-1}\mathbf{b})$ and the constraint coefficients under the entering variable $(= \boldsymbol{\alpha}^j = \mathbf{B}^{-1}\mathbf{P}_j)$.

Note that in carrying out the revised simplex computation, it will be helpful initially to summarize the computations of steps 1 and 2 in the tableau form shown.

Example 4.2-1. We shall solve the Reddy Mikks model by the revised method. The same example was solved by the regular (primal) simplex method in Section 3.2. You are encouraged to compare the computations of both methods to convince yourself that the two methods are basically equivalent.

The Reddy Mikks model (in standard form) is summarized here. We use x_1 and x_2 in place of x_E and x_I for convenience. Also, the slacks are represented by x_3, x_4, x_5, and x_6.

$$\text{maximize } z = 3x_1 + 2x_2$$

subject to

$$\begin{aligned}
x_1 + 2x_2 + x_3 \qquad\qquad\qquad &= 6\\
2x_1 + x_2 \qquad + x_4 \qquad\qquad &= 8\\
-x_1 + x_2 \qquad\qquad + x_5 \qquad &= 1\\
x_2 \qquad\qquad\qquad + x_6 &= 2\\
x_1, x_2, \ldots, x_6 \geq 0 &
\end{aligned}$$

Starting Solution

$$\begin{aligned}
\mathbf{X}_B &= (x_3, x_4, x_5, x_6)^T\\
\mathbf{C}_B &= (0, 0, 0, 0)\\
\mathbf{B} &= (\mathbf{P}_3, \mathbf{P}_4, \mathbf{P}_5, \mathbf{P}_6) = \mathbf{I}\\
\mathbf{B}^{-1} &= \mathbf{I}
\end{aligned}$$

First Iteration

Step 1: Computation of $z_j - c_j$ for nonbasic $\mathbf{P}_1$ and $\mathbf{P}_2$.

$$\begin{aligned}
\mathbf{Y} = \mathbf{C}_B\mathbf{B}^{-1} &= (0, 0, 0, 0)\mathbf{I} = (0, 0, 0, 0)\\
(z_1 - c_1, z_2 - c_2) &= \mathbf{Y}(\mathbf{P}_1, \mathbf{P}_2) - (c_1, c_2)\\
&= (0, 0, 0, 0)\begin{pmatrix} 1 & 2\\ 2 & 1\\ -1 & 1\\ 0 & 1 \end{pmatrix} - (3, 2)\\
&= (-3, -2)
\end{aligned}$$

In terms of the simplex tableau of Chapter 3, the computations are represented as

Basic	x_1	x_2	x_3	x_4	x_5	x_6	Solution
z	-3	-2	0	0	0	0	0

(Notice that $z_j - c_j$ automatically equals zero for all basic variables.) Thus $\mathbf{P}_1$ is the entering vector.

Step 2: Determination of the leaving vector given that $\mathbf{P}_1$ enters the basis.

$$\mathbf{X}_B = \mathbf{B}^{-1}\mathbf{b} = \mathbf{I}\mathbf{b} = \mathbf{b} = \begin{pmatrix} 6 \\ 8 \\ 1 \\ 2 \end{pmatrix}$$

$$\boldsymbol{\alpha}^1 = \mathbf{B}^{-1}\mathbf{P}_1 = \mathbf{I}\mathbf{P}_1 = \mathbf{P}_1 = \begin{pmatrix} 1 \\ 2 \\ -1 \\ 0 \end{pmatrix}$$

In terms of the tableau of Chapter 3, the computations for steps 1 and 2 can be summarized as follows:

Basic	x_1	x_2	x_3	x_4	x_5	x_6	Solution
z	-3	-2	0	0	0	0	0
x_3	1						6
x_4	2						8
x_5	-1						1
x_6	0						2

Thus

$$\theta = \min\{6/1, 8/2, -, -,\} = 4, \quad \text{corresponding to } x_4$$

As a result, $\mathbf{P}_4$ is the leaving vector.

Step 3: Determination of the next basis inverse. Since $\mathbf{P}_1$ replaces $\mathbf{P}_4$ and $\boldsymbol{\alpha}^1 = (1, 2, -1, 0)^T$, we have

$$\boldsymbol{\xi} = \begin{pmatrix} -1/2 \\ +1/2 \\ -(-1/2) \\ 0/2 \end{pmatrix} = \begin{pmatrix} -1/2 \\ 1/2 \\ 1/2 \\ 0 \end{pmatrix}$$

and

$$\mathbf{B}_{\text{next}}^{-1} = \mathbf{E}\mathbf{B}^{-1} = \mathbf{E}\mathbf{I} = \mathbf{E} = \begin{pmatrix} 1 & -1/2 & 0 & 0 \\ 0 & 1/2 & 0 & 0 \\ 0 & 1/2 & 1 & 0 \\ 0 & 0 & 0 & 1 \end{pmatrix}$$

The new basis is associated with the basic vector

$$\mathbf{X}_B = (x_3, x_1, x_5, x_6)$$
$$\mathbf{C}_B = (0, 3, 0, 0)$$

Second Iteration

Step 1: Computation of $z_j - c_j$ for nonbasic $\mathbf{P}_2$ and $\mathbf{P}_4$.

$$\mathbf{C}_B\mathbf{B}^{-1} = (0, 3, 0, 0)\begin{pmatrix} 1 & -1/2 & 0 & 0 \\ 0 & 1/2 & 0 & 0 \\ 0 & 1/2 & 1 & 0 \\ 0 & 0 & 0 & 1 \end{pmatrix} = (0, 3/2, 0, 0)$$

$$(z_2 - c_2, z_4 - c_4) = (0, 3/2, 0, 0)\begin{pmatrix} 2 & 0 \\ 1 & 1 \\ 1 & 0 \\ 1 & 0 \end{pmatrix} - (2, 0) = (-1/2, 3/2)$$

Thus $\mathbf{P}_2$ is the entering vector.

Step 2: Determination of the leaving vector given that $\mathbf{P}_2$ enters the basis.

$$\mathbf{X}_B = \mathbf{B}^{-1}\mathbf{b} = \begin{pmatrix} 1 & -1/2 & 0 & 0 \\ 0 & 1/2 & 0 & 0 \\ 0 & 1/2 & 1 & 0 \\ 0 & 0 & 0 & 1 \end{pmatrix}\begin{pmatrix} 6 \\ 8 \\ 1 \\ 2 \end{pmatrix} = \begin{pmatrix} 2 \\ 4 \\ 5 \\ 2 \end{pmatrix}$$

$$\boldsymbol{\alpha}^2 = \mathbf{B}^{-1}\mathbf{P}_2 = \begin{pmatrix} 1 & -1/2 & 0 & 0 \\ 0 & 1/2 & 0 & 0 \\ 0 & 1/2 & 1 & 0 \\ 0 & 0 & 0 & 1 \end{pmatrix}\begin{pmatrix} 2 \\ 1 \\ 1 \\ 1 \end{pmatrix} = \begin{pmatrix} 3/2 \\ 1/2 \\ 3/2 \\ 1 \end{pmatrix}$$

Steps 1 and 2 computations can be summarized in tableau form as follows:

Basis	x_1	x_2	x_3	x_4	x_5	x_6	Solution
z	0	$-1/2$	0	3/2	0	0	
x_3		3/2					2
x_1		1/2					4
x_5		3/2					5
x_6		1					2

Thus

$$\theta = \min\left\{\frac{2}{3/2}, \frac{4}{1/2}, \frac{5}{3/2}, \frac{2}{1}\right\} = 4/3$$

corresponding to x_3. As a result, $\mathbf{P}_3$ is the leaving vector.

Step 3: Determination of the next basis inverse. Since $\mathbf{P}_2$ replaces $\mathbf{P}_3$ and $\boldsymbol{\alpha}^2 = (3/2, 1/2, 3/2, 1)^T$, we have

$$\boldsymbol{\xi} = \begin{pmatrix} +1/(3/2) \\ -(1/2)/(3/2) \\ -(3/2)/(3/2) \\ -1/(3/2) \end{pmatrix} = \begin{pmatrix} 2/3 \\ -1/3 \\ -1 \\ -2/3 \end{pmatrix}$$

$$\mathbf{B}_{\text{next}}^{-1} = \begin{pmatrix} 2/3 & 0 & 0 & 0 \\ -1/3 & 1 & 0 & 0 \\ -1 & 0 & 1 & 0 \\ -2/3 & 0 & 0 & 1 \end{pmatrix}\begin{pmatrix} 1 & -1/2 & 0 & 0 \\ 0 & 1/2 & 0 & 0 \\ 0 & 1/2 & 1 & 0 \\ 0 & 0 & 0 & 1 \end{pmatrix}$$

$$= \begin{pmatrix} 2/3 & -1/3 & 0 & 0 \\ -1/3 & 2/3 & 0 & 0 \\ -1 & 1 & 1 & 0 \\ -2/3 & 1/3 & 0 & 1 \end{pmatrix}$$

The new basis is associated with the basic vector

$$\mathbf{X}_B = (x_2, x_1, x_5, x_6)$$
$$\mathbf{C}_B = (2, 3, 0, 0)$$

Third Iteration

Step 1: Computation of $z_j - c_j$ for $\mathbf{P}_3$ and $\mathbf{P}_4$.

$$\mathbf{C}_B\mathbf{B}^{-1} = (2, 3, 0, 0)\begin{pmatrix} 2/3 & -1/3 & 0 & 0 \\ -1/3 & 2/3 & 0 & 0 \\ -1 & 1 & 1 & 0 \\ -2/3 & 1/3 & 0 & 1 \end{pmatrix} = (1/3, 4/3, 0, 0)$$

$$(z_3 - c_3, z_4 - c_4) = (1/3, 4/3, 0, 0)\begin{pmatrix} 1 & 0 \\ 0 & 1 \\ 0 & 0 \\ 0 & 0 \end{pmatrix} - (0, 0) = (1/3, 4/3)$$

Since all $z_j - c_j \geq 0$, the last basis is optimal.

Optimal Solution

$$\begin{pmatrix} x_2 \\ x_1 \\ x_5 \\ x_6 \end{pmatrix} = \mathbf{B}^{-1}\mathbf{b} = \begin{pmatrix} 2/3 & -1/3 & 0 & 0 \\ -1/3 & 2/3 & 0 & 0 \\ -1 & 1 & 1 & 0 \\ -2/3 & 1/3 & 0 & 1 \end{pmatrix}\begin{pmatrix} 6 \\ 8 \\ 1 \\ 2 \end{pmatrix} = \begin{pmatrix} 4/3 \\ 10/3 \\ 3 \\ 2/3 \end{pmatrix}$$

$$\mathbf{z} = \mathbf{C}_B\mathbf{X}_B = (2, 3, 0, 0)\begin{pmatrix} 4/3 \\ 10/3 \\ 3 \\ 2/3 \end{pmatrix} = 38/3$$

◀

Exercise 4.2-2

(a) In Example 4.2-1, consider the basis $\mathbf{B}_* = (\mathbf{P}_2, \mathbf{P}_1, \mathbf{P}_5, \mathbf{P}_4)$. Generate $\mathbf{B}_*^{-1}$ from the optimal basis $(\mathbf{P}_2, \mathbf{P}_1, \mathbf{P}_5, \mathbf{P}_6)$ and check if it is feasible and/or optimal.
[*Ans.* $\mathbf{B}_*$ is feasible and nonoptimal. $(x_2, x_1, x_5, x_4) = (2, 2, 1, 2)$, $z_3 - c_3 = 3$, and $z_6 - c_6 = -4$.]

(b) Show how the revised *dual* simplex computations can be carried out by using matrix manipulations (in place of the Gauss–Jordan row operations as given in Section 3.4).
[*Ans.* The starting basis equals **I**. The steps at each iteration are as follows:

Step 1: Compute $\mathbf{X}_B = \mathbf{B}^{-1}\mathbf{b}$, the current values of the basic variables. If $\mathbf{X}_B \geq \mathbf{0}$, the solution is feasible; stop. Otherwise, select the leaving variable x_r as the one having the most negative value among all the elements of $\mathbf{X}_B$.

Step 2

(a) Compute $z_j - c_j = \mathbf{C}_B\mathbf{B}^{-1}\mathbf{P}_j - c_j$ for all the nonbasic variables x_j.

(b) For all the nonbasic variables x_j, compute the constraint coefficients α_r^j associated with the row of the leaving variable x_r using the formula

$$\alpha_r^j = (\text{row of } \mathbf{B}^{-1} \text{ associated with } x_r) \times \mathbf{P}_j$$

(c) The entering variable is associated with

$$\theta = \min_{j} \left\{ \left| \frac{z_j - c_j}{\alpha_r^j} \right|, \alpha_r^j < 0 \right\}$$

(If all $\alpha_r^j \geq 0$, no feasible solution exists.)

Step 3: Obtain the new basis by interchanging the entering and leaving vectors $\mathbf{P}_j$ and $\mathbf{P}_r$ using the familiar formula

$$\mathbf{B}_{\text{next}}^{-1} = \mathbf{E}\mathbf{B}^{-1}$$

Set $\mathbf{B}^{-1} = \mathbf{B}_{\text{next}}^{-1}$ and go to step 1.
(See Example 5.6-2 for an application of this procedure.)

4.3 SUMMARY

In the revised simplex method, computations at each iteration are obtained from the current inverse $\mathbf{B}^{-1}$ and the original data of the problem. Thus the adverse effect of machine round-off error can be minimized by controlling the round-off error in computing $\mathbf{B}^{-1}$. Additionally, the revised algorithm may lead to fewer computations than in the regular tableau algorithm, depending on the relationship between the number of constraints and the number of variables. Other than that, we should keep in mind that the revised method utilizes the exact same steps used with the regular tableau algorithm.

SELECTED REFERENCES

BAZARAA, M., J. JARVIS, and H. SHERALI, *Linear Programming and Network Flows*, Wiley, New York, 1990.

DANTZIG, G., *Linear Programming and Extensions*, Princeton University Press, Princeton, N.J., 1963.

MURTY, K., *Linear Programming*, Wiley, New York, 1983.

PROBLEMS

Section	Assigned Problems
4.1.1	4–1, 4–2
4.1.2	4–3 to 4–10
4.1.3	4–11 to 4–16
4.2.1	4–17 to 4–19
4.2.2	4–20 to 4–33

☐ **4–1** Express the following program in the standard form that is suitable for the application of the matrix version of the primal simplex method. Identify **A**, **C**, **b**, and **X** for each problem.

(a) Minimize $z = 2x_1 + 5x_2$
subject to

$$\begin{aligned} 3x_1 + 2x_2 &\le 5 \\ 4x_1 - x_2 &\ge 2 \\ x_1, x_2 &\ge 0 \end{aligned}$$

(b) Maximize $z = 6x_1 + 2x_2 + 3x_3$
subject to

$$\begin{aligned} 5x_1 + 2x_2 + 4x_3 &= 20 \\ 3x_1 - x_2 + 2x_3 &\le 15 \\ x_1, x_2, x_3 &\ge 0 \end{aligned}$$

(c) Maximize $z = 3x_1 + 2x_2 + 5x_3$
subject to

$$\begin{aligned} 7x_1 + 3x_2 - x_3 &\le 15 \\ 2x_1 - 2x_2 + 3x_3 &\le 20 \\ x_1 + x_2 + x_3 &\le 5 \\ x_1, x_2, x_3 &\ge 0 \end{aligned}$$

☐ **4–2** Develop the standard form for applying the revised dual simplex method to part (a) in Problem 4–1.

☐ **4–3** Show graphically whether each of the following matrices forms a basis.

$$B_1 = \begin{pmatrix} 1 & 2 \\ 2 & 3 \end{pmatrix}, \qquad B_2 = \begin{pmatrix} 1 & 2 \\ 2 & 1 \end{pmatrix}$$

$$B_3 = \begin{pmatrix} 2 & -4 \\ -1 & 2 \end{pmatrix}, \qquad B_4 = \begin{pmatrix} 1 & 5 \\ 2 & 10 \end{pmatrix}$$

☐ **4–4** Solve Problem 4–3 algebraically.

☐ **4–5** Show graphically whether the following systems of equations have a unique solution, no solution, or an infinity of solutions. For unique solutions, indicate whether the values of x_1 and x_2 are positive, zero, or negative.

(a) $\begin{pmatrix} 5 & 4 \\ 1 & -3 \end{pmatrix}\begin{pmatrix} x_1 \\ x_2 \end{pmatrix} = \begin{pmatrix} 1 \\ 1 \end{pmatrix}$ (b) $\begin{pmatrix} 2 & -2 \\ 1 & 3 \end{pmatrix}\begin{pmatrix} x_1 \\ x_2 \end{pmatrix} = \begin{pmatrix} 1 \\ 3 \end{pmatrix}$

(c) $\begin{pmatrix} 2 & 4 \\ 1 & 3 \end{pmatrix}\begin{pmatrix} x_1 \\ x_2 \end{pmatrix} = \begin{pmatrix} -2 \\ -1 \end{pmatrix}$ (d) $\begin{pmatrix} 2 & 4 \\ 1 & 2 \end{pmatrix}\begin{pmatrix} x_1 \\ x_2 \end{pmatrix} = \begin{pmatrix} 6 \\ 3 \end{pmatrix}$

(e) $\begin{pmatrix} -2 & 4 \\ 1 & -2 \end{pmatrix}\begin{pmatrix} x_1 \\ x_2 \end{pmatrix} = \begin{pmatrix} 2 \\ 1 \end{pmatrix}$ (f) $\begin{pmatrix} 1 & -2 \\ 0 & 0 \end{pmatrix}\begin{pmatrix} x_1 \\ x_2 \end{pmatrix} = \begin{pmatrix} 1 \\ 1 \end{pmatrix}$

☐ **4–6** Consider the system of equations

$$\mathbf{P}_1 x_1 + \mathbf{P}_2 x_2 + \mathbf{P}_3 x_3 + \mathbf{P}_4 x_4 = \mathbf{b}$$

where

$$\mathbf{P}_1 = \begin{pmatrix} 1 \\ 2 \\ 3 \end{pmatrix}, \quad \mathbf{P}_2 = \begin{pmatrix} 0 \\ 2 \\ 1 \end{pmatrix}, \quad \mathbf{P}_3 = \begin{pmatrix} 1 \\ 4 \\ 2 \end{pmatrix}, \mathbf{P}_4 = \begin{pmatrix} 2 \\ 0 \\ 0 \end{pmatrix}, \quad \mathbf{b} = \begin{pmatrix} 3 \\ 4 \\ 2 \end{pmatrix}$$

Indicate whether the following vector combinations form a basis.

(a) $(\mathbf{P}_1, \mathbf{P}_2, \mathbf{P}_3)$
(b) $(\mathbf{P}_1, \mathbf{P}_2, \mathbf{P}_4)$
(c) $(\mathbf{P}_2, \mathbf{P}_3, \mathbf{P}_4)$

☐ **4–7** Consider the following linear program:

$$\text{maximize } c_1x_1 + c_2x_2 + c_3x_3 + c_4x_4$$

subject to

$$\mathbf{P}_1x_1 + \mathbf{P}_2x_2 + \mathbf{P}_3x_3 + \mathbf{P}_4x_4 = \mathbf{b}$$
$$\text{all } x \geq 0$$

The vectors $\mathbf{P}_1$, $\mathbf{P}_2$, $\mathbf{P}_3$, and $\mathbf{P}_4$ are shown in Figure 4-3. Assume that the basis associated with the current iteration is given as

$$\mathbf{B} = (\mathbf{P}_1, \mathbf{P}_2)$$

(a) If the vector $\mathbf{P}_3$ enters the basis, which of the current two basic vectors must leave for the resulting basic solution to be feasible?
(b) Can the vector $\mathbf{P}_4$ be part of a feasible basis?

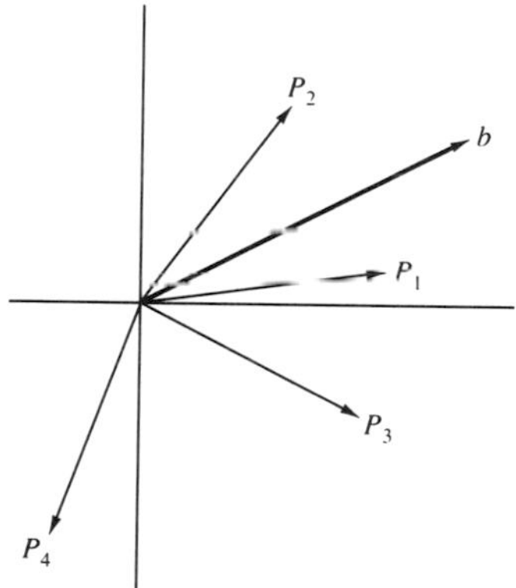

Figure 4-3

☐ **4–8** Consider the following system of linear equations in which all $x_j \geq 0$.

$$\begin{pmatrix} 2 & 3 & 1 & 0 \\ 1 & 2 & 0 & 1 \end{pmatrix} \begin{pmatrix} x_1 \\ x_2 \\ x_3 \\ x_4 \end{pmatrix} = \begin{pmatrix} 6 \\ 4 \end{pmatrix}$$

Determine all its *feasible* extreme points by evaluating all its basic feasible solutions. What is the relationship between the numbers of basic solutions and extreme points?

☐ **4–9** Determine all the feasible extreme points and their corresponding basic solutions for the following system of linear equations.

$$\begin{aligned} 3x_1 + 6x_2 + 5x_3 + x_4 \qquad\quad &= 12 \\ 2x_1 + 4x_2 + x_3 \qquad + 2x_5 &= 8 \\ x_1, x_2, x_3, x_4, x_5 \geq 0 \end{aligned}$$

□ **4–10** Consider a linear programming problem in which the variable x_k is unrestricted in sign. Prove that by replacing x_k by $x_k' - x_k''$, where x_k' and x_k'' are nonnegative variables, then in any of the simplex iterations (including the optimum) it is never possible to have *both* x_k' and x_k'' as *basic* variables, nor is it possible that these two variables can replace one another in an *alternative* optimum solution.

□ **4–11** Consider the following linear program expressed in the standard form:

$$\text{maximize } z = 3x_1 + 2x_2 + 5x_3$$

subject to

$$\begin{aligned} x_1 + 2x_2 + \ x_3 + x_4 \qquad\qquad &= 30 \\ 3x_1 \qquad + 2x_3 \qquad + x_5 \qquad &= 60 \\ x_1 + 4x_2 \qquad\qquad\qquad + x_6 &= 20 \\ x_1, x_2, \ldots, x_6 \geq 0 & \end{aligned}$$

The following matrices represent the inverses and their corresponding basic variables associated with different simplex iterations of the problem. Compute the associated *constraint equations* of each iteration and determine the corresponding basic variables and their values.

$$\text{(a) } (x_4, x_3, x_6); \begin{pmatrix} 1 & -1/2 & 0 \\ 0 & 1/2 & 0 \\ 0 & 0 & 1 \end{pmatrix}$$

$$\text{(b) } (x_2, x_3, x_1); \begin{pmatrix} 1/4 & -1/8 & 1/8 \\ 3/2 & -1/4 & -3/4 \\ -1 & 1/2 & 1/2 \end{pmatrix}$$

$$\text{(c) } (x_2, x_3, x_6); \begin{pmatrix} 1/2 & -1/4 & 0 \\ 0 & 1/2 & 0 \\ -2 & 1 & 1 \end{pmatrix}$$

□ **4–12** In Problem 4–11, suppose that the objective function is given as

$$\text{maximize } z = 3x_1 + 2x_2 + 5x_3 - x_4 + 4x_5$$

Determine whether or not the bases in parts (a), (b), and (c) are optimal.

□ **4–13** Consider the following linear program expressed in the standard form:

$$\text{maximize } z = 4x_1 + 14x_2 - 2x_3$$

subject to

$$\begin{aligned} 2x_1 + 7x_2 + x_3 \qquad &= 21 \\ 7x_1 + 2x_2 \qquad + x_4 &= 21 \\ x_1, x_2, x_3, x_4 \geq 0 & \end{aligned}$$

Each of the following cases provides an inverse matrix and its corresponding basic variables for the LP given. Determine whether or not each basic solution is feasible and/or optimal.

(a) (x_2, x_4); $\begin{pmatrix} 1/7 & 0 \\ -2/7 & 1 \end{pmatrix}$

(b) (x_2, x_3); $\begin{pmatrix} 0 & 1/2 \\ 1 & -7/2 \end{pmatrix}$

(c) (x_2, x_1); $\begin{pmatrix} 7/45 & -2/45 \\ -2/45 & 7/45 \end{pmatrix}$

(d) (x_1, x_4); $\begin{pmatrix} 1/2 & 0 \\ -7/2 & 1 \end{pmatrix}$

☐ **4–14** Consider the following linear program expressed in the standard form:

$$\text{minimize } z = 2x_1 + x_2$$

subject to

$$\begin{aligned} 3x_1 + x_2 - x_3 \quad\quad &= 3 \\ 4x_1 + 3x_2 \quad - x_4 \quad &= 6 \\ x_1 + 2x_2 \quad\quad + x_5 &= 3 \\ x_1, x_2, x_3, x_4, x_5 &\geq 0 \end{aligned}$$

(a) Compute the entire simplex tableau associated with the following inverse matrix.

$$\text{basic variables} = (x_1, x_2, x_5); \quad \text{inverse} = \begin{pmatrix} 3/5 & -1/5 & 0 \\ -4/5 & 3/5 & 0 \\ 1 & -1 & 1 \end{pmatrix}$$

(b) Determine whether the iteration in part (a) is optimal and feasible.

☐ **4–15** Consider the following linear program expressed in the standard form:

$$\text{maximize } z = 5x_1 + 12x_2 + 4x_3$$

subject to

$$\begin{aligned} x_1 + 2x_2 + x_3 + x_4 &= 10 \\ 2x_1 - x_2 + 3x_3 \quad &= 2 \\ x_1, x_2, x_3, x_4 &\geq 0 \end{aligned}$$

Each of the following inverses is associated with a *basic feasible* solution and only one of them represents the optimal solution. Show how you can identify the optimal solution.

(a) (x_4, x_3); $\begin{pmatrix} 1 & -1/3 \\ 0 & 1/3 \end{pmatrix}$

(b) (x_2, x_1); $\begin{pmatrix} 2/5 & -1/5 \\ 1/5 & 2/5 \end{pmatrix}$

(c) (x_2, x_3); $\begin{pmatrix} 3/7 & -1/7 \\ 1/7 & 2/7 \end{pmatrix}$

☐ **4–16** The final optimal tableau of a maximization linear programming problem with three constraints of type ($\leq$) and two unknowns (x_1, x_2) is

Basic	x_1	x_2	s_1	s_2	s_3	Solution
z	0	0	0	3	2	?
s_1	0	0	1	1	−1	2
x_2	0	1	0	1	0	6
x_1	1	0	0	−1	1	2

The variables s_1, s_2, and s_3 are all slack variables. Find the associated value of the objective function z.

☐ **4–17** The matrix **A** and its inverse $\mathbf{A}^{-1}$ are given as follows:

$$\mathbf{A} = \begin{pmatrix} 2 & 1 & 0 \\ 0 & 2 & 0 \\ 4 & 0 & 1 \end{pmatrix}, \qquad \mathbf{A}^{-1} = \begin{pmatrix} 1/2 & -1/4 & 0 \\ 0 & 1/2 & 0 \\ -2 & 1 & 1 \end{pmatrix}$$

If the second and third columns of **A** are replaced by $(5, -1, 4)^T$ and $(1, 2, 1)^T$, find the new inverse by using the product form introduced in Section 4.2.1.

☐ **4–18** In Problem 4–17, suppose that the third column of **A** is replaced by the sum of the first two columns. This change will make **A** singular. Show how the product form method discovers that the new matrix is singular.

☐ **4–19** Invert each of the following matrices by using the product form:

$$\text{(a)} \begin{pmatrix} 1 & 0 & 1 \\ 0 & 2 & 0 \\ 1 & 2 & 3 \end{pmatrix} \qquad \text{(b)} \begin{pmatrix} 1 & 0 & 3 \\ 4 & 1 & 2 \\ 1 & 3 & 0 \end{pmatrix}$$

☐ **4–20** Given the general linear programming problem with m equations and $(m + n)$ unknowns, what is the maximum number of *adjacent* extreme points that can be reached from a nondegenerate extreme point of the corresponding convex set?

☐ **4–21** In applying the feasibility condition of the simplex method, suppose that $x_r = 0$ is a basic variable and x_j is the entering variable. Why is it necessary to have $(\mathbf{B}^{-1}\mathbf{P}_j)_r > 0$ for x_r to be the leaving variable? What is the fallacy if $(\mathbf{B}^{-1}\mathbf{P}_j)_r \le 0$?

☐ **4–22** In applying the feasibility condition of the simplex method, what are the conditions for a degenerate solution to appear for the first time in the next iteration? For continuing to obtain a degenerate solution in the next iteration? For removing degeneracy in the next iteration? Express the answer mathematically.

☐ **4–23** What are the relationships between extreme points and basic solutions under each of the following conditions: (a) nondegeneracy; (b) degeneracy? What is the maximum possible number of simplex iterations that can be performed at the same extreme point?

☐ **4–24** Consider the problem, max $z = \mathbf{CX}$ subject to $\mathbf{AX} \le \mathbf{b}$, where $\mathbf{b} \ge \mathbf{0}$ and $\mathbf{X} \ge \mathbf{0}$. Suppose that the entering vector $\mathbf{P}_j$ is such that at least one element of

$\mathbf{B}^{-1}\mathbf{P}_j$ is greater than zero. If $\mathbf{P}_j$ is replaced by $\beta\mathbf{P}_j$, where β is a positive scalar, and provided that x_j remains the entering variable, find the relationships between the values of x_j corresponding to $\mathbf{P}_j$ and $\beta\mathbf{P}_j$.

☐ **4–25** Answer Problem 4–24 if, in addition, **b** is replaced by $\gamma\mathbf{b}$, where γ is a positive scalar.

☐ **4–26** Prove that for the minimization case, a nonbasic vector $\mathbf{P}_j$ can improve the current solution only if $z_j - c_j$ is greater than zero.

☐ **4–27** Consider the linear programming problem defined in Problem 4–24. After obtaining the optimum solution, it is suggested that a nonbasic variable x_j can be made basic (profitable) by reducing the requirements per unit of x_j for the different resources to $1/\beta$ of their original values, where β is a scalar greater than 1. Since the requirements per unit are reduced, it is expected that the profit per unit of x_j will be reduced to $1/\beta$ of its original value. Will these changes make x_j a profitable variable? What should be recommended for x_j to be an attractive variable?

☐ **4–28** Given the linear programming problem,

$$\text{maximize } z = \mathbf{CX}$$

subject to

$$(\mathbf{A}, \mathbf{I})\mathbf{X} = \mathbf{b}, \qquad \mathbf{X} \geq 0$$

where **X** is an $(m + n)$ column vector. Let $\{\mathbf{P}_1, \mathbf{P}_2, \ldots, \mathbf{P}_m\}$ be the vectors corresponding to a *basic* solution, and let $\{c_1, c_2, \ldots, c_m\}$ be the coefficients in the objective function associated with these vectors. If $\{c_1, \ldots, c_m\}$ is changed to $\{d_1, \ldots, d_m\}$, show that $z_j - c_j$ for the *basic* variables will remain equal to zero and interpret the result.

☐ **4–29** Solve the following problem by the revised simplex method:

$$\text{maximize } z = 6x_1 - 2x_2 + 3x_3$$

subject to

$$\begin{aligned} 2x_1 - x_2 + 2x_3 &\leq 2 \\ x_1 \qquad + 4x_3 &\leq 4 \\ x_1, x_2, x_3 &\geq 0 \end{aligned}$$

☐ **4–30** Solve the following problem by the revised simplex method:

$$\text{maximize } z = 2x_1 + x_2 + 2x_3$$

subject to

$$\begin{aligned} 4x_1 + 3x_2 + 8x_3 &\leq 12 \\ 4x_1 + x_2 + 12x_3 &\leq 8 \\ 4x_1 - x_2 + 3x_3 &\leq 8 \\ x_1, x_2, x_3 &\geq 0 \end{aligned}$$

□ **4–31** Solve the following problem by the revised simplex method:

$$\text{minimize } z = 2x_1 + x_2$$

subject to

$$\begin{aligned} 3x_1 + x_2 &= 3 \\ 4x_1 + 3x_2 &\geq 6 \\ x_1 + 2x_2 &\leq 3 \\ x_1, x_2 &\geq 0 \end{aligned}$$

□ **4–32** Solve the following problems by the *revised dual* simplex method outlined in Exercise 4.2-2(b).

(a) Minimize $z = 2x_1 + 3x_2$
subject to

$$\begin{aligned} 2x_1 + 3x_2 &\leq 30 \\ x_1 + 2x_2 &\geq 10 \\ x_1, x_2 &\geq 0 \end{aligned}$$

(b) Minimize $z = 5x_1 + 6x_2$
subject to

$$\begin{aligned} x_1 + x_2 &\geq 2 \\ 4x_1 + x_2 &\geq 4 \\ x_1, x_2 &\geq 0 \end{aligned}$$

□ **4–33** Solve the following problems by applying the revised simplex to the "two-phase" procedure.

(a) The example in Section 3.3.1.
(b) Problem 3–27.

Chapter 5

Linear Programming: Duality, Sensitivity, and Parametric Analysis

This chapter introduces the new topic of duality in linear programming. Aside from its immense theoretical interest, duality is a key concept in the development of the important practical topic of sensitivity and parametric analysis. We have dealt with sensitivity analysis in Chapters 2 and 3 at an elementary level. We will now use duality to cover the topic in depth. In addition, duality theory forms the basis for the development of new and efficient computational techniques, which will be presented in Chapter 7.

5.1 DEFINITION OF THE DUAL PROBLEM

The **dual** is an LP problem that is derived mathematically from a given primal LP model. The dual and primal problems are very closely related to the extent that the optimum simplex solution of either problem *automatically* yields the optimum solution to the other problem.

In most LP treatments, the dual is defined for various forms of the primal depending on the types of the constraints, the signs of the variables, and the sense of the optimization. Our experience shows that beginners often become confused by the details of these definitions. More important, the use of these multiple definitions may lead to inconsistent interpretations of the data in the simplex tableau, particularly with regard to the signs of the dual variables.

In this book we introduce a *single* definition of the dual problem that automatically subsumes all the forms of the primal. It is based on the fact that the LP problem must be put in the standard form (see Section 4.1.1) before it is solved by either the primal or dual simplex method. As such, by defining the dual problem from the standard form, the results will be consistent with the information contained in the simplex tableau. Keep in mind, however, that the single definition we give here is *general* in the sense that it automatically accounts for *all* the forms given in the other LP treatments.

The general *standard* form of the primal is defined as

$$\text{maximize or minimize } z = \sum_{j=1}^{n} c_j x_j$$

subject to

$$\sum_{j=1}^{n} a_{ij} x_j = b_i, \qquad i = 1, 2, \ldots, m$$

$$x_j \geq 0, \qquad j = 1, 2, \ldots, n$$

Note that the n variables, x_j, include the surplus, slacks, and artificials. For the purpose of constructing the dual, we arrange the coefficients of the primal schematically as shown in Table 5-1.

The diagram shows that the dual is obtained symmetrically from the primal according to the following rules:

1. For every primal constraint there is a dual variable.
2. For every primal variable there is a dual constraint.
3. The constraint coefficients of a primal variable form the left-side coefficients of the corresponding dual constraint; and the objective coefficient of the same variable becomes the right side of the dual constraint. (See, e.g., the tinted column under x_j.)

Table 5-1

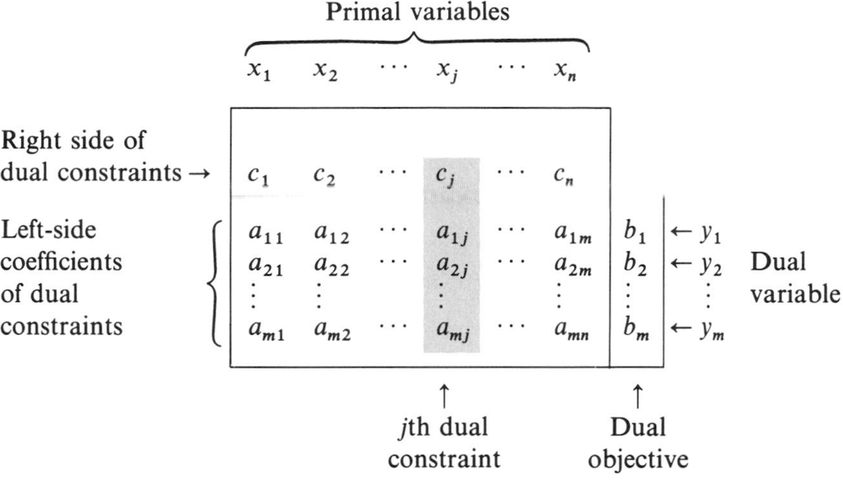

Table 5-2

Standard Primal Objective[a]	Dual Objective	Dual Constraints	Dual Variables
Maximization	Minimization	$\geq$	Unrestricted
Minimization	Maximization	$\leq$	Unrestricted

[a] All primal constraints are equations and all variables are nonnegative.

These rules indicate that the dual problem will have m variables ($y_1, y_2, \ldots, y_m$) and n constraints (corresponding to $x_1, x_2, \ldots, x_n$).

We now turn our attention to determining the remaining elements of the dual problem: the sense of optimization, the type of constraints, and the sign of the dual variables. This information is summarized in Table 5-2 for the maximization and minimization types of the standard form. Recall again that the standard primal form requires all constraints to be equations (with nonnegative right side if the primal simplex method is used to solve the primal problem) and all the variables to be nonnegative.

The following examples are designed to illustrate the use of these rules and, more important, to show that our definition incorporates all forms of the primal.

Example 5.1-1

Primal

$$\text{Maximize } z = 5x_1 + 12x_2 + 4x_3$$

subject to

$$\begin{aligned} x_1 + 2x_2 + x_3 &\leq 10 \\ 2x_1 - x_2 + 3x_3 &= 8 \\ x_1, x_2, x_3 &\geq 0 \end{aligned}$$

Standard Primal

$$\text{Maximize } z = 5x_1 + 12x_2 + 4x_3 + 0x_4$$

subject to

$$\begin{aligned} x_1 + 2x_2 + x_3 + x_4 &= 10 \\ 2x_1 - x_2 + 3x_3 + 0x_4 &= 8 \\ x_1, x_2, x_3, x_4 &\geq 0 \end{aligned}$$

Notice that x_4 is a slack in the first constraint; hence, it has zero coefficients in the objective function and the second constraint.

Dual

$$\text{Minimize } w = 10y_1 + 8y_2$$

subject to

$$\begin{aligned} x_1&: \quad y_1 + 2y_2 \geq 5 \\ x_2&: \quad 2y_1 - y_2 \geq 12 \\ x_3&: \quad y_1 + 3y_2 \geq 4 \\ x_4&: \quad y_1 + 0y_2 \geq 0 \qquad \text{(implies that } y_1 \geq 0) \\ &\quad y_1, y_2 \text{ unrestricted} \end{aligned}$$

Observe that "y_1 unrestricted" is dominated by $y_1 \geq 0$, the dual constraint associated with x_4. Thus, eliminating the redundancy, the dual problem should read as

$$\text{minimize } w = 10y_1 + 8y_2$$

subject to

$$\begin{aligned} y_1 + 2y_2 &\geq 5 \\ 2y_1 - y_2 &\geq 12 \\ y_1 + 3y_2 &\geq 4 \\ y_1 &\geq 0 \\ y_2 &\text{ unrestricted} \end{aligned}$$

◀

Exercise 5.1-1

Indicate the *changes* in the dual shown if its primal is minimization instead of maximization. [*Ans.* Changes are: Maximize w, first three constraints are of the type $\leq$, and $y_1 \leq 0$.]

Example 5.1-2

Primal

$$\text{Minimize } z = 15x_1 + 12x_2$$

subject to

$$\begin{aligned} x_1 + x_2 &\geq 1.5 \\ 2x_1 + 3x_2 &\leq 5 \\ x_1, x_2 &\geq 0 \end{aligned}$$

The primal problem above can be solved by either the primal simplex (using an artificial and a slack starting variable) or directly by the dual simplex method. The selection of the specific method of solution will have an effect on how the optimal dual solution is obtained from the optimal solution of the primal. We consider both cases.

Standard Model When Primal Simplex Is Used to Solve Primal

$$\text{Minimize } z = 15x_1 + 12x_2$$

subject to

$$\begin{aligned} x_1 + \ \ x_2 - x_3 \qquad &= 1.5 \\ 2x_1 + 4x_2 \qquad + x_4 &= 5 \\ x_1, x_2, x_3, x_4 &\geq 0 \end{aligned}$$

Dual

$$\text{Maximize } z = 1.5y_1 + 5y_2$$

subject to

$$\begin{aligned} y_1 + 2y_2 &\leq 15 \\ y_1 + 4y_2 &\leq 12 \\ -y_1 \qquad &\leq 0 \quad (\text{or } y_1 \geq 0) \\ y_2 &\leq 0 \\ y_1, y_2 &\text{ unrestricted (redundant)} \end{aligned}$$

Standard Model When Dual Simplex Is Used to Solve Primal

$$\text{Minimize } z = 15x_1 + 12x_2$$

subject to

$$\begin{aligned} -x_1 - \ \ x_2 + x_3 \qquad &= -1.5 \\ 2x_1 + 4x_2 \qquad + x_4 &= \quad 5 \\ x_1, x_2, x_3, x_4 &\geq 0 \end{aligned}$$

Dual

$$\text{Maximize } z = -1.5y_1 + 5y_2$$

subject to

$$\begin{aligned} -y_1 + 2y_2 &\leq 15 \\ -y_1 + 4y_2 &\leq 12 \\ y_1 \qquad &\leq 0 \\ y_2 &\leq 0 \\ y_1, y_2 &\text{ unrestricted (redundant)} \end{aligned}$$

You will notice that the two duals are consistent, since the coefficients of y_1 in one dual have the opposite sign of the same coefficients in the other dual. However, the distinction is necessary because the simplex tableau results (which are used to interpret the dual problem solution) are directly dependent on the way the standard form is defined before the primal or the dual simplex method is applied. This fine detail may be lost when we try to use the general definitions given in other LP treatments. ◀

Example 5.1-3

Primal

$$\text{Maximize } z = 5x_1 + 6x_2$$

subject to

$$\begin{aligned} x_1 + 2x_2 &= 5 \\ -x_1 + 5x_2 &\geq 3 \\ 4x_1 + 7x_2 &\leq 8 \\ x_1 &\text{ unrestricted} \\ x_2 &\geq 0 \end{aligned}$$

Standard Primal

Let $x_1 = x_1' - x_1''$, where $x_1', x_1'' \geq 0$. Then the standard primal becomes

$$\text{maximize } z = 5x_1' - 5x_1'' + 6x_2$$

subject to

$$\begin{aligned} x_1' - x_1'' + 2x_2 \qquad\qquad &= 5 \\ -x_1' + x_1'' + 5x_2 - x_3 \qquad &= 3 \\ 4x_1' - 4x_1'' + 7x_2 \qquad + x_4 &= 8 \\ x_1', x_1'', x_2, x_3, x_4 &\geq 0 \end{aligned}$$

Dual

$$\text{Minimize } w = 5y_1 + 3y_2 + 8y_3$$

subject to

$$\begin{aligned} \left.\begin{aligned} y_1 - y_2 + 4y_3 &\geq 5 \\ -y_1 + y_2 - 4y_3 &\geq -5 \end{aligned}\right\} &\quad \text{(imply that } y_1 - y_2 + 4y_3 = 5\text{)} \\ 2y_1 + 5y_2 + 7y_3 \geq 6 & \\ -y_2 \geq 0 &\quad \text{(implies that } y_2 \leq 0\text{)} \\ y_3 \geq 0 & \end{aligned}$$

$$y_1 \text{ unrestricted}$$

$$y_2, y_3 \text{ unrestricted} \quad \text{(redundant)}$$

Observe that the first and second dual constraints can (*but need not*) be replaced by the equation $y_1 - y_2 + 4y_3 = 5$. This will always be the case when the primal variable is unrestricted, meaning that an unrestricted primal variable will always lead to a dual *equation* (rather than inequality). The result is true whether the primal represents maximization or minimization. ◀

Exercise 5.1-2

Indicate the changes in the dual just shown if the objective is minimization and the first constraint is of the type "$\geq$."

[*Ans.* Maximize w, first three constraints are of the type "$\leq$," and $y_1 \geq 0$, $y_2 \geq 0$, $y_3 \leq 0$.]

If you investigate the foregoing examples carefully, you will be able to devise all the general rules that are traditionally presented in conjunction with the definition of the dual. This, however, will lead to a variety of conditions, particularly in connection with the signs of the dual variables (as you already saw in the examples). However, if you follow the two simple rules we gave in Table 5-2, you will never concern yourself with such problems. Also, remember that the preparation of the standard form does not really represent additional work, since it is always used in the starting simplex iteration.

Exercise 5.1-3

Show that the dual constraint associated with an *artificial* variable (R_i) in the standard form of the primal is always redundant. Hence it is never necessary to consider the dual constraint associated with an artificial variable.

[*Ans.* The dual constraint of artificial variable R_i is $y_i \geq -M$ in case of primal *maximization* and $y_i \leq M$ in case of primal *minimization*. Both are redundant, since M can assume as large a value as desired.]

We now provide a general matrix definition of the dual problem based on the following standard primal LP model:

$$\text{maximize } z = \mathbf{C}_{\text{I}}\mathbf{X}_{\text{I}} + \mathbf{C}_{\text{II}}\mathbf{X}_{\text{II}}$$

subject to

$$\mathbf{AX}_{\text{I}} + \mathbf{IX}_{\text{II}} = \mathbf{b}$$
$$\mathbf{X}_{\text{I}} \geq \mathbf{0}, \quad \mathbf{X}_{\text{II}} \geq \mathbf{0}$$

Let $\mathbf{Y} = (y_1, y_2, \ldots, y_m)$ be the dual vector. The rules in Table 5-2 yield the following dual:

$$\text{minimize } w = \mathbf{Yb}$$

subject to

$$\mathbf{YA} \geq \mathbf{C}_{\text{I}}$$
$$\mathbf{Y} \geq \mathbf{C}_{\text{II}}$$
$$\mathbf{Y} \text{ unrestricted vector}$$

Note that $\mathbf{Y} \geq \mathbf{C}_{\text{II}}$ may override the unrestricted status of $\mathbf{Y}$.

If the primal problem is changed to minimization, the dual problem sense of optimization is changed to maximization and the first two sets of constraints are changed to $\leq$ with $\mathbf{Y}$ remaining unrestricted.

5.2 SOLUTION OF THE DUAL PROBLEM

In this section we show the relationship between the solutions of the primal and dual problems. As illustrated below, the optimum simplex tableau associated with one problem (primal or dual) directly provides complete information about the optimal solution to the other problem.

5.2.1 RELATIONSHIP BETWEEN PRIMAL AND DUAL OBJECTIVE VALUES

The objective values in a pair of primal–dual problems must satisfy the following relationships:

1. For any pair of *feasible* primal and dual solutions

$$\begin{pmatrix}\text{objective value in} \\ \textit{maximization}\text{ problem}\end{pmatrix} \leq \begin{pmatrix}\text{objective value in} \\ \textit{minimization}\text{ problem}\end{pmatrix}$$

2. At the *optimum* solution for both problems

$$\begin{pmatrix}\text{objective value in} \\ \textit{maximization}\text{ problem}\end{pmatrix} = \begin{pmatrix}\text{objective value in} \\ \textit{minimization}\text{ problem}\end{pmatrix}$$

Observe carefully that these two results say nothing about which problem is primal and which is dual. It is the sense of optimization (maximization and minimization) that matters in this case.

To prove the validity of these results, let $(\mathbf{X}_\mathrm{I}, \mathbf{X}_\mathrm{II})$ and $\mathbf{Y}$ be the *feasible* primal and dual solutions corresponding to the primal–dual definitions given in matrix form at the end of Section 5.1. Then, premultiplying the primal constraints by $\mathbf{Y}$, we get

$$\mathbf{YAX}_\mathrm{I} + \mathbf{YX}_\mathrm{II} = \mathbf{Yb} \equiv w$$

Now, postmultiplying the dual constraints by $\mathbf{X}_\mathrm{I}$ and $\mathbf{X}_\mathrm{II}$, we get

$$\mathbf{YAX}_\mathrm{I} \geq \mathbf{C}_\mathrm{I}\mathbf{X}_\mathrm{I}$$

$$\mathbf{YX}_\mathrm{II} \geq \mathbf{C}_\mathrm{II}\mathbf{X}_\mathrm{II}$$

(Observe that $\mathbf{X}_\mathrm{I} \geq 0$ and $\mathbf{X}_\mathrm{II} \geq 0$; hence the direction of the inequality remains unchanged.) Then, adding the two constraints yields

$$\mathbf{YAX}_\mathrm{I} + \mathbf{YX}_\mathrm{II} \geq \mathbf{C}_\mathrm{I}\mathbf{X}_\mathrm{I} + \mathbf{C}_\mathrm{II}\mathbf{X}_\mathrm{II} \equiv z$$

Since the left-hand sides of the w and z identities above are equal, we conclude that

$$z \leq w$$

which proves the first result given above.

Now to show that $z = w$ at the optimum solutions, observe that z is associated with maximization, whereas w is associated with minimization. This means that z seeks the highest value among all *feasible* $(\mathbf{X}_\mathrm{I}, \mathbf{X}_\mathrm{II})$ and w seeks the lowest value among all *feasible* $\mathbf{Y}$. Since $z \leq w$ for *all* feasible solutions (including the optima), the two problems will reach optimality only when max z = min w.

Example 5.2-1. Consider the following pair of primal and dual problems:

Primal	Dual
Minimize $z = 5x_1 + 2x_2$	Maximize $w = 3y_1 + 5y_2$
subject to	subject to
$x_1 - x_2 \geq 3$	$y_1 + 2y_2 \leq 5$
$2x_1 + 3x_2 \geq 5$	$-y_1 + 3y_2 \leq 2$
$x_1, x_2 \geq 0$	$y_1, y_2 \geq 0$
Feasible solution:	*Feasible solution*:
$x_1 = 3, x_2 = 0$	$y_1 = 3, y_2 = 1$
Objective value:	*Objective value*:
$z = 5 \times 3 + 2 \times 0 = 15$	$w = 3 \times 3 + 5 \times 1 = 14$

The feasible solutions given above are determined by inspecting (trial and error) the constraints of both problems. The objective value in the maximization problem (dual) is less than the objective value in the minimization problem (primal). This result means that

$$14 \leq (\min z = \max w) \leq 15$$

Since the range (14 to 15) is relatively narrow, we can actually think of the two feasible solutions above as being *near optimal.* In essence, the given inequality can be used to test the "goodness" of the feasible solutions. If the two limits happen to be equal, the corresponding solutions are optimal. ◀

Exercise 5.2-1

In Example 5.2-1, determine whether or not the following solutions are optimal.

(a) $(x_1 = 3, x_2 = 1; y_1 = 4, y_2 = 1)$
[*Ans.* Even though $z = w = 17$, the solutions are not optimal because they are not feasible.]

(b) $(x_1 = 4, x_2 = 1; y_1 = 1, y_2 = 0)$
[*Ans.* No, because $z = 22 \neq w = 3$, even though the solutions are feasible.]

(c) $(x_1 = 3, x_2 = 0; y_1 = 5, y_2 = 0)$
[*Ans.* Yes, because the solutions are feasible *and* $z = w = 15$.]

5.2.2 OPTIMAL DUAL SOLUTION

The optimal dual solution can be determined directly from the optimal primal tableau. We verify this result using the primal and dual problems in matrix form given at the end of Section 5.1:

Standard Primal

$$\text{Maximize } z = \mathbf{C}_{\text{I}}\mathbf{X}_{\text{I}} + \mathbf{C}_{\text{II}}\mathbf{X}_{\text{II}}$$

subject to

$$\mathbf{AX}_{\text{I}} + \mathbf{IX}_{\text{II}} = \mathbf{b}$$
$$\mathbf{X}_{\text{I}}, \mathbf{X}_{\text{II}} \geq \mathbf{0}$$

Dual

$$\text{Minimize } w = \mathbf{Yb}$$

subject to

$$\mathbf{YA} \geq \mathbf{C}_{\text{I}}$$
$$\mathbf{Y} \geq \mathbf{C}_{\text{II}}$$
$$\mathbf{Y} \text{ unrestricted vector}$$

Suppose that $\mathbf{B}$ is the optimal *primal* basis and let $\mathbf{C}_B$ be its associated objective function coefficients, then

$$\mathbf{Y} = \mathbf{C}_B \mathbf{B}^{-1}$$

is the optimal *dual* solution. To show that this result is true, we need to verify the following two requirements:

1. $\mathbf{Y} = \mathbf{C}_B \mathbf{B}^{-1}$ is a feasible dual solution.
2. max z in the primal equals min w in the dual.

The dual solution $\mathbf{Y} = \mathbf{C}_B \mathbf{B}^{-1}$ is feasible if it satisfies the dual constraints $\mathbf{YA} \geq \mathbf{C}_{\text{I}}$ and $\mathbf{Y} \geq \mathbf{C}_{\text{II}}$. By the optimality of the primal, we have $z_j - c_j \geq 0$ for all j (see the revised simplex in Section 4.3); that is,

$$\mathbf{C}_B \mathbf{B}^{-1}\mathbf{A} - \mathbf{C}_{\text{I}} \geq \mathbf{0} \qquad \text{and} \qquad \mathbf{C}_B \mathbf{B}^{-1} - \mathbf{C}_{\text{II}} \geq \mathbf{0}$$

By letting $\mathbf{Y} = \mathbf{C}_B \mathbf{B}^{-1}$, we immediately see that the dual constraints are satisfied.

The second requirement is verified by showing that $z = w$ for $\mathbf{Y} = \mathbf{C}_B \mathbf{B}^{-1}$. This follows directly because

$$w = \mathbf{Yb} = \mathbf{C}_B \mathbf{B}^{-1}\mathbf{b}$$
$$z = \mathbf{C}_B \mathbf{X}_B = \mathbf{C}_B \mathbf{B}^{-1}\mathbf{b}$$

The discussion above relating the primal optimality and the dual constraints feasibility leads to an interesting observation. While the primal problem is seeking optimality, the dual problem is automatically seeking feasibility. This observation is actually the basis for the development of the dual simplex method (Section 3.3), which starts better than optimal and continues to maintain optimality at all iterations while seeking feasibility. At the iteration where feasibility is reached the process ends.

Exercise 5.2-2

Consider the following linear program:

$$\text{maximize } z = 5x_1 + 12x_2 + 4x_3$$

subject to

$$x_1 + 2x_2 + x_3 \leq 5$$
$$2x_1 - x_2 + 3x_3 = 2$$
$$x_1, x_2, x_3 \geq 0$$

In each of the following cases, first verify that the basis **B** is feasible for the primal. Then, using $\mathbf{Y} = \mathbf{C}_B\mathbf{B}^{-1}$, compute the associated dual values and verify whether the dual solution is optimal.

(a) $\mathbf{B} = (\mathbf{P}_{s_1}, \mathbf{P}_3)$, where s_1 is the slack in the first constraint.
[*Ans.* **B** is feasible. $\mathbf{Y} = (0, 4/3)$ is not optimal because the first and second *dual* constraints are not satisfied.]

(b) $\mathbf{B} = (\mathbf{P}_2, \mathbf{P}_3)$
[*Ans.* **B** is feasible. $\mathbf{Y} = (40/7, -4/7)$ is not optimal because at least the first dual constraint is not satisfied.]

(c) $\mathbf{B} = (\mathbf{P}_1, \mathbf{P}_2)$
[*Ans.* **B** is feasible. $\mathbf{Y} = (29/5, -2/5)$ is optimal because all dual constraints are satisfied *and* $w = z = 141/5$.]

(d) $\mathbf{B} = (\mathbf{P}_1, \mathbf{P}_3)$
[*Ans.* **B** is *not* feasible. Note, however, that the associated $\mathbf{Y} = (7, -1)$ satisfies all dual constraints and also the condition $z = w = 31$; yet it is not optimal because **B** is infeasible.]

The optimal dual solution can be secured directly from the objective row of the optimal primal tableau given below. (See Section 4.2.2 for the details of deriving this tableau.)

Basic	$\mathbf{X}_{\text{I}}$	$\mathbf{X}_{\text{II}}$	Solution
z	$\mathbf{C}_B\mathbf{B}^{-1}\mathbf{A} - \mathbf{C}_{\text{I}}$	$\mathbf{C}_B\mathbf{B}^{-1} - \mathbf{C}_{\text{II}}$	$\mathbf{C}_B\mathbf{B}^{-1}\mathbf{b}$
$\mathbf{X}_B$	$\mathbf{B}^{-1}\mathbf{A}$	$\mathbf{B}^{-1}$	$\mathbf{B}^{-1}\mathbf{b}$

The coefficients under $\mathbf{X}_{\text{II}}$ in the z-row are given by $\mathbf{C}_B\mathbf{B}^{-1} - \mathbf{C}_{\text{II}}$. Thus, if the starting basic vector $\mathbf{X}_{\text{II}}$ consists of all slacks, $\mathbf{C}_{\text{II}} = \mathbf{0}$ and the z-row coefficients of $\mathbf{X}_{\text{II}}$ will yield the dual values directly. Else, it would be necessary to add $\mathbf{C}_{\text{II}}$ to $\mathbf{C}_B\mathbf{B}^{-1} - \mathbf{C}_{\text{II}}$ to secure the dual solution.

The observation above is useful only if we are using the regular simplex tableau. In the case of the revised simplex, the dual values are secured directly from the formula $\mathbf{Y} = \mathbf{C}_B\mathbf{B}^{-1}$.

Example 5.2-2. The primal and dual problems of Example 5.1-1 are listed below.

Primal	Dual
Maximize $z = 5x_1 + 12x_2 + 4x_3$	Minimize $w = 10y_1 + 8y_2$
subject to	subject to
$x_1 + 2x_2 + x_3 \le 10$	$y_1 + 2y_2 \ge 5$
$2x_1 - x_2 + 3x_3 = 8$	$2y_1 - y_2 \ge 12$
$x_1, x_2, x_3 \ge 0$	$y_1 + 3y_2 \ge 4$
	$y_1 \ge 0$, y_2 unrestricted

The optimal primal tableau is given below.

	$\mathbf{X}_I$			$\mathbf{X}_{II}$		
Basic	x_1	x_2	x_3	x_4	R	Solution
z	0	0	3/5	29/5	$-2/5+M$	274/5
x_2	0	1	$-1/5$	2/5	$-1/5$	12/5
x_1	1	0	7/5	1/5	2/5	26/5

Since $\mathbf{X}_{II} = (x_4, R)^T$ and $\mathbf{C}_{II} = (0, -M)$, we have from the tableau above:

$$\mathbf{C}_B\mathbf{B}^{-1} - \mathbf{C}_{II} = (29/5, -2/5 + M)$$

Thus we get

$$\begin{aligned}\mathbf{Y} = (y_1, y_2) = \mathbf{C}_B\mathbf{B}^{-1} &= (29/5, \ -2/5 + M) + (0, \ -M) \\ &= (29/5, \ -2/5)\end{aligned}$$

You will notice that the same result is obtained by using the revised simplex computations as follows:

$$\mathbf{Y} = \mathbf{C}_B\mathbf{B}^{-1} = (12, 5)\begin{pmatrix} \frac{2}{5} & -\frac{1}{5} \\ \frac{1}{5} & \frac{2}{5} \end{pmatrix} = \left(\frac{29}{5}, -\frac{2}{5}\right)$$

Notice that $\mathbf{C}_B$ consists of the objective coefficient of x_2 (= 12) followed by that of x_1 (= 5) because $\mathbf{X}_B = (x_2, x_1)^T$ per their order in the basic column.

We can just as well determine the optimal *primal* solution directly from the *optimal dual tableau*. All we have to do is to solve the dual problem first, then follow a procedure similar to the one given above to obtain the optimal primal solution. The point to be made is that it may be advantageous computationally to solve the dual in place of the primal. Since the amount of computation in the simplex computation is primarily a function of the number of constraints, it may be more efficient to solve the dual, from which the primal solution is obtained. The discussion points to a possible advantage of the dual problem. ◀

Computer Drill

Use TORA to solve the dual of Example 5.2-2 and verify that the optimal dual tableau yields the optimal primal solution ($x_1 = 26/5, x_2 = 12/5$).

5.3 ECONOMIC INTERPRETATION OF THE DUAL PROBLEM

In Sections 2.1.2 and 3.6.3 we used intuitive arguments to define two LP economic indicators: **dual prices** and **reduced costs**. Specifically, we stated that *dual prices* represent the worth per unit of the LP resources. The *reduced costs*, on the other hand, represent the increase in the marginal return or the decrease in the per unit cost of resource needed to make an LP activity (variable) just profitable.

This section uses the primal–dual problems to shed light on the exact economic meaning of *dual prices* and *reduced costs*. The interpretation will prove useful in two aspects:

1. Providing a fundamental understanding of the LP model as an economic input–output system.
2. Allowing efficient implementation of sensitivity or postoptimal analysis.

The first aspect is addressed in this section. Sensitivity analysis will be covered in the next section.

For the purpose of providing an economic interpretation of the dual problem, we use the following (nonmatrix) definitions of the primal and dual problems.

Primal	Dual
Maximize $z = \sum_{j=1}^{n} c_j x_j$ subject to $\sum_{j=1}^{n} a_{ij} x_j = b_i, \quad i = 1, 2, \ldots, m$ $x_j \geq 0, \quad j = 1, 2, \ldots, n$	Minimize $w = \sum_{i=1}^{m} b_i y_i$ subject to $\sum_{i=1}^{m} a_{ij} y_i \geq c_j, \quad j = 1, 2, \ldots, n$ y_i unrestricted, $\quad i = 1, 2, \ldots, m$

Economically, we can think of the primal model in this manner. The coefficient c_j represents the *marginal* profit of activity j whose level equals x_j units. The objective function $z = \sum_{j=1}^{m} c_j x_j$ thus represents the profit of all activities. The model has m resources. Resource i has a level b_i that is allocated at the rate a_{ij} units per unit of activity j. The left side $\sum_{j=1}^{n} a_{ij} x_j$ represents the usage of resource i by all activities. We now use the definition above to explain the meaning of the economic indicators *dual prices* and *reduced costs.*

5.3.1 DUAL PRICES

In Section 5.2.1 we showed that at the optimal solution of both the primal and the dual, we have

$$z = w$$

or

$$\sum_{j=1}^{n} c_j x_j = \sum_{i=1}^{m} b_i y_i$$

We can obtain an economic interpretation of the dual variables y_i using the following dimensional analysis. Since the left side of the equation represents dollars (return) and b_i represents units (amount) of resource i, then y_i, by the equation above, must represent dollars per unit of resource i as the following dimensional analysis shows:

$$\$(\text{return}) = \sum_{i=1}^{m} (\text{units of resource } i)(\$/\text{unit of resource } i)$$

The dual variables y_i thus represent the *worth per unit* of resource i. In the literature, y_i are usually referred to as **dual prices** (sometimes the name **shadow prices** is also used).

The dimensional analysis above leads to an interesting observation. We have explained in Section 5.2.1 that for nonoptimal *feasible* primal and dual solutions, we have

$$z < w$$

By virtue of the economic interpretation given to the dual values, this inequality indicates that

$$\sum_{j=1}^{n} c_j x_j < \sum_{i=1}^{m} b_i y_i$$

or

$$(\text{profit}) < (\text{worth of resources})$$

The inequality says that as long as the total return of all the activities is less than the worth of the resources of the model, the corresponding (primal and dual) feasible solutions cannot be optimal. Optimality (maximum return) is reached only when the resources have been exploited fully; that is, when the total return equals the total worth of the resources ($z = w$). Alternatively, we can think of the LP model as an input–output system with the resources and return representing the input and the output elements, respectively. The system remains *unstable* (nonoptimal) as long as the input (worth of resources) exceeds the output (return), with stability taking place when the two quantities are equal.

Example 5.3-1. In Example 5.2-2, the dual prices $y_1 = 29/5$ and $y_2 = -2/5$ provide the worth per unit of resources 1 and 2 associated with constraints 1 and 2, respectively. The given dual prices thus indicate that for each unit increase in resource 1, the value of the profit z will increase by 29/5. On the other hand, it does not pay to increase resource 2 because its worth per unit is negative ($= -2/5$). In fact, it is advantageous in this case to decrease resource 2. This may appear illogical because one would aspire to increase a resource rather than decrease it. However, constraint 2 ($2x_1 - x_2 + 3x_3 = 8$) is not a conventional resource-type constraint, which accounts for its nonconventional behavior. ◀

The statements above regarding the use of the dual prices as worth per unit of the resources must be qualified. Specifically, there is a limit on how far a resource may be increased or decreased while maintaining the given worth per unit. We have seen in Section 3.6.4 that there is an allowable range of variation in the amounts of the resources beyond which the given dual prices cease to be applicable. In Section 5.5 we show how postoptimal or sensitivity analysis is used to deal with changes in resources outside the allowable ranges.

Computer Drill

Use TORA to determine the optimal dual prices of the primal of Example 5.1-2 by examining the optimal primal tableau. In particular, you will notice that if the problem is solved by the primal simplex method, you will get the dual solution $y_1 = 12$, $y_2 = 0$, whereas the solution by the dual simplex method will yield $y_1 = -12$, $y_2 = 0$. Despite the sign difference in the value of y_1, the dual price for constraint 1 still equals 12 in both cases. The reason for this is that in the starting tableau of the dual simplex method the first constraint equation is multiplied by -1, which means that the right-hand side of constraint 1 is -1.5 (compared with 1.5 in the primal simplex starting solution). Hence increasing the right-hand-side value above 1.5 in the primal simplex case is exactly equivalent to decreasing it below -1.5 in the dual simplex case.

Exercise 5.3-1

Use the optimal $\mathbf{B}^{-1}$ obtained from the computer drill above and its associated $\mathbf{C}_B$ to verify that the answers can be obtained from the vector $\mathbf{C}_B\mathbf{B}^{-1}$.

5.3.2 REDUCED COSTS

We have seen from the details of the revised simplex method in Section 4.2 that the objective equation coefficient of variable x_j in any iteration is given by

$$z_j - c_j = \mathbf{C}_B\mathbf{B}^{-1}\mathbf{P}_j - c_j$$

Alternatively, using $\mathbf{Y} = \mathbf{C}_B\mathbf{B}^{-1}$ as the associated dual values we obtain

$$\begin{aligned} z_j - c_j &= \mathbf{YP}_j - c_j \\ &= \sum_{i=1}^{m} a_{ij}y_i - c_j \end{aligned}$$

This relationship says that the objective equation coefficient $z_j - c_j$ of variable x_j in the primal tableau equals the difference between the left- and right-hand sides of the jth dual constraint. The equation yields interesting economic interpretations of the LP model, which we reveal by using dimensional analysis.

Since c_j of the primal represents the per unit return of activity j, its units may be represented as dollars per unit of activity j. For consistency, the quantity $\sum_{i=1}^{m} a_{ij}y_i$ also must have the dimension of dollars per unit of activity j. However, since c_j and $\sum_{i=1}^{m} a_{ij}y_i$ appear with opposite signs, the quantity $\sum_{i=1}^{m} a_{ij}y_i$ must stand for "cost." Now, by definition, a_{ij} is the amount of resource i consumed by 1 unit of activity j. As a result y_i must represent the **imputed cost** per unit of resource i and we can think of $\sum_{i=1}^{m} a_{ij}y_i$ as the total imputed cost of all the resources used to produce 1 unit of activity j. Now, depending on whether the cost $z_j = \sum_{i=1}^{m} a_{ij}y_i$ exceeds the return c_j, the explanation above leads to the following dimensional analysis of the equation for $z_j - c_j$:

$$\$(\text{profit or loss})/\text{unit} = \$(\text{cost})/\text{unit} - \$(\text{return})/\text{unit}$$

The maximization optimality condition of the (revised) simplex method (Sections 3.2.2 and 4.3) says that the level of a currently unused activity j (i.e., nonbasic $x_j = 0$) should be increased above zero level only if its objective coefficient $z_j - c_j$ is negative. This condition is justified economically as follows: From the interpretation of $z_j - c_j$, the optimality condition stipulates that

$$\begin{pmatrix}\text{imputed cost of used} \\ \text{resources per unit of } j\end{pmatrix} - \begin{pmatrix}\text{return per} \\ \text{unit of } j\end{pmatrix} < 0$$

or

$$\begin{pmatrix}\text{imputed cost of used} \\ \text{resources per unit of } j\end{pmatrix} < \begin{pmatrix}\text{return per} \\ \text{unit of } j\end{pmatrix}$$

Thus, as long as the return per unit exceeds the imputed cost of used resources, more resources should be allocated to the activity to take advantage of the profit potential. This, in essence, means that the level of activity j, x_j, must be increased above zero level.

You will notice that when we admit an activity j into the solution (make its variable basic), we increase its level to the point where its $z_j - c_j$ reduces to zero. This is equivalent to exploiting the profitability of the activity to the fullest extent, since any further increase will simply result in increasing the imputed cost beyond the potential return of the activity.

You can see now why in maximization models an activity with $z_j - c_j > 0$ should remain at zero level. The fact that its imputed cost of used resources is higher than its return makes it economically unattractive.

For those activities that are at zero level in the optimal solution (nonbasic variables), the quantity $z_j - c_j$ is referred to in the literature as the **reduced cost** per unit of activity j. According to the explanation given above (and in Sections 2.1.2 and 3.6.5), this quantity represents the amount by which the economic standing of the activity must be improved in order to make the activity more attractive economically (i.e., increase its level from zero to a positive value). Such a result can happen in two ways:

1. Increasing the activity's marginal return, c_j.
2. Decreasing the activity's consumption of the limited resources, $\sum_{i=1}^{m} a_{ij} y_i$.

The first option may not always be feasible, since profit margins are normally dictated by the market and competition conditions. The second option truly reflects the commitment of the economic entity to *improving* its operation primarily through a reduction in the use of limited resources. In essence, the second option deals with removing possible inefficiencies in the operation of the system under consideration.

The dual values y_i can be used as indicators of where the second option should be implemented. In effect, since y_i represents the imputed cost of using 1 unit of resource i per unit of activity j, the resources having relatively high values of y_i should receive priority in any improvement studies.

Example 5.3-2. Consider the product-mix problem in which each of three products is processed on three different operations. The limits on the available time for the three operations are 430, 460, and 420 minutes daily and the profits per unit of the three products are \$3, \$2, and \$5. The times in minutes per unit on the three operations are given as follows:

	Product 1	Product 2	Product 3
Operation 1	1	2	1
Operation 2	3	0	2
Operation 3	1	4	0

The LP model is written as

$$\text{maximize } z = 3x_1 + 2x_2 + 5x_3 \qquad \text{(daily profit)}$$

subject to

$$\left.\begin{aligned} \text{operation 1:} \quad & 1x_1 + 2x_2 + 1x_3 \leq 430 \\ \text{operation 2:} \quad & 3x_1 + 0x_2 + 2x_3 \leq 460 \\ \text{operation 3:} \quad & 1x_1 + 4x_2 + 0x_3 \leq 420 \end{aligned}\right\} \qquad \left(\begin{array}{c} \text{limits on} \\ \text{daily usages} \\ \text{of operations} \end{array}\right)$$

$$x_j \geq 0, j = 1, 2, 3$$

Given x_4, x_5, and x_6 are the slacks of the three constraints, the optimal basic vector $\mathbf{X}_B$ and the associated basis $\mathbf{B}$ are obtained by the primal revised simplex method as (verify!):

$$\mathbf{X}_B = (x_2, x_3, x_6)^T$$

$$\mathbf{B}^{-1} = \begin{pmatrix} 1/2 & -1/4 & 0 \\ 0 & 1/2 & 0 \\ -2 & 1 & 1 \end{pmatrix}$$

Thus

$$\mathbf{C}_B = (2, 5, 0)$$

and the dual prices are computed as

$$\mathbf{Y} = (y_1, y_2, y_3) = \mathbf{C}_B \mathbf{B}^{-1} = (1, 2, 0)$$

We notice that the optimal mix does not include product 1 ($x_1 = 0$). This means that product 1 is not profitable, which occurs because the imputed cost of product 1 is larger than its unit profit; that is, $z_1 > c_1$. Since $z_1 = 1y_1 + 3y_2 + 1y_3$ and $c_1 =$ \$3, we can make x_1 profitable by decreasing the value of z_1. This result can be accomplished by reducing the usages by product 1 of the three operations times. These usages are given by the coefficients of y_1, y_2, and y_3 in the expression for z_1.

The dual prices $y_1 = 1$, $y_2 = 2$, and $y_3 = 0$ mean that a reduction in the usage of operation 3 will not be effective, since its imputed cost per unit, y_3, is zero. Thus, considering operations 1 and 2, we notice that y_2 $(= 2)$ is larger than y_1 $(= 1)$. As a result, it may be more attractive to give higher priority to reducing the usage of operation 2.

Suppose that we are interested in determining the amount of reduction in the usage of operation 2 that will make product 1 just profitable. To do so, let r_2 represent reduction in minutes per unit of product 1 on operation 2. In this case,

$$\begin{aligned} z_1 = y_1 + (3 - r_2)y_2 + y_3 &= 1(1) + (3 - r_2)(2) + 1(0) \\ &= 7 - 2r_2 \end{aligned}$$

Product 1 becomes just profitable when c_1 just exceeds z_1; that is, $c_1 > z_1$ or $7 - 2r_2 < 3$, which yields $r_2 > 2$. This means that the usage of operation 2 must be reduced by more than 2 minutes to make product 1 profitable. ◀

Exercise 5.3-2

In Example 5.3-2, suppose that the per unit usage of operation 2 cannot be reduced by more than 1.75 minutes. Determine the additional reduction in the usage of operation 1 that will make x_1 just profitable.
[*Ans.* .5 minute.]

5.4 COMPLEMENTARY SLACKNESS

If you investigate the matrix version of the simplex tableau, you will discover the following results regarding the *optimal* primal and dual solutions.

1. If at the optimum a primal variable x_j has $z_j - c_j > 0$, then x_j must be nonbasic and hence at zero level.

2. If at the optimum a dual variable y_i has a positive value, the ith primal constraint $\sum_{j=1}^{n} a_{ij} x_j \leq b_i$ must be satisfied in equation form because its associated slack must be zero.

Let us translate this information mathematically. We note that $z_j - c_j$ represents the difference between the left and right sides of the dual constraint and hence must represent the dual surplus variable. If we assume that v_j and s_i are the surplus and slack variables for the jth dual and ith primal constraints, then

$$v_j = z_j - c_j = \sum_{i=1}^{m} a_{ij} y_i - c_j$$

$$s_i = b_i - \sum_{j=1}^{n} a_{ij} x_j$$

The result given may thus be summarized as follows:

1. When $v_j > 0$, $x_j = 0$.
2. When $y_i > 0$, $s_i = 0$.

We can express both conditions in a compact form as follows. For the optimal primal and dual solutions,

$$v_j x_j = y_i s_i = 0 \qquad \text{for all } i \text{ and } j$$

Equivalently, we have

$$x_j\left(\sum_{i=1}^{m} a_{ij} y_i - c_j\right) = 0, \qquad j = 1, 2, \ldots, n$$

$$y_i\left(b_i - \sum_{j=1}^{n} a_{ij} x_j\right) = 0, \qquad i = 1, 2, \ldots, m$$

We make use of the observations above to state the following theorem:

Complementary Slackness Theorem: *A pair of primal and dual **feasible** solutions x_j ($j = 1, 2, \ldots, n$) and y_i ($i = 1, 2, \ldots, m$) are optimal to their respective problems if, and only if, the following conditions are satisfied*:

$$y_i\left(b_i - \sum_{j=1}^{n} a_{ij} x_j\right) = y_i s_i = 0, \qquad i = 1, 2, \ldots, m$$

$$x_j\left(\sum_{i=1}^{m} a_{ij} y_i - c_j\right) = x_j v_j = 0, \qquad j = 1, 2, \ldots, n$$

where s_i and v_j are the slack and surplus variables associated with the primal and dual constraints.

The application of the complementary slackness theorem particularly arises in the development of the **primal–dual algorithm** for solving LPs that start both nonoptimal and infeasible. It is also used for the development of the **out-of-kilter algorithm** in network flow models.

Example 5.4-1. Consider the model of Example 5.3-2. We can use the complementary slackness theorem to verify that the basic vector $\mathbf{X}_B = (x_2, x_3, x_6)^T$ is optimal as follows: The corresponding primal and dual solutions are

$$(x_1, x_2, x_3) = (0, 100, 230)$$
$$(y_1, y_2, y_3) = (1, 2, 0)$$

These solutions are *feasible* because they yield

$$(s_1, s_2, s_3) = (0, 0, 20)$$
$$(v_1, v_2, v_3) = (4, 0, 0)$$

which are all nonnegative (verify by direct substitution in the primal and dual constraints). The solutions $(x_1, x_2, x_3) = (0, 100, 230)$ and $(y_1, y_2, y_3) = (1, 2, 0)$ are also optimal because they satisfy the complementary slackness conditions $y_i s_i = 0$ $(i = 1, 2, 3)$ and $v_j x_j = 0$ $(j = 1, 2, 3)$. ◀

5.5 POSTOPTIMAL OR SENSITIVITY ANALYSIS

In Section 3.6 we studied the determination of the ranges of variation that will keep a current solution both optimal and infeasible. This section goes a step farther. If certain changes take place in the parameters of the original model, would the optimal solution change? And if it does, can we compute the new optimum without having to solve the problem completely anew? This is what postoptimal analysis attempts to do. You will find out that in many cases, the new optimal solution can be obtained without too much additional computational effort.

The crux of the postoptimal analysis lies in investigating the general simplex tableau given in matrix form. Given the following LP problem in standard form:

$$\text{maximize } z = \mathbf{C}_\text{I}\mathbf{X}_\text{I} + \mathbf{C}_\text{II}\mathbf{X}_\text{II}$$

subject to

$$\mathbf{AX}_\text{I} + \mathbf{IX}_\text{II} = \mathbf{b}$$
$$\mathbf{X}_\text{I}, \mathbf{X}_\text{II} \geq \mathbf{0}$$

Assume that $\mathbf{B}$ is the current basis and let $\mathbf{C}_B$ and $\mathbf{X}_B$ be its associated elements as defined throughout this chapter. Given the dual values $\mathbf{Y} = \mathbf{C}_B\mathbf{B}^{-1}$, the corresponding general simplex iteration is

Basic	$\mathbf{X}_\text{I}$	$\mathbf{X}_\text{II}$	Solution
z	$\mathbf{YA} - \mathbf{C}_\text{I}$	$\mathbf{Y} - \mathbf{C}_\text{II}$	$\mathbf{C}_B\mathbf{B}^{-1}\mathbf{b}$
$\mathbf{X}_B$	$\mathbf{B}^{-1}\mathbf{A}$	$\mathbf{B}^{-1}$	$\mathbf{B}^{-1}\mathbf{b}$

Carefully observe that once $\mathbf{B}$, $\mathbf{C}_B$, and $\mathbf{X}_B$ are known, the *entire tableau* can be computed using $\mathbf{B}^{-1}$ *and the original data of the problem.* Postoptimal analysis is based precisely on this observation.

Normally, in postoptimal analysis we are interested in studying the effect of changing the objective function coefficients $\mathbf{C}_\text{I}$ and $\mathbf{C}_\text{II}$ and/or the available amounts of the resources $\mathbf{b}$. Look at the tableau above and note that changes in $\mathbf{C}_\text{I}$, $\mathbf{C}_\text{II}$, and $\mathbf{b}$ have no effect whatsoever on $\mathbf{B}$ or $\mathbf{B}^{-1}$. The reason is that $\mathbf{B}$ is comprised of columns of (**A**, **I**) and as long as (**A**, **I**) remains unchanged, **B** will remain unaffected. So the first thing we want to do in postoptimal analysis is to test whether or not a change from ($\mathbf{C}_{\text{I}}$, $\mathbf{C}_{\text{II}}$) to ($\mathbf{D}_{\text{I}}$, $\mathbf{D}_{\text{II}}$) and/or a change from **b** to **d** will keep the current basis **B** both optimal and feasible. Thus, under the assumption of no change in **B**, all we have to do is to replace $\mathbf{C}_B$ with the new $\mathbf{D}_B$ and **b** with **d** and then recompute the objective row (using $\mathbf{Y} = \mathbf{D}_B\mathbf{B}^{-1}$) and the right-hand side ($= \mathbf{B}^{-1}\mathbf{d}$). If none of the new objective row coefficients violate optimality and none of the new right-hand-side coefficients become negative, then **B** remains optimal and feasible at the new values $\mathbf{B}^{-1}\mathbf{d}$. Otherwise, depending on whether optimality or feasibility (or both) has been violated, additional computations will be needed to obtain the new solution.

To summarize the discussion above, postoptimal analysis falls into one of three categories.

1. Changes in the objective coefficients ($\mathbf{C}_{\text{I}}$, $\mathbf{C}_{\text{II}}$) can only affect optimality.
2. Changes in the right-hand side **b** can only affect feasibility.
3. Simultaneous changes in ($\mathbf{C}_{\text{I}}$, $\mathbf{C}_{\text{II}}$) and **b** can affect both optimality and feasibility.

The additional computations needed to obtain a new solution correspondingly fall into one of three procedures.

1. If the tableau becomes *nonoptimal*, apply the *primal* simplex method to the *new* tableau until optimality is reached (or there is evidence that the new solution is unbounded).
2. If the tableau becomes *infeasible*, apply the *dual* simplex method to the *new* tableau until feasibility is restored (or there is evidence that the new solution remains infeasible).
3. If the tableau becomes both *nonoptimal and infeasible*, first apply the primal simplex to the new tableau without regard to infeasibility. Once optimality is reached, apply the dual simplex method to recover feasibility. This procedure essentially combines procedures 1 and 2 in a sequential fashion.

You probably are wondering if postoptimal analysis will be extended to cover changes in the (technological) constraint coefficients **A** of the LP model. Keep in mind that **B** is composed of column vectors in (**A**, **I**). If the changes in **A** do not affect **B**, that is, the changes take place only in nonbasic column vectors, **B** remains unaffected, and from the general simplex tableau given above, the changes in **A** in this case will affect only the objective row and hence optimality. On the other hand, if the changes in **A** affect the column vectors of **B**, watch out! The current inverse $\mathbf{B}^{-1}$ will no longer be valid and the essence of the simplex tableau is "literally shattered." Of course, we can go ahead and attempt to recompute a new $\mathbf{B}^{-1}$ from the new **B**. However, there is no prior assurance that the new **B** will be a basis at all. But even if it is, recomputing $\mathbf{B}^{-1}$ may be a tedious task, hence defeating the purpose of carrying out postoptimal analysis. In summary, changes in the technological matrix **A** do not lend themselves neatly to postoptimal analysis. Thus, except in the case where the change is made in a *non*basic column vector of **A**, it is more advisable to solve the problem anew.

We now provide the details of the three procedures. The Reddy Mikks problem, which we summarize below for convenience, will be used to illustrate all three procedures. It is more convenient, mainly for the sake of compactness, to summarize the computations in the familiar simplex tableau format. The shaded matrix in the optimal primal tableau below defines the inverse $\mathbf{B}^{-1}$. The optimal basic vector $\mathbf{X}_B$ is $(x_2, x_1, x_5, x_6)^T$.

Reddy Mikks Primal	Reddy Mikks Dual
Maximize $z = 3x_1 + 2x_2$ subject to $x_1 + 2x_2 \leq 6$ $2x_1 + x_2 \leq 8$ $-x_1 + x_2 \leq 1$ $x_2 \leq 2$ $x_1, x_2 \geq 0$	Minimize $w = 6y_1 + 8y_2 + y_3 + 2y_4$ subject to $y_1 + 2y_2 - y_3 \geq 3$ $2y_1 + y_2 + y_3 + y_4 \geq 2$ $y_1, y_2, y_3, y_4 \geq 0$

Optimal Primal Tableau

Basic	x_1	x_2	x_3	x_4	x_5	x_6	Solution
z	0	0	1/3	4/3	0	0	38/3
x_2	0	1	2/3	−1/3	0	0	4/3
x_1	1	0	−1/3	2/3	0	0	10/3
x_5	0	0	−1	1	1	0	3
x_6	0	0	−2/3	1/3	0	1	2/3

(As you proceed through the remainder of this section, it will be convenient to keep in front of you a copy of the information given. Henceforth, we refer to the optimal primal solution as the *current* solution.)

Exercise 5.5-1

Identify the basis **B** associated with optimal tableau above using the data of the original Reddy Mikks primal problem. Verify that $\mathbf{BB}^{-1} = \mathbf{I}$.

$$\left[\textit{Ans.}\ \mathbf{B} = \begin{pmatrix} 2 & 1 & 0 & 0 \\ 1 & 2 & 0 & 0 \\ 1 & -1 & 1 & 0 \\ 1 & 0 & 0 & 1 \end{pmatrix} \right]$$

5.5.1 CHANGES AFFECTING OPTIMALITY

Optimality of the simplex solution is affected only in one of three ways.

1. The objective coefficients $(\mathbf{C}_{\text{I}}, \mathbf{C}_{\text{II}})$ are changed.
2. The resource usage of a nonbasic activity (i.e., a nonbasic column vector in **A**) is changed.

3. A new activity is added to the model.

The three cases are explained below.

A. Changes in the Objective Coefficients

From the definition of the general simplex tableau, changes in $(\mathbf{C}_\text{I}, \mathbf{C}_\text{II})$ only require recomputing the objective row of the optimal tableau. As an illustration, suppose that in the Reddy Mikks model the objective function is changed from $z = 3x_1 + 2x_2$ to $z = 5x_1 + 4x_2$. Given the current optimal $\mathbf{X}_B = (x_2, x_1, x_5, x_6)$, then

$$\mathbf{C}_B = (4, 5, 0, 0)$$

$$\mathbf{Y} = (y_1, y_2, y_3, y_4)$$

$$= \mathbf{C}_B\mathbf{B}^{-1} = (4, 5, 0, 0)\begin{pmatrix} 2/3 & -1/3 & 0 & 0 \\ -1/3 & 2/3 & 0 & 0 \\ -1 & 1 & 1 & 0 \\ -2/3 & 1/3 & 0 & 1 \end{pmatrix}$$

$$= (1, 2, 0, 0)$$

Now, we compute the new z-row coefficients using

$$\{z_j - c_j\} = (\mathbf{YA} - \mathbf{C}_\text{I}, \mathbf{Y} - \mathbf{C}_\text{II})$$

where $\mathbf{C}_\text{I} = (5, 4)$ and $\mathbf{C}_\text{II} = (0, 0, 0, 0)$. Observe carefully that $\mathbf{C}_\text{I}$ and $\mathbf{C}_\text{II}$ are determined from the new objective function.

Actually, $\mathbf{YA} - \mathbf{C}_\text{I}$ and $\mathbf{Y} - \mathbf{C}_\text{II}$ are nothing but the difference between the left and right sides of the corresponding dual constraints and we can proceed to compute the individual $(z_j - c_j)$ for all j in this manner. [Notice that it is not necessary to recompute $(z_j - c_j)$ for current basic vectors since they are always equal to zero. Why? Explain mathematically.] We will use the matrix notation here, however.

$$(z_3 - c_3, z_4 - c_4) = (1, 2, 0, 0)\begin{pmatrix} 1 & 0 \\ 0 & 1 \\ 0 & 0 \\ 0 & 0 \end{pmatrix} - (0, 0) = (1, 2)$$

The new objective row should thus appear as

Basic	x_1	x_2	x_3	x_4	x_5	x_6	Solution
z	0	0	1	2	0	0	22

The z-equation coefficients are all nonnegative and hence the current solution remains unchanged; namely, $x_1 = 10/3$, $x_2 = 4/3$. The only change occurs in the value of z, which now must equal $5 \times (10/3) + 4 \times (4/3) = 22$.

Exercise 5.5-2

Recompute the z-equation coefficients in each of the following cases. What general observation do you have regarding the objective coefficients of the basic variables? Specifically, could they ever differ from zero?

(a) $z = 6x_1 + 4x_2$

[*Ans.* z-equation coefficients $= (0, 0, 2/3, 8/3, 0, 0)$.]

(b) $z = 5x_1 + 5x_2$
[*Ans.* z-equation coefficients = (0, 0, 5/3, 5/3, 0, 0). The general observation is that the coefficients of the basic variables *always* remain zero, indicating that the corresponding *dual* constraint must be satisfied in equation form. This observation means that it is necessary to recompute the coefficients of the nonbasic variables only.]

Let us consider another example in which changes in the objective function will result in nonoptimality. Suppose that

$$z = 4x_1 + x_2$$

then

$$(y_1, y_2, y_3, y_4) = \mathbf{C}_B\mathbf{B}^{-1} = (1, 4, 0, 0)\begin{pmatrix} 2/3 & -1/3 & 0 & 0 \\ -1/3 & 2/3 & 0 & 0 \\ -1 & 1 & 1 & 0 \\ -2/3 & 1/3 & 0 & 1 \end{pmatrix}$$

$$= (-2/3, 7/3, 0, 0)$$

You can verify that the new z-equation becomes

Basic	x_1	x_2	x_3	x_4	x_5	x_6	Solution
z	0	0	−2/3	7/3	0	0	44/3

Since x_3 has a negative coefficient, x_3 must enter the solution and optimality is recovered by applying the primal simplex method. Table 5-3 shows that the new optimum is reached in one iteration. The first iteration is the same as the current optimum iteration, with the exception of the z-equation.

The revised simplex method could have been used to secure the optimum above. We use the regular tableau form only for compactness.

Table 5-3

Iteration	Basic	x_1	x_2	x_3	x_4	x_5	x_6	Solution
1 (starting)	z	0	0	−2/3	7/3	0	0	44/3
x_3 enters	x_2	0	1	2/3	−1/3	0	0	4/3
x_2 leaves	x_1	1	0	−1/3	2/3	0	0	10/3
	x_5	0	0	−1	1	1	0	3
	x_6	0	0	−2/3	1/3	0	1	2/3
2 (optimal)	z	0	1	0	2	0	0	16
	x_3	0	3/2	1	−1/2	0	0	2
	x_1	1	1/2	0	1/2	0	0	4
	x_5	0	3/2	0	1/2	1	0	5
	x_6	0	1	0	0	0	1	2

Exercise 5.5-3

Consider the optimum in Table 5-3, which yields the optimum solution given $z = 4x_1 + x_2$ subject to the original constraints of the Reddy Mikks model.

(a) Recompute the z-equation given $z = 4x_1 + (3/2)x_2$.
[*Ans.* Since the change occurs only in x_2, which is nonbasic, the dual values remain (0, 2, 0, 0) and only the coefficient of x_2 will change in the z-equation. Its value is 1/2, which means that x_2 will remain zero and the solution will be unchanged.]

(b) Will the given solution remain optimal when $z = 3x_1 + 2x_2$?
[*Ans.* Recompute dual values, since the coefficient of basic x_1 changes. This yields $(y_1, y_2, y_3, y_4) = (0, 3/2, 0, 0)$. The z-equation coefficients of nonbasic x_2 and x_4 are $-1/2$ and 3/2. All others equal zero. Thus x_2 enters and x_3 leaves.]

B. Changes in Activity's Usage of Resources

A change in an activity's usage of resources can affect only the optimality of the solution, since it affects the left side of its dual constraint. However, we must restrict this statement to activities that are currently *nonbasic*. A change in the constraint coefficients of basic activities will affect the inverse and could lead to complications in the computations. We shall thus restrict our presentation to changes in nonbasic activities. The easiest way to handle changes in basic activities is to solve the problem *anew*. Although methods exist for handling changes in a *single* constraint coefficient of a basic activity, the "quality" of the information they yield is not on a par with what one gets from other postoptimal analysis procedures.

Let us consider the Reddy Mikks model with $z = 4x_1 + x_2$. Its optimal solution is shown in Table 5-3. Activity x_2 is nonbasic, and we can consider modifying its constraint coefficients. Suppose that the usages by activity 2 of raw materials A and B are 4 and 3 tons instead of 2 and 1 tons. The associated dual constraint is

$$\mathbf{4}y_1 + \mathbf{3}y_2 + y_3 + y_4 \geq 1$$

(Note that the right side equals the coefficient of x_2 in $z = 4x_1 + x_2$.) Since the objective function remains unchanged, the dual values remain the same as given in Table 5-3. We thus have in the z-equation.

$$z_2 - c_2 = 4(0) + 3(2) + 1(0) + 1(0) - 1 = 5$$

Since it is ≥ 0, the proposed change does not affect the optimum solution in Table 5-3.

Exercise 5.5-4

Indicate whether the following changes in the constraint coefficients of x_2 will affect the optimal solution in Table 5.3.

(a) Usage of raw materials A and B is 4 and 2 tons.
[*Ans.* No, because the new $z_2 - c_2$ is 3.]

(b) Usage of raw materials A and B is 2 and 1/4 tons.
[*Ans.* Yes, because the new x_2-coefficient is $-1/2$.]

Instead of considering separately how the new optimum solution is obtained when the change results in nonoptimality (such as in case b), we present next the case of adding a completely new activity. Its treatment will automatically include this situation.

C. Addition of a New Activity

In the original Reddy Mikks model (with $z = 3x_1 + 2x_2$), suppose that we are interested in producing a cheaper brand of exterior paint, which uses 3/4 ton of each of raw materials A and B per ton of the new paint. The relationship between interior and exterior paints as expressed in the third constraint will remain binding except that now *both* types of exterior paint must be considered in the new constraint. The profit per ton of the new paint is $1\frac{1}{2}$ (thousand dollars).

Let x_7 equal the tons of new paint produced. The original model is modified as follows:

$$\text{maximize } z = 3x_1 + 2x_2 + \mathbf{(3/2)}\boldsymbol{x_7}$$

subject to

$$\begin{aligned} x_1 + 2x_2 + \mathbf{(3/4)}\boldsymbol{x_7} &\le 6 \\ 2x_1 + x_2 + \mathbf{(3/4)}\boldsymbol{x_7} &\le 8 \\ -x_1 + x_2 - \mathbf{1}\boldsymbol{x_7} &\le 1 \\ x_2 &\le 2 \\ x_1, x_2, x_7 &\ge 0 \end{aligned}$$

The addition of a new activity is equivalent to combining the analysis of making changes in the objective and the resource usages. We can think of x_7 as if it were part of the original model with *all zero* coefficients, which are now changed as shown in the foregoing model. This case is equivalent to saying that x_7 is nonbasic.

The first thing to do is to check the corresponding dual constraint:

$$(3/4)y_1 + (3/4)y_2 - y_3 \ge 3/2$$

Since x_7 is regarded as a nonbasic variable in the original tableau, the dual values remain unchanged. Thus the coefficient of x_7 in the current optimal tableau is

$$(3/4)(1/3) + (3/4)(4/3) - (1)(0) - 3/2 = -1/4$$

This means that the current solution will improve if x_7 becomes positive.

The *current optimal tableau* is modified by creating an x_7-column in the left side with its z-equation coefficient equal to $-1/4$. The associated constraint coefficients are computed as

$$\mathbf{B}^{-1}\mathbf{P}_7 = \begin{pmatrix} 2/3 & -1/3 & 0 & 0 \\ -1/3 & 2/3 & 0 & 0 \\ -1 & 1 & 1 & 0 \\ -2/3 & 1/3 & 0 & 1 \end{pmatrix} \begin{pmatrix} 3/4 \\ 3/4 \\ -1 \\ 0 \end{pmatrix} = \begin{pmatrix} 1/4 \\ 1/4 \\ -1 \\ -1/4 \end{pmatrix}$$

Table 5-4 gives the iterations for the new solution.

Table 5-4

Iteration	Basic	x_1	x_2	x_7	x_3	x_4	x_5	x_6	Solution
1 (starting)	z	0	0	−1/4	1/3	4/3	0	0	38/3
x_7 enters	x_2	0	1	1/4	2/3	−1/3	0	0	4/3
x_2 leaves	x_1	1	0	1/4	−1/3	2/3	0	0	10/3
	x_5	0	0	−1	−1	1	1	0	3
	x_6	0	0	−1/4	−2/3	1/3	0	1	2/3
2 (optimal)	z	0	1	0	1	1	0	0	14
	x_7	0	4	1	8/3	−4/3	0	0	16/3
	x_1	1	−1	0	−1	1	0	0	2
	x_5	0	4	0	5/3	−1/3	1	0	25/3
	x_6	0	1	0	0	0	0	1	2

Exercise 5.5-5

Suppose that the objective and constraint coefficients of x_7 were given respectively as 1, 1/2, 1, −1, and 0. Will it be profitable to produce the new product?
[*Ans.* No, because the z-equation coefficient of x_7 is 1/2.]

You may have already noticed that a new activity cannot be admitted into the solution unless it improves the objective value (e.g., in Table 5-4 the optimum value of z increased from $12\frac{2}{3}$ to 14 as a result of incorporating x_7 in the optimum solution). This result is in contrast to the addition of a new constraint (Section 5.5.2B), where a new constraint can never improve the optimum objective value. Indeed, if the additional constraint violates the current optimum, it must worsen the optimum value of z.

5.5.2 CHANGES AFFECTING FEASIBILITY

Feasibility of the simplex solution is affected in one of two ways:

1. The right-hand-side vector **b** is changed.
2. A new constraint is added to the model.

A. Changes in the Right-Hand Side

Suppose that in the Reddy Mikks model, the daily availability of raw material A is changed from 6 tons to 7 tons. How is the current solution affected?

We know from the simplex computations that changes in the right-hand-side vector **b** can affect only the right-hand of the tableau. In other words,

$$\mathbf{X}_B = \mathbf{B}^{-1}\mathbf{b}$$

Thus, in our example, new $\mathbf{b} = (7, 8, 1, 2)^T$ and

$$\mathbf{X}_B = \begin{pmatrix} x_2 \\ x_1 \\ x_5 \\ x_6 \end{pmatrix} = \begin{pmatrix} 2/3 & -1/3 & 0 & 0 \\ -1/3 & 2/3 & 0 & 0 \\ -1 & 1 & 1 & 0 \\ -2/3 & 1/3 & 0 & 1 \end{pmatrix} \begin{pmatrix} 7 \\ 8 \\ 1 \\ 2 \end{pmatrix} = \begin{pmatrix} 2 \\ 3 \\ 2 \\ 0 \end{pmatrix}$$

Since $\mathbf{X}_B$ remains nonnegative, the basis **B** remains unchanged. However, the values of the variables are changed to $x_1 = 3$, $x_2 = 2$, $x_5 = 2$, $x_3 = x_4 = x_5 = 0$. The new value of z is $3(3) + 2(2) = 13$.

Exercise 5.5-6

Suppose that in addition to the change in availability of material A, the maximum limit on the daily demand of interior paint (x_2) is increased from 2 tons to 3 tons. Check if the current (basic) variables remain feasible and find the new values of the variables.
[*Ans.* The basic variables remain unchanged. $x_1 = 3$, $x_2 = 2$, $x_5 = 2$, $x_6 = 1$, $x_3 = x_4 = 0$.]

Let us now consider an example of what happens when the current basic variable becomes infeasible. Suppose that the daily availabilities of materials A and B are 7 tons and 4 tons instead of 6 tons and 8 tons. The right side of the tableau is computed as follows:

$$\mathbf{X}_B = \begin{pmatrix} x_2 \\ x_1 \\ x_5 \\ x_6 \end{pmatrix} = \begin{pmatrix} 2/3 & -1/3 & 0 & 0 \\ -1/3 & 2/3 & 0 & 0 \\ -1 & 1 & 1 & 0 \\ -2/3 & 1/3 & 0 & 1 \end{pmatrix} \begin{pmatrix} \mathbf{7} \\ \mathbf{4} \\ 1 \\ 2 \end{pmatrix} = \begin{pmatrix} 10/3 \\ 1/3 \\ -2 \\ -4/3 \end{pmatrix} = \begin{pmatrix} \text{new right} \\ \text{side of} \\ \text{the tableau} \end{pmatrix}$$

The changes will make x_5 and x_6 negative, meaning that the current solution is infeasible. We must thus use the dual simplex method to recover feasibility.

The following optimal primal tableau shows the *new* right side with tinted overlay. All the remaining elements are unchanged.

Basic	x_1	x_2	x_3	x_4	x_5	x_6	Solution
z	0	0	1/3	4/3	0	0	23/3
x_2	0	1	2/3	−1/3	0	0	10/3
x_1	1	0	−1/3	2/3	0	0	1/3
x_5	0	0	[−1]	1	1	0	−2
x_6	0	0	−2/3	1/3	0	1	−4/3

Notice that the new value of z is $3(1/3) + 2(10/3) = 23/3$.

The tableau is optimal (all coefficients in the z-equation are ≥ 0) but infeasible (at least one basic variable is negative). The application of the *dual* simplex method shows that the leaving and entering variables are x_5 and x_3. This leads to the following tableau:

Basic	x_1	x_2	x_3	x_4	x_5	x_6	Solution
z	0	0	0	5/3	1/3	0	7
x_2	0	1	0	1/3	2/3	0	2
x_1	1	0	0	1/3	−1/3	0	1
x_3	0	0	1	−1	−1	0	2
x_6	0	0	0	−1/3	−2/3	1	0

This tableau is both optimal and feasible. The new solution is $x_1 = 1$, $x_2 = 2$, and $z = 7$. Although the feasible solution was recovered in one iteration, in general the dual simplex method may require more than one iteration to reach feasibility.

Exercise 5.5-7
Consider the Reddy Mikks model as *originally* given. Suppose that the daily availability of raw material A is 3 tons (instead of 6 tons). Show that the current solution becomes infeasible and determine the entering and leaving variables in the first dual simplex iteration.
[*Ans.* New right-side elements $= (-2/3, 13/3, 6, 8/3) = (x_2, x_1, x_5, x_6)$. Dual simplex: x_2 leaves and x_4 enters.]

B. Addition of a New Constraint

The addition of a new constraint can result in one of two conditions:

1. The constraint is satisfied by the current solution, in which case the constraint is *redundant* and its addition will thus not change the solution.
2. The constraint is not satisfied by the current solution. In this case the new solution is obtained by using the dual simplex method.

To illustrate these cases, suppose that the daily demand on exterior paint does not exceed 4 tons. A new constraint of the form

$$x_1 \leq 4$$

must be added to the model. Since the current solution ($x_1 = 10/3$, $x_2 = 4/3$) obviously satisfies the new constraint, it is labeled redundant, and the current solution remains unchanged.

Now suppose that the maximum demand on exterior paint is 3 tons instead of 4 tons. Then the new constraint becomes $x_1 \leq 3$, which is not satisfied by the current solution $x_1 = 10/3$ and $x_2 = 4/3$.

Here is what we do to recover feasibility. First, put the new constraint in the standard form by augmenting a slack or a surplus variable if necessary. Then substitute out any of the current basic variables in the constraint in terms of the (current) nonbasic variables. The final step is to augment the "modified" constraint to the current optimum tableau and apply the dual simplex to recover feasibility.

Using x_7 as a slack, we find that the standard form of $x_1 \leq 3$ is

$$x_1 + x_7 = 3, \qquad x_7 \geq 0$$

Now, in the current solution x_1 is a basic variable and we must substitute it out in terms of the nonbasic variables. In the x_1-equation of the current optimal tableau, we have

$$x_1 - (1/3)x_3 + (2/3)x_4 = 10/3$$

Thus the new constraint expressed in terms of the current nonbasic variables becomes

$$(10/3) + (1/3)x_3 - (2/3)x_4 + x_7 = 3$$

or

$$(1/3)x_3 - (2/3)x_4 + x_7 = -1/3$$

(The negative right side indicates infeasibility since, given $x_3 = x_4 = 0$, $x_7 = -1/3$, which violates the requirement $x_7 \geq 0$.)

The modified constraint is now augmented to the current optimal tableau as given next. The augmentation to the tableau is shown by tinted overlay. The remaining elements are taken directly from the current optimum tableau:

Basic	x_1	x_2	x_3	x_4	x_5	x_6	x_7	Solution
z	0	0	1/3	4/3	0	0	0	38/3
x_2	0	1	2/3	−1/3	0	0	0	4/3
x_1	1	0	−1/3	2/3	0	0	0	10/3
x_5	0	0	−1	1	1	0	0	3
x_6	0	0	−2/3	1/3	0	1	0	2/3
x_7	0	0	1/3	−2/3	0	0	1	−1/3

By the dual simplex, x_7 leaves the solution and x_4 enters. This yields the following optimal feasible tableau:

Basic	x_1	x_2	x_3	x_4	x_5	x_6	x_7	Solution
z	0	0	1	0	0	0	2	12
x_2	0	1	1/2	0	0	0	−1/2	3/2
x_1	1	0	0	0	0	0	1	3
x_5	0	0	−1/2	0	1	0	3/2	5/2
x_6	0	0	−1/2	0	0	1	1/2	1/2
x_4	0	0	−1/2	1	0	0	−3/2	1/2

The new solution has a worse optimum value of z than before the constraint is augmented. This is always expected, since the addition of a new nonredundant constraint can never improve the value of z.

Exercise 5.5-8

Suppose that each of the following constraints is added to the Reddy Mikks model. Determine whether the added constraint is nonredundant. If so, express the nonredundant constraint in terms of the nonbasic variables of the current solution and identify the entering and leaving variables of the dual simplex method.

(a) $x_2 \leq 2$

[*Ans.* The constraint is redundant.]

(b) $x_1 + x_2 \leq 4$
[*Ans.* $-(1/3)x_3 - (1/3)x_4 + x_7 = -2/3$. x_7 leaves and x_3 enters.]
(c) $2x_1 + 3x_2 \geq 11$
[*Ans.* $(4/3)x_3 + (1/3)x_4 + x_7 = -1/3$. No feasible solution exists.]

The idea of adding constraints, one at a time, to a current optimum tableau is sometimes used to reduce the computational burden in solving linear programs. As we noted in Chapter 3, the amount of computations in the simplex method depends primarily on the number of constraints. We can effectively reduce the number of constraints in a model as follows. First, we identify the **secondary constraints**, which are the constraints we suspect are the least restrictive in the optimum solution. The model is then solved subject to the remaining (primary) constraints. The secondary constraints are then augmented to the resulting optimum tableau, one at a time, until a solution is encountered that satisfies all secondary constraints not augmented in the tableau. A computational advantage is realized when a large number of secondary constraints are not augmented to the simplex tableau.

5.5.3 CHANGES AFFECTING OPTIMALITY AND FEASIBILITY

Suppose that we consider the following *simultaneous* changes in Reddy Mikks model:

1. The objective function is changed to $z = x_1 + 4x_2$.
2. The right-hand side is changed to $(7, 4, 1, 2)^T$.

The two types of changes lead to the following tableau (verify!):

Basic	x_1	x_2	x_3	x_4	x_5	x_6	Solution
z	0	0	7/3	−2/3	0	0	41/3
x_2	0	1	2/3	−1/3	0	0	10/3
x_1	1	0	−1/3	2/3	0	0	1/3
x_5	0	0	−1	1	1	0	−2
x_6	0	0	−2/3	1/3	0	1	−4/3

The tableau is both nonoptimal and infeasible.

First, we work on restoring optimality without regard to feasibility. Thus x_4 enters the solution, and any of the variables x_2, x_1, x_5, or x_6 can leave the solution. The only stipulation in the general case is that the pivot element be different from zero. Using x_1 as the leaving variable, we find that the tableau becomes

Basic	x_1	x_2	x_3	x_4	x_5	x_6	Solution
z	1	0	2	0	0	0	14
x_2	1/2	1	1/2	0	0	0	7/2
x_4	3/2	0	−1/2	1	0	0	1/2
x_5	−3/2	0	−1/2	0	1	0	−5/2
x_6	−1/2	0	−1/2	0	0	1	−3/2

The last tableau is now optimal but infeasible. Applications of the dual simplex method require x_5 to leave and x_1 to enter as the following tableau shows:

Basic	x_1	x_2	x_3	x_4	x_5	x_6	Solution
z	0	0	5/3	0	2/3	0	37/3
x_2	0	1	1/3	0	1/3	0	8/3
x_4	0	0	−1	1	1	0	−2
x_1	1	0	1/3	0	−2/3	0	5/3
x_6	0	0	−1/3	0	−1/3	1	−2/3

Now we let x_4 leave and x_3 enter, which gives

Basic	x_1	x_2	x_3	x_4	x_5	x_6	Solution
z	0	0	0	5/3	7/3	0	9
x_2	0	1	0	1/3	2/3	0	2
x_3	0	0	1	−1	−1	0	2
x_1	1	0	0	1/3	−1/3	0	1
x_6	0	0	0	−1/3	−2/3	1	0

The last tableau is now optimal and feasible.

5.6 PARAMETRIC LINEAR PROGRAMMING

Parametric linear programming is a natural extension of the postoptimal analysis procedure. It investigates the changes in the optimum LP solution due to *predetermined continuous* variations in the model's parameters, such as the availability of resources or changes in marginal profits or costs. In the oil industry, for example, where LP has tremendously successful applications, it is normal to investigate changes in the optimal LP solution resulting from changes in the availability and quality of crude oils.

The predetermined functions representing changes in the model's coefficients need *not* be linear, for this has nothing to do with *linear* programming. Figure 5-1 depicts functions that can typically represent changes in availability of resources. About the

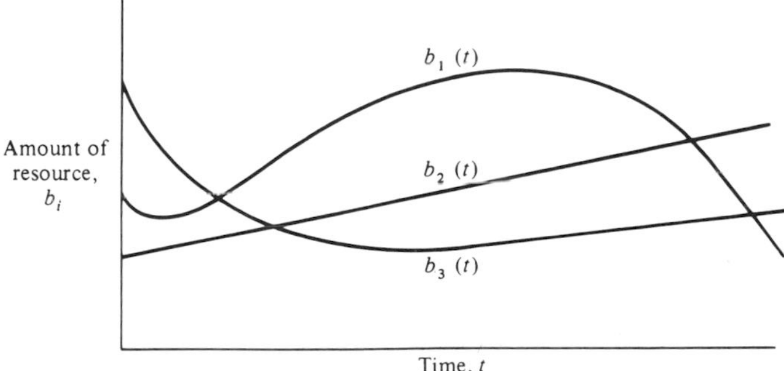

Figure 5-1

only advantage of utilizing linear function is that the computations become less cumbersome. For this reason, and not to be sidetracked with computational details, the remainder of this section concentrates on the use of linear functions only. Keep in mind, however, that any (single-variable) nonlinear function can be approximated by a piecewise linear function (see Section 20.2.1). Nevertheless, we show throughout the section how nonlinearity can be handled directly and also point to possible computational difficulties.

As in sensitivity analysis, we consider the following types of variation:

1. Variation in objective coefficients **C**.
2. Variation in resources availability **b**.
3. Variation in constraint coefficients $\mathbf{P}_j$.
4. Simultaneous changes in **C**, **b**, and $\mathbf{P}_j$.

Suppose that t is the parameter with which the different coefficients vary. The general idea of parametric programming is to compute the optimal solution at $t = 0$. Then, using the optimality and feasibility conditions of the primal/dual simplex methods, we find the range of t for which the solution at $t = 0$ remains optimal and feasible. Suppose that this range is given by $(0, t_1)$. This means that any increase in t beyond t_1 will result in an infeasible and/or nonoptimal solution. Thus, at $t = t_1$, we determine a new solution that will remain optimal and feasible from $t = t_1$ to $t = t_2$, where $t_2 > t_1$. The process is then repeated at $t = t_2$ and a new solution is obtained. Eventually, a point on the scale t is reached beyond which the solution either does not change or does not exist. This is where the parametric analysis ends.

We shall now show how the critical values $t_1, t_2, \ldots$ and their associated solutions are determined. We shall consider the different changes separately.

5.6.1 CHANGES IN C

Let $\mathbf{C}(t)$ represent the parameterized objective vector as a function of t. For simplicity, assume that $t \geq 0$. Suppose that $\mathbf{B}_i$ represents the optimal basis at the critical value t_i. We show now how the next critical value t_{i+1} and its optimal basis are determined. Initially, we start at $t = t_0 = 0$ with $\mathbf{B}_0$ as the associated optimal basis.

Let ${}^i\mathbf{X}_B$ be the optimal basic vector at t_i and define $\mathbf{C}_B(t)$ as its associated coefficients of $\mathbf{C}(t)$. As we can see from Section 5.5.1, changes in **C** can affect only the optimality of the current solution. Thus the solution

$${}^i\mathbf{X}_B = \mathbf{B}_i^{-1}\mathbf{b}$$

remains optimal for all $t \geq t_i$ for which all $z_j(t) - c_j(t)$ remain nonnegative (maximization).

Mathematically, this is expressed as

$$\mathbf{C}_B(t)\mathbf{B}_i^{-1}\mathbf{P}_j - c_j(t) \geq 0, \qquad \text{for all } j$$

These inequalities are satisfied for the range of t from t_i to t_{i+1}, where t_{i+1} is determined as the largest t beyond which at least one of the given inequalities is violated. Note that *nothing* is specified in the inequalities that requires $\mathbf{C}(t)$ to vary *linearly* with t. Any function is acceptable. The prime difficulty with using nonlinear functions is that the numerical evaluation of the inequalities may be cumbersome. It may even require the use of some type of numerical method to obtain the results.

Example 5.6-1

$$\text{Maximize } z = (3 - 6t)x_1 + (2 - 2t)x_2 + (5 + 5t)x_3$$

subject to

$$\begin{aligned} x_1 + 2x_2 + x_3 &\le 40 \\ 3x_1 \qquad + 2x_3 &\le 60 \\ x_1 + 4x_2 \qquad &\le 30 \\ x_1, x_2, x_3 &\ge 0 \end{aligned}$$

The parameter t is assumed nonnegative.

According to the problem,

$$\mathbf{C}(t) = (3 - 6t,\ 2 - 2t,\ 5 + 5t)$$

We start at $t = t_0 = 0$. The associated optimal tableau follows, where the slacks are represented by x_4, x_5, and x_6.

Optimal Solution at $t = t_0 = 0$

Basic	x_1	x_2	x_3	x_4	x_5	x_6	Solution
z	4	0	0	1	2	0	160
x_2	−1/4	1	0	1/2	−1/4	0	5
x_3	3/2	0	1	0	1/2	0	30
x_6	2	0	0	−2	1	1	10

Thus

$$^0\mathbf{X}_B = \begin{pmatrix} x_2 \\ x_3 \\ x_6 \end{pmatrix} = \begin{pmatrix} 5 \\ 30 \\ 10 \end{pmatrix} \quad \text{and} \quad \mathbf{B}_0^{-1} = \begin{pmatrix} 1/2 & -1/4 & 0 \\ 0 & 1/2 & 0 \\ -2 & 1 & 1 \end{pmatrix}$$

Now we determine the first critical value $t = t_1$. The parameterized objective coefficients of $^0\mathbf{X}_B$ are

$$\mathbf{C}_B(t) = (2 - 2t,\ 5 + 5t,\ 0)$$

Consequently,

$$\mathbf{C}_B(t)\mathbf{B}_0^{-1} = (1 - t,\ 2 + 3t,\ 0)$$

The values of $z_j(t) - c_j(t)$ for $j = 1, 4,$ and 5 (nonbasic x_j) are thus given by

$$\{\mathbf{C}_B(t)\mathbf{B}_0^{-1}\mathbf{P}_j - c_j(t)\}_{j=1,4,5} = (1 - t,\ 2 + 3t,\ 0)\begin{pmatrix} 1 & 1 & 0 \\ 3 & 0 & 1 \\ 1 & 0 & 0 \end{pmatrix} - (3 - 6t,\ 0,\ 0)$$

$$= (4 + 14t,\ 1 - t,\ 2 + 3t)$$

Given $t \ge 0$, the solution $^0\mathbf{X}_B$ (or basis $\mathbf{B}_0^{-1}$) remains optimal as long as the conditions $4 + 14t \ge 0$, $1 - t \ge 0$, and $2 + 3t \ge 0$ are satisfied. The second inequality shows that t must not exceed 1. (All others are satisfied for all $t \ge 0$.) This means that $t_1 = 1$ is the next critical value and that $^0\mathbf{X}_B$ remains optimal for the range $(t_0, t_1) = (0, 1)$.

Exercise 5.6-1

Suppose that t is allowed to assume positive, zero, or negative values (instead of $t \geq 0$ only), what is the range of t for which ${}^0\mathbf{X}_B$ remains optimal?
[*Ans.* ${}^0\mathbf{X}_B$ remains optimal for $-2/7 \leq t \leq 1$.]

At $t = 1$, we notice that $z_4(t) - c_4(t) = 0$. For $t > 1$, $z_4(t) - c_4(t) < 0$. This means that for $t > 1$, x_4 must enter the basic solution, in which case x_2 must leave (see the optimal table at $t = t_0 = 0$). At $t = 1$, entering x_4 into the basic solution will result in an alternative solution. (Why?) This new solution will remain optimal for the next range (t_1, t_2), where t_2 is the next critical value to be evaluated. We first determine the alternative basis $\mathbf{B}^{-1}$ and then determine the next critical value t_2.

Alternative Optimal Basis at $t = t_1 = 1$

Since $\mathbf{P}_4$ and $\mathbf{P}_2$ are the entering and leaving vectors, we have (see Section 4.3):

$$\boldsymbol{\alpha}^4 = \mathbf{B}_0^{-1}\mathbf{P}_4 = \begin{pmatrix} 1/2 & -1/4 & 0 \\ 0 & 1/2 & 0 \\ -2 & 1 & 1 \end{pmatrix}\begin{pmatrix} 1 \\ 0 \\ 0 \end{pmatrix} = \begin{pmatrix} 1/2 \\ 0 \\ -2 \end{pmatrix}$$

$$\boldsymbol{\xi} = \begin{pmatrix} +1/(1/2) \\ 0/(1/2) \\ -(-2)/(1/2) \end{pmatrix} = \begin{pmatrix} 2 \\ 0 \\ 4 \end{pmatrix}$$

Thus the new basis inverse is given by

$$\mathbf{B}_1^{-1} = \begin{pmatrix} 2 & 0 & 0 \\ 0 & 1 & 0 \\ 4 & 0 & 1 \end{pmatrix}\begin{pmatrix} 1/2 & -1/4 & 0 \\ 0 & 1/2 & 0 \\ -2 & 1 & 1 \end{pmatrix} = \begin{pmatrix} 1 & -1/2 & 0 \\ 0 & 1/2 & 0 \\ 0 & 0 & 1 \end{pmatrix}$$

and

$${}^1\mathbf{X}_B = \begin{pmatrix} x_4 \\ x_3 \\ x_6 \end{pmatrix} = \begin{pmatrix} 1 & -1/2 & 0 \\ 0 & 1/2 & 0 \\ 0 & 0 & 1 \end{pmatrix}\begin{pmatrix} 40 \\ 60 \\ 30 \end{pmatrix} = \begin{pmatrix} 10 \\ 30 \\ 30 \end{pmatrix}$$

We now proceed to compute the next critical value t_2. For $\mathbf{X}_B^1$, we have

$$\mathbf{C}_B(t)\mathbf{B}_1^{-1} = (0, 5 + 5t, 0)\mathbf{B}_1^{-1} = \left(0, \frac{5 + 5t}{2}, 0\right)$$

The values of $z_j(t) - c_j(t)$ for $j = 1, 2$, and 5 are given by

$$\left(0, \frac{5 + 5t}{2}, 0\right)\begin{pmatrix} 1 & 2 & 0 \\ 3 & 0 & 1 \\ 1 & 4 & 0 \end{pmatrix} - (3 - 6t, 2 - 2t, 0) = \left(\frac{9 + 27t}{2}, -2 + 2t, \frac{5 + 5t}{2}\right)$$

The basis $\mathbf{B}_1$ remains optimal as long as all $z_j(t) - c_j(t) \geq 0$. This condition is satisfied for all $t \geq 1$. Thus $t_2 = \infty$. (Notice that the optimality conditions automatically "remember" that ${}^1\mathbf{X}_B$ is optimal for a range of t that starts from the last critical value $t_1 = 1$. This will always be the case with parametric computations.)

The optimal solutions for the entire range of t can be summarized as shown in the following table. Notice that the value of z is obtained by direct substitution in the objective function.

t	x_1	x_2	x_3	z
$0 \le t \le 1$	0	5	30	$160 + 140t$
$t \ge 1$	0	0	30	$150 + 150t$

◀

Exercise 5.6-2

Consider Example 5.6-1.

(a) Suppose that the objective function is changed to

$$\text{maximize } z = (3 + 18t)x_1 + (2 - 4t)x_2 + (5 + 3t)x_3$$

Find t_1 and indicate which basic variable in ${}^0\mathbf{X}_B$ leaves the solution and which one enters to obtain the alternative basic solution ${}^1\mathbf{X}_B$. (Note that at $t = 0$, the optimum tableau is as given for $t = t_0 = 0$.)

[*Ans.* $t_1 = 8/25$; x_1 enters and x_6 leaves.]

(b) Repeat part (a) if the objective function is expressed in terms of the following *nonlinear* parameterization:

$$\text{maximize } z = (3 + 2t^2)x_1 + (2 - 2t^2)x_2 + (5 - t)x_3$$

[*Ans.* $t_1 = 1$. x_4 enters and x_2 leaves. See Figure 5-2 for a graphic representation of $z_j(t) - c_j(t)$. This example is designed to illustrate the computational inconvenience that accompanies the use of nonlinear parameterization.]

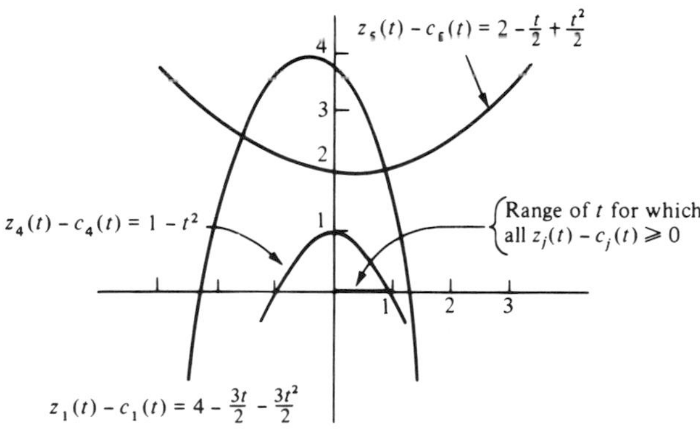

Figure 5-2

5.6.2 CHANGES IN *b*

Let $\mathbf{b}(t)$ represent the parameterized right-side vector as a function of t. As in Section 5.6.1, define $\mathbf{B}_i$ and ${}^i\mathbf{X}_B$ as the basis and the basic vector at the critical value t_i.

Section 5.5.2 shows that changes in the vector $\mathbf{b}$ can affect only the feasibility of the solution. Thus the solution ${}^i\mathbf{X}_B$ remains feasible as long as the condition

$$\mathbf{B}_i^{-1}\mathbf{b}(t) \geq \mathbf{0}$$

is satisfied. The following example shows how the successive critical values are determined.

Example 5.6-2

$$\text{Maximize } z = 3x_1 + 2x_2 + 5x_3$$

subject to

$$\begin{aligned} x_1 + 2x_2 + x_3 &\le 40 - t \\ 3x_1 \qquad + 2x_3 &\le 60 + 2t \\ x_1 + 4x_2 \qquad &\le 30 - 7t \\ x_1, x_2, x_3 &\ge 0 \end{aligned}$$

Assume that $t \ge 0$.

At $t = t_0 = 0$, the problem is identical to that of Example 5.6-1 at $t = 0$. Thus

$$^0\mathbf{X}_B = \begin{pmatrix} x_2 \\ x_3 \\ x_6 \end{pmatrix} = \begin{pmatrix} 5 \\ 30 \\ 10 \end{pmatrix} \quad \text{and} \quad \mathbf{B}_0^{-1} = \begin{pmatrix} 1/2 & -1/4 & 0 \\ 0 & 1/2 & 0 \\ -2 & 1 & 1 \end{pmatrix}$$

The first critical value t_1 is detemined by considering

$$\mathbf{B}_0^{-1}\mathbf{b}(t) \ge 0$$

This gives

$$\begin{pmatrix} x_2 \\ x_3 \\ x_6 \end{pmatrix} = \begin{pmatrix} 1/2 & -1/4 & 0 \\ 0 & 1/2 & 0 \\ -2 & 1 & 1 \end{pmatrix} \begin{pmatrix} 40 - t \\ 60 + 2t \\ 30 - 7t \end{pmatrix} = \begin{pmatrix} 5 - t \\ 30 + t \\ 10 - 3t \end{pmatrix} \ge \begin{pmatrix} 0 \\ 0 \\ 0 \end{pmatrix}$$

These inequalities are satisfied for $t \le 10/3$. Thus $t_1 = 10/3$ and the basis $\mathbf{B}_0$ remains feasible for the range $(t_0, t_1) = (0, 10/3)$.

Although the basis $\mathbf{B}_0$ remains unchanged for $0 \le t \le 10/3$, the values of the associated basic variables x_2, x_3, and x_6 will be given by $x_2 = 5 - t$, $x_3 = 30 + t$, and $x_6 = 10 - 3t$. The value of z is $2(5 - t) + 5(30 + t) = 160 + 3t$, $0 \le t \le 10/3$.

At $t = t_1 = 10/3$, x_6 equals zero. Any increase in t beyond $10/3$ will make x_6 negative. Thus, at the critical value $t_1 = 10/3$, an alternative basis $\mathbf{B}_1$ can be obtained by applying the *dual simplex method* with x_6 as the leaving variable. We use the matrix procedure outlined in Exercise 4.2-2(b) to determine the new basis.

Alternative Basis at $t = t_1 = 10/3$

Since the leaving variable is already known $(= x_6)$, we need to determine the entering variable only to compute $\mathbf{B}^{-1}$. Given $^0\mathbf{X}_B = (x_2, x_3, x_6)^T$, $\mathbf{C}_B = (2, 5, 0)$, and $\mathbf{C}_B\mathbf{B}_0^{-1} = (1, 2, 0)$, then $(z_j - c_j)$ for $j = 1, 4$, and 5 are given by

$$\{\mathbf{C}_B\mathbf{B}_0^{-1}\mathbf{P}_j - c_j\} = (1, 2, 0)\begin{pmatrix} 1 & 1 & 0 \\ 3 & 0 & 1 \\ 1 & 0 & 0 \end{pmatrix} - (3, 0, 0) = (4, 1, 2)$$

Next we compute α_r^j for $j = 1, 4$, and 5, and $x_r = x_6$ as

$$\begin{aligned} (\alpha_6^1, \alpha_6^4, \alpha_6^5) &= (\text{row of } \mathbf{B}_0^{-1} \text{ associated with } x_6)(\mathbf{P}_1, \mathbf{P}_4, \mathbf{P}_5) \\ &= (\text{third row of } \mathbf{B}_0^{-1})(\mathbf{P}_1, \mathbf{P}_4, \mathbf{P}_5) \\ &= (-2, 1, 1)\begin{pmatrix} 1 & 1 & 0 \\ 3 & 0 & 1 \\ 1 & 0 & 0 \end{pmatrix} = (2, -2, 1) \end{aligned}$$

Thus, for $j = 1, 4$, and 5

$$\theta = \min \{-, |1/-2|, -\} = 1/2, \qquad \text{corresponding to } x_4$$

As a result, $\mathbf{P}_4$ is the entering vector.

We now determine $\mathbf{B}_1^{-1}$ by interchanging the entering and leaving vectors $\mathbf{P}_4$ and $\mathbf{P}_6$. Thus

$$\alpha^4 = \mathbf{B}_0^{-1}\mathbf{P}_4 = \begin{pmatrix} 1/2 \\ 0 \\ -2 \end{pmatrix}$$

$$\xi = \begin{pmatrix} -(1/2)/(-2) \\ -0/(-2) \\ +1/(-2) \end{pmatrix} = \begin{pmatrix} 1/4 \\ 0 \\ -1/2 \end{pmatrix}$$

$$\mathbf{B}_1^{-1} = \mathbf{E}\mathbf{B}_0^{-1} = \begin{pmatrix} 1 & 0 & 1/4 \\ 0 & 1 & 0 \\ 0 & 0 & -1/2 \end{pmatrix} \begin{pmatrix} 1/2 & -1/4 & 0 \\ 0 & 1/2 & 0 \\ -2 & 1 & 1 \end{pmatrix} = \begin{pmatrix} 0 & 0 & 1/4 \\ 0 & 1/2 & 0 \\ 1 & -1/2 & -1/2 \end{pmatrix}$$

with ${}^1\mathbf{X}_B = (x_2, x_3, x_4)^T$.

The next critical value t_2 is determined by considering

$$\mathbf{B}_1^{-1}\mathbf{b}(t) \geq 0$$

which yields

$$\begin{pmatrix} x_2 \\ x_3 \\ x_4 \end{pmatrix} = \begin{pmatrix} 0 & 0 & 1/4 \\ 0 & 1/2 & 0 \\ 1 & -1/2 & -1/2 \end{pmatrix} \begin{pmatrix} 40 - t \\ 60 + 2t \\ 30 - 7t \end{pmatrix} = \begin{pmatrix} \dfrac{30 - 7t}{4} \\ 30 + t \\ \dfrac{-10 + 3t}{2} \end{pmatrix} \geq \begin{pmatrix} 0 \\ 0 \\ 0 \end{pmatrix}$$

Thus $\mathbf{B}_1$ remains feasible for $10/3 \leq t \leq 30/7$.

At $t = t_2 = 30/7$, an alternative basis, in which x_2 is the leaving variable, can be obtained by applying the dual simplex method.

Alternative Basis at $t = t_2 = 30/7$

To determine the entering variable (given x_2 is the leaving variable), we compute the ratios of the dual simplex.

Given ${}^1\mathbf{X}_B = (x_2, x_3, x_4)^T$, $\mathbf{C}_B = (2, 5, 0)$, and $\mathbf{C}_B\mathbf{B}^{-1} = (0, 5/2, 1/2)$, then $(z_j - c_j)$ for $j = 1, 5$, and 6 are given by

$$\{\mathbf{C}_B\mathbf{B}_1^{-1}\mathbf{P}_j - c_j\} = (0, 5/2, 1/2) \begin{pmatrix} 1 & 0 & 0 \\ 3 & 1 & 0 \\ 1 & 0 & 1 \end{pmatrix} - (3, 0, 0)$$

$$= (5, 5/2, 1/2)$$

Next we compute α_r^j for $j = 1, 5$, and 6 and $x_r = x_2$ as

$$(\alpha_2^1, \alpha_2^5, \alpha_2^6) = (\text{first row of } \mathbf{B}_1^{-1})(\mathbf{P}_1, \mathbf{P}_5, \mathbf{P}_6)$$

$$= (0, 0, 1/4) \begin{pmatrix} 1 & 0 & 0 \\ 3 & 1 & 0 \\ 1 & 0 & 1 \end{pmatrix}$$

$$= (1/4, 0, 1/4)$$

Since all $\alpha_r^j \geq 0$, the problem has no feasible solution for $t > 30/7$ and the parametric analysis ends at $t = t_2 = 30/7$.

The optimal feasible solution for the entire range of t may thus be summarized as follows:

t	x_1	x_2	x_3	z
$0 \leq t \leq 10/3$	0	$5 - t$	$30 + t$	$160 + 3t$
$10/3 \leq t \leq 30/7$	0	$\dfrac{30 - 7t}{4}$	$30 + t$	$165 + \dfrac{3}{2}t$
$t > 30/7$	(no feasible solution)			

◀

Exercise 5.6-3

In Example 5.6-2, find the first critical value t_1 and the vectors of $\mathbf{B}_1$ in each of the following cases.

(a) $\mathbf{b}(t) = (40 + 2t, 60 - 3t, 30 + 6t)^T$
[*Ans.* $t_1 = 10$, $\mathbf{B}_1 = (\mathbf{P}_2, \mathbf{P}_3, \mathbf{P}_4)$.]

(b) $\mathbf{b}(t) = 40 - t, 60 + 2t, 30 - 5t)^T$
[*Ans.* $t_1 = 5$, $\mathbf{B}_1 = (\mathbf{P}_5, \mathbf{P}_3, \mathbf{P}_6)$.]

5.6.3 CHANGES IN $\mathbf{P}_j$

We shall assume that $\mathbf{P}_j$ is a nonbasic vector in the optimal solution at $t = 0$. If it is basic, the situation would not lend itself neatly to parametric analysis because the basis $\mathbf{B}_0$ will be affected directly.

Let $\mathbf{P}_j(t)$ be the parameterized vector. From Section 5.5.1 we know that variation in a nonbasic vector can affect the optimality of that vector only. The vector $\mathbf{P}_j$ will enter the solution only when its $z_j - c_j$ becomes negative (maximization). Thus a current basis $\mathbf{B}_i$ remains optimal as long as the condition

$$z_j(t) - c_j = \mathbf{C}_B \mathbf{B}_i^{-1} \mathbf{P}_j(t) - c_j \geq 0$$

is satisfied. This inequality thus can be used to determine the next critical value t_{i+1}.

Observe that at $t = t_{i+1}$, an alternative optimal basis $\mathbf{B}_{i+1}$ can be obtained by introducing $\mathbf{P}_j$ into the basis. For $t > t_{i+1}$, $\mathbf{P}_j$ must be the entering vector. At this point it will not be possible to carry out the parametric analysis any further, since $\mathbf{P}_j$ will be in the basis and the resulting situation becomes rather complex. For this reason we limit our attention to determining one critical value t_{i+1} given the basis $\mathbf{B}_i$ at $t = t_i$.

Example 5.6-3. In Example 5.6-1, x_1 is nonbasic at $t = 0$. Suppose that

$$\mathbf{P}_1(t) = \begin{pmatrix} 1 + t \\ 3 - 2t \\ 1 + 3t \end{pmatrix}$$

is the only parameterized vector in the problem. The solution in Example 5.6-1 shows that

$$\mathbf{B}_0^{-1} = \begin{pmatrix} 1/2 & -1/4 & 0 \\ 0 & 1/2 & 0 \\ -2 & 1 & 1 \end{pmatrix}, \qquad {}^0\mathbf{X}_B = \begin{pmatrix} x_2 \\ x_3 \\ x_6 \end{pmatrix}$$

Consequently,

$$\begin{aligned} z_1(t) - c_1 &= \mathbf{C}_B \mathbf{B}_0^{-1} \mathbf{P}_1(t) - c_1 \\ &= (2, 5, 0) \begin{pmatrix} 1/2 & -1/4 & 0 \\ 0 & 1/2 & 0 \\ -2 & 1 & 1 \end{pmatrix} \begin{pmatrix} 1 + t \\ 3 - 2t \\ 1 + 3t \end{pmatrix} - 3 \\ &= 4 - 3t \end{aligned}$$

As a result, $\mathbf{B}_0$ will be optimal as long as $\mathbf{P}_1$ remains nonbasic. This will be the case when the condition $4 - 3t \geq 0$ is satisfied. The critical value t_1 is thus equal to 4/3.

We can obtain the alternative solution at $t = t_1$ by introducing $\mathbf{P}_1$ into the basis and dropping $\mathbf{P}_6$. However, we will be unable to carry out the parametric analysis for $\mathbf{P}_1$ as soon as it enters the basis. ◀

From the practical standpoint, the parametric analysis of nonbasic vectors only does not generally yield useful information. Normally, the parametrization of the different vectors is specified prior to solving the problem for any value of t. Clearly, it will be impossible to carry out any parametric analysis if any of the vectors in the current basis are parameterized. We specifically stress this point here since in practice, managers or decision makers could not care less whether an activity of the model is "basic" or "nonbasic." This is a technical language. All they really want to know is whether parametric analysis can be carried out in such situations, and the answer generally is "no!" This presentation is designed to show you why this answer is justifiable.

Exercise 5.6-4

Find t_1 in Example 5.6-3 assuming that $\mathbf{P}_1(t)$ is given by

$$(1 - 2t, 3 + 3t, 1 - 4t)^T$$

[*Ans.* $\mathbf{B}_0$ remains optimal for all $t \geq 0$. This means that the solution remains unaffected by the parameterization of $\mathbf{P}_1$.]

5.6.4 SIMULTANEOUS CHANGES IN C AND b

In this section we combine the parameterizations of **C** and **b** so that they are allowed to occur simultaneously. The idea is quite simple. For a given optimal basis $\mathbf{B}_i$, we check the optimality and feasibility separately by applying the procedures given in Sections 5.6.1 and 5.6.2. Let t' and t'' be the next critical values for optimality and feasibility, respectively. We have three cases:

1. If $t' < t''$, $\mathbf{B}_i$ will become nonoptimal first and the next basis $\mathbf{B}_{i+1}$ is obtained at $t_{i+1} = t'$ by using the regular simplex method (see Section 5.6.1).
2. If $t'' < t'$, $\mathbf{B}_i$ will become infeasible first and the next basis $\mathbf{B}_{i+1}$ is obtained at $t_{i+1} = t''$ by using the dual simplex method (see Section 5.6.2).
3. If $t' = t''$, $\mathbf{B}_i$ will become both nonoptimal and infeasible at $t_{i+1} = t' = t''$. In this situation we need to alternate between the use of the *primal* and *dual* simplex methods. (See Section 5.5.3 for an illustration for determining the next basis $\mathbf{B}_{i+1}$.)

Example 5.6-4. This example will combine the parameterization of **C** and **b** as specified in Examples 5.6-1 and 5.6-2. You must carefully note that combining the parameterization of $\mathbf{C}(t)$ and $\mathbf{b}(t)$ does not generally result in superimposing the critical values obtained by considering each parameterization separately.

$$\text{Maximize } z = (3 - 6t)x_1 + (2 - 2t)x_2 + (5 + 5t)x_3$$

subject to

$$\begin{aligned} x_1 + 2x_2 + x_3 &\leq 40 - t \\ 3x_1 + 2x_3 &\leq 60 + 2t \\ x_1 + 4x_2 &\leq 30 - 7t \\ x_1, x_2, x_3 &\geq 0 \end{aligned}$$

Optimal Basis at $t = t_0 = 0$

From Example 5.6-1, we have

$$^{0}\mathbf{X}_B = \begin{pmatrix} x_2 \\ x_3 \\ x_6 \end{pmatrix}, \qquad \mathbf{B}^{-1} = \begin{pmatrix} 1/2 & -1/4 & 0 \\ 0 & 1/2 & 0 \\ -2 & 1 & 1 \end{pmatrix}$$

Optimality: $\mathbf{B}_0$ remains optimal as long as $z_j(t) - c_j(t)$, $j = 1, 4, 5$, remain nonnegative. That is,

$$\begin{aligned} \{z_j(t) - c_j(t)\}_{j=1,4,5} &= (4 + 14t, 1 - t, 2 + 3t) \\ &\geq (0, 0, 0) \end{aligned}$$

(Verify these expressions. They are the same as in Example 5.6-1.) These conditions yield $t' = 1$.

Feasibility: $\mathbf{B}_0$ remains feasible as long as

$$\begin{pmatrix} x_2 \\ x_3 \\ x_6 \end{pmatrix} = \mathbf{B}_0^{-1}\mathbf{b}(t) = \begin{pmatrix} 5 - t \\ 30 + t \\ 10 - 3t \end{pmatrix} \geq \begin{pmatrix} 0 \\ 0 \\ 0 \end{pmatrix}$$

(Verify the computations!) The feasibility is satisfied for $t \leq 10/3$ and $t'' = 10/3$.

Optimality and Feasibility: $t_1 = \min\{t', t''\} = t' = 1$, which indicates that $\mathbf{B}_0$ will become nonoptimal first. We thus compute the alternative optimum at $t_1 = 1$ using the regular simplex method.

Alternative Basis at $t = t_1 = 1$

As seen from the optimality conditions, x_4 is the entering variable in the alternative solution. To determine the leaving variable, we carry out the following computations.

$$\boldsymbol{\alpha}^4 = \mathbf{B}_0^{-1}\mathbf{P}_4 = \begin{pmatrix} 1/2 & -1/4 & 0 \\ 0 & 1/2 & 0 \\ -2 & 1 & 1 \end{pmatrix}\begin{pmatrix} 1 \\ 0 \\ 0 \end{pmatrix} = \begin{pmatrix} 1/2 \\ 0 \\ -2 \end{pmatrix}$$

$$\begin{pmatrix} x_2 \\ x_3 \\ x_6 \end{pmatrix}_{t=1} = \mathbf{B}_0^{-1}\mathbf{b}(1) = \begin{pmatrix} 5 - 1 \\ 30 + 1 \\ 10 - 3 \times 1 \end{pmatrix} = \begin{pmatrix} 4 \\ 31 \\ 7 \end{pmatrix}$$

Thus, for x_2, x_3, and x_6,

$$\theta = \min\left(\frac{4}{1/2}, -, -\right) = 8$$

which means that x_2 is the leaving variable.

The new basis $\mathbf{B}_1$ is thus obtained from $\mathbf{B}_0$ by interchanging $\mathbf{P}_2$ and $\mathbf{P}_4$. Thus

$$\mathbf{X}_B = (x_4, x_3, x_6)^T$$

$$\mathbf{B}_1^{-1} = \begin{pmatrix} 2 & 0 & 0 \\ 0 & 1 & 0 \\ 4 & 0 & 1 \end{pmatrix}\begin{pmatrix} 1/2 & -1/4 & 0 \\ 0 & 1/2 & 0 \\ -2 & 1 & 1 \end{pmatrix}$$

$$= \begin{pmatrix} 1 & -1/2 & 0 \\ 0 & 1/2 & 0 \\ 0 & 0 & 1 \end{pmatrix}$$

Next we compute the new critical value of $t(= t_2)$.

Optimality:

$$\{z_j(t) - c_j(t)\}_{j=1,2,5} = \left(\frac{9 + 27t}{2}, -2 + 2t, \frac{5 + 5t}{2}\right)$$
$$\geq (0, 0, 0)$$

(Verify the computations!) Thus $\mathbf{B}_1$ remains optimal for all $t \geq 1$, which means that $t' = \infty$.

Feasibility:

$$\begin{pmatrix} x_4 \\ x_3 \\ x_6 \end{pmatrix} = \mathbf{B}_1^{-1}\mathbf{b}(t) = \begin{pmatrix} 10 - 2t \\ 30 + t \\ 30 - 7t \end{pmatrix} \geq \begin{pmatrix} 0 \\ 0 \\ 0 \end{pmatrix}$$

(Verify the computations!) Thus $\mathbf{B}_1$ remains feasible for $t \leq 30/7$ and $t'' = 30/7$.

Optimality and Feasibility: $t_2 = \min\{t', t''\} = 30/7$. Thus $\mathbf{B}_1$ becomes infeasible first.

Alternative Basis at $t = t_2 = 30/7$

The alternative basis is determined by the dual simplex method with x_6 as the leaving variable. To determine the entering variable, we consider the following computations. For $j = 1, 2, 5$, we have

$$\{z_j(t) - c_j(t)\}_{t=30/7} = [9/2 + (27/2)(30/7),\ -2 + 2(30/7),\ 5/2 + (5/2)(30/7)]$$
$$= (62.36,\ 6.57,\ 13.21)$$

$$(\alpha_6^1, \alpha_6^2, \alpha_6^5) = (0, 0, 1)\begin{pmatrix} 1 & 2 & 0 \\ 3 & 0 & 1 \\ 1 & 4 & 0 \end{pmatrix} = (1, 4, 0)$$

Since all $\alpha_r^j \geq 0$, no feasible solutions exist for $t > 30/7$ and the parametric analysis is complete.

The optimum solution for the entire range of t is summarized as

t	x_1	x_2	x_3	z
$0 \leq t \leq 1$	0	$5 - t$	$30 + t$	$7t^2 + 143t + 160$
$1 \leq t \leq 30/7$	0	0	$30 + t$	$5t^2 + 155t + 150$
$t > 30/7$	(No feasible solution)			

You will notice that the critical value $t = 10/3$, which was obtained when $b(t)$ was considered separately (Example 5.6-2), is not encountered when both $\mathbf{b}(t)$ and $\mathbf{C}(t)$ are considered simultaneously. This is the reason we mentioned earlier that the problem cannot be analyzed by superimposing the critical values obtained when $\mathbf{b}(t)$ and $\mathbf{C}(t)$ are considered separately. ◀

5.7 SUMMARY

In this chapter the dual problem is defined and its role in providing an elegant economic interpretation of the LP problem as a resource allocation model is discussed. Postoptimal or sensitivity analysis is fully explained from the standpoint of duality. Parametric analysis, which is a natural extension of the sensitivity problem is covered in depth. Both sensitivity and parametric analysis give the LP solution a dynamic dimension that enhances its use in practice.

SELECTED REFERENCES

BRADLEY, S., A. HAX, and T. MAGNANTIC, *Applied Mathematical Programming*, Addison-Wesley, Reading, Mass., 1977.

HADLEY, G., *Linear Programming*, Addison-Wesley, Reading, Mass., 1962.

LUENBERGER, D. G., *Introduction to Linear and Nonlinear Programming*, Addison-Wesley, Reading, Mass., 1973.

MURTY, K., *Linear Programming*, Wiley, New York, 1983.

PROBLEMS

Section	Assigned Problems
5.1	5–1 to 5–4
5.2.1	5–5 to 5–10
5.2.2	5–11 to 5–23
5.3	5–24 to 5–27
5.4	5–28 to 5–30
5.5.1	5–31 to 5–39
5.5.2	5–40 to 5–46
5.5.3	5–47, 5–48
5.6.1	5–49 to 5–53
5.6.2	5–54 to 5–56
5.6.3	5–57, 5–58
5.6.4	5–59 to 5–64

☐ **5–1** Write the duals using the standard form of the primal simplex method:

(a) Maximize $z = -5x_1 + 2x_2$
subject to

$$\begin{aligned} -x_1 + x_2 &\leq -2 \\ 2x_1 + 3x_2 &\leq 5 \\ x_1, x_2 &\geq 0 \end{aligned}$$

(b) Minimize $z = 6x_1 + 3x_2$
subject to

$$\begin{aligned} 6x_1 - 3x_2 + x_3 &\geq 2 \\ 3x_1 + 4x_2 + x_3 &\geq 5 \\ x_1, x_2, x_3 &\geq 0 \end{aligned}$$

(c) Maximize $z = 5x_1 + 6x_2$
subject to

$$\begin{aligned} x_1 + 2x_2 &= 5 \\ -x_1 + 5x_2 &\geq 3 \\ x_1 &\text{ unrestricted} \\ x_2 &\geq 0 \end{aligned}$$

(d) Minimize $z = 3x_1 + 4x_2 + 6x_3$
subject to

$$\begin{aligned} x_1 + x_2 &\geq 10 \\ x_1, x_3 &\geq 0 \\ x_2 &\leq 0 \end{aligned}$$

(e) Maximize $z = x_1 + x_2$
subject to

$$\begin{aligned} 2x_1 + x_2 &= 5 \\ 3x_1 - x_2 &= 6 \\ x_1, x_2 &\text{ unrestricted} \end{aligned}$$

☐ **5–2** Write the duals using the standard form of the dual simplex method:

(a) Minimize $z = 2x_1 + 3x_2$
subject to

$$5x_1 - 2x_2 \le 3$$
$$7x_1 + 3x_2 \ge 2$$
$$x_1, x_2 \ge 0$$

(b) Minimize $z = 5x_1 + 6x_2 + x_3$
subject to

$$2x_1 + 3x_2 + 2x_3 \ge 5$$
$$5x_1 - x_2 + 6x_3 \ge 4$$
$$x_1 \ge 0, x_2 \ge 0, x_3 \ge 0$$

☐ **5–3** Consider the following problem:

$$\text{minimize } z = x_1 + 2x_2 - 3x_3$$

subject to

$$-x_1 + x_2 + x_3 = 5$$
$$12x_1 - 9x_2 + 9x_3 \ge 8$$
$$x_1, x_2, x_3 \ge 0$$

The (primal) simplex solution of this problem requires the use of artificial variables in both constraints. Show that the dual problems obtained from the standard primal before and after the artificials are added are exactly the same. As a result, the artificial variables can lead only to redundant constraints.

☐ **5–4** Repeat Problem 5–3 given that the objective function is replaced by

$$\text{maximize } z = 5x_1 - 6x_2 + 7x_3$$

☐ **5–5** Section 5.2.1 proves that $z \le w$ for any pair of *feasible* primal and dual solutions. Where does the proof make use of the requirement that both the primal and dual solutions must be feasible?

☐ **5–6** In each of the LPs in Problem 5–1, find (by inspection) a pair of feasible primal and dual solutions. Use the information to estimate a range for the optimal objective value of the primal and the dual problems.

☐ **5–7** Repeat Problem 5–6 for the LPs in Problem 5–2.

☐ **5–8** Consider the primal problem:

$$\text{maximize } z = 3x_1 + 2x_2 + 5x_3$$

subject to

$$x_1 + 2x_2 + x_3 \le 500$$
$$3x_1 + 2x_3 \le 460$$
$$x_1 + 4x_2 \le 420$$
$$x_1, x_2, x_3 \ge 0$$

Write the dual problem for the primal. Without carrying out the simplex method computations on either the primal or the dual problem, estimate a range for the optimum value of the objective function.

□ **5–9** For the following pairs of primal–dual problems, determine whether the listed solutions are optimal:

Primal	Dual
Minimize $z = 2x_1 + 3x_2$ subject to $2x_1 + 3x_2 \leq 30$, $x_1 + 2x_2 \geq 10$, $x_1 - x_2 \geq 0$, $x_1, x_2 \geq 0$	Maximize $w = 30y_1 + 10y_2$ subject to $2y_1 + y_2 + y_3 \leq 2$, $3y_1 + 2y_2 - y_3 \leq 3$, $y_1 \leq 0, y_2 \geq 0, y_3 \geq 0$

(a) $(x_1 = 10, x_2 = 10/3; y_1 = 0, y_2 = 1, y_3 = 1)$.
(b) $(x_1 = 20, x_2 = 10; y_1 = 1, y_2 = 4, y_3 = 0)$.
(c) $(x_1 = 10/3, x_2 = 10/3; y_1 = 0, y_2 = 5/3, y_3 = 1/3)$.

□ **5–10** Consider the following problem:

$$\text{minimize } z = 3x_1 + 4x_2 - 5x_3$$

subject to

$$\begin{aligned} 2x_1 + 3x_2 - 5x_3 &\geq 10 \\ x_1 - 2x_2 - 3x_3 &\leq 8 \\ x_1, x_2, x_3 &\geq 0 \end{aligned}$$

The dual problem is defined as

$$\text{maximize } w = 10y_1 + 8y_2$$

subject to

$$\begin{aligned} 2y_1 + y_2 &\leq 3 \\ 3y_1 - 2y_2 &\leq 4 \\ -5y_1 + 3y_2 &\leq -5 \\ y_1, y_2 &\geq 0 \end{aligned}$$

(a) Consider the following pairs of (feasible or infeasible) solutions:

x_1	x_2	x_3	y_1	y_2
5	0	0	1	0
6	1	0	3	1
8	2	1	2	2
2	1	3	7/6	2/3

Estimate a range for the optimal value of z.

(b) Verify that the following two solutions are optimal for the primal and dual problems:

$$(x_1, x_2, x_3) = (0, 10/3, 0), (y_1, y_2) = (4/3, 0)$$

☐ **5–11** Consider the following linear program:

$$\text{maximize } z = 5x_1 + 2x_2 + 3x_3$$

subject to

$$x_1 + 5x_2 + 2x_3 = 30$$
$$x_1 - 5x_2 - 6x_3 \leq 40$$
$$x_1, x_2, x_3 \geq 0$$

The optimal solution is given by:

Basic	x_1	x_2	x_3	R	x_4	Solution
z	0	23	7	$5 + M$	0	150
x_1	1	5	2	1	0	30
x_4	0	-10	-8	-1	1	10

(a) Write the associated dual problem.
(b) Using the information in the optimal tableau above, find the optimal dual solution.
(c) Define $\mathbf{X}_B$, $\mathbf{C}_B$, and $\mathbf{B}$ associated with the optimal primal solution, then obtain $\mathbf{B}^{-1}$ directly from $\mathbf{B}$. Use this information to determine the optimal dual solution.

☐ **5–12** Consider the following linear program:

$$\text{maximize } z = x_1 + 5x_2 + 3x_3$$

subject to

$$x_1 + 2x_2 + x_3 = 3$$
$$2x_1 - x_2 = 4$$
$$x_1, x_2, x_3 \geq 0$$

(a) Write the associated dual problem.
(b) Suppose that the optimal primal basic solution is $\mathbf{X}_B = (x_1, x_3)^T$. Determine the optimal dual solution, including the optimal value of the objective function.

☐ **5–13** Consider the following linear program:

$$\text{maximize } z = 2x_1 + 4x_2 + 4x_3 - 3x_4$$

subject to

$$x_1 + x_2 + x_3 = 4$$
$$x_1 + 4x_2 + x_4 = 8$$
$$x_1, x_2, x_3, x_4 \geq 0$$

(a) Write the associated dual problem.

(b) Verify that $\mathbf{X}_B = (x_2, x_3)^T$ is optimal by computing $(z_j - c_j)$ for all nonbasic x_j.

(c) Find the associated optimal dual solution from the appropriate $z_j - c_j$ computed in part (b).

☐ **5–14** An LP model consists of two variables x_1 and x_2 and three constraints of the type $\leq$. The primal simplex method is used to solve the problem. Given s_1, s_2, and s_3 are the slack starting basic solution, the optimal basic vector is given as

$$\mathbf{X}_B = (s_1, x_2, x_1)^T$$

with the associated inverse given as

$$\mathbf{B}^{-1} = \begin{pmatrix} 1 & 1 & -1 \\ 0 & 1 & 0 \\ 0 & -1 & 1 \end{pmatrix}$$

The optimal primal and dual solutions are given as

$$\mathbf{X}_B = (s_1, x_2, x_1)^T = (2, 6, 2)^T$$
$$\mathbf{Y} = (y_1, y_2, y_3) = (0, 3, 2)$$

Determine the associated optimal value of the objective function.

☐ **5–15** Find the *optimal objective value* of the following problem by inspecting only its dual. (Do not solve the dual by the simplex method.)

$$\text{minimize } z = 10x_1 + 4x_2 + 5x_3$$

subject to

$$5x_1 - 7x_2 + 3x_3 \geq 50$$
$$x_1, x_2, x_3 \geq 0$$

☐ **5–16** Find a solution to the following set of inequalities by using the dual problem.

$$\begin{aligned} 2x_1 + 3x_2 &\leq 12 \\ -3x_1 + 2x_2 &\leq -4 \\ 3x_1 - 5x_2 &\leq 2 \\ x_1 &\text{ unrestricted} \\ x_2 &\geq 0 \end{aligned}$$

[*Hint*: Augment the trivial objective function maximize $z = 0x_1 + 0x_2$ to the inequalities, then solve the dual.]

☐ **5–17** Solve the following problem by considering its dual:

$$\text{minimize } z = 5x_1 + 6x_2 + 3x_3$$

subject to

$$\begin{aligned} 5x_1 + 5x_2 + 3x_3 &\geq 50 \\ x_1 + x_2 - x_3 &\geq 20 \\ 7x_1 + 6x_2 - 9x_3 &\geq 30 \end{aligned}$$

$$\begin{aligned} 5x_1 + 5x_2 + 5x_3 &\geq 35 \\ 2x_1 + 4x_2 - 15x_3 &\geq 10 \\ 12x_1 + 10x_2 \quad &\geq 90 \\ x_2 - 10x_3 &\geq 20 \\ x_1, x_2, x_3 &\geq 0 \end{aligned}$$

Compare the number of constraints in the two problems.

☐ **5–18** Consider the following problem:

$$\text{minimize } w = 6y_1 + 7y_2 + 3y_3 + 5y_4$$

subject to

$$\begin{aligned} 5y_1 + 6y_2 - 3y_3 + 4y_4 &\geq 12 \\ y_2 - 5y_3 - 6y_4 &\geq 10 \\ 2y_1 + 5y_2 + y_3 + y_4 &\geq 8 \\ y_1, y_2, y_3, y_4 &\geq 0 \end{aligned}$$

(a) Indicate *three* different methods for solving this problem, and give the complete starting tableau in each case.
(b) Compute the maximum number of possible iterations in each of the three cases.
(c) Which of the foregoing methods would you use, and why?

☐ **5–19** Given that a linear programming problem has an unbounded solution, why is it that its dual must necessarily be infeasible?

☐ **5–20** Consider the problem:

$$\text{maximize } z = 8x_1 + 6x_2$$

subject to

$$\begin{aligned} x_1 - x_2 &\leq 3/5 \\ x_1 - x_2 &\geq 2 \\ x_1, x_2 &\geq 0 \end{aligned}$$

Show that both the primal and the dual problems have no feasible space. Hence it is not always true that when one problem is infeasible, its dual is unbounded. (Notice the important difference between the argument in this problem and the one in Problem 5–19.)

☐ **5–21** Consider the following problem:

$$\text{minimize } w = y_1 - 5y_2 + 6y_3$$

subject to

$$\begin{aligned} 2y_1 \quad + 4y_3 &\geq 50 \\ y_1 + 2y_2 \quad &\geq 30 \\ y_3 &\geq 10 \\ y_1, y_2, y_3 &\text{ unrestricted} \end{aligned}$$

Show that the solution to this problem is unbounded by showing that the dual is infeasible and the primal is feasible. Suppose that the primal problem is not checked for feasibility. Would it be possible to make this conclusion? Why?

☐ **5–22** Consider the following primal problem:

$$\text{maximize } z = -2x_1 + 3x_2 + 5x_3$$

subject to

$$x_1 - x_2 + x_3 \leq 15$$
$$x_1, x_2, x_3 \geq 0$$

Show by inspection that the dual is infeasible. What can be said about the solution to the primal?

☐ **5–23** For the linear programming problem defined in Section 5.2.2, let the given basis be optimal. Prove that for any vector

$$\mathbf{P}_k = \begin{pmatrix} a_{1k} \\ a_{2k} \\ \vdots \\ a_{mk} \end{pmatrix}, \qquad k = 1, 2, \ldots, m + n$$

the following relationship holds.

$$\sum_{j=1}^{m} c_j \alpha_j^k = \sum_{i=1}^{m} y_i^* a_{ik}$$

where $\alpha_j^k = (\mathbf{B}^{-1}\mathbf{P}_k)_j$ and y_i^* is the corresponding optimal dual value.

☐ **5–24** A company produces leather jackets and handbags. A jacket requires 8 square meters of leather and a handbag uses only 3 square meters. The labor requirements for the two products are 12 hours and 4 hours, respectively. The purchase price of leather is \$8 per square meter and the labor cost is estimated at \$15 an hour. The current weekly supplies of leather and labor are limited to 1200 square meters and 1800 hours. The company sells the jackets and handbags at \$350 and \$120, respectively. The objective is to determine the production schedule that maximizes the net revenue. The company is contemplating an expansion of its production. What is the maximum purchase price the company should pay for leather? For labor?

☐ **5–25** Consider Problem 2–29 (Chapter 2). Interpret the dual prices of the problem.

☐ **5–26** Consider Problem 3–34 (Chapter 3). The problem has at least one alternative solution. Interpret the dual prices and the reduced costs for two alternative optima.

□ **5–27** Consider Problem 2–28 (Chapter 2). Products 3 and 4 are not in the optimum solution. Make suggestions that will make it possible for these variables to be positive in the optimum solution. Since the LP model has two constraints only, would there be any conditions under which the model will produce more than two products?

□ **5–28** Consider the linear program

$$\text{maximize } z = 5x_1 + 12x_2 + 4x_3$$

subject to

$$\begin{aligned} x_1 + 2x_2 + x_3 &\leq 10 \\ 2x_1 - x_2 + 3x_3 &= 8 \\ x_1, x_2, x_3 &\geq 0 \end{aligned}$$

You are given the information that x_1 and x_2 are positive in the optimal solution. Use the complementary slackness theorem to find the optimal dual solution.

□ **5–29** Consider the linear program in Problem 5–28.

(a) Write the dual problem and then solve it graphically.
(b) Use the information in part (a) and the complementary slackness theorem to obtain the optimal solution of the primal problem.

□ **5–30** Show how the optimal values of the slack variables in the dual problem can be obtained *directly* from the optimal primal tableau. Apply the procedure to Example 5.2-2, and check the result by substituting the optimal dual variables in the dual constraints.

□ **5–31** Consider the product-mix model of Example 5.3-2. Determine the optimal solution when the profit function is changed as follows:

(a) $z = 4x_1 + 2x_2 + x_3$.
(b) $z = 3x_1 + 4x_2 + 2x_3$.
(c) $z = 3x_2 + x_3$.
(d) $z = 2x_1 + 2x_2 + 8x_3$.
(e) $z = 5x_1 + 2x_2 + 5x_3$.

□ **5–32** Consider Problem 5–11. For each of the following objective functions, find the new optimum solution by using the sensitivity analysis procedure:

(a) Maximize $z = 12x_1 + 5x_2 + 2x_3$.
(b) Minimize $z = 2x_2 - 5x_3$.

□ **5–33** Consider Problem 5–12. For each of the following objective functions, find the optimum solution by using the sensitivity analysis procedure:

(a) Maximize $z = 2x_1 + x_2 + 4x_3$.
(b) Minimize $z = x_1 - 2x_2 + x_3$.

□ **5–34** Consider Problem 5–13. For each of the following objective functions, find the new optimum solution by using the sensitivity analysis procedure:

(a) Minimize $z = 4x_1 - 3x_2 - 4x_3 + x_4$.
(b) Maximize $z = 2x_1 + 5x_2 + 2x_3 + 4x_4$.

□ **5–35** In the product-mix model of Example 5.3-2, suppose that a fourth product is scheduled on the original three operations. The new product has the following data:

Operation	1	2	3
Minutes per Unit	3	2	4

Determine the optimal solution when the profit per unit of the new product is given by (a) \$5; (b) \$10.

□ **5–36** In the product-mix model of Example 5.3-2, determine the necessary increase in the profit coefficient of product 1 that will make it profitable.

□ **5–37** In the product-mix model in Example 5.3-2, the first product is not in the optimal mix even though x_1 has a higher marginal profit than x_2. Market conditions do not permit increasing the marginal profit of x_1. Thus it is decided to improve the profitability of product 1 by reducing its usages of the times of the three operations. Indicate whether the following changes will improve the profitability of x_1.

(a) Change the usages per unit of product 1 from (1, 3, 1) to (1, 2, 3).
(b) Change the usages to (1/2, 7/2, 2).
(c) Change the usages to (1, 1, 5).

□ **5–38** Consider Problem 5–12. Check whether a new variable x_4 will improve the optimum value of z assuming that its objective and constraint coefficients are as given. If so, find the new optimum solution:

(a) (5; 2, 2).
(b) (4; 1, 1).
(c) (3; 4, 6).
(d) (5; 3, 3).

□ **5–39** Consider Problem 5–13. Check whether a new variable x_5 will improve the optimum value of z assuming that its objective and constraint coefficients are as given below. If so, find the new optimum solution:

(a) (5; 1, 2).
(b) (6; 2, 3).
(c) (10; 2, 5).
(d) (15; 3, 3).

□ **5–40** Consider Problem 5–11. Suppose that the technological coefficients of x_2 are $(5 - \theta, -5 + \theta)$ instead of $(5, -5)$, where θ is a nonnegative parameter. Find the values of θ for which the solution to Problem 5–11 remains optimal.

□ **5–41** In the product-mix model of Example 5.3-2, determine the optimal solution when the time limits (in minutes) of the daily usages of the operations are changed as shown by the following vectors.

(a) $\begin{pmatrix} 420 \\ 460 \\ 440 \end{pmatrix}$ (b) $\begin{pmatrix} 500 \\ 400 \\ 600 \end{pmatrix}$ (c) $\begin{pmatrix} 300 \\ 800 \\ 200 \end{pmatrix}$ (d) $\begin{pmatrix} 300 \\ 400 \\ 150 \end{pmatrix}$

□ **5–42** Consider Problem 5–11. Suppose that the right side of the constraints becomes $(30 + \theta, 40 - \theta)$, where θ is a nonnegative parameter. Determine the values of θ for which the basic solution in Problem 5–11 remains feasible.

□ **5–43** In Problem 5–42, find the new optimal solution when $\theta = 10$.

□ **5–44** In Problem 5–41, suppose that it is necessary to add a fourth operation to all the products of the product-mix problem. The maximum production rate based on 480 minutes a day is *either* 120 units of product 1, 480 units of product 2, *or* 240 units of product 3. Determine the optimal solution assuming that the daily capacity of the fourth operation is limited by (a) 570 minutes; (b) 548 minutes.

□ **5–45** Consider Problem 5–12. Check whether each of the following constraints will affect the current optimum solution. If so, find the new solution:

(a) $x_1 + x_2 \leq 2$.
(b) $2x_1 + 4x_2 \geq 10$.
(c) $2x_1 + x_2 = 6$.
(d) $x_1 + x_2 + x_3 \leq 2$.

□ **5–46** Consider Problem 5–13. Check whether each of the following constraints will affect the current solution. If so, find the new solution:

(a) $x_1 + x_2 + x_3 \leq 5$.
(b) $2x_1 + x_2 - x_4 \geq 4$.
(c) $x_1 + 2x_2 + x_3 + x_4 \leq 4$.
(d) $x_1 + x_4 = 1$.

□ **5–47** Consider the problem

$$\text{maximize } z = 2x_2 - 5x_3$$

subject to

$$\begin{aligned} x_1 \quad\quad + x_3 &\geq 2 \\ 2x_1 + x_2 + 6x_3 &\leq 6 \\ x_1 - x_2 + 3x_3 &= 0 \\ x_1, x_2, x_3 &\geq 0 \end{aligned}$$

(a) Given that the optimum basic solution is (x_2, x_4, x_1), where x_4 is the surplus of the first constraint, solve the problem.
(b) Suppose that the right-hand side of the primal is changed from (2, 6, 0) to (2, 10, 5). Find the new optimal solution.
(c) Suppose that the coefficients of x_2 and x_3 in the objective function are changed from $(2, -5)$ to $(1, 1)$. Find the new solution.
(d) Find the new solution given parts (b) and (c) are considered simultaneously.

□ **5–48** Consider Example 5.3-2. Find the new optimum solution for each of the following simultaneous changes:

(a) Objective function: maximize $z = 5x_1 + 3x_2 + 4x_3$
Right-hand side: $(420, 460, 440)^T$

(b) Objective function: maximize $z = 4x_1 + 3x_2 + 2x_3$
Right-hand side: $(300, 800, 600)^T$
(c) Objective function: maximize $z = 2x_1 + x_2 + 3x_3$
Right-hand side: $(300, 400, 150)^T$

☐ **5–49** Solve Example 5.6-1 assuming that the objective function is given by
(a) $z = (3 + 3t)x_1 + 2x_2 + (5 - 6t)x_3$.
(b) $z = (3 - 2t)x_1 + (2 + t)x_2 + (5 + 2t)x_3$
(c) $z = (3 + t)x_1 + (2 + 2t)x_2 + (5 - t)x_3$.

☐ **5–50** Consider the example in Section 3.3.1A. Suppose that the objective function becomes

$$\text{minimize } z = (4 - t)x_1 + (1 - 3t)x_2 + (2 - 2t)x_5$$

where x_5 is an additional variable whose constraint coefficients in the original problem are 2, 2, and 5, respectively. Study the variations in the optimal solution with t. Assume that $t \geq 0$.

☐ **5–51** The analysis in this chapter has always assumed that the optimal solution of the problem at $t = 0$ is obtained by the regular simplex method. In some problems, however, it may be more convenient to obtain the optimal solution by the dual simplex method of Section 3.4. Indicate how parametric analysis can be carried out in this case.

☐ **5–52** In the problem introduced in Section 3.4 (dual simplex method), suppose that the objective function is given by

$$z = (3 + t)x_1 + (2 + 4t)x_2$$

Study the variation in the optimal solution with $t \geq 0$.

☐ **5–53** Solve Example 5.6-1 assuming that the objective function is given by

$$z = (3 + 3t)x_1 + 2x_2 + (5 - 6t)x_3$$

where t is a nonnegative parameter.

☐ **5–54** Solve Example 5.6-2 assuming that the right-hand side of the constraints is given by

$$\mathbf{b}(t) = \begin{pmatrix} 430 \\ 460 \\ 420 \end{pmatrix} + t \begin{pmatrix} 500 \\ 100 \\ -200 \end{pmatrix}$$

where t is a nonnegative parameter.
[*Hint*: $\mathbf{B}_0^{-1}$ as given in Example 5.6-2 remains feasible for the new $\mathbf{b}(0) = (430, 460, 420)^T$.]

☐ **5–55** In Problem 5–50 suppose instead that the right-hand side of the constraints is given by

$$\mathbf{b}(t) = \begin{pmatrix} 3 \\ 6 \\ 4 \end{pmatrix} + t\begin{pmatrix} 3 \\ 2 \\ -1 \end{pmatrix}$$

Study the variation in the optimal solution with t. Assume that $t \geq 0$.

☐ **5–56** In Problem 5–52, suppose instead that the right-hand side of the constraints is given by

$$\mathbf{b}(t) = \begin{pmatrix} 3 + 2t \\ 6 - t \\ 3 - 4t \end{pmatrix}$$

Study the variation in the optimal solution with t, $t \geq 0$.

☐ **5–57** The linear programming problem

$$\text{maximize } z = 3x_1 + 6x_2$$

subject to

$$\begin{aligned} x_1 \qquad &\leq 4 \\ 3x_1 + 2x_2 &\leq 18 \\ x_1, x_2 &\geq 0 \end{aligned}$$

has the solution

Basic	x_1	x_2	x_3	x_4	Solution
z	6	0	0	3	54
x_3	1	0	1	0	4
x_2	3/2	1	0	1/2	9

where x_3 and x_4 are slack variables. Let

$$c_2(t) = 6 - 4t$$

$$\mathbf{b}(t) = \begin{pmatrix} 4 \\ 18 \end{pmatrix} + t\begin{pmatrix} 8 \\ -24 \end{pmatrix}$$

$$\mathbf{P}_1(t) = \begin{pmatrix} 1 \\ 3 \end{pmatrix} + t\begin{pmatrix} 2 \\ -3 \end{pmatrix}$$

whereas c_1 and $\mathbf{P}_2$ remain as given in the original problem.

If the foregoing parametric functions are introduced *simultaneously*, find the range of t for which the solution remains basic, feasible, and optimal. Assume that $t \geq 0$.

☐ **5–58** In Problem 5–57, suppose that

$$z = (3 + \alpha)x_1 + (6 - \alpha)x_2$$

$$\mathbf{P}_1(\beta) = \begin{pmatrix} 1 + \beta \\ 3 - \beta \end{pmatrix}$$

whereas **b** remains unparameterized, where α and β are real parameters. Find the relationship between α and β that will always keep the solution in Problem 5–57 optimal.

☐ **5–59** Suppose that the parameterization of z and **b** given in Problems 5–53 and 5–54 are considered simultaneously. Study the variations in the optimal solution with t.

☐ **5–60** Suppose that the parameterization of z and **b** as given in Problems 5–50 and 5–55 are considered simultaneously. Study the variation in the optimal solution with t.

☐ **5–61** Consider the following problem:

$$\text{maximize } z = (2 + t)x_1 + (4 - t)x_2 + (4 - 2t)x_3 + (-3 + 3t)x_4$$

subject to

$$\begin{aligned} x_1 + x_2 + x_3 \qquad &= 4 - t \\ 2x_1 + 4x_2 \qquad + x_4 &= 8 - t \\ x_1, x_2, x_3, x_4 &\geq 0 \end{aligned}$$

where t is a nonnegative parameter. Obtain the optimal solution for $t = 0$ using x_3 and x_4 for the starting basic solution. Then study the variation of the optimal solution with t.

☐ **5–62** Consider the problem

$$\text{maximize } z = (4 - 10t)x_1 + (8 - 4t)x_2$$

subject to

$$\begin{aligned} x_1 + x_2 &\leq 4 \\ 2x_1 + x_2 &\leq 3 - t \\ x_1, x_2 &\geq 0 \end{aligned}$$

Study the variations in the optimal solution with the parameter t, where $-\infty < t < \infty$. Notice that t may assume negative values in this case.

☐ **5–63** Consider the unparameterized version of Problem 5–57. Suppose that the objective function and the right-hand side vary with the parameter t according to

$$z = (3 + t - t^2)x_1 + (6 - 2t - t^2)x_2$$

$$\mathbf{b}(t) = \begin{pmatrix} 4 + t^2 \\ 18 - 2t^2 \end{pmatrix}$$

Study the variation in the optimal solution with the parameter $t (t \geq 0)$. What are the difficulties involved in dealing with the nonlinear functions?

Chapter 6

Linear Programming: Transportation Model

This chapter presents the transportation model and its variants. In the obvious sense, the model deals with the determination of a minimum-cost plan for transporting a single commodity from a number of sources (e.g., factories) to a number of destinations (e.g., warehouses). The model can be extended in a direct manner to cover practical situations in the areas of inventory control, employment scheduling and personnel assignment, among others.

The transportation model is basically a linear program that can be solved by the regular simplex method. However, its special structure allows the development of a solution procedure, called the transportation technique, that is computationally more efficient.

The transportation technique can be, and often is, presented in an elementary manner that appears completely detached from the simplex method. However, we must emphasize that the "new" technique essentially follows the *exact* steps of the simplex method.

6.1 DEFINITION AND APPLICATIONS OF THE TRANSPORTATION MODEL

In this section we present the standard definition of the transportation model. We then describe variants of the model that extend its scope of application to a wider class of real-life problems.

In the direct sense, the transportation model seeks the determination of a transportation plan of a *single* commodity from a number of sources to a number of destinations. The data of the model include

1. Level of supply at each source and amount of demand at each destination.
2. The *unit* transportation cost of the commodity from each source to each destination.

Since there is only one commodity, a destination can receive its demand from one or more sources. The objective of the model is to determine the amount to be shipped from each source to each destination such that the total transportation cost is minimized.

The basic assumption of the model is that the transportation cost on a given route is directly proportional to the number of units transported. The definition of "unit of transportation" will vary depending on the "commodity" transported. For example, we may be speaking of a unit of transportation as each of the steel beams needed to build a bridge. Or we may use a truckload of the commodity as a unit of transportation. In either case, the units of supply and demand must be consistent with our definition of a "transported unit."

Figure 6-1 depicts the transportation model as a network with m sources and n destinations. A *source* or a *destination* is represented by a **node**. The **arc** joining a source and a destination represents the route through which the commodity is transported. The amount of supply at source i is a_i and the demand at destination j is b_j. The *unit* transportation cost between source i and destination j is c_{ij}.

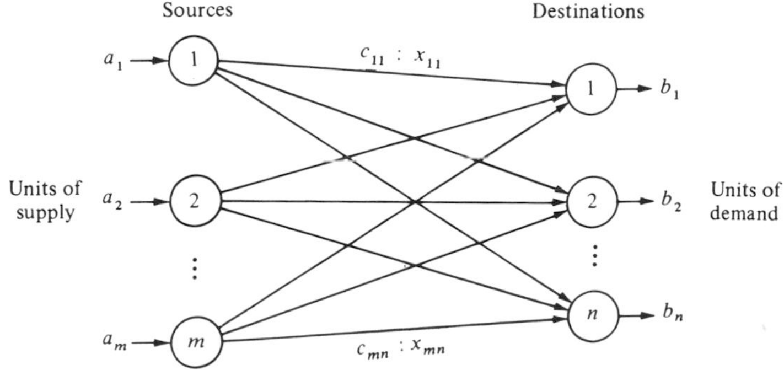

Figure 6-1

Let x_{ij} represent the amount transported from source i to destination j; then the LP model representing the transportation problem is given generally as

$$\text{minimize } z = \sum_{i=1}^{m} \sum_{j=1}^{n} c_{ij} x_{ij}$$

subject to

$$\sum_{j=1}^{n} x_{ij} \leq a_i, \qquad i = 1, 2, \ldots, m$$

$$\sum_{i=1}^{m} x_{ij} \geq b_j, \qquad j = 1, 2, \ldots, n$$

$$x_{ij} \geq 0, \qquad \text{for all } i \text{ and } j$$

The first set of constraints stipulates that the sum of the shipments *from* a source cannot exceed its supply; similarly, the second set requires that the sum of the shipments *to* a destination must satisfy its demand.

The model just described implies that the total supply $\sum_{i=1}^{m} a_i$ must at least equal the total demand $\sum_{j=1}^{n} b_j$. When the total supply *equals* the total demand ($\sum_{i=1}^{m} a_i = \sum_{j=1}^{n} b_j$), the resulting formulation is called a **balanced transportation model**. It differs from the model above only in the fact that all constraints are equations; that is,

$$\sum_{j=1}^{n} x_{ij} = a_i, \qquad i = 1, 2, \ldots, m$$

$$\sum_{i=1}^{m} x_{ij} = b_j, \qquad j = 1, 2, \ldots, n$$

In real life it is not necessarily true that supply equal demand or, for that matter, exceed it. However, a transportation model can always be balanced. The balancing, in addition to its usefulness in modeling certain practical situations, is important for the development of a solution method that fully exploits the special structure of the transportation model. The following two examples present the idea of balancing as well as its practical implications.

Example 6.1-1 (Standard Transportation Model). The MG Auto Company has plants in Los Angeles, Detroit, and New Orleans. Its major distribution centers are located in Denver and Miami. The capacities of the three plants during the next quarter are 1000, 1500, and 1200 cars. The quarterly demands at the two distribution centers are 2300 and 1400 cars. The train transportation cost per car per mile is approximately 8 cents. The mileage chart between the plants and distribution centers is as follows:

	Denver	Miami
Los Angeles	1000	2690
Detroit	1250	1350
New Orleans	1275	850

The mileage chart can be translated to cost per car at the rate of 8 cents per mile. This yields the following costs (rounded to the closest dollar), which represent c_{ij} in the general model:

	Denver (1)	Miami (2)
Los Angeles (1)	80	215
Detroit (2)	100	108
New Orleans (3)	102	68

Using numeric codes to represent the plants and distribution centers, we let x_{ij} represent the number of cars transported from source i to destination j. Since the total supply (= 1000 + 1500 + 1200 = 3700) happens to equal the total demand (= 2300 + 1400 = 3700), the resulting transportation model is *balanced*. Hence the following LP model presenting the problem has all *equality* constraints:

$$\text{minimize } z = 80x_{11} + 215x_{12} + 100x_{21} + 108x_{22} + 102x_{31} + 68x_{32}$$

subject to

$$\begin{aligned}
x_{11} + x_{12} \qquad\qquad\qquad\qquad\qquad\qquad &= 1000\\
+ x_{21} + x_{22} \qquad\qquad\qquad &= 1500\\
+ x_{31} + x_{32} &= 1200\\
x_{11} \qquad + x_{21} \qquad\quad + x_{31} \qquad\quad &= 2300\\
+ x_{12} \qquad + x_{22} \qquad\quad + x_{32} &= 1400\\
x_{ij} \geq 0, \qquad \text{for all } i \text{ and } j&.
\end{aligned}$$

A more compact method for representing the transportation model is to use what we call the **transportation tableau.** It is a matrix form with its rows representing the sources and its columns the destinations. The cost elements c_{ij} are summarized in the northeast corner of the matrix cell (i, j). The MG model can thus be summarized as shown in Table 6-1.

We shall see in the next section that the transportation tableau is the basis for the development of the special simplex-based method for solving the transportation problem. ◀

Exercise 6.1-1

Suppose that it is desired not to ship any cars from the Detroit plant to the Denver distribution center. How can this condition be incorporated in the MG model?

[*Ans.* Assign a very high unit transportation cost, M, to the Detroit–Denver route; compare the penalty method, Section 3.3.1.]

The MG model happened to have equal supply and demand. Example 6.1-2 demonstrates how a transportation model can always be balanced. Keep in mind that the main reason for wanting to balance the transportation problem (i.e., converting all the constraints to equations) is that it allows the development of an efficient computational procedure based on the tableau representation illustrated in Table 6-1.

Table 6-1

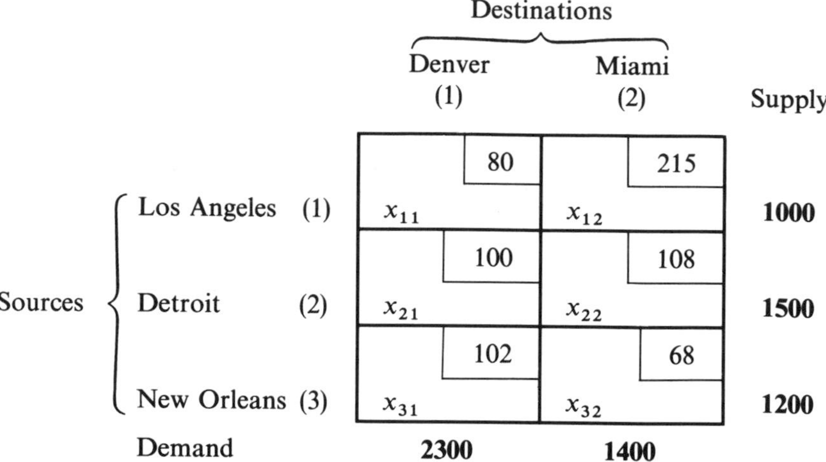

		Destinations: Denver (1)	Destinations: Miami (2)	Supply
Sources	Los Angeles (1)	80; x_{11}	215; x_{12}	**1000**
	Detroit (2)	100; x_{21}	108; x_{22}	**1500**
	New Orleans (3)	102; x_{31}	68; x_{32}	**1200**
	Demand	**2300**	**1400**	

Example 6.1-2 (Balanced Transportation Model). In Example 6.1-1, suppose that the Detroit plant capacity is 1300 cars (instead of 1500). The situation is said to be **unbalanced** because the total supply (= 3500) does not equal the total demand (= 3700). Stated differently, this unbalanced situation means that it will not be possible to fill *all* the demand at the distribution centers. Our objective is to reformulate the transportation model in a manner that will distribute the shortage quantity (= 3700 − 3500 = 200 cars) optimally among the distribution centers.

Since demand exceeds supply, a fictitious or **dummy source** (plant) can be added with its capacity equal to 200 cars. The dummy plant is allowed, under normal conditions, to ship its "production" to all distribution centers. Physically, the amount shipped to a destination from a dummy plant will represent the shortage quantity at that destination.

The only information missing for the completion of the model is the unit "transportation" costs from the dummy plant to the destinations. Since the plant does not exist, no physical shipping will occur and the corresponding unit transportation cost is zero. We may look at the situation differently, however, by saying that a penalty cost is incurred for every unsatisfied demand unit at the distribution

Table 6-2

	Denver	Miami	
Los Angeles	80	215	**1000**
Detroit	100	108	**1300**
New Orleans	102	68	**1200**
Dummy Plant	0	0	**200**
	2300	**1400**	

Table 6-3

	Denver	Miami	Dummy Distribution Center	
Los Angeles	80	215	0	**1000**
Detroit	100	108	0	**1500**
New Orleans	102	68	0	**1200**
	1900	**1400**	**400**	

centers. In this case the unit transportation costs will equal the unit penalty costs at the various destinations.

Table 6-2 summarizes the balanced model under the new capacity restriction of the Detroit plant. The dummy plant (shown by a tint overlay) has a capacity of 200 cars.

In a similar manner, if the supply exceeds the demand, we can add a fictitious or **dummy destination** that will absorb the difference. For example, suppose in Example 6.1-1 that the demand at Denver drops to 1900 cars. Table 6-3 summarizes the model with the dummy distribution center. Any cars shipped from a plant to a dummy distribution center represent a *surplus* quantity at that plant. The associated unit transportation cost is zero. However, we can charge a *storage* cost for holding the cars at the plant, in which case the unit transportation cost will equal the unit storage cost.

Exercise 6.1-2

(a) Will it ever be necessary to add both a dummy source and a dummy destination to produce a balanced transportation model?
[*Ans.* No.]

(b) In Table 6-2 suppose that the penalty costs for each unreceived car at Denver and Miami are $200 and $260. Change the model to include this information.
[*Ans.* The unit transportation cost in the dummy row should be 200 and 260 instead of 0.]

(c) Interpret the solution in Table 6-2 if the number of cars "shipped" from the dummy plant to Denver and Miami are 150 and 50, respectively.
[*Ans.* The orders at Denver and Miami will be 150 and 50 cars short.]

(d) In Table 6-3, suppose that the Detroit plant must ship out *all* its production of 1500 cars. How can we implement this restriction?
[*Ans.* Assign a very high cost M to the Detroit–dummy distribution center route.]

(e) In each of the following cases, indicate whether a dummy source or destination should be added to balance the model.

(1) $a_1 = 10, a_2 = 5, a_3 = 4, a_4 = 6$
$b_1 = 10, b_2 = 5, b_3 = 7, b_4 = 9$
[*Ans.* Add a dummy source with capacity of 6 units.]

(2) $a_1 = 30, a_2 = 44$
$b_1 = 25, b_2 = 30, b_3 = 10$
[*Ans.* Add a dummy destination with demand 9 units.]

The application of the transportation model is not limited to the problem of "transporting" commodities between geographical sources and destinations. The following two examples illustrate the use of the transportation model in other unrelated area. The next section presents the assignment model, which deals with the assignment of jobs to machines or personnel.

Example 6.1.3. (Production-Inventory Model). A company is developing a master plan for the production of an item over a 4-month period. The demands for the four months are 100, 200, 180, and 300 units, respectively. A current month's demand may be satisfied by

1. Excess production in an earlier month held in stock for later consumption.
2. Production in the current month.
3. Excess production in a later month backordered for preceding months.

The variable production cost per unit in any month is \$4.00. A unit produced for later consumption will incur a holding (or storage) cost at the rate of \$.50 per unit per month. Backordered items incur a penalty cost of \$2.00 per unit per month.

The production capacity for manufacturing the item varies monthly. The estimates for the next four months are 50, 180, 280, and 270 units, respectively.

The objective is to devise the minimum-cost production–inventory plan.

This problem can be formulated as a "transportation" model. The equivalence between the elements of the production and the transportation systems is established as follows:

Transportation System	Production System
1. Source i	1. Production period i
2. Destination j	2. Demand period j
3. Supply at source i	3. Production capacity of period i
4. Demand at destination j	4. Demand per period j
5. Transportation cost from source i to destination j	5. Production and inventory cost from period i to j

Table 6-4 summarizes the problem as a transportation model. The unit "transportation" cost from period i to period j is

$$c_{ij} = \begin{cases} \text{production cost in } i, & i = j \\ \text{production cost in } i + \text{holding cost from } i \text{ to } j, & i < j \\ \text{production cost in } i + \text{penalty cost from } i \text{ to } j, & i > j \end{cases}$$

The definition of c_{ij} indicates that production in period i for the same period ($i = j$) equals the unit production cost only. If period i produces for future periods j ($i < j$), an additional holding cost is incurred. Similarly, production in i to fill backorders in previous periods j ($i > j$) incurs an additional penalty cost. For example,

$$c_{11} = \$4$$
$$c_{24} = 4 + (.5 + .5) = \$5$$
$$c_{41} = 4 + (2 + 2 + 2) = \$10$$

◀

Table 6-4

Period		Period 1	2	3	4	Capacity
	1	4.	4.5	5.	5.5	**50**
	2	6.	4.	4.5	5.	**180**
	3	8.	6.	4.	4.5	**280**
	4	10	8.	6.	4.	**270**
Demand		**100**	**200**	**180**	**300**	

Exercise 6.1-3
In Table 6-4, suppose that the holding costs per unit change with the periods and are given by \$.4, and \$.3, and \$.7 for periods 1, 2, and 3. The penalty costs remain unchanged. Recompute c_{ij} in Table 6-4.
[*Ans.* c_{ij} by row are (4, 4.4, 4.7, 5.4), (6, 4, 4.3, 5.0), (8, 6, 4, 4.7), and (10, 8, 6, 4).]

The optimal solution of the model (obtained by TORA) is shown in Figure 6-2. It shows that 50 units of the demand for period 1 must be satisfied by a backorder production in period 2. Meanwhile, 70 units of the demand for period 2 are satisfied by a backorder production in period 3. This solution may appear economically unacceptable, since period 2 provides a backorder production for period 1 and simultaneously receives a backorder production from period 3. The argument can be refuted by observing that, in period 2, we have no choice but to provide period 1 with 50 backorder units because period 1's production capacity (= 50 units) is not sufficient to cover its own demand (= 100 units).

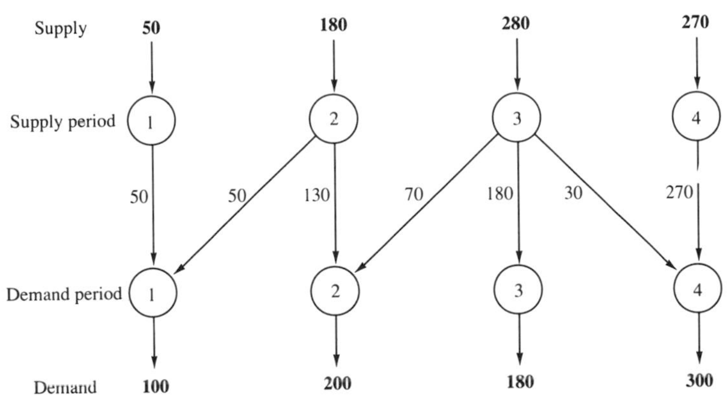

Figure 6-2

Example 6.1-4 (Caterer Problem). A caterer is contracted to provide clean napkins for N consecutive days. The demand for day i is given as d_i napkins. There are three sources from which the daily demand may be satisfied:

1. Buy new napkins at the price of a dollars each.

2. Send end-of-day soiled napkins to a fast next-day cleaning service (napkins sent at the end of day i are received at the start of day $i + 1$) at the cost of b dollars each.
3. Send end-of-day soiled napkins to a slow 3-day cleaning service (napkins sent at the end of day i are received at the start of day $i + 3$) at the cost of c dollars each.

The classical caterer problem actually paraphrases an airplane engine repair problem, where we have the options of buying new engines or overhauling used ones (see Problem 6–11).

In the direct sense, the situation does not appear to follow the format of the classical transportation problem. However, we will show that with some insight, the problem can be formulated using the transportation model. The following 7-day data are used to illustrate the procedure:

Day, i	1	2	3	4	5	6	7
Demand, d_i	240	120	140	200	180	140	220

The cost parameters a, b, and c are given by \$1.20, \$.60, and \$.30, respectively.

The overall idea is to consider seven destination nodes, each representing a day in the planning period. The demand at each of these destinations is as given above. As for the sources, we notice that at the end of each day we will have soiled napkins equal to the number of clean napkins demanded for that day. Thus we have seven sources with the respective amounts of supply again equal to the amounts listed above. We need an extra source to account for the supply of new napkins. Conceivably, all the demands for the 7-day period may be satisfied from the new napkins source. As a result, the amount of supply at the new-napkins source may be set equal to the sum of the demands for all the destinations (= 1240 napkins). To allow the option of not using all new napkins, a disposal destination node with a demand of 1240 napkins is added to the model. Actually, since it is cheaper to recycle soiled napkins, it will never be necessary to use new napkins to fill the demands of all seven days. However, from the optimization standpoint, such a detail is unimportant because all excess new napkins will be sent to the disposal destination.

Table 6-5 summarizes the transportation model consisting of eight sources and eight destinations. All the routes from the current period to any back periods are clearly not feasible and hence must be blocked by assigning each of them a very high cost M. The unit "transportation costs" from all eight sources to the disposal destination is zero. The remaining unit costs are established as follows. It will cost \$1.20 between source 1 (new napkins) and each of the seven destinations of the model. For sources 2 through 8 (days 1 through 7), the unit cost from node i to each of nodes $i + 1$ and $i + 2$ is \$.60 and from node i to each of nodes $i + 3, i + 4, \ldots, 7$ is \$.30 (fast and slow services, respectively). Note carefully the significance of the route i to $i + 2$. It represents sending soiled napkins at the end of day i, receiving them at the start of day $i + 1$ (fast service) and "storing" them for use on day $i + 2$. A similar interpretation can be made for the slow service routes. ◀

Exercise 6.1-4

Suppose that a clean napkin costs an additional 2-cent storage cost per day if not used on the same day it is received from the laundry. Revise the cost elements in Table 6-5.
[*Ans.* Replace the second .60 in each row with .62 and the second and higher .30 with .32.]

Table 6-5

	1	2	3	4	5	6	7	Disposal	
New	1.20	1.20	1.20	1.20	1.20	1.20	1.20	0	**1240**
1	M	.60	.60	.30	.30	.30	.30	0	**240**
2	M	M	.60	.60	.30	.30	.30	0	**120**
3	M	M	M	.60	.60	.30	.30	0	**140**
4	M	M	M	M	.60	.60	.30	0	**200**
5	M	M	M	M	M	.60	.60	0	**180**
6	M	M	M	M	M	M	.60	0	**140**
7	M	M	M	M	M	M	M	0	**220**
	240	**120**	**140**	**200**	**180**	**140**	**220**	**1240**	

Table 6-6

Period	New Napkins	Laundry Service Fast	Laundry Service Slow	Disposal
1	240	180	60	0
2	20	60	60	0
3	0	140	0	0
4	0	120	80	0
5	0	140	0	40
6	0	140	0	0
7	0	0	0	220

The optimum solution of the problem (obtained by TORA) is summarized in Figure 6-3. These data can be summarized in a ready-to-use format as shown in Table 6-6. Observe the interpretation of the solution regarding the laundry service. For example, at the end of day 1, 180 soiled napkins are sent to fast service, 100 of which are used on day 2 and the remaining 80 napkins are stored for use in day 3. This information is shown in Figure 6-3 by a 100-napkin arc from node 1 to node 2 and 80-napkin arc from node 1 to node 3.

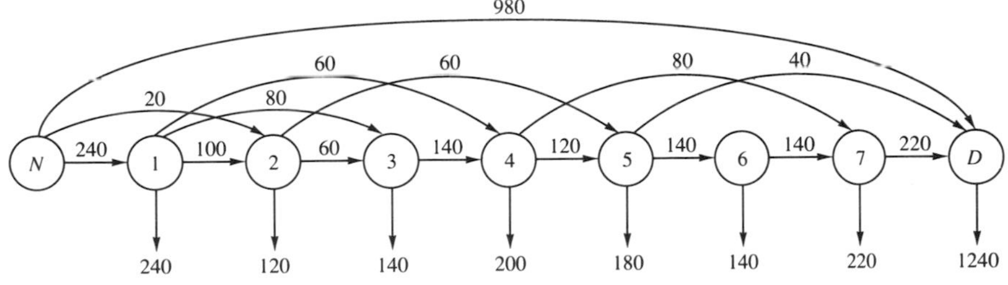

Figure 6-3

6.2 SOLUTION OF THE TRANSPORTATION PROBLEM

In this section we introduce the details for solving the transportation model. The method uses the steps of the simplex method directly and differs only in the details of implementing the optimality and feasibility conditions.

6.2.1 THE TRANSPORTATION TECHNIQUE

The basic steps of the transportation technique are

Step 1: Determine a starting feasible solution.

Step 2: Determine an entering variable from among the nonbasic variables. If all such variables satisfy the optimality condition (of the simplex method), stop; otherwise, go to step 3.

Step 3: Determine a leaving variable (using the feasibility condition) from among the variables of the current basic solution; then find the new basic solution. Return to step 2.

These steps will be considered in detail. The vehicle of explanation is the problem in Table 6-7. The unit transportation cost c_{ij} is in dollars. The supply and demand are given in number of units.

Table 6-7

	Destination 1	2	3	4	Supply
Source 1	x_{11} [10]	x_{12} [0]	x_{13} [20]	x_{14} [11]	**15**
2	x_{21} [12]	x_{22} [7]	x_{23} [9]	x_{24} [20]	**25**
3	x_{31} [0]	x_{32} [14]	x_{33} [16]	x_{34} [18]	**5**
Demand	**5**	**15**	**15**	**10**	

A. Determination of the Starting Solution

The general definition of the transportation model in Section 6.1 requires that $\sum_{i=1}^{m} a_i = \sum_{j=1}^{n} b_j$. This requirement results in one dependent equation, which means that the transportation model has only $m + n - 1$ independent equations. Thus, as in the simplex method, a starting basic feasible solution must include $m + n - 1$ basic variables.

Normally, if the transportation model is formulated as a simplex tableau, it would be necessary to utilize artificial variables to secure a starting basic solution. However, when the transportation tableau is used, a starting basic feasible solution can be obtained easily and directly. We present a procedure called the **northwest-corner rule** for this purpose. Two other procedures, called **least-cost** method and **Vogel's approximation**, are presented in Section 6.2.2. These procedures usually provide better starting solutions in the sense that the associated values of the objective function are smaller.

The *northwest corner* method starts by allocating the maximum amount allowable by the supply and demand to the variable x_{11} (the one in the northwest corner of the tableau). The satisfied column (row) is then crossed out, indicating that the remaining variables in the crossed-out column (row) equal zero. If a column and a row are satisfied simultaneously, *only one* (either one) may be crossed out. This condition guarantees locating *zero* basic variables, if any, automatically. (See Table 6-9 for an illustration.) After adjusting the amounts of supply and demand for all uncrossed-out rows and columns, the maximum feasible amount is allocated to the first uncrossed-out element in the new column (row). The process is completed when *exactly* one row *or* one column remains uncrossed out.

The procedure just described is now applied to the example in Table 6-7.

1. $x_{11} = 5$, which crosses out column 1. Thus no further allocation can be made in column 1. The amount left in row 1 is 10 units.
2. $x_{12} = 10$, which crosses out row 1 and leaves 5 units in column 2.
3. $x_{22} = 5$, which crosses out column 2 and leaves 20 units in row 2.
4. $x_{23} = 15$, which crosses out column 3 and leaves 5 units in row 2.
5. $x_{24} = 5$, which crosses out row 2 and leaves 5 units in column 4.
6. $x_{34} = 5$, which crosses out row 3 *or* column 4. Since only one row or one column remains uncrossed out, the process ends.

The resulting starting basic solution is given in Table 6-8. The *basic* variables are $x_{11} = 5$, $x_{12} = 10$, $x_{22} = 5$, $x_{23} = 15$, $x_{24} = 5$, and $x_{34} = 5$. The remaining variables are *nonbasic* at zero level. The associated transportation cost is

$$5 \times 10 + 10 \times 0 + 5 \times 7 + 15 \times 9 + 5 \times 20 + 5 \times 18 = \$410$$

When both a column and a row are satisfied simultaneously, the next variable to be added to the basic solution will necessarily be at the zero level. Table 6-9 illustrates this point where column 2 and row 2 are satisfied simultaneously. If column 2 is crossed out, x_{23} becomes basic at zero level in the next step, since the remaining supply for row 2 is now zero. (This case is shown in Table 6-9.) If, instead, row 2 is crossed out, x_{32} would be the zero basic variable.

Table 6-8

	1	2	3	4	
1	**5**	**10**			**15**
2		**5**	**15**	**5**	**25**
3				**5**	**5**
	5	**15**	**15**	**10**	

Table 6-9

	1	2	3	4	
1	5	5			~~10~~ ~~5~~
2		5	0		~~5~~ 0
3			8	7	15
	~~5~~	~~10~~ ~~5~~	8	7	

The starting solutions in Tables 6-8 and 6-9 include the proper number of basic variables, namely, $m + n - 1 = 6$. The northwest-corner rule always yields the proper number of basic variables.

B. Determination of Entering Variable (Method of Multipliers)

The entering variable is determined by using the optimality condition of the simplex method. As explained later in this section, the computations of the objective equation coefficients is based on the primal–dual relationships presented in Section 5.2. We first present the mechanics of the method and then provide a rigorous explanation of the procedure based on duality theory. Another method, called the **stepping-stone** procedure, is also available for determining the entering variable. Although the computations in the two methods are exactly equivalent, the stepping-stone method gives the impression that the procedure is completely unrelated to the simplex method.

In the method of multipliers we associate the multipliers u_i and v_j with row i and column j of the transportation tableau. For each *basic* variable x_{ij} in the current solution, the multipliers u_i and v_j must satisfy the following equation:

$$u_i + v_j = c_{ij}, \qquad \text{for each } basic \text{ variable } x_{ij}$$

These equations yield $m + n - 1$ equations (because there are only $m + n - 1$ basic variables) in $m + n$ unknowns. The values of the multipliers can be determined from these equations by assuming an *arbitrary* value for *any one* of the multipliers (usually u_1 is set equal to zero) and then solving the $m + n - 1$ equations in the remaining $m + n - 1$ unknown multipliers. Once this is done, the evaluation of each nonbasic variable x_{pq} is given by

$$\bar{c}_{pq} = u_p + v_q - c_{pq}, \qquad \text{for each } nonbasic \text{ variable } x_{pq}$$

(These values will be the same regardless of the arbitrary choice of the value of u_1. See the next Computer Drill below.) The entering variable is then selected as the nonbasic variable with the *most positive* $\bar{c}_{pq}$ (compare with the minimization optimality condition of the simplex method.

If we apply this procedure to the nonbasic variables in Table 6-8 (current solution), the equations associated with the basic variables are given as

$$\begin{aligned}
x_{11}&: \quad u_1 + v_1 = c_{11} = 10 \\
x_{12}&: \quad u_1 + v_2 = c_{12} = 0 \\
x_{22}&: \quad u_2 + v_2 = c_{22} = 7 \\
x_{23}&: \quad u_2 + v_3 = c_{23} = 9 \\
x_{24}&: \quad u_2 + v_4 = c_{24} = 20 \\
x_{34}&: \quad u_3 + v_4 = c_{34} = 18
\end{aligned}$$

By letting $u_1 = 0$, the values of the multipliers are successively determined as $v_1 = 10$, $v_2 = 0$, $u_2 = 7$, $v_3 = 2$, $v_4 = 13$, and $u_3 = 5$. The evaluations of the nonbasic variables are thus given as follows:

$$\begin{aligned}
x_{13}&: \quad \bar{c}_{13} = u_1 + v_3 - c_{13} = 0 + 2 - 20 = -18 \\
x_{14}&: \quad \bar{c}_{14} = u_1 + v_4 - c_{14} = 0 + 13 - 11 = 2 \\
x_{21}&: \quad \bar{c}_{21} = u_2 + v_1 - c_{21} = 7 + 10 - 12 = 5 \\
x_{31}&: \quad \bar{c}_{31} = u_3 + v_1 - c_{31} = 5 + 10 - 0 = \boxed{15} \\
x_{32}&: \quad \bar{c}_{32} = u_3 + v_2 - c_{32} = 5 + 0 - 14 = -9 \\
x_{33}&: \quad \bar{c}_{33} = u_3 + v_3 - c_{33} = 5 + 2 - 16 = -9
\end{aligned}$$

Since x_{31} has the most positive $\bar{c}_{pq}$, it is selected as the entering variable.

The equations $u_i + v_j - c_{ij}$, which we use for determining the multipliers, have such a simple structure that it is really unnecessary to write them explicitly. It is usually much simpler to determine the multipliers directly from the transportation tableau by noting that u_i of row i and v_j of column j add up to c_{ij} when row i and column j intersect in a cell containing a *basic* variable x_{ij}. Once u_i and v_j are determined, we can compute $\bar{c}_{pq}$ for all nonbasic x_{pq} by adding u_p of row p and v_q of column q and then subtracting c_{pq} in the cell at the intersection of row p and column q.

Computer Drill

Use TORA's user-guided option to view the iteration that corresponds to the computation above. You will notice that TORA computes u_i and v_j by starting with $v_4 \equiv 0$ (in place of $u_1 \equiv 0$). Although the values of u_i and v_j are different, the resulting $\bar{c}_{ij}$, and hence the entering variable ($= x_{31}$), remain the same. The drill shows that any u_i and v_j can be assigned an arbitrary value. (See also Problem 6–41.)

Computer Drill

Enter the transportation model in Table 6-7 as a regular LP model with 12 variables and 7 (equality) constraints (actually, 6 constraints because one constraint is redundant). (You will find it helpful to use the user-defined variable names x11, x12, ...) Choose the primal simplex with the M-starting solution. Now use the "next iteration (user-guided)" option and successively select the entering variables as 1, 2, 6, 7, 8, and 12 corresponding to x_{11}, x_{12}, x_{22}, x_{23}, x_{24}, and x_{34}, respectively. The leaving variable in each case is selected using the default choice. You will discover at the end that the objective row yields the same values of $\bar{c}_{pq}$ given above. The drill demonstrates that computations using the multipliers u_i and v_j produce the same results as the simplex method.

C. Determination of Leaving Variable (Loop Construction)

This step is equivalent to applying the feasibility condition in the simplex method. However, since all the constraint coefficients in the original transportation model are either zero or 1, the (positive) ratios of the feasibility condition will always have their denominator equal to 1. Thus the values of the basic variables will give the associated ratios directly.

For the purpose of determining the minimum ratio, we construct a *closed loop* for the current entering variable (x_{31} in the current iteration). The loop starts and ends at the designated nonbasic variable. It consists of *successive* horizontal and vertical (connected) segments whose end points must be basic variables, except for the end points that are associated with the entering variable. This means that every corner element of the loop must be a cell containing a basic variable. Table 6-10 illustrates a loop for the entering variable x_{31} given the basic solution in Table 6-8. This loop may be defined in terms of the basic variables as $x_{31} \rightarrow x_{11} \rightarrow x_{12} \rightarrow x_{22} \rightarrow x_{24} \rightarrow x_{34} \rightarrow x_{31}$. *It is immaterial whether the loop is traced in a clockwise or counterclockwise direction.* Observe that for a given basic solutions, only *one unique* loop can be constructed for each nonbasic variable.

We can see from Table 6-10 that if x_{31} (the entering variable) is increased by one unit, then, to maintain the feasibility of the solution, the *corner* basic variables of the x_{31}-loop must be adjusted as follows. Decrease x_{11} by one unit, increase x_{12} by one unit, decrease x_{22} by one unit, increase x_{24} by one unit, and finally decrease x_{34} by one unit. This process is summarized by plus ⊕ and minus ⊖ signs in the appropriate corners in Table 6-10. The change will keep the supply and demand restrictions satisfied.

The leaving variable is selected from among the corner variables of the loop that will decrease when the entering variable x_{31} increases above zero level. These are indicated in Table 6-10 by the variables in the squares labeled by minus signs ⊖. From Table 6-10, x_{11}, x_{22}, and x_{34} are the basic variables that will decrease when x_{31} increases. The leaving variable is then selected as the one having the *smallest* value, since it will be the first to reach zero value and any further decrease will cause

Table 6-10

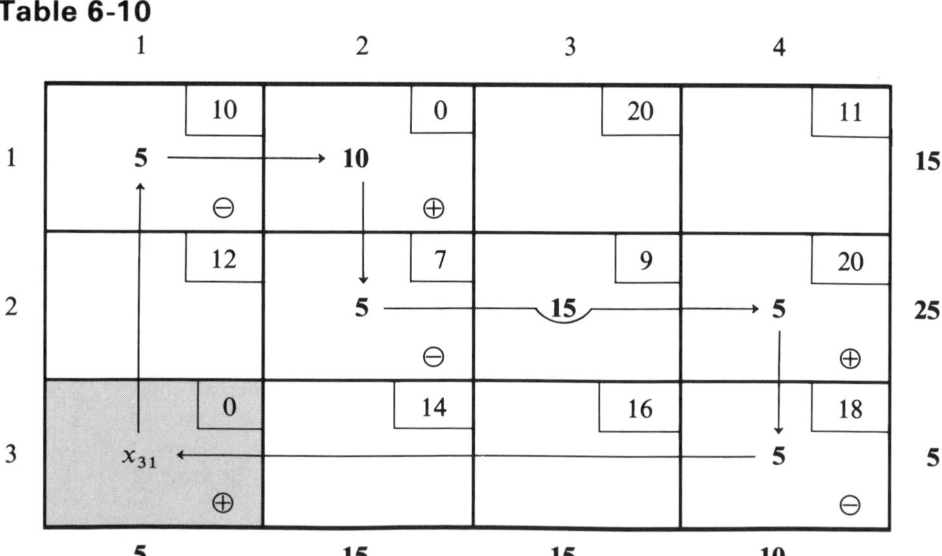

	1	2	3	4	
1	[10] 5 ⊖	[0] 10 ⊕	[20]	[11]	15
2	[12]	[7] 5 ⊖	[9] 15	[20] 5 ⊕	25
3	[0] x_{31} ⊕	[14]	[16]	[18] 5 ⊖	5
	5	15	15	10	

Table 6-11

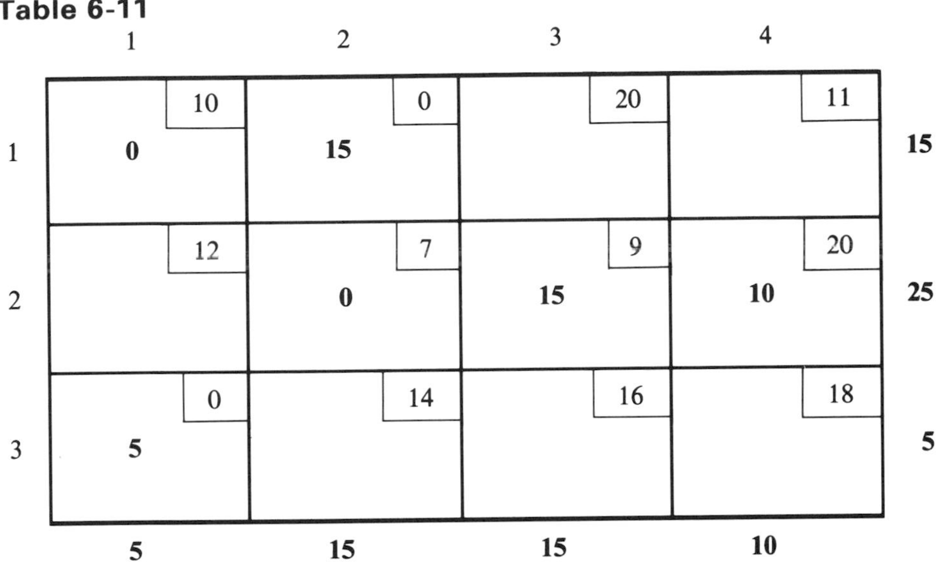

	1	2	3	4	
1	10 **0**	0 **15**	20	11	**15**
2	12	7 **0**	9 **15**	20 **10**	**25**
3	0 **5**	14	16	18	**5**
	5	**15**	**15**	**10**	

it to be negative (compare the feasibility condition of the simplex method where the leaving variable is associated with the minimum ratio). In this example the three ⊖-variables x_{11}, x_{22}, and x_{34} have the same value (= 5), in which case any *one* of them can be selected as a leaving variable. Suppose that x_{34} is taken as the leaving variable, then the value of x_{31} is increased to 5 and the values of the *corner* (basic) variables are adjusted accordingly (i.e., each is increased or decreased by 5, depending on whether it has ⊕ or ⊖ associated with it). The new solution is summarized as shown in Table 6-11. Its new cost is $0 \times 10 + 15 \times 0 + 0 \times 7 + 15 \times 9 + 10 \times 20 + 5 \times 10 = \$335$. This cost differs from the one associated with the starting solution in Table 6-8 by $410 - 335 = \$75$, which is equal to the number of units assigned to x_{31} (= 5) multiplied by $\bar{c}_{31}$ (= \$15).

The basic solution in Table 6-11 is degenerate, since the basic variables x_{11} and x_{22} are zero. Degeneracy, however, needs no special provisions, and the zero basic variables are treated as any other positive basic variables.

The new basic solution in Table 6-11 is now checked for optimality by computing the *new* multipliers as shown in Table 6-12. The values of $\bar{c}_{pq}$ are given by the numbers in the *southwest* corner of each nonbasic cell. The nonbasic variable x_{21} with the largest positive $\bar{c}_{pq}$ thus enters the solution. The closed loop associated with x_{21} shows that either x_{11} or x_{22} can be the leaving variable. We arbitrarily select x_{11} to leave the solution.

Exercise 6.2-1

Verify the values of u_i, v_j, and $\bar{c}_{pq}$ in Table 6-12.

Table 6-13 shows the new basic solution that follows from Table 6-12 (x_{21} enters and x_{11} leaves). The new values of u_i, v_j, and $\bar{c}_{pq}$ are computed anew. Table 6-13 gives the entering and leaving variables as x_{14} and x_{24}, respectively. By effecting this change in Table 6-13, we obtain the new solution in Table 6-14. Since all the $\bar{c}_{pq}$ in Table 6-14 are *nonpositive*, the optimum solution has been attained (compare with the minimization optimality condition of the simplex method).

The optimal solution is summarized as follows. Ship 5 units from (source) 1 to (destination) 2 at $5 \times 0 = \$0$, 10 units from 1 to 4 at $10 \times 11 = \$110$, 10 units from

Table 6-12

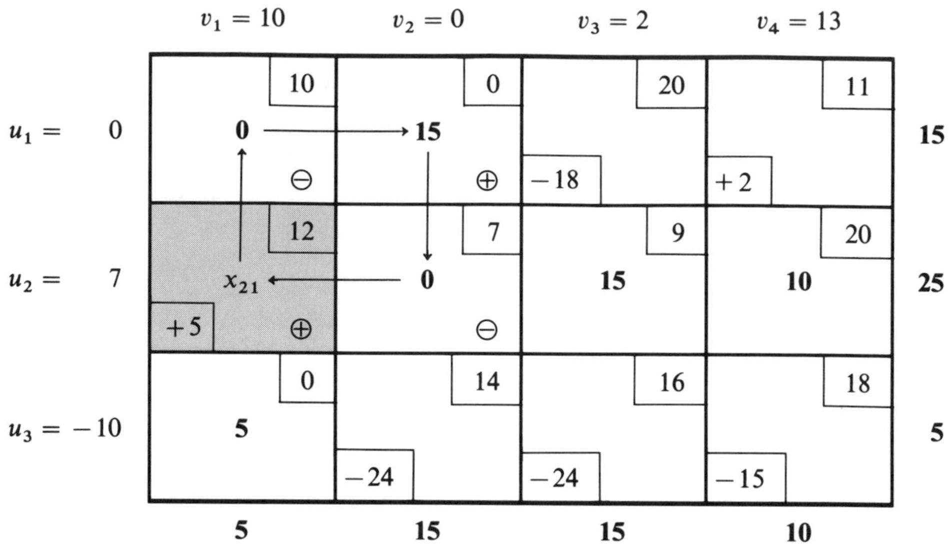

	$v_1 = 10$	$v_2 = 0$	$v_3 = 2$	$v_4 = 13$	
$u_1 = 0$	10; **0** ⊖	0; **15** ⊕	20; −18	11; +2	**15**
$u_2 = 7$	12; x_{21} ⊕; +5	7; **0** ⊖	9; **15**	20; **10**	**25**
$u_3 = -10$	0; **5**	14; −24	16; −24	18; −15	**5**
	5	**15**	**15**	**10**	

Table 6-13

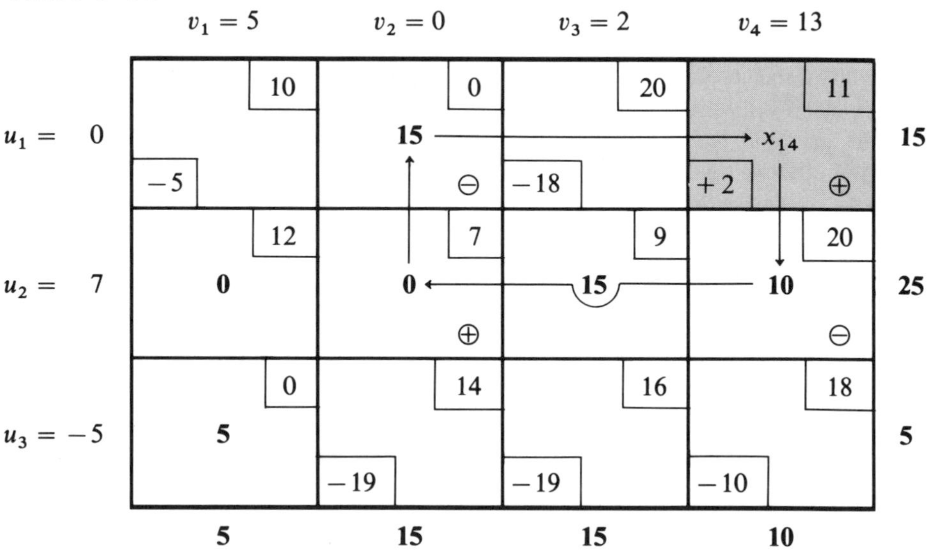

	$v_1 = 5$	$v_2 = 0$	$v_3 = 2$	$v_4 = 13$	
$u_1 = 0$	10; −5	0; **15** ⊖	20; −18	11; x_{14} ⊕; +2	**15**
$u_2 = 7$	12; **0**	7; **0** ⊕	9; **15**	20; **10** ⊖	**25**
$u_3 = -5$	0; **5**	14; −19	16; −19	18; −10	**5**
	5	**15**	**15**	**10**	

2 to 2 at 10 × 7 = \$70, 15 units from 2 to 3 at 15 × 9 = \$135, and 5 units from 3 to 1 at 5 × 0 = \$0. The total transportation cost of the schedule is \$315.

Exercise 6.2-2

Consider the transportation problem discussed above.

(a) Compute the improvements (decreases) in the value of the objective function in each of the following cases by using the values of $\bar{c}_{pq}$ directly.

(1) Solution moves from Table 6-10 to Table 6-11.
[*Ans.* 5 × 15 = \$75.]

(2) Solution moves from Table 6-12 to Table 6-13.
[*Ans.* 0 × 5 = \$0.]

Table 6-14

	$v_1 = 5$	$v_2 = 0$	$v_3 = 2$	$v_4 = 11$	
$u_1 = 0$	10 / −5	0 / **5**	20 / −18	11 / **10**	**15**
$u_2 = 7$	12 / **0**	7 / **10**	9 / **15**	20 / −2	**25**
$u_3 = -5$	0 / **5**	14 / −19	16 / −19	18 / −12	**5**
	5	**15**	**15**	**10**	

(3) Solution moves from Table 6-13 to Table 6-14.
[*Ans.* $10 \times 2 = \$20$.]

(b) In Table 6-12, determine the change (increase or decrease) in the value of the objective function when each of the following nonbasic variables is forced to enter the basic solution.

(1) x_{13}. [*Ans.* +\$270.]
(2) x_{14}. [*Ans.* −\$20.]
(3) x_{32}. [*Ans.* +\$120.]
(4) x_{33}. [*Ans.* +\$120.]
(5) x_{34}. [*Ans.* \$75.]

Computer Drill

(a) Modify the unit transportation cost in column 1 (destination D1) of Table 6-7 by adding the amount 10 to each unit cost in that column. Solve the new problem by TORA and observe that the optimum transportation schedule remains unchanged except for the value of z, which increases by $5 \times 10 = 50$.

(b) Repeat part (a), this time adding the amount 10 to the unit costs of *all* the routes. The optimum transportation schedule will also remain unchanged, but the value of z will increase by $45 \times 10 = 450$.

D. Explanation of the Method of Multipliers As a Simplex Method†

The relationship between the method of multipliers and the simplex method can be established by showing that $\bar{c}_{pq}$, as defined, directly equals the coefficients of the objective equation in the simplex tableau associated with the current iteration. We have seen from the primal–dual computations in Section 5.2 that, given the dual

† The remainder of this section assumes knowledge of duality theory (Chapter 5). It may be skipped without loss of continuity.

Table 6-15

		Source 1 Variables			Source 2 Variables			
	z	x_{11}	x_{12}	x_{13}	x_{21}	x_{22}	x_{13}	R.H.S.
Objective equation	1	$-c_{11}$	$-c_{12}$	$-c_{13}$	$-c_{21}$	$-c_{22}$	$-c_{23}$	0
Sources constraints	0	1	1	1				a_1
	0				1	1	1	a_2
Destinations constraints	0	1			1			b_1
	0		1			1		b_2
	0			1			1	b_3

values of the current iteration, the objective equation coefficients are obtained by taking the difference between the left and right sides of the dual constraints. This relationship will be used to show that the multipliers method is essentially equivalent to the simplex method. Indeed, the multipliers u_i and v_j are nothing but the dual variables.

To show how the general dual problem is obtained for the transportation model, consider first the special case of $m = 2$ and $n = 3$ given in Table 6-15. Let the dual variables be u_1 and u_2 for the sources constraints and v_1, v_2, and v_3 for the destinations constraints. The dual problem becomes (see Section 5.1)

$$\text{maximize } w = (a_1u_1 + a_2u_2) + (b_1v_1 + b_2v_2 + b_3v_3)$$

subject to

$$\begin{aligned}
u_1 \quad + v_1 \qquad\qquad &\le c_{11} \\
u_1 \qquad\quad + v_2 \qquad &\le c_{12} \\
u_1 \qquad\qquad\quad + v_3 &\le c_{13} \\
u_2 + v_1 \qquad\qquad &\le c_{21} \\
u_2 \qquad\quad + v_2 \qquad &\le c_{22} \\
u_2 \qquad\qquad\quad + v_3 &\le c_{23} \\
u_1, u_2, v_1, v_2, v_3 \text{ unrestricted} &
\end{aligned}$$

The special structure of the dual constraints results from the special arrangement of the "1" and "0" elements in the primal problem. Each constraint includes one u-variable and one v-variable only. Also, for each dual constraint, the subscripts of u and v match the double subscripts of the c-element. Thus, in general, if u_i and v_j are the dual variables corresponding to the constraints of the ith source and the jth destination ($i = 1, 2, \ldots, m; j = 1, 2, \ldots, n$) the corresponding dual problem is given by

$$\text{maximize } w = \sum_{i=1}^{m} a_i u_i + \sum_{j=1}^{n} b_j v_j$$

subject to

$$\begin{aligned}
u_i + v_j \le c_{ij}, \qquad &\text{for all } i \text{ and } j \\
u_i \text{ and } v_j &\text{ unrestricted}
\end{aligned}$$

According to Section 5.2, the objective equation coefficients (and hence the evaluation of the nonbasic variables) are found by substituting the current values of the dual variables in the dual constraints and then taking the difference between its left- and right-hand sides. The values of the dual variables can be determined by observing that the dual constraints corresponding to a basic variable must be satisfied as strict equations; that is,

$$u_i + v_j = c_{ij}, \qquad \text{for every } \textit{basic} \text{ variable } x_{ij}$$

which gives $m + n - 1$ equations. Therefore, by assuming an arbitrary value for u_1 ($= 0$), the remaining multipliers can be determined.

The coefficient of nonbasic variable x_{pq} in the objective equation is now given by the difference between the left- and right-hand sides of the corresponding dual constraint, that is, $u_p + v_q - c_{pq}$. Since the transportation problem is a *minimization* problem, the entering variable is the one with the largest *positive* $u_p + v_q - c_{pq}$.

The relationship between the method of multipliers and simplex methods should be clear now. Indeed, at the optimum iteration the multipliers give the *optimal* dual values directly. From Section 5.2, these values should yield the same optimum objective value in the primal and dual. The simplex multipliers associated with the *optimal* solution in Table 6-14 are $u_1 = 0$, $u_2 = 7$, $u_3 = -5$, $v_1 = 5$, $v_2 = 0$, $v_3 = 2$, and $v_4 = 11$. The corresponding value of the dual objective function is

$$\begin{aligned}\sum_{i=1}^{3} a_i u_i + \sum_{j=1}^{4} b_j v_j &= (15 \times 0 + 25 \times 7 + 5 \times -5) \\ &\quad + (5 \times 5 + 15 \times 0 + 15 \times 2 + 10 \times 11) \\ &= 315\end{aligned}$$

which is the same as in the primal.

In the foregoing discussion, an arbitrary value is assigned to one of the dual variables (e.g., $u_1 = 0$), which indicates that the simplex multipliers associated with a given basic solution are not unique. This may appear inconsistent with the results in Chapter 5, where the dual values must be unique. Problem 6–41 resolves this apparent paradox and shows that there is actually no inconsistency.

6.2.2 IMPROVED STARTING SOLUTION

The northwest-corner method presented in Section 6.2.1 does not necessarily produce a "good" starting solution for the transportation model. In this section we present two procedures that determine the starting solution by selecting "cheap" routes of the model.

A. The Least-Cost Method

The procedure is as follows. Assign as much as possible to the variable with the smallest *unit* cost in the entire tableau. (Ties are broken arbitrarily.) Cross out the satisfied row or column. (As in the *northwest-corner* method, if both a column and a row are satisfied simultaneously, only one may be crossed out.) After adjusting the supply and demand for all *un*crossed-out rows and columns, repeat the process by

Table 6-16

	1	2	3	4	
1	(10) **0**	(0) **15**	(20)	(11) **0**	**15**
2	(12)	(7)	(9) **15**	(20) **10**	**25**
3	(0) **5**	(14)	(16)	(18)	**5**
	5	**15**	**15**	**10**	

assigning as much as possible to the variable with the smallest uncrossed-out unit cost. The procedure is complete when exactly one row *or* one column remains uncrossed out.

The transportation problem in Table 6-7 is used again to illustrate the application of the least-cost method. Table 6-16 gives the resulting starting solution. The steps of the solution are as follows; x_{12} and x_{31} are the variables associated with the smallest unit costs ($c_{12} = c_{31} = 0$). Breaking the tie arbitrarily, select x_{12}. The associated supply and demand units give $x_{12} = 15$, which satisfies both row 1 and column 2. By crossing out column 2, the supply left in row 1 is zero. Next, x_{31} has the smallest uncrossed-out unit cost. Thus $x_{31} = 5$ satisfies both row 3 and column 1. By crossing out row 3, the demand in column 1 is zero. The smallest uncrossed-out element is $c_{23} = 9$. The supply and demand units give $x_{23} = 15$, which crosses out column 3 and leaves 10 units of supply in row 2. The smallest uncrossed-out element is $c_{11} = 10$. Since the remaining supply in row 1 and the remaining demand in column 1 are both zero, $x_{11} = 0$. By crossing out column 1, the supply "left" in row 1 is zero. The remaining basic variables are obtained, respectively, as $x_{14} = 0$ and $x_{24} = 10$. Then the total cost that is associated with this solution is $0 \times 10 + 15 \times 0 + 0 \times 11 + 15 \times 9 + 10 \times 20 + 5 \times 0 = \$335$, which is better (smaller) than the one provided by the northwest-corner method.

Exercise 6.2-3

Rework this problem assuming that the least-cost method starts with an assignment to x_{31} instead of x_{12} (both c_{31} and c_{12} equal zero), and compare the resulting starting solution with the one given.

[*Ans.* The positive variables are the same. The only difference occurs in the assignment of the zero variables. This is not a general result, however.]

B. Vogel's Approximation Method (VAM)

This method is a heuristic and usually provides a better starting solution than the northwest or the least-cost methods. In fact, VAM generally yields an optimum, or close to optimum, starting solution.

The steps of the procedure are as follows.

Step 1: Evaluate a penalty for each row (column) by subtracting the *smallest* cost element in the row (column) from the *next smallest* cost element in the same row (column).

Step 2: Identify the row or column with the largest penalty, breaking ties arbitrarily. Allocate as much as possible to the variable with the least cost in the selected row or column. Adjust the supply and demand and cross out the satisfied row *or* column. If a row and a column are satisfied simultaneously, only one of them is crossed out and the remaining row (column) is assigned a zero supply (demand). *Any row or column with zero supply or demand should not be used in computing future penalties (in step 3).*

Step 3

(a) If exactly one row or one column remains uncrossed out, stop.

(b) If only one (column) with *positive* supply (demand) remains uncrossed out, determine the basic variables in the row (column) by the least-cost method.

(c) If all uncrossed-out rows and columns have (assigned) zero supply and demand, determine the *zero* basic variables by the least-cost method. Stop.

(d) Otherwise, recompute the penalties for the uncrossed-out rows and columns, then go to step 2. (Notice that the rows and columns with assigned zero supply and demand should not be used in computing these penalties.)

We apply VAM to the problem in Table 6-7. Table 6-17 shows the first set of row and column penalties. Since row 3 has the largest penalty (= 14) and since $c_{31} = 0$ is the least unit cost in the same row, the quantity 5 is assigned to x_{31}. Row 3 and column 1 are satisfied simultaneously. Assume that column 1 is crossed out. The remaining supply for row 3 is zero.

Table 6-17

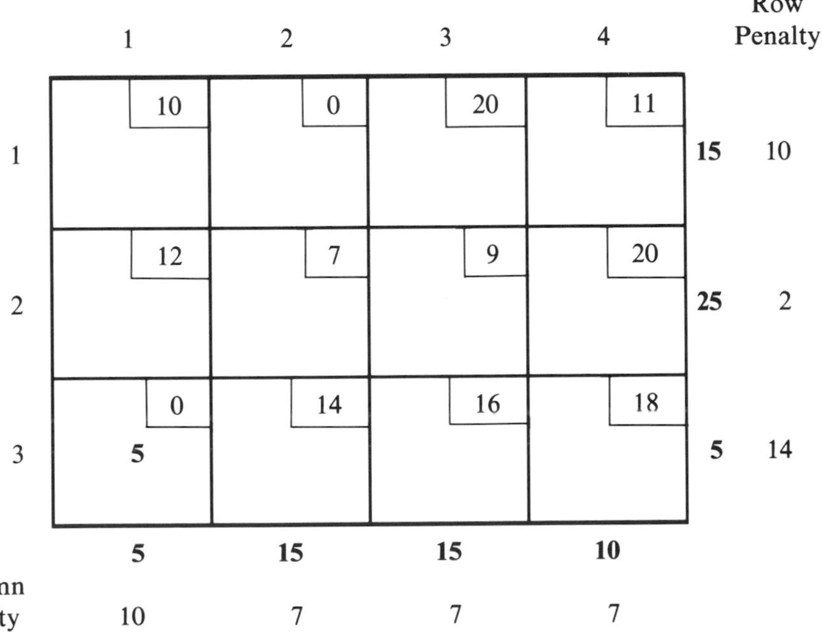

	1	2	3	4		Row Penalty
1	10	0	20	11	**15**	10
2	12	7	9	20	**25**	2
3	0 / **5**	14	16	18	**5**	14
	5	**15**	**15**	**10**		
Column Penalty	10	7	7	7		

Table 6-18

	1	2	3	4		Row Penalty
1	10	0	20	11	15	11
2	12	7	9 **15**	20	**25 10**	2
3	0 **5**				**5 0**	—
	5	**15**	**15**	**10**		
Column Penalty	—	7	11	9		

Table 6-18 shows the new set of penalties after crossing out column 1 in Table 6-17. (Notice that row 3 with zero supply is not used in computing the penalties.) Row 1 and column 3 have the same penalties. By selecting column 3 arbitrarily, the amount 15 is assigned to x_{23}, which crosses out column 3 and adjusts the supply in row 2 to 10.

Successive applications of VAM yield $x_{22} = 10$ (cross out row 2), $x_{12} = 5$ (cross out column 2), $x_{14} = 10$ (cross out row 1), and $x_{34} = 0$. (Verify.) The cost of the program is $315, which happens to be optimal.

The given version of VAM breaks ties between penalties arbitrarily. However, breaking of ties may be crucial in rendering a good starting solution. For example, in Table 6-18, if row 1 is selected instead of column 3, a worse starting solution results. (Verify that this solution is $x_{12} = 15$, $x_{23} = 15$, $x_{24} = 10$, $x_{31} = 5$, which will yield a total cost of $335.) The complete VAM procedure provides details for breaking some of these ties advantageously. (See N. Reinfeld and W. Vogel, *Mathematical Programming*, Prentice Hall, Englewood Cliffs, N.J., 1958.)

Exercise 6.2-4

Rework the problem by VAM after replacing the value of c_{12} by 2 (instead of zero). For the purpose of this problem, when a column and a row are satisfied simultaneously, always cross out the row.

[*Ans.* The successive assignments are $x_{31} = 5$, $x_{23} = 15$, $x_{22} = 10$, $x_{14} = 10$, $x_{12} = 5$, and $x_{11} = 0$.]

6.3 THE ASSIGNMENT MODEL

Consider the situation of assigning m jobs (or workers) to n machines. A job i (= 1, 2, ..., m) when assigned to machine j (= 1, 2, ..., n) incurs a cost c_{ij}. The objective is

Table 6-19

		Machine				
		1	2	...	n	
Job	1	c_{11}	c_{12}	...	c_{1n}	**1**
	2	c_{21}	c_{22}	...	c_{2n}	**1**
	⋮	⋮	⋮		⋮	⋮
	m	c_{m1}	c_{m2}	...	c_{mn}	**1**
		1	**1**	...	**1**	

to assign the jobs to the machines (one job per machine) at the least total cost. The situation is known as the **assignment problem**.

The formulation of this problem may be regarded as a special case of the transportation model. Here jobs represent "sources" and machines represent "destinations." The supply available at each source is 1; that is, $a_i = 1$ for all i. Similarly, the demand required at each destination is 1; that is, $b_j = 1$ for all j. The cost of "transporting" (assigning) job i to machine j is c_{ij}. If a job cannot be assigned to a certain machine, the corresponding c_{ij} is taken equal to M, a very high cost. Table 6-19 gives a general representation of the assignment model.

Before the model can be solved by the transportation technique, it is necessary to balance the problem by adding fictitious jobs or machines, depending on whether $m < n$ or $m > n$. It will thus be assumed that $m = n$ without loss of generality.

The assignment model can be expressed mathematically as follows. Let

$$x_{ij} = \begin{cases} 0, & \text{if the } i\text{th job is } \textit{not} \text{ assigned to the } j\text{th machine} \\ 1, & \text{if the } i\text{th job is assigned to the } j\text{th machine} \end{cases}$$

The model is thus given by

$$\text{minimize } z = \sum_{i=1}^{n} \sum_{j=1}^{n} c_{ij} x_{ij}$$

subject to

$$\sum_{j=1}^{n} x_{ij} = 1, \qquad i = 1, 2, \ldots, n$$

$$\sum_{i=1}^{n} x_{ij} = 1, \qquad j = 1, 2, \ldots, n$$

$$x_{ij} = 0 \quad \text{or} \quad 1$$

To illustrate the assignment model, consider the problem in Table 6-20 with three jobs and three machines. The initial solution (using the northwest-corner rule) is degenerate. This will always be the case in the assignment model regardless of the method used to obtain the starting basis. In fact, the solution will continue to be degenerate at every iteration.

The special structure of the assignment model allows the development of an efficient solution technique called the **Hungarian method**. This method will be illustrated by the example just presented.

Table 6-20

		Machine 1	Machine 2	Machine 3	
Job	1	1 (5)	(7)	(9)	1
	2	(14)	1 (10)	(12)	1
	3	(15)	(13)	1 (16)	1
		1	1	1	

The optimal solution of the assignment model remains the same if a constant is added or subtracted to any row or column of the cost matrix. This is proved as follows. If p_i and q_j are subtracted from the ith row and the jth column, the new cost elements become $c'_{ij} = c_{ij} - p_i - q_j$. This yields the new objective function

$$z' = \sum_i \sum_j c'_{ij} x_{ij} = \sum_i \sum_j (c_{ij} - p_i - q_j) x_{ij}$$
$$= \sum_i \sum_j c_{ij} x_{ij} - \sum_i p_i \sum_j x_{ij} - \sum_j q_j \sum_i x_{ij}$$

Since $\sum_j x_{ij} = \sum_i x_{ij} = 1$, we get $z' = z -$ constant. This shows that the minimization of the original objective function z yields the same solution as the minimization of z'.

This idea indicates that if one can create a new c'_{ij}-matrix with zero entries, and if these zero elements or a subset thereof constitute a feasible solution, this feasible solution is optimal, because the cost cannot be negative.

In Table 6-20 the zero elements are created by subtracting the smallest element in each row (column) from the corresponding row (column). If one considers the rows first, the new c'_{ij}-matrix is shown in Table 6-21.

The last matrix can be made to include more zeros by subtracting $q_3 = 2$ from the third column. This yields Table 6-22.

The squares in Table 6-22 give the feasible (and hence optimal) assignment (1, 1), (2, 3), and (3, 2), costing 5 + 12 + 13 = 30. Notice that this cost is equal to $p_1 + p_2 + p_3 + q_3$.

Table 6-21

		1	2	3	
$\lVert c'_{ij} \rVert =$	1	0	2	4	$p_1 = 5$
	2	4	0	2	$p_2 = 10$
	3	2	0	3	$p_3 = 13$

Table 6-22

$\|c'_{ij}\| =$	1	2	3
1	[0]	2	2
2	4	0	[0]
3	2	[0]	1

Table 6-23

	1	2	3	4
1	1	4	6	3
2	9	7	10	9
3	4	5	11	7
4	8	7	8	5

Unfortunately, it is not always possible to obtain a feasible assignment as in the example. Further rules are thus required to find the optimal solution. These rules are illustrated by the example shown in Table 6-23.

Now, carrying out the same initial steps as in the previous example, one gets Table 6-24.

A feasible assignment to the zero elements is not possible in this case. The procedure then is to draw a *minimum* number of lines through some of the rows and columns such that all the zeros are crossed out. Table 6-25 shows the application of this rule.

The next step is to select the *smallest* uncrossed-out element (= 1 in Table 6-25). This element is subtracted from every *un*crossed-out element and added to every element at the intersection of two lines. This yields Table 6-26, which gives the optimal assignment (1, 1), (2, 3), (3, 2), and (4, 4). The corresponding total cost is $1 + 10 + 5 + 5 = 21$.

Table 6-24

	1	2	3	4
1	0	3	2	2
2	2	0	0	2
3	0	1	4	3
4	3	2	0	0

Table 6-25

	1	2	3	4
1	0	3	2	2
2	2	0	0	2
3	0	1	4	3
4	3	2	0	0

(Lines drawn through column 1 and rows 2 and 4.)

Table 6-26

	1	2	3	4
1	[0]	2	1	1
2	3	0	[0]	2
3	0	[0]	3	2
4	4	2	0	[0]

It should be noted that if the optimal solution was not obtained in the preceding step, the given procedure of drawing lines should be repeated umtil a feasible assignment is achieved.

Computer Drill

Apply the transportation technique to the problem in Table 6-23 and show that it yields the same solution. Hence conclude that the assignment model can be solved directly by the transportation technique.

Explanation of the Hungarian Algorithm As a Simplex Method†

The motivation for the Hungarian method can be explained in terms of the simplex method. As in the transportation method, the dual of the assignment model is given as

$$\text{maximize } w = \sum_{i=1}^{n} u_i + \sum_{i=1}^{n} v_j$$

subject to

$$u_i + v_j \leq c_{ij}, \qquad i, j = 1, 2, \ldots, n$$

$$u_i, v_j \text{ unrestricted}, \qquad i, j = 1, 2, \ldots, n$$

An obvious feasible dual solution is given by

$$p_i = \min_{j=1,2,\ldots,n} \{c_{ij}\}, \qquad i = 1, 2, \ldots, n$$

$$q_j = \min_{i=1,2,\ldots,n} \{c_{ij} - p_i\}, \qquad j = 1, 2, \ldots, n$$

What this solution says is that p_i is the smallest value in row i and q_j is the smallest value in column j after p_i has been subtracted from the successive row. In essence, the dual values p_i and q_j are computed as illustrated in Tables 6-21 and 6-22.

If $p_i + q_j = c_{ij}$ (or equivalently, $p_i + q_j - c_{ij} = 0$), then according to the simplex method theory (Section 5.2) the objective coefficient of x_{ij} in the corresponding simplex tableau is a candidate for being an optimal basic variable. Actually, the result is also evident by the complementary slackness theorem (Section 5.4), which states that optimal u_i, v_j, and x_{ij} must satisfy

$$(u_i + v_j - c_{ij})x_{ij} = 0, \qquad i, j = 1, 2, \ldots, n$$

---

† This material may be skipped without loss of continuity.

It then follows that if after subtracting p_i and q_j (as we did in Tables 6-21 and 6-22) the resulting entries having $p_i + q_j - c_{ij} = 0$ yield a feasible assignment, we have the optimal solution.

If the process of determining p_i and q_j does not result in a feasible assignment, it would be necessary to seek a different set of dual values that continue to satisfy the complementary slackness theorem and yet provide a feasible assignment. Such is achieved by using the proposed procedure of covering all the zero elements with a minimum number of lines. We shall not provide the details of this (somewhat involved) proof which, generally, is a variation of the application of the complementary slackness theorem.

6.4 THE TRANSSHIPMENT MODEL

The standard transportation model assumes that the *direct* route between a source and a destination is a *minimum-cost* route. Thus, in Example 6.1-1, the mileage table from the three plants to the two distribution centers gives the *shortest routes* between the sources and destinations. This means that preparatory calculations involving the determination of the shortest routes must be carried out before the unit costs of the standard transportation model can be determined. These calculations can be carried out by applying the *shortest-route algorithm* (see Section 7.2) to desired pairs of nodes.

An alternative procedure to the use of the regular transportation model (with embedded shortest-route algorithm) is the so-called **transshipment model**. The new model has the added feature of allowing the transported units from *all* sources to potentially pass through intermediate or *transient* nodes before ultimately reaching their designated destinations. In effect, the new algorithm combines both the regular transportation algorithm and the shortest route algorithm into one procedure. We illustrate the new method by means of an example.

Figure 6-4 represents two automobile plants, two distribution centers, and three dealers. The supply amounts at the two plants, nodes 1 and 2, are 1000 and 1200, respectively. Cars are shipped to dealers 5, 6, and 7 through distribution centers 3 and 4. The demands at the three dealers are 800, 900, and 300, respectively. In terms of the arc connections in Figure 6-4, nodes 1 and 2 are characterized by outgoing arcs only, whereas node 7 is characterized by incoming arcs only. All the remaining

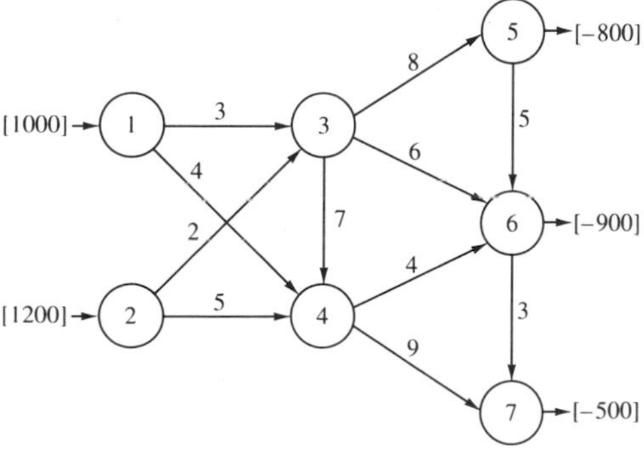

Figure 6-4

Table 6-27

	x_{13}	x_{14}	x_{23}	x_{24}	x_{34}	x_{35}	x_{36}	x_{46}	x_{47}	x_{56}	x_{67}	
	3	4	2	5	7	8	6	4	9	5	3	min
node 1	1	1										= 1000
node 2			1	1								= 1200
node 3	−1		−1		1	1	1					= 0
node 4		−1		−1	−1			1	1			= 0
node 5						−1				1		= −800
node 6							−1	−1		−1	1	= −900
node 7									−1		−1	= −500

nodes have both incoming and outgoing arcs. In this respect, nodes 1 and 2 are *pure supply* points and node 7 is a *pure demand* point. All the remaining nodes are *transshipment* nodes because, conceivably, the entire supply amount $(= 1000 + 1200 = 2200)$ could pass through any of these nodes before eventually reaching its designated destinations.

Having defined what we mean by transshipping, we now show how the model is constructed. First, we express the model as a regular linear program and then show how the formulation is converted equivalently into a transportation model. Let x_{ij} be the amount shipped from node i to node j; then the LP model is given as shown in Table 6-27.

Each constraint in the formulation above is associated with a node. The constraint equation simply represents the conservation of flow in and out of the node: namely,

$$\text{total sum of input flow} = \text{total sum of output flow}$$

Actually, the equations in Table 6-27 correspond directly to

$$\text{total sum of output flow} - \text{total sum of input flow} = 0$$

In this manner the right-hand side of each equation becomes positive for supply nodes 1 and 2 and negative for demand nodes 5, 6, and 7. Otherwise, all other equations will have a zero right-hand side, as shown above.

Observe the special arrangement of the $+1$ and -1 coefficients in Table 6-27. Each variable x_{ij} has a $+1$ in row i and -1 in row j. This special structure is typical of the problems that can be represented by the transshipment model, as we show below.

The transshipment LP model in Table 6-27 can be converted into the transportation model format as follows. The equations associated with nodes 1, 2, and 7 can be written in the following forms:

$$\begin{aligned}
\text{node 1:}&\quad x_{13} + x_{14} = 1000\\
\text{node 2:}&\quad x_{23} + x_{24} = 1200\\
\text{node 7:}&\quad x_{47} + x_{67} = \ \ 500
\end{aligned}$$

As for the remaining nodes (3, 4, 5, and 6), we rewrite each equation in the following manner:

$$\begin{aligned}
\text{node 3:}&\quad x_{34} + x_{35} + x_{36} = x_{13} + x_{23}\\
\text{node 4:}&\quad x_{46} + x_{47} = x_{14} + x_{24} + x_{34}
\end{aligned}$$

node 5: $x_{56} = x_{35} - 800$
node 6: $x_{67} = x_{36} + x_{46} + x_{56} - 900$

Next, we add a dummy nonnegative variable x_{ii} to each side of equation i, $i = 3, 4,$ 5, and 6. We thus get

$$\begin{aligned}
&\text{node 3:} \quad \mathbf{x}_{33} + x_{34} + x_{35} + x_{36} = \mathbf{x}_{33} + x_{13} + x_{23}\\
&\text{node 4:} \quad \mathbf{x}_{44} + x_{46} + x_{47} = \mathbf{x}_{44} + x_{14} + x_{24} + x_{34}\\
&\text{node 5:} \quad \mathbf{x}_{55} + x_{56} = \mathbf{x}_{55} + x_{35} - 800\\
&\text{node 6:} \quad \mathbf{x}_{66} + x_{67} = \mathbf{x}_{66} + x_{36} + x_{46} + x_{56} - 900
\end{aligned}$$

If we let B be a sufficiently large value, the equation above may then be replaced with

$$\begin{aligned}
&x_{33} + x_{34} + x_{35} + x_{36} = B\\
&x_{13} + x_{23} + x_{33} = B\\
&x_{44} + x_{46} + x_{47} = B\\
&x_{14} + x_{24} + x_{34} + x_{44} = B\\
&x_{55} + x_{56} = B\\
&x_{35} + x_{55} = 800 + B\\
&x_{66} + x_{67} = B\\
&x_{36} + x_{46} + x_{56} + x_{66} = 900 + B
\end{aligned}$$

We are able to use the same value B in all the equations correctly because the variables x_{ii}, $i = 3, 4, 5$, and 6, are arbitrary. Actually, if you regard x_{ii} as a slack variable and select B large enough so it will represent a nonrestrictive upper bound on each of the left-hand-side sums above, the equations above will be valid. In effect, we can safely estimate B as being at least equal to the sum of all the shipments that may possibly pass through any of the nodes in the network; that is,

$$B \geq 1000 + 1200 = 2200$$

The amount B is usually referred to as the **buffer**.

The last set of equations, together with those of nodes 1, 2, and 7, directly define the transportation model in Table 6-28 (verify!). The resulting model has the following properties:

1. Nodes 1 and 2 are "pure" supply points and hence appear only as source rows.
2. Node 7 is a "pure" demand point and hence appears only as a destination column.
3. All transshipping nodes (3, 4, 5, and 6) appear as both sources and demand points.
4. The amounts of supply and demand for all transshipping nodes are each inflated by the buffer amount B (≥ 2200).

The properties above actually represent the rules for the development of the transshipment tableau directly from a network similar to the one given in Figure 6-4.

Letting $B = 2200$ and using the cost values shown in Table 6-28, we obtain the optimal solution shown in Figure 6-5 using TORA. Distribution node 3 receives 1200 cars from plant node 2 and distribution node 4 receives 1000 cars from plant

Table 6-28

	3	4	5	6	7	
1	3 x_{13}	4 x_{14}	M	M	M	1000
2	2 x_{23}	5 x_{24}	M	M	M	1200
3	0 x_{33}	7 x_{34}	8 x_{35}	6 x_{36}	M	B
4	M	0 x_{44}	M	4 x_{46}	9 x_{47}	B
5	M	M	0 x_{55}	5 x_{56}	M	B
6	M	M	M	0 x_{66}	3 x_{67}	B
	B	B	$800 + B$	$900 + B$	500	

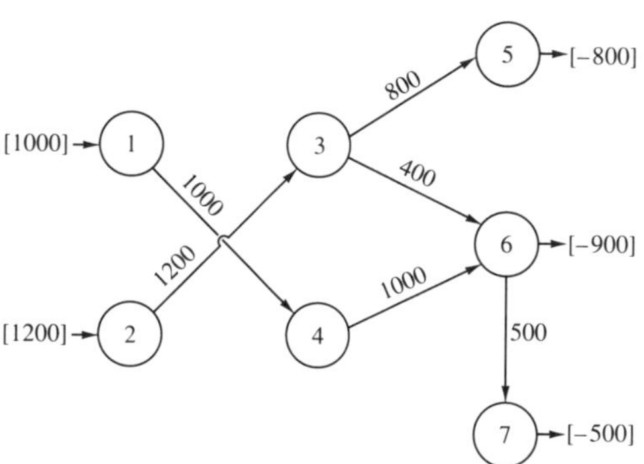

Figure 6-5

node 1. Of the 1200 cars received at node 3, 800 units are sent to fulfill the demand of dealer node 5 and 400 to dealer node 6. Dealer node 6 also receives 1000 cars from distribution node 4, keeps 900 cars for the local demand and sends the excess 500 cars to dealer node 7. Nodes 3, 4, and 6 in the figure demonstrate the concept of transshipping in the network.

Exercise 6.4-1

Modify the transshipment model in Figure 6-4 to account for the following change: Distribution center 3 has an extra supply of 20 cars and dealers 6 and 7 require 10 additional cars each.

[*Ans.* $B = 2220$, supply of row 3 in the transshipment tableau is $20 + B$, and demands in the columns of nodes 6 and 7 are $910 + B$ and 510, respectively.]

Exercise 6.4-2

Verify algebraically that based on the LP model in Table 6-27, the amounts of supply and demand in Table 6-28 may be equivalently changed as follows:

Node	1	2	3	4	5	6	7
Supply Units	1000	1200	B	B	$-800+B$	$-900+B$	—
Demand Units	—	—	B	B	B	B	500

We next show how a problem that initially appears unrelated to the transshipment model can be converted to that format through proper manipulation.

Example 6.4-1 (Employment Scheduling). An employment agency must provide the following semiskilled laborers over the next 5 months:

Month	1	2	3	4	5
Number of Laborers	100	120	80	170	50

Because of the fluctuation in demand, it may be more economical to keep more laborers than needed during some months of the planning horizon. The company estimates that the cost of recruiting and maintaining the laborers is a function of their length of stay with the agency. The following table summarizes these estimates:

Length of Employment Period (months)	1	2	3	4	5
Cost per Laborer (dollars)	100	130	180	220	250

We first formulate the problem as a linear program; then by using proper algebraic manipulations, we show that the resulting model is equivalent to a transshipment problem. Let x_{ij} be the number of laborers hired at the *start* of period i and terminated at the *start* of period j. For example, x_{12} is the number hired for one period at the start of month 1 and x_{36} is the number hired at the start of month 3 and terminated at the start of month 6 (or, equivalently, the end of month 5). Figure 6-6 defines the feasible arcs of the problem. Notice that node 6 is added to allow us to define the variables that terminate at the end of the planning horizon (end of

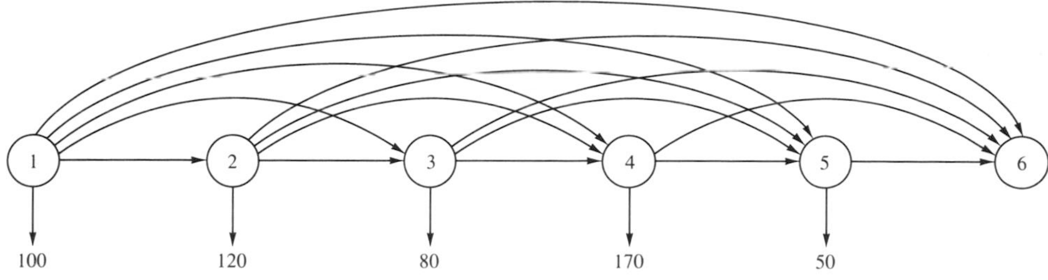

Figure 6-6

Table 6-29

	x_{12}	x_{13}	x_{14}	x_{15}	x_{16}	x_{23}	x_{24}	x_{25}	x_{26}	x_{34}	x_{35}	x_{36}	x_{45}	x_{46}	x_{56}	
	100	130	180	220	250	100	130	180	220	100	130	180	100	130	100	min
(1)	1	1	1	1	1											≥ 100
(2)		1	1	1	1	1	1	1	1							≥ 120
(3)			1	1	1		1	1	1	1	1	1				≥ 80
(4)				1	1			1	1		1	1	1	1		≥ 170
(5)					1				1			1		1	1	≥ 50

Table 6-30

x_{12}	x_{13}	x_{14}	x_{15}	x_{16}	x_{23}	x_{24}	x_{25}	x_{26}	x_{34}	x_{35}	x_{36}	x_{45}	x_{46}	x_{56}	S_1	S_2	S_3	S_4	S_5	
100	130	180	220	250	100	120	180	220	100	130	180	100	130	100						min
1	1	1	1	1											−1					100
	1	1	1	1	1	1	1	1								−1				120
		1	1	1		1	1	1	1	1	1						−1			80
			1	1			1	1		1	1	1	1					−1		170
				1				1			1		1	1					−1	50

month 5 or, equivalently, the beginning of fictitious month 6). The associated LP model is summarized in Table 6-29.

Let S_1, S_2, S_3, S_4, and S_5 be the surplus variables associated with constraints 1, 2, 3, 4, and 5 in Table 6-29. The problem will thus appear as shown in Table 6-30.

The last LP does not have the format of a transshipment model. However, the equations can be transformed readily to the transshipment format by carrying out the following algebraic manipulations:

Leave equation (1) unchanged.
Replace (2) with (2) − (1).
Replace (3) with (3) − (2).
Replace (4) with (4) − (3).
Replace (5) with (5) − (4).
Add a new equation that corresponds to −(5).

The resulting (equivalent) LP is shown in Table 6-31. Notice that the new formulation has the structure of a transshipment model (each column has exactly one "+1" and one "−1"; compare with the LP in Table 6-27).

If we replace S_1 with x_{21}, S_2 with x_{32}, S_3 with x_{43}, S_4 with x_{54}, and S_5 with x_{65}, the LP in Table 6-31 will directly translate into the transshipment model as shown in Table 6-32. The amount of the buffer B can be taken equal to the sum of all the

Table 6-31

x_{12}	x_{13}	x_{14}	x_{15}	x_{16}	x_{23}	x_{24}	x_{25}	x_{26}	x_{34}	x_{35}	x_{36}	x_{45}	x_{46}	x_{56}	S_1	S_2	S_3	S_4	S_5	
100	130	180	220	250	100	130	180	220	100	130	180	100	130	100						min
1	1	1	1	1											−1					100
−1					1	1	1	1							1	−1				20
	−1				−1				1	1	1					1	−1			−40
		−1				−1			−1			1	1				1	−1		90
			−1				−1			−1		−1		1				1	−1	−120
				−1				−1			−1		−1	−1					1	−50

Table 6-32

	1	2	3	4	5	6	
1	0	100	130	180	220	250	**100 + B**
2	0	0	100	130	180	220	**20 + B**
3	M	0	0	100	130	180	**B**
4	M	M	0	0	100	130	**90 + B**
5	M	M	M	0	0	100	**B**
6	M	M	M	M	0	0	**B**
	B	**B**	**40 + B**	**B**	**120 + B**	**50 + B**	

demands during the entire planning horizon, namely, $B = 520$. By using the procedure given at the start of this section to define the buffer B, the amounts of supply and demand of the model in Table 6-32 can be shown to be as follows (verify!):

Node	1	2	3	4	5	6
Supply Units	$100 + B$	$20 + B$	B	$90 + B$	B	B
Demand Units	B	B	$40 + B$	B	$120 + B$	$50 + B$

These values follow directly from the way the LP equations are defined. As such, the LP and the transshipment formulations must yield identical results (verify using TORA). ◀

Exercise 6.4-3

Verify algebraically that based on the LP model in Table 6-30, the amounts of supply and demand in Table 6-32 may be equivalently changed as follows:

Node	1	2	3	4	5	6
Supply Units	$100 + B$	$20 + B$	$-40 + B$	$90 + B$	$-120 + B$	$-50 + B$
Demand Units	B	B	B	B	B	B

The optimum solution of the problem is summarized graphically in Figure 6-7. It requires the following hiring and firing policy:

Hired at the Start of Period	Fired at the Start of Period	Number of Laborers
1	5	100
2	5	20
4	6	50

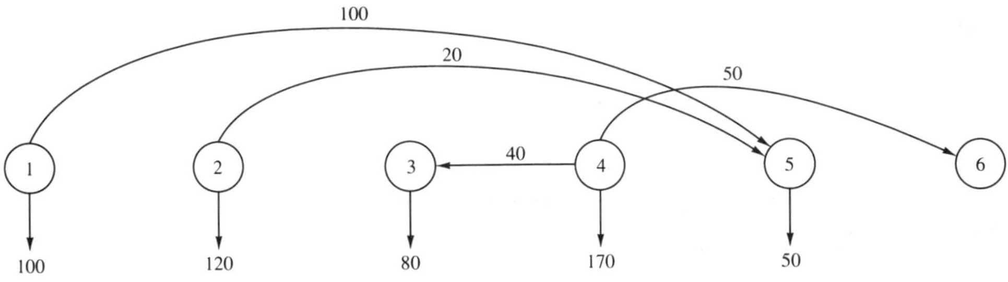

Figure 6-7

Notice that the solution gives $x_{43} = 40$. By definition, x_{43} is actually the surplus variable S_3 and its positive value indicates that for the given cost figures, it is more economical to retain an extra 40 laborers above the 80 laborers needed during period 3.

Exercise 6.4-4

Show how the solution in Figure 6-7 satisfies the demand requirements for the 5-month planning horizon.

6.5 SUMMARY

In the obvious sense, the transportation model deals with transporting goods among geographical locations. However, this chapter introduces applications that extend the utility of the model to other nonconventional areas, including the production-inventory model, the caterer problem, the assignment problem, and the employment scheduling problem.

The transportation model is a special LP whose special structure allows the development of an efficient computational technique for solving the problem. The technique is based directly on the use of duality theory in linear programming. Related models also include the assignment and the transshipment problems.

The transportation model and its variants are but one class of the generalized network models that will be covered in Chapter 8. In practice, network models appear to have tremendous success in solving real-life problems. Indeed, some recent surveys report that as much as 70% of the real-world mathematical programming problems may be treated as network or network-related problems.

SELECTED REFERENCES

BAZARAA, M., J. JARVIS, and H. SHERALI, *Linear Programming and Network Flows*, 2nd ed., Wiley, New York, 1990.

DANTZIG, G., *Linear Programming and Extensions*, Princeton University Press, Princeton, N.J., 1963.

ELMAGHRABY, S. E., *The Design of Production Systems*, Reinhold, New York, 1966, Chapter 4.

PHILLIPS, D., and A. GARCIA-DIAZ, *Fundamentals of Network Analysis*, Prentice Hall, Englewood Cliffs, N.J., 1981.

PROBLEMS

Section	Assigned Problems
6.1	6–1 to 6–11
6.2.1	6–12 to 6–22, 6–41, 6–42
6.2.2	6–23 to 6–25
6.3	6–26 to 6–32
6.4	6–33 to 6–40

☐ **6–1** Three electric power plants with capacities of 25, 40, and 30 million kilowatt hour (kWh) supply electricity to three cities whose maximum demands are estimated at 30, 35, and 25 million kWh. The costs in dollars of selling power to the different cities per million kWh are as follows:

		City		
		1	2	3
Plant	1	600	700	400
	2	320	300	350
	3	500	480	450

During the month of August, there is a 20% increase in demand at each of the three cities. To meet the excess demand, the power company must purchase additional electricity from another network at a premium flat price of $1000 per million kWh. This network, however, is not linked to city 3. Formulate the problem as a transportation problem for the purpose of establishing the most economical distribution plan from the standpoint of the power company. Solve with TORA and interpret the solution.

☐ **6–2** The National Parks Service is receiving bids for logging at three pine forest locations. The three locations include 10 thousand, 20 thousand, and 30 thousand acres. A single bidder can bid for at most 50% of the acreage in all locations. Four bidders have submitted their per acre bids in dollars for the three locations according to the following table.

		Location		
		1	2	3
Bidder	1	520	430	570
	2	—	510	495
	3	650	—	710
	4	180	210	240

How much acreage should be assigned to each bidder to maximize the total sum of revenue? Solve with TORA and interpet the solution.

☐ **6–3** Three refineries with maximum daily capacities of 6 million, 5 million, and 8 million gallons of gasoline supply three distribution areas with daily demands of 4 million, 8 million, and 7 million gallons. Gasoline is transported to the three distribution areas through a network of pipelines. The transportation cost is estimated based on the length of the pipeline at about 1 cent per 100 gallons per mile. The mileage table summarized here shows that refinery 1 is not connected to distribution area 3. Formulate the problem as a transportation model. Solve with TORA and interpret the solution.

		Distribution Area		
		1	2	3
Refinery	1	120	180	—
	2	300	100	80
	3	200	250	120

☐ **6–4** In Problem 6–3, suppose that the capacity of refinery 3 is reduced to 6 million gallons. Also, distribution area 1 must receive all its demand, and any shortage at areas 2 and 3 will result in a penalty of 5 cents per gallon. Formulate the problem as a transportation model. Solve with TORA and interpret the solution.

☐ **6–5** In Problem 6–3, suppose that the daily demand at area 3 drops to 4 million gallons. Any surplus production at refineries 1 and 2 must be diverted to other distribution areas by trucks. The resulting average transportation costs per 100 gallons are $1.50 from refinery 1 and $2.20 from refinery 2. Refinery 3 can divert its surplus gasoline to other chemical processes within the plant. Formulate the problem as a transportation model. Solve with TORA and interpret the solution.

☐ **6–6** Cars are shipped by truck from three distribution centers to five dealers. The shipping cost is based on the mileage between sources and destinations. This cost is independent of whether the truck makes the trip with a partial or a full load. The following table summarizes the mileage between the distribution centers and the dealers as well as the monthly supply and demand figures estimated in *number* of cars. Each truck can carry a maximum of 18 cars. Given that the transportation cost per truck mile is $10, formulate the problem as a transportation model. Solve with TORA and interpret the solution.

		Dealers					Supply
		1	2	3	4	5	
Distribution Centers	1	100	150	200	140	35	**400**
	2	50	70	60	65	80	**200**
	3	40	90	100	150	130	**150**
Demand		**100**	**200**	**150**	**160**	**140**	

☐ **6–7** The MG Company produces four different models, which we refer to for simplicity as M1, M2, M3, and M4. The Detroit plant produces models M1, M2, and M4. Models M1 and M2 only are produced in New Orleans. The Los Angeles plant manufactures models M3 and M4. The capacities of the various plants and the demands of the distribution centers are given here according to model type.

	Model				
	M1	M2	M3	M4	Totals
Plant					
Los Angeles	—	—	700	300	1000
Detroit	500	600	—	400	1500
New Orleans	800	400	—	—	1200
Distribution center					
Denver	700	500	500	600	2300
Miami	600	500	200	100	1400

The mileage chart is the same as given in Example 6.1-1. For simplicity, we assume that the transportation rate remains 8 cents per car per mile for all models. Suppose that it is possible to substitute a percentage of the demand for one model from the supply for another according to the following table:

Distribution Center	Percentage of Demand	Interchangeable Models
Denver	10	M1, M2
	20	M3, M4
Miami	10	M1, M3
	5	M2, M4

Formulate the problem as a transportation model. Solve using TORA and interpret the solution.

[*Hint*: Add four new destinations corresponding to the new combinations (M1, M2), (M3, M4), (M1, M3), and (M2, M4). The demands at the new destinations are determined from the given percentages.]

☐ **6–8** Consider the problem of assigning four different categories of machines and five types of tasks. The number of machines available in the four categories are 25, 30, 20, and 30. The number of jobs in the five tasks are 20, 20, 30, 10, and 25. Machine category 4 cannot be assigned to task type 4. For the unit costs given, formulate a mathematical model for determining the optimal assignment of machines to tasks. Solve using TORA and interpret the solution.

		Task Type				
		1	2	3	4	5
Machine Category	1	10	2	3	15	9
	2	5	10	15	2	4
	3	15	5	14	7	15
	4	20	15	13	—	8

☐ **6–9** The demand for a perishable item over the next 4 months is 500, 630, 200, and 230 tons, respectively. The supply capacities for the successive months of the planning period are 400, 300, 420, and 380 tons and the corresponding prices per ton are \$100, \$140, \$120, and \$150, respectively. Because the item is perishable, a current month's purchase must be totally consumed within 3 months (including the current month). It is estimated that the storage cost per ton per month is about \$3. Again, the nature of the item does not allow backordering. Formulate the problem as a transportation model. Solve using TORA and interpret the solution.

□ **6–10** The demand for a special small engine over the next five periods is 200, 150, 300, 250, and 400 units. The manufacturer supplying the engines has different production capacities estimated at 180, 230, 430, 300, and 300 units for the five periods. Backordering is not allowed, but the manufacturer may use overtime production to fill the demand, if necessary. Overtime capacity for each period is estimated at half the capacity of the regular production. The production costs per unit for the five periods are \$100, \$96, \$115, \$102, and \$105, respectively. The overtime cost per engine is 50% higher than the regular production cost. If an engine is produced now for use in later periods, there is an additional storage cost of \$4 per engine per period. Set up the problem as a transportation model. Use TORA to solve the model and then interpret the solution.

□ **6–11** Periodic preventive maintenance is carried out on aircraft engines where an important component must be replaced. The numbers of aircraft scheduled for such maintenance over the next 6 months are estimated at 200, 180, 300, 198, 230, and 290, respectively. All maintenance work is done during the first 2 days of the month. A used component may be replaced with a new or an overhauled component. The overhauling of used components may be done in the local repair facility, where they will be ready for use at the beginning of the next month, or may be sent to the central repair shop, where a delay of 4 months (including the month in which maintenance takes place) is expected. The repair cost in the local shop is \$120 per component. At the central facility, the cost is only \$35. An overhauled part that is not used in the same month in which it is received will incur an additional storage cost of \$1.50 per unit per month. New components may be purchased in the first month of the planning horizon at \$200 each with a 5% price increase every 2 months. Formulate the problem as a transportation model. Solve by TORA and interpret the results.

□ **6–12** Apply the northwest-corner rule to find the starting solution for each of the following transportation models. Balance the model where necessary.

(a) $a_1 = 20, a_2 = 30, a_3 = 40$
$b_1 = 25, b_2 = 40, b_3 = 28.$

(b) $a_1 = 30, a_2 = 35, a_3 = 45$
$b_1 = 15, b_2 = 17, b_3 = 40, b_4 = 15.$

□ **6–13** Apply the northwest-corner rule to find a starting solution for each of the following transportation models. Indicate whether or not the solution is degenerate. Balance the model where necessary.

(a) $a_1 = 10, a_2 = 5, a_3 = 4, a_4 = 6$
$b_1 = 10, b_2 = 5, b_3 = 7, b_4 = 3.$

(b) $a_1 = 1, a_2 = 16, a_3 = 7, a_4 = 8$
$b_1 = 3, b_2 = 4, b_3 = 5, b_4 = 2, b_5 = 8.$

(c) $a_1 = 10, a_2 = 3, a_3 = 7$
$b_1 = 14, b_2 = 3, b_3 = 4, b_4 = 9.$

□ **6–14** Consider the basic solution in Table 6-11.

(a) Determine the loop associated with each nonbasic variable.

(b) If each nonbasic variable is used as an entering variable, determine the associated leaving variable. At what level does each nonbasic variable enter the solution?

(c) For each case in part (b), determine the *total* increase or decrease in the value of the objective function.

□ **6–15** Solve the following transportation models whose starting solutions are degenerate. Use the northwest-corner method to find the starting solution. (The numbers in the box give c_{ij}.)

(a)

0	2	1	**5**
2	1	5	**10**
2	4	3	**5**
5	**5**	**10**	

(b)

0	4	2	**8**
2	3	4	**5**
1	2	0	**6**
7	**6**	**6**	

(c)

—	3	5	**4**
7	4	9	**7**
1	8	6	**19**
5	**6**	**19**	

□ **6–16** In the following transportation problem, the total demand exceeds total supply. Suppose that the penalty costs per unit of unsatisfied demand are 5, 3, and 2 for destinations 1, 2, and 3. Find the optimal solution.

5	1	7	**10**
6	4	6	**80**
3	2	5	**15**
75	**20**	**50**	

□ **6–17** In Problem 6–16, suppose that there are no penalty costs and the demand at destination 3 must be satisfied exactly. Reformulate the problem and find the optimal solution.

□ **6–18** In the unbalanced transportation problem given, if a unit from source i is not shipped out (to one of the destinations), a storage cost must be incurred. Let the storage costs per unit at sources 1, 2, and 3 be 5, 4, and 3. If, in addition, all the supply at source 2 must be shipped out to make room for a new product, find the optimal solution.

1	2	1	**20**
0	4	5	**40**
2	3	3	**30**
30	**20**	**20**	

□ **6–19** In a (3×3) transportation problem let x_{ij} be the amount shipped from source i to destination j and c_{ij} the corresponding per unit transportation cost. The supplies at sources 1, 2, and 3 are 15, 30, and 85 units, and the demands at destinations 1, 2, and 3 are 20, 30, and 80 units. Assume that the starting solution obtained by the northwest-corner method gives the *optimal* basic solution to the problem. Let the associated values of the multipliers for sources 1, 2, and 3 be -2, 3, and 5, and those for destinations 1, 2, and 3 be 2, 5, and 10.

(a) Find the total optimal transportation cost.

(b) What are the smallest values of c_{ij} for the nonbasic variables that will keep the solution optimal?

□ **6–20** The transportation problem given here has the indicated *degenerate* basic solution. It is required to minimize the transportation costs. Let the multipliers corresponding to this basic solution be 1, -1 for sources 1 and 2 and -1, 2, -5 for destinations 1, 2, and 3. Let

$$c_{ij} = i + j\theta, \qquad -\infty < \theta < \infty$$

for *all* the *zero* (basic and nonbasic) variables, where c_{ij} is the cost *per unit* shipped from source i to destination j.

(a) If the solution is the optimal, what is the corresponding value of the objective function? (Answer this part in two different ways.)

(b) Under the conditions in part (a), find the single value of θ for which the solution is basic and optimal.

10			**10**
	20	**20**	**40**
10	**20**	**20**	

□ **6–21** Solve this problem by the transportation technique and the simplex method and show that there is a one-to-one correspondence between the iterations of the two methods. Find the starting solution by the northwest-corner method.

1	0	2	**4**
3	5	4	**6**
1	2	3	**10**
3	**5**	**12**	

□ **6–22 (Sensitivity Analysis).** Consider the optimal transportation tableau in Table 6-14. In each of the following cases, determine the change in the amounts of the supply and demand that will keep the current solution feasible.

(a) Source 1 and destination 1.

(b) Source 2 and destination 1.

(c) Source 2 and destination 4.

(d) Source 3 and destination 4.

[*Hint*: Suppose that we change the supply and demand at source i and destination j from a_i and b_j to $a_i + \Delta$ and $b_j + \Delta$, where Δ is unrestricted. If x_{ij} is currently basic, Δ is added directly to the current value of x_{ij} and the solution remains feasible as long as the new value of x_{ij} remains nonnegative. If x_{ij} is nonbasic, construct its loop and from it determine the adjustment in the values of basic variables at the corners of the loop that will keep the solution feasible while netting the value of the nonbasic x_{ij} from Δ to zero.]

☐ **6–23** Solve each of the following transportation models by using the northwest-corner method, least-cost method, and Vogel's approximation method to obtain the starting solution. Compare the computations.

(a)

1	2	6	**7**
0	4	2	**12**
3	1	5	**11**
10	**10**	**10**	

(b)

5	1	8	**12**
2	4	0	**14**
3	6	7	**4**
9	**10**	**11**	

☐ **6–24** Find the starting solution in the following transportation problem by the (a) northwest-corner method; (b) the least-cost method; (c) Vogel's approximation method. Obtain the optimal solution by using the best starting solution.

10	20	5	7	**10**
13	9	12	8	**20**
4	15	7	9	**30**
14	7	1	0	**40**
3	12	5	19	**50**
60	**60**	**20**	**10**	

☐ **6–25** Solve the following unbalanced transportation problem using VAM to find the starting solution; demand at destination 1 must be shipped from source 4.

5	1	0	**20**
3	2	4	**10**
7	5	2	**15**
9	6	0	**15**
5	**10**	**15**	

☐ **6–26** Show by the method of multipliers (Section 6.2.1) that the solution in Table 6-26 is optimal.

☐ **6–27** Solve the following assignment models.

(a)

3	8	2	10	3
8	7	2	9	7
6	4	2	7	5
8	4	2	3	5
9	10	6	9	10

(b)

3	9	2	3	7
6	1	5	6	6
9	4	7	10	3
2	5	4	2	1
9	6	2	4	6

☐ **6–28** Consider the problem of assigning four operators to four machines. The assignment costs in dollars are given. Operator 1 cannot be assigned to machine 3. Also, operator 3 cannot be assigned to machine 4. Find the optimal assignment.

		Machine 1	Machine 2	Machine 3	Machine 4
Operator	1	5	5	—	2
	2	7	4	2	3
	3	9	3	5	—
	4	7	2	6	7

□ **6–29** Suppose that in Problem 6–28 a fifth machine is made available. Its respective assignment costs (in dollars) to the four operators are 2, 1, 2, and 8. The new machine replaces an existing one if the replacement can be justified economically. Reformulate the problem as an assignment model and find the optimal solution. In particular, is it economical to replace one of the existing machines? If so, which one?

□ **6–30** An airline has two-way flights between two cities A and B. The crew based in city A (B) and flying to city B (A) must return to city A (B) on a later flight either on the same day or a following day. An A-based crew can return on an A-destined flight only if there is at least 90 minutes between the arrival time at B and the departure time of the A-destined flight. The objective is to pair the flights so as to minimize the total layover time by all the crews. Solve the problem as an assignment model using the timetable given below.

[*Note*: The complete formulation of a similar problem is given in R. Ackoff and M. Sasieni, *Fundamentals of Operations Research*, Wiley, New York, 1968, pp. 143–145.]

Flight	From A	To B	Flight	From B	To A
1	6:00	8:30	10	7:30	9:30
2	8:15	10:45	20	9:15	11:15
3	13:30	16:00	30	16:30	18:30
4	15:00	17:30	40	20:00	22:00

□ **6–31** Figure 6-8 gives a schematic layout of a shop with its existing work centers shown by squares 1, 2, 3, and 4. Four new work centers are to be added to the shop at the locations designated by circles a, b, c, and d. The objective is to assign the new centers to the proposed locations in a manner that will minimize the total materials handling traffic between the existing centers and the proposed ones. The table below summarizes the frequency of trips between the new centers and the old ones. Materials handling equipment travels along the rectangular aisles intersecting at the locations of the centers. For example, the one-way travel distance between centers 1 and b is $30 + 20 = 50$ meters. Formulate the problem as an assignment model. Solve by TORA and interpret the solution.

		New Center 1	New Center 2	New Center 3	New Center 4
Existing Center	1	10	2	4	3
	2	7	1	6	5
	3	0	8	9	2
	4	11	4	0	7

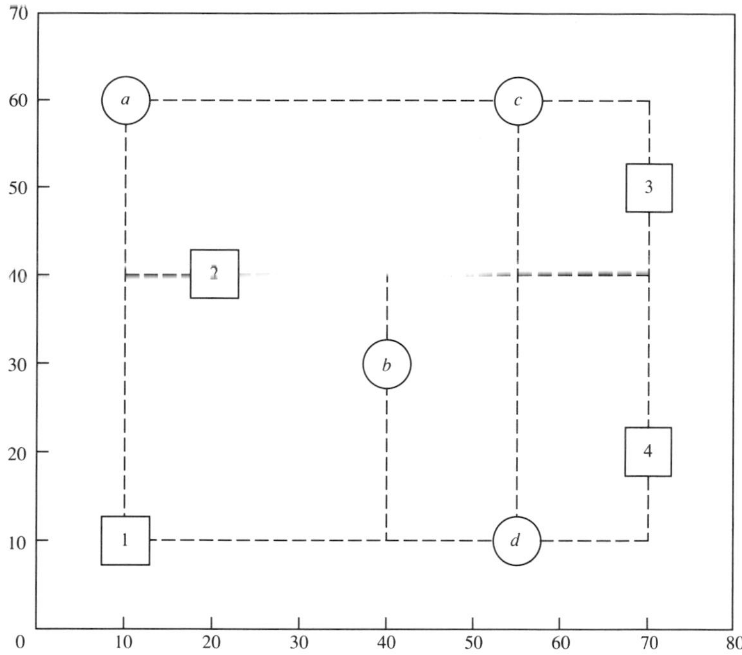

Figure 6-8

☐ **6–32** A business executive who is stationed in city A must make six round trips between cities A and B according to the following schedule:

Departure Date from City A	Return Date to City A
Monday, June 3	Friday, June 7
Monday, June 10	Wednesday, June 12
Monday, June 17	Friday, June 21
Tuesday, June 25	Friday, June 28

The basic price of a round-trip air ticket between A and B is \$400. A discount of 25% is granted if the dates of arrival and departure span a weekend (Saturday and Sunday). If the stay in B lasts more than 21 days, a 30% discount can be obtained. A one-way ticket from A to B (or B to A) costs \$250. How should the executive purchase the tickets? Solve by TORA.

☐ **6–33** The network in Figure 6-9 depicts the shipping routes from nodes 1 and 2 to nodes 5 and 6 by way of nodes 3 and 4. The unit shipping costs are shown on the respective arcs.

(a) Write the associated LP model.
(b) Write the associated transshipment model specifying the size of the buffer and the amounts of supply and demand.
(c) Convert the transshipment model in part (b) into a regular transportation model with exactly two sources and two destinations.
(d) Show how the solution of part (c) provides a feasible solution for the original network.

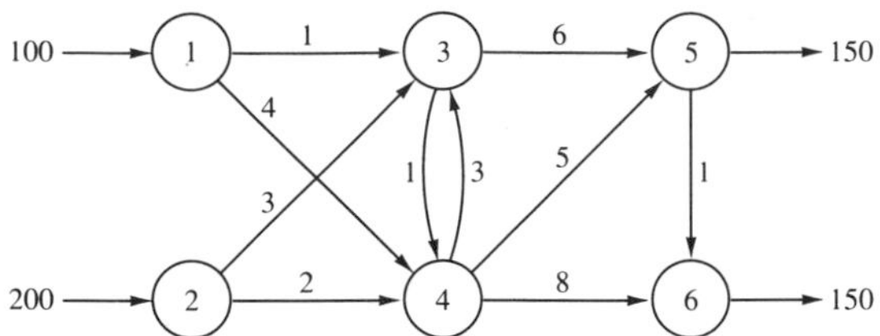

Figure 6-9

□ **6–34** Consider the employment scheduling model of Example 6.4-1. Reformulate the model and provide the optimal solution for each of the following cases (use TORA):

(a)

Month	1	2	3	4	5
Number of Laborers	300	180	90	170	200

(b)

Month	1	2	3	4	5
Number of Laborers	200	220	300	50	240

□ **6–35** Reformulate the employment scheduling model in Example 6.4-1 assuming that employment must last at least two months. Obtain the optimum solution.

□ **6–36** Reformulate the employment scheduling model assuming that employment lasts between one and three months only. Obtain the optimum solution.

□ **6–37** The network in Figure 6-10 shows the routes for shipping cars from three plants (nodes 1, 2, and 3) to five dealers (nodes 6 through 10) by way of two distribution centers (nodes 4 and 5). Assume that the unit shipping cost from node i to node j is c_{ij}. Answer the following:

(a) Set up the associated transshipment model for the problem in Figure 6-10.

(b) Reformulate the model assuming that transshipping is allowed among the dealers.

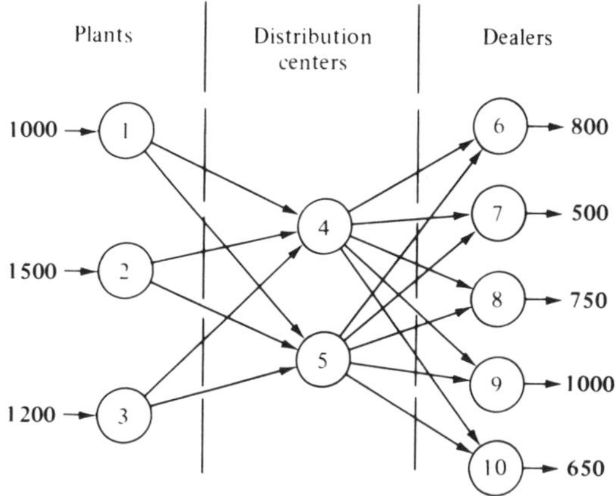

Figure 6-10

(c) Reformulate the model assuming that distribution center 4 will sell 240 cars directly to customers.

☐ **6–38 (Shortest-Route Problem).** Find the shortest route between nodes 1 and 7 of the network in Figure 6-11 by formulating the problem as a transshipment model. The distances between the different nodes are indicated on the network.

[*Hint*: Node 1 has a net supply of 1 unit and node 7 has a net demand of 1 unit.]

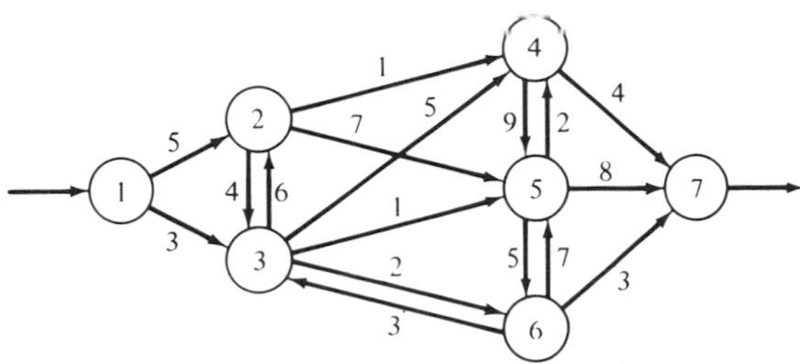

Figure 6-11

☐ **6–39** Consider the transportation problem where two factories are supplying three retail stores with a certain commodity. The number of units available at factories 1 and 2 are 200 and 300; those demanded at stores 1, 2, and 3 are 100, 200, and 50. Rather than ship directly from sources to destinations, it is decided to investigate the possibility of transshipment. Find the optimal shipping schedule. The transportation costs per unit are given.

		Factory 1	Factory 2	Store 1	Store 2	Store 3
Factory	1	0	6	7	8	9
	2	6	0	5	4	3
Store	1	7	2	0	5	1
	2	1	5	1	0	4
	3	8	9	7	6	0

☐ **6–40** Consider Figure 6-12, which represents an oil pipeline network. The different nodes represent pumping and/or receiving stations. The lengths in miles of the

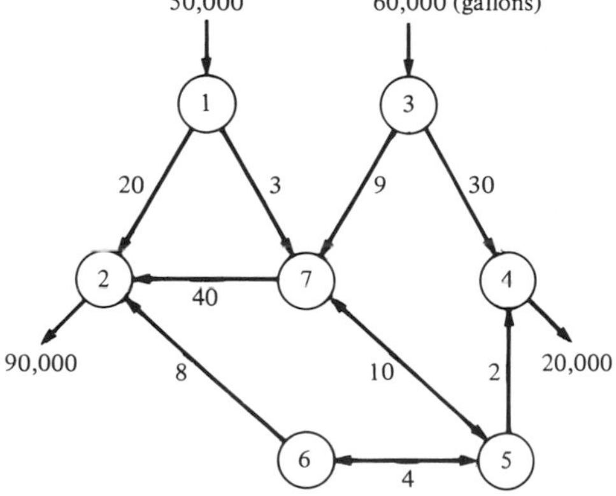

Figure 6-12

different segments of the network are shown on the respective arcs. Construct the transshipment model for determining the least-cost transportation schedule between pumping stations 1 and 3 and receiving stations 2 and 4. The amounts of supply and demand are shown directly in the network. Assume the transportation cost per gallon pumped through the pipeline to be directly proportional to the length of the pipeline between the source and destination.

□ **6–41** In the transportation model, one of the dual variables assumes an arbitrary value. Thus, for the same basic solution, the values of the associated dual variables are not unique. This appears to contradict the theory of linear programming where the dual values are determined by the product of the vector of the objective coefficients for the basic variables and the associated inverse basic matrix (see Section 5.2.2).

Show that for the transportation model, although a given inverse matrix is uniquely defined, the vector of *basic* objective coefficients may not be unique for the same problem. Specifically, show that if c_{ij} is changed to $c_{ij} + k$ for all i and j, where k is a constant, the optimal values of x_{ij} remain the same. Thus an arbitrary assignment of a value to a dual variable is implicitly equivalent to assuming that a certain constant k is added to all c_{ij}.

□ **6–42 (Unbalanced Transportation Problem).** Consider the problem

$$\text{minimize } z = \sum_{i=1}^{m} \sum_{j=1}^{n} c_{ij} x_{ij}$$

subject to

$$\sum_{j=1}^{n} x_{ij} \geq a_i, \qquad i = 1, 2, \ldots, m \tag{1}$$

$$\sum_{i=1}^{m} x_{ij} \geq b_j, \qquad j = 1, 2, \ldots, n \tag{2}$$

$$x_{ij} \geq 0 \qquad \text{for all } i \text{ and } j$$

It may be logical to assume that, at the optimum, inequality (1) *or* (2) will certainly be satisfied in equation form depending on whether $\sum a_i \geq \sum b_j$ or $\sum a_i \leq \sum b_j$, respectively. A counterexample to this hypothesis is

1	1	2	**5**
6	5	1	**6**
2	**7**	**1**	

Show that the application of the suggested procedure yields the "optimum" solution $x_{11} = 2$, $x_{12} = 3$, $x_{22} = 4$, and $x_{23} = 2$ with $z = 27$, which is worse than the feasible solution $x_{11} = 2$, $x_{12} = 7$, and $x_{23} = 6$ with $z = 15$. [Note that this counterexample is due to A. Charnes, F. Glover, and D. Klingman, "A Note on a Distribution Problem," *Operations Research*, Vol. 18, 1970, pp. 1213–1216.]

Chapter 7

Linear Programming: Additional Topics

In Chapters 3 and 4 we presented the computational techniques of linear programming, including the primal and dual simplex methods both in tableau and matrix forms. Duality theory, sensitivity analysis and parametric programming were presented in Chapter 5. In this chapter we present additional topics of linear programming that include the **bounded variables** technique, the **decomposition principle**, and the most recent development in linear programming, **Karmarkar's interior-point algorithm**.

7.1 BOUNDED VARIABLES PRIMAL SIMPLEX METHOD

Applications of linear programming exist where, in addition to the regular constraints, some (or all) variables are bounded from above and below. In this case the problem appears as

$$\text{maximize } z = \mathbf{CX}$$

subject to

$$(\mathbf{A}, \mathbf{I})X = \mathbf{b}$$
$$\mathbf{L} \le \mathbf{X} \le \mathbf{U}$$

where

$$\mathbf{U} = \begin{pmatrix} u_1 \\ u_2 \\ \vdots \\ u_{n+m} \end{pmatrix} \quad \text{and} \quad \mathbf{L} = \begin{pmatrix} l_1 \\ l_2 \\ \vdots \\ l_{n+m} \end{pmatrix}, \qquad \mathbf{U} \ge \mathbf{L} \ge 0$$

The elements of **L** and **U** for an unbounded variable are 0 and ∞.

The problem can be solved by the regular simplex method, in which case the constraints are put in the form

$$(\mathbf{A}, \mathbf{I})\mathbf{X} = \mathbf{b}$$
$$\mathbf{X} + \mathbf{X}' = \mathbf{U}$$
$$\mathbf{X} - \mathbf{X}'' = \mathbf{L}$$
$$\mathbf{X}, \mathbf{X}', \mathbf{X}'' \ge \mathbf{0}$$

where $\mathbf{X}'$ and $\mathbf{X}''$ are slack and surplus variables. This problem includes $3(m + n)$ variables and $3m + 2n$ constraint equations. However, the size can be reduced considerably through the use of special techniques that ultimately reduce the constraints to the set

$$(\mathbf{A}, \mathbf{I})\mathbf{X} = \mathbf{b}$$

Consider first the lower-bound constraints. The effect of these constraints can be accounted for by using the substitution

$$\mathbf{X} = \mathbf{L} + \mathbf{X}''$$

to eliminate **X** from all the remaining constraints. The new variables of the problem thus become $\mathbf{X}'$ and $\mathbf{X}''$. There is no fear in this case that **X** may violate the nonnegativity constraint, since both **L** and $\mathbf{X}''$ are nonnegative.

The real difficulty occurs with the upper-bounded variables. A substitution similar to that of the lower-bound case is incorrect, since there is no guarantee that $\mathbf{X} = \mathbf{U} - \mathbf{X}'$ will remain nonnegative. This difficulty is overcome by using a simplex method variation that accounts for the upper bounds implicitly.

The upper-bounded problem may be written as

$$\text{maximize } z = \mathbf{CX}$$

subject to

$$(\mathbf{A}, \mathbf{I})\mathbf{X} = \mathbf{b}$$
$$\mathbf{X} + \mathbf{X}' = \mathbf{U}$$
$$\mathbf{X}, \mathbf{X}' \ge \mathbf{0}$$

It is assumed that **b** is a nonnegative vector so that the problem is initially primal-feasible, hence we will present the **primal simplex method for bounded variables.**

Rather than include the constraints

$$\mathbf{X} + \mathbf{X}' = \mathbf{U}$$

in the simplex tableau, one can account for their effect by modifying the feasibility condition of the simplex method. The optimality condition remains the same as in the primal simplex method.

The basic idea for modifying the feasibility condition of the primal simplex method is that a variable becomes infeasible if it becomes negative or exceeds its upper bound. The nonnegativity condition is treated exactly as in the primal simplex method. The upper-bound condition requires special provisions that will allow a basic variable to become *nonbasic at its upper bound.* (Compare with the primal simplex method, where all the nonbasic variables are at zero level.) Also, when a nonbasic variable is selected to enter the solution, its entering value should not exceed its upper bound. Thus, in developing the new feasibility condition, two main points must be considered:

1. The nonnegativity and upper-bound constraints for the entering variable.
2. The nonnegativity and upper-bound constraints for those basic variables that may be affected by introducing the entering variable.

To develop these ideas mathematically, consider the linear programming problem without the upper bounds. At every iteration, one guarantees that the solution is feasible as follows. Let x_j be a nonbasic variable at *zero* level that is selected to enter the solution. (Later it is shown that every nonbasic variable can always be put at zero level.) Let $(\mathbf{X}_B)_i = (\mathbf{X}_B^*)_i$ be the ith variable of the current basic solution $\mathbf{X}_B$. Thus introducing x_j into the solution gives

$$(\mathbf{X}_B)_i = (\mathbf{X}_B^*)_i - \alpha_i^j x_j$$

where α_i^j is the ith element of $\boldsymbol{\alpha}^j = \mathbf{B}^{-1}\mathbf{P}_j$ and $\mathbf{P}_j$ is the vector of $(\mathbf{A}, \mathbf{I})$ corresponding to x_j.

Now, x_j remains feasible if

$$0 \leq x_j \leq u_j \tag{i}$$

whereas $(\mathbf{X}_B)_i$ remains feasible if

$$0 \leq (\mathbf{X}_B^*)_i - \alpha_i^j x_j \leq (\mathbf{U}_B)_i, \qquad i = 1, 2, \ldots, m \tag{ii}$$

Since the introduction of x_j into the solution implies that it must be nonnegative, condition (i) is taken care of by observing the upper bound on x_j. Next, consider condition (ii). From the nonnegativity condition

$$(\mathbf{X}_B)_i = (\mathbf{X}_B^*)_i - \alpha_i^j x_j \geq 0$$

it follows that only $\alpha_i^j > 0$ may cause $(\mathbf{X}_B)_i$ to be negative. Let θ_1 represent the maximum value of x_j resulting from this condition. Thus

$$\theta_1 = \min_i \left\{ \frac{(\mathbf{X}_B^*)_i}{\alpha_i^j}, \alpha_i^j > 0 \right\}$$

This actually is the same as the feasibility condition of the regular simplex method.

If we let $\mathbf{U}_B$ be the upper-bound vector for current basic variables $\mathbf{X}_B$, then to guarantee that $(\mathbf{X}_B)_i$ will not exceed its upper bound, it is necessary that the following condition be satisfied:

$$(\mathbf{X}_B)_i = (\mathbf{X}_B^*)_i + (-\alpha_i^j)x_j \le (\mathbf{U}_B)_i$$

This condition can be violated only if α_i^j is negative. Thus, by letting θ_2 represent the maximum value of x_j resulting from this condition, we get

$$\theta_2 = \min_i \left\{ \frac{(\mathbf{U}_B)_i - (\mathbf{X}_B^*)_i}{-\alpha_i^j}, \ \alpha_i^j < 0 \right\}$$

Let θ denote the maximum value of x_j that does not violate any of the conditions above. Then

$$\theta = \min \{\theta_1, \theta_2, u_j\}$$

It is noticed that an old basic variable $(\mathbf{X}_B)_i$ can become nonbasic only if the introduction of the entering variable x_j at level θ causes $(\mathbf{X}_B)_i$ to become zero or to reach its upper bound. This means that if $\theta = u_j$, x_j cannot be made basic, since no $(\mathbf{X}_B)_i$ can be dropped from the solution, and thus x_j should remain nonbasic *at its upper bound.* (If $\theta = u_j = \theta_1 = \theta_2$, the tie may be broken arbitrarily.)

In the foregoing derivation, the entering variable x_j is assumed to be at zero level before it is introduced into the solution. To maintain the validity of this condition, every nonbasic variable x_k at upper bound can be put at zero level by using the substitution

$$x_k = u_k - x_k'$$

where $0 \le x_k' \le u_k$.

Using these ideas, we can effect the changes in the current basic solution as follows. Let $(\mathbf{X}_B)_r$ be the variable corresponding to $\theta = \min \{\theta_1, \theta_2, u_j\}$; then

1. If $\theta = \theta_1$, $(\mathbf{X}_B)_r$ leaves the solution and x_j enters by using the Gauss–Jordan procedure of the simplex method.
2. If $\theta = \theta_2$, $(\mathbf{X}_B)_r$ leaves and x_j enters by using the Gauss–Jordan procedure; then $(\mathbf{X}_B)_r$ being nonbasic at its upper bound must be substituted out by using $(\mathbf{X}_B)_r = u_r - (\mathbf{X}_B)_r'$.
3. If $\theta = u_j$, x_j is substituted at its upper bound $u_j - x_j'$ but remains nonbasic.

Example 7.1-1. Consider the following problem:

$$\text{maximize } z = 3x_1 + 5y + 2x_3$$

subject to

$$x_1 + y + 2x_3 \le 14$$
$$2x_1 + 4y + 3x_3 \le 43$$
$$0 \le x_1 \le 4, \quad 7 \le y \le 10, \quad 0 \le x_3 \le 3$$

Since y has a positive lower bound, it must be substituted at its lower bound. Let $y = x_2 + 7$; then $0 \le x_2 \le 10 - 7 = 3$, and the starting tableau becomes

Basic	x_1	x_2	x_3	x_4	x_5	Solution
z	-3	-5	-2	0	0	35
x_4	1	1	2	1	0	7
x_5	2	4	3	0	1	15

First Iteration

Select x_2 as the entering variable ($z_2 - c_2 = -5$). Thus

$$\boldsymbol{\alpha}^2 = \begin{pmatrix} 1 \\ 4 \end{pmatrix} > \mathbf{0}$$

and

$$\theta_1 = \min \{7/1, 15/4\} = 3.75$$

Since all $\alpha_i^2 > 0$, it follows that $\theta_2 = \infty$. Thus $\theta = \min \{3.75, \infty, 3\} = 3$.

Because $\theta = u_2$, x_2 is substituted at its upper limit but it remains nonbasic. Thus, putting $x_2 = u_2 - x_2' = 3 - x_2'$, the new tableau becomes

Basic	x_1	x_2'	x_3	x_4	x_5	Solution
z	-3	5	-2	0	0	50
x_4	1	-1	2	1	0	4
x_5	2	-4	3	0	1	3

Second Iteration

Select x_1 as the entering variable ($z_1 - c_1 = -3$). Thus

$$\boldsymbol{\alpha}^1 = \begin{pmatrix} 1 \\ 2 \end{pmatrix}$$

$$\theta_1 = \min \{4/1, 3/2\} = 3/2, \quad \text{corresponding to } x_5$$

$$\theta_2 = \infty$$

Hence $\theta = \min \{3/2, \infty, 4\} = 3/2$. Since $\theta = \theta_1$, introduce x_1 and drop x_5. This yields

Basic	x_1	x_2'	x_3	x_4	x_5	Solution
z	0	-1	5/2	0	3/2	109/2
x_4	0	1	1/2	1	$-1/2$	5/2
x_1	1	-2	3/2	0	1/2	3/2

Third Iteration

Sclcct x_2' as the entering variable. Given

$$\boldsymbol{\alpha}^2 = \begin{pmatrix} 1 \\ -2 \end{pmatrix}$$

$$\theta_1 = 5/2$$

$$\theta_2 = \frac{4 - 3/2}{-(-2)} = 5/4, \quad \text{corresponding to } x_1$$

Thus $\theta = \min\{5/2, 5/4, 3\} = 5/4$. Since $\theta = \theta_2$, introduce x_2' into the basis and drop x_1; then substitute x_1 out at its upper bound $(4 - x_1')$. Thus, by removing x_1 and introducing x_2', the tableau becomes

Basic	x_1	x_2'	x_3	x_4	x_5	Solution
z	−1/2	0	7/4	0	5/4	215/4
x_4	1/2	0	5/4	1	−1/4	13/4
x_2'	−1/2	1	−3/4	0	−1/4	−3/4

Now, by substituting for $x_1 = 4 - x_1'$, the final tableau becomes

Basic	x_1'	x_2'	x_3	x_4	x_5	Solution
z	1/2	0	7/4	0	5/4	223/4
x_4	−1/2	0	5/4	1	−1/4	5/4
x_2'	1/2	1	−3/4	0	−1/4	5/4

which is now optimal and feasible.

The optimal solution in terms of the original variables x_1, x_2, and x_3 is found as follows. Since $x_1' = 0$, it follows that $x_1 = 4$. Also, since $x_2' = 5/4$, $x_2 = 3 - 5/4 = 7/4$ and $y = 7 + 7/4 = 35/4$. Finally, x_3 equals 0. These values yield $z = 223/4$, as shown in the optimal tableau. ◀

It might be beneficial at this point to study the effect of the upper bounding technique on the development of the simplex tableau. Specifically, it is required to define $\{z_j - c_j\}$ and the basic solution at every iteration. This will be presented here in matrix notation.

Let $\mathbf{X}_u$ represent the basic *and* nonbasic variables in $\mathbf{X}$ that have been substituted at their upper bound. Also, let $\mathbf{X}_z$ be the remaining basic *and* nonbasic variables. Suppose that the order of the vectors of $(\mathbf{A}, \mathbf{I})$ corresponding to $\mathbf{X}_z$ and $\mathbf{X}_u$ are given by the matrices $\mathbf{D}_z$ and $\mathbf{D}_u$, and let the vector $\mathbf{C}$ of the objective function be partitioned correspondingly to give $(\mathbf{C}_z, \mathbf{C}_u)$. The equations of the linear programming problem at any iteration then become

$$\begin{pmatrix} 1 & -\mathbf{C}_z & -\mathbf{C}_u \\ 0 & \mathbf{D}_z & \mathbf{D}_u \end{pmatrix} \begin{pmatrix} z \\ \mathbf{X}_z \\ \mathbf{X}_u \end{pmatrix} = \begin{pmatrix} 0 \\ \mathbf{b} \end{pmatrix}$$

Instead of dealing with two types of variables, $\mathbf{X}_z$ and $\mathbf{X}_u$, $\mathbf{X}_u$ is put at zero level by using the substitution

$$\mathbf{X}_u = \mathbf{U}_u - \mathbf{X}_u'$$

where $\mathbf{U}_u$ is a subset of $\mathbf{U}$ representing the upper bounds for the variables in $\mathbf{X}_u$. This gives

$$\begin{pmatrix} 1 & -\mathbf{C}_z & \mathbf{C}_u \\ \mathbf{0} & \mathbf{D}_z & -\mathbf{D}_u \end{pmatrix} \begin{pmatrix} z \\ \mathbf{X}_z \\ \mathbf{X}_u' \end{pmatrix} = \begin{pmatrix} \mathbf{C}_u\mathbf{U}_u \\ \mathbf{b} - \mathbf{D}_u\mathbf{U}_u \end{pmatrix}$$

The optimality and the feasibility conditions can be developed more easily now, since all nonbasic variables are at zero level. However, it is still necessary to check that no basic or nonbasic variable will exceed its upper bound.

Define $\mathbf{X}_B$ as the basic variables of the current iteration, and let $\mathbf{C}_B$ represent the elements corresponding to $\mathbf{X}_B$ in $\mathbf{C}$. Also, let $\mathbf{B}$ be the basic matrix corresponding to $\mathbf{X}_B$. The current solution is determined from

$$\begin{pmatrix} 1 & -\mathbf{C}_B \\ 0 & \mathbf{B} \end{pmatrix}\begin{pmatrix} z \\ \mathbf{X}_B \end{pmatrix} = \begin{pmatrix} \mathbf{C}_u \mathbf{U}_u \\ \mathbf{b} - \mathbf{D}_u \mathbf{U}_u \end{pmatrix}$$

By inverting the partitioned matrix as in Section 4.1.3, the current basic solution is given by

$$\begin{pmatrix} z \\ \mathbf{X}_B \end{pmatrix} = \begin{pmatrix} 1 & \mathbf{C}_B \mathbf{B}^{-1} \\ \mathbf{0} & \mathbf{B}^{-1} \end{pmatrix}\begin{pmatrix} \mathbf{C}_u \mathbf{U}_u \\ \mathbf{b} - \mathbf{D}_u \mathbf{U}_u \end{pmatrix} = \begin{pmatrix} \mathbf{C}_u \mathbf{U}_u + \mathbf{C}_B \mathbf{B}^{-1}(\mathbf{b} - \mathbf{D}_u \mathbf{U}_u) \\ \mathbf{B}^{-1}(\mathbf{b} - \mathbf{D}_u \mathbf{U}_u) \end{pmatrix}$$

By using

$$\mathbf{b}' = \mathbf{b} - \mathbf{D}_u \mathbf{U}_u$$

the complete simplex tableau corresponding to any iteration is (compare with Section 4.1.3).

Basic	$\mathbf{X}_z^T$	$\mathbf{X}_u'^T$	Solution
z	$\mathbf{C}_B \mathbf{B}^{-1}\mathbf{D}_z - \mathbf{C}_z$	$-\mathbf{C}_B \mathbf{B}^{-1}\mathbf{D}_u + \mathbf{C}_u$	$\mathbf{C}_B \mathbf{B}^{-1}\mathbf{b}' + \mathbf{C}_u \mathbf{U}_u$
$\mathbf{X}_B$	$\mathbf{B}^{-1}\mathbf{D}_z$	$-\mathbf{B}^{-1}\mathbf{D}_u$	$\mathbf{B}^{-1}\mathbf{b}'$

The arrangement of this tableau is the same as the one presented in Section 4.1.3. For the z-equation, the left-hand side coefficients yield $z_j - c_j$, the optimality indicator for all the nonbasic variables in $\mathbf{X}_z$ and $\mathbf{X}_u'$, and its right-hand side yields the corresponding value of z. The constraint coefficients $\mathbf{B}^{-1}(\mathbf{D}_z, -\mathbf{D}_u)$ give the corresponding $\{\boldsymbol{\alpha}\}$ for the nonbasic variables. Finally, the right-hand side of the constraint equations $\mathbf{B}^{-1}\mathbf{b}'$ gives directly the values of $\mathbf{X}_B$.

Exercise 7.1-1

Consider the optimal tableau of Example 7.1-1. Compute the optimal inverse $\mathbf{B}^{-1}$; then show how the entire tableau can be generated from $\mathbf{B}^{-1}$ and the original data of the problem by using the matrix representation shown. Can $\mathbf{B}^{-1}$ be identified directly from the optimal tableau of Example 7.1-1?

[*Ans.* $\mathbf{B} = (\mathbf{P}_4, \mathbf{P}_2')$, $\mathbf{B}^{-1} = \begin{pmatrix} 1 & -1/4 \\ 0 & -1/4 \end{pmatrix}$. Yes, $\mathbf{B}^{-1}$ is located under the variables of the starting solution.]

7.2 DECOMPOSITION ALGORITHM

The special structure of certain large linear programs may allow the determination of the optimal solution by first decomposing the problem into smaller subproblems and then solving the subproblems almost independently. The procedure has the

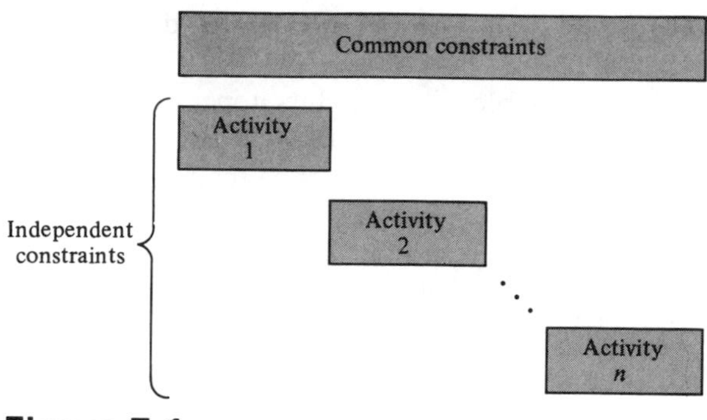

Figure 7-1

advantage of making it possible to solve large-scale problems that otherwise may be computationally infeasible.

A typical situation can arise in the planning of production facilities at the corporate level. Although each facility may have its own independent constraints, the different activities are usually tied together at the corporate level by budgetary constraints. The two types of constraints are referred to as *common* and *independent* restrictions.

Figure 7-1 demonstrates a typical structure of an LP model that can be solved by decomposing the problem into smaller subproblems. Note that the independent constraints of the n activities do not overlap. In the absence of the common constraints, the different activities will be completely independent of one another.

Let $\mathbf{D}_j$ ($j = 1, 2, \ldots, n$) be the technology matrix of the jth activity (e.g., production facility) and let $\mathbf{X}_j$ represent the vector of the corresponding variables. Let the resources of the jth activity be given by the vector $\mathbf{b}_j$. It follows that each set of independent constraints can be written as†

$$\mathbf{D}_j\mathbf{X}_j = \mathbf{b}_j, \qquad j = 1, 2, \ldots, n$$

For the common constraints, let $\mathbf{A}_j$ be the technological matrix of the jth activity and let $\mathbf{b}_0$ be its corresponding resources vector. This gives

$$\mathbf{A}_1\mathbf{X}_1 + \mathbf{A}_2\mathbf{X}_2 + \cdots + \mathbf{A}_n\mathbf{X}_n = \mathbf{b}_0$$

Further, let $\mathbf{C}_j$ represent the vector of the objective function coefficients for the jth activity. Thus the complete problem becomes

$$\text{maximize } z = \mathbf{C}_1\mathbf{X}_1 + \mathbf{C}_2\mathbf{X}_2 + \cdots + \mathbf{C}_n\mathbf{X}_n$$

subject to

$$\begin{aligned}
\mathbf{A}_1\mathbf{X}_1 + \mathbf{A}_2\mathbf{X}_2 + \cdots + \mathbf{A}_n\mathbf{X}_n &= \mathbf{b}_0 \\
\mathbf{D}_1\mathbf{X}_1 \qquad\qquad\qquad\qquad &= \mathbf{b}_1 \\
\mathbf{D}_2\mathbf{X}_2 \qquad\qquad\quad &= \mathbf{b}_2 \\
\ddots \qquad\qquad &\;\;\vdots \\
\mathbf{D}_n\mathbf{X}_n &= \mathbf{b}_n \\
\mathbf{X}_j \geq \mathbf{0}, \quad \text{for all } j &
\end{aligned}$$

† Slack variables are added as necessary to change inequality constraints into equalities. In this case, the resulting slacks and coefficients are assumed to be part of $\mathbf{X}_j$ and $\mathbf{D}_j$.

If the size of $\mathbf{A}_j$ is $(r_0 \times m_j)$ and that of $\mathbf{D}_j$ is $(r_j \times m_j)$, the problem has $\sum_{j=0}^{n} r_j$ constraints and $\sum_{j=0}^{n} m_j$ variables.

The **decomposition principle** as applied to the preceding problem will now be discussed. It is assumed that each of the convex sets

$$\mathbf{D}_j \mathbf{X}_j = \mathbf{b}_j, \qquad \mathbf{X}_j \geq \mathbf{0}, \qquad j = 1, 2, \ldots, n$$

is bounded. Thus, if $\hat{\mathbf{X}}_j^k$, $k = 1, 2, \ldots, K_j$, are the extreme points of the jth set, every point $\mathbf{X}_j$ in this set can be expressed as a convex combination of these extreme points. This means that, for $\beta_j^k \geq 0$ and $\sum_{k=1}^{K_j} \beta_j^k = 1$,

$$\mathbf{X}_j = \sum_{k=1}^{K_j} \beta_j^k \hat{\mathbf{X}}_j^k, \qquad j = 1, 2, \ldots, n$$

These new equations imply the complete solution space defined by the sets $\mathbf{D}_j \mathbf{X}_j = \mathbf{b}_j$ and $\mathbf{X}_j \geq \mathbf{0}$, $j = 1, 2, \ldots, n$. It is thus possible to eliminate the constraints of the subproblems and reformulate the original problem in the following equivalent form, which we shall call the **master problem**:

$$\text{maximize } z = \sum_{k=1}^{K_1} \mathbf{C}_1 \hat{\mathbf{X}}_1^k \beta_1^k + \sum_{k=1}^{K_2} \mathbf{C}_2 \hat{\mathbf{X}}_2^k \beta_2^k + \cdots + \sum_{k=1}^{K_n} \mathbf{C}_n \hat{\mathbf{X}}_n^k \beta_n^k$$

subject to

$$\begin{aligned}
\sum_{k=1}^{K_1} \mathbf{A}_1 \hat{\mathbf{X}}_1^k \beta_1^k + \sum_{k=1}^{K_2} \mathbf{A}_2 \hat{\mathbf{X}}_2^k \beta_2^k + \cdots + \sum_{k=1}^{K_n} \mathbf{A}_n \hat{\mathbf{X}}_n^k \beta_n^k &= \mathbf{b}_0 \\
\sum_{k=1}^{K_1} \beta_1^k \qquad\qquad\qquad\qquad\qquad\qquad\qquad\qquad &= 1 \\
\sum_{k=1}^{K_2} \beta_2^k \qquad\qquad\qquad\qquad\qquad &= 1 \\
\ddots \qquad\qquad\qquad\qquad &\;\vdots \\
\sum_{k=1}^{K_n} \beta_n^k &= 1
\end{aligned}$$

$$\beta_j^k \geq 0, \qquad \text{for all } j \text{ and } k$$

Since $\hat{\mathbf{X}}_j^k$ are the "known" extreme points of the set $\mathbf{D}_j \mathbf{X}_j = \mathbf{b}_j$, $\mathbf{X}_j \geq \mathbf{0}$, the new decision variables of the modified problem become β_j^k. Once the optimal values of β_j^k for all j and k are determined, the optimal solution to the original problem is obtained by recognizing that

$$\mathbf{X}_j = \sum_{k=1}^{K_j} \beta_j^k \hat{\mathbf{X}}_j^k$$

Exercise 7.2-1

In each of the following cases, express the solution space as a convex combination of its extreme points.

(a) Solution space in Figure 3-4.
[*Ans.* $(\bar{x}_1, \bar{x}_2) = \beta_1(0, 0) + \beta_2(0, 2) + \beta_3(4, 0)$, where $\beta_1, \beta_2, \beta_3 \geq 0$ and $\beta_1 + \beta_2 + \beta_3 = 1$.]

(b) Solution space in Figure 3-5.
[*Ans.* $(\bar{x}_1, \bar{x}_2) = \beta_1(0, 0) + \beta_2(4, 0) + \beta_3(3, 1) + \beta_4(0, 5/2)$, where $\beta_1, \beta_2, \beta_3, \beta_4 \geq 0$ and $\beta_1 + \beta_2 + \beta_3 + \beta_4 = 1$.]

(c) Solution space in Figure 3-6.

[*Ans.* The solution space is unbounded. Hence it is not possible to determine $(\bar{x}_1, \bar{x}_2)$ in terms of the extreme points. However, if we augment the artificial restriction $x_2 \geq M$, where M is very large, then we can represent the solution space as

$$(\bar{x}_1, \bar{x}_2) = \beta_1(0, 0) + \beta_2(10, 0) + \beta_3(20, 10) + \beta_4(20, M) + \beta_5(0, M)$$

where $\beta_1 + \beta_2 + \beta_3 + \beta_4 + \beta_5 = 1$ and $\beta_1, \beta_2, \beta_3, \beta_4, \beta_5 \geq 0$.]

To solve the *master* problem by the (revised) simplex method, we need to determine the entering and leaving vectors. But to do so, it appears, at first thought, that all the extreme points $\hat{\mathbf{X}}_j^k$ must be known in advance. Fortunately, this is not the case. What the decomposition algorithm does is recognize that we need only identify the one extreme point (from among all $\hat{\mathbf{X}}_j^k$) that is associated with the entering variable. Once done, we can determine *numerically* all the elements of the entering vector as well as its objective equation coefficient. The leaving vector can then be determined by using the feasibility condition of the simplex method.

The overall idea of the decomposition algorithm thus involves two principal phases:

1. Convert the original problem into a master problem by implicitly expressing the solution space of each subproblem as a convex combination of its extreme points.
2. Generate the column vector associated with the entering vector and use this information to determine the leaving vector.

The second-phase operation is commonly referred to as **column generation** because it generates the elements of entering vector.

We now show how these ideas can be expressed mathematically. Let $\mathbf{B}$ be the current basis of the *master* problem and $\mathbf{C}_B$ the vector of the corresponding coefficients in the objective function. Thus, according to the revised simplex method, the current solution is optimal if for all nonbasic $\mathbf{P}_j^k$,

$$z_j^k - c_j^k = \mathbf{C}_B \mathbf{B}^{-1} \mathbf{P}_j^k - c_j^k \geq 0$$

where, from the definition of the master problem,

$$c_j^k = \mathbf{C}_j \hat{\mathbf{X}}_j^k \qquad \text{and} \qquad \mathbf{P}_j^k = \begin{array}{l} r_0\{ \\ \\ n \left\{ \begin{array}{l} \\ \\ \\ \\ \end{array} \right. \end{array} \begin{pmatrix} \mathbf{A}_j \hat{\mathbf{X}}_j^k \\ 0 \\ \vdots \\ 1 \\ \vdots \\ 0 \end{pmatrix} \begin{array}{l} \\ \\ \\ \leftarrow (r_0 + j)\text{th place} \\ \\ \\ \end{array}$$

The expression for $z_j^k - c_j^k$ can be simplified as follows. Let

$$\mathbf{B}^{-1} = (\overbrace{\mathbf{R}_0}^{r_0} \mid \overbrace{\mathbf{V}_1, \mathbf{V}_2, \ldots, \mathbf{V}_j, \ldots, \mathbf{V}_n}^{n})$$

where $\mathbf{R}_0$ is the matrix of size $(r_0 + n) \times r_0$ consisting of the first r_0 columns of $\mathbf{B}^{-1}$, and $\mathbf{V}_j$ is the $(r_0 + j)$th column of the same matrix $\mathbf{B}^{-1}$. Thus

$$\begin{aligned} z_j^k - c_j^k &= (\mathbf{C}_B \mathbf{R}_0 \mathbf{A}_j \hat{\mathbf{X}}_j^k + \mathbf{C}_B \mathbf{V}_j) - \mathbf{C}_j \hat{\mathbf{X}}_j^k \\ &= (\mathbf{C}_B \mathbf{R}_0 \mathbf{A}_j - \mathbf{C}_j) \hat{\mathbf{X}}_j^k + \mathbf{C}_B \mathbf{V}_j \end{aligned}$$

If the current solution is not optimal, the vector $\mathbf{P}_j^k$ having the smallest (most negative) $z_j^k - c_j^k < 0$ is selected to enter the solution. The important point is that $z_j^k - c_j^k$ cannot be evaluated numerically until all the elements of $\mathbf{P}_j^k$ are known. On the other hand, $\mathbf{P}_j^k$ cannot be evaluated numerically until the corresponding extreme point $\hat{\mathbf{X}}_j^k$ is known. This leads to the key point that the evaluation of $z_j^k - c_j^k$ (and hence the selection of the entering variable) depends on the determination of $\hat{\mathbf{X}}_j^k$.

Instead of determining all the extreme points for all the n sets, the problem can be reduced to determining the extreme point $\hat{\mathbf{X}}_j^{k*}$ in every set j that will yield the smallest $z_j^k - c_j^k$. Let

$$\rho_j = \min_k \{z_j^k - c_j^k\} = z_j^{k*} - c_j^{k*}$$

and let $\rho = \min_j \{\rho_j\}$. Consequently, if $\rho < 0$, the variable β_j^{k*} corresponding to ρ is selected as the entering variable. Otherwise, if $\rho \geq 0$, the optimal solution is attained.

The extreme point $\hat{\mathbf{X}}_j^{k*}$ is determined by solving the linear programming problem:

$$\text{minimize } z_j - c_j$$

subject to

$$\mathbf{D}_j \mathbf{X}_j = \mathbf{b}_j$$
$$\mathbf{X}_j \geq 0$$

The superscript k is suppressed for the following reason. Since by assumption the set $\mathbf{D}_j \mathbf{X}_j = \mathbf{b}_j$, $\mathbf{X}_j \geq \mathbf{0}$, is bounded, the minimum value of $z_j - c_j$ is also bounded and must occur at an extreme point of the set. This automatically gives the required extreme point $\hat{\mathbf{X}}_j^{k*}$.

Now, as shown previously,

$$z_j^k - c_j^k = (\mathbf{C}_B \mathbf{R}_0 \mathbf{A}_j - \mathbf{C}_j)\hat{\mathbf{X}}_j^k + \mathbf{C}_B \mathbf{V}_j$$

Since $\mathbf{C}_B \mathbf{V}_j$ is a constant independent of k, the linear programming problem becomes

$$\text{minimize } w_j = (\mathbf{C}_B \mathbf{R}_0 \mathbf{A}_j - \mathbf{C}_j)\mathbf{X}_j$$

subject to

$$\mathbf{D}_j \mathbf{X}_j = \mathbf{b}_j$$
$$\mathbf{X}_j \geq \mathbf{0}$$

It thus follows that

$$\rho_j = w_j^* + \mathbf{C}_B \mathbf{V}_j$$

where w_j^* is the optimum value of w_j. As stated, the variable β_j^k corresponding to $\rho = \min_j \{\rho_j\}$ is then selected to enter the solution. (Notice that the extreme point corresponding to β_j^k is automatically known at this point.)

The leaving variable is determined in the usual manner by using the feasibility condition of the revised simplex method. At the iteration when ρ becomes non-negative, the optimal solution to the original problem is given by

$$\mathbf{X}_j^* = \sum_{k=1}^{K_j} \beta_j^{k*} \hat{\mathbf{X}}_j^k, \qquad j = 1, 2, \ldots, n$$

where β_j^{k*} is the optimal solution to the modified problem and $\hat{\mathbf{X}}_j^{k*}$ is the corresponding extreme point.

The decomposition algorithm is summarized by the following steps:

Step 1: Reduce the original problem to the modified form in terms of the new variables β_j^k.

Step 2: Find an initial basic feasible solution to the modified problem. If such a solution is not immediately obvious, use the artificial variables technique (see Section 3.2.3) to secure an initial basis.

Step 3: For the current iteration, find $\rho_j = w_j^* + \mathbf{C}_B \mathbf{V}_j$ for each subproblem j and then determine $\rho = \min_j \{\rho_j\}$. If $\rho \geq 0$, the current solution is optimal and the process is terminated; otherwise,

Step 4: Introduce the variable β_j^k corresponding to ρ into the basic solution. Determine the leaving variable and then compute the next $\mathbf{B}^{-1}$. Go to step 3.

Example 7.2-1

$$\text{Maximize } z = 3x_1 + 5x_2 + x_3 + x_4$$

subject to

$$\begin{aligned} x_1 + x_2 + x_3 + \;\; x_4 &\leq 40 \\ 5x_1 + x_2 \qquad\qquad\quad &\leq 12 \\ x_3 + \;\; x_4 &\geq \;\, 5 \\ x_3 + 5x_4 &\leq 50 \\ x_1, x_2, x_3, x_4 &\geq 0 \end{aligned}$$

By augmenting the slacks S_1, S_2, S_3, and S_4 to the constraints, the information of the problem can be summarized as follows:

x_1	x_2	S_2	x_3	x_4	S_3	S_4	S_1	
3	5	0	1	1	0	0		
1	1	0	1	1	0	0	1	40
5	1	1						12
			1	1	−1	0		5
			1	5	0	1		50

The problem can be decomposed into two subproblems, $j = 1, 2$. For $j = 1$,

$$\mathbf{X}_1 = (x_1, x_2, S_2)^T, \qquad \mathbf{C}_1 = (3, 5, 0)$$
$$\mathbf{A}_1 = (1, 1, 0), \qquad \mathbf{D}_1 = (5, 1, 1)$$
$$b_1 = 12$$

For $j = 2$,

$$\mathbf{X}_2 = (x_3, x_4, S_3, S_4)^T, \qquad \mathbf{C}_2 = (1, 1, 0, 0)$$
$$\mathbf{A}_2 = (1, 1, 0, 0), \qquad \mathbf{D}_2 = \begin{pmatrix} 1 & 1 & -1 & 0 \\ 1 & 5 & 0 & 1 \end{pmatrix}$$
$$\mathbf{b}_2 = (5, 50)^T$$

The slack variable S_1 does not constitute a subproblem in the sense given above. Thus it is treated separately, as will be shown.

Let R_1 and R_2 be artificial variables. The starting solution for the modified problem is thus given as follows.

β_1^1	β_1^2	$\dots$	$\beta_1^{K_1}$	β_2^1	β_2^2	$\dots$	$\beta_2^{K_2}$	S_1	R_1	R_2	
$\mathbf{C}_1\hat{\mathbf{X}}_1^1$	$\mathbf{C}_1\hat{\mathbf{X}}_1^2$	$\dots$	$\mathbf{C}_1\hat{\mathbf{X}}_1^{K_1}$	$\mathbf{C}_2\hat{\mathbf{X}}_2^1$	$\mathbf{C}_2\hat{\mathbf{X}}_2^2$	$\dots$	$\mathbf{C}_2\hat{\mathbf{X}}_2^{K_2}$	0	$-M$	$-M$	
$\mathbf{A}_1\hat{\mathbf{X}}_1^1$	$\mathbf{A}_1\hat{\mathbf{X}}_1^2$	$\dots$	$\mathbf{A}_1\hat{\mathbf{X}}_1^{K_1}$	$\mathbf{A}_2\hat{\mathbf{X}}_2^1$	$\mathbf{A}_2\hat{\mathbf{X}}_2^2$	$\dots$	$\mathbf{A}_2\hat{\mathbf{X}}_2^{K_2}$	1	0	0	40
1	1	$\dots$	1	0	0	$\dots$	0	0	1	0	1
0	0	$\dots$	0	1	1	$\dots$	1	0	0	1	1
Subproblem 1				Subproblem 2				Starting basic solution			

Exercise 7.2-2

If the first (common) constraints of the original problem is $\geq$ instead of $\leq$, indicate how the tableau will be affected.
[*Ans.* Augment an artificial variable to the first equation and change the coefficient of S_1 to -1.]

The information of the starting basic solution is as follows.

$$\mathbf{X}_B = (S_1, R_1, R_2)^T = (40, 1, 1)^T$$

$$\mathbf{B} = \mathbf{B}^{-1} = \begin{pmatrix} 1 & 0 & 0 \\ 0 & 1 & 0 \\ 0 & 0 & 1 \end{pmatrix}, \qquad \mathbf{C}_B = (0, -M, -M)$$

$$\mathbf{R}_0 = \begin{pmatrix} 1 \\ 0 \\ 0 \end{pmatrix}, \qquad \mathbf{V}_1 = \begin{pmatrix} 0 \\ 1 \\ 0 \end{pmatrix}, \qquad \mathbf{V}_2 = \begin{pmatrix} 0 \\ 0 \\ 1 \end{pmatrix}$$

Consequently, $\mathbf{C}_B\mathbf{R}_0 = 0$.

First Iteration

The linear program corresponding to subproblem $j = 1$ is

$$\text{minimize } w_1 = (\mathbf{C}_B\mathbf{R}_0\mathbf{A}_1 - \mathbf{C}_1)\mathbf{X}_1$$

subject to

$$\mathbf{D}_1\mathbf{X}_1 = b_1, \ \mathbf{X}_1 \geq \mathbf{0}$$

Since

$$w_1 = [(0)(1, 1, 0) - (3, 5, 0)]\begin{pmatrix} x_1 \\ x_2 \\ S_2 \end{pmatrix} = -3x_1 - 5x_2$$

the problem becomes

$$\text{minimize } w_1 = -3x_1 - 5x_2$$

subject to

$$(5, 1, 1)\begin{pmatrix} x_1 \\ x_2 \\ S_2 \end{pmatrix} = 12$$

$$x_1, x_2, S_2 \geq 0$$

The optimal solution (obtained by the simplex method) is

$$\hat{\mathbf{X}}_1^1 = (0, 12, 0)^T, \qquad w_1^* = -60$$

Thus $\rho_1 = w_1^* + \mathbf{C}_B \mathbf{V}_1 = -60 - M$.

The linear program for $j = 2$ is given as

$$\text{minimize } w_2 = [(0)(1, 1, 0, 0) - (1, 1, 0, 0)]\begin{pmatrix} x_3 \\ x_4 \\ S_3 \\ S_4 \end{pmatrix} = -x_3 - x_4$$

subject to

$$\begin{pmatrix} 1 & 1 & -1 & 0 \\ 1 & 5 & 0 & 1 \end{pmatrix}\begin{pmatrix} x_3 \\ x_4 \\ S_3 \\ S_4 \end{pmatrix} = \begin{pmatrix} 5 \\ 50 \end{pmatrix}$$

$$x_3, x_4, S_3, S_4 \geq 0$$

This has the optimal solution

$$\hat{\mathbf{X}}_2^1 = (50, 0, 45, 0)^T, \qquad w_2^* = -50$$

Thus $\rho_2 = w_2^* + \mathbf{C}_B \mathbf{V}_2 = -50 - M$.

The solution of the two subproblems thus gives $\rho = \min \{\rho_1, \rho_2\} = \rho_1$. Since $\rho = -60 - M < 0$, the variable β_1^1 corresponding to $\hat{\mathbf{X}}_1^1$ enters the solution.

The leaving variable is determined by applying the feasibility condition of the revised simplex method. It is noticed that

$$\mathbf{P}_1^1 = \begin{pmatrix} \mathbf{A}_1 \hat{\mathbf{X}}_1^1 \\ 1 \\ 0 \end{pmatrix} = \begin{bmatrix} (1, 1, 0)\begin{pmatrix} 0 \\ 12 \\ 0 \end{pmatrix} \\ 1 \\ 0 \end{bmatrix} = \begin{pmatrix} 12 \\ 1 \\ 0 \end{pmatrix}$$

Thus $\boldsymbol{\alpha}$ for $\mathbf{P}_1^1$ is

$$\boldsymbol{\alpha} = (\alpha_{S_1}, \alpha_{R_1}, \alpha_{R_2})^T = \mathbf{B}^{-1}\mathbf{P}_1^1 = (12, 1, 0)^T$$

Subsequently, $\theta = \min \{40/12, 1/1, —\} = 1$, which corresponds to R_1. Thus R_1 is the leaving variable.

The formula in Section 4.2.1 is used to determine $\mathbf{B}_{\text{next}}^{-1}$; that is,

$$\mathbf{B}_{\text{next}}^{-1} = \mathbf{E}\mathbf{B}^{-1} = \begin{pmatrix} 1 & -12 & 0 \\ 0 & 1 & 0 \\ 0 & 0 & 1 \end{pmatrix}\begin{pmatrix} 1 & 0 & 0 \\ 0 & 1 & 0 \\ 0 & 0 & 1 \end{pmatrix} = \begin{pmatrix} 1 & -12 & 0 \\ 0 & 1 & 0 \\ 0 & 0 & 1 \end{pmatrix}$$

By letting $\mathbf{B}^{-1} = \mathbf{B}_{\text{next}}^{-1}$, the new basic solution is thus given as

$$\mathbf{X}_B = (S_1, \beta_1^1, R_2)^T = \mathbf{B}^{-1}(40, 1, 1)^T = (28, 1, 1)^T$$

The coefficient of β_1^1 in the modified objective function is $c_1^1 = \mathbf{C}_1\hat{\mathbf{X}}_1^1 = 60$. This gives $\mathbf{C}_B = (0, 60, -M)$. Since

$$\mathbf{R}_0 = \begin{pmatrix} 1 \\ 0 \\ 0 \end{pmatrix}, \qquad \mathbf{V}_1 = \begin{pmatrix} -12 \\ 1 \\ 0 \end{pmatrix}, \qquad \mathbf{V}_2 = \begin{pmatrix} 0 \\ 0 \\ 1 \end{pmatrix}$$

it follows that $\mathbf{C}_B\mathbf{R}_0 = 0$.

Second Iteration

j = 1: The objective function is $w_1 = -3x_1 - 5x_2$. Thus the solution space $\mathbf{D}_1\mathbf{X}_1 = b_1$, $\mathbf{X}_1 \geq 0$ yields exactly the same optimal solution vector $\mathbf{X}_1^1$ as in the first iteration. Since the corresponding extreme points have been considered previously, the first subproblem yields no new information at this point. [Actually, $\rho_1 = 0$ (verify!) because β_1^1 is a basic variable.]

j = 2: The objective function is $w_2 = -x_3 - x_4$. The solution space $\mathbf{D}_2\mathbf{X}_2 = \mathbf{b}_2$, $\mathbf{X}_2 \geq 0$, yields the optimal solution

$$\hat{\mathbf{X}}_2^2 = (50, 0, 45, 0)^T, \qquad w_2^* = -50$$

$$\rho_2 = w_2^* + \mathbf{C}_B\mathbf{V}_2 = -50 - M$$

(Notice that $\hat{\mathbf{X}}_2^2$ is the same as $\hat{\mathbf{X}}_2^1$. Yet, unlike $\hat{\mathbf{X}}_1^1$, β_2^1 is not a basic variable. The superscript 2 is used with $\hat{\mathbf{X}}_2^2$ for notational convenience, i.e., to represent the second iteration.) Since $\rho = \rho_2 < 0$, β_2^2 enters the solution.

The leaving variable is now determined. Consider

$$\mathbf{P}_2^2 = \begin{pmatrix} \mathbf{A}_2\hat{\mathbf{X}}_2^2 \\ 0 \\ 1 \end{pmatrix} = \begin{bmatrix} (1, 1, 0, 0)\begin{pmatrix} 50 \\ 0 \\ 45 \\ 0 \end{pmatrix} \\ 0 \\ 1 \end{bmatrix} = \begin{pmatrix} 50 \\ 0 \\ 1 \end{pmatrix}$$

$$\boldsymbol{\alpha} = (\alpha_{S_1}, \alpha_{\beta_1{}^1}, \alpha_{R_2})^T = \mathbf{B}^{-1}\mathbf{P}_2^2 = (50, 0, 1)^T$$

Subsequently, $\theta = \min\{28/50, —, 1/1\} = 14/25$. Thus S_1 is the leaving variable.

Next, compute $\mathbf{B}_{\text{next}}^{-1}$ and the new basic solution. Thus

$$\mathbf{B}^{-1} = \begin{pmatrix} 1/50 & 0 & 0 \\ 0 & 1 & 0 \\ -1/50 & 0 & 1 \end{pmatrix}\begin{pmatrix} 1 & -12 & 0 \\ 0 & 1 & 0 \\ 0 & 0 & 1 \end{pmatrix} = \begin{pmatrix} 1/50 & -12/50 & 0 \\ 0 & 1 & 0 \\ -1/50 & 12/50 & 1 \end{pmatrix}$$

$$\mathbf{X}_B = (\beta_2^2, \beta_1^1, R_2)^T = (14/25, 1, 11/25)^T$$

Since $c_2^2 = \mathbf{C}_2\hat{\mathbf{X}}_2^2 = 50$, it follows that $\mathbf{C}_B = (50, 60, -M)$. Also,

$$\mathbf{R}_0 = \begin{pmatrix} 1/50 \\ 0 \\ -1/50 \end{pmatrix}, \qquad \mathbf{V}_1 = \begin{pmatrix} -12/50 \\ 1 \\ 12/50 \end{pmatrix}, \qquad \mathbf{V}_2 = \begin{pmatrix} 0 \\ 0 \\ 1 \end{pmatrix}$$

Consequently, $\mathbf{C}_B\mathbf{R}_0 = 1 + M/50$.

Third Iteration

$j = 1$: $w_1 = (M/50 - 2)x_1 + (M/50 - 4)x_2$. The associated optimum solution is $\hat{\mathbf{X}}_1^3 = (0, 0, 12)^T$, which is the same as $\hat{\mathbf{X}}_1^1$.

$j = 2$: $w_2 = (M/50)(x_3 + x_4)$. The associated optimum solution is $\hat{\mathbf{X}}_2^3 = (5, 0, 0, 45)^T$ and $w_2^* = M/10$ with $\rho_2 = w_2^* + \mathbf{C}_B\mathbf{V}_2 = -9M/10$.

This iteration differs from the preceding two in that S_1 is now nonbasic and hence must be checked for the possibility of being a candidate for the entering variable. Consider

$$z_{S_1} - c_{S_1} = \mathbf{C}_B\mathbf{B}^{-1}\mathbf{P}_{S_1} - c_{S_1}$$
$$= \left(1 + \frac{M}{50}, 48 - \frac{12M}{50}, -M\right)(1, 0, 0)^T - 0 = 1 + \frac{M}{50}$$

This shows that S_1 cannot improve the solution. Thus $\rho = \rho_2 = -9M/10$ and β_2^3 associated with $\hat{\mathbf{X}}_2^3$ enters the solution.

To determine the leaving variable, consider

$$\mathbf{P}_2^3 = \begin{bmatrix} (1, 1, 0, 0)\begin{pmatrix}5\\0\\0\\45\end{pmatrix} \\ 0 \\ 1 \end{bmatrix} = \begin{pmatrix}5\\0\\1\end{pmatrix}$$

$$\boldsymbol{\alpha} = (\alpha_{\beta_2}^2, \alpha_{\beta_1}^1, \alpha_{R_2})^T = \mathbf{B}^{-1}\mathbf{P}_2^3 = (1/10, 0, 9/10)^T$$

This gives

$$\theta = \min\left\{\frac{14/25}{1/10}, —, \frac{11/25}{9/10}\right\} = 22/45$$

which shows that R_2 is the leaving variable. The new solution is thus given by

$$\mathbf{B}^{-1} = \begin{pmatrix} 1 & 0 & -1/9 \\ 0 & 1 & 0 \\ 0 & 0 & 10/9 \end{pmatrix}\begin{pmatrix} 1/50 & -12/50 & 0 \\ 0 & 1 & 0 \\ -1/50 & 12/50 & 0 \end{pmatrix}$$
$$= \begin{pmatrix} 1/45 & -12/45 & -5/45 \\ 0 & 1 & 0 \\ -1/45 & 12/45 & 50/45 \end{pmatrix}$$

$$\mathbf{X}_B = (\beta_2^2, \beta_1^1, \beta_2^3)^T = (23/45, 1, 22/45)^T$$

Since $\mathbf{C}_2^3 - \mathbf{C}_2\hat{\mathbf{X}}_2^3 - 5$, it follows that $\mathbf{C}_B - (50, 60, 5)$. Hence $\mathbf{C}_B\mathbf{R}_0 - 1$ (verify!).

Fourth Iteration

$j = 1$: $w_1 = -2x_1 - 4x_2$. This gives the same solution as in the first iteration.

$j = 2$: $w_2 = 0x_3 + 0x_4$. Thus $w_2^* = 0$ and $\rho_2 = 48$.

Slack S_1: $z_{S_1} - c_{S_1} = 1 - 0 = 1$.

This information shows that the last basic is optimal.

The optimal solution to the original problem is

$$\mathbf{X}_1^* = (x_1, x_2, S_2)^T = \beta_1^1 \hat{\mathbf{X}}_1^1 = (1)(0, 12, 0)^T = (0, 12, 0)^T$$

$$\begin{aligned}\mathbf{X}_2^* = (x_3, x_4, S_3, S_4)^T &= \beta_2^2 \hat{\mathbf{X}}_2^2 + \beta_2^3 \hat{\mathbf{X}}_2^3 \\ &= (23/45)(50, 0, 45, 0)^T + (22/45)(5, 0, 0, 45)^T \\ &= (28, 0, 23, 22)^T\end{aligned}$$

All the remaining variables equal zero. ◄

7.3 KARMARKAR INTERIOR-POINT ALGORITHM

As shown throughout the preceding chapters, the simplex method obtains the optimum solution by moving "cautiously" along edges of the solution space that connect adjacent corners or extreme points. Although in practice the simplex method has served well in solving very large problems, theoretically the computational basis of the technique can result in an exponential growth in the number of iterations needed to reach the optimum solution. In fact, researchers have constructed LP problems with n variables in which all 2^n extreme points are encountered before the optimum is attained.†

Attempts to produce a computationally efficient procedure that "cuts" across the interior of the solution space, rather than moves along the edges, were unsuccessful until 1984, when N. Karmarkar produced a polynomial-time algorithm. The effectiveness of the algorithm appears to be in the solution of extremely large LP problems. (As you will see below, the amount of computation associated with very small problems can be rather tedious and voluminous.)

We start by introducing the main idea of the Karmarkar method and then provide the computational details of the algorithm.

7.3.1 BASIC IDEA OF THE INTERIOR-POINT ALGORITHM

Consider the following (obviously trivial) example:

$$\text{maximize } z = x_1$$

subject to

$$0 \le x_1 \le 2$$

By letting x_2 represent a slack variable, the problem can be rewritten as

$$\text{maximize } z = x_1$$

† Try the following problem using TORA: maximize $z = x_1 + x_2$ subject to $x_1 \le 1$, $2x_1 + x_2 \le 3$, $x_1, x_2 \ge 0$. The solution is attained after all $2^2 = 4$ feasible extreme points have been examined.

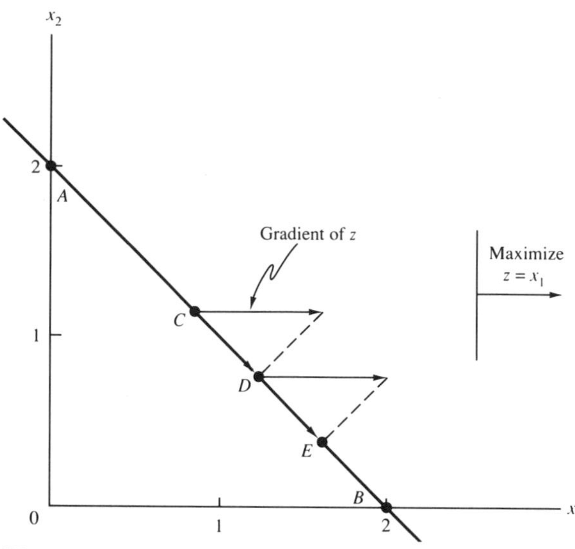

Figure 7-2

subject to

$$x_1 + x_2 = 2$$
$$x_1, x_2 \geq 0$$

Figure 7-2 depicts the problem. The solution space is given by the line segment AB. The direction of increase in z is in the positive direction of x_1.

Let us start with any arbitrary *interior* (nonextreme) point C in the feasible space (line AB). We then observe that the **gradient** of the objective function (maximize $z = x_1$) at C is the direction of fastest increase in z. If we locate an arbitrary point along the gradient and then project it perpendicularly on the feasible space (line AB), we obtain the new point D. From the standpoint of the value of z, the new point D is better than the starting point C. Such improvement is obtained by moving in the direction of the **projected gradient** CD. If we repeat the same procedure at D, we will determine a new point E that is closer to the optimum at B. Conceivably, if we move (very cautiously) in the direction of the projected gradient, we will "stumble" over the optimum point B. You will notice that if we are minimizing z (instead of maximizing), the procedure of the projected gradient will correctly move us *away* from point B toward the optimum at point A ($x_1 = 0$).

The steps given above hardly qualify for defining an algorithm in the normal sense, but the idea is intriguing! What we need are some modifications that will guarantee that (1) the steps generated along the projected gradient will not "overshoot" the optimum point at B, and (2) in the general n-dimensional case, the direction created by the projected gradient will not cause an "entrapment" of the algorithm at a nonoptimum point. This, basically, is what Karmarkar's interior-point algorithm accomplishes.

7.3.2 INTERIOR-POINT ALGORITHM

Several variants of Karmarkar's algorithm are now in circulation. Our presentation follows the original algorithm advanced by the developer of the technique.

Karmarkar assumes that the linear programming problem is given in the following special form:

$$\text{minimize } z = \mathbf{CX}$$

subject to

$$\mathbf{AX} = \mathbf{0}$$
$$\mathbf{1X} = 1$$
$$\mathbf{X} \geq \mathbf{0}$$

In essence, all the constraints are homogeneous equations except for the constraint $\mathbf{1X} = \sum_{j=1}^{n} x_j = 1$, which defines an n-dimensional simplex. The validity of Karmarkar's algorithm rests on satisfying two conditions:

1. $\mathbf{X} = \left(\frac{1}{n}, \frac{1}{n}, \ldots, \frac{1}{n}\right)$ satisfies $\mathbf{AX} = \mathbf{0}$
2. $\min z = 0$

Karmarkar provides algebraic transformations for converting the general LP problem to the form given above. The following example illustrates how a general LP may be put in the homogeneous form $\mathbf{AX} = \mathbf{0}$ with $\mathbf{1X} = 1$. It also shows how the transformation results in $\mathbf{X} = (1/n, 1/n, \ldots, 1/n)$ being a feasible solution of $\mathbf{AX} = \mathbf{0}$ (condition 1 above). The transformation needed to produce $\min z = 0$ (condition 2 above) will not be presented here because it involves tedious details.

Example 7.3-1. Consider the problem

$$\text{maximize } z = y_1 + y_2$$

subject to

$$y_1 + 2y_2 \leq 2$$
$$y_1, y_2 \geq 0$$

The constraint $y_1 + 2y_2 \leq 2$ is converted into an equation by augmenting a slack variable $y_3 \geq 0$ to yield

$$y_1 + 2y_2 + y_3 = 2$$

Now define

$$y_1 + y_2 + y_3 \leq U$$

where U is selected sufficiently large so that it will not eliminate any feasible points in the original solution space. In our example, as can be determined from the constraint $y_1 + 2y_2 + y_3 = 2$, $U = 5$ will be adequate. Augmenting a slack variable $y_4 \geq 0$, we obtain

$$y_1 + y_2 + y_3 + y_4 = 5$$

We can homogenize the constraint $y_1 + 2y_2 + y_3 = 2$ by multiplying the right-hand side by $(y_1 + y_2 + y_3 + y_4)/5$, since the latter fraction equals 1. This yields, after simplification,

$$3y_1 + 8y_2 + 3y_3 - y_4 = 0$$

To convert $y_1 + y_2 + y_3 + y_4 = 5$ to the simplex form, we simply define the new variable $x_i = y_i/5$, $i = 1, 2, 3, 4$. We thus obtain the following LP model:

$$\text{maximize } z = 5x_1 + 5x_2$$

subject to

$$\begin{aligned} 3x_1 + 8x_2 + 3x_3 - x_4 &= 0 \\ x_1 + x_2 + x_3 + x_4 &= 1 \\ x_j \geq 0, \quad j &= 1, 2, 3, 4 \end{aligned}$$

Finally, we can ensure that the center $\mathbf{X} = (1/n, 1/n, \ldots, 1/n)$ of the simplex is a feasible point for homogeneous equations by subtracting from the left-hand side of each equation an artificial variable whose coefficient equals the algebraic sum of all the left-hand-side constraint coefficients. The artificial variables are then added to the simplex equation and are penalized appropriately in the objective function. In our example, the artificial x_5 is augmented as follows:

$$\text{maximize } z = 5x_1 + 5x_2 - Mx_5$$

subject to

$$\begin{aligned} 3x_1 + 8x_2 + 3x_3 - x_4 - 13x_5 &= 0 \\ x_1 + x_2 + x_3 + x_4 + x_5 &= 1 \\ x_j \geq 0, \quad j &= 1, 2, \ldots, 5 \end{aligned}$$

For this system of equations, the new simplex center $(1/5, 1/5, \ldots, 1/5)$ is feasible for the homogeneous equation. The value M in the objective function is chosen sufficiently large to drive x_5 to zero (compare with the M-method, Section 3.3.1). ◀

We are now ready to present the main steps of the algorithm. Figure 7-3(a) provides a typical illustration of the solution space in three dimensions with the homogeneous set $\mathbf{AX} = \mathbf{0}$ consisting only of one equation. By definition, the solution space consisting of the line segment AB lies entirely in the simplex $\mathbf{1X} = 1$ and passes through the feasible interior point (1/3, 1/3, 1/3). In a similar fashion, Figure 7-3(b) provides an illustration of the solution space ABC in four dimensions with the homogeneous set again consisting of one constraint only. In this case, the center of the simplex is given by (1/4, 1/4, 1/4, 1/4).

Karmarkar's principal idea, as illustrated in Section 7.3.1, is to start from an interior point represented by the center of the simplex and then advance in the direction of the *projected gradient* to determine a new solution point. The new point must satisfy an important condition: It must be strictly an interior point, meaning that all its coordinates must be positive. This condition, as we will see shortly, is essential for the algorithm to be valid.

For the new solution point to be strictly positive, it must not lie on the boundaries of the simplex. (In terms of Figure 7-3, points A and B in three dimensions and lines AB, BC, and AC in three dimensions must be excluded.) To accomplish this task, a sphere with its center coinciding with that of the simplex is inscribed "tightly" inside the simplex. In the n-dimensional case, the radius r of this sphere equals $1/\sqrt{n(n-1)}$. Now a smaller sphere with radius αr $(0 < \alpha < 1)$ will be a subset of the "tight" sphere and any point in the intersection of the smaller sphere with the homogeneous system $\mathbf{AX} = \mathbf{0}$ will be an interior point, with all its coordinates being

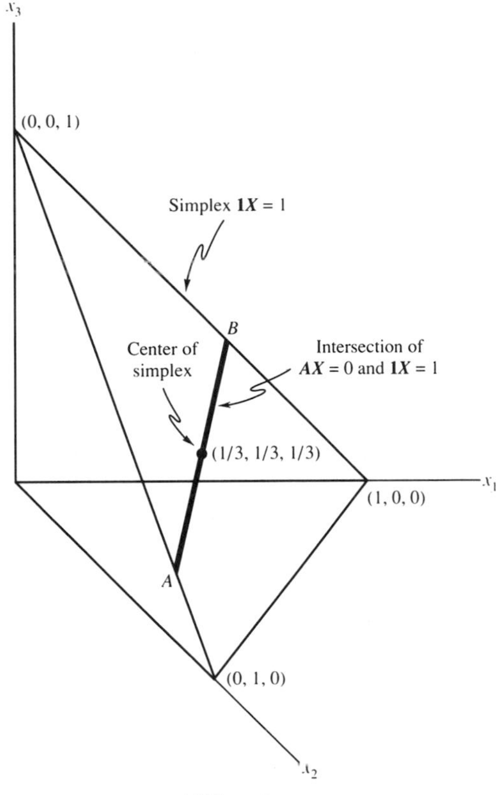

(a) Three dimensions

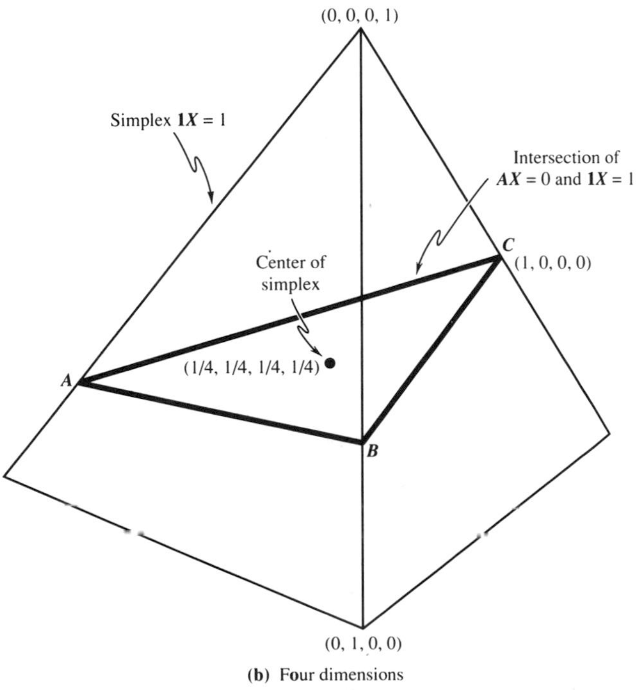

(b) Four dimensions

Figure 7-3

strictly positive. Thus we can move "as far as possible" in this restricted space (intersection of $\mathbf{AX} = \mathbf{0}$ and the αr-sphere) along the projected gradient to determine the new (necessarily improved) solution point.

The new solution point determined by the procedure above will no longer be at the center of the simplex. For the procedure to be iterative, we need to find a way to bring the *new* solution point to the center of a simplex. Karmarkar satisfies this requirement by proposing the following intriguing idea, called **projective transformation**. Let

$$y_i = \frac{x_i/x_{ki}}{\sum_{j=1}^{n} x_i/x_{kj}}, \qquad i = 1, 2, \ldots, n$$

where x_{ki} is the ith element of the current solution point $\mathbf{X}_k$. The transformation is valid, since all $x_{ki} > 0$ by design. You will also notice that $\sum_{i=1}^{n} y_i = 1$, or $\mathbf{1Y} = 1$, by definition. This transformation is equivalent to

$$\mathbf{Y} = \frac{\mathbf{D}_k^{-1}\mathbf{X}}{\mathbf{1D}_k^{-1}\mathbf{X}}$$

where $\mathbf{D}_k$ is a *diagonal* matrix whose ith diagonal elements equal x_{ki}. The transformation maps the X-space onto the Y-space uniquely because we can directly show that the equation above yields

$$\mathbf{X} = \frac{\mathbf{D}_k\mathbf{Y}}{\mathbf{1D}_k\mathbf{Y}}$$

By definition, min $\mathbf{CX} = 0$. It follows that $\mathbf{1D}_k\mathbf{Y}$ must be positive, in which case our original linear program can be written as

$$\text{minimize } z = \mathbf{CD}_k\mathbf{Y}$$

subject to

$$\mathbf{AD}_k\mathbf{Y} = \mathbf{0}$$
$$\mathbf{1Y} = 1$$
$$\mathbf{Y} \geq \mathbf{0}$$

This transformed problem has the same format as the original problem. We can thus start with the simplex center $\mathbf{Y} = (1/n, 1/n, \ldots, 1/n)$ and repeat the iterative step explained earlier. After each iteration, we can compute the values of the original $\mathbf{X}$ variables from the $\mathbf{Y}$ solution.

We are now in a position to show how the new solution point can be determined for the transformed problem. Essentially, our problem at any iteration k is given by

$$\text{maximize } z = \mathbf{CD}_k\mathbf{Y}$$

subject to

$$\mathbf{AD}_k\mathbf{Y} = \mathbf{0}$$
$$\mathbf{Y} \text{ lies in the } \alpha r\text{-sphere}$$

Since the αr-sphere is a subset of the space of the constraints $\mathbf{1X} = 1$ and $\mathbf{X} \geq \mathbf{0}$, these two constraints can be dispensed with. The optimum solution of the problem above can be shown to be

$$\mathbf{Y}_{\text{new}} = \mathbf{Y}_{\text{current}} + \alpha r \frac{\mathbf{c}_p}{\|\mathbf{c}_p\|}$$

where $\mathbf{Y}_{\text{current}} = (1/n, 1/n, \ldots, 1/n)^t$ and $\mathbf{c}_p$ is the projected gradient, which can be shown to be computed as follows:

$$\mathbf{c}_p = [\mathbf{I} - \mathbf{P}^t(\mathbf{P}\mathbf{P}^t)^{-1}\mathbf{P}](\mathbf{C}\mathbf{D}_k)^t$$

with $\mathbf{P} = \begin{pmatrix} \mathbf{A}\mathbf{D}_k \\ \mathbf{1} \end{pmatrix}$.

We emphasize that the specific selection of α is crucial in producing a "potent" algorithm. Normally, we would like to select α as large as possible to acquire large jumps in the solution. However, by choosing α too large, we may "dangerously" come too close to the prohibited boundaries of the simplex. There is no known general answer to this problem. Karmarkar suggests the use of $\alpha = (n - 1)/3n$.

Summary of the Algorithm

The steps of Karmarkar's algorithm may now be summarized as follows:

Step 0: Start with the solution point $\mathbf{X}_0 = (1/n, 1/n, \ldots, 1/n)$ and compute $r = \sqrt{1/n(n-1)}$ and $\alpha = (n - 1)/3n$.

General Step k: Define

$$\mathbf{D}_k = \text{diag}\,\{x_{k1}, \ldots, x_{kn}\}$$

$$\mathbf{P} = \begin{pmatrix} \mathbf{A}\mathbf{D}_k \\ \mathbf{1} \end{pmatrix}$$

and compute

$$\mathbf{Y}_{\text{new}} = \left(\frac{1}{n}, \ldots, \frac{1}{n}\right)^t + \alpha r \frac{\mathbf{c}_p}{\|\mathbf{c}_p\|}$$

$$\mathbf{X}_{k+1} = \frac{\mathbf{D}_k \mathbf{Y}_{\text{new}}}{\mathbf{1}\mathbf{D}_k \mathbf{Y}_{\text{new}}}$$

where $\mathbf{c}_p = [\mathbf{I} - \mathbf{P}^t(\mathbf{P}\mathbf{P}^t)^{-1}\mathbf{P}](\mathbf{c}\mathbf{D}_k)^t$.

Example 7.3-2. Consider the following linear program, which is already in the format specified by the Karmarkar algorithm.

$$\text{Minimize } z = x_1 - 2x_2$$

subject to

$$\begin{aligned} x_1 - 2x_2 + x_3 &= 0 \\ x_1 + x_2 + x_3 &= 1 \\ x_1, x_2, x_3 &\geq 0 \end{aligned}$$

The example satisfies all the conditions of Karmarkar's algorithm; namely, $X = (1/3,\ 1/3,\ 1/3)$ satisfies $x_1 - 2x_2 + x_3 = 0$ and the optimum value of z [corresponding to the optimum solution (2/3, 1/3, 0)] is zero.

Iteration 0

$$\mathbf{X}_0 = \left(\frac{1}{3}, \frac{1}{3}, \frac{1}{3}\right), \qquad r = \frac{1}{\sqrt{6}}, \qquad \alpha = \frac{2}{9}, \qquad z = \frac{-1}{3} = -.33333$$

Iteration 1

$$\mathbf{D}_0 = \begin{pmatrix} 1/3 & 0 & 0 \\ 0 & 1/3 & 0 \\ 0 & 0 & 1/3 \end{pmatrix}$$

$$\mathbf{cD}_0 = (1/3 \quad -2/3 \quad 0)$$

$$\mathbf{AD}_0 = (1 \quad -2 \quad 1)\begin{pmatrix} 1/3 & 0 & 0 \\ 0 & 1/3 & 0 \\ 0 & 0 & 1/3 \end{pmatrix} = (1/3 \quad -2/3 \quad 1/3)$$

$$\mathbf{P} = \begin{pmatrix} 1/3 & -2/3 & 1/3 \\ 1 & 1 & 1 \end{pmatrix}$$

$$(\mathbf{PP}^t)^{-1} = \begin{pmatrix} 2/3 & 0 \\ 0 & 3 \end{pmatrix}^{-1} = \begin{pmatrix} 3/2 & 0 \\ 0 & 1/3 \end{pmatrix}$$

$$\mathbf{c}_p = \left[\begin{pmatrix} 1 & 0 & 0 \\ 0 & 1 & 0 \\ 0 & 0 & 1 \end{pmatrix} - \begin{pmatrix} 1/3 & 1 \\ -2/3 & 1 \\ 1/3 & 1 \end{pmatrix}\begin{pmatrix} 3/2 & 0 \\ 0 & 1/3 \end{pmatrix}\begin{pmatrix} 1/3 & -2/3 & 1/3 \\ 1 & 1 & 1 \end{pmatrix}\right]\begin{pmatrix} 1/3 \\ -2/3 \\ 0 \end{pmatrix}$$

$$= (1/6, 0, -1/6)^t$$

$$\|\mathbf{c}_p\| = \sqrt{(1/6)^2 + 0 + (1/6)^2} = .2357$$

$$\frac{\alpha r}{\|\mathbf{c}_p\|} = \frac{(2/9)(1/\sqrt{6})}{.2357} = .384901$$

$$\mathbf{Y}_{\text{new}} = \left(\frac{1}{3}, \frac{1}{3}, \frac{1}{3}\right)^t + .384901\left(\frac{1}{6}, 0, \frac{-1}{6}\right)^t$$

$$= (.397483, .333333, .269183)^t$$

We now compute $\mathbf{X}_1$, the solution associated with $\mathbf{Y}_{\text{new}}$. Since $\mathbf{D}_0$ has equal diagonal elements (= 1/3) and the fact that $\mathbf{1Y} = 1$, the formula $\mathbf{X}_1 = \mathbf{D}_0\mathbf{Y}_{\text{new}}/\mathbf{1D}_0\mathbf{Y}_{\text{new}}$ yields $\mathbf{X}_1 = \mathbf{Y}_{\text{new}} = (.397483,\ .333333,\ .269183)^t$. The corresponding value of $z = -.269183$, which is better than the preceding solution $\mathbf{X}_0$, for which $z = -.33333$.

Observe that if α is taken larger than the current value of 2/9, the solution will move faster toward the optimum point (2/3, 1/3, 0). In fact, if we take $\alpha = 1$, the resulting $\mathbf{Y}_{\text{new}}$ will provide the optimum value directly. However, we *cannot* do this because $x_3 = 0$ will invalidate the assumption on which the projective transformation **Y** is based. This observation provides a glimpse at one of the uncertainties that is inherent in the interior-point algorithm.

Iteration 2

$$\mathbf{D}_1 = \text{diag}\ \{.397485,\ .333333,\ .269182\}$$

$$\mathbf{cD}_1 = (.397485,\ -.666666,\ 0)$$

$$\mathbf{AD}_1 = (1,\ -2,\ 1)\begin{pmatrix} .397485 & 0 & 0 \\ 0 & .333333 & 0 \\ 0 & 0 & .269182 \end{pmatrix}$$

$$= (.397485,\ -.666666,\ .269182)$$

$$\mathbf{P} = \begin{pmatrix} .397845 & -.666666 & .269182 \\ 1 & 1 & 1 \end{pmatrix}$$

$$\mathbf{c}_p = (.132402,\ .018152,\ -.150555)^t$$

$$\|\mathbf{c}_p\| = .201312$$

$$\frac{\alpha r}{\|\mathbf{c}_p\|} = \frac{(2/9)(1/\sqrt{6})}{.201312} = .450653$$

$$\mathbf{Y}_{\text{new}} = \left(\frac{1}{3}, \frac{1}{3}, \frac{1}{3}\right)^t + .450653(.132402,\ .018152,\ -.150555)^t$$

$$= (.393001,\ .341514,\ .265486)^t$$

Now, to compute $\mathbf{X}_2$, we have

$$\mathbf{D}_1\mathbf{Y}_{\text{new}} = \begin{pmatrix} .156212 \\ .113838 \\ .071464 \end{pmatrix}, \qquad \mathbf{1D}_1\mathbf{Y}_{\text{new}} = .341514$$

$$\mathbf{X}_2 = \frac{\mathbf{D}_1\mathbf{Y}_{\text{new}}}{\mathbf{1D}_1\mathbf{Y}_{\text{new}}} = \begin{pmatrix} .457411 \\ .333333 \\ .209256 \end{pmatrix}$$

$$z = .20934$$

Repeated application of the steps of the algorithm will move the solution closer to the optimum point (2/3, 1/3, 0). Karmarkar does provide an additional step for rounding the optimal solution to the optimum extreme point. The details of this step will not be presented here, however. ◀

7.4 SUMMARY

Both the upper bounding and the decomposition algorithm are designed primarily to improve the computational efficiency. The upper bounding algorithm is particularly important because it allows us to consider the associated constraints implicitly, thus increasing the efficiency of computations. Upper bounding will also be of major importance when we solve the integer programming problem by the branch-and-bound procedure.

Karmarkar interior-point algorithm offers a fresh look at the solution of linear programs where the iterations are constructed to "shoot" through the interior of the solution space. The simple example we solved in this chapter indicates a tremendous volume of computations. However, Karmarkar has been claiming significant successes in solving very large problems. Despite the elegance of the interior-point algorithm, the computational advantage of the method will remain in doubt until a feasible commercial code becomes accessible.

SELECTED REFERENCES

BAZARAA, M., J. JARVIS, and H. SHERALI, *Linear Programming and Network Flows*, 2nd ed., Wiley, New York, 1990.

LASDON, L., *Optimization Theory for Large Systems*, Macmillan, New York, 1970.

KARMARKAR, N., "A New Polynomial Algorithm for Linear Programming," *Combinatorica*, Vol. 4, pp. 373–395, 1984.

KARMARKAR, N., "Methods and Applications for Efficient Resource Allocation," *United States Patent 4,744,028*, May 10, 1988.

NICKELS, W., W. RODDER, L. XU, and H. J. ZIMMERMANN, "Intelligent Gradient Search in Linear Programming," *European Journal of Operational Research*, Vol. 22, pp. 293–303, 1985.

PROBLEMS

Section	Assigned Problems
7.1	7–1 to 7–6
7.2	7–7 to 7–10
7.3	7–11, 7–12

☐ **7–1** Consider the following linear program:

$$\text{maximize } z = 2x_1 + x_2$$

subject to

$$x_1 + x_2 \leq 3$$
$$0 \leq x_1 \leq 2, 0 \leq x_2 \leq 2$$

(a) Solve the problem graphically and trace the sequence of extreme points leading to the optimum solution.
(b) Solve the problem by the upper-bound primal simplex and show that the method produces the same sequence of extreme points before reaching the optimum (use TORA to generate the iterations).
(c) How does the upper-bound simplex method recognize the extreme points?

☐ **7–2** Solve the following problem by using the bounded primal simplex method:

$$\text{maximize } z = 6x_1 + 2x_2 + 8x_3 + 4x_4 + 2x_5 + 10x_6$$

subject to

$$8x_1 + x_2 + 8x_3 + 2x_4 + 2x_5 + 4x_6 \leq 13$$
$$0 \leq x_j \leq 1, j = 1, 2, \ldots, 6$$

☐ **7–3** Apply the bounded primal simplex method to the following problems.

(a) Minimize $z = 6x_1 - 2x_2 - 3x_3$
subject to

$$2x_1 + 4x_2 + 2x_3 \leq 8$$
$$x_1 - 2x_2 + 3x_3 \leq 7$$
$$0 \leq x_1 \leq 2, 0 \leq x_2 \leq 2, 0 \leq x_3 \leq 1$$

(b) Maximize $z = 3x_1 + 5x_2 + 2x_3$
subject to

$$x_1 + 2x_2 + 2x_3 \leq 10$$
$$2x_1 + 4x_2 + 3x_3 \leq 15$$
$$0 \leq x_1 \leq 4, 0 \leq x_2 \leq 3, 0 \leq x_3 \leq 3$$

☐ **7–4** Solve the following problems by the bounded primal simplex method:

(a) Maximize $z = 3x_1 + 2x_2 - 2x_3$
subject to

$$2x_1 + x_2 + x_3 \leq 8$$
$$x_1 + 2x_2 \quad x_3 \geq 3$$
$$1 \leq x_1 \leq 3, 0 \leq x_2 \leq 3, 2 \leq x_3$$

(b) Maximize $z = x_1 + 2x_2$
subject to

$$-x_1 + 2x_2 \geq 0$$
$$3x_1 + 2x_2 \leq 10$$
$$-x_1 + x_2 \leq 1$$
$$1 \leq x_1 \leq 3, 0 \leq x_2 \leq 1$$

(c) Maximize $z = 4x_1 + 2x_2 + 6x_3$
subject to

$$4x_1 - x_2 \leq 9$$
$$-x_1 + x_2 + 2x_3 \leq 8$$
$$-3x_1 + x_2 + 4x_3 \leq 12$$
$$1 \leq x_1 \leq 3, 0 \leq x_2 \leq 5, 0 \leq x_3 \leq 2$$

☐ **7–5** In Section 7.1 the lower bounds are accounted for by using the substitution $\mathbf{X} - \mathbf{X}'' = \mathbf{L}$. Show mathematically how the effect of lower bounds can be considered directly by modifying the feasibility condition of the primal simplex method. Apply the new condition to Problem 7–4.

☐ **7–6 (Bounded Dual Simplex Method).** The dual simplex method can be modified to apply to the bounded variables LP problem as follows. Given the upper-bound constraint $x_j \leq u_j$, for all j (if u_j is not finite, replace it with a sufficiently large upper bound M), the LP problem is converted into a dual feasible form by using the substitution $x_j = u_j - x'_j$, if necessary.

Step 1: If any current basic variable $(\mathbf{X}_B)_i$ exceeds its upper bound, use the substitution $(\mathbf{X}_B)_i = (\mathbf{U}_B)_i - (\mathbf{X}_B)'_i$. Go to step 2.

Step 2: If all basic variables are feasible, stop. Otherwise, select the leaving variable x_r as the basic variable having the most negative value. Go to step 3.

Step 3: Select the entering variable using the optimality condition of the regular dual simplex method. Go to step 4.

Step 4: Carry out a change of basis, then go to step 1.

Apply the procedure to the following problem:

$$\text{minimize } z = -3x_1 - 2x_2 + 2x_3$$

subject to

$$\begin{aligned} 2x_1 + x_2 + x_3 &\leq 8 \\ -x_1 + 2x_2 + x_3 &\geq 13 \\ 0 \leq x_1 \leq 2,\ 0 \leq x_2 \leq 3,\ &0 \leq x_3 \leq 1 \end{aligned}$$

□ **7–7** Apply the decomposition principle to the following problem:

$$\text{maximize } z = 6x_1 + 7x_2 + 3x_3 + 5x_4 + x_5 + x_6$$

subject to

$$\begin{aligned} x_1 + x_2 + x_3 + x_4 + x_5 + x_6 &\leq 50 \\ x_1 + x_2 &\leq 10 \\ x_2 &\leq 8 \\ 5x_3 + x_4 &\leq 12 \\ x_5 + x_6 &\geq 5 \\ x_5 + 5x_6 &\leq 50 \\ x_1, x_2, \ldots, x_6 &\geq 0 \end{aligned}$$

□ **7–8** Solve the following problem by the decomposition algorithm:

$$\text{maximize } z = x_1 + 3x_2 + 5x_3 + 2x_4$$

subject to

$$\begin{aligned} 2x_1 + x_2 &\leq 9 \\ 5x_1 + 3x_2 + 4x_3 &\geq 10 \\ x_1 + 4x_2 &\leq 8 \\ x_3 - 5x_4 &\leq 4 \\ x_3 + x_4 &\leq 10 \\ x_1, x_2, x_3, x_4 &\geq 0 \end{aligned}$$

□ **7–9** Indicate the necessary changes in the decomposition algorithm to apply it to minimization problems. Then solve the problem:

$$\text{minimize } z = 5x_1 + 3x_2 + 8x_3 - 5x_4$$

subject to

$$\begin{aligned} x_1 + x_2 + x_3 + x_4 &\geq 25 \\ 5x_1 + x_2 \qquad\qquad &\leq 20 \\ 5x_1 - x_2 \qquad\qquad &\geq 5 \\ x_3 + x_4 &= 20 \\ x_1, x_2, x_3, x_4 &\geq 0 \end{aligned}$$

☐ **7–10** Solve the following problem using the decomposition algorithm:

$$\text{minimize } z = 10y_1 + 2y_2 + 4y_3 + 8y_4 + y_5$$

subject to

$$\begin{aligned} y_1 + 4y_2 - y_3 \qquad\qquad &\geq 8 \\ 2y_1 + y_2 + y_3 \qquad\qquad &\geq 2 \\ 3y_1 \qquad + y_4 + y_5 &\geq 4 \\ y_1 \qquad + 2y_4 - y_5 &\geq 10 \\ y_1, y_2, \ldots, y_5 &\geq 0 \end{aligned}$$

[*Hint*: Consider the dual of the problem.]

☐ **7–11** Carry out one additional iteration in Example 7.3-2 and show that the solution is moving toward optimum $z = 0$.

☐ **7–12** Carry out three iterations of Karmarkar's algorithm.

$$\text{Maximize } z = -4x_1 + x_3 - x_4$$

subject to

$$\begin{aligned} -2x_1 + 2x_2 + x_3 - x_4 &= 0 \\ x_1 + x_2 + x_3 + x_4 &= 1 \\ x_1, x_2, x_3 . x_4 &\geq 0 \end{aligned}$$

Chapter 8

Network Models

In Chapter 6 we limited our attention to transportation (or distribution) problems that deal with shipping commodities between sources and destinations at minimum transportation costs. The transportation model (and its variants) is but one of the many problems that can be represented and solved as a network. To be specific, consider the following situations:

a. Design of offshore natural-gas pipeline network connecting wellheads in the Gulf of Mexico with an onshore delivery point with the objective of minimizing the cost of constructing the pipeline.

b. Determination of the shortest route joining two cities in an existing network of roads.

c. Determination of the maximum annual capacity in tons of a coal slurry pipeline network joining the coal mines in Wyoming with the power plants in Houston. (Slurry pipelines transport coal by pumping water through suitably designed pipes operating between the coal mines and the desired destination.)

d. Determination of the *minimum-cost* flow schedule from oil fields to refineries and finally to distribution centers. Crude oils and gasoline products can be shipped via tankers, pipelines, and/or trucks. In addition to maximum supply availability at the oil fields and minimum demand requirements at the distribution centers, restrictions on the capacity of the refineries and the modes of transportation must be taken into account.

A study of this representative list reveals that network optimization problems can generally be modeled by one of four models:

1. Minimal spanning tree model (situation a).
2. Shortest-route model (situation b).
3. Maximum-flow model (situation c).
4. Minimum-cost capacitated network model (situation d).

The examples cited above deal with the determination of distances and material flow in a literal sense. There are many applications where the variables of the problem can represent other properties such as inventory or money flow. Examples illustrating these situations will be given in this chapter.

The network models listed can be represented and, in principle, solved as linear programs (see Section 8.5.2). However, the tremendous number of variables and constraints that normally accompanies a typical network model makes it inadvisable to solve network problems directly by the simplex method. The special structure of these problems allows the development of highly efficient algorithms, which in most cases are based on linear programming theory.

From the practical standpoint, the minimum-cost capacitated network model enjoys a wide variety of applications. Indeed, both the shortest-route and maximum-flow problem can be formulated as special cases of the capacitated transportation model. These points will be addressed throughout the chapter.

8.1 NETWORK DEFINITIONS

A network consists of a set of **nodes** linked by **arcs** or **branches**. Associated with each arc is a flow of some type. For example, in a transportation network, cities represent nodes and highways represent arcs, with traffic representing the arc flow. The standard notation for describing a network G is $G = (\mathbf{N}, \mathbf{A})$, where $\mathbf{N}$ is the set of nodes and $\mathbf{A}$ is the set of arcs. The network in Figure 8-1 comprised of five nodes and eight arcs is thus described by

$$\mathbf{N} = \{1, 2, 3, 4, 5\}$$
$$\mathbf{A} = \{(1, 3), (1, 2), (2, 3), (2, 4), (2, 5), (3, 4), (3, 5), (4, 5)\}$$

Associated with each network is a flow of some type (e.g., oil products flow in a pipeline network and traffic flows in a transportation network). In general, the flow

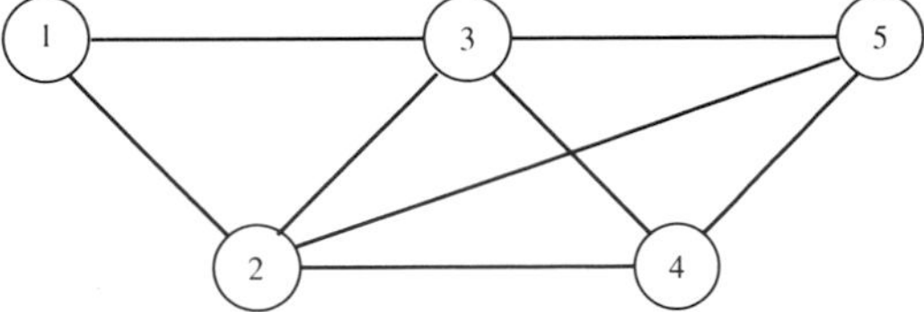

Figure 8-1

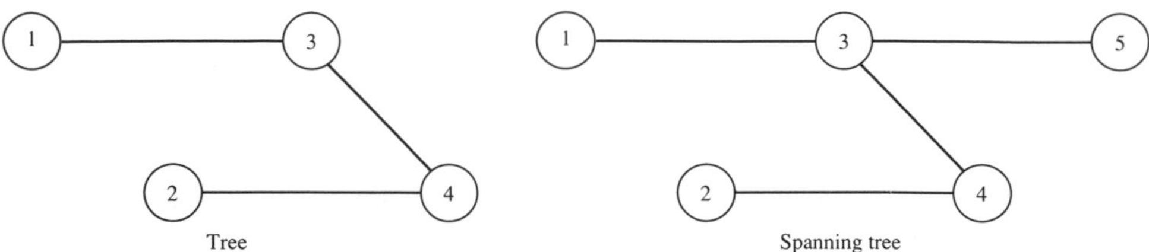

Figure 8-2

in an arc is limited by its **capacity**, which may be finite or infinite. An arc is said to be **directed** or **oriented** if it allows positive flow in one direction and zero flow in the opposite direction. A **directed network** is thus a network with all directed arcs.

A **path** is a sequence of distinct arcs that join the two nodes regardless of the orientation of the individual arcs. For example, in Figure 8-1, arcs (1, 3), (3, 2), and (2, 4) represent a path from node 1 to node 4. A path will form a **loop** or a **cycle** if it connects a node to itself. For example, in Figure 8-1, the arcs (2, 3), (3, 4), and (4, 2) form a loop. A **directed loop** (or a **circuit**) is a loop in which all the arcs have the same direction or orientation.

A **connected network** is a network in which every two distinct nodes are linked by a path as demonstrated by the network in Figure 8-1. A **tree** is a connected network that may involve only a subset of the nodes and a **spanning tree** is a connected network that includes all the nodes in the network with no loops. Figure 8-2 defines a tree and a spanning tree for the network in Figure 8-1.

8.2 MINIMAL SPANNING TREE PROBLEM

Consider the situation in which it is desired to create a network of paved roads that link a number of rural towns. Because of budget limitations, the miles of constructed roads must be the absolute minimum that allows direct or indirect traffic linkage among the different towns.

The situation above can be represented by a network in which towns represent nodes and proposed roads represent arcs. The resulting model is typical of the so-called *minimal spanning tree* problem, where it is desired to determine the spanning tree that results in the smallest sum of the connecting arcs. In effect, the minimal spanning tree deals with finding the most "efficient" connections among all the nodes in the network, which, by definition, cannot include any loops or cycles.

The minimal spanning tree algorithm calls for starting with *any* node and joining it to the *closest* node in the network. The resulting two nodes then form a *connected set*, C, with the remaining nodes comprising the *unconnected set*, $\bar{C}$. Next, we choose a node from the unconnected set that is *closest* (has the shortest arc length) to *any* node in the connected set. The chosen node is then removed from the unconnected set and joined to the connected set. The process is repeated until the unconnected set becomes empty (or equivalently, until all the nodes are moved from $\bar{C}$ to set C). A tie may be broken arbitrarily. Ties, however, point to the existence of alternative solutions.

Example 8.2-1. The Midwest TV Cable Company is in the process of planning a network for providing cable TV service to five new housing development areas.

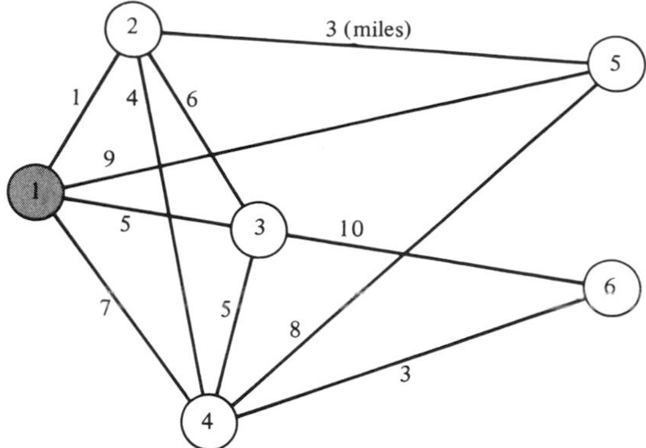

Figure 8-3

The cable system network is summarized in Figure 8-3. The numbers associated with each branch represent the miles of cable needed to connect any two locations. Node 1 represents the cable TV relay station and the remaining nodes (2 through 6) represent the five development areas. A missing branch between two nodes implies that it is prohibitively expensive or physically impossible to connect the associated development areas. It is required to determine the links that will result in the use of minimum cable miles while guaranteeing that all areas are connected (directly or indirectly) to the cable TV station.

The graphical solution is summarized in Figure 8-4 by iterations. The procedure can be started from any node, always ending up with the same optimum solution. In the cable TV example, it is logical to start the computations with node 1. Thus node 1 represents the initial set of "connected nodes." The corresponding set of "unconnected nodes" is represented by nodes 2, 3, 4, 5, and 6. Symbolically, we write this as

$$C = \{1\}, \qquad \bar{C} = \{2, 3, 4, 5, 6\}$$

Iteration 1

Node 1 must be connected to node 2, the closest node in $\bar{C} = \{2, 3, 4, 5, 6\}$. Iteration 1 of Figure 8-4 thus shows that

$$C = \{1, 2\}, \qquad \bar{C} = \{3, 4, 5, 6\}$$

Iteration 2

Nodes 1 and 2 (set C) are now linked permanently. In iteration 2 we select a node in $\bar{C} = \{3, 4, 5, 6\}$ that is closest to a node in $C = \{1, 2\}$. Since the shortest distance occurs between nodes 2 and 5 (see iteration 2 of Figure 8-4), we have

$$C = \{1, 2, 5\}, \qquad \bar{C} = \{3, 4, 6\}$$

Iteration 3

Iteration 3 of Figure 8-4 gives the distances from the nodes of $C = \{1, 2, 5\}$ to all the nodes in $\bar{C} = \{3, 4, 6\}$. Thus nodes 2 and 4 are connected, which yields

$$C = \{1, 2, 4, 5\}, \qquad \bar{C} = \{3, 6\}$$

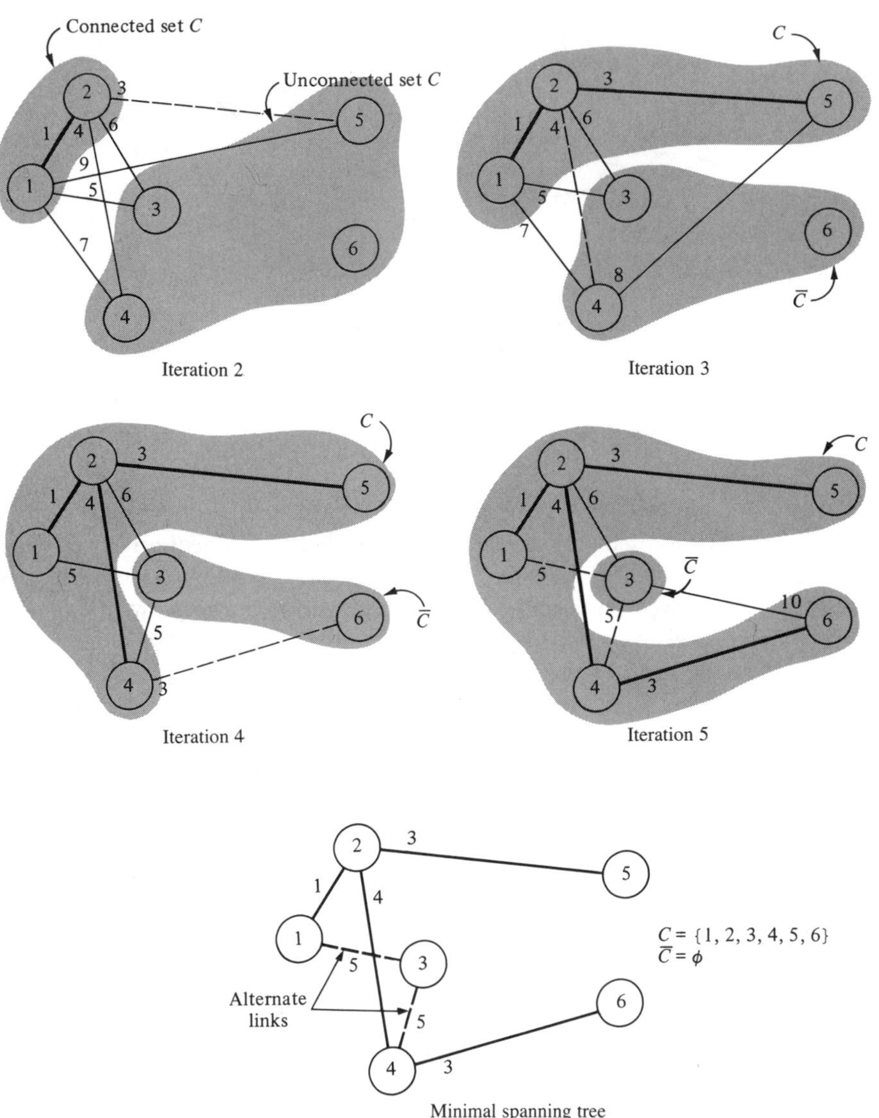

Figure 8-4

Iteration 4

Iteration 4 of Figure 8-4 shows that nodes 4 and 6 must be connected. Thus we obtain

$$C = \{1, 2, 4, 5, 6\}, \qquad \bar{C} = \{3\}$$

Iteration 5

In iteration 5 we have a tie that may be broken arbitrarily. This means that we can connect 1 and 3 *or* 4 and 3. Both (alternative) solutions lead to

$$C = \{1, 2, 3, 4, 5, 6\}, \qquad \bar{C} = \emptyset$$

Since all the nodes are connected, the procedure is complete. The minimum cable miles that are used to connect the development areas to the TV station equal $1 + 3 + 4 + 3 + 5 = 16$ miles. ◀

Exercise 8.2-1
Solve Example 8.2-1 using node 4 as the initial connected set; that is, initial $C = \{4\}$. Follow the graphical procedure of Figure 8-4.
[*Ans.* The successive iterations will lead to connecting 4 to 6, 4 to 2, 2 to 1, 2 to 5, and finally, 1 to 3 or 4 to 3. This is the same solution obtained previously, thus demonstrating that the specific choice of the initial set C is arbitrary.]

8.3 SHORTEST-ROUTE PROBLEM

In the obvious sense, the shortest-route problem deals with determining the *connected* arcs in a transportation network that collectively comprise the shortest distance between a source and a destination. In this section we present other types of applications that can be modeled and solved as a shortest-route problem. The applications are followed by a presentation of the solution algorithms.

8.3.1 EXAMPLES OF THE SHORTEST-ROUTE APPLICATIONS

Example 8.3-1 (Three-Jug Puzzle).† You are presented with an 8-gallon jug filled with some fluid. You are also given two empty 5-gallon and 3-gallon jugs. It is desired to divide the fluid into two equal 4-gallon portions by pouring back and forth among the three jugs. No other measuring devices are allowed.

We use network representation to model this situation. A node is defined to represent the amounts of fluid in the 8-gallon, 5-gallon, and 3-gallon jugs, respectively. We use the notation (a, b, c) to summarize the definition of the node. For example, node (8, 0, 0) means that the 8-gallon jug is full and the 5-gallon and 3-gallon jugs are empty. If we pour fluid from the 8-gallon jug to fill the 5-gallon jug, we will be reaching node (3, 5, 0). The node (8, 0, 0) actually represents the initial state of the system before any dividing has taken place, whereas node (3, 5, 0) represents a possible node along the path that will eventually lead us to the desired solution (4, 4, 0). Our objective is to find the path (sequence of nodes) that takes us from the initial state, node (8, 0, 0), to the final solution, node (4, 4, 0). Observe that no combination other than (4, 4, 0) will give the desired final solution because the third jug has a capacity of 3 gallons only.

The "length" of the arc joining various nodes will be taken to represent the number of fluid-pouring operations needed to reach one node from another. For example, the length of the arc from node (8, 0, 0) to node (3, 5, 0) is 1 because only

† You probably have come across this puzzle previously. Our objective is to show how network representation can be used to systematize the solution procedure. One of my students, after being exposed to the solution of this problem in my networks class, was able to make use of the same logical process to solve a problem in his methods and standards class (see Problem 8–6).

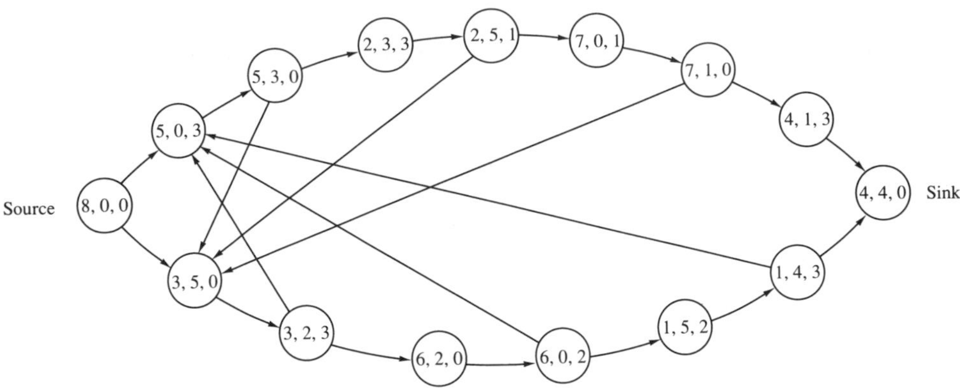

Figure 8-5

one operation is needed to change the state of the node. Our objective, of course, is to find the shortest path from the initial node (8, 0, 0) to final node (4, 4, 0). Thus the model falls in the category of the shortest-route algorithm.

Figure 8-5 presents all the *promising* nodes that can lead from node (8, 0, 0) to the final node (4, 4, 0). Each arc in the network corresponds to exactly one "pouring" operation; hence each has a nominal length of 1 unit. The optimal solution requires seven pouring operations and is (obviously) given by the following sequence:

$$(8, 0, 0) \rightarrow (3, 5, 0) \rightarrow (3, 2, 3) \rightarrow (6, 2, 0) \rightarrow (6, 0, 2) \rightarrow (1, 5, 2) \rightarrow (1, 4, 3) \rightarrow (4, 4, 0)$$ ◀

Example 8.3-2 (Equipment Replacement). A car rental company is developing a replacement plan for its fleet over the next 5 years. A car must be in service for at least 1 year before replacement is considered. Table 8-1 summarizes the replacement cost per car (in thousands of dollars) as a function of time and the number of years in operation. The cost includes purchasing, salvage, operating, and maintenance.

This problem can be represented by a network as follows. Each year is represented by a node. The "length" of an arc joining two nodes equals the associated replacement cost given in Table 8-1. Figure 8-6 depicts the network. The problem reduces to finding the shortest "route" from node 1 to node 5.

The shortest "route" can be determined using the algorithm we will present in Section 8.3.2. The optimal solution will yield the route $1 \rightarrow 2 \rightarrow 5$ with a total cost of $4 + 8.1 = 12.1$ (thousands of dollars). This means that each car should be replaced in year 2 and discarded in year 5. ◀

Table 8-1

Year	1	2	3	4	5
1		4.0	5.4	9.8	13.7
2			4.3	6.2	8.1
3				4.8	7.1
4					4.9

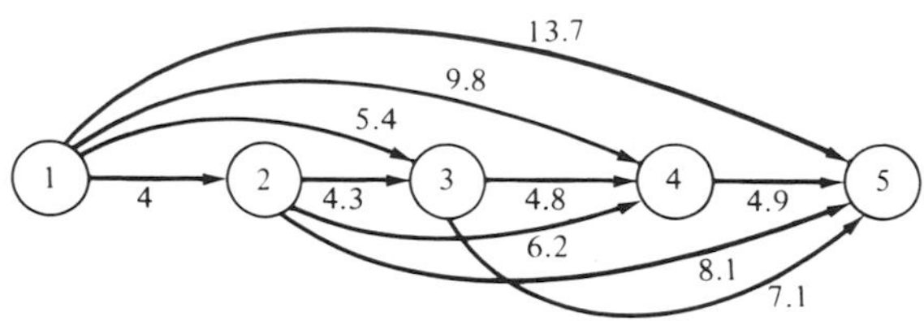

Figure 8-6

Example 8.3-3 (Most Reliable Route). I. Q. Smart has to drive daily between residence and place of work. Having just taken a class in network analysis, Smart was able to determine the shortest route to work. Unfortunately, the shortest route was heavily patrolled by police.

With all the fines paid for speeding violations, the shortest route obviously was not a good choice. Smart thus decided to choose a route that maximizes the probability of *not* being stopped by police. Observing all the feasible road segments, the associated probabilities were compiled as given on the different arcs (road segments) of Figure 8-7.

Investigating the probability information, Smart realized that the total probability of *not* being stopped by police on a given route equals the product of the probabilities associated with the road segments comprising the chosen route. For example, the probability associated with the route $1 \to 2 \to 3 \to 5 \to 7$ is $.2 \times .6 \times .3 \times .25 = .009$. Although it is possible to compute all such probabilities (eight different routes in this case), Smart decided to convert the problem to a shortest-route model by using the following conversion. Letting $P_{1k} = P_1 \times P_2 \times \cdots \times P_k$ be the probability of not being stopped in the specific route $(1, k)$, then

$$\log P_{1k} = \log P_1 + \log P_2 + \cdots + \log P_k$$

A maximization of P_{1k} is algebraically equivalent to maximizing $\log P_{1k}$ and, consequently, to maximizing the *sum* of the logarithms of the individual probabilities along the chosen route. Since $\log P_j \leq 0$, $j = 1, 2, \ldots, k$, *maximizing* the sum of $\log P_j$ is equivalent to *minimizing* the sum of $(-\log P_j)$. Table 8-2 summarizes the probabilities of Figure 8-7 and their logarithms. Figure 8-8 now expresses Smart's problem as a shortest-route model.

The "shortest route" in Figure 8-8 is defined by the nodes $1 \to 3 \to 5 \to 7$ with a corresponding distance of 1.1707. Thus $\log P_7 = -1.1707$, or $P_7 = .0675$. This means that the maximum probability of not being stopped by police is only .0675. ◀

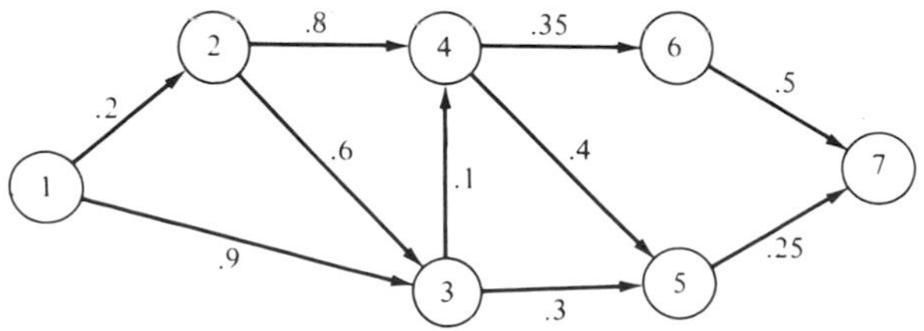

Figure 8-7

Table 8-2

Road Segment (i, j)	P_{ij}	$\log P_{ij}$	$-\log P_{ij}$
(1, 2)	.2	−.69897	.69897
(1, 3)	.9	−.04576	.04576
(2, 3)	.6	−.22185	.22185
(2, 4)	.8	−.09691	.09691
(3, 4)	.1	−1.0	1.0
(3, 5)	.3	−.52288	.52288
(4, 5)	.4	−.39794	.39794
(4, 6)	.35	−.45593	.45593
(5, 7)	.25	−.60206	.60206
(6, 7)	.5	−.30103	.30103

Exercise 8.3-1

Suppose that the information in Figure 8-7 represents the probabilities of being stopped by police. Can the same type of analysis be used to choose the route with the *smallest* probability of being stopped?

[*Ans.* No, because the probability of being stopped on a route no longer equals the product of the probabilities of the individual road segments. Specifically, it will equal the complement of the probability of *not* being stopped.]

8.3.2 SHORTEST-ROUTE ALGORITHMS

This section presents two algorithms for finding the shortest route in **acyclic** and **cyclic** networks. A network is said to be acyclic if it contains no loops; otherwise, it is cyclic. Of the two algorithms we present below, the cyclic algorithm is more general in the sense that it subsumes the acyclic case. The acyclic algorithm is more efficient, however, because it entails fewer computations.

A. Acyclic Algorithm

The acyclic algorithm is based on the use of **recursive computations**, which is the basis for the dynamic programming calculations in Chapter 10. The steps of the algorithm are explained via a numeric example.

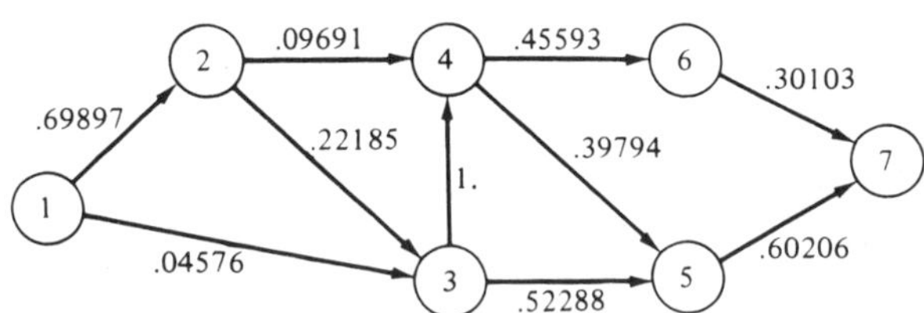

Figure 8-8

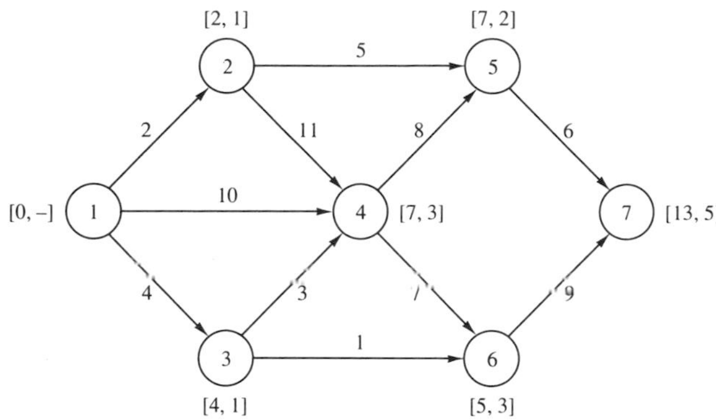

Figure 8-9

Example 8.3-4. Consider the network in Figure 8-9. Node 1 is the starting node (source or origin) and node 7 is the terminal point (sink or destination). The distances d_{ij} between nodes i and j are given directly on each arc. For example, $d_{12} = 2$. The network is acyclic because it includes no loops.

Let

$$u_j = \textit{shortest} \text{ distance from node 1 to node } j$$

where $u_1 = 0$ by definition. The values of u_j, $j = 1, 2, \ldots, n$, are computed recursively using the following formula

$$u_j = \min_i \left\{ \begin{array}{c} \text{shortest distance } u_i \text{ to an } \textit{immediately preceding} \text{ node } i \\ \textit{plus} \\ \text{distance } d_{ij} \text{ between present node } j \text{ and its predecessor } i \end{array} \right\}$$
$$= \min_i \{u_i + d_{ij}\}$$

The recursive formula requires that the shortest distance u_j to node j be computed only after we have computed the shortest distance u_i to each predecessor node i linked to j by a direct arc.

In the final solution of the shortest-route model, it is not sufficient to only determine u_j of node j. Concurrently, we must also identify the nodes encountered along the route. To achieve this goal, we use a **labeling procedure** that associates the following label with node j:

$$\text{node } j \text{ label} = [u_j, n]$$

where n is the node *immediately preceding* j that leads to the shortest distance u_j; that is,

$$u_j = \min_i \{u_i + d_{ij}\}$$
$$= u_n + d_{nj}$$

By definition, the label at node 1 is [0, —], indicating that node 1 is the source.

The computations proceed in stages, with each stage identified with a distinct node. Table 8-3 provides the sequence of the computations leading to the final solution. The computations can also be summarized directly on the network, as shown in Figure 8-9.

Table 8-3

Node j	Computation of u_j	Label
1	$u_1 \equiv 0$	[0, —]
2	$u_2 = u_1 + d_{12} = 0 + 2 = 2$, from 1	[2, 1]
3	$u_3 = u_1 + d_{13} = 0 + 4 = 4$, from 1	[4, 1]
4	$u_4 = \min\{u_1 + d_{14}, u_2 + d_{24}, u_3 + d_{34}\}$	
	$= \min\{0 + 10, 2 + 11, \mathbf{4 + 3}\} = 7$, from 3	[7, 3]
5	$u_5 = \min\{u_2 + d_{25}, u_4 + d_{45}\}$	
	$= \min\{\mathbf{2 + 5}, 7 + 8\} = 7$, from 2	[7, 2]
6	$u_6 = \min\{u_3 + d_{36}, u_4 + d_{46}\}$	
	$= \min\{\mathbf{4 + 1}, 7 + 7\} = 5$, from 3	[5, 3]
7	$u_7 = \min\{u_5 + u_{57}, u_6 + d_{67}\}$	
	$= \min\{\mathbf{7 + 6}, 5 + 9\} = 13$, from 5	[13, 5]

The optimum route is obtained starting from node 7 and tracing backward through the nodes using the labels' information. The following sequence demonstrates the procedure:

$$(7) \to [13, 5] \to (5) \to [7, 2] \to (2) \to [2, 1] \to (1)$$

The algorithm, in fact, provides the shortest distance between node 1 and every other node in the network. ◀

Exercise 8.3-2

(a) In Figure 8-9, compute shortest distance and its designated route to each of the following nodes.

(1) Node 4

[*Ans.* $u_4 = 7, 1 \to 3 \to 4$.]

(2) Node 6

[*Ans.* $u_6 = 5, 1 \to 3 \to 6$.]

(b) Recompute the shortest route in Figure 8-9 when each of the following changes is effected independently.

(1) Node 4 is connected to 7 by an arc of length 5.

[*Ans.* $u_7 = 12, 1 \to 3 \to 4 \to 7$.]

(2) Node 5 is reached from 6 by an arc of length 2.

[*Ans.* $u_7 = 13, 1 \to 2 \to 5 \to 7$ or $1 \to 3 \to 6 \to 5 \to 7$.]

B. Cyclic (Dijkstra's) Algorithm

The acyclic algorithm will not perform correctly if the network happens to include any directed loops. To demonstrate this point, consider the network in Figure 8-10, where a directed loop is formed by nodes 2, 3, and 4. With the rules of the acyclic algorithm, it will be impossible to evaluate any of the loop nodes 2, 3, and 4 because the algorithm requires computing u_i for all the nodes leading into node j before u_j can be evaluated.

The cyclic algorithm differs from the acyclic algorithm in that it allows as many chances as may be needed to reevaluate a node. When it becomes evident that the shortest distance to a node has been reached, the node is excluded from further

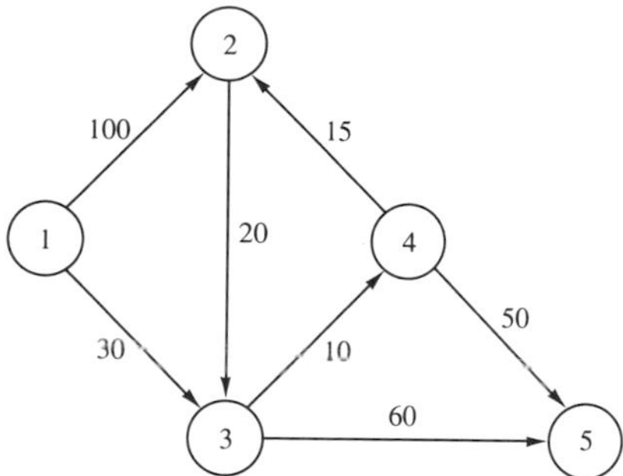

Figure 8-10

consideration. The process ends when the destination or sink node has been evaluated.

The cyclic algorithm (also known as **Dijkstra's algorithm**) uses two types of labels: temporary and permanent. Both labels utilize the same format used with the acyclic algorithm: namely, $[d, n]$, where d is the shortest distance *so far available* for a current node, and n is the immediate predecessor node responsible for realizing the distance d. The algorithm starts with the source node carrying the *permanent* label [0, —]. Next we consider *all* the nodes that can be reached directly from the source node and then determine their associated labels. The newly created labels are designated as *temporary*. The next permanent label is selected from among all current temporary labels as the one having the smallest d in the label $[d, n]$ (ties are broken arbitrarily). The process is now repeated for the last node that has been designated permanent. In such a case, a temporary label of a node may be changed only if the new label yields a smaller distance d.

Let us apply the procedure to the network in Figure 8-10. A basic assumption of the algorithm is that all the distances in the network are nonnegative.

Iteration 0: Node 1 carries the *permanent* label [0, —].

Iteration 1: Nodes 2 and 3, which can be reached directly from node 1 (the last permanently labeled node), now carry the *temporary* labels [0 + 100, 1] and [0 + 30, 1], or [100, 1] and [30, 1], respectively.

Among the current temporary labels, node 3 has the smallest distance $d = 30$ ($= \min\{100, 30\}$). Thus node 3 is permanently labeled.

Iteration 2: Nodes 4 and 5 can be reached from the last permanently labeled node (node 3) and their temporary labels are [30 + 10, 3] and [30 + 60, 3] (or [40, 3] and [90, 3]), respectively. At this point, we have the three temporary labels [100, 1], [40, 3], and [90, 3] associated with nodes 2, 4, and 5, respectively. Temporarily labeled node 4 has the smallest $d = 40$ ($= \min\{100, 40, 90\}$) and hence its label [40, 3] is converted to the permanent status.

Iteration 3: From node 4, we now label node 2 with the new temporary label [40 + 15, 4] = [55, 4], which replaces the old temporary label [100, 1]. Next, node 5 is labeled temporarily with [40 + 50, 4] = [90, 4]. The temporary labels now include [55, 4] and [90, 4] associated with nodes 2 and 5, respectively. We thus label node 2 permanently with [55, 4].

The only remaining node is the sink node 5, which converts its [90, 4] into a permanent label, thus completing the procedure.

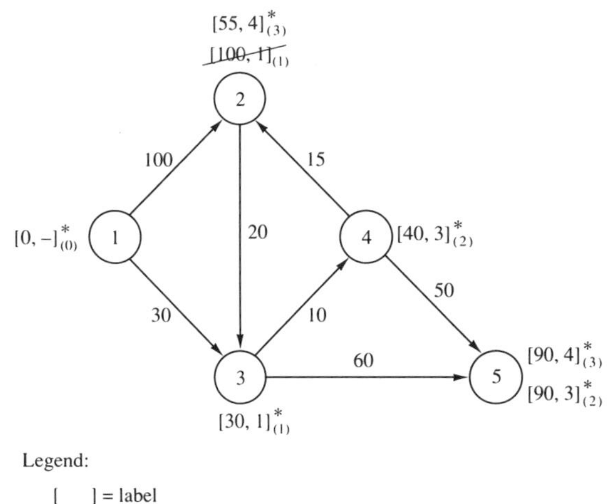

Figure 8-11

The computational steps above are summarized graphically in Figure 8-11. Observe that the calculations are based on the recursion concept employed with the acyclic algorithm. The prime difference between the two algorithms occurs in that a node in the cyclic algorithm may be (temporarily) labeled regardless of whether or not all the nodes directly leading into it have been labeled.

The solution in Figure 8-11 provides the shortest distance to each node in the network together with its route.

Exercise 8.3-3

In Figure 8-11, determine the shortest distance and its designated route for each of the following nodes:

(1) Node 2

[*Ans.* $D_2 = 55, 1 \to 3 \to 4 \to 2$.]

(2) Node 5

[*Ans.* $D_5 = 90, 1 \to 3 \to 4 \to 5$.]

Computer Drill

Use TORA's shortest-route algorithm to solve the acyclic model of Example 8.3-4. Compare TORA's iterations (which are based on the cyclic algorithm) with those of the acyclic iterations in Example 8.3-4.

8.3.3 THE SHORTEST-ROUTE PROBLEM VIEWED AS A TRANSSHIPMENT MODEL

We can formulate the shortest-route problem as a transshipment model (see Section 6.4). We can think of the shortest-route network as a transportation model with one source and one destination. The supply at the source is one unit and the demand at the destination is also one unit. The one unit will flow from the source to the destination through the admissable routes of the network. The objective is to minimize the distance traveled by the unit flow from the source to the destination.

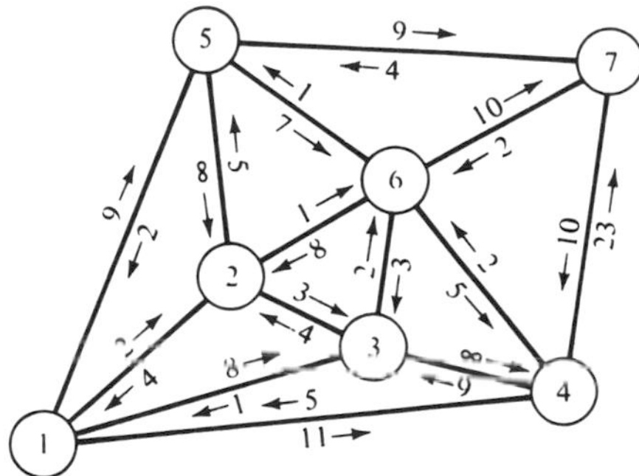

Figure 8-12

To illustrate the construction of the model, we consider the network of Figure 8-12. Unlike the algorithms in Section 8.3.2, which automatically computes the shortest distances between node 1 and all the other nodes, the transshipment model computes the shortest distance between two nodes only. Thus, assuming that we are interested in determining the shortest distance between nodes 1 and 7, Table 8-4 gives the associated transshipment model of the problem. Note that the buffer stock B (see Section 6.4) equals 1, since at any time during transshipment no more than one unit can pass through any of the nodes of the network. Note also that node 1 does not appear as a destination, since it is the (main) source for the network. Similarly, node 7 cannot act as a source, since it represents the final destination of the unit flow. The "transportation costs" equal the associated distances. Blocked

Table 8-4

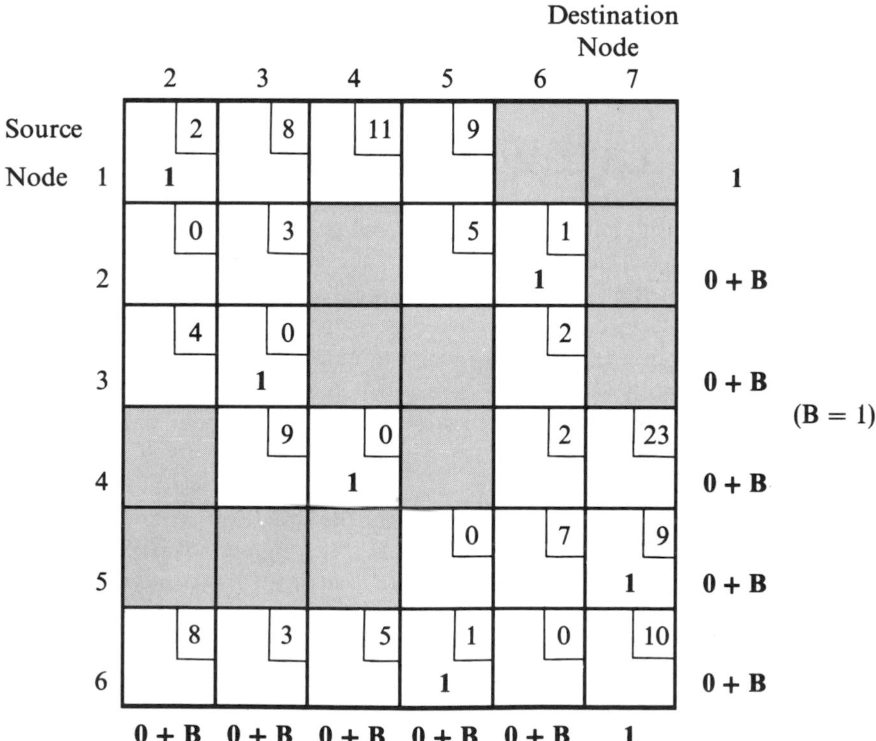

Source Node \ Destination Node	2	3	4	5	6	7	
1	2 **1**	8	11	9	(blocked)	(blocked)	**1**
2	0	3	(blocked)	5	1 **1**	(blocked)	**0 + B**
3	4	0 **1**	(blocked)	(blocked)	2	(blocked)	**0 + B**
4	(blocked)	9	0 **1**	(blocked)	2	23	**0 + B**
5	(blocked)	(blocked)	(blocked)	0	7	9 **1**	**0 + B**
6	8	3	5	1 **1**	0	10	**0 + B**
	0 + B	**0 + B**	**0 + B**	**0 + B**	**0 + B**	**1**	

(B = 1)

cells imply that the corresponding route does not exist and must be assigned a very high cost M when solving the model. Finally, the distance from a node to itself is zero.

Table 8-4 also gives the optimum solution, which is obtained by using the transportation technique (Section 6.2.1). The table shows that

$$x_{12} = 1, \quad x_{26} = 1, \quad x_{33} = 1, \quad x_{44} = 1, \quad x_{57} = 1, \quad x_{65} = 1$$

The values of $x_{33} = x_{44} = 1$ do not contribute to the solution, since they connect nodes 3 and 4 to themselves. The remaining values can be arranged in the order

$$x_{12} = 1, \quad x_{26} = 1, \quad x_{65} = 1, \quad x_{57} = 1$$

which shows that the optimal route is $1 \rightarrow 2 \rightarrow 6 \rightarrow 5 \rightarrow 7$, as obtained previously. (The optimality condition of the transportation will show that an alternate optimum solution exists between nodes 1 and 7. Verify.)

Exercise 8.3-4

Show how you can construct the transshipment model associated with finding the shortest route between nodes 6 and 4.

[*Ans.* The transshipment model will have six sources and six destinations, with no row associated with node 4 (destination node) and no column with node 6 (source node). All nodes will each have one unit of supply or demand.]

If you investigate Table 8-4, you will discover that it has the structure of an assignment model. (Section 6.3). This suggests that it may be possible to formulate the assignment problem as a shortest-route problem. Although this is true, the involved computations are usually more tedious than solving the assignment model directly. The relationship is theoretically interesting, however.

8.4 MAXIMAL-FLOW PROBLEM

In this section we consider the situation in which a source node and a destination node are linked through a network of finite capacity arcs. The network is unidirectional in the sense that the flow starts at the source node and leaves at the destination node. However, an arc (i, j) may have two distinct capacities, depending on whether the flow is from i to j or from j to i. For example, if the network deals with traffic flow in city streets, a one-way street will have a positive capacity in one direction and a zero capacity in the other direction. On the other hand, a two-way street may have different capacities in the opposite directions if the two directions do not include the same number of lanes.

An example of the maximal-flow problem is the situation where a number of refineries are connected to distribution terminals through a network of pipelines. Booster and pumping stations are mounted on the pipelines to move the oil products to the distribution terminals. The objective of analyzing the situation is to maximize the flow between the refineries and the terminals under the capacity restrictions of the refineries and the pipelines.

Figure 8-13 depicts the refinery maximal-flow problem. Nodes 1, 2, and 3 represent the refineries with nodes 7 and 8 representing the terminals. The remaining

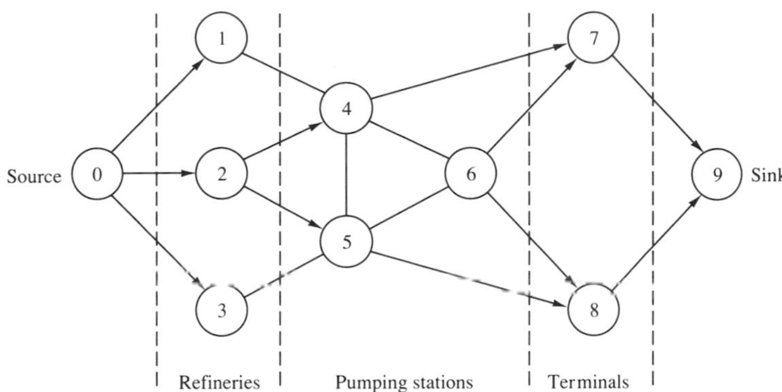

Figure 8-13

nodes represent the pumping stations. Since the maximal-flow model requires only one source node and one destination node, nodes 0 and 9 are added to represent such end points. The capacities of the arcs from the source node 0 can be taken equal to the outputs of the different refineries. On the other hand, the capacities from the distribution terminals to sink node 9 may represent the demands for the oil product. It is assumed in this situation that the pipeline transports only one type of oil product at a time.

The network in Figure 8-13 has some arcs with positive capacities in one direction only. These arcs are shown on the figure with arrows. As for the pumping stations 4, 5, and 6, flow may occur in either direction, possibly with different capacities, depending on the design of the pipeline network.

We use a special notation to represent the bidirectional flow on an arc. For an arc with end nodes i and j, the notation (a, b) signifies that the flow capacity from i to j is a, and that from j to i is b. For example, in Figure 8-13, the capacities from node 0 (source) to the refineries is represented as $(c_1, 0)$, $(c_2, 0)$, and $(c_3, 0)$, where c_1, c_2, and c_3 are the capacities (per unit time) of refineries 1, 2, and 3. In the case of the arcs connecting the pumping stations, both a and b may be positive.

The basic idea of the maximal-flow algorihm is to find a **breakthrough path** that links the source node to the sink node such that the capacity of each arc on the path is positive. The maximum flow along this path must then equal the *smallest* capacity, c^*, of all the arcs comprising the path. We then modify the arc capacities (a, b) along the path to $(a - c^*, b + c^*)$ or $(a + c^*, b - c^*)$ depending on whether the flow on arc (i, j) is $i \to j$ or $j \to i$, respectively. The modification is intended to indicate that the flow c^* has been "committed." The process of finding breakthrough paths from source to sink is repeated until it becomes evident that no further breakthroughs are possible. The maximal flow then equals the sum of the c^*-values determined in the successive iterations.

The requirement that (a, b) be modified to $(a - c^*, b + c^*)$ or $(a + c^*, b - c^*)$ is crucial because it allows future cancellation of a *previously committed* flow c^*, when necessary. By *adding* c^* to the opposite direction of a committed flow, we now have an instrument for "remembering" how much flow can be canceled at a later iteration. The networks in Figure 8-14(a) illustrate this point. All arcs have the capacity (5, 0), indicating a one-way flow in the direction $i \to j$ with a maximum capacity of 5. The first iteration (arbitrarily) identifies the breakthrough path $1 \to 2 \to 3 \to 4$, which results in modifying the capacities of arcs (1, 2), (2, 3), and (3, 4) from (5, 0) to (0, 5) because $c^* = 5$, as shown in Figure 8-14(b). Next, in Figure 8-14(b) we identify the

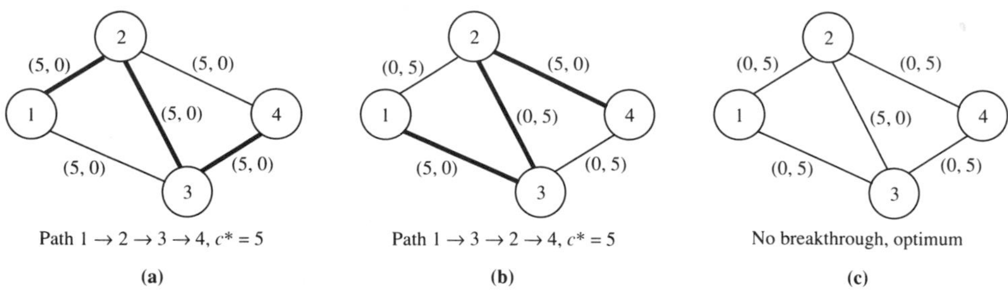

Figure 8-14

breakthrough path $1 \to 3 \to 2 \to 4$. Notice that arcs (1, 3) and (2, 4) have the capacity (5, 0) and arc (3, 2) has the capacity (0, 5), which shows a positive flow in the direction $3 \to 2$. This path yields $c^* = 5$ and results in the network of Figure 8-14(c). Observe carefully that what happened in the transition from (b) to (c) is nothing but a cancellation of a previously committed flow in the direction $2 \to 3$. In essence, the algorithm recognizes that the arc (2, 3) should not be used and that the maximum flow is achieved by using the two paths $1 \to 2 \to 4$ and $1 \to 3 \to 4$. The algorithm is able to "remember" that a flow has been committed previously only through the use of the modifications $(a - c^*, b + c^*)$ and $(a + c^*, b - c^*)$ explained earlier.

Example 8.4-1. Consider the network in Figure 8-15. Only arc (3, 4) has capacities in both directions. We will systematize the procedure for determining a breakthrough path as follows. Starting at node 1, we can choose either node 2, node 3, or node 4 as the next node to be linked to current node 1. The selection is based on a heuristic that calls for linking to the node that has the highest arc capacity from the current node. (In the case of a tie, we will select the first *ordered* node in the tie set.) Thus, from node 1, we link to node 3 because it has the highest arc capacity $(= \max\{20, 30, 10\})$. We indicate the selection by labeling node 3 with [30, 1], which represents the flow capacity (= 30) of the *just added* arc originating at node 1. (At the source node 1, the label $[\infty, —]$ indicates an infinite starting capacity with no predecessor node.)

Next, at node 3 we can link to either node 4 (flow capacity = 10) or to node 5 (flow capacity = 20). Node 2 is excluded because it shows a zero flow capacity in the direction $3 \to 2$. Thus, according to our heuristic, we link 3 to 5 and label 5 with [20, 3]. Since 5 is the sink node, the breakthrough path $1 \to 3 \to 5$ has been constructed. The maximum flow along this path is determined directly from the labels as

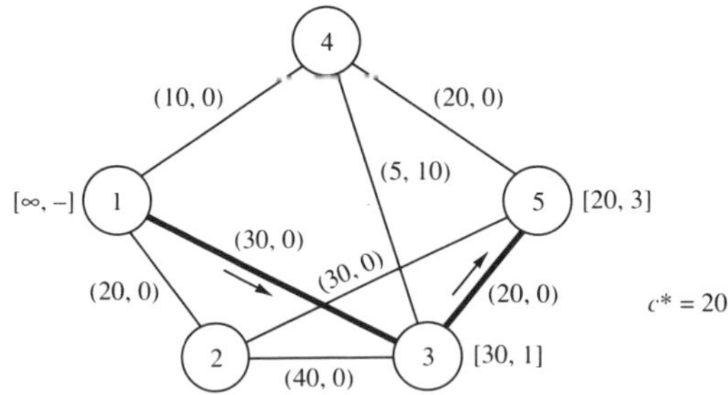

Figure 8-15

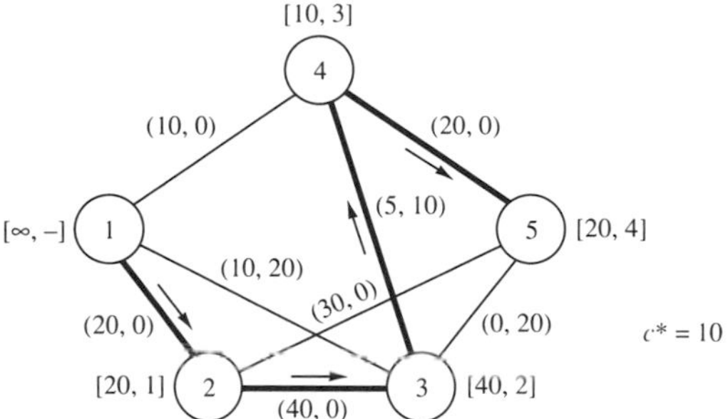

Figure 8-16

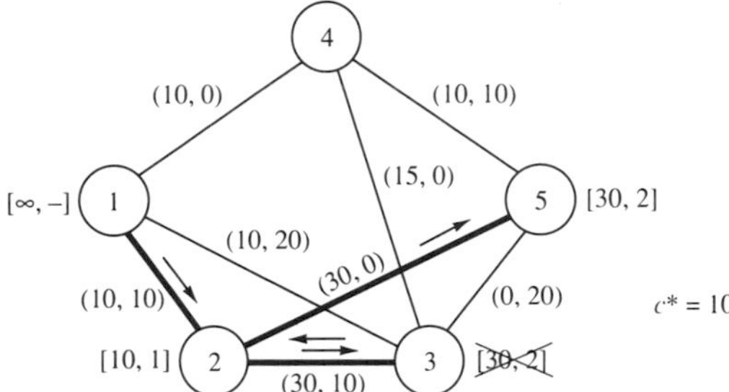

Figure 8-17

$c^* = \min\{\infty, 30, 20\} = 20$.† Figure 8-16 adjusts the flows (a, b) along the path $1 \to 3 \to 5$ that reflects a committed flow of $c^* = 20$; namely, we change (30, 0) of arc (1, 3) to (10, 20) and (20, 0) of arc (3, 5) to (0, 20).

The procedure is repeated for the modified flows in Figure 8-16. Keep in mind that once a node is labeled, it cannot be relabeled again during the same iteration. Thus, as shown in Figure 8-16, nodes 1, 2, 3, 4, and 5 are labeled with [∞, —], [20, 1], [40, 2], [10, 3] and [20, 4], respectively. The maximum flow along the path $1 \to 2 \to 3 \to 4 \to 5$ is $c^* = \min\{20, 40, 10, 20\} = 10$, which results in the modified flow capacities in Figure 8-17.

In Figure 8-17, the breakthrough path is $1 \to 2 \to 5$ with $c^* = 10$. Notice that at node 1 a tie exists between nodes 2, 3, and 4 because all three nodes have the same flow capacity (= 10). According to our rule of thumb we select the first *ordered* node in the tie set: namely, node 2. At node 2, the same rule leads to node 3. However, from node 3 we cannot label node 4 or node 5 because of the zero capacity from 3 to 4 and from 3 to 5 (node 1 is already labeled and hence cannot be relabeled). We thus **backtrack** from 3 to 2 and cross out 3 so that it will not be labeled again during the current iteration. At node 2, we label node 5 with [30, 2], which gives us the breakthrough path $1 \to 2 \to 5$ with $c^* = 10$. The modified flow is given in Figure 8-18. It is important to notice that, in general, the *backtracking* process should be applied repeatedly until we either secure a breakthrough path or until the backtracking step takes us back to the source node. In the latter case, no further breakthrough paths are possible, signifying the end of the procedure.

---

† You can, if you wish, change the labeling procedure so that the flow through the most recently added node will equal the minimum of the incoming arc capacity and the flow through its immediate predecessor (as recorded by its label). In this manner, c^* will be on hand when the sink node is reached.

Figures 8-18 through 8-20 complete the procedure because the modified flow in Figure 8-20 shows that no breakthrough paths exist (all modified flow capacities from node 1 are zero). We can now obtain the optimal flow in the network by subtracting the modified flows (a^*, b^*) in Figure 8-20 from the original flow (a, b) in Figure 8-15.

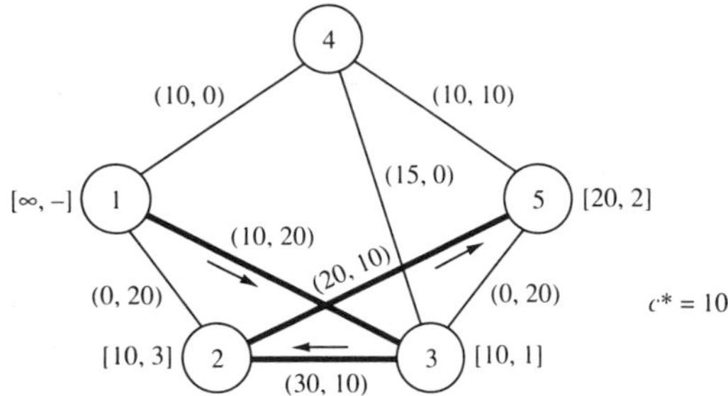

Figure 8-18

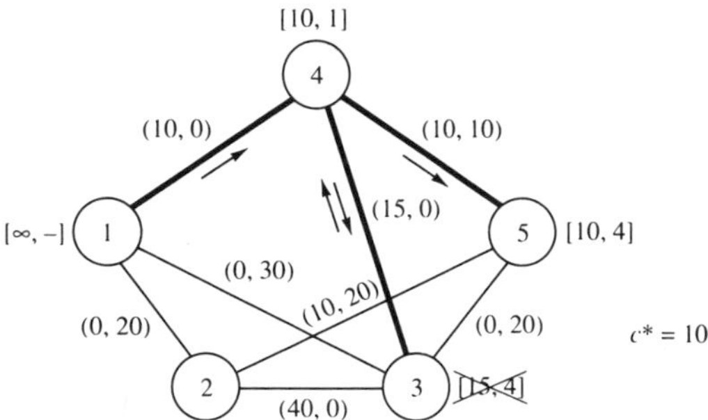

Figure 8-19

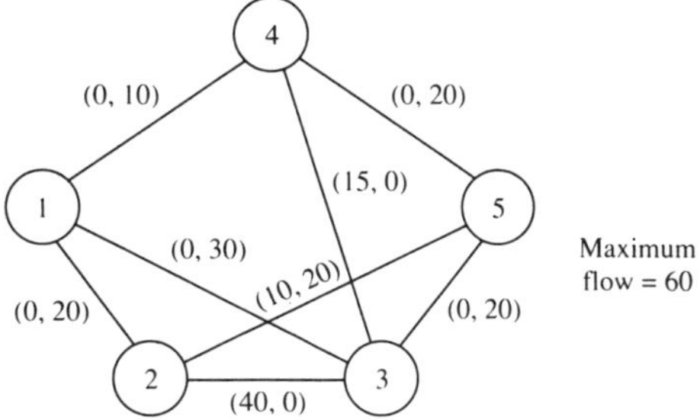

Figure 8-20

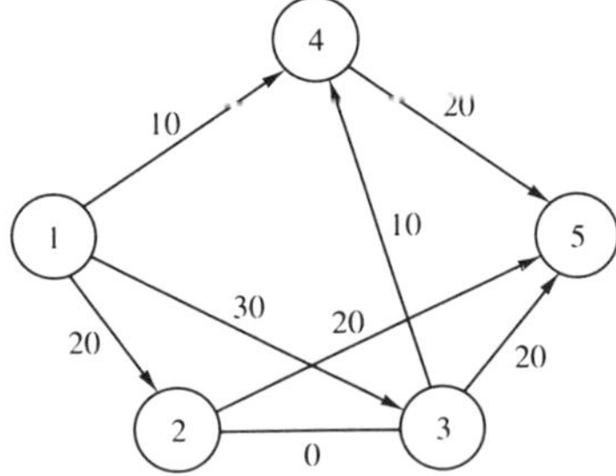

Figure 8-21

If $(a - a^*) > 0$, a flow in the amount $(a - a^*)$ occurs in the direction $i \to j$; otherwise, if $b - b^* > 0$, a flow of $(b - b^*)$ occurs in the direction $j \to i$. It is impossible to have both $(a - a^*)$ and $(b - b^*)$ greater than zero simultaneously. The use of this rule yields the flow given in Figure 8-21. The maximum flow in the network is the sum of the flow out of the source node or into the sink node (= 60). ◀

Exercise 8.4-1

(a) Determine the surplus capacity for all the arcs in Figure 8-21.
[*Ans.* Arc (2, 3) = 40, arc (4, 3) = 5.]

(b) Determine the amount of flow through nodes 2, 3, and 4 in Figure 8-21.
[*Ans.* Node 2 = 20, node 3 = 30, node 4 = 20.]

(c) In the network in Figure 8-15, would it be advantageous (from the standpoint of increasing the maximal flow) to increase the flow capacities in the directions $3 \to 5$ and $4 \to 5$?
[*Ans.* No, node 1 still represents a bottleneck.]

Computer Drill

Use TORA to verify the labeling procedure given in Example 8.4-1.

At this point, it is appropriate to discuss the role of using **cuts** in the solution of the maximal-flow problem. A *cut* in a connected network defines a set of arcs that when set to zero capacity will disrupt the flow between the source and destination nodes. In this case we say that the **capacity of the cut** equals the sum of the capacities of its associated arcs. As illustrations, following is a set of cuts for the network in Figure 8-15.

Cut-Set Arcs	Capacity
(1, 2), (1, 3), (1, 4)	10 + 30 + 20 = 60
(2, 5), (3, 5), (4, 5)	30 + 20 + 20 = 70
(2, 3), (2, 5), (1, 3), (1, 4)	30 + 30 + 30 + 10 = 100

Intuitively, we can determine the maximum flow by enumerating *all* the cuts in the network. The cut with the smallest capacity provides the desired maximum flow. This intuitive result has actually been proved using the so-called **maximum-flow minimum-cut theorem**, which states that the maximum flow in the network equals the capacity of its minimal cut. [See Ford and Fulkerson (1962) for more details.]

8.5 MINIMUM-COST CAPACITATED FLOW PROBLEM

The minimum-cost capacitated flow problem represents a general class of network models that subsumes the transportation, transshipment, assignment, and maximum-flow problems as special cases. We first illustrate this type of problem and then discuss its specialization to the specific cases mentioned above.

Example 8.5-1. A company manufactures a basic chemical compound that is used by other manufacturers to produce a variety of paint products. The company owns two plants and is contracted by two suppliers to provide the raw material. The contract calls for a minimum delivery of 500 and 750 tons of raw material per month from suppliers 1 and 2 at the respective prices of $200 and $210 per ton. It takes 1.2 tons of raw material to manufacture 1 ton of the basic chemical compound. The transportation costs per ton from the suppliers to the two plants are summarized below.

Supplier	Plant 1	Plant 2
1	$10	$12
2	9	13

The production capacities and the cost per ton at the two plants are given below.

Plant	Production Cost/Ton	Minimum Capacity (tons)	Maximum Capacity (tons)
1	$25	400	800
2	28	450	900

The monthly demands at the two centers are 660 tons and 800 tons. The transportation costs per ton between the plants and the distribution centers are given below.

	Transportation Costs/Ton	
Plant	D1	D2
1	3	4
2	5	2

Figure 8-22 provides the network representing the problem. The source node is given by node 1. Arcs (1, 2) and (1, 3) represent the two suppliers. The minimum arc capacities reflect the minimum shipment guaranteed for each supplier. Since these arcs have no upper bounds, their capacities are summarized as (500, ∞) and (750, ∞). The purchase prices per ton for the two suppliers are $200 and $210, respectively.

To introduce the plant's capacity in the model, each plant is represented by two nodes, which may be viewed as the input and output points of the plant. The arcs linking the input and output nodes carry the capacities (400, 800) and (450, 900).

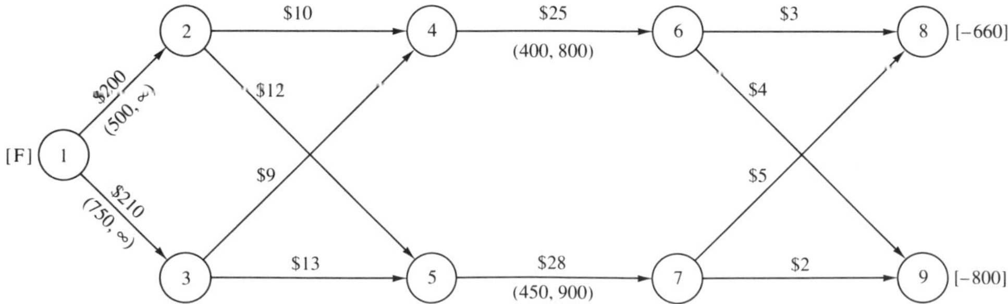

Figure 8-22

The output nodes of the plants (nodes 6 and 7) link to the distribution nodes (nodes 8 and 9) via the transportation arcs (6, 8), (6, 9), (7, 8), and (7, 9). These arcs are similar to the transportation arcs coming into the plants at nodes 4 and 5.

The demands at the distribution nodes 8 and 9 are represented by [−660] and [−800], respectively. Correspondingly, the amount of supply at source node 1 is specified as [F]. For the problem to yield a feasible solution, the supply amount must equal the total demand. However, we must take into account the fact that the suppliers are dealing with tons of raw material, whereas the distribution centers are dealing with tons of the chemical compound. This discrepancy can be reconciled by using a factor of 1.2 to convert the raw material into equivalent chemical compound. For example, the capacities of arcs (1, 2) and (1, 3) should be replaced with $(500/1.2, \infty)$ and $(750/1.2, \infty)$. In this case, the unit purchase costs from the two suppliers should be scaled up to $\$200 \times 1.2$ and $\$210 \times 1.2$. A similar scaling applies to the transportation costs from nodes 2 and 3 to nodes 4 and 5. With this conversion, we can specify the supply amount at source node 1 as $660 + 800 = 1460$ (chemical compound) tons.

The solution of the network in Figure 8-22 should yield optimal allocation of supplies to the two plants as well as the allocation of each plant's output to the two distribution centers. The objective is to minimize the net cost of the entire operation. ◀

The example in Figure 8-22 is actually a generalization of the transshipment problem we studied in Chapter 6. The main difference is that arcs may be capacitated. Additionally, transshipping nodes (i.e., nodes 2, 3, 4, 5, 6, and 7 in Figure 8-22) may also have their external flow. For example, in Figure 8-22, external flows at nodes 6 and 7 may be used to represent local sales of the chemical compound.

8.5.1 SPECIAL CASES OF THE CAPACITATED NETWORK MODEL

The capacitated network model discussed above can be shown to represent the following models as special cases:

1. The transportation/assignment/transshipment model.
2. The shortest-route model.
3. The maximum-flow model.

The capacitated model can be specialized to describe the transportation (or assignment) model by effecting the following changes:

1. Source nodes are connected directly to the destination nodes.
2. All arc lower-bound capacities are set equal to zero.
3. All arc upper-bound capacities are set equal to infinity.

The transshipment model requires the same changes as the transportation model except that transported units may be shipped from a source to a destination by way of one or more transshipping nodes, as illustrated in Section 6.4.

The shortest-route model discussed in Section 8.3 is a special case of the capacitated network model in the following manner:

1. The source node ships [+1] unit and the destination node receives [−1] unit.

2. All arcs have zero lower-bound and infinite upper-bound capacities.
3. The cost per unit of flow on each arc should now represent the distance between nodes.

The objective of the shortest-route model is to "ship" 1 unit of flow from the source to the destination node at minimum cost (distance).

Finally, the maximum-flow model (Section 8.4) can be expressed as a capacitated network in the following manner:

1. The upper-bound capacity of an arc is used to represent the maximum flow in the arc (the lower bound is set equal to zero).
2. All arcs are assumed to have zero cost per unit of flow.
3. The amount shipped from the source node and the amount received at the destination node are set equal to $[+F]$ and $[-F]$ units, respectively. The value of F should be chosen sufficiently high to allow the maximum flow to be realized in the network.
4. A direct arc is used to link the source node to the destination node. The purpose of this arc is to carry the surplus amount of F that does not flow through the network. This arc must be uncapacitated. Additionally, it must be assigned a unit flow cost sufficiently high, thus forcing the optimization process to send as much flow as possible through the arcs of the original network. Such a procedure will achieve a realization of the maximum flow in the capacitated network.

8.5.2 LINEAR PROGRAMMING FORMULATION

The capacitated model can be expressed as a linear program. Let x_{ij} be the amount of flow on arc (i, j) and assume that c_{ij} is its associated unit cost. Each node corresponds to a constraint that conserves the balance of flow at the node. Assuming that $[b_j]$ $(-[b_j])$ represents the amount of supply (demand) at node j, and given (l_{ij}, u_{ij}) as the capacities of arc (i, j), the linear program is given as:

$$\text{minimize } z = \sum_{i=1}^{n} \sum_{j=1}^{n} c_{ij} x_{ij}$$

subject to

$$\sum_{k=1}^{n} x_{ik} - \sum_{k=1}^{n} x_{ki} = b_i \qquad \text{for all i}$$

$$l_{ij} \leq x_{ij} \leq u_{ij} \qquad \text{for all } i \text{ and } j$$

As we explained in Section 7.1, the lower bound l_{ij} on arc (i, j) can always be accounted for by using the substitution $x_{ij} = l_{ij} + y_{ij}$. In this case the new variables of the problem will be the variables y_{ij}, whose upper bounds are now given by $u_{ij} - l_{ij}$. As such, there is no loss in generality when we assume that the capacitated network variables are bounded from above only (with zero lower bound).

Of course, we can solve the linear program directly by using the simplex algorithm presented in Chapter 3. However, like the transportation model in Chapter 6, the special structure of the capacitated network allows us to use a variation of the regular simplex method that is computationally more efficient. The new computational technique is based on the use of duality theory. However, as in the transportation algorithm, the new algorithm uses the exact same step of the simplex method, giving rise to the suggestive name *network simplex method.*

8.5.3 CAPACITATED NETWORK SIMPLEX METHOD

The steps of the network simplex method are exactly the same as in the simplex method for upper-bounded variables (Section 7.1). Differences occur only in the computational details, which are designed to exploit the special structure of the network problem.

Before providing the details of the algorithm, notice that for the capacitated network to have a feasible solution, it is necessary that the net sum of all supply and demand units equal zero; that is,

$$\sum_{j=1}^{n} b_j = 0$$

This condition can always be satisfied by adding a dummy source or a dummy destination as we do in the transportation model. The dummy source (destination) node should be connected to every destination (source) node in the network with zero unit-flow cost and infinite upper-bound capacity. Keep in mind that the condition above does not guarantee a feasible solution because the capacities of the arcs may preclude the existence of a feasible solution.

The iterations of the network simplex method are associated with basic feasible solutions only, exactly as in the regular primal simplex method. A basic solution of the capacitated network is characterized by recognizing that an n-node network corresponds to a set of n constraints. However, since the net sum of supply and demand units must equal zero, one of these constraints must be redundant. This means that a basic solution for the network problem must include $n - 1$ basic variables. If you study the definition of a spanning tree (Section 8.1), you will discover that it always includes $n - 1$ connecting arcs, with no subset of these arcs forming a loop. In fact, it can be proved that a spanning tree solution corresponds to a basic solution of the capacitated LP model, and vice versa. This result is the key idea for the development of the network simplex method.

The steps of the network simplex method are summarized as follows:

Step 0: Find a starting feasible spanning tree (basic) solution. If no feasible solution exists, stop.

Step 1: Determine an entering arc (variable) using the optimality condition of the simplex method. If none exists, stop; else go to step 2.

Step 2: Determine the leaving arc (variable) using the feasibility condition of the upper-bounded simplex method. Change the spanning tree (basis), then go to step 1.

The details of the steps above are best illustrated by a numerical example. You will find it helpful to review the upper-bounded simplex method (Section 7.1) at this point.

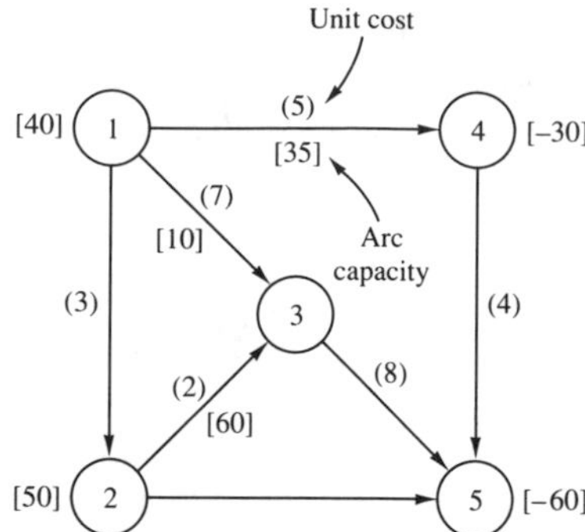

Figure 8-23

Example 8.5-2. Consider the capacitated network in Figure 8-23. The model is already balanced because the sum of all supply and demand units is zero. We first start by presenting the LP associated with the problem. This formulation will be needed in explaining the optimality condition of the network algorithm.

	x_{12}	x_{13}	x_{14}	x_{23}	x_{25}	x_{35}	x_{45}		
Min	3	7	5	2	1	8	4		Dual Variables
Node 1	1	1	1					40	w_1
Node 2	−1			1	1			50	w_2
Node 3		−1		−1		1		0	w_3
Node 4			−1				1	−30	w_4
Node 5					−1	−1	−1	−60	w_5
Upper Bounds	∞	10	35	60	30	∞	∞		

Notice that with the exception of the upper bounds, the main constraints of the LP model have the basic structure of a transshipment problem (see Section 6.4). This special structure will allow us to develop the optimality condition based on the dual problem, exactly as we did in the transportation algorithm (Section 6.2).

Our first task is to find a starting *feasible* spanning tree. In our example, the starting solution in Figure 8-24 is obtained by inspection. Normally, we should be implementing an artificial variable technique to find such a solution. However, since

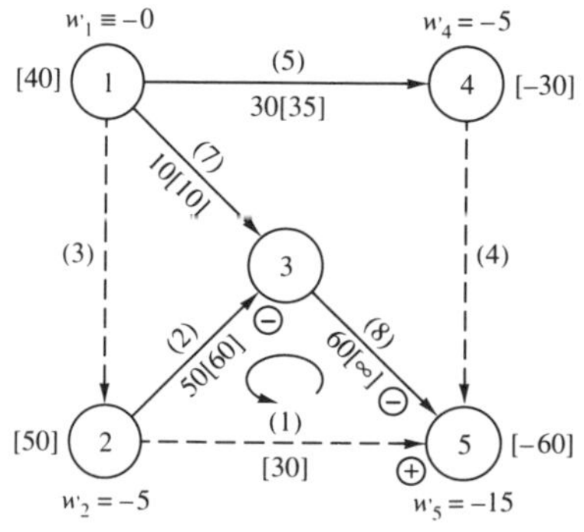

$z_{12} - c_{12} = 0 - (-5) - 3 = 2$

$z_{25} - c_{25} = -5 - (-15) - 1 = \boxed{9}$

$z_{45} - c_{43} = -5 - (-15) - 4 = 6$

Arc (2, 5) reaches its upper bound at 30

Substitute $x_{25} = 30 - x'_{25}$

Figure 8-24

this technique is very much in the spirit of the M-method and the two-phase method presented in Section 3.3.1, we will not provide this detail here [see Bazaraa et al. (1990, pp. 440–446)].

The spanning tree in Figure 8-24 shows that arcs (1, 3), (1, 4), (2, 3), and (3, 5) (with feasible flows of 30, 10, 50, and 60 units, respectively) define the basic variables. Correspondingly, arcs (1, 2), (2, 5), and (4, 5) define the nonbasic variables. Our objective now is to decide whether the present solution can be improved by increasing the flow above zero in one of the nonbasic arcs. We perform this task by computing the objective coefficient $z_{ij} - c_{ij}$ for each nonbasic arc (i, j). The associated computations are based on the use of the dual problem, exactly as we did in the transportation model (see the end of Section 6.2.1). Specifically, the dual variables associated with the main constraints (excluding the upper bounds) of the network LP problem produce the following general dual problem:

$$\text{maximize } w = \sum_{i=1}^{n} b_i w_i$$

subject to

$$w_i - w_j \leq c_{ij} \qquad \text{for all defined } i \text{ and } j$$
$$w_i \text{ unrestricted in sign} \qquad \text{for all } i = 1, 2, \ldots, n$$

where w_i and b_i are the dual variable and demand units associated with node (constraint) i and c_{ij} is the unit cost coefficient associated with arc (i, j). From the theory of LP (complementary slackness), we have

$$w_i - w_j = c_{ij} \qquad \text{for all basic arc } (i, j)$$

Since one of the original LP constraints is redundant, it follows that we can assign an arbitrary value to one of the dual variables w_i associated with node i. (Compare with the transportation algorithm, Section 6.2.1.) In this example we will set $w_1 = 0$. Implementing the equation above to the spanning tree in Figure 8-24, we form the following equations:

$w_1 = 0$, by definition
arc (1, 3): $w_1 - w_3 = 7$, hence $w_3 = -7$
arc (1, 4): $w_1 - w_4 = 5$, hence $w_4 = -5$
arc (2, 3): $w_2 - w_3 = 2$, hence $w_2 = -5$
arc (3, 5): $w_3 - w_5 = 8$, hence $w_5 = -15$

We now can evaluate $z_{ij} - c_{ij}$ for all nonbasic arcs (i, j) by using the following equation (compare with the transportation algorithm, Section 6.2.1):

$$z_{ij} - c_{ij} = w_i - w_j - c_{ij}$$

This gives

arc (1, 2): $z_{12} - c_{12} = w_1 - w_2 - c_{12} = 0 - (-5) - 3 = 2$
arc (2, 5): $z_{25} - c_{25} = w_2 - w_5 - c_{25} = (-5) - (-15) - 1 = 9 \leftarrow$
arc (4, 5): $z_{45} - c_{45} = w_4 - w_5 - c_{45} = (-5) - (-15) - 4 = 6$

From the optimality condition of the simplex method, (2, 5) must be the entering arc.

From Figure 8-24 we observe that nonbasic arc (2, 5) forms a loop with basic arcs (2, 3) and (3, 5) (by the definition of the spanning tree, no other loop can be formed).

Since we aim to increase the flow in arc (2, 5), we must adjust the arcs of the loop by an equal amount to maintain the feasibility of the solution. The manner of adjusting the flow around the loop is straightforward. The positive orientation (+) of the loop should be in the direction of flow of the entering nonbasic arc, that is, from node 2 to node 5 because we are increasing the flow in that arc. We then assign (+) or (−) to the remaining arcs of the loop depending on whether the flow in each arc agrees with or opposes the positive orientation of the loop. The application of this procedure results in the sign convention shown in Figure 8-24.

Our next task now is to determine the maximum level of flow in the entering arc (2, 5). This level must be selected such that:

1. None of the current basic arcs forming the loop will have a negative flow or a flow that exceeds its capacity.
2. The flow in the entering arc will not exceed its capacity.

Applying these conditions to loop [(2, 5), (2, 3), (3, 5)], we notice the following:

1. Since arc (2, 3) has (−) orientation, its flow cannot be decreased by more than 50 units. For the same reason, the flow across arc (3, 5) cannot be decreased by more than 60 units.
2. Since the capacity of arc (2, 5) is 30, the maximum flow in arc (2, 5) is 30 units.

From the conditions above, the maximum flow in arc (2, 5) is min {50, 60, 30} = 30, which corresponds to its upper bound. Using the same rules in Section 7.1, arc (2, 5) must then remain nonbasic at its upper bound. In this case we use the substitution

$$x_{25} = 30 - x'_{25}$$

where $0 \le x'_{25} \le 30$. If you examine the LP formulation above, you will notice that such a substitution will affect the constraints of nodes 2 and 5 only, together with the coefficient of x_{25} in the objective function. To be specific, consider the following constraints:

$$\begin{aligned} &\text{node 2 constraint:} & x_{23} + x_{25} &= 50 \\ &\text{node 5 constraint:} & -x_{35} - x_{25} &= -60 \end{aligned}$$

The substitution $x_{25} = 30 - x'_{25}$ will thus yield

$$\begin{aligned} &\text{node 2 constraint:} & x_{23} - x'_{25} &= 20 \\ &\text{node 5 constraint:} & -x_{35} + x'_{25} &= -30 \end{aligned}$$

Simultaneously, the coefficient of x'_{25} in the objective function will be -1 in place of 1. This information is shown in Figure 8-25 by changing the supply and demand units at nodes 2 and 5 to [20] and [−30], changing the orientation of arc (2, 5) to (5, 2), and changing the unit cost of (5, 2) to −1. An asterisk (*) is used on arc (5, 2) to indicate the upper bound substitution.

The result of this change in the network is that all the nonbasic arcs are again at zero level, and we can start the computations of a new iteration in the same manner given above. In Figure 8-25 we recompute the dual values w_i, starting with $w_1 = 0$. We then compute $z_{ij} - c_{ij}$ for the nonbasic arcs (1, 2), (4, 5), and (5, 2) [notice the orientation of arc (5, 2)]. The computations show that (4, 5) is the entering arc (verify!). This arc forms the loop [(4, 5), (1, 3), (1, 4), (4, 5)]. The orientation of the loop produces the sign convention shown in Figure 8-25, which shows that an

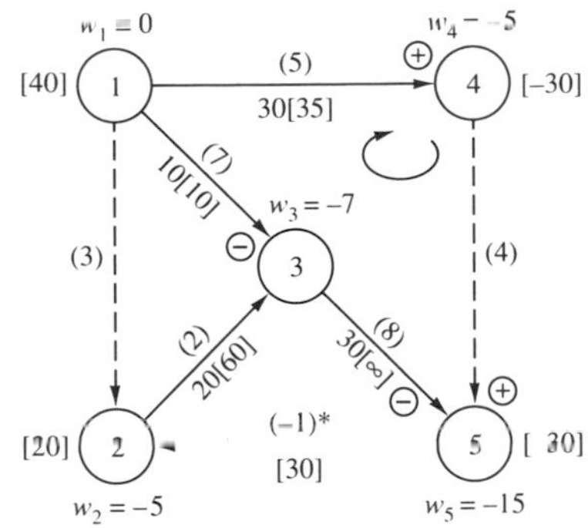

$z_{12} - c_{12} = 0 - (-5) - 3 = 2$
$z_{52} - c_{52} = -15 - (-5) - (-1) = -9$
$z_{45} - c_{45} = -5 - (-15) - 4 = \boxed{6}$

Arc (4, 5) becomes basic at level 5

Arc (1, 4) becomes nonbasic at upperbound

Substitute $x_{14} = 35 - x'_{14}$
Reduce each of x_{13} and x_{35} by 5

Figure 8-25

increase in the flow of nonbasic arc (4, 5) must be coupled simultaneously with decreases in basic arcs (1, 3) and (3, 5) and an increase in basic arc (1, 4). We can see from the capacity and nonnegativity limits that:

1. There is no upper bound on the capacity of nonbasic arc (4, 5).
2. Basic arc (1, 4) flow can be increased by at most $35 - 30 = 5$ units.
3. Basic arc (1, 3) flow can be decreased by at most 10 units.
4. Basic arc (3, 5) flow can be decreased by at most 30 units.

Combining all of these restrictions, we conclude that the flow in nonbasic arc (4, 5) can be increased by 5 units, in which case basic arc (1, 4) must leave the basis (spanning tree) and become nonbasic at its upper bound of 35. In this case we use the substitution $x_{14} = 35 - x'_{14}$. This substitution will result in the network shown in Figure 8-26 (verify the supply and demand values [35] and [−25] at nodes 1 and 4). The (basic) spanning tree now consists of arcs (1, 3), (2, 3), (3, 5), and (4, 5), with arcs (1, 2), (4, 1), and (5, 2) being nonbasic.

The computations of w_i and $z_{ij} - c_{ij}$ in Figure 8-26 show that nonbasic arc (1, 2) must enter the basic solution at level 5, simultaneously forcing basic arc (1, 3) to become nonbasic at its lower (zero) bound (verify). This results in the new spanning tree shown in Figure 8-27. By repeating the same type of computation on Figure 8-27, all $z_{ij} - c_{ij}$ for the nonbasic variables are shown to be negative, thus indicating that the current iteration is optimum. The flows across arcs (1, 4) and (2, 5) are

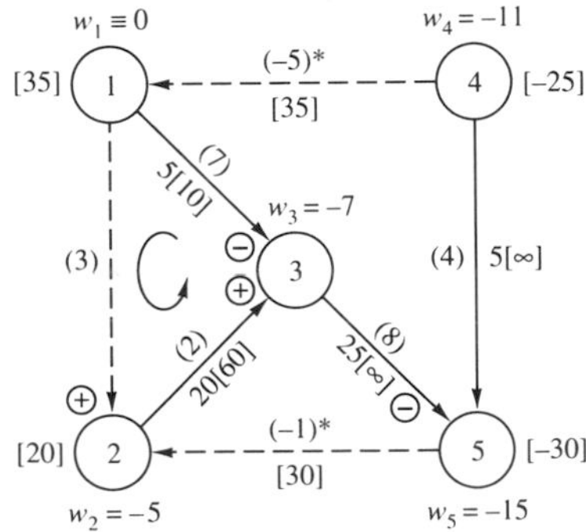

$z_{12} - c_{12} = 0 - (-5) - 3 = \boxed{2}$
$z_{41} - c_{41} = -11 - 0 - (-5) = -6$
$z_{52} - c_{52} = -15 - (-5) - (-1) = -9$

Arc (1, 2) enters at level 5
Arc (1, 3) leaves at level 0

Increase x_{23} by 5

Figure 8-26

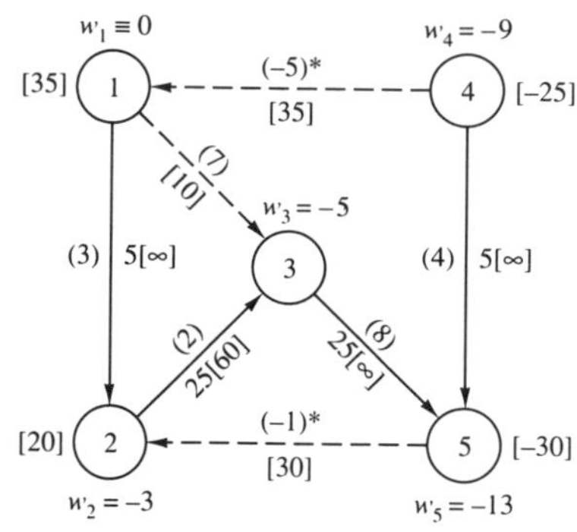

$z_{13} - c_{13} = 0 - (-5) - 7 = -2$
$z_{41} - c_{41} = -9 - 0 - (-5) = -4$
$z_{52} - c_{52} = -13 - (-3) - (-1) = -9$

Optimum solution:

$x_{12} = 5,\ x_{13} = 0$
$x_{14} = 35 - 0 = 35$
$x_{23} = 25$
$x_{25} = 30 - 0 = 30$
$x_{35} = 25,\ x_{45} = 5$

Figure 8-27

determined by back substitution, as

$$x_{14} = 35 - x_{41} = 35 - 0 = 35$$
$$x_{25} = 30 - x_{52} = 30 - 0 = 35$$

where x_{41} and x_{52} actually equal x'_{14} and x'_{25} obtained from upper-bound substitutions. ◀

8.6 SUMMARY

In this chapter we presented a number of applications of network modeling, including the minimal spanning tree, the shortest-route algorithm, the maximum-flow model, and the general capacitated network. Although special algorithms for each network model were presented, the discussion shows that the capacitated network simplex method subsumes most of these special solution algorithms. Nevertheless, the specialized algorithms do offer computational advantages over the network simplex method.

Another algorithm for solving the capacitated network model is the **out-of-kilter** method. This algorithm is a combined primal–dual method designed to exploit the special structure of the model.

Another type of network analysis is the PERT–CPM technique. This technique seeks the determination of a feasible schedule of the individual activities in complex projects. In the next chapter we present the details of this important type of network analysis.

SELECTED REFERENCES

BAZARAA, M., J. JARVIS, and H. SHERALI, *Linear Programming and Network Flow*, 2nd ed., Wiley, New York, 1990.

FORD, L., and D. FULKERSON, *Flows in Networks*, Princeton University Press, Princeton, N.J., 1962.

KENNINGTON, J., and R. HELGASON, *Algorithms for Network Programming*, Wiley-Interscience, New York, 1980.

MANDL, C., *Applied Network Optimization*, Academic Press, Orlando, Fla., 1979.

PHILLIPS, D., and A. GARCIA-DIAZ, *Fundamentals of Network Analysis*, Prentice Hall, Englewood Cliffs, N.J., 1981.

PROBLEMS

Section	Assigned Problems
8.1	8–1
8.2	8–2 to 8–5
8.3	8–6 to 8–12
8.4	8–13 to 8–17
8.5	8–18 to 8–25

☐ **8–1** For each network in Figure 8-28 determine the following: (a) a path, (b) a loop, (c) directed loop or a circuit, (d) a tree, and (e) a spanning tree.

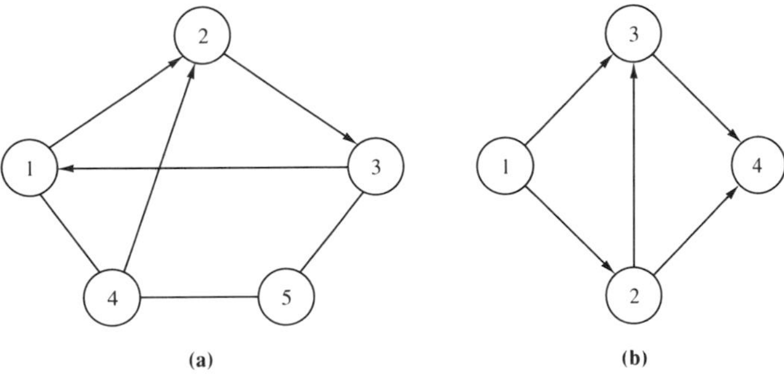

Figure 8-28

☐ **8–2** Find the minimal spanning tree of the network in Figure 8-3 under each of the following *independent* conditions:

(a) Nodes 5 and 6 are linked by a 2-mile cable.
(b) Nodes 2 and 5 cannot be linked.
(c) Nodes 2 and 6 are linked by a 4-mile cable.
(d) The cable between nodes 1 and 2 is 8 miles long.
(e) Nodes 3 and 5 are linked by a 2-mile cable.
(f) Node 2 cannot be connected directly to nodes 3 and 5.

☐ **8–3** Suppose that it is desired to establish a cable communication network that links the major cities shown in Figure 8-29. Determine how the cities are connected such that the total used cable mileage is minimized.

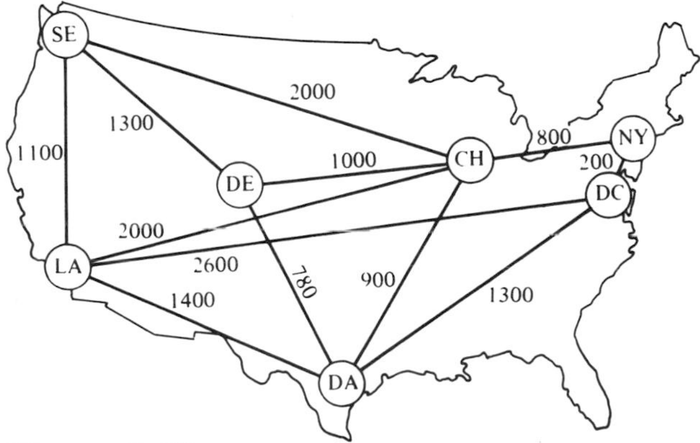

Figure 8-29

☐ **8–4** Figure 8-30 shows the mileage of the feasible links connecting nine offshore natural-gas wellheads with an onshore delivery point. Since the location of wellhead 1 is the closest to shore, it is equipped with sufficient pumping and storage capacity to pump the output of the remaining eight wells to the delivery point. Determine the pipeline network linking all the wellheads to the delivery point that will minimize the total pipeline miles.

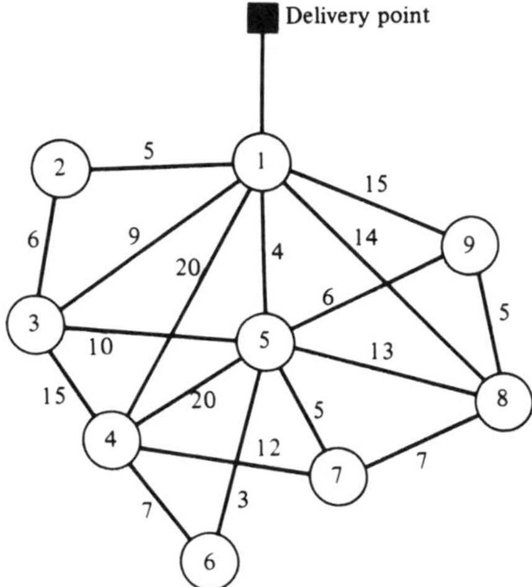

Figure 8-30

☐ **8–5** In Figure 8-30, suppose that the wellheads can be divided into two groups, depending on gas pressure: a high-pressure group, which includes wells 2, 3, 4, and 6, and a low-pressure group, which includes wells 5, 7, 8, and 9. Because of the pressure difference it is not possible to link wellheads from the two groups. However, both groups are connected to the delivery point through wellhead 1. Determine the optimum pipeline network that will connect all wellheads to the delivery point.

☐ **8–6** An "old-fashioned" electric toaster has two hand-operated hinged doors that open downward. A slice of bread is toasted one side at a time by opening one of the doors with one hand and placing the slice with the other hand. Each door is held shut by a spring. After one side is toasted, the slice is turned over to toast the other side. It is desired to determine the sequence of operations (placing, toasting, turning, and removing slices) needed to toast three slices of bread in the shortest possible time. Assume the following elemental times:

Operation	Time (seconds)
Placing one slice in either side	3
Toasting one side	30
Turning one slice that is already in toaster	1
Removing one slice from either side	3

☐ **8–7** Reconstruct the equipment replacement model assuming that a car must be kept in service for at least 2 years before replacement is considered.

☐ **8–8** The network in Figure 8-31 represents the distances in miles between various cities i, $i = 1, 2, \ldots, 8$. Find the shortest routes between the following pairs of cities:

(a) City 1 and city 8.
(b) City 1 and city 6.
(c) City 4 and city 8.
(d) City 2 and city 6.

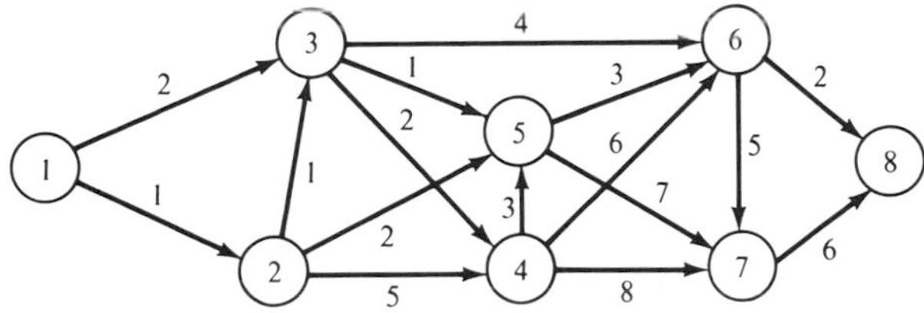

Figure 8-31

☐ **8–9** A truck must deliver concrete from a ready-mix plant to a construction site. The network in Figure 8-32 represents the available routes between the plant and the site. Each route is designated with two pieces of information (d, t), where d is the length of the route and t the time the truck takes to cross the road segment. The speed of the truck on each segment is decided by the condition of the road as well as the number and durations of the stop lights. What is the best route from plant to site?

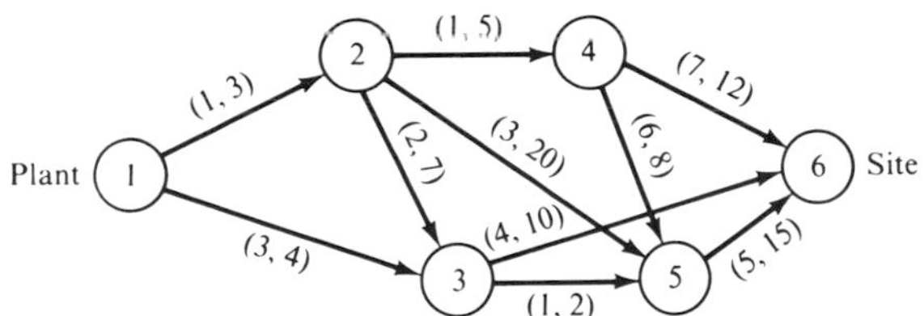

Figure 8-32

☐ **8–10** Determine the shortest route between node 1 and every other node for the network in Figure 8-33.

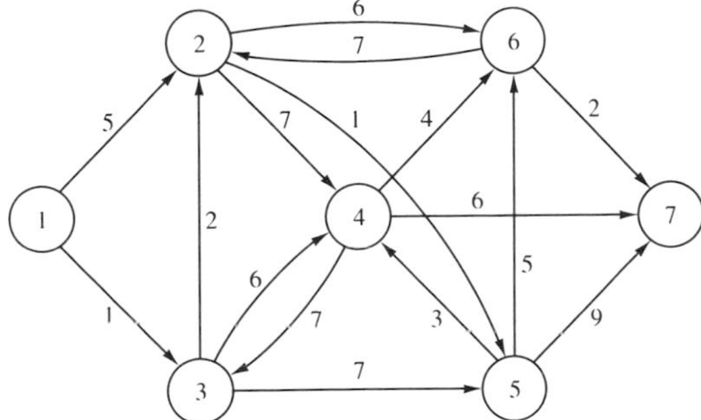

Figure 8-33

☐ **8–11** Determine the shortest route between node 1 and every other node for the network in Figure 8-34.

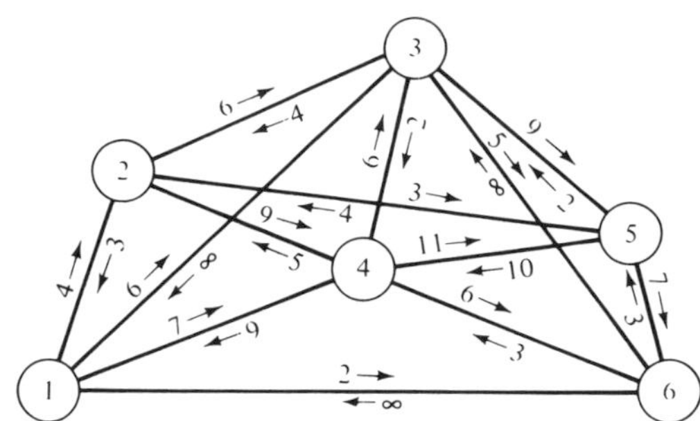

Figure 8-34

☐ **8–12** Express the shortest-route problem of the network in Figure 8-34 as a transshipment model, assuming that the shortest route is to be found between the following pairs of nodes.

(a) Nodes 1 and 5.
(b) Nodes 6 and 3.
(c) Nodes 2 and 6.

☐ **8–13** Three refineries send their gasoline product to two terminals. The capacities of the refineries are estimated at 200,000, 250,000, and 300,000 bbl per day. The demands at the terminals are known to be 400,000 and 450,000 bbl per day. Any demand that cannot be satisfied from the refineries is acquired from other sources. The gasoline product is transported to the terminals via a network of pipelines that are boosted by three pumping stations. Figure 8-35 summarizes the links of the network together with the capacity of each pipeline. How much flow should be passing through each pumping station?

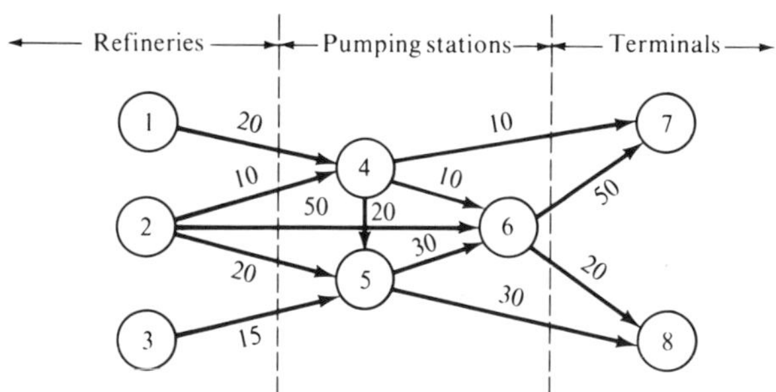

Figure 8-35

☐ **8–14** Consider a version of the transportation problem in which the objective is to maximize the *amounts* transported between m sources and n destinations. Although the sources may have ample supply to satisfy the demand, the limited capacity of the routes connecting the sources and destinations may impede fulfilling the demand completely. Our objective is to determine the shipping schedule that will maximize the *amount* transported (rather than minimize the transportation cost) by expressing the problem as a flow network.

The following table provides the amounts of supply a_i and demand b_j at sources i and destinations j. The maximum capacity c_{ij} of the (i, j) route is given by the (i, j)th element of the tableau. Empty squares indicate that the corresponding route does not exist. Find the schedule that ships the most amounts between the sources and destinations.

		Destination j 1	2	3	4	a_i
Source i	1	30	5		40	**20**
	2			5	90	**20**
	3	20	40	10	10	**200**
	b_j	**200**	**10**	**60**	**20**	

☐ **8–15** Solve Problem 8–14 assuming that transshipment is allowed between sources 1, 2, and 3 with a maximum two-way capacity of 50 units each. Also, transshipment is allowed between destinations 1, 2, 3, and 4 with a maximum two-way capacity of 50 units. What is the effect of transshipping on the unsatisfied demands at the different destinations?

☐ **8–16** Determine the maximum flow between nodes 1 and 5 for the network in Figure 8-36.

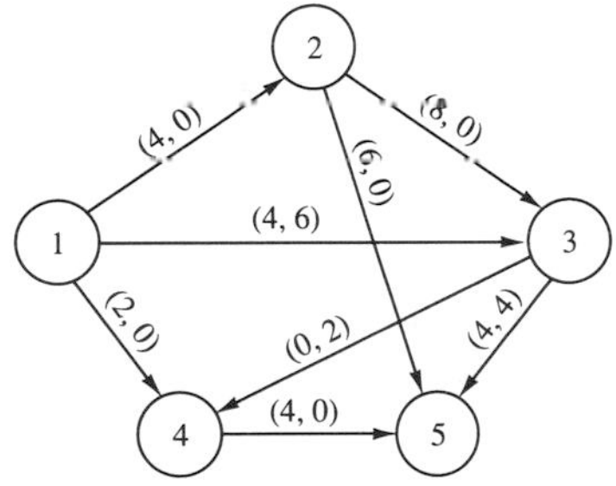

Figure 8-36

☐ **8–17** In Problem 8–13, identify four different cuts. Show that the capacity of these cuts at least equals the maximal flow in Problem 8–13.

☐ **8–18** A product is manufactured in any of four periods according to the following data:

Period	Demand (units)	Production Unit Cost	Holding Unit Cost
1	100	$24	1
2	110	26	2
3	95	21	1
4	125	24	2

Assume that no backordering is allowed. It is desired to minimize the total production and inventory costs for all four periods.

(a) Formulate the problem as an LP model and use TORA to obtain the optimum.
(b) Formulate the problem as a regular transportation model and solve with TORA.
(c) Formulate the problem as a network model and solve using the network simplex method.

☐ **8–19** Repeat Problem 8–18 assuming that backordering is allowed. The penalty cost for backordering is \$1.5 per unit per period.

☐ **8–20** Repeat Problem 8–18 assuming that items can be held in inventory for no more than one period.

☐ **8–21** Repeat Problem 8–18 assuming that both inventory and backordering cannot exceed one period.

☐ **8–22** Consider the following transportation model with no bounds:

			Supply
1	0	5	**10**
2	3	2	**20**
4	2	4	**30**
15	**20**	**25**	

Demand

Formulate the problem as a network model, then show that the network simplex method produces exactly the same computations as in Chapter 6.

☐ **8–23** Solve Example 8.5-1 (Figure 8-22) using the network simplex method.

☐ **8–24** Consider the following transportation model.

5	8	4	9	3	**8**
6	9	12	8	13	**14**
3	−2	0	3	3	**18**
10	14	8	10	13	**4**
16	**6**	**14**	**4**	**4**	

Suppose that no more than 10 units can be transported on any route. Express the problem as a network and solve by the network simplex method.

Chapter 9

Integer Linear Programming

Integer linear programming (ILP) essentially deals with linear programs in which some or all of the variables assume integer or discrete values. An ILP is said to be **mixed** or **pure** depending on whether some or all the variables are restricted to integer values.

Although several algorithms have been developed for ILP, none of these methods are totally reliable from the computational standpoint, particularly as the number of integer variables increases. Unlike LP, where problems with thousands of variables and thousands of constraints can be solved in a reasonable amount of time, computational experience with ILP, after more than 30 years of development, remains elusive.

The computational difficulty with available ILP algorithms has led users to find other means to "solve" the problem. One such approach is to solve the model as a continuous LP and then **round** the optimum solution to the closest feasible integer values. However, there is no guarantee in this case that the resulting *rounded* solution will satisfy the constraints. This is *always true* if the original ILP has one or more *equality* constraints. From the theory of linear programming, a rounded solution in this case cannot be feasible, since it implies that the same basis (with all nonbasic variables at zero level) can yield two distinct solutions.

The infeasibility created by rounding may be tolerated, since, in general, the (estimated) parameters of the problems are not exact. But there are typical *equality* constraints in integer problems where the parameters are exact. The multiple-choice constraint $x_1 + x_2 + \cdots + x_n = 1$, where $x_j = (0, 1)$ for all j, is but one example. Under such conditions, rounding cannot be used, and an exact algorithm becomes essential.

To emphasize further the inadequacy of rounding in general, note that although integer variables are commonly thought of as representing a discrete number of objects (e.g., machines, men, ships), other types represent quantifications of some codes. Thus a decision to finance or not to finance a project can be represented by the binary variable $x = 0$ if the project is rejected or $x = 1$ if it is accepted. In this case it is nonsensical to deal with fractional values of x, and the use of rounding as an approximation is logically unacceptable.

To enhance the importance of problems in which "coded" variables are used, the next section presents typical applications in this area. This will also serve to illustrate the importance of integer programming in general.

9.1 ILLUSTRATIVE APPLICATIONS OF INTEGER PROGRAMMING

In this section a number of integer programming applications are presented. Some of these applications are concerned with the direct formulation of the problem. Another important contribution is the use of integer programming to reformulate "ill-constructed" models into the acceptable format of mathematical programming models. In this case the available techniques can be used to solve problems that otherwise may be difficult to tackle.

9.1.1 CAPITAL BUDGETING PROBLEM

Five projects are being considered for execution over the next 3 years. The expected returns for each project and the yearly expenditures (in thousands of dollars) are tabulated below.

The problem seeks to decide which of the five projects should be executed over the 3-year planning period. In this regard, the problem reduces to a "yes–no" decision for each project. This decision is coded numerically as a binary variable, where

Project	Expenditures for: Year 1	Year 2	Year 3	Returns
1	5	1	8	20
2	4	7	10	40
3	3	9	2	20
4	7	4	1	15
5	8	6	10	30
Available funds	25	25	25	

the value 1 represents "yes" and the value 0 represents "no." We formalize the decision problem by defining the binary variable x_j to represent the jth project. The associated model then becomes

$$\text{maximize } z = 20x_1 + 40x_2 + 20x_3 + 15x_4 + 30x_5$$

subject to

$$\begin{aligned}
5x_1 + 4x_2 + 3x_3 + 7x_4 + 8x_5 &\leq 25 \\
1x_1 + 7x_2 + 9x_3 + 4x_4 + 6x_5 &\leq 25 \\
8x_1 + 10x_2 + 2x_3 + x_4 + 10x_5 &\leq 25 \\
x_j = 0, 1, \qquad j = 1, 2, \ldots, 5 &
\end{aligned}$$

The optimum continuous (LP) solution, obtained by imposing the upper bounds $x_j \leq 1$, for all j, yields $x_1 = .5789$, $x_2 = x_3 = x_4 = 1$, and $x_5 = .7368$. This solution obviously is not meaningful because x_1 and x_5 assume fractional values. Attempting to use rounding to obtain a solution is also meaningless because x_j is defined originally as a numeric code for the "yes–no" decision. As such, fractional values have no physical relevance with respect to the original model. Actually, the optimum integer solution for the model is $x_1 = x_2 = x_3 = x_4 = 1$, with $x_5 = 0$ and $z = 105$.

9.1.2 FIXED-CHARGE PROBLEM

In a typical production planning problem involving N products, the production cost for product j may consist of a fixed cost (charge) K_j independent of the amount produced and a variable cost c_j per unit. Thus, if x_j is the production level of product j, its production cost function may be written as

$$C_j(x_j) = \begin{cases} K_j + c_j x_j, & x_j > 0 \\ 0, & x_j = 0 \end{cases}$$

The objective criterion then becomes

$$\text{minimize } z = \sum_{j=1}^{N} C_j(x_j)$$

This criterion is nonlinear in x_j because of the discontinuity at the origin. This makes z untractable from the analytic standpoint.

The problem can be made "more" manageable analytically by introducing auxiliary binary variables. Let

$$y_j = \begin{cases} 0, & x_j = 0 \\ 1, & x_j > 0 \end{cases}$$

These conditions can be expressed in the form of a single (linear) constraint as

$$x_j \leq My_j$$

where $M > 0$ is sufficiently large to render $x_j \leq M$ redundant with respect to any active constraint of the problem. Thus the objective criterion may be written as

$$\text{minimize } z = \sum_{j=1}^{N} (c_j x_j + K_j y_j)$$

subject to

$$0 \leq x_j \leq My_j, \qquad \text{all } j$$
$$y_j = 0 \text{ or } 1, \qquad \text{all } j$$

To show that $x_j \leq My_j$ is a proper constraint, notice that if $x_j > 0$, $y_j = 1$ and the fixed charge K_j is added in the objective function. If $x_j = 0$, y_j is either zero or one, but since $K_j > 0$ and z is minimized, y_j must be at zero level.

It is interesting that the original fixed-charge problem has nothing to do with integer programming. Yet the "transformed" problem becomes a zero–one mixed integer problem. The transformation is introduced only for analytic convenience. Indeed, the added binary variables are "extraneous" in the sense that they do not reveal any new information about the solution. For example, $y_j = 1$ in the optimal solution is already implied by $x_j > 0$.

9.1.3 JOB-SHOP SCHEDULING PROBLEM

Consider the sequencing problem involving the completion of n different operations on a *single* machine in the minimum possible time. Each end product goes through a sequence of different operations whose order must be preserved. Also, each of these end products may have to meet a delivery date.

The problem thus has three types of constraints: (1) sequencing, (2) noninterference, and (3) delivery date. The second type guarantees that no two operations are processed (on one machine) simultaneously.

Consider the first type. Let x_j be the time (beginning from the zero datum) for starting operation j. Let a_j be the processing time required to finish operation j. If operation i is to precede operation j, the resulting sequencing constraint is

$$x_i + a_i \leq x_j$$

Consider next the noninterference constraints. For operations i and j not to occupy the machine simultaneously, we have

$$\textit{either} \quad x_i - x_j \geq a_j \quad \textit{or} \quad x_j - x_i \geq a_i$$

depending, respectively, on whether j precedes i or i precedes j in the optimal solution.

The presence of the **either–or constraints** poses a problem, since the model is no longer in the linear programming format (i.e., the either–or constraint results in a nonconvex solution space). This difficulty is overcome by introducing the binary variable y_{ij} defined by

$$y_{ij} = \begin{cases} 0, & \text{if operation } j \text{ precedes operation } i \\ 1, & \text{if operation } i \text{ precedes operation } j \end{cases}$$

For M sufficiently large, the "either–or" constraints become equivalent to the two *simultaneous* constraints

$$My_{ij} + (x_i - x_j) \geq a_j \qquad \text{and} \qquad M(1 - y_{ij}) + (x_j - x_i) \geq a_i$$

The significance of the new transformation is that if in the optimal solution $y_{ij} = 0$, the second constraint becomes redundant. In the meantime the first constraint remains active. Similarly, if $y_{ij} = 1$, the second but not the first constraint becomes active. The introduction of the binary variable y_{ij} has thus reduced these constraints to a form where mixed integer linear programming can be applied.

The delivery dates can be met by adding the following constraints. Suppose that operation j must be completed by time d_j, then

$$x_j + a_j \leq d_j$$

Now, if t is the total time required to finish all n operations, the problem becomes

$$\text{minimize } z = t$$

subject to

$$x_j + a_j \leq t, \quad j = 1, 2, \ldots, n$$

together with the sequencing, noninterference, and delivery constraints developed.

9.1.4 DICHOTOMIES

Suppose that in a certain situation, it is required that *any* k out of m constraints may be active. However, the specific constraints that must be imposed are not known in advance. This situation can be effected as follows. Let the m constraints be of the form

$$g_i(x_1, x_2, \ldots, x_n) \leq b_i, \qquad i = 1, 2, \ldots, m$$

Define

$$y_i = \begin{cases} 0, & \text{if the } i\text{th constraint is active} \\ 1, & \text{if the } i\text{th constraint is inactive} \end{cases}$$

Thus any k out of the m constraints are guaranteed to be active if, for M sufficiently large,

$$g_i(x_1, x_2, \ldots, x_n) \leq b_i + My_i, \qquad i = 1, 2, \ldots, m$$

and

$$y_1 + y_2 + \cdots + y_m = m - k$$

where $y_i = 0$ or 1 for all i. This shows for $m - k$ constraints the associated right-hand side will be of the form $b_i + M$, which makes the constraint redundant. It is important to note that the formulation will select the set of *active* constraints that yields the best objective value.

A related situation occurs when the right-hand side of a single constraint is required to assume *one* of several values; that is,

$$g(x_1, x_2, \ldots, x_n) \le b_1, b_2, \ldots, \text{or } b_r$$

This can be achieved by transforming the constraint to

$$g(x_1, x_2, \ldots, x_n) \le \sum_{k=1}^{r} b_k y_k$$

and

$$y_1 + y_2 + \cdots + y_r = 1$$

where

$$y_k = \begin{cases} 1, & \text{if } b_k \text{ is the right-hand side} \\ 0, & \text{if otherwise} \end{cases}$$

Another application of integer programming for the approximation of a nonlinear single-variable function is given in Section 20.2.1.

9.2 SOLUTION METHODS OF INTEGER PROGRAMMING

In LP, the simplex method is based on recognizing that the optimum occurs at an extreme point of the solution space. This powerful result essentially reduces the search for the optimum from an infinite to a finite number of candidate solutions. On the other hand, ILP starts with a finite number of solution points (assume a bounded pure ILP). Yet the integer nature of the variables makes it difficult to devise an effective algorithm that searches directly among the feasible integer points of the solution space. In view of this difficulty, researchers have developed a solution procedure that is based on exploiting the tremendous success in solving LP problems. The strategy for this procedure can be summarized in three steps:

1. Relax the solution space of the integer problem by ignoring the integer restrictions altogether. This step converts the ILP into a regular LP.
2. Solve the resulting "relaxed" LP model and identify its (continuous) optimum point.
3. Starting from the continuous optimum point, add special constraints that will iteratively force the optimum extreme point of the resulting LP model toward the desired integer restrictions.

The reason we start the search for the ILP optimum at the continuous LP optimum is that there is an improved chance that both solutions will be located close to one another, hence increasing the possibility of locating the integer solution quickly. The essence of the proposed procedure is that it solves successive LP problems, which is more manageable computationally than dealing directly with ILP problems.

There are two methods for generating the special constraints that will force the optimum solution of the relaxed LP problem toward the desired integer solution:

1. Branch-and-bound.
2. Cutting plane.

In both methods, the added constraints effectively eliminate portions of the relaxed solution space, *but never any of the feasible integer points.* Unfortunately, neither of the two methods can be claimed to be uniformly effective in solving ILPs. Nevertheless, branch-and-bound methods are far more successful computationally than are the cutting-plane methods. For this reason most commercial codes are based on the use of the branch-and-bound procedure.

Another technique for solving binary (zero–one) integer programs is the so-called **implicit enumeration** method. This method was introduced in 1965 after both the branch-and-bound and cutting had been in circulation for at least 5 years and was presented as a "new direction" for solving the general ILP through conversion to binary ILP. We will show later, however, that implicit enumeration is actually a special case of the more general branch-and-bound method.

Historically, the cutting-plane methods were the first to be introduced in the OR literature. However, we will start our presentation with the branch-and-bound procedure because of its practical importance.

9.3 BRANCH-AND-BOUND ALGORITHM

It will be more convenient at this point to explain the basics of the branch-and-bound algorithm (B&B) by means of a numeric example. The example will be followed by a summary of the steps of the algorithm.

Example 9.3-1 (Basics of B&B). Consider the following ILP:

$$\text{maximize } z = 5x_1 + 4x_2$$

subject to

$$x_1 + x_2 \leq 5$$
$$10x_1 + 6x_2 \leq 45$$
$$x_1, x_2 \geq 0 \text{ and integer}$$

In Figure 9-1 the ILP solution space is shown by dots. The associated LP solution space, LP0, is defined by dropping the integer constraints. The optimum LP0 solution is given in Figure 9-1 as $x_1 = 3.75$, $x_2 = 1.25$, and $z = 23.75$.

The B&B procedure is based on dealing with the LP problem only. Since the optimum LP solution ($x_1 = 3.75$, $x_2 = 1.25$, $z = 23.75$) does not satisfy the integer requirements, the B&B algorithm calls for "modifying" the LP solution space in a manner that should eventually allow us to identify the ILP optimum. First, we

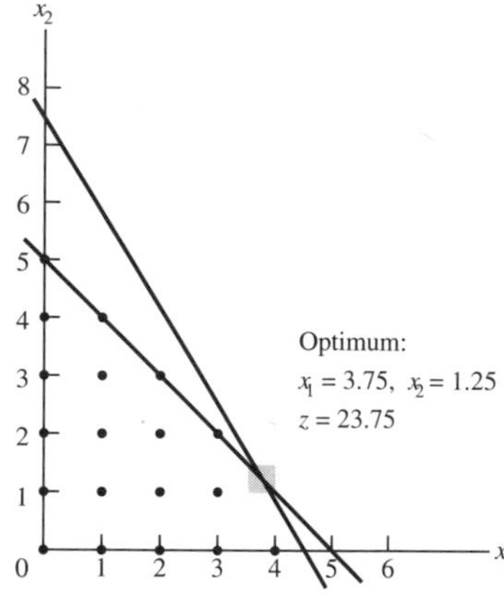

Figure 9-1

select one of the variables whose current value at the optimum LP0 solution violates the integer requirement. Selecting x_1 (= 3.75) arbitrarily, we observe that the region ($3 < x_1 < 4$) of the LP0 solution space cannot, by definition, include any feasible ILP solutions. We can thus modify the LP solution space by eliminating this nonpromising region, which, in essence, is equivalent to replacing the original LP0 space with two LP spaces, LP1 and LP2, defined as follows:

1. LP1 space = LP0 space + ($x_1 \leq 3$).
2. LP2 space = LP0 space + ($x_1 \geq 4$).

Figure 9-2 shows LP1 and LP2 graphically. You will notice that the two spaces contain the same integer feasible points of the ILP model. This means that from the standpoint of the original ILP problem, dealing with LP1 and LP2 is the same as dealing with the original LP0. The main difference is that the selection of the new bounding constraints ($x_1 \leq 3$ and $x_1 \geq 4$) will now improve the chance of forcing the optimum extreme points of LP1 and LP2 toward satisfying the integer requirements. Additionally, the fact that the bounding constraints are in the "immediate vicinity" of the continuous LP0 optimum will increase their chances of producing "good" integer solutions.

As can be seen in Figure 9-2, since the new restrictions $x_1 \leq 3$ and $x_1 \geq 4$ are mutually exclusive, LP1 and LP2 must be dealt with as two separate linear programs. This dichotomization gives rise to the concept of **branching** in the B&B algorithm. In effect, branching signifies partitioning a current solution space into

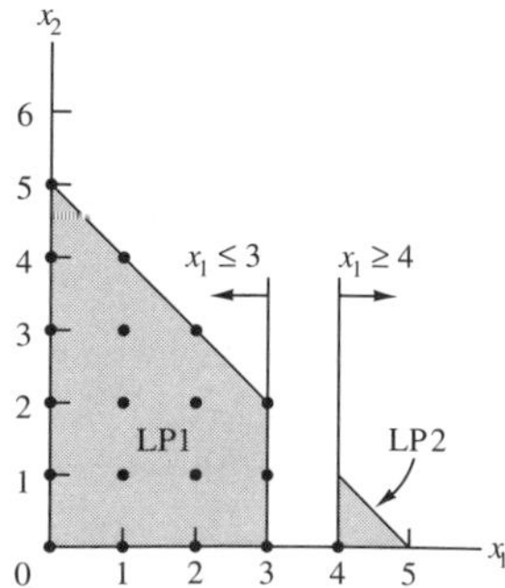

Figure 9-2

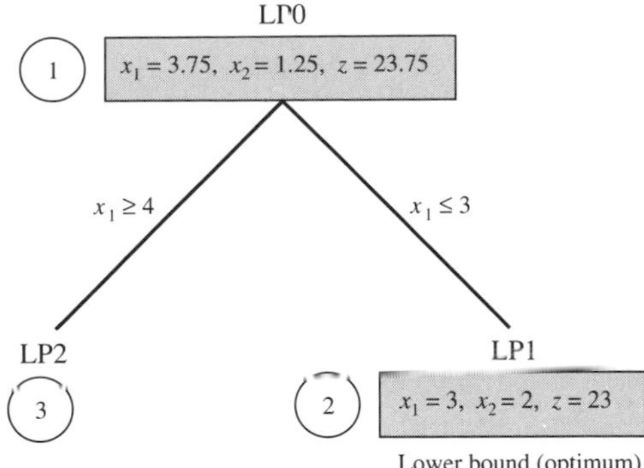

Figure 9-3

mutually exclusive subspaces. Figure 9-3 demonstrates the creation of LP1 and LP2 from LP. The associated branches are defined by the constraints $x_1 \leq 3$ and $x_1 \geq 4$, in which case x_1 is referred to as the **branching variable**.

We know that the optimum ILP must lie in either LP1 or LP2. However, in the absence of the graphical solution space, we have no way of determining where the optimum may be. Consequently, our only option is to investigate *both* problems. We do so by working with one problem at a time (LP1 or LP2). Suppose that we arbitrarily select LP1 associated with $x_1 \leq 3$. In effect, we solve the following problem:

$$\text{maximize } z = 5x_1 + 4x_2$$

subject to

$$\begin{aligned} x_1 + x_2 &\leq 5 \\ 10x_1 + 6x_2 &\leq 45 \\ x_1 &\leq 3 \\ x_1, x_2 &\geq 0 \end{aligned}$$

As stated above, LP1 is the same as LP0 with the added *upper-bound* restriction $x_1 \leq 3$. We can thus apply the primal upper-bounding algorithm (Section 7.1) to solve the problem. This will yield the new optimum solution

$$x_1 = 3, \qquad x_2 = 2, \quad \text{and} \quad z = 23$$

Since the solution happens to satisfy the integer requirements, we say that LP1 has been **fathomed**, which means that LP1 cannot produce any *better* ILP solutions and hence need not be investigated any further.

The attainment of a feasible integer solution at an early stage of the computations is crucial to enhancing the efficiency of the B&B algorithm. Such a solution sets a **lower bound** on the optimum objective value of the ILP problem, which in turn can be used to automatically discard any unexplored subproblems (such as LP2) that do not yield a *better* integer solution. In terms of our example, LP1 produces the lower bound $z = 23$. This means that any *improved* integer solution must have a z-value higher than 23. However, since the optimum solution of the (original) LP0 problem has $z = 23.75$ and *since all the coefficients of the objective function happen to be integers*, it follows that no subproblem emanating from LP0 can produce a value of z that is better than 23. As a result, we can, without further investigation, discard

LP2. In this case LP2 is said to be *fathomed* because it cannot yield a better integer solution.

From the discussion above, we see that a subproblem is *fathomed* if one the following conditions is satisfied:

1. The subproblem yields a feasible integer solution of the ILP problem.
2. The subproblem cannot yield a better solution than the best available lower (z-value) bound of the ILP problem. (A special case of this condition is that the subproblem will have no feasible solution at all.)

In our example, LP1 and LP2 are fathomed by conditions 1 and 2, respectively. Since there are no more subproblems to be investigated, the procedure ends and the optimum integer solution of the ILP problem is the one associated with the current lower bound: namely, $x_1 = 3$, $x_2 = 2$, and $z = 23$.

If you investigate the procedure outlined above, you will discover that a number of questions remain unanswered:

1. At LP0, could we have selected x_2 as the branching variable in place of x_1?
2. When selecting the next subproblem to be investigated, could we have solved LP2 first instead of LP1?

The answer to both questions is "yes," but the ensuing computational details could differ dramatically. We illustrate this point by referring to Figure 9-3. Suppose that we decided to investigate LP2 first. Figure 9-4 gives the resulting solution as $x_1 = 4$, $x_2 = .8333$, $z = 23.3333$ (verify using TORA). Since $x_2 = .83333$ is noninteger, LP2 must be investigated further by creating LP3 and LP4 using the respective branches $x_2 \geq 0$ and $x_2 \geq 1$. This means that

$$\text{LP3 space} = \text{LP0 space} + (x_1 \geq 4) + (x_2 \leq 0)$$
$$\text{LP4 space} = \text{LP0 space} + (x_1 \geq 4) + (x_2 \geq 1)$$

At this point we have three subproblems to choose from: LP1, LP3, and LP4. (You will notice again that these three subproblems include all the feasible integer solutions of the original ILP problem.) Selecting LP4 arbitrarily, we discover that it has no feasible solution and hence it is fathomed. Next, we (arbitrarily) select LP3 for investigation. Its solution is given by $x_1 = 4.5$, $x_2 = 0$, and $z = 22.5$. Since $x_1 = 4.5$ is noninteger, we create two subproblems, LP5 and LP6, from LP4 by using the restrictions $x_1 \leq 4$ and $x_1 \geq 5$, respectively. We thus get

$$\text{LP5 space} = \text{LP0 space} + (x_1 \geq 4) + (x_2 \leq 0) + (x_1 \leq 4)$$
$$\text{LP6 space} = \text{LP0 space} + (x_1 \geq 4) + (x_2 \leq 0) + (x_1 \geq 5)$$

Now we have LP1, LP5, and LP6 to deal with and we arbitrarily select LP6 for investigation. Since LP6 has no feasible solution, it is fathomed. Next, we select LP5, whose optimum solution ($x_1 = 4$, $x_2 = 0$, $z = 20$) satisfies the integer requirements. Alas, we finally encountered an integer solution that sets a lower bound ($z = 20$) on the optimum integer solution! Unfortunately, this lower bound is both "too weak" and "too late" to be useful. The only remaining node, LP1, is fathomed next with $z = 23$, which immediately sets a new lower bound. Since there are no more subproblems to be investigated, the last lower bound associates the optimum ILP solution with LP1.

The solution sequence in Figure 9-4 is deliberately selected to be a worst-case scenario, to demonstrate one of the main weaknesses of the B&B algorithm.

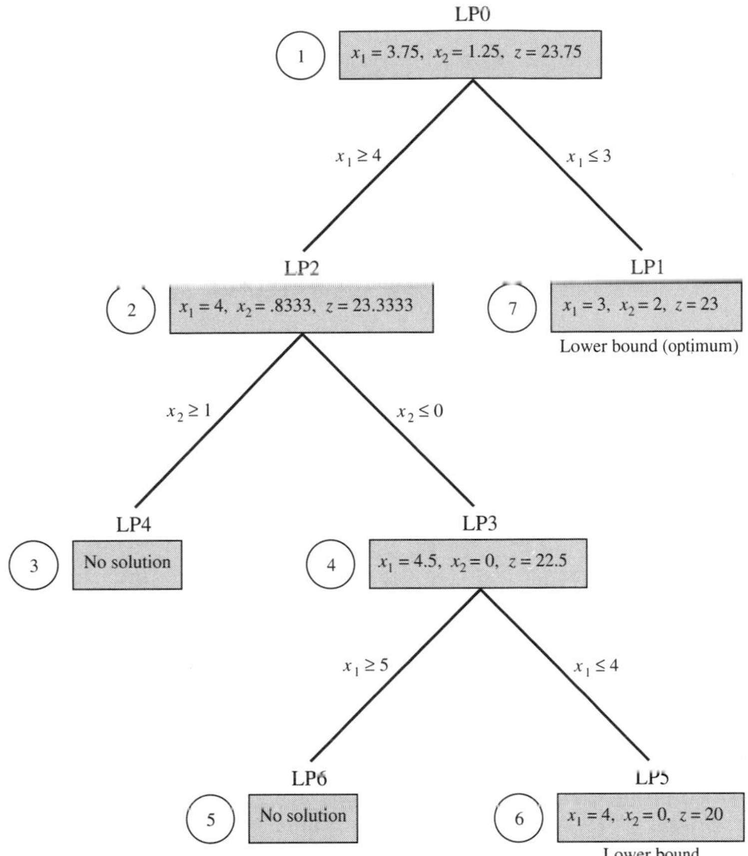

Figure 9-4

Namely, at a given subproblem, how do we select the branching variable, and among all the unexplored subproblems, which subproblem should be investigated next? You will notice that in Figure 9-3, we happen to "stumble" over a good lower bound at the first subproblem LP1, which allows us to fathom LP2 without further investigation. In essence, the ILP problem is solved by investigating one subproblem only. In Figure 9-4, we had to solve six subproblems before verifying optimality. The extreme case in Figure 9-4 is not unusual and may well be encountered in real situations. Although many heuristics exist for enhancing the ability of the B&B algorithm to "look ahead" and make a best "guess" as to whether or not a given branch will lead to an improved ILP solution, the fact remains that there is no solid theory that can be claimed to yield uniformly consistent results for the solution of the general ILP problem. ◀

We now summarize the steps of the B&B algorithm. Assuming a maximization problem, define z as the lower bound on the optimum integer ILP solution. Initially, set $z = -\infty$ and $i = 0$.

Step 1: Fathoming/Bounding. Select LPi as the next subproblem to be investigated. Solve LPi and attempt to fathom it using the appropriate conditions.

(a) If LPi is fathomed (solution inferior, infeasible or integer), update the lower bound z if a better ILP solution is encountered; otherwise, select a new subproblem

i and repeat step 1. If all subproblems have been investigated, stop; the optimum ILP is associated with the last lower bound $\underline{z}$, if any. Otherwise,

(b) If LPi is not fathomed, go to step 2 to effect branching of LPi.

Step 2: Branching. Select one of the variables x_j whose optimum value x_j^* in the LPi solution does not satisfy the integer restriction. Eliminate the region $[x_j^*] < x_j < [x_j^*] + 1$ (where [A] defines the largest integer $\leq$ A) by creating two LP subproblems corresponding to the following two mutually exclusive constraints

$$x_j \leq [x_j^*] \qquad \text{and} \qquad x_j \geq [x_j^*] + 1$$

Go to step 1.

Exercise 9.3-1

Modify the B&B algorithm to fit minimization problems.
[*Ans.* Replace the lower bound $\underline{z}$ with an upper bound $\bar{z}$. Initially, $\bar{z} = +\infty$. All the other details remain unchanged.]

Computer Drill

Solve the problem in Example 9.3-1 by starting with x_2 as the branching variable. Use TORA, with the MODIFY option of upper and lower bounds, to solve the resulting subproblems. Start the procedure by solving the subproblem associated with the upper bound $x_2 \leq [x_2^*]$.

The B&B algorithm is applicable to both pure and mixed integer problems. If a variable is not restricted to integer values, we simply never select it as a branching variable. For example, suppose that in Example 9.3-1 only variable x_1 is restricted to integer values, meaning that x_2 is continuous. In this case, since LP1 in Figure 9-3 yields an integer value of x_1 (= 3), the associated z-value provides a legitimate lower bound $\underline{z} = 23$. It is not possible, however, to fathom LP2 at this point based on this information alone, since the optimum value of z for the original ILP may now assume a fractional value. We thus must solve LP2. As can be seen from Figure 9-4, LP2 yields an integer value of x_1 (= 4) as desired. This means that LP2 is fathomed. However, since $z = 23.3333$ for LP2, the new lower bound is $\underline{z} = 23.3333$. The process ends at this point with LP2 yielding the desired optimum solution.

Exercise 9.3-2

Suppose that we start in Figure 9-3 by solving LP2. Is the information obtained from LP2 sufficient to fathom LP1 without actually having to solve its associated linear program?
[*Ans.* No, because LP1 is fathomed based on its optimum objective value ($z = 23$) relative to the current lower bound $\underline{z} = 23.3333$.]

Computations in Branch-and-Bound Methods

Practical computer codes based on the branch-and-bound technique differ from the outline given above mainly in the details of selecting the branching variables at a node and the sequence in which the subproblems are examined. These rules are based on heuristics developed through experimentation.

A basic disadvantage of the B&B algorithm given above is that it is necessary to solve a complete linear program at each node. In large problems, this could be very time consuming, particularly when the only information needed at the node may be its optimum objective value. This point is clarified by realizing that once a "good" bound is obtained, "many" nodes can be discarded from the knowledge of their optimum objective values.

The preceding point led to the development of a procedure whereby it may be unnecessary to solve all the subproblems of the branch-and-bound tree. The idea is to "estimate" an *upper* bound (assume a maximization problem) on the optimum objective value at each node. Should this upper bound become smaller than the objective value associated with the best available integer solution, the node is discarded. The main advantage is that the upper bounds can be estimated quickly with minimal computations. The general idea is to estimate the **penalties** (i.e., the deterioration in the objective value) resulting from enforcing the conditions $x_k \leq [\beta_k]$ and $x_k \geq [\beta_k] + 1$. This can be achieved by augmenting each of these constraints to the optimum tableau at the node (with which x_k is associated). Then, *under the assumption of no change in basis*, the required penalty can be estimated directly from the objective function coefficients (see Problem 9–32).

Although the penalties are easy to compute, their values may not necessarily be proportional to the *true* degradation in the objective value. In other words, they do not provide a tight upper bound and hence may not be effective. Various attempts to "strengthen" these penalties have been made. The most interesting of these is the one using information from the cutting methods (see Section 9.4). Nevertheless, even these "strengthened" penalties appear to be ineffective computationally, particularly when the size of the problem increases. It appears that commercial codes have abandoned the use of simple penalties in favor of heuristics that proved, through experimentation with large and complex problems, to be quite effective [see Taha (1975, pp. 165 171)].

In spite of the drawbacks of branch-and-bound methods, it can be stated that, to date, these methods are the most effective in solving integer programs of practical sizes. Indeed, all available commercial codes are based on the branch-and-bound method. This does *not* mean, however, that *every* integer program can be solved by a branch-and-bound method. It only means that when the choice is between a cutting method and a branch-and-bound method, the latter has generally proved superior.

9.4 CUTTING-PLANE ALGORITHMS

The concept of the cutting plane will first be illustrated by an example. Consider the integer linear programming problem

$$\text{maximize } z = 7x_1 + 9x_2$$

subject to

$$\begin{aligned} -x_1 + 3x_2 &\leq 6 \\ 7x_1 + x_2 &\leq 35 \end{aligned}$$

$$x_1, x_2 \text{ nonnegative integers}$$

The optimal continuous solution (ignoring the integer condition) is shown graphically in Figure 9-5. This is given by $z = 63$, $x_1 = 9/2$, and $x_2 = 7/2$, which is noninteger.

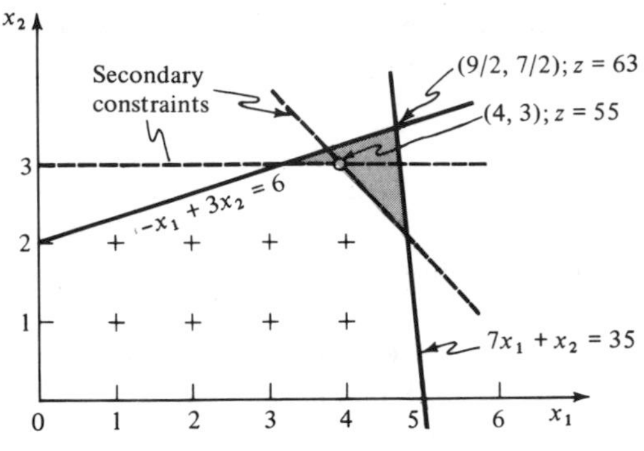

Figure 9-5

The idea of the cutting-plane algorithm is to change the convex set of the solution space so that the appropriate extreme point becomes all-integer. Such changes in the boundaries of the solution space should result still in a convex set. Also, this change should be made without "slicing off" *any* of the feasible *integer* solutions of the original problem. Figure 9-5 shows how two secondary constraints are added to the problem with the new extreme point (4, 3) giving the integer optimal solution. Notice that the area sliced off from the original solution space (shaded area) does not include any integer values.

The following analysis shows how the secondary constraints are developed systematically for the pure and mixed integer problems.

9.4.1 THE FRACTIONAL (PURE INTEGER) ALGORITHM

A basic requirement for the application of this algorithm is that all the coefficients and the right-hand-side constant of each constraint must be integer. For example, the constraint

$$x_1 + \frac{1}{3} x_2 \leq \frac{13}{2}$$

must be transformed to

$$6x_1 + 2x_2 \leq 39$$

where no fractions are present. The latter is achieved by multiplying both sides of the original constraint by the least common multiple of the denominators.

The foregoing requirement is imposed since, as will be shown later, the pure integer algorithm does not differentiate between the regular and slack variables of the problem in the sense that all variables must be integers. The presence of fractional coefficients in the constraints thus may not allow the slack variables to assume integer values. In this case, the fractional algorithm may indicate that no feasible solution exists, even though the problem may have a feasible integer solution in terms of *non*slack variables. (See Problem 9–20 for an illustration of this case.)

The details of the algorithm will be discussed now. First, the relaxed LP problem is solved, that is, disregarding the integer condition. If the optimal solution happens to be integer, there is nothing more to be done. Otherwise, the secondary constraints that will force the solution toward the integer solution are developed as follows. Let the final optimal tableau for the linear program be given by

Basic	x_1	$\cdots$	x_i	$\cdots$	x_m	w_1	$\cdots$	w_j	$\cdots$	w_n	Solution
z	0	$\cdots$	0	$\cdots$	0	$\bar{c}_1$	$\cdots$	$\bar{c}_j$	$\cdots$	$\bar{c}_n$	β_0
x_1	1	$\cdots$	0	$\cdots$	0	α_1^1	$\cdots$	α_1^j	$\cdots$	α_1^n	β_1
$\vdots$	$\vdots$		$\vdots$		$\vdots$	$\vdots$		$\vdots$		$\vdots$	$\vdots$
x_i	0	$\cdots$	1	$\cdots$	0	α_i^1	$\cdots$	α_i^j	$\cdots$	α_i^n	β_i
$\vdots$	$\vdots$		$\vdots$		$\vdots$	$\vdots$		$\vdots$		$\vdots$	$\vdots$
x_m	0	$\cdots$	0	$\cdots$	1	α_m^1	$\cdots$	α_m^j	$\cdots$	α_m^n	β_m

The variables x_i ($i = 1, 2, \ldots, m$) represent the basic variables and the variables w_j ($j = 1, 2, \ldots, n$) are the nonbasic variables. These variables have been arranged as such for convenience.

Consider the ith equation where the basic variable x_i assumes a noninteger value.

$$x_i = \beta_i - \sum_{j=1}^{n} \alpha_i^j w_j, \qquad \beta_i \text{ noninteger} \qquad (\textit{source row})$$

Any such equation will be referred to as a **source row**. Since, in general, the coefficients of the objective function can be made integer, the variable z is also integer and the z-equation may be selected as a source row. Indeed, the convergence proof of the algorithm requires that z be integer.

Let

$$\beta_i = [\beta_i] + f_i$$
$$\alpha_i^j = [\alpha_i^j] + f_{ij}$$

where $N = [a]$ is the largest integer such that $N \leq a$. It follows that $0 < f_i < 1$ and $0 \leq f_{ij} < 1$; that is, f_i is a strictly positive fraction and f_{ij} is a nonnegative fraction. For example,

a	$[a]$	$f = a - [a]$
$1\frac{1}{2}$	1	1/2
$-2\frac{1}{3}$	-3	2/3
-1	-1	0
$-2/5$	-1	3/5

The source row thus yields

$$f_i - \sum_{j=1}^{n} f_{ij} w_j = x_i - [\beta_i] + \sum_{j=1}^{n} [\alpha_i^j] w_j$$

For *all* the variables x_i and w_j to be integer, the right-hand side of the equation must be integer, which in turn implies that the left-hand side must also be integer.

Given $f_{ij} \geq 0$ and $w_j \geq 0$ for all i and j, it follows that $\sum_{j=1}^{n} f_{ij} w_j \geq 0$. Consequently,

$$f_i - \sum_{j=1}^{n} f_{ij} w_j \leq f_i < 1$$

Since $f_i - \sum_{j=1}^{n} f_{ij} w_j$ must be integer by construction, a *necessary* condition for satisfying integrality becomes

$$f_i - \sum_{j=1}^{n} f_{ij} w_j \leq 0$$

The last constraint can be put in the form

$$S_i = \sum_{j=1}^{n} f_{ij} w_j - f_i \qquad (\textit{fractional cut})$$

where S_i is a nonnegative slack variable that by definition must be an integer. This constraint equation defines the **fractional cut**. From the last tableau, $w_j = 0$ and thus $S_i = -f_i$, which is infeasible. This means that the new constraint is not satisfied by the given solution. The dual simplex method (Section 3.4) can then be used to clear the infeasibility, which is equivalent to cutting off the solution space toward the optimal integer solution.

The new tableau after adding the fractional cut will thus become

Basic	x_1	$\dots$	x_i	$\dots$	x_m	w_1	$\dots$	w_j	$\dots$	w_n	S_i	Solution
z	0	$\dots$	0	$\dots$	0	$\bar{c}_1$	$\dots$	$\bar{c}_j$	$\dots$	$\bar{c}_n$	0	β_0
x_1	1	$\dots$	0	$\dots$	0	α_1^1	$\dots$	α_1^j	$\dots$	α_1^n	0	β_1
$\vdots$	$\vdots$		$\vdots$		$\vdots$	$\vdots$		$\vdots$		$\vdots$	$\vdots$	$\vdots$
x_i	0	$\dots$	1	$\dots$	0	α_i^1	$\dots$	α_i^j	$\dots$	α_i^n	0	β_i
$\vdots$	$\vdots$		$\vdots$		$\vdots$	$\vdots$		$\vdots$		$\vdots$	$\vdots$	$\vdots$
x_m	0	$\dots$	0	$\dots$	1	α_m^1	$\dots$	α_m^j	$\dots$	α_m^n	0	β_m
S_i	0	$\dots$	0	$\dots$	0	$-f_{i1}$	$\dots$	$-f_{ij}$	$\dots$	$-f_{in}$	1	$-f_i$

If the new solution (after applying dual simplex method) is integer, the process ends. Otherwise, a new fractional cut is constructed from the *resulting* tableau and the dual simplex method is used again to clear the infeasibility. This procedure is repeated until an integer solution is achieved. However, if at any iteration the dual simplex algorithm indicates that no feasible solution exists, the problem has no feasible *integer* solution.

The algorithm is referred to as the **fractional method** because all the nonzero coefficients of the generated cut are less than one.

The fractional algorithm may indicate, at first thought, that the size of the simplex tableau can become very large as new cuts are augmented to the problem. This is not true. In fact, the total number of constraints in the *augmented* problem cannot exceed the number of variables in the original problem, that is, $(m + n)$. This result follows, since if the augmented problem includes more than $(m + n)$ constraints, one or more of the slack variables S_i associated with the fractional cuts must become basic. In this case the associated equations become redundant and may be dropped from the tableau completely.

The fractional algorithm has two disadvantages:

1. The round-off errors that evolve in automatic calculations will most likely distort the original data, particularly with the increase in problem size.
2. The solution of the problem remains infeasible in the sense that no *integer* solution can be obtained until the optimal integer solution is reached. This means that there will be no "good" integer solution in store if the calculations are stopped prematurely prior to the attainment of the optimal (integer) solution.

The first difficulty is overcome by the development of an **all-integer integer algorithm**. The algorithm starts with an initial all-integer tableau (i.e., all the coefficients are integers) suitable for the application of the dual simplex algorithm. Special cuts are then constructed such that their addition to the tableau will preserve the integrality of all the coefficients. However, the fact that the solution remains infeasible until the integer optimal solution is reached still presents a disadvantage.

The second difficulty was considered by developing cutting-plane algorithms that start integer and feasible but nonoptimal. The iterations continue to be feasible and integer until the optimum solution is reached. In this respect, this algorithm is **primal-feasible** as compared with the fractional algorithm, which is **dual-feasible**. The primal algorithms do not appear to be computationally promising, however.

Example 9.4-1. Consider the problem that was solved graphically at the beginning of this section. The optimal continuous solution is given by

Basic	x_1	x_2	x_3	x_4	Solution
z	0	0	28/11	15/11	63
x_2	0	1	7/22	1/22	7/2
x_1	1	0	−1/22	3/22	9/2

Since the solution is noninteger, a fractional cut is added to the tableau. Generally, any of the constraint equations corresponding to a noninteger solution can be selected to generate the cut. However, as a rule of thumb, we usually choose the equation corresponding to $\max_i\{f_i\}$. Since both equations in this problem have the same value of f_i, that is, $f_1 = f_2 = 1/2$, either one may be used. Consider the x_2-equation. This gives

$$x_2 + \frac{7}{22}x_3 + \frac{1}{22}x_4 = 3\tfrac{1}{2}$$

or

$$x_2 + \left(0 + \frac{7}{22}\right)x_3 + \left(0 + \frac{1}{22}\right)x_4 = \left(3 + \frac{1}{2}\right)$$

Hence the corresponding fractional cut is given by

$$S_1 - \frac{7}{22}x_3 - \frac{1}{22}x_4 = -\frac{1}{2}$$

This gives the new tableau

Basic	x_1	x_2	x_3	x_4	S_1	R.H.S.
z	0	0	28/11	15/11	0	63
x_2	0	1	7/22	1/22	0	$3\frac{1}{2}$
x_1	1	0	$-1/22$	3/22	0	$4\frac{1}{2}$
S_1	0	0	$-7/22$	$-1/22$	1	$-1/2$

The dual simplex method yields

Basic	x_1	x_2	x_3	x_4	S_1	Solution
z	0	0	0	1	8	59
x_2	0	1	0	0	1	3
x_1	1	0	0	1/7	$-1/7$	$4\frac{4}{7}$
x_3	0	0	1	1/7	$-22/7$	$1\frac{4}{7}$

Since the solution is still noninteger, a new cut is constructed. The x_1-equation is written as

$$x_1 + \left(0 + \frac{1}{7}\right)x_4 + \left(-1 + \frac{6}{7}\right)S_1 = \left(4 + \frac{4}{7}\right)$$

which gives the cut

$$S_2 - \frac{1}{7}x_4 - \frac{6}{7}S_1 = -\frac{4}{7}$$

Adding this constraint to the last tableau, we get

Basic	x_1	x_2	x_3	x_4	S_1	S_2	R.H.S.
z	0	0	0	1	8	0	59
x_2	0	1	0	0	1	0	3
x_1	1	0	0	1/7	$-1/7$	0	$4\frac{4}{7}$
x_3	0	0	1	1/7	$-22/7$	0	$1\frac{4}{7}$
S_2	0	0	0	$-1/7$	$-6/7$	1	$-4/7$

The dual simplex method now yields

Basic	x_1	x_2	x_3	x_4	S_1	S_2	Solution
z	0	0	0	0	2	7	55
x_2	0	1	0	0	1	0	3
x_1	1	0	0	0	-1	1	4
x_3	0	0	1	0	-4	1	1
x_4	0	0	0	1	6	-7	4

which gives the optimal integer solution $z = 55$, $x_1 = 4$, $x_2 = 3$.

The reader can verify graphically that the addition of the developed cuts "cuts" the solution space as desired (see Figure 9-5). The first cut

$$S_1 - \frac{7}{22}x_3 - \frac{1}{22}x_4 = -\frac{1}{2}$$

can be expressed in terms of x_1 and x_2 only by using the appropriate substitution as follows:

$$S_1 - \frac{7}{22}(6 + x_1 - 3x_2) - \frac{1}{22}(35 - 7x_1 - x_2) = -\frac{1}{2}$$

or

$$S_1 + x_2 = 3$$

which is equivalent to

$$x_2 \leq 3$$

Similarly, for the second cut,

$$S_2 - \frac{1}{7}x_4 - \frac{6}{7}S_1 = -\frac{4}{7}$$

the equivalent constraint in terms of x_1 and x_2 is

$$x_1 + x_2 \leq 7$$

Figure 9-5 shows that the addition of these two constraints will result in the new (optimal) extreme point (4, 3).

Exercise 9.4-1

Consider the Reddy Mikks model, whose solution is given in Example 3.2-1. Suppose that all the variables are integers. Determine the cuts associated with the basic variables x_E, x_I, s_3, and s_4 and express them in terms of x_E and x_I only.

[*Ans.* x_I: $2/3s_1 + 2/3s_2 \geq 1/3$, or $2x_E + 2x_I \leq 9$.

x_E: Same cut as x_I.

s_3: No cut is possible, since s_3 is already integer.

s_4: $1/3s_1 + 1/3s_2 \geq 2/3$, or $x_E + x_I \leq 4$.]

Strength of the Fractional Cut

The foregoing development indicates that the specific inequality defining a cut depends directly on the "source row" from which it is generated. Thus different inequality cuts may be generated from the same simplex tableau. The question naturally arises: Which cut is the "strongest"? Strength could be measured in terms of how deep the inequality cuts into the solution space. This result can be expressed mathematically as follows. Consider the two inequalities

$$\sum_{j=1}^{n} f_{ij} w_j \geq f_i \tag{1}$$

and

$$\sum_{j=1}^{n} f_{kj} w_j \geq f_k \tag{2}$$

Cut (1) is said to be stronger than (2) if $f_i \geq f_k$ and $f_{ij} \leq f_{kj}$, for all j, with the strict inequality holding at least once.

This definition of strength is difficult to implement computationally. Thus empirical rules reflecting this definition are devised. Two such rules call for generating the cut from the source row that has (1) $\max_i\{f_i\}$ or (2) $\max_i\{f_i/\sum_{j=1}^{n} f_{ij}\}$. The second rule is more effective, since it more closely represents the definition of strength given.†

Example 9.4-2. In Example 9.4-1, the optimum continuous solution is $z = 63$, $x_1 = 9/2$, and $x_2 = 7/2$. Since z is already integer, its equation cannot be taken as a source row. According to the empirical rules given, since $f_1 = f_2 = 1/2$, the rule is nonconclusive about which source row may be better. But to apply the second rule, it is necessary to develop all the coefficients of the respective fractional cuts from each source row. The cuts from the x_1-row and x_2-row are

$$x_1\text{-row:}\quad \frac{21}{22}x_3 + \frac{3}{22}x_4 \geq \frac{1}{2}$$

$$x_2\text{-row:}\quad \frac{7}{22}x_3 + \frac{1}{22}x_4 \geq \frac{1}{2}$$

Since

$$\frac{1/2}{7/22 + 1/22} > \frac{1/2}{21/22 + 3/22}$$

the x_2-equation is selected as a source row.

The selection of the x_2-equation as a source row in Example 9.4-1 was only accidental. To show that this was a proper choice, the two cuts (from the x_1-row and x_2-row) are compared. In Example 9.4-1, the cut from the x_2-row expressed in terms of x_1 and x_2 is given by

$$x_2 \leq 3$$

By following a similar substitution, the cut from the x_1-row is expressed as

$$x_2 < 10/3$$

The first cut is more *restrictive* and hence stronger than the second cut. One must caution, however, that the given rules, being empirical, may not generally yield the strongest cut. ◀

---

† Other rules that are based on information in the objective function row may also be found in Taha (1975, pp. 184–185).

Exercise 9.4-2
In Exercise 9.4-1, determine the strongest of the resulting cuts by using the criterion above; then plot the cuts on the (x_E, x_I)-space to illustrate the concept of cut strength graphically.
[*Ans.* The s_4-cut is the strongest. In the graphical space, it cuts the deepest into the solution space.]

9.4.2 THE MIXED ALGORITHM

Let x_k be an integer variable of the mixed problem. Again, as in the pure integer case, consider the x_k-equation in the optimal continuous solution. This is given by

$$x_k = \beta_k - \sum_{j=1}^{n} \alpha_k^j w_j = [\beta_k] + f_k - \sum_{j=1}^{n} \alpha_k^j w_j \qquad \textit{(source row)}$$

or

$$x_k - [\beta_k] = f_k - \sum_{j=1}^{n} \alpha_k^j w_j$$

Because some of the w_j variables may not be restricted to integer values in this case, it is incorrect to use the fractional cut developed in the preceding section. But a new cut can be devised based on the same general idea.

For x_k to be integer, either $x_k \le [\beta_k]$ or $x_k \ge [\beta_k] + 1$ must be satisfied. From the source row, these conditions are equivalent to

$$\sum_{j=1}^{n} \alpha_k^j w_j \ge f_k \tag{1}$$

$$\sum_{j=1}^{n} \alpha_k^j w_j \le f_k - 1 \tag{2}$$

Let

$$J^+ = \text{set of subscripts } j \text{ for which } \alpha_k^j \ge 0$$
$$J^- = \text{set of subscripts } j \text{ for which } \alpha_k^j < 0$$

Then, from (1) and (2), we get

$$\sum_{j \subset J^+} \alpha_k^j w_j \ge f_k \tag{3}$$

$$\frac{f_k}{f_k - 1} \sum_{j \in J^-} \alpha_k^j w_j \ge f_k \tag{4}$$

Since (1) and (2), and hence (3) and (4), cannot occur simultaneously, it follows that (3) and (4) can be combined into one constraint of the form

$$S_k - \left\{ \sum_{j \in J^+} \alpha_k^j w_j + \frac{f_k}{f_k - 1} \sum_{j \in J^-} \alpha_k^j w_j \right\} = -f_k \qquad \textit{(mixed cut)}$$

where $S_k \ge 0$ is a nonnegative slack variable. The last equation is the required **mixed cut**, and it represents a necessary condition for x_k to be integer. Since all $w_j = 0$ at the current optimal tableau, it follows that the cut is infeasible. The dual simplex method is thus used to clear the infeasibility.

The mixed cut is developed without taking advantage of the fact that some of the

w_j variables may be integer. If this is taken into account, the following stronger cut will result:

$$S_k = -f_k + \sum_{j=1}^{n} \lambda_j w_j$$

where

$$\lambda_j = \begin{cases} \alpha_k^j & \text{if } \alpha_k^j \geq 0 \text{ and } w_j \text{ is nonintegral} \\ \dfrac{f_k}{f_k - 1}\alpha_k^j & \text{if } \alpha_k^j < 0 \text{ and } w_j \text{ is nonintegral} \\ f_{kj} & \text{if } f_{kj} \leq f_k \text{ and } w_j \text{ is integral} \\ \dfrac{f_k}{1 - f_k}(1 - f_{kj}) & \text{if } f_{kj} > f_k \text{ and } w_j \text{ is integral} \end{cases}$$

The derivation of this formula is found in Taha (1975, p. 200).

Example 9.4-3. Consider Example 9.4-1. Suppose that x_1 only is restricted to integer values. From the x_1-equation,

$$x_1 - \frac{1}{22}x_3 + \frac{3}{22}x_4 = \left(4 + \frac{1}{2}\right)$$

$$J^- = \{3\}, \qquad J^+ = \{4\}, \qquad f_1 = 1/2$$

Hence the mixed cut is given by

$$S_1 - \left\{\frac{3}{22}x_4 + \left(\frac{\frac{1}{2}}{\frac{1}{2} - 1}\right)\left(-\frac{1}{22}\right)x_3\right\} = -\frac{1}{2}$$

or

$$S_1 - \frac{1}{22}x_3 - \frac{3}{22}x_4 = -\frac{1}{2}$$

Adding this to the last tableau gives

Basic	x_1	x_2	x_3	x_4	S_1	R.H.S.
z	0	0	28/11	15/11	0	63
x_2	0	1	7/22	1/22	0	7/2
x_1	1	0	−1/22	3/22	0	9/2
S_1	0	0	−1/22	−3/22	1	−1/2

Now, applying the dual simplex method yields

Basic	x_1	x_2	x_3	x_4	S_1	Solution
z	0	0	23/11	0	10	58
x_2	0	1	10/33	0	−1/3	10/3
x_1	1	0	−1/11	0	1	4
x_4	0	0	1/3	1	−22/3	11/3

which yields the optimal solution $z = 58$, $x_1 = 4$, and $x_2 = 10/3$ with x_1 an integer as required. ◀

Exercise 9.4-3

Consider Example 9.4-3.

(a) Suppose that x_2 is integer also. Develop its mixed cut from the last tableau of the example.
[*Ans.* $S_2 - 10/33x_3 - 1/6S_1 = -1/3$.]

(b) In the original problem before the x_1-cut is added, if both x_1 and x_2 are integers, then x_3 and x_4 must also be integers. Develop a mixed cut from the x_1-row by using the definition of λ_j given and compare it with the fractional cut for x_1. (Notice that in both cases all the variables x_1, x_2, x_3, and x_4 are integers.)
[*Ans.* Mixed cut: $-1/2 + 1/22x_3 + 3/22x_4 \geq 0$
Fractional cut: $-1/2 + 21/22x_3 + 3/22x_4 \geq 0$
The mixed cut is stronger.]

Computations in Cutting Methods

Although only two types of cuts are presented in this book, several other cuts have been developed, with each new cut alleviating some of the computational difficulties associated with the others. However, no single cut can be considered uniformly superior from the computational standpoint.

Although in some isolated cases of specially structured problems cuts have proven effective, the general consensus among practitioners is that cutting methods cannot be relied on to solve integer problems regardless of size. Experience has shown that some rather small problems could not be solved by the cutting methods. In fact, cases have been reported in which a random change in the order of the constraints has converted a computationally easy problem into a rather formidable one.

Perhaps the general conclusion concerning cutting methods is that they alone cannot be used effectively to solve the general integer problem. However, ideas may be, and indeed have been, borrowed from these methods to enhance the effectiveness of other types of solution techniques [see Taha (1975, pp. 160–161)]. Also, cutting planes have been used within the context of the B&B algorithm to expedite moving the solution of each subproblem toward the desired integer solution.

9.5 ZERO–ONE INTEGER PROBLEM

Any integer variable can be equivalently expressed in terms of a number of pure **zero–one (binary)** variables. The simplest way to accomplish this is as follows. Let $0 \leq x \leq n$ be an integer variable where n is an integer upper bound. Then, given that $y_1, y_2, \ldots,$ and y_n are zero–one variables,

$$x = y_1 + y_2 + \cdots + y_n$$

is an exact binary representation of all feasible values of x. Another more economical representation in which the number of binary variables is usually less than

n is given by

$$x = y_0 + 2y_1 + 2^2 y_2 + \cdots + 2^k y_k$$

where k is the smallest integer satisfying $2^{k+1} - 1 \geq n$.

The fact that every integer problem can be made binary together with the computational simplicity of dealing with zero–one variables (each variable has two values only) has directed attention to exploiting these properties to develop an efficient algorithm.

In this section we present a new algorithm that is designed specifically for solving the binary problem. The new method, called the **additive algorithm**, is actually a variation of the more general B&B method presented in Section 9.3. It is interesting that the original version of the additive algorithm was not presented in this context. One reason for this "confusion" is that the original algorithm does not involve the solution of any linear programs, as the B&B procedure does. In fact, the only arithmetic operations needed in the algorithm are addition and subtraction, hence the name *additive algorithm.*

Our presentation of the additive algorithm will be in the context of the B&B algorithm, with the objective of demonstrating that the additive algorithm is actually a special case of the B&B technique.

9.5.1 THE ADDITIVE ALGORITHM

For the purpose of this algorithm, the continuous version of the zero–one problem must start dual-feasible, that is, optimal but not feasible. Moreover, all the constraints must be of the type ($\leq$), thus ruling out explicit equations. This format can always be achieved as follows. Let the problem be of the minimization type (there is no loss in generality here) and define it as

$$\text{minimize } z = \sum_{j=1}^{n} c_j x_j$$

subject

$$\sum_{j=1}^{n} a_{ij} x_j + S_i = b_i, \qquad i = 1, 2, \ldots, m$$

$$x_j = 0 \text{ or } 1, \qquad j = 1, 2, \ldots, n$$

$$S_i \geq 0, \qquad i = 1, 2, \ldots, m$$

where S_i is the slack variable associated with the ith constraint. The continuous version of the foregoing problem is dual-feasible if every $c_j \geq 0$. Any $c_j < 0$ can be converted to the desired format by complementing the variable x_j, that is, by substituting $x_j = 1 - x_j'$, where x_j' is a binary variable, in the objective function and constraints. If, in addition to dual feasibility, the problem is primal-feasible, nothing more need to be done, since the minimum, in terms of the new variables, is achieved by assigning zero values to all the variables. However, if it is primal infeasible, the additive algorithm is used to find the optimum.

The general idea of the additive algorithm is to enumerate all 2^n possible solutions of the problem. However, it recognizes that some solutions can be discarded automatically without being investigated implicitly. Hence, in the final analysis, only a portion of the 2^n solutions need be investigated explicitly.

In terms of the given zero–one problem, this idea is implemented as follows. Initially, assume that all the variables are at zero level. This is logical, since all $c_j \geq 0$. Since the corresponding solution is not feasible (i.e., some slack variables S_i may be negative), it will be necessary to elevate some variables to level one. The procedure calls for elevating one (or perhaps more) variable at a time, provided there is evidence that this step will be moving the solution toward feasibility, that is, making $S_i \geq 0$ for all i. A number of tests have been developed to ensure the proper selection of the variables to be elevated to level one. These are first presented by means of a numerical example and later formalized mathematically.

Example 9.5-1

$$\text{Maximize } x_0 = 3x'_1 + 2x'_2 - 5x'_3 - 2x'_4 + 3x'_5$$

subject to

$$\begin{aligned}
x'_1 + x'_2 + x'_3 + 2x'_4 + x'_5 &\leq 4\\
7x'_1 \qquad\quad + 3x'_3 - 4x'_4 + 3x'_5 &\leq 8\\
11x'_1 - 6x'_2 \qquad\quad + 3x'_4 - 3x'_5 &\geq 3\\
x'_j = 0 \quad \text{or} \quad 1 \qquad \text{for all } j&
\end{aligned}$$

This problem is converted into the *minimization* form, in which all variables have nonnegative coefficients in the objective function. First, convert the objective function to minimization form by multiplying x_0 by -1. This leaves x'_1, x'_2, and x'_5 with negative coefficients and x'_3 and x'_4 with positive coefficients. Thus the substitution

$$x'_j = \begin{cases} 1 - x_j, & j = 1, 2, 5 \\ x_j, & j = 3, 4 \end{cases}$$

converts all the objective function coefficients to nonnegative values as desired. After the third constraint is changed to ($\leq$), the problem is put in the following convenient form (z is the objective value of the *converted* problem).

x_1	x_2	x_3	x_4	x_5	S_1	S_2	S_3	R.H.S.
3	2	5	2	3	0	0	0	z
−1	−1	1	2	−1	1	0	0	1
−7	0	3	−4	−3	0	1	0	−2
11	−6	0	−3	−3	0	0	1	−1

Since initially all $x_j = 0$, the values of slacks are

$$(S_1^0, S_2^0, S_3^0) = (1, -2, -1)$$

[The superscript (0) represents the starting iteration.] The associated objective value is $z^0 = 0$.

It is evident now that the starting solution is not feasible, since S_2^0 and S_3^0 are negative. Thus at least one x_j variable must be elevated to level one. Such a variable must move the solution closer to feasibility, and this can be indicated by the values of the slacks. By investigating the variables at level zero, we see that all the *constraint* coefficients of x_3 corresponding to the negative slacks are *nonnegative*. Thus

x_3, if elevated to level 1, can only worsen the infeasibility. This means that x_3 must remain at zero level. Although each of x_1, x_2, and x_4 cannot *individually* bring feasibility, a combination of them at level one may lead to feasible values of the slacks. Thus these variables cannot be excluded (as in the case of x_3) at this point. On the other hand, if x_5 is set equal to one, a feasible solution is achieved. Thus the procedure calls for elevating x_5 to level one. This yields

$$(S_1^1, S_2^1, S_3^1) = [S_1^0 - (-1), S_2^0 - (-3), S_3^0 - (-3)] = (2, 1, 2)$$

with $x_5 = 1$ and $z^1 = 3$. Since this is a feasible solution, it is stored as the best available so far. Thus $\bar{z} = z^1 = 3$ is an upper bound on any future feasible solution. In other words, from here on, we are interested only in feasible solutions with objective values *better* (smaller) than $\bar{z}$ (compare with the B&B algorithm).

At this point it is instructive to introduce the foregoing procedure as a branch-and-bound method. Figure 9-6 shows the initial node (0), which represents the problem for which all $x_j = 0$. Two branches emanate from this node. These are associated with $x_5 = 0$ and $x_5 = 1$. By selecting the branch $x_5 = 1$, we obtain the feasible solution at node (1) with $\bar{z} = 3$.

Because all the coefficients of the objective function are positive and since the objective is to minimize z, any branch emanating from node (1) cannot yield a better objective value. In this case the branch $x_5 = 1$ is **fathomed**. Since $x_5 = 0$ is the only remaining branch in the tree, its associated solution must be considered (compare with the branch-and-bound algorithm). This leads to node (2), Figure 9-6, with its solution given by

$$(S_1^2, S_2^2, S_3^2) = (1, -2, -1)$$

with $z^2 = 0$ and all the binary variables equal to zero.

You may wonder about the difference between the solutions at nodes (0) and (2). There is no difference so far as the *values* of the variables and objective function are concerned. But there is the important difference that at node (0) any of the variables x_1, x_2, x_3, x_4, and x_5 is **free** to assume a zero or one value, whereas at node (2) x_5 is fixed at level zero. Thus, in choosing the branching variable at (2), only x_1, x_2, x_3, or x_4 may be considered.

The selection of a variable to be elevated to one at node (2) follows the same logic used at node (0). However, there is now the additional information that no *free* variable should assume a value of 1 if it leads to an objective value greater than or equal to $\bar{z}$. Thus elevating x_3 to level one is not promising because this will worsen both optimality (it yields $z = 5 > \bar{z}$) and feasibility (it makes the slacks more negative). Also, x_1 may be discarded because $c_1 = 3$ cannot lead to a *better* objective value than $\bar{z}$. Thus a choice must be made between x_2 and x_4. Neither variable can

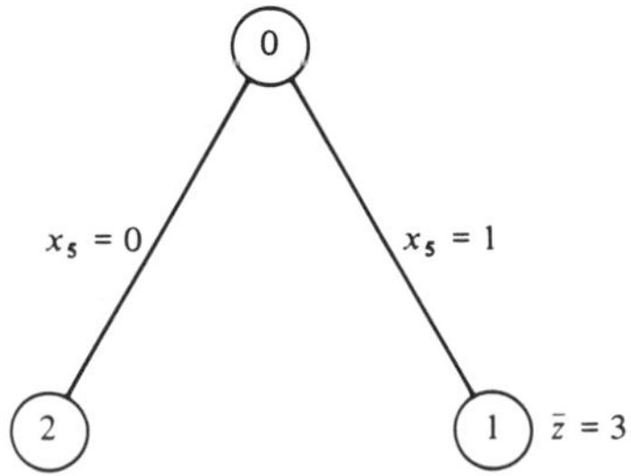

Figure 9-6

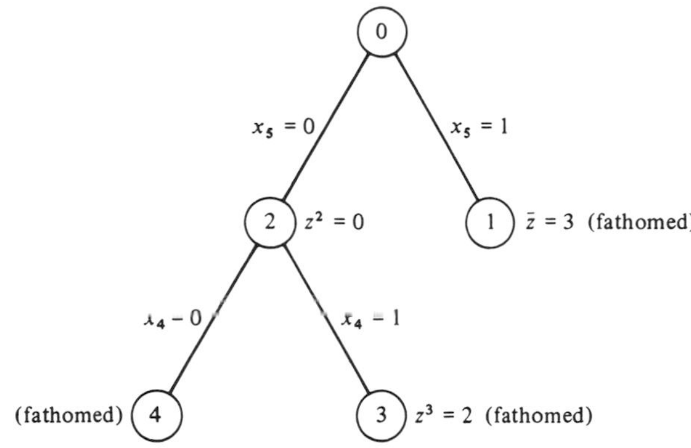

Figure 9-7

individually bring feasibility. In this case a choice is made based on an empirical measure. Define for each *free* variable x_j

$$v_j = \sum_{\text{all } i} \min\{0, S_i - a_{ij}\}$$

This actually may be regarded as a "measure" of the total infeasibility resulting from elevating the free variable x_j to level one. The branching variable selected is the one with the smallest v. Now, for x_2 and x_4,

$$v_2 = 0 + (-2 - 0) + 0 = -2$$
$$v_4 = (1 - 2) + 0 + 0 = \boxed{-1}$$

Hence x_4 is selected as the branching variable, and $x_4 = 1$ leads to node (3), Figure 9-7, where

$$(S_1^3, S_2^3, S_3^3) = (1 - 2, -2 + 4, -1 + 3) = (-1, 2, 2)$$

with $z^3 = 2$.

Node (3) is now defined by $x_5 = 0$ and $x_4 = 1$ so that x_1, x_2, and x_3 are the only free variables at (3). Since $c_1 = 3$, $c_2 = 2$, and $c_3 = 5$, elevating x_1, x_2, or x_3 to level one cannot yield a better objective value than $\bar{z}$, since they yield $z = 2 + 3$, $2 + 2$, and $2 + 5$. Hence x_1, x_2, and x_3 are excluded. Since *all* the free variables are non-promising, no further branching can be effected from node (3) and hence it is fathomed.

The only remaining node is (4). Since it is defined by $x_5 = 0$ and $x_4 = 0$,

$$(S_1^4, S_2^4, S_3^4) = (1, -2, -1)$$

with $z^4 = 0$. Again x_1, x_2, and x_3 are the free variables. The variable x_3 is non-promising from both optimality and feasibility viewpoints. The remaining variables x_1 and x_2 cannot make the solution at (4) feasible. Thus no branching variables exist at (4) and (4) is fathomed. Since no more unfathomed nodes exist in Figure 9-6, the solution is given by node (1) with $z = 3$ and $x_5 = 1$, and all the remaining variables equal zero. This solution can be translated in terms of the original variables to give $x'_1 = x'_2 = 1$, $x'_3 = x'_4 = x'_5 = 0$, with $x_0 = 5$. ◀

It was stated earlier that the foregoing procedure enumerates (implicitly or explicitly) all 2^n of the problems. This result is illustrated for the examples just presented as follows. The fathoming of node (1) means that all the binary solutions in which $x_5 = 1$ have been accounted for. There are $2^{5-1} = 16$ such solutions. Also, node (3) is fathomed. Since it is defined by $x_5 = 0$ and $x_4 = 1$, the number of solutions accounted for at node (3) is $2^{5-2} = 8$. Similarly, node (4) is fathomed, and this accounts for $2^{5-2} = 8$ solutions. Thus, by considering all fathomed nodes together, a total of $16 + 8 + 8 = 2^5$ solutions have been considered, which is the total number of possible binary solutions. One observes that the solutions counted at the different *fathomed* nodes are nonredundant, since the path (branches) leading to each of these nodes is unique.

It is interesting that only 5 (out of 32) solutions are investigated explicitly in the example above. This is why the procedure is sometimes referred to as **implicit enumeration.**

The zero–one branch-and-bound tree (e.g., Figure 9-7) can be represented for data manipulation in a very simple manner. To accomplish this, the following definitions are needed.

1. *Free variable.* At any node of the tree, a binary variable is called free if it is not fixed by any of the branches leading to this node. In Figure 9-7, node (3) has x_1, x_2, and x_3 as free variables. A free variable is initially at zero level but may be elevated to level one if this can improve the infeasibility of the problem.
2. *Partial solution.* A partial solution provides a specific binary assignment for some of the variables in the sense that it fixes the values of one or more variables at zero or one. A convenient way to summarize this information for the purpose of the (branch-and-bound) algorithm is to express the partial solution as an *ordered* set. Let J_t represent the partial solution at the tth node (or iteration), and let the notation $+j$ $(-j)$ represent $x_j = 1$ $(x_j = 0)$. Thus the elements of J_t consist of the subscripts of the fixed variables with the plus (minus) sign signifying that the variable is one (zero). The set J_t must be *ordered* in the sense that each new element is always augmented *on the right* of the partial solution.

Partial solutions can be used to define the nodes in the branch-and-bound tree, since the branches leading to a node actually represent a partial binary assignment to some variables. In Figure 9-7, the nodes are represented as follows:

Node (0): $J_0 = \varnothing$
Node (1): $J_1 = \{5\}$
Node (2): $J_2 = \{-5\}$
Node (3): $J_3 = \{-5, 4\}$
Node (4): $J_4 = \{-5, -4\}$

Actually, the use of partial solutions eliminates the need for recording generated nodes by means of the branch-and-bound tree. This means that partial solutions can be generated successively from one another. The procedure for generating successive partial solutions (nodes) will be illustrated by the example in Figure 9-7. First, the rules for fathoming are summarized. A partial solution is said to be fathomed if

1. It cannot lead to a better value of the objective function.
2. It cannot lead to a feasible solution.

A fathomed partial solution means that it is not promising to further branch its associated node, since all the solutions that could be generated from the node are either inferior or infeasible.

The solution of Example 9.5-1 starts with $J_0 = \varnothing$, meaning that all the binary variables are free. Now $x_5 = 1$ leads to $J_1 = \{5\}$, which is feasible. From the special structure of the problem, J_1 is fathomed. At this point the next partial solution is generated by complementing the *rightmost positive* element of J_1. This gives $J_2 = \{-5\}$.† Essentially, J_2 means that the branch $x_5 = 1$ has been considered (fathomed) and hence its complement branch $x_5 = 0$ must now be considered. According to the tests given in Example 9.5-1, J_2 is not fathomed, since $x_4 = 1$ can be augmented. This yields $J_3 = \{-5, 4\}$. Now J_3 is fathomed and J_4 is obtained by complementing the rightmost element of J_3. This yields $J_4 = \{-5, -4\}$. Again, J_4 is fathomed, but since all its elements are negative, the enumeration is complete.

Actually, the general rule for generating the next partial solution from a *fathomed* one is as follows. If *all* the elements of a *fathomed* partial solution are negative, the enumeration is complete. Otherwise, select the rightmost *positive* element, complement it, and *then delete all the (negative) elements to its right.* For example, if $J_t = \{1, 5, 4, -3, 2, 6, -7, -8\}$ is fathomed, $J_{t+1} = \{1, 5, 4, -3, 2, -6\}$. We can see the significance of the negative elements. Since the additive algorithm always adds variables at level one, a negative element means that a *preceding* partial solution (in which this element was positive) must have been fathomed. Thus, when all the elements of a *fathomed* partial solution are negative, the associated variables would have been considered at both zero and one levels. As a result, there are no more branches to consider and the enumeration is complete.

It is important to notice that the *order* of the elements in a partial solution is crucial in properly enumerating all the solutions. Thus $\{1, -3\}$ is not the same as $\{-3, 1\}$, since the first implies that the node reached by $x_1 = 1$ and $x_3 = 1$ has been fathomed whereas in the second the node reached by $x_3 = 1$ only has been fathomed.

The general version of the additive algorithm is now presented by using the concept of partial solutions. The exclusion tests used to fathom partial solutions and augment new variables at level one are also generalized for the zero–one problem.

Consider the following general binary problem:

$$\text{minimize } z = \sum_{j=1}^{n} c_j x_j, \qquad \text{all } c_j \geq 0$$

subject to

$$\sum_{j=1}^{n} a_{ij} x_j + S_i = b_i, \qquad i = 1, 2, \ldots, m$$

$$x_j = 0 \text{ or } 1, \qquad \text{for all } j$$

$$S_i \geq 0, \qquad \text{for all } i$$

Let J_t be the partial solution at node t (initially, $J_0 \equiv \varnothing$, which means that all variables are free) and assume z^t is the associated value of z while $\bar{z}$ is the current best upper bound (initially $\bar{z} = \infty$).

Test 1: For any free variable x_r, if $a_{ir} \geq 0$ for *all* i corresponding to $S_i^t < 0$, then x_r cannot improve the infeasibility of the problem and must be discarded as nonpromising.

---

† The process of complementing the *rightmost positive* element is sometimes called **backtracking**. In the case of J_1, the solution "backtracks" along the branch $x_5 = 1$, and then "moves down" along the branch $x_5 = 0$ to reach J_2 (see Figure 9-7).

Test 2: For any free variable x_r, if

$$c_r + z^t \geq \bar{z}$$

then x_r cannot lead to an improved solution and hence must be discarded.

Test 3: Consider the ith constraint

$$a_{i1}x_1 + a_{i2}x_2 + \cdots + a_{in}x_n + S_i = b_i$$

for which $S_i^t < 0$. Let N_t define the set of *free* variables not discarded by tests 1 and 2. None of the free variables in N_t are promising if for at least one $S_i^t < 0$, the following condition is satisfied:

$$\sum_{j \in N_t} \min\{0, a_{ij}\} > S_i^t$$

This actually says that the set N_t cannot lead to a feasible solution and hence must be discarded altogether. In this case, J_t is said to be fathomed.

Test 4: If $N_t \neq \varnothing$, the branching variable x_k is selected as the one corresponding to

$$v_k^t = \max_{j \in N_t}\{v_j^t\}$$

where

$$v_j^t = \sum_{i=1}^{m} \min\{0, S_i^t - a_{ij}\}$$

If $v_k^t = 0$, $x_k = 1$ together with J_t yields an *improved* feasible solution. In this case, J_{t+1}, which is defined by J_t with $\{k\}$ augmented on the right, is fathomed. Otherwise, the foregoing tests are applied again to J_{t+1} until the enumeration is completed, that is, until *all* the elements of the *fathomed* partial solution are negative.

Example 9.5-2. As a way of summarizing the preceding generalized procedure, Example 9.5-1 is presented by using the new "bookkeeping" method.

Iteration 0

For $J_0 = \varnothing$, $\bar{z} = \infty$,

$$(S_1^0, S_2^0, S_3^0) = (1, -2, -1), \; z^0 = 0$$

x_3 is excluded by test 1. By test 3, $N_0 = \{1, 2, 4, 5\}$ cannot be abandoned because

$$S_2\colon \quad -7 - 4 - 3 = -14 < -2$$
$$S_3\colon \quad -6 - 3 - 3 = -12 < -1$$

By test 4,

$$v_1^0 = 0 + 0 + (-1 - 11) = -12$$
$$v_2^0 = 0 + (-2 - 0) + 0 = -2$$
$$v_4^0 = (1 - 2) + 0 + 0 = -1$$
$$v_5^0 = 0 + 0 + 0 + 0 = \boxed{0}$$

Hence, $k = 5$.

Iteration 1

For $J_1 = \{5\}, \bar{z} = 3$,

$$(S_1^1, S_2^1, S_3^1) = (1 + 1, -2 + 3, -1 + 3) = (2, 1, 2), z^1 = 3$$

Since it is feasible, $\bar{z} = z^1 = 3$. Thus J_1 is fathomed.

Iteration 2

For $J_2 = \{-5\}, \bar{z} = 3$

$$(S_1^2, S_2^2, S_3^2) = (1, -2, -1), z^2 = 0$$

Test 1 excludes x_3. Test 2 excludes x_1 and x_3. By test 3, $N_2 = \{2, 4\}$ cannot be abandoned. By test 4, $v_2^2 = -2$ and $v_4^2 = \boxed{-1}$. Hence $k = 4$.

Iteration 3

For $J_3 = \{-5, 4\}$ $\bar{z} = 3$,

$$(S_1^3, S_2^3, S_3^3) = (-1, 2, 2), z^3 = 2$$

Test 1 excludes x_3. Test 2 excludes x_1, x_2, and x_3. Since $N_3 = \varnothing$, J_3 is fathomed.

Iteration 4

For $J_4 = \{-5, -4\}, \bar{z} = 3$

$$(S_1^4, S_2^4, S_3^4) = (1, -2, -1), z^4 = 0$$

Test 1 excludes x_3. Test 2 excludes x_1 and x_3. Test 3 indicates $N_4 = \{2\}$ must be abandoned. Thus J_4 is fathomed. Since all the elements of J_4 are negative, the enumeration is complete and J_1 is optimal. ◀

9.5.2 ZERO-ONE POLYNOMIAL PROGRAMMING

Consider the problem

$$\text{maximize } z = f(x_1, \ldots, x_n)$$

subject to

$$g_i(x_1, \ldots, x_n) \le b_i, \qquad i = 1, 2, \ldots, m$$
$$x_j = 0 \quad \text{or} \quad 1, \qquad j = 1, 2, \ldots, n$$

Assume that f and g_i are polynomials with the kth term generally represented by $d_k \prod_{j=1}^{n_k} x_j^{a_{kj}}$, where a_{kj} is a positive constant exponent and d_k is a constant.

The seemingly highly nonlinear problem shown can be converted into a linear form, which can then be solved as a zero–one linear program. Since x_j is a binary variable, $x_j^{a_{kj}} = x_j$ for any positive exponent a_{kj}. (If $a_{kj} = 0$, obviously the variable x_j will not be present in the kth term.) This means that the kth term can be written as $d_k \prod_{j=1}^{n_k} x_j$.

Let $y_k = \prod_{j=1}^{n_k} x_j$, then y_k is also a binary variable and the kth term of the polynomial reduces to the linear term $d_k y_k$. However, to ensure that $y_k = 1$ when all

$x_j = 1$ and zero otherwise, the following constraints must be added† for each y_k.

$$\sum_{j=1}^{n_k} x_j - (n_k - 1) \leq y_k \tag{1}$$

$$\frac{1}{n_k} \sum_{j=1}^{n_k} x_j \geq y_k \tag{2}$$

If all $x_j = 1$, $\sum_{j=1}^{n_k} x_j = n_k$ and constraint (1) yields $y_k \geq 1$, and constraint (2) gives $y_k \leq 1$; that is, $y_k = 1$. On the other hand, if at least one $x_j = 0$, then $\sum_{j=1}^{n_k} x_j < n_k$ and constraints (1) and (2), respectively, yield $y_k \geq -(n_k - 1)$ and $y_k < 1$ with the only feasible value given by $y_k = 0$.

Example 9.5-3. The foregoing linear transformation is illustrated by the following problem:

$$\text{maximize } z = 2x_1x_2x_3^3 + x_1^2x_2$$

subject to

$$5x_1 + 9x_2^2x_3 \leq 15$$

$$x_1, x_2, \text{ and } x_3 \text{ binary}$$

Let $y_1 = x_1x_2x_3$, $y_2 = x_1x_2$, and $y_3 = x_2x_3$. The problem becomes

$$\text{maximize } z = 2y_1 + y_2$$

subject to

$$\begin{aligned} 5x_1 + 9y_3 &\leq 15 \\ x_1 + x_2 + x_3 - 2 &\leq y_1 \\ \tfrac{1}{3}(x_1 + x_2 + x_3) &\geq y_1 \\ x_1 + x_2 - 1 &\leq y_2 \\ \tfrac{1}{2}(x_1 + x_2) &\geq y_2 \\ x_2 + x_3 - 1 &\leq y_3 \\ \tfrac{1}{2}(x_2 + x_3) &\geq y_3 \end{aligned}$$

where y_1, y_2, y_3, x_1, x_2, and x_3 are binary variables. ◀

Computations in Implicit Enumeration

The main difference between the B&B algorithm in Section 9.3 and the additive algorithm presented here is the manner in which a partial solution is fathomed at a node. In the B&B algorithm, we (partially or completely) solve an LP problem. In the additive algorithm, we rely on some heuristics that exploit the binary nature of the integer variables. In this regard, the additive algorithm is essentially a B&B algorithm.

The effectiveness of the additive algorithm is highly dependent on the strength of its fathoming tests. Unfortunately, these tests are not sufficient to produce a compu-

† A more efficient procedure that does not require the addition of these constraints and deals directly with the converted linear system of the polynomial problem has been developed by H. Taha, "A Balasian-Based Algorithm for Zero–One Polynomial Programming," *Management Science*, Vol. 18, 1972, pp. B328–B343. This procedure extends the Balas algorithm to the polynomial problem in a straightforward manner.

tationally feasible algorithm. Successful computer codes are based on much stronger tests. Perhaps the most effective of these is the so-called **surrogate** (or substitute) **constraint**. Rather than scan the constraints one at a time, a surrogate constraint seeks to "combine" all the original constraints of the problem into one constraint and does not eliminate any of the original feasible (integer) points of the problem. The new constraint is devised such that it has the potential to reveal information that cannot be conveyed by any of the original constraints considered separately (see Problem 9-33).

Reported computational experiences indicate that the use of the surrogate constraint is effective in improving the computation time. However, because implicit enumeration investigates (implicitly or explicitly) all 2^n binary points, the solution time varies almost exponentially with the number of variables n. This limits the number of variables that can be handled by this method. Although successful cases have been reported for rather large problems (having special structures), it is safe to conclude that, in general, only problems with up to 100 variables can be solved in a reasonable amount of computation time.

One particular observation about the additive algorithm is that the computation time is data-dependent. The specific ordering of the variables and constraints may have a direct effect on the efficiency of the algorithm. For example, the constraints should be ordered with the most restrictive at the top, while the variables could be arranged according to an ascending order of their (nonnegative) objective coefficients. Both conditions are favorable to producing "faster" fathoming of partial solutions.

The general conclusion is that the implicit enumeration method still does not provide the answer to the computational problem in integer programming. It appears that the branch-and-bound methods (Secton 9.3) will continue to dominate, particularly when large practical problems are attempted.

9.6 SUMMARY

As can be inferred from the discussion in this chapter, the most important factor affecting computations in integer programming is the number of variables. This situation is more pronounced in branch-and-bound method. Consequently, in formulating an integer model, it is advantageous to reduce the number of integer variables as much as possible. This may be effected, in general, by

1. Approximating integer variables by continuous ones.
2. Restricting the feasible ranges of the integer variables.
3. Eliminating the use of auxiliary binary variables (e.g., as in the fixed-charge problem) by devising more direct solution methods.
4. Avoiding nonlinearity in the model.

These ideas should help in alleviating the computational problem.

Experience with integer codes shows that a user will be disappointed if he or she expects to feed in input data to the computer and then await the answer at the output end of the machine. In a typical integer code, manual intervention during the computations is almost mandatory. The codes are usually equipped with a number of options, each with a specific advantage in handling the integer problem. The user then plans a strategy for tackling the problem. By monitoring the intermediate information extracted from the machine, one decides whether to continue the same course of action or to select another option. In other words, human judgment during the calculations is needed to ensure that the program is progressing satisfactorily.

The importance of the integer problem in practice is not yet matched by the development of efficient solution methods. This problem is due primarily to the inherent difficulty in dealing with integer computations in general. The current intensive research may eventually lead to a breakthrough. It is more likely, however, that this breakthrough will be achieved by the development of extremely powerful and highly accurate digital computers rather than by the development of more theoretical methods.

SELECTED REFERENCES

GARFINKEL, R., and G. NEMHAUSER, *Integer Programming*, Wiley, New York, 1972.

SALKIN, H., *Integer Programming*, Addison-Wesley, Reading, Mass., 1975.

PARKER, R., and R. RARDIN, *Discrete Optimization*, Academic Press, Orlando, Fla., 1988.

TAHA, H., *Integer Programming: Theory, Applications and Computations*, Academic Press, New York, 1975.

PROBLEMS

Section	Assigned Problems
9.1	9–1 to 9–12
9.2	None
9.3	9–13 to 9–18, 9–31
9.4.1	9–19 to 9–22
9.4.2	9–23 to 9–26
9.5	9–27 to 9–30, 9–32

☐ **9–1** Consider the problem

$$\text{maximize } z = 20x_1 + 10x_2 + 10x_3$$

subject to

$$2x_1 + 20x_2 + 4x_3 \le 15$$
$$6x_1 + 20x_2 + 4x_3 = 20$$
$$x_1, x_2, x_3 \text{ nonnegative integers}$$

Solve the problem as a (continuous) linear program; then show that it is impossible to obtain a feasible integer solution by using simple rounding.

☐ **9–2** An investment company is presented with five investment opportunities, with the following expenses and returns (in thousands of dollars):

Investment	1	2	3	4	5
Expenses	8	4	6	3	9
Returns	32	21	24	15	16

The total capital available for investment is \$25,000. If the company's investment portfolio includes investment 2, it must also select investment 4. Investments 2 and 3, on the other hand, are mutually exclusive. Formulate the problem as a zero–one ILP.

☐ **9–3** Truck deliveries are made to five locations. A total of six routes are available. The following informaton summarizes the location that can be reached by each route:

Route 1: 1, 2, 3, 4
Route 2: 1, 3, 4, 5
Route 3: 1, 2, 5
Route 4: 2, 3, 5
Route 5: 1, 2, 3
Route 6: 1, 3, 5

The delivery distances to the five locations are 10, 5, 9, 13, and 6 miles, respectively. It is desired to make exactly one delivery to each location.

Formulate an ILP model that will result in the shortest total distance routing.

☐ **9–4** Consider the production planning problem where 2000 units of a certain product are manufactured on three machines. The setup costs, the production costs per unit, and the maximum production capacity for each machine are tabulated below. The objective is to minimize the total production cost of the required lot.

Machine	Setup Cost	Production Cost/Unit	Capacity (units)
1	100	10	600
2	300	2	800
3	200	5	1200

Formulate the problem as an integer programming problem.

☐ **9–5** In an oil-well-drilling problem there are two attractive drilling sites for reaching four targets (or possible oil wells). The preparation costs at each site and the cost of drilling from site i to target j ($i = 1, 2$; $j = 1, 2, 3, 4$) are given. The objective is to determine the best site for each target so that the total cost is minimized.

	Drilling Cost to Target				
Site	1	2	3	4	Preparation Cost
1	2	1	8	5	5
2	4	6	3	1	6

Formulate the problem as an integer programming model.

☐ **9–6** A development company owns 90 acres of land in a growing metropolitan area where it intends to construct office buildings and a shopping center. The developed property is rented for 7 years, after which time it is sold. The sale price for each building is estimated at 10 times its operating net income in the last year of rental. The company estimates that the project will include a 4.5-million-square-foot shopping center. The master plan calls for constructing three high-rise and four garden office buildings.

The company is faced with a scheduling problem. If a building is completed too early, it may stay vacant; if it is completed too late, potential tenants may be lost to other projects. The demand for office space over the next 7 years estimate based on appropriate market studies is

	Demand (thousands of square feet)	
Year	High-Rise Space	Garden Space
1	200	100
2	220	110
3	242	121
4	266	133
5	293	146
6	322	161
7	354	177

The following table lists the proposed capacities of the seven buildings:

Garden	Capacity (square feet)	High-Rise Buildings	Capacity (square feet)
1	60,000	1	350,000
2	60,000	2	450,000
3	75,000	3	350,000
4	75,000		

The gross rental income is estimated at \$18 per square foot. The operating expenses are \$3.75 and \$4.75 per square foot for garden and high-rise buildings, respectively. The associated construction costs are \$70 and \$105 per square foot, respectively. Both construction cost and rental income are estimated to increase at a rate roughly equal to the inflation rate.

How should the company schedule the construction of the seven buildings?

☐ **9–7** In a National Collegiate Athletic Association (NCAA) women's gymnastic meet consisting of four events (vault, uneven bars, balance beam, and floor exercises), each team may enter the competition with six gymnasts per event. A gymnast is evaluated on a scale of 1 to 10. The total score for a team is determined by summarizing the top five individual scores for each event. An entrant may participate as a specialist in one event or an all-arounder in all four events, but never both. A specialist is allowed to compete in at most three events. Of the six participants allowed for each event, at least four must be all-arounders.

How should a coach select her gymnastic team?

☐ **9–8 (Delivery Problem).** Consider the situation in which orders from m different destinations are delivered from a central warehouse. Each destination receives its order in one delivery. Feasible routes are assigned to different carriers, and each carrier may combine at most r orders. Suppose that there are n feasible routes with each route specifying the destinations to which orders are delivered. Assume further that the cost of the jth route is c_j. Overlapping is expected so that the same destination can be reached by more than one carrier. Formulate the problem as an integer model.

□ **9–9 (Quadratic Assignment).** Consider the assignment of n plants to n different locations. The volume of goods transported between plants i and j is d_{ij}, and the cost of transporting one unit from location p to location q is c_{pq}. Formulate the problem as an integer model so as to minimize the total transportation costs.

□ **9–10** Consider the job-shop scheduling problem involving eight operations on a single machine with a total of two end products. The sequencing of operations is shown in Figure 9-8. Let b_j be the processing time for the jth operation ($j = 1, 2, \ldots, 8$). Delivery dates for products 1 and 2 are restricted by d_1 and d_2 time units measured from the zero datum. Since each operation requires a special machine setup, it is assumed that any operation once started must be completed before a new operation can be undertaken.

Formulate the problem as a mixed integer programming model to minimize the total processing time on the machine while satisfying all the pertinent constraints.

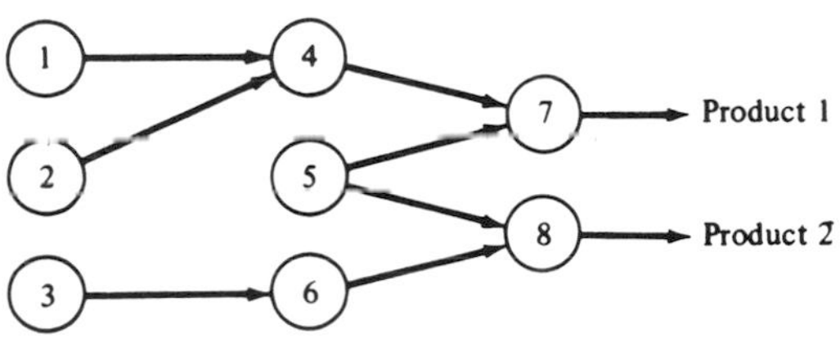

Figure 9-8

□ **9–11** Show how the nonconvex solution spaces (shaded areas in Figure 9-9) can be represented by simultaneous constraints.

Find the optimum solution that maximizes $z = 2x_1 + 3x_2$ subject to the solution space given in Figure 9-9(a).

[*Hint*: Use "either–or" constraints.]

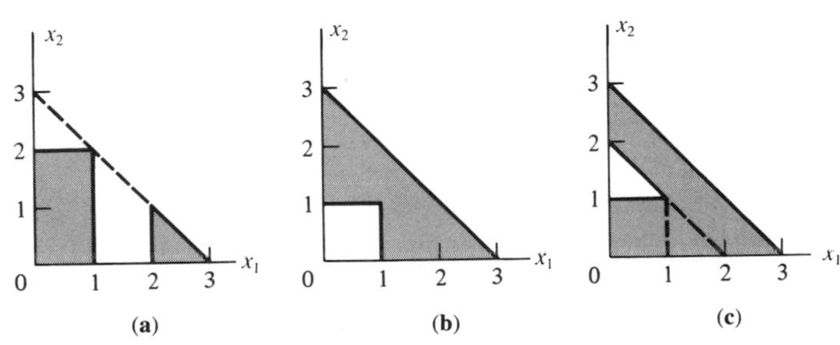

Figure 9-9

□ **9–12** Show how the solution space indicated by the shaded area in Figure 9-10 can be expressed as simultaneous mixed integer constraints.

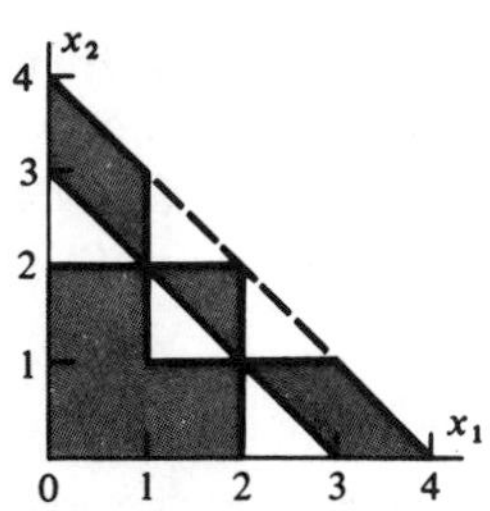

Figure 9-10

☐ **9–13** Solve Example 9.3-1. Start with x_2 as the branching variable in place of x_1.

☐ **9–14** Solve the following problems by the B&B algorithm. (For convenience, always select x_1 as the branching variable at node 0.)

(a) Maximize $z = 3x_1 + 2x_2$
subject to

$$2x_1 + 2x_2 \leq 9$$
$$3x_1 + 3x_2 \leq 18$$
$$x_1, x_2 \geq 0 \text{ and integer}$$

(b) Maximize $z = 2x_1 + 3x_2$
subject to

$$5x_1 + 7x_2 \leq 35$$
$$4x_1 + 9x_2 \leq 36$$
$$x_1, x_2 \geq 0 \text{ and integer}$$

(c) Maximize $z = x_1 + x_2$
subject to

$$2x_1 + 5x_2 \leq 16$$
$$6x_1 + 5x_2 \leq 30$$
$$x_1, x_2 \geq 0 \text{ and integer}$$

(d) Minimize $z = 5x_1 + 4x_2$
subject to

$$4x_1 + 2x_2 \geq 6$$
$$2x_1 + 3x_2 \geq 8$$
$$x_1, x_2 \geq 0 \text{ and integer}$$

(e) Maximize $z = 5x_1 + 7x_2$
subject to

$$2x_1 + x_2 \leq 13$$
$$5x_1 + 9x_2 \leq 41$$
$$x_1, x_2 \geq 0 \text{ and integer}$$

☐ **9–15** Repeat Problem 9–14 assuming that x_2 only is restricted to integer values.

□ **9–16** Show graphically that the following problem has no feasible integer solution:

$$\text{maximize } z = 2x_1 + x_2$$

subject to

$$10x_1 + 10x_2 \leq 9$$
$$10x_1 + 5x_2 \geq 1$$
$$x_1, x_2 \geq 0 \text{ and integer}$$

Verify the result by using the B&B algorithm.

□ **9–17** Consider the following *cargo-loading* problem, where five items are to be loaded on a vessel. The weight w_i and the volume v_i per unit of the different items as well as their corresponding values r_i are tabulated as follows:

Item i	w_i	v_i	r_i
1	5	1	4
2	8	8	7
3	3	6	6
4	2	5	5
5	7	4	4

The maximum cargo weight and volume are given by $W = 112$ and $V = 109$, respectively. It is required to determine the most valuable cargo load in discrete units of each item.

Formulate the problem as an integer programming model and then solve by the branch-and-bound method.

□ **9–18** Solve the following problem by the B&B algorithm.

(a) Maximize $z = 18x_1 + 14x_2 + 8x_3 + 4x_4$
subject to

$$15x_1 + 12x_2 + 7x_3 + 4x_4 + x_5 \leq 37$$
$$x_j = (0, 1), \quad j = 1, 2, \ldots, 5$$

(b) Maximize $z = x_1 + 2x_2 + 5x_3$
subject to

$$|-x_1 + 10x_2 - 3x_3| \geq 15$$
$$2x_1 + x_2 + x_3 \leq 10$$
$$x_1, x_2, x_3 \geq 0$$

□ **9–19** Solve Problem 9–16 by the fractional algorithm.

□ **9–20** Consider the problem

$$\text{maximize } z = x_1 + 2x_2$$

subject to

$$x_1 + x_2/2 \leq 13/4$$
$$x_1, x_2 \text{ nonnegative integers}$$

Show that the fractional algorithm does not yield a feasible solution unless the coefficients *and* the right-hand side of the constraint are integers. Then find the optimal solution.

☐ **9–21** Solve the fractional algorithm

$$\text{maximize } z = 4x_1 + 6x_2 + 2x_3$$

subject to

$$\begin{aligned} 4x_1 - 4x_2 &\leq 5 \\ -x_1 + 6x_2 &\leq 5 \\ -x_1 + x_2 + x_3 &\leq 5 \end{aligned}$$

$$x_1, x_2, x_3 \text{ nonnegative integers}$$

Compare the rounded optimal solution and the integer optimal solution.

☐ **9–22** Solve by the fractional algorithm

$$\text{maximize } z = 3x_1 + x_2 + 3x_3$$

subject to

$$\begin{aligned} -x_1 + 2x_2 + x_3 &\leq 4 \\ 4x_2 - 3x_3 &\leq 2 \\ x_1 - 3x_2 + 2x_3 &\leq 3 \end{aligned}$$

$$x_1, x_2, x_3 \text{ nonnegative integers}$$

Compare the rounded optimal solution and the integer optimal solution.

☐ **9–23** Construct the *first* mixed cut and its stronger version for the following problem and compare the two cuts. By examining the coefficients of the cuts, what is the effect of machine round-off error if the problem is solved by the computer?

$$\text{Maximize } z = 5x_1 + 8x_2 + 6x_3$$

subject to

$$\begin{aligned} 2x_1 + 6.3x_2 + x_3 &\leq 11 \\ 9x_1 + 6x_2 + 10x_3 &\leq 28 \\ x_2 &\geq 0 \end{aligned}$$

$$x_1 \text{ and } x_3 \text{ nonnegative integers}$$

☐ **9–24** Solve Problem 9–21 by the mixed algorithm assuming that x_1 and x_3 are the only integer variables.

☐ **9–25** Solve Problem 9–22 by the mixed algorithm assuming that x_1 and x_3 are the only integer variables.

☐ **9–26** Show that the stronger mixed cut (given at the end of Section 9.4.2) when applied to the *pure* integer problem is stronger than the fractional cut (Section 9.4.1) developed from the same source row. Discuss the use of this cut in solving the pure integer problem. In particular, does the pure problem remain pure integer after the first cut is applied?

□ **9–27** In Problem 9–22, suppose that all the variables are binary. Find the optimal solution by the additive algorithm.

□ **9–28** In Problem 9–16, assume that x_1 and x_2 are binary variables. Show how the additive algorithm can be used to discover that the problem has no feasible (integer) solution.

□ **9–29** Solve the capital budgeting model in Section 9.1.1 by using the additive algorithm.

□ **9–30** Suggest some modifications that will give stronger exclusion tests for the additive algorithm.

□ **9–31** Solve the following problem assuming that only one of the given constraints holds.

$$\text{Maximize } z = x_1 + 2x_2 - 3x_3$$

subject to

$$\begin{aligned} 20x_1 + 15x_2 - x_3 &< 10 \\ 12x_1 - 3x_2 + 4x_3 &\leq 20 \\ x_1, x_2, x_3 &\text{ binary} \end{aligned}$$

□ **9–32 (Penalties).** Suppose that the basic variable associated with the current node of a maximization branch-and-bound algorithm is defined by

$$x_k = \beta_k - \sum_{j=1}^{n} \alpha_k^j w_j$$

Branching is effected by the two constraints $x_k - [\beta_k] \leq 0$ and $x_k - [\beta_k] - 1 \geq 0$. Let P_d and P_u be the lower bounds on the true degradation in the optimum objective value as a result of activating the first and second constraints. Show (by using the dual simplex algorithm) that, under the assumption of *no change in basis*,

$$P_d = \min_{j \in J^+} \left\{ \frac{(z_j - c_j) f_k}{\alpha_k^j} \right\}$$

$$P_u = \min_{j \in J^-} \left\{ \frac{(z_j - c_j)(f_k - 1)}{\alpha_k^j} \right\}$$

where $(z_j - c_j)$ is the objective coefficient of the jth nonbasic variable at the current node, $f_k = \beta_k - [\beta_k]$, and J^+ (J^-) is the set of nonbasic subscripts for which $\alpha_k^j > 0$ ($\alpha_k^j < 0$). Consequently, the true degradation in the objective value is *at least* equal to $\bar{P} = \min\{P_d, P_u\}$. This means that given z is the optimum objective value at the current node, $z - \bar{P}$ gives an upper bound (assume a maximization problem) on the optimum objective values at the two nodes emanating from the current node. Thus, if $z - \bar{P}$ is less than the best available lower bound, the current node is fathomed.

☐ **9–33 (Surrogate Constraint).** Assume that the set of constraints for the zero–one problem is given in matrix form as $\mathbf{AX} \leq \mathbf{b}$. Let $\boldsymbol{\mu} \geq \mathbf{0}$ be a row vector of nonnegative multipliers. Defin the surrogate constraint as

$$\boldsymbol{\mu}(\mathbf{AX} - \mathbf{b}) \leq 0$$

Show that

(a) All the feasible binary solutions of $\mathbf{AX} \leq \mathbf{b}$ are also feasible with respect to the surrogate constraint.

(b) If the surrogate constraint is infeasible, then the original constraints $\mathbf{AX} \leq \mathbf{b}$ are also infeasible.

Chapter 10

Dynamic (Multistage) Programming

Dynamic programming (DP) is a mathematical procedure designed primarily to improve the computational efficiency of select mathematical programming problems by decomposing them into smaller, and hence computationally simpler, subproblems. Dynamic programming typically solves the problem in **stages**, with each stage involving exactly one optimizing variable. The computations at the different stages are linked through **recursive computations** in a manner that yields a feasible optimal solution to the *entire* problem.

The name *dynamic programming* probably evolved because of its use with applications involving decision making over time (such as inventory problems). However, other situations in which time is not a factor are also solved by DP. For this reason, a more apt name may be **multistage programming**, since the procedure typically determines the solution in stages.

The main unifying theory in DP is the **principle of optimality**. It basically dictates how a properly decomposed problem may be solved in stages (rather than as one entity) through the use of recursive computations.

The subtle concepts used in DP together with the unfamiliar mathematical notations are often a source of confusion, especially to a beginner. However, our experience shows that frequent exposure to DP formulations and solutions will, with some effort, enable a beginner to comprehend these subtle concepts. When this happens, DP becomes amazingly simple and clear.

10.1 ELEMENTS OF THE DP MODEL: THE CAPITAL BUDGETING EXAMPLE

A corporation is entertaining proposals from its three plants for possible expansion of facilities. The corporation is budgeting $5 million for allocation to all three plants. Each plant is requested to submit its proposals giving total cost (c) and total revenue (R) for each proposal. Table 10-1 summarizes the costs and revenues (in millions of dollars). The zero-cost proposals are introduced to allow for the possibility of not allocating funds to individual plants. The goal of the corporation is to maximize the total revenue resulting from the allocation of the $5 million to the three plants.

A straightforward, and perhaps naïve, way to solve the problem is by exhaustive enumeration. The problem has $3 \times 4 \times 2 = 24$ possible solutions, some of which are infeasible because they require more capital than the $5 million available. The idea of exhaustive enumeration is to compute the total cost for each of the 24 combinations. If it does not exceed the available capital, its total revenue is computed. The optimum solution is the feasible combination yielding the highest total revenue. For example, proposals 2, 3, and 1 for plants 1, 2, and 3 cost $4 million ($<5$) and yield a total revenue of $14 million. On the other hand, the combination comprising proposals 3, 4, and 2 is infeasible because it costs $7 million.

Let us examine the drawbacks of exhaustive enumeration.

1. Each combination defines a decision policy for the *entire* problem, and hence the enumeration of all possible combinations may not be feasible computationally for problems of moderate and large size.
2. The infeasible combinations cannot be detected a priori, thus leading to computational inefficiency.
3. Available information regarding previously investigated combinations is not used to eliminate future inferior combinations.

Table 10-1

	Plant 1		Plant 2		Plant 3	
Proposal	c_1	R_1	c_2	R_2	c_3	R_3
1	0	0	0	0	0	0
2	1	5	2	8	1	3
3	2	6	3	9	—	—
4	—	—	4	12	—	—

The DP algorithm that we present here is designed to alleviate all the difficulties just noted.

10.1.1 DP MODEL

In DP, computations are carried out in stages by breaking down the problem into subproblems. Each subproblem is then considered separately with the objective of reducing the volume and complexity of computations. However, since the subproblems are interdependent, a procedure must be devised to link the computations in a manner that guarantees that a feasible solution for each stage is also feasible for the entire problem.

A **stage** in DP is defined as the portion of the problem that possesses a set of mutually exclusive alternatives from which the best alternative is to be selected. In terms of the capital budgeting example, each plant defines a stage with the first, second, and third stages having three, four, and two alternatives, respectively. These stages are *interdependent* because all three plants must compete for a *limited* budget. For example, choosing proposal 1 for plant 1 will leave \$5 million for plants 2 and 3, whereas choosing proposal 2 for plant 1 will leave \$4 million only for plants 2 and 3.

The basic idea of DP is practically to eliminate the effect of interdependence between stages by associating a *state* definition with each stage. A **state** is normally defined to reflect the status of the constraints that bind all the stages together. In the capital budgeting example, we define the states for stages 1, 2, and 3 as follows:

x_1 = amount of capital allocated to stage 1
x_2 = amount of capital allocated to stages 1 and 2
x_3 = amount of capital allocated to stages 1, 2, and 3

We now show how the given definitions of *stages* and *states* are used to decompose the capital budgeting problem into three computationally separate subproblems.

First note that the values of x_1 and x_2 are not known exactly, but must lie somewhere between 0 and 5. In fact, because the costs of the different proposals are discrete, x_1 and x_2 may only assume the values 0, 1, 2, 3, 4, or 5. On the other hand, x_3, which is the total capital allocated to *all* three stages, is equal to 5.

The way we solve the problem is to start with stage (plant) 1. We obtain *conditional* decisions for that stage that answer the following question: Given a specific value of x_1 (= 0, 1, 2, 3, 4, or 5), what would be the best alternative (proposal) for stage 1? The computations for stage 1 are straightforward. Given the value of x_1, we choose the best proposal whose cost does not exceed x_1. The following table summarizes the *conditional* decisions for stage 1.

If Available Capital x_1 Equals:	Then, the Resulting Optimal Proposal Is:	And the Total Revenue of Stage 1 Is:
0	1	0
1	2	5
2	3	6
3	3	6
4	3	6
5	3	6

So far, we do not know the exact value of x_1. However, by the time we reach stage 3, such information will be available to us, and the problem will then reduce to reading the proper entries in the table.

Exercise 10.1-1

In the preceding table, is it possible that $x_1 > 2$ can be optimal in the final solution? [*Ans.* No, because $x_1 > 2$ represents overspending for stage 1.]

We now consider stage 2 calculations. These calculations also seek a *conditional* optimal solution for stage 2 as a function of the state x_2. However, they differ from those of stage 1 in that the state x_2 now defines the capital to be allocated to stage 1 *and* stage 2. Such a definition will guarantee that a decision made for stage 2 will be automatically feasible for stage 1. The idea now is to choose the alternative in stage 2 given x_2 that yields the best revenue for stages 1 and 2. The following formula summarizes the nature of the computations for stage 2:

$$\begin{pmatrix}\text{best revenue}\\ \text{for stages}\\ \text{1 and 2 given}\\ \text{state } x_2\end{pmatrix} = \max_{\substack{\text{all feasible}\\ \text{alternatives}\\ \text{of stage 2}\\ \text{given } x_2}} \left\{\begin{pmatrix}\text{revenue of}\\ \text{the feasible}\\ \text{alternative}\\ \text{for stage 2}\end{pmatrix} + \begin{pmatrix}\text{best revenue}\\ \text{for stage 1}\\ \text{given its}\\ \text{state } x_1\end{pmatrix}\right\}$$

where $x_1 = x_2 -$ capital allocated to given alternative of stage 2.

The basic idea of the formula is that a specific choice of an alternative for stage 2 will affect the capital remaining for stage 1, namely, x_1. Thus, by considering *all* the feasible alternatives of stage 2, we are automatically accounting for all the combinations that are possible for stages 1 and 2. Notice that the second term of the right side in the equation is obtained directly from the summary table for stage 1.

We now provide the details for stage 2 computations.

$x_2 = 0$

The only feasible alternative for stage 2 given $x_2 = 0$ is proposal 1 whose cost and revenue are both equal to zero. Thus the application of the formula yields

$$\begin{pmatrix}\text{best revenue}\\ \text{given } x_2 = 0\end{pmatrix} = 0 + 0 = 0$$

corresponding to proposal 1.

$x_2 = 1$

For $x_2 = 1$, we only have one feasible alternative for stage 2; namely, proposal 1, which costs zero and yields a revenue of zero. The remaining proposals are infeasible because they cost at least 2. We thus have

$$\begin{pmatrix}\text{best revenue}\\ \text{given } x_2 = 1\end{pmatrix} = 0 + 5 = 5$$

corresponding to proposal 1.

Notice that $x_1 = x_2 -$ cost of proposal $1 = 1 - 0 = 1$. In the summary table of stage 1, we find that the best revenue given $x_1 = 1$ is 5. Notice also that all we need from the calculations in stage 1 is the best revenue associated with given x_1. In other words we do not really care about the *specific proposal* selected at stage 1.

$x_2 = 2$

Here we have two feasible alternatives: proposals 1 and 2 costing 0 and 2 and yielding revenues of 0 and 8, respectively. Thus the values of x_1 corresponding to proposals 1 and 2 are $2 - 0 = 2$ and $2 - 2 = 0$. The corresponding best revenues from stage 1 given $x_1 = 2$ and $x_1 = 0$ are 6 and zero, respectively. We thus get

$$\begin{pmatrix}\text{best revenue}\\ \text{given } x_2 = 2\end{pmatrix} = \max\{0 + 6, 8 + 0\} = 8$$

corresponding to proposal 2.

$x_2 = 3$

Feasible alternatives are proposals 1, 2, and 3. The corresponding values of x_1 are $3 - 0 = 3$, $3 - 2 = 1$, and $3 - 3 = 0$, respectively. Thus we have

$$\begin{pmatrix}\text{best revenue}\\ \text{given } x_2 = 3\end{pmatrix} = \max\{0 + 6, 8 + 5, 9 + 0\} = 13$$

corresponding to proposal 2.

$x_2 = 4$

Feasible alternatives are proposals 1, 2, 3, and 4. The corresponding values of x_1 are $4 - 0 = 4$, $4 - 2 = 2$, $4 - 3 = 1$, and $4 - 4 = 0$, respectively, which leads to

$$\begin{pmatrix}\text{best revenue}\\ \text{given } x_2 = 4\end{pmatrix} = \max\{0 + 6, 8 + 6, 9 + 5, 12 + 0\} = 14$$

corresponding to proposal 2 or 3

$x_2 = 5$

We have the same feasible alternatives as in $x_2 = 4$. The corresponding values of x_1 are 5, 3, 2, and 1, respectively. Thus

$$\begin{pmatrix}\text{best revenue}\\ \text{given } x_2 = 5\end{pmatrix} = \max\{0 + 6, 8 + 6, 9 + 6, 12 + 5\} = 17$$

corresponding to proposal 4.

We can summarize stage 2 computation as follows:

If Available Capital x_2 Is:	Then, the Resulting Optimal Proposal Is:	And the Total Revenue for Stages 1 and 2 Is:
0	1	0
1	1	5
2	2	8
3	2	13
4	2 or 3	14
5	4	17

Stage 3 is now considered. The formula for computing the best revenue is similar to that of stage 2 except that x_2 and x_1 are replaced by x_3 and x_2. Similarly, stage 2 and stage 1 are replaced by stage 3 and stage 2. Notice, however, that unlike x_1 or x_2, x_3 now has a single specific value; namely, $x_3 = 5$. Since stage 3 has two proposals whose cost does not exceed 5, both proposals are feasible. The values of x_2 corresponding to proposals 1 and 2 are $5 - 0 = 5$ and $5 - 1 = 4$, respectively. Using the summary table for stage 2 together with x_2, we then obtain

$$\begin{pmatrix}\text{best revenue}\\ \text{given } x_3 = 5\end{pmatrix} = \max\{0 + 17, 3 + 14\} = 17$$

corresponding to 1 or 2.

Now that we have completed all the computations, we can *read* the optimal solution directly. Starting from stage 3, we can choose either proposal 1 or 2. If we choose proposal 1, which costs 0, then x_2 for stage 2 will be $5 - 0 = 5$. From the summary table of stage 2, we see that the optimal alternative given $x_2 = 5$ is proposal 4. Since proposal 4 of stage 2 costs 4, we have $x_1 = x_2 - 4 = 5 - 4 = 1$. Again, from the summary table of stage 1, we obtain proposal 2 as the optimal alternative for stage 1.

By combining all the answers for the three stages, an optimal solution calls for selecting proposal 2 for plant 1, proposal 4 for plant 2, and proposal 1 for plant 3. The total cost is 5 and the optimal revenues is 17. Another two solutions can be determined by considering the alternate optimal proposal at stage 3.

Exercise 10.1-2

Identify the remaining two alternate optima for the foregoing example.
[*Ans.* (3, 2, 2) and (2, 3, 2).]

If you study the given procedure carefully, you will find that the computations are actually *recursive.* Thus stage 2 computations are based on stage 1 computations. Similarly, stage 3 computations make use of stage 2 computations only. In other words, the computations at a current stage utilize a summary information from the immediately preceding stage. This summary provides the optimal revenues of *all* stages previously considered. In using this summary, we never concern ourselves about the specific decisions taken in the preceding stages. Indeed, all *future* decisions are selected optimally without recourse to previously made decisions. This special property constitutes the **principle of optimality**, which is the basis for the validity of DP computations.

To express the recursive equation mathematically, we introduce the following symbols. Let

$R_j(k_j)$ = revenue of alternative k_j at stage j

$f_j(x_j)$ = optimal return of stages 1, 2, ..., and j given the state x_j

We thus write the recursive equations for the capital budgeting example as

$$f_1(x_1) = \max_{\substack{\text{feasible} \\ \text{proposals } k_1}} \{R_1(k_1)\}$$

$$f_j(x_j) = \max_{\substack{\text{feasible} \\ \text{proposals } k_j}} \{R_j(k_j) + f_{j-1}(x_{j-1})\}, \qquad j = 2, 3$$

There is an important point that we need to clarify regarding the mathematical accuracy of this recursive equation. First, note that $f_j(x_j)$ is a function of the argument x_j only. This requires that the right side of the recursive equation be expressed in terms of x_j rather than x_{j-1}. This is accomplished by recalling that

$$x_{j-1} = x_j - c_j(k_j)$$

where $c_j(k_j)$ is the cost of alternative k_j at stage j.

Another point deals with expressing the feasibility of the proposals mathematically. Specifically, a proposal k_j is feasible if its cost $c_j(k_j)$ does not exceed the state of the system x_j at stage j.

Taking these two points into account, we can write the DP recursive equations as

$$f_1(x_1) = \max_{c_1(k_1) \le x_1} \{R_1(k_1)\}$$

$$f_j(x_j) = \max_{c_j(k_j) \le x_j} \{R_j(k_j) + f_{j-1}[x_j - c_j(k_j)]\}, \qquad j = 2, 3$$

The implementation of the recursive equations is usually done in a standard tabular form as the following computations illustrate. We must point out, however, that it is always tempting to do the tabular computations in a mechanical fashion without truly understanding *why* they are done. To avoid falling into this trap, we suggest that you always try to relate the tabular computations entries to the corresponding mathematical symbols in the recursive equation.

Stage 1

$$f_1(x_1) = \max_{\substack{c_1(k_1) \le x_1 \\ k_1 = 1, 2, 3}} \{R_1(k_1)\}$$

	$R_1(k_1)$			Optimal Solution	
x_1	$k_1 = 1$	$k_1 = 2$	$k_1 = 3$	$f_1(x_1)$	k_1^*
0	**0**	—	—	0	1
1	0	**5**	—	5	2
2	0	5	**6**	6	3
3	0	5	**6**	6	3
4	0	5	**6**	6	3
5	0	5	**6**	6	3

Stage 2

$$f_2(x_2) = \max_{\substack{c_2(k_2) \le x_2 \\ k_2 = 1, 2, 3, 4}} \{R_2(k_2) + f_1[x_2 - c_2(k_2)]\}$$

	$R_2(k_2) + f_1[x_2 - c_2(k_2)]$				Optimal Solution	
x_2	$k_2 = 1$	$k_2 = 2$	$k_2 = 3$	$k_2 = 4$	$f_2(x_2)$	k_2^*
0	$0 + 0 = \mathbf{0}$	—	—	—	0	1
1	$0 + 5 = \mathbf{5}$	—	—	—	5	1
2	$0 + 6 = 6$	$8 + 0 = \mathbf{8}$	—	—	8	2
3	$0 + 6 = 6$	$8 + 5 = \mathbf{13}$	$9 + 0 = 9$	—	13	2
4	$0 + 6 = 6$	$8 + 6 = \mathbf{14}$	$9 + 5 = \mathbf{14}$	$12 + 0 = 12$	14	2 or 3
5	$0 + 6 = 6$	$8 + 6 = 14$	$9 + 6 = 15$	$12 + 5 = \mathbf{17}$	17	4

Stage 3

$$f_3(x_3) = \max_{\substack{c_3(k_3) \le x_3 \\ k_3 = 1, 2}} \{R_3(k_3) + f_2[x_3 - c_3(k_3)]\}$$

	$R_3(k_3) + f_2[x_3 - c_3(k_3)]$		Optimum Solution	
x_3	$k_3 = 1$	$k_3 = 2$	$f_3(x_3)$	k_3^*
5	$0 + 17 = \mathbf{17}$	$3 + 14 = \mathbf{17}$	17	1 or 2

The optimum solution can now be read directly from the foregoing tableaus starting with stage 3. For $x_3 = 5$, the optimal proposal is either $k_3^* = 1$ or $k_3^* = 2$. Consider $k_3^* = 1$ first. Since $c_3(1) = 0$, this leaves $x_2 = x_3 - c_3(1) = 5$ for stages 2 and 1. Now, stage 2 shows that $x_2 = 5$ yields $k_2^* = 4$. Since $c_2(4) = 4$, this leaves $x_1 = 5 - 4 = 1$. From stage 1, $x_1 = 1$ gives $k_1^* = 2$. Thus an optimal combination of proposals for stages 1, 2, and 3 is (2, 4, 1). Figure 10-1 shows how all the alternative optima are determined systematically.

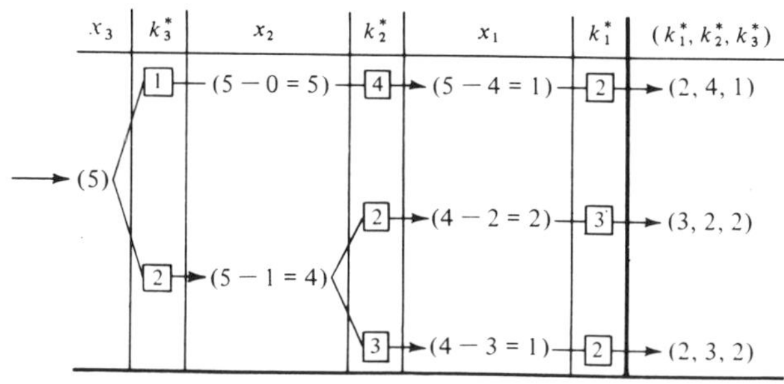

Figure 10-1

Exercise 10.1-3

(a) In each of the following cases, which relate to the capital budgeting example, determine the optimum solution of the problem.

(1) $x_3 = 2$.

[*Ans.* $f_3(2) = 8$, and the optimal proposals are (1, 2, 1) or (2, 1, 2).]

(2) $x_3 = 3$.

[*Ans.* $f_3(3) = 13$, and the optimal proposals are (2, 2, 1).]

(b) Suppose that the costs of the proposals include fractions of \$.1 million rather than being rounded to the closest million dollars as in the example above. How would this change in data affect the tabular computations?

[*Ans.* x_1 and x_2 must assume discrete values in steps of .1, that is, 0, .1, .2, ..., 4.9, 5, thus increasing the number of table entries at stages 1 and 2 by approximately 10 times.]

10.1.2 BACKWARD RECURSIVE EQUATION

In Section 10.1.1 the computations are carried out in the order

$$f_1 \rightarrow f_2 \rightarrow f_3$$

This method of computations is known as the **forward procedure** because the computations advance from the first to the last stage. However, when you study most DP literature, you will find out that the recursive equation is set up such that the computations start at the last stage and then "proceed" backward to stage 1. This method is called the **backward procedure**.

The main difference between the forward and backward methods occurs in the way we define the *state* of the system. To be specific, let us reconsider the capital budgeting example. For the backward procedure, we define the states y_j as

y_1 = amount of capital allocated to stages 1, 2, and 3
y_2 = amount of capital allocated to stages 2 and 3
y_3 = amount of capital allocated to stage 3

To appreciate the difference between the definition of states x_j and y_j in the forward and backward methods, the two definitions are summarized graphically in Figure 10-2.

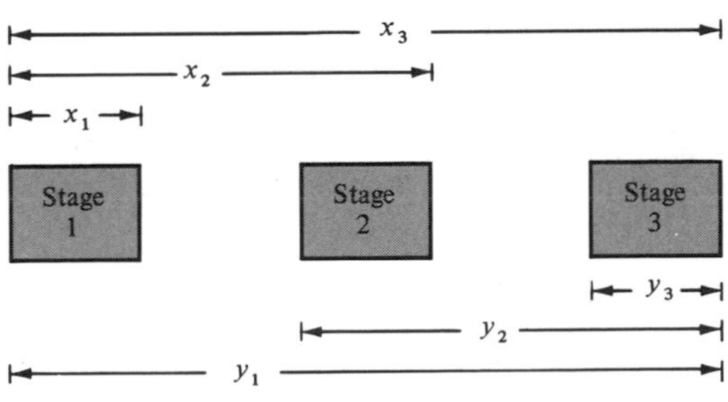

Figure 10-2

Now define

$f_3(y_3)$ = optimal revenue for stage 3 given y_3
$f_2(y_2)$ = optimal revenue for stages 2 *and* 3 given y_2
$f_1(y_1)$ = optimal revenue for stages 1, 2, *and* 3 given y_1

The backward recursive equation is thus written as

$$f_3(y_3) = \max_{\substack{k_3 \\ c_3(k_3) \le y_3}} \{R_3(k_3)\}$$

$$f_j(y_j) = \max_{\substack{k_j \\ c_j(k_j) \le y_j}} \{R_j(k_j) + f_{j+1}[y_j - c_j(k_j)]\}, \qquad j = 1, 2$$

The order of stage computations is thus $f_3 \to f_2 \to f_1$. The computations are now carried out as follows

Stage 3

$$f_3(y_3) = \max_{\substack{c_3(k_3) \le y_3 \\ k_3 = 1,\, 2}} \{R_3(k_3)\}$$

	$R_3(k_3)$		Optimum Solution	
y_3	$k_3 = 1$	$k_3 = 2$	$f_3(y_3)$	k_3^*
0	**0**	—	0	1
1	0	**3**	3	2
2	0	**3**	3	2
3	0	**3**	3	2
4	0	**3**	3	2
5	0	**3**	3	2

Stage 2

$$f_2(y_2) = \max_{\substack{c_2(k_2) \le y_2 \\ k_2 = 1,\, 2,\, 3,\, 4}} \{R_2(k_2) + f_3[y_2 - c_2(k_2)]\}$$

	$R_2(k_2) + f_3[y_2 - c_2(k_2)]$				Optimum Solution	
y_2	$k_2 = 1$	$k_2 = 2$	$k_2 = 3$	$k_2 = 4$	$f_2(y_2)$	k_2^*
0	0 + 0 = **0**	—	—	—	0	1
1	0 + 3 = **3**	—	—	—	3	1
2	0 + 3 = 3	8 + 0 = **8**	—	—	8	2
3	0 + 3 = 3	8 + 3 = **11**	9 + 0 = 9	—	11	2
4	0 + 3 = 3	8 + 3 = 11	9 + 3 = **12**	12 + 0 = **12**	12	3 or 4
5	0 + 3 = 3	8 + 3 = 11	9 + 3 = 12	12 + 3 = **15**	15	4

Stage 1

$$f_1(y_1) = \max_{\substack{c_1(k_1) \leq y_1 \\ k_1 = 1, 2, 3}} \{R_1(k_1) + f_2[y_1 - c_1(k_1)]\}$$

	$R_1(k_1) + f_2[y_1 - c_1(k_1)]$			Optimum Solution	
y_1	$k_1 = 1$	$k_1 = 2$	$k_1 = 3$	$f_1(y_1)$	k_1^*
5	0 + 15 = 15	5 + 12 = **17**	6 + 11 = **17**	17	2 or 3

The optimal solution is determined by starting with y_1 at stage 1 and proceeding to y_3 at stage 3. Naturally, the solutions are identical with those of the forward method (verify).

Exercise 10.1-4
Compute $f_1(y_1)$ for $y_1 = 3$ and $y_1 = 4$ and find the corresponding optimum proposals.
[*Ans.* $f_1(3) = 13$, optimal proposals for stages 1, 2, and 3 are 2, 2, and 1. $f_1(4) = 16$ and the optimal proposals are 2, 2, and 2.]

You may wonder why the backward recursive formulation is needed at all, particularly in that the forward formulation appears more logical and certainly more straightforward. This conclusion is true for the preceding example, since the specific assignment of stages to plants is nonconsequential. In this respect, the forward and backward formulations are in fact computationally equivalent. There are situations, however, where it would make a difference, from the standpoint of computational efficiency, which formulation is used. This is particularly so in problems involving decision making over time, such as inventory and production planning. In this case the stages are designated based on the strict chronological order of the time periods they represent; and the efficiency of computations will depend on whether the forward or backward formulation is used (see Example 10.3-5).

Apparently, experience with DP computations has shown that the backward formulations are generally more efficient. In fact, most of the DP literature is presented in terms of the backward formulation regardless of whether or not it contributes to computational efficiency. Following this tradition, all the presentations in the remainder of this chapter will be based on the backward formulation. The forward formulation will be used only when a comparison is warranted or when the forward formulation offers special advantages. (See Section 14.3.5 for an illustrative application in the area of inventory.)

10.2 MORE ON THE DEFINITION OF THE STATE

The *state* of the system is perhaps the most important concept in a dynamic programming model. It represents the "link" between (successive) stages so that when each stage is optimized *separately*, the resulting decision is automatically feasible for the *entire* problem. Moreover, it allows one to make optimum decisions for the remaining stages without having to check the effect of future decisions on decisions previously made.

The definition of the state is usually the most subtle concept in dynamic programming formulations. There is no easy way to define the state, but clues can usually be found by asking the following two questions:

1. What relationships bind the stages together?
2. What information is needed to make feasible decisions at the current stage without checking the feasibility of decisions made at previous stages?

The following examples are introduced to help you understand the definition of the state.

Example 10.2-1. Consider the capital budgeting problem. As indicated in Section 10.1, each plant represents a stage for which a decision is made. The alternatives are given by the decision variable k_j at stage j, which designates a specific expansion plan. In this case the return function is $R_j(k_j)$.

What defines the state at stage j? Note that the stages are "linked" by the fact that all the plants (stages) are competing for a share of the limited capital C. This suggests that the state should be defined in terms of capital allocation.

Experience has shown that a beginner in dynamic programming will usually define the state at stage j as "the amount of capital allocated to stage j." To see why this definition is *not* correct, consider the manner in which the problem will be solved. The definition of the state should allow one to make a feasible decision for the current stage without checking the decisions made for previous stages. The definition of state given indicates only that the amount allocated to stage j can be as small as zero or as high as the total available capital C. This is not sufficient information to guarantee a feasible decision for the current stage. For example, suppose that it is decided to allocate $.4C$ dollars to the current stage. The feasibility of this decision is not guaranteed without checking the preceding stages to ensure that their total capital allocation did not exceed $C - .4C = .6C$ dollars. This shows that the current stage is not optimized independently, contrary to the basic idea of dynamic programming.

Assume the backward formulation and consider the definition of the state at stage j as "the amount of capital allocated to stages $j, j + 1, \ldots,$ and N," where N is the total number of plants. This definition is correct, since the difference between the capital allocated to stages $j, j + 1, \ldots, N$—that is, the state of the system at stage j—and the capital allocated to stages $j + 1, j + 2, \ldots, N$—that is, the state of the system at stage $(j + 1)$—gives the amount of capital to be allocated to stage j only. This, as we saw in Section 10.1.3, allows us to make a feasible decision for stage j without checking the previous stages. ◀

The capital budgeting problem represents a typical *allocation* problem in which a resource (or, generally, resources) is distributed (optimally) among a number of activities (stages). The definition of the state of the system for all allocation problems is generally the same: namely, the amount of the resource allocated to a successive number of stages starting from the last stage. Other types of problems do not fall into this category, however, and require a different definition of the state of the system. Two examples are presented here.

Example 10.2-2. A contractor wishes to determine the size of a labor force during each of the next 5 weeks. The minimum number of workers needed for each week is given. Additional cost is incurred when workers are hired or fired and when workers are idle. The costs of hiring, firing, and idleness per worker are known. The objective is to decide how many workers should be hired or fired each week in order to minimize the total cost.

In looking at this situation from the dynamic programming standpoint, the first element to identify is the stage. Since a decision is to be made for each week, each period (week) represents a stage.

The second element to be defined is the alternatives (decision variables) associated with each stage. In this example the decision variable is the number of workers hired or fired in the period. The return function is represented by the cost of hiring or firing and the cost of idleness.

The third and most important element is the state of the system at a given stage. Unlike allocation problems, no explicit constraint ties the stages together. However, a clue for defining the state can be found by asking the question: What information is needed from all previously considered stages (periods) to make a decision for the current stage without having to examine any of the decisions previously made? With some reflection, we note that the number of workers available at the end of the preceding stage (period) provides sufficient information to decide how many to hire or fire in the current stage. Consequently, the number of workers at the end of the preceding stage defines the state of the system at the current stage. In other words, knowing how many were hired or fired in each of the previously considered stages (i.e., previous decisions) is of no consequence in making the decision for the current stage. The only important information is how many workers are on hand before the current decision is made. This information is available from the definition of the state of the system. Stated differently, the state of the system summarizes all the information needed to make a feasible decision for the current stage. ◀

Example 10.2-3. Consider an equipment replacement situation where at the end of each year a decision is made to keep a machine another year or replace it immediately. If a machine is kept longer, its realized profit declines. On the other hand, replacing a machine incurs the cost of a replacement. The problem is to decide when a machine should be replaced to maximize the total net profit.

In this problem, stage j represents year j. The alternatives at each stage are either to keep the machine or to replace it. Now you should ask: What is the relationship between two successive stages? What information is needed from the preceding stages to make a decision (keep or replace) in the current stage? The answer is: the age of the machine. Thus the state of the system at a stage is defined as the age of the machine at the beginning of the associated period.

10.3 EXAMPLES OF DP MODELS AND COMPUTATIONS

This section presents further examples of dynamic programming models. The first four examples involve both model formulations and computations. The last example introduces a comparison between the forward and backward recursive equations.

(Other examples pertaining to DP applications in inventory and Markovian processes are presented in Chapters 14 and 18.)

As you study this section, make sure that you have a clear understanding of the basic elements of the model: (1) stages, (2) states at each stage, and (3) decision alternatives (proposals) at each stage. As we indicated previously, the concept of *state* is usually the most subtle. Our experience indicates that an understanding of the concept of state is enhanced by trying to "question the validity" of the way it is defined in the book. Try a different definition that may appear "more logical" and use it in the recursive computations. You will eventually discover that the definition given here is not incorrect and, in most cases, may be the only correct definition. In the process you will also gain insight into what the concept of state is all about.

Example 10.3-1 (Cargo-Loading Problem).† Consider loading a vessel with stocks of N items. Each unit of item i has a weight w_i and a value $v_i (i = 1, 2, \ldots, N)$. The maximum cargo weight is W. It is required to determine the most valuable cargo load without exceeding the maximum weight of the vessel. Specifically, consider the following special case of three items and assume that $W = 5$.

i	w_i	v_i
1	2	65
2	3	80
3	1	30

Note that the optimal solution to this example can be obtained by inspection. A typical problem usually involves a large number of items and hence the solution would not be as obvious. See the discussion immediately following the end of this example.

Consider the general problem of N items first. If k_i is the number of units of item i, the problem becomes

$$\text{maximize } v_1 k_1 + v_2 k_2 + \cdots + v_N k_N$$

subject to

$$w_1 k_1 + w_2 k_2 + \cdots + w_N k_N \leq W$$
$$k_i \text{ nonnegative integer}$$

If k_i is not restricted to integer values, the solution is easily determined by the simplex method. In fact, since there is only one constraint, only one variable will be basic and the problem reduces to selecting the item i for which $v_i W/w_i$ is maximum. Since linear programming is not applicable here, the problem will be attempted by dynamic programming. It must be noted that this problem is also typical of the type that can be solved by integer programming techniques (see Chapter 9).

The DP model is constructed by first considering its three basic elements:

1. *Stage* j is represented by item j, $j = 1, 2, \ldots, N$.
2. *State* y_j at stage j is the total weight assigned to stages $j, j + 1, \ldots, N$; $y_1 = W$ and $y_j = 0, 1, \ldots, W$ for $j = 2, 3, \ldots, N$.

---

† This problem is known also as the **knapsack** or the **flyaway kit** problem.

3. *Alternative* k_j at stage j is the *number* of units of item j. The value of k_j may be as small as zero or as large as $[W/w_j]$, where $[W/w_j]$ is the largest integer included in (W/w_j).

There is a striking similarity between this problem and the capital budgeting example of Section 10.1, since both are of the resource allocation type. About the only difference is that the alternatives in the cargo-loading model are not given directly as in the capital budgeting model.

Let

$$f_j(y_j) = \text{optimal value of stages } j, j+1, \ldots, N \text{ given the state } y_j$$

The (backward) recursive equation is thus given as

$$f_N(y_N) = \max_{\substack{k_N = 0, 1, \ldots, [y_N/w_N] \\ y_N = 0, 1, \ldots, W}} \{v_N k_N\}$$

$$f_j(y_j) = \max_{\substack{k_j = 0, 1, \ldots, [y_j/w_j] \\ y_j = 0, 1, \ldots, W}} \{v_j k_j + f_{j+1}(y_j - w_j k_j)\}, \qquad j = 1, 2, \ldots, N-1$$

Note that the maximum *feasible* value of k_j is given by $[y_j/w_j]$. This limit will automatically delete all infeasible alternatives for a given value of the state y_j.

Exercise 10.3-1

Establish the relationship between $R_j(k_j)$ and $c_j(k_j)$ in the capital budgeting model of Section 10.1 and the corresponding elements in the cargo-loading model.
[*Ans.* $R_j(k_j)$ corresponds to $v_j k_j$ and $c_j(k_j)$ is equivalent to $w_j k_j$.]

For the special example given, stage computations are performed as follows.

Stage 3

$$f_3(y_3) = \max_{k_3}\{30k_3\}, \qquad \max k_3 = [5/1] = 5$$

	$30k_3$						Optimal Solution	
	$k_3 = 0$	1	2	3	4	5		
y_3	$v_3 k_3 = 0$	30	60	90	120	150	$f_3(y_3)$	k_3^*
0	0	—	—	—	—	—	0	0
1	0	30	—	—	—	—	30	1
2	0	30	60	—	—	—	60	2
3	0	30	60	90	—	—	90	3
4	0	30	60	90	120	—	120	4
5	0	30	60	90	120	150	150	5

Stage 2

$$f_2(y_2) = \max_{k_2}\{80k_2 + f_3(y_2 - 3k_2)\}, \qquad \max k_2 = [5/3] = 1$$

	$80k_2 + f_3(y_2 - 3k_2)$		Optimum Solution	
	$k_2 = 0$	1		
y_2	$v_2 k_2 = 0$	80	$f_2(y_2)$	k_2^*
0	0 + 0 = 0	—	0	0
1	0 + 30 = 30	—	30	0
2	0 + 60 = 60	—	60	0
3	0 + 90 = 90	80 + 0 = 80	90	0
4	0 + 120 = 120	80 + 30 = 110	120	0
5	0 + 150 = 150	80 + 60 = 140	150	0

Stage 1

$$f_1(y_1) = \max_{k_1}\{65k_1 + f_2(y_1 - 2k_1)\}, \qquad \max k_1 = [5/2] = 2$$

	$65k_1 + f_2(y_1 - 2k_1)$			Optimum Solution	
	$k_1 = 0$	1	2		
y_1	$v_1 k_1 = 0$	65	130	$f_1(y_1)$	k_1^*
0	0 + 0 = 0	—	—	0	0
1	0 + 30 = 30	—	—	30	0
2	0 + 60 = 60	65 + 0 = 65	—	65	1
3	0 + 90 = 90	65 + 30 = 95	—	95	1
4	0 + 120 = 120	65 + 60 = 125	130 + 0 = 130	130	2
5	0 + 150 = 150	65 + 90 = 155	130 + 30 = 160	160	2

Given $y_1 = W = 5$, the associated optimum solution is $(k_1^*, k_2^*, k_3^*) = (2, 0, 1)$, with a total value of 160.

Notice that at stage 1, it is sufficient to construct the table for $y_1 = 5$ only. However, by computing the entire table for $y_1 = 0, 1, 2, 3, 4$, and 5, it is possible to study changes in the optimal solution when the maximum weight allocation is reduced below $W = 5$. This is a form of sensitivity analysis that the DP computations provide automatically. ◀

Exercise 10.3-2

Find the optimal solution to the cargo-loading problem in each of the following cases.

(1) $W = 3$.

[*Ans.* $(k_1^*, k_2^*, k_3^*) = (1, 0, 1)$; total value = 95.]

(2) $W = 4$.

[*Ans.* $(k_1^*, k_2^*, k_3^*) = (2, 0, 0)$; total value = 130.]

It may appear that the knapsack problem can be solved in general by computing the ratios v_j/w_j for all the variables k_j, and then assigning the largest integer quantities to the variables successively in the order of their ratios until the resource is exhausted. (This procedure actually produces the optimal solution in Example 10.3-1.) Unfortunately, this is not always true, as the following counterexample shows.

$$\text{Maximize } 17k_1 + 72k_2 + 35k_3$$

subject to

$$10k_1 + 41k_2 + 20k_3 \leq 50$$
$$k_1, k_2, k_3 \text{ nonnegative integers}$$

The ratios for k_1, k_2, and k_3 are 1.7, 1.756, and 1.75. Since k_2 has the largest ratio, it is assigned the largest value allowed by the constraint, that is, $k_2 = [50/41] = 1$. The remaining amount of the resource is now $50 - 41 = 9$, which is not sufficient to assign any positive integer values to k_1 or k_3. Thus the trial solution is $k_1 = k_3 = 0$, and $k_2 = 1$ with the objective value equal to 72. This is not optimal, since the feasible solution ($k_1 = 1, k_2 = 0, k_3 = 2$) yields a better objective value equal to 87.

Example 10.3-2 (Reliability Problem). Consider the design of an electronic device consisting of three main components. The three components are arranged in series so that the failure of one component will cause the failure of the entire device. The reliability (probability of no failure) of the device can be improved by installing standby units in each component. The design calls for using one or two standby units, which means that each main component may include up to three units in parallel. The total capital available for the design of the device is \$10,000. The data for the reliability $R_j(k_j)$ and cost $c_j(k_j)$ for the jth component ($j = 1, 2, 3$) given k_j parallel units are summarized next. The objective is to determine the number of parallel units, k_j, in component j that will maximize the reliability of the device without exceeding the allocated capital.

	$j = 1$		$j = 2$		$j = 3$	
k_j	R_1	c_1	R_2	c_2	R_3	c_3
1	.6	1	.7	3	.5	2
2	.8	2	.8	5	.7	4
3	.9	3	.9	6	.9	5

By definition the total reliability R of a device of N series components and k_j parallel units in component j ($j = 1, 2, \ldots, N$) is the *product* of the individual realiabilities. The problem thus becomes

$$\text{maximize } R = \prod_{j=1}^{N} R_j(k_j)$$

subject to

$$\sum_{j=1}^{N} c_j(k_j) \leq C$$

where C is the total capital available. (Notice that the alternative $k_j = 0$ is meaningless in this problem.)

The reliability problem is similar to the capital budgeting problem in Section 10.1 with the exception that the return function R is the *product*, rather than the sum, of the returns of the individual components. The recursive equation is thus based on **multiplicative** rather than **additive decomposition.**

The elements of the DP model are defined as follows.

1. *Stage j* represents main component j.
2. *State* y_j is the total capital assigned to components $j, j+1, \ldots, N$.
3. *Alternative* k_j is the number of parallel units assigned to main component j.

Let $f_j(y_j)$ be the total optimal reliability of components $j, j+1, \ldots, N$, given the capital y_j. The recursive equations are written as

$$f_N(y_N) = \max_{\substack{k_N \\ c_N(k_N) \le y}} \{R_N(k_N)\}$$

$$f_j(y_j) = \max_{\substack{k_j \\ c_j(k_j) \le y_j}} \{R_j(k_j) \cdot f_{j+1}(y_j - c_j(k_j))\}, \qquad j = 1, 2, \ldots, N-1$$

As we have seen previously, the amount of computations at stage j depends directly on the number of values assumed for the state y_j. We show here how we can compute tighter limits on the values of y_j.

Starting with stage 3, since main component 3 must include at least one (parallel) unit, we find that y_3 must at least equal $c_3(1) = 2$. By the same reasoning y_3 cannot exceed $10 - (3 + 1) = 6$; otherwise, the remaining capital will not be sufficient to provide main components 1 and 2 with at least one (parallel) unit each. Following the same reasoning, we see that $y_2 = 5, 6, \ldots,$ or 9, and $y_1 = 6, 7, \ldots,$ or 10. (Verify!)

Stage 3

$$f_3(y_3) = \max_{k_3 = 1, 2, 3} \{R_3(k_3)\}$$

	$R_3(k_3)$			Optimal Solution	
	$k_3 = 1$	$k_3 = 2$	$k_3 = 3$		
y_3	$R = .5, c = 2$	$R = .7, c = 4$	$R = .9, c = 5$	$f_3(y_3)$	k_3^*
2	.5	—	—	.5	1
3	.5	—	—	.5	1
4	.5	.7	—	.7	2
5	.5	.7	.9	.9	3
6	.5	.7	.9	.9	3

Stage 2

$$f_2(y_2) = \max_{k_3=1,2,3} \{R_2(k_2) \cdot f_3[y_2 - c_2(k_2)]\}$$

	$R_2(k_2) \cdot f_3[y_2 - c_2(k_2)]$			Optimal Solution	
	$k_2 = 1$	$k_2 = 2$	$k_2 = 3$		
y_2	$R = .7, c = 3$	$R = .8, c = 5$	$R = .9, c = 6$	$f_2(y_2)$	k_2^*
5	.7 × .5 = .35	—	—	.35	1
6	.7 × .5 = .35	—	—	.35	1
7	.7 × .7 = .49	.8 × .5 = .40	—	.49	1
8	.7 × .9 = .63	.8 × .5 = .40	.9 × .5 = .45	.63	1
9	.7 × .9 = .63	.8 × .7 = .56	.9 × .5 = .45	.63	1

Stage 1

$$f_1(y_1) = \max_{k_1=1,2,3} \{R_1(k_1) \cdot f_2[y_1 - c_1(k_1)]\}$$

	$R_1(k_1) \cdot f_2[y_1 - c_1(k_1)]$			Optimal Solution	
y_1	$R = .6, c = 1$	$R = .8, c = 2$	$R = .9, c = 3$	$f_1(y_1)$	k_1^*
6	.6 × .35 = .210	—	—	.210	1
7	.6 × .35 = .210	.8 × .35 = .280	—	.280	2
8	.6 × .49 = .294	.8 × .35 = .280	.9 × .35 = .315	.315	3
9	.6 × .63 = .378	.8 × .49 = .392	.9 × .35 = .315	.392	2
10	.6 × .63 = .378	.8 × .63 = .504	.9 × .49 = .441	.504	2

The optimal solution given $C = 10$ is $(k_1^*, k_2^*, k_3^*) = (2, 1, 3)$ with $R = .504$. ◀

Exercise 10.3-3

Suppose that a *fourth* main component is added (in series) to the electronic device. The costs and reliabilities of using one, two, or three parallel units in the new component are $R_4(1) = .4$, $c_4(1) = 1$; $R_4(2) = .8$, $c_4(2) = 3$; and $R_4(3) = .95$, $c_4(3) = 7$.

(a) Determine the limits on the values of y_4, y_3, y_2, and y_1.
[*Ans.* $1 \le y_4 \le 4$, $3 \le y_3 \le 6$, $6 \le y_2 \le 9$, $7 \le y_1 \le 10$.]

(b) Does the definition of states in (a) require recomputing the optimal solutions at all stages?
[*Ans.* Yes, because stage 4 must be computed first, thus affecting computations at stages 3, 2, and 1.]

(c) Can you find the optimal solution to the entire problem utilizing directly the computations given for the three stages?
[*Ans.* Yes, but this will require redefining stage 4 as stage 0. Since the order of the components in the device is irrelevant, we can pretend that the new component precedes component 1, numbering it as stage 0. Under this condition, the values of the states are limited by $2 \le y_3 \le 5$, $5 \le y_2 \le 8$, $6 \le y_1 \le 9$, and $7 \le y_0 \le 10$.]

(d) Compute $f_0(y_0)$ and k_0^* as defined in part (c) and find the optimal solution to the four-component problem given $C = 10$.
[*Ans.* $f_0(7) = .084$, $k_0^* = 1$; $f_0(8) = .112$, $k_0^* = 1$; $f_0(9) = .168$, $k_0^* = 2$; $f_0(10) = .224$, $k_0^* = 2$. The optimal solution given $C = 10$ is $(k_0^*, k_1^*, k_2^*, k_3^*) = (2, 2, 1, 1)$ with $R = .224$.]

Example 10.3-3 (Optimal Subdivision Problem). Consider the mathematical problem of dividing a quantity q (> 0) into N parts. The objective is to determine the optimum subdivision of q that will maximize the product of the N parts.

Let z_j be the jth portion of q ($j = 1, 2, \ldots, N$). The problem is thus expressed as

$$\text{maximize } p = \prod_{j=1}^{N} z_j$$

subject to

$$\sum_{j=1}^{N} z_j = q, \quad z_j \geq 0 \qquad \text{for all } j$$

The DP formulation of this problem is very similar to the reliability model of Example 10.3-2. The main difference occurs in that the variables z_j are continuous, a condition that requires the use of calculus for optimizing each stage's problem.

The elements of the DP model are defined as

1. *Stage* j represents the jth portion of q.
2. *State* y_j is the portion of q allocated to stages $j, j + 1, \ldots, N$.
3. *Alternative* z_j is the portion of q allocated to stage j.

Let $f_j(y_j)$ be the optimum value of the objective function for stages $j, j + 1, \ldots, N$ given the state y_j. The recursive equations are thus given as

$$f_N(y_N) = \max_{z_N \leq y_N} \{z_N\}$$
$$f_j(y_j) = \max_{z_j \leq y_j} \{z_j \cdot f_{j+1}(y_j - z_j)\}, \qquad j = 1, 2, \ldots, N - 1$$

Stage N

$$f_N(y_N) = \max_{z_N \leq y_N} \{z_N\}$$

Since z_N is a linear function, $\max_{z_N \leq y_N}\{z_N\} = y_N$, which occurs at $z_N^* = y_N$. We can summarize this stage's optimum solution using the form we used in the preceding examples:

	Optimum Solution	
State	$f_N(y_N)$	z_N^*
y_N	y_N	y_N

Stage N − 1

$$f_{N-1}(y_{N-1}) = \max_{z_{N-1} \leq y_{N-1}} \{z_{N-1} \cdot f_N(y_{N-1} - z_{N-1})\}$$

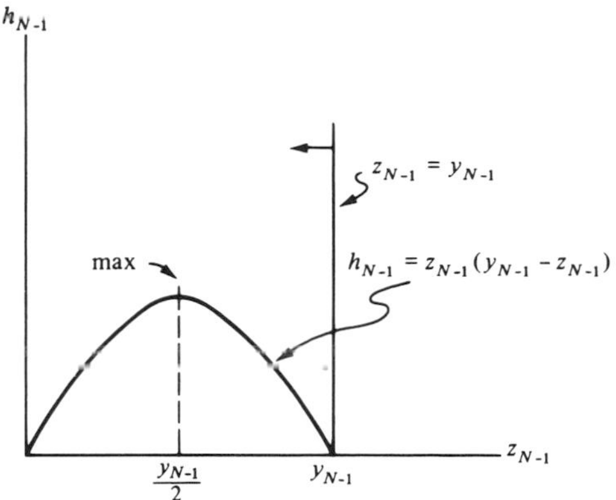

Figure 10-3

Since $f_N(y_N) = y_N$, we have

$$f_N(y_{N-1} - z_{N-1}) = y_{N-1} - z_{N-1}$$

Thus, by substituting for f_N, the problem for stage $N - 1$ reduces to maximizing $h_{N-1} = z_{N-1} f_N(y_{N-1} - z_{N-1}) = z_{N-1}(y_{N-1} - z_{N-1})$ given $z_{N-1} \le y_{N-1}$. (This is precisely the same procedure that we follow in the case of tabular computations.) Figure 10-3 shows what the optimization problem entails by plotting the function h_{N-1} in terms of z_{N-1} together with the feasible region $z_{N-1} \le y_{N-1}$. The optimum feasible solution occurs at $z^*_{N-1} = y_{N-1}/2$. The point $z^*_{N-1} = y_{N-1}/2$ is obtained by differentiating h_{N-1} with respect to z_{N-1}. Since $z^*_{N-1} = y_{N-1}/2$ is feasible, that is, satisfies the condition $z_{N-1} \le y_{N-1}$, it is the optimum solution.†

The value of $f_{N-1}(y_{N-1})$ is obtained by substituting $z_{N-1} = y_{N-1}/2$ in h_{N-1}. The resulting optimum solution is thus given by

	Optimum Solution	
State	$f_{N-1}(y_{N-1})$	z^*_{N-1}
y_{N-1}	$(y_{N-1}/2)^2$	$(y_{N-1}/2)$

Stage j

$$f_j(y_j) = \max_{z_j \le y_j} \{z_j \cdot f_{j+1}(y_j - z_j)\}$$

We can now use *induction* to show that the optimum solution at stage j ($j = 1, 2, \ldots, N$) is summarized as

	Optimum Solution	
State	$f_j(y_j)$	z^*_j
y_j	$\left(\frac{y_j}{N-j+1}\right)^{N-j+1}$	$\left(\frac{y_j}{N-j+1}\right)$

† This simple procedure is applicable here because, among other conditions, h_{N-1} is a concave function. It becomes more involved when these conditions are not satisfied. See Chapter 19 on classical optimization theory for more clarification of this statement.

By inspecting the general solution at stage j, we can obtain the optimum values of z_j given $y_1 = q$ as follows.

$$y_1 = q \rightarrow z_1 = \frac{q}{N} \rightarrow y_2 = \frac{N-1}{N} q \rightarrow \cdots \rightarrow y_j = \frac{N-j+1}{N} q \rightarrow z_j = \frac{q}{N}$$

Thus the general solution is

$$z_1^* = z_2^* = \cdots = z_j^* = \cdots = z_N^* = \frac{q}{N}$$

and the optimum value of the objective function

$$p = f_1(q) = (q/N)^N$$

This example demonstrates that DP does not give specifics about *how* each stage's problem is optimized. The use of calculus to solve these subproblems has nothing to do with dynamic programming. Note, however, that the decomposition of the "master" problem to smaller subproblems normally simplifies the computations associated with the optimization process. This is the main objective of DP. ◀

Exercise 10.3-4

In Example 10.3-3, suppose that the objective function is $p = \prod_{j=1}^{N} a_j z_j$ and the constraint is $\sum_{j=1}^{N} b_j z_j = q$. Write the recursive equation.
[*Ans.* $f_j(y_j) = \max_{z_j \leq y_j/b_j}\{a_j z_j \cdot f_{j+1}(y_j - b_j z_j)\}$ for $j = 1, 2, \ldots, N$, where $f_{N+1} \equiv 1$. The state y_j is defined as the portion of q allocated to stages $j, j+1, \ldots,$ and N.]

Example 10.3-4 (Work Force Size). A contractor needs to decide on the size of his work force over the next 5 weeks. Estimates of the *minimum* force size b_i for the 5 weeks are 5, 7, 8, 4, and 6 workers for $i = 1, 2, 3, 4,$ and 5, respectively.

The contractor can maintain the required minimum number of workers by exercising the options of hiring and firing. However, additional hiring cost is incurred every time the work force size of the current week exceeds that of last week. On the other hand, if the contractor maintains a work force for any week that exceeds the minimum requirement, an excess cost is incurred for that week.

Let y_j represent the number of workers for the jth week. Define $C_1(y_j - b_j)$ as the excess cost when y_j exceeds b_j, and $C_2(y_j - y_{j-1})$ as the cost of hiring new workers $(y_j > y_{j-1})$. The contractor's data show that

$$C_1(y_j - b_j) = 3(y_j - b_j), \qquad j = 1, 2, \ldots, 5$$

$$C_2(y_j - y_{j-1}) = \begin{cases} 4 + 2(y_j - y_{j-1}), & y_j > y_{j-1} \\ 0, & y_j \leq y_{j-1} \end{cases}$$

Note that the definition of C_2 implies that firing $(y_j \leq y_{j-1})$ incurs no additional cost.

If the initial work force y_0 at the beginning of the first week is 5 workers, it is required to determine the optimum sizes of the work force for the 5-week planning horizon.

The definition of *stages* in this example is obvious: Each week represents a stage. However, the definition of the *state* is not as obvious. In all the preceding examples, the definitions of the states are similar because all these examples are of the resource allocation type in which a single resource is distributed optimally among the stages. Our present example is different and we must thus find an appropriate definition of the state.

Recall that the prime objective of the state is to provide sufficient information about all previously considered stages so that future *optimal feasible* decisions can be made without any consideration of how previous decisions were made. In the contractor's problem, the size of the work force at the end of the last week provides sufficient information to make proper feasible decisions for all the remaining weeks. Consequently, the state at stage j is defined by y_{j-1}.

The only remaining element of the DP model is the definition of alternatives at stage j. This is obviously given by y_j, the work force size at stage j.

To summarize, the elements of the DP model are given as

1. *Stage* j represents the jth week.
2. *State* y_{j-1} at stage j is the number of workers at the end of stage $j - 1$.
3. *Alternative* y_j is the number of workers in week j.

Let $f_j(y_{j-1})$ be the optimal cost for periods (weeks) $j, j + 1, \ldots, 5$, given y_{j-1}. The recursive equations are then written as

$$f_5(y_4) = \min_{y_5 = b_5} \{C_1(y_5 - b_5) + C_2(y_5 - y_4)\}$$

$$f_j(y_{j-1}) = \min_{y_j \geq b_j} \{C_1(y_j - b_j) + C_2(y_j - y_{j-1}) + f_{j+1}(y_j)\}, \qquad j = 1, 2, 3, 4$$

Before we carry out the tabular computations, we need to define the possible values for y_1, y_2, y_3, y_4, and y_5. Since $j = 5$ is the last period and since firing does not incur any cost, y_5 must equal the minimum required number of workers b_5; that is, $y_5 = b_5 = 6$. On the other hand, since b_4 $(= 4) < b_5$ $(= 6)$, the contractor may maintain $y_4 = 4$, 5, or 6, depending on which level will yield the lowest cost. Following similar reasoning, we can conclude that $y_3 = 8$, $y_2 = 7$ or 8, and $y_1 = 5$, 6, 7, or 8. The initial work force size y_0 is 5, as given by the problem.

Stage 5

$b_5 = 6$

	$C_1(y_5 - 6) + C_2(y_5 - y_4)$	Optimum Solution	
y_4	$y_5 = 6$	$f_5(y_4)$	y_5^*
4	$3(0) + 4 + 2(2) = 8$	8	6
5	$3(0) + 4 + 2(1) = 6$	6	6
6	$3(0) + 0 = 0$	0	6

Stage 4

$b_4 = 4$

	$C_1(y_4 - 4) + C_2(y_4 - y_3) + f_5(y_4)$			Optimum Solution	
y_3	$y_4 = 4$	5	6	$f_4(y_3)$	y_4^*
8	$0 + 0 + 8 = 8$	$3(1) + 0 + 6 = 9$	$3(2) + 0 + 0 = 6$	6	6

Stage 3

$$b_3 = 8$$

	$C_1(y_3 - 8) + C_2(y_3 - y_2) + f_4(y_3)$	Optimum Solution	
y_2	$y_3 = 8$	$f_3(y_2)$	y_3^*
7	$0 + 4 + 2(1) + 6 = 12$	12	8
8	$0 + 0 + 6 = 6$	6	8

Stage 2

$$b_2 = 7$$

	$C_1(y_2 - 7) + C_2(y_2 - y_1) + f_3(y_2)$		Optimum Solution	
y_1	$y_2 = 7$	$y_2 = 8$	$f_2(y_1)$	y_2^*
5	$0 + 4 + 2(2) + 12 = 20$	$3(1) + 4 + 2(3) + 6 = 19$	19	8
6	$0 + 4 + 2(1) + 12 = 18$	$3(1) + 4 + 2(2) + 6 = 17$	17	8
7	$0 + 0 + 12 = 12$	$3(1) + 4 + 2(1) + 6 = 15$	12	7
8	$0 + 0 + 12 = 12$	$3(1) + 0 + 6 = 9$	9	8

Stage 1

$$b_1 = 5$$

	$C_1(y_1 - 5) + C_2(y_1 - y_0) + f_2(y_1)$				Optimum Solution	
y_0	$y_1 = 5$	6	7	8	$f_1(y_0)$	y_1^*
5	$0 + 0 + 19 = 19$	$3(1) + 4 + 2(1) + 17 = 26$	$3(2) + 4 + 2(2) + 12 = 26$	$3(3) + 4 + 2(3) + 9 = 28$	19	5

The optimal solution is obtained as follows:

$$y_0 = 5 \rightarrow y_1^* = 5 \rightarrow y_2^* = 8 \rightarrow y_3^* = 8 \rightarrow y_4^* = 6 \rightarrow y_5^* = 6$$

This solution can be translated to the following plan.

Week j	Minimum Requirement b_j	y_j	Decision
1	5	5	No hiring or firing
2	7	8	Hire 3 workers
3	8	8	No hiring or firing
4	4	6	Fire 2 workers
5	6	6	No hiring or firing

◀

Exercise 10.3-5

Consider the preceding work force size example.

(a) Suppose that the minimum requirements b_j are 6, 5, 3, 6, and 8 for $j = 1, 2, 3, 4$, and 5. Determine all possible values of y_j.
[*Ans.* $y_5 = 8$, $y_4 = 6, 7$, or 8, $y_3 = 3, 4, 5, 6, 7$, or 8, $y_2 = 5, 6, 7$, or 8, and $y_1 = 6, 7$, or 8.]

(b) If $y_0 = 3$ instead of 5, find the new optimum solution.
[*Ans.* Same optimum values of y_i except that $f_1(y_0) = 27$.]

Example 10.3-5 (Forward and Backward Recursive Equations). A farmer owns k sheep. Once every year he decides how many to sell and how many to keep. If he sells, his profit per sheep is p_i in year i. If he keeps, the number of sheep kept in year i will be doubled in year $(i + 1)$. He will sell out completely at the end of n years.

This highly simplified example is designed to illustrate the potential advantages of using backward recursive equations in comparison with the forward method. In general, the forward and backward methods will lead to different computational efficiencies when the stages of the model must be ordered in a specific sequential order. This happens to be the case in this example (also Example 10.3-4), where stage j represents year j. Thus the stages must be considered in the chronological order of the years they represent (compare with Examples 10.3-1 through 10.3-3, where the assignment of stages can be arbitrary).

We first develop the forward and backward recursive equations, and then make a computational comparison between the two methods. The prime difference between the two formulations stems from the definition of state. To facilitate understanding of this point, the problem is summarized graphically in Figure 10-4. For year j, let x_j and y_j represent the number of sheep kept and the number sold, respectively. Define $z_j = x_j + y_j$. Then from the conditions of the problem,

$$z_1 = 2x_0 = 2k$$
$$z_j = 2x_{j-1}, \qquad j = 1, 2, \ldots, n$$

The state of the model at stage j may be described by z_j, the number of sheep available at the end of stage j for allocation to stages $j + 1, j + 2, \ldots, n$; or by x_j, the number of sheep available at the beginning of stage $j + 1$ after the decisions at stages $1, 2, \ldots, j$ have been made. The first definition will result in the use of the backward recursive equations, and the second will lead to the use of the forward formulation.

Backward Formulation

Let $f_j(z_j)$ be the optimum profit for stages $j, j + 1, \ldots,$ and given z_j. The recursive equations are thus given as

$$f_n(z_n) = \max_{y_n = z_n \leq 2^n k} \{p_n y_n\}$$

$$f_j(z_j) = \max_{y_j \leq z_j \leq 2^j k} \{p_j y_j + f_{j+1}(2[z_j - y_j])\}, \qquad j = 1, 2, \ldots, n - 1$$

Notice that y_j and z_j are nonnegative integers. Also, y_j, the amount sold at the end of period j, must be less than or equal to z_j. The upper limit of z_j is $2^j k$ (where k is the initial size of the flock), which will occur if no sales take place.

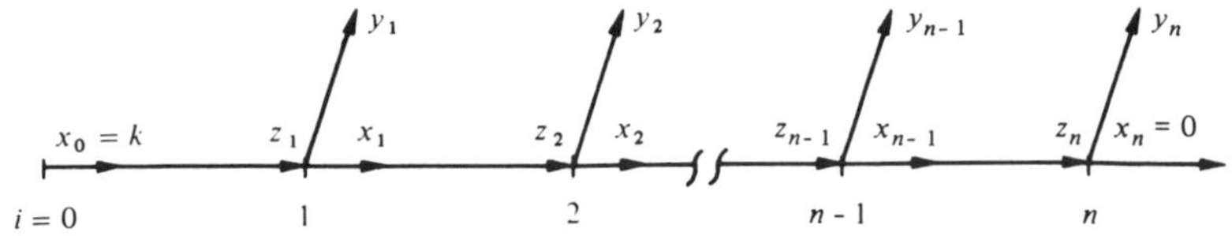

y_1 y_2 y_{n-1} y_n

$x_0 = k$ z_1 x_1 z_2 x_2 z_{n-1} x_{n-1} z_n $x_n = 0$

$i = 0$ 1 2 $n-1$ n

Figure 10-4

Forward Formulation

Let $g_j(x_j)$ be the optimum profit accumulated from stages 1, 2, ..., j given x_j (where x_j is the size of the flock at the beginning of stage $j + 1$). The recursive is thus given as

$$g_1(x_1) = \max_{y_1 = 2k - x_1} \{p_1 y_1\}$$

$$g_j(x_j) = \max_{\substack{y_j \leq 2^j k - x_j \\ (x_j + y_j)/2 \text{ integer}}} \left\{p_j y_j + g_{j-1}\left(\frac{y_j + x_j}{2}\right)\right\}, \qquad j = 2, 3, \ldots, n$$

A comparison of the two formulations shows that during the course of computation, expressing x_{j-1} in terms of x_j is more difficult than is expressing z_{j+1} in terms of z_j. Namely, $x_{j-1} = (x_j + y_j)/2$ requires that the right side be integer, whereas $z_{j+1} = 2(z_j - y_j)$ does not have such a restriction. Thus, in the case of the forward formulation, the values of y_j and x_j satisfying

$$y_j \leq 2^j k - x_j$$

must additionally satisfy an integrality condition resulting from transforming x_{j-1} to x_j. The example illustrates the computational difficulties that are normally associated with the forward formulation. ◀

10.4 PROBLEM OF DIMENSIONALITY IN DYNAMIC PROGRAMMING

In all the dynamic programming problems presented thus far, the states of the system have been described by one variable only. In general, these states may consist of n (≥ 1) variables in which case the dynamic programming model is said to have a multidimensional state vector.

An increase in the state variables signifies an increase in the number of evaluations for the different alternatives at each stage. This is especially true in the case of tabular computations. Since most dynamic programming computations are done on the digital computers, such an increase in the state variables may tax the computer memory and increase the computation time. This problem is known as the **problem of dimensionality** (or the **curse of dimensionality**, as it is called by R. Bellman), and it presents a serious obstacle in solving medium- and large-sized dynamic programming problems.

To illustrate the concept of multidimensional states, consider the following example.

Example 10.4-1. In a house-to-house advertising campaign, D dollars and M labor-hours are available for conducting the canvass in N districts. The net return from the jth district is estimated by $R_j(d_j, m_j)$, where d_j is the amount of dollars spent and m_j is the amount of labor hours devoted to the district. The objective is to determine d_j and m_j for each district j in order to maximize the total returns without exceeding available dollars and labor hours.

In the backward recursive equation, the states of the system at any stage j should be described by the amount of capital and labor hours that are allocated to stages j, $j+1, \ldots, N$. This means that the states should be represented by a two-dimensional vector (D_j, M_j), where D_j and M_j represent the capital and labor hours available at stage j for stages $j, j+1, \ldots, N$. Let $f_j(D_j, M_j)$ be the optimal return for stages j through N inclusive given D_j and M_j. The recursive equation is thus given by

$$f_N(D_N, M_N) = \max_{\substack{0 \le d_N \le D_N \\ 0 \le m_N \le M_N}} \{R_N(d_N, m_N)\}$$

$$f_j(D_j, M_j) = \max_{\substack{0 \le d_j \le D_j \\ 0 \le m_j \le M_j}} \{R_j(d_j, m_j) + f_{j+1}(D_j - d_j, M_j - m_j)\}, \qquad j = 1, 2, \ldots, N-1$$

The computations of $f_j(D_j, M_j)$ and (d_j^*, m_j^*) become more difficult in this case, since we have to account for all the feasible combinations of d_j and m_j. The computer storage requirements and computation time increase rather rapidly with the number of state variables at each stage. Some ramifications and approximation methods have been explored, however, which may partially compensate for the effect of the increase in the number of state variables [see White (1969)]. The bulk of the computational difficulties still persists, however, and will probably continue to do so irrespective of the tremendous advancement in the capabilities of modern digital computers. ◀

10.5 SOLUTION OF LINEAR PROGRAMS BY DYNAMIC PROGRAMMING

The general linear programming problem

$$\text{maximize } z = c_1 x_1 + c_2 x_2 + \cdots + c_n x_n$$

subject to

$$\begin{aligned}
a_{11}x_1 + a_{12}x_2 + \cdots + a_{1n}x_n &\le b_1 \\
a_{21}x_1 + a_{22}x_2 + \cdots + a_{2n}x_n &\le b_2 \\
\vdots \qquad\qquad\qquad & \quad \vdots \\
a_{m1}x_1 + a_{m2}x_2 + \cdots + a_{mn}x_n &\le b_m \\
x_1, x_2, \ldots, x_n &\ge 0
\end{aligned}$$

can be formulated as a dynamic programming model. Each activity j ($j = 1, 2, \ldots, n$) may be regarded as a stage. The level of activity $x_j (\ge 0)$ represents the alternatives at stage j. Since x_j is continuous, each stage possesses an infinite number of alternatives within the feasible space. For reasons to be stated shortly, it is assumed that all $a_{ij} \geq 0$.

The linear programming problem is an allocation problem. Thus, similar to the examples of Section 10.3, the states may be defined as the amounts of resources to be allocated to the current stage and the succeeding stages. (This will result in a backward recursive equation.) Since there are m resources, the states must be represented by an m-dimensional vector. (In the examples of Section 10.3, each problem has one constraint and hence one state variable.)

Let $(B_{1j}, B_{2j}, \ldots, B_{mj})$ be the states of the system at stage j, that is, the amounts of resources 1, 2, ..., m, allocated to stage $j, j+1, \ldots, n$. Using the backward recursive equation, we let $f_j(B_{1j}, B_{2j}, \ldots, B_{mj})$ be the optimum value of the objective function for stages (activities) $j, j+1, \ldots, n$ given the states $B_{1j}, \ldots, B_{mj}$. Thus

$$f_n(B_{1n}, B_{2n}, \ldots, B_{mn}) = \max_{\substack{0 \leq a_{in}x_n \leq B_{in} \\ i=1,2,\ldots,m}} \{c_n x_n\}$$

$$f_j(B_{1j}, B_{2j}, \ldots, B_{mj}) = \max_{\substack{0 \leq a_{ij}x_j \leq B_{ij} \\ i=1,\ldots,m}} \{c_j x_j + f_{j+1}(B_{1j} - a_{1j}x_j, \ldots, B_{mj} - a_{mj}x_j)\}, \quad j = 1, 2, \ldots, n-1$$

where $0 \leq B_{ij} \leq b_i$ for all i and j.

Example 10.5-1. Consider the following linear programming problem:

$$\text{maximize } z = 2x_1 + 5x_2$$

subject to

$$\begin{aligned} 2x_1 + x_2 &\leq 430 \\ 2x_2 &\leq 460 \\ x_1, x_2 &\geq 0 \end{aligned}$$

Because there are two resources, the states of the equivalent dynamic programming model are described by two variables only. Let (v_j, w_j) describe the states at stage j ($j = 1, 2$). Thus

$$f_2(v_2, w_2) = \max_{\substack{0 \leq x_2 \leq v_2 \\ 0 \leq 2x_2 \leq w_2}} \{5x_2\}$$

Since $x_2 \leq \min\{v_2, w_2/2\}$ and $f_2(x_2 \mid v_2, w_2) = 5x_2$, then

$$f_2(v_2, w_2) = \max_{x_2} f_2(x_2 \mid v_2, w_2) = 5 \min\left(v_2, \frac{w_2}{2}\right)$$

and $x_2^* = \min(v_2, w_2/2)$.

Now

$$\begin{aligned} f_1(v_1, w_1) &= \max_{0 \leq 2x_1 \leq v_1} \{2x_1 + f_2(v_1 - 2x_1, w_1)\} \\ &= \max_{0 \leq 2x_1 \leq v_1} \left\{2x_1 + 5 \min\left(v_1 - 2x_1, \frac{w_1}{2}\right)\right\} \end{aligned}$$

Since this is the last stage, $v_1 = 430$, $w_1 = 460$. Thus $x_1 \le v_1/2 = 215$ and

$$
\begin{aligned}
f_1(x_1 \mid v_1, w_1) &= f_1(x_1 \mid 430, 460) \\
&= 2x_1 + 5 \min\left(430 - 2x_1, \frac{460}{2}\right) \\
&= 2x_1 + \begin{cases} 5(230), & 0 \le x_1 \le 100 \\ 5(430 - 2x_1), & 100 \le x_1 \le 215 \end{cases} \\
&= \begin{cases} 2x_1 + 1150 & 0 \le x_1 \le 100 \\ -8x_1 + 2150, & 100 \le x_1 \le 215 \end{cases}
\end{aligned}
$$

Hence, for the given ranges of x_1,

$$
\begin{aligned}
f_1(v_1, w_1) = f_1(430, 460) &= \max_{x_1}(2x_1 + 1150, \ -8x_1 + 2150) \\
&= 2(100) + 1150 = -8(100) + 2150 = 1350
\end{aligned}
$$

which is achieved at $x_1^* = 100$.

To obtain x_2^*, notice that

$$
\begin{aligned}
v_2 &= v_1 - 2x_1 = 430 - 200 = 230 \\
w_2 &= w_1 - 0 = 460
\end{aligned}
$$

Hence

$$
x_2^* = \min\left(v_2, \frac{w_2}{2}\right) = \min(230, 460/2) = 230
$$

Thus the optimal solution is $z = 1350$, $x_1 = 100$, $x_2 = 230$. ◀

In Example 10.5-1 all the constraint coefficients are nonnegative. If some of the coefficients are negative, then for a constraint of the type ($\le$) it is no longer true that the right-hand side will give the largest value of the state variable. This problem will be more pronounced if the solution happens to be unbounded. The general conclusion then is that dynamic programming is not adequate for solving the general linear programming problem. Perhaps this emphasizes the point that dynamic programming is based on so powerful an optimization principle that it is computationally infeasible for some problems. A case in point is the absence of a general computer code for (even a subclass of) dynamic programming problems.

10.6 SUMMARY

The chapter shows that DP is a procedure designed primarily to enhance the computational efficiency of solving certain mathematical programs by decomposing them into smaller, hence more manageable, problems. We must stress, however, that the principle of optimality provides a well-defined *framework* for solving the problem in stages; but it is "vague" about how each stage should be optimized. In this respect, the principle of optimality is sometimes regarded as being too powerful to be useful in practice; for although a problem can be decomposed properly, a numerical answer still may not be attainable because of the complexity of the optimization process at each stage. We must point out, however, that in spite of this disadvantage, the solution of many problems has been facilitated greatly through the use of DP.

There are several important topics that are not covered in this chapter. Notable among them are methods for reducing dimensionality (or number of state variables), infinite-stage systems, and probabilistic dynamic programming. The last topic is covered in Chapters 14 and 18 as applications of inventory and Markovian decision models. The remaining topics are available in specialized books.

SELECTED REFERENCES

BEIGHTLER, C., D. PHILLIPS, and D. WILDE, *Foundations of Optimization*, 2nd ed., Prentice Hall, Englewood Cliffs, N.J., 1979.

BELLMAN, R., and S. DREYFUS, *Applied Dynamic Programming*, Princeton University Press, Princeton, N.J., 1962.

DENARDO, E., *Dynamic Programming Theory and Applications*, Prentice Hall, Englewood Cliffs, N.J., 1982.

DREYFUS, S., and A. LAW, *The Art and Theory of Dynamic Programming*, Academic Press, New York, 1977.

HADLEY, G., *Nonlinear and Dynamic Programming*, Addison-Wesley, Reading, Mass., 1964.

WHITE, D. J., *Dynamic Programming*, Holden-Day, San Francisco, 1969.

PROBLEMS

Section	Assigned Problems
10.1 and 10.2	10–1 to 10–5
10.3	10–6 to 10–22
10.4	10–23 to 10–25
10.5	10–26, 10–28

☐ **10–1** Consider the capital budgeting problem of Section 10.1. Suppose that plant 3 and plant 1 are renamed as plant 1 and plant 3, respectively, so that the new plant 1 now has the data of old plant 3, and vice versa. Resolve the problem and show that the new designations have no effect on the optimal solution.

☐ **10–2** Consider the capital budgeting example in Section 10.1. Develop the forward DP model associated with cases (a) and (b) and find the optimum solution. Assume that the total available is $8 million.

(a)

	Plant 1		Plant 2		Plant 3	
Proposal	c_1	R_1	c_2	R_2	c_3	R_3
1	3	5	3	4	0	0
2	4	6	4	5	2	3
3	—	—	5	8	3	5
4	—	—	—	—	6	9

(b)

Proposal	Plant 1 c_1	Plant 1 R_1	Plant 2 c_2	Plant 2 R_2	Plant 3 c_3	Plant 3 R_3	Plant 4 c_4	Plant 4 R_4
1	0	0	1	1.5	0	0	0	0
2	3	5	3	5	1	2.1	2	2.8
3	4	7	4	6	—	—	3	3.6

□ **10–3** Formulate Problem 10–2 as a DP model using the backward recursive equation and obtain the solution. Compare the computations with those of Problem 10–2.

□ **10–4** A student must select ten elective courses from four different departments. She must choose at least one course from each department. Her objective is to "allocate" the ten courses to the four departments so as to maximize her "knowledge" in the four fields. She realizes that if she takes over a certain number of courses in one department, her knowledge about the subject will not increase appreciably either because the material becomes too complicated for her comprehension or because the courses repeat themselves. She thus measures her learning ability as a function of the number of courses she takes in each department on a 100-point scale and produces the following chart. (It is assumed that the course groupings satisfy the prerequisites for each department.) Formulate the problem as a dynamic programming model using both the forward and backward recursive equations.

	Number of Courses									
Department	1	2	3	4	5	6	7	8	9	10
I	25	50	60	80	100	100	100	100	100	100
II	20	70	90	100	100	100	100	100	100	100
III	40	60	80	100	100	100	100	100	100	100
IV	10	20	30	40	50	60	70	80	90	100

□ **10–5** Solve Problem 10–4 by using the forward and backward recursive equations of DP. Define the states and their feasible range of values for each stage.

□ **10–6** Resolve Example 10.3-1 by using the following data.

(a) $w_1 = 4, v_1 = 70; w_2 = 1, v_2 = 20; w_3 = 2, v_3 = 40; W = 6.$

(b) $w_1 = 1, v_1 = 30; w_2 = 2, v_2 = 60; w_3 = 3, v_3 = 80; W = 4.$

□ **10–7** In Example 10.3-2, suppose that there are four main components with the following data.

m_i	$i = 1$ R	$i = 1$ c	$i = 2$ R	$i = 2$ c	$i = 3$ R	$i = 3$ c	$i = 4$ R	$i = 4$ c
1	.8	3	.9	3	.6	2	.7	4
2	.82	5	—	—	.8	4	.75	5
3	—	—	—	—	—	—	.95	7

Let $C = 15$. Define the feasible range for the values of the state variables at each of the four stages. Then find the optimal solution.

☐ **10–8** Formulate and solve the forward DP model of the following resource allocation problem:

$$\text{maximize } z = 2x_1 + 3x_2 + 4x_3$$

subject to

$$2x_1 + 2x_2 + 3x_3 \leq 4$$
$$x_1, x_2, x_3 \geq 0 \text{ and integers}$$

☐ **10–9** Solve Problem 10–8 by the DP backward recursive equation.

☐ **10–10** Solve the work force size problem of Example 10.3-4 assuming that the minimum requirements b_j and the initial work force size y_0 are given as follows:

(a) $b_1 = 6, b_2 = 5, b_3 = 3, b_4 = 6, b_5 = 8$, and $y_0 = 5$.
(b) $b_1 = 8, b_2 = 4, b_3 = 7, b_4 = 8, b_5 = 2$, and $y_0 = 6$.

☐ **10–11 (Shortest-Route Problem).** The network given in Figure 10-5 gives different routes for reaching city B from city A passing through a number of other cities. The lengths of the individual routes are shown on the arrows. It is required to determine the shortest route from A to B. Formulate the problem as a dynamic programming model. Explicitly define the stages, states, and return function; then find the optimal solution.

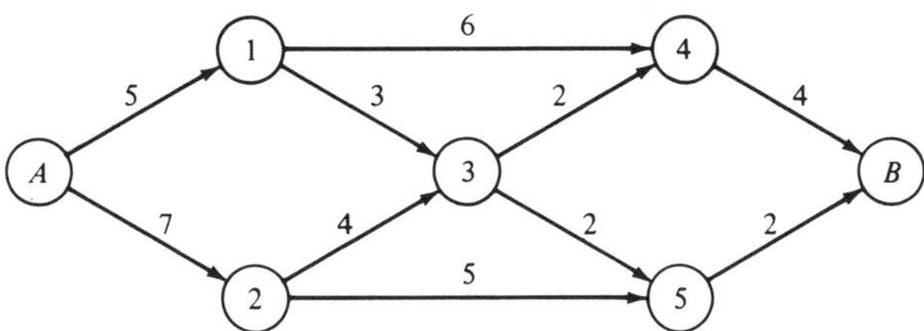

Figure 10-5

☐ **10–12** Formulate the following problem as a dynamic programming model:

$$\text{maximize } z = (x_1 + 2)^2 + x_2 x_3 + (x_4 - 5)^2$$

subject to

$$x_1 + x_2 + x_3 + x_4 \leq 5$$
$$x_i \text{ nonnegative integer}$$

Find the optimum solution. What is the optimum solution if the right-hand side of the constraint is 3 instead of 5?

☐ **10–13** Solve the following problem by dynamic programming:

$$\text{minimize } \sum_{i=1}^{10} y_i^2$$

subject to

$$\prod_{i=1}^{10} y_i = 8, \quad y_i > 0$$

☐ **10–14** An equipment rental business is considering the investment of an initial capital C in buying two types of equipment. If x is the amount of money invested in type I, the corresponding profit at the end of the first year is $g_1(x)$, and the profit from type II is $g_2(C - x)$. The company's policy is to salvage equipment after one year. The salvage values for type I and type II at period t are $p_t x$ and $q_t(C - x)$, where $0 < p_t < 1$ and $0 < q_t < 1$. At the end of each year the company reinvests the returns from salvaging the equipment. This is repeated over the next N years, with the same return functions g_1 and g_2 holding for every year.

Formulate the problem as a dynamic programming model by the backward method, then solve using the following data for $N = 5$.

t	1	2	3	4	5
p_t	.5	.9	.4	.5	.9
q_t	.6	.1	.5	.7	.5

Assume that $C = \$10{,}000$, $g_1(z) = .5z$, and $g_2(z) = .7z$.

☐ **10–15** Solve Problem 10–14 if in addition to the return from salvaging equipment 80% of the profit in period t is reinvested in period $t + 1$.

☐ **10–16** Solve Problem 10–14 for $N = 3$, $g_1(z) = .6(z - 1)^2$, $g_2(z) = .5z^2$, and $C = \$10{,}000$. Use the values of p_t and q_t for the first three periods in Problem 10–14.

☐ **10–17** Formulate the dynamic recursive equation for the problem:

$$\min_{\substack{y_i \\ i=1,2,\ldots,n}} \{\max[f(y_1), f(y_2), \ldots, f(y_n)]\}$$

subject to

$$\sum_{i=1}^{n} y_i = C, \qquad y_i \geq 0$$

Then solve, assuming that $n = 3$, $C = 10$, and

$$\begin{aligned} f(y_1) &= y_1 + 5 \\ f(y_2) &= 5y_2 + 3 \\ f(y_3) &= y_3 - 2 \end{aligned}$$

☐ **10–18** Solve Example 10.3-5 by the forward and backward formulations. Assume that $x_0 = 2$, $N = 3$, and $p_1 = 16$, $p_2 = 4$, $p_3 = 4$.

☐ **10–19** An investor decides to invest in a savings account. At the end of each year a decision is made as to how much to spend and how much to reinvest. The return on investment is α ($\alpha > 1$) and the satisfaction derived from spending an amount y_i in period i is measured by $g(y_i)$. Formulate the problem as a dynamic programming model by the forward and backward formulations. Assuming that the initial capital available is C and $g(y_i) = by_i$, where b is a constant, find the optimal solution to the problem.

□ **10–20** Solve Problem 10–19 assuming $g(y_i) = b\sqrt{y_i}$.

□ **10–21** Consider the following equipment replacement problem over N years. The new equipment costs C dollars and its salvage value T years hence is $S(T) = N - T$ for $N \geq T$ and zero for $N < T$. The annual profit for T-year-old equipment is $P(T) = N^2 - T^2$, for $N \geq T$, and zero otherwise. Formulate the problem as a dynamic programming model, then solve, assuming that $N = 3$, $C = 10$, and the present equipment is 2 years old.

□ **10–22** Solve Problem 10–21 assuming that $P(T) = N/(1 + T)$, $C = 6$, $N = 4$, and the equipment is 1 year old.

□ **10–23** Consider the cargo-loading problem presented in Example 10.3-1. Suppose that in addition to the weight limitation W, there is also the volume limitation V. Formulate the problem as a dynamic programming model given v_i is the volume per unit of item i. The remaining information is the same as in Example 10.3-1.

□ **10–24** Consider the transportation problem (Chapter 6) with m sources and n destinations. Let a_i be the amount available at source i, $i = 1, 2, \ldots, m$, and let b_j be the amount demanded at destination j, $j = 1, 2, \ldots, n$. If the cost of transporting x_{ij} units from source i to destination j is $h_{ij}(x_{ij})$, formulate the problem as a dynamic programming model.

□ **10–25** Solve the following linear programming problem by dynamic programming. Assume all the variables to be nonnegative integers.

$$\text{Maximize } z = 8x_1 + 7x_2$$

subject to

$$2x_2 + x_2 \leq 8$$
$$5x_1 + 2x_2 \leq 15$$
$$x_1 \text{ and } x_2 \text{ nonnegative integers}$$

□ **10–26** Solve the following linear programming problem using dynamic programming:

$$\text{maximize } z = 4x_1 + 14x_2$$

subject to

$$2x_1 + 7x_2 \leq 21$$
$$7x_1 + 2x_2 \leq 21$$
$$x_1, x_2 \geq 0$$

□ **10–27** Solve the following nonlinear problem by dynamic programming:

$$\text{maximize } z = 7x_1^2 + 6x_1 + 5x_2^2$$

subject to

$$x_1 + 2x_2 \leq 10$$
$$x_1 - 3x_2 \leq 9$$
$$x_1, x_2 \geq 0$$

Because the second constraint involves a negative coefficient, some computational difficulty is expected if the backward dynamic programming formulation is used. Show that in this example such a difficulty can be eliminated by using the forward formulation (i.e., starting with x_1, whose constraint coefficients are positive).

□ **10–28** A retail store handles a particular item that has been exhibiting fluctuating purchasing and sales prices. On December 1 of each year, the store manager develops a plan for the upcoming year for the acquisition and sales of the item. The item can be ordered during the month for use at the start of the following month. Although there is no specific limit on the size of the order that can be placed each month, the policy of the store stipulates that the maximum capital tied to the inventory of the item at any one time may never exceed $15,000. The store manager has compiled the following list for the purchasing and sales prices of the item over the next 12 months:

Month	Unit Purchasing Price	Unit Sales Price
1	$30	$33
2	31	33
3	33	37
4	32	35
5	32	34
6	32	31
7	31	31
8	30	31
9	31	32
10	31	34
11	30	35
12	30	34

The stock level as of December 31 is 200 units.

How should the item be handled over the next year?

PART II

PROBABILISTIC MODELS

THIS PART INCLUDES CHAPTERS 11 THROUGH 18. Chapter 11 deals with data representation in OR, including histogramming and fitting raw data to theoretical distributions and forecasting future trends. Chapter 12 presents decision theory and games. PERT-CPM techniques are detailed in Chapter 13. Chapter 14 covers traditional inventory models as well as MRP and JIT systems. Basic queueing models and their use within the context of decision models are presented in Chapters 15 and 16. Chapter 17 on simulation is oriented toward the actual development of simulation models using the SIMNET II language. In Chapter 18 we present the Markovian decision process.

The materials in this part require only a first course in mathematical statistics and calculus. Additional prerequisites for Markovian decision processes are presented in the chapter's appendix. Dynamic programming (Chapter 10) is an important prerequisite for some inventory models in Chapter 14 and the Markovian decision process in Chapter 18. Linear programming is used in Chapters 12 (games theory), Chapter 14 (production and inventory control), and Chapter 18. However, the associated sections may be skipped without loss of continuity.

Chapter 11

Data Representation in Operations Research

When we study inventory in Chapter 14, we will be dealing with deterministic versus probabilistic and stationary versus nonstationary demands. In the development of queueing models in Chapter 15, we will use certain probability distributions, such as Poisson arrivals and exponential service times. How does the operations research analyst decide on the nature of such input data in real situations? The answer lies in analyzing the raw data of the system under study.

In this chapter we present statistical techniques designed to transform raw data into forms that are suitable for analytic use in OR models. These techniques deal with estimation of probability distribution and with forecasting methods. Although the details of these techniques are covered generically in most statistics books, our presentation differs in that it explains the procedures from the standpoint of their use in operations research models, thus providing an appreciation of how these models are implemented in practice.

11.1 NATURE OF DATA IN OR

From the standpoint of the development of OR models, input data may fall into one of two broad categories:

1. **Deterministic**, in which data are assumed to be known with certainty.
2. **Probabilistic**, where data exhibit *random* variations.

OR models dealing with deterministic data are usually much simpler than those involving probabilistic data. Unfortunately, in real life, most situations exhibit random variations. However, if the "degree" of randomness is not "severe," it may be possible to use deterministic approximation adequately. In this section we show how the probabilistic nature of data may be assessed using appropriate statistics. These statistics may then be the basis for justifying the use of deterministic approximation.

11.1.1 MEAN AND VARIANCE OF A DATA SET

The first step toward characterizing the nature of a set of raw data is to compute their mean and variance. The **mean** or **average** value is a representation of the *central tendency* of the data whereas the **variance** is a measure of the *spread* or *random variation* around the mean value. In essence, the mean value is what we use as representation of data if we decide to approximate it by a constant (deterministic) value. On the other hand, the variance is a measure of the *degree of uncertainty*, in the sense that the larger the value of the variance, the more inclined we will be to think of the variable as being probabilistic rather than deterministic.

The formulas for computing the mean and variance differ depending on the type of variable with which we are dealing. Essentially, in operations research, we deal with two types of statistical variables:

1. Observation based.
2. Time based.

Examples of **observation-based** variables include waiting time in a queue, size of an inventory order, and time between arrivals at a service facility. **Time-based** variables are characterized by the fact that each value is a function of time. For example, when we speak of the size of a queue, we must associate with it the time period over which the given queue size is maintained.

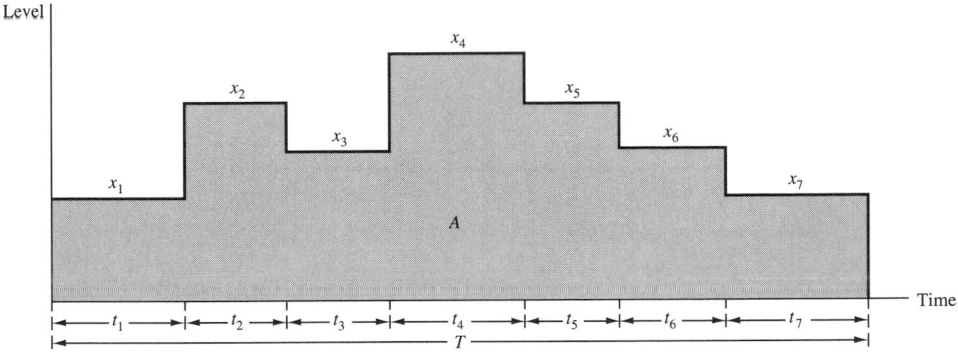

Figure 11-1

Let $x_1, x_2, \ldots, x_n$ be a set of n data points of an observation-based variable; then the mean $\bar{x}$ and variance S^2 are computed as follows:

$$\bar{x} = \frac{\sum_{i=1}^{n} x_i}{n}$$

$$S^2 = \frac{\sum_{i=1}^{n}(x_i - \bar{x})^2}{n-1} = \frac{\sum_{i=1}^{n} x_i^2 - n\bar{x}^2}{n-1}$$

(observation-based variable)

As for the time-based variable, the computation of the mean and variance requires expressing the variation in the variable as a function of time. Figure 11-1 gives a typical example of the variation of a time-based variable over a period of T time units. In general, let x_i be the value of the time-based variable over a time period t_i ($i = 1, 2, \ldots, n$) and assume that $T = \sum_{i=1}^{n} t_i$. Then the mean and variance are computed as

$$\bar{x} = \frac{\sum_{i=1}^{n} x_i t_i}{T} = \frac{A}{T}$$

$$S^2 = \frac{\sum_{i=1}^{n}(x_i - \bar{x})^2 t_i}{T} = \frac{\sum_{i=1}^{n} x_i^2 t_i}{T} - \bar{x}^2$$

(time-based variable)

Informally speaking, we say that a variable can be regarded as being (approximately) deterministic if its standard deviation S (the square root of the variance) is "reasonably" small compared to its mean value $\bar{x}$. In such a case the variable will assume the "deterministic" value $\bar{x}$. On the other hand, if the standard deviation is too large to be ignored, we must conclude that the variable x_i is drawn from a random population. Strictly speaking, we should use a proper statistical procedure that tests the hypothesis that the standard deviation of the population from which the sample is drawn is zero. In a practical sense, however, the analyst may be able to judge the nature of the data by examining the mean and variance. This argument is plausible when the sample size n is sufficiently large.

Example 11.1-1. Consider the set of data in Table 11-1, which represents the service time (in minutes) for a sample of 60 customers. The nature of the variable indicates that it is observation based.

Table 11-1

.7	.4	3.4	4.8	2.0	1.0	5.5	6.2	1.2	4.4
1.5	2.4	3.4	6.4	3.7	4.8	2.5	5.5	.3	8.7
2.7	.4	2.2	2.4	.5	1.7	9.3	8.0	4.7	5.9
.7	1.6	5.2	.6	.9	3.9	3.3	.2	.2	4.9
9.6	1.9	9.1	1.3	10.6	3.0	.3	2.9	2.9	4.8
8.7	2.4	7.2	1.5	7.9	11.7	6.3	3.8	6.9	5.3

From these data we have

$$\sum_{j=1}^{60} x_j = 236.2 \quad \sum_{j=1}^{60} x_j^2 = 1455.56$$

Hence we get

$$\bar{x} = \frac{236.2}{60} = 3.937$$

$$S^2 = \frac{1455.56 - 60 \times 3.937^2}{60 - 1} = 8.91$$

◀

Example 11.1-2. Consider the data in Table 11-2 that represent the change in queue length, q, with time, t, in minutes. L_q is a time-based variable.

Table 11-2

Time, t	Queue Length, L_q
0	0
5.5	1
12	2
13	1
16	0
24	2
25	0

For the purpose of computing the mean and variance, the data in Table 11-2 can be summarized as

i	Time Interval, t_i	L_{qi}
1	5.5	0
2	6.5	1
3	1.0	2
4	3.0	1
5	8.0	0
6	1.0	2

We thus get

$$T = 25 \text{ minutes}$$

$$A = \sum_{i=1}^{6} t_i L_{qi} = 13.5$$

$$\sum_{i=1}^{6} t_i L_{qi}^2 = 17.5$$

The mean and variance are then computed as

$$\bar{L}_q = \frac{13.5}{25} = .54 \text{ customer}$$

$$S = \sqrt{\frac{17.5}{25} - .54^2} = .639 \text{ customer}$$

The value of the standard deviation S is larger than the mean $\bar{L}_q$. Hence it is not advisable in this case to assume that L_q is (approximately) deterministic. ◀

In some models a knowledge of $\bar{x}$ and S^2 may be sufficient to complete the analysis of the model (see, e.g., the P-K queueing model in Section 15.6). In other situations it may be necessary to estimate the probability distribution associated with x_i before the model can be analyzed. Most probabilistic inventory models (Chapter 14) and many queueing models (Chapter 15) fall into this category. In the next section we provide procedures for estimating probability distributions based on raw data.

11.1.2 EMPIRICAL PROBABILITY DISTRIBUTIONS

Although raw data may give us information about each individual observation, they do not give a descriptive interpretation of the nature of the data. The mean and variance computed in Section 11.1.1 provide the simplest forms of a descriptive representation of raw data. A more apt way of summarizing raw data is to use frequency histograms. A **frequency histogram** is constructed by dividing range of the raw data values into nonoverlapping intervals. Given the boundaries of interval i (I_{i-1}, I_i), the frequency in the ith interval is determined as the count (or tally) of all raw data values, x, that fall in the range $I_{i-1} \leq x \leq I_i$. The following two examples illustrate the procedure for the observation-based and time-based variables.

Example 11.1-3 (Observation-Based Histogram). Consider the data in Table 11-1. Table 11-3 provides the frequency count for the given data using intervals of width 1 minute each. It is important to notice that the selection of the interval width is a crucial factor in capturing the shape of the empirical distribution. Although there are no hard rules for determining the interval width, a general rule of thumb is to use between 10 and 20 intervals to cover the range of the raw data. In practice it may be necessary to try different interval widths before a proper selection is made. (The interactive capability of TORA should prove useful in this regard.)

The relative frequency, f_i, in Table 11-3 is summarized graphically in Figure 11-2. The *cumulative* relative frequency, F_i, for the same data is shown in Figure 11-3.

Table 11-3

Interval	Observations Tally	Observed Frequency, n_i	Relative Frequency, f_i	Cumulative Relative Frequency, F_i
[0, 1)	~~||||~~ ~~||||~~ |	11	.1833	.1833
[1, 2)	~~||||~~ |||	8	.1333	.3166
[2, 3)	~~||||~~ ||||	9	.1500	.4666
[3, 4)	~~||||~~ ||	7	.1167	.5833
[4, 5)	~~||||~~ |	6	.1000	.6833
[5, 6)	~~||||~~	5	.0833	.7666
[6, 7)	||||	4	.0667	.8333
[7, 8)	||	2	.0333	.8666
[8, 9)	|||	3	.0500	.9166
[9, 10)	|||	3	.0500	.9666
[10, 11)	|	1	.0167	.9833
[11, 12)	|	1	.0167	1.0000
	Totals	60	1.0000	

Note that in continuous variables, each interval is replaced by its midpoint. We can then use linear interpolation for approximating intermediate values.

The resulting relative frequency histograms provide the so-called **empirical distributions**. These distributions provide more descriptive information about the population from which the sample of raw data is taken. In particular, we can now

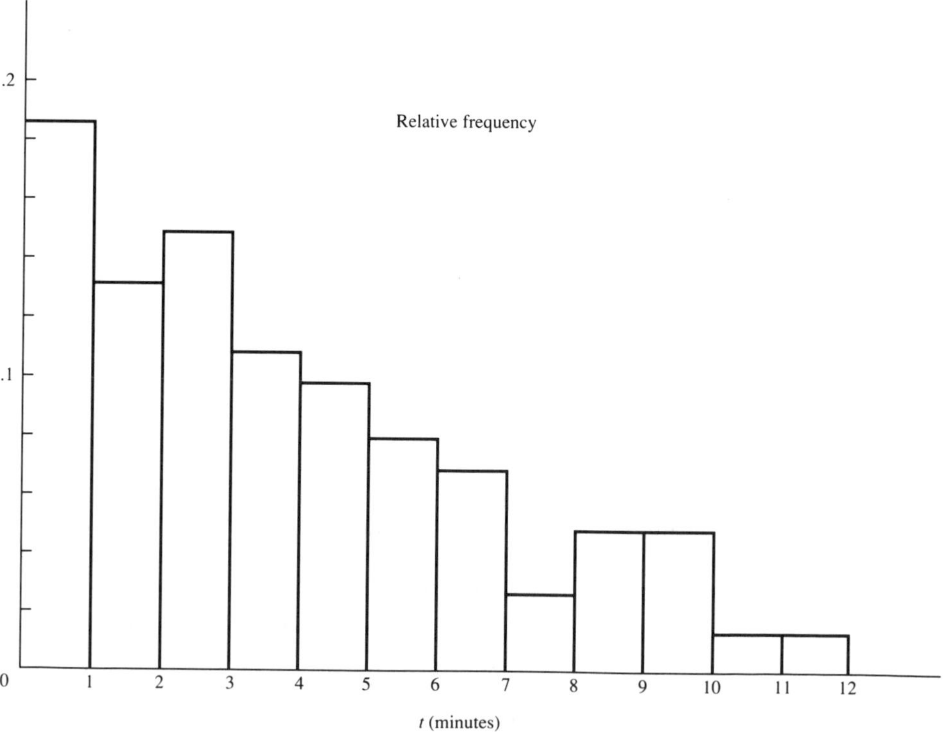

Figure 11-2

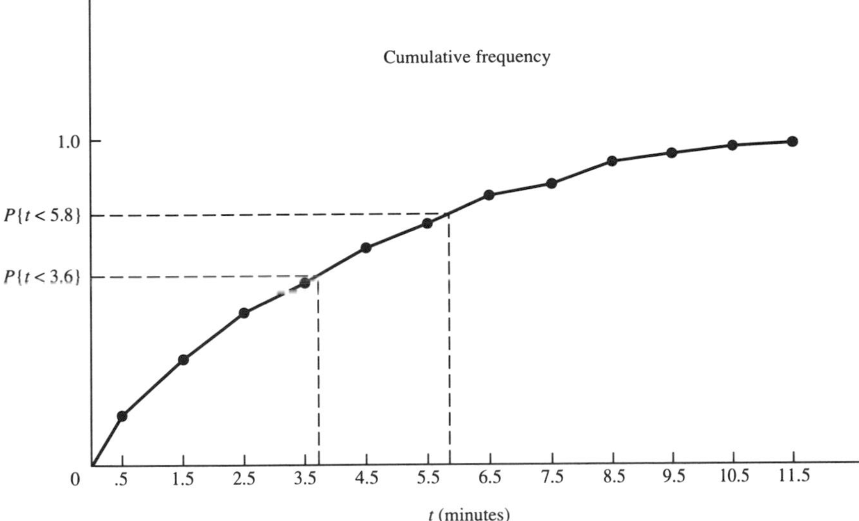

Figure 11-3

draw probability conclusions about the population. As an illustration, the probability that the service time lies between 3.6 and 5.8 minutes is defined as

$$P\{3.6 < t < 5.8\} = P\{t < 5.8\} - P\{t < 3.6\}$$

Both $P\{t < 5.8\}$ and $P\{t < 3.6\}$ can be estimated by linear interpolation as shown in Figure 11-3. ◀

Although useful descriptive information can be drawn from empirical distributions, the format of such distributions may not be suitable for direct use with operations research models. For example, a number of queueing models (Chapter 16) are developed based on the assumption that interarrival and service times are exponential. This means that such models cannot be implemented unless we can verify that the empirical distributions satisfy the exponential assumptions. In the next section we provide the details of the statistical procedure called **goodness of fit**, which is designed to test the hypothesis that empirical distributions are drawn from given theoretical distributions.

Example 11.1-4 (Time-Based Histogram). Consider the data in Table 11-2, representing the time-based variable L_q. In this case the observed frequency is obtained by weighting each L_q data point with the length of time the associated value is maintained. For example, $L_q = 0$ is maintained for the length of time $5.5 + 8 = 13.5$ minutes. The following table summarizes the resulting time-based histogram.

L_q	Weighted Frequency, n_i	Relative Frequency, F_i
0	$5.5 + 8 = 13.5$	.54
1	$6.5 + 3 = 9.5$	.38
2	$1.0 + 1.0 = 2.0$	.08
Totals	25.0	1.00

◀

11.1.3 GOODNESS-OF-FIT TESTS

A quick way to check whether a set of raw data fits a given theoretical distribution is to compare graphically the cumulative empirical distribution with the corresponding cumulative density function of the proposed theoretical distribution. If the two functions do not show excessive deviation, there is a good chance that the theoretical distribution fits the raw data.

To illustrate this procedure, consider the empirical distribution in Figure 11-3. Suppose that we wish to test whether the data are drawn from an exponential distribution. The first task ahead of us is to specify the hypothesized theoretical distribution. Since $\bar{x} = 3.937$ minutes, the proposed exponential distribution is given as

$$f(t) = \frac{1}{3.937} e^{-t/3.937} = .254e^{-.254t}, \qquad t > 0$$

and the associated cumulative density function is computed as

$$F(T) = \int_0^T f(t)\, dt = 1 - e^{-.254T}, \qquad T > 0$$

Figure 11-4 compares $F(T)$ and the empirical cumulative distribution of Figure 11-3. A cursory examination of the graph suggests that the exponential distribution may yield a reasonable fit. Actually, the idea of comparing the empirical and theoretical distributions is the basis for the **Kolmogrov–Smirnov (K–S) test**. This test, which is applicable only to continuous random variables, utilizes a statistic for accepting or rejecting the hypothesized distribution at a specified significance level.

Another statistical test, which applies to both discrete and continuous random variables, is the **chi-square test**. The test is based on comparing the probability density functions, rather than the cumulative density functions as in the K–S test. The first step in the chi-square procedure is to construct a frequency histogram as shown in Section 11.1.2. By plotting the relative frequency histogram, we can visually decide which of the known theoretical density functions best fits the histogrammed data. For example, the histogram in Figure 11-2 appears to resemble an exponential density function.

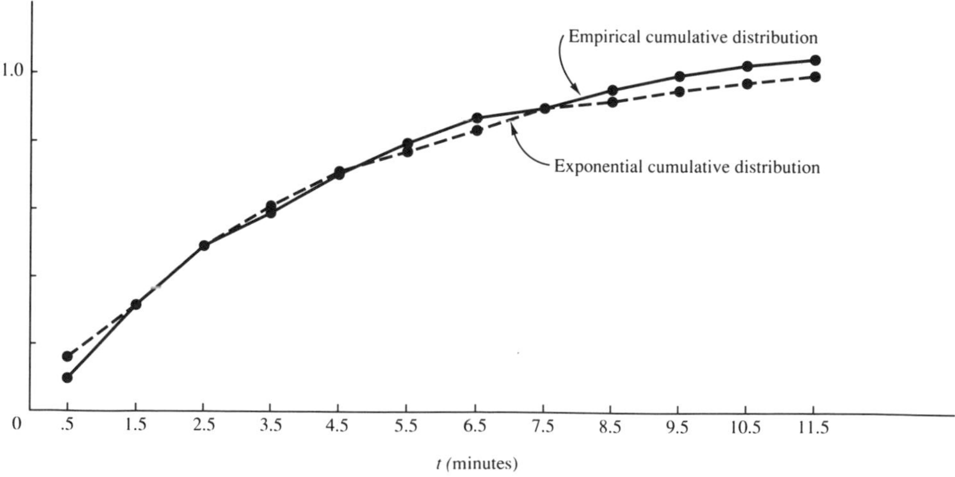

Figure 11-4

The chi-square test is based on measuring the "amount" of deviation between the empirical and the theoretical density functions. To accomplish this task, let $[I_{i-1}, I_i]$ represent the boundaries of interval i as defined in the empirical distribution and assume that $f(t)$ is the hypothesized theoretical density function. Given a sample of raw data of size n, the theoretical frequency associated with interval i is then computed as

$$n_i = n \int_{I_{i-1}}^{I_i} f(t)\, dt, \qquad i = 1, 2, \ldots, m$$

where m is the number of cells used in constructing the empirical density function.

Given n_i as computed above and assuming that O_i is the observed empirical frequency in cell i, a measure of the deviation between the empirical and observed frequencies is computed as

$$\chi^2 = \sum_{i=1}^{m} \frac{(O_i - n_i)^2}{n_i}$$

where χ^2 tends to be asymptotically chi-square as the number of intervals $m \to \infty$. The number of degrees of freedom of the chi-square is $m - k - 1$, where k is the number of parameters that are estimated from the raw data for use in defining the theoretical distribution. For example, in order to use the exponential as the hypothesized theoretical distribution corresponding to the empirical histogram in Figure 11-2, it is necessary to estimate the mean value of the exponential random variable from the raw data. This means that $k = 1$ in the case of the exponential distribution.

Letting $\chi^2_{m-k-1,\,1-\alpha}$ be the chi-square value for $m - k - 1$ degrees of freedom and α level of significance, the null hypothesis stating that the observed raw data are drawn from the theoretical distribution $f(t)$ is accepted if $\chi^2 < \chi^2_{m-k-1,\,1-\alpha}$; otherwise, the hypothesis is rejected.

Example 11.1-5. We apply the chi-square test to the empirical density function in Figure 11-2. The null hypothesis is an exponential distribution. The mean of the exponential distribution is estimated from the data in Table 11-3 as

$$\begin{aligned}\bar{t} &= \sum_{i=1}^{12} \bar{t}_i f_i \\ &= .5 \times .1833 + 1.5 \times .1333 + 2.5 \times .15 + \cdots + 11.5 \times .0167 \\ &= 3.934 \text{ minutes}\end{aligned}$$

Notice that $\bar{t}_i$ is the midpoint of interval i.

Given $\bar{t} = 3.934$, the hypothesized exponential density function is given as

$$\begin{aligned}f(t) &= \frac{1}{3.934} e^{-t/3.934} \\ &= .254e^{-.254t}, \qquad t > 0\end{aligned}$$

For cell i we obtain the theoretical frequency as

$$n_i = n \int_{I_{i-1}}^{I} f(t)\, dt$$

Table 11-4

Interval	Observed Frequency, O_i	Theoretical Frequency, n_i	$\frac{(O_i - n_i)^2}{n_i}$
[0, 1)	11	13.47	.453
[1, 2)	8	10.44	.570
[2, 3)	9	8.10	.100
[3, 4)	7	6.28	.083
[4, 5)	6	4.87	
[5, 6)	5	3.88	
[6, 7)	4	2.93	
[7, 8)	2	2.27	
[8, 9)	3 } 25	1.76 } 21.71	.499
[9, 10)	3	1.37	
[10, 11)	1	1.06	
[11, 12)	1	.82	
[12, ∞)	0	2.75	
Totals	$n = 60$	$n = 60$	χ^2-value = 1.705

Given $n = 60$, it follows that

$$n_i = 60(e^{-.254I_{i-1}} - e^{-.254I_i})$$

Table 11-4 summarizes the computations needed to calculate the χ^2 value. As a rule of thumb, it is recommended that the expected theoretical frequency in any interval be no less than 5. This usually is resolved by combining successive intervals until the rule is satisfied. In Table 11-4 the rule requires forming a single interval with the limits $[4, \infty)$.

The effective number of cells in Table 11-4 is $m = 5$. Since we estimated one parameter from the observed data, the chi-square degrees of freedom equal $5 - 1 - 1 = 3$. If we assume a significance level $\alpha = .05$, the critical value is obtained from the chi-square tables as $\chi^2_{3,.95} = 7.81$. Since the test value (= 1.705) is less than $\chi^2_{3,.95}$, we accept the hypothesis that the sample is drawn from the hypothesized exponential distribution. This means that we can now use the theoretical distribution

$$f(t) = .254e^{-.254t}, \qquad t > 0$$

in place of the empirical distribution of Figure 10-4. ◀

11.1.4 SUMMARY OF COMMON DISTRIBUTIONS

In Section 11.1.3, we explained how the chi-square test is used to fit empirical data into theoretical distributions. In this section we provide a summary of common theoretical distributions. The objective is to familiarize the reader with the shapes and properties of such distributions for the purpose of implementing them in practice.

Let $f(x)$ and $F_x(X)$ be the *probability density function* (pdf) and the *cumulative density function* (CDF) of the random variable x, where x is assumed to be defined over the domain $[a, b]$. The two functions possess the following properties:

$$\int_a^b f(x)\,dx = 1$$

$$F_x(X) = \int_a^X f(x)\,dx, \qquad a < X < b$$

$$\text{mean} = \int_a^b xf(x)\,dx$$

$$\text{variance} = \int_a^b (x - \text{mean})^2 f(x)\,dx$$

We now provide a brief description of common probability distributions.

A. Uniform Distribution

$$f(x) = \frac{1}{b-a}, \qquad a \le x \le b$$

$$F_x(X) = \frac{X-a}{b-a}, \qquad 0 \le X \le b \qquad \text{[uniform, UN(a, b)]}$$

$$\text{mean} = \frac{b+a}{2}$$

$$\text{variance} = \frac{(b-a)^2}{12}$$

The uniform pdf is shown in Figure 11-5.

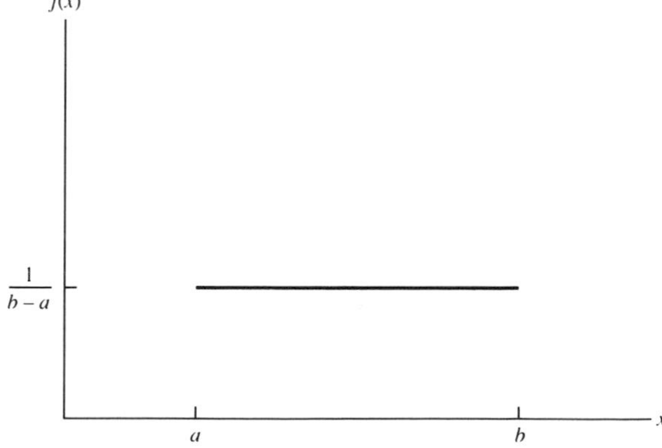

Figure 11-5

B. Negative Exponential Distribution

$$f(x) = \mu e^{-\mu x}, \qquad x > 0, \mu > 0$$
$$F_x(X) = 1 - e^{-\mu X}, \qquad X > 0$$
$$\text{mean} = \frac{1}{\mu} \qquad \text{[exponential, EX}(1/\mu)]$$
$$\text{variance} = \frac{1}{\mu^2}$$

The exponential pdf is given in Figure 11-6. This distribution has important applications in queueing theory (Chapter 15). It is also strongly related to the Erlang and Poisson distributions.

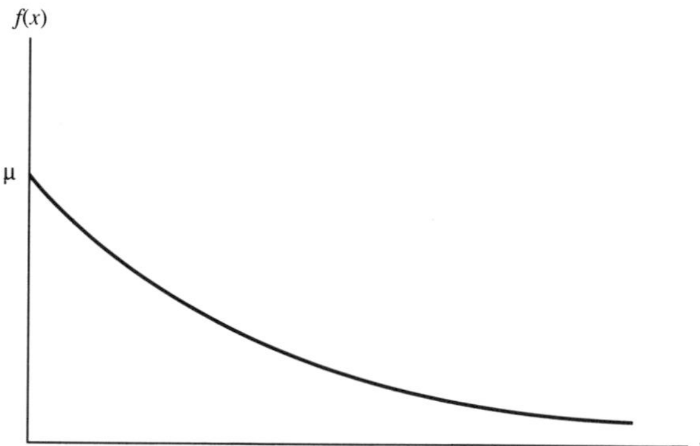

Figure 11-6

C. Erlang and Gamma Distributions

$$f(x) = \frac{\mu}{\Gamma(\alpha)} (\mu x)^{\alpha-1} e^{-\mu x}, \qquad x > 0, \mu > 0, \alpha > 0$$
$$F_x(X) = \begin{cases} 1 - e^{-\mu X} \sum_{i=0}^{\alpha-1} \frac{(\mu X)^i}{i!}, & X > 0, \alpha \text{ integer} \\ \text{no closed form if } \alpha \text{ is noninteger} \end{cases} \qquad \text{[Erlang and gamma, GA}(\alpha, 1/\mu)]$$
$$\text{mean} = \frac{\alpha}{\mu}$$
$$\text{variance} = \frac{\alpha}{\mu^2}$$

If the shape parameter α is a positive integer, the distribution is known as **Erlang**. Otherwise, noninteger values of α define the general **gamma** distribution. The Erlang distribution is the convolution (sum) of α independent and identically distributed exponentials with mean $1/\mu$. Typical gamma/Erlang distributions are illustrated in Figure 11-7.

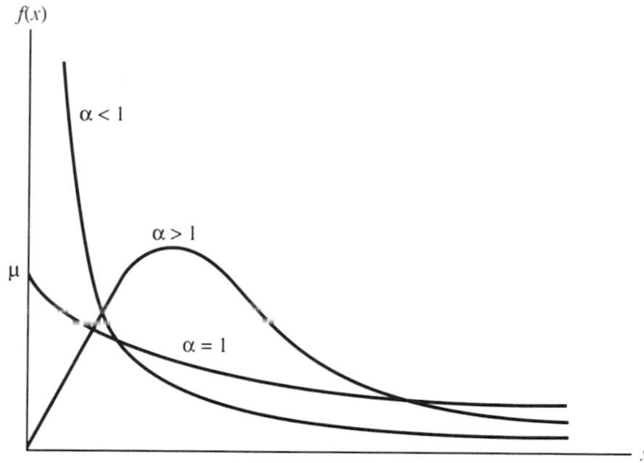

Figure 11-7

D. Normal Distribution

$$f(x) = \frac{1}{\sqrt{2\pi\sigma^2}} e^{-(x-\mu)^2/2\sigma^2}, \qquad -\infty < x < \infty$$

$F_x(X)$ has no closed form [normal, NO(μ, σ)]

mean $= \mu$

variance $= \sigma^2$

Figure 11-8 illustrates the normal pdf. Since $F_x(X)$ has no closed form, normal tables are usually given for the standard case with mean zero and standard deviation 1. The conversion of any normal random variable x to the standard normal is effected by using the formula

$$z = \frac{x - \mu}{\sigma}$$

This conversion allows the use of standard normal tables with any normal random variable.

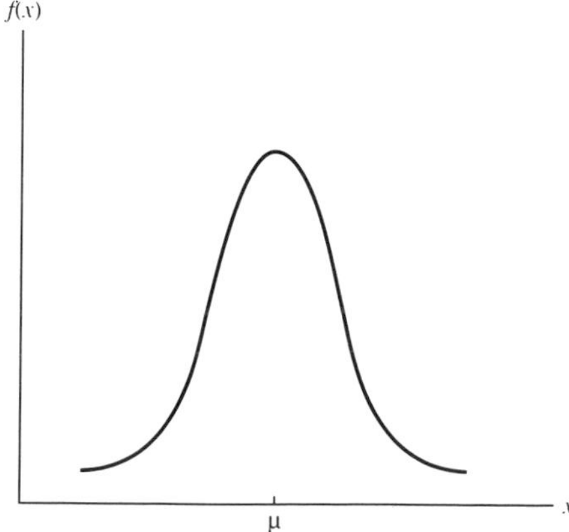

Figure 11-8

E. Lognormal Distribution

$$f(x) = \frac{1}{x\sqrt{2\pi\sigma^2}} e^{-(\ln x - \mu)^2/2\sigma^2}, \qquad x > 0$$

$F_x(X)$ has no closed form [lognormal, LN(μ, σ)]

mean $= e^{\mu + \sigma^2/2}$

variance $= e^{2\mu + \sigma^2}(e^{\sigma^2} - 1)$

Figure 11-9 shows a typical lognormal density function. A random variable x is said to follow a lognormal density function if, and only if, $\ln x$ follows a normal distribution with mean μ and variance σ^2.

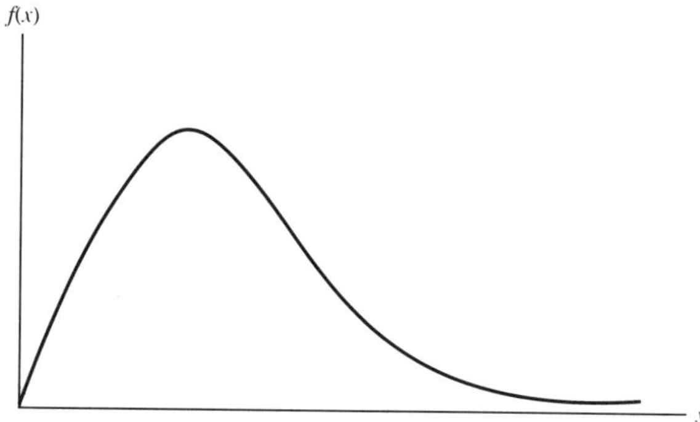

Figure 11-9

F. Weibull Distribution

$$f(x) = \alpha\mu(\mu x)^{\alpha - 1} e^{-(\mu x)^\alpha}, \qquad x > 0, \alpha > 0, \mu > 0$$

$$F_x(X) = 1 - e^{-(\mu X)^\alpha}, \qquad X > 0$$

mean $= \dfrac{1}{\alpha\mu}\Gamma(1/\alpha)$ [Weibull, WE(α, $1/\mu$)]

variance $= \dfrac{1}{\alpha\mu^2}\left[2\Gamma(2/\alpha) - \dfrac{1}{\alpha}\Gamma^2(1/\alpha)\right]$

For $\alpha = 1$, the Weibull density function reduces to the negative exponential. The Weibull density function shown in Figure 11-10 resembles that of the gamma for the various parameters α.

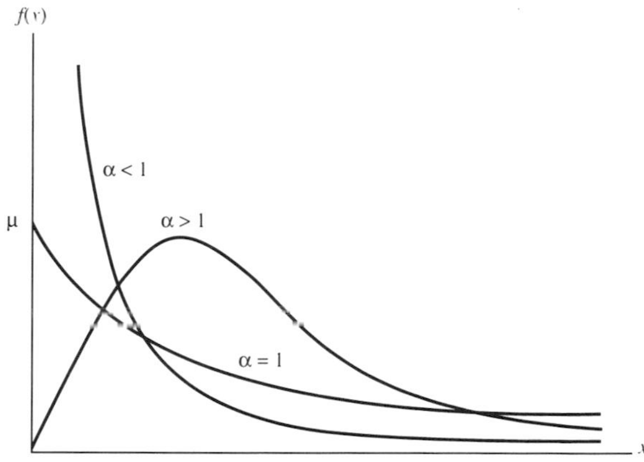

Figure 11-10

G. Beta Distribution

$$f(x) = \frac{\Gamma(\alpha + \beta)}{\Gamma(\alpha)\Gamma(\beta)} x^{\alpha-1}(1-x)^{\beta-1}, \qquad 0 < x < 1$$

$F_x(X)$ has no closed form

[beta, BE(α, β)]

$$\text{mean} = \frac{\alpha}{\alpha + \beta}$$

$$\text{variance} = \frac{\alpha\beta}{(\alpha+\beta)^2(\alpha+\beta+1)}$$

The given beta random variable is defined over the range (0, 1) only. A transformation over any range (a, b) can be effected by using the relationship $y = a + (b - a)x$. Figure 11-11 provides examples of the beta density function for different values of α/β with $\alpha \geq 1$ and $\beta \geq 1$. A variety of shapes can be obtained for other values of α and β.

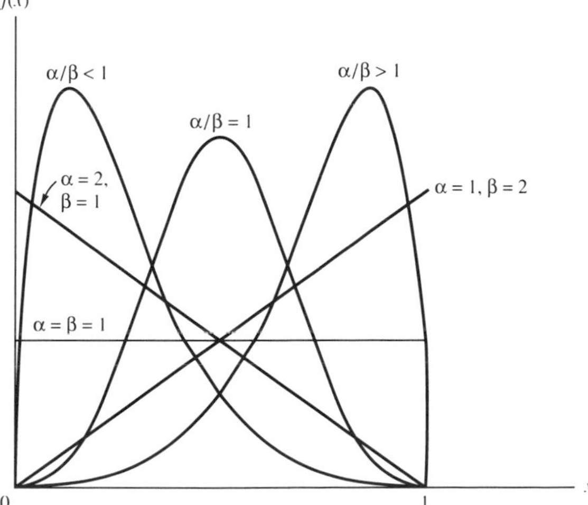

Figure 11-11

H. Triangular Distribution

$$f(x) = \begin{cases} \dfrac{2(x-a)}{(b-a)(c-a)}, & a \le x \le b \\ \dfrac{2(c-x)}{(c-b)(c-a)}, & b \le x \le c \end{cases}$$

$$F_x(X) = \begin{cases} \dfrac{(X-a)^2}{(b-a)(c-a)}, & a \le X \le b \\ 1 - \dfrac{(c-X)^2}{(c-b)(c-a)}, & b \le X \le c \end{cases} \qquad \text{[triangular, TR(a, b, c)]}$$

$$\text{mean} = \frac{a+b+c}{3}$$

$$\text{variance} = \frac{a^2 + b^2 + c^2 - ab - ac - bc}{18}$$

The triangular distribution illustrated in Figure 11-12 is defined once the three parameters a, b, c ($a \le b \le c$) are known. This makes the distribution particularly useful as an initial approximation of situations for which no reliable data are available. As an illustration it is relatively easy to estimate the durations of activities in a project using the three estimates: optimistic (a), most likely (b), and pessimistic (c).

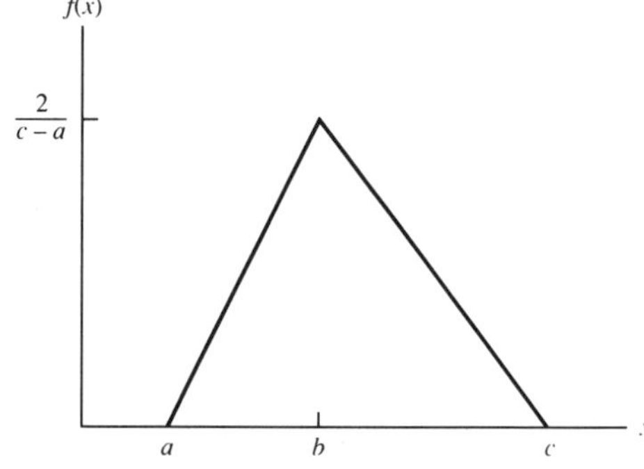

Figure 11-12

I. Poisson Distribution

The Poisson distribution describes a discrete random variable. For this reason we use $p(x)$ and $P_x(X)$ in place of $f(x)$ and $F_x(X)$ used with the continuous distribution.

$$p(x) = \frac{\lambda^x e^{-\lambda}}{x!}, \qquad x = 0, 1, 2, \ldots$$

$P_x(X)$ has no closed form [Poisson, PO(λ)]

mean $= \lambda$

variance $= \lambda$

Figure 11-13 illustrates a typical Poisson distribution. Notice that the range of values extends to infinity. The Poisson is used in queueing models (Chapter 15) to describe the *number* of occurrences (arrivals or departures) in a given time period, in which case λ would represent the number of occurrences per unit time. The Poisson is affiliated with the exponential in the sense that if x represents the *number* of Poisson occurrences in a given time period, then the time interval between *successive* occurrences is exponential. In this case the mean of the Poisson is λ per unit time, whereas that of the exponential is $1/\lambda$ time units.

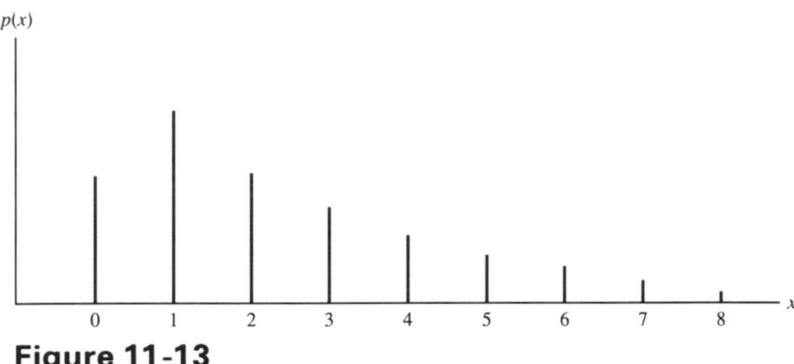

Figure 11-13

J. Other Distributions

The distributions summarized above are the ones that are referenced in coming chapters of this book. There are a number of other distributions that also arise in practice. These additional distributions are summarized in Figure 11-14 in the form of a self-explanatory chart that shows the relationships among different density functions. Other details regarding each distribution may be found in specialized books in the area of probability and statistics.

11.1.5 NONSTATIONARITY OF DATA

The discussion above shows how empirical distributions are used to describe data variability. In real situations, such distributions may change with time. For example, in inventory (Chapter 14), the demand for an item may experience seasonal variations; and in queueing (Chapter 15), the rate of arrival of cars at a busy intersection may vary with the time of the day. Such types of variation lead to the so-called *nonstationary* distributions; that is, probabilistic distributions that vary with time.

Ideally, from the standpoint of OR application, we would be interested in determining how the probability distribution changes with time over a specified planning horizon. However, this goal is not practical. For even if such distributions can be determined adequately, their implementation within available OR models (with the exception of simulation) is practically impossible, mainly because most implementable probabilistic OR models assume that data are stationary.

In view of the complexity of nonstationary models, the only open course of action is to use approximation. In this regard, there are two types of approximation: (1) use of a single distribution as a conservative representation of the behavior of the system over an entire planning horizon, and (2) treatment of data under the condition of *assumed certainty* by ignoring random variations. An example of the first

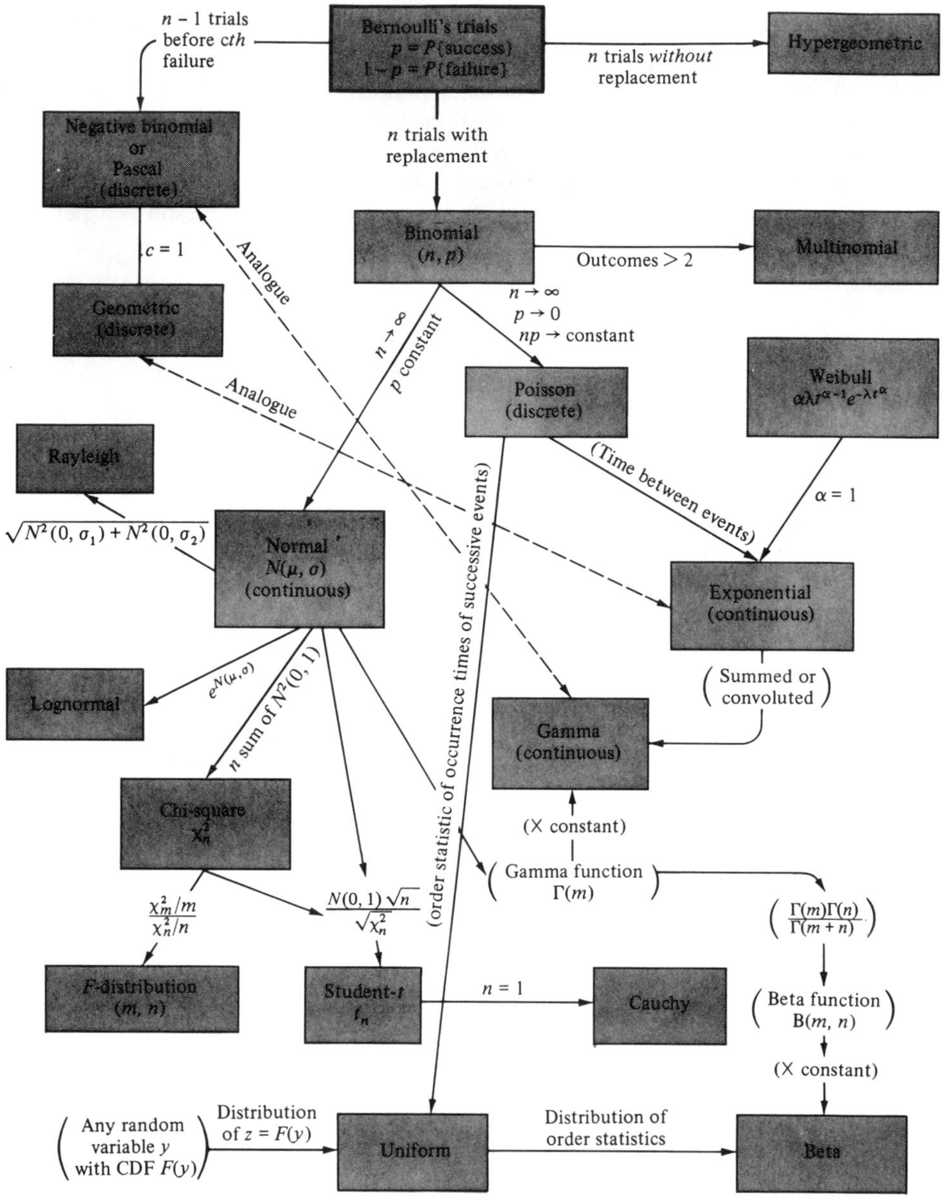

$n - 1$ trials before cth failure

Bernoulli's trials
$p = P\{\text{success}\}$
$1 - p = P\{\text{failure}\}$

n trials *without* replacement

Hypergeometric

Negative binomial or Pascal (discrete)

n trials with replacement

Binomial (n, p)

Outcomes > 2

Multinomial

$c = 1$

Analogue

Geometric (discrete)

$n \to \infty$
$p \to 0$
$np \to$ constant

$n \to \infty$
p constant

Weibull
$\alpha\lambda t^{\alpha-1}e^{-\lambda t^{\alpha}}$

Poisson (discrete)

Analogue

Rayleigh

(Time between events)

$\alpha = 1$

$\sqrt{N^2(0, \sigma_1) + N^2(0, \sigma_2)}$

Normal
$N(\mu, \sigma)$
(continuous)

(order statistic of occurrence times of successive events)

Exponential (continuous)

Summed or convoluted

$e^{N(\mu, \sigma)}$

Lognormal

n sum of $N^2(0, 1)$

Gamma (continuous)

Chi-square
χ_n^2

($\times$ constant)

Gamma function
$\Gamma(m)$

$\dfrac{\chi_m^2/m}{\chi_n^2/n}$

$\dfrac{N(0,1)\sqrt{n}}{\sqrt{\chi_n^2}}$

$\left(\dfrac{\Gamma(m)\Gamma(n)}{\Gamma(m+n)}\right)$

F-distribution (m, n)

Student-t
t_n

$n = 1$

Cauchy

Beta function
$B(m, n)$

($\times$ constant)

Any random variable y with CDF $F(y)$

Distribution of $z = F(y)$

Uniform

Distribution of order statistics

Beta

Source: This chart was developed by Roy E. Lave, Jr., while at Stanford University.

Figure 11-14

approximation is the use of rush-hour traffic at an intersection as a conservative representation of traffic flow. The second type of approximation is demonstrated by replacing the probabilistic distribution of demand at a given point in time by its *mean* value, thus ignoring the uncertainty in the data. This type of approximation is useful when the data exhibit a trend or seasonal variation.

Of the two types of approximation given above, the first type is straightforward, and hence needs no further elaboration. As for the second type, there are various **forecasting methods** that are specially designed to detect the existence of trends or seasonal variations in data, and are particularly suited for analyzing demand data in inventory models. These methods are discussed in the next section.

11.2 FORECASTING TECHNIQUES

Forecasting is based on the use of past data of a variable to predict its future performance. In this regard, past data are usually given in the form of a **time series** that summarizes the changes in the values of the variable as a function of time. A basic assumption in the application of forecasting techniques is that the performance of past data will continue to recur in (at least) the immediate future. Empirical evidence indicates that this assumption is valid in many real situations, particularly when the time series represents a long history of the variable under review.

Figure 11-15 depicts the most common patterns of variations exhibited by time series: (a) random fluctuations with no trend, (b) random fluctuations with a trend, (c) random fluctuations with seasonal pattern, and (d) random fluctuations with a trend and a seasonal pattern. In forecasting, we are less concerned with the random fluctuations than we are with trends and seasonal patterns of variation. Unfortunately, it is not a simple task to differentiate between random variations and the other types (trends and seasonal patterns). The most common procedure for checking the nature of the time series is to plot the historical data against time. By visually examining the resulting graph, we can normally obtain an initial assessment of the nature of the data with regard to random and seasonal and trend fluctuations.

In this section we present three forecasting models: (1) regression analysis, (2) moving average, and (3) exponential smoothing. The first model is particularly suited for detecting trends in data. In the moving average and exponential smooth-

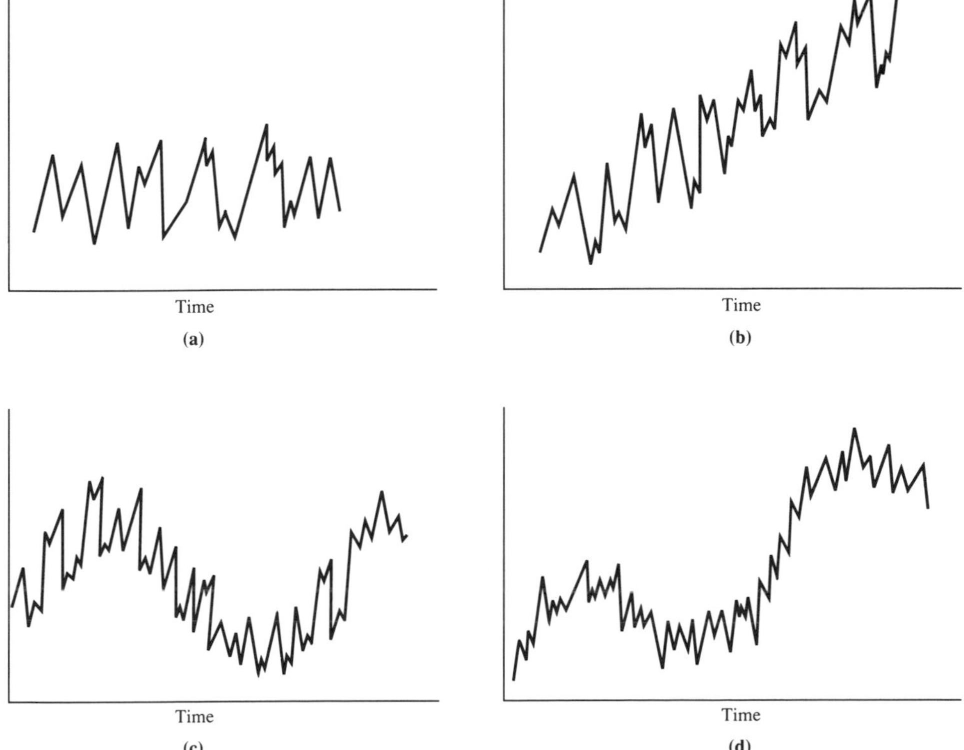

Figure 11-15

ing models, the effect of random fluctuations is masked, which better reveals the trend and/or seasonal variations in the historical data.

11.2.1 REGRESSION MODEL

The simplest form of the regression model assumes a linear trend with time. By letting $\hat{y}$ represent the estimated value of the variable at time t, the linear regression model is given as

$$\hat{y} = a + bt$$

The constants a and b are determined from the raw data based on the **least-squares criterion** as follows. Let the raw data be represented by (y_i, t_i), where y_i is the actual demand at time t_i, $i = 1, 2, \ldots, n$. Define

$$S = \sum_{i=1}^{n} (y_i - a - bt_i)^2$$

as the sum of the square of deviations between the observed and estimated demand values. The values of a and b are determined by solving the necessary conditions for the minimization of S; that is,

$$\frac{\partial S}{\partial a} = -2 \sum_{i=1}^{n} (y_i - a - bt_i) = 0$$

$$\frac{\partial S}{\partial b} = -2 \sum_{i=1}^{n} (y_i - a - bt_i)t_i = 0$$

After some algebraic manipulations, the two equations above yield

$$b = \frac{\sum_{i=1}^{n} y_i t_i - n\bar{y}\bar{t}}{\sum_{i=1}^{n} t_i^2 - n\bar{t}^2}$$

$$a = \bar{y} - b\bar{t}$$

where

$$\bar{t} = \frac{\sum_{i=1}^{n} t_i}{n}$$

$$\bar{y} = \frac{\sum_{i=1}^{n} y_i}{n}$$

The procedure calls for estimating b first, following which a may be determined.

The estimates of a and b given above are valid for any probabilistic distribution of y. However, under certain assumptions (the most important of which is that y_i is normal with a constant standard deviation) a confidence interval can be determined for a and b, and hence for y.

We can test how well $\hat{y}$ fits the raw data by computing the **correlation coefficient** r using the formula

$$r = \frac{\sum_{i=1}^{n} y_i t_i - n\bar{y}\bar{t}}{\sqrt{(\sum_{i=1}^{n} t_i^2 - n\bar{t}^2)(\sum_{i=1}^{n} y_i^2 - n\bar{y}^2)}}$$

where $-1 \leq r \leq 1$. A perfect linear fit occurs when $r = \pm 1$. In general, the closer the value of $|r|$ to 1, the better the linear fit. On the other hand, $r = 0$ signifies that there is a likelihood that y and t are independent. It is important to note, however, that $r = 0$ is a necessary but not sufficient condition for independence, in the sense that two *dependent* variables may have $r = 0$.

Example 11.2-1. The following table summarizes the demand for an inventory item (in number of units) over a 24-month period.

Month, t	Demand, y	Month, t	Demand, y
1	46	13	54
2	56	14	42
3	54	15	64
4	43	16	60
5	57	17	70
6	56	18	66
7	67	19	57
8	62	20	55
9	50	21	52
10	56	22	62
11	47	23	70
12	56	24	72

We thus obtain

$$\sum_{i=1}^{24} y_i t_i = 17{,}842, \qquad \sum_{i=1}^{24} t_i = 300, \qquad \sum_{i=1}^{24} t_i^2 = 4900,$$

$$\sum_{i=1}^{24} y_i = 1374, \qquad \sum_{i=1}^{24} y_i^2 = 80{,}254$$

so that

$$\bar{t} = 12.5, \qquad \bar{y} = 57.25$$

and

$$b = \frac{17{,}842 - 24 \times 57.25 \times 12.5}{4900 - 24 \times (12.5)^2} = .58$$

$$a = 57.25 - .58 \times 12.5 = 50$$

The forecast (estimated value) of future demand may thus be determined from the equation

$$\hat{y} = 50 + .58t$$

For example, at $t = 25$, $\hat{y} = 50 + .58(25) = 64.5$ units.

The correlation coefficient is computed as

$$r = \frac{17{,}842 - 24 \times 57.25 \times 12.5}{\sqrt{(4900 - 24 \times 12.5^2)(80{,}254 - 24 \times 57.25^2)}} = .493$$

The value of $r = .493$ indicates that the regression line $\hat{y} = 50 + .58t$ does not provide a good fit for the observed data. A reasonable fit normally occurs in the range $.75 \leq |r| \leq 1$. ◀

11.2.2 MOVING AVERAGE MODEL

The moving average model estimates next period's demand as the average of the actual demand of the last m periods; that is,

$$\hat{y}_{t+1} = \frac{y_t + y_{t-1} + \cdots + y_{t-m+1}}{m}$$

There are no definite rules for selecting the exact value of m. In practice, a value in the range 2 to 10 is acceptable. If m is too small, cyclic variations may not be detected. On the other hand, if m is too large, cyclic variations may be over-suppressed. The nature of the computations in the moving average model indicates that the procedure cannot be initialized until an accumulation of at least m historical data points are available.

The forecast for any future period t, $t + 1$, $t + 2$, ..., is taken equal to $\hat{y}_t$. This result follows from the nature of the model which bases future estimates on actual demand data. We can thus see that the model is appropriate only for short-term forecasts.

Example 11.2-2. The moving average procedure is applied to the data of Example 11.2-1. The following table summarizes the application of the procedure using $m = 3$.

Month	Demand	Moving Average	Month	Demand	Moving Average
1	46	—	13	54	52.33
2	56	—	14	42	50.67
3	54	52	15	64	53.33
4	43	51	16	60	55.33
5	57	51.33	17	70	64.67
6	56	52	18	66	65.33
7	67	60	19	57	64.33
8	62	61.17	20	55	59.33
9	50	59.17	21	52	54.67
10	56	56	22	62	56.33
11	47	51	23	70	61.33
12	56	53	24	72	68

Based on the data above, the forecast for the future months (25, 26, ...) is computed as

$$\hat{Y}_{24+t} = \frac{62 + 70 + 72}{3} = 68 \text{ units}, \qquad t = 1, 2, 3, \ldots$$

11.2.3 EXPONENTIAL SMOOTHING

The disadvantage of the moving average model is that it places the same weight on all the observations comprising the average. Normally, the most recent observation should carry a larger weight than the most distant past observation. Exponential smoothing is designed to alleviate this problem. Specifically, given the previous data points $y_1, y_2, \ldots,$ and y_t, an estimate, $\hat{y}_{t+1}$, for period $t + 1$ is thus computed as

$$\hat{y}_{t+1} = \alpha y_t + \alpha(1 - \alpha)y_{t-1} + \alpha(1 - \alpha)^2 y_{t-2} + \cdots$$

where α is called the smoothing constant, $0 < \alpha < 1$. The formula shows that distant data points carry an increasingly smaller weight than the most recent ones. The formula for computing $\hat{y}_{t+1}$ can be expressed in the following recursive form

$$\hat{y}_{t+1} = \alpha y_t + (1 - \alpha)\hat{y}_t$$

This formula is easier to work with than is the original formula.

The selection of the value of the smoothing constant is crucial in producing "reliable" forecasts. In practice, the value of α is chosen between 0.1 and 0.3.

As in the case of the moving average model, forecasts for future demands $\hat{y}_{t+i}$, $i = 1, 2, \ldots$ are all equal to $\hat{y}_{t+1}$. This result again indicates that the model is suitable for making short-term forecasts.

Example 11.2-3. In this example we apply exponential smoothing to the data of Example 11.2-1 using $\alpha = .1$. Notice that the successive values are computed recursively so that $\hat{y}_{t+1}$ is computed from $\hat{y}_t$ and y_t, that is,

$$\hat{y}_{t+1} = \alpha y_t + (1 - \alpha)\hat{y}_t$$

The procedure starts with $\hat{y}_1 = y_1$.

From the computations in Table 11-5, we can estimate $\hat{y}_{25}$ as

$$\begin{aligned}\hat{y}_{25} &= \alpha y_{24} + (1 - \alpha)\hat{y}_{24} \\ &= .1(72) + .9(57.63) = 59.07 \text{ units}\end{aligned}$$

This forecast is considerably different from that of the moving average model (= 68 units) and the regression model (= 64.5 units). ◀

Table 11-5

Month, i	Demand, y_i	Estimated $\hat{y}_i$	Month, i	Demand, y_i	Estimated $\hat{y}_i$
1	46	—	13	54	.1(56) + .9(51.63) = 52.07
2	56	46	14	42	.1(54) + .9(52.07) = 52.26
3	54	.1(56) + .9(46) = 47	15	64	.1(42) + .9(52.26) = 51.23
4	43	.1(54) + .9(47) = 47.7	16	60	.1(64) + .9(51.23) = 52.5
5	57	.1(43) + .9(47.7) = 47.23	17	70	.1(60) + .9(525) = 53.26
6	56	.1(57) + .9(47.23) = 48.21	18	66	.1(70) + .9(53.26) = 54.93
7	67	.1(56) + .9(48.21) = 48.98	19	57	.1(66) + .9(54.93) = 56.04
8	62	.1(67) + .9(48.98) = 50.79	20	55	.1(57) + .9(56.04) = 56.14
9	50	.1(62) + .9(50.79) = 51.91	21	52	.1(55) + .9(56.14) = 56.02
10	56	.1(50) + .9(51.91) = 51.72	22	62	.1(52) + .9(56.02) = 55.62
11	47	.1(56) + .9(51.72) = 52.15	23	70	.1(62) + .9(55.62) = 56.26
12	56	.1(47) + .9(52.15) = 51.63	24	72	.1(70) + .9(56.26) = 57.63

Figure 11-16 combines plots of the raw data, the regression line of Example 11.2-1, the moving averages model (Example 11.2-2), and the exponential smoothing model (Example 11.2-3), all as a function of time. The regression line suppresses all the fluctuations in demand and simply shows the long-term trend of demand. On the other hand, the moving average and the exponential smoothing models suppress the extreme random fluctuations in data, yet maintain the short-term variations.

Figure 11-16

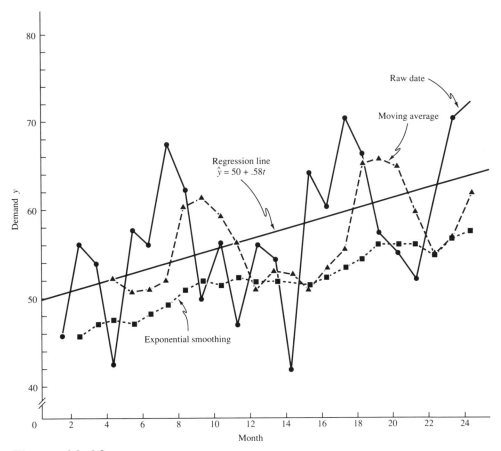

Notice, however, that the exponential smoothing lags behind the regression and moving average models. The reason for this is that our exponential model does not allow for trends explicitly in this case. Other models exist that account for this characteristic, hence leading to better forecasts. [See Silver and Peterson (1985), pp. 97–126 for more details.]

11.3 SUMMARY

In this chapter we explain how raw data can be summarized in forms that are suitable for use in OR models. The discussion shows that certain approximations may be necessary before the data can be employed with OR models. In particular, it is indicated that probabilistic-nonstationarity may be the most difficult of all data representations. In such cases it is recommended that either stationarity be assumed or the random variations be suppressed. The overall conclusion from this chapter is that data analysis and summarization represent a crucial phase in the development, solution, and implementation of OR models.

SELECTED REFERENCES

Brown, R. G., *Smoothing, Forecasting, and Prediction of Discrete Time Series*, Prentice Hall, Englewood Cliffs, N.J., 1972.

KACHIGAN, S., *Statistical Analysis*, Radius Press, New York, 1986.
LINDGREN, B., *Statistical Theory*, 2nd ed., Macmillan, New York, 1968.
PARZEN, E., *Modern Probability Theory and Its Applications*, 2nd ed., Wiley, New York, 1960.

PROBLEMS

Section	Assigned Problems
11.1	11–1 to 11–5
11.2	11–6 to 11–11

☐ **11–1** Identify the following variables as either time-based or observation-based:
(a) Inventory level of an item.
(b) Number of pallets transported by a conveyor belt.
(c) Number of defective items in an inspected lot.
(d) Order quantity of an inventory item.
(e) Number of cars in a parking lot.
(f) Time between arrivals at a service facility.

☐ **11–2** The following data represent the interarrival times (in minutes) at a service facility:

4.3	3.4	.9	.7	5.8	3.4	2.7	7.8
4.4	.8	4.4	1.9	3.4	3.1	5.1	1.4
.1	4.1	4.9	4.8	15.9	6.7	2.1	2.3
2.5	3.3	3.8	6.1	2.8	5.9	2.1	2.8
3.4	3.1	.4	2.7	.9	2.9	4.5	3.8
6.1	3.4	1.1	4.2	2.9	4.6	7.2	5.1
2.6	.9	4.9	2.4	4.1	5.1	11.5	2.6
2.1	10.3	4.3	5.1	4.3	1.1	4.1	6.7
2.2	2.9	5.2	8.2	1.1	3.3	2.1	7.3
3.5	3.1	7.9	.9	5.1	6.2	5.8	1.4
.5	4.5	6.4	1.2	2.1	10.7	3.2	2.3
3.3	3.3	7.1	6.9	3.1	1.6	2.1	1.9

(a) Estimate the mean and variance.
(b) Develop histograms using cell widths of .5 minute, 1.0 minute, and 1.5 minutes.
(c) Compare graphically the cumulative distributions of the empirical data and that of a corresponding exponential distribution.
(d) Test the hypothesis that the resulting histogram represents an exponential distribution. Use a 95% confidence level.

☐ **11–3** Consider the following sample, which represents the time period (in seconds) needed to transmit messages.

25.8	67.3	35.2	36.4	58.7
47.9	94.8	61.3	59.3	93.4
17.8	34.7	56.4	22.1	48.1
48.2	35.8	65.3	30.1	72.5
5.8	70.9	88.9	76.4	17.3
77.4	66.1	23.9	23.8	36.8
5.6	36.4	93.5	36.4	76.7
89.3	39.2	78.7	51.9	63.6
89.5	58.6	12.8	28.6	82.7
38.7	71.3	21.1	35.9	29.2

Test the hypothesis that these data are drawn from a uniform distribution at a 95% confidence level given the following information:

(a) The interval of the distribution is between 0 and 100.

(b) The interval of the distribution is between a and b, where a and b are unknown parameters.

(c) The interval of the distribution is between a and 100, where a is an unknown parameter.

☐ **11–4** An automatic device is used to record the volume of traffic at a busy intersection. The device records the time a car arrives at the intersection on a continuous time scale, starting from a zero datum. The following table provides the arrival times (in minutes) for the first 60 cars. (Normally, the data required for determining the arrivals distribution may be collected over a period of days or weeks. However, we cannot reproduce a full set of data here because of space limitations.)

Arrival	Arrival Time (minutes)	Arrival	Arrival Time (minutes)	Arrival	Arrival Time (minutes)	Arrival	Arrival Time (minutes)
1	5.2	16	67.6	31	132.7	46	227.8
2	6.7	17	69.3	32	142.3	47	233.5
3	9.1	18	78.6	33	145.2	48	239.8
4	12.5	19	86.6	34	154.3	49	243.6
5	18.9	20	91.3	35	155.6	50	250.5
6	22.6	21	97.2	36	166.2	51	255.8
7	27.4	22	97.9	37	169.2	52	256.5
8	29.9	23	111.5	38	169.5	53	256.9
9	35.4	24	116.7	39	172.4	54	270.3
10	35.7	25	117.3	40	175.3	55	275.1
11	44.4	26	118.2	41	180.1	56	277.1
12	47.1	27	124.1	42	188.8	57	278.1
13	47.5	28	127.4	43	201.2	58	283.6
14	49.7	29	127.6	44	218.4	59	299.8
15	67.1	30	127.8	45	219.9	60	300.0

Construct a suitable histogram to test the hypothesis that the interarrival time is drawn from an exponential distribution. Use a 95% confidence level.

☐ **11–5** The following data represent the changes in the length of a queue as a function of time in minutes (starting from the zero datum).

Time	Queue Length	Time	Queue Length
0	0	20.8	1
1.5	1	22.3	0
2.5	2	24.5	1
3.7	3	26.8	2
4.1	2	27.5	1
4.8	3	29.9	2
5.9	4	32.5	3
7.2	3	35.1	2
8.9	4	40.6	3
9.3	3	42.7	4
10.8	2	50.3	3
11.9	1	52.1	2
14.1	2	55.7	3
15.7	3	58.9	2
18.9	2	59.3	1

(a) Estimate the average length and variance of the queue length.
(b) Construct a histogram of the queue length.

☐ **11–6** Consider the data of Examples 11.2-1, 11.2-2, and 11.2-3. Forecast the demand for the item in period 30 using
(a) Regression.
(b) Moving average.
(c) Exponential smoothing.

☐ **11–7** In Example 11.2-2, recompute the moving average based on $m = 6$ (as compared with $m = 3$ in the example). What effect does the larger m have with regard to suppressing the fluctuations in demand?

☐ **11–8** In Example 11.2-3, use $\alpha = .3$ to reapply the exponential smoothing. What effect does the larger value of α have on the smoothed demand?

☐ **11–9** The following set of data represents the quarterly changes in demand for an item over the next 3 months.

Quarter	Demand	Quarter	Demand	Quarter	Demand
1	100	5	124	9	140
2	128	6	115	10	129
3	114	7	118	11	132
4	120	8	123	12	130

(a) Apply the following forecasting techniques of the data:
(i) Regression.
(ii) Moving average with base $m = 3$.
(iii) Exponential smoothing with $\alpha = .1$.

(b) Provide forecasts for the demand in quarters 13, 14, and 15 based on the three methods.

☐ **11–10** The number of visitors at a tourist area over the past 10 years is given below.

Year	1980	1981	1982	1983	1984	1985	1986	1987	1988	1989
Car	1042	1182	1224	1338	1455	1613	1644	1699	1790	1885
Air	500	522	540	612	715	790	840	900	935	980

Analyze the data for the purpose of forecasting the future number of visitors.

☐ **11–11** The following time series represents the sales (in millions of dollars) for a department store.

Year	1981	1982	1983	1984	1985	1986	1987	1988	1989	1990
Sales	21	22.3	23.2	24	24.9	25.6	26.6	27.4	28.5	29.6

(a) Estimate the regression line for the data.
(b) Use regression and moving average to estimate the sales in 1991.
(c) Use exponential smoothing with $\alpha = .2$ to forecast the sales for 1991.

Chapter 12

Decision Theory and Games

In Chapters 2 through 10, all decision models are formulated and solved assuming the availability of *perfect* information. This is usually referred to as decision making under **certainty**. For example, in a product-mix problem, the profit per unit, c_j, of the jth product is assumed to be a fixed real value. If x_j is the decision variable representing the level of production for product j, the total profit contribution of the jth product is $c_j x_j$, which again is fixed for a given value of x_j.

The availability of *partial* or *imperfect* information about a problem leads to two new categories of decision-making situations:

1. Decisions under **risk**.
2. Decisions under **uncertainty**.

In the first category, the degree of ignorance about the data is expressed in terms of a probability density function, whereas in the second category no probability density function can be secured. In other words, from the standpoint of data availability, *certainty* and *uncertainty* represent the two extreme cases, and *risk* is the "in-between" situation.

To illustrate risk and uncertainty situations, consider the product-mix example just cited. Under *risk* conditions, the profit c_j will no longer be a fixed value; rather, it is a random variable whose exact numerical value is unknown but can be represented in terms of a probability density function, $f(c_j)$. Thus it does not make sense to talk about c_j without associating some probability statement with it. The profit contribution of the jth variable $c_j x_j$ is also a random variable whose exact value, for a given value of x_j, is unknown.

Under the condition of *uncertainty*, the probability density function $f(c_j)$ is either unknown or cannot be determined. Actually, uncertainty does *not* imply *complete* ignorance about the problem. For example, the decision maker may possess the partial information that c_j is equal to one of three values: c'_j, c''_j, and c'''_j. However, as long as no probabilities can be associated with these three values, the situation is regarded as decision making under uncertainty.

The degree of ignorance about data bears directly on how a problem is modeled and solved. For example, suppose that the product-mix problem has a total of n products. Under the assumption of certainty it makes sense to use $z = c_1x_1 + c_2x_2 + \cdots + c_nx_n$ as an objective criterion to be maximized subject to proper restrictions. However, under the assumption of risk, the same criterion would be of little value without some type of a probability statement, since z is actually a random variable. The criterion given becomes completely inadequate under the assumption of uncertainty, since the *specific* values of c_j are not known. This simple illustration indicates that insufficient data lead to a more complex decision model and, inevitably, a less satisfactory solution.

Unfortunately, the insufficiency of data has resulted in several, often inconsistent, approaches for quantifying and solving a decision model. There is almost universal acceptance of the criterion of maximizing profit (or minimizing its antithesis, cost) under conditions of certainty. However, several criteria exist in risk and uncertainty situations. For example, under risk the maximization of *expected* profit is sometimes acceptable, but it cannot be applied to every situation. Other criteria range from being completely conservative to being completely permissive. The situation becomes worse under uncertainty.

In most decision models, the problem resolves to selecting a best course(s) of action from a number (possibly infinite) of available options. This was shown in the models in Chapters 2 through 10. However, none of these models assume that decisions are being made in an environment where the system itself is trying to "defeat" the decision maker. To be specific, suppose one is making a decision that depends on whether it would or would not rain. In this case, the decision maker does not expect nature to be a malevolent opponent.

In decisions under uncertainty, competitive situations exist in which two (or more) opponents are working in conflict, with each opponent trying to gain at the expense of the other(s). These situations are distinguished from customary decision making under uncertainty by the fact that the decision maker is working against an *intelligent* opponent. The theory governing these types of decision problems is known as the **theory of games**.

12.1 DECISIONS UNDER RISK

Decisions under risk are usually based on one of the following criteria:

1. Expected value (of profit or loss).
2. Combined expected value and variance.
3. Known aspiration level.
4. Most likely occurrence of a future state.

Each of these criteria will now be explained in detail.

12.1.1 EXPECTED VALUE CRITERION

A natural extension of decisions under certainty is the use of expected value criterion, where it is desired to maximize expected profit (or minimize expected cost). This criterion may be expressed in terms of either *actual* money or its **utility**. To illustrate the difference between actual money and its utility, suppose that an investment of \$20,000 will result in a gross profit of either zero or \$100,000 with equal probabilities. Based on the expected value of *money*, the individual's expected net gain is $100{,}000 \times .5 + 0 \times .5 - 20{,}000 = \$30{,}000$. Using this result alone, one would find that the "optimum" decision is to invest the \$20,000. However, this decision may not be acceptable to all potential investors. For example, investor *A* may argue that because of the scarcity of liquid cash, the loss of \$20,000 could lead to bankruptcy. Consequently, *A* may elect not to enter into this arrangement. Investor *B*, on the other hand, has a surplus of dormant capital that far exceeds any need for liquid money and, consequently, is willing to undertake the venture. What is being illustrated here is the importance of the decision maker's *attitude* toward the worth or utility of money. This point can be dramatized by considering investor *A*'s situation again. Suppose that investor *A* would in no case be willing to risk the loss of more than \$5000. Suppose further that *A* has two ventures: Invest \$20,000 and obtain a \$100,000 gross profit with probability .5 and \$0 with probability .5, or invest \$5000 and obtain a \$23,000 gross profit with probability .5 and \$0 with probability .5. This information now shows that investor *A* has no choice but to select the second alternative even though its *expected* net profit of \$6500 is much smaller than the \$30,000 expected from the first alternative.

The main result from the illustration is that utility need not be directly proportional to actual money values. Unfortunately, although guidelines for establishing **utility curves** (i.e., actual money versus its utility) have been developed, utility is a rather subtle concept that cannot be quantified easily. In actual practice, the effect of utility may be expressed in terms of additional constraints that reflect the behavior of the decision maker. This point is illustrated by the maximum limit on the dollar loss investor *A* is willing to accept. In other words, it is not advisable to use expected money value as the only criterion for reaching a decision. Rather, it should serve only as a guide, and the final decision should ultimately be made by considering all the pertinent factors that affect the decision maker's attitude toward the utility of money.

Whether utility or actual money is used in computing expected values, the following drawback is usually cited against the use of the expected value criterion. Expectation implies that the same decision should be repeated a sufficiently large number of times before realizing the net value computed from the expectation formula. Mathematically, this result is expressed as follows. Let z be a random variable with expected value $E\{z\}$ and variance σ^2. If $(z_1, z_2, \ldots, z_n)$ is a random sample of n observed values of z, the sample average $\bar{z} = (z_1 + z_2 + \cdots + z_n)/n$ has a variance σ^2/n. Thus, as $n \to \infty$ (i.e., n becomes very large), $\sigma^2/n \to 0$ and $\bar{z}$ approaches $E\{z\}$. In other words, as the sample size becomes sufficiently large, the difference between the sample average and the expected value tends to zero. Thus, to use the expected value properly in comparing alternatives, one must expect the same decision process to be repeated a sufficiently large number of times. Otherwise, if the process is repeated a small number of times, the sample average $\bar{z}$ may differ considerably from $E\{z\}$. The main conclusion here then is that the use of expectation may be misleading for decisions that are applied only a few number of times.

Example 12.1-1. A preventive maintenance policy requires making decisions about when a machine (or a piece of equipment) should be serviced on a regular basis in order to minimize the cost of sudden breakdown. If the time horizon is specified in terms of equal time periods, the decision entails determining the optimal number of periods between two successive maintenances. If preventive maintenance is applied too frequently, the maintenance cost will increase while the cost of sudden breakdown will decrease. A compromise between the two extreme cases calls for balancing the costs of preventive maintenance and sudden breakdown.

Since we cannot predict in advance when a machine may break down, it is necessary to compute the probability that a machine would break down in a given period t. This is where the element of "risk" enters in the decision process.

The decision situation can be summarized as follows. A machine in a group of n machines is serviced when it breaks down. At the end of T periods, preventive maintenance is performed by servicing all n machines. The decision problem is to determine the optimum T that minimizes the total cost per period of servicing broken machines and applying preventive maintenance.

Let p_t be the probability that a machine would break down in period t, and let n_t be the random variable representing the number of broken machines in the same period. Further, assume that c_1 is the cost of repairing a broken machine and c_2 the preventive maintenance cost per machine.

The application of the expected value criterion to this example is reasonable if one can expect the machines to remain in operation for a large number of periods. The expected cost per period can be written as

$$EC(T) = \frac{c_1 \sum_{t=1}^{T-1} E\{n_t\} + c_2 n}{T}$$

where $E\{n_t\}$ is the expected number of broken machines in period t. Since n_t is a binomial random variable with parameter (n, p_t), $E\{n_t\} = np_t$. Thus

$$EC(T) = \frac{n(c_1 \sum_{t=1}^{T-1} p_t + c_2)}{T}$$

The necessary conditions for T^* to minimize $EC(T)$ are

$$EC(T^* - 1) \geq EC(T^*) \quad \text{and} \quad EC(T^* + 1) \geq EC(T^*)$$

Thus, by starting with a small value of T, computation of $EC(T)$ is continued until the foregoing conditions are satisfied.

To illustrate this point, suppose that $c_1 = \$100$, $c_2 = \$10$, and $n = 50$. The values of p_t are tabulated below. The table shows that preventive maintenance is applied to all machines every three ($= T^*$) time periods.

	T	p_T	$\sum_{t=1}^{T-1} p_t$	$EC(T)$	
	1	.05	0	\$500	
	2	.07	.05	375	
$T^* \rightarrow$	**3**	.10	.12	**366.7**	$\leftarrow EC(T^*)$
	4	.13	.22	400	
	5	.18	.35	450	

◀

Exercise 12.1-1

In Example 12.1-1, suppose that the net worth of production per machine per period is $\$a$ and that it is desired to maximize the expected profit per period, $EP(T)$. Assume that the profit is computed as the difference between the net production worth and the cost of machine breakdown and maintenance.

(a) Write the general expression for $EP(T)$.
[*Ans.* $EP(T) = n(a - c_2 - c_1 \sum_{t=1}^{T-1} P_t)/T$.]

(b) Write the necessary condition for determining T^* based on maximizing $EP(T)$.
[*Ans.* $EP(T^*) \geq EP(T^* - 1)$ and $EP(T^*) \geq EP(T^* + 1.)$]

12.1.2 EXPECTED VALUE–VARIANCE CRITERION

In Section 12.1.1 we indicated that the expected value criterion is suitable mainly for making "long-run" decisions. The same criterion can be modified to improve its applicability to "short-run" decision problems by considering the following observation. If z is a random variable with variance σ^2, the sample average $\bar{z}$ has a variance σ^2/n, where n is the sample size. Thus, as σ^2 becomes smaller, the variance of $\bar{z}$ also becomes smaller and the probability that $\bar{z}$ approaches $E\{z\}$ becomes larger. This means that it is advantageous to develop a criterion that maximizes expected profit and, simultaneously, minimizes the variance of the profit. This is actually equivalent to considering two goals in the same criterion. A possible criterion reflecting this objective is

$$\text{maximize } E\{z\} - K \operatorname{var}\{z\}$$

where z is a random variable representing profit and K is a prespecified constant.†

† It may be argued that the criterion should be replaced with max $E\{z\} - K\sqrt{\operatorname{var}\{z\}}$. In this manner, the units of $E\{z\}$ and $\sqrt{\operatorname{var}\{z\}}$ will be consistent.

The constant K is sometimes referred to as **risk aversion factor**. It is actually a weighting factor that indicates the "degree of importance" of var$\{z\}$ relative to $E\{z\}$. For example, a decision maker particularly sensitive to large reductions in profit below $E\{z\}$ may choose K much larger than one. This arrangement will weigh the variance heavily and hence will result in a decision that reduces the chances of having low profit.

It is interesting that the new criterion is compatible with the use of utility in decision making, since the risk aversion factor K is an indicator of the decision maker's attitude toward excessive deviation from the expected values. This intuitive argument has a mathematical basis, and, using Taylor's series expansion, one can show that the first three terms in the expected utility function produce a criterion similar to the one just given (see Problem 12–7).

Example 12.1-2. The expected value–variance criterion is applied to Example 12.1-1. To do so, we need to compute the variance of the cost per period, that is, the variance of

$$C_T = \frac{c_1 \sum_{t=1}^{T-1} n_t + nc_2}{T}$$

C_T is a random variable because n_t ($t = 1, \ldots, T - 1$) is a random variable. Since n_t is binomial with mean np_t and variance $np_t(1 - p_t)$, it follows that

$$\begin{aligned} \text{var}\{C_T\} &= \left(\frac{c_1}{T}\right)^2 \sum_{t=1}^{T-1} \text{var}\{n_t\} \\ &= \left(\frac{c_1}{T}\right)^2 \sum_{t=1}^{T-1} np_t(1 - p_t) = n\left(\frac{c_1}{T}\right)^2 \left\{\sum_{t=1}^{T-1} p_t - \sum_{t=1}^{T-1} p_t^2\right\} \end{aligned}$$

Since $E\{C_T\} = EC(T)$, as given in Example 12.1-1, the criterion becomes

$$\text{minimize } EC(T) + K \text{ var}\{C_T\}$$

The function $EC(T)$ is *added* to K var$\{C_T\}$, since $EC(T)$ is a cost function. With $K = 1$, the criterion becomes

$$\text{minimize } EC(T) + \text{var}\{C_T\} = n\left\{\left(\frac{c_1}{T} + \frac{c_1^2}{T^2}\right) \sum_{t=1}^{T-1} p_t - \left(\frac{c_1}{T}\right)^2 \sum_{t=1}^{T-1} p_t^2 + \frac{c_2}{T}\right\}$$

Using the same information as that in Example 12.1-1, we can set up the following table to give $T^* = 1$, which indicates that preventive maintenance must be applied every period.

It is interesting that, for the same data, the expected value–variance criterion has resulted in a more conservative decision that applies preventive maintenance every period compared with every third period in Example 12.1-1.

T	p_T	p_T^2	$\sum_{t=1}^{T-1} p_t$	$\sum_{t=1}^{T-1} p_t^2$	$EC(T) + \text{var}\{C_T\}$
1	.05	.0025	0	0	**500.00**
2	.07	.0049	.05	.0025	6312.50
3	.10	.0100	.12	.0074	6622.22
4	.13	.0169	.22	.0174	6731.25
5	.18	.0324	.35	.0343	6764.00

◀

Exercise 12.1-2

Write the expected value–variance criterion associated with Exercise 12.1-1.
[*Ans.* Maximize $EP(T) - nK(c_1/T)^2\{\sum_{t+1}^{T-1} p_t - \sum_{t=1}^{T-1} p_t^2\}$.

12.1.3 ASPIRATION-LEVEL CRITERION

The aspiration-level criterion does not yield an optimal decision in the sense of maximizing profit or minimizing cost. Rather, it is a means of determining *acceptable* courses of action. Consider, for example, the situation where a person advertises a used car for sale. On receiving an offer, the seller must decide, within a reasonable time span, whether it is acceptable or not. In this respect, the seller sets a price limit below which the car will not be sold. This is the **aspiration level**, which will allow the seller to accept the first offer that satisfies it. Such a criterion may not yield the optimum, for a later offer may be higher than the one accepted.

In making a decision in the used-car example, there was no mention of a probability distribution. Why then is the aspiration-level criterion classified as a technique for making decisions under risk? It can be argued that in selecting the aspiration level, the owner of the car is aware of the market values of similar cars. This is equivalent to saying that the owner has a "feeling" of the distribution of used-car prices. Admittedly, this does not provide a formal definition of a probability density function, but there is a basis here for collecting data that can be used to develop such a function. Indeed, one must assume that this is the case, since complete ignorance about the distribution may cause the owner to set the aspiration level too high, in which case no offer would be acceptable, or too low, in which case the owner may not collect a fair value for the car. In any case, one of the advantages of using aspiration-level method is that it may not be necessary to define the probability density function exactly.

This illustration pinpoints to the usefulness of the aspiration-level criterion when *all* alternative courses of action are *not* available at the time the decision is made. This need not be the only situation where this criterion is used. Consider, for example, the situation in which a service facility (say, a laundry, a restaurant, or a barbershop) can be operated at different service rates. A high service rate, although it will provide fast service for customers, may be too costly for the owner. Conversely, slow service may not be as costly but could result in lost customers and hence in reduced profit. The objective is to determine the "optimum" level at which service may be performed.

In situations such as the foregoing, it is usually possible to determine the probability distributions for the arrivals of customers and their service times. Because such facilities supposedly operate for a long period of time, it appears ideal to determine the optimum service level based on minimizing the *expected* total cost (Section 12.1.1) of the facility per unit time. This includes the expected cost of operating the facility plus the expected cost of customer inconvenience, both being a function of the service level so that the higher is the first, the lower will be the second, and vice versa. However, this criterion becomes impractical because of the difficulty of estimating a cost for customer "inconvenience." Many intangible factors cannot be expressed readily in terms of cost, since they depend on the customer's behavior and attitude.

The aspiration-level criterion may apply here. For example, one may decide to select the service level such that the service facility is idle only $\alpha\%$ of the time, while simultaneously requiring that the expected waiting time per customer does not exceed β time units. The parameters α and β are aspiration levels that the decision maker may determine based on a concept of running an "efficient" facility and a knowledge of the customer's behavior. Notice that α and β assume implicit cost values for operating the service facility and for the waiting time of customers, which, if known, could be used in the expected cost model. However, one can see that the determination of α and β is not as demanding as determining cost parameters.

Example 12.1-3. Suppose that the demand x per period on a certain commodity is given by the continuous probability density function $f(x)$. If the amount stocked at the beginning of the period is not sufficient, shortage may occur. If too much is stocked, extra inventory will be held at the end of the period. Both situations are costly. The first reflects loss of potential profit and loss of customers' goodwill; the second reflects an increase in the cost of storing and maintaining the inventory.

Presumably, one would like to balance these two conflicting costs. Since it is generally difficult to estimate the cost of shortage, we may wish to determine the level of stock such that the *expected* shortage quantity does not exceed A_1 units and the *expected* excess quantity does not exceed A_2 units. Mathematically, this is expressed as follows. Let I be the stock level to be determined. Thus

$$\text{expected shortage quantity} = \int_I^\infty (x - I)f(x)\,dx \leq A_1$$

$$\text{expected excess quantity} = \int_0^I (I - x)f(x)\,dx \leq A_2$$

In general, the selection of the aspiration levels A_1 and A_2 may not yield feasible values for I. In this case it would be necessary to relax one of the two restrictions in order to achieve feasibility.

To illustrate the example numerically, suppose that $f(x)$ is given by the distribution

$$f(x) = \begin{cases} \dfrac{20}{x^2}, & 10 \leq x \leq 20 \\ 0, & \text{otherwise} \end{cases}$$

It follows that

$$\int_I^{20} (x - I)f(x)\,dx = \int_I^{20} (x - I)\frac{20}{x^2}\,dx = 20\left\{\ln\frac{20}{I} + \frac{I}{20} - 1\right\}$$

$$\int_{10}^{I} (I - x)f(x)\,dx = \int_{10}^{I} (I - x)\frac{20}{x^2}\,dx = 20\left\{\ln\frac{10}{I} + \frac{I}{10} - 1\right\}$$

Thus the aspiration level criteria simplify to

$$\ln I - \frac{I}{20} \geq \ln 20 - \frac{A_1}{20} - 1 = 1.996 - \frac{A_1}{20}$$

$$\ln I - \frac{I}{10} \geq \ln 10 - \frac{A_2}{20} - 1 = 1.302 - \frac{A_2}{20}$$

The aspiration levels A_1 and A_2 must be such that the two inequalities can be satisfied simultaneously for at least one value of I.

For example, if $A_1 = 2$ and $A_2 = 4$, the inequalities become

$$\ln I - \frac{I}{20} \geq 1.896$$

$$\ln I - \frac{I}{10} \geq 1.102$$

The value of I must be between 10 and 20, since these are the limits of the demand. The following table shows that the two conditions are satisfied simultaneously for $13 \leq I \leq 17$. Thus any of these values provides an answer to the problem.

I	10	11	12	**13**	**14**	**15**	**16**	**17**	18	19	20
$\ln I - I/20$	1.8	1.84	1.88	**1.91**	1.94	1.96	1.97	1.98	1.99	1.99	1.99
$\ln I - I/10$	1.3	1.29	1.28	1.26	1.24	1.21	1.17	**1.13**	1.09	1.04	.99

◀

Exercise 12.1-3

Consider Example 12.1-3.

(a) Indicate if the following combinations of A_1 and A_2 will yield a feasible solution. If so, find the answer.

(1) $A_1 = A_2 = 3$ [*Ans.* $12 \leq I \leq 16$.]

(2) $A_1 = A_2 = 1$ [*Ans.* No feasible solution.]

(b) Suppose that $f(x) = 1/10$, $0 \leq x \leq 10$. Determine a general expression for determining a feasible range for I given the levels of aspiration A_1 and A_2.

[*Ans.* $\text{Max}\{0, 10 - \sqrt{20A_1}\} \leq I \leq \min\{10, \sqrt{20A_2}\}$, provided that the lower limit does not exceed the upper limit. If it does, no feasible solution exists.]

12.1.4 MOST LIKELY FUTURE CRITERION

This criterion is based on converting the probabilistic situation into a deterministic situation by replacing the random variable with the single value that has the highest probability of occurrence. For example, suppose that the profit per unit of a jth product is c_j, whose (discrete) probability density function is $p_j(c_j)$. Let c_j^* be defined such that $p_j(c_j^*) = \max p_j(c_j)$ for all c_j. Then c_j^* is treated as the "deterministic" value representing the per unit profit for the jth product.

This criterion may be thought of as a simplification of the more complex decision under risk. Such a simplification is done not for mere analytic convenience, but primarily for recognizing that, from the practical standpoint, the most probable future provides adequate information for making the decision. For example, there is always a positive probability (small as it may be) that an airplane may crash; yet most passengers fly under the assumption that air travel is always safe.

We must warn against the pitfalls of using the most probable future criterion. Suppose that the random variable under consideration assumes a large number of values each of which has a small probability of occurrence, say, .05, or less. Or consider the case where several values of the random variable occur with the same probability. In both cases, the most likely future criterion becomes inadequate for making a "sound" decision.

12.1.5 EXPERIMENTAL DATA IN DECISIONS UNDER RISK

In developing the criteria for decisions under risk, it is assumed that the probability distributions are known or can be secured. In this respect, these probabilities are referred to as **prior probabilities**.

It is sometimes possible to perform an experiment on the system under study and, depending on the outcomes of the experiment, modify the *prior* probabilities to reflect the availability of new information about the system. The new probabilities are known as the **posterior probabilities**.

Example 12.1-4. A typical situation in which experimentation is used occurs in inspection procedures. Suppose that a manufacturer produces a product in lots of fixed sizes. Because of occasional malfunctions in the production process, bad lots with an unacceptable number of defectives may be produced. Past experience indicates that the probability of producing bad lots is .05, in which case the probability of producing a good lot is .95. These are the prior probabilities. For convenience, let $\theta = \theta_1$ $(= \theta_2)$ indicate that the lot is good (bad), so that

$$P\{\theta = \theta_1\} = .95 \qquad \text{and} \qquad P\{\theta = \theta_2\} = .05$$

The manufacturer realizes that a penalty may result from shipping out a bad lot. However, based on the prior probabilities, the probability of producing a bad lot appears sufficiently small to warrant a random selection of any of the available lots for shipping (compare the most likely future criterion, Section 12.1.4).

The decision above is made without sampling from the shipped lot. If, on the other hand, the manufacturer makes the decision *after* testing a sample from the lot, the additional information may lead to a different conclusion. For example, suppose that a test sample of two items is taken from the lot. The outcomes of the test may then be

z_1: Both items are good.
z_2: One item is good.
z_3: Both items are defective.

Because the sample is drawn either from a good or a bad lot, the conditional probabilities $P\{z_j | \theta_i\}$ are assumed available. The ultimate objective is to use these probabilities together with the prior probabilities to compute the required posterior probabilities which are defined by $P\{\theta_i | z_j\}$, that is, the probability of selecting either a good or a bad lot ($\theta = \theta_1$ or θ_2) given the outcome z_j of the experiment. These probabilities will be the basis for making a decision depending on the outcome of the sample test.

To show how the posterior probabilities $P\{\theta_i | z_j)$ are computed from the prior probabilities $P\{\theta_i\}$ and the conditional probabilities $P\{z_j | \theta_j\}$, assume a general case in which $\theta = \theta_1, \theta_2, \ldots,$ or θ_m and $z = z_1, z_2, \ldots,$ or z_n. Since

$$P\{z_j\} = \sum_{i=1}^{m} P\{\theta_i, z_j\} = \sum_{i=1}^{m} P\{z_j | \theta_i\} P\{\theta_i\}$$

the posterior probabilities are given by

$$P\{\theta_i \mid z_j\} = \frac{P\{\theta_i, z_j\}}{P\{z_j\}} = \frac{P\{z_j \mid \theta_i\}P\{\theta_i\}}{\sum_{i=1}^{m} P\{z_j \mid \theta_i\}P\{\theta_i\}}$$

These probabilities are also known as **Bayes's probabilities.**

Returning now to the numerical example, we suppose that the percentage of defectives in a good lot is 4%, while a bad lot has 15% defective items. Then based on a binomial distribution and a sample of size 2, the conditional probabilities of an outcome z_j given a lot is good or bad are as follows:

$$\begin{aligned}
P\{z_1 \mid \theta_1\} &= C_2^2(.96)^2(.04)^0 = .922\\
P\{z_2 \mid \theta_1\} &= C_1^2(.96)^1(.04)^1 = .0768\\
P\{z_3 \mid \theta_1\} &= C_0^2(.96)^0(.04)^2 = .0016\\
P\{z_1 \mid \theta_2\} &= C_2^2(.85)^2(.15)^0 = .7225\\
P\{z_2 \mid \theta_2\} &= C_1^2(.85)^1(.15)^1 = .255\\
P\{z_3 \mid \theta_2\} &= C_0^2(.85)^0(.15)^2 = .0225
\end{aligned}$$

These probabilities can be summarized conveniently as shown in the following table:

$P\{z_j \mid \theta_i\} =$

	z_1	z_2	z_3
θ_1	.922	.0768	.0016
θ_2	.7225	.255	.0225

Given $P\{\theta = \theta_1\} = .95$ and $P\{\theta = \theta_2\} = .05$, the joint probabilities

$$P\{\theta_i, z_j\} = P\{z_j \mid \theta_i\}P\{\theta_i\}$$

can be determined from the foregoing table by multiplying its first row by .95 and its second row by .05. Thus we obtain

$P\{\theta_i, z_j\} =$

	z_1	z_2	z_3
θ_1	.8759	.07296	.00152
θ_2	.036125	.01275	.001125

Next, we determine $P\{z_j\}$ by using the formula

$$P\{z_j\} = \sum_{i=1}^{2} P\{\theta_i, z_j\}$$

This is equivalent to summing the columns of the last table. Thus we obtain

$$P\{z_1\} = .912025, \qquad P\{z_2\} = .08571, \qquad P\{z_3\} = .002645$$

Finally, we obtain the posterior probabilities by using the formula

$$P\{\theta_i \mid z_j\} = \frac{P\{\theta_i, z_j\}}{P\{z_j\}}$$

These probabilities are computed by dividing the columns of the last table by the associated $P\{z_j\}$. Thus we obtain the following table:

$P\{\theta_i \mid z_j\} =$	z_1	z_2	z_3
θ_1	.96039	.85124	.57467
θ_2	.03961	.14876	.42533

It is interesting to see how the posterior probabilities can affect the final decision depending on the outcome z_j of the test. If both items tested are good ($z = z_1$), the probability that the lot is good is .96039. If both are bad ($z = z_3$), it is almost equally likely that the lot is good or bad. This shows that the final decision can be affected by the outcome z_j. ◀

Exercise 12.1-4

In Example 12.1-4, suppose that the test is applied to a sample of size 1. Specify the outcomes of the test and compute the posterior probabilities using the data of the example.
[*Ans.* There are two outcomes z_1 and z_2, representing whether the tested item is good or bad. $P\{\theta_1 \mid z_1\} = .955474$, $P\{\theta_1 \mid z_2\} = .835165$, $P\{\theta_2 \mid z_1\} = .044526$, and $P\{\theta_2 \mid z_2\} = .164835$.]

We now illustrate how the posterior probabilities are used in decision making.

Example 12.1-5. In Example 12.1-4, suppose that the manufacturer ships lots to two customers, *A* and *B*. The contracts specify that the percentage of defectives for *A* and *B* should not exceed 5 and 8, respectively. A penalty of \$100 is incurred per percentage point above the maximum limit. On the other hand, supplying better quality lots will cost the manufacturer \$80 per percentage point. Assuming that a sample of size 2 is inspected prior to shipping, how should the manufacturer decide where to ship an inspected lot?

There are two possible actions for this problem, namely,

a_1: Ship the lot to customer *A*.

a_2: Ship the lot to customer *B*.

Letting θ_1 and θ_2 represent the two types with 4% and 15% defectives, we can develop a cost matrix as follows:

$C(a, \theta) =$	θ_1	θ_2
a_1	\$80	\$1000
a_2	\$320	\$700

Action a_1 specifies that customer *A* will accept lots with 5% defectives without penalty. If the lot has 4% defective ($= \theta_1$) it will cost the manufacturer $(5 - 4) \times \$80 = \$80$ for supplying a better quality than needed, but if the lot has 15% defectives ($= \theta_2$), a penalty of $(15 - 5) \times \$100 = \$1000$ will be incurred. A similar reasoning is used to obtain the cost elements of action a_2 (verify!).

We notice now that the decision-making process must be a function of the outcomes z_1, z_2, and z_3 of the sample test. In other words, we must decide which action is preferable (less costly) given that the outcome of the test is two good items, one good item, or two bad items. We shall base our decision on minimization of expected costs. A general formula for computing expected costs is

$$E\{a_k | z_j\} = \sum_{\theta_i} C(a_k, \theta_i)P\{\theta_i | z_j\}$$

Case 1: The outcome is z_1 (two good items):

$$E\{a_1 | z_1\} = 80 \times .96039 + 1000 \times .03961 = \mathbf{\$116.44}$$
$$E\{a_2 | z_1\} = 320 \times .96039 + 700 \times .03961 = \$335.05$$

Thus, if the outcome is z_1, the decision is to ship the lot to customer A, since a_1 yields the lower expected cost.

Case 2: The outcome is z_2 (one good item):

$$E\{a_1 | z_2\} = 80 \times .85124 + 1000 \times .14876 = \mathbf{\$216.86}$$
$$E\{a_2 | z_2\} = 320 \times .85124 + 700 \times .14876 = \$376.53$$

Again, as in case 1, the lot should be shipped to customer A if the outcome of the test indicates one good item.

Case 3: The outcome is z_3 (two defective items):

$$E\{a_1 | z_3\} = 80 \times .57467 + 1000 \times .42533 = \mathbf{\$471.30}$$
$$E\{a_2 | z_3\} = 320 \times .57467 + 700 \times .42533 = \$481.63$$

Thus, in this case also, the lot should be shipped to customer A.

The general decision for the problem, then, is that all lots should be shipped to customer A regardless of the outcome of the test. ◀

Exercise 12.1-5
Use the data of Example 12.1-5 to determine the optimal decision in Exercise 12.1-4.
[*Ans.* Ship lots to A regardless of the outcome of the test.]

12.2 DECISION TREES

In Section 12.1 we presented decision criteria for evaluating what may be termed as "single-stage" alternatives, in the sense that no future decisions will depend on the decision taken now. In this section we consider a "multiple-stage" decision process in which dependent decisions are made in tandem. A graphical representation of the decision problem can be made by using a **decision tree**. This representation facilitates the decision-making process. The following example illustrates the basics of the decision tree procedure.

Example 12.2-1.† A company has the options now of building a full-size plant or a small plant that can be expanded later. The decision depends primarily on future demands for the product the plant will manufacture. The construction of a full-size plant can be justified economically if the level of demand is high. Otherwise,

† This example is adapted from J. F. Magee, "Decision Trees for Decision Making," *Harvard Business Review*, July–August 1964, pp. 126–138.

it may be advisable to construct a small plant now and then decide in two years whether it should be expanded.

The multistage decision problem arises here because if the company decides to build a small plant now, a future decision must be made in two years regarding expansion. In other words, the decision process involves two stages: a decision now regarding the size of the plant, and a decision two years from now regarding expansion (assuming that it is decided to construct a small plant now).

Figure 12-1 summarizes the problem as a *decision tree*. It is assumed that the demand can be either high or low. The decision tree has two types of nodes: a square (□) represents a *decision point* and a circle (○) stands for a *chance event*. Thus, starting with node 1 (a decision point), we must make a decision regarding the size of the plant. Node 2 is a chance event from which two branches representing low and high demand emanate depending on the conditions of the market. These conditions will be represented by associating probabilities with each branch. Node 3 is also a chance event from which two branches representing high and low demands emanate.

Logically, the company will consider possible future expansion of the small plant only if the demand over the first two years turns out to be high. This is the reason node 4 represents a decision point with its two emanating branches representing the "expansion" and "no expansion" decisions. Again, nodes 5 and 6 are chance events, and the branches emanating from each represent high and low demands.

The data for the decision tree must include (1) the probabilities associated with the branches emanating from the chance events and (2) the revenues associated with different alternatives of the problem. Suppose that the company is interested in studying the problem over a 10-year period. A market survey indicates that the probabilities of having high and low demands over the next 10 years are .75 and .25, respectively. The immediate construction of a large plant will cost $5 million and a

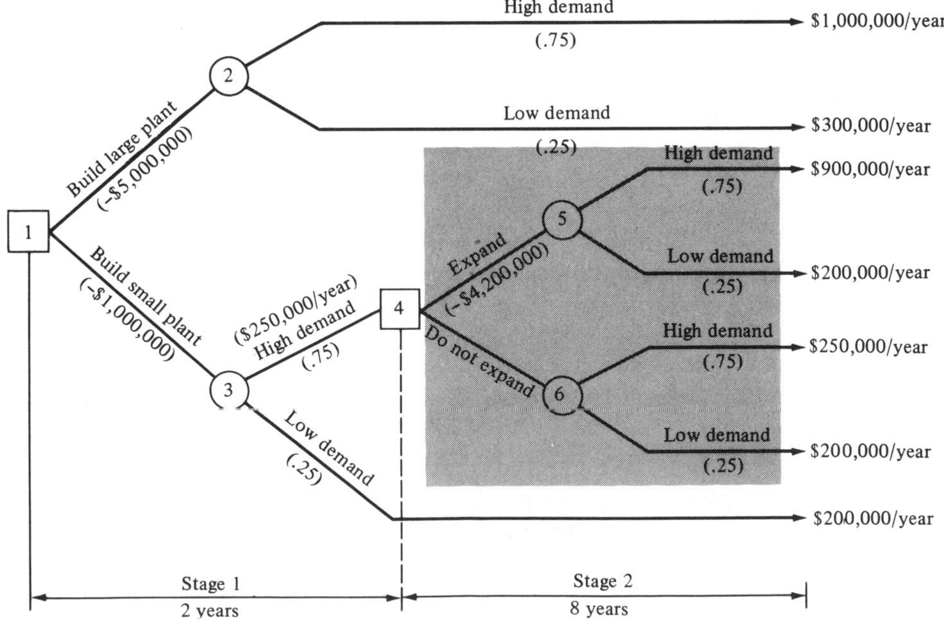

Figure 12-1

small plant will cost only \$1 million. The expansion of the small plant 2 years from now is estimated to cost \$4.2 million. Estimates of annual income for each of the alternatives are given as follows.

1. Full-size plant and high (low) demand will yield \$1,000,000 (\$300,000) annually.
2. Small plant and low demand will yield \$200,000 annually.
3. Small plant and high demand will yield \$250,000 for each of the 10 years.
4. Expanded small plant with high (low) demand will yield \$900,000 (\$200,000) annually.
5. Small plant with no expansion and high demand in the first two years followed by low demand will yield \$200,000 in each of the remaining 8 years.

These data are summarized in Figure 12-1. We are now ready to evaluate the alternatives. The final decision must tell us what to do at both of the decision nodes 1 and 4.

The evaluation of the alternatives is based on the use of the expected value criterion. The computations start at stage 2 and then move backward to stage 1. Thus, for the last 8 years, we can evaluate the two alternatives at node 4 as follows:

$$E\{\text{net profit} \mid \text{expansion}\} = (900{,}000 \times .75 + 200{,}000 \times .25) \times 8 - 4{,}200{,}000 = \$1{,}600{,}000$$

$$E\{\text{net profit} \mid \text{no expansion}\} = (250{,}000 \times .75 + 200{,}000 \times .25) \times 8 = \mathbf{\$1{,}900{,}000}$$

Thus, at node 4, the decision calls for no expansion, and the associated expected net profit is \$1,900,000.

We can now replace all the branches emanating from node 4 by a single branch with an expected net profit of \$1,900,000, representing the net profit for the *last 8 years.* We now make stage 1 computations corresponding to node 1 as follows:

$$E\{\text{net profit} \mid \text{large plant}\} = (1{,}000{,}000 \times .75 + 300{,}000 \times .25) \times 10 - 5{,}000{,}000 = \mathbf{\$3{,}250{,}000}$$

$$E\{\text{net profit} \mid \text{small plant}\} = (1{,}900{,}000 + 500{,}000) \times .75 + 2{,}000{,}000 \times .25 - 1{,}000{,}000 = \$1{,}300{,}000$$

Thus the optimal decision at node 1 is to build a full-size plant now. Making this decision now obviously eliminates the need for considering the alternatives at node 4. ◀

Exercise 12.2-1

In Example 12.2-1, suppose that demand during the last 8 years can be high, medium, or low, with probabilities .7, .2, and .1, respectively. The annual incomes are summarized as follows:

1. Expanded small plant with high, medium, and low demands will yield annual income of \$900,000, \$600,000, and \$200,000.
2. Nonexpanded small plant with high, medium, and low demand will yield annual income of \$400,000, \$280,000, and \$150,000.

Determine the optimal decision at node 4.

[*Ans.* $E\{\text{net profit} \mid \text{expansion}\} = \$1{,}960{,}000$ and $E\{\text{net profit} \mid \text{no expansion}\} = \$2{,}808{,}000$. Hence do not expand at node 4.]

12.3 DECISIONS UNDER UNCERTAINTY

This section introduces a number of criteria for making decisions under uncertainty under the assumption that no probability distributions are available. The methods to be presented here include

1. The Laplace criterion.
2. The Minimax criterion.
3. The Savage criterion.
4. The Hurwicz criterion.

The major difference among these criteria is reflected by how conservative the decision maker is in dealing with the prevailing uncertainty conditions. For example, the Laplace criterion is based on more optimistic conditions than the minimax criterion. Also, the Hurwicz criterion can be adjusted to reflect attitudes ranging from the most optimistic to the most pessimistic. In this respect, the criteria, even though they are quantitative in nature, reflect a subjective appraisal of the environment in which the decision is made. Unfortunately, there are no general guidelines as to which criterion should be implemented, since the (changing) mood of the decision maker dictated by the uncertainty of the situation may be an important factor in choosing a suitable criterion.

In the foregoing criteria, it is assumed that the decision maker does not have an *intelligent* opponent. In this case, "nature" is said to be the opponent and there is no reason to believe that "nature" *aims* at inflicting losses on the decision maker.

Situations exist, however, where "nature" is replaced by an intelligent opponent whose interests conflict with those of the decision maker. For example, in a war, opposing armies represent intelligent opponents. The existence of this new element requires special provisions in designing a suitable criterion. **Game theory**, presented in Section 12.4, handles this case.

The information utilized in making decisions under uncertainty is usually summarized in the form of a matrix with its rows representing possible **actions** and its columns representing possible future **states** of the system. Consider, for example, the situation where a company is faced with a labor strike. Depending on the length of the strike, a level of inventory for a certain item must be maintained. The future states of the system (columns) are represented by the possible length of the strike, and the actions (rows) are represented by the level of inventory that should be maintained. This means that an action represents a possible decision.

Associated with each action and each future state is an outcome that evaluates the gain (or loss) resulting from taking such action when a given future state occurs. Thus, if a_i represents the ith action ($i = 1, 2, \ldots, m$) and θ_j represents the jth future state ($j = 1, 2, \ldots, n$), then $v(a_i, \theta_j)$ will represent the associated outcome. In general, $v(a_i, \theta_j)$ may be a continuous function of a_i and θ_j. Under discrete conditions, this information is arranged as shown next in the matrix. This representation will be the basis for developing the criteria for decisions under uncertainty.

	θ_1	θ_2	$\cdots$	θ_n
a_1	$v(a_1, \theta_1)$	$v(a_1, \theta_2)$	$\cdots$	$v(a_1, \theta_n)$
a_2	$v(a_2, \theta_1)$	$v(a_2, \theta_2)$	$\cdots$	$v(a_2, \theta_n)$
$\vdots$	$\vdots$	$\vdots$		$\vdots$
a_m	$v(a_m, \theta_1)$	$v(a_m, \theta_2)$	$\cdots$	$v(a_m, \theta_n)$

12.3.1 LAPLACE CRITERION

This criterion is based on what is known as the **principle of insufficient reason.** Since the probabilities associated with the occurrence of $\theta_1, \theta_2, \ldots,$ and θ_n are unknown, we do not have enough information to conclude that these probabilities will be different. For if this is not the case, we should be able to determine these probabilities, and the situation will no longer be a decision under uncertainty. Thus, because of insufficient reason to believe otherwise, the states $\theta_1, \theta_2, \ldots,$ and θ_n are equally likely to occur. When this conclusion is established, the problem is converted into a decision under risk, where one selects the action a_i yielding the largest *expected* gain. That is, select the action a_i^* corresponding to

$$\max_{a_i}\left\{\frac{1}{n}\sum_{j=1}^{n} v(a_i, \theta_j)\right\}$$

where $1/n$ is the probability that θ_j $(j = 1, 2, \ldots, n)$ occurs.

Example 12.3-1. A recreational facility must decide on the level of supplies it must stock to meet the needs of its customers during one of the holidays. The exact number of customers is not known, but it is expected to be in one of four categories: 200, 250, 300, or 350 customers. Four levels of supplies are thus suggested, with level i being ideal (from the viewpoint of incurred costs) if the number of customers falls in category i. Deviation from the ideal levels results in additional costs either because extra supplies are stocked needlessly or because demand cannot be satisfied. The following table provides these costs in thousands of dollars.

		Customer Category			
		θ_1	θ_2	θ_3	θ_4
Supplies Level	a_1	5	10	18	25
	a_2	8	7	8	23
	a_3	21	18	12	21
	a_4	30	22	19	15

The Laplace principle assumes that $\theta_1, \theta_2, \theta_3,$ and θ_4 are equally likely to occur. Thus the associated probabilities are given by $P\{\theta = \theta_j\} = 1/4, j = 1, 2, 3, 4,$ and the expected costs for the different actions $a_1, a_2, a_3,$ and a_4 are

$$E\{a_1\} = (1/4)(5 + 10 + 18 + 25) = 14.5$$
$$E\{a_2\} = (1/4)(8 + 7 + 8 + 23) = \mathbf{11.5}$$
$$E\{a_3\} = (1/4)(21 + 18 + 12 + 21) = 18.0$$
$$E\{a_4\} = (1/4)(30 + 22 + 19 + 15) = 21.5$$

Thus the best level of inventory according to Laplace criterion is specified by a_2. ◀

Exercise 12.3-1
Suppose it is decided that customer category 4 is not a feasible possibility, determine the optimal supply in Example 12.3-1. [*Ans.* a_2.]

12.3.2 MINIMAX (MAXIMIN) CRITERION

This is the most conservative criterion, since it is based on making the best out of the worst possible conditions. That is, if the outcome $v(a_i, \theta_j)$ represents loss for the decision maker, then, for a_i, the worst loss regardless of what θ_j may be is $\max_{\theta_j}\{v(a_i, \theta_j)\}$. The **minimax criterion** then selects the action a_i associated with $\min_{a_i} \max_{\theta_j}\{v(a_i, \theta_j)\}$. In a similar manner, if $v(a_i, \theta_j)$ represents gain, the criterion selects the action a_i associated with $\max_{a_i} \min_{\theta_j}\{v(a_i, \theta_j\}$. This is called the **maximin criterion.**

Example 12.3-2. Consider Example 12.3-1. Since $v(a_i, \theta_j)$ represents cost, the minimax criterion is applicable. The computations are summarized in the matrix. The minimax strategy is a_3.

$v(a_j, \theta_j) =$

	θ_1	θ_2	θ_3	θ_4	$\max_{\theta_j}\{v(a_i, \theta_j)\}$
a_1	5	10	18	25	25
a_2	8	7	8	23	23
a_3	21	18	12	21	**21** ← minimax value
a_4	30	22	19	15	30

◀

Exercise 12.3-2
Apply the minimax criterion to Exercise 12.3-1.
[*Ans.* The minimax value = 8, corresponding to a_2.]

12.3.3 SAVAGE MINIMAX REGRET CRITERION

The minimax criterion of Section 12.3.2 is extremely conservative, to the extent that it may sometimes lead to illogical conclusions. Consider the following *loss* matrix, which is usually quoted as a classic example for justifying the need for the Savage "less conservative" criterion.

$v(a_i, \theta_j) =$

	θ_1	θ_2
a_1	$11,000	$90
a_2	$10,000	$10,000

A minimax criterion applied to this matrix yields a_2. But intuitively we are tempted to choose a_1, since there is a chance that if $\theta = \theta_2$ only $90 will be lost, whereas it is certain that a_2 will yield a loss of $10,000 whether $\theta = \theta_1$ or θ_2.

The Savage criterion "rectifies" this point by constructing a new loss matrix in which $v(a_i, \theta_j)$ is replaced by $r(a_i, \theta_j)$, which is defined by

$$r(a_i, \theta_j) = \begin{cases} \max\limits_{a_k}\{v(a_k, \theta_j)\} - v(a_i, \theta_j), & \text{if } v \text{ is profit} \\ v(a_i, \theta_j) - \min\limits_{a_k}\{v(a_k, \theta_j)\}, & \text{if } v \text{ is loss} \end{cases}$$

This means that $r(a_i, \theta_j)$ is the difference between the best choice in column θ_j and the values of $v(a_i, \theta_j)$ in the same column. In essence, $r(a_i, \theta_j)$ is a representation of the "regret" of the decision maker as a result of missing the best choice corresponding to a given future state θ_j. The function $r(a_i, \theta_j)$ is referred to as the **regret matrix**.

To show how the new elements $r(a_i, \theta_j)$ produce a logical conclusion for the foregoing example, consider

$$r(a_i, \theta_j) = \begin{array}{c|cc} & \theta_1 & \theta_2 \\ \hline a_1 & \$1000 & \$0 \\ a_2 & \$0 & \$9910 \end{array}$$

The minimax criterion yields a_1, as is expected.

Notice that whether $v(a_i, \theta_j)$ is a profit or a loss function, $r(a_i, \theta_j)$ is a regret function which, in both cases, represents loss. Thus only the minimax (and not the maximin) criterion can be applied to $r(a_i, \theta_j)$.

Example 12.3-3. Consider Example 12.3-1. The given matrix represents costs. The corresponding regret matrix given here is determined by subtracting 5, 7, 8, and 15 from columns 1, 2, 3, and 4, respectively.

$r(a_i, \theta_j) =$

	θ_1	θ_2	θ_3	θ_4	$\max_{\theta_j}\{r(a_i, \theta_j)\}$
a_1	0	3	10	10	10
a_2	3	0	0	8	**8** ← minimax value
a_3	16	11	4	6	16
a_4	25	15	11	0	25

Although the same minimax criterion is used to determine the best action (a_2 in this case), the use of $r(a_i, \theta_j)$ has resulted in a different solution from that in Example 12.3-2. ◀

Exercise 12.3-3

Resolve Example 12.3-3 assuming that a_2 is not a possibility.
[*Ans.* The minimax of $r(a_i, \theta_j) = 10$, corresponding to a_1.]

12.3.4 HURWICZ CRITERION

This criterion represents a range of attitudes from the most optimistic to the most pessimistic. Under the most optimistic conditions, one would choose the action yielding $\max_{a_i} \max_{\theta_j}\{v(a_i, \theta_j)\}$. [It is assumed that $v(a_i, \theta_j)$ represents gain or profit.] Similarly, under the most pessimistic conditions, the chosen action corresponds to $\max_{a_i} \min_{\theta_j}\{v(a_i, \theta_j)\}$. The Hurwicz criterion strikes a balance between extreme pessimism and extreme optimism by weighing the above two conditions by the respective weights α and $(1 - \alpha)$, where $0 \le \alpha \le 1$. That is, if $v(a_i, \theta_j)$ represents profit, select the action that yields

$$\max_{a_i}\{\alpha \max_{\theta_j} v(a_i, \theta_j) + (1 - \alpha)\min_{\theta_j} v(a_i, \theta_j)\}$$

For the case where $v(a_i, \theta_j)$ represents cost, the criterion selects the action that yields

$$\min_{a_i}\{\alpha \min_{\theta_j} v(a_i, \theta_j) + (1-\alpha)\max_{\theta_j} v(a_i, \theta_j)\}$$

The parameter α is known as the index of optimism: when $\alpha = 1$, the criterion is "too" optimistic; when $\alpha = 0$, it is "too" pessimistic. A value of α between zero and one can be selected depending on whether the decision maker leans toward pessimism or optimism. In the absence of a strong feeling one way or the other, a value $\alpha = 1/2$ seems to be a reasonable choice.

Example 12.3-4. The Hurwicz principle is applied to Example 12.3-1. It is assumed that $\alpha = 1/2$. The necessary calculations are shown in the table that follows. The optimum solution is given by either a_1 or a_2.

	$\min_{\theta_j} v(a_i, \theta_j)$	$\max_{\theta_j} v(a_i, \theta_j)$	$\alpha \min_{\theta_j} v(a_i, \theta_j) + (1-\alpha)\max_{\theta_j} v(a_i, \theta_j)$
a_1	5	25	**15** $\leftarrow \min_{a_i}$
a_2	7	23	**15**
a_3	12	21	16.5
a_4	15	30	22.5

◀

Exercise 12.3-4

Resolve Example 12.3-4 assuming that $\alpha = .75$.
[*Ans.* Choose a_1 with a value of 10.]

12.4 GAME THEORY

In Section 12.3 the criteria for decisions under uncertainty are developed under the assumption that "nature" is the opponent. In this respect, nature is not malevolent. This section deals with decisions under uncertainty involving two or more *intelligent* opponents in which each opponent aspires to optimize his own decision at the expense of the other opponents. Typical examples include launching advertisement campaigns for competing products and planning war tactics for opposing armies.

In game theory, an opponent is referred to as a **player**. Each player has a number of choices, finite or infinite, called **strategies**. The **outcomes** or **payoffs** of a game are summarized as functions of the different strategies for each player. A game with two players, where a gain of one player *equals* a loss to the other, is known as **two-person zero-sum game**. In such a game it suffices to express the outcomes in terms of the payoff to one player. A matrix similar to the one used in Section 12.3 is usually used to summarize the payoffs to the player whose strategies are given by the rows of the matrix. This section will deal primarily with two-person zero-sum games.

Example 12.4-1. To illustrate the definitions of a *two-person zero-sum* game, consider a coin-matching situation in which each of the two players A and B selects a head (H) or a tail (T). If the outcomes match (i.e., H and H, or T and T), player A wins \$1.00 from player B. Otherwise, A loses \$1.00 to B.

In this game each player has two strategies (H or T), which yield the following 2×2 game matrix expressed in terms of the payoff to A:

		Player B H	T
Player A	H	1	-1
	T	-1	1

The "optimal" solution to such a game may require each player to play a **pure strategy** (e.g., either H or T) or a mixture of pure strategies. The latter case is known as **mixed strategy** selection. ◀

12.4.1 OPTIMAL SOLUTION OF TWO-PERSON ZERO-SUM GAMES

The selection of a criterion for solving a decision problem depends largely on the available information. Games represent the ultimate case of lack of information in which intelligent opponents are working in a conflicting environment. The result is that a very conservative criterion, called the **minimax-maximin** criterion, is usually proposed for solving two-person zero-sum games. This criterion was introduced in Section 12.3.2. The main difference is that "nature" is not regarded as an active (or malevolent) opponent, whereas in game theory each player is intelligent and hence actively tries to defeat his opponent.

To accommodate the fact that each opponent is working against the other's interest, the minimax criterion selects each player's (mixed or pure) strategy that yields the *best* of the *worst* possible outcomes. An optimal solution is said to be reached if neither player finds it beneficial to alter his strategy. In this case, the game is said to be **stable** or in a state of equilibrium.

Since the game matrix is usually expressed in terms of the payoff to player A (whose strategies are represented by the rows), the (conservative) criterion calls for A to select the strategy (mixed or pure) that maximizes his minimum gain, the minimum being taken over all the strategies of player B. By the same reasoning, player B selects the strategy that minimizes his maximum losses. Again, the maximum is taken over all A's strategies.

The following example illustrates the computations of the minimax and maximin values of a game.

Example 12.4-2. Consider the following payoff matrix, which represents player A's gain. The computations of the minimax and maximin values are shown on the matrix.

		Player B 1	2	3	4	Row Minimum
Player A	1	8	2	9	5	2
	2	6	**5**	7	18	**5** Maximin
	3	7	3	-4	10	-4
Column Maximum		8	**5** Minimax	9	18	

When player A plays his first strategy, he may gain 8, 2, 9, or 5, which depends on player B's selected strategy. He can guarantee, however, a gain of at least min $\{8, 2, 9, 5\} = 2$ regardless of B's selected strategy. Similarly, if A plays his second strategy, he is guaranteed an income of at least $\min\{6, 5, 7, 18\} = 5$, and if he plays his third strategy, he is guaranteed an income of at least $\min\{7, 3, -4, 10\} = -4$. Thus the minimum value in each row represents the minimum gain guaranteed A if he plays his pure strategies. These are indicated in the matrix by "row minimum." Now, player A, by selecting his second strategy, is maximizing his minimum gain. This gain is given by $\max\{2, 5, -4\} = 5$. Player A's selection is called the **maximin strategy**, and his corresponding gain is called the **maximin** (or **lower**) **value** of the game.

Player B, on the other hand, wants to minimize her losses. She realizes that, if she plays her first pure strategy, she can lose no more than $\max\{8, 6, 7\} = 8$ regardless of A's selections. A similar argument can also be applied to the three remaining strategies. The corresponding results are thus indicated in the matrix by "column maximum." Player B will then select the strategy that minimizes her maximum losses. This is given by the second strategy and her corresponding loss is given by $\min\{8, 5, 9, 18\} = 5$. Player B's selection is called the **minimax strategy** and her corresponding loss is called the **minimax** (or **upper**) **value** of the game. ◀

From the conditions governing the minimax criterion, the minimax (upper) value is *greater than* or *equal to* the maximum (lower) value (see Problem 12–24). In the case where the equality holds, that is, minimax value = maximin value, the corresponding pure strategies are called "optimal" strategies and the game is said to have a **saddle point**. The value of the game, given by the common entry of the optimal pure strategies, is equal to the maximin and the minimax values. "Optimality" here signifies that neither player is tempted to change his or her strategy, since the opponent can counteract by selecting another strategy yielding less attractive payoff. In general, the value of the game must satisfy the inequality

$$\text{maximin (lower) value} \leq \text{value of the game} \leq \text{minimax (upper) value}$$

In the preceding example, maximin value = minimax value = 5. This implies that the game has a saddle point which is given by the entry (2, 2) of the matrix. The value of the game is thus equal to 5. Notice that neither player can improve his position by selecting any other strategy.

12.4.2 MIXED STRATEGIES

The preceding section shows that the existence of a saddle point immediately yields the optimal pure strategies for the game. Some games do not have saddle points, however. For example, consider the following zero-sum game:

		B 1	2	3	4	Row Minimum
A	1	5	−10	9	0	−10
	2	6	7	8	1	1
	3	8	7	15	2	**2** Maximin
	4	3	4	−1	4	−1
Column Maximum		8	7	15	**4** Minimax	

The minimax value (= 4) is greater than the maximin value (= 2). Hence the game does not have a saddle point and the pure maximin-minimax strategies are not optimal. This is true, since each player can improve his payoff by selecting a different strategy. In this case, the game is said to be **unstable.**

The failure of the minimax-maximin (pure) strategies, in general, to give an optimal solution to the game has led to the idea of using mixed strategies. Each player, instead of selecting a pure strategy only, may play all his strategies according to a predetermined set of probabilities. Let $x_1, x_2, \ldots, x_m$ and $y_1, y_2, \ldots, y_n$ be the row and column probabilities by which A and B, respectively, select their pure strategies. Then

$$\sum_{i=1}^{m} x_i = \sum_{j=1}^{n} y_j = 1$$

$$x_i, y_j \geq 0, \qquad \text{for all } i \text{ and } j$$

Thus if a_{ij} represents the (i, j)th entry of the game matrix, x_i and y_i will appear as in the following matrix:

			B		
		y_1	y_2	$\cdots$	y_n
	x_1	a_{11}	a_{12}	$\cdots$	a_{1n}
A	x_2	a_{21}	a_{22}	$\cdots$	a_{2n}
	$\vdots$	$\vdots$	$\vdots$		$\vdots$
	x_m	a_{m1}	a_{m2}	$\cdots$	a_{mn}

The solution of the mixed strategy problem is based also on the minimax criterion given in Section 12.4.1. The only difference is that A selects x_i that maximize the smallest *expected* payoff in a column, whereas B selects y_j that minimize the largest *expected* payoff in a row. Mathematically, the minimax criterion for a mixed strategy case is given as follows. Player A selects x_i ($x_i \geq 0$, $\sum_{i=1}^{m} x_i = 1$) that will yield

$$\max_{x_i}\left\{\min\left(\sum_{i=1}^{m} a_{i1}x_i, \sum_{i=1}^{m} a_{i2}x_i, \ldots, \sum_{i=1}^{m} a_{in}x_i\right)\right\}$$

and player B selects y_j ($y_j \geq 0$, $\sum_{j=1}^{n} y_j = 1$) that will yield

$$\min_{y_j}\left\{\max\left(\sum_{j=1}^{n} a_{1j}y_j, \sum_{j=1}^{n} a_{2j}y_j, \ldots, \sum_{j=1}^{n} a_{mj}y_j\right)\right\}$$

These values are referred to as the maximin and the minimax expected payoffs, respectively.

As in the pure strategies case, the relationship

$$\text{minimax expected payoff} \geq \text{maximin expected payoff}$$

holds. When x_i and y_j correspond to the optimal solution, the equality holds and the resulting values become equal to the (optimal) expected value of the game. This result follows from the **minimax theorem** and is stated here without proof (see Problem 12–31). If x_i^* and y_j^* are the optimal solutions for both players, each payoff element a_{ij} will be associated with the probability $(x_i^* y_j^*)$. Thus the optimal expected value of the game is

$$v^* = \sum_{i=1}^{m} \sum_{j=1}^{n} a_{ij} x_i^* y_j^*$$

There are several methods for solving two-person zero-sum games for the optimal values of x_i and y_j. This section presents two methods only. The graphical method for solving $(2 \times n)$ or $(m \times 2)$ games is presented in Section 12.4.3, and the general linear programming method for solving any $(m \times n)$ game is presented in Section 12.4.4.

12.4.3 GRAPHICAL SOLUTION OF $(2 \times N)$ AND $(M \times 2)$ GAMES

Graphical solutions are only applicable to games in which at least one of the players has two strategies only. Consider the following $(2 \times n)$ games.

				B	
		y_1	y_2	$\cdots$	y_n
A	x_1	a_{11}	a_{12}	$\cdots$	a_{1n}
	$x_2 = 1 - x_1$	a_{21}	a_{22}	$\cdots$	a_{2n}

It is assumed that the game does not have a saddle point.

Since A has two strategies, it follows that $x_2 = 1 - x_1$; $x_1 \geq 0$, $x_2 \geq 0$. His expected payoffs corresponding to the *pure* strategies of B are given by

B's Pure Strategy	A's Expected Payoff
1	$(a_{11} - a_{21})x_1 + a_{21}$
2	$(a_{12} - a_{22})x_1 + a_{22}$
$\vdots$	
n	$(a_{1n} - a_{2n})x_1 + a_{2n}$

This shows that A's average payoff varies linearly with x_1.

According to the minimax criterion for mixed strategy games, player A should select the value of x_1 that maximizes his minimum expected payoffs. This may be done by plotting the straight lines as functions of x_1. The following example illustrates the procedure.

Example 12.4-3. Consider the following (2×4) game.

				B	
		1	2	3	4
A	1	2	2	3	−1
	2	4	3	2	6

This game does not have a saddle point. Thus A's expected payoffs corresponding to B's pure strategies are given as follows.

B's Pure Strategies	A's Expected Payoff
1	$-2x_1 + 4$
2	$-x_1 + 3$
3	$x_1 + 2$
4	$-7x_1 + 6$

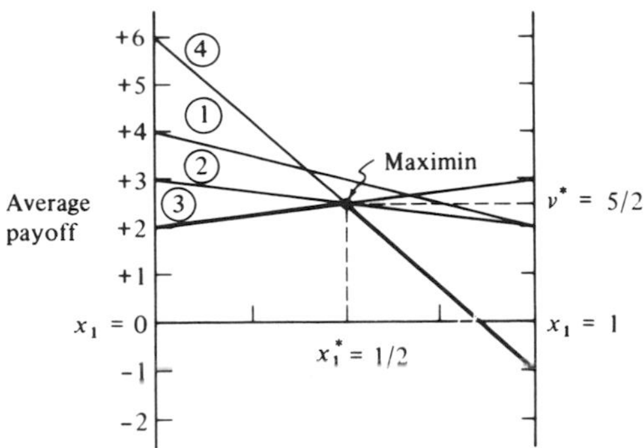

Figure 12-2

These four straight lines are then plotted as functions of x_1 as shown in Figure 12-2. The maximin occurs at $x_1^* = 1/2$. This is the point of intersection of *any* two of the lines 2, 3, and 4. Consequently, A's optimal strategy is ($x_1^* = 1/2$, $x_2^* = 1/2$), and the value of the game is obtained by substituting for x_1 in the equation of any of the lines passing through the maximin point. This gives

$$v^* = \begin{cases} -1/2 + 3 = 5/2 \\ 1/2 + 2 = 5/2 \\ -7(1/2) + 6 = 5/2 \end{cases}$$

To determine B's optimal strategies, it should be noticed that three lines pass through the maximin point. This is an indication that B can mix all three strategies. Any two lines having *opposite* signs for their slopes define an alternative optimum solution. Thus, of the three combinations (2, 3), (2, 4), and (3, 4), the combination (2, 4) must be excluded as nonoptimal.

The first combination (2, 3) implies that $y_1^* = y_4^* = 0$. Consequently, $y_3 = 1 - y_2$ and B's average payoffs corresponding to A's pure strategies are given as follows:

A's Pure Strategy	B's Expected Payoff
1	$-y_2 + 3$
2	$y_2 + 2$

Thus y_2^* (corresponding to minimax point) can be determined from

$$-y_2^* + 3 = y_2^* + 2$$

This gives $y_2^* = 1/2$. Notice that by substituting $y_2^* = 1/2$ in B's expected payoffs given, the minimax value is 5/2, which equals the value of the game v^*, as should be expected.

The remaining combination (3, 4) can be treated similarly to obtain an alternative optimal solution. Any weighted average of the combinations (2, 3) and (3, 4) will also yield a new optimal solution that mixes all the three strategies 2, 3, and 4. The treatment of this case is left as an exercise for the reader (see Problem 12–27). ◀

Exercise 12.4-1

Consider Example 12.4-3.

(a) Determine B's pure strategies that can be deleted without affecting the optimal solution.
[*Ans.* Delete B's strategies 1 and 2.]

(b) If B's third pure strategy is eliminated, determine the optimal solution.
[*Ans.* A saddle point optimal solution occurs with each player selecting his second pure strategy.]

Example 12.4-4. Consider the following (4×2) game:

		B 1	B 2
A	1	2	4
	2	2	3
	3	3	2
	4	-2	6

This game does not have a saddle point. Let y_1 and y_2 $(= 1 - y_1)$ be B's mixed strategies. Thus

A's Pure Strategy	B's Expected Payoff
1	$-2y_1 + 4$
2	$-y_1 + 3$
3	$y_1 + 2$
4	$-8y_1 + 6$

These four lines are plotted in Figure 12-3. In this case the minimax point is determined as the lowest point of the upper envelope. The value of y_1^* is obtained as the point of intersection of lines 1 and 3. This yields $y_1^* = 2/3$ and $v^* = 8/3$.

The lines intersecting at the minimax point correspond to A's pure strategies 1 and 3. This indicates that $x_2^* = x_4^* = 0$. Consequently, $x_1 - 1 - x_3$ and A's average payoffs corresponding to B's pure strategies are

B's Pure Strategy	A's Expected Payoff
1	$-x_1 + 3$
2	$2x_1 + 2$

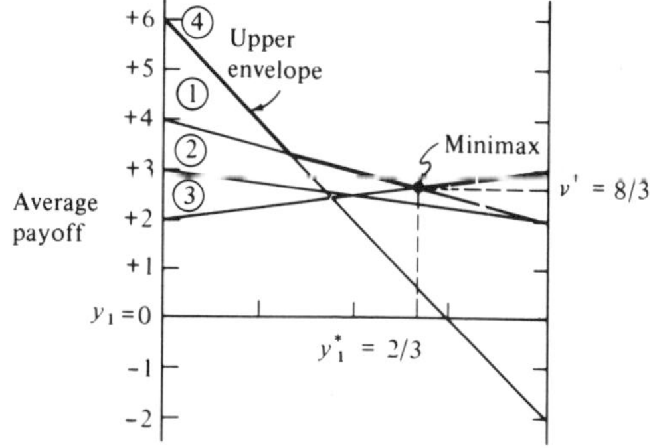

Figure 12-3

The point x_1^* is determined by solving

$$-x_1^* + 3 = 2x_1^* + 2$$

This gives $x_1^* = 1/3$. Thus A's optimal strategies are $x_1^* = 1/3$, $x_2^* = 0$, $x_3^* = 2/3$, $x_4^* = 0$. This yields $v^* = 8/3$, as before. ◀

Exercise 12.4-2

(a) In Example 12.4-4, determine A's pure strategies that are strictly dominated by others.
[*Ans.* Strategy 2 is strictly dominated by strategy 1.]

(b) If A's pure strategy 1 is deleted in Example 12.4-4, determine the new optimal solution for A and B.
[*Ans.* Player A plays 2 and 3 with equal probabilities and player B plays his two strategies also with equal probabilities.]

12.4.4 SOLUTION OF $(M \times N)$ GAMES BY LINEAR PROGRAMMING

Game theory bears a strong relationship to linear programming, since every finite two-person zero-sum game can be expressed as a linear program and, conversely, every linear program can be represented as a game. In fact, G. Dantzig (1963, p. 24) states that J. von Neumann, father of game theory, when first introduced to the simplex method of linear programming in 1947, immediately recognized this relationship and further pinpointed and stressed the concept of *duality* in linear programming. This section illustrates the solution of game problems by linear programming. It is especially useful for games with large matrices.

Section 12.4.2 shows that A's optimum mixed strategies satisfy

$$\max_{x_i}\left\{\min\left(\sum_{i=1}^{m} a_{i1}x_i, \sum_{i=1}^{m} a_{i2}x_i, \ldots, \sum_{i=1}^{m} a_{in}x_i\right)\right\}$$

subject to the constraints

$$x_1 + x_2 + \cdots + x_m = 1$$
$$x_i \geq 0, \qquad i = 1, 2, \ldots, m$$

This problem can be put in the linear programming form as follows. Let

$$v = \min\left(\sum_{i=1}^{m} a_{i1}x_i, \sum_{i=1}^{m} a_{i2}x_i, \ldots, \sum_{i=1}^{m} a_{in}x_i\right)$$

then the problem becomes (see Example 2.3-3)

$$\text{maximize } z = v$$

subject to

$$\sum_{i=1}^{m} a_{ij}x_i \geq v, \qquad j = 1, 2, \ldots, n$$

$$\sum_{i=1}^{m} x_i = 1$$

$$x_i \geq 0, \qquad \text{for all } i$$

where v represents the value of the game in this case.

The linear programming formulation can be simplified by dividing all $(n + 1)$ constraints by v. This division is correct as long as $v > 0$. Otherwise, if $v < 0$, the direction of the inequality constraints must be reversed. If $v = 0$, the division is illegitimate. This point presents no special problem, since a positive constant K can be added to all the entries of the payoff matrix, thus guaranteeing that the value of the game for the "modified" matrix is greater than zero. The *true* value of the game is determined by subtracting K from the *modified* value of the game. In general, if the maximin value of the game is nonnegative, the value of the game is greater than zero (provided that the game has no saddle point).

Thus, assuming that $v > 0$, the constraints of the linear program become

$$\begin{aligned}
a_{11}\frac{x_1}{v} + a_{21}\frac{x_2}{v} + \cdots + a_{m1}\frac{x_m}{v} &\geq 1 \\
a_{12}\frac{x_1}{v} + a_{22}\frac{x_2}{v} + \cdots + a_{m2}\frac{x_m}{v} &\geq 1 \\
\vdots \qquad\qquad\qquad\qquad &\ \vdots \\
a_{1n}\frac{x_1}{v} + a_{2n}\frac{x_2}{v} + \cdots + a_{mn}\frac{x_m}{v} &\geq 1 \\
\frac{x_1}{v} + \frac{x_2}{v} + \cdots + \frac{x_m}{v} &= \frac{1}{v}
\end{aligned}$$

Let $X_i = x_i/v$, $i = 1, 2, \ldots, m$. Since

$$\max v \equiv \min \frac{1}{v} = \min\{X_1 + \cdots + X_m\}$$

the problem becomes

$$\text{minimize } z = X_1 + X_2 + \cdots + X_m$$

subject to

$$\begin{aligned}
a_{11}X_1 + a_{21}X_2 + \cdots + a_{m1}X_m &\geq 1 \\
a_{12}X_1 + a_{22}X_2 + \cdots + a_{m2}X_m &\geq 1 \\
\vdots \qquad\qquad\qquad &\ \vdots \\
a_{1n}X_1 + a_{2n}X_2 + \cdots + a_{mn}X_m &\geq 1 \\
X_1, X_2, \ldots, X_m &\geq 0
\end{aligned}$$

Player B's problem is given by

$$\min_{y_j}\left\{\max\left(\sum_{j=1}^{n} a_{1j}y_j, \sum_{j=1}^{n} a_{2j}y_j, \ldots, \sum_{j=1}^{n} a_{mj}y_j\right)\right\}$$

subject to

$$\begin{aligned}
y_1 + y_2 + \cdots + y_n &= 1 \\
y_j \geq 0, \qquad j &= 1, 2, \ldots, n
\end{aligned}$$

This can also be expressed as a linear program as follows:

$$\text{maximize } w = Y_1 + Y_2 + \cdots + Y_n$$

subject to

$$\begin{aligned} a_{11}Y_1 + a_{12}Y_2 + \cdots + a_{1n}Y_n &\le 1 \\ a_{21}Y_1 + a_{22}Y_2 + \cdots + a_{2n}Y_n &\le 1 \\ \vdots \qquad\qquad\qquad & \quad \vdots \\ a_{m1}Y_1 + a_{m2}Y_2 + \cdots + a_{mn}Y_n &\le 1 \\ Y_1, Y_2, \ldots, Y_n &\ge 0 \end{aligned}$$

where

$$w = \frac{1}{v}, \qquad Y_j = \frac{y_j}{v}, \qquad j = 1, 2, \ldots, n$$

Notice that B's problem is actually the dual of A's problem. Thus the optimal solution of one problem automatically yields the optimal solution to the other. Player B's problem can be solved by the regular simplex method, and player A's problem is solved by the dual simplex method. The choice of either method will depend on which problem has a smaller number of constraints, which in turn depends on the number of pure strategies for each player.

Example 12.4-5. Consider the following (3 × 3) game:

		B 1	2	3	Row Minimum
A	1	3	−1	−3	−3
	2	−3	3	−1	−3
	3	−4	−3	3	−4
Column Maximum		3	3	3	

Since the maximin value is −3, it is possible that the value of the game may be negative or zero. Thus a constant K, which is at *least* equal to the negative of the maximin value, is added to all the elements of the matrix; that is, $K \ge 3$. Let $K = 5$. The preceding matrix becomes

		B 1	2	3
A	1	8	4	2
	2	2	8	4
	3	1	2	8

B's linear programming problem is thus given as

$$\text{maximize } w = Y_1 + Y_2 + Y_3$$

subject to

$$\begin{aligned} 8Y_1 + 4Y_2 + 2Y_3 &\le 1 \\ 2Y_1 + 8Y_2 + 4Y_3 &\le 1 \\ 1Y_1 + 2Y_2 + 8Y_3 &\le 1 \\ Y_1, Y_2, Y_3 &\ge 0 \end{aligned}$$

The final optimal tableau for this problem is given by

Basic	Y_1	Y_2	Y_3	S_1	S_2	S_3	Solution
w	0	0	0	5/49	11/196	1/14	45/196
Y_1	1	0	0	1/7	−1/14	0	1/14
Y_2	0	1	0	−3/98	31/196	−1/14	11/196
Y_3	0	0	1	−1/98	−3/98	1/7	5/49

Thus, for the original problem,

$$v^* = \frac{1}{w} - K = 196/45 - 5 = -29/45$$

$$y_1^* = \frac{Y_1}{w} = \frac{1/14}{45/196} = 14/45$$

$$y_2^* = \frac{Y_2}{w} = \frac{11/196}{45/196} = 11/45$$

$$y_3^* = \frac{Y_3}{w} = \frac{5/49}{45/196} = 20/45$$

The optimal strategies for A are obtained from the dual solution to the problem above. This is given by

$$z = w = 45/196, \quad X_1 = 5/49, \quad X_2 = 11/196, \quad X_3 = 1/14$$

Hence

$$x_1^* = X_1/z = 20/45, \quad x_2^* = X_2/z = 11/45, \quad x_3^* = X_3/z = 14/45$$

You can verify that these optimal strategies satisfy the minimax theorem. ◀

12.5 SUMMARY

In this chapter a number of decision criteria are discussed for problems with imperfect data. Although some applications have already been presented, Chapters 13 through 18 provide more applications to project scheduling, inventory, Markov processes, queueing, and simulation. You will notice that the decision models in most of these applications are based on the *expected value* criterion. This point requires some explanation. As stated throughout the chapter, the expected value criterion may not be applicable in certain situations, particularly those where the decision is not repeated a sufficiently large number of times. However, part of the reason for the wide use of expectations is purely traditional. Perhaps also the fact that the expected value criterion is analytically simple makes it particularly appealing to decision makers. For example, the minimax criterion is generally more complex than the expected value criterion.

You should realize that some of the applications in the following chapters may not justify the use of the expected value criterion and, as such, be on the alert to question whether each of these applications is proper. In this respect, different interpretations of the decision problem may give rise to different conclusions about the use of a suitable criterion.

We shall not attempt to compare the applications of the given decision criteria to the different problems we present in Chapter 12, as this may detract from concentrating on the basic elements of the situation for which a decision is made. In general, the use of the expected value criterion should be regarded as an illustration of the application of decision criteria.

SELECTED REFERENCES

DANTZIG, G. B., *Linear Programming and Extensions*, Princeton University Press, Princeton, N.J., 1963.

LUCE, R., and H. RAIFFA, *Games and Decisions*, Wiley, New York, 1957.

MORRIS, W., *The Analysis of Management Decisions*, Irwin, Homewood, Ill., 1964.

WILLIAMS, J., *The Compleat Strategyst*, rev. ed., McGraw-Hill, New York, 1966.

PROBLEMS

Section	Assigned Problems
12.1	12–1 to 12–14, 12–35
12.2	12–15 to 12–18
12.3	12–19 to 12–21
12.4	12–22 to 12–34

□ **12–1** Solve Example 12.1-1 assuming that $c_1 = 200$, $c_2 = 15$, and $n = 30$. The probabilities are given by

$$P_t = \begin{cases} 0.03, & t = 1 \\ P_{t-1} + .01, & t = 2, 3, \ldots, 10 \\ .13, & t = 11, 12, \ldots \end{cases}$$

□ **12–2** In a manufacturing process, lots having 8%, 10%, 12%, or 14% defectives are produced according to the respective probabilities .4, .3, .25, and .05. Three customers have contracts to receive lots from the manufacturer. The contracts specify that the percentages of defectives in lots shipped to customers A, B, and C should not exceed 8, 12, and 14, respectively. If a lot has a higher percentage of defectives than stipulated, a penalty of $100 per percentage point is incurred. On the other hand, supplying better quality than required costs the manufacturer $50 per percentage point. If the lots are not inspected prior to shipment, which customer should have the highest priority for receiving the order?

□ **12–3** Daily demand for loaves of bread at a grocery store are given by the following probability distribution:

x	100	150	200	250	300
$p(x)$	.20	.25	.30	.15	.10

If a loaf is not sold the same day, it can be disposed of at 15 cents at the end of the day. Otherwise, the price of a fresh loaf is 49 cents. The cost per loaf to the store is

25 cents. Assuming that the stock level is restricted to one of the demand levels, how many loaves should be stocked daily?

☐ **12–4** An automatic machine produces α (thousands of) units of a certain product per day. As α increases, the proportion of defectives p goes up. The probability density function of p in terms of α is given by

$$f(p) = \begin{cases} \alpha p^{\alpha - 1}, & 0 \leq p \leq 1 \\ 0, & \text{otherwise} \end{cases}$$

Each defective item incurs a loss of \$50. A good item produces a profit of \$5. Determine the value of α that maximizes expected profit.

☐ **12–5** The outer diameter d of a cylinder that is processed on an automatic machine has upper and lower tolerance limits of $d + t_U$ and $d - t_L$. If the machine is set at d, the produced diameters can be described by a normal distribution with mean d and standard deviation σ. Cylinders with oversized diameters can be reworked at c_1 dollars per cylinder. Undersized cylinders must be salvaged at a loss of c_2 per cylinder. Determine the best setting of the machine.

☐ **12–6** In production processes, maintenance action is periodically applied to cutting tools. If the tool is not sharpened frequently, the percentage of defective items increases. In the meantime, an increase in the frequency of sharpening a tool increases the cost of maintenance. Ideally, a balance between the two extreme costs is desired.

In a typical process, let S_U and S_L represent the upper and lower limits allowed for a measurable dimension machined by the tool. Let $\mu(t)$ be the average of the process at time t after the tool is sharpened, where $\mu(0)$ represents the ideal setting of the machine. Each time the tool is sharpened, a cost c_1 is incurred. A defective item costs c_2 to be reworked. Suppose that the output of the process can be described by a normal distribution with mean $\mu(t)$ and variance σ (σ is independent of time), and that a lot of size Q is to be manufactured at the rate α items per unit time. Determine an expression for the expected cost of sharpening the tool and reworking defectives as a function of the time T that must elapse before maintenance is applied. Show that the optimal value of T is independent of Q and interpret the result. Then determine a numerical value for T by using the data, $c_1 = 10$, $c_2 = 48.85$, $\alpha = 10$, $\mu(t) = \mu(0) + t$, and $\sigma = 1$.

[*Hint*: Approximate the number of times a tool is sharpened during the production of Q by $Q/\alpha T$. Also, numerical integration may be needed to obtain a numerical value of T.]

☐ **12–7** Let x be a random variable representing cost and let $f(x)$ be its probability density function. Suppose that $U(x)$ is the utility function of x. Show that the expected value of $U(x)$, $E\{U(x)\}$, can be expanded as a series around the point $E\{x\}$ and that the resulting expansion can be approximated by

$$E\{U(x)\} \cong U(E\{x\}) + K \text{ var}\{x\}$$

Determine the expression for K and show that K assumes a positive value if x represents loss and a negative value if x represents profit.

[*Note*: This result is consistent with the derivation of the expected value–variance criterion, Section 12.1.2.]

☐ **12–8** Solve Problem 12–4 by applying the expected value–variance criterion. Compare the optimal solution for the following risk aversion factors: $K = 1, 2$, and 5.

☐ **12–9** The demand for an item is described by the following probability density function:

x	0	1	2	3	4	5
$p(x)$	.1	.15	.4	.15	.1	.1

Determine the stock level so that the probability of running out of stock does not exceed .45. If the average shortage and surplus quantities must not exceed 1 and 2 units, respectively, determine the stock level.

☐ **12–10** In Problem 12–9, suppose that the expected shortage quantity must be strictly less than the expected surplus quantity by at least one unit. Determine the inventory level.

☐ **12–11** In Problem 12–2, suppose that a sample of size $n = 20$ is inspected before each lot is shipped to customers. If four defectives are found in the sample, compute the posterior probabilities of the lot having 8%, 10%, 12%, and 14% defectives. By using the new probabilities, determine which customer has the lowest expected cost.

☐ **12–12** Electronic components are received from two vendors. Vendor *A* supplies 75% of the components known to include 1% defectives. Vendor *B*'s components include 2% defectives. When a sample of size 5 is inspected, only one defective component is found. By using this information, determine the posterior probability that the components are delivered from vendor *A*. From vendor *B*.

☐ **12–13** Consider the following payoff (profit) matrix:

	θ_1	θ_2	θ_3	θ_4
a_1	10	20	−20	13
a_2	12	14	0	15
a_3	7	2	18	9

The a priori probabilities of θ_1, θ_2, θ_3, and θ_4 are .2, .1, .3, and .4. An experiment is conducted and its outcomes z_1 and z_2 are described by the following probabilities:

	θ_1	θ_2	θ_3	θ_4
z_1	.1	.2	.7	.4
z_2	.9	.8	.3	.6

(a) Determine the best action when no data are used.
(b) Determine the best action when the experimental data are used.

☐ **12–14** The probability that it will rain during the rainy season of the year is .7. A fisherman wants to decide whether or not to go fishing tomorrow. The conditional probability that rain is forecast given that it is the rainy season is .85. Find the probability that it will not rain tomorrow given that rain is forecast.

☐ **12–15** The daily demand for loaves of bread in a grocery store can assume one of the following values: 100, 120, or 130 loaves with probabilities .2, .3, and .5. The owner of the store is thus limiting her alternatives to stocking one of the indicated four levels. If she stocks more than she can sell in the same day, she must dispose of the remaining loaves at a discount price of 55 cents/loaf. Assuming that she pays 60 cents per loaf and sells it for $1.05, find the optimum stock level by using a decision tree representation.

☐ **12–16** In Problem 12–15, suppose that the owner wishes to consider her decision problem over a 2-day period. Her alternatives for the second day are determined as follows. If the demand in day 1 is equal to the amount stocked, she will continue to order the same quantity on the second day. Otherwise, if the demand exceeds the amount stocked, she will have the options to order higher levels of stock on the second day. Finally, if day 1's demand is less than the amount stocked, she will have the options to order any of the lower levels of stock for the second day. Express the problem as a decision tree and find the optimum solution using the cost data given in Problem 12–15.

☐ **12–17** Solve Example 12.2-1 assuming that the annual interest rate is 10% and that decisions are made based on the expected value of *discounted* income.

☐ **12–18** In Example 12.2-1, suppose that a third alternative is added which will allow us to expand the small plant to a medium-size plant. This option can be exercised regardless of whether the demand is high or low during the first 2 years. Thus if the 2-year demand is high, the company has three options: (i) expand the plant fully (cost = $4,200,000), (ii) expand it moderately (cost = $2,800,000), or (iii) do not expand it at all. On the other hand, if the demand is low, the company can expand the plant moderately or elect not to expand it at all. Estimates of annual income for the different alternatives are given as follows:

(i) High demand in the first 2 years and medium-size expansion will yield $700,000 ($250,000) for each of the remaining 8 years if the demand is high (low).
(ii) Low demand in the first 2 years and medium-size expansion will yield $600,000 ($300,000) for each of the remaining 8 years if the demand is high (low).
(iii) Low demand in the first 2 years and no expansion will yield $300,000 ($400,000) for each of the remaining 8 years if the demand is high (low).

The remaining data are as given in Example 12.2-1. Determine the optimal decision based on the optimal value criterion.

☐ **12–19** Consider the following payoff (profit) matrix.

	θ_1	θ_2	θ_3	θ_4	θ_5
a_1	15	10	0	−6	17
a_2	3	14	8	9	2
a_3	1	5	14	20	−3
a_4	7	19	10	2	0

No probabilities are known for the occurrence of the nature states. Compare the solutions obtained by each of the following criteria:

(a) Laplace.
(b) Maximin.
(c) Savage.
(d) Hurwicz (assume that $\alpha = .5$).

☐ **12–20** One of N machines is to be selected for producing a lot whose size Q could assume any value between Q^* and Q^{**} ($Q^* < Q^{**}$). The production cost for machine i is

$$C_i = K_i + c_i Q$$

Solve the problem by each of the following criteria:

(a) Laplace.
(b) Minimax.
(c) Savage.
(d) Hurwicz (assume that $\alpha = .5$).

☐ **12–21** Give numerical answers for Problem 12–20 given that $Q^* = 1000$, $Q^{**} = 4000$, and

Machine i	K_i	C_i
1	100	5
2	40	12
3	150	3
4	90	8

☐ **12–22** (a) Find the saddle point and the value of the game for each of the following two games. The payoff is for player A.

(1)

	B			
A	8	6	2	8
	8	9	4	5
	7	5	3	5

(2)

	B			
A	4	−4	−5	6
	−3	−4	−9	−2
	6	7	−8	−9
	7	3	−9	5

(b) Find the range of values for "p" and "q" that will render the entry (2, 2) a saddle point in the following games.

	B		
A	1	q	6
	p	5	10
	6	2	3

	B		
A	2	4	5
	10	7	q
	4	p	6

☐ **12–23** Indicate whether the values of the following games are greater than, less than, or equal to zero.

(c)

	B			
A	1	9	6	0
	2	3	8	4
	−5	−2	10	−3
	7	4	−2	−5

	B			
A	3	7	−1	3
	4	8	0	−6
	6	−9	−2	4

	B			
A	−1	9	6	8
	−2	10	4	6
	5	3	0	7
	7	−2	8	4

	B		
A	3	6	1
	5	2	3
	4	2	−5

☐ **12–24** Let a_{ij} be the (i, j)th element of the payoff matrix with m and n strategies, respectively. Prove that

$$\max_i \min_j a_{ij} \leq \min_j \max_i a_{ij}$$

☐ **12–25** Two companies A and B are promoting two competing products. Each product currently controls 50% of the market. Because of recent modifications in the two products, the two companies are now preparing to launch a new advertisement campaign. If no advertisement is made by either of the two companies, the present status of the market shares will remain unchanged. However, if either company launches a stronger campaign, the other company will certainly lose a proportional percentage of its customers. A survey of the market indicated that 50% of the potential customers can be reached through television, 30% through newspapers, and the remaining 20% through radio. The objective of each company is to select the appropriate advertisement media.

Formulate the problem as a two-person zero-sum game. Does the problem have a saddle point?

☐ **12–26** Consider the game

		B 1	2	3
A	1	5	50	50
	2	1	1	0.1
	3	10	1	10

Verify that the strategies (1/6, 0, 5/6) for player A and (49/54, 5/54, 0) for player B are optimal and find the value of the game.

☐ **12–27** In Example 12.4-3, show that combination (2, 4) for player B does not yield optimal values for y_j, whereas combination (3, 4) yields the optimal solution. Develop a general expression for all the alternative solutions to the problem.

☐ **12–28** Solve the following games graphically.

	B			
A	1	3	−3	7
	2	5	4	−6

	B	
A	1	2
	5	6
	−7	9
	−4	−3
	2	1

	B		
A	1	2	5
	8	4	7
	−1	5	−6

☐ **12–29** Consider Colonel Blotto's game, where the Colonel and his enemy are trying to take over two strategic locations. The regiments available for Blotto and his enemy are 2 and 3, respectively. Both sides will distribute their regiments between the two locations. Let n_1 and n_2 be the number of regiments allocated by Colonel Blotto to locations 1 and 2, respectively. Also, let m_1 and m_2 be his enemy's allocations to the respective locations. The payoff of Blotto is computed as follows. If $n_1 > m_1$, he receives $m_1 + 1$, and if $n_2 > m_2$, he receives $m_2 + 1$. On the other hand, if $n_1 > m_1$, he loses $n_1 + 1$, and if $n_2 < m_2$, he loses $n_2 + 1$. Finally, if the number of regiments from both sides are the same, each side gets zero. Formulate the problem as a two-person zero-sum game and then solve by linear programming.

☐ **12–30** Verify that *B*'s problem is defined by the linear programming problem given in Section 12.4.4.

☐ **12–31** Prove the minimax theorem by using the relationship between the values of the objective function in the primal and the dual problems of the linear programming problem.

☐ **12–32** Verify that the linear programming solution to Example 12.4-5 satisfies the minimax theorem.

☐ **12–33** Consider the two-finger "Morra" game. Each player shows one or two fingers and simultaneously makes a guess of the number of fingers his opponent has. The player making the correct guess wins an amount equal to the total number of fingers shown by the two players. In all other cases, the game is a draw. Formulate the problem as a two-person zero-sum game and then solve by linear programming.

☐ **12–34** Solve the following games by linear programming:

(a)

		B	
A	−1	1	1
	2	−2	2
	3	3	−3

(b)

		B		
A	1	2	−5	3
	−1	4	7	2
	5	−1	1	9

☐ **12–35** In the airline industry, working hours are ruled by agreements between unions and the companies. For example, the maximum length of tour of duty may be limited to 16 hours for Boeing-747 flights and 14 hours for Boeing-707 flights. Whenever these limits are exceeded because of unexpected delays, the crew must be replaced by a fresh crew. The airlines maintain reserve crews for such eventualities. The average annual cost of a reserve crew member is estimated at $30,000. On the other hand, an overnight delay due to unavailability of reserve crew could cost as much as $50,000 for each delay. A crew member is on call 4 days a week for 12 consecutive hours. The member may not be called upon during the remaining 3 days of the week. The B-747 crew can be served by two B-707 crews.

The following table summarizes the callout probabilities for reserve crews based on 3-year historical data.

Trip Category	Trip Hours	Probability of Callout of a Reserve Crew B-747	B-707
1	14	.014	.072
2	13	.0	.019
3	$12\frac{1}{2}$	.0	.006
4	12	.016	.006
5	$11\frac{1}{2}$	.003	.003
6	11	.002	.003

As an illustration, the data indicate that for 14 hour-long trips, the probability of a callout is .014 for B-747 and .072 for B-707.

A typical *peak* day schedule is shown here as a function of the time of day.

Time of Day	Aircraft	Trip Category
8:00	707	3
9:00	707	6
	707	2
10:00	707	3
11:00	707	2
	707	4
15:00	747	6
16:00	747	4
19:00	747	1

The present reserve crew policy calls for using two (seven-member) crews between 5:00 and 11:00, four crews between 11:00 and 17:00, and two crews between 17:00 and 23:00.

Evaluate the effectiveness of the present reserve crew policy. Specifically, is the present reserve crew size too large, too small, or just right?

Chapter 13

Project Scheduling by PERT-CPM

A **project** defines a combination of interrelated activities that must be executed in a certain order before the entire task can be completed. The activities are interrelated in a logical sequence in the sense that some activities cannot start until others are completed. An **activity** in a project is usually viewed as a job requiring time and resources for its completion. In general, a project is a one-time effort; that is, the same sequence of activities may not be repeated in the future.

In the past, the scheduling of a project (over time) was done with little planning. The best-known "planning" tool then was the **Gantt bar chart**, which specifies the start and finish times for each activity on a horizontal time scale. Its disadvantage is that the interdependency between the different activities (which mainly controls the progress of the project) cannot be determined from the bar chart. The growing complexities of today's projects have demanded more systematic and more effective planning techniques with the objective of optimizing the efficiency of executing the project. Efficiency here implies effecting the utmost reduction in the time required to complete the project while accounting for the economic feasibility of using available resources.

Project management has evolved as a new field with the development of two analytic techniques for planning, scheduling, and controlling of projects. These are the **critical path method (CPM)** and the **project evaluation and review technique (PERT)**. The two techniques were developed by two different groups almost simultaneously (1956–1958). CPM was first developed by E. I. du Pont de Nemours & Company as an application to construction projects and was later extended to a more advanced status by Mauchly Associates; PERT was developed for the U.S. Navy by a consulting firm for scheduling the research and development activities for the Polaris missile program.

PERT and CPM are basically time-oriented methods in the sense that they both lead to the determination of a time schedule. Although the two methods were developed independently, they are strikingly similar. Perhaps the most important difference is that originally the time estimates for the activites were assumed deterministic in CPM and probabilistic in PERT. Today, PERT and CPM actually comprise one technique and the differences, if any, are only historical. Consequently, both techniques will be referred to as "project scheduling" techniques.

Project scheduling by PERT–CPM consists of three basic phases: **planning**, **scheduling**, and **controlling**.

The planning phase is initiated by breaking down the project into distinct activities. The time estimates for these activities are then determined, and a network (or arrow) diagram is constructed with each of its arcs (arrows) representing an activity. The entire arrow diagram gives a graphic representation of the interdependencies between the activities of the project. The construction of the arrow diagram as a planning phase has the advantage of studying the different jobs in detail, perhaps suggesting improvements before the project is actually executed. More important will be its use to develop a schedule for the project.

The ultimate objective of the scheduling phase is to construct a time chart showing the start and finish times for each activity as well as its relationship to other activities in the project. In addition, the schedule must pinpoint the critical (in view of time) activities that require special attention if the project is to be completed on time. For the noncritical activities, the schedule must show the amount of slack or float times that can be used advantageously when such activities are delayed or when limited resources are to be used effectively.

The final phase in project management is project control. This includes the use of the arrow diagram and the time chart for making periodic progress reports. The network may thus be updated and analyzed, and, if necessary, a new schedule is determined for the remaining portion of the project.

13.1 ARROW (NETWORK) DIAGRAM REPRESENTATIONS

The arrow diagram represents the interdependencies and precedence relationships among the activities of the project. An **arrow** is commonly used to represent an

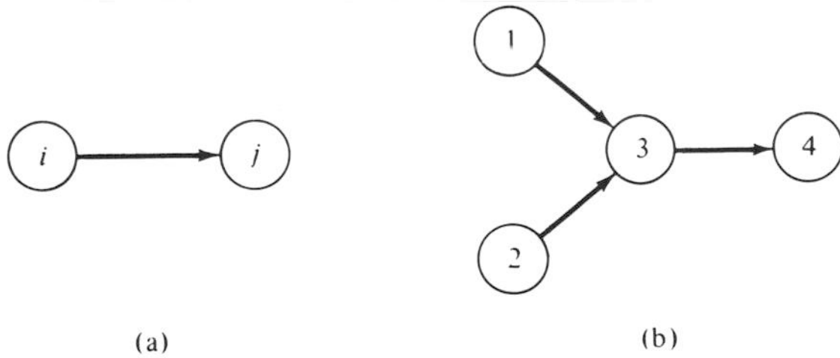

Figure 13-1

activity, with its head indicating the direction of progress in the project. The precedence relationship between the activities is specified by using events. An **event** represents a point in time that signifies the completion of some activities and the beginning of new ones. The beginning and end points of an activity are thus described by two events usually known as the *head* and *tail* events. Activities originating from a certain event cannot start until the activities terminating at the same event have been completed. In network theory terminology, each activity is represented by a directed arc and each event is represented by a node. The length of the arc need not be proportional to the duration of the activity nor does it have to be drawn as a straight line.

Figure 13-1(a) shows an example of a typical representation of an activity (i, j) with its tail event i and its head event j. Figure 13-1(b) shows another example, where activities (1, 3) and (2, 3) must be completed before activity (3, 4) can start. The direction of progress in each activity is specified by assigning a smaller number to the tail event compared with the number of its head event. This procedure is especially convenient for automatic computations and hence will be adopted throughout this chapter.

The rules for constructing the arrow diagram will be summarized now.

Rule 1. *Each activity is represented by one and only one arrow in the network.*

No single activity can be represented twice in the network. This is to be differentiated from the case where one activity is broken down into segments, in which case each segment may be represented by a separate arrow. For example, laying down a pipe may be done in sections rather than as one job.

Rule 2. *No two activities can be identified by the same head and tail events.*

A situation like this may arise when two or more activities can be performed concurrently. An example is shown in Figure 13-2(a), where activities A and B have the same end events. The procedure is to introduce a **dummy** activity either between A and one of the end events or between B and one of the end events. The modified representations, after introducing the dummy D, are shown in Figure 13-2(b). As a result of using D, activities A and B can now be identified by unique end events. It must be noted that a dummy activity does not consume time or resources.

Dummy activities are also useful in establishing logic relationships in the arrow diagram that cannot otherwise be represented correctly. Suppose that in a certain project jobs A and B must precede C while job E is preceded by job B only. Figure 13-3(a) shows the incorrect way, since, although the relationship among A, B, and C is correct, the diagram implies that E must be preceded by both A and B. The

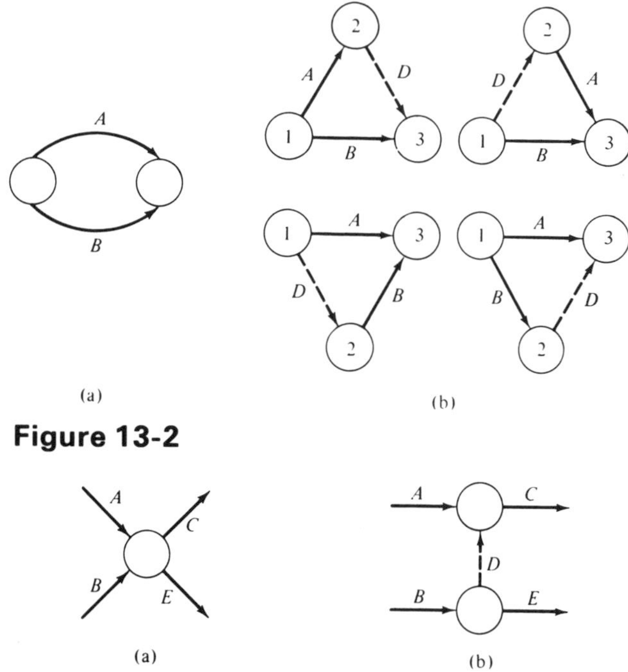

Figure 13-3

correct representation using the dummy D is shown in Figure 13-3(b). Since D consumes no time (or resources), the precedence relationships indicated are satisfied.

Rule 3. *To ensure the correct precedence relationship in the arrow diagram, the following questions must be answered as every activity is added to the network.*

(a) *What activities must be completed immediately before this activity can start?*

(b) *What activities must follow this activity?*

(c) *What activities must occur concurrently with this activity?*

This rule is self-explanatory. It actually allows for checking (and rechecking) the precedence relationships as one progresses in the development of the network.

Example 13.1-1. Construct the arrow diagram comprising activities A, B, $C, \ldots,$ and L such that the following relationships are satisfied.

1. A, B, and C, the first activities of the project, can start simultaneously.
2. A and B precede D.
3. B precedes E, F, and H.
4. F and C precede G.
5. E and H precede I and J.
6. C, D, F, and J precede K.
7. K precedes L.
8. I, G, and L are the terminal activities of the project.

The resulting arrow diagram is shown in Figure 13-4. The dummy activities D_1 and D_2 are used to establish correct precedence relationships. D_3 is used to identify

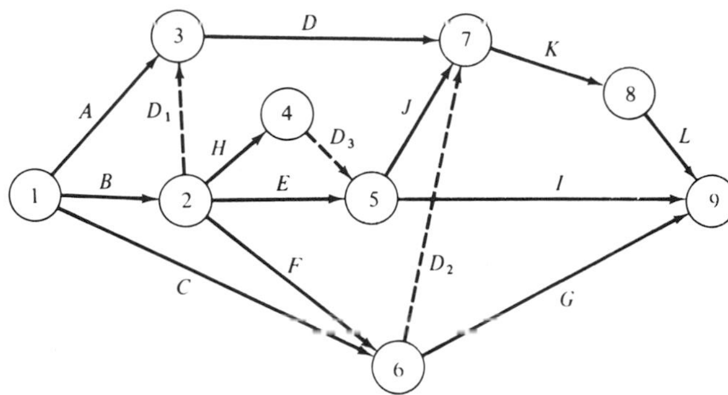

Figure 13-4

activities E and H with unique end events. The events of the project are numbered such that their ascending order indicates the direction of progress in the project. ◀

Exercise 13.1-1

Consider Example 13.1-1.

(a) Indicate the effect of adding each of the following activities on the precedence relationships in the network. All cases are considered independently.
  (1) Dummy (3, 5).
    [*Ans.* A precedes I and J.]
  (2) Dummy (3, 4).
    [*Ans.* Same as in (1).]
  (3) Dummy (5, 6).
    [*Ans.* E and H precede G.]
  (4) Dummy (3, 6).
    [*Ans.* A precedes G.]

(b) Indicate how each of the following additional relationships can be incorporated in the network.
  (1) Activities A and B precede G.
    [*Ans.* Add dummy (3, 6).]
  (2) Activity D precedes G.
    [*Ans.* Insert dummy between end of D and node 7, then connect end of D and node 6 by a dummy activity.]
  (3) Activity C precedes D.
    [*Ans.* Insert dummy between end of C and node 6, then connect end of C and node 3 by a dummy activity.]

13.2 CRITICAL PATH CALCULATIONS

The application of PERT–CPM should ultimately yield a schedule specifying the start and completion dates of each activity. The arrow diagram represents the first step toward achieving that goal. Because of the interaction among the different activities, the determination of the start and completion times requires special computations. These calculations are performed directly on the arrow diagram using simple arithmetic. The end result is to classify the activities of the project as **critical** or **noncritical**. An activity is said to be critical if a delay in its start will cause a delay in the completion date of the entire project. A noncritical activity is such that the time between its earliest start and its latest completion dates (as allowed by the project) is longer than its actual duration. In this case the noncritical activity is said to have a **slack** or **float** time.

The advantage of pinpointing the critical activities and determining the floats will be discussed in Section 13.3. This section mainly presents the methods for obtaining this information.

13.2.1 DETERMINATION OF THE CRITICAL PATH

A critical path defines a *chain* of critical activities that connects the start and end events of the arrow diagram. In other words, the critical path identifies all the critical activities of the project. The method of determining such a path is illustrated by a numerical example.

Example 13.2-1. Consider the network in Figure 13-5 that starts at node 0 and terminates at node 6. The time required to perform each activity is indicated on the arrows.

The critical path calculations include two phases. The first phase is called the **forward pass**, where calculations begin from the "start" node and move to the "end" node. At each node a number is computed representing the earliest occurrence time of the corresponding event. These numbers are shown in Figure 13-5 in squares □. The second phase, called the **backward pass**, begins calculations from the "end" node and moves to the "start" node. The number computed at each node (shown in triangles △) represents the latest occurrence time of the corresponding event. The forward pass is considered now.

Let ES_i be the **earliest start time** of all the activities emanating from event i. Thus ES_i represents the earliest occurrence time of event i. If $i = 0$ is the "start" event, then conventionally, for the critical path calculations, $ES_0 = 0$. Let D_{ij} be the duration of activity (i, j). The forward pass calculations are thus obtained from the formula

$$ES_j = \max_i \{ES_i + D_{ij}\}, \qquad \text{for all } (i, j) \text{ activities defined}$$

where $ES_0 = 0$. Thus, to compute ES_j for event j, ES_i for the tail events of *all* the incoming activities (i, j) must be computed first.

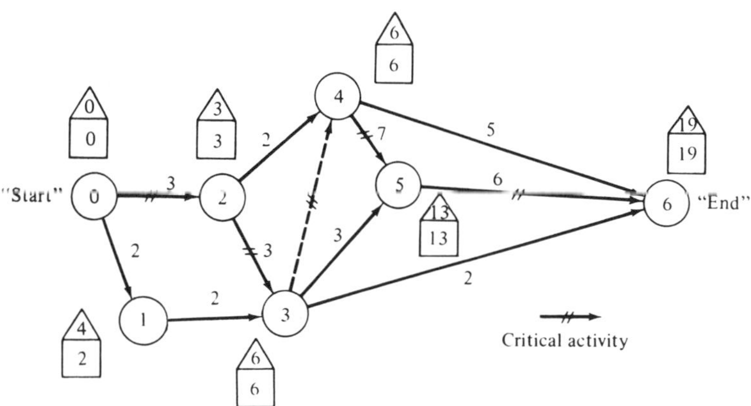

Figure 13-5

The forward pass calculations applied to Figure 13-5 start with $ES_0 = 0$, as shown in the square above event 0. Since there is only one incoming activity (0, 1) to event 1 with $D_{01} = 2$,

$$ES_1 = ES_0 + D_{01} = 0 + 2 = 2$$

which is entered in the square associated with event 1. Next, we consider event 2. [Notice that event 3 cannot be considered at this point, since ES_2 (event 2) is not yet known.] Thus

$$ES_2 = ES_0 + D_{02} = 0 + 3 = 3$$

which is entered in the square associated with event 2. The next event to be considered is 3. Since there are two incoming activities, (1, 3) and (2, 3), we have

$$ES_3 = \max_{i=1,2} \{ES_i + D_{i3}\} = \max\{2 + 2, 3 + 3\} = 6$$

which, again, is entered in the square of event 3.

The procedure continues in the same manner until ES_j is computed for all j. Thus

$$ES_4 = \max_{i=2,3} \{ES_i + D_{i4}\} = \max\{3 + 2, 6 + 0\} = 6$$
$$ES_5 = \max_{i=3,4} \{ES_i + D_{i5}\} = \max\{6 + 3, 6 + 7\} = 13$$
$$ES_6 = \max_{i=3,4,5} \{ES_i + D_{i6}\} = \max\{6 + 2, 6 + 5, 13 + 6\} = 19$$

These calculations complete the forward pass.

The backward pass starts from the "end" event. The objective of this phase is to compute LC_i, the **latest completion time** for all the activities coming into event i. Thus, if $i = n$ is the "end" event, $LC_n = ES_n$ initiates the backward pass. In general, for any node i,

$$LC_i = \min_j \{LC_j - D_{ij}\}, \qquad \text{for all } (i, j) \text{ activities defined}$$

The values of LC (entered in the triangles $\triangle$) are determined as follows.

$$LC_6 = ES_6 = 19$$
$$LC_5 = LC_6 - D_{56} = 19 - 6 = 13$$
$$LC_4 = \min_{j=5,6} \{LC_j - D_{4j}\} = \min\{13 - 7, 19 - 5\} = 6$$
$$LC_3 = \min_{j=4,5,6} \{LC_j - D_{3j}\} = \min\{6 - 0, 13 - 3, 19 - 2\} = 6$$
$$LC_2 = \min_{j=3,4} \{LC_j - D_{2j}\} = \min\{6 - 3, 6 - 2\} = 3$$
$$LC_1 = LC_3 - D_{13} = 6 - 2 = 4$$
$$LC_0 = \min_{j=1,2} \{LC_j - D_{0j}\} = \min\{4 - 2, 3 - 3) = 0$$

The backward pass calculations are now complete.

The critical path activities can now be identified by using the results of the forward and backward passes. An activity (i, j) lies on the **critical path** if it satisfies the following three conditions:

$$ES_i = LC_i \tag{1}$$
$$ES_j = LC_j \tag{2}$$
$$ES_j - ES_i = LC_j - LC_i = D_{ij} \tag{3}$$

These conditions actually indicate that there is no float or slack time between earliest start (completion) and the latest start (completion) of the critical activity. In the arrow diagram these activities are characterized by the numbers in □ and △ being the same at each of the head and the tail events *and* that the difference between the number in □ (or △) at the head event and the number in □ (or △) at the tail event is equal to the duration of the activity.

Activities (0, 2), (2, 3), (3, 4), (4, 5), and (5, 6) define the critical path in Figure 13-5. Actually, the critical path represents the shortest duration needed to complete the project. Notice that activities (2, 4), (3, 5), (3, 6), and (4, 6) satisfy conditions (1) and (2) for critical activities but not condition (3). Hence they are not critical. Notice also that the critical path must form a chain of *connected* activities that spans the network from "start" to "end." ◀

Exercise 13.2-1

For the network in Figure 13-5, determine the critical path(s) for each of the following (independent) cases.

(a) $D_{01} = 4$.
[*Ans.* (0, 2, 3, 4, 5, 6) and (0, 1, 3, 4, 5, 6).]

(b) $D_{36} = 15$.
[*Ans.* (0, 2, 3, 6).]

13.2.2 DETERMINATION OF THE FLOATS

Following the determination of the critical path, the floats for the noncritical activities must be computed. Naturally, a critical activity must have zero float. In fact, this is the main reason it is critical.

Before showing how floats are determined, it is necessary to define two new times that are associated with each activity. These are the **latest start** (*LS*) and the **earliest completion** (*EC*) times, which are defined for activity (i, j) by

$$LS_{ij} = LC_j - D_{ij}$$
$$EC_{ij} = ES_i + D_{ij}$$

There are two important types of floats: **total float** (*TF*) and **free float** (*FF*). The total float TF_{ij} for activity (i, j) is the difference between the maximum time available to perform the activity $(= LC_j - ES_i)$ and its duration $(= D_{ij})$; that is,

$$TF_{ij} = LC_j - ES_i - D_{ij} = LC_j - EC_{ij} = LS_{ij} - ES_i$$

The free float is defined by assuming that all the activities start as early as possible. In this case FF_{ij} for activity (i, j) is the excess of available time $(= ES_j - ES_i)$ over its duration $(= D_{ij})$; that is,

$$FF_{ij} = ES_j - ES_i - D_{ij}$$

The critical path calculations together with the floats for the noncritical activities can be summarized in the convenient form shown in Table 13-1. Columns (1), (2), (3), and (6) are obtained from the network calculations of Example 13.2-1. The remaining information can be determined from the foregone formulas.

Table 13-1 gives a typical summary of the critical path calculations. It includes all the information necessary to construct the time chart. Notice that a critical activity,

Table 13-1

		Earliest		Latest			
		Start	Completion	Start	Completion		
Activity (i, j) (1)	Duration D_{ij} (2)	□ ES_i (3)	EC_{ij} (4)	LS_{ij} (5)	△ LC_j (6)	Total Float TF_{ij} (7)	Free Float FF_{ij} (8)
(0, 1)	2	0	2	2	4	2	0
(0, 2)	3	0	3	0	3	0[a]	0
(1, 3)	2	2	4	4	6	2	2
(2, 3)	3	3	6	3	6	0[a]	0
(2, 4)	2	3	5	4	6	1	1
(3, 4)	0	6	6	6	6	0[a]	0
(3, 5)	3	6	9	10	13	4	4
(3, 6)	2	6	8	17	19	11	11
(4, 5)	7	6	13	6	13	0[a]	0
(4, 6)	5	6	11	14	19	8	8
(5, 6)	6	13	19	13	19	0[a]	0

[a] Critical activity.

and only a critical activity, must have zero *total* float. The free float must also be zero when the total float is zero. The converse is not true, however, in the sense that a *non*critical activity may have zero free float. For example, in Table 13-1, the noncritical activity (0, 1) has zero free float.

Exercise 13.2-2

In Table 13-1, verify the given values of the free and total floats for each of the following activities.

(a) Activity (0, 1).
(b) Activity (3, 4).
(c) Activity (4, 6).

13.3 CONSTRUCTION OF THE TIME CHART AND RESOURCE LEVELING

The end product of network calculations is the construction of the time chart (or schedule). This time chart can be converted easily into a calendar schedule for convenient use in the execution of the project.

The construction of the time chart must be made within the limitations of the available resources, since it may not be possible to execute concurrent activities because of personnel and equipment limitations. This is the point where the total floats for the noncritical activity become useful. By shifting a noncritical activity (back and forth) between its maximum allowable limits, one may be able to lower the maximum resource requirements. In any case, even in the absence of limited resources, it is common practice to use total floats to level resources over the duration of the entire project. In essence this would mean a more steady work force compared to the case where the work force (and equipment) would vary drastically from one day to the next.

The procedure for constructing the time chart will be illustrated by Example 13.1-1. Example 13.3-2 will then show how resource leveling can be effected for the same project.

Example 13.3-1. In this example the time chart for the project given in Example 13.2-1 will be constructed.

The information necessary to construct the time chart is summarized in Table 13-1. The first step is to consider the scheduling of the critical activities. Next, the noncritical activities are considered by indicating their *ES* and *LC* time limits on the chart. The critical activities are shown with solid lines. The time ranges for the noncritical activities are shown by dashed lines, indicating that such activities may be scheduled within those ranges *provided that the precedence relationships are not disturbed.*

Figure 13-6 shows the time chart corresponding to Example 13.2-1. The dummy activity (3, 4) consumes no time and hence is shown by a vertical line. The numbers shown with the noncritical activities represent their durations.

The roles of the *total* and *free* floats in scheduling noncritical activities is explained in terms of two general rules:

1. If the total float *equals* the free float, the noncritical activity can be scheduled *anywhere* between its earliest start and latest completion times (dashed time spans in Figure 13-6).
2. If the free float is *less than* the total float, the starting of the noncritical activity can be delayed relative to its earliest start time by no more than the amount of its free float without affecting the scheduling of its *immediately* succeeding activities.

In our example, rule 2 applies to activity (0, 1) only, whereas all others are scheduled according to rule 1. The reason is that activity (0, 1) has *zero* free float. Thus, if the starting time for (0, 1) is not delayed beyond its earliest start time ($t = 0$), the immediately succeeding activity (1, 3) can be scheduled anywhere between its earliest start time ($t = 2$) and latest completion time ($t = 6$). On the other hand, if the starting time of (0, 1) is delayed beyond $t = 0$, the earliest start time of (1, 3) must be delayed relative to its earliest start time by at least the same amount. For example, if (0, 1) starts at $t = 1$, it terminates at $t = 3$ and (1, 3) can then be scheduled anywhere

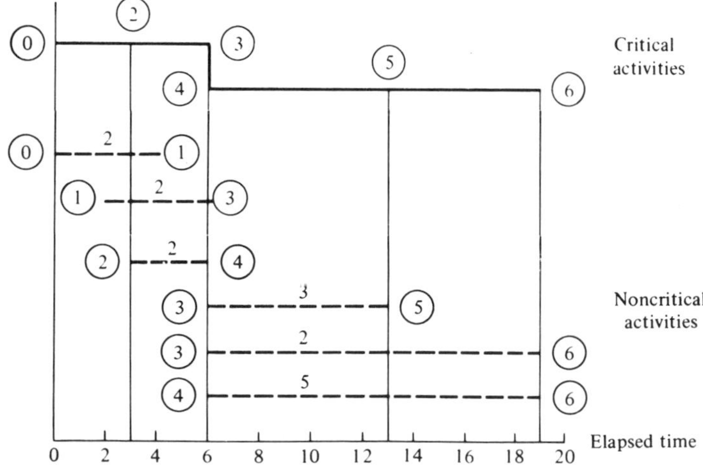

Figure 13-6

between $t = 3$ and $t = 6$. This type of restriction does not apply to any of the remaining noncritical activities because they all have equal total and free floats. We can also see this result in Figure 13-6, since (0, 1) and (1, 2) are the only two tandem activities whose permissible time spans overlap.

In essence, having the free float less than the total float gives us a warning that the scheduling of the activity should not be finalized without first checking its effect on the start times of the *immediately* succeeding activities. This valuable information can be secured only through the use of critical path computations. ◀

Exercise 13.3-1

The following cases represent the total and free floats (TF and FF) for a noncritical activity. Indicate the maximum delay in the starting time of the activity relative to its earliest start time that will allow all the immediately succeeding activities to be scheduled anywhere between their earliest and latest completion times.

(a) $TF = 10, FF = 10, D = 4$.
[*Ans.* Delay = 10.]

(b) $TF = 10, FF = 5, D = 4$.
[*Ans.* Delay = 5.]

(c) $TF = 10, FF = 0, D = 4$.
[*Ans.* Delay = 0.]

(d) $TF = 10, FF = 3, D = 4$.
[*Ans.* Delay = 3.]

Example 13.3-2. In Example 13.3-1 suppose that the following worker requirements are specified for the different activities. It is required to develop a time schedule that will level the worker requirements during the project duration. [Note that activities (0, 1) and (1, 3) require no manual labor, which is indicated by assigning zero number of men to each activity. As a result, the scheduling of (0, 1) and (1, 3) can be made independently of the resource leveling procedure.]

Activity	Number of Workers	Activity	Number of Workers
0, 1	0	3, 5	2
0, 2	5	3, 6	1
1, 3	0	4, 5	2
2, 3	7	4, 6	5
2, 4	3	5, 6	6

Figure 13-7(a) shows the personnel requirements over time if the noncritical activities are scheduled as early as possible, and Figure 13-7(b) shows the same requirements if these activities are scheduled as late as possible. The dashed line shows the requirements for the critical activities that must be satisfied if the project is to be completed on time. [Notice that activities (0, 1) and (1, 3) require no resources.]

The project requires at least 7 workers, as indicated by the requirements of the critical activity (2, 3). The earliest scheduling of the noncritical activities requires a maximum of 10 men, while the latest scheduling of the same activities sets the maximum requirements at 12 workers, which means that the maximum requirements depend on how the floats of the noncritical activities are used. In Figure 13-7, however, regardless of how the floats are allocated, the maximum requirement cannot be fewer than 10 workers, since the range for activity (2, 4) coincides with the time for the critical activity (2, 3). The work force requirement using the earliest

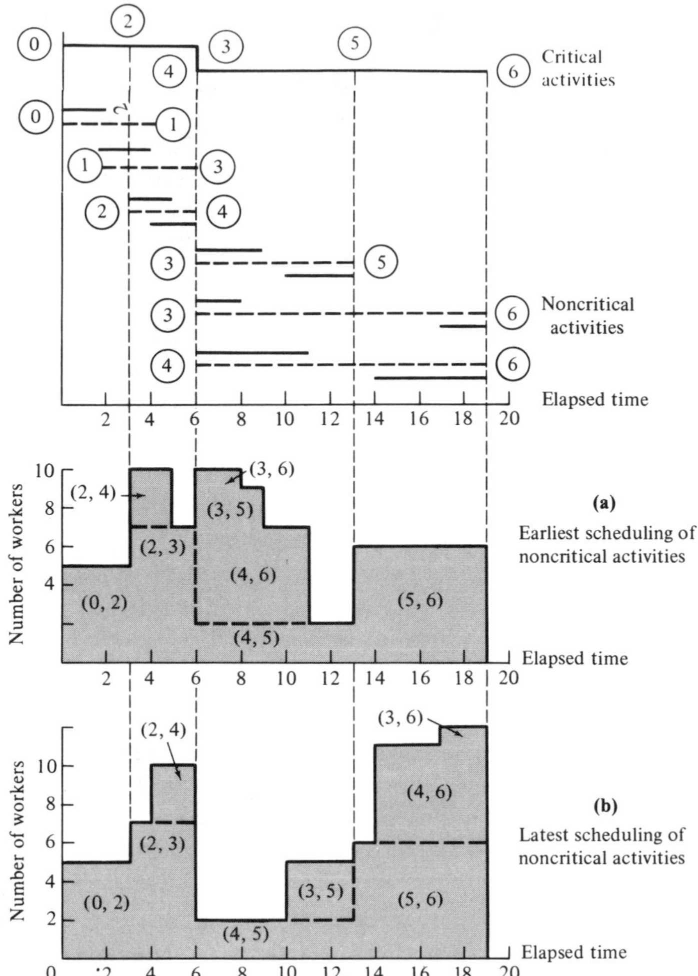

Figure 13-7

scheduling can be improved by rescheduling activity (3, 5) at its latest possible time and activity (3, 6) immediately after activity (4, 6) is completed. This new requirement is shown in Figure 13-8. The new schedule has now resulted in a smoother allocation of resources.

In some projects the objective may be to keep the maximum resource utilization below a certain limit rather than merely leveling the resources. If this objective cannot be accomplished by rescheduling the noncritical activities, it will be necessary to expand the time for some of the critical activities, thus reducing the required daily level of the resource. ◀

Because of mathematical complexity, no technique has yet been developed that will yield the *optimum* solution to the resource leveling problem, that is, minimization of the maximum required resources for the project at any point in time. Rather, heuristic programs similar to the one just outlined are actually used. These programs take advantage of the different floats for the noncritical activities.

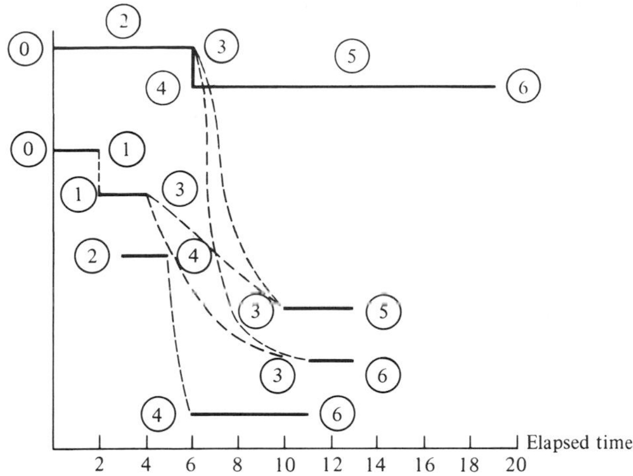

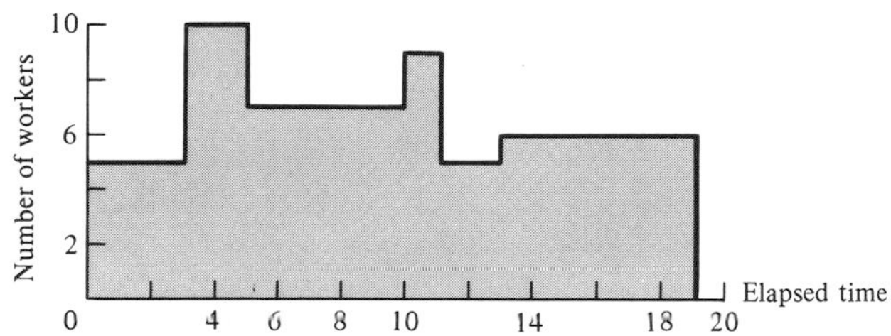

Figure 13-8

Exercise 13.3-2

In Example 13.3-2, suppose that activities (0, 1) and (1, 3) require 8 and 2 workers, respectively. Indicate the changes in Figure 13-7 in each of the following cases.

(a) Both activities are scheduled as early as possible.
[*Ans.* Changes in the number of workers are 13 for $0 \leq t < 2$, 7 for $2 \leq t < 3$, and 12 for $3 \leq t < 4$.]

(b) Both activities are scheduled as late as possible.
[*Ans.* Changes in the number of workers are 13 for $2 \leq t < 3$, 15 for $3 \leq t < 4$, and 12 for $4 \leq t < 6$.]

13.4 PROBABILITY AND COST CONSIDERATIONS IN PROJECT SCHEDULING

The analysis in Sections 13.1, 13.2, and 13.3 does not take into account the case where time estimates for the different activities are probabilistic. Also, it does not consider explicitly the cost of schedules. This section will thus present both the probability and cost aspects in project scheduling.

13.4.1 PROBABILITY CONSIDERATIONS IN PROJECT SCHEDULING

Probability considerations are incorporated in project scheduling by assuming that the time estimate for each activity is based on three different values:

a = **optimistic time**, which will be required if execution goes extremely well
b = **pessimistic time**, which will be required if everything goes badly
m = **most likely time**, which will be required if execution is normal

The range specified by the optimistic and pessimistic estimates (a and b, respectively) supposedly must enclose every possible estimate of the duration of the activity. The most likely estimate m need not coincide with the midpoint $(a + b)/2$ and may occur to its left or to its right. Because of these properties it is *intuitively* justified that the duration for each activity may follow a beta distribution with its unimodal point occurring at m and its end points at a and b. Figure 13-9 shows the three cases of the beta distribution, which are (a) symmetric, (b) skewed to the right, and (c) skewed to the left.

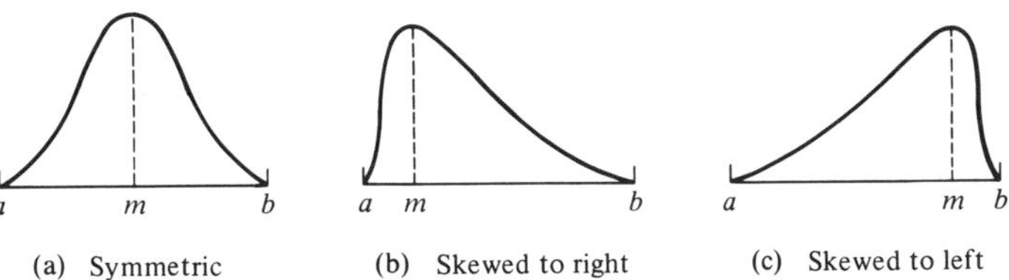

(a) Symmetric (b) Skewed to right (c) Skewed to left

Figure 13-9

The expressions for the mean $\bar{D}$ and variance V of the beta distribution are developed as follows.† The midpoint $(a + b)/2$ is assumed to weigh half as much as the most likely point m. Thus $\bar{D}$ is the arithmetic means of $(a + b)/2$ and $2m$; that is,

$$\bar{D} = \frac{(a + b)/2 + 2m}{3} = \frac{a + b + 4m}{6}$$

The range (a, b) is assumed to enclose about 6 standard deviations of the distribution, since about 90% or more of *any* probability density function lies within 3 standard deviations of its mean. Thus

$$V = \left(\frac{b - a}{6}\right)^2$$

† The validity of the beta distribution assumption has been challenged. The expressions for $\bar{D}$ and V developed below cannot be satisfied for the beta distribution unless certain restrictive relationships among a, b, and m exist. (See F. Grubbs, "Attempts to Validate Certain PERT Statistics or 'Picking on PERT'," *Operations Research*, Vol. 10, 1962, pp. 912–915.) However, the expressions for $\bar{D}$ and V are based on intuitive arguments regardless of the original beta distribution assumption. Later it will be shown that the network analysis is based on the central limit theorem, which assumes normality regardless of the parent distribution of individual activities. In this respect, whether the real distribution is beta or not seems to be unimportant. The question as to whether $\bar{D}$ and V are the true measures of the parent (unknown) distribution still remains unanswered, however.

The network calculations given in Sections 13.1, 13.2, and 13.3 can now be applied directly, with $\bar{D}$ replacing the single estimate D.

It is now possible to estimate the probability of occurrence of each event in the network. Let μ_i be the earliest occurrence time of event i. Since the times of the activities summing up to i are random variables, μ_i is also a random variable. Assuming that all the activities in the network are statistically independent, one obtains the mean and variance of μ_i as follows. If there is only one path leading from the "start" event to event i, $E\{\mu_i\}$ is given by the sum of the expected durations $\bar{D}$ for the activities along this path, and $\text{var}\{\mu_i\}$ is the sum of the variances of the same activities. Complications arise, however, where more than one path leads to the same event. In this case, if the *exact* $E\{\mu_i\}$ and $\text{var}\{\mu_i\}$ are to be computed, one must first develop the statistical distribution for the longest of the different paths (i.e., the distribution of the maximum of several random variables) and then find its expected value and variance. This problem is rather difficult in general and a simplifying assumption is introduced that computes $E\{\mu_i\}$ and $\text{var}\{\mu_i\}$ as those of the path to event i having the largest sum of *expected* activity durations. If two or more paths have the same $E\{\mu_i\}$, the one with the largest $\text{var}\{\mu_i\}$ is selected, since it reflects greater uncertainty and hence more conservative results. To summarize, $E\{\mu_i\}$ and $\text{var}\{\mu_i\}$ are given for the selected path by

$$E\{\mu_i\} = ES_i$$
$$\text{var}\{\mu_i\} = \sum_k V_k$$

where k defines the activities along the longest path leading to i.

The idea is that μ_i is the sum of independent random variables and hence, according to the central limit theorem, μ_i is approximately normally distributed with the mean $E\{\mu_i\}$ and variance $\text{var}\{\mu_i\}$. Since μ_i represents the earliest occurrence time, event i will meet a certain scheduled time ST_i (specified by the analyst) with probability

$$P\{\mu_i \leq ST_i\} = P\left\{\frac{\mu_i - E\{\mu_i\}}{\sqrt{\text{var}\{\mu_i\}}} \leq \frac{ST_i - E\{\mu_i\}}{\sqrt{\text{var}\{\mu_i\}}}\right\} = P\{z \leq K_i\}$$

where z is the standard normal distribution with mean zero and variance one and

$$K_i = \frac{ST_i - E\{\mu_i\}}{\sqrt{\text{var}\{\mu_i\}}}$$

It is common practice to compute the probability that event i will occur no later than its LC_i. Such probabilities will thus represent the chance that the succeeding events will occur within their (ES_i, LC_i) durations.

Example 13.4-1. Consider the project of Example 13.2-1. To avoid repeating the critical path calculations, the values of a, b, and m shown in Table 13-2 are selected such that $\bar{D}_{ij}$ will have the same value as its corresponding D_{ij} in Example 13.2-1.

The mean $\bar{D}_{ij}$ and variance V_{ij} for the different activities are given in Table 13-3.

The probabilities are given in Table 13-4. The information in the ST_i column is part of the input data. The values of ST_i can be replaced by LC_i to obtain the probabilities that none of the activities will be delayed beyond its latest occurrence time.

Table 13-2

Activity (i, j)	Estimated Times (a, b, m)	Activity (i, j)	Estimated Times (a, b, m)
(0, 1)	(1, 3, 2)	(3, 5)	(1, 7, 2.5)
(0, 2)	(2, 8, 2)	(3, 6)	(1, 3, 2)
(1, 3)	(1, 3, 2)	(4, 5)	(6, 8, 7)
(2, 3)	(1, 11, 1.5)	(4, 6)	(3, 11, 4)
(2, 4)	(.5, 7.5, 1)	(5, 6)	(4, 8, 6)

Table 13-3

Activity	$\bar{D}_{ij}$	V_{ij}	Activity	$\bar{D}_{ij}$	V_{ij}
(0, 1)	2	.11	(3, 5)	3	1.00
(0, 2)	3	1.00	(3, 6)	2	.11
(1, 3)	2	.11	(4, 5)	7	.11
(2, 3)	3	2.78	(4, 6)	5	1.78
(2, 4)	2	1.36	(5, 6)	6	.44

Table 13-4

Event	Path	$E\{\mu_i\}$	$\text{var}\{\mu_i\}$	ST_i	K_i	$P\{z \le K_i\}$
1	(0, 1)	2	.11	4	6.03	1.000
2	(0, 2)	3	1.00	2	−1.000	.159
3	(0, 2, 3)	6	3.78	5	−.514	.304
4	(0, 2, 3, 4)	6	3.78	6	.000	.500
5	(0, 2, 3, 4, 5)	13	3.89	17	2.028	.987
6	(0, 2, 3, 4, 5, 6)	19	4.33	20	.480	.684

The information under the path column is obtained directly from the network. It defines the *longest* path from event 0 to event *i*.

After computing $E\{\mu_i\}$ and $\text{var}\{\mu_i\}$, the calculations of K_i and $P\{z \le K_i\}$ are straightforward. The probabilities associated with the realization of each event can then be computed. These probabilities provide information about where resources are needed most to reduce the probability of delays in execution of the project. ◀

13.4.2 COST CONSIDERATIONS IN PROJECT SCHEDULING

The cost aspect is included in project scheduling by defining the cost–duration relationship for each activity in the project. Costs are defined to include direct elements only. Indirect costs cannot be included. Their effect will be included in the final analysis, however. Figure 13-10 shows a typical straight-line relationship used

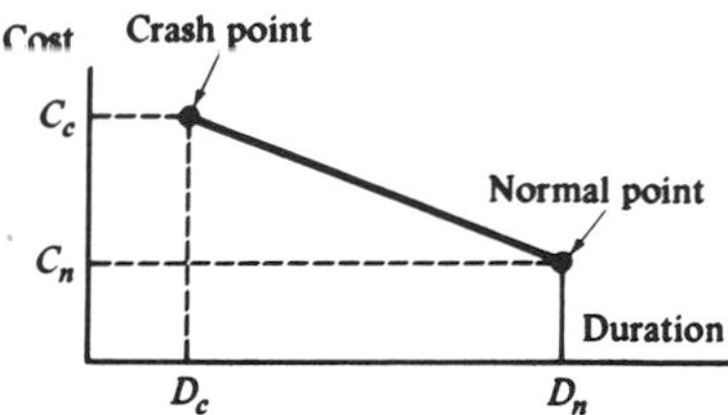

Figure 13-10

with most projects. The point (D_n, C_n) represents the duration D_n and its associated cost C_n if the activity is executed under **normal** conditions. The duration D_n can be compressed by increasing the allocated resources and hence by increasing the direct costs. There is a limit, called **crash** time, beyond which no further reduction in the duration can be effected. At this point any increase in resources will only increase the costs without reducing the duration. The crash point is indicated in Figure 13-10 by the point (D_c, C_c).

The straight-line relationship is used mainly for convenience, since it can be determined for each activity from the knowledge of the normal and crash points only, that is, (D_n, C_n) and (D_c, C_c). A nonlinear relationship will complicate the calculations. There is one exceptional case, however, where the nonlinear relationship can be approximated by a *piecewise* linear curve as shown in Figure 13-11. Under such conditions, the activity can be broken down into a number of subactivities each corresponding to one of the line segments. Notice the increasing slopes of the line segments as we move from the normal point to the crash point. If this condition is not satisfied, the approximation is invalid.

After defining the cost–time relationships, the activities of the project are assigned their normal durations. The corresponding critical path is then computed and the associated (direct) costs are recorded. The next step is to consider reducing the duration of the project. Since such a reduction can be effected only if the duration of a critical activity is reduced, attention must be paid to such activities alone. To achieve a reduction in the duration at the least possible cost, one must compress as much as possible the critical activity having the smallest cost–time slope.

The amount by which an activity can be compressed is limited by its crash time. However, other limits must be taken into account before the exact compression amount can be determined. The details of these limits are discussed in Example 13.4-2.

The result of compressing an activity is a new schedule perhaps with a new critical path. The cost of the new schedule must be greater than that of the immediately preceding one. The new schedule must now be considered for compression by selec-

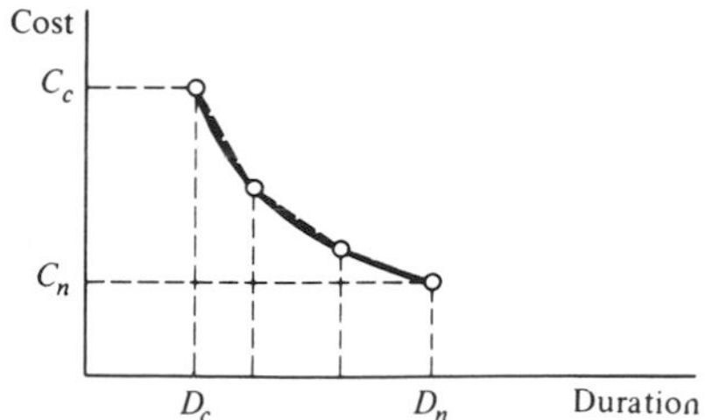

Figure 13-11

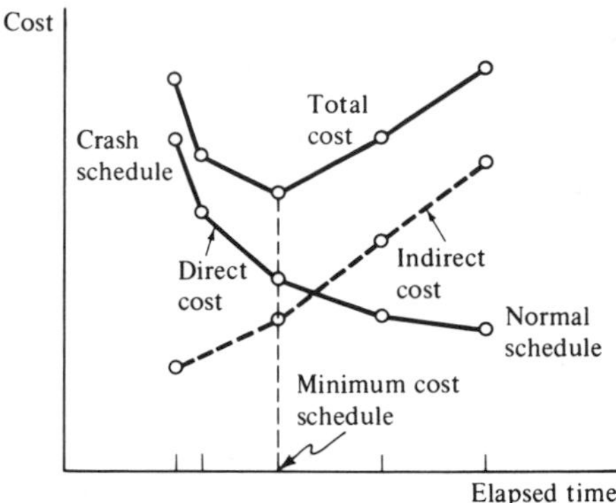

Figure 13-12

ting the (uncrashed) critical activity with the least slope. The procedure is repeated until all *critical* activities are at their crash times. The final result of these calculations is a cost–time curve for the various schedules and their corresponding costs. A typical curve is shown by a solid line in Figure 13-12. As indicated earlier, it represents the direct costs only.

It is logical to assume that as the duration of the project increases, the *in*direct costs must also increase as shown in Figure 13-12 by a dashed curve. The sum of these two costs (direct + indirect) gives the total cost of the project. The optimum schedule corresponds to the minimum total cost.

Example 13.4-2. Consider the network in Figure 13-13. The normal and crash points for each activity are given in Table 13-5. It is required to compute the different minimum-cost schedules that can occur between normal and crash times.

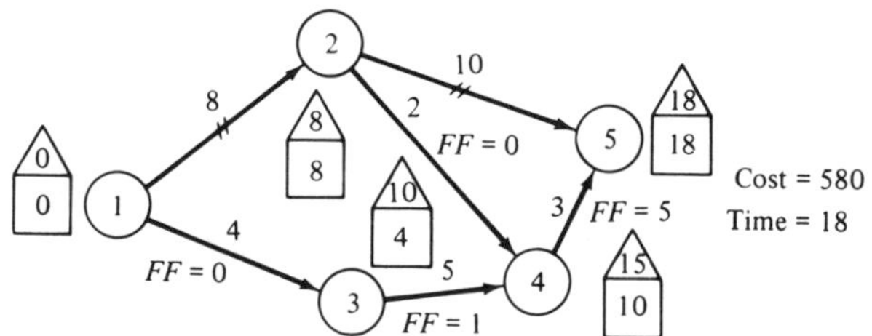

Figure 13-13

Table 13-5

Activity (i, j)	Normal Duration	Normal Cost	Crash Duration	Crash Cost
(1, 2)	8	100	6	200
(1, 3)	4	150	2	350
(2, 4)	2	50	1	90
(2, 5)	10	100	5	400
(3, 4)	5	100	1	200
(4, 5)	3	80	1	100

Table 13-6

Activity	Slope
(1, 2)	50
(1, 3)	100
(2, 4)	40
(2, 5)	60
(3, 4)	25
(4, 5)	10

The analysis in this problem is dependent mainly on the cost–time slopes for the various activities, which can be computed using the formula

$$\text{slope} = \frac{C_c - C_n}{D_n - D_c}$$

The slopes for the activities of the network are summarized in Table 13-6.

The first step in the calculation procedure is to assume that all activities occur at normal times. The network in Figure 13-13 shows the critical path calculations under normal conditions. Activities (1, 2) and (2, 5) constitute the critical path. The time of the project is 18 and its associated (normal) cost is 580.

The second step is to reduce the time of the project by compressing (as much as possible) the critical activity with the least slope. For the network in Figure 13-13 there are only two critical activities, (1, 2) and (2, 5). Activity (1, 2) is selected for compression because it has the smaller slope. According to the time–cost curve, this activity can be compressed by two time units, a limit that is specified by its crash point (henceforth called **crash limit**). However, compressing a critical activity to its crash point would not necessarily mean that the duration of the entire project will be reduced by an equivalent amount. This result follows, since, as the critical activity is compressed, a *new* critical path may develop. At this point we must discard the old critical activity and pay attention to the activities of the new critical path.

One way of predicting whether a new critical path will develop before reaching crash point is to consider the free floats for the noncritical activities. By definition, these free floats are independent of the start times of the other activities. Thus if during the compression of a critical activity a *positive* free float becomes zero, this critical activity is not to be compressed without further checking because there is a *possibility* that this zero free float activity may become critical. Thus, in addition to the *crash limit*, one must consider the **free float limit**.

To determine the free float limit, we need first to reduce the duration of the critical activity selected for compression by *one* time unit. Then, by recomputing the free floats for all the noncritical activities, we note which of these activities have reduced their *positive* free floats by *one* time unit. The smallest free float (before reduction) of all such activities determines the required free float limit.

By applying this to the network of Figure 13-13, the free floats (FF) are shown on the respective activities. A reduction of activity (1, 2) by one time unit will drop the free float of activity (3, 4) from one to zero. The free float of activity (4, 5) will remain unchanged at 5. Thus FF-limit = 1. Since the crash limit for (1, 2) is 2, its **compression limit** equals the minimum of its crash and FF-limits, that is, $\min\{2, 1\} = 1$. The new schedule is shown in Figure 13-14. The corresponding project time is 17 and its associated cost is equal to that of the previous schedule

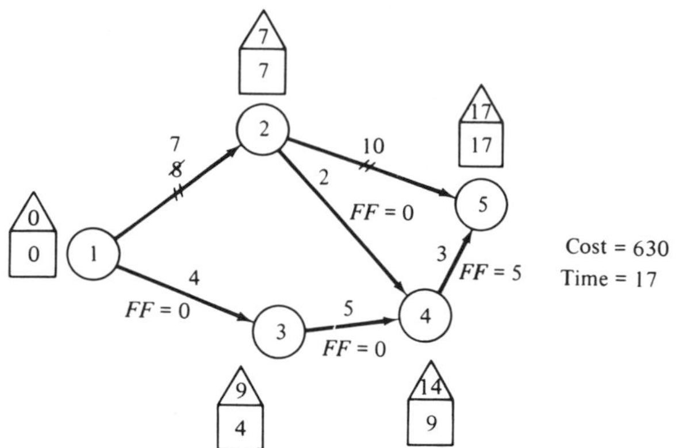

Figure 13-14

plus the additional cost of the compressed time, that is, $580 + (18 - 17) \times 50 = 630$. Although the free float determines the compression limit, the critical path remains the same. Thus it is *not* always true that a new critical path will arise when the compression limit is specified by the FF-limit.

Since activity (1, 2) is still the best candidate for compression, its corresponding crash and FF-limits are computed. However, since the crash limit for activity (1, 2) is equal to 1, it is not necessary to compute the FF-limit because any positive FF is at least equal to 1. Consequently, activity (1, 2) is compressed by one unit, thus reaching its crash limit. The resulting computations are shown in Figure 13-15, which also shows that the critical path remains unchanged. The time of the project is 16 and its associated cost is $630 + (17 - 16) \times 50 = 680$.

Activity (1, 2) can no longer be compressed. Hence activity (2, 5) is selected for compression. Now

$$\text{crash limit} = 10 - 5 = 5$$

$$\text{FF-limit} = 4, \text{ corresponding to activity } (4, 5)$$

$$\text{compression limit} = \min\{5, 4\} = 4$$

The resulting computations are shown in Figure 13-16. There are two critical paths now: (1, 2, 5) and (1, 3, 4, 5). The time for the new project is 12, and its cost is $680 + (16 - 12) \times 60 = 920$.

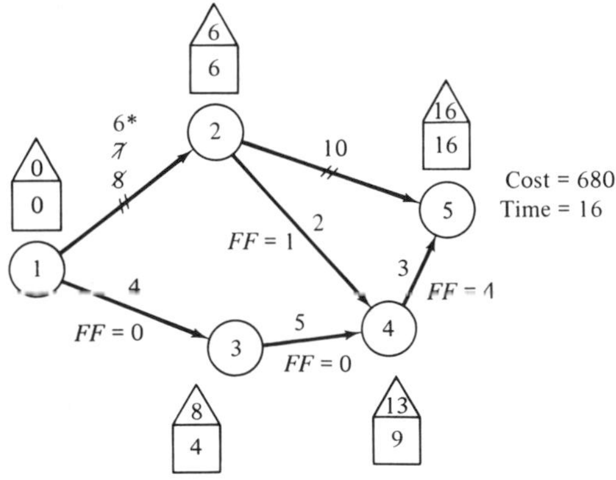

*Signifies that activity has reached its crash limit.

Figure 13-15

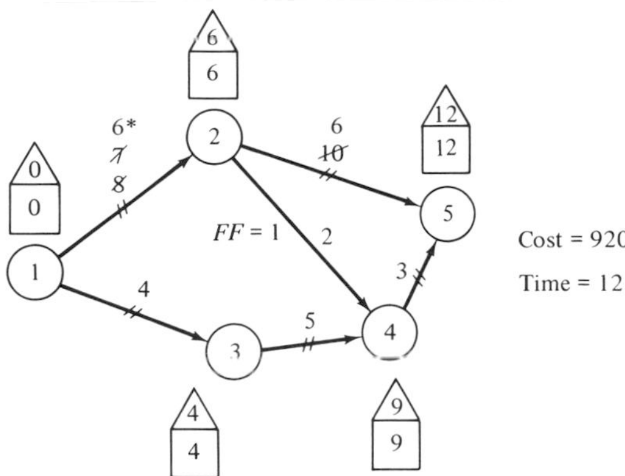

*Signifies that activity has reached its crash limit.

Figure 13-16

The appearance of two critical paths indicates that to reduce the time of the project, it will be necessary to reduce the time of the two critical paths simultaneously. The previous rule for selecting the critical activities to be compressed still applies here. For path (1, 2, 5), activity (2, 5) can be compressed by one time unit. For path (1, 3, 4, 5), activity (4, 5) has the least slope and its crash limit is 2. Thus the crash limit for the two paths is equal to $\min\{1, 2\} = 1$. The FF-limit is determined for this case by taking the minimum of the FF-limits obtained by considering each critical path separately. However, since the crash limit is equal to 1, the FF-limit need not be computed.

The new schedule is shown in Figure 13-17. Its time is 11 and its cost is $920 + (12 - 11) \times (10 + 60) = 990$.

The two critical paths of the project remain the same. Since all the activities on the critical path (1, 2, 5) are at crash time, it is no longer possible to reduce the time of the project. The schedule in Figure 13-17 thus gives the crash schedule.

A summary of these computations is given in Figure 13-18, which represents the direct cost of the project. By adding the indirect costs corresponding to each schedule, we can compute the minimum total cost (or optimum) schedule. ◀

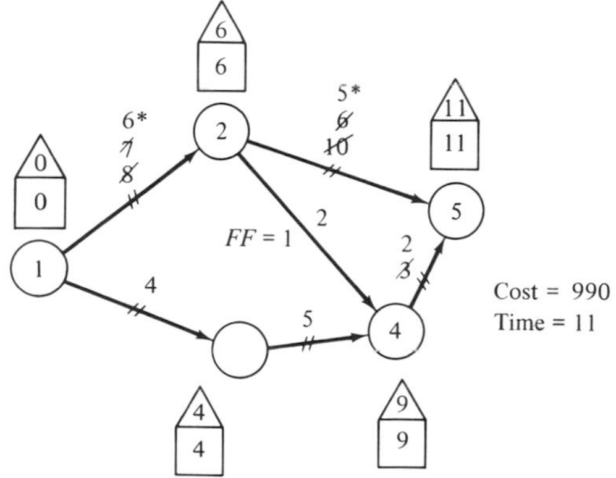

*Signifies that activity has reached its crash limit.

Figure 13-17

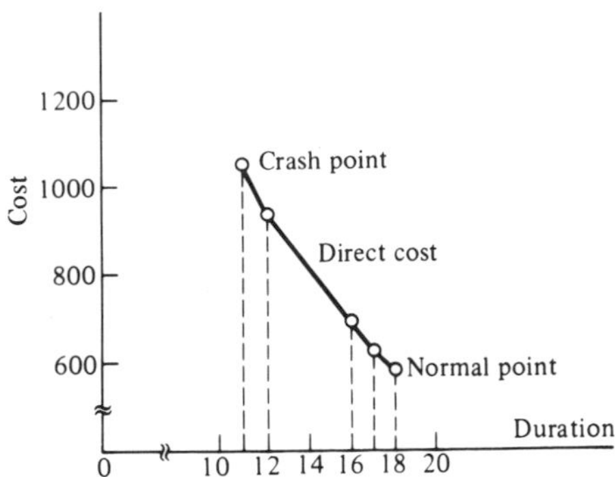

Figure 13-18

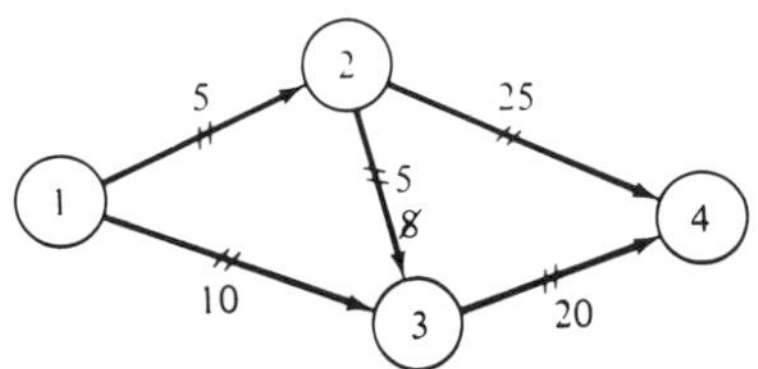

Figure 13-19

Example 13.4-2 summarizes all the rules for compressing activities under the given conditions. There are cases, however, where one may have to expand an already compressed activity before the duration of the entire project can be reduced. Figure 13-19 illustrates a typical case. There are three critical paths: (1, 2, 3, 4), (1, 2, 4), and (1, 3, 4). Activity (2, 3) has been compressed from its normal time 8 to its present time 5. The duration of the project may be reduced by simultaneously reducing one of the activities on each of the critical paths (1, 2, 4) and (1, 3, 4) or by simultaneously compressing activities (1, 2) and (3, 4) and expanding activity (2, 3). The alternative with the smallest *net* sum of slopes is selected. Notice that if activities (1, 2) and (3, 4) are compressed and activity (2, 3) is expanded, the *net* sum of slopes is the sum of the slopes for activities (1, 2) and (3, 4) *minus* the slope for activity (2, 3). In all other cases where there are no expandable activities, the net sum is equal to the sum of the slopes of the compressed activities.

If expansion is necessary, then, in addition to the crash limit and the FF-limit, the expansion limit must also be taken into account. This is equal to the normal time of the activity minus its present compressed time. The compression limit is thus the minimum of the crash limit, the FF-limit, and the expansion limit.

An Alternative Procedure for Detecting New Critical Paths

In Example 13.4-2 the FF-limit was used to detect the possibility of having new critical paths. If the FF-limit is large and equal to the compression limit, we can reduce the duration of the project in large steps. In essence, this procedure has the advantage of minimizing the number of schedules computed between the normal and crash points, which possibly means that the *main* computations of the project are minimized. However, the determination of the FF-limits requires additional computations that increase especially with the increase in the number of critical paths in the project. Consequently, there is no guarantee that the use of the FF-limit method would yield minimum computations.

Another method has thus been developed that completely eliminates the need for the FF-limit.† It is indicated in Example 13.4-2 that if the crash limit is equal to 1, the FF-limit need not be computed, since any positive FF is at least equal to 1. The new procedure thus calls for reducing the duration of the project by one time unit at each cycle of the computations. This is done again by compressing the activity having the least slope. The procedure is repeated on the new schedule—and the new critical path(s), if any—until the crash schedule is attained. Notice that the new method compresses the project duration by one time unit each cycle. Thus, if there are n time units between normal and crash schedules, we should expect a total of n cycles of computations.

There is no conclusive evidence as to which of the methods just described is computationally more efficient. However, for hand computations the non-FF-limit method seems more convenient. You are asked in Problem 13-17 to resolve Example 13.4-2 using the new method and hence compare the amount of computations in each cycle.

13.5 PROJECT CONTROL

There is a tendency among some PERT–CPM users to think that the arrow diagram can be discarded as soon as the time schedule is developed. This is not so. In fact, an important use of the arrow diagram occurs during the execution phase of the project. It seldom happens that the planning phase will develop a time schedule that can be followed exactly during the execution phase. Quite often some of the jobs are delayed or expedited, which naturally depends on actual work conditions. As soon as such disturbances occur in the original plan, it becomes necessary to develop a new time schedule for the remaining portion of the project. This section outlines a procedure for monitoring and controlling the project during the execution phase.

It is important to follow the progress of the project on the arrow diagram rather than solely on the time schedule. The time schedule is used principally to check if each activity is on time. The effect of a delay in a certain activity on the remaining portion of the project can best be traced on the arrow diagram.

Suppose that as the project progresses over time, it is discovered that delay in some activities necessitates developing a completely new schedule. How can the new schedule be obtained using the present arrow diagram? The immediate requirement is to update the arrow diagram by assigning zero values to the durations of the completed activities. Partially completed activities are assigned times equivalent to their unfinished portions. Changes in the arrow diagram such as addition or deletion of any future activities must also be made. By repeating the usual computations on the arrow diagram with its new time elements, we can determine the new time schedule and possible changes in the duration of the project. Such information is used until it is again necessary to update the time schedule. In real situations, many

† There exist other more efficient methods for effecting minimum computations between the normal and crash schedules. The rules for such methods are somewhat complex, however. [See, for example, Moder and Phillips (1970, Chap. 9).]

revisions of the time schedule are usually required at the early stages of the execution phase. A stable period follows in which little revision of the current schedule may be required.

13.6 SUMMARY

Critical path computations are quite simple, yet they provide valuable information that simplifies the scheduling of complex projects. The result is that PERT–CPM techniques enjoy tremendous popularity among practitioners in the field. The usefulness of the techniques is further enhanced by the availability of specialized computer systems for executing, analyzing, and controlling network projects.

SELECTED REFERENCES

ELMAGHRABY, S., *Activity Networks*, Wiley, New York, 1977.

MODER, J., and C. PHILLIPS, *Project Management with CPM and PERT*, 2nd ed., Van Nostrand Reinhold, New York, 1970.

PROBLEMS

Section	Assigned Problems
13.1	13–1 to 13–4
13.2	13–5 to 13–11
13.3	13–12 to 13–14
13.4.1	13–15
13.4.2	13–16 to 13–18

☐ **13–1** Construct the arrow diagram comprising activities *A*, *B*, *C*, ..., *P* that satisfies the following precedence relationships.

(i) *A*, *B*, and *C*, the first activities of the project, can start simultaneously.
(ii) Activities *D*, *E*, and *F* start immediately after *A* is completed.
(iii) Activities *I* and *G* start after both *B* and *D* are completed.
(iv) Activity *H* starts after both *C* and *G* are completed.
(v) Activities *K* and *L* succeed activity *I*.
(vi) Activity *J* succeeds both *E* and *H*.
(vii) Activities *M* and *N* succeed *F* but cannot start until *E* and *H* are completed.
(viii) Activity *O* succeeds *M* and *I*.
(ix) Activity *P* succeeds *J*, *L*, and *O*.
(x) Activities *K*, *N*, and *P* are the terminal jobs of the project.

☐ **13–2** The footings of a building can be completed in four consecutive sections. The activities for each section include digging, placing steel, and pouring concrete. The digging of one section cannot start until the preceding one is completed. The same restriction applies to pouring concrete. Develop a network for the project.

☐ **13–3** Consider Problem 13–2. After digging all sections, plumbing work can be started but only 10% of the job can be completed before *any* concrete is poured. After each section of the footings is completed, an additional 5% of the plumbing can be started provided that the preceding 5% portion is complete. Construct the activity network.

☐ **13–4** An opinion survey involves designing and printing questionnaires, hiring and training personnel, selecting participants, mailing questionnaires, and analyzing the data. Construct a network for this project. Specify all the assumptions made.

☐ **13–5** Table 13-7 provides the data for building a new house. Construct the associated network model and carry out the critical path computations.

Table 13-7

Activity	Description	Immediate Predecessor(s)	Duration (days)
A	Clear site	—	1
B	Bring utilities to site	—	2
C	Excavate	*A*	1
D	Pour foundation	*C*	2
E	Outside plumbing	*B, C*	6
F	Frame house	*D*	10
G	Electric wiring	*F*	3
H	Lay floor	*G*	1
I	Lay roof	*F*	1
J	Inside plumbing	*E, H*	5
K	Shingling	*I*	2
L	Outside sheathing insulation	*F, J*	1
M	Install windows and outside doors	*F*	2
N	Brick work	*L, M*	4
O	Insulate walls and ceiling	*G, J*	2
P	Cover walls and ceiling	*O*	2
Q	Insulate roof	*I, P*	1
R	Finish interior	*P*	7
S	Finish exterior	*I, N*	7
T	Landscape	*S*	3

☐ **13–6** For the purpose of preparing its next year's budget, a company must gather information from its sales, production, accounting, and treasury departments. Table 13-8 indicates the activities and their durations. Prepare the network model of the problem and carry out the critical path computations.

Table 13-8

Activity	Description	Immediate Predecessor(s)	Duration (days)
A	Forecast sales volume	—	10
B	Study competitive market	—	7
C	Design item and facilities	*A*	5
D	Prepare production schedules	*C*	3
E	Estimate cost of production	*D*	2
F	Set sales price	*B, E*	1
G	Prepare budget	*E, F*	14

Table 13-9

Activity	Description	Immediate Predecessor(s)	Duration (days)
A	Select music	—	21
B	Learn music	*A*	14
C	Make copies and buy books	*A*	14
D	Tryouts	*B*, *C*	3
E	Rehearsals	*D*	70
F	Solo rehearsals	*D*	70
G	Rent candelabra	*D*	14
H	Buy candles	*G*	1
I	Set up and decorate candelabra	*H*	1
J	Buy decorations	*D*	1
K	Set up decorations	*J*	1
L	Order choir robe stoles	*D*	7
M	Press robes	*L*	7
N	Check out PA system	*D*	7
O	Select music tracks	*N*	14
P	Set up PA system	*O*	1
Q	Final rehearsal	*E*, *F*, *P*	1
R	Choir party	*Q*, *I*, *K*	1
S	Final program	*M*, *R*	1

Table 13-10

Activity	Description	Immediate Predecessor(s)	Duration (days)
A	Job review	—	1
B	Advise customers of temporary outage	*A*	.5
C	Requisition stores	*A*	1
D	Scout job	*A*	.5
E	Secure poles and materials	*C*, *D*	3
F	Distribute poles	*E*	3.5
G	Pole location coordination	*D*	.5
H	Restake	*G*	.5
I	Dig holes	*H*	3
J	Frame and set poles	*F*, *I*	4
K	Cover old conductors	*F*, *I*	1
L	Pull new conductors	*J*, *K*	2
M	Install remaining material	*L*	2
N	Sag conductor	*L*	2
O	Trim trees	*D*	2
P	Deenergize and switch lines	*B*, *M*, *N*, *O*	.1
Q	Energize and phase new line	*P*	.5
R	Clean up	*Q*	1
S	Remove old conductor	*Q*	1
T	Remove old poles	*S*	2
U	Return material to stores	*I*	2

□ **13–7** The activities involved in a candlelight choir service are given in Table 13-9. Prepare the network model and carry out the critical path computations.

□ **13–8** Table 13-10 summarizes the activities for relocating ("reconductoring") 1700 feet of 13.8-kilovolt overhead primary line due to the widening of the road section in which the line is presently installed. Draw the network model and carry out the critical path computations.

□ **13–9** The activities for buying a new car are summarized in Table 13-11. Draw the network model and carry out the critical path computations.

Table 13-11

Activity	Description	Immediate Predecessor(s)	Duration (days)
A	Conduct feasibility study	—	3
B	Find potential customer for present car	*A*	14
C	List possible models	*A*	1
D	Research all possible models	*C*	3
E	Conduct interviews with mechanics	*C*	1
F	Collect dealer propaganda	*C*	2
G	Compile and organize all pertinent information	*D, E, F*	1
H	Choose top three models	*G*	1
I	Test-drive all three choices	*H*	3
J	Gather warranty and financing information	*H*	2
K	Choose one car	*I, J*	2
L	Compare dealers and choose dealer	*K*	2
M	Search for desired color and options	*L*	4
N	Test-drive chosen model once again	*L*	1
O	Purchase new car	*B, M, N*	3

□ **13–10** Determine the critical path(s) for projects (a) and (b) (Figure 13-20).

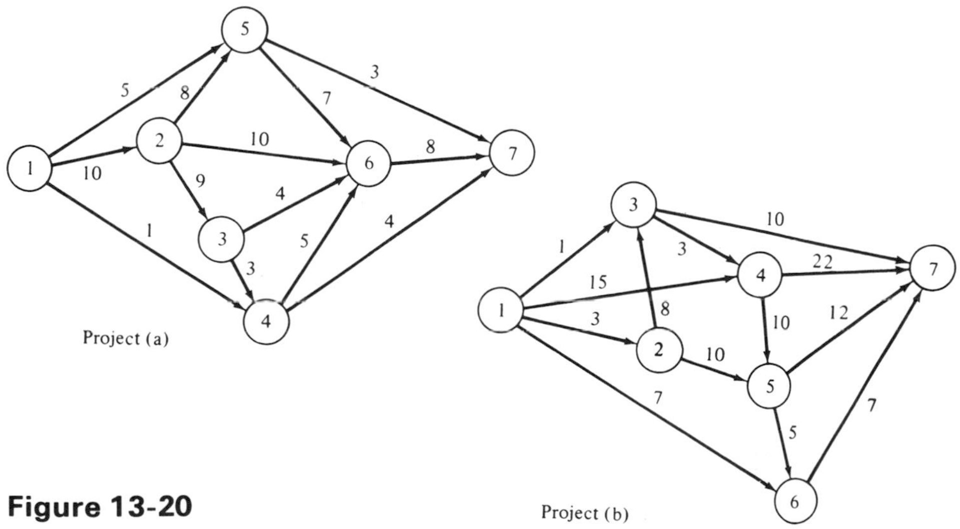

Figure 13-20

☐ **13–11** In Problem 13–10, compute the total and free floats and summarize the critical path calculations using the format in Table 13-1.

☐ **13–12** In Problem 13-10, using the results of Problem 13-11, construct the corresponding time charts assuming no limits on the resources.

☐ **13–13** Construct the time schedule for Problem 13–5.

☐ **13–14** Construct the time schedule for Problem 13–6.

☐ **13–15** Suppose that in Problem 13–10 the following personnel requirements are specified for the various activities of projects (a) and (b).

Project (a):

Activity	Number of Workers	Activity	Number of Workers
1, 2	5	3, 6	9
1, 4	4	4, 6	1
1, 5	3	4, 7	10
2, 3	1	5, 6	4
2, 5	2	5, 7	5
2, 6	3	6, 7	2
3, 4	7		

Project (b):

Activity	Number of Workers	Activity	Number of Workers
1, 2	1	3, 7	9
1, 3	2	4, 5	8
1, 4	5	4, 7	7
1, 6	3	5, 6	2
2, 3	1	5, 7	5
2, 5	4	6, 7	3
3, 4	10		

Find the minimum number of workers (as a function of the project time) required during the scheduling of the project. Using resource leveling, estimate the maximum number of workers required.

☐ **13–16** In Problem 13–10, suppose that the estimates (a, b, m) are given as shown in the tables. Find the probabilities that the different events will occur without delay.

Project (a):

Activity	(a, b, m)	Activity	(a, b, m)
1, 2	(5, 8, 6)	3, 6	(3, 5, 4)
1, 4	(1, 4, 3)	4, 6	(4, 10, 8)
1, 5	(2, 5, 4)	4, 7	(5, 8, 6)
2, 3	(4, 6, 5)	5, 6	(9, 15, 10)
2, 5	(7, 10, 8)	5, 7	(4, 8, 6)
2, 6	(8, 13, 9)	6, 7	(3, 5, 4)
3, 4	(5, 10, 9)		

Project (b):

Activity	(a, b, m)	Activity	(a, b, m)
1, 2	(1, 4, 3)	3, 7	(12, 14, 13)
1, 3	(5, 8, 7)	4, 5	(10, 15, 12)
1, 4	(6, 9, 7)	4, 7	(8, 12, 10)
1, 6	(1, 3, 2)	5, 6	(7, 11, 8)
2, 3	(3, 5, 4)	5, 7	(2, 8, 4)
2, 5	(7, 9, 8)	6, 7	(5, 7, 6)
3, 4	(10, 20, 15)		

☐ **13–17** Solve Example 13.4-2 without using the FF limit method, that is, by compressing the project duration one unit at a time, and compare with the computations in Example 13.4-2.

☐ **13–18** In Problem 13–10, given the following data for the direct costs of the normal and crash durations, find the different minimum cost schedules between the normal and crash points.

Project (a):

Activity	Normal		Crash	
(i, j)	Duration	Cost	Duration	Cost
1, 2	5	100	2	200
1, 4	2	50	1	80
1, 5	2	150	1	180
2, 3	7	200	5	250
2, 5	5	20	2	40
2, 6	4	20	2	40
3, 4	3	60	1	80
3, 6	10	30	6	60
4, 6	5	10	2	20
4, 7	9	70	5	90
5, 6	4	100	1	130
5, 7	3	140	1	160
6, 7	3	200	1	240

Project (*b*):

Activity (i, j)	Normal		Crash	
	Duration	Cost	Duration	Cost
1, 2	4	100	1	400
1, 3	8	400	5	640
1, 4	9	120	6	180
1, 6	3	20	1	60
2, 3	5	60	3	100
2, 5	9	210	7	270
3, 4	12	400	8	800
3, 7	14	120	12	140
4, 5	15	500	10	750
4, 7	10	200	6	220
5, 6	11	160	8	240
5, 7	8	70	5	110
6, 7	10	100	2	180

Chapter 14

Inventory Models

Inventories deal with maintaining sufficient stocks of goods (e.g., parts and raw materials) that will ensure a smooth operation of a production system or a business activity. Traditionally, inventory has been viewed by business and industry as a necessary evil: too little of it may cause costly interruptions in the operation of the system, and too much of it can ruin the competitive edge and profitability of the business. From that standpoint the only effective way of coping with inventory is to minimize its adverse impact by striking a "happy medium" between the two extreme cases. This attitude toward inventory remained prevalent throughout the Western industrialized nations until the post–World War II era, when Japan successfully implemented the now renowned just-in-time (JIT) system, which effectively called for a (nearly) stockless production environment. It is important to remember, however, that JIT is more than an inventory control system in the traditional sense. It is a total philosophy that aims at eliminating inventory through quality improvement and reduction of waste. In essence, JIT regards inventory as being the result of deficiencies in the production components, such as product design, quality control, equipment selection, material management, and others. By eliminating such deficiencies, the production process can be balanced and the dependence of the production flow on inventory is minimized or eliminated.

The JIT system is particularly suited for highly repetitive assembly manufacturing (e.g., its most successful implementation has been in the automobile industry). As such, the need for the traditional inventory control techniques for other types of production systems will continue to be in demand for a long time to come.

In this chapter we address both the traditional and the JIT treatments of inventory control. Since JIT is more a philosophy than a quantitative approach, the discussion in this chapter concentrates primarily on describing how the system works. Traditional inventory techniques, on the other hand, abound in the literature and will thus be discussed in more depth in this presentation.

14.1 THE ABC INVENTORY SYSTEM

In most real-life situations, inventory management usually involves a large number of items ranging in price from relatively inexpensive to possibly very expensive units. Since inventory in reality represents idle capital, it is natural that inventory control be exercised on items that are significantly responsible for the increase in capital cost. Thus routine items, such as bolts and nuts, contribute insignificantly to capital cost when compared with items involving expensive spare parts.

Experience has shown that only a relatively small number of inventory items usually incurs a major share of capital cost. Such items are the ones that must be subject to close inventory control.

The ABC system is a simple procedure that can be used to isolate the items that require special attention in terms of inventory control. The procedure calls for plotting percent of total inventory items against the percent of total dollar value of these items for a given time period (usually one year). Figure 14-1 illustrates a typical ABC curve.

The idea of the procedure is to determine the percent of items that contribute 80% of the cumulative dollar value. These items are classified as group A, and they normally constitute about 20% of all the items. Class B items are those corresponding to percent dollar values between 80% and 95%. They normally comprise about 25% of all the items. The remaining items constitute class C.

Class A items represent small quantities of expensive items and must be subject to tight inventory control. Class B items are next in order where a moderate form of inventory control can be applied. Finally class C items should be given the lowest priority in the application of any form of inventory control. Usually, the order size of expensive class A items is expected to be low to reduce the associated capital cost. On the other hand, the order size for class C can be quite large.

The ABC analysis is usually the first step that must be applied in an inventory control situation. Once the important inventory items are identified, models of the types to be presented in the succeeding sections can be used to decide on the ideal way of controlling inventory.

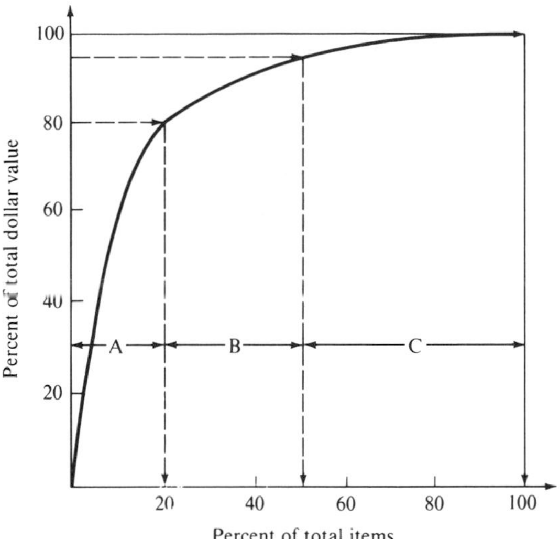

Figure 14-1

14.2 A GENERALIZED INVENTORY MODEL

The ultimate objective of any inventory model is to answer two questions:

1. How much to order?
2. When to order?

The answer to the first question is expressed in terms of what we call the **order quantity**. It represents the optimum amount that should be ordered every time an order is placed and may vary with time depending on the situation under consideration. The answer to the second question depends on the type of the inventory system. If the system requires **periodic review** at equal time intervals (e.g., every week or month), the time for acquiring a new order usually coincides with the beginning of each time interval. If, on the other hand, the system is of the **continuous review** type, a **reorder point** is usually specified by the *inventory level* at which a new order must be placed.

We can thus express the solution of the general inventory problem as follows:

1. *Periodic review case.* Receive a new order of the amount specified by the *order quantity* at equal intervals of time.

2. *Continuous review case.* When the inventory level reaches the *reorder point*, place a new order whose size equals the *order quantity*.

The order quantity and reorder point are normally determined by minimizing the total inventory cost that can be expressed as a function of these two variables. We can summarize the total cost of a general inventory model as a function of its principal components in the following manner:

$$\begin{pmatrix}\text{total}\\ \text{inventory}\\ \text{cost}\end{pmatrix} = \begin{pmatrix}\text{purchasing}\\ \text{cost}\end{pmatrix} + \begin{pmatrix}\text{setup}\\ \text{cost}\end{pmatrix} + \begin{pmatrix}\text{holding}\\ \text{cost}\end{pmatrix} + \begin{pmatrix}\text{shortage}\\ \text{cost}\end{pmatrix}$$

The **purchasing cost** becomes an important factor when the commodity unit price becomes dependent on the size of the order. This situation is normally expressed in terms of a **quantity discount** or a **price break**, where the unit price of the item decreases with the increase of ordered quantity. The **setup cost** represents the fixed charge incurred when an order is placed. Thus, to satisfy the demand for a given time period, the (more frequent) ordering of smaller quantities will result in a higher setup cost during the period than if the demand is satisfied by placing larger (and hence less frequent) orders. The **holding cost**, which represents the costs of carrying inventory in stock (e.g., interest on invested capital, storage, handling, depreciation, and maintenance), normally increases with the level of inventory. Finally, the **shortage cost** is a penalty incurred when we run out of stock of a needed commodity. It generally includes costs due to loss of customer's goodwill as well as potential loss in income.

Figure 14-2 illustrates the variation of the four cost components of the general inventory model as a function of the inventory level. The optimum inventory level corresponds to the minimum total cost of all four components. Note, however, that an inventory model need not include all four types of costs, either because some of the costs are negligible or will render the total cost function too complex for mathematical analysis. In practice, however, we can delete a cost component only if its effect on the total cost model is negligible. This point should be kept in mind as you study the various models we present in this chapter.

The foregoing general inventory model appears simple enough. Why, then, do we have large varieties of models whose methods of solutions range from the use of simple calculus to the sophisticated applications of dynamic and mathematical programming? The answer lies principally in whether the demand for the item is deterministic (known with certainty) or probabilistic (described by a probability density). Figure 14-3 illustrates the different classifications for demand as they are normally assumed in inventory models. A **deterministic demand** may be **static**, in the sense that the consumption rate remains constant with time, or **dynamic**, where the demand is known with certainty but varies from one time period to the next. The **probabilistic demand** has two similar classifications: the **stationary** case, in which the

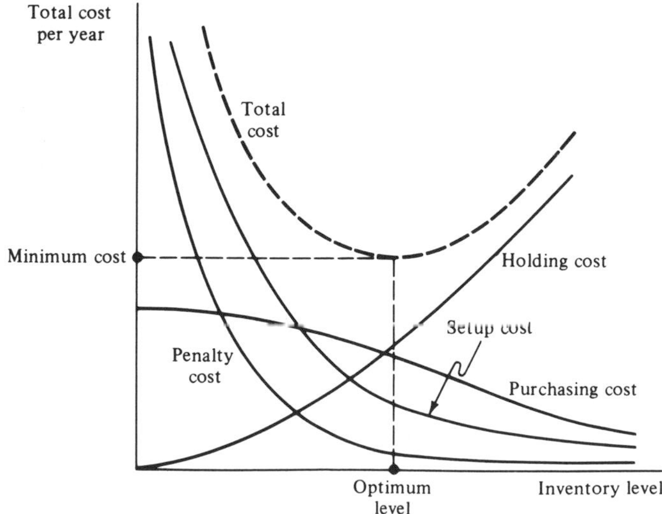

Figure 14-2

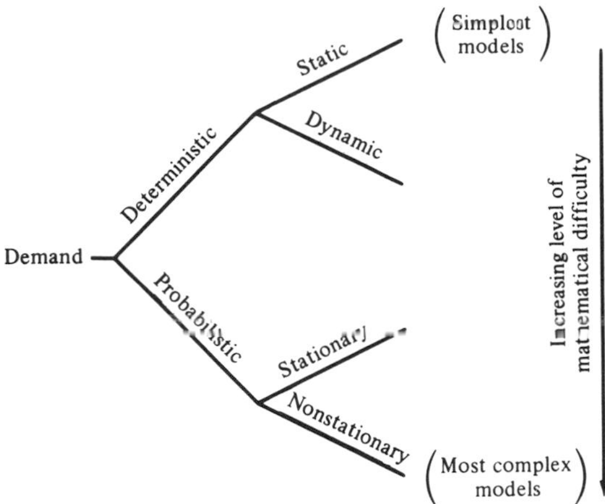

Figure 14-3

demand probability density function remains unchanged over time; and the **nonstationary** case, where the probability density function varies with time.

It is rare that a deterministic static demand would occur in real life. We may thus regard this situation as a simplifying case. For example, although demand for staple items, such as bread, may vary from day to day, the variations may be small and negligible with the result that a static demand assumption may not be too far from reality.

The most accurate representation of demand can perhaps be made by *probabilistic nonstationary* distributions. However, from the mathematical standpoint, the resulting inventory model will be rather complex, especially as the time horizon for the problem increases. Figure 14-3 illustrates this point by showing that the mathematical complexity of the inventory models increases as we move away from the assumption of deterministic static demand to the probabilistic nonstationary demand. Indeed, we can think of the classifications in Figure 14-3 as representing different *levels of abstraction* in demand.

The first level assumes that the probability distribution of demand is stationary over time. That is, the same probability density function is used to represent the demand for all periods over which the study is made. The implication of this assumption is that the effects of seasonal trends in demand, if any, will not be included in the model.

The second level of simplification recognizes the variations in demand between different periods. However, rather than utilize probability distributions, the *average* demand is used to represent the requirements of each period. This simplification has the effect of ignoring the element of risk in the inventory situation. Yet it allows the analyst to consider seasonal trends in demand that for analytic and computational difficulties cannot be included in a probabilistic model. In other words, there appears to be some kind of trade-off between using stationary probability distributions and variable but known demands under the assumption of "assumed certainty."

The third level of simplification eliminates both elements of risk and variability in demand. Thus the demand at any period is assumed equal to the average of the (assumedly) *known* demands for all periods under consideration. The result of this simplification is that demand may be represented as a *constant* rate per unit time.

Although the type of demand is a principal factor in the design of the inventory model, the following factors may also influence the way the model is formulated.

1. *Delivery lags or lead times.* When an order is placed, it may be delivered instantaneously, or it may require some time before delivery is effected. The time between the placement of an order and its receipt is called delivery lag or lead time, which may be deterministic or probabilistic.
2. *Stock replenishment.* Although an inventory system may operate with delivery lags, the actual replenishment of stock may occur instantaneously or uniformly. Instantaneous replenishment can occur when the stock is purchased from outside sources. Uniform replenishment may occur when the product is manufactured locally within the organization. In general, a system may operate with positive delivery lag and also with uniform stock replenishment.
3. *Time horizon.* The time horizon defines the period over which the inventory level will be controlled. This horizon may be finite or infinite, depending on the time period over which demand can be forecast reliably.
4. *Number of supply echelons.* An inventory system may consist of several (rather than one) stocking points. In some cases these stocking points are organized such that one point acts as a supply point for others. This type of operation may be repeated at different levels so that a demand point may again become a new supply point. The situation is usually referred to as a multiechelon system.
5. *Number of items.* An inventory system may involve more than one item (commodity). This case is of interest mainly if some kind of interaction exists between the different items. For example, the items may compete for limited floor space or limited total capital.

14.3 DETERMINISTIC MODELS

It is extremely difficult to develop a general inventory model that accounts for all variations in real systems. Indeed, even if a sufficiently general model can be formulated, it may not be analytically solvable. The models presented in this section are thus meant to be illustrative of some inventory systems. It is unlikely these models will fit a real situation exactly, but the objective of the presentation is to provide different ideas that can be adapted to specific inventory systems.

Five models are discussed in this section. Most of them deal with a single inventory item. Only one treats the effect on the solution of including several competing items. The main difference among these models is whether demand is static or dynamic. The type of cost function is also important in formulating and solving the models. You will notice the diverse methods of solution, which include classical optimization and linear and dynamic programming. These examples underscore the importance of using different optimization techniques in solving inventory models.

14.3.1 SINGLE-ITEM STATIC MODEL (EOQ)

The simplest type of inventory model occurs when demand is constant over time with instantaneous replenishment and no shortages. Figure 14-4 illustrates the

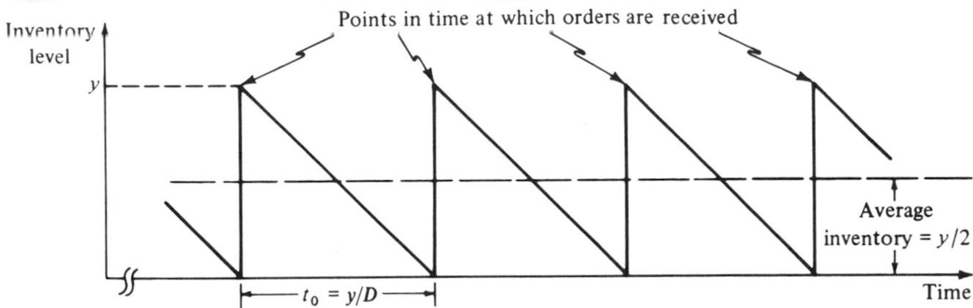

Figure 14-4

variation of the inventory level. It is assumed that demand occurs at the rate D (per unit time). The highest level of inventory occurs when the order quantity y is delivered. (Delivery lag is assumed a known constant.) The inventory level reaches zero level y/D time units after the order quantity y is received.

The smaller the order quantity y, the more frequent will be the placement of new orders. However, the average level of inventory held in stock will be reduced. On the other hand, larger order quantities indicate larger inventory level but less frequent placement of orders (see Figure 14-5). Because there are costs associated with placing orders and holding inventory in stock, the quantity y is selected to allow a compromise between the two types of costs. This is the basis for formulating the inventory model.

Let K be the setup cost incurred every time an order is placed and assume that the holding cost per unit inventory *per unit time* is h. Hence the total cost *per unit time* TCU as a function of y may be written as

$$\begin{aligned}\text{TCU}(y) &= \text{setup cost/unit time} + \text{holding cost/unit time}\\ &= \frac{K}{y/D} + h\left(\frac{y}{2}\right)\end{aligned}$$

As seen from Figure 14-4, the length of each inventory cycle is $t_0 = y/D$ and the *average* inventory in stock is $y/2$.

The optimum value of y is obtained by minimizing TCU(y) with respect to y. Thus, assuming that y is a continuous variable, we have

$$\frac{d\text{TCU}(y)}{dy} = -\frac{KD}{y^2} + \frac{h}{2} = 0$$

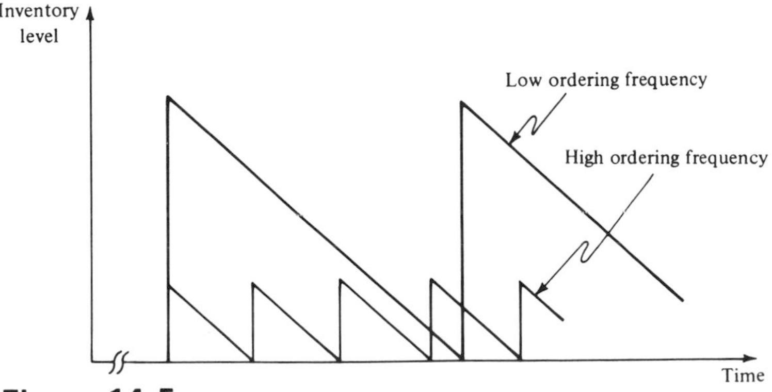

Figure 14-5

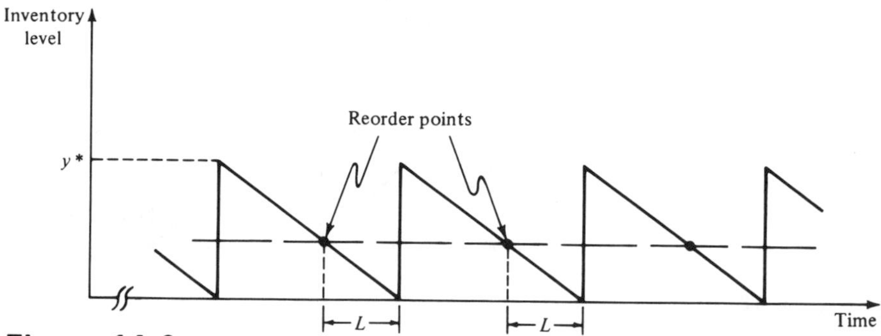

Figure 14-6

which yields the optimum order quantity as

$$y^* = \sqrt{\frac{2KD}{h}}$$

[It can be proved that y^* minimizes TCU(y) by showing that the second derivative at y^* is strictly positive.] The order quantity is usually referred to as **Wilson's economic lot size** or simply the **economic order quantity (EOQ)**.

The optimum policy of the model calls for ordering y^* units every $t_0^* = y^*/D$ time units. The optimum cost TCU(y^*) obtained by direct substitution is $\sqrt{2KDh}$.

Most practical situations usually have a (positive) **lead time** (or time lag) L from the point at which the order is placed until it is actually delivered. The ordering policy of the foregoing model thus must specify the **reorder point**. Figure 14-6 illustrates the situation where reordering occurs L time units before delivery is expected. This information may be translated conveniently for practical implementation by simply specifying the *reorder point*, which is the *level of inventory* at reordering. In practice, the situation is equivalent to observing continuously the level of inventory until the reorder point is reached. Perhaps this is why the EOQ model is sometimes classified as a **continuous review model**. Notice that as the system "stabilizes," the lead time L, for the purpose of analysis, may always be taken less than the cycle length t_0^*. The next example illustrates this point.

Example 14.3-1. The daily demand D for a commodity is approximately 100 units. Every time an order is placed, a fixed cost K of \$100 is incurred. The daily holding cost h per unit inventory is \$.02. If the lead time is 12 days, determine the economic lot size and the reorder point.

From the earlier formulas, the economic lot size is

$$y^* = \sqrt{\frac{2KD}{h}} = \sqrt{\frac{2 \times 100 \times 100}{.02}} = 1000 \text{ units}$$

The associated optimum cycle length is thus given as

$$t_0^* = \frac{y^*}{D} = \frac{1000}{100} = 10 \text{ days}$$

Since the lead time is 12 days and the cycle length is 10 days, reordering occurs when the level of inventory is sufficient to satisfy the demand for two (= 12 − 10) days. Thus the quantity $y^* = 1000$ is ordered when the level of inventory reaches $2 \times 100 = 200$ units.

Notice that the "effective" lead time is taken equal to 2 days rather than 12 days. This result occurs because the lead time is longer than t_0^*. However, after the system stabilizes (it takes two cycles in this example), the situation may be treated as if the lead time is $L - nt_0^*$, where n is the largest integer not exceeding L/t_0^*. Situations such as this exhibit more than one outstanding order at a time. ◀

Exercise 14.3-1

For Example 14.3-1, determine the reorder point in each of the following cases.

(a) Lead time = 15 days. [*Ans.* 500 units.]
(b) Lead time = 23 days. [*Ans.* 300 units.]
(c) Lead time = 8 days. [*Ans.* 800 units.]
(d) Lead time = 10 days. [*Ans.* Zero units.]

The assumptions of the model may not be satisfied for some real situations because demand may be probabilistic. A "crude" procedure has evolved among practitioners that, while retaining the simplicity of applying the economic lot size model, does not completely ignore the effect of probabilistic demand. The idea is quite simple and calls for superimposing a (constant) buffer stock on the inventory level throughout the entire planning horizon. The size of the buffer is determined such that the probability of running out of stock *during lead time L* does not exceed a prespecified value. Suppose that $f(x)$ is the density function of demand *during lead time*. Suppose further that the probability of running out of stock during L must not exceed α. Then the buffer size B is determined from

$$P\{x \geq B + LD\} \leq \alpha$$

where LD represents the consumption during L. The inventory variation with the buffer is illustrated in Figure 14-7.

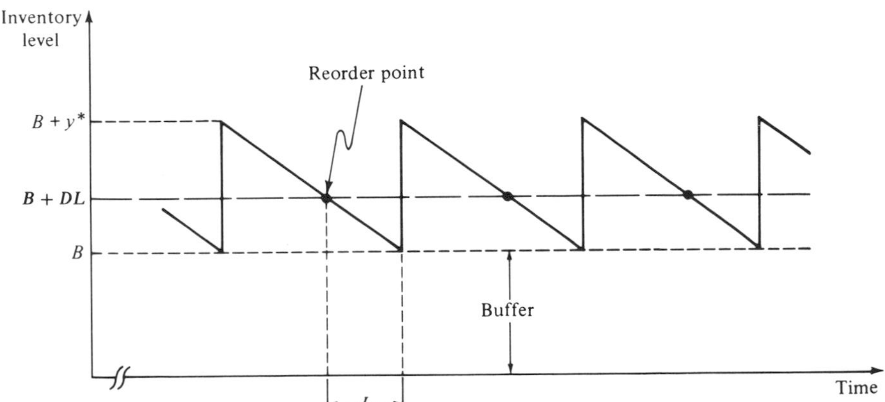

Figure 14-7

Example 14.3-2. Suppose that the demand in Example 14.3-1 is actually an approximation of a probabilistic situation in which the *daily* demand is normal with mean $\mu = 100$ and standard deviation $\sigma = 10$. Determine the size of the buffer stock such that the probability of running out of stock during lead time is at most .05.

From Example 14.3-1, lead time equals 2 days. Because the daily demand is normal, the lead time demand x_L is also normal, with mean $\mu_L = 2 \times 100 = 200$

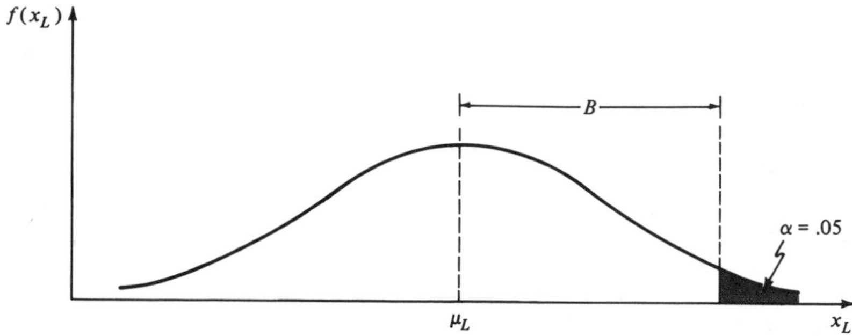

Figure 14-8

units and standard deviation $\sigma_L = \sqrt{2 \times 10^2} = 14.14$. Figure 14-8 illustrates the relationship between the distribution of x_L and the buffer size B.

It then follows that

$$P\{x_L \geq \mu_L + B\} \leq \alpha$$

or

$$P\left\{\frac{x_L - \mu_L}{\sigma_L} \geq \frac{B}{\sigma_L}\right\} \leq \alpha$$

or

$$P\left\{\frac{x_L - \mu_L}{\sigma_L} \geq \frac{B}{14.14}\right\} \leq .05$$

From standard tables, this gives $B/14.14 \geq 1.64$ or $B \geq 23.2$. ◀

Exercise 14.3-2

For Example 14.3-2, determine the buffer stock B in each of the following cases, assuming that the *daily* demand is normal with mean 100 units and variance 30.

(a) Lead time = 15 days. [*Ans.* $\mu_L = 500$, $\sigma_L = 12.25$, $B \geq 20.1$.]
(b) Lead time = 23 days. [*Ans.* $\mu_L = 300$, $\sigma_L = 9.49$, $B \geq 15.6$.]
(c) Lead time = 8 days. [*Ans.* $\mu_L = 800$, $\sigma_L = 15.49$, $B \geq 25.4$.]
(d) Lead time = 10 days. [*Ans.* $\mu_L = \sigma_L = 0$, $B = 0$.]

It is interesting in Example 14.3-2 that the size of B is independent of the mean μ_L. This result is generally expected, since the important factor is the standard deviation. Indeed, if the standard deviation is zero (deterministic case), the buffer size should be zero.

There is no reason to believe that the combined result of superimposing the technique for determining B on the technique for determining EOQ is necessarily optimal or near optimal. The fact that some pertinent information is initially ignored, only to be used completely independently at a later stage of the calculations, is sufficient to refute optimality. In fact, the cost of holding the buffer B may merely be considered the "price" for not employing all the information simultaneously in the analysis.

To appreciate the effect of including the probabilistic demand directly in a *continuous review* model, Section 14.4.1 presents a typical case. As should be expected, the new model is necessarily much more complex than the present one. You are encouraged to compare the two models.

Variations of the EOQ model allow for shortage and uniform (rather than instantaneous) stock replenishment over time. The latter is typical of some production systems where the stock replenishment rate is a function of the production rate. The inventory models in these situations again balance the holding and setup costs. If shortage occurs, a penalty cost is included also in the total cost function. In general, the shortage cost is assumed proportional to the average shortage quantity. Because the analysis of these situations is very similar to the one just given, their details are not presented here. Problems 14-7, 14-10, and 14-13 present the basic results of these models.

14.3.2 SINGLE-ITEM STATIC MODEL WITH PRICE BREAKS

In the models in Section 14.3.1, the purchasing cost per unit time is neglected in the analysis because it is constant and hence should not affect the level of inventory. It often happens, however, that the purchasing price per unit may depend on the size of the quantity purchased. This situation usually occurs in the form of discrete **price breaks** or **quantity discounts**. In such cases, the purchasing price should be considered in the inventory model.

Consider the inventory model with instantaneous stock replenishment and no shortage. Assume that the cost per unit is c_1 for $y < q$ and c_2 for $y \geq q$, where $c_1 > c_2$ and q is the quantity above which a price break is granted. The total cost per cycle will now include the purchasing cost in addition to the setup and holding costs.

The total cost *per unit time* for $y < q$ is

$$\text{TCU}_1(y) = Dc_1 + \frac{KD}{y} + \frac{h}{2}y$$

For $y \geq q$ this cost is

$$\text{TCU}_2(y) = Dc_2 + \frac{KD}{y} + \frac{h}{2}y$$

These two functions are shown graphically in Figure 14-9(a). Disregarding the effect of price breaks for the moment, we let y_m be the quantity at which the minimum values of TCU_1 and TCU_2 occur. Then

$$y_m = \sqrt{\frac{2KD}{h}}$$

The cost functions TCU_1 and TCU_2 in Figure 14-9(a) reveal that the determination of the optimum order quantity y^* depends on where q, the price break point, falls with respect to the three zones I, II, and III shown in the figure. These zones are defined by determining q_1 ($> y_m$) from the equation

$$\text{TCU}_1(y_m) = \text{TCU}_2(q_1)$$

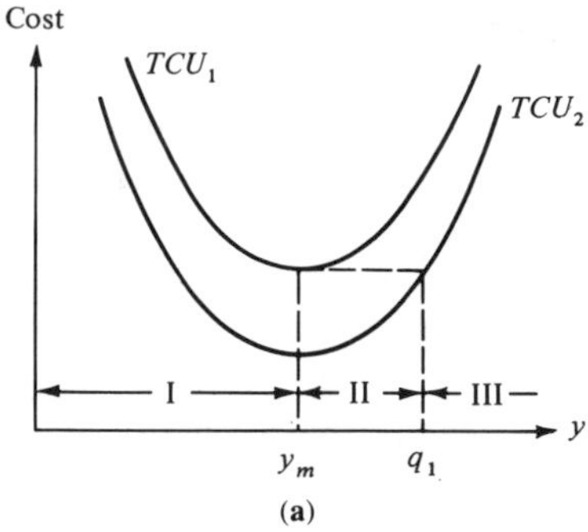

(a)

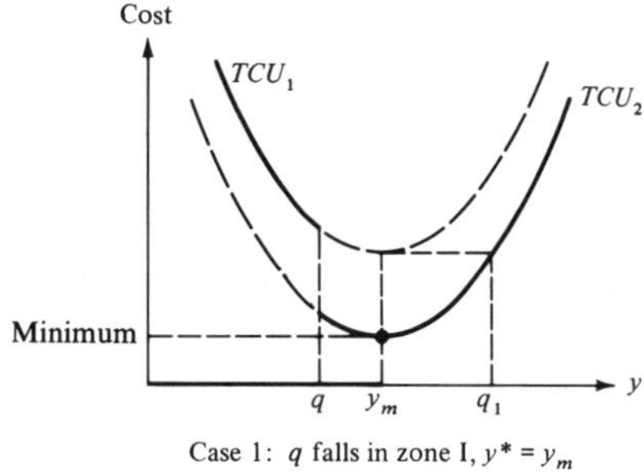

Case 1: q falls in zone I, $y^* = y_m$

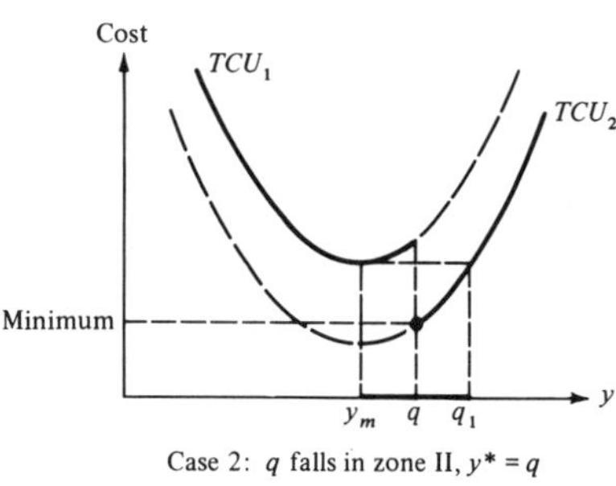

Case 2: q falls in zone II, $y^* = q$

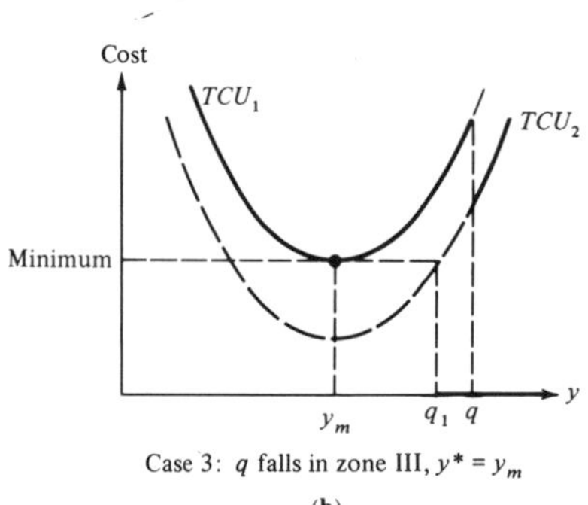

Case 3: q falls in zone III, $y^* = y_m$

(b)

Figure 14-9

Since y_m is known $(= \sqrt{2KD/h})$, the solution of the equation will yield the value of q_1. In this case the zones are defined as follows.

$$\begin{aligned} \text{zone I:} \quad & 0 \le q < y_m \\ \text{zone II:} \quad & y_m \le q < q_1 \\ \text{zone III:} \quad & q \ge q_1 \end{aligned}$$

Figure 14-9(b) provides a graphical solution for each case, depending on whether q falls in zone I, II, or III. We thus summarize the optimum order quantity y^* as follows:

$$y^* = \begin{cases} y_m, & \text{if } 0 \le q < y_m \quad \text{(zone I)} \\ q, & \text{if } y_m \le q < q_1 \quad \text{(zone II)} \\ y_m, & \text{if } q \ge q_1 \quad \text{(zone III)} \end{cases}$$

The procedure for determining y^* may thus be summarized as follows:

1. Determine $y_m = \sqrt{2KD/h}$. If $q < y_m$ (zone I), then $y^* = y_m$, and the procedure ends. Otherwise,

2. Determine q_1 from the equation $\text{TCU}_1(y_m) = \text{TCU}(q_1)$ and decide whether q falls in zone II or zone III.

a. If $y_m \le q < q_1$ (zone II), then $y^* = q$.
b. If $q \ge q_1$ (zone III), then $y^* = y_m$.

Example 14.3-3. Consider the inventory model with the following information. $K = \$10$, $h = \$1$, $D = 5$ units, $c_1 = \$2$, $c_2 = \$1$, and $q = 15$ units. First compute y_m; thus

$$y_m = \sqrt{\frac{2KD}{h}} = \sqrt{\frac{2 \times 10 \times 5}{1}} = 10 \text{ units}$$

Since $q > y_m$, it is necessary to check whether q is in zone II or III. The value of q_1 is computed from

$$\text{TCU}_1(y_m) = \text{TCU}_2(q_1)$$

or

$$c_1 D + \frac{KD}{y_m} + \frac{hy_m}{2} = c_2 D + \frac{KD}{q_1} + \frac{hq_1}{2}$$

Substitution yields

$$2 \times 5 + \frac{10 \times 5}{10} + \frac{1 \times 10}{2} = 1 \times 5 + \frac{10 \times 5}{q_1} + \frac{1 \times q_1}{2}$$

or

$$q_1^2 - 30q_1 + 100 = 0$$

This yields $q_1 = 26.18$ or $q_1 = 3.82$. By definition, q_1 is selected as the larger value. Since $y_m < q < q_1$, q is in zone II. It follows that $y^* = q = 15$ units. The associated total cost per unit time is thus computed as

$$\text{TCU}(y^*) = \text{TCU}_2(15) = c_2 D + \frac{KD}{15} + \frac{h \times 15}{2}$$

$$= 1 \times 5 + \frac{10 \times 5}{15} + \frac{1 \times 15}{2} = \$15.83/\text{day}$$

◀

Exercise 14.3-3

In Example 14.3-3, determine y^* and the total cost *per cycle* in each of the following cases.
(a) $q = 30$. [*Ans.* $y^* = 10$, cost/cycle = \$40.]
(b) $q = 5$. [*Ans.* $y^* = 10$, cost/cycle = \$30.]

14.3.3 MULTIPLE-ITEM STATIC MODEL WITH STORAGE LIMITATION

This model considers the inventory system including n (> 1) items that are competing for a limited storage space. This limitation represents an interaction between the different items and may be included in the model as a constraint.

Let A be the maximum storage area available for the n items and assume that the storage area requirements per unit of the ith item is a_i. If y_i is the amount ordered of the ith item, the storage requirements constraint becomes

$$\sum_{i=1}^{n} a_i y_i \leq A$$

Assume that each item is replenished instantaneously and that there is no quantity discount. Assume further that no shortages are allowed. Let D_i, K_i, and h_i be, respectively, the demand rate per unit time, the setup cost, and the holding cost per unit time corresponding to the ith item. The inventory costs associated with each item should be essentially the same as in the case of an equivalent single-item model. The problem thus becomes

$$\text{minimize TCU}(y_1, \ldots, y_n) = \sum_{i=1}^{n}\left(\frac{K_i D_i}{y_i} + \frac{h_i y_i}{2}\right)$$

subject to

$$\sum_{i=1}^{n} a_i y_i \leq A$$

$$y_i > 0, \qquad \text{for all } i$$

The general solution of this problem is obtained by the Lagrange multipliers method.† However, before this is done, it is necessary to check whether the constraint is active by checking whether the unconstrained value

$$y_i^* = \sqrt{\frac{2K_i D_i}{h_i}}$$

satisfies the storage constraint. If it does, the constraint is said to be inactive or redundant and may be neglected.

If the constraint is not satisfied by the values of y_i^*, it must be active. In this case, we must find new optimal values of y_i that satisfy the storage constraint in *equality* sense.‡ This result is accomplished by first formulating the Lagrangian function as

$$\begin{aligned} L(\lambda, y_1, y_2, \ldots, y_n) &= \text{TCU}(y_1, \ldots, y_n) - \lambda\left(\sum_{i=1}^{n} a_i y_i - A\right) \\ &= \sum_{i=1}^{n}\left(\frac{K_i D_i}{y_i} + \frac{h_i y_i}{2}\right) - \lambda\left(\sum_{i=1}^{n} a_i y_i - A\right) \end{aligned}$$

where λ (< 0) is the Lagrange multiplier.

The optimum values of y_i and λ can be found by equating the respective first partial derivatives to zero. This gives

$$\frac{\partial L}{\partial y_i} = \frac{K_i D_i}{y_i^2} + \frac{h_i}{2} - \lambda a_i = 0$$

$$\frac{\partial L}{\partial \lambda} = -\sum_{i=1}^{n} a_i y_i + A = 0$$

---

† See Chapter 19 for a complete analysis of the Lagrangian method.

‡ This procedure happens to yield the correct answer because $\text{TCU}(y_1, \ldots, y_n)$ is convex and the problem has a single constraint that is linear (convex solution space). The procedure may not be correct under other conditions or when there is more than one constraint. See Section 19.2.2A.

The second equation implies that y_i^* must satisfy the storage constraint in equality sense.

From the first equation,

$$y_i^* = \sqrt{\frac{2K_i D_i}{h_i - 2\lambda^* a_i}}$$

Notice that y_i^* is dependent on λ^*, the optimal value of λ. Also, for $\lambda^* = 0$, y_i^* gives the solution of the unconstrained case.

The value λ^* can be found by systematic trial and error. Since by definition $\lambda < 0$ for the minimization case, by trying successive negative values of λ the value of λ^* should result in simultaneous values of y_i^* that satisfy the given constraint in equality sense. Thus the determination of λ^* automatically yeilds y_i^*.

Example 14.3-4. Consider the inventory problem with three items ($n = 3$). The parameters of the problem are shown in the table.

Item i	K_i	D_i	h_i	a_i
1	\$10	2 units	\$.3	1 ft^2
2	5	4 units	.1	1 ft^2
3	15	4 units	.2	1 ft^2

Assume that the total available storage area is given by $A - 25$ ft^2.

Given the formula

$$y_i^* = \sqrt{\frac{2K_i D_i}{h_i - 2\lambda^* a_i}}$$

the following table is constructed:

λ	y_1	y_2	y_3	$\sum_{i=1}^{3} a_i y_i - A$
0	11.5	20.0	24.5	+31
−.05	10.0	14.1	17.3	+16.4
−.10	9.0	11.5	14.9	+10.4
−.15	8.2	10.0	13.4	+ 6.6
−.20	7.6	8.9	12.2	+ 3.7
−.25	7.1	8.2	11.3	+ 1.6
−.30	6.7	7.6	10.6	− 0.1

For $A = 25$ ft^2, the storage constraint is satisfied in equality sense for some value of λ between $-.25$ and $-.3$. This value is equal to λ^* and may be estimated by linear interpolation. The corresponding values of y_i should thus yield y_i^* directly. Since from the table λ^* appears very close to $-.3$, optimal y_i^* are approximately given by

$$y_1^* = 6.7, \quad y_2^* = 7.6, \quad \text{and} \quad y_3^* = 10.6$$

If $A \geq 56$ $(= 11.5 + 20.0 + 24.5)$, the unconstrained values of y_i corresponding to $\lambda = 0$ yield y_i. In this case the constraint is inactive.

Exercise 14.3-4

Consider Example 14.3-4. Using the second table, determine the range of λ in which λ^* falls assuming that the area A is given as follows.

(a) $A = 45 \text{ ft}^2$. [*Ans.* $0 > \lambda^* > -.05$.]
(b) $A = 30 \text{ ft}^2$. [*Ans.* $-.15 > \lambda^* > -.2$.]
(c) $A = 20 \text{ ft}^2$. [*Ans.* $\lambda^* < -.3$.]

14.3.4 *N*-PERIOD PRODUCTION SCHEDULING MODEL

Consider the problem of scheduling production over N successive periods. The demands for the different periods are variable but deterministic. These demands may be met by either fluctuating inventory while keeping production constant or fluctuating production while keeping inventory constant, or a combination of both. Fluctuations in production can be achieved by working overtime, and fluctuation in inventory may be met by holding positive stock on hand or by allowing a backlog of unfilled demand. The objective here is to determine the production schedule for all N periods that minimizes the total relevant costs.

This model assumes zero setup cost in every period. In general, shortages are allowed except that all backlogged demand must be filled by the Nth period. This situation can be represented as a transportation model (see Chapter 6). In particular, by noting the special characteristics of the model for the case where no shortage is allowed, the problem can be solved in an easy way without having to apply the iterative procedure of the transportation technique.

Define the following symbols for period i, $i = 1, \ldots, N$.

c_i = production cost per unit during regular time
d_i = production cost per unit during overtime, $c_i < d_i$
h_i = holding cost per unit forwarded from period i to period $i + 1$
p_i = shortage cost per unit demanded in period i and filled in period $i + 1$
a_{Ri} = production capacity (number of units) during regular time
a_{Ti} = production capacity (number of units) during overtime
b_i = demand (number of units)

Notice that c_i, the per unit production cost during regular time, is less than d_i, the per unit production cost during overtime, as shown graphically in Figure 14-10(a). The situation may be generalized to the case where there are k levels of

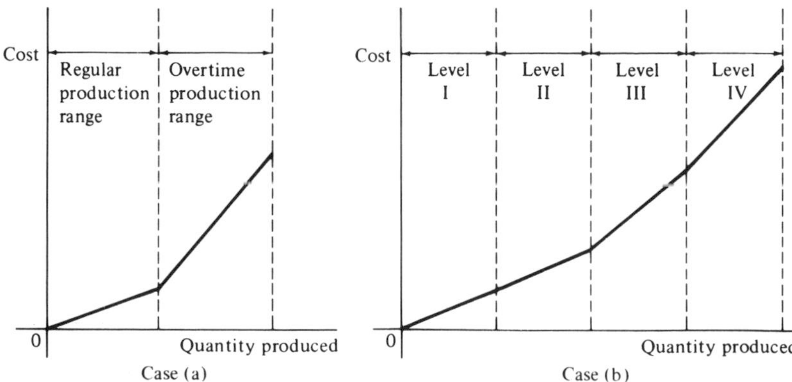

Figure 14-10

production such that the per unit production cost increases with the level of production. A typical illustration is shown in Figure 14-12(b). Under such conditions, the production cost function is said to have increasing marginal costs. Mathematically, the function is said to be convex.

This restriction on the production cost function must be maintained; otherwise, the following model will not be applicable. This point will be justified later after the details of the model have been presented.

A. No Shortage Model

First, consider the case where no shortage is allowed in the system. According to the terminology of the transportation model (Chapter 6), the *sources* are represented by the regular and overtime productions for the various periods. The *destinations* are given by the demands for the respective periods. The per unit *transportation cost* from any source to any destination is represented by the corresponding per unit production plus holding costs.

The complete cost matrix for the equivalent transportation model (assuming no shortages) is given in Table 14-1.

The surplus column is used to balance the transportation model; that is, $S = \sum_i a_i - \sum_j b_j$. This is based on the reasonable assumption that the demand is always less than the production capacity of the system. (The cost per unit in the surplus column is equal to zero.) Since no shortage is allowed, a current production period cannot be used to satisfy the demands for its preceding periods. Table 14-1 implements this restriction by using shaded squares, which is actually equivalent to assigning a very large per unit cost.

Because no backorders are allowed in this model, it is necessary to include the restriction that for every period k, the cumulative amount of demand up to and including that period does not exceed the corresponding cumulative amount of production; that is,

$$\sum_{i=1}^{k} (a_{Ri} + a_{Ti}) \geq \sum_{j=1}^{k} b_j, \qquad \text{for } k = 1, 2, \ldots, N$$

Table 14-1

Demand Period j

Production Period i	1	2	3	...	N	Surplus	
R_1	c_1	$c_1 + h_1$	$c_1 + h_1 + h_2$		$c_1 + h_1 + \cdots + h_{N-1}$	0	a_{R1}
T_1	d_1	$d_1 + h_1$	$d_1 + h_1 + h_2$		$d_1 + h_1 + \cdots + h_{N-1}$	0	a_{T1}
R_2		c_2	$c_2 + h_2$		$c_2 + h_2 + \cdots + h_{N-1}$	0	a_{R2}
T_2		d_2	$d_2 + h_2$		$d_2 + h_2 + \cdots + h_{N-1}$	0	a_{T2}
$\vdots$							$\vdots$
R_N					c_N		a_{RN}
T_N					d_N	0	a_{TN}
	b_1	b_2	b_3	...	b_N	S	

The solution of the problem is greatly simplified by its formulation as a transportation model. Since the demand at period i should be satisfied before those at periods $i + 1$, $i + 2$, ..., N, and because of the special condition imposed on the production cost function, it will not be necessary to use the regular transportation algorithm in solving the problem. Instead, the demand for period 1 is first satisfied by successively assigning as much as possible to the cheapest entries of the first column (period 1). The new values of a_i are then updated to reflect the *remaining* capacities for the different periods. Next, period 2 is considered and its demand is satisfied in the cheapest possible way within the new capacity limitations. The process is continued until the demand for period N is satisfied.†

Because of the increasing marginal costs in the production cost function, the regular production capacity will be exhausted before overtime production can start. If this condition is not satisfied, the transportation model will not be applicable since this might yield meaningless results (such as using overtime production before regular production is exhausted).

Example 14.3-5. Consider a four-period production scheduling problem with the following data:

Period i	Capacity (units) a_{Ri}	Capacity (units) a_{Ti}	Demand (units) b_i
1	100	50	120
2	150	80	200
3	100	100	250
4	200	50	200
Totals	550	280	770

The production costs are identical for all the periods; that is, $c_i = 2$ and $d_i = 3$ for all i. The holding cost is also constant for all periods and is given by $h_i = 0.1$ for all i. The cost functions are assumed identical for all periods only for simplicity.

The equivalent transportation model is shown in Table 14-2. The number in the top right-hand corner of each square represents the "transportation" costs; those in the middle of the squares (boldface numbers) represent the solution.

Notice the logic of the solution. For column 1, square (R_1, 1) has the smallest cost per unit (= 2). The maximum amount that can be assigned to this square is 100 units, which exhausts the supply of R_1. The remaining demand units for period 1 can be satisfied by assigning 20 units to square (T_1, 1). This leaves a supply of 30 units for T_1. Next, consider column 2. Square (R_2, 2) has the smallest cost (= 2). A maximum of 150 units can be assigned to it, which will exhaust the R_2-supply. The next smallest cost in column 2 occurs in square (R_1, 2). Since the R_1-supply is zero now, square (T_2, 2), with the next smallest cost element in the same column, must be considered. By assigning 50 units to this square, the demand for period 2 is satisfied. This leaves 30 units in the T_2-supply. The indicated procedure is continued until the demand for period 4 (column 4) is satisfied.

† For a proof of the optimality of this procedure, see S. M. Johnson, "Sequential Production Planning over Time at Minimum Cost," *Management Science*, Vol. 3, 1957, pp. 435–437.

Table 14-2

	1	2	3	4	Surplus	
R_1	[2] **100**	[2.1]	[2.2]	[2.3]	[0]	~~100~~
T_1	[3] **20**	[3.1]	[3.2] **20**	[3.3]	[0] **10**	~~50~~ ~~30~~ ~~10~~
R_2		[2] **150**	[2.1]	[2.2]	[0]	~~150~~
T_2		[3] **50**	[3.1] **30**	[3.2]	[0]	~~80~~ ~~30~~
R_3			[2] **100**	[2.1]	[0]	~~100~~
T_3			[3] **100**	[3.1]	[0]	~~100~~
R_4				[2] **200**	[0]	~~200~~
T_4				[3]	[0] **50**	~~50~~
	~~120~~ ~~20~~	~~200~~ ~~50~~	~~250~~ ~~150~~ ~~50~~ ~~20~~	~~200~~	~~60~~ ~~10~~	

You can verify that this solution is optimal by using the optimality condition of the transportation algorithm (see Section 6.2.1). This is accomplished in the usual manner by computing the simplex multipliers for the present solution and then checking for optimality (see Problem 14–21). Notice, however, that the given "optimal" solution is degenerate. ◀

Exercise 14.3-5

Consider the optimal solution of Example 14.3-5 as given in Table 14-2.

(a) Determine the following amounts.
  (1) Production in period 1 for 1.
  [*Ans.* 120 units.]
  (2) Production in period 1 for 2.
  [*Ans.* None.]
  (3) Production in period 1 for 3.
  [*Ans.* 20 units.]
  (4) Regular and overtime production in period 1.
  [*Ans.* 100 units regular time and 40 units overtime.]
  (5) Inventory carried from period 1 to 3.
  [*Ans.* 20 units.]
  (6) Inventory carried from period 2 to 3.
  [*Ans.* 30 units.]
  (7) Inventory carried from period 3 to 4.
  [*Ans.* None.]

(b) Suppose that 55 additional units are needed in period 4. Determine how they should be produced.
  [*Ans.* Produce 50 overtime units in period 4 and 5 overtime units in period 1.]

B. Shortage Model

Now consider a generalization of the model in which shortages are allowed. It is assumed that backlogged demand must be filled by the end of the N-period horizon.

Table 14-2 can be modified readily to include the effect of backlogging by introducing the appropriate unit "transportation" costs in the blocked routes. For example, if p_i is the shortage cost per unit demanded in period i and filled in period $i + 1$, the unit transportation costs corresponding to squares (R_N, 1) and T_N, 1) are given by $\{c_N + p_1 + p_2 + \cdots + p_{N-1}\}$ and $\{d_N + p_1 + \cdots + p_{N-1}\}$, respectively.

It would seem reasonable that the solution procedure used with the no-shortage case would also apply to the new situation, where shortage is allowed. Unfortunately, this is not true. To justify this claim, the following numerical example is designed to show that the preceding procedure may generally yield an inferior solution.

Example 14.3-6. Consider a three-period model where regular and overtime production are used. The production capacities for the three periods are as follows:

	Production Capacity (units)	
Period	Regular	Overtime
1	15	10
2	15	0
3	20	15

The production cost per unit is 5 for regular production and 10 for overtime production. The holding and shortage costs per unit are given by 1 and 2, respectively. The demand units for the three periods are 20, 35, and 15, respectively.

The equivalent transportation model is given in Table 14-3. Period 2 has no overtime production, since its corresponding capacity is zero.

Table 14-3

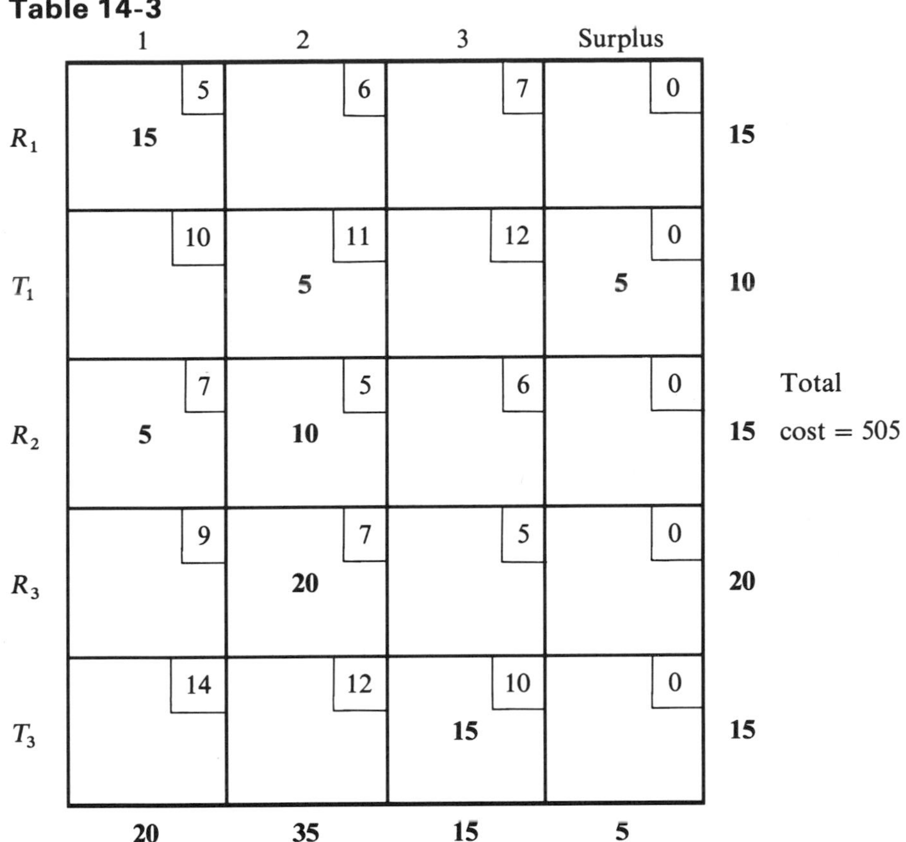

	1	2	3	Surplus	
R_1	5 **15**	6	7	0	**15**
T_1	10	11 **5**	12	0 **5**	**10**
R_2	7 **5**	5 **10**	6	0	**15**
R_3	9	7 **20**	5	0	**20**
T_3	14	12	10 **15**	0	**15**
	20	**35**	**15**	**5**	

Total cost = 505

Table 14-3 also shows the solution of the problem obtained by using the foregoing procedure. Thus, for column 1, 15 units are assigned to $(R_1, 1)$ and 5 units to $(R_2, 1)$. (Notice that the cheapest route is selected from among *all* the entries of the column under consideration.) Next, consider column 2. Assign 10 units to $(R_2, 2)$, 20 units to $(R_3, 2)$, and 5 units to $(T_1, 2)$. Finally, in column 3, assign 15 units to $(T_3, 3)$. The total cost associated with the schedule is $5 \times 15 + 5 \times 7 + 5 \times 11 + 10 \times 5 + 20 \times 7 + 15 \times 10 = 505$.

It can be shown that the solution in Table 14-3 does not satisfy the optimality condition of the transportation algorithm. In fact, Table 14-4 gives the optimal solution to this problem. The associated total cost in this case is $15 \times 5 + 5 \times 10 + 5 \times 11 + 15 \times 5 + 5 \times 7 + 10 \times 12 + 15 \times 5 = 485$. ◀

Example 14.2-6 shows that the simple procedure of satisfying the demands for the successive periods does not yield an optimal solution for the shortage model. Consequently, we would have to apply the general transportation algorithm to obtain the optimal solution.

14.3.5 SINGLE-ITEM *N*-PERIOD DYNAMIC EOQ MODEL

In this model it is assumed that demand is known with certainty, but may vary from one period to the next. Also, the inventory level is reviewed periodically. A delivery

Table 14-4

	1	2	3	Surplus	
R_1	[5] **15**	[6]	[7]	[0]	**15**
T_1	[10] **5**	[11] **5**	[12]	[0]	**10**
R_2	[7]	[5] **15**	[6]	[0]	**15**
R_3	[9]	[7] **5**	[5] **15**	[0]	**20**
T_3	[14]	[12] **10**	[10]	[0] **5**	**15**
	20	**35**	**15**	**5**	

Total cost = 485

lag (expressed as a fixed number of periods) is allowed but with instantaneous replenishment at the beginning of the delivery period. The model assumes no shortages. The ultimate objective of the dynamic model is the same as in all inventory models: determination of a delivery schedule that will minimize the total costs of production (or purchasing) and inventory holding.

This model is sometimes referred to as the **dynamic economic order quantity** (EOQ) because it is a refinement of the static EOQ model presented in Section 14.3.1. Indeed, if the fluctuations in demand among the different periods are not "too pronounced," the computationally simple static EOQ model should be used as a reasonable approximation. In this case the demand rate D is estimated as the average demand among the N periods of the dynamic model.

The dynamic EOQ is applicable to situations where the demand for an item varies periodically or seasonally. An important variation of this application evolves out of the use of the so-called **materials requirement planning** (**MRP**) to provide a timely delivery of required materials for the different stages of the production process.

In this section we start by describing how the MRP approach results in a typical N-period dynamic inventory model. Following this motivational presentation, we then present a number of methods for solving the model. You will notice that unlike the static EOQ model, the dynamic EOQ can deal only with a finite planning horizon. Given the fact that we must predict the variations in future demands, it is not unreasonable to assume that such forecasts will be valid only over a finite future horizon.

A. Materials Requirement Planning (MRP) Application

The basic idea of the MRP approach can best be described by an example. Suppose that the quarterly demand over the next year for two final models, M1 and M2, of a given product are 100 and 150 units, respectively. Deliveries of quarterly lots are promised at the end of each quarter. The production lead time for M1 is 2 months, and that of M2 is 1 month only (e.g., the first lots of M1 and M2 must start production at the beginning of February and March, respectively, for delivery at the end of March). Both models use a common subassembly S at the rate of 2 units per unit of the final product. The lead time for the manufacturing of the subassembly is 1 month.

Figure 14-11 summarizes production schedules associated with the two models. The schedules start with the quarterly demand (solid arrows) for M1 and M2 occurring at the end of March, June, September, and December (months 3, 6, 9, and 12). Given the lead times of 2 and 1 months for M1 and M2, the dashed arrows then show the planned starts of each production lot. In order for the production to start on schedule, it is necessary that the subassembly S be delivered at these points in time. This means that the start of a production lot for either M1 or M2 must coincide with the delivery of a subassembly lot. This information is shown in Figure 14-11 by the solid arrows corresponding to the subassembly (S) chart. The corresponding demand quantities are computed directly on the basis of 2 : 1 for both M1 and M2 (each unit of M1 or M2 requires 2 units of S). Using a production lead time of 1 month, the production schedule for S associated with M1 and M2 can then be determined as shown by the dashed arrows. The next step now is to determine the

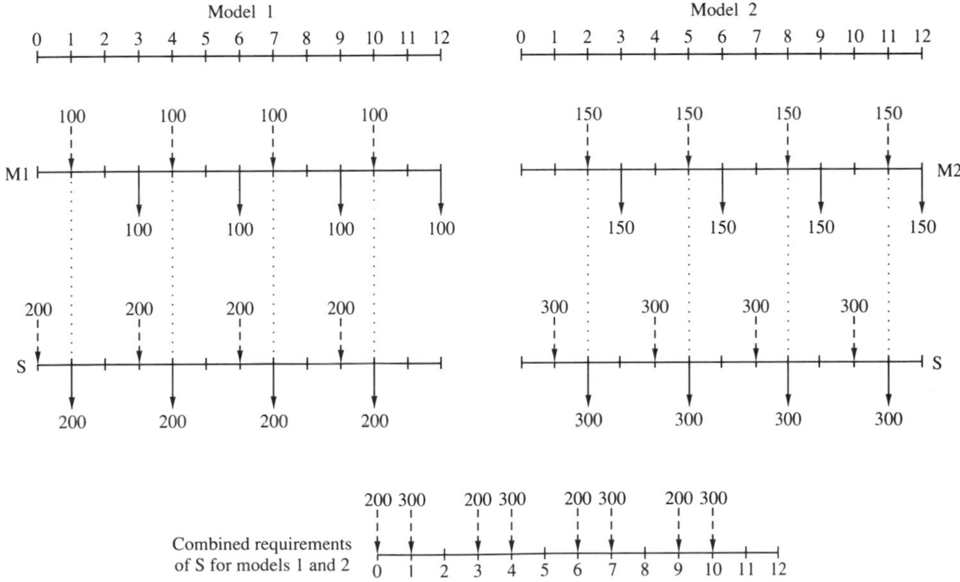

Figure 14-11

total production schedule of S by combining the two subassembly charts of M1 and M2 into one chart as shown in Figure 14-11. The resulting variable demand schedule is typical of the situation that can be solved by the dynamic EOQ algorithms, which we present below.

In a typical MRP situation, the material requirements may involve several levels of subassembly with each level yielding a combined chart similar to the one demonstrated by S above. In such a case each level will result in a separate application of the dynamic EOQ model. It is interesting to notice that the main products (e.g., M1 and M2) may start with perfectly uniform demands with time, yet the interaction between the final products and the subassemblies, together with the effect of production lead times could result in variable or dynamic demands over the course of the planning horizon. The fact that the final product schedule is the key factor in deciding how production/purchasing should take place in the preceding production stages gives rise to the suggestive name **pull system**, as opposed to the **push system**, in which inventory items are distributed, possibly in a multiechelon fashion, from a central location (e.g., a warehouse) to demand points (e.g., retailers).

B. Solution Algorithms

In this section we present two types of solution algorithms: a dynamic programming (DP) model and a heuristic model. The DP model is based on the principles we presented in Chapter 10, and although it guarantees optimality, typically it involves lengthy computations even on the computer. The heuristic approach, when applicable, is fast and efficient computationally and, according to computational experiences, yields very good solutions.

Dynamic Programming Model

Define for period i, $i = 1, 2, \ldots, N$,

z_i = amount ordered
D_i = amount demanded
x_i = entering inventory (at the beginning of period i)
h_i = holding cost per unit of inventory carried forward from period i to period $i + 1$
K_i = setup cost
$c_i(z_i)$ = marginal purchasing (production) cost function given z_i

Let

$$C_i(z_i) = \begin{cases} 0, & z_i = 0 \\ K_i + c_i(z_i), & z_i > 0 \end{cases}$$

The function $c_i(z_i)$ is of interest only if the unit purchasing cost varies from one period to the next or if there are price breaks.

Since no shortages are allowed, the objective is to determine the optimal values of z_i that minimize the sum of the setup, purchasing, and holding costs for all N periods. The holding cost is assumed proportional to

$$x_{i+1} = x_i + z_i - D_i$$

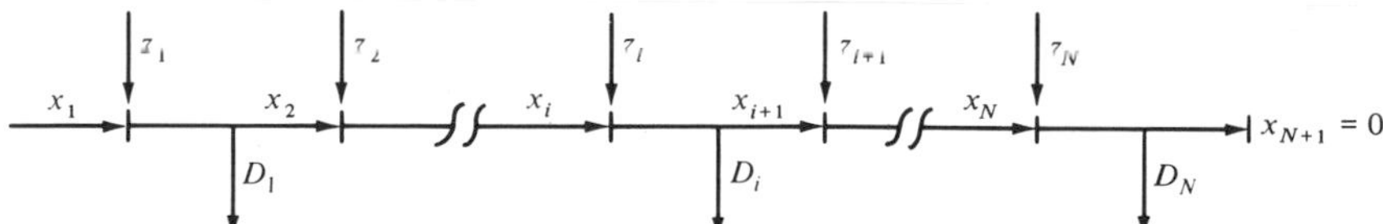

Figure 14-12

which is the amount of inventory carried forward from i to $i + 1$. As a result, the holding cost for period i is $h_i x_{i+1}$. The assumption is introduced only for simplicity, since the model may be readily extended to cover any holding cost function $H_i(x_{i+1})$ by replacing $h_i x_{i+1}$ by $H_i(x_{i+1})$. By the same token, holding cost may be based on x_i or $(x_i + x_{i+1})/2$.

The development of the dynamic programming model is simplified by depicting the problem schematically as shown in Figure 14-12. Each period represents a stage. Using the backward recursive equation, we define the states of the system at stage i as the amount of entering inventory x_i. Let $f_i(x_i)$ be the minimum inventory cost for periods $i, i + 1, \ldots$, and N. The complete recursive equation is given by

$$f_N(x_N) = \min_{\substack{z_N + x_N = D_N \\ z_N \geq 0}} \{C_N(z_N)\}$$

$$f_i(x_i) = \min_{\substack{D_i \leq x_i + z_i \leq D_i + \cdots + D_N \\ z_i \geq 0}} \{C_i(z_i) + h_i(x_i + z_i - D_i) + f_{i+1}(x_i + z_i - D_i)\},$$

$$i - 1, 2, \ldots, N - 1$$

The forward recursive equation can be developed by defining the states at stage i as the amount of inventory at the end of period i. From Figure 14-12, these states are given by x_{i+1}. At any stage, the values of x_{i+1} are limited by

$$0 \leq x_{i+1} \leq D_{i+1} + \cdots + D_N$$

Thus, in the extreme case, the amount z_i in period i may be ordered large enough so that the remaining inventory x_{i+1} will satisfy the demand for all the remaining periods.

Let $f_i(x_{i+1})$ be the minimum inventory cost for periods $1, 2, \ldots$, and i given x_{i+1}, the amount of inventory at the end of period i. The complete recursive equation is then given by

$$f_1(x_2) = \min_{0 \leq z_1 \leq D_1 + x_2} \{C_1(z_1) + h_1 x_2\}$$

$$f_i(x_{i+1}) = \min_{0 \leq z_i \leq D_i + x_{i+1}} \{C_i(z_i) + h_i x_{i+1} + f_{i-1}(x_{i+1} + D_i - z_i)\},$$

$$i = 2, 3, \ldots, N$$

The forward and backward formulations of the model are computationally equivalent. However, the forward algorithm, as indicated later, will prove useful in developing an important special case of the preceding model. The following numerical example is thus used to illustrate the computational procedure of the forward algorithm. The procedure for the backward algorithm is left as an exercise (see Problem 14–28).

Exercise 14.3-6

Suppose that the holding cost in period i is based on the *average* inventory during the period. Write the expressions for the holding cost as they should appear in the forward and backward recursive equations.

[*Ans.* Backward: $h_i\left(x_i + z_i - \frac{D_i}{2}\right)$, forward: $h_i\left(x_{i+1} + \frac{D_i}{2}\right)$.]

Example 14.3-7. Consider a three-period inventory situation with discrete units and dynamic deterministic demand. The data for the problem are as follows:

Period i	Demand D_i	Setup Cost K_i	Holding Cost h_i
1	3 units	\$3.00	\$1.00
2	2 units	7.00	3.00
3	4 units	6.00	2.00

The entering inventory x_1 to period 1 is 1 unit. Suppose that the marginal purchasing cost is \$10 per unit for the first 3 units and \$20 for each additional unit. Then

$$c_i(z_i) = \begin{cases} 10z_i, & 0 \le z_i \le 3 \\ 30 + 20(z_i - 3), & z_i \ge 4 \end{cases}$$

The stage calculations for the forward algorithm are as follows.

Stage 1: $D_1 = 3, 0 \le x_2 \le 2 + 4 = 6$

		$f_1(z_1 \mid x_2) = C_1(z_1) + h_1x_2$							Optimal Solution	
		$z_1 = 2$	3	4	5	6	7	8		
x_2	h_1x_2	$C_1(z_1) = 23$	33	53	73	93	113	133	$f_1(x_2)$	z_1^*
0	0	23							23	2
1	1		34						34	3
2	2			55					55	4
3	3				76				76	5
4	4					97			97	6
5	5						118		118	7
6	6							139	139	8

Since $x_1 = 1$, the smallest value of z_1 is $D_1 - x_1 = 3 - 1 = 2$.

Stage 2: $D_2 = 2, 0 \le x_3 \le 4$

		$f_2(z_2 \mid x_3) = C_2(z_2) + h_2 x_3 + f_1(x_3 + D_2 - z_2)$							Optimal Solution	
		$z_2 = 0$	1	2	3	4	5	6		
x_3	$h_2 x_3$	$C_2(z_2) = 0$	17	27	37	57	77	97	$f_2(x_3)$	z_2^*
0	0	0 + 55 = 55	17 + 34 = 51	27 + 23 = 50					50	2
1	3	3 + 76 = 79	20 + 55 = 75	30 + 34 = 64	40 + 23 = 63				63	3
2	6	6 + 97 = 103	23 + 76 = 99	33 + 55 = 88	43 + 34 = 77	63 + 23 = 86			77	3
3	9	9 + 118 = 127	26 + 97 = 123	36 + 76 = 112	46 + 55 = 101	66 + 34 = 100	86 + 23 = 109		100	4
4	12	12 + 139 = 151	29 + 118 = 147	39 + 97 = 136	49 + 76 = 125	69 + 55 = 124	89 + 34 = 123	109 + 23 = 132	123	5

Stage 3: $D_3 = 4, x_4 = 0$

		$f_3(z_3 \mid x_4) = C_3(z_3) + h_3 x_4 + f_2(x_4 + D_3 - z_3)$					Optimal Solution	
		$z_3 = 0$	1	2	3	4		
x_4	$h_3 x_4$	$C_3(z_3) = 0$	16	26	36	56	$f_3(x_4)$	z_3^*
0	0	0 + 123 = 123	16 + 100 = 116	26 + 77 = 103	36 + 63 = 99	56 + 50 = 106	99	3

The solution is given as $z_1^* = 2$, $z_2^* = 3$, and $z_3^* = 3$, which costs a total of \$99. ◀

Exercise 14.3-7

Consider Example 14.3-7.

(a) Does it make sense to have $x_4 > 0$?
[*Ans.* No, because it is nonoptimal to terminate the planning horizon with positive inventory.]

(b) In each of the following (independent) cases, determine the feasible ranges for z_1, z_2, z_3, x_2, and x_3. (You will find it helpful to depict each case as in Figure 14-12.)
(1) $x_1 = 4$ and all other data remain unchanged
[*Ans.* $0 \le z_1 \le 5, 0 \le z_2 \le 5, 0 \le z_3 \le 4, 1 \le x_2 \le 6, 0 \le x_3 \le 4$.]
(2) $x_1 = 0$, $D_1 = 5$, $D_2 = 4$, and $D_3 = 5$
[*Ans.* $5 \le z_1 \le 14, 0 \le z_2 \le 9, 0 \le z_3 \le 5, 0 \le x_2 \le 9, 0 \le x_3 \le 5$.]

Special Case with Constant or Decreasing Marginal Costs

The dynamic programming model can be used with *any* cost functions. An important special case of this model occurs when for period i both the purchasing (production) cost *per unit* and the holding cost *per unit* are *constant* or *decreasing* functions of z_i and x_{i+1}, respectively. In this case the cost function is said to yield constant or decreasing *marginal* cost. Typical illustrations of such cost functions are shown in Figure 14-13. Mathematically, these functions are concave. Case (a) shows

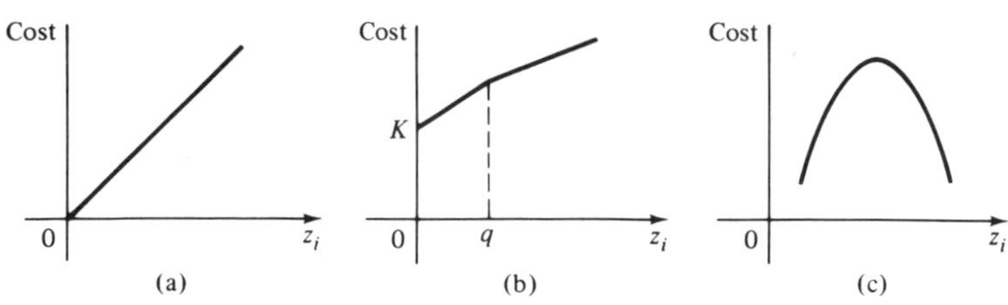

Figure 14-13

the situation of constant marginal cost. Case (b) is typical of many production (or purchasing) cost functions where, regardless of the amount produced, a setup cost K is charged. A constant marginal cost is then incurred; but if quantity discount or price break is allowed at $z_i = q$, the marginal cost for $z_i > q$ becomes smaller. Finally, case (c) illustrates a general concave function.

Under the conditions just stipulated, it can be proved that:†

1. Given the initial inventory $x_1 = 0$, then at any period i of the N-period model, it is optimal to have a positive quantity z_i^* *or* a positive entering inventory x_i^* but not both; that is, $z_i^* x_i^* = 0$.‡
2. The amount z_i ordered at any period i is optimal only if it is zero *or* satisfies the *exact* demand of one or more succeeding periods. These succeeding periods are such that if the demand in period $i + m$ ($< N$) is satisfied by z_i^*, then the demands for periods, $i, i + 1, \ldots$, and $i + m - 1$ must also be satisfied by z_i^*.

The first property (theorem) implies that for any period i, it is not economical to bring in inventory and place an order at the same time. For, suppose that the *least* marginal cost of acquiring and holding *one* additional unit from a previous period i' to the present period i'' ($i' < i''$) is b', while the marginal cost of ordering one more unit at i'' is b''. If $b'' \leq b'$, the amount ordered at i'' can be increased to cover the exact demand at i'' without an increase in the associated total costs as compared with the case where this demand is satisfied from period i'. This result follows because of the nonincreasing marginal costs. Hence having $x_i'' z_i'' = 0$ will yield a solution that is *at least* as good as any other solution. On the other hand, if $b'' > b'$, it is more economical to increase the order in i' to cover the demand in i' and i'' so that the amount ordered in i'' is equal to zero. This conclusion follows again because of the nonincreasing marginal costs. The implication here then is that the condition $x_i z_i = 0$ will not yield any worse solution provided that the marginal costs are constant or decreasing and the initial inventory is zero. The second property, which calls for ordering the exact amount for one or more periods, follows immediately from the first property.

---

† For details of the proof, see H. Wagner and T. Whitin, "Dynamic Version of the Economic Lot Size Model," *Management Science*, Vol. 5, 1958, pp. 89–96. The original proofs by Wagner and Whitin, however, are developed under the restrictive assumption that the per unit purchasing costs are *constant* and *identical* for all periods. This was later improved by A. F. Veinott, Jr., of Stanford University, to include concave cost functions for each period.

‡ In this special case, the initial inventory x_1 can always be taken equal to zero. If $x_1 > 0$, this amount can be written off from the demands of the successive periods until it is exhausted. Under such conditions, the periods for which the demands have been satisfied are still included in the problem; this time with zero demands. In such a case it is possible to have both z_i and x_i equal to zero.

The properties described, when applicable, will result in a simplified computational procedure, which is still based on the general dynamic programming algorithms presented. This point is explained by using the forward algorithm.

Since by the second property the amount of inventory at the end of period i, that is, x_{i+1}, must satisfy the exact requirements of one or more successive periods, it follows that the number of state values of the system at any period is determined by the number of succeeding *periods* (rather than by the number of *units* demanded in the succeeding periods as in the general model). For example, let $N = 5$ with demands 10, 15, 20, 50, and 70, respectively. Then at the *end* of the third period (stage), the number of state values (x_4) in the general model will be $50 + 70 + 1 = 121$, whereas in the new model it will reduce to three (the remaining number of periods plus one), since x_4 could be 0, 50, or 120 only. A similar argument based on the first property also shows that the number of alternatives z_i are much smaller in the new model. The result is that the computational effort is reduced tremendously in the new model.

Example 14.3-8. Consider a four-period model with the following data:

Period i	D_i	K_i
1	76	$ 98
2	26	114
3	90	185
4	67	70

The holding cost per unit per period is constant and equal to $1.00. Also the purchasing cost per unit is equal to $2.00 for all the periods. The initial inventory x_1 is 15 units. (The per unit holding and purchasing costs are taken the same over all the periods only for simplicity.)

The solution is obtained by using the same forward algorithm except that the values of states x_{i+1} and the values of alternatives z_i are determined according to the new properties. Since $x_1 = 15$, the demand for the first period is decreased by an equivalent amount and thus equals $76 - 15 = 61$.

Stage 1: $D_1 = 61$

		$f_1(z_1 \mid x_2) = C_1(z_1) + h_1 x_2$				Optimal Solution	
		$z_1 = 61$	87	177	244		
x_2	$h_1 x_2$	$C_1(z_1) = 220$	272	452	586	$f_1(x_2)$	z_1^*
0	0	220	—	—	—	220	61
26	26	—	298	—	—	298	87
116	116	—	—	568	—	568	177
183	183	—	—	—	769	769	244
Order in 1 for:		1	1, 2	1, 2, 3	1, 2, 3, 4		

Stage 2: $D_2 = 26$

		$f_2(z_2 \mid x_3) = C_2(z_2) + h_2 x_3 + f_1(x_3 + D_2 - z_2)$				Optimal Solution	
		$z_2 = 0$	26	116	183		
x_3	$h_2 x_3$	$C_2(z_2) = 0$	166	346	480	$f_2(x_3)$	z_2^*
0	0	0 + 298 = 298	166 + 220 = 386	—	—	298	0
90	90	90 + 568 = 586	—	436 + 220 = 656	—	656	116
157	157	157 + 769 = 926	—	—	637 + 220 = 857	857	183
Order in 2 for:		—	2	2, 3	2, 3, 4		

Stage 3: $D_3 = 90$

		$f_3(z_3 \mid x_4) = C_3(z_3) + h_3 x_4 + f_2(x_4 + D_3 - z_3)$			Optimal Solution	
		$z_3 = 0$	90	157		
x_4	$h_3 x_4$	$C_3(z_3) = 0$	365	499	$f_3(x_4)$	z_3^*
0	0	0 + 656 = 656	365 + 298 = 663	—	656	0
67	67	67 + 857 = 924	—	566 + 298 = 864	864	157
Order in 3 for:		—	3	3, 4		

Stage 4: $D_4 = 67$

		$f_4(z_4 \mid x_5) = C_4(z_4) + h_4 x_5 + f_3(x_3 + D_4 - z_4)$		Optimal Solution	
		$z_4 = 0$	67		
x_5	$h_4 x_5$	$C_4(z_4) = 0$	204	$f_4(x_5)$	z_4^*
0	0	0 + 864 = 864	204 + 656 = 860	860	67
Order in 4 for:		—	4		

The optimal policy is thus given by $z_1^* = 61$, $z_2^* = 116$, $z_3^* = 0$, and $z_4^* = 67$, at a total cost of \$860. ◀

Exercise 14.3-8

In Example 14.3-8, determine the feasible ranges for z_1 in each of the following cases.

(a) $x_1 = 10$ and all the remaining data are unchanged.
[*Ans.* $z_1 = 66, 92, 182$, or 249.]

(b) $x_1 = 80$ and all the remaining data are unchanged.
[*Ans.* $z_1 = 0, 22, 112$, or 179.]

(c) $D_1 = 70$, $D_2 = 25$, $D_3 = 80$, $D_4 = 70$, and $x_1 = 10$.
[*Ans.* $z_1 = 60, 85, 165$, or 235.]

A special case of the *concave* cost model described above occurs when the production cost for a period is defined by the linear function

$$C_i(z_i) = K_i + c_i z_i, \qquad i = 1, 2, \ldots, N$$

provided that $c_{i+1} \le c_i$ for all i, that is, $c_1 \ge c_2 \ge \cdots \ge c_N$. Under this new condition, the forward algorithm for the concave cost model can be modified such that further savings in computations are possible. To avoid confusion, the names "original" and "modified" algorithms will be used to refer to the forward algorithms associated, respectively, with the concave cost model and the model to be presented shortly.

In the original algorithm each stage i computes the optimal policy by considering ordering in period i for future periods up to an including period j; that is, $i \le j \le N$. The modified algorithm defines each stage i such that for period i, the optimal policy is determined by considering ordering in each of the preceding periods, k, for periods up to and including period i; $1 \le k \le i$. This is expressed mathematically as†

$$f_i = \min \begin{cases} C_1 + h_1(D_2 + \cdots + D_i) + \cdots + h_{i-1}D_i & \text{(order in 1)} \\ C_2 + h_2(D_3 + \cdots + D_i) + \cdots + h_{i-1}D_i + f_1 & \text{(order in 2)} \\ \vdots & \\ C_{i-1} + h_{i-1}D_i + f_{i-2} & \text{(order in } i-1) \\ C_i + f_{i-1} & \text{(order in } i) \end{cases}$$

where

f_i = minimum total cost for periods 1 through i, inclusive, $i = 1, 2, \ldots, N$
C_k = total ordering cost (setup + purchasing) for ordering in period k the amount $z_k = D_k + \cdots + D_i$ for periods k through i, $k \le i$

To start with, and without taking advantage of the special feature of the cost function $C_i(z_i)$, the amount of computations in the modified model is less than that in the original one.‡ This result follows because the modified model does not consider explicitly the case where no orders are placed at the different stages. The computations using the modified algorithm may be further reduced by making use of the following theorem.

Planning Horizon Theorem. *In the modified forward algorithm, if for period i^* the minimum cost occurs such that the demand at i^* is satisfied by ordering in a previous period $i^{**} < i^*$, then for all future periods $i > i^*$ it is sufficient to compute the optimal program based on ordering in periods i^{**}, $i^{**} + 1, \ldots, i$ only. In particular, if the optimal policy calls for ordering in i^* for the same period i^* (i.e., $i^* = i^{**}$), then for any future period $i > i^*$ it will always be optimal to order in i^* regardless of future demands. In this case, i^* is said to mark the beginning of a planning horizon.*

---

† In the modified model, the state of the system x_i is suppressed, since this corresponds directly to the number of the preceding periods, that is, i. The same reasoning could have been used with the original model.

‡ The maximum number of entries are $\{N(N + 1) + (N - 1)N\}/2 = N^2$ in the original table and $N(N + 1)/2$ in the modified one.

This theorem implies two important implications:

1. During the course of computations, the calculations may be truncated so that the entries for periods $k < i^{**}$ need not be considered. This should lead to computational savings.
2. For the special case where $i^* = i^{**}$, in addition to truncating the computations at i^*, future periods starting with i^* may be considered completely independently of all previous periods. Moreover, it is always optimal to order in i^* regardless of future demands.

When i^{**} is strictly less than i^*, it is not always true that ordering will occur in i^{**}. Indeed, future demands may call for a change in the optimal policy. In this case it will not be possible to break down the problem into independent planning horizons. To avoid confusion, i^{**} will be referred to as the starting period of a *subhorizon* whenever $i^{**} < i^*$.

Example 14.3-9. Consider a six-period inventory model with the following data:

i	D_i	K_i	h_i
1	10	20	1
2	15	17	1
3	7	10	1
4	20	20	3
5	13	5	1
6	25	50	1

The purchasing cost per unit is 2 for all the periods.

The computations for this example are summarized in Table 14-5. These computations are carried out on a row-by-row basis starting with row 1. Each column represents a decision alternative defining the period k in which the demands for periods $k, k+1, \ldots, i$ are filled, $1 \leq k \leq i$. Each row represents the limiting period up to which the demand is filled. Thus, for each i, the optimum value f_i, as defined for the modified algorithm, is obtained by considering all feasible decision alternatives k $(\leq i)$ and then selecting the alternative yielding minimum cumulative cost. For example, given $i = 3$, we have three options: (1) order in 1 for 1, 2, and 3, (2) order in 2 for 2 and 3, and (3) order in 3 for 3. The entries of the table above its main diagonal are infeasible, since no backorders are allowed.

To illustrate the use of planning horizons (and subhorizons), in row 3 f_3 occurs under period 2. This means that it is optimal at this point to order for period 3 (and period 2) in period 2. This is equivalent to saying that $i^{**} = 2$ and $i^* = 3$. According to the theorem, for all $i > 3$ the calculations may go back only to period 2. Period 2 thus marks the beginning of a *sub*horizon. Moving to row 4, we see that f_4 occurs under period 4 signifying it is optimal to order for period 4 in period 4. Thus $i^{**} = i^* = 4$ and $i = 4$ marks the beginning of a planning horizon, which signifies that in the succeeding rows the entries under periods 1, 2, 3 should not be computed. Continuing in this manner, we see in Table 14-1 that another planning horizon commences in period 5, with the result that in the computations in row 6 only the entries under periods 5 and 6 need be computed. Thus periods 1, 4, and 5 mark the beginnings of the three planning horizons of the problem. The advantages

Table 14-5

		$k = 1$[a]	$k = 2$	$k = 3$	$k = 4$	$k = 5$	$k = 6$
$i = 1$	(1)[b]	20					
	(2)	$10 \times 2 = 20$					
	(3)	0					
	(4)	0					
		$f_1 \rightarrow 40^*$					
$i = 2$	(1)	20	17				
	(2)	$(10 + 15) \times 2 = 50$	$15 \times 2 = 30$				
	(3)	15×1	0				
	(4)	0	$f_1 = 40$				
		$f_2 \rightarrow 85^*$	87				
$i = 3$	(1)	20	17	10			
	(2)	$(10 + 15 + 7) \times 2 = 64$	$(15 + 7) \times 2 = 44$	$7 \times 2 = 14$			
	(3)	$22 \times 1 + 7 \times 1 = 29$	$7 \times 1 = 7$	0			
	(4)	0	$f_1 = 40$	$f_2 = 85$			
		113	$f_3 \rightarrow 108^*$	109			
$i = 4$	(1)		17	10	20		
	(2)		$(15 + 7 + 20) \times 2 = 84$	$(7 + 20) \times 2 = 54$	$20 \times 2 = 40$		
	(3)		$27 \times 1 + 20 \times 1 = 47$	$20 \times 1 = 20$	0		
	(4)		$f_1 = 40$	$f_2 = 85$	$f_3 = 108$		
			188	169	$f_4 \rightarrow 168^*$		
$i = 5$	(1)				20	5	
	(2)				$(20 + 13) \times 2 = 66$	$13 \times 2 = 26$	
	(3)				$13 \times 3 = 39$	0	
	(4)				$f_3 = 108$	$f_4 = 168$	
					233	$f_5 \rightarrow 199^*$	
$i = 6$	(1)					5	50
	(2)					$(13 + 25) \times 2 = 76$	$25 \times 2 = 50$
	(3)					$25 \times 1 = 25$	0
	(4)					$f_4 = 168$	$f_5 = 199$
						$f_6 \rightarrow 274^*$	299

[a] Place order in period k for periods up to and including i.
[b] (1) Setup cost; (2) purchasing cost; (3) holding cost; (4) optimum total cost from preceding periods.

of the planning horizon theorem must be clear now, since all the blank entries below the main diagonal of the table represent computational savings.

The optimal solution is obtained by considering the last row in Table 14-1. f_6 indicates that it is optimal to order in 5 the amount $z_5 = 38$ for 5 and 6. Thus from row 4 $(= 5 - 1)$, f_4 requires ordering $z_4 = 20$ for period 4 alone. Again, in row 3 $(= 4 - 1)$, f_3 calls for ordering in 2 the amount $z_2 = 22$ for 2 and 3. Finally, the amount $z_1 = 10$ is ordered in period 1. The total cost is 274 for the entire problem. ◀

Exercise 14.3-9

In Example 14.3-9, determine the optimal solution (directly from Table 14-3) assuming that the inventory problem includes the first five periods only.

[*Ans.* Order 13 units in 5 for 5, 20 units in 4 for 4, 22 units in 2 for 2 and 3, and 10 units in 1 for 1.]

(Silver-Meal) Heuristic Model

The heuristic model to be presented here is used as an approximation of the DP model *provided that the unit production/purchasing costs are identical and constant for all the periods.* This represents a slight restriction over the DP model given above where any concave cost function is allowable. In the heuristic, however, it is permissible to have different setup and holding costs for the different periods. With this restriction, the variable production cost is ignored and the heuristic is designed to balance the setup and inventory holding costs only.

The decision variable in the heuristic is defined as the number of successive periods whose demand can be "lumped" into a single production or purchasing lot for the purpose of balancing the setup cost against the inventory holding cost. For example, in a 10-period model with demands of 10, 20, 30, 20, 10, 40, 70, 80, 10, and 30 units, respectively, a typical decision may call for producing 60 units in period 1 (to cover periods 1, 2, and 3), 140 units in period 4, and 120 units in period 8. The nature of this decision is the same as in the DP model.

Let T represent the number of successive periods starting at period i for which replenishment is made; then the heuristic aims at determining T that minimizes the total associated cost per period. Thus define

$$\begin{aligned} \text{TC}(T \mid i) &= \text{setup plus holding cost for } T \text{ successive periods starting at } i \\ &= K_i + \sum_{j=0}^{T-1} H_{i+j} D_{i+j+1}, \qquad T > 1 \end{aligned}$$

where K_i represents the setup cost in period i, D_{i+j} is the demand in period $i + j$, and

$$H_{i+j} = h_i + h_{i+1} + \cdots + h_{i+j-1}$$

The cost h_{i+k} is the inventory unit holding cost from period $i + k$ to period $i + k + 1$. The cost elements K and h and the demand D actually have the same definitions as in the DP model. The associated unit cost per period given i is thus given as

$$\text{TCU}(T \mid i) = \frac{\text{TC}(T \mid i)}{T}$$

For the purpose of computations, the formula for $TC(T \mid i)$ can be expressed recursively as

$$TC(1 \mid i) = K_i$$
$$TC(T \mid i) = TC(T-1 \mid i) + H_{i+T-1}D_T$$
$$= TC(T-1 \mid i) + (h_i + h_{i+1} + \cdots + h_{i+T-2})D_T, \qquad T = 2, 3, \ldots, N$$

The problem is solved iteratively starting at $i = 1$. This means that the procedure starts by determining the number of successive periods whose demand can be satisfied from period 1. Such is achieved by continuing to evaluate $TCU(T \mid 1)$ for successive incremental values of T $(=1, 2, 3, \ldots)$ as long as $TCU(T \mid 1)$ shows a net decrease in value with each incremental value of T. Suppose that $T = T^*$ is the first value of T at which $TCU(T \mid 1)$ shows an increase. In this case $T = T^* - 1$ is a local minimum point and we conclude that according to the heuristic, the first replenishment should encompass periods 1, 2, …, and $T^* - 1$, which gives $T_1 = T^* - 1$. The second iteration starts by resetting the datum of the problem to period T^*, meaning that period T^* now assumes the role of period 1 in the first iteration. This iterative process is repeated as many times as necessary until the entire planning horizon is covered.

Example 14.3-10. The heuristic is applied to the model in Example 14.3-9. Notice that since the production cost remains unchanged (= \$2), the heuristic is properly applicable to this situation. The successive iterations are detailed below.

Iteration 1: ($i = 1$, $K_1 = \$20$). This iteration starts at period $t = 1$. The computations below show that a local minimum occurs at $t = 3$ yielding $T^* = 3$. The first lot produced in period 1 must thus cover the demands for periods 1, 2, and 3. The next iteration will now start at $i = 4$.

Period t	T	D_t	$TC(T \mid 1)$	$TCU(T \mid 1) = TC(T \mid 1)/T$	
1	1	10	20	20/1 = 20.00	
2	2	15	20 + 1 × 15 = 35	35/2 = 17.50	
3	3	7	35 + (1 + 1) × 7 = 49	49/3 = **16.33**	← T^*
4	4	20	49 + (1 + 1 + 1) × 20 = 109	109/4 = 27.25	

Iteration 2: ($i = 4$, $K_4 = \$20$). The computations below show that a local minimum occurs at $t = 4$, which yields $T^* = 1$. This means that period 4 will supply itself only. The next iteration will then start at $i = 5$.

Period t	T	D_t	$TC(T \mid 4)$	$TCU(T \mid 4) = TC(T \mid 4)/T$	
4	1	20	20	20/1 = **20**	← T^*
5	2	13	20 + 3 × 13 = 59	59/2 = 29.5	

Iteration 3: ($i = 5$, $K_5 = \$5$). The computations below show that a local minimum occurs at $t = 5$, which yields $T^* = 1$. This means that period 5 will supply itself only. The next iteration will then start at $i = 6$. However, since this is the last period of the planning horizon, no further calculations are needed and period 6 must supply itself only.

Period t	T	D_t	TC(T | 5)	TCU(T | 5) = TC(T | 5)/T	
5	1	13	5	5/1 = **5**	← T^*
6	2	25	5 + 1 × 25 = 30	30/2 = 15	

The table below compares the heuristic and the DP solutions. Observe that the variable production cost of the DP model has been deleted from the DP cost values in Table 14-5 to allow a proper comparison between the two models.

	Heuristic		DP	
Period	Amount Produced	Cost ($)	Amount Produced	Cost ($)
1	32	49	10	20
2	—	—	22	24
3	—	—	—	—
4	20	20	20	20
5	13	5	38	30
6	25	50	—	—
Totals	90	$124	90	$94

The heuristic gives a production schedule that costs about 32% more than that of the DP model ($124 as opposed to $94). This "inadequate" performance of the heuristic may be the result of the specific data used in the problem. Specifically, the extreme irregularities of the setup costs K for periods 5 and 6 are to blame for this poor performance. Generally, in a typical situation, one does not expect such extreme variations in the setup costs from one period to the next. On the other hand, the example shows that the heuristic does not have the capability to "look ahead" for better scheduling opportunities. For example, it is evident that by ordering in period 5 for periods 5 and 6 (instead of ordering for each separately as recommended by the heuristic) we can save $25, which will bring the total heuristic cost to $99 (or about 5.3% above the DP cost). Apparently, the heuristic has been shown to perform well for the more well-behaved cases that are typical of real-life situations. ◀

14.4 PROBABILISTIC MODELS

In this section we present different (single-item) inventory models with probabilistic demand. The first model extends the deterministic continuous review model (Section 14.3.1) by directly including the probabilistic demand in the formulation. The remaining formulations are categorized under single- and multiple-period models. In the multiple-period models, the distribution of demand is either stationary or nonstationary. Most multiperiod models with stationary demand may be easily extended to the nonstationary case, but the associated computations, especially in the nonstationary case, are almost prohibitive. However, if stationary demand and infinite horizon are assumed, closed-form solutions may usually be obtained for the models.

The basic decision criterion used with probabilistic inventory models in this chapter is the minimization of *expected* costs (or equivalently maximization of expected profit). As mentioned in Chapter 12, other criteria could be used as well. However, since the objective is to concentrate on the development of the inventory problem itself, no other criteria will be discussed here.

14.4.1 A CONTINUOUS REVIEW MODEL

In this section we introduce a probabilistic model in which the stock is reviewed continuously and an order of size y is placed every time the stock level reaches a certain reorder point R. The objective is to determine the optimum values of y and R that minimize the total expected inventory costs per unit time. In this model, one year represents a unit of time.

The inventory fluctuations corresponding to this situation are depicted in Figure 14-14. A cycle is defined as the time period between two successive arrivals of orders. The assumptions of the model are

1. Lead time between the placement of an order and its receipt is stochastic.
2. Unfilled demand during lead time is backlogged.
3. The distribution of demand during lead time is independent of the time at which it occurs.
4. There is no more than one outstanding order at a time.

Let

$r(x \mid t)$ = conditional PDF of demand x during lead time t, $x > 0$

$s(t)$ = PDF of lead time t, $t > 0$

$f(x)$ = absolute PDF of demand x during lead time $= \int_0^\infty r(x \mid t)s(t)\, dt$

y = amount *ordered* per cycle

D = expected total demand per year

h = holding cost per unit per year

p = shortage cost per unit per year

The total annual cost for this model includes the average setup cost, the expected holding cost, and the expected shortage cost. The average setup cost is given by (DK/y), where (D/y) is the approximate number of orders per year and K is the setup cost per order.

The expected holding cost is calculated based on the expected net inventory level at the beginning and end of a cycle. The expected stock level at the end of an

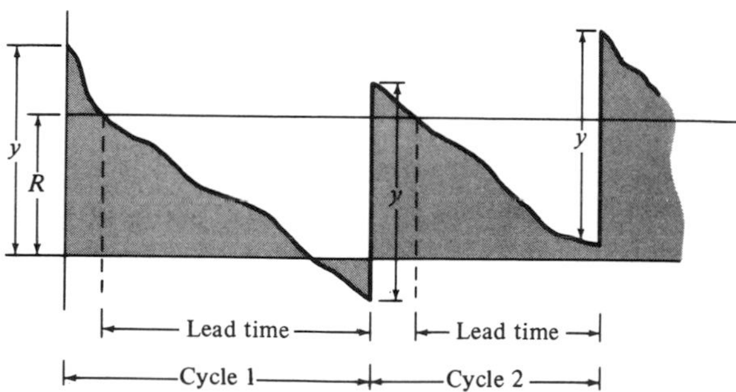

Figure 14-14

inventory cycle is equal to $E\{R - x\}$. At the beginning of the cycle (right after an order of size y is received), the expected stock level is $y + E\{R - x\}$. Thus the average inventory per cycle (and hence per year) is given by

$$\bar{H} = \frac{(y + E\{R - x\}) + E\{R - x\}}{2} = \frac{y}{2} + E\{R - x\}$$

Now, given $f(x)$ as defined,

$$E\{R - x\} = \int_0^\infty (R - x)f(x)\,dx = R - E\{x\}$$

Notice that the expression for $\bar{H}$ neglects the case where $R - E\{x\}$ is negative (shortage quantity). This approximation is one of the simplifying assumptions of the model.

Let S be the shortage quantity per cycle. Then

$$S(x) = \begin{cases} 0, & x \le R \\ x - R, & x > R \end{cases}$$

Consequently, the expected shortage quantity per cycle is

$$\bar{S} = \int_0^\infty S(x)f(x)\,dx = \int_R^\infty (x - R)f(x)\,dx$$

Since there are approximately (D/y) orders per year, the expected annual shortage is then equal to $(D\bar{S}/y)$.

The total annual cost of the system is thus given by

$$\text{TAC}(y, R) = \frac{DK}{y} + h\left(\frac{y}{2} + R - E\{x\}\right) + \frac{pD\bar{S}}{y}$$

Notice that the shortage cost $(pD\bar{S}/y)$ is assumed proportional to the shortage quantity only without taking the shortage time into account. This approximation again is another simplifying assumptions in the model, since in the case of backlog, shortage cost is also a function of shortage time.

The solution for optimal y^* and R^* is obtained from

$$\frac{\partial \text{TAC}}{\partial y} = -\left(\frac{DK}{y^2}\right) + \frac{h}{2} - \frac{pD\bar{S}}{y^2} = 0$$

$$\frac{\partial \text{TAC}}{\partial R} = h - \left(\frac{pD}{y}\right)\int_R^\infty f(x)\,dx = 0$$

From the first equation,

$$y^* = \sqrt{\frac{2D(K + p\bar{S})}{h}} \tag{1}$$

and from the second equation,

$$\int_{R^*}^\infty f(x)\,dx = \frac{hy^*}{pD} \tag{2}$$

An explicit general solution for y^* and R^* is not possible in this case. A convenient numerical method is thus used to solve equations (1) and (2). The following procedure, due to Hadley and Whitin (1963), is proved to converge in a finite number of iterations, provided that a solution exists.

In equation (1), $\bar{S}$ at *least* equals zero, which shows that the *smallest* value of y^* is $\sqrt{2DK/h}$, a result that is achieved when $\bar{S} = 0$ (or $R \to \infty$). Now, at $R = 0$, equation (1) gives

$$y^* = \hat{y} = \sqrt{\frac{2D(K + pE\{x\})}{h}}$$

and equation (2) gives

$$y^* = \tilde{y} = \frac{pD}{h}$$

It can be proved (Hadley and Whitin, 1963, pp. 169–174) that if $\tilde{y} \geq \hat{y}$, the optimal values of y and R exist and are unique. In such a case these values are computed as follows. Compute the first trial value of y^* as $y_1 = \sqrt{2DK/h}$. Next use equation (2) to compute the value of R_1 corresponding to y_1. By using R_1, a new trial value y_2 is obtained from equation (1). Next, R_2 is computed from equation (2) by using y_2. This procedure is repeated until two successive values of R are approximately equal. At this point, the last values computed for y and R will yield y^* and R^*.

Example 14.4-1. Let $K = \$100$, $D = 1000$ units, $p = \$10$, and $h = \$2$ and assume that the demand during lead time follows a uniform distribution over the range 0 to 100.

To check whether the problem has a feasible solution, consider

$$\hat{y} = \sqrt{\frac{2D(K + pE\{x\})}{h}} = \sqrt{\frac{2 \times 1000(100 + 10 \times 50)}{2}}$$
$$= 774.5$$

and

$$\tilde{y} = \frac{pD}{h} = \frac{10 \times 1000}{2} = 5000$$

Since $\tilde{y} > \hat{y}$, a unique solution for y^* and R^* exists.

Now

$$\bar{S} = \int_R^\infty (x - R)f(x)\,dx = \int_R^{100} (x - R)\frac{1}{100}\,dx$$
$$= \frac{R^2}{200} - R + 50 \tag{3}$$

From equation (3),

$$y^* = \sqrt{\frac{2D(K + p\bar{S})}{h}} = \sqrt{\frac{2 \times 1000(100 + 10\bar{S})}{2}}$$
$$= \sqrt{100{,}000 + 10{,}000\bar{S}} \tag{4}$$

where $\bar{S}$ is as given by (3). From equation (4),

$$\int_{R^*}^{100} \frac{1}{100}\,dx = \frac{2y^*}{10 \times 1000}$$

or

$$R^* = 100 - \frac{y^*}{50} \tag{5}$$

Equation (5) is used to compute R_i for a given value of y_i, and equation (4) is used to compute y_{i+1} for a given value of R_i.

Iteration 1

$$y_1 = \sqrt{\frac{2DK}{h}} = \sqrt{\frac{2 \times 1000 \times 100}{2}} = 316$$

$$R_1 = 100 - \frac{316}{50} = 93.68$$

Iteration 2

$$\bar{S} = \frac{R_1^2}{200} - R_1 + 50 = .19971$$

$$y_2 = \sqrt{100{,}000 + 10{,}000 \times .19971} = 319.37$$

Hence

$$R_2 = 100 - \frac{319.37}{50} = 93.612$$

Iteration 3

$$\bar{S} = \frac{R_2^2}{200} - R_2 + 50 = .20403$$

$$y_3 = \sqrt{100{,}000 + 10{,}000 \times .20403} = 319.43$$

Thus

$$R_3 = 100 - \frac{319.43}{50} = 93.611$$

Since R_2 and R_3 are approximately equal, the approximate optimal solution is given by

$$R^* \cong 93.61 \qquad \text{and} \qquad y^* \cong 319.4$$

◀

Exercise 14.4-1

In Example 14.4-1, determine the following values based on the assumptions of the model.

(a) The approximate number of orders per year.
[*Ans.* Three orders.]

(b) The annual setup cost.
[*Ans.* \$300.]

(c) The expected holding cost per year.
[*Ans.* \$406.62.]

(d) The expected shortage cost per year.
[*Ans.* \$6.39.]

(e) The probability of running out of stock during lead time.
[*Ans.* .0639.]

14.4.2 SINGLE-PERIOD MODELS

The single-period inventory models occur when an item is ordered once only to satisfy the demand of a specific period. For example, a style item becomes obsolete and hence may not be reordered. In this section the single-period models will be investigated under different conditions, including instantaneous and uniform demand with and without setup cost. It is assumed that stock replenishment occurs instantaneously. The optimal inventory level will be derived based on the minimization of expected inventory costs, which include the ordering (setup + purchasing or production), holding, and shortage. Because the demand is probabilistic, the purchasing (production) cost per unit, although constant, becomes an effective factor in the cost function.

A. Instantaneous Demand, No Setup Cost

In the models with instantaneous demand, it is assumed that the total demand is filled at the beginning of the period. Thus, depending on the amount demanded D, the inventory position right after demand occurs may be either positive (surplus) or negative (shortage). These two cases are shown in Figure 14-15.

From Figure 14-15, given y, the amount on hand after an order is received, the holding inventory is generally given by

$$H(y) = \begin{cases} y - D & \text{for } D < y \\ 0, & \text{for } D \geq y \end{cases}$$

The shortage inventory is given by

$$G(y) = \begin{cases} 0, & \text{for } D < y \\ D - y, & \text{for } D \geq y \end{cases}$$

Let x be the amount on hand before an order is placed. Define $f(D)$ as the PDF of demand, and let h and p be the holding and shortage costs per unit per period. Further, let c be the purchasing cost per unit. If we assume that y is continuous and

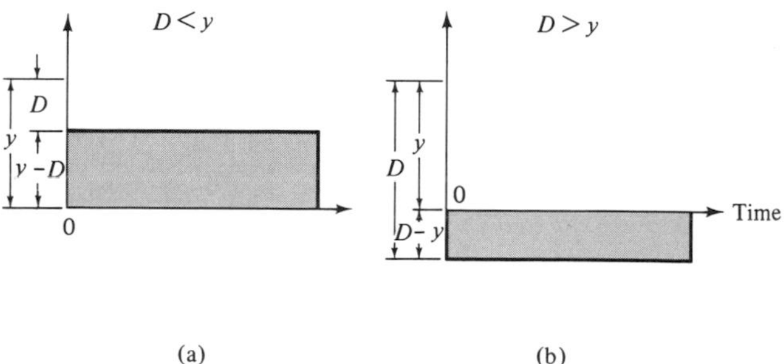

Figure 14-15

no setup cost is incurred, the expected cost for the period is then given by

$$\begin{aligned}
E\{C(y)\} &= \text{purchasing cost} + E\{\text{holding cost}\} + E\{\text{shortage cost}\}\\
&= c(y - x) + h \int_0^\infty H(y)f(D)\,dD + p \int_0^\infty G(y)f(D)\,dD\\
&= c(y - x) + h\left\{\int_0^y (y - D)f(D)\,dD + 0\right\} + p\left\{0 + \int_y^\infty (D - y)f(D)\,dD\right\}\\
&= c(y - x) + h \int_0^y (y - D)f(D)\,dD + p \int_y^\infty (D - y)f(D)\,dD
\end{aligned}$$

The optimal value of y is obtained by equating the first derivative of $E\{C(y)\}$ to zero. Thus

$$\frac{\partial E\{C(y)\}}{\partial y} = c + h \int_0^y f(D)\,dD - p \int_y^\infty f(D)\,dD = 0$$

Since

$$\int_y^\infty f(D)\,dD = 1 - \int_0^y f(D)\,dD$$

the equation gives

$$\int_0^{y^*} f(D)\,dD = \frac{p - c}{p + h}$$

The value of y^* is defined only if $p \geq c$. If $p < c$, this is interpreted as discarding the inventory system completely. Now

$$\frac{\partial^2 E\{C(y)\}}{\partial y^2} = (h + p)f(y^*) > 0$$

shows that y^* corresponds to a minimum point. Graphically, the function $E\{C(y)\}$ should appear as shown in Figure 14-16. In such cases $E\{C(y)\}$ is convex. Since y^* is unique, it must give a global minimum. The policy adopted is thus called a **single critical number policy**.

According to the condition given, the value of y^* is selected such that the probability $D \leq y^*$ is equal to

$$q = \frac{p - c}{p + h}, \qquad p > c$$

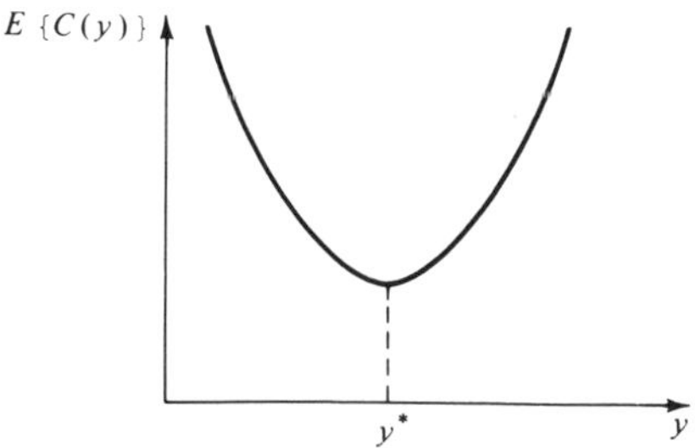

Figure 14-16

The optimal ordering policy given x is on hand before an order is placed is given by

$$\begin{array}{ll} \text{if } y^* > x, & \text{order } y^* - x \\ \text{if } y^* \leq x, & \text{do not order} \end{array}$$

Example 14.4-2. Consider the one-period model with $h = \$.5$, $p = \$4.5$, and $c = \$.5$. The demand density function is given by

$$f(D) = \begin{cases} 1/10, & 0 \leq D \leq 10 \\ 0, & D > 10 \end{cases}$$

Thus

$$q = \frac{p - c}{p + h} = \frac{4.5 - .5}{4.5 + .5} = .8$$

and

$$P\{D \leq y^*\} = \int_0^{y^*} f(D)\, dD = \int_0^{y^*} \frac{1}{10}\, dD = \frac{y^*}{10}$$

or

$$y^* = 8$$

This solution is illustrated graphically in Figure 14-17. ◀

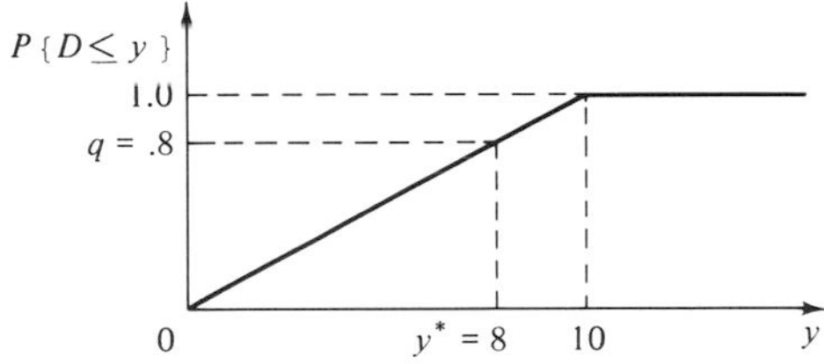

Figure 14-17

Exercise 14.4-2
Consider Example 14.4-2.
(a) Determine the order quantity in each of the following cases.
  (1) Initial inventory = 5 units.
  [*Ans.* Order 3 units.]
  (2) Initial inventory = 10 units.
  [*Ans.* Do not order.]
(b) Determine the probability of not running out of stock during the period.
  [*Ans.* 0.8.]

Suppose now that demand occurs in discrete rather than in continuous units. Then

$$E\{C(y)\} = c(y - x) + h \sum_{D=0}^{y} (y - D) f(D) + p \sum_{D=y+1}^{\infty} (D - y) f(D)$$

In the discrete case, the necessary conditions for a minimum are given by

$$E\{C(y - 1)\} \geq E\{C(y)\} \qquad \text{and} \qquad E\{C(y + 1)\} \geq E\{C(y)\}$$

Thus

$$E\{C(y-1)\} = c(y-1-x) + h\sum_{D=0}^{y-1}(y-1-D)f(D) + p\sum_{D=y}^{\infty}(D-y+1)f(D)$$

$$= c(y-x) + h\sum_{D=0}^{y-1}(y-D)f(D) + p\sum_{D=y}^{\infty}(D-y)f(D)$$

$$- h\sum_{D=0}^{y-1} f(D) + p\sum_{D=y}^{\infty} f(D) - c$$

$$= E\{C(y)\} + p - c - (h+p)\sum_{D=0}^{y-1} f(D)$$

Therefore,

$$E\{C(y-1)\} - E\{C(y)\} = p - c - (h+p)P\{D \le y-1\} \ge 0$$

or

$$P\{D \le y-1\} \le \frac{p-c}{p+h}$$

Similarly, it can be shown that $E\{C(y+1)\} \ge E\{C(y)\}$ yields

$$P\{D \le y\} \ge \frac{p-c}{p+h}$$

Thus y^* must satisfy

$$P\{D \le y^*-1\} \le \frac{p-c}{p+h} \le P\{D \le y^*\}$$

Example 14.4-3. Consider the single-period model with $h = \$1.00$, $p = \$4.00$, and $c = \$2.00$. The demand density function is given by

D	0	1	2	3	4	5
$f(D)$	.10	.20	.25	.20	.15	.10

The critical ratio is

$$q = \frac{p-c}{p+h} = \frac{4-2}{4+1} = 0.4$$

The optimal solution is obtained by constructing the following table:

y	0	1	2	3	4	5
$P\{D \le y\}$	.10	.30	.55	.75	.90	1.00

↑ $q = .4$ (between .30 and .55)

Since

$$P\{D \le 1\} = .3 < .4 < .55 = P\{D \le 2\}$$

the optimal value is given by $y^* = 2$. ◀

Exercise 14.4-3

In Example 14.4-3, determine the optimal inventory level in each of the following cases.

(a) $p = \$6$, $c = \$2$, and $h = \$1$.
[*Ans.* $y^* = 3$.]

(b) $p = \$10$, $c = \$8$, and $h = \$2$.
[*Ans.* $y^* = 1$.]

B. Uniform Demand, No Setup Cost

In this case demand occurs uniformly (rather than instantaneously) during the period as shown in Figure 14-18. Assuming that y is a continuous variable, we find that the expected total cost for this model is given by

$$E\{C(y)\} = c(y - x) + h\left\{\int_0^y \left(y - \frac{D}{2}\right) f(D)\, dD + \int_y^\infty \frac{y^2}{2D} f(D)\, dD\right\}$$
$$+ p \int_y^\infty \frac{(D - y)^2}{2D} f(D)\, dD$$

where c, h, and p are as defined in Section 14.4.2A. Taking the first derivative and equating it to zero, we get

$$c + h\left(\int_0^y f(D)\, dD + \int_0^\infty \frac{y}{D} f(D)\, dD\right) - p \int_0^\infty \left(\frac{D - y}{D}\right) f(D)\, dD = 0$$

or

$$\int_0^{y^*} f(D)\, dD + y^* \int_{y^*}^\infty \frac{f(D)}{D}\, dD = \frac{p - c}{p + h} = q$$

This policy is also of the single critical number type, since $E\{C(y)\}$ is convex.

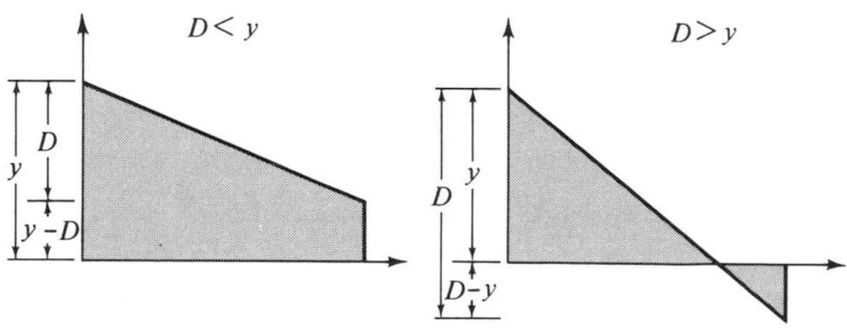

Average holding inventory = $y - \frac{D}{2}$

Average shortage inventory = 0

(a)

Average holding inventory = $\frac{y^2}{2D}$

Average shortage inventory = $\frac{(D-y)^2}{2D}$

(b)

Figure 14-18

Example 15.4-4. Consider Example 14.4.2. Since

$$f(D) = \frac{1}{10}, \qquad 0 \le D \le 10$$

then

$$\int_0^{y^*} \frac{1}{10}\, dD + y^* \int_{y^*}^{10} \frac{1}{10D}\, dD = .8$$

or

$$(1/10)(y^* - y^* \ln y^* + 2.3y^*) = 0.8$$

or

$$3.3y^* - y^* \ln y^* - 8 = 0$$

The solution of this equation is obtained by trial and error and is given by $y^* = 4.5$. Notice the difference between this result and the one given in the case of instantaneous demand. ◀

C. Instantaneous Demand, Setup Cost—(*s*-*S* Policy)

Consider the model in Section 14.4.2A with the exception that the setup cost K will be taken into account. Let $E\{\bar{C}(y)\}$ be the total expected cost of the system inclusive of the setup cost. Thus

$$\begin{aligned} E\{\bar{C}(y)\} &= K + c(y - x) + h \int_0^y (y - D)f(D)\, dD + p \int_y^\infty (D - y)f(D)\, dD \\ &= K + E\{C(y)\} \end{aligned}$$

The minimum value of $E\{C(y)\}$ is shown in Section 14.4.2A to occur at y^*, satisfying

$$\int_0^{y^*} f(D)\, dD = \frac{p - c}{p + h}$$

Since K is constant, the minimum value of $E\{\bar{C}(y)\}$ must also occur at y^*. The curves $E\{C(y)\}$ and $E\{\bar{C}(y)\}$ are shown in Figure 14-19. The new symbols s and S

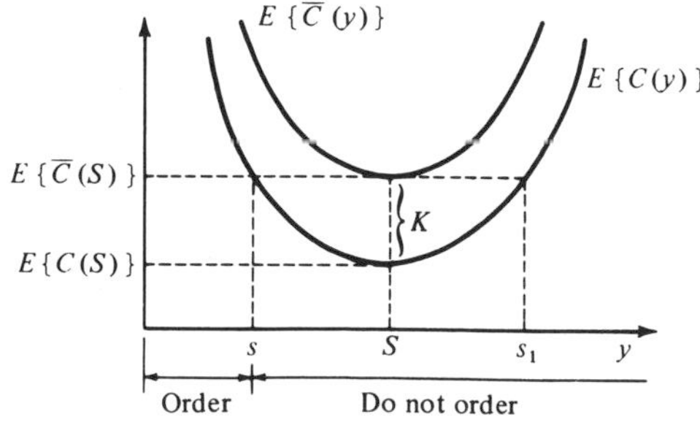

Figure 14-19

are defined in the figure for use later in the analysis. The value of S is equal to y^*, and the value of s is determined from

$$E\{C(s)\} = E\{\bar{C}(S)\} = K + E\{C(S)\}$$

such that $s < S$. (Notice that this equation must yield another value $s_1 > S$, which may be disregarded.)

The question now is: Given x, the amount on hand before the order is placed, how much should be ordered, if any? This question is investigated under three conditions:

1. $x < s$.
2. $s \leq x \leq S$.
3. $x > S$.

Case 1: $x < s$. Since x is already on hand, its equivalent cost is given by $E\{C(x)\}$. If any additional amount $y - x$ $(y > x)$ is ordered, the corresponding cost given y is $E\{\bar{C}(y)\}$, which includes the setup cost K. It follows from Figure 14-19 that, for all $x < s$,

$$\min_{y > x} E\{\bar{C}(y)\} = E\{\bar{C}(S)\} < E\{C(x)\}$$

Thus the optimal inventory level must reach $y^* = S$ and the amount ordered must equal to $S - x$.

Case 2: $s \leq x \leq S$. Again, from Figure 14-19,

$$E\{C(x)\} \leq \min_{y > x} E\{\bar{C}(y)\} = E\{\bar{C}(S)\}$$

Thus it is no more costly not to order in this case. Hence $y^* = x$.

Case 3: $x > S$. From Figure 14-19, for $y > x$,

$$E\{C(x)\} < E\{\bar{C}(y)\}$$

which again indicates that it is less costly not to order and hence $y^* = x$.

This policy is called the s-S policy and is summarized as follows:

$$\begin{array}{ll} \text{if } x < s, & \text{order } S - x \\ \text{if } x \geq s, & \text{do not order} \end{array}$$

The optimality of the s-S policy follows from the fact that the cost function is convex. In general, when this property is not satisfied, the s-S policy will cease to be optimal.

Example 14.4-5. Consider Example 14.4-2. Let $K = \$25$ and assume a zero initial inventory. Since $y^* = 8$, it follows that $S = 8$. To determine the value of s, consider

$$\begin{aligned} E\{C(y)\} &= .5(y - x) + .5 \int_0^y \frac{1}{10}(y - D)\, dD + 4.5 \int_y^{10} \frac{1}{10}(D - y)\, dD \\ &= .5(y - x) + .05\left[yD - \frac{D^2}{2}\right]_0^y + .45\left[\frac{D^2}{2} - Dy\right]_y^{10} \\ &= .25y^2 - 4.0y + 22.5 - .5x \end{aligned}$$

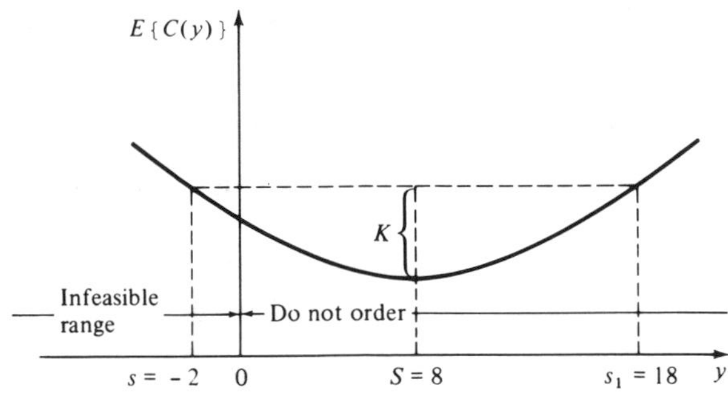

Figure 14-20

The equation

$$E\{C(s)\} = K + E\{C(S)\}$$

thus gives

$$.25s^2 - 4.0s + 22.5 - .5x = 25 + .25S^2 - 4.0S + 22.5 - .5x$$

Setting $S = 8$, we obtain the equation

$$s^2 - 16s - 36 = 0$$

whose solution is

$$s = -2 \quad \text{or} \quad 18$$

The value of $s = 18$ (which is greater than S) should be disregarded. Since the remaining value is negative ($= -2$), s has no feasible value [notice that $E\{C(y)\}$ is defined for nonnegative values of y only]. The optimal solution thus calls for not ordering at all. Clearly, this does not follow the s-S policy, since s is undefined.† The current situation is illustrated graphically in Figure 14-20. This usually occurs when the cost function is flat or when the setup cost K is large compared with the other costs. ◀

Exercise 14.4-4

Find the optimal solution ordering policy of Example 14.4-5 assuming that the setup cost is $5.

[*Ans.* If inventory is below 3.53 units, order up to 8 units.]

14.4.3 MULTIPERIOD MODELS

In this section probabilistic models are considered for the multiperiod (finite or infinite) case under different combinations of the following conditions:

1. Backlogging and no backlogging of demand.
2. Zero and positive delivery lags.

---

† Conventionally, if $s < 0$, s is set equal to zero and the given s-S policy becomes applicable.

The models are developed mainly for the finite horizon case. Models with infinite periods will be derived from the finite case by taking the limit as the number of periods tends to infinity. It is assumed that no setup cost is incurred in any period. The inclusion of setup costs in the multiperiod case generally leads to difficult computations. As will be shown, all multiperiod models are formulated by dynamic programming.

Although in all previous inventory models the optimal policy is determined by minimizing a cost function, solutions in this section are based on the maximization of a profit function. The objective is to familiarize the reader with the application of the maximization (profit) criterion as an alternative to the minimization (cost) criterion.

Unlike the single-period models, a multiperiod model should take into account the discounted value of money. Thus if α (< 1) is the discount factor per period, an amount of money S after n periods ($n \geq 1$) is equivalent to $\alpha^n S$ now.

The following models are developed under the assumption that the demand distribution is stationary for all periods. In the finite horizon case, stationary models may be extended to cover nonstationary distributions by replacing demand density function $f(D)$ by $f_i(D_i)$, where i designates the period.

A. Backlog, Zero Delivery Lag

Let the finite planning horizon be limited to N periods. Define

$F_i(x_i)$ = maximum total expected profit for periods $i, i+1, \ldots, N$, given that x_i is the amount on hand before an order is placed in the ith period

Using the symbols of the preceding section and assuming that r is the revenue per unit, we can formulate the problem as a (backward) dynamic programming model as follows:

$$F_i(x_i) = \max_{y_i \geq x_i} \Bigg(-c(y_i - x_i) + \int_0^{y_i} [rD - h(y_i - D)] f(D)\, dD + \int_{y_i}^{\infty} [ry_i + \alpha r(D - y_i) - p(D - y_i)] f(D)\, dD + \alpha \int_0^{\infty} F_{i+1}(y_i - D) f(D)\, dD \Bigg), \qquad i = 1, 2, \ldots, N$$

with $F_{N+1}(y_N - D) \equiv 0$. Notice that x_i may be negative, since the unfilled demand is backlogged. The quantity $\alpha r(D - y_i)$ in the second integral is included for the following reason. The amount $(D - y_i)$ represents the unfilled demand in the ith period that must be filled in the $(i + 1)$st period. The discounted return is thus $\alpha r(D - y_i)$.

The recursive equation can basically be solved by dynamic programming. However, this procedure is extremely difficult in this case. An important case can be analyzed, however, by considering the infinite period model with its recursive equation given by

$$F(x) = \max_{y \geq x} \Bigg(-c(y - x) + \int_0^{y} [rD - h(y - D)] f(D)\, dD + \int_{y}^{\infty} [ry + \alpha r(D - y) - p(D - y)] f(D)\, dD + \alpha \int_0^{\infty} F(y - D) f(D)\, dD \Bigg)$$

where x and y are the inventory levels for each period before and after an order is received.

The optimal policy for the infinite period case is of the single critical number type. Thus

$$\frac{\partial(\cdot)}{\partial y} = -c - h \int_0^y f(D)\, dD + \int_y^\infty [(1-\alpha)r + p] f(D)\, dD$$
$$+ \alpha \int_0^\infty \frac{\partial F(y-D)}{\partial y} f(D)\, dD = 0$$

The value of

$$\frac{\partial F(y-D)}{\partial y}$$

is determined as follows. If there are δ (> 0) units more on hand at the start of the next period, the profit for the next period will increase by $c\delta$, for this much less has to be ordered. Consequently, the

$$\frac{\partial F(y-D)}{\partial y} = c$$

This equation thus becomes

$$-c - h \int_0^y f(D)\, dD + \left((1-\alpha)r + p\right)\left(1 - \int_0^y f(D)\, dD\right) + \alpha c \int_0^\infty f(D)\, dD = 0$$

which reduces to

$$\int_0^{y^*} f(D)\, dD = \frac{p + (1-\alpha)(r-c)}{p + h + (1-\alpha)r}$$

The optimal policy for each period given its entering inventory x is

$$\text{if } x < y^*, \quad \text{order } y^* - x$$
$$\text{if } x \geq y^*, \quad \text{do not order}$$

It is stated here, without proof, that if in the finite model y_i^* represents the optimal inventory level for period i, the following relationship is always satisfied:

$$y_N^* \leq y_{N-1}^* \leq \cdots \leq y_i^* \leq \cdots \leq y_1^* \leq y^*$$

where y^* is the single critical value in the infinite model. In the finite model the optimal policy calls for ordering less as one comes closer to the end of the horizon. In the meantime, none of the critical values y_i^* can exceed the optimal value y^* in the infinite model.

B. No Backlog, Zero Delivery Lag

This model is similar to the backlog case except when the demand D exceeds the inventory level y_i, in which case the next period will start with $x_{i+1} = 0$. This means that the unfilled demand is lost and hence does not result in any revenue.

The N-period (finite) recursive equation for the no backlog case is thus given by

$$F_i(x_i) = \max_{y_i \geq x_i}\left(-c(y_i - x_i) + \int_0^{y_i} [rD - h(y_i - D)]f(D)\, dD \right.$$
$$+ \int_{y_i}^{\infty} [ry_i - p(D - y_i)]f(D)\, dD + \alpha\left[\int_0^{y_i} F_{i+1}(y_i - D)f(D)\, dD \right.$$
$$\left.\left. + \int_{y_i}^{\infty} F_{i+1}(0)f(D)\, dD\right]\right), \qquad i = 1, 2, \ldots, N$$

with $F_{N+1} \equiv 0$.

It is also difficult to solve this problem by dynamic programming. The corresponding infinite period model is easy to solve, however, since it is of the single critical number type. Thus we get

$$F(x) = \max_{y \geq x}\left(-c(y - x) + \int_0^{y} [rD - h(y - D)]f(D)\, dD \right.$$
$$+ \int_{y}^{\infty} [ry - p(D - y)]f(D)\, dD$$
$$\left. + \alpha\left[\int_0^{y} F(y - D)f(D)\, dD + \int_{y}^{\infty} F(0)f(D)\, dD\right]\right)$$

Taking the first derivative and equating to zero, we obtain

$$-c - h\int_0^{y} f(D)\, dD + (r + p)\int_{y}^{\infty} f(D)\, dD + \alpha\int_0^{y} \frac{\partial F(y - D)}{\partial y} f(D)\, dD = 0$$

and using the result

$$\frac{\partial F(y - D)}{\partial y} = c$$

we obtain

$$\int_0^{y^*} f(D)\, dD = \frac{r + p - c}{h + r + p - \alpha c}$$

In this model, as in the preceding one, the relationship

$$y_N^* \leq y_{N-1}^* \leq \cdots \leq y_i^* \leq \cdots \leq y_1^* \leq y^*$$

holds, where y_i^* corresponds to the optimal inventory level of period i in the finite model.

C. Backlog, Positive Delivery Lag

In this model it is assumed that an order placed at the beginning of period i will be received k periods later; that is, at period $i + k$, $k \geq 1$. The delivery lag k is assumed constant for all the periods.

Let $z, z_1, \ldots, z_{k-1}$ be the amounts due in (as a result of previous decisions) at the beginning of periods $i, i + 1, \ldots, i + k - 1$ (see Figure 14-21). Let $y = x + z$ be the amount of inventory at the beginning of period i, where x is the entering inventory

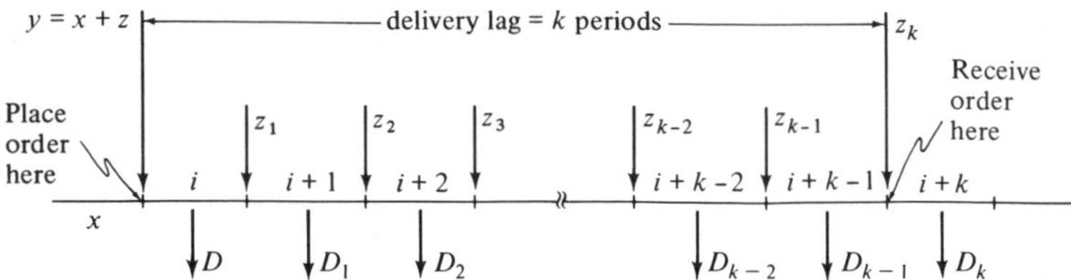

Figure 14-21

(possibly negative because of backlogging) in period i. At period i, the decision variable is represented by z_k, the amount ordered now to be received k periods later.

Define $F_i(y, z_1, \ldots, z_{k-1})$ as the present worth of the maximum expected profit for periods $i, i+1, \ldots, N$ given $y, z_1, \ldots,$ and z_{k-1}. Thus

$$F_i(y, z_1, \ldots, z_{k-1}) = \max_{z_k \geq 0}\left\{-cz_k + L(y) + \alpha \int_0^\infty F_{i+1}(y + z_1 - D, z_2, \ldots, z_k) f(D)\, dD\right\}, \qquad i = 1, 2, \ldots, N$$

where $F_{N+1} \equiv 0$ and

$$L(y) = \int_0^y [rD - h(y - D)] f(D)\, dD + \int_y^\infty [ry + (\alpha r - p)(D - y)] f(D)\, dD$$

Here $L(y)$ represents the expected revenue minus the holding and penalty costs for period i.

The optimal policy for this model can be expressed in terms of $(y + z_1 + \cdots + z_{k-1})$. This is advantageous computationally, since it reduces the dimensions of the state of the system to one only.

Consider first the special case of a finite horizon consisting of k periods starting with period i. Since z_k is received at the beginning of period $i + k$, it has no effect on the holding and penalty costs or the revenue during the k-period horizon. Let C_k represent the present worth of the expected revenue during the k-period horizon exclusive of the ordering cost cz_k. Thus

$$C_k = L(y) + \alpha E\{L(y + z_1 - D)\} + \alpha^2 E\{L(y + z_1 + z_2 - D - D_1)\} + \cdots + \alpha^{k-1} E\left\{L\left(y + \sum_{j=1}^{k-1} z_j - D - \sum_{j=1}^{k-2} D_j\right)\right\}$$

where D is the demand for period i and D_j is the demand for period $i + j$. The operator "E" is the expectation operator.

Since all the demands are independent and identically distributed, each with PDF $f(D)$, the random variable $s_m = D + D_1 + \cdots + D_{m-1}$, $m = 2, 3, \ldots, k - 1$, is the m-fold convolution of D (see Section 10.10). Let $f_m(s_m)$ be the PDF of s_m. Then

$$E\left\{L\left(y + \sum_{j=1}^{m} z_j - D - \sum_{j=1}^{m-1} D_j\right)\right\} = \int_0^\infty L\left(y + \sum_{j=1}^{m} z_j - s_m\right) f_m(s_m)\, ds_m$$

The expression for C_k is a constant independent of z_k.

To compute the net revenue for period $i + k$, let

$$u = y + (z_1 + \cdots + z_{k-1}) + z_k$$

and

$$v = y + (z_1 + \cdots + z_{k-1}) = u - z_k$$

$s_{k+1} = D + D_1 + \cdots D_k$ represents the demand for periods $i, i + 1, \ldots, i + k$. The holding and shortage inventories for period $i + k$ are thus given by $(u - s_{k+1})$ and $(s_{k+1} - u)$. Consequently, the net revenue (not accounting for the ordering cost cz_k) for period $i + k$ is given by

$$L_{k+1}(u) = \left[\int_0^u \{rs_{k+1} - h(u - s_{k+1})\} f_{k+1}(s_{k+1})\, ds_{k+1} + \int_u^\infty \{ru + (\alpha r - p)(s_{k+1} - u)\} f_{k+1}(s_{k+1})\, ds_{k+1} - A\right]$$

where A is a constant representing the expected revenue for periods $i, i + 1, \ldots, i + k - 1$.

Let $g_i(v)$ define the optimal expected profit for periods $i + k, \ldots, N$. Then

$$g_i(v) = \max_{u \ge v}\left\{-c(u - v) + \alpha^k L_{k+1}(u) + \alpha \int_0^\infty g_{i+1}(u - D) f(D)\, dD\right\}$$

The expected optimum revenue for periods $i, i + 1, \ldots, N$ is equal to the sum of the expected optimum revenues for periods $i, i + 1, \ldots, i + k - 1$ and for periods $i + k, i + k + 1, \ldots, N$; $N \ge k$. Since $v = y + z_1 + \cdots + z_{k-1}$, by definition the statement implies that

$$F_i(y, z_1, \ldots, z_{k-1}) = C_k + g_i(y + z_1 + \cdots + z_{k-1})$$

Since C_k is a constant, the optimization problem using f_i must be equivalent to the optimization problem using g_i. The advantage is that the new problem is described by one state $v = y + z_1 + \cdots + z_{k-1}$, which is computationally more attractive. The solution of the modified problem is essentially the same as that of the zero lag case discussed in Section 14.4.3A.

In the infinite horizon case the modified problem becomes

$$g(v) = \max_{u \ge v}(-c(u - v) + \alpha^k L_{k+1}(u) + \alpha E\{g(u - D)\})$$

This, as shown in Section 14.4.3A, yields a unique optimal value u^*, which is obtained from

$$\frac{\partial(\cdot)}{\partial u} = -c + \alpha^k L'_{k+1}(u) + \alpha c = 0$$

This gives

$$\int_0^{u^*} f_{k+1}(s_{k+1})\, ds_{k+1} = \frac{p + (1 - \alpha)(r - c\alpha^{-k})}{h + p + (1 - \alpha)r}$$

The optimal policy at any period i is

if $u^* \ge v$, order $u^* - v$

if $u^* < v$, do not order

At period i, the value of v is already known. (See the definition of v.) Also, for $k = 0$, that is, no delivery lag, the result reduces to the same one as that given for the zero delivery lag model (Section 14.4.3A).

D. No Backlog, Positive Delivery Lag

With the same symbols as in Section 14.4.3C, the model for the no backlog case becomes

$$F_i(y, z_1, \ldots, z_{k-1}) = \max_{z_k \geq 0}\Bigg[-cz_k + \int_0^y \{rD - h(y - D)\} f(D)\, dD + \int_y^\infty \{ry - p(D - y)\} f(D)\, dD + \alpha \int_0^y F_{i+1}(y - D + z_1, z_2, \ldots, z_k) f(D)\, dD + \alpha \int_y^\infty F_{i+1}(z_1, z_2, \ldots, z_k) f(D)\, dD\Bigg], \quad i = 1, 2, \ldots, N$$

with $F_{N+1} \equiv 0$.

In general, the dynamic programming solution of this model is very difficult for $k > 1$, since this results in a dimensionality problem that increases with k.

14.5 JUST-IN-TIME (JIT) MANUFACTURING SYSTEM

The name "just-in-time" is suggestive of what the JIT system entails: a manufacturing system that ideally operates with a very small inventory at all times. Such a goal is achieved by designing a production system in which required materials are made available on the production floor exactly when they are needed. Perhaps the best way to understand the JIT system is first to describe how it operates in practice. Ideally, the JIT system is suited for high-volume repetitive assembly or manufacturing processes in which the input materials of one operation are the output materials of one or more immediately preceding operations.

The JIT system is based on the use of **containers** and **cards**. A container is used to house the smallest number of parts that guarantees smooth operation at the production stage where it is needed. A card is used to authorize the movement of containers (empty or full) between successive production stages or the production of a container of parts at a given production stage. Figure 14-22 depicts the movement

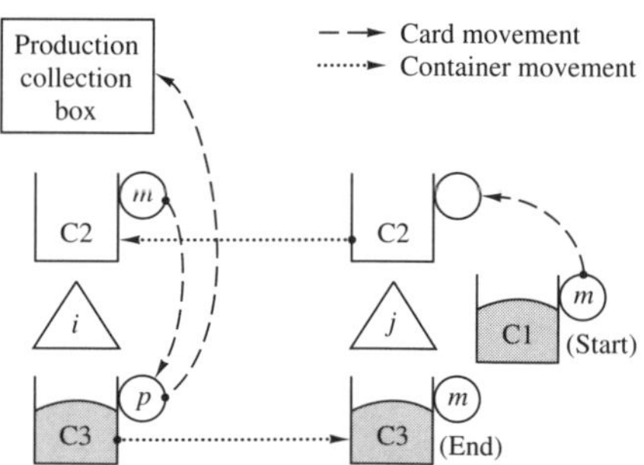

Figure 14-22

of cards and containers between two production stages i and j. The figure assumes that stage j has just started to use the parts in container C1. Such a container, as we will see shortly, must have a move (m) card attached to it. At the instant stage j starts to use C1, its m-card is removed and attached to an empty container C2 at the same stage. This action authorizes C2 to be moved to the immediately preceding stage i for replenishment. At i, a full container C3 carrying a production (p) card must be waiting. Thus, upon the receipt of C2, its m-card is removed and attached to C3, whose p-card must in turn be removed and placed in a production collection box. This collection box authorizes the start of a new production lot at i, which upon completion will be placed in empty container C2 with the p-card from the collection box attached to it. Container C3, which now has an m-card, is moved to station j. This action completes the movement of cards and containers initiated by the use of full container C1 at j. You will notice the following:

1. No container is moved between stages unless an m-card is attached to it.
2. No production is initiated at a stage unless a p-card is placed in the production collection box of that stage.

These two rules guarantee that production (in container-size lots) at a stage is initiated only in response to the start of consumption of an equal container at the succeeding stage. By keeping the container size sufficiently small, we are practically eliminating the work-in-process inventory. Notice also that the only inventory attached to the production system exists only on the production floor.

The JIT system, like the MRP system (Section 14.3.5A), is a **pull** system, in which the demand at a succeeding stage j initiates the production of an equal amount at the immediately preceding stage.

The JIT system normally starts by assigning a number of m- and p-cards as well as a number of containers to each production stage. Clearly, the larger the number of cards and containers, the higher the corresponding in-process inventory on the production floor. The basic premise of the JIT system is to reduce both cards and containers to a minimum. Indeed, the basic philosophy of the JIT system is that inventory is an indicator of inefficiency in the production or assembly line. For this reason, it is necessary always to seek improvements in product quality, equipment and personnel performance, and procedures to uncover, and hence eliminate, the sources of problems. Such improvements will then result in reducing dependency on in-process inventory. In JIT, improvements are measured in terms of the number of cards and containers that can be removed from the production floor while maintaining a smooth operation of the production line.

One of the major requirements for a successful implementation of JIT is that the setup cost associated with lot productions (full containers) must be reasonably small. This requirement follows from the fact that production lot sizes in JIT are necessarily small, and hence are produced more frequently. A reduction in the setup times is thus one of the main goals of effecting improvements in the JIT manufacturing system.

14.6 SUMMARY

An inventory problem deals with making optimum decisions regarding *how much* and *when* to order an inventory item. In this chapter we have presented a variety of models that deal with different inventory situations, including different assumptions regarding the cost parameters, the deterministic versus the probabilistic nature of the demand, and backordering, backlogging, and lead times. The simplest model is associated with static deterministic demands and the more complex ones are associated with the probabilistic inventory situations.

The majority of models presented in this chapter assume a *push* inventory system, in which items are produced first for later distribution to customers. The MRP and JIT systems, on the other hand, are *pull* systems, where production in one stage is initiated in response to a demand at a succeeding stage. The JIT system differs from the MRP system, however, in that the first aims at reducing the in-process inventory to a minimum by balancing the successive production stages.

SELECTED REFERENCES

HADLEY, G., and T. WHITIN, *Analysis of Inventory Systems*, Prentice Hall, Englewood Cliffs, N.J., 1963.

LOVE, S., *Inventory Control*, McGraw-Hill, New York, 1979.

SILVER, E., and R. PETERSON, *Decision Systems for Inventory Management and Production Planning*, 2nd ed., Wiley, New York, 1985.

TERSINE, R., *Principles of Inventory and Materials Management*, North-Holland, New York, 1982.

PROBLEMS

Section	Assigned Problems
14.1	14–1
14.3.1	14–2 to 14–14
14.3.2	14–15 to 14–18
14.3.3	14–19, 14–20
14.3.4	14–21 to 14–25
14.3.5	14–26 to 14–34
14.4.1	14–35 to 14–37
14.4.2	14–38 to 14–50
14.4.3	14–51 to 14–59

☐ **14–1** A small manufacturing company keeps 10 items, I1 through I10, in stock. The following table provides the cost per unit and annual usage of each item.

Item	Unit Cost	Annual Usage	Item	Unit Cost	Annual Usage
I1	\$.05	2,500	I6	\$.35	3,500
I2	.20	1,500	I7	.45	20,000
I3	.10	6,700	I8	.95	8,500
I4	.15	120,000	I9	.10	6,500
I5	.75	50,000	I10	.60	80,000

Apply the ABC analysis to this inventory situation. Which items should be given the tightest inventory control?

☐ **14–2** In each of the following cases, stock is replenished instantaneously and no shortage is allowed. Find the economic lot size, the associated total cost, and the length of time between two orders.

(a) $K = \$100$, $h = \$.05$, $D = 30$ units/day.
(b) $K = \$50$, $h = \$.05$, $D = 30$ units/day.
(c) $K = \$100$, $h = \$.01$, $D = 40$ units/day.
(d) $K = \$100$, $h = \$.04$, $D = 20$ units/day.

☐ **14–3** A company currently replenishes its stock of a certain item by ordering enough supply to cover a 1-month demand. The annual demand of the item is 1500 units. It is estimated that it costs \$20 every time an order is placed. The holding cost per unit inventory per month is \$2 and no shortage is allowed.

(a) Determine the optimal order quantity and the time between orders.
(b) Determine the difference in annual inventory costs between the optimal policy and the current policy of ordering a 1-month supply 12 times a year.

☐ **14–4** A company stocks an item that is consumed at the rate of 50 units per day. It costs the company \$20 each time an order is placed. A unit inventory held in stock for 1 week will cost \$.70. Determine the optimum number of orders (rounded to the closest integer) that the company has to place each year. Assume that the company has a standing policy of not allowing shortages in demand.

☐ **14–5** In each case in Problem 14–2, determine the reorder point assuming that the lead time is

(1) 14 days.
(2) 40 days.

☐ **14–6** Suppose that the demand distribution per unit time for the four cases in Problem 14–2 is normal with mean $\mu = D$ and constant variance $\sigma^2 = 9$. By using the information in Problem 14–5, determine the buffer stock in each case such that the probability of stock out during lead time is at most .02.

[*Hint*: For the purpose of estimating the variance of demand during lead time, approximate the cycle length t_0 by its closest integer value.]

☐ **14–7** In the model in Figure 14-4 (Section 14.3.1), suppose that stock is replenished uniformly (rather than instantaneously) at the rate a. Consumption occurs at the uniform rate D at every point in time. If y is the order size and no shortage is allowed, show that

(a) Maximum inventory level at any point in time is $y(1 - D/a)$.
(b) Total cost per unit time given y is

$$\text{TCU}(y) = \frac{KD}{y} + \frac{h}{2}\left(1 - \frac{D}{a}\right)y$$

(c) The economic lot size is

$$y^* = \sqrt{\frac{2KD}{h(1 - D/a)}}, \quad \text{provided } a > D$$

(d) Show how the economic lot size of Section 14.3.1 may be derived directly from part (c).

[*Hint*: Instantaneous replenishment is equivalent to letting a tend to infinity.]

☐ **14–8** Solve Problem 14–2 assuming that the stock is replenished uniformly at the rate $a = 50$ per unit time.

☐ **14–9** A company can produce an item or buy it from a contractor. If it is produced locally, it will cost $20 each time the machines are set up. The production rate is 100 units per day. If it is bought from a contractor, it will cost $15 each time an order is placed. The cost of maintaining the item in stock, whether bought or produced, is $.02 a day. The company's usage of the item is estimated at 26,000 units annually. Assuming that the company operates with no shortage, should they buy or produce?

☐ **14–10** In the model of Figure 14-4 (Section 14.3.1), suppose that shortage is allowed and that shortage cost per unit per unit time is p. If w is the shortage quantity and y is the amount ordered, show that:

(a) Total cost per unit time given y and w is

$$\text{TCU}(y, w) = \frac{KD}{y} + \frac{h(y - w)^2 + pw^2}{2y}$$

(b) $y^* = \sqrt{\dfrac{2KD(p + h)}{ph}}$

(c) $w^* = \sqrt{\dfrac{2KDh}{p(p + h)}}$

☐ **14–11** A stock can be replenished instantaneously upon order. Demand occurs at the constant rate of 50 items per unit time. A fixed cost of $400 is incurred each time an order is placed. Although shortage is allowed, it is the company's policy that the shortage quantity not exceed 20 units. In the meantime, because of budget limitation, no more than 200 units can be ordered at a time. Find the relationship between the implied holding and the shortage cost per unit under optimal conditions.

☐ **14–12** Show how the results of the model in Figure 14-4 may be derived from the results in Problem 14–10.

☐ **14–13** Generalize the models in Problems 14–7 and 14–10 into a single model in which both uniform replenishment and shortages are present. Show that the following results apply.

(a) $\text{TCU}(y, w) = \dfrac{KD}{y} + \dfrac{h\{y(1 - D/a) - w\}^2 + pw^2}{2(1 - D/a)y}$

(b) $y^* = \sqrt{\dfrac{2KD(p + h)}{ph(1 - D/a)}}$

(c) $w^* = \sqrt{\dfrac{2KDh(1 - D/a)}{p(p + h)}}$

☐ **14–14** Show that the model in Problem 14–13 may be specialized to produce directly the results of any of the preceding models.

☐ **14–15** An item is consumed at the rate of 30 items per day. The holding cost per unit time is $.05 and the setup cost is $100. Suppose that no shortage is allowed and

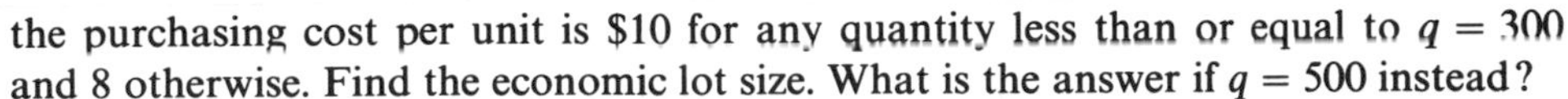

the purchasing cost per unit is \$10 for any quantity less than or equal to $q = 300$ and 8 otherwise. Find the economic lot size. What is the answer if $q = 500$ instead?

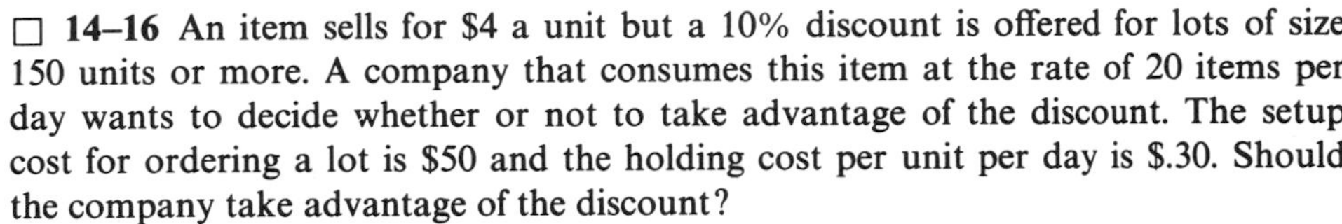

☐ **14–16** An item sells for \$4 a unit but a 10% discount is offered for lots of size 150 units or more. A company that consumes this item at the rate of 20 items per day wants to decide whether or not to take advantage of the discount. The setup cost for ordering a lot is \$50 and the holding cost per unit per day is \$.30. Should the company take advantage of the discount?

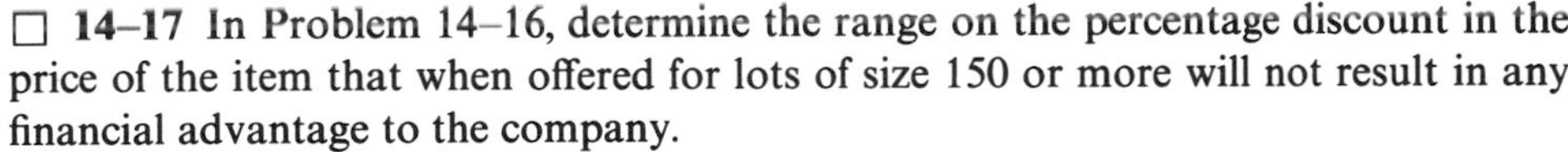

☐ **14–17** In Problem 14–16, determine the range on the percentage discount in the price of the item that when offered for lots of size 150 or more will not result in any financial advantage to the company.

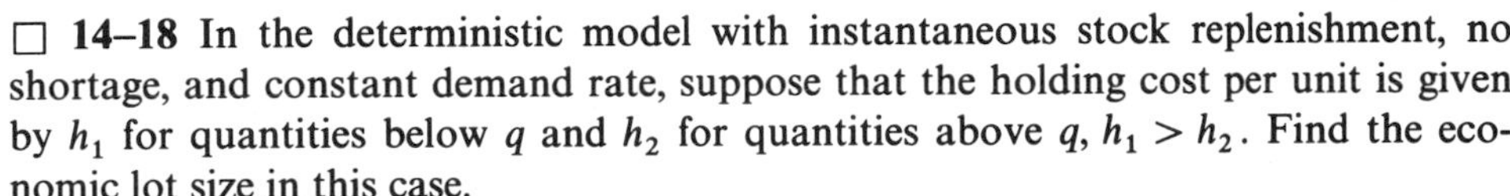

☐ **14–18** In the deterministic model with instantaneous stock replenishment, no shortage, and constant demand rate, suppose that the holding cost per unit is given by h_1 for quantities below q and h_2 for quantities above q, $h_1 > h_2$. Find the economic lot size in this case.

☐ **14–19** Four different items are kept in store for continuous use in a manufacturing process. The demand rates are constant for the four items. Shortage is not allowed and stock may be replenished instantaneously upon request. Let d_i be the annual amount demanded for the ith item ($i = 1, 2, 3, 4$). In terms of the regular symbols introduced in the chapter, the data of the problem are given by

Item i	K_i	D_i	h_i	d_i
1	100	10	.1	10,000
2	50	20	.2	5,000
3	90	5	.2	7,500
4	20	10	.1	5,000

Find the economic lot sizes for the four products, assuming that the total number of orders per year (for the four items) cannot exceed 200 orders.

☐ **14–20** Solve Problem 14–19 assuming that there is a limit $C = \$10{,}000$ on the amount of capital to be invested in inventory at any time. Let c_i be the cost per unit of the ith item, where $c_i = 10$, 5, 10, and 10, for $i = 1$, 2, 3, and 4. Disregard the restriction on the number of orders per year.

☐ **14–21** Show that the solution of Example 14.3-5 is optimal by showing that the optimality condition of the transportation technique (Section 6.2.3) is satisfied.

☐ **14–22** Solve Example 14.3-5 if production costs for the periods are as follows:

Period	R	T
1	2	3
2	3	4
3	3	5
4	1	2

☐ **14–23** An item is manufactured to meet known demand for four periods. The following table summarizes the costs and demand requirements.

	Production Cost per Unit in:			
Production Range (units)	Period 1	Period 2	Period 3	Period 4
1–3	1	2	2	3
4–11	1	4	5	4
12–15	2	4	7	5
16–25	5	6	10	7
Holding cost per unit to next period	2	5	3	—
Total demand	11	4	17	29

Find the optimal solution indicating the number of units to be produced in each of the four periods. Suppose that 10 additional units are needed in period 4. In which periods should they be produced?

☐ **14–24** The demand for a product in the next five periods may be filled by regular production, overtime production, and subcontracting. Subcontracting may be used only if overtime capacity is not sufficient. The following data give the supply and demand figures for the five periods.

Period	Maximum Number of Supply Units			
i	Regular Time	Overtime	Subcontracting	Demand
1	100	50	30	153
2	40	60	80	300
3	90	80	70	159
4	60	50	20	134
5	70	50	100	203

The production cost is the same for all periods and is given by 1, 2, and 3 per unit for regular time, overtime, and subcontracting, respectively. The holding cost from period i to period $i + 1$ is .5. A penalty cost of 2 per unit per period is incurred for late delivery. Find the optimal solution.

[*Hint*: This problem requires backordering.]

☐ **14–25** Repeat Problem 14–24 assuming that holding and backordering are each limited to a maximum of one period only.

☐ **14–26** In Figure 14-11, determine the combined requirements of part P for both models in each of the following independent cases:

(a) Lead time for M1 is one period only.

(b) Lead time for M1 is three periods.

☐ **14–27** Solve Example 14.3-7 assuming an initial inventory $x_1 = 4$.

☐ **14–28** Solve Example 14.3-7 by the backward recursive equation of dynamic programming.

☐ **14–29** Solve the following four-period deterministic inventory problem.

Period i	Demand D_i	Setup Cost K_i	Holding Cost h_i
1	5	5	1
2	7	7	1
3	11	9	1
4	3	7	1

The purchasing cost per unit is 1 for the first six units and 2 for any additional units.

☐ **14–30** Solve Example 14.3-8 assuming an initial inventory $x_1 = 80$ units.

☐ **14–31** Solve the following 10-period deterministic inventory problem. Assume an initial inventory of 50 units.

Period i	Demand D_i	Purchasing Cost c_i	Holding Cost h_i	Setup Cost K_i
1	150	6	1	100
2	100	6	1	100
3	20	4	2	100
4	40	4	1	200
5	70	6	2	200
6	90	8	3	200
7	130	4	1	300
8	180	4	4	300
9	140	2	2	300
10	50	6	1	300

☐ **14–32** Solve the following five-period deterministic inventory problem by the modified forward algorithm.

Period i	Demand D_i	Holding Cost h_i	Setup Cost K_i
1	50	1	80
2	70	1	70
3	100	1	60
4	30	1	80
5	60	1	60

The ordering cost function specifies a per unit cost of 20 for the first 30 items and 10 for any additional units (quantity discount).

☐ **14–33** Solve Problem 14–31 assuming a constant purchasing cost $c_i = 6$ for all the periods. Identify the planning horizons and the subhorizons for the problem.

☐ **14–34** Solve Problem 14–33 using the heuristic algorithm and compare the results with those of the DP model.

☐ **14–35** Solve Example 14.4-1 assuming that the pdf of demand during lead time is given by

$$f(x) = \begin{cases} 1/50, & 0 \leq x \leq 50 \\ 0, & \text{otherwise} \end{cases}$$

All the other parameters remain the same as in Example 14.4-1.

☐ **14–36** Find the optimal solution for the continuous review model of Section 14.4-1, assuming that $f(x)$ is normal with mean 100 and variance 4. Assume that $D = 10{,}000$, $h = 2$, $p = 4$, and $K = 20$.

☐ **14–37** In Problem 14–35, suppose that

$$f(x) = \begin{cases} 1/10, & 20 \leq x \leq 30 \\ 0, & \text{otherwise} \end{cases}$$

with all the other parameters remaining unchanged. Compare the values of R^* and y^* in this problem with those of Problem 14–35 and interpret the result.

[*Hint*: In both problems $E\{x\}$ is the same, but the variance in this problem is smaller.]

☐ **14–38** The demand for an item during a single period occurs according to an exponential distribution with mean 10 units. Assuming that the demand occurs instantaneously at the beginning of the period and that the per unit holding and penalty costs for the period are 1 and 3, respectively. The purchasing cost is 2 per unit. Find the optimal order quantity given an initial inventory of 2 units. What is the optimal order quantity if the initial inventory is 5 units?

☐ **14–39** For the discrete case derivation given in Section 14.4.2A, prove that at the optimal solution

$$P\{D \leq y\} \geq \frac{p - c}{p + h}$$

☐ **14–40** Solve Problem 14–38 assuming that the demand occurs according to a Poisson distribution with mean 10 units.

☐ **14–41** The purchasing cost per unit of a product is \$10 and its holding cost per unit per period is \$1. If the order quantity is 4 units, find the permissible range of p under optimal conditions given the following demand pdf:

D	0	1	2	3	4	5	6	7	8
$f(D)$	.05	.1	.1	.2	.25	.15	.05	.05	.05

☐ **14–42** Suppose that in Problem 14–38 the penalty cost p cannot be estimated easily. Consequently, it is decided to determine the order quantity such that the probability of shortage is at most equal to .1. What is the order quantity in this case? Assuming that all the remaining parameters are as given in Problem 14–38, what is the implied penalty cost under optimal conditions?

□ **14–43** Consider a one-period inventory model with zero setup cost and zero initial inventory. Let c be the ordering cost per unit and let r and v be the selling price and salvage values per unit ($v < c < r$). The demand D is described by a *discrete* pdf $f(D)$. Find the expression for the total expected *profit* as a function of the order quantity and derive the condition for selecting the optimal value. Assume zero holding and penalty costs.

□ **14–44** Solve Problem 14–38 assuming that the demand occurs uniformly over the period.

□ **14–45** Solve Problem 14–38 assuming that the demand is discrete and occurs uniformly over the period. Derive the general condition for the optimal order quantity given discrete demand units.

□ **14–46** Solve Problem 14–41 assuming that the demand occurs uniformly over the period.

□ **14–47** Find the optimal ordering policy for a one-period model with instantaneous demand given that the demand occurs according to the following pdf:

$$f(D) = \begin{cases} 1/5, & 5 \le D \le 10 \\ 0, & \text{otherwise} \end{cases}$$

The cost parameters are $h = 1.0$, $p = 5.0$, and $c = 3.0$; the setup cost is $K = 5.0$. Assume an initial inventory of 10 units. What is the general ordering policy in this case?

□ **14–48** Repeat Problem 14–47 assuming that

$$f(D) = \begin{cases} e^{-D}, & D > 0 \\ 0, & \text{otherwise} \end{cases}$$

and zero initial inventory.

□ **14–49** In the single-period model of Section 14.4.2A, suppose instead that profit is to be maximized. Given that r is the selling price per unit and using the information in Section 14.4.2A, develop an expression for the total expected *profit* and find the optimal order quantity.

Suppose that $r = 3$, $c = 2$, $p = 4$, $h = 1$. If a setup cost $K = 10$ is included in the problem, find the optimal ordering policy given that the pdf of demand is uniform for $0 \le D \le 10$.

□ **14–50** Consider a one-period model where it is desired to maximize the expected profit per period. The demand occurs instantaneously at the *end* of the period. Let r and v be the per unit selling price and salvage value, respectively. Using the notation of the chapter, develop the expression for the expected profit and then find the optimal solution. Assume that the unfilled demand at the end of the period is lost.

☐ **14–51** Consider a *two*-period probabilistic inventory model with a backlog and zero delivery lag. Let the demand pdf be given by

$$f(D) = \begin{cases} 1/10, & 0 \le D \le 10 \\ 0, & \text{otherwise} \end{cases}$$

The cost parameters per unit are

$$\begin{aligned} \text{selling price} &= 2 \\ \text{purchasing price} &= 1 \\ \text{holding cost} &= .1 \\ \text{penalty cost} &= 3 \\ \text{discount factor} &= .8 \end{aligned}$$

Find the optimal ordering policy that will maximize the expected profit over the two periods. Use the dynamic programming formulation.

☐ **14–52** By expanding the recursive equation for the infinite horizon model in Section 14.4.3A, show that $f(x)$ is concave. Hence there exists a single critical number y^* for all periods.

☐ **14–53** Consider an infinite horizon probabilistic inventory model for which the demand pdf per period is given by

$$f(D) = \begin{cases} .08D & 0 \le D \le 5 \\ 0, & \text{otherwise} \end{cases}$$

The per unit parameters are

$$\begin{aligned} \text{selling price} &= 10 \\ \text{purchasing price} &= 8 \\ \text{penalty cost} &= 1 \\ \text{discount factor} &= .9 \end{aligned}$$

Find the optimal ordering policy that maximizes the expected profit given that unfilled demand is backlogged and zero delivery lag.

☐ **14–54** Solve Problem 14–51 assuming no backlog.

☐ **14–55** Solve Problem 14–53 assuming no backlog.

☐ **14–56** Consider an infinite horizon inventory model. Rather than developing the optimal policy based on maximization of profit, it is developed based on minimization of expected costs. Using the regular symbols in the chapter, develop an expression for the expected cost and then find the optimal solution. Assume that

$$\text{holding cost for } x \text{ units} = hx^2$$
$$\text{penalty cost for } x \text{ units} = px^2$$

Also assume that there is no delivery lag and that all unfilled demand is backlogged.

Show that for the special case where $h = p$, the optimal solution is independent of the specific PDF of demand.

☐ **14–57** Repeat Problem 14–56 assuming no backlog of unfilled demand. In this case, however, when $h = p$, the optimal solution depends on the pdf of demand.

☐ **14–58** Consider a five-period probabilistic inventory model with backlogged demand. Given a delivery lag of three periods and that the pdf of demand per period is exponential with mean one, give a detailed procedure describing how the order quantities for periods 4 and 5 can be determined. Assume, for simplicity, that the receipts for periods 1, 2, and 3 all equal zero and that the initial inventory at the beginning of period 1 equals x_1.

☐ **14–59** Consider an infinite horizon probabilistic inventory model with the following pdf for the demand per period:

$$f(D) = \begin{cases} e^{-D}, & D > 0 \\ 0, & \text{otherwise} \end{cases}$$

If the parameters are $r = 10$, $c = 5$, $p = 15$, $h = 1$, and $\alpha = .9$, find the optimal policy assuming backlog and a two-period delivery lag.

Chapter 15

Queueing Models

Imagine the following situations:

1. Shoppers waiting in front of checkout stands in a supermarket.
2. Cars waiting at a stoplight.
3. Patients waiting at an outpatient clinic.
4. Planes waiting for takeoff in an airport.
5. Broken machines waiting to be serviced by a repairman.
6. Letters waiting to be typed by a secretary.
7. Programs waiting to be processed by a digital computer.

What these situations have in common is the phenomenon of waiting. It would be most convenient if we could be offered these services, and others like it, without the "nuisance" of having to wait. But like it or not, waiting is part of our daily life, and all we should hope to achieve is to reduce its inconvenience to bearable levels.

The waiting phenomenon is the direct result of *randomness* in the operation of service facilities. In general, the customer's arrival and service time are not known in advance; for otherwise the operation of the facility could be scheduled in a manner that would eliminate waiting completely.

Our objective in studying the operation of a service facility under random conditions is to secure some characteristics that measure the performance of the system under study. For example, a logical measure of performance is how long a customer is expected to wait before being serviced. Another measure is the percentage of time the service facility is not used. The first measure looks at the system from the customer's standpoint, whereas the second measure evaluates the degree of utilization of the facility. We can intuitively see that the larger the customer's waiting time, the smaller is the percentage of time the facility would remain idle, and vice versa. These measures of performance may thus be used to select the level of service (or service rate) that will strike a reasonable balance between the two conflicting situations.

This chapter discusses a number of queueing models that account for a variety of service operations. The ultimate objective of solving these models is to determine the characteristics that measure the performance of the system. We then show in Chapter 16 how this information can be used in seeking an "optimal" design for the service facility.

15.1 BASIC ELEMENTS OF THE QUEUEING MODEL

From the standpoint of a queueing model, a waiting line situation is created in the following manner. As customers arrive at the facility, they join a waiting line (or a queue). The server chooses a customer from the waiting line to begin service. Upon the completion of a service, the process of choosing a new (waiting) customer is repeated. It is assumed that no time is lost between the completion of a serivce and the admission of a new customer into the facility.

The principal actors in a queueing situation are the **customer** and the **server**. In queueing models, the interaction between the customer and the server are of interest only in as far as it relates to the *period of time* the customer needs to complete a service. Thus, from the standpoint of customer arrivals, we are interested in the time intervals that separate *successive* arrivals. Also, in the case of service, it is the service time per customer that counts in the analysis.

In queueing models, customer arrivals and service times are summarized in terms of probability distributions normally referred to as **arrivals** and **service time distributions**. These distributions may represent situations where customers arrive and are served *individually* (e.g., banks or supermarkets). In other situations, customers may arrive and/or be served in groups (e.g., restaurants). The latter case is normally referred to as **bulk queues**.

Although the patterns of arrivals and departures are the main factors in the analysis of queues, other factors also figure importantly in the development of the models. The first factor is the manner of choosing customers from the waiting line to start service. This is referred to as the **service discipline**. The most common discipline is the FCFS rule (first come, first served). LCFS (last come, first served) and SIRO (service in random order) may also arise in practical situations. We must also add that whereas service discipline regulates the selection of customers from a waiting line, it is also possible that customers arriving at a facility may be put in **priority queues** such that those with a higher priority will receive preference to start service first. The specific selection of customers from each priority queue may, however, follow any service discipline.

The second factor deals with the design of the facility and the execution of service. The facility may include more than one server, thus allowing as many customers as the number of servers to be serviced simultaneously (e.g., bank tellers). In this case, all servers offer the same service and the facility is said to have **parallel servers**. On the other hand, the facility may comprise a number of series stations through which the customer may pass before service is completed (e.g., processing of a product on a sequence of machines). The resulting situations are normally known as **queues in series** or **tandem queues**. The most general design of a service facility includes both series and parallel processing station. This results in what we call **network queues**.

The third factor concerns admissible **queue size**. In certain situations, only a limited number of customers may be allowed, possibly because of space limitation (e.g., car spaces allowed in a drive-in bank). Once the queue fills to capacity, newly arriving customers may not join the queue.

The fourth factor deals with the nature of the source from which calls for service (arrivals of customers) are generated. The **calling source** may be capable of generating a finite number of customers or (theoreticlly) infinitely many customers. A finite source exists when an arrival affects the rate of arrival of new customers. In a machine shop with a total of M machines, the calling source before any machine breaks down consists of M potential customers. Once a machine breaks down, it becomes a customer and hence incapable of generating new calls until it is repaired. A distinction must be made between the machine shop situation and others where the "cause" for generating calls is limited, yet capable of generating infinity of arrivals. For example, in a typing pool, the number of users is finite, yet each user could generate any number of arrivals, since a user generally need not wait for the completion of previously submitted material before generating new ones.

Queueing models representing situations in which human beings take the roles of customers and/or servers must be designed to account for the effect of **human behavior**. A "human" server may speed up the rate of service when the waiting line builds up in size. A "human" customer may **jockey** from one waiting line to another in hopes of reducing the waiting time (the next time you are in a bank or a supermarket you may kill your waiting time by observing this jockeying phenomenon). Some "human" customers also may **balk** from joining a waiting line altogether because they *anticipate* a long delay, or they may **renege** *after* being in the queue for a while because their wait has been too long. (Note that in terms of human behavior, a long wait for one person may not be as long as for another.)

Undoubtedly, there are other traits of human behavior that exist in everyday queueing situations. Yet from the standpoint of the queueing *model*, these traits can be accounted for only if they can be quantified in a manner that allows their mathematical inclusion in the model. Also, queueing models cannot account for the *individual* behavior of customers in the sense that all customers in a queue are expected to "behave" equally while in the facility. Thus a "chatty" customer is considered an odd case and his or her behavior is ignored in the design of the system. On the other hand, if the majority of customers happen to be unduly talkative, a *realistic* design of the service facility must be based on the fact that this habit, wasteful as it may be, is an integral part of the operation. A logical way for including the effect of this habit is to increase the service time per customer.

We now see that the basic elements of a queueing model depend on the following factors:

1. Arrivals distribution (single or bulk arrivals).
2. Service-time distributions (single or bulk service).
3. Design of service facility (series, parallel, or network stations).
4. Service discipline (FCFS, LCFS, SIRO) and service priority.
5. Queue size (finite or infinite).
6. Calling source (finite or infinite).
7. Human behavior (jockeying, balking, and reneging).

There are as many queueing models as there are variations on the factors listed. In this chapter we consider a number of models that appear useful in practical applications. The next section shows that the Poisson and exponential distributions play an important role in representing the arrivals and service times in many queueing situations. The succeeding sections then present the selected queueing models and their solutions.

15.2 ROLE OF THE POISSON AND EXPONENTIAL DISTRIBUTIONS

Consider the queueing situation in which the arrivals and departures (events) occurring during an interval of time are controlled by the following conditions:

Condition 1: The probability of an event (arrival or departure) occurring between t and $t + s$ depends *only* on the length of s, meaning that the probability does not depend on t or the number of events occurring during the time period $(0, t)$. (Mathematically, we say that the probability function has **stationary independent** increments.)

Condition 2: The probability of an event occurring during a very small time interval h is positive but less than one.

Condition 3: At most one event can occur during a very small time interval h.

In the remainder of this section we show that the given three conditions describe a process in which the *count* of events during a given time interval is *Poisson*, and equivalently the *time* interval between successive events is *exponential.* In such a case, we say that the conditions represent a **Poisson process.**

Define:

$p_n(t)$ = probability of n events occurring during time t

Then, by condition 1, the probability of no event occurring during $t + h$ is

$$p_0(t + h) = p_0(t)p_0(h)$$

For $h > 0$ and sufficiently small, condition 2 indicates that $0 < p_0(h) < 1$. Under these conditions, the equation above has the following solution

$$p_0(t) = e^{-\alpha t}, \qquad t \geq 0$$

where α is a positive constant. [See Parzen (1962, pp. 121–123) for details of the proof.]

We now show that for the process described by $p_n(t)$, the time interval between successive events is exponential. Using the known relationship between the exponential and the Poisson, we can then conclude that $p_n(t)$ must be Poisson.

Let

$f(t)$ = probability density function (pdf) of the time interval t between the occurrence of *successive events,* $t \geq 0$

Suppose that T is the time interval since the occurrence of the last event; then the following probability statement is valid:

$$P\begin{Bmatrix}\text{interevent time} \\ \text{exceeds } T\end{Bmatrix} = P\begin{Bmatrix}\text{no events} \\ \text{occur during } T\end{Bmatrix}$$

This statement translates to

$$\int_T^\infty f(t)\, dt = p_0(T)$$

Substituting for $p_0(T)$ as derived above, we get

$$\int_T^\infty f(t)\, dt = e^{-\alpha T}, \qquad T > 0$$

or

$$\int_0^T f(t)\, dt = 1 - e^{-\alpha T}, \qquad T > 0$$

Taking the derivative of both sides with respect to T, we get

$$f(t) = \alpha e^{-\alpha t}, \qquad t \geq 0 \qquad \text{(exponential)}$$

which is an **exponential distribution** with mean $E\{t\} = 1/\alpha$ time units.

Given that $f(t)$ is an exponential distribution, probability theory (see Figure 11-14) tells us that $p_n(t)$ must be a **Poisson distribution**, that is,

$$p_n(t) = \frac{(\alpha t)^n e^{-\alpha t}}{n!}, \qquad n = 0, 1, 2, \ldots \qquad \text{(Poisson)}$$

The mean value of n during a given period t is $E\{n \mid t\} = \alpha t$ events. This means that α represents the *rate* at which events occur.

The conclusion from the results above is that if the *time interval* between successive events is exponential with mean $1/\alpha$ time units, then the *number* of events in a given time period must be Poisson with mean rate of occurrence (events per unit time) α. The converse is also true.

The Poisson is a **completely random process** because it has the property that the time interval remaining until the occurrence of the next event is totally independent of the time interval that has elapsed since the occurrence of the last event. This property is equivalent to proving the following probability statement

$$P\{t > T + S \mid t > S\} = P\{t > T\}$$

where S is the time interval since the occurrence of the last event. Since t is exponential, we have

$$\begin{aligned} P\{t > T + S \mid t > S\} &= \frac{P\{t > T + S \mid t > S\}}{P\{t > S\}} = \frac{P\{t > T + S\}}{P\{t > S\}} \\ &= \frac{e^{-\alpha(T+S)}}{e^{-\alpha S}} = e^{-\alpha T} \\ &= P\{t > T\} \end{aligned}$$

This property is referred to as **forgetfulness** or **lack of memory** of the exponential, which is the basis for showing that the Poisson distribution is completely random.

Another distinguishing characteristic of the Poisson is that it is the only distribution whose mean and variance are equal. This property is sometimes used as an initial indicator of whether or not a sample data is drawn from a Poisson distribution.

Example 15.2-1. A service machine always has a standby unit for immediate replacement upon failure. The time to failure of the machine or its standby unit is exponential with mean 10 hours. Failures thus occur at the rate of .1 event per hour.

The exponential distribution of the time to failure is thus given as

$$f(t) = .1e^{-.1t}, \qquad t > 0$$

whereas the Poisson distribution of the number of failures during a period T is given as

$$p_n(T) = \frac{(.1T)^n e^{-.1T}}{n!}, \qquad n = 0, 1, 2, \ldots$$

Suppose that we are interested in computing the probability that a failure will take place within 5 hours. This probability is given as

$$\begin{aligned} P\{t < 5\} &= \int_0^5 f(t)\, dt \\ &= 1 - e^{-.5} = .393 \end{aligned}$$

Alternatively, the probability that a failure will occur after 6 hours from now given the last failure took place 3 hours earlier, makes use of the forgetfulness property of the exponential and is given by

$$P\{t > 9 \mid t > 3\} = P\{t > 6\} = e^{-.1 \times 6} = .549$$

The relationship between the Poisson and the exponential is demonstrated by computing the probability that no failures will take place during a 1-day (24-hour) period; that is,

$$p_0(24) = \frac{(.1 \times 24)^0 e^{-.1 \times 24}}{0!} = e^{-2.4} = .091$$

Observe that $p_0(24)$ is equivalent to having an interfailure time of at least 24 hours; that is,

$$P\{t > 24\} = \int_{24}^{\infty} .1e^{-.1t}\, dt = e^{-2.4}$$

◀

Exercise 15.2-1

In Example 15.2-1, determine

(a) The average number of failures in 1 week assuming service is offered 24 hours a day.
[*Ans.* 16.8 failures.]

(b) The probability of at least one failure in a 24-hour period.
[*Ans.* .909.]

15.3 PURE BIRTH AND PURE DEATH PROCESSES

In this section we consider two special processes. In the first process, customers arrive and never leave and in the second process customers are withdrawn from an initial stock. In both cases the processes of arrival and withdrawal occur in a completely random fashion. The two situations are referred to as **pure birth** and **pure death** processes.

15.3.1 PURE BIRTH MODEL

Consider the situation of issuing birth certificates for newborn babies. These certificates are normally kept as permanent records in a central office administered by the state health department. There is every reason to believe that the birth of new babies, and hence the issuing of birth certificates, is a completely random process that can be described by a Poisson distribution. Using the information in Section 15.2 and assuming that λ is the rate at which birth certificates are issued, the pure birth process of having n arrivals (birth certificates) during the time period t is described by the following Poisson distribution:

$$p_n(t) = \frac{(\lambda t)^n e^{-\lambda t}}{n!}, \qquad n = 0, 1, 2, \ldots \qquad \text{(Pure Birth)}$$

where λ is the rate of arrival per unit time with the expected number of arrivals during t being equal to λt.

Example 15.3-1. Suppose that births in a state are spaced over time according to an exponential distribution with one birth occurring every 7 minutes on the average.

Since the average interarrival (interbirth) time is 7 minutes, the birthrate in the state is computed as

$$\lambda = \frac{24 \times 60}{7} = 205.7 \text{ births/day}$$

The number of births in the state per year is given as

$$\lambda t = 205.7 \times 365 = 75{,}080 \text{ births/year}$$

The probability of no births in any one day is computed as

$$p_0(1) = \frac{(205.7 \times 1)^0 e^{-205.7 \times 1}}{0!} \simeq 0$$

Suppose that we are interested in the probability of issuing 45 birth certificates by the end of a period of 3 hours given that 35 certificates were issued in the first 2 hours. We observe that since births occur according to a Poisson process, the required probability reduces to having $45 - 35 = 10$ births in one $(= 3 - 2)$ hour. Given $\lambda = 60/7 = 8.57$ births/hour, we get

$$p_{10}(1) = \frac{(8.57 \times 1)^{10} e^{-8.57 \times 1}}{10!} = .11172$$

Queueing formulas similar to the one given above normally involve tedious computations. It is thus advisable to use the TORA software to carry out these calculations. Figure 15-1 provides the program output for the pure birth model with $\lambda t = (8.57 \times 1) = 8.57$. The results give $p_n(t)$ and cumulative $p_n(t)$ for different values of n. ◀

```
Problem title: Example 15.3-1
Scenario 1 — Pure Birth Model
------------------------------------------------------------
Poisson with Lambda*t =          8.57000
------------------------------------------------------------
Values of p(n) for n=0 to 23, else p(n) < .00001

  0 0.00019   1 0.00163   2 0.00697   3 0.01990   4 0.04264
  5 0.07308   6 0.10439   7 0.12780   8 0.13691   9 0.13036
 10 0.11172  11 0.08704  12 0.06216  13 0.04098  14 0.02509
 15 0.01433  16 0.00768  17 0.00387  18 0.00184  19 0.00083
 20 0.00036  21 0.00015  22 0.00006  23 0.00002

Cumulative values of p(n) for n=0 to 23

  0 0.00019   1 0.00182   2 0.00878   3 0.02868   4 0.07132
  5 0.14441   6 0.24879   7 0.37659   8 0.51350   9 0.64387
 10 0.75559  11 0.84263  12 0.90479  13 0.94577  14 0.97086
 15 0.98519  16 0.99287  17 0.99674  18 0.99858  19 0.99941
 20 0.99977  21 0.99991  22 0.99997  23 0.99999
```

Figure 15-1

Exercise 15.3-1

In Example 15.3-1, suppose that the clerk who enters the information from the birth certificates into a computer normally waits until at least five certificates have accumulated. What is the probability that the clerk will be inputting a new batch every hour?
[*Ans.* $p_{n \geq 5}(1) = .92868$.]

15.3.2 PURE DEATH MODEL

Consider the situation of stocking N units of an item at the start of the week to meet customers' demand during the week. If we assume that customer demand occurs at the rate μ units per day and that the demand process is completely random, the associated probability of having n items *remaining* in stock after time t is given by the following **truncated Poisson** distribution:

$$p_n(t) = \frac{(\mu t)^{N-n} e^{-\mu t}}{(N-n)!}, \qquad n = 1, 2, \ldots, N$$

$$p_0(t) = 1 - \sum_{n=1}^{N} p_n(t) \qquad \text{(Pure Death)}$$

Example 15.3-2. At the beginning of each week, 15 units of an inventory item are stocked for use during the week. Withdrawals from stock occur only during the first 6 days (business is closed on Sundays) and follows a Poisson distribution with mean 3 units/day. When the stock level reaches 5 units, a new order of 15 units is placed for delivery at the beginning of next week. Because of the nature of the item, all units left at the end of the week are discarded.

We can analyze this situation in a number of ways. First, we recognize that the consumption rate is $\mu = 3$ units per day. Suppose that we are interested in computing the probability of having 5 units (the reorder level) on day t; that is,

$$p_5(t) = \frac{(3t)^{15-5} e^{-3t}}{(15-5)!}, \qquad t = 1, 2, \ldots, 6$$

As an illustration of the computations, the following results are obtained from TORA using $\mu t = 3, 6, 9, \ldots$, and 18.

t (days)	1	2	3	4	5	6
μt	3	6	9	12	15	18
$p_5(t)$	.0008	.0413	.1186	.1048	.0486	.015

Note that $p_5(t)$ represents the probability of reordering *on* day t. This probability peaks at $t = 3$ and then declines as we advance through the week. If we are interested in the probability of reordering *by* day t, we must compute the cumulative probability of having 5 units *or* less on day t; that is,

$$p_{n \leq 5}(t) = p_0(t) + p_1(t) + \cdots + p_5(t)$$

Again, using TORA we get

t (days)	1	2	3	4	5	6
μt	3	6	9	12	15	18
$p_{n \leq 5}(t)$	.0011	.0839	.4126	.7576	.9301	.9847

We can see from the table that the probability of placing the order *by* day t increases monotonically with t.

Another piece of information that is important in analyzing the situation is determining the average number of inventory units that will be discarded at the end of the week. This is done by computing the expected number of units available on day 6; that is,

$$E\{n \mid t = 6\} = \sum_{n=0}^{15} np_n(6)$$

The following table summarizes the computations given $\mu t = 18$.

n	0	1	2	3	4	5	6	7	8	9	10	11
$p_n(6)$	.792	.0655	.0509	.0368	.0245	.015	.0083	.0042	.0018	.0007	.0002	.0001

and $p_n(6) \cong 0$ for $n = 12$, 13, 14, and 15. Thus, computing the average, we get

$$E\{n \mid t = 6\} = .5537 \text{ unit}$$

This means that, on the average, less than 1 unit will be discarded at the end of each week. ◀

Exercise 15.3-2

In Example 15.3-2, determine

(a) The probability that the stock is depleted after 3 days.
[*Ans.* $p_0(3) = .04147$.]

(b) The probability that an inventory unit will be withdrawn by the end of the fourth day given that the last unit was withdrawn at the end of the third day.
[*Ans.* $P\{\text{time between withdrawals} \leq 1\} = .9502$.]

(c) The probability that the time remaining until the next withdrawal is at most 1 day given that the last withdrawal occurs a day earlier.
[*Ans.* Same as in part (b).]

(d) The average inventory held in stock at the end of the second day.
[*Ans.* $E\{n \mid t = 2\} = 9.0011$ units.]

(e) The probability that no withdrawals occur during the first day.
[*Ans.* $p_{15}(1) = .0498$.]

15.4 QUEUES WITH COMBINED ARRIVALS AND DEPARTURES

In this section we study queueing situations that combine both the arrivals and departures processes. We restrict our attention to waiting lines where customers are

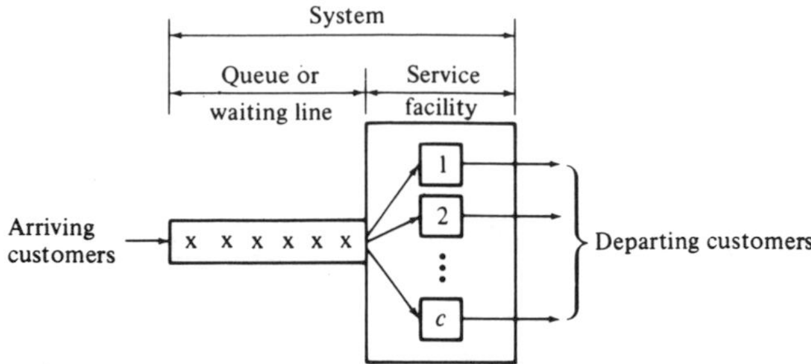

Figure 15-2

served by c *parallel* servers so that c customers can be serviced simultaneously. All servers offer equal services from the viewpoint of the time it takes to service each customer. Figure 15-2 represents the parallel queueing system schematically. Note that the number of customers in the *system* at any point in time is defined to include those in *queue* and in *service*.

A notation that is particularly suited for summarizing the main characteristics of *parallel* queues has been universally standardized in the following format,

$$(a/b/c):(d/e/f)$$

where the symbols a, b, c, d, e, and f stand for basic elements of the model as follows (see Section 15.1).

$a \equiv$ arrivals distribution
$b \equiv$ service time (or departures) distribution
$c \equiv$ number of parallel servers ($c = 1, 2, \ldots, \infty$)
$d \equiv$ service discipline (e.g., FCFS, LCFS, SIRO)
$e \equiv$ maximum number allowed in *system* (in queue + in service)
$f \equiv$ size of calling source

The standard notation replaces the symbols a and b for arrivals and departures by the following codes.

$M \equiv$ Poisson (or Markovian) arrival or departure distribution (or equivalently exponential interarrival or/service-time distribution)
$D \equiv$ constant or deterministic interarrival or service time
$E_k \equiv$ Erlangian or gamma distribution of interarrival or service time distribution with parameter k
$GI \equiv$ general independent distribution of arrivals (or interarrival time)
$G \equiv$ general distribution of departures (or service time)

To illustrate the notation, consider

$$(M/D/10):(GD/N/\infty)$$

Here we have Poisson arrivals, constant service time, and 10 parallel servers in the facility. The service discipline is general (GD) in the sense that it could be FCFS, LCFS, SIRO, or whatever procedure the servers may use to decide on the order in which customers are chosen from the queue to start service. Regardless of how many customers arrive at the facility, the system (queue + service) can hold only a maximum of N customers; all others must seek service elsewhere. Finally, the source generating the arriving customers has an infinite capacity.

The standard notation described was initially devised by D. G. Kendall (1953) in the form $(a/b/c)$ and is known in the literature as the **Kendall notation**. Later, A. M. Lee (1966) added the symbols d and e to the Kendall notation. In this book we find it convenient to augment the Kendall–Lee notation by use of the symbol f, representing the capacity of calling source.

The ultimate objective of analyzing queueing situations is to develop measures of performance for evaluating the real systems. However, since any queueing system operates as a function of time, we must decide in advance whether we are interested in analyzing the system under **transient** or **steady-state** conditions. Transient conditions prevail when the behavior of the system continues to depend on time. Thus the pure birth and death processes (Section 15.3) always operate under transient conditions. On the other hand, queues with combined arrivals and departures start under transient conditions and gradually reach steady state after a *sufficiently large* time has elapsed, provided that the parameters of the system permit reaching steady state (e.g., a queue with arrival rate λ higher than its departure rate μ will never reach steady state regardless of elapsed time, since the queue size will increase with time). We note that transient analysis is quite complex mathematically and hence will not be considered in this presentation.

The remainder of this section first develops a steady-state model for the generalized Poisson queue with c parallel servers. The main result obtained from this model is the determination of the steady-state probabilities of having n customers in the system. These probabilities are then used to develop the measures of performance of the generalized queueing model.

15.4.1 GENERALIZED POISSON MODEL

The generalized model developed in this section applies to Poisson queues with state-dependent arrival and departure rates. In Section 15.5 we specialize the results of the developed model to specific Poisson queueing situations.

Before providing the details of the generalized model, we explain what we mean by *state-dependent* arrival and service rates. Consider a machine shop with a total of N machines. The rate of machine breakdown is a function of the number of machines that are in working condition; that is, if λ is the rate of breakdown *per machine*, the rate of breakdown in the entire shop given n ($\leq N$) machines are operative is $n\lambda$. In a similar manner, if a facility has c parallel servers and given that μ is the service rate *per server*, then given that n is the number of customers in the system (in queue + in service), the rate of departure from the entire facility is $n\mu$ if $n < c$ and $c\mu$ if $n \geq c$.

The two examples above demonstrate how in the generalized queueing model the rates of arrival and departure may be functions of the state of the system represented by number of customers, n. We thus use the notation λ_n and μ_n to define the arrival and departure rates as a function of n.

The immediate goal of the generalized model is to derive an expression for p_n, the steady-state probability of n customers in system, as a function of λ_n and μ_n. Given p_n, we show in Section 15.4.2 how the system's measures of performance (e.g., expected number waiting and expected utilization of the service facility) can be evaluated directly.

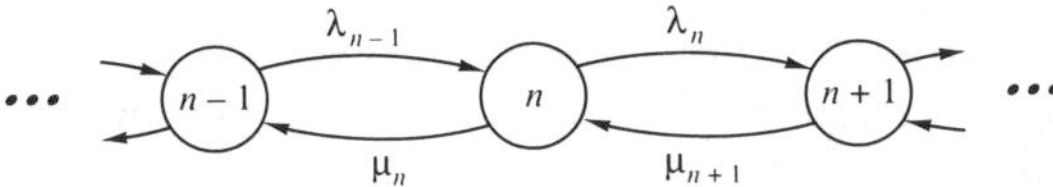

Figure 15-3

The derivation of an expression for p_n is achieved by using the so-called **transition-rate diagram**. From the definition of the Poisson process given in Section 15.2, given there are n in the system at any time t, the number in the system at the end of a sufficiently small time interval h, will be either $n - 1$ or $n + 1$, depending on whether a departure or an arrival takes place during h (note that the probability of *more than one event* occurring during h tends to zero as $h \to 0$). We thus say that in a Poisson process, state n can only communicate with states $n - 1$ and $n + 1$. Figure 15-3 illustrates the situation by using a transition rate diagram in which the arrows represent the transition among the states n, $n - 1$, and $n + 1$. The values associated with each arrow represent the transition rate between the states. For example, the rate from state $n - 1$ to state n is the arrival rate λ_{n-1}, where λ_{n-1} is a function of the *originating* state $n - 1$. On the other hand, the rate of transition from state n to state $n - 1$ is the departure rate μ_n which, again, is a function of the originating state n. In a similar manner, the arrival rate λ_n and the departure rate μ_{n+1} provides the transition rates between states n and $n + 1$.

Under steady-state condition, the *expected* rates of flow into and out of state n must be equal. Since state n communicates with $n - 1$ and $n + 1$ only, the transition rates from all other states $(0, 1, 2, \ldots, n - 2, n + 2, n + 3, \ldots)$ must be zero. We thus have

$$\begin{aligned}\begin{pmatrix}\text{expected rate of}\\ \text{flow into state } n\end{pmatrix} &= 0(p_0 + \cdots + p_{n-2}) + \lambda_{n-1}p_{n-1} + \mu_{n+1}p_{n+1} + 0(p_{n+2} + \cdots)\\ &= \lambda_{n-1}p_{n-1} + \mu_{n+1}p_{n+1}\end{aligned}$$

Similarly,

$$\begin{pmatrix}\text{expected rate of}\\ \text{flow out of state } n\end{pmatrix} = (\lambda_n + \mu_n)p_n$$

Equating the two rates, we get the so-called **balance equation**:

$$\lambda_{n-1}p_{n-1} + \mu_{n+1}p_{n+1} = (\lambda_n + \mu_n)p_n, \qquad n = 1, 2, \ldots$$

The equation above is valid only for $n > 0$. To obtain the balance equation for $n = 0$, consider the transition rate diagram in Figure 15-4. In this case state 0 communicates with state 1 only. We thus get

$$\lambda_0 p_0 = \mu_1 p_1, \qquad n = 0$$

The given balance equations are solved recursively starting with p_1, and proceeding by induction to determine p_n. From the balance equation for $n = 0$, we get

$$p_1 = \frac{\lambda_0}{\mu_1} p_0$$

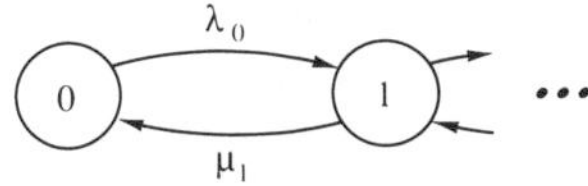

Figure 15-4

Next for $n = 1$, we have

$$\lambda_0 p_0 + \mu_2 p_2 = (\lambda_1 + \mu_1)p_1$$

substituting $p_1 = (\lambda_0/\mu_1)p_0$, and simplifying, we get (verify!)

$$p_2 = \frac{\lambda_1 \lambda_0}{\mu_2 \mu_1} p_0$$

In general, we can show by induction that

$$p_n = \frac{\lambda_{n-1}\lambda_{n-2} \cdots \lambda_0}{\mu_n \mu_{n-1} \cdots \mu_1} p_0, \qquad n = 1, 2, \ldots$$

The value of p_0 is determined from the following equation:

$$\sum_{n=0}^{\infty} p_n = 1$$

Example 15.4-1. Consider a single-server queueing situation in which the arrival and departure rates are constant and given by $\lambda_n = 3$ arrivals per hour and $\mu_n = 8$ departures per hour for all $n \geq 0$.

To compute p_n for $n \geq 0$, we notice that

$$p_n = \left(\frac{\lambda}{\mu}\right)^n p_0 = \left(\frac{3}{8}\right)^n p_0 = (.375)^n p_0, \qquad n = 0, 1, 2, \ldots$$

We determine p_0 from the equation $\sum_{n=0}^{\infty} p_n = 1$, which yields

$$p_0 + .375p_0 = .375^2 p_0 + \cdots = 1$$

or

$$p_0(1 + .375 + .375^2 + \cdots) = 1$$

Using the formula for the sum of a geometric series, we get

$$p_0\left(\frac{1}{1 - .375}\right) = 1$$

which gives $p_0 = .625$. We can then use the formula $p_n = .375^n p_0$ to determine p_n for $n = 1, 2, \ldots$ as listed below.

n	0	1	2	3	4	5	6	7	≥ 8
p_n	.625	.234	.088	.033	.012	.005	.002	.001	0

◀

Exercise 15.4-1

(a) In Example 15.4-1, determine the steady-state probability of having no one in the system assuming that the arrival and departure rates per hour are 4 and 5, respectively.
[*Ans.* $p_0 = .2$.]

(b) In part (a), what is the probability that the system will not be empty?
[*Ans.* .8.]

15.4.2 STEADY-STATE MEASURES OF PERFORMANCE

In this section we show that once the steady-state probability p_n of n customers in the system is determined, we can compute the steady-state measures of performance of the queueing situation in a straightforward manner. Such measures of performance may then be used to analyze the operation of the queueing situation for the purpose of making recommendations about the design of the system. Prominent among these measures of performance are the expected number of customers waiting, the expected waiting time per customer, and the expected utilization of the service facility.

Let

L_s = expected number of customers in *system*
L_q = expected number of customers in *queue*
W_s = expected waiting time in *system*
W_q = expected waiting time in *queue*

Recall that the *system* comprises both the *queue* and the *service facility*.

Suppose that we are considering a service facility with c parallel servers. Then from the definition of p_n, we obtain

$$L_s = \sum_{n=0}^{\infty} np_n$$

$$L_q = \sum_{n=c+1}^{\infty} (n-c)p_n$$

A strong relationship exists between L_s and W_s (also L_q and W_q) so that either measure is automatically determined from the other. Let λ_{eff} be the *effective* average arrival rate (independent of the number in the system n); then

$$L_s = \lambda_{\text{eff}} W_s$$
$$L_q = \lambda_{\text{eff}} W_q$$

The value of λ_{eff} is determined from the state-dependent λ_n and the probabilities p_n as

$$\lambda_{\text{eff}} = \sum_{n=0}^{\infty} \lambda_n p_n$$

A direct relationship also exists between W_s and W_q. By definition,

$$\begin{pmatrix}\text{expected waiting}\\ \text{time in system}\end{pmatrix} = \begin{pmatrix}\text{expected waiting}\\ \text{time in queue}\end{pmatrix} + \begin{pmatrix}\text{expected service}\\ \text{time}\end{pmatrix}$$

Given that μ is the service rate per busy server, the expected service time is $1/\mu$, and we get

$$W_s = W_q + \frac{1}{\mu}$$

Multiplying both sides by λ_{eff}, we obtain

$$L_s = L_q + \frac{\lambda_{\text{eff}}}{\mu}$$

The expected utilization of a service facility is defined as a function of the average number of busy servers. Since the difference between L_s and L_q must equal the expected number of busy servers, we obtain

$$\begin{pmatrix}\text{expected number of} \\ \text{busy servers}\end{pmatrix} = \bar{c} = L_s - L_q = \frac{\lambda_{\text{eff}}}{\mu}$$

The percent utilization of a service facility with c parallel servers is thus computed as

$$\text{percent utilization} = \frac{\bar{c}}{c} \times 100$$

In summary, given p_n we can compute the system's measures of performance in the following order:

$$p_n \rightarrow L_s = \sum_{n=0}^{\infty} n p_n \rightarrow W_s = \frac{L_s}{\lambda_{\text{eff}}} \rightarrow W_q = W_s - \frac{1}{\mu} \rightarrow L_q = \lambda_{\text{eff}} W_q \rightarrow \bar{c} = L_s - L_q$$

Example 15.4-2. In Example 15.4-1 we use the probabilities p_n to compute the model's measures of performance. First, observe that $\lambda_n = \lambda = 3$ arrivals per hour for all $n \geq 0$. Thus the average arrival rate is computed as $\lambda_{\text{eff}} = 3(p_0 + p_1 + p_2 + \cdots) = 3$ arrivals per hour. Now,

$$\begin{aligned} L_s = \sum_{n=0}^{\infty} n p_n &= 0 \times .625 + 1 \times .234 + 2 \times .088 + 3 \times .033 \\ &\quad + 4 \times .012 + 5 \times .005 + 6 \times .002 + 7 \times .001 \\ &= .6 \text{ customer} \end{aligned}$$

Using the formula $L_s = \lambda_{\text{eff}} W$, we get the waiting time in the system as

$$W_s = \frac{L_s}{\lambda_{\text{eff}}} = \frac{.6}{3} = .2 \text{ hour}$$

From this we get the expected waiting time in queue as

$$W_q = W_s - \frac{1}{\mu} = .2 - \frac{1}{8} = .075 \text{ hour}$$

The expected number in queue is then computed as

$$L_q = \lambda_{\text{eff}} W_q = 3 \times .075 = .225 \text{ customer}$$

Finally, since the facility has only one server, we have $c = 1$ and the percent utilization is computed as

$$\begin{aligned}\text{percent utilization} &= \frac{\bar{c}}{c} \times 100\\ &= \frac{L_s - L_q}{1} \times 100\\ &= \frac{.6 - .225}{1} \times 100 = 37.5\%\end{aligned}$$

◄

Exercise 15.4-2

In Example 15.4-2, compute the following.

(a) The expected number in the queue using p_n directly.
[*Ans.* .225.]

(b) The expected number of customers in the service facility.
[*Ans.* $L_s - L_q = .375$.]

(c) The percentage of time the server is idle.
[*Ans.* $p_0 = .625$.]

15.5 SPECIALIZED POISSON QUEUES

In this section we use the results of the generalized model given in Section 15.4.1 to study specialized Poisson queues. Each model is described in terms of the extended Kendall notation presented in Section 15.4. Since the derivation of p_n in Section 15.4.1 is completely independent of the queue discipline, it is appropriate to use the symbol GD (general discipline) in the Kendall notation.

15.5.1 $(M/M/1):(GD/\infty/\infty)$

This is a single-server model with no limit on the capacity of either the system or the calling source. It is assumed that arrival rates are independent of the number in the system; that is, $\lambda_n = \lambda$ for all n. Similarly, it is assumed that the single server in the system completes services at a constant rate; that is, $\mu_n = \mu$ for all n. In effect, the present model has Poisson arrivals and departures with mean rates λ and μ, respectively. From Section 15.4.2, it follows that $\lambda_{\text{eff}} = \lambda$.

Defining $\rho = \lambda/\mu$, the expression for p_n in the generalized model reduces to

$$p_n = \rho^n p_0, \qquad n = 0, 1, 2, \ldots$$

We determine p_0 by using the fact that the sum of all p_n for $n = 0, 1, 2, \ldots$ equals 1, we get

$$p_0(1 + \rho + \rho^2 + \cdots) = 1$$

If we assume that $\rho < 1$, then

$$p_0\left(\frac{1}{1 - \rho}\right) = 1$$

or

$$p_0 = 1 - \rho$$

We thus get the following general formula:

$$p_n = (1 - \rho)\rho^n, \qquad n = 0, 1, 2, \ldots \qquad (M/M/1):(GD/\infty/\infty)$$

which is a **geometric distribution.**

The mathematical requirement $\rho < 1$ needed to ensure the convergence of the geometric series $(1 + \rho + \rho^2 + \cdots)$ leads to an intuitive argument. Essentially, $\rho < 1$ means that $\lambda < \mu$, which states that the arrival rate must be strictly less than the service rate in the facility in order for the system to reach stability (steady-state conditions). This makes sense because under other conditions, the queue size could build up indefinitely.

The measure L_s can be derived in the following manner:

$$\begin{aligned} L_s &= \sum_{n=0}^{\infty} np_n = \sum_{n=0}^{\infty} n(1 - \rho)\rho^n \\ &= (1 - \rho)\rho \frac{d}{d\rho} \sum_{n=0}^{\infty} \rho^n \\ &= (1 - \rho)\rho \frac{d}{d\rho}\left(\frac{1}{1 - \rho}\right) \\ &= \frac{\rho}{1 - \rho} \end{aligned}$$

Note that the convergence of $\sum_{n=0}^{\infty} \rho^n$ is ensured because $\rho < 1$. Using the relationships given earlier, we obtain all the basic measures of performance as

$$\begin{aligned} L_s &= E\{n\} = \frac{\rho}{1 - \rho} \\ L_q &= L_s - \frac{\lambda}{\mu} = \frac{\rho^2}{1 - \rho} \\ W_s &= \frac{L_s}{\lambda} = \frac{1}{\mu(1 - \rho)} \\ W_q &= \frac{L_q}{\lambda} = \frac{\rho}{\mu(1 - \rho)} \end{aligned}$$

Example 15.5-1. In a car-wash service facility, information gathered indicates that cars arrive for service according to a Poisson distribution with mean 4 per hour. The time for washing and cleaning each car varies but is found to follow an exponential distribution with mean 10 minutes per car. The facility cannot handle more than one car at a time.

To analyze this situation using the results of the $(M/M/1):(GD/\infty/\infty)$, we must assume that the calling source is so large that it can be considered infinite. Moreover, there is enough parking space to accommodate all arriving cars.

For the given situation we have $\lambda = 4$ cars per hour and $\mu = 60/10 = 6$ cars per hour. Since $\rho = \lambda/\mu = 4/6$ is less than 1, the system can operate under steady-state conditions. The output of the model is shown in Figure 15-5. The value of $L_q = 1.33$ cars gives us an idea about how many cars are waiting on the average when a customer arrives. We realize, however, that L_q represents an expected value so that the number of waiting cars at any point in time may be larger or smaller than 1.333 cars. Thus we may be interested in determining the number of parking spaces in a manner that associates a reasonable probability for an arriving car to find a parking space. For example, suppose that we need to provide enough parking spaces so that an arriving car will find an empty space at least 90% of the time. Letting s represent the desired number of parking spaces, the requirement is equivalent to saying that the number of customers *in the system* should be at least one less than the maximum number that the entire system (s parking spaces plus one server) can hold. The condition thus reduces to

$$p_0 + p_1 + \cdots + p_s \geq .9$$

From Figure 15-5 the cumulative value of p_n is .86831 for $n = 4$ and .91221 for $n = 5$. This means that the number of parking spaces s should equal at least 5.

```
Problem title: Example 15.5-1
Scenario 1 — (M/M/1):(GD/*/*)
------------------------------------------------------------------------
Lambda =     4.00000                    Lambda eff =     4.00000
Mu =         6.00000                    Rho =            0.66667

Ls =         2.00000                    Lq =             1.33333
Ws =         0.50000                    Wq =             0.33333
------------------------------------------------------------------------
Values of p(n) for n=0 to 25, else p(n) < .00001

 0 0.33333   1 0.22222   2 0.14815   3 0.09877   4 0.06584
 5 0.04390   6 0.02926   7 0.01951   8 0.01301   9 0.00867
10 0.00578  11 0.00385  12 0.00257  13 0.00171  14 0.00114
15 0.00076  16 0.00051  17 0.00034  18 0.00023  19 0.00015
20 0.00010  21 0.00007  22 0.00004  23 0.00003  24 0.00002
25 0.00001

Cumulative values of p(n) for n=0 to 25

 0 0.33333   1 0.55556   2 0.70370   3 0.80247   4 0.86831
 5 0.91221   6 0.94147   7 0.96098   8 0.97399   9 0.98266
10 0.98844  11 0.99229  12 0.99486  13 0.99657  14 0.99772
15 0.99848  16 0.99898  17 0.99932  18 0.99955  19 0.99970
20 0.99980  21 0.99987  22 0.99991  23 0.99994  24 0.99996
25 0.99997
```

Figure 15-5

We can obtain more information about the operation of the car-wash facility. For example, the percentage of time the facility is idle equals the probability of having no cars in the facility; that is, $p_0 \cong .33$, meaning that the facility is idle 33% of the time. On the other hand, the expected waiting time from the moment the car arrives until it leaves may be useful in determining the convenience of service from the customers' standpoint. From Figure 15-5, we have $W_s = .5$ hour. This appears quite long and the manager of the facility should think of means to speed up the service rate.
◀

Exercise 15.5-1

In Example 15.5-1:

(a) Determine the probability that an arriving car must wait prior to being washed.
[*Ans.* .6667.]

(b) If there are six parking spaces outside the facility, determine the probability an arriving car will not find a parking space.
[*Ans.* $p_{n \geq 7} = .05853$.]

Waiting-Time Distribution Based on FCFS Service Discipline

In the analysis of the $(M/M/1):(GD/\infty/\infty)$, the derivation of p_n is shown to be completely independent of the service discipline. This means that W_s and W_q, the *expected* waiting times in system and in queue, are also completely independent of the service discipline, since they can be determined from $W_s = L_s/\lambda$ and $W_q = L_q/\lambda$.

Although the *expected* waiting time is independent of the service discipline, its probability density function (distribution) does depend on the type of service discipline used. Thus although the distributions may differ depending on the service discipline, their expected values remain unchanged. We illustrate here how the pdf of the waiting time is derived for the queueing model above based on the FCFS discipline. Let τ be the amount of time a person *just arriving* must wait in the *system*, that is, until the service is completed. Based on FCFS service discipline, if there are n customers in the system ahead of an arriving customer, then

$$\tau = t'_1 + t_2 + \cdots + t_{n+1}$$

where t'_1 is the time needed for the customer actually in service to complete service and $t_2, t_3, \ldots, t_n$ are the service times for the $n - 1$ customers in queue. The time t_{n+1} thus represents the service time for the arriving customer.

Let $w(\tau \mid n + 1)$ be the conditional pdf of τ given n customers in the system ahead of the arriving customer. Since t_i, for all i, is exponentially distributed, by the forgetfulness property (Section 15.2), t'_1 will also have the same exponential distribution as $t_2, t_3, \ldots, t_{n+1}$. Consequently, τ is the sum of $n + 1$ identically distributed and independent exponential distributions. From probability theory $w(\tau \mid n + 1)$ must be gamma-distributed with parameters $(\mu, n + 1)$. Thus

$$w(\tau) = \sum_{n=0}^{\infty} w(\tau \mid n + 1)p_n = \sum_{n=0}^{\infty} \frac{\mu(\mu\tau)^n e^{-\mu\tau}}{n!}(1 - \rho)\rho^n$$

$$= (1 - \rho)\mu e^{-\mu\tau} \sum_{n=0}^{\infty} \frac{(\lambda\tau)^n}{n!} = \mu(1 - \rho)e^{-\mu(1-\rho)\tau}, \qquad \tau > 0$$

which is an exponential distribution with mean

$$E\{\tau\} = \frac{1}{\mu(1-\rho)}$$

The mean $E\{\tau\}$ actually equals W_s, the expected waiting time in the system.

Knowledge of the distribution of waiting time can provide information that is not attainable otherwise. For example, we can obtain an idea about the "reliability" of W_s in indicating the actual time customers wait by computing the probability that customers will wait more than $W_s = 1/\mu(1-\rho)$; that is,

$$\begin{aligned} P\{\tau > W_s\} &= 1 - \int_0^{W_s} w(\tau)\, d\tau \\ &= e^{-\mu(1-\rho)W_s} \\ &= e^{-1} \cong .368 \end{aligned}$$

Thus, under FCFS discipline, 36.8% of the customers will wait more than the average waiting time W_s. Naturally, this probability will change with the service discipline and, intuitively, should be higher for the SIRO and LCFS disciplines.

Exercise 15.5-2

In Example 15.5-1, find the following:

(a) The standard deviation of the waiting time in the system.
[*Ans.* Standard deviation = .5.]

(b) The probability that the waiting time in the system will vary by half a standard deviation around the mean value.
[*Ans.* Probability = .3834.]

15.5.2 $(M/M/1):(GD/N/\infty)$

The only difference between this model and the $(M/M/1):(GD/\infty/\infty)$ model is that the maximum number of customers allowed in the system is N (maximum queue length $= N - 1$). This means that once N customers are in the system, new arrivals either balk or are not permitted to join the queue. In terms of the generalized model, this situation translates to

$$\lambda_n = \begin{cases} \lambda, & n = 0, 1, 2, \ldots, N-1 \\ 0, & n = N, N+1, \ldots \end{cases}$$

$$\mu_n = \mu \qquad \text{for all } n = 0, 1, 2, \ldots$$

Letting $\rho = \lambda/\mu$, we thus get

$$p_n = \begin{cases} \rho^n p_0, & n \le N \\ 0, & n > N \end{cases}$$

The value of p_0 is determined from the equation

$$\sum_{n=0}^{N} p_n = 1, \quad \text{which yields} \quad p_0(1 + \rho + \rho^2 + \cdots + \rho^N) = 1$$

or

$$p_0 = \begin{cases} \dfrac{1-\rho}{1-\rho^{N+1}}, & \rho \neq 1 \\ \dfrac{1}{N+1}, & \rho = 1 \end{cases}$$

The formulas for p_n may then be summarized as

$$p_n = \begin{cases} \dfrac{1-\rho}{1-\rho^{N+1}}\rho^n, & \rho \neq 1 \\ \dfrac{1}{N+1}, & \rho = 1 \end{cases} \quad n = 0, 1, 2, \ldots, N \qquad (M/M/1):(GD/N/\infty)$$

Note that $\rho = \lambda/\mu$ need *not* be less than 1 as in the case of the $(M/M/1):(GD/\infty/\infty)$. Intuitively, we see this result because the number allowed in the system is controlled by the queue length ($= N - 1$), not by the relative rates of arrival and departure, λ and μ.

Using p_n above, we find that the expected number in the system is computed as follows:

$$\begin{aligned} L_s = E\{n\} &= \sum_{n=0}^{N} np_n \\ &= \frac{1-\rho}{1-\rho^{N+1}} \sum_{n=0}^{N} n\rho^n \\ &= \frac{1-\rho}{1-\rho^{N+1}} \rho \frac{d}{d\rho}\left(\frac{1-\rho^{N+1}}{1-\rho}\right) \\ &= \frac{\rho\{1-(N+1)\rho^N + N\rho^{N+1}\}}{(1-\rho)(1-\rho^{N+1})} \end{aligned}$$

or

$$L_s = \begin{cases} \dfrac{\rho\{1-(N+1)\rho^N + N\rho^{N+1}\}}{(1-\rho)(1-\rho^{N+1})}, & \rho \neq 1 \\ \dfrac{N}{2}, & \rho = 1 \end{cases}$$

The measures L_q, W_s, and W_q can be derived from L_s once the effective arrival rate λ_{eff} is determined. From Section 15.4.2 we have

$$\lambda_{\text{eff}} = \lambda(p_0 + p_1 + \cdots + p_{N-1}) + 0p_N$$

We thus get

$$\lambda_{\text{eff}} = \lambda(1 - p_N)$$

The formula for λ_{eff} makes sense because the probability of a customer *not* being able to join the system is p_N. Thus the ratio of customers that can join the system is $(1 - p_N)$, directly leading to the formula for λ_{eff}. Using L_s and λ_{eff}, we then obtain

$$L_q = L_s - \frac{\lambda_{\text{eff}}}{\mu} = L_s - \frac{\lambda(1 - p_N)}{\mu}$$

$$W_q = \frac{L_q}{\lambda_{\text{eff}}} = \frac{L_q}{\lambda(1 - p_N)}$$

$$W_s = W_q + \frac{1}{\mu} = \frac{L_s}{\lambda(1 - p_N)}$$

It can be shown that

$$\lambda_{\text{eff}} = \mu(L_s - L_q) = \lambda(1 - p_N)$$

(see Problem 15–58).

Example 15.5-2. Consider the car-wash facility of Example 15.5-1. Suppose that the facility has a total of four parking spaces. If the parking lot is full, newly arriving cars balk to seek service elsewhere.

Noting that $N = 4 + 1 = 5$, we find that the TORA output of the model is as given in Figure 15-6. A first piece of information that may interest the owner of the facility is to know how many customers are lost because of the limited parking space. Essentially, this would be equivalent to determining the value of λp_N or, equivalently, $\lambda - \lambda_{\text{eff}}$. From Figure 15-6,

$$\lambda - \lambda_{\text{eff}} = 4 - 3.8075 = .1925 \text{ car per hour}$$

```
Problem title: Example 15.5-2
Scenario 1 — (M/M/1):(GD/5/*)
-----------------------------------------------------------------
Lambda =     4.00000               Lambda eff =  3.80752
Mu =         6.00000               Rho =         0.66667

Ls =         1.42256               Lq =          0.78797
Ws =         0.37362               Wq =          0.20695
-----------------------------------------------------------------
Values of p(n) for n=0 to 5, else p(n) < .00001

  0 0.36541   1 0.24361   2 0.16241   3 0.10827   4 0.07218
  5 0.04812

Cumulative values of p(n) for n=0 to 5

  0 0.36541   1 0.60902   2 0.77143   3 0.87970   4 0.95188
  5 1.00000
```

Figure 15-6

or, based on an 8-hour day, the facility loses approximately 2 ($\simeq 8 \times .1925$) cars per day on the average or, $(2/4 \times 8) \times 100 = 6.25\%$ of all arriving cars per day. A decision regarding enlarging the parking lot beyond four spaces should thus be based on the "worth" of lost business.

The expected total time from the moment of arrival until a car is washed is $W_s = .3736$ hour (approximately 22 minutes), which is down from $W_s \simeq 30$ minutes when all arriving cars are allowed to join the facility (Example 15.5-1). This reduction of about 25% is achieved at the expense of losing an average of 6.25% of all arriving cars per day because of the unavailability of parking spaces. ◀

Exercise 15.5-3

In Example 15.5-2, compute:

(a) The probability that an arriving car will start service immediately upon arrival.
[*Ans.* .36541.]

(b) The expected waiting time until a service starts.
[*Ans.* 12.4 minutes.]

(c) The expected number of parking spaces occupied.
[*Ans.* .7879 space.]

15.5.3 $(M/M/c):(GD/\infty/\infty)$

In this model customers arrive at a constant rate λ and a maximum of c customers may be serviced simultaneously. The service rate per busy server is also constant and equal to μ. From Section 15.4.2, we get $\lambda_{\text{eff}} = \lambda$.

The ultimate effect of using c parallel servers is to "speed up" the rate of service by allowing simultaneous services. If the number of customers in the system, n, equals or exceeds c, the combined departure rate from the facility is $c\mu$. Else, if n is less than c, the service rate is $n\mu$. Thus, in terms of the generalized model (Section 15.4.1), we have

$$\lambda_n = \lambda, \qquad n \geq 0$$

$$\mu_n = \begin{cases} n\mu, & n \leq c \\ c\mu, & n \geq c \end{cases}$$

We thus compute p_n for $n \leq c$ as

$$p_n = \frac{\lambda^n}{\mu(2\mu)(3\mu)\cdots(n\mu)}\, p_0$$

$$= \frac{\lambda^n}{n!\mu^n}\, p_0$$

and for $n \geq c$, we have

$$p_n = \frac{\lambda^n}{\mu(2\mu)\cdots(c-1)\mu\underbrace{(c\mu)(c\mu)\cdots(c\mu)}_{(n-c)\text{ times}}}\, p_0$$

$$= \frac{\lambda^n}{c!c^{n-c}\mu^n}\, p_0$$

If we let $\rho = \lambda/\mu$, the value of p_0 is determined from $\sum_{n=0}^{\infty} p_n = 1$, which gives

$$p_0 = \left\{\sum_{n=0}^{c-1} \frac{\rho^n}{n!} + \frac{\rho^c}{c!} \sum_{n=c}^{\infty} \frac{\rho^{n-c}}{c^{n-c}}\right\}^{-1} = \left\{\sum_{n=0}^{c-1} \frac{\rho^n}{n!} + \frac{\rho^c}{c!} \sum_{j=0}^{\infty} \left(\frac{\rho}{c}\right)^j\right\}^{-1}$$

$$= \left\{\sum_{n=0}^{c-1} \frac{\rho^n}{n!} + \frac{\rho^c}{c!} \left(\frac{1}{1-\rho/c}\right)\right\}^{-1}, \qquad \frac{\rho}{c} < 1$$

Thus

$$p_n = \begin{cases} \left(\dfrac{\rho^n}{n!}\right) p_0, & 0 \le n \le c \\ \left(\dfrac{\rho^n}{c^{n-c} c!}\right) p_0, & n > c \end{cases} \qquad (M/M/c):(GD/\infty/\infty)$$

$$p_0 = \left\{\sum_{n=0}^{c-1} \frac{\rho^n}{n!} + \frac{\rho^c}{c!(1-\rho/c)}\right\}^{-1}$$

where

$$\frac{\rho}{c} < 1 \qquad \text{or} \qquad \frac{\lambda}{\mu c} < 1$$

The expression for L_q is obtained as follows:

$$L_q = \sum_{n=c}^{\infty} (n-c) p_n = \sum_{k=0}^{\infty} k p_{k+c} = \sum_{k=0}^{\infty} \frac{k\rho^{k+c}}{c^k c!} p_0$$

$$= p_0 \frac{\rho^c}{c!} \frac{\rho}{c} \sum_{k=0}^{\infty} k\left(\frac{\rho}{c}\right)^{k-1} = p_0 \frac{\rho^c}{c!} \frac{\rho}{c} \left[\frac{1}{(1-\rho/c)^2}\right]$$

$$= \left[\frac{\rho^{c+1}}{(c-1)!(c-\rho)^2}\right] p_0 = \left[\frac{c\rho}{(c-\rho)^2}\right] p_c$$

We thus get

$$L_q = \frac{\rho^{c+1}}{(c-1)!(c-\rho)^2} p_0 = \left[\frac{c\rho}{(c-\rho)^2}\right] p_c$$

$$L_s = L_q + \rho$$

$$W_q = \frac{L_q}{\lambda}$$

$$W_s = W_q + \frac{1}{\mu}$$

The computations associated with this model may be tedious. Morse (1958, p. 103) gives two useful approximations for p_0 and L_q. For ρ much smaller than 1,

$$p_0 \cong 1 - \rho \qquad \text{and} \qquad L_q \cong \frac{\rho^{c+1}}{c^2}$$

and for ρ/c very close to 1,

$$p_0 \cong \frac{(c-\rho)(c-1)!}{c^c} \qquad \text{and} \qquad L_q \cong \frac{\rho}{c-\rho}$$

Example 15.5-3. A small town is being serviced by two cab companies. Each of the two companies owns two cabs and are known to share the market almost equally. This is evident by the fact that calls arrive at each company's dispatching office at the rate of 10 per hour. The average time per ride is 11.5 minutes. Arrival of calls follows a Poisson distribution, whereas ride times are exponential.

The two companies were recently bought by an investor. The first action after taking over the two companies was to try to consolidate the two companies into one dispatching office in hope of providing faster service for customers. However, the new owner noticed that the utilization (ratio of hourly arriving calls to rides) for each company is

$$100\,\frac{\lambda}{c\mu} = \frac{100 \times 10}{2 \times (60/11.5)} = 95.8\%$$

(Note that each cab represents a server.) As a result, the cost of relocating the two companies in one office may not be justifiable because each of the current dispatching offices appears "quite busy," as evidenced by the high utilization factor.

To analyze the new owner's problem, we need in essence to make a comparison between the following two situations:

1. Two independent queues each of the type $(M/M/2):(GD/\infty/\infty)$ with $\lambda = 10$ calls per hour and $\mu = 5.217$ rides per hour.
2. One queue of the type $(M/M/4):(GD/\infty/\infty)$ with $\lambda = 2 \times 10 = 20$ calls per hour and $\mu = 5.217$ rides per hour.

Note that in both situations, μ represents the number of rides a *single* cab can provide per hour.

The utilization factor in the second situation is

$$\frac{100\lambda}{c\mu} = \frac{100 \times 20}{4 \times 5.217} = 95.8\%$$

which, of course, remains equal to the utilization factors when the two dispatching offices remain unconsolidated. This result seems to confirm the owner's suspicion that the consolidation is unjustified. However, if we consider other measures of performance, the picture will become different. Specifically, let us compute the expected waiting time until a customer gets a cab. Figures 15-7 provides the TORA outputs for the two scenarios.

The results show that $W_q = 2.161$ hours for the two-queue situation and 1.048 hours for the consolidated case. This means that the expected waiting time until a

Problem title: Example 15.5-3
Comparative measures: Nbr of scenarios = 2

Nbr	c	Lambda	Mu	l'da_eff	Ls	Ws	Lq	Wq
1	2	10.000	5.217	10.000	23.531	2.353	21.614	2.161
2	4	20.000	5.217	20.000	24.786	1.239	20.952	1.048

Figure 15-7

cab arrives is reduced by about 50%. The conclusion then is that **pooling of services** should normally result in a more effective operation in terms of offering faster service to the customer, even if the utilization of the separate facilities is high (i.e., 95.8% in our example). (Of course, the owner has more to be concerned about since, even after consolidating the two companies, waiting more than one hour for a 10-minute taxi ride is a bit much! Obviously, the fleet size needs to be increased.) ◀

Exercise 15.5-4

In Example 15.5-3, use TORA to find:

(a) The probability that *all* cabs in each of the two companies are "on call."
[*Ans.* .938.]

(b) The percentage of time *all* cabs in the consolidated company are "on call."
[*Ans.* .9093. It is interesting that the percentage of full occupancy is smaller when the two companies are consolidated into one pool, even though the waiting time W_q is halved.]

(c) Expected number of idle cabs for the two situations.
[*Ans.* .083 and .166.]

15.5.4 $(M/M/c):(GD/N/\infty)$, $c \leq N$

This queueing situation differs from $(M/M/c):(GD/\infty/\infty)$ in that a limit N is set on the capacity of the system (i.e., maximum queue size $= N - c$). In terms of the generalized model (Section 15.4.1), λ_n and μ_n for the current model are given by

$$\lambda_n = \begin{cases} \lambda, & 0 \leq n < N \\ 0, & n \geq N \end{cases}$$

$$\mu_n = \begin{cases} n\mu, & 0 \leq n \leq c \\ c\mu, & c \leq n \leq N \end{cases}$$

Substituting for λ_n and μ_n in the general expression for p_n and noting that $\rho = \lambda/\mu$, we get

$$p_n = \begin{cases} \dfrac{\rho^n}{n!}\, p_0, & 0 \leq n \leq c \\[2ex] \dfrac{\rho^n}{c!\,c^{n-c}}\, p_0, & c \leq n \leq N \end{cases} \qquad (M/M/c):(GD/N/\infty)$$

where

$$p_0 = \begin{cases} \left[\displaystyle\sum_{n=0}^{c-1} \frac{\rho^n}{n!} + \frac{\rho^c(1 - (\rho/c)^{N-c+1})}{c!(1 - \rho/c)}\right]^{-1}, & \rho/c \neq 1 \\[3ex] \left[\displaystyle\sum_{n=0}^{c-1} \frac{\rho^n}{n!} + \frac{\rho^c}{c!}(N - c + 1)\right]^{-1}, & \rho/c = 1 \end{cases}$$

Note that the only difference between p_n in this model and $(M/M/c):(GD/\infty/\infty)$ occurs in the expression for p_0. Note also that the *utilization factor* ρ/c need not be less than 1.

Next, we compute L_q as

$$L_q = \sum_{n=c+1}^{N} (n-c)p_n = \sum_{j=1}^{N-c} jp_{j+c} = p_0 \frac{\rho^c}{c!}\frac{\rho}{c}\sum_{j=1}^{N-c} j\left(\frac{\rho}{c}\right)^{j-1}$$

$$= p_0 \frac{\rho^{c+1}}{(c-1)!(c-\rho)^2}\left\{1-\left(\frac{\rho}{c}\right)^{N-c} - (N-c)\left(\frac{\rho}{c}\right)^{N-c}\left(1-\frac{\rho}{c}\right)\right\}$$

We thus have

$$L_q = \begin{cases} p_0 \dfrac{\rho^{c+1}}{(c-1)!(c-\rho)^2}\left\{1-\left(\dfrac{\rho}{c}\right)^{N-c} - (N-c)\left(\dfrac{\rho}{c}\right)^{N-c}\left(1-\dfrac{\rho}{c}\right)\right\}, & \rho/c \neq 1 \\ p_0 \dfrac{\rho^c(N-c)(N-c+1)}{2c!}, & \rho/c = 1 \end{cases}$$

$$L_s = L_q + (c - \bar{c}) = L_q + \frac{\lambda_{\text{eff}}}{\mu}$$

where

$$\bar{c} = \text{expected number of idle servers} = \sum_{n=0}^{c} (c-n)p_n$$

$$\lambda_{\text{eff}} = \lambda(1-p_N) = \mu(c-\bar{c})$$

Notice the interpretation of λ_{eff} in this case. Since $(c-\bar{c})$ represents the expected number of busy channels, $\mu(c-\bar{c})$ represents the actual number served per unit time and hence the effective arrival rate.

Example 15.5-4. In the consolidated cab company problem (Example 15.5-3), although the expected waiting time is excessive, the owner is unable to obtain funds for the purchase of additional cabs. To alleviate the problem of excessive waiting, however, the dispatching office is instructed to apologize to prospective customers for the unavailability of cabs once the waiting list reaches 16 customers.

To study the effect of the owner's decision on the waiting time, we realize that having a waiting list of 16 customers is equivalent to having 16 + 4 = 20 customers in the system, since the company has 4 cabs (servers). The queueing model thus reduces to $(M/M/4):(GD/20/\infty)$, where $\lambda = 20$ per hour and $\mu = 5.217$ per hour. The TORA output of the model is given in Figure 15-8.

The expected waiting time W_q before setting a limit on the capacity of the system was 1.05 hours, which is three times higher than the new expected waiting time of .303 hour ($\cong$ 18 minutes). Note that this remarkable reduction is achieved at the expense of losing about 3.4% of potential customers ($p_{20} = .03433$). Of course, the

```
Problem title: Example 15.5-4
Scenario 1 — (M/M/4):(GD/20/*)
_____________________________________________________________
Lambda =    20.00000                 Lambda eff =  19.31347
Mu =         5.21700                 Rho =          3.83362

Ls =         9.55634                 Lq =           5.85431
Ws =         0.49480                 Wq =           0.30312
_____________________________________________________________
Values of p(n) for n=0 to 20, else p(n) < .00001

 0 0.00753   1 0.02886   2 0.05531   3 0.07068   4 0.06774
 5 0.06492   6 0.06222   7 0.05963   8 0.05715   9 0.05478
10 0.05250  11 0.05031  12 0.04822  13 0.04622  14 0.04429
15 0.04245  16 0.04068  17 0.03899  18 0.03737  19 0.03582
20 0.03433

Cumulative values of p(n) for n=0 to 20

 0 0.00753   1 0.03638   2 0.09169   3 0.16237   4 0.23011
 5 0.29503   6 0.35726   7 0.41689   8 0.47404   9 0.52882
10 0.58132  11 0.63163  12 0.67985  13 0.72607  14 0.77036
15 0.81281  16 0.85349  17 0.89249  18 0.92986  19 0.96567
20 1.00000
```

Figure 15-8

result does not say how much effect, in the long run, the possible loss of customer's goodwill will have on the operation. ◀

Exercise 15.5-5

In Example 15.5-4 find

(a) The expected number of idle cabs.
[*Ans.* $\bar{c} = .298$.]

(b) The probability that a calling customer will be told that no cabs are available.
[*Ans.* $p_{20} = .03433$.]

15.5.5 $(M/M/\infty):(GD/\infty/\infty)$—SELF-SERVICE MODEL

In this model, the number of servers is unlimited because the customer is also the server. This normally is the case in self-service facilities. A typical example is taking the written part of a driver's license test. We must caution, however, that situations such as self-service gas stations or 24-hour banks do not fall under this model's category. This conclusion follows because in these situations, the servers really are the gas pump and the bank computer, even though the customer is the one who operates the equipment.

Again, in terms of the generalized model, we have

$$\lambda_n = \lambda, \quad \text{for all } n \geq 0$$
$$\mu_n = n\mu, \quad \text{for all } n \geq 0$$

Direct substitution in the expression for p_n yields

$$p_n = \frac{\lambda^n}{n!\,\mu^n} p_0 = \frac{\rho^n}{n!} p_0$$

Table 15-1

Measure	$\rho = .1$				$\rho = 9$			
	$M/M/10$	$M/M/20$	$M/M/50$	$M/M/\infty$	$M/M/10$	$M/M/20$	$M/M/50$	$M/M/\infty$
W_s	.1	.1	.1	.1	1.6	1.0	1.0	1.0
W_q	$.25 \times 10^{-18}$	$.18 \times 10^{-40}$	0	0	.668	.0001	$.6 \times 10^{-22}$	0
L_s	.1	.1	.1	.1	15.02	9.0	9.0	9.0
L_q	$.25 \times 10^{-18}$	$.18 \times 10^{-40}$	0	0	6.02	.0092	$.56 \times 10^{-21}$	0
p_0	.90484	.90484	.90484	.90484	.00007	.00012	.00012	.00012

Since $\sum_{n=0}^{\infty} p_n = 1$, it follows that

$$p_0 = \frac{1}{1 + \rho + \dfrac{\rho^2}{2!} + \cdots} = \frac{1}{e^{\rho}} = e^{-\rho}$$

As a result,

$$p_n = \frac{e^{-\rho}\rho^n}{n!}, \qquad n = 0, 1, 2, \ldots \qquad (M/M/\infty):(GD/\infty/\infty)$$

which is Poisson with mean $E\{n\} = \rho$. We also have

$$L_s = E\{n\} = \rho$$
$$W_s = \frac{1}{\mu}$$
$$L_q = W_q = 0$$

Note that $W_q = 0$ because of the self-service requirement. This is the reason W_s is equal to the mean service time $1/\mu$.

The results of the $(M/M/\infty):(GD/\infty/\infty)$ can be used to approximate those of the $(M/M/c):(GD/\infty/\infty)$ as c increases "sufficiently." The advantage is obvious, since the computations are much simpler in the $(M/M/\infty)$ model.

We demonstrate the relative accuracy of the approximation by presenting samples of the measures of performance for both models for different values of c and $\rho\ (= \lambda/\mu)$. Table 15-1 summarizes the results. (The last three elements of the Kendall notation are deleted for convenience.)

The computations show that as ρ becomes small (i.e., λ much less than μ), the $(M/M/\infty)$ model is a close approximation of the $(M/M/c)$ model even for c as small as 10.

15.5.6 $(M/M/R):(GD/K/K)$, $R < K$—MACHINE SERVICING MODEL

This model assumes that R repairpersons are available for servicing a total of K machines. Since a broken machine cannot generate new calls while in service, the model is an example of a finite calling source.

The model is a special case of the generalized model. If we define λ as the rate of breakdown *per machine*, we have

$$\lambda_n = \begin{cases} (K-n)\lambda, & 0 \le n \le K \\ 0, & n \ge K \end{cases}$$

$$\mu_n = \begin{cases} n\mu, & 0 \le n \le R \\ R\mu, & R \le n \le K \\ 0, & n > K \end{cases}$$

Substituting for λ_n and μ_n in the expression for p_n, we get (verify!)

$$p_n = \begin{cases} \binom{K}{n}\rho^n p_0, & 0 \le n \le R \\ \binom{K}{n}\dfrac{n!\rho^n}{R!R^{n-R}} p_0, & R \le n \le K \end{cases} \qquad (M/M/R):(GD/K/K)$$

$$p_0 = \left\{ \sum_{n=0}^{R} \binom{K}{n}\rho^n + \sum_{n=R+1}^{K} \binom{K}{n} \frac{n!\rho^n}{R!R^{n-R}} \right\}^{-1}$$

The other measures are given by

$$L_q = \sum_{n=R+1}^{K} (n-R)p_n$$

$$L_s = L_q + (R - \bar{R}) = L_q + \frac{\lambda_{\text{eff}}}{\mu} \qquad (R > 1)$$

where

$$\bar{R} = \text{expected number of idle repairpersons} = \sum_{n=0}^{R} (R-n)p_n$$

$$\lambda_{\text{eff}} = \mu(R - \bar{R}) = \lambda(K - L_s)$$

The second expression for λ_{eff} is obtained as follows. Since the arrival rate given n machines in the system is $\lambda(K-n)$ (where λ is the rate of breakdown per machine), under steady-state conditions

$$\lambda_{\text{eff}} = E\{\lambda(K-n)\} = \lambda(K - L_s)$$

The results apply to the case of a single repairperson simply by putting $R = 1$. In this case it can be shown that

$$L_q = K - \left(1 + \frac{1}{\rho}\right)(1 - p_0)$$

$$L_s = K - \frac{1 - p_0}{\rho} \qquad (R = 1)$$

```
Problem title: Example 15.5-6
Comparative measures: Nbr of scenarios = 4
```

Nbr	c	Lambda	Mu	l'da_eff	Ls	Ws	Lq	Wq
1	1	0.500	5.000	4.998	12.004	2.402	11.004	2.202
2	2	0.500	5.000	8.816	4.368	0.495	2.604	0.295
3	3	0.500	5.000	9.767	2.466	0.252	0.513	0.052
4	4	0.500	5.000	9.950	2.100	0.211	0.110	0.011

Figure 15-9

Example 15.5-5. A machine shop includes a total of 22 machines. On the average, an operative machine breaks down once every 2 hours. It takes 12 minutes on the average to effect a repair. The owner is interested in determining the number of repairpersons needed to keep the shop running "reasonably" smoothly.

We can analyze the situation by investigating the efficiency of the operation as a function of the number of repairpersons. Using TORA with $\lambda = .5$ breakdown per hour and $\mu = 5$ repairs per hour, Figure 15-9 summarizes some of the model's results as a function of $R = 1, 2, 3$, and 4.

In Figure 15-9, L_s essentially represents the average number of broken machines at any time. The *productivity* of the shop may thus be computed as the average number of working machines divided by the total number of machines in the shop. The following table summarizes the results (verify!).

Repairpersons, R	1	2	3	4
Shop Productivity (%)	45.44	80.15	88.79	90.45

Looking at these results, we see that by increasing the number of repairpersons from 1 to 2, the productivity of the shop jumps from the unacceptable level of 45.44% to the reasonable level of 80.15%. The marginal increase in productivity resulting from increasing R from 2 to 3 or from 3 to 4 is not as pronounced. We can thus conclude that the number of repair persons should at least equal 2. Any increase beyond this level should be based on the economics of increase in production as opposed to the added expenses of hiring extra repairpersons. This point will be discussed in more detail in Chapter 16.

In the computations in Figure 15-9, it may appear perplexing that λ_{eff}, the average rate of machine breakdown in the shop, increases with R. Observe that as the number of repair persons R increases, machines will be operative more often, thus increasing the frequency of making further repair calls. In fact, we can "dramatize" this point by citing the extreme case of having no repair persons at all, in which case λ_{eff} will be zero once all the machines are down. This example serves to demonstrate that λ_{eff} cannot be used in the present model as a measure of the effectiveness of the repair service. ◀

Exercise 15.5-6

In Example 15.5-5 with $R = 4$:

(a) Show how λ_{eff} is computed.

(b) Compute the expected number of idle repairpersons.
[*Ans.* 2.01.]

(c) Compute the probability that all repairpersons are busy.
[*Ans.* .1545.]

15.6 NON-POISSON QUEUES

Queueing models in which the arrival and/or departure process do not follow the Poisson assumptions lead to highly complex and, perhaps less tractable, analytical results. In general, it is advisable in such cases to use simulation as the tool for analyzing these situations (see Chapter 17).

In this section, we present one of the few non-Poisson queues for which analytic results are available. It deals with the $(M/G/1):(GD/\infty/\infty)$ in which the service time is described by a general probability distribution with mean $E\{t\}$ and variance $\text{var}\{t\}$. Unfortunately, the analysis of this situation is rather restricted in the sense that it does not provide a tractable analytic expression for the probabilities p_n. Instead, the results of this model only provide the basic measures of performance, including L_s, L_q, W, and W_q.

Let λ be arrival rate at the single-server facility, and given $E\{t\}$ and $\text{var}\{t\}$ as the mean and variance of the service-time distribution, it can be shown using sophisticated probability/Markov chain analysis that

$$L_s = \lambda E\{t\} + \frac{\lambda^2(E^2\{t\} + \text{var}\{t\})}{2(1 - \lambda E\{t\})} \qquad (M/G/1):(GD/\infty/\infty)$$

where $\lambda E\{t\} < 1$. This expression is known as the **Pollaczek–Khintchine (P–K) formula**. From this formula we can obtain other measures of performance, such as

$$W_s = \frac{L_s}{\lambda}$$

$$L_q = L - \lambda E\{t\}$$

$$W_q = \frac{L_q}{\lambda}$$

Note that the service rate $\mu = 1/E\{t\}$. The value of $\lambda_{\text{eff}} = \lambda$ in this model.

For the case where the service time is approximately constant, $\text{var}\{t\} = 0$ and the P–K formula reduces to

$$L_s = \rho + \frac{\rho^2}{2(1 - \rho)} \qquad (M/D/1):(GD/\infty/\infty)$$

where $\rho = \lambda/\mu$ and μ is the constant service rate.

If the service time is Erlang with parameters m and μ, meaning that $E\{t\} = 1/\mu$ and $\text{var}\{t\} = 1/m\mu^2$. The P–K formula yields

$$L = \rho + \frac{1 + m}{2m}\left(\frac{\rho}{1 - \rho}\right) \qquad (M/E_m/1):(GD/\infty/\infty)$$

Example 15.6-1. Suppose that in the car wash facility (Example 15.5-1), the washing is done by automatic machines, so that the service time may be considered the same and constant for all cars. The washing machine cycle takes 10 minutes exactly.

To analyze the situation, we note that $\lambda = 4$ per hour (see Example 15.5-1). On the other hand, since the service time is constant, we have $E\{t\} = 10/60 = 1/6$ hour and $\text{var}\{t\} = 0$. Thus

$$L_s = 4(1/6) + \frac{4^2[(1/6)^2 + 0]}{2(1 - 4/6)} = 1.333 \text{ cars}$$

$$L_q = 1.333 - (4/6) = .667 \text{ car}$$

$$W_s = \frac{1.333}{4} = .333 \text{ hour}$$

$$W_q = \frac{.667}{4} = .167 \text{ hour}$$

(You may also use TORA to obtain the results above.)

It is interesting that even though the arrival and departure rates ($\lambda = 4$ and $\mu = 1/E\{t\} = 6$) in this example exactly equal those of Example 15.5-1, where both arrivals and departures are Poisson, the expected waiting times are lower in the current situation, where service time is constant. Namely, we have

	Poisson Arrivals and Departures	Poisson Arrivals and Constant Service Time
W_s	.5 hour	.333 hour
W_q	.333 hour	.167 hour

This conclusion makes sense because a constant service time indicates *more certainty* in the operation of the facility, with the result that the expected waiting time is reduced. ◀

15.7 QUEUES WITH PRIORITIES FOR SERVICE

In queueing models with priority, it is assumed that several parallel queues are formed in front of the facility with each queue accounting for customers belonging to certain order of priority. If the facility has m queues, we assume that queue 1 has the highest priority for service, and queue m includes customers with lowest priority. Rates of arrival and service may vary for the different priority queues. However, we shall assume that customers within each queue are served on FCFS basis.

Priority service may follow one of two rules:

1. **Preemptive** rule, where the service of a lower-priority customer may be interrupted in favor of an arriving customer with higher priority.
2. **Nonpreemptive** rule, where a customer, once in service, will leave the facility only after the service is completed and regardless of the priority of newly arriving customers.

This section will not treat the preemptive case. Two nonpreemptive models applicable to single and multiple servers are presented. The single-server model assumes Poisson arrivals and arbitrary service distributions. In the multiple-server case, both arrivals and departures follow the Poisson distribution. The symbol NPRP is used with the Kendall notation to represent the nonpreemptive discipline; M_i and G_i stand for Poisson and arbitrary distributions.

15.7.1 $(M_i/G_i/1):(NPRP/\infty/\infty)$

Let $F_i(t)$ be the CDF of the arbitrary service time distribution for the ith queue ($i = 1, 2, \ldots, m$) and let $E_i\{t\}$ and $\text{var}_i\{t\}$ be the mean and variance, respectively. Let λ_i be the arrival rate at the ith queue per unit time.

Define $L_q^{(k)}$, $L_s^{(k)}$, $W_q^{(k)}$, and $W_s^{(k)}$ in the usual manner except that they now represent the measures of the kth queue. Then the results of this situation are given by

$$W_q^{(k)} = \frac{\sum_{i=1}^{m} \lambda_i(E_i^2\{t\} + \text{var}_i\{t\})}{2(1 - S_{k-1})(1 - S_k)}$$

$$L_q^{(k)} = \lambda_k W_q^{(k)} \qquad (M_i/G_i/1):(NPRP/\infty/\infty)$$

$$W_s^{(k)} = W_q^{(k)} + E_k\{t\}$$

$$L_s^{(k)} = L_q^{(k)} + \rho_k$$

where

$$\rho_k = \lambda_k E_k\{t\}$$

$$S_k = \sum_{i=1}^{k} \rho_i < 1, \qquad k = 1, 2, \ldots, m$$

$$S_0 \equiv 0$$

Notice that W_q, the expected waiting time in the queue for *any* customer regardless of priority, is given by

$$W_q = \sum_{k=1}^{m} \frac{\lambda_k}{\lambda} W_q^{(k)}$$

where $\lambda = \sum_{i=1}^{m} \lambda_i$ and λ_k/λ is the relative weight of $W_q^{(k)}$. A similar result applies to W_s.

Example 15.7-1. Jobs arrive at a production facility in three categories: rush order, regular order, and low-priority order. Although rush jobs are processed prior to any other job and regular jobs take precedence over low-priority orders, any job, once started, must be completed before a new job is taken in. Arrival of orders from the three categories are Poisson with means 4, 3, and 1 per day. The respective service rates are constant and equal to 10, 9, and 5 per day.

In this queueing situation, we have three nonpreemptive priority queues. Assume that queues 1, 2, and 3 represent the three job categories in the order given in the description of the problem. We thus have

$$\rho_1 = \lambda_1 E\{t_1\} = 4(1/10) = .4$$
$$\rho_2 = 3(1/9) = .333$$
$$\rho_3 = 1(1/5) = .2$$

We also have

$$S_1 = \rho_1 = .4$$
$$S_2 = \rho_1 + \rho_2 = .733$$
$$S_3 = \rho_1 + \rho_2 + \rho_3 = .933$$

Since $S_3 > 1$, the system can reach steady-state conditions.

We can thus compute the expected waiting time in each queue as follows. Since

$$\sum_{i=1}^{m} \lambda_i(E_i^2\{t\} + \text{var}_i\{t\}) = 4[(1/10)^2 + 0] + 3[(1/9)^2 + 0] + 1[(1/5)^2 + 0] = .117$$

we get

$$W_q^1 = \frac{.117}{2(1-0)(1-.4)} = .0975 \text{ day} \cong 2.34 \text{ hours}$$

$$W_q^2 = \frac{.117}{2(1-.4)(1-.733)} = .365 \text{ day} \cong 8.77 \text{ hours}$$

$$W_q^3 = \frac{.117}{2(1-.733)(1-.933)} = 3.27 \text{ days} \simeq 78.5 \text{ hours}$$

The expected overall waiting time for *any* customer regardless of priority is given by

$$W_q = \frac{4 \times 2.34 + 3 \times 8.77 + 1 \times 78.5}{4 + 3 + 1} = 14.27 \text{ hours}$$

We can also obtain the average number of jobs awaiting processing in each priority queue.

$$L_q^1 = 4 \times .0975 = .39 \text{ job}$$
$$L_q^2 = 3 \times .365 = 1.095 \text{ jobs}$$
$$L_q^3 = 1 \times 3.27 = 3.27 \text{ jobs}$$

◀

15.7.2 $(M_i/M/c):(NPRP/\infty/\infty)$

This model assumes that all customers have the same service time distribution regardless of their priorities and that all c channels have identical exponential service distribution with service rate μ. The arrivals at the kth priority queue occur according to a Poisson distribution with an arrival rate λ_k, $k = 1, 2, \ldots, m$. It can be shown for the kth queue that

$$W_q^{(k)} = \frac{E\{\xi_0\}}{(1 - S_{k-1})(1 - S_k)}, \qquad k = 1, 2, \ldots, m$$

where $S_0 \equiv 0$ and

$$S_k = \sum_{i=1}^{k} \frac{\lambda_i}{c\mu} < 1, \qquad \text{for all } k$$

$$E\{\xi_0\} = \frac{1}{\mu c\left[\rho^{-c}(c-\rho)(c-1)!\sum_{n=0}^{c-1}\frac{\rho^n}{n!} + 1\right]}, \qquad \rho = \frac{\lambda}{\mu}$$

Example 15.7-2. To illustrate the computations in the model, suppose that we have three priority queues with arrival rates $\lambda_1 = 2$, $\lambda_2 = 5$, and $\lambda_3 = 10$ per day. There are two servers and the service rate is 10 per day. Both arrivals and departures follow Poisson distributions.

$$S_1 = \frac{\lambda_1}{c\mu} = \frac{2}{2 \times 10} = .1$$

$$S_2 = S_1 + \frac{\lambda_2}{c\mu} = .1 + \frac{5}{2 \times 10} = .35$$

$$S_3 = S_2 + \frac{\lambda_3}{c\mu} = .35 + \frac{10}{2 \times 10} = .85$$

Since all $S_i < 1$, steady state can be reached.

Now, by definition

$$\rho = \frac{\lambda_1 + \lambda_2 + \lambda_3}{\mu} = \frac{17}{10} = 1.7$$

Hence

$$E\{\xi_0\} = \frac{1}{10 \times 2\{(1.7)^{-2}(2-1.7)(1!)(1+1.7)+1\}} = .039$$

Thus

$$W_q^{(1)} = \frac{.039}{(1-.1)} = .0433$$

$$W_q^{(2)} = \frac{.039}{(1-.1)(1-.35)} = .0665$$

$$W_q^{(3)} = \frac{.039}{(1-.35)(1-.85)} = .4$$

The waiting time in the queue for *any* customer is then given by

$$W_q = \frac{\lambda_1}{\lambda} W_q^{(1)} + \frac{\lambda_2}{\lambda} W_q^{(2)} + \frac{\lambda_3}{\lambda} W_q^{(3)}$$

$$= \frac{2}{17}(.0433) + \frac{5}{17}(.0665) + \frac{10}{17}(.4) = .26$$

Finally, the expected number waiting in the queue for the entire system is given by

$$L_q = \lambda W_q = 17 \times .26 = 4.42$$

◀

15.8 TANDEM OR SERIES QUEUES

This section considers Poisson queues with service stations arranged in series so that the customer must pass through all stations before completing service. We first present the simple case of two series stations where no queues are allowed. Next, we present an important result for serial Poisson queues with no queue limit.

15.8.1 TWO-STATION SERIES MODEL WITH ZERO QUEUE CAPACITY

As an example of the analysis of queues in series, consider a simplified one-channel queueing system consisting of two series stations as shown in Figure 15-10. A customer arriving for service must go through station 1 and station 2. Service times at each station are exponentially distributed with the same service rate μ. Arrivals occur according to a Poisson distribution with rate λ. No queues are allowed in front of station 1 or station 2.

Construction of the model requires first that the states of the system at any point in time be identified. This is accomplished as follows. Each station may be either free or busy. Station 1 is said to be blocked if the customer in this station completes service before station 2 becomes free. Let the symbols 0, 1, and b represent the free, busy, and blocked states, respectively. Let i and j represent the states of station 1 and station 2. Then the states of the system are given by

$$\{(i, j)\} = \{(0, 0), (1, 0), (0, 1), (1, 1), (b, 1)\}$$

Define $p_{ij}(t)$ as the probability that the system is in state (i, j) at time t. The transition probabilities between times t and $t + h$ (h is a small positive increment in time) are summarized as shown in Table 15-2. The empty squares indicate that transitions between the indicated states at t and $t + h$ are impossible ($= 0$).

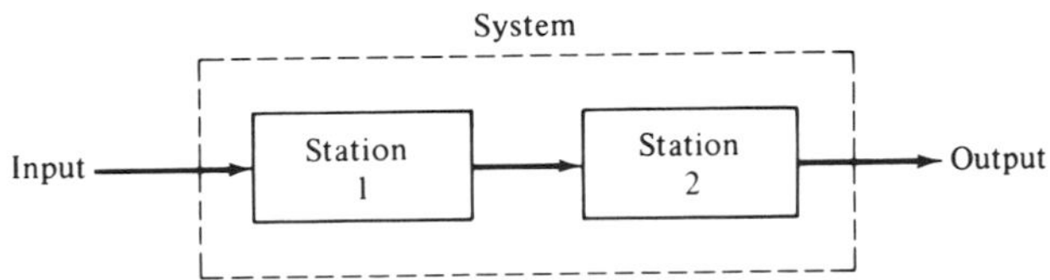

Figure 15-10

Table 15-2

	States at $(t + h)$: $(0, 0)$	$(0, 1)$	$(1, 0)$	$(1, 1)$	$(b, 1)$
States at t: $(0, 0)$	$1 - \lambda h$		λh		
$(0, 1)$	$\mu h(1 - \lambda h)$	$1 - \mu h - \lambda h$		$\lambda h(1 - \mu h)$	
$(1, 0)$		$\mu h(1 - \lambda h)$	$1 - \mu h$		
$(1, 1)$		$\mu h(1 - \lambda h)$	μh	$(1 - \mu h)(1 - \mu h)$	μh
$(b, 1)$		$\mu h(1 - \lambda h)$			$1 - \mu h$

The following equations can now be established (neglecting the terms in h^2):

$$p_{00}(t+h) = p_{00}(t)(1-\lambda h) + p_{01}(t)(\mu h)$$
$$p_{01}(t+h) = p_{01}(t)(1-\mu h-\lambda h) + p_{10}(t)(\mu h) + p_{b1}(t)(\mu h)$$
$$p_{10}(t+h) = p_{00}(t)(\lambda h) + p_{10}(t)(1-\mu h) + p_{11}(t)(\mu h)$$
$$p_{11}(t+h) = p_{01}(t)(\lambda h) + p_{11}(t)(1-2\mu h)$$
$$p_{b1}(t+h) = p_{11}(t)(\mu h) + p_{b1}(t)(1-\mu h)$$

By rearranging the terms and taking the appropriate limits, the steady-state equations are given by

$$\begin{aligned} p_{01} - \rho p_{00} &= 0 \\ p_{10} + p_{b1} - (1+\rho)p_{01} &= 0 \\ \rho p_{00} + p_{11} - p_{10} &= 0 \\ \rho p_{01} - 2p_{11} &= 0 \\ p_{11} - p_{b1} &= 0 \end{aligned}$$

One of these equations is redundant. Hence adding the condition

$$p_{00} + p_{01} + p_{10} + p_{11} + p_{b1} = 1$$

the solution for p_{ij} is given by

$$p_{00} = \frac{2}{A}$$
$$p_{01} = \frac{2\rho}{A}$$
$$p_{10} = \frac{\rho^2 + 2\rho}{A}$$
$$p_{11} = p_{b1} = \frac{\rho^2}{A}$$

where

$$A = 3\rho^2 + 4\rho + 2$$

The expected number in the system may then be obtained as

$$L_s = 0p_{00} + 1(p_{01} + p_{10}) + 2(p_{11} + p_{b1}) = \frac{5\rho^2 + 4\rho}{A}$$

Example 15.8-1. A two-station subassembly line is operated by a conveyor belt system. The size of the assembled product does not permit storing more than one unit in each station. The product arrives to the subassembly line from another production facility according to a Poisson distribution with mean 10 per hour. The assembly times at stations 1 and 2 are exponential with mean 5 minutes each. All arriving items that cannot enter the assembly line directly are diverted to other subassembly lines.

Since $\lambda = 10$ per hour and $\mu = 60/5 = 12$ per hour, we have $\rho = \lambda/\mu = 10/12 = .833$. We can compute all the probabilities by noting that

$$A = 3(.833)^2 + 4(.833) + 2 = 7.417$$

Thus

$$p_{00} = \frac{2}{7.417} = .2697$$

$$p_{01} = \frac{2 \times .833}{7.417} = .2247$$

$$p_{10} = \frac{.833^2 + 2 \times .833}{7.417} = .3183$$

$$p_{11} = p_{b1} = \frac{.833^2}{7.417} = .0936$$

The probability that an arriving item will enter station 1 is $p_{00} + p_{01} = .2697 + .2247 = .4944$ so that the effective arrival rate is $\lambda_{\text{eff}} = .4944 \times 10 = 4.944$ jobs per hour. Since

$$L_s = \frac{5 \times .833^2 + 4 \times .833}{7.417} = .917$$

it follows that the waiting time in the system is

$$W_s = \frac{L_s}{\lambda_{\text{eff}}} = \frac{.917}{4.944} = .185 \text{ hour}$$

Observe that W_s represents the expected service time per item since no queues are allowed. We note that an item can be serviced in an average time of $5 + 5 = 10$ minutes or .167 hour provided that station 1 is not blocked. Thus the difference between W_s $(= .185)$ and .167 may actually be regarded as the average time an item waits because of the blockage of state 2; that is, $.185 - .167 = .018$ hour or 1.08 minutes. ◀

Exercise 15.8-1

In the two-station series-queues model of Example 15.8-1, determine a general condition relating λ and μ such that the probability of an arriving item joining station 1 directly is higher than the probability of the item being diverted to other subassembly lines.
[*Ans.* $\lambda < .816\mu$.]

15.8.2 *k*-STATION SERIES MODEL WITH INFINITE QUEUE CAPACITY

In this section we state without proof a theorem that is applicable to a k-station series with unlimited interqueue capacity. [See Saaty (1961, Secs. 12-2 to 12-4) for the proof.]

Consider a system with k stations in series, as shown in Figure 15-11. Assume that arrivals at station 1 are generated from an infinite population according to a

Figure 15-11

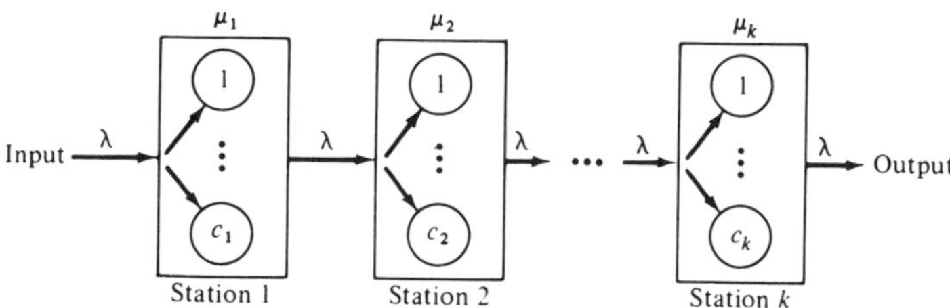

Figure 15-12

Poisson distribution with mean arrival rate λ. Serviced units will move successively from one station to the next until they are discharged from station k. Service time distribution at each station i is exponential with mean rate μ_i, $i = 1, 2, \ldots, k$. Further, there is no queue limit at any station.

Under these conditions, it can be proved that, for all i, the output from station i (or, equivalently, the input to station $i + 1$) is Poisson with mean rate λ and that each station may be treated *independently* as $(M/M_i/1):(GD/\infty/\infty)$. This means that for the ith station, the steady-state probabilities p_{n_i} are given by

$$p_{n_i} = (1 - \rho_i)\rho_i^{n_i}, \qquad n_i = 0, 1, 2, \ldots$$

for $i = 1, 2, \ldots, k$, where n_i is the number in the system consisting of station i only. Steady-state results will exist only if $\rho_i = \lambda/\mu_i < 1$.

The same result can be extended to the case where station i includes c_i parallel servers, each with the same exponential service rate μ_i per unit time (see Figure 15-12). In this case each station may be treated independently as $(M/M_i/c_i):(GD/\infty/\infty)$ with mean arrival rate λ. Again, the steady-state results of Section 15.5.1 will prevail only if $\lambda < c_i\mu_i$, for $i = 1, 2, \ldots, k$.

Example 15.8-2. In a production line with five series stations, jobs arrive at station 1 according to a Poisson distribution with mean rate $\lambda = 20$ per hour. The production time in each station is exponential with mean 2 minutes. The output from station i is used as input to station $i + 1$. The portion of good items produced at station i is taken as α_i of the total input to the same station. The remaining portion, $(1 - \alpha_i)$, is defective and is discarded as scrap.

Suppose that we are interested in the size of the storage space between successive stations that will accommodate all incoming items 100β percent of the time. The probability p_{n_i} of n_i items in station i is given by

$$p_{n_i} = (1 - \rho_i)\rho_i^{n_i}$$

where $\rho_i = \lambda_i/\mu_i$. Thus the storage requirement is satisfied if the storage space for station i accommodates $N_i - 1$ items, where N_i is determined from

$$\sum_{n_i=1}^{N_i} p_{n_i} = \sum_{n_i=1}^{N_i} (1 - \rho_i)\rho_i^{n_i} \geq \beta, \qquad i = 1, 2, \ldots, 5$$

Upon simplification, we get (verify)

$$N_i \geq \frac{\ln(1-\beta)}{\ln \rho_i} - 1, \qquad i = 1, 2, \ldots, 5$$

Suppose that $\alpha_i = .9$; then

$$\begin{aligned}
\lambda_1 &= \lambda = 20 \\
\lambda_2 &= \alpha_1 \lambda_1 = 20\alpha_1 = 18 \\
\lambda_3 &= \alpha_2 \alpha_1 \lambda_1 = 20\alpha_1\alpha_2 = 16.2 \\
\lambda_4 &= 20\alpha_1\alpha_2\alpha_3 = 14.58 \\
\lambda_5 &= 20\alpha_1\alpha_2\alpha_3\alpha_4 = 13.12
\end{aligned}$$

Since $\mu_i = \mu = 30$ per hour, we have

$$\rho_1 = .67, \quad \rho_2 = .6, \quad \rho_3 = .54, \quad \rho_4 = .486, \quad \rho_5 = .437$$

If we want to establish storage for all incoming items 99% of the time (i.e., $\beta = .99$), the limits on N_i can thus be computed as

$$N_1 \geq 10.499 \ (\cong 11), \quad N_2 \geq 8, \quad N_3 \geq 6.47 \ (\cong 7),$$
$$N_4 \geq 5.38 \ (\cong 6), \quad N_5 \geq 4.57 \ (\cong 5)$$ ◀

Exercise 15.8-2

In Example 15.8-2, find the expected number of defective items that will accumulate each day from all stations.
[*Ans.* Approximately 197 items.]

15.9 SUMMARY

Queueing theory provides models for analyzing the operation of service facilities in which arrival and/or service of customers occur randomly. The numerical examples introduced throughout the chapter show that queueing analysis yields results that may not be obvious intuitively.

The Poisson and exponential distributions play important roles in queueing analysis. They characterize service facilities in which both arrivals and service are *completely random.* Although other distributions can be implemented in queueing models, the analysis is much more complex than in the Poisson queues. Additionally, the complexity of the analysis does not permit securing as much information as in the Poisson models.

The big question regarding queueing theory is how good it is in practice. The limitations imposed by the mathematical analysis seem to make it difficult to find real applications that fit the model. Nevertheless, many successful queueing applications have been reported over the years. In Chapter 16 we address this point by presenting the use of queueing theory in practice.

SELECTED REFERENCES

Gross, D., and C. Harris, *Fundamentals of Queueing Theory*, 2nd ed., Wiley, New York, 1985.

HALL, R., *Queueing Methods for Service and Manufacturing*, Prentice Hall, Englewood Cliffs, N.J., 1991.
KENDALL, D. G., "Stochastic Processes Occurring in the Theory of Queues and Their Analysis by the Method of Markov Chains," *Annals of Mathematical Statistics*, Vol. 24, pp. 338–354, 1953.
LEE, A., *Applied Queueing Theory*, Macmillan, Toronto, Canada, 1966.
MORSE, P., *Queues, Inventories, and Maintenance*, Wiley, New York, 1958.
PARZEN, E., *Stochastic Processes*, Holden-Day, San Francisco, 1962.
SAATY, T., *Elements of Queueing Theory*, McGraw-Hill, New York, 1961.

NUMERICAL PROBLEMS†

Section	Assigned Problems
15.1	15–1 to 15–4
15.2	15–5 to 15–8
15.3.1	15–9 to 15–12
15.3.2	15–13 to 15–15
15.4	15–16, 15–18
15.5.1	15–19 to 15–23
15.5.2	15–24 to 15–27
15.5.3	15–28 to 15–32
15.5.4	15–33, 15–34
15.5.5	15–35, 15–36
15.5.6	15–37 to 15–39
15.6	15–40 to 15–42
15.7	15–43 to 15–45
15.8	15–46 to 15–50

□ **15–1** In each of the following situations, identify the basic elements of the queueing model (i.e., customer, server, design of the facility, service discipline, and limits on the calling source and queue).

(a) Shoppers in front of checkout stands in a supermarket.
(b) Cars waiting at a stop light.
(c) An outpatient clinic.
(d) Planes taking off in an airport.
(e) Toll gates on a superhighway.
(f) A computer center.
(g) 24-hour bank tellers.

□ **15–2** Study the following system and identify all the associated queueing situations. For each situation, define the customers, the server(s), the service discipline, the service time, the maximum queue length, and the calling source.

Orders for jobs are received at a workshop for processing. Upon receipt, the supervisor decides whether it is a rush job or a regular job. Some of these orders require use of one type of machine, of which several are available. The remaining orders are processed in a two-stage production line, of which only two are available.

† You are encouraged to use TORA whenever possible in all the problems of this chapter.

In each of the two groups, one facility is especially assigned to handle rush jobs. Jobs arriving at any facility are processed in order of arrival. Completed orders are shipped upon arrival from a terminal shipping zone having a limited capacity.

Sharpened tools for the different machines are supplied from a central tool crib, where operators exchange old tools for new ones. When a machine breaks down, a repairperson is called from the service pool to attend it. Machines working on rush orders always receive priorities both in acquiring new tools from the crib and in receiving repair service.

☐ **15–3** In Problem 15–1, describe what constitutes the interarrival and service time distributions for each queueing situation.

☐ **15–4** Discuss the possibilities of balking, reneging, and/or jockeying, if any, in each of the following situations.

(a) Customers awaiting service in a multiteller bank.
(b) Legal cases awaiting trial dates in a court.
(c) Individuals lining up in front of several elevators in a large building.
(d) Planes awaiting takeoff on a runway.

☐ **15–5** Customers arrive in a Poisson stream at a state revenue office. The rate of arrival between 8:00 A.M. and 10:00 P.M. is 20 per hour. Compute the following:

(a) The average number of arriving customers during the 2-hour period.
(b) The probability that no customer will arrive between 8:00 and 8:10.
(c) The probability that one customer will arrive between 8:10 and 8:20 given that no customers have arrived between 8:00 and 8:10.

☐ **15–6** Customers arrive at a restaurant according to a Poisson distribution at the rate of 20 per hour. The restaurant opens for business at 11:00 A.M. Find the following:

(a) The probability of having 20 customers in the restaurant at 11:12 A.M. given that there were 18 at 11:07 A.M.
(b) The probability a new customer will arrive between 11:28 and 11:30 A.M. given that the last customer arrived at 11:25 A.M.

☐ **15–7** Consider the following probabilities taken from a Poisson distribution with $\lambda = 2$ arrivals/hour and $t = 1$ hour.

n	0	1	2	3	4	5	6	7	8	9
p_n	.135	.271	.271	.181	.090	.036	.012	.003	.001	.0002

Show numerically that the mean and variance of the distribution equal $\lambda t = 2$, a unique property of the Poisson distribution.

☐ **15–8** During a very small time interval h, at most one arrival can occur. The probability of an arrival occurring is directly proportional to h with the proportionality constant equal to 2. Determine the following:

(a) The average time between two successive arrivals.
(b) The probability that no arrivals occurs during a period of .5 time unit.
(c) The probability that time between two successive arrivals is at least 3 time units.

(d) The probability that the time between two successive arrivals is at most 2 time units.

☐ **15–9** Two employees, Ann and Jim, of a fast-food restaurant play the following game while waiting for customers to arrive. Jim pays Ann 1 cent if the next customer does not arrive within 1 minute; otherwise, Ann pays Jim 1 cent. Determine Jim's expected gain in an 8-hour period assuming that the customers arrive according to a Poisson distribution with mean rate one per minute.

☐ **15–10** Consider Problem 15–9. Suppose the game is such that Jim would pay Ann 1 cent if the next customer arrives after 1.5 minutes, whereas Ann would pay Jim 1 cent if the next customer's arrival is within 1 minute. Determine Jim's expected winnings in an 8-hour period.

☐ **15–11** Customers arrive at a facility according to a Poisson distribution at the rate of two an hour. Find the following:

(a) The average number of customers arriving in an 8-hour period.
(b) The probability that there will be at least one customer in a 1-hour period.

☐ **15–12** Books previously ordered arrive at a university library according to a Poisson distribution at the rate of 25 books per day. Each shelf in the stacks can hold 100 books. Determine the following:

(a) The expected number of shelves that will be stacked with new books each month.
(b) The probability that more than 10 bookcases will be needed each month given that a bookcase has five shelves.

☐ **15–13** Inventory is withdrawn from a stock of 80 items according to a Poisson distribution at the rate of 5 items a day.

(a) Find the probability that 10 items are withdrawn during the first 2 days.
(b) Determine the probability that no items are left at the end of 4 days.
(c) Determine the *average* number of items withdrawn over a 4-day period.

☐ **15–14** A machine shop has just stocked 10 spare parts for the repair of a machine. Stock replenishments of size 10 pieces each take place every 7 days. The Poisson breakdown of the machine occurs three times a week on the average. Determine the probability that the machine will remain broken because of the unavailability of parts for 2 days, for 5 days.

☐ **15–15** Demand for an item occurs according to a Poisson distribution with mean 3 a day. The maximum stock level is 25 items, which occurs on each Monday, immediately after a new order is received. The order size thus depends on the number of units left at the end of work week on Saturday (the business is closed on Sundays). Determine the following:

(a) The *average* weekly size of the orders.
(b) The probability of incurring shortage in demand after 4 working days.
(c) The probability that the weekly order size will exceed 5 units.

☐ **15–16** In a queueing situation, the system can hold no more than 4 customers. The arrival rate is $\lambda = 10$ per hour and the departure rate is $\mu = 5$ per hour. Both rates are independent of the number in the system n. Assume that the arrival and departure processes follow a Poisson distribution. Draw the complete transition-rate diagram; then determine the following:

(a) The set of balance equations describing the system.
(b) The steady-state probabilities.
(c) The expected number in the system L_s.
(d) The effective arrival rate λ_{eff}.
(e) The expected waiting time in the queue W_q.

□ **15–17** Repeat Problem 15–16 assuming that $\lambda_n = 10 - n$, $n = 0, 1, 2, 3$ and $\mu_n = 5 + n/2$, $n = 1, 2, 3, 4$. This situation is equivalent to reducing the arrival rate and increasing the service rate as the number in the system, n, increases.

□ **15–18** Repeat Problem 15–16 for a simplified single-queue model in which the service mechanism that allows only *one* customer in the system. Customers who arrive while the facility is busy leave and never return. Assume that customers arrive according to a Poisson distribution with mean λ per unit time and that the service time is exponential with mean value equal to $1/\mu$ time units.

□ **15–19** A fast-food restaurant has *one* drive-in window. It is estimated that cars arrive according to a Poisson distribution at the rate of 2 every 5 minutes and that there is enough space to accommodate a line of 10 cars. Other arriving cars can wait outside this space, if necessary. It takes 1.5 minutes on the average to fill an order, but the service time actually varies according to an exponential distribution. Determine the following:

(a) The probability that the facility is idle.
(b) The expected number of customers waiting but currently not being served.
(c) The expected waiting time until a customer can place his order at the window.
(d) The probability that the waiting line will exceed the capacity of the space leading to the drive-in window.

□ **15–20** Cars arrive at a toll gate on a freeway according to a Poisson distribution with mean 90 per hour. Average time for passing through the gate is 38 seconds. Drivers complain of the long waiting time. Authorities are willing to decrease the passing time through the gate to 30 seconds by introducing new automatic devices. This can be justified only if under the old system the number of waiting cars exceeds 5. In addition, the percentage of the gate's idle time under the new system should not exceed 10%. Can the new device be justified?

□ **15–21** Customers arrive at a one-window drive-in bank according to a Poisson distribution with mean 10 per hour. Service time per customer is exponential with mean 5 minutes. There are three spaces in front of the window, including that for the car being serviced. Other arriving cars can wait outside these three spaces.

(a) What is the probability that an arriving customer can enter one of the three spaces in front of the window?
(b) What is the probability that an arriving customer will have to wait outside the three spaces?
(c) How long is an arriving customer expected to wait before starting service?
(d) How many car spaces should be provided in front of the window so that an arriving customer can wait in front of the window at least 20% of the time?

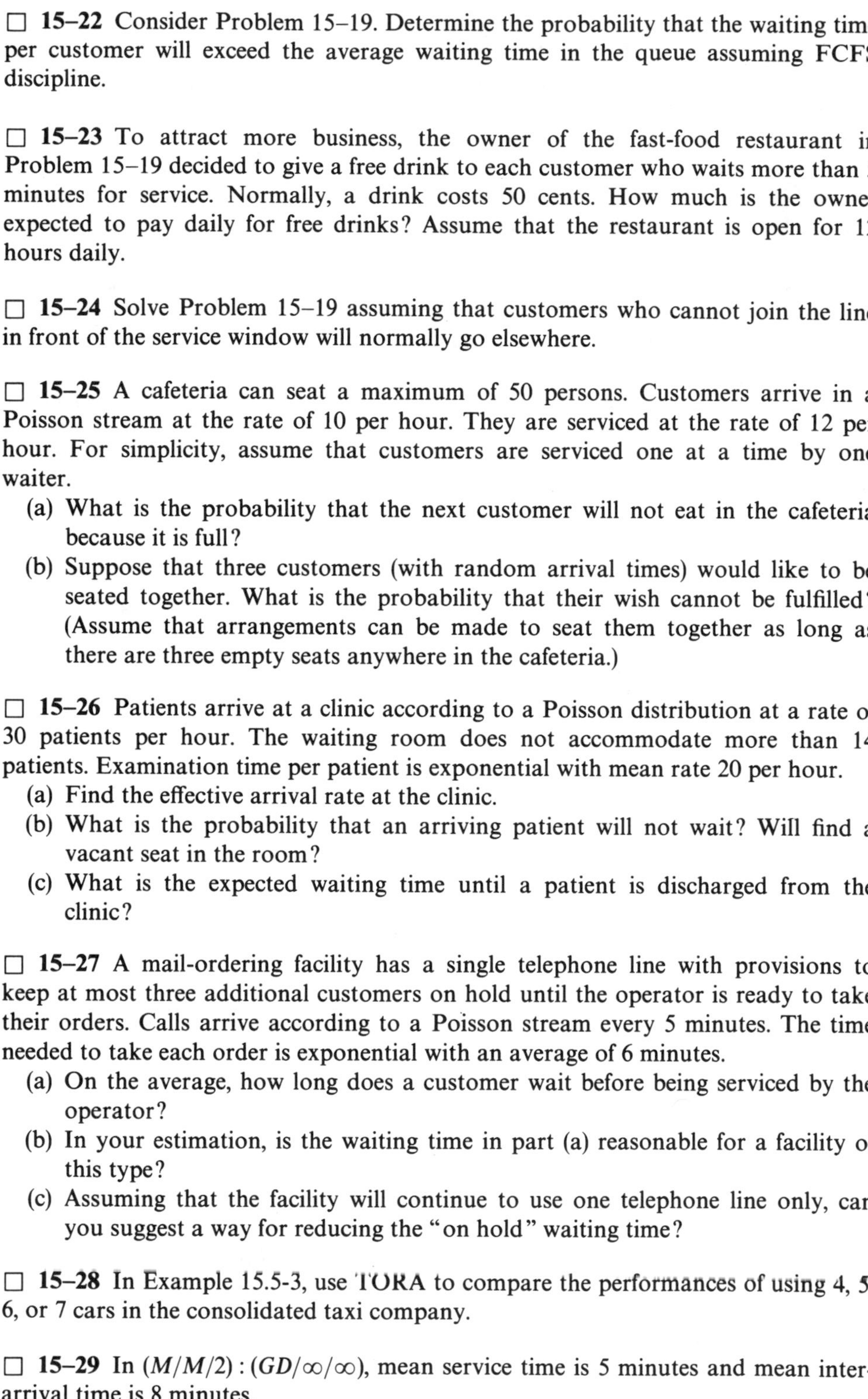

□ **15–22** Consider Problem 15–19. Determine the probability that the waiting time per customer will exceed the average waiting time in the queue assuming FCFS discipline.

□ **15–23** To attract more business, the owner of the fast-food restaurant in Problem 15–19 decided to give a free drink to each customer who waits more than 5 minutes for service. Normally, a drink costs 50 cents. How much is the owner expected to pay daily for free drinks? Assume that the restaurant is open for 12 hours daily.

□ **15–24** Solve Problem 15–19 assuming that customers who cannot join the line in front of the service window will normally go elsewhere.

□ **15–25** A cafeteria can seat a maximum of 50 persons. Customers arrive in a Poisson stream at the rate of 10 per hour. They are serviced at the rate of 12 per hour. For simplicity, assume that customers are serviced one at a time by one waiter.

(a) What is the probability that the next customer will not eat in the cafeteria because it is full?
(b) Suppose that three customers (with random arrival times) would like to be seated together. What is the probability that their wish cannot be fulfilled? (Assume that arrangements can be made to seat them together as long as there are three empty seats anywhere in the cafeteria.)

□ **15–26** Patients arrive at a clinic according to a Poisson distribution at a rate of 30 patients per hour. The waiting room does not accommodate more than 14 patients. Examination time per patient is exponential with mean rate 20 per hour.

(a) Find the effective arrival rate at the clinic.
(b) What is the probability that an arriving patient will not wait? Will find a vacant seat in the room?
(c) What is the expected waiting time until a patient is discharged from the clinic?

□ **15–27** A mail-ordering facility has a single telephone line with provisions to keep at most three additional customers on hold until the operator is ready to take their orders. Calls arrive according to a Poisson stream every 5 minutes. The time needed to take each order is exponential with an average of 6 minutes.

(a) On the average, how long does a customer wait before being serviced by the operator?
(b) In your estimation, is the waiting time in part (a) reasonable for a facility of this type?
(c) Assuming that the facility will continue to use one telephone line only, can you suggest a way for reducing the "on hold" waiting time?

□ **15–28** In Example 15.5-3, use TORA to compare the performances of using 4, 5, 6, or 7 cars in the consolidated taxi company.

□ **15–29** In $(M/M/2):(GD/\infty/\infty)$, mean service time is 5 minutes and mean inter-arrival time is 8 minutes.

(a) What is the probability of a delay?
(b) What is the probability of at least one of the servers being idle?
(c) What is the probability that both servers are idle?

☐ **15–30** A computer center is equipped with three digital computers, all of the same type and capability. The number of users in the center at any time is equal to 10. For *each* user, the time for writing and inputting a program is exponential with mean rate .5 per hour. The execution time per program is exponentially distributed with mean rate 2 per hour. Assuming that the center is in operation on a full-time basis, and neglecting the effect of computer downtime, find the following.

(a) The probability that a program is not executed immediately upon receipt at the center.
(b) The average time until a program is released from the center.
(c) The average number of programs awaiting execution.
(d) The expected number of idle computers.
(e) The percentage of time the computer center is idle.
(f) The average percentage of idleness *per computer*.

☐ **15–31** An airport terminal services three types of customers: those arriving from rural areas, those arriving from suburban areas, and the transit customers who are changing planes at the airport. The arrivals distribution for each of the three groups is assumed Poisson with mean arrival rates 10, 5, and 7 per hour, respectively. Assuming that all customers require the same type of service at the terminal and that the service time is exponential with mean rate 10 per hour, how many counters should be provided at the terminal under each of the following conditions?

(a) The expected waiting time in the system per customer does not exceed 15 minutes.
(b) The expected number of customers in the system is at most 10.
(c) The probability that all counters are idle does not exceed .11.

☐ **15–32** In a bank customers arrive in a Poisson stream with mean 36 per hour. The service time per customer is exponential with mean .035 hour. Assuming that the system can accommodate at most 30 customers at a time, how many tellers should be provided under each of the following conditions?

(a) The probability of having more than 3 customers waiting is less than .20.
(b) The expected number in the system does not exceed 3.

☐ **15–33** In a parking lot there are 10 parking spaces only. Cars arrive according to a Poisson distribution with mean 10 per hour. The parking time is exponentially distributed with mean 10 minutes. Find the following.

(a) The expected number of empty parking spaces.
(b) The probability that an arriving car will not find a parking space.
(c) The effective arrival rate of the system.

☐ **15–34** For $(M/M/5):(GD/20/\infty)$, suppose that $\lambda = 1/3$ and $\mu = 1/12$. Use TORA to verify that $\lambda_{\text{eff}} = \mu(L_s - L_q) = \mu(c - \bar{c}) = \lambda(1 - p_{20})$, where $c = 5$ and $\bar{c}$ is the expected number of idle channels.

☐ **15–35** Verify the computations in Table 15-1 by using TORA.

☐ **15–36** In a self-service facility arrivals occur according to a Poisson distribution with mean 50 per hour. Service time per customer is exponentially distributed with mean 5 minutes.

(a) Find the expected number of customers in service.
(b) What is the percentage of time the facility is idle?

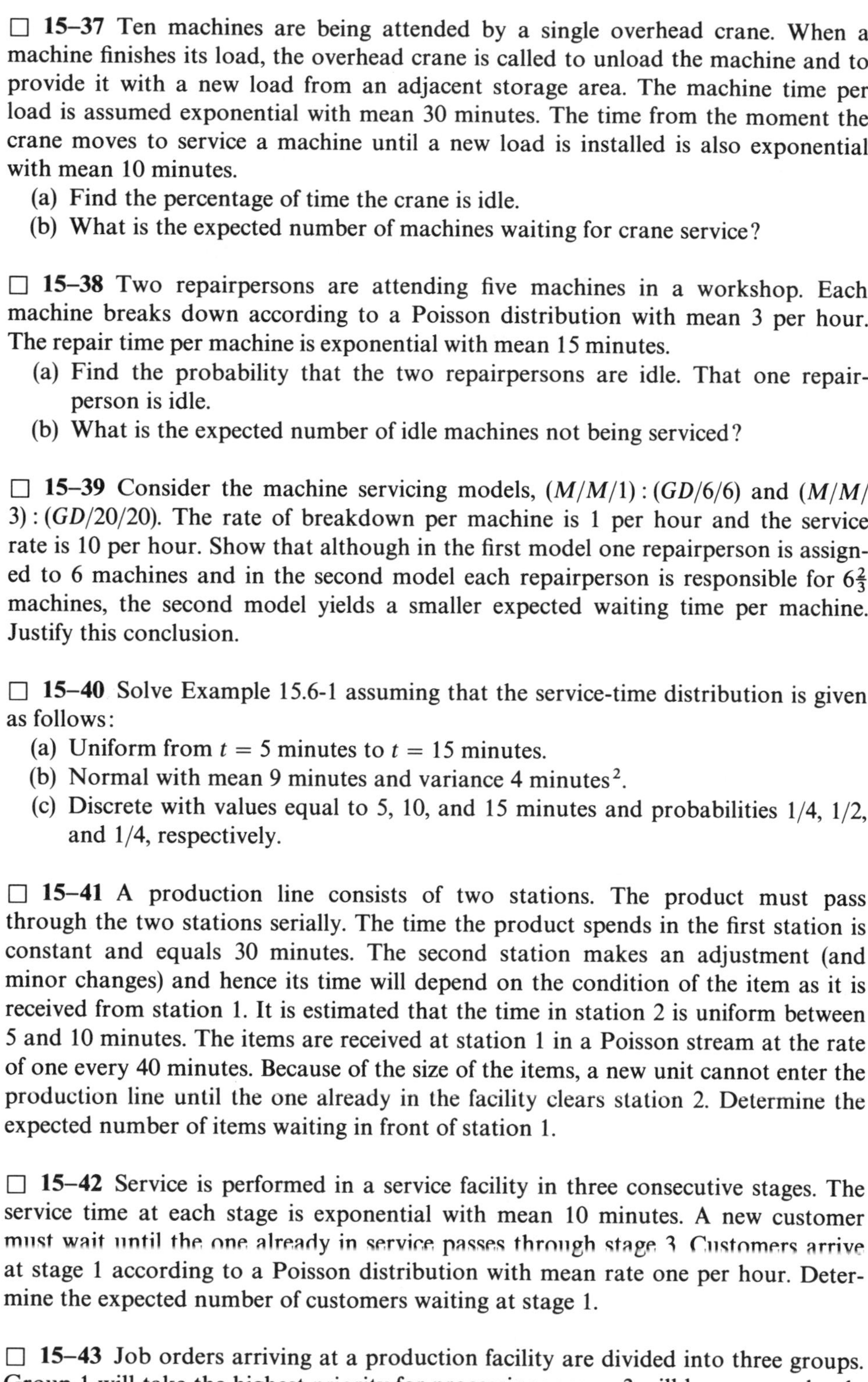

☐ **15–37** Ten machines are being attended by a single overhead crane. When a machine finishes its load, the overhead crane is called to unload the machine and to provide it with a new load from an adjacent storage area. The machine time per load is assumed exponential with mean 30 minutes. The time from the moment the crane moves to service a machine until a new load is installed is also exponential with mean 10 minutes.

(a) Find the percentage of time the crane is idle.

(b) What is the expected number of machines waiting for crane service?

☐ **15–38** Two repairpersons are attending five machines in a workshop. Each machine breaks down according to a Poisson distribution with mean 3 per hour. The repair time per machine is exponential with mean 15 minutes.

(a) Find the probability that the two repairpersons are idle. That one repairperson is idle.

(b) What is the expected number of idle machines not being serviced?

☐ **15–39** Consider the machine servicing models, $(M/M/1):(GD/6/6)$ and $(M/M/3):(GD/20/20)$. The rate of breakdown per machine is 1 per hour and the service rate is 10 per hour. Show that although in the first model one repairperson is assigned to 6 machines and in the second model each repairperson is responsible for $6\frac{2}{3}$ machines, the second model yields a smaller expected waiting time per machine. Justify this conclusion.

☐ **15–40** Solve Example 15.6-1 assuming that the service-time distribution is given as follows:

(a) Uniform from $t = 5$ minutes to $t = 15$ minutes.

(b) Normal with mean 9 minutes and variance 4 minutes^2.

(c) Discrete with values equal to 5, 10, and 15 minutes and probabilities 1/4, 1/2, and 1/4, respectively.

☐ **15–41** A production line consists of two stations. The product must pass through the two stations serially. The time the product spends in the first station is constant and equals 30 minutes. The second station makes an adjustment (and minor changes) and hence its time will depend on the condition of the item as it is received from station 1. It is estimated that the time in station 2 is uniform between 5 and 10 minutes. The items are received at station 1 in a Poisson stream at the rate of one every 40 minutes. Because of the size of the items, a new unit cannot enter the production line until the one already in the facility clears station 2. Determine the expected number of items waiting in front of station 1.

☐ **15–42** Service is performed in a service facility in three consecutive stages. The service time at each stage is exponential with mean 10 minutes. A new customer must wait until the one already in service passes through stage 3. Customers arrive at stage 1 according to a Poisson distribution with mean rate one per hour. Determine the expected number of customers waiting at stage 1.

☐ **15–43** Job orders arriving at a production facility are divided into three groups. Group 1 will take the highest priority for processing; group 3 will be processed only if there are no waiting orders from groups 1 and 2. It is assumed that a job once admitted to the facility must be completed before any new job is taken in. Orders from groups 1, 2, and 3 occur according to Poisson distributions with means 4, 3, and 2 per day, respectively. The service times for the three groups are *constant* with rates 10, 9, and 10 per day, respectively. Find the following.

(a) The expected waiting time in the system for each of the three queues.
(b) The expected waiting time in the system for *any* customer.
(c) The expected number of waiting jobs in each of the three groups.
(d) The expected number waiting in the system.

☐ **15–44** Repeat Problem 15–43 given that the service-time distributions are *exponential* with service rates 10, 9, and 10 per day, respectively.

☐ **15–45** Suppose in Problem 15–43 that there are three production facilities in parallel. The service-time distribution for each facility is negative exponential with mean 5 minutes. Find the expected number of waiting jobs in each group. What is the total number of waiting jobs?

☐ **15–46** Repeat Problem 15–45 assuming that there are five production facilities in parallel and compare the results.

☐ **15–47** In a production line suppose that there are k stations in series (Figure 15-13). Assume that jobs arrive at station 1 from an infinite source according to a Poisson distribution with mean rate λ per unit time. The output from station i is used as input to station $i + 1$. Because there are defective items at each station, the percentage of good items from station i is equal to $100\alpha_i$, $0 \leq \alpha_i \leq 1$. The remaining percentage $100(1 - \alpha_i)$ represents the defectives at station i. Assume that service time distribution at station i is exponential with mean rate μ_i per unit time.

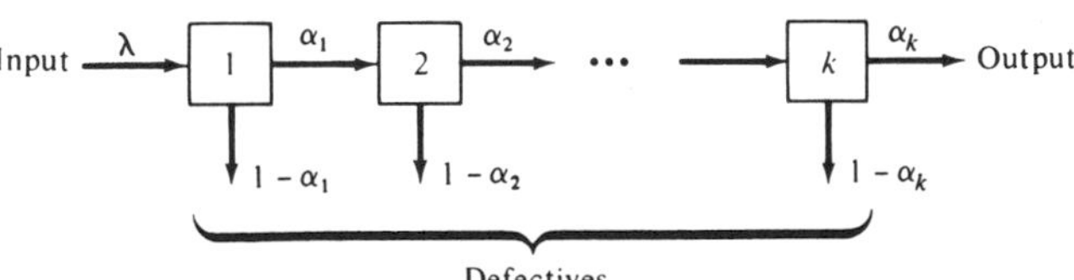

Figure 15-13

(a) Derive a general expression for determining storage space associated with each station i such that all the arriving (good) items can be accommodated β% of the time.
(b) Let $\lambda = 20$ items per hour and $\mu_i = 30$ items per hour for all stations. Percentage of defectives at each station may be assumed constant and equal to 10%. Give a numerical answer for part (a) given $k = 5$ and $\beta = 95\%$.
(c) Using the data in part (b), what is the expected number of defective items from all stations during a period of T hours?

☐ **15–48** Suppose in Problem 15–47 that there is one rework station associated with each station in the production line, as shown in Figure 15-14. Defective items are reworked in these "rework" stations and are sent to the station succeeding the one from which they arrive. Assume that for the ith rework station the service-time distribution is exponential with mean rate γ_i and that the percentage of items that can be reworked successfully is equal to δ_i%.

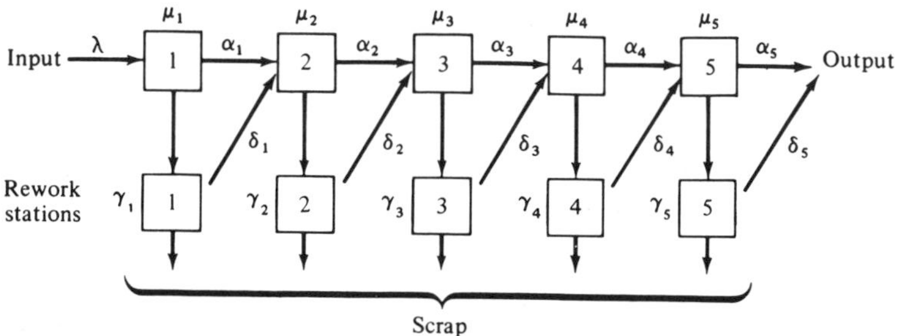

Figure 15-14

(a) Answer part (b) in Problem 15–47 if in addition, $\gamma_i = 4$ items per hour for all i and $\delta_i = 1/(i + 1)$, $i = 1, 2, \ldots, 5$.
(b) How much space must be provided for each rework station to accommodate all incoming defectives 90% of the time?
(c) What is the average number of defective items in each rework station (queue + in service)?
(d) What is the expected waiting time until an arriving item at station 1 is released from station $k = 5$?
(e) Answer parts (a), (b), (c), and (d) assuming that $\delta_i = 1$ for all i.

☐ **15–49** In Problem 15–48 suppose that all the rework stations are pooled into parallel channels (Figure 15-15). The service-time distribution for each channel is exponential with the same rate γ. Assume that the percentage of reworked items at each channel is equal to δ and the output from the pooled facility is distributed back to the respective production stations according to the same input ratios to the facility.

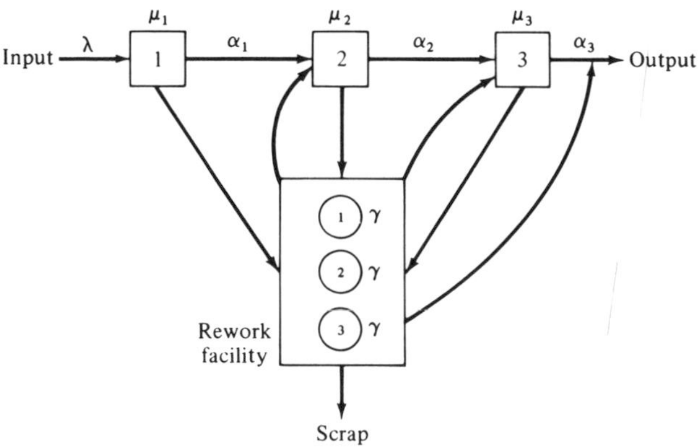

Figure 15-15

Let $k = 3$, $\gamma = 10$, $\mu_i = 15$ for all i, $\alpha_i = 1/2i$, $i = 1, 2, 3$, $\gamma = 10$, and $\delta = 90\%$. Find the following.

(a) The probability of having three items in the production line.
(b) The probability of having two or more items in the rework facility.
(c) The average number of items awaiting processing at each production line station.

(d) The expected waiting time for an arriving item that does not go through a rework facility until it is released from station k.

(e) The expected number in the entire system comprising both production line and rework facility.

☐ **15–50** Repeat Problem 15–49 assuming that $\delta = 75\%$. All the remaining information is unchanged.

THEORETICAL PROBLEMS

Section	Assigned Problems
15.2	15–51, 15–52
15.3	15–53, 15–54
15.4	15–55
15.5.1	15–56, 15–57
15.5.2	15–58, 15–59
15.5.3	15–60, 15–63
15.5.4	15–64, 15–65
15.6	15–66, 15–67
15.8	15–68

☐ **15–51** Prove that the *minimum* of n independent exponential random variables with means $1/\mu_i$, $i = 1, 2, \ldots, n$ is also exponential.

☐ **15–52** Prove that for the exponential distribution with mean $1/\mu$

$$P\{t < T + h \mid t > T\} \cong \mu h$$

where $h > 0$ is sufficiently small.

☐ **15–53** Prove that the mean and variance of the Poisson distribution in Section 15.3.1 are equal and have the value λt.

☐ **15–54** Repeat Problem 15–53 for the truncated Poisson in Section 15.3.2.

☐ **15–55** For the generalized model (Section 15.4.1), suppose that

$$\lambda_n = \lambda \quad \text{and} \quad \mu_n = n^\alpha \mu$$

where λ, μ, and α are given positive constants. This model represents the case where the server regulates output according to the number of customers n in the system. The constant α is known as the "pressure" coefficient. Find the steady-state difference equations describing the system and then solve, showing that

$$p_0 = \frac{1}{Q}$$

$$p_n = \frac{(\lambda/\mu)^n}{(n!)^\alpha Q}, \qquad n = 1, 2, \ldots$$

where

$$Q = \sum_{n=0}^{\infty} \frac{(\lambda/\mu)^n}{(n!)^\alpha}$$

☐ **15–56** For $(M/M/1):(GD/\infty/\infty)$ show that

(a) The expected number in the queue given that the queue is not empty $= 1/(1-\rho)$.

(b) The expected waiting time in the queue for those who have to wait $= 1/(\mu-\lambda)$.

☐ **15–57** Show that for $(M/M/1):(FCFS/\infty/\infty)$, the distribution of waiting time in the queue is

$$w_q(T) = \begin{cases} 1-\rho, & T=0 \\ \mu\rho(1-\rho)e^{-(\mu-\lambda)T}, & T>0 \end{cases}$$

where $\rho = \lambda/\mu$. Then find W_q by using the expression for $w_q(T)$.

☐ **15–58** For $(M/M/1):(GD/N/\infty)$ (Section 15.5.2), show that the two expressions for λ_{eff} are equivalent, namely,

$$\lambda_{\text{eff}} = \lambda(1-p_N) = \mu(L_s - L_q)$$

☐ **15–59** For the $(M/M/1):(GD/N/\infty)$, prove the formula for p_n and L_s when $\rho = 1$.

☐ **15–60** For $(M/M/c):(FCFS/\infty/\infty)$, show that the pdf of waiting time in the queue is given by

$$w_q(T) = \begin{cases} 1 - \dfrac{\rho^c p_0}{(c-1)!(c-\rho)}, & T=0 \\ \dfrac{\mu\rho^c e^{-\mu(c-\rho)T}}{(c-1)!}\, p_0, & T>0 \end{cases}$$

☐ **15–61** In Problem 15–60, show that

$$P\{T>y\} = P\{T>0\}e^{-(c\mu-\lambda)y}$$

where $P\{T>0\}$ is the probability that an arriving customer must wait.

☐ **15–62** For $(M/M/c):(FCFS/\infty/\infty)$, show that the pdf of waiting time in the system is given by

$$w(\tau) = \mu e^{-\mu\tau} + \frac{\rho^c \mu e^{-\mu\tau} p_0}{(c-1)!(c-1-\rho)} \left\{ \frac{1}{c-\rho} - e^{-\mu(c-1-\rho)\tau} \right\}$$

for $\tau \geq 0$.

[*Hint*: τ is the convolution of the waiting in queue T (Problem 15–60) and the service-time distribution.]

☐ **15–63** For $(M/M/c):(GD/\infty/\infty)$ show that

(a) The probability that someone is waiting $= [\rho/(c-\rho)]p_c$.

(b) The expected number in the queue if it is given that it is not empty $= c/(c-\rho)$.

(c) The expected waiting time in queue for customers who have to wait $= 1/\mu(c-\rho)$.

☐ **15–64** For $(M/M/c):(GD/N/\infty)$, derive the steady-state equations describing the situation for $N = c$; then show that the expression for p_n is given by

$$p_n = \begin{cases} \dfrac{\rho^n}{n!} p_0, & n = 0, 1, 2, \ldots, c \\ 0, & \text{otherwise} \end{cases}$$

where

$$p_0 = \left\{ \sum_{n=0}^{c} \frac{\rho^n}{n!} \right\}^{-1}$$

☐ **15–65** For the $(M/M/c):(GD/N/\infty)$, prove the formulas for p_0 and L_s when $\rho = c$.

☐ **15–66** (a) In a service facility with c parallel serviers, assume that customers arrive according to a Poisson distribution with mean rate λ. Rather than assuming that any customer can join any free server, customers will be assigned to the different servers on a rotational basis so that the first arriving customer is assigned to server 1, the second customer to server 2, and so on. After the cycle is completed for all c servers, the assignment starts again by considering server 1. Find the pdf of interarrival time at each server.

(b) Suppose in part (a) that customers are assigned randomly to the different servers according to the probabilities α_i, where $\alpha_i \geq 0$, and $\alpha_1 + \alpha_2 + \cdots + \alpha_c = 1$. Find the pdf of interarrival time at each server.

☐ **15–67** Show that for exponential service time with mean $1/\mu$, the P–K formula for L_s (Section 15.6) reduces to the corresponding formula for $(M/M/1):(GD/\infty/\infty)$.

☐ **15–68** Rework the model in Section 15.8 assuming three tandem stations. Assume all the remaining conditions to be the same as in the two-station model.

Chapter 16

Queueing Theory in Practice

The models in Chapter 15 provide results that *describe* the behavior of a number of queueing situations. The use of these results in the context of a decision model for the purpose of designing systems is not inherent in queueing theory. This chapter bridges the gap between queueing theory results and their use within the framework of a decision model.

16.1 SELECTION OF APPROPRIATE QUEUEING MODEL

The use of queueing theory in practice involves two major aspects:

1. Selection of the appropriate mathematical model that will represent the real system adequately with the objective of determining the system's measures of performance.

2. Implementation of a decision model based on the system's measures of performance for the purpose of designing the service facility.

The selection of a specific model for analyzing a queueing situation, be it analytically or by simulation, is principally determined by the distributions of arrivals and service times. In practice, the determination of these distributions entails observing the queueing system during operation and recording the pertinent data. Two questions normally arise regarding the collection of the necessary data:

1. *When* to observe the system?
2. *How* to collect the data?

Most queueing situations have what are called *busy periods*, during which the system's arrival rate increases in comparison with other times of the day. A typical variation in the arrival rate appears as shown in Figure 16-1. For example, incoming and outgoing traffic on a main highway leading into a city reaches its peak during rush hours around 8:00 A.M. and 5:00 P.M. In situations like these it will be necessary to collect the data during the busy periods. This may be a conservative attitude, but we must keep in mind that congestion in queueing systems takes place during busy periods. As such the system must be designed to account for these extreme conditions.

Collecting the data regarding arrivals and departures can be achieved in one of two ways:

1. Measuring the clock time between successive arrivals (departures) to obtain the interarrival (service) times.
2. Counting the number of arrivals (departures) during a selected time unit (e.g., an hour).

The first method is designed to yield the distributions of interarrival or service times, and the second method yields the distributions of the number of arrivals or departures. In most analytic queueing models, we can describe the input and output processes by either the *number* of events (arrivals or departures) or the *time* between events (interarrival or service time).

The mechanism for collecting data may be based on the use of a stopwatch technique or an automatic recording device. An automatic device appears essential when the arrivals occur at a high rate. The use of a manual technique in this case will probably result in distortion of data.

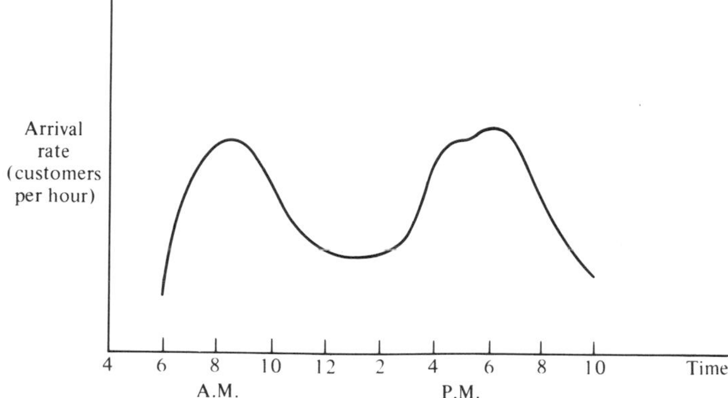

Figure 16-1

After gathering the data in the manner just outlined, the information must be summarized in a meaningful way that would allow us to determine the associated distribution. This is normally achieved by first summarizing the observations in the form of a frequency histogram as detailed in Section 11.1.2. We can then suggest a theoretical distribution that fits the data observed (e.g., Poisson, exponential, normal). A statistical test can then be applied to test the "goodness of fit" of the proposed distribution (see Section 11.1.3 for details). If the resulting distribution happens to fit the exponential-Poisson assumptions required of most usable queueing models, we may then be able to utilize most of the results of Chapter 15 to represent the practical situation. Otherwise, it may be necessary to seek other analysis tools to complete the study. Simulation (Chapter 17) is particularly suited for investigating "ill-behaved" queueing situations that cannot be analyzed by standard queueing theory models.

16.2 QUEUEING DECISION MODELS

The selection of a suitable queueing model as outlined in Section 16.1 can only provide us with measures of performance that describe the behavior of the system under investigation. The next step is to devise *decision* models that can be used in optimizing the design of the queueing system. In the general spirit of operations research, we would be interested in developing decision models that minimize the total costs associated with the operation of the queueing situation.

In general, a cost model in queueing seeks to balance the conflicting costs of waiting against the cost of increasing the level of service. Figure 16-2 summarizes this result. As the level of service increases, the cost of service goes up and, conversely, the cost of customer waiting time goes down. The optimum service level occurs where the sum of the two costs is a minimum.

The nature of some queueing situations may preclude the use of cost decision models. In particular, the cost of waiting is usually the most difficult to determine. To clarify this point, we categorize queueing situations into the following three broad categories:

1. *Human systems.* Both the server and the customer are human beings, as in the operation of a supermarket, a restaurant, or a bank.

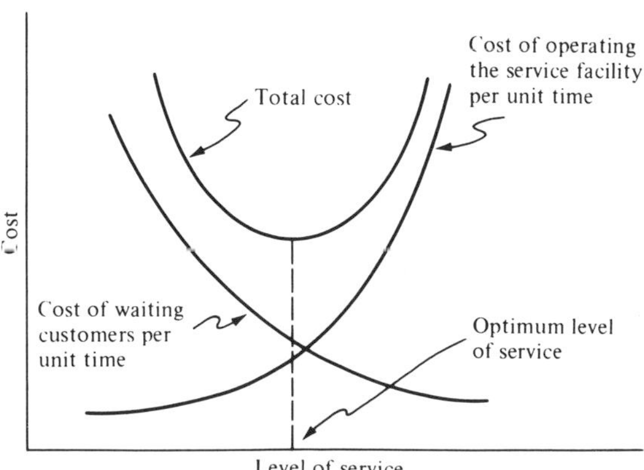

Figure 16-2

2. *Semiautomatic systems.* Only the customer or the server is a human being, as in the machine repair situation in which the broken machine is the customer and the mechanic is the server.

3. *Automatic systems.* Both the customer and the server are not human beings, as in a computer center where the programs are the customers and the central processing unit is the server.

In this categorization, the degree of human involvement in the operation of the facility is generally a measure of the degree of difficulty of implementing cost models. In this regard, human systems are the most obscure primarily because of the difficulty of estimating the cost of waiting. Actually, human systems includes two types: the first type refers to those situations in which the interests of the customer and server are mutual, and the second type includes systems where the interests may be in conflict. An illustration of the first type is the tool crib situation in a machine shop. Here the customers are the operators seeking tool replacement and the servers are the clerks handling the delivery of tools. In this situation, both the customer and the server work toward maintaining an acceptable productivity level. Under this premise, waiting essentially translates to loss in production, which, in most cases, is readily quantifiable.

The case of a human system where the interests of the customer and server are not mutual is exemplified by a bank or a grocery store operation. In these two systems it is difficult to place monetary values on the cost of waiting. Indeed, the "cost" of waiting for the *same* individuals may vary depending on the queueing situation they happen to be in. For example, an individual may be irritated at the thought of waiting more than a couple of minutes in a fast-food line but may be willing to wait more than half an hour to see a favorite movie. (Those of us who have waited between 1 and 2 hours in Disney's EPCOT Center would agree that excessive wait can be tolerated dramatically in anticipation of a perhaps fulfilling experience.)

What we are trying to demonstrate is the fact that not all queueing models can be optimized using cost models. In such cases one must seek other means for making design decisions. For example, in a fast-food restaurant, one would design the facility to appease customers by limiting the average waiting time to 2 or 3 minutes, per customer expectation. This type decision model is based on the use of an **aspiration level** which the service facility must satisfy. Thus an average wait of 2 minutes is the level we *aspire* to fulfill for our customers.

Although the use of aspiration levels to design a queueing system is not "as clean cut" as using an optimization cost model, the procedure does fill a void. In the remaining sections we detail both the cost and aspiration-level models.

16.2.1 Cost Models

Cost models, as shown in Figure 16-2, basically balance the following two types of conflicting costs:

1. Cost of offering the service.
2. Cost of delay in offering the service.

The first cost reflects the server's point of view, whereas the second cost represents that of the customer. In this section we apply the cost model to two situations: the first deals with determining the optimum service rate in a single-server facility and the second determines the optimum number of parallel servers in a multiserver facility.

A. Optimum Service Rate

This model deals with a single-server situation in which the arrival rate λ is known. It is desired to determine the optimum service rate μ based on an appropriate cost model. Let

$$\text{EOC}(\mu) = \text{expected cost of operating the facility per unit time given } \mu$$
$$\text{EWC}(\mu) = \text{expected cost of waiting per unit time}$$

We thus seek to determine the value of μ that minimizes the sum of these two costs.

The specific forms of EOC and EWC as a function of μ depend on the situation under study. For example, these functions may be linear or nonlinear. They may also be continuous or discrete, depending on the characteristic of μ.

Example 16.2-1. A printing company is in the process of acquiring a high-speed commercial copier to meet increasing demand for its copying service. The following table summarizes the specifications of different models:

Copier Model Number	Operating Cost (per hour)	Speed (sheets per minute)
1	\$15	30
2	\$20	36
3	\$24	50
4	\$27	66

Jobs arrive at the company in a Poisson stream at the rate of four jobs per 24-hour day. The size of each job is random but is estimated to average about 10,000 sheets per job. Contracts with the customers specify a penalty cost for late completion at the rate of \$80 per day per job.

Using an average job size of 10,000 sheets, the service rates of the different model copiers may be summarized as follows:

Model	Service Rate, μ (jobs/day)
1	4.32
2	5.18
3	7.20
4	9.50

The computations above are illustrated by the following example. For model 1,

$$\text{time per average job} = \frac{10{,}000}{30} \times \frac{1}{60} = 5.56 \text{ hours}$$

$$\text{corresponding service rate} = \frac{24}{5.56} = 4.32 \text{ jobs/day}$$

An appropriate cost model for the situation recognizes that μ occurs in four discrete values, corresponding to the four different models. This indicates that the optimum service rate can be obtained by comparing the corresponding total costs.

The determination of the total cost associated with each model is achieved as follows. Using a day (24 hours) to represent unit time, the cost of operating the facility per day is given as

$$\text{EOC}_i = 24C_i, \qquad i = 1, 2, 3, 4$$

where C_i is the hourly operating cost of model i. The cost of waiting per day, on the other hand, requires some thinking. Since the contracts specify an \$80 per day penalty for delayed jobs, we can express this cost element as

$$\text{EWC}_i = 80L_{si}$$

where L_{si} is average number of unfinished jobs given model i. The total cost function thus reduces to

$$\text{ETC}_i = 24C_i + 80L_{si}$$

We can determine the values of L_{si}, the expected number in system for model i, from the formulas of the $(M/M/1):(GD/\infty/\infty)$ (Section 15.5.1) or by using TORA. The following table summarizes the results:

Model i	λ_i	μ_i	L_{si}
1	4	4.32	13.50
2	4	5.18	4.39
3	4	7.20	2.25
4	4	9.50	1.73

Using this information, we compute ETC_i for $i = 1, 2, 3, 4$, as shown below. All costs are per day.

Model i	EOC_i	EWC_i	ETC_i
1	\$360.00	\$1000.00	\$1360.00
2	480.00	271.20	751.20
3	**576.00**	**100.00**	**676.00**
4	648.00	58.16	706.16

The computations show that model 3 has the lowest total cost per day. ◀

B. Optimum Number of Servers

The model above can be extended to the case of determining the optimum number of parallel servers in a facility. Given c is the number of parallel servers, the problem reduces to determining c that minimizes

$$\text{ETC}(c) = \text{EOC}(c) + \text{EWC}(c)$$

The optimum value of c must satisfy the following necessary conditions:

$$\text{ETC}(c-1) \geq \text{ETC}(c) \quad \text{and} \quad \text{ETC}(c+1) \geq \text{ETC}(c)$$

As an application of these conditions, consider the following cost functions:

$$\text{EOC}(c) = C_1 c$$
$$\text{EWC}(c) = C_2 L_s(c)$$

where

C_1 = cost per additional server per unit time
C_2 = cost per unit waiting time per customer
$L_s(c)$ = expected number of customers in the system given c

Applying the given necessary conditions, we obtain

$$L_s(c) - L_s(c+1) \leq \frac{C_1}{C_2} \leq L_s(c-1) - L_s(c)$$

The value of C_1/C_2 now indicates where the search for optimum c should start.

Example 16.2-2. In a tool crib facility, requests for tool exchange occur according to a Poisson distribution with mean 17.5 requests per hour. Each clerk in the facility can handle an average of 10 requests per hour. The cost of adding a new clerk to the facility is estimated at \$6 an hour. The cost of lost production per waiting machine per hour is estimated at \$30 an hour. How many clerks should staff the facility?

The determination of optimum c is achieved by carrying out the computations as shown below [note that $L_s(1) = \infty$, since $\lambda > \mu$].

c	$L_s(c)$	$L_s(c-1) - L_s(c)$	
1	∞	—	
2	7.467	∞	
3	2.217	5.25	
4	1.842	.375	$\leftarrow C_1/C_2 = .2$
5	1.769	.073	
6	1.754	.015	
7	1.75	.004	

Since $C_1/C_2 = 6/30 = .2$, we have

$$L_s(4) - L_s(5) = .073 < .2 < .375 = L_s(3) - L_s(4)$$

Consequently, optimum $C = 4$ clerks. ◀

Exercise 16.2-1
In Example 16.2-2, find the optimal c given $C_1 = \$10$ and $C_2 = \$20$.
[*Ans.* $c = 3$.]

16.2.2 ASPIRATION-LEVEL MODEL

The aspiration-level model recognizes the difficulty of estimating cost parameters, and hence it is based on a more straightforward analysis. It makes direct use of the

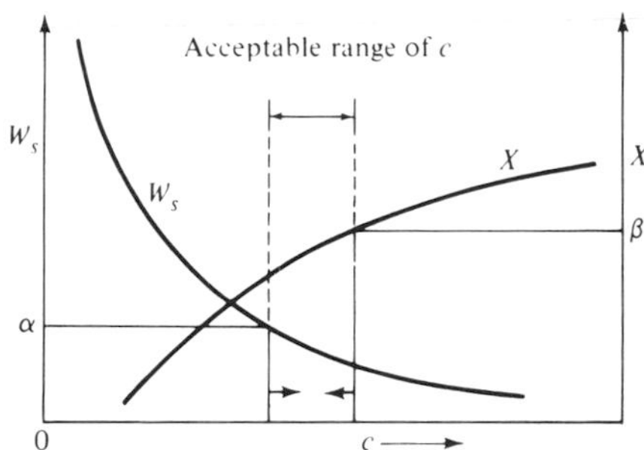

Figure 16-3

operating characteristics of the system in deciding on the "optimal" values of the design parameters. Optimality here is viewed in the sense of satisfying certain aspiration levels set by the decision maker. These aspiration levels are defined as the upper limits on the values of the conflicting measures that the decision maker wishes to balance.

In the multiple-server model where it is required to determine the optimum value of the number of servers c, the two conflicting measures may be taken as

1. The expected waiting time in the system W_s.
2. The percentage of servers' idle time X.

These two measures reflect the aspirations of customer and server. Let the levels of aspiration (upper limits) for W_s and X be given by α and β. Then the aspiration-level method may be expressed mathematically as follows.

Determine the number of servers c such that

$$W_s \leq \alpha \qquad \text{and} \qquad X \leq \beta$$

The expression for W_s is known from the analysis of $(M/M/c):(GD/\infty/\infty)$. The expression for X is given by

$$X = \frac{100}{c} \sum_{n=0}^{c} (c-n)p_n = 100\left(1 - \frac{\rho}{c}\right)$$

The solution of the problem may be determined more readily by plotting W_s and X against c as shown in Figure 16-3. By locating α and β on the graph, we can immediately determine an acceptable range of c that satisfies both restrictions. Naturally, if these two conditions are not satisfied simultaneously, it would be necessary to relax one or both restrictions before a decision is made.

Example 16.2-3. In Example 16.2-2, suppose that it is desired to determine the number of clerks such that the expected waiting time until a tool is received remains below 20 minutes. Simultaneously, it is required that the percentage of time that the clerks are idle does not exceed 15%.

The table below summarizes W_s and X for different values of c. As c increases, W_s decreases and X increases.

c	1	2	3	4	5	6	7	8
W_s (minutes)	∞	25.6	7.6	6.3	6.1	6.0	6.0	6.0
X (%)	0	12.5	41.7	56.3	65.0	70.8	75.0	78.0

For W_s to stay below 20 minutes, we must have *at least* 3 clerks. On the other hand, keeping the clerks busy 85% of the time requires limiting their number to a *maximum* of 2 clerks. Thus the two aspiration levels cannot be satisfied simultaneously and one of the two conditions must be relaxed if we are to find a feasible solution.

We notice that a substantial drop in W_s occurs as c increases from 2 to 3. Further increases have little effect on the value of W_s. In terms of X, increasing c from 2 to 3 more than triples the percentage of idle time for the clerks. Thus the choice between $c = 2$ and $c = 3$ should be made in view of whether it is "worthwhile" to reduce the machine's idle time from 25.6 minutes to 7.6 minutes even though the idle time of the clerks will increase from 12.5% to 41.7%. ◀

To assist in making a specific decision in the case of the aspiration-level method, we can compute a range on the cost parameter C_2 resulting from the selection of c for given aspiration levels. We specifically select C_2 instead of C_1 because it is usually more difficult to estimate the cost of waiting in most waiting line models. The procedure we give here thus assumes that C_1, the incremental cost associated with acquiring an additional server, can be estimated without too much difficulty.

From the cost model in Section 16.2.1B, optimum c must satisfy

$$L_s(c) - L_s(c+1) \le \frac{C_1}{C_2} \le L_s(c-1) - L_s(c)$$

Thus, under optimal conditions, C_2 falls in the range

$$\frac{C_1}{L_s(c-1) - L_s(c)} \le C_2 \le \frac{C_1}{L_s(c) - L_s(c+1)}$$

We illustrate the application of the method by the following example.

Example 16.2-4. In Example 16.2-3 we can estimate ranges on C_2 for $c = 2$ and $c = 3$. Using $C_1 = \$6$ as given in Example 16.2-2, we get the following results. (See the table in Example 16.2-2 for the values of L_s.)

$c = 2$

$$\frac{6}{\infty} \le C_2 \le \frac{6}{5.25}$$

which gives

$$0 \le C_2 \le \$1.14$$

$c = 3$

$$\frac{6}{5.25} \le C_2 \le \frac{6}{.375}$$

or

$$\$1.14 \le C_2 \le \$16$$

Perhaps the ranges on C_2 given $c = 2$ and $c = 3$ can help us make a more selective choice between using 2 or 3 clerks. For $c = 2$, the range on C_2 indicates that the worth of a machine waiting for a tool cannot exceed \$1.14 in terms of lost production. This estimate regarding the worth of the machine appears very low. Alternatively, for $c = 3$ an upper limit of \$16 on the value of C_2 appears more reasonable. It is thus more logical to use 3 clerks instead of 2. ◀

16.3 SUMMARY

In this chapter we have presented three types of difficulty in applying queueing theory in practice.

1. Difficulty of modeling queueing situations mathematically, especially those in which the customer and/or server are human beings.
2. Difficulty of obtaining usable analytic results for certain mathematical models.
3. Difficulty of estimating cost parameters.

For the cases where it is difficult to estimate the cost parameters, it may be more effective to replace the cost model with an appropriate aspiration level model. Simulation is also recommended as an alternative tool for analyzing complex queueing situations for which no mathematical models are readily available.

SELECTED REFERENCES

HALL, R. W., *Queueing Methods for Service and Manufacturing*, Prentice Hall, Englewood Cliffs, N.J., 1991.

PROBLEMS

Section	Assigned Problems
16.1	16–1
16.2	16–2 to 16–12
16.2.2	16–13 to 16–15

☐ **16–1** The following table summarizes data representing number of arrivals n per hour and the associated frequency of occurrences f_n. Test the hypothesis that the data are generated from a Poisson stream. If the hypothesis is accepted, write down the Poisson density function that you would use in analyzing the queueing situation.

n	0	1	2	3	4	5	6	7	8	≥ 9
f_n	6	15	22	24	15	9	4	3	2	0

☐ **16–2** Classify the queueing situation in Problem 15–1 (Chapter 15) as *human*, *semiautomatic*, and *automatic*. In the *human* system, indicate whether the interests of the customer and the server are mutual.

☐ **16–3** Consider the $(M/M/1):(GD/\infty/\infty)$ model with arrival and departure rates λ and μ. Define

c_1 = cost per unit increase in μ per unit time
c_2 = cost of waiting per unit waiting time per customer

(a) Develop a general cost model for the problem.
(b) Determine optimal μ that minimizes the cost function in part (a).

☐ **16–4** Apply the result in Problem 16–3 to the following situation: Jobs arrive at a machine shop according to a Poisson stream at the rate of 10 a day. An automatic machine represents the bottleneck in the shop. It is estimated that a unit increase in the production rate of the machine will cost \$100 per week. Delayed jobs normally result in lost business, which is estimated to be \$200 per job per week. Determine the optimum speed of the machine in units of the production rate.

☐ **16–5** Inventory stock is depleted and replenished according to Poisson distributions. Mean times between depletions and replenishments are equal to $1/\mu$ and $1/\lambda$, respectively. This process may be viewed as an $(M/M/1):(GD/\infty/\infty)$ queueing model.

Suppose that every unit of time that inventory is out of stock, a penalty cost C_2 is incurred. Also, every unit of time that n items of inventory are on hand, a holding cost $C_1 n$ is incurred, where $C_2 > C_1$.
(a) Find an expression for *expected* total cost per unit time.
(b) What is the optimal value of $\rho = \lambda/\mu$?

☐ **16–6** Consider the cost parameters defined in Problem 16–3. Suppose that we consider the $(M/M/1):(GD/N/\infty)$ model where a maximum of N customers are in the system. Additionally, define

c_3 = cost per unit time per additional unit increase in N
c_4 = cost incurred per lost customer for those who cannot join because all N spaces in the system are taken

Develop a general cost model for this situation.

☐ **16–7** A company sells two franchized models of restaurant. Model A has a capacity of 80 customers, whereas model B can accommodate 100 customers. The monthly cost of operating model A is \$10,000 and that of B is \$12,000. A prospective investor wants to set up a restaurant. The owner estimates that customers will arrive according to a Poisson distribution at the rate of 30 per hour. Model A will offer service at the rate of 20 customers per hour, and model B will serve 35 customers per hour. Once the restaurant is filled to capacity, new arrivals would normally leave without seeking service. The lost business per customer per day is estimated at about \$8.00. A delay in serving those customers waiting inside the restaurant is estimated to cost the owner about \$.40 per customer per hour due to the loss in customers' goodwill. Which model should the owner choose? Assume that the restaurant will be open for 10 hours daily.

☐ **16–8** Verify the result

$$L_s(c) - L_s(c+1) \le \frac{C_1}{C_2} \le L_s(c-1) - L_s(c)$$

given in Section 16.2.1B for the optimal number of servers c.

☐ **16–9** In Example 16.2-2 suppose that for $(M/M/c):(GD/\infty/\infty)$, $\lambda = 10$ and $\mu = 3$. The costs are $C_1 = 5$ and $C_2 = 25$. Find the number of servers that must be used to minimize total expected costs.

□ **16–10** Two repairpersons are being considered for attending 10 machines in a workshop. The first repairperson will be paid at the rate of $6.00 per hour and can repair machines at the rate of 5 per hour. The second repairperson will be paid $10.00 per hour but can repair machines at the rate of 8 per hour. It is estimated that machine downtime cost is $16.00 per hour.

Assuming that machines break down according to a Poisson distribution with mean 4 per hour and the repair time is exponentially distributed, which repairperson should be hired?

□ **16–11** A particular pipeline booster unit that operates continuously on a 24 hour basis requires service at exponential time intervals with mean time between breakdowns equal to 20 hours. A repairperson can service a broken booster on the average in 10 hours with exponential service time. At a station with 10 boosters and two repairpersons on duty at all times, each repairperson draws a salary of $7.00 an hour. Pipeline schedule losses are estimated to be $15.00 per hour per broken pump. The company is considering hiring an additional repairperson.

(a) Determine the cost savings per hour achieved by hiring the additional repairperson.
(b) What is the schedule loss in dollars per breakdown with two repairpeople on duty?
(c) What is the schedule loss in dollars per breakdown with three repairpeople on duty?

□ **16–12** A company leases a WATS line for telephone service in all states for $2000 a month. The office is open 200 working hours per month. At all other times the WATS line service is used for other purposes and is not available for company business. Access to the WATS line during business hours is extended to 100 executives, each of whom may need the line at any time, but on an average of twice per 8-hour day (assume exponential time between calls). An executive will always wait for the WATS line if it is busy at an estimated inconvenience cost of 1 cent per minute of waiting. It is assumed that no additional needs for calls will arise while the executive waits for a given call. The normal cost of calls (not using the WATS line) averages 50 cents per minute and the duration of each call is exponential with mean 6 minutes. The company is considering leasing (at the same price) a second WATS line to assist in handling the heavy traffic of calls.

(a) Is the single WATS line saving the company money over a "no WATS line" system? How much is the company gaining or losing per month over the "no WATS line" system?
(b) Should the company lease a second WATS line? How much would it gain or lose over the single WATS line system by leasing a second line?

□ **16–13** A shop utilizes 10 identical machines. The profit per machine is $4.00 per hour of operation. Each machine breaks down on the average once every 7 hours. One person can repair a machine in 4 hours on the average, but the actual repair time varies according to an exponential distribution. The repairperson's salary is $6.00 an hour. Determine the following:

(a) The number of repairpersons that will minimize the total cost.
(b) The number of repairpersons needed so that the expected number of broken machines is less than 4.
(c) The number of repairpersons needed so that the expected delay time until a machine is repaired is less than 4 hours.

☐ **16–14** A state-run child abuse center operates from 9:00 A.M. to 9:00 P.M. daily. Calls reporting cases of child abuse arrive, as expected, in a completely random fashion. The accompanying table gives the number of calls recorded on an hourly basis over a period of 7 days.

Starting Hour	Total Number of Calls During Given Hour						
	Day 1	Day 2	Day 3	Day 4	Day 5	Day 6	Day 7
9:00	4	6	8	4	5	3	4
10:00	6	5	5	3	6	4	7
11:00	3	9	6	8	4	7	5
12:00	8	11	10	5	15	12	9
13:00	10	9	8	7	10	16	6
14:00	8	6	10	12	12	11	10
15:00	10	9	12	4	10	6	8
16:00	8	6	9	14	12	10	7
17:00	5	10	10	8	10	10	9
18:00	5	4	6	5	6	7	5
19:00	3	4	6	2	3	4	5
20:00	4	3	2	2	2	3	4
21:00	1	2	1	3	3	5	3

The table does not include lost calls resulting from the caller receiving a busy signal. For those calls that are actually received, each call lasts randomly for up to 12 minutes with an average of 7 minutes. Past calls show that the center has been experiencing a 15% annual rate of increase in telephone calls.

The center would like to determine the number of telephone lines that must be installed to provide adequate service now and in the future. In particular, special attention is given to reducing the adverse effect of a caller receiving a busy signal.

☐ **16–15** A manufacturing company employs three trucks for transporting materials among six departments. Truck users have been demanding that a fourth truck be added to the fleet to alleviate the problem of excessive delays.

The trucks do not have a "home" station from which they can be called. Instead, management considers it more efficient to keep the trucks in (semi-) continuous motion about the factory. A department requesting the use of a truck must await its arrival in the vicinity. If the truck is available, it will respond to the call. Otherwise, the department must await the appearance of another truck.

Data collected regarding the number of calls from all departments are

Number of Calls per Hour	Frequency	Number of Calls per Hour	Frequency
0	30	7	47
1	90	8	30
2	99	9	20
3	102	10	12
4	120	11	10
5	100	12	4
6	60		

The service time for each department (in minutes) is approximately the same. The following table summarizes a typical service-time histogram for one of the departments.

Service Time t	Frequency
$0 \leq t < 10$	61
$10 \leq t < 20$	34
$20 \leq t < 30$	15
$30 \leq t < 40$	5
$40 \leq t < 50$	8
$50 \leq t < 60$	4
$60 \leq t < 70$	4
$70 \leq t < 80$	3
$80 \leq t < 90$	2
$90 \leq t < 100$	2

What type of recommendation would you make for the management?

PROJECTS

The following projects are suggestions for possible areas of queueing theory applications. You should keep in mind that you may not be able to find a mathematical model that fits the system you are studying. This is expected! What we hope to accomplish by attempting to investigate real-life problems is to gain firsthand experience in the use of queueing theory in practice. *Ideally*, the analysis of a queueing system should proceed in the following orderly manner:

1. Gather data.
2. Test the goodness of fit of the empirical distributions.
3. Select a proper mathematical model and determine its measures of performance.
4. Apply an appropriate decision model.

As you work with a real-life situation, you may discover that progress cannot be made, particularly in step 3, where it may be difficult to find a proper mathematical model. When this happens, you should determine the reasons for these difficulties and study the possibility of circumventing them. A clear recognition of such difficulties should help in realizing the limitations of using queueing theory in practice.

Project 1: Select a parking lot around the campus of your college or university. Model the situation as a queueing system for the purpose of determining the number of parking spaces.

Project 2: Study the checkout counters at the university library with the objective of determining the best design of the facility from the standpoint of selecting the service mechanism and the number of clerks.

Project 3: Study the queueing systems of the cashiers in the university cafeteria with the objective of determining the number of cashiers as well as the layout of the facility.

Project 4: Study the mass transit system on your campus at one of the busy bus stops with the purpose of determining how often a bus should pass through the station selected.

Project 5: Study the operation of a drive-in bank with the objective of determining the number of tellers.

Chapter 17

Simulation Modeling with SIMNET II†

† The material in this chapter is excerpted from Hamdy A. Taha, *Simulation with SIMNET II*, SimTec, Inc., Fayetteville, Ark., 1990.

In the first four editions of this book, the subject of simulation was treated in the form of general concepts only. Now with the availability of powerful microcomputers, it is more apt to experience the use of simulation in more concrete terms. This chapter introduces the SIMNET II simulation language (developed by the author). The presentation will allow you to develop and execute typical simulation models using the SIMNET II software provided with the Instructor's Manual of this book.

Because of space limitation, the present software does not include the full capabilities of the expanded student version. Full details of this version and the full microcomputer version, as well as of the mainframe and minicomputer versions, can be found in the references of this chapter.

The statistical methods of gathering data in simulation are presented in Section 17.15 as an integral part of SIMNET II.

17.1 INTRODUCTION

Simulation is the next best thing to observing a real system. In simulation, we use computer models to (literally) imitate the behavior of the real situation as a function of time. As the simulation advances with time, pertinent statistics are gathered about the simulated system in very much the same way it is carried out in real life. Perhaps the main difference is that in simulation we need to pay attention to the system only when changes in statistics take place. Such changes are associated with the occurrence of **events**. For example, in a bank operation, pertinent events include arrivals at and departures from the facility, since these are only points in time at which the length of the queue and/or the (idle/busy) status of the tellers may change. In effect, simulation is performed by "jumping" on the time scale from one event to the next. This is the reason for describing this type of modeling as **discrete event simulation**.

Model development in simulation can be based on one of two approaches: **next-event scheduling** or **process operation**. Although both approaches are based on the common concept of collecting statistics when an event occurs, the main difference occurs in the amount of details that the user must provide. The next-event scheduling approach normally requires extensive modeling effort, whereas the process approach automates most of the modeling effort on behalf of the user. The trade-off is that process simulation may not be as flexible as the next-event scheduling approach. On the other hand, process-oriented models are usually more compact and easier to implement.

The execution of simulation models typically involves tremendous computations, mostly of a repetitive nature. As such, computers are an essential tool for carrying out these computations. A number of specialized computer languages have been developed to alleviate the programming burden of developing simulation models. These languages are designed based on either the *next-event scheduling* or the *process approach* described above. SIMSCRIPT is the oldest of the next-event scheduling languages. Process languages include SIMNET, SIMAN, SLAM, and GPSS. The last three languages allow the use of external FORTRAN or C inserts to account for the modeling logic that cannot be coded directly by the language facilities. SIMNET modeling capabilities, on the other hand, are sufficiently powerful to eliminate the need for using external FORTRAN or C inserts.

In this chapter we provide the modeling details of SIMNET II via modular applications. The statistical aspects of the **simulation experiment** form an integral part of the design of SIMNET II and will thus be covered during the course of the presentation.

17.2 SIMNET MODELING FRAMEWORK

The design of SIMNET II is based on the general idea that discrete simulation models may be viewed in some form or another as queueing systems. In this context, the language is based on a **network approach** that utilizes three suggestive nodes: a **source** from which transactions (customers) arrive, a **queue** where waiting takes place, if necessary, and a **facility** where service is performed. A fourth node, called **auxiliary**, is added to enhance the modeling capabilities of the language.

Nodes in SIMNET II are connected by **branches**. As the transactions traverse the branches, they perform important functions that include (1) controlling transaction flow anywhere in the network, (2) collecting pertinent statistics, and (3) performing arithmetic calculations.

During the simulation execution, SIMNET II keeps track of the transactions by placing them in **files**. A file can be thought of as a two-dimensional array with each row being used to store information about a unique transaction. The columns of the array represent the **attributes** that allow the modeler to keep track of the characteristics of each transaction. This means that attributes are *local* variables that move with their respective transactions wherever they go in the model network.

SIMNET II uses three types of files:

1. Event calendar.
2. Queue.
3. Facility.

The **event calendar** (or **E.FILE** as it is called in SIMNET II) is the principal file that drives the simulation. It automatically keeps track of an updated list of the model's events in their proper *chronological* order. The operations of the queues and facilities require that they be associated with special files whose function is different from that of the E.FILE. These special files, once defined by the modeler, are automatically maintained by SIMNET II.

17.3 STATEMENT REPRESENTATION OF SIMNET II NODES

Information about the characteristics and operation of SIMNET II nodes are coded in **statements** acceptable to the SIMNET II processor. The following is the general format of a node statement:

```
node identifier; field 1; field 2; ...; field m:
```

The **node identifier** consists of an arbitrary user-defined name (12 characters maximum) followed by one of the codes *S, *Q, *F, or *A, which identify the name as either a source, a queue, a facility, or an auxiliary. The node identifier is then followed by a number of fields separated by semicolons with the last field terminating with a colon. Each field carries information that is needed for the operation of the node. All fields are *positional* in the sense that their order must be preserved in order for the processor to recognize their information content. If a field is not used or is defaulted, its order is preserved by inserting successive semicolons. For example, the statement

```
ARRIVE   *S;10;;;;LIM=500:
```

identifies a source node named ARRIVE, for which the value 10 shown in the first field identifies the time between successive arrivals. Fields 2, 3, and 4 assume *default* values (to be described later), whereas field 5 shows that the maximum number of creations from ARRIVE is limited to 500 transactions.

The default fields of a statement can be suppressed and the position of the nondefaulted fields directly identified by prefixing each with the code /n/, where n is the field number. For example, the statement above may be written equivalently as

```
ARRIVE   *S;10;/5/LIM=500:
```

We will show later that /n/ can be replaced more conveniently with descriptive reserved words or single letters.

Coding in SIMNET II is free formatted as well as upper/lowercase insensitive. A statement may be segmented among any number of successive lines by terminating each line with an ampersand (&). For example, the statement above may be written as

```
ARRIVE  *S;10;/5/LI&          !line 1 of ARRIVE
                     M=500:   !line 2 of ARRIVE
```

A SIMNET II line may include a **comment**, which is recognized by an exclamation mark (!) prefix. Any text that follows ! is treated as a comment and is ignored by the SIMNET II processor.

The remainder of this section defines the various fields of SIMNET II's four nodes.

17.3.1 SOURCE NODE

The source node is used to create the arrival of transactions into the network. The definitions of its fields and its graphic symbol are given in Figure 17-1. The information in parentheses describes the type of data to be used in the field.

SNAME *S;F1;F2;F3;MULT = F4;LIM = F5;F6;F7;*T:

	Field Identifier		Default
F1		Interarrival time (expression)[a]	0
F2		Occurrence time of first creation (expression)	0
F3		Mark attribute number with the attribute automatically carrying creation time if F3 > 0 or serial number if F3 < 0 (constant)	none
F4	/m/	Simultaneous transactions per single creation (constant or variable)[b,c]	1
F5	/L/	Limit on number of creations if F5 > 0 or limit on time of creation if F5 < 0 (constant or variable)[b]	∞
F6	/s/	Output select rule (see Section 17.7.2)	none
F7	/r/	Resources returned by source (see Section 17.10)	none
*T		List of nodes reached from source by direct transfer (see Section 17.7.3)[d]	none

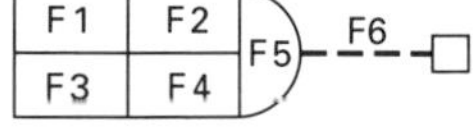

[a] SIMNET II mathematical expression (see Section 17.4)

[b] For fields F4 through F7, the field number n in the field identifier notation /n/ may be replaced with the descriptive words /Multiple/, /Limit/, /Select/, and /Resources/ or /M/, /L/, /S/, and /R/, respectively.

[c] Variable may be a nonsubscripted or an array element (see Section 17.4).

[d] The asterisk may be replaced by the descriptive word GOTO-.

Figure 17-1

In this section we concentrate on fields F1 through F5 with an introduction to the use of the transfer field *T. The other fields are covered later in the sections designated in Figure 17-1.

Example 17.3-1 (Source Node Illustrations). (a) Individual customers upon arrival at a car registration facility are assigned serial numbers that identify the order in which they will receive service. The interarrival time is exponential with mean 12 minutes. The first customer usually arrives about 10 minutes after the facility opens.

The source statement defining the situation is as follows:

```
CUSTMRS  *S;EX(12);10;-1:
```

The name given to the source is CUSTMRS. Field 1 carries the information EX(12), which designates the time between successive arrivals as a random sample taken from an EXponential distribution with mean 12. (The reserved symbol EX is recognized by SIMNET II as representing the exponential distribution. See Table 17-5 for a summary of the random functions available in SIMNET II.) The second field designates the arrival time of the *first* customer as 10 (starting from the zero datum). In general, any mathematical expression (see Section 17.4) may be used in the first two fields. The third field contains the value -1, indicating that attribute 1 will automatically carry the serial numbers 1, 2, 3, ... for the successive arrivals. In SIMNET II attributes are designated by the reserved array $A(\cdot)$, so that -1 in field 3 signifies that $A(1) = 1, 2, 3, \ldots$ for the successive arrivals. Since the third field ends with a colon, all the remaining fields are defaulted.

(b) TV units arrive every 5 minutes for packaging. It is desired to keep track of the arrival time of each transaction in attribute 2. The following statements are equivalent:

```
TVS  *S;5;;2;*PKGNG:
TVS  *S;5;;2;goto-PKGNG:
```

The creation time for the first TV unit is 0 because field F2 is defaulted. As a result, A(2) for the successive customers will assume the respective values 0, 5, 10, 15, ... as requested by field F3(= 2). The transactions leaving sources TVS will be *transferred* to a queue (buffer) node named PKGNG as shown by the *T field. Note that *T is a *floating* field in the sense that it *always* occupies the *last* field of the node regardless of the number of default fields that may precede it.

(c) A mill is contracted to receive 100 truckloads of logs. Each truckload includes 50 logs. The mill processes the logs one at a time. The arrivals of trucks at the mill are spaced 45 minutes apart.

```
TRKS  *S;45;/m/MULT=50;LIM=100;*MILL:
```

The LIM-field indicates that source TRKS will generate 100 transactions (trucks), following which it will literally go dormant. As each transaction leaves TRKS, it will be *replaced* by 50 *identical* transactions representing the logs as shown in the MULT-field. ◀

17.3.2 QUEUE NODE

Queues serve to house waiting transactions. In the obvious sense, an arriving transaction that cannot be serviced immediately must wait in a queue until the facility

QNAME *Q;F1(SUBF1);F2(SUBF2);F3;F4;F5;*T:			
	Field Identifier		Default
F1		Maximum queue size (constant or variable)[a]	∞
SUBF1		Initial number in queue (constant or variable)	0
F2		Number of waiting transactions required to create *one* leaving transaction (constant or variable)	1
SUBF2		Rule for computing the attributes of the leaving transactions when F2 > 1: SUM, PROD, FIRST, LAST, HI(#), LO(#), where # is an attribute number (see Table 17-1)	LAST
F3	/d/	Queue discipline: FIFO, LIFO, RAN, HI(#), LO(#), where # is an attribute number (see Table 17-2)	FIFO
F4	/s/	Output select rule (see Section 17.7.2)[b]	none
F5	/r/	Resources returned by queue (see Section 17.10)	none
*T		List of nodes reached from queue by direct transfer (see Section 17.7.3)[c]	none

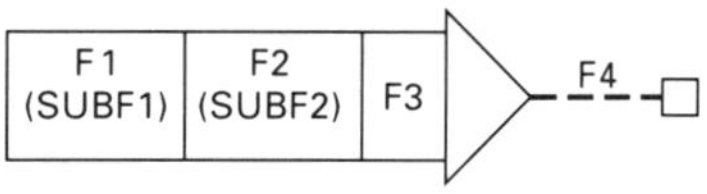

[a] Variable may be nonsubscripted or array elements (see Section 17.4).
[b] For fields F4 and F5, the field number n in the field identifier notation /n/ may be replaced with the descriptive words /Discipline/, /Select/, and /Resources/ or /D/, /S/, and /R/, respectively.
[c] The asterisk may be replaced with the descriptive word GOTO-.

Figure 17-2

becomes available. There are other applications of queues that will be introduced later in the chapter.

In SIMNET II, a queue size may be finite or infinite and the initial number waiting at the start of the simulation may be zero or positive. Transactions waiting in a queue may leave, according to one of a number of queue disciplines, and the queue itself may act as an **accumulator**, whereby a specified number of waiting transactions are replaced by *one* leaving transaction. In such a case the modeler must specify how the attributes of the leaving transactions are obtained from those of the accumulated ones. This information, as well as the descriptions of the various fields of a queue node, are summarized in Tables 17-1 and 17-2 and Figure 17-2.

Example 17.3-2 (Queue Node Illustrations). (a) Rush and regular jobs arrive at a shop randomly with rush jobs taking priority for processing.

A direct way to represent this situation is to associate the job type with an attribute. Let A(1) = 0 and A(1) = 1 identify the regular and rush jobs, respectively. These

Table 17-1
Rules for Computing Exiting Transaction Attributes in an Accumulating Queue

Rule	Description
SUM	Sum of the attributes of the accumulated transactions
PROD	Product of the attributes of the accumulated transactions
FIRST	Attributes of the first of the accumulated transactions
LAST	Attributes of the last of the accumulated transactions
HI(#)	Attributes of the transaction having the highest A(#) among all accumulated transactions
LO(#)	Attributes of the transaction having the lowest A(#) among all accumulated transactions

Table 17-2
Queue Discipline Codes

Discipline	Leaving Transaction
FIFO	First in, first out
LIFO	Last in, first out
RAN	RANdom selection
HI(#)	Transaction having the HIghest Attribute A(#), where # is an integer constant
LO(#)	Transaction having the LOwest Attribute A(#)

jobs are then ordered in a queue named JOBQ according to the following statement:

```
JOBQ  *Q;;;HI(1):
```

The queue discipline HI(1) requires that all transactions be ordered in descending order of the value of A(1). This means that rush jobs with A(1) = 1 will be placed at the head of the queue as desired. Notice that field 1 is defaulted, signifying that queue JOBQ has an infinite capacity.

If the values assigned to A(1) are switched around so that A(1) = 0 represents the rush job, the queue discipline must be changed to LO(1) as follows:

```
JOBQ  *Q;;;LO(1):
```

(b) Units of a product are packaged four to a carton. The buffer area can hold a maximum of 75 units. Initially, the buffer is holding 30 units.

Letting QUNIT represent the buffer, the associated statement is given as

```
QUNIT  *Q;75(30);4:
```

The first field sets the maximum queue capacity (= 75) and the initial number in the system (= 30). The queue discipline is FIFO because field 3 is defaulted. Field 2 indicates that four product units will be converted to a single carton. By default, the attributes of the "carton" transaction will equal those of the LAST of the four "unit" transactions forming the carton (see Figure 17-1). ◀

17.3.3 FACILITY NODE

A facility node is where service is performed. In SIMNET II, a facility has a finite capacity representing the number of parallel servers. During the simulation, each server may be busy or idle. The general format of the node statement and the description of its fields are given in Figure 17-3.

FNAME *F;F1;F2;F3(SUBF3);F4;F5;*T:

	Field Identifier		Default
F1		Rule for selecting an input *queue* (see Section 17.7.2)	none
F2		Service time (expression)[a]	0
F3		Number of parallel servers (constant or variable)[b]	1
SUBF3		Initial number of busy servers (constant or variable)	0
F4	/s/	Output select rule (see Section 17.7.2)[c]	none
F5	/r/	Resource(s) acquired/released by facility (see Section 17.10)	none
*T		List of nodes reached from facility by direct transfer (see Section 17.7.3)[d]	none

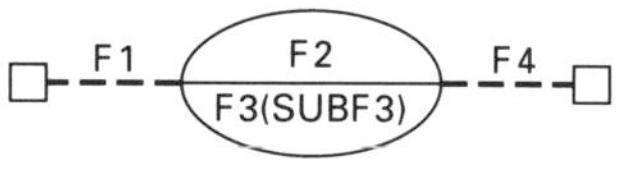

[a] SIMNET II mathematical expression (see Section 17.4).
[b] Variable may be a nonsubscripted or an array element (see Section 17.4).
[c] For fields F4 and F5, the field number n in the field identifier notation /n/ may be replaced with the descriptive words /Select/ and /Resources/ or /S/ and /R/, respectively.
[d] The asterisk may be replaced with the descriptive word GOTO-.

Figure 17-3

Example 17.3-3 (Facility Node Illustrations). (a) A facility has one server who happens to be busy at the start of the simulation. The service time is 15 minutes. Units completing the service are removed (TERMinated) from the system.

Using the name SRVR, the SIMNET II statement is given as

```
SRVR  *F;;15;1(1);*TERM:
```

Field 1 is not needed in this situation because it normally deals with multiple queue input to the facility, which we discuss in Section 17.7.2. In field 2 the value 15 provides the service time in the facility. This field may also be any mathematical expression. Field 3 shows that the facility has one server that is initially busy. The *T field shows that the completed transaction will be TERMinated by using *TERM (or goto-TERM). The symbol TERM is a reserved word of SIMNET II. It is not a node but simply a code that will cause the transaction to "vanish" from the system.

(b) A facility has three parallel servers, two of which are initially busy. The service time is exponential with mean 3 [EX(3)].

The associated statement is given as

```
SRVR  *F;;EX(3);3(2):
```

(c) A small shop has one machine and 10 waiting jobs, in addition to the job that is currently being processed. The processing time per job is exponential with mean 30 minutes.

The network representing this situation is shown below, where the symbol ᗡ following the facility represents TERM.

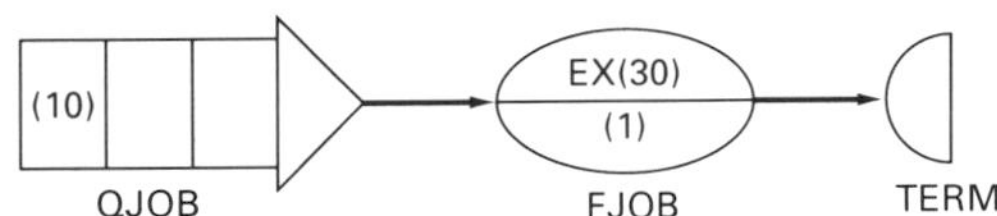

The associated SIMNET II statements are

```
QJOB  *Q;(10):
FJOB  *F;;EX(30);(1);*TERM:
```

We could have ended the QJOB statement with the transfer field *FJOB (or goto-FJOB) to indicate that the transaction leaving QJOB will go to FJOB. However, as we explain in Section 17.7.1, this is not necessary, since the routing in this case is dictated by the fact that the QJOB statement immediately precedes that of FJOB.

In the network above, since FJOB is initially busy, as indicated by the entry (1) in field 3, the facility will automatically process its resident job using a sample from EX(30) as its processing time. After the job leaves FJOB to be TERMinated, the facility will *automatically* "look back" and draw a new job from QJOB. This process is repeated until all 10 jobs are processed. ◀

17.3.4 AUXILIARY NODE

An auxiliary is an infinite capacity node that will always accept all incoming transactions. The node is designed to enhance the modeling capability of the language. It is mostly suited for representing delays. Also, auxiliary is the only node that can enter itself, a characteristic that is particularly useful in simulating repetitive actions (or loops). Figure 17-4 provides a description of the fields of the auxiliary node.

ANAME *A;F1;F2;F3;*T:			
	Field Identifier		Default
F1		Delay time (expression)[a]	0
F2	/s/	Rule for selecting output node (see Section 17.7.2)[b]	none
F3	/r/	Resource(s) released by auxiliary (see Section 17.10)	none
F4		List of nodes reached from auxiliary by direct transfer (see Section 17.7.3)[c]	none

[a] SIMNET II mathematical expression (see Section 17.4).
[b] For fields F2 and F3, the field number n in the field identifier notation /n/ may be replaced with the descriptive words /Select/ and /Resources/ or /S/ and /R/, respectively.
[c] The asterisk may be replaced with the descriptive word GOTO-.

Figure 17-4

Example 17.3-4 (Auxiliary Node Illustration). Job applicants arrive at an employment office every EX(25) minutes. Each applicant must fill out a form and then wait to be interviewed. It takes approximately 15 minutes to complete the form.

The network segment and statements describing the arrival, completing the form, and waiting are given below.

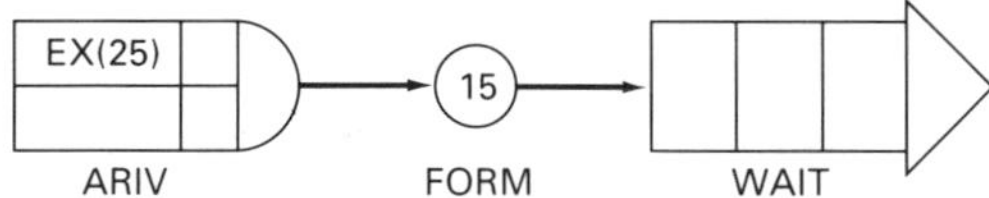


```
ARIV   *S;EX(25):
FORM   *A;15:
WAIT   *Q:
```

The model assumes that the forms are immediately accessible to the arriving applicants. This is the reason for representing the process of filling out the form by the infinite capacity auxiliary FORM. If the forms were to be completed with the assistance of a clerk, the auxiliary FORM would have to be replaced with a single-server facility preceded by a queue. ◀

17.3.5 BASIC RULES FOR THE OPERATION OF NODES

This section summarizes a number of SIMNET II rules for the operation of the source, queue, facility, and auxiliary. Violations of these rules will be detected by the SIMNET II processor and an appropriate error message given.

1. A source may not be entered by any other node, including another source.

2. A queue may not feed *directly* into another queue, nor can it feed back into itself.

3. Facilities may follow one another without intervening queues. However, a facility may not feed directly into itself.

4. An auxiliary is the only node that can feed directly into itself, thus allowing the simulation of loops.

5. A transaction will skip a queue if the queue is not full and its successor node accepts the transaction, even if the queue happens to have waiting transactions when the skipping transaction arrives.

6. If a facility is preceded by a queue, the facility will automatically attempt to draw from the waiting transactions immediately upon the completion of a service. If the queue happens to be empty, the facility will go dormant until it is "revived" by a newly arriving transaction.

7. Movement of transactions in and out of the queue can only be caused by *other* nodes. The queue itself is not capable of initiating this movement.

8. When facilities follow one another in tandem or when the intervening buffers (queues) have limited capacities, a transaction completing service in one of the facilities will be **blocked** if its successor node is a full (finite) queue or a busy facility. The **unblocking** will take place automatically in a chain effect when the cause of blocking subsides.

The rules above will suffice for the time being to get us started with modeling in SIMNET II. Other rules will be introduced later in the chapter.

17.4 SIMNET II MATHEMATICAL EXPRESSIONS

Mathematical expressions are used in certain fields of nodes, such as the interarrival time in a source. They may also be used with arithmetic assignments and conditions.

The rules for constructing and evaluating mathematical expressions in SIMNET II are the same as in FORTRAN. The arithmetic operators include addition (+), subtraction (−), multiplication (*), division (/), and exponentiation (**). An expression may include any legitimate combination of the following elements:

1. User-defined nonsubscripted or subscripted (array) variables.
2. All familiar algebraic and trigonometric functions (see Table 17-3).

Table 17-3
SIMNET II Intrinsic Functions[a]

Algebraic	
Single argument:	INT, ABS, EXP, SQRT, SIGN, LOG, LOG10
Double arguments:	MOD
Multiple arguments:	MAX, MIN
Trigonometric (single argument)	
Regular:	SIN, COS, TAN
Arc:	ASIN, ACOS, ATAN
Hyperbolic:	SINH, COSH, TANH

[a] Arguments may be any SIMNET II mathematical expressions.

3. SIMNET II simulation variables that define the status of the simulation during execution (see Table 17-4).
4. SIMNET II random samples from probabilistic distributions (see Table 17-5).
5. SIMNET II special functions (see Table 17-6).

Names of user-defined variables may be of any length, although only the first 12 characters are recognizable by the SIMNET II processor. The name may include

Table 17-4
SIMNET II Simulation Variables

Variable	Definition
LEN(auxiliary)	Current number of transactions residing in an auxiliary node
LEN/HLEN/LLEN/ALEN (file name)	Current/highest/lowest/average LENgth of a queue, or facility
VAL/HVAL/LVAL/AVAL (variable name)	Current/highest/lowest/average VALue of a statistical variable (see Section 17.8.4)
LEV/HLEV/LLEV/ALEV (resource name)	Current/highest/lowest/average LEVel of a resource (see Section 17.10)
COUNT(node, resource, or variable name)	Number of transactions that departed a node since the start of the simulation or the number of updates of a resource or a variable
RUN.LEN	Length of current run
TR.PRD	Length of transient period
CUR.TIME	Current simulation time
OBS	Current statistical OBServation number (see Section 17.15)
NOBS	Total number of observations per run
RUN	Current statistical RUN number (see Section 17.15)
NRUNS	Total number of runs
AQWA(queue name)	Average wait in queue for *all* customers including those who do not wait
AQWP(queue name)	Average wait in queue for those who must wait
AFBL(facility name)	Average blockage in a facility
AFTB(facility name)	Average blockage time in a facility
AFIT(facility name)	Average time facility is idle
AFBT(facility name)	Average time facility is busy
ARTU(resource name)	Average resource units in transit
ARTT(resource name)	Average time a resource is in transit
ARBT(resource name)	Average time a resource is busy (in use)
ARIT(resource name)	Average time a resource is idle
AFRQ(variable name, cell #)[a]	Absolute histogram frequency of cell # of a variable
RFRQ(variable name, cell #)[a]	Relative histogram frequency of cell # of a variable
NTERM(node name)	Number of transactions terminated from a node
NDEST(node name)	Number of transactions destroyed from a node

[a] Cell # may be any mathematical expression. For an N-cell histogram, cells 0 and N + 1 represent the underflow and overflow cells, respectively.

Table 17-5
SIMNET II Random Functions

Function[a]	Definition
BE(arg1, arg2, RS)	[0, 1] BEta sample with shape parameters α = arg1 and β = arg2
BI(arg1, arg2, RS)	BInomial sample with parameter n = arg1 and p = arg2
DI(arg1, RS)	DIscrete Probability sample (see Section 17.13.2) if arg1 > 0 or linearly-interpolated sample if arg1 < 0
EX(arg1, RS)	EXponential sample with mean $1/\mu$ = arg1
GA(arg1, arg2, RS)	GAmma sample with shape parameters α = arg1 and $1/\mu$ = arg2; if α is a positive integer, the sample is Erlang
GE(arg1, RS)	GEometric sample with parameter p = arg1
LN(arg1, arg2, RS)	LogNormal sample corresponding to a normal distribution with mean μ = arg1 and standard deviation σ = arg2
NE(arg1, arg2, RS)	NEgative binomial with parameters c = arg1 and p = arg2
NO(arg1, arg2, RS)	NOrmal sample with mean μ = arg1 and standard deviation σ = arg2
PO(arg1, RS)	POisson sample with mean λ = arg1
RND(RS)	[0, 1] random sample
TR(arg1, arg2, arg3, RS)	TRiangular sample in the interval [arg1, arg3] with mode arg2
UN(arg1, arg2, RS)	UNiform sample in the interval [arg1, arg2]
WE(arg1, arg2, RS)	WEibull sample with shape parameters α = arg1 and μ = arg2

[a] See Section 11.1.4 for definitions of α, β, n, p, μ, σ, and λ. Arguments arg1, arg2, and arg3 and random stream RS may be any mathematical expressions. RS must assume a nonzero integer value in the range [−50, +50] corresponding to SIMNET II 50 random streams. If RS is negative, the **antithetic** [0, 1] random number 1 − R is used.

intervening blanks but must exclude the following special symbols:

: , ; ( ) { } + − * / = < > $ & % ? !

These symbols are used to represent specific operations in SIMNET II. Array variables may represent one or two subscripts only. The following examples are typical of SIMNET II's nonsubscripted and array variables:

```
nbr_of_machines
TIME BET ARVL
Sample(I*(J+K)**2)
SCORE(Sample(I+J),MAX(K,nbr_of_machines))
```

Table 17-6
SIMNET II Special Variables

Variable[a]	Definition
TL(arg1, arg2)	Value of a dependent variable obtained from Table Lookup number arg1 given the value of the independent variable is arg2. If arg1 < 0, TL is automatically determined by linear interpolation. (See Section 17.13.3.)
FUN(arg1)	Mathematical expression number arg1 obtained from a predefined list of expressions. (See Section 17.13.6.)
FFUN(arg1, arg2)	Mathematical expression in location (arg1, arg2) obtained from a predefined two-dimensional array list of expressions. (See Section 17.13.6.)

[a] arg1 and arg2 may be any mathematical expressions that may be truncated to integer values depending on usage.

The subscripts of the single and double arrays named Sample and SCORE may be any mathematical expressions, which will be automatically truncated to integer values if necessary.

The algebraic and trigonometric functions accepted by SIMNET II are listed in Table 17-3. The arguments of these functions may be any legitimate mathematical expressions. All given functions have the same properties as in FORTRAN.

SIMNET II simulation variables provide access to all simulation parameters and statistics during execution. Simulation statistics are provided in the form of current, highest, lowest, and average values. For example, LEN(QQ), HLEN(QQ), LLEN(QQ), and ALEN(QQ) define the current, highest, lowest, and average LENgth of a queue named QQ. Table 17-4 describes the SIMNET II simulation variables that can be accessed during execution. These variables may be used directly within any mathematical expression.

Table 17-5 describes the random functions available in SIMNET II. You should refer to Section 11.1.4 for a mathematical description of these functions and their arguments. All arguments can be represented by a SIMNET II mathematical expression. The default value of the **random number stream**, RS, is 1.

The last element of a mathematical expression includes SIMNET II special variables. These variables include table look-ups TL(arg1, arg2) and mathematical functions FUN(arg1) and FFUN(arg1, arg2). Table 17-6 provides definitions of these special variables.

17.5 LAYOUT OF SIMNET II MODEL

Although SIMNET II statements are free formatted, the segments of the model must follow a specific organization. Figure 17-5 shows the layout of a SIMNET II model.

$PROJECT;model name;date;analyst name:
$DIMENSION;ENTITY(m),array 1,array 2,. . . ,array n:
$ATTRIBUTES; (descriptive names of attributes):

Definitions Segment:
$VARIABLES: (definitions of statistical variables):
$SWITCHES: (definitions of logic switches):
$RESOURCES: (definitions of scarce resources):

Model Logic Segment:
$BEGIN:
(model logic statements)
$END:

Control Segment:
$RUN-LENGTH=(run length):
$TRACE=(limits of simulation period to be traced):
$TRANSIENT-PERIOD=(transient period length):
$RUNS=(number of runs in a single simulation session):
$OBS/RUN=(number of statistical observations per run):

Initial Data Segment:
$DISCRETE-PDFS: (definitions of discrete probability functions):
$INITIAL-ENTRIES: (attributes of initial queue entries):
$TABLE-LOOKUPS: (definitions of table lookup functions):
$ARRAYS: (initial values of array variables):
$CONSTANTS: (initial values of nonsubscripted variables):
$FUNCTIONS: (definitions of mathematical expressions):
$PRE-RUN: (pre-execution arithmetic and READ/WRITE assignments):

$PLOT=(list of model elements to be plotted):
$STOP:

Figure 17-5

Reserved labels are prefixed with $ and are used to identify the different statements within the segments of the model. $PROJECT and $DIMENSION are *mandatory* statements that always occupy the first and second statements of the model. The $PROJECT statement provides general information about the model. The $DIMENSION statement allocates memory dynamically to the model's files (queues, facilities, and the E.FILE) and user-defined arrays. In particular, the dimension m of ENTITY is an *estimate* of the maximum number of transactions that can be in the system at any time. Any number of single- and double-subscripted arrays may be defined and the statement may occupy more than one line, if necessary. The only restriction on the use of $DIMENSION is that attributes be defined by the reserved array name A(·). As an illustration, the statement

$DIMENSION; ENTITY(50),A(5),sample(50, 3):

indicates that the maximum number of transactions during execution is estimated not to exceed 50 and each transaction will have five attributes. The double-subscripted array sample (50, 3) is defined to have 50 rows and three columns.

The optional $ATTRIBUTES statement is used when it is desired to assign descriptive names to the elements of the A(·) array. For example, suppose that the $DIMENSION statement specifies the attributes array as A(5), meaning that each transaction will have five attributes. The statement

```
$ATTRIBUTES;Type,ser_nbr(2),,Prod_time:
```

signifies the following equivalences:

```
A(1)=Type
A(2)=Ser_nbr(1)
A(3)=Ser_nbr(2)
A(5)=Prod_time.
```

Notice that the name of A(4) has been defaulted, which means that it has no descriptive name.

The **definitions segment** of the model defines the model's statistical variables (Section 17.8.4), logic switches (Section 17.9), and resources (Section 17.10). All three types of statements are optional in the sense that a model may not make use of any of them.

The **logic segment** includes the code that describes the simulated system using the nodes and branches of SIMNET II. This segment will be the subject matter of the majority of this chapter.

The **control segment** provides information related to how output results are gathered during execution (see Section 17.15). Finally, the **initial data segment** provides all the data needed to initialize the simulation run (see Section 17.13).

Example 17.5-1 (Multiserver Queueing Model). Customers arrive randomly at a three-clerk post office. The interarrival time is exponential with mean 5 minutes. The service time is also exponential with mean 10 minutes. All arriving customers form one waiting line and are served by free clerks on a FIFO basis.

Figure 17-6 provides the network representation of the model together with the complete SIMNET II statements. As you proceed through the explanation of this model, you will find it helpful to refer to the definitions of the nodes summarized in Figures 17-1 through 17-4 earlier in this chapter.

The $DIMENSION statement estimates that at most 30 transactions (customers) will be in the model at any one time. If during execution this estimate is exceeded,

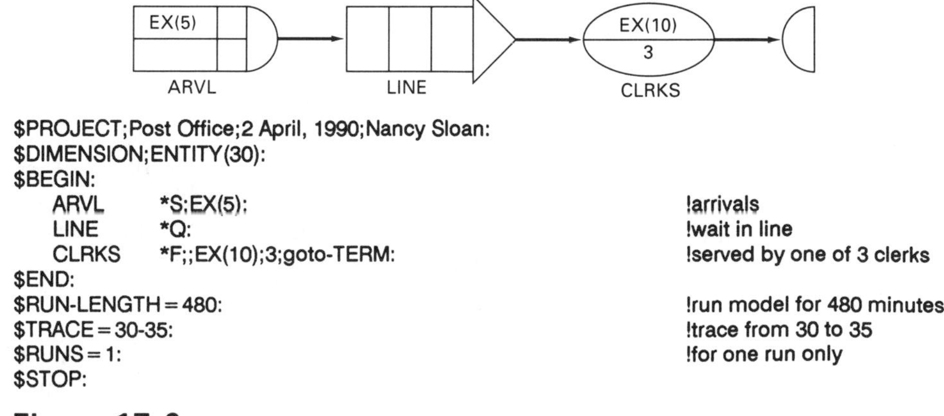


```
$PROJECT;Post Office;2 April, 1990;Nancy Sloan:
$DIMENSION;ENTITY(30):
$BEGIN:
    ARVL     *S;EX(5):                          !arrivals
    LINE     *Q:                                !wait in line
    CLRKS    *F;;EX(10);3;goto-TERM:            !served by one of 3 clerks
$END:
$RUN-LENGTH=480:                                !run model for 480 minutes
$TRACE=30-35:                                   !trace from 30 to 35
$RUNS=1:                                        !for one run only
$STOP:
```

Figure 17-6

SIMNET II will give an error message. In this case, the $DIMENSION of ENTITY must be increased.

The present model does not use $ATTRIBUTES, $VARIABLES, $SWITCHES, or $RESOURCES as evidenced by the absence of these statements.

The logic of the model is represented by the statements enclosed between $BEGIN and $END. Transactions are automatically created by source ARVL by randomly sampling the interarrival time EX(5) with the first arrival taking place at time 0 (default of field 2). Arriving transactions will enter queue LINE if all three clerks are busy. Otherwise, the queue is skipped. When a transaction completes a service, it will be TERMinated. At this point, facility CLRKS will look back at queue LINE and bring in the first-in-line transaction (queue discipline is FIFO by default). Notice that the route of the transaction is defined automatically by the sequence ARVL-LINE-CLRKS because of the physical order of the statements in the model. This is the reason we did not use a transfer field with ARVL and LINE. (Later, in Section 17.7, we will give a complete account of how transactions are routed in the network.) The control data of the model shows that it will be executed for one run of length 480 minutes.

The standard output of the model is given in Figure 17-7. Queue LINE has an infinite capacity (designated by asterisks) and an IN : OUT ratio of 1 : 1 signifying that each exiting transaction corresponds to *one* waiting transaction (default for field 2 of LINE). The AVERAGE LENGTH of 1.30 transactions represents the average number of waiting transactions over the entire length of the run. The MIN/

```
                        ****************************************
                        *                                      *
                        *     S I M N E T  OUTPUT REPORT       *
                        *                                      *
                        ****************************************

PROJECT: Post office      RUN LENGTH =      480.00           NBR RUNS =     1
DATE: 2 April 1990        TRANSIENT PERIOD =          .00    OBS/RUN =      1
ANALYST: Nancy Sloan      TIME BASE/OBS =       480.00

              *** I N D E P E N D E N T   R U N S   D A T A ***
*** RUN  1:
                                  ---------------------
                                       Q U E U E S
                                  ---------------------

           CAPA-   IN:OUT    AVERAGE  MIN/MAX/   AV. DELAY  AV. DELAY  % ZERO WAIT
           CITY    RATIO     LENGTH   LAST LEN   (ALL)      (+VE WAIT) TRANSACTION
LINE       ****     1: 1       1.30   0/ 12/  0       6.51      15.63        58.00
                                  ---------------------
                                    F A C I L I T I E S
                                  ---------------------

           NBR   MIN/MAX/    AV. GROSS  AVERAGE   AVERAGE     AVERAGE   AVERAGE
           SRVRS LAST UTILZ  UTILIZ     BLOCKAGE  BLKGE TIME  IDLE TIME BUSY TIME
CLRKS       3     0/  3/  1     1.9931     .0000        .00      8.48     16.78

*** TRANSACTIONS COUNT AT T =      480.0 OF RUN   1:
NODE          IN       OUT    RESIDING    SKIPPING    UNLINKED/LINKED    TERMINATED
                                          (BLOCKED)   (DESTROYED)
 *S:
 ARVL                   96                            (     0)                  0
 *Q:
 LINE          40       40         0          56             0/     0           0
 *F:
 CLRKS         96       95         1     (     0)     (     0)                 95
```

Figure 17-7

MAX/LAST LEN column provides the minimum, maximum, and last length of LINE (= 0, 12, 0, respectively) that occur during the run. The average waiting time of *all* transactions (including those that do not wait) is given by AV. DELAY(ALL) = 6.51 minutes. The next column AV. DELAY(+VE WAIT) shows the average waiting time for those that *must* wait as 15.63 minutes. Finally, the last column indicates that 58% of the transactions arriving from source ARVL skip LINE, meaning that they do not experience any waiting at all.

Facility CLRKS has three parallel servers. The second column shows that CLRKS starts empty, reaches a maximum of three busy clerks, and ends the simulation with one busy server. The average gross utilization (third column) indicates that on the average 1.9931 servers (out of 3) were busy throughout the run, thus reflecting a gross percent utilization of $(1.9931/3) \times 100 = 66.4\%$. The AVERAGE BLOCKAGE records the average *nonproductive* occupancy of the facility (expressed in number of servers) that are the result of either waiting for resources (see Section 17.10) or being blocked by a succeeding finite queue or facility. Neither condition applies to our example, thus resulting in zero average blockage. In general, the *net* utilization of a facility is the difference between its average gross utilization and its average blockage. The AVERAGE BLKGE TIME represents the average time a facility remains in a blocked state (= 0 in this example). The next-to-last column represents the average length of time a facility remains idle between busy periods. In our example, when no customers are in the system, each clerk remains idle about 8.48 minutes. The last column provides the average block of time a facility stays busy before it reverts to the idle state. Actually, the average busy time can never be less than the average service time per server. In our example, the average busy time is 16.78 minutes. Since the average service time per transaction is 10 minutes [service time = EX(10)], we conclude that *on the average* each server attends to $16.78/10 = 1.678$ customers before becoming idle for 8.48 minutes.

The transactions count given at the end of the report provides a complete history of the flow of transactions during the run. This summary can be helpful in spotting irregularities in the model. For example, a queue buildup may indicate a possible bottleneck. In our example, during the 480-minute run, 96 transactions are created by source ARVL, 40 of which experienced some waiting in queue LINE and the remaining 56 skipped the queue. Facility CLRKS received 96 customers and released 95 with 1 transaction remaining unprocessed at the end of the run. The remaining entries in the count are all zeros. In particular, the UNLINKED/LINKED column is used only when the model experiences file manipulations (see Section 17.12.3). The (BLOCKED) and (DESTROYED) columns will show positive values whenever a facility is blocked or when transactions are destroyed (vanish from the system). Neither case applies to our example.

In addition to the standard output exemplified in Figure 17-7, the user may also produce tailored output using SIMNET II WRITE facility. The WRITE statement is not covered in this limited presentation, however. ◀

17.6 MODEL DEBUGGING IN SIMNET II

Debugging in SIMNET II may be carried out in batch mode or interactively. The batch mode is invoked by including the *control* statement

```
$TRACE=t1-t2
```

```
                    *** S I M N E T   TRACE REPORT ***

Time            Action
-----           ------
  30.0368       Exit ARVL
                  File   next ARVL       creation at T =       42.6198
                  Enter LINE        -- CUR.LEN =   1

  32.2512       Exit CLRKS
                  Terminate transaction
                  Make server in CLRKS      idle -- CUR.UTILIZ =    2
                  Leave LINE        -- CUR.LEN =    0
                  Enter CLRKS       -- CUR.UTILIZ =    3
                  File departure from CLRKS      at T =       33.4242

  33.4242       Exit CLRKS
                  Terminate transaction
                  Make server in CLRKS      idle -- CUR.UTILIZ =    2
```

Figure 17-8

where t1 and t2 are real values that represent the lower and upper bounds of the time interval to be traced. Figure 17-8 provides a segment of the trace report for the multiple-server model in Example 17.5-1, resulting from placing the statement $TRACE = 30-35: immediately following the $RUN-LENGTH statement. The trace report automatically provides all the details of the simulation in the specified interval. In particular, observe how facility CLRKS at T = 32.25 upon becoming idle will "look back" at queue LINE and draw the waiting transaction.

Batch trace reports, though useful, are characteristically voluminous in content and size. Selective debugging can be achieved interactively using the SIMNET II interactive debugger. Details of the interactive debugger are given in Taha (1990).

17.7 TRANSACTION ROUTING IN SIMNET II

Transactions are routed among the various nodes of the network by using:

1. Next-node sequencing.
2. Node's select field.
3. Node's transfer field *T (or goto-field).
4. Branches (*B) emanating from the node.

In this section we provide the details of the first three types. Branching, which represents a very important element of the SIMNET II model, is presented separately in Section 17.8.

17.7.1 NEXT-NODE ROUTING

As demonstrated in the preceding section, next-node routing calls for sending the current node's transaction to the immediately succeeding node. There are two exceptions to this rule:

1. The design of SIMNET II automatically blocks transactions from entering a source node regardless of the type of node that physically precedes it (including another source).

2. A queue node is not allowed to feed *directly* into a succeeding queue node. If two queues happen to be listed sequentially in a model, we can avoid triggering an execution error by separating them by the reserved word $SEGMENT as the following example illustrates:

```
Q1       *Q:
$SEGMENT:
Q2       *Q:
```

17.7.2 SELECT ROUTING

Each of SIMNET II's four nodes has a **select field** (see Figures 17-1 through 17-4) that can be used to route transactions conditionally. In particular, a facility has both input and output select fields because it is the only node that is capable of automatically "looking back" at a set of predecessor queues for the purpose of drawing a transaction. What the select field does is to allow a transaction to be routed *from* or *to* one of several candidate nodes, depending on their conditions. For example, a facility looking back at a set of predecessor queues may draw a transaction from the longest of these queues. Another example is that of a transaction, leaving a node which may visit several destination nodes in a specific preferred order.

Table 17-7 summarizes SIMNET II's select rules categorized into three groups. Group A applies to all nodes and to TERMinate. Groups B and C apply to queues and facilities only.

Table 17-7
List of Select Rules

Rule	Description
A. All nodes and TERM	
[format: rule($node_1$, $node_2$, ..., $node_m$)]:	
POR	Preferred ORder of scanning
ROT	ROTational order of scanning
RAN	RANdom order of scanning
B. Queues and facilities	
[format: rule($file_1$, $file_2$, ..., $file_m$)]:	
HAU(LAU)	Highest(Lowest) Average Utilization = max(min) {average file length}
HAI(LAI)	Highest(Lowest) Average Idleness = total capacity – LAU (HAU)
HAD(LAD)	Highest(Lowest) Delay in file
HTE(LTE)	Highest(Lowest) Time file has been Empty
C. Queues and facilities	
[format: rule($file_{11} \pm file_{12} \pm \ldots, \ldots, file_{m1} \pm file_{m2} \pm \ldots$)]:	
HBC(LBC)	Highest(Lowest) Busy Capacity; that is, file length
HIC(LIC)	Highest(Lowest) Idle Capacity = file capacity – LBC (HBC)

The select field formats for groups A and B are given as

rule(node$_1$,node$_2$, . . . ,node$_m$)

For example, ROT(Q1,Q2,TERM) means that transactions leaving the node will be assigned to Q1, Q2, and TERM on a strict rotational basis. Similarly, HTE(F1,F2) will send the transaction to either facility F1 or F2, depending on which one has been empty (idle) the longest. Observe that the select rule is placed in the appropriate field of the node from which the transaction is leaving, as explained in Figures 17-1 through 17-4.

The rules in group C have the format

rule(file$_{11}$ ±file$_{12}$±. . . , . . . ,file$_{m1}$ ±file$_{m2}$±. . .)

which bases the selection on the *algebraic* sum of the busy or idle capacities of *groups* of files. In this case, the transaction will be sent to the "lead" file in each summation group. For example, the select field

LBC(Q1+F1,Q2−Q1,Q4)

will send the transaction from the current node to Q1, Q2, or Q4, depending on which one yields

MIN(LEN(Q1)+LEN(F1),LEN(Q2)−LEN(Q1),LEN(Q4))

If a tie exists, the first node in order is selected.

The following examples demonstrate the use of the select rule.

1. SS *S;UN(10,20);/s/POR(Q1,Q2,A1):

Transactions leaving source SS will scan the nodes Q1, Q2, and A1 in the given order and will choose the *first* node that admits the transaction.

2. FF *F;HBC(Q1,Q2,Q3);EX(10);3;LBC(F3,Q4,Q5):

Facility FF uses both its *input* and *output* select fields. The input select rule in field 2 stipulates that when FF "looks back" at queues Q1, Q2, and Q3, it will attempt to draw a transaction from the queue with the largest length (HBC). On the other hand, a transaction leaving FF will select F3, Q4, or Q5 according to the LBC rule; that is, depending on which one has the smallest length.

Example 17.7-1 (Bank Model). Cars arrive at a two-window drive-in bank according to an exponential interarrival time with mean 2 minutes. A car chooses the right or left lane, depending on which lane is shorter. The service time in either lane is UN(3, 4) minutes. The space in each lane, excluding the window, can accommodate at most three cars.

The model network and statements are given in Figure 17-9. Transactions are created from source CARS every EX(2) minutes. Field 6 of CARS carries the select rule LBC(QL+WL,QR+WR), indicating that an arriving transaction will enter QL if the number of cars in the left lane (including the window) does not exceed that of the right lane. Otherwise, the right lane is selected. Notice that the "next-node" ordering of source CARS and queue QL is overridden by the select rule of CARS. On the other hand, a transaction leaving QL uses the next-node sequencing to route itself to WL. The same logic applies to QR and WR.

Incidentally, if both QL and QR happen to be full to capacity [LEN(QL) = 3 and LEN(QR) = 3], transactions arriving from CARS will have nowhere to go and will

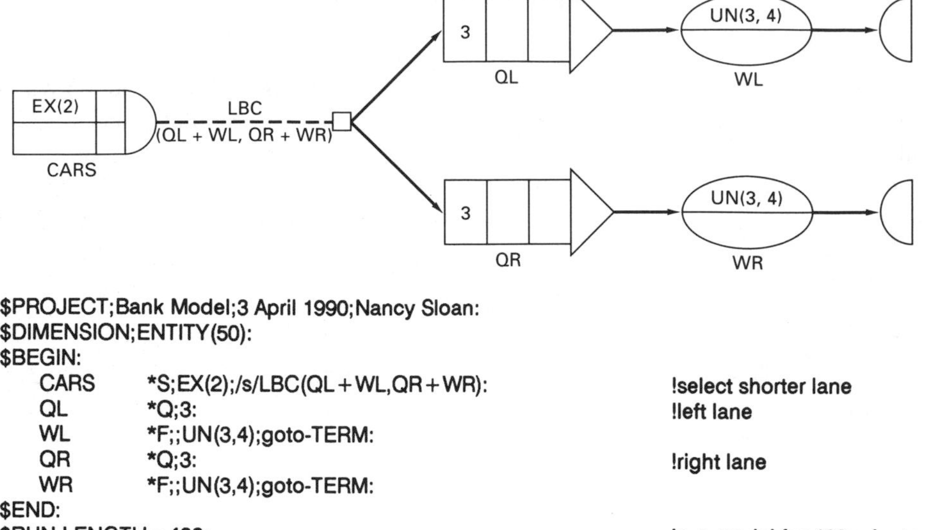


```
$PROJECT;Bank Model;3 April 1990;Nancy Sloan:
$DIMENSION;ENTITY(50):
$BEGIN:
    CARS    *S;EX(2);/s/LBC(QL+WL,QR+WR):     !select shorter lane
    QL      *Q;3:                              !left lane
    WL      *F;;UN(3,4);goto-TERM:
    QR      *Q;3:                              !right lane
    WR      *F;;UN(3,4);goto-TERM:
$END:
$RUN-LENGTH=480:                               !run model for 480 minutes
$RUNS=1:                                       !for one run only
$STOP:
```

Figure 17-9

be destroyed by the system. Later, when we study branching in Section 17.8, we show how alternative routes can be constructed for these "unwanted" transactions. ◀

17.7.3 DIRECT TRANSFER ROUTING (*T OR GOTO-FIELD)

The *T or goto-field allows the modeler to exercise additional control over the routing of the transactions in a network. The *T field uses either of the following two formats:

*node name/transfer type, node name/transfer type, . . . , repeats
goto-node name/transfer type, node name/transfer type, . . . , repeats

The transfer types are summarized in Table 17-8. The remainder of this section provides illustrative examples of the use of the *T field.

Table 17-8
Type of Transfer Routing

SIMNET II Symbol	Usage
A	Always or unconditional transfer (*default*)
P	Probabilistic transfer
D	Dependent transfer
E	Exclusive transfer
L	Last choice transfer

We have used the **always** (A) transfer with TERM in Example 17.7-1 with the symbol A suppressed because it is the default type. A-transfer signifies that the transaction will *always* attempt to enter the designated node. **Probabilistic** (P) transfers select a succeeding node based on a given set of discrete probabilities whose sum must add up to 1. For example, *N1/.2,N2/.3,N3/.5 indicates that nodes N1, N2, and N3 will be entered 20%, 30%, and 50% of the time. The actual selection is done randomly using an internal (0, 1) random number.

Dependent (D) transfer specifies that the node associated with D will not be taken unless *at least* one of the nodes preceding it in the *T-field has been taken. Thus it would be meaningless to place D at the top of the *T list. As an illustration, in the code *N1,N2/.2,N3/.8,N4/D,N5/D, nodes N4 and N5 cannot be entered unless at least one of the preceding nodes N1, N2, or N3 is taken. Note that D-set may include more than one node.

Exclusive (E) transfer works like a D-transfer in the sense that its node(s) cannot be entered unless at least one of the preceding nodes in the *T field has been entered. It differs in one aspect. If any of the E-nodes cannot be entered, all the preceding nodes in the *T field will be blocked as well. This type of transfer is useful when it is necessary to enter two nodes *simultaneously*. For example, *N1,N2/E will result in either entering both N1 and N2 or neither one of the two. Notice that *N1,N2/D may result in N1 only being taken.

The **last choice** (L) transfer is associated with exactly one node, which must be placed at the bottom of the list. The idea of the L-transfer is that its node will be taken only if *none* of the nodes that precede it in the *T field are taken. As an illustration of L-transfer, consider the bank model in Example 17.7-1. Since queues QL or QR have finite capacities, a transaction leaving source CARS will be destroyed if both QL and QR are full. However, if we assume that the customer who cannot enter one of the two lanes will go inside the bank for service, the situation can be modeled by changing the source node to read

```
CARS   *S;EX(2);/s/LBC(QL+WL,QR+WR);*QIN/L:
```

Queue QIN represents the inside of the bank. If the transaction cannot enter QL or QR, it will go to QIN as a last choice.

Example 17.7-2 (TV Inspection). Television units arrive on a conveyor belt from an assembly line at the rate of 5 units per hour for inspection. The inspection time is UN(10,15) minutes. Statistics show that 20% of inspected units must be adjusted and then sent back for reinspection. The adjustment time is UN(6,8) minutes.

The model network and statements are given in Figure 17-10. Notice the manner in which the transaction route is specified. The route TVS–QINSP–FINSP is dictated by the next-node sequencing. The probabilistic transfer from FINSP will randomly send 20% of the transactions to QADJ and the remaining 80% to TERM. When adjustment is completed in FADJ, the default A-transfer will route the transaction back to QINSP as desired. The given model assumes that a TV unit can be adjusted any number of times. Later, we will study modeling capabilities that allow us to control the number of times adjustments are done. ◀

Example 17.7-3 (Synchronized Parallel Workstations). In the final stage of automobile manufacturing, a car moving on a transporter is situated between two parallel workstations to allow work to be done on both the left and

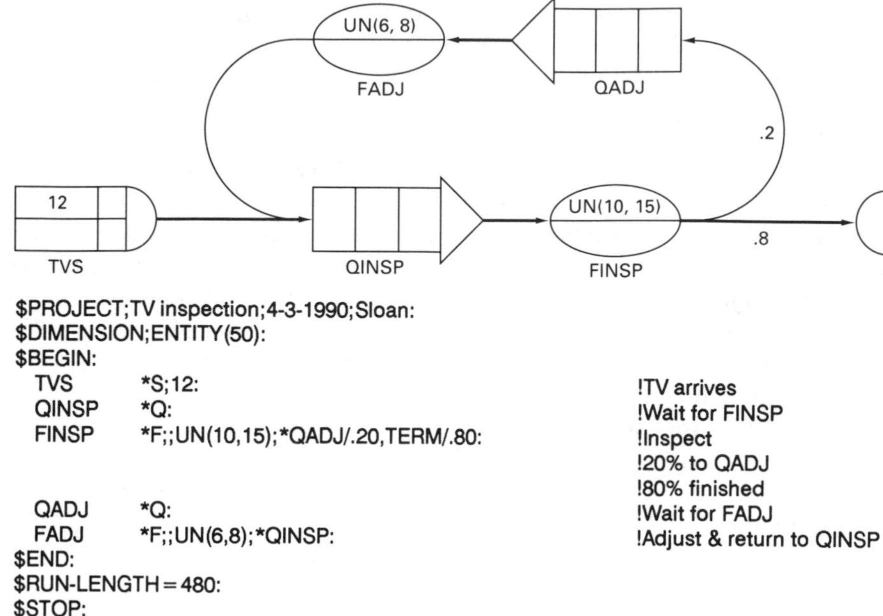


```
$PROJECT;TV inspection;4-3-1990;Sloan:
$DIMENSION;ENTITY(50):
$BEGIN:
  TVS      *S;12:                                  !TV arrives
  QINSP    *Q:                                     !Wait for FINSP
  FINSP    *F;;UN(10,15);*QADJ/.20,TERM/.80:       !Inspect
                                                   !20% to QADJ
                                                   !80% finished
  QADJ     *Q:                                     !Wait for FADJ
  FADJ     *F;;UN(6,8);*QINSP:                     !Adjust & return to QINSP
$END:
$RUN-LENGTH=480:
$STOP:
```

Figure 17-10

right sides of the car simultaneously. The operation times for the left and right sides are UN(18,20) and UN(20,30) minutes, respectively. When both operations are completed, the transporter moves the car outside the stations area. Transporters arrive at the stations area every UN(20,30) minutes.

The model network and statements are given in Figure 17-11. When the transporter leaves queue WAIT, it will split into two copies corresponding to the two stations RST and LST. However, to simulate the transporter movement, both RST and LST must start operation at the same instant in time. This is achieved by

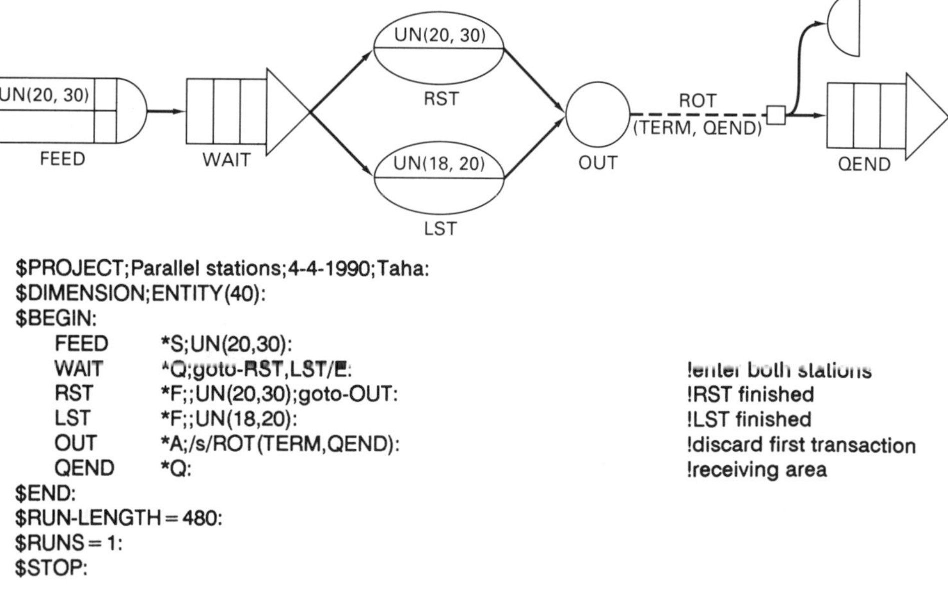


```
$PROJECT;Parallel stations;4-4-1990;Taha:
$DIMENSION;ENTITY(40):
$BEGIN:
   FEED    *S;UN(20,30):
   WAIT    *Q;goto-RST,LST/E:                 !enter both stations
   RST     *F;;UN(20,30);goto-OUT:            !RST finished
   LST     *F;;UN(18,20):                     !LST finished
   OUT     *A;/s/ROT(TERM,QEND):              !discard first transaction
   QEND    *Q:                                !receiving area
$END:
$RUN-LENGTH=480:
$RUNS=1:
$STOP:
```

Figure 17-11

defining the transfer field from queue WAIT as *RST,LST/E. The exclusive transfer condition guarantees that transactions will not leave WAIT unless *both* RST and LST are idle.

The movement of the transporter out of the workstations area must coincide with the longer completion time of facilities LST and RST. The modeling of this condition is accomplished by channeling transactions from both facilities to a zero-delay auxiliary named OUT. When the two transactions leave OUT, we dispose of the first by sending it to TERM. The second will represent the movement of the transporter to the storage area named QEND. The use of select condition ROT(TERM,QEND) with auxiliary OUT will accomplish this task. ◀

17.8 BRANCHES IN SIMNET II

Branches route transactions among nodes in a manner similar to that of direct transfer (Section 17.7.3). However, we use branches in place of direct transfer when we are interested in performing any of the following functions:

1. Checking logical conditions that must be satisfied before the next node is entered.
2. Executing arithmetic assignments.
3. Executing **special assignments** that control the flow of transactions in the network.
4. Collecting data on (user-defined) statistical variables.
5. Returning resources to their base stock.

The information listed above appears in the successive fields of a branch using the format in Figure 17-12. Fields F1/SUBF1, F2, F3, and F4 are explained below. The remaining F5 field dealing with resources is covered in Section 17.10.

***B;F1/SUBF1;F2?;F3%;F4%;F5:**

	Field Identifier		Default
F1		Name of destination node	(error)
SUBF1		Branch type (see Table 17-9)	A
F2	/c/	Condition(s) with AND/OR (field must end with ?)[a]	none
F3	/a/	Assignment(s) (field must end with %)	none
F4	/v/	List of statistical variables (field must end with %) (see Section 17.8.4)	none
F5	/r/	Resources returned by branch (see Section 17.10)	none

[a] For fields F2 through F5, field number n in the notation /n/ of field identifier may be replaced by the descriptive words /Conditions/, /Assignments/, /Variables/, and /Resources/ or /C/, /A/, /V/, and /R/, respectively.

Figure 17-12

Table 17-9
Types of Branches

SIMNET II Symbol	Usage
S	Select branch
A	Always branch (default)
C	Conditional branch
P	Probabilistic branch
E	Exclusive branch
D	Dependent branch
L	Last choice branch

17.8.1 Branch Types (SUBF1)

The branch types in subfield SUBF1 include the same list used with direct transfer (Table 17-8). Additionally, SIMNET II uses select (S) branches to accommodate the transaction routed via the select field of the node. It also uses conditional (C) branches to specify that certain logical conditions must be satisfied before a branch is traversed. Table 17-9 gives a summary of all branch types.

The routing of transactions using the A-, P-, E-, D-, and L-branches follows the same rules introduced in Section 17.7.3 in connection with direct transfer. Specifically, the L-branch must be at the bottom of the list with the E- and D-branches immediately preceding it. The A- and P-branches may appear in any order ahead of the D-, E-, and L-branches.

We now describe the remaining two types of branching: select and conditional. **Select** (S) branching is used when it is necessary to associate branch actions (checking conditions, executing assignments, etc.) with the transaction routed by the select field of the node (see Section 17.7.2). This point is illustrated by the following example. Consider the situation where transactions arriving from a source SS would select the *shorter* of two queues named Q1 and Q2. During the first 100 time units of the simulation, Q1 and Q2 will not be accessible and all transactions must go to queue Q3. Figure 17-13 describes this model segment. The select condition LBC(Q1,Q2) routes transactions to the shorter of Q1 and Q2. However, before

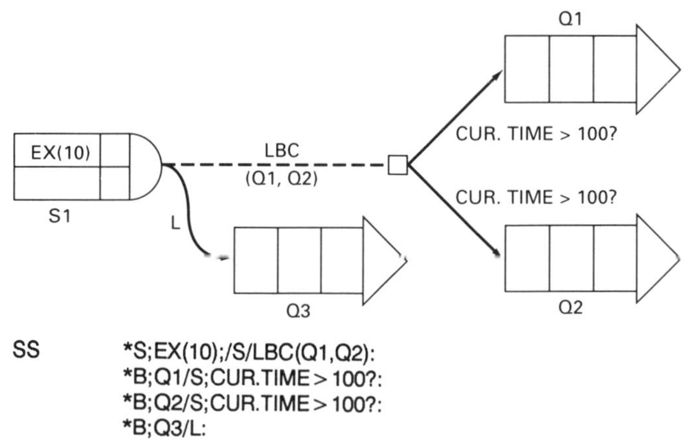

Figure 17-13

entering either queue, SIMNET II will check for an S-branch from SS with a destination node that matches that selected by LBC(Q1,Q2). This means that when Q1 is selected by LBC, the S-branch to Q1 will be checked automatically. Since the branch carries the condition CUR.TIME > 100?, Q1 will not be entered until that condition is satisfied. The same logic applies when Q2 is selected by LBC. Notice that the L-branch from source SS is used to route the transactions to Q3 during the first 100 time units.

Since the select field of a node is acted upon prior to considering the branches, SIMNET II expects the S-branches to be placed at the top of the branches list. This follows because S-branches are the first ones to be checked by SIMNET II.

Conditional (C) branching is used when it is necessary to check specified conditions before a branch can be taken. Such conditional branches may be grouped into distinct sets of one or more *adjoining* branches where each set is identified by associating a specified positive integer value of C to all its member branches. In this case, C will represent the *maximum* number of branches to be taken conditionally from its corresponding set. Figure 17-14 demonstrates the idea of forming conditional sets. Node NN has eight conditional branches representing four distinct sets. The first set consisting of the first two branches (nodes N1 and N2) has C = 1, which indicates that at most *one* of these two branches can be taken. The second set also consists of two branches (nodes N3 and N4) but has C = 2. In this case, both branches can be taken if their conditions are satisfied. The third set consists of one branch only (node N5) with C = 1, meaning that the branch may be taken provided its condition is

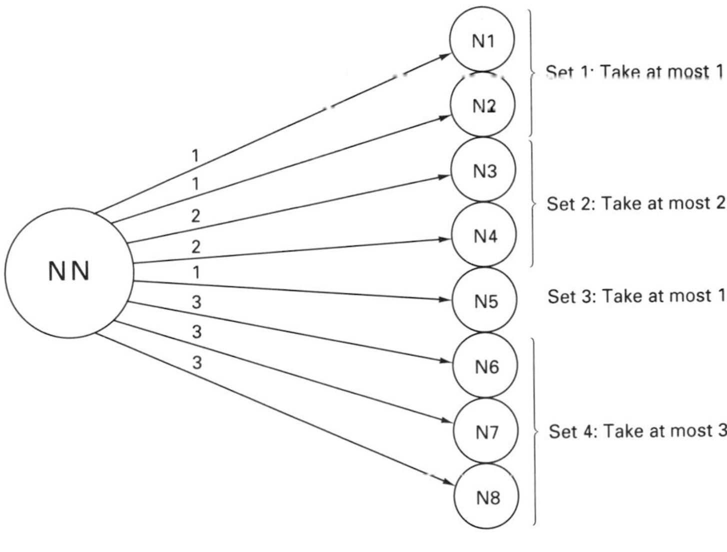

Node NN statement:

```
*B;N1/1;conditions1?:
*B;N2/1;conditions2?:
*B;N3/2;conditions3?:
*B;N4/2;conditions4?:
*B;N5/1;conditions5?:
*B;N6/3;conditions6?:
*B;N7/3;conditions7?:
*B;N8/3;conditions8?:
```

Figure 17-14

satisfied. (Notice that set 3 is distinct from set 1, even though both have C = 1.) Finally, the fourth set consists of three branches (nodes N6, N7, and N8) with C = 3, which signifies that a maximum of three branches may be taken from this set.

Note that SIMNET II scans the branches, and hence each set's branches, in the order in which they are listed. At the point where the maximum number of branches C is reached, the remaining branches *in the set*, if any, are automatically skipped. For example, in set 1 with C = 1, if the branch to N1 can be taken, the second branch to N2 will be skipped. Notice that it is conceivable that none of the branches from a set would be taken depending on their conditions. Notice also that although sets 1 and 3 have the same C(= 1), the two sets are treated totally independently because they are separated by a distinct set.

In SIMNET II, branches of any type and in any number may emanate from the same node. These branches may also be ordered sequentially in any manner with two exceptions:

1. The S-branches must always be placed at the top of the list because they must be synchronized with the node's select field, which is acted on prior to considering any branches.
2. The L-branch, if any, must be at the bottom of the list, preceded by D and/or E branches, if any.

17.8.2 BRANCH CONDITION (F2)

The general format for the conditions field of a branch is as follows:

condition 1,AND/OR, . . . ,AND/OR,condition m?

The field must terminate with ?. As is conventional, AND is evaluated prior to OR. However, we can override this rule by grouping the condition using braces { } as we will illustrate below. The conditions themselves may be arithmetic or logical. Arithmetic conditions have the following general format:

left expression(=,>,<,>=,<=, or <>)right expression

Logical conditions involve logical switch operations and are discussed in Section 17.9.

Examples of Arithmetic Conditions

1. (A(I)+SAMPLE(J))**2<SUM,and,LEN(QQ)=0?
2. {{V(I)>J,or,K<M},and,XX=LEN(QQ)}?

Note that in example 2, the braces {·} can be used to group the conditions in any way desired.

By definition, a conditional C-branch *must* carry conditions. Some of the other types of branches may also carry conditions optionally. Table 17-10 summarizes this information.

17.8.3 BRANCH ASSIGNMENTS (F3)

The assignment field F3 of a branch is where all SIMNET II assignments are executed. The field may hold any number of assignments according to the following format:

assignment 1,assignment 2, . . . ,assignment m%

Table 17-10
Applicability of Conditions Field to Branch Type

Branch type	Conditions Field Accepted?
A	No
E	No
D	No
C	Yes—mandatory
P	Yes—optional
S	Yes—optional
L	Yes—optional

The field must terminate with %. Assignments in the same field are executed sequentially so that a current assignment may affect the computations in the ones that follow it.

SIMNET II assignments will be executed only by a transaction in motion. In other words, if the branch conditions (field 2) are not satisfied or if the node reached by the branch cannot be entered (e.g., a busy facility), then the branch cannot be taken and none of its assignments, nor, for that matter, any of its fields will be activated.

Assignments may be executed unconditionally or conditionally. They may also be executed within loops. In the remainder of this section we introduce the syntax of conditional and loop assignments.

A. Conditional Assignment

SIMNET II provides the following of conditional statement:

IF,*conditions*,THEN,*assignments*,ELSE,*assignments*,ENDIF

The IF-ENDIF statements may be nested to any depth. The following examples illustrate the use of the conditional assignment:

```
1. IF,{A(1)=1,OR,SUM=0},AND,K=LEN(QQ),
     THEN,A(1)=A(1)+1,SUM=(K+1)**2,
   ENDIF
2. IF,A(K**2+2)>0,
     THEN,SAMPL(I+J)=0,
     ELSE,I=LEN(QQ),J=I+1,
   ENDIF
3. IF,XX-1<SQRT(MAX(YY,0)),
     THEN,XX=YY,
   ENDIF
4. IF,I=1,
     THEN,K=K+1,
             IF,K>2,THEN,J=1,A(K**2)=1,ENDIF,
     ELSE,
             IF,K<= 2,THEN,J=0,ENDIF,
   ENDIF
```

Example 17.8-1 (Bus Loading/Unloading Model). Buses arrive at a station every EX(30) minutes. The number of passengers on the bus is usually between 20 and 50, uniformly distributed. Between 2 and 6 passengers, uniformly distributed, leave the bus at the station and from 1 to 8 passengers, also uniformly distributed, are usually waiting to board the bus. It takes UN(3,8) seconds per passenger to leave the bus and UN(4,7) seconds to board it. The maximum capacity of the bus is 50 passengers.

The basic idea of the model is to determine how many passengers are on the bus upon arrival and how many will leave at the station. We then let the leaving passengers exit the bus, one at a time, by using a **simulated loop**. Next, we determine the number of passengers that can board the bus and then load them on one by one. The determination of the bus load upon arrival and the number of passengers to leave and board at the station is achieved by realizing that a uniform *discrete* sample in the closed interval [a,b] is given as INT(UN(a,b + 1)), where INT is the integer function (see Table 17-3).

Figure 17-15 gives the network model and its associated statements. The branch emanating from BUS is of the A-type (default). It computes the busload (n_on) when it arrives and the number of passengers that will leave (n_off). The loop around auxiliary UNLD simulates the unloading of passengers. The first branch is

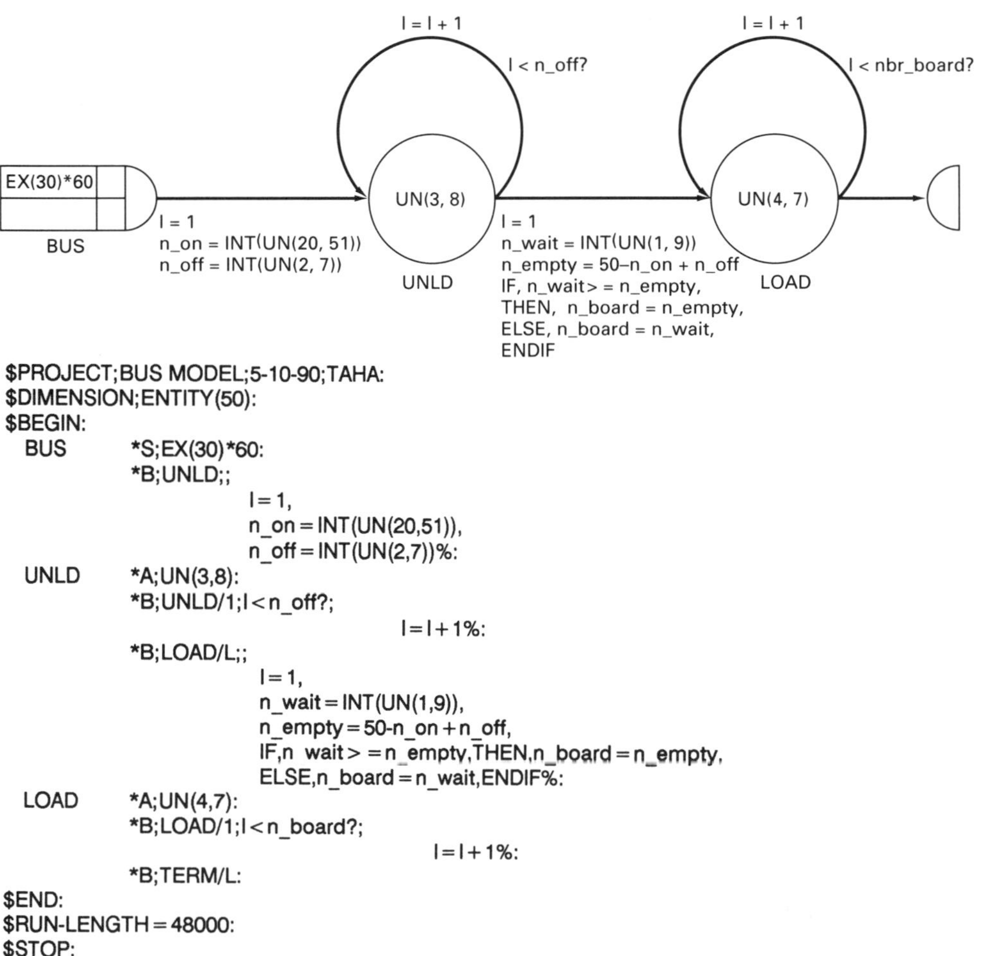


```
$PROJECT;BUS MODEL;5-10-90;TAHA:
$DIMENSION;ENTITY(50):
$BEGIN:
  BUS      *S;EX(30)*60:
           *B;UNLD;;
                      I=1,
                      n_on=INT(UN(20,51)),
                      n_off=INT(UN(2,7))%:
  UNLD     *A;UN(3,8):
           *B;UNLD/1;I<n_off?;
                                    I=I+1%:
           *B;LOAD/L;;
                      I=1,
                      n_wait=INT(UN(1,9)),
                      n_empty=50-n_on+n_off,
                      IF,n_wait>=n_empty,THEN,n_board=n_empty,
                      ELSE,n_board=n_wait,ENDIF%:
  LOAD     *A;UN(4,7):
           *B;LOAD/1;I<n_board?;
                                    I=I+1%:
           *B;TERM/L:
$END:
$RUN-LENGTH=48000:
$STOP:
```

Figure 17-15

taken conditionally back to UNLD if the loop's index I is less than n_off. Each round will also increment the index I by 1. After the loop has been satisfied, the L-branch (last choice) will take the transaction to auxiliary LOAD, which simulates the loading process. To do so, we first determine the number of empty seats (n_empty) and the number waiting (n_wait). The number that will board (n_board) will then equal the smaller of n_empty and n_wait. Observe that n_board can be determined *equivalently* as

```
n_board=MIN(INT(UN(1,9)),50-n_on+n_off)
```

The procedure we used in the example above is intended to demonstrate the use of IF-ENDIF, however.

B. Loop Assignment

The Loop assignment allows the execution of repetitive assignments in a manner similar to the DO-loop in FORTRAN. The general format of the loop statement is as follows:

```
FOR, index=limit 1,TO,limit 2,STEP,step size,DO,
        assignment 1,
        assignment 2,
             :
        assignment m,
NEXT
```

The *index* may be any nonsubscripted variable. The parameters *limit 1*, *limit 2*, and *step size* of the loop may be any SIMNET II mathematical expressions with the *step size* assuming a positive or a negative value. If (STEP, *step size*,) is not specified, a default value of 1 will be assumed.

There are no restrictions on the use of the FOR-NEXT statement. The statement may also be nested to any desired depth.

SIMNET II offers the following two *special assignments* (borrowed from C language) that can be used within the FOR-NEXT loop:

1. LOOP=BREAK will cause an immediate break away from the loop exactly as if *index* has exceeded *limit 2*.
2. LOOP=CONTINUE will cause a skipping of the remaining assignments for the current cycle of the loop.

The following example illustrates the use of FOR-NEXT:

```
IF,I=J,THEN,
        FOR,K=1,TO,J+4,DO,
                IF,K=10,THEN,LOOP=BREAK,ENDIF,
                IF,K=12,THEN,A(1)=A(2),ENDIF,
                FOR,L=K+2,TO,1,STEP,-1,DO,
                        nbr_jobs=nbr_jobs+1,
                NEXT,
        NEXT,
ELSE,
        nbr_jobs=nbr_jobs-1,
        FOR,K=1,TO,3,DO,
                A(K)=A(K+1),
        NEXT,
ENDIF
```

17.8.4 STATISTICAL VARIABLES (F4)

SIMNET II supports three types of user-defined statistical variables:

1. **Observation-based** (OBS.BASED) variables are the familiar ones whose average is obtained by summing the observation values and then dividing the sum by the number of observations (see Section 11.1.1).
2. **Time-based** (TIME.BASED) variables are those whose values are time-dependent. A description of this variable is given in Section 11.1.1.
3. **Run-end** (RUN.END) variables are those variables that are meaningful only at the very end of the simulation run. Examples of this type are percentages and cumulative amounts.

Before statistical observations can be collected, the variables themselves must be defined by name, type, observation value, and histogram data. This task is accomplished by using the $VARIABLES statement in the definition segment of the model as given in Figure 17-5. The general format of this statement is as follows:

```
$VARIABLES: Variable name;Type;value;n/u/w:
                 :
                 :
              repeats
```

The variable name is user defined and may include up to 12 characters. Its type may be either OBS.BASED (default), TIME.BASED, or RUN.END. The observation value must be defined according to the definitions in Table 17-11. If a histogram is desired, its specifications must be defined in terms of n, the number of histogram cells, u, the upper limit on the first cell, and w, the cell width. A default of n/u/w signifies that a histogram is not desired. Normally, it may be necessary to experiment with different values of n, u, and w before a suitable histogram is produced.

In Table 17-11 the observation value TRANSIT(#) is particularly useful in computing time intervals between two points in the network. This is normally accomplished by assigning the current clock time CUR.TIME to attribute A(#) at a

Table 17-11
Statistical Variables

Observation Value	Definition
1. All Types (OBS.BASED, TIME.BASED, and RUN.END)	
Expression	Any legitimate SIMNET II mathematical expression
2. OBS.BASED only	
TRANSIT(#)	Value equal to CUR.TIME − A(#), where # is any SIMNET II expression (> 0) that is truncated to an integer value, if necessary
BET.ARVL	Time interval between successive arrivals of transactions at the point in the network where the variable is computed
ARVL.TIME	Arrival time of transactions at the point in the network where the variable is computed
FIRST	Time of the *first* arrival at the point in the network where the variable is computed

desired start point in the network. Later, when the transaction reaches its desired end point, it will be carrying A(#) with it. TRANSIT(#) then computes the elapsed time by subtracting A(#) from the current clock time CUR.TIME.

The following examples illustrate how statistical variables are defined:

```
$VARIABLES:  SYS TIME;OBS.BASED;TRANSIT(I+J):
             PERCENTAGE;RUN.END;(B(1)+C(1))/N*100:
             INV LEVEL;TIME.BASED;I;20/10/8:
             T BET BLKGE;OBS.BASED;BET.ARVL:
             Late_t(1-3);OBS.BASED;compl_time DUE(J):
```

Notice, in particular, the definition of the **indexed variable** Late_t(1 − 3). This definition refers to three variables Late_t(1), Late_t(2), and Late_t(3). Such variables may be computed in the model (fourth field of a branch) by replacing the index with any mathematical expression. For example, Late_t(I + J) is acceptable so long as I + J assumes one of the values 1, 2, or 3.†

Once the RUN.END and TIME.BASED variables are defined under $VARIABLES, the collection of their statistics is totally automated within SIMNET II. The collection of OBS.BASED variables, on the other hand, necessitates placing their names in the fourth field of the appropriate branch by using the following format:

```
variable1 name,variable2 name, ...%
```

The field must terminate with %.

Example 17.8-2 (Car Wash Facility). Cars arrive at a one-bay car wash facility every EX(10) minutes. Arriving cars line up in a single lane that can accommodate five waiting cars. If the lane is full, arriving cars will balk and go elsewhere. It takes UN(10,15) minutes to wash a car. It is desired to compute two statistics: the time a car spends in the facility until it is washed, and the time interval between successive balks.

Figure 17-16 gives the network model and its associated statements. When source ARIV creates a transaction, it will automatically set its A(1) = CUR.TIME (because field 3 of ARIV is marked with 1). The first branch from ARIV will attempt to take the transaction to queue LANE. However, if LANE is full, the transaction will take the L-branch to TERM, signifying that the car is balking. The statistical variable BET BALKS has the observation type BET.ARVL and is computed on the branch to TERM. This variable will automatically keep track of the time between balks. Transactions completing WASH will compute SYS TIME before being terminated. In essence, SYS TIME measures the time interval from the moment a transaction is created at ARIV until it leaves facility WASH.

Figure 17-17 shows the segment of the SIMNET II output pertaining to the statistical variables. The symbol (O) preceding the name indicates that the variable is OBS.BASED. [The symbols (T) and (E) are used with TIME.BASED and RUN.END variables.] Notice that the standard deviation is a highly biased estimate because of the high dependence of data in the simulation experiment. As such,

† The complete version of SIMNET II additionally allows the indexing of all nodes, resources, and switches in a general manner.

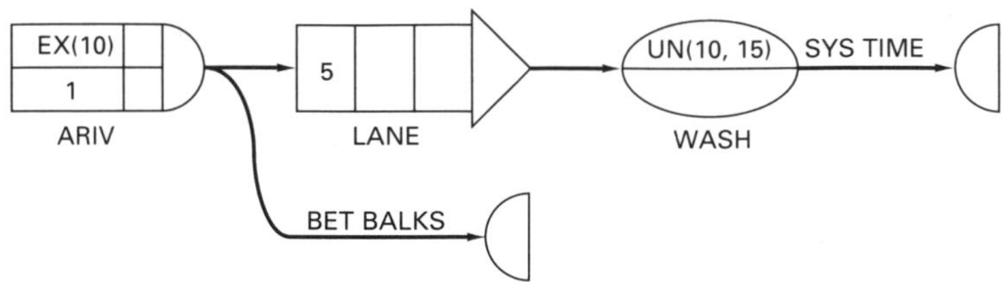


```
$PROJECT;Car Wash Model;8 April 1990;Taha:
$DIMENSION:ENTITY(20),A(1):
$VARIABLES:SYS TIME;obs.based;TRANSIT(1):
            BET BALKS;obs.based;BET.ARVL:
$BEGIN:
  ARIV      *S;EX(10);;1:                        !Mark A(1)=CUR.TIME
            *B;LANE:                             !Enter lane if not full
            *B;TERM/L;/v/BET BALKS%:             !Else, balk
  LANE      *Q,5:                                !Lane capacity = 5 cars
  WASH      *F;;UN(10,15):                       !Wash car
            *B;TERM;/v/SYS TIME%:                !Compute SYS TIME
$END:
$RUN-LENGTH=480:
$STOP:
```

Figure 17-16

```
                      ---------------------
                       V A R I A B L E S
                      ---------------------

              UPDATES  AV. VALUE   STD DEV  MIN VALUE  MAX VALUE  LAST UPDATE
(O)SYS TIME      38       41.61     21.75      12.33      77.74        73.42
(O)BET BALKS      9       17.15     21.40        .68      71.29         1.21
```

Figure 17-17

this measure should not be used in any statistical inference test. It simply gives a "rough" estimate of the spread of the variable around the average value. (See Section 17.15 for further details.) ◀

17.9 LOGIC SWITCHES

Queues in SIMNET II act as buffers where transactions may be stored indefinitely. Until now we have learned that an incoming transaction may skip a queue if the successor node will accept it (e.g., an idle facility). Additionally, a facility completing a service will "look back" at a preceding queue and attempt to draw a transaction from it. This essentially means that movements of transactions in and out of a queue are automatically controlled by the conditions of *other* nodes in the network, but never by the queue itself.

It often happens in simulation modeling that we would want to override this automatic external control over the queue operation. For example, a machine maintenance shutdown can be simulated by "blocking" its in-path from the queue preceding it, so that no transaction can be drawn when the facility looks back at the queue. Eventually, when maintenance is completed we can "revive" the machine by releasing a waiting transaction from the queue. SIMNET II's logic switches are designed to provide this function by allowing the modeler to exercise selective control over the operation of the queue. Additionally, as will be explained below, the ON/OFF state of a switch can be used as a regular logical condition that controls the flow across a branch.

A logic switch is defined by using the $SWITCHES statement as follows:

```
$SWITCHES:  switch name;initial state;queue 1,queue 2, ....
                 :
            repeats
```

The switch name is user defined and may include up to 12 characters. The *initial state* of the switch (at the beginning of the simulation) may be either ON or OFF. The list of queue names represents those queues that the switch controls. For example, the statement

```
$SWITCHES:  SW;ON;Q1,Q2:
```

indicates that switch SW is initially ON and that it controls the queues named Q1 and Q2. We will explain shortly what we mean by "control of queues."

Modeling of the switch operation is achieved by using **special assignments** of the form

```
Switch name=ON
Switch name=OFF
```

These special assignments are implemented in two distinct ways:

1. As conditions that check the current state of the switch (ON or OFF).
2. As assignments that reverse the state of the switch (ON to OFF or OFF to ON).

In the first case, the condition may be integrated (with AND/OR) in the second field of a branch or in the IF-ENDIF statement. In the second case, the assignment is used in the third field of a branch, possibly within the context of the conditional IF-ENDIF statement. Essentially, the *special assignments* are implemented as if they were regular arithmetic conditions or assignments, with the understanding that they perform special functions in the simulation as we will now explain.

The use of the switch as a *condition* may be regarded simply as a binary (0–1) test. On the other hand, its use as an assignment allows us to control the operation of the queues listed in the definition of the switch. Specifically, when the assignment, switch name=ON, is executed, the SIMNET II processor, in addition to reverting the state of switch to ON, *will automatically attempt to push the first waiting transaction out of each of the queues listed in the definition of the switch.* If the queue happens to be empty or if the node succeeding the queue cannot be entered (e.g., branch condition not satisfied or facility busy), no action is taken on that queue.

Keep in mind that pushing transactions out of a designated queue by a switch can take place only if the switch is turned ON by executing an assignment on a branch. This means that an *initial* ON-state of a switch as given by its $SWITCHES definition will not result in any action and should be recognized only as a mere definition.

Similarly, execution of switch name = OFF may only alter the state of the switch but will have no effect on its designated queue(s).

The proposed operation of the switches is referred to in SIMNET II as **remote control**, because it allows control over the queues from a remote area in the network.

Example 17.9-1 (Machine Maintenance). Jobs arrive for processing at a machine every EX(11) minutes. The processing time is EX(12) minutes. After every 8 hours of operation, the machine must be shut down for maintenance. It takes UN(15,20) minutes to carry out the maintenance.

Figure 17-18 provides the network model and associated statements. The model includes two *disjointed* segments. The first segment simulates the maintenance cycle of the machine, whereas the second segment represents the machine operation. The exit end of queue QJOBS feeding into MACHINE is controlled by a switch named SW using the condition SW = ON? on the branch leading to facility MACHINE. Transactions will be permitted to leave QJOBS only if SW is ON. Initially, SW is ON per its definition in $SWITCHES which will satisfy the condition SW = ON?, thus allowing jobs from QJOBS to enter MACHINE. Note that the use of SW = ON? as a condition is essential in this case.

The state of the switch is controlled by the maintenance segment. Source SS sends one transaction to auxiliary DELAY where it is delayed 8 hours representing the operation time of MACHINE. The transaction exiting DELAY signifies that MACHINE is due for maintenance. It thus executes the assignment SW = OFF to prevent new transactions from leaving QJOB. The maintenance transaction then

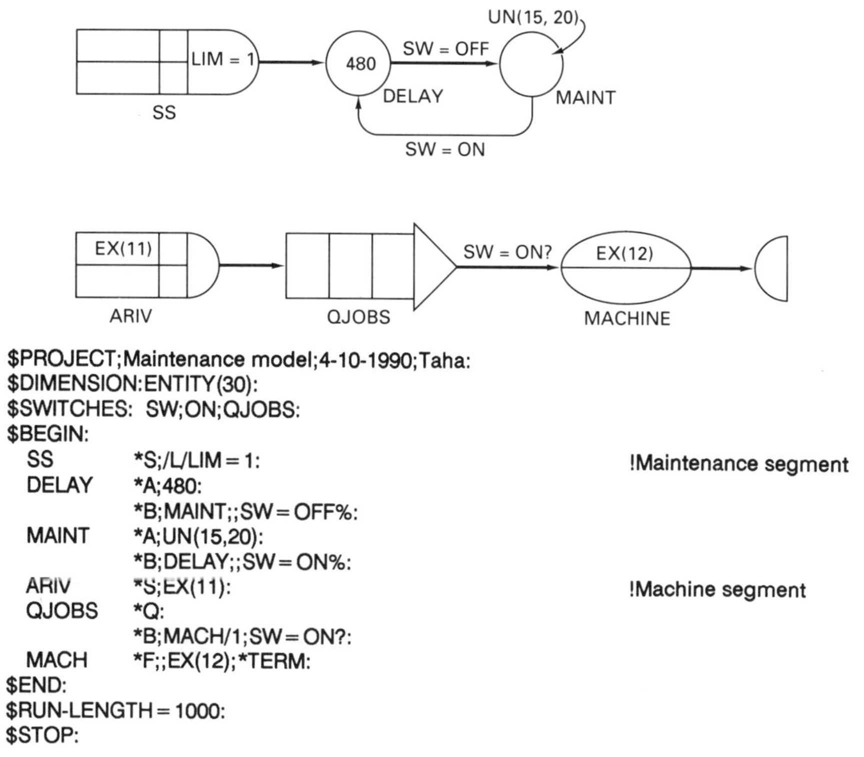


```
$PROJECT;Maintenance model;4-10-1990;Taha:
$DIMENSION:ENTITY(30):
$SWITCHES: SW;ON;QJOBS:
$BEGIN:
  SS       *S;/L/LIM=1:                                  !Maintenance segment
  DELAY    *A;480:
           *B;MAINT;;SW=OFF%:
  MAINT    *A;UN(15,20):
           *B;DELAY;;SW=ON%:
  ARIV     *S;EX(11):                                    !Machine segment
  QJOBS    *Q:
           *B;MACH/1;SW=ON?:
  MACH     *F;;EX(12);*TERM:
$END:
$RUN-LENGTH=1000:
$STOP:
```

Figure 17-18

moves into auxiliary MAINT representing the time period needed to complete the maintenance. When the transaction exits MAINT, it reenters auxiliary DELAY to repeat the cycle. On its way there, it will execute the assignment SW=ON, which will then attempt to push a waiting job out of QJOBS into MACHINE, as desired. If QJOBS happens to be empty at the time SW=ON is executed, the assignment will simply act to unblock QJOBS so that a newly arriving job can skip the queue and enter MACHINE. ◀

17.10 RESOURCES IN SIMNET II

In SIMNET II a resource is a scarce item that may be shared among facility nodes. For example, two machines attended by a single operator may be modeled by defining the operator as a resource and the two machines as separate facilities. Allocation of a resource to facilities may be based on a specified set of priorities. In such a case a higher-priority facility may preempt resources from lower-priority facilities.

We first consider the case where no priority classes are specified. In this case, the definition of the resources follows the format below:

```
$RESOURCES:  resource name;initial level(facility 1, ...,facility m):
                  :
             repeats
```

Figure 17-19 depicts the graphical symbol of the resource. Note that a resource is not a node; rather, it is a definition similar to that of a switch or of a statistical variable.

The following are examples of resource definitions:

```
$RESOURCES:  R1,5(F1,F2,F3):
             R2,(F3,F4):
```

The initial level of resource R1 is 5 units and it can be allocated to facilities F1, F2, and F3. Resource R2 has an initial level of *one* unit by default and may be allocated to facilities F3 and F4.

In the absence of preemption privileges, a transaction entering a facility can only satisfy its needs from the **base stock**, that is, from the unused resource units. If the resource is not immediately available, the transaction will simply wait *in the facility* until the base stock is replenished, possibly by resource units that are freed by the system. In such a case a facility waiting for a resource is said to be in a state of **resource blockage**.

An increase in the base stock of a resource during the simulation will automatically trigger a scan of its associated facilities. Once a facility in a state of resource blockage has satisfied its needs of the resources, it will immediately start servicing its transaction.

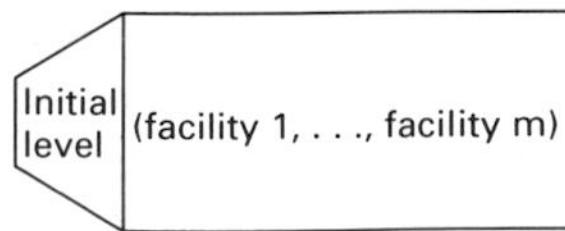

Figure 17-19

Resources can be acquired only by a facility, but may be freed or released at the *exit end* of any node or branch. Information controlling the acquisition and release of a resource is placed in the resource field of the node or branch using the following standard format:

```
resource1_name(a,b,c,d),resource2_name(a,b,c,d), ...
```

where

a = units of the resource to be acquired by a *facility* prior to commencement of service (default = 1)
b = transit time needed to move a units from base stock to *facility* (default = 0)
c = units of the resource to be returned to base stock from the *exit* end of a node or a branch (default = 1)
d = transit time needed to return c units to base stock (default = 0)

The elements a, b, c, and d may be any SIMNET II mathematical expression. Observe that a and b are meaningful only in the case of a facility because *a resource may be acquired only by a facility.* In all other cases, the elements a and b are ignored by the SIMNET II processor and might as well be defaulted in these cases.

The following examples illustrate resource fields:

1. `F1 *F;;EX(5);/r/R1(,5,J+1,),R2:`

Facility F1 uses two resources named R1 and R2. It needs a = 1 unit of R1 (default), which will take b = 5 time units to arrive from base stock. *After service is completed,* c = J + 1 units will be returned to base stock in d = 0 time units. Resource R2 has all default values and hence uses a = 1, b = 0, c = 1, and d = 0.

2. `AX *A;UN(2,3);/r/R1(,,3,A(1)+J):`

Auxiliary AX will return c = 3 units of R1 to base stock in d = A(1) + J time units. Elements a and b, which are defaulted, are ignored because they are meaningful only in the case of a facility.

In dealing with allocation of resources to facilities, the following rules are observed:

1. Partial allocation of the request for any one resource is not permissible in the sense that a facility must acquire all of its request of any one resource at the same time.
2. When a facility requests more than one resource, the resources are acquired *one at a time* with the facility remaining in a state of **resource blockage** until *all* its request is filled.

Example 17.10-1 (Waste Disposal Model I). A food-processing plant produces waste material that must be hauled to dumping grounds. The plant employs four trucks for this operation. Piles of solid waste are discharged from the plant every 6 minutes. It takes two piles to make one truckload. Two mechanical loaders, each operated by a human operator, are used to load the trucks. The loading times for the two loaders are EX(10) and EX(12) minutes. The operator must spend about 3.5 minutes between loads to prepare the loader for the next truck. The trip to dumping grounds takes UN(15,20) minutes, with the return trip taking UN(10,15) minutes only. The time needed to unload the truck is approximately 5 minutes.

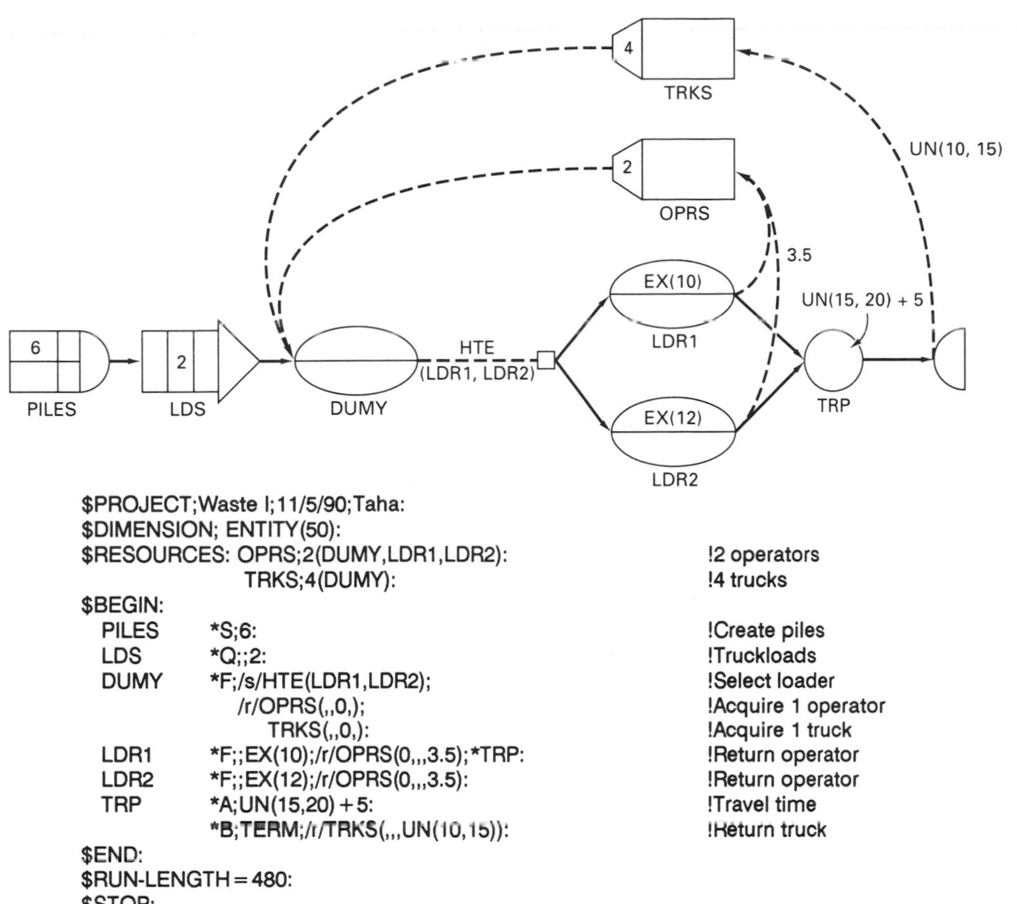


```
$PROJECT;Waste I;11/5/90;Taha:
$DIMENSION; ENTITY(50):
$RESOURCES: OPRS;2(DUMY,LDR1,LDR2):                 !2 operators
                TRKS;4(DUMY):                       !4 trucks
$BEGIN:
  PILES     *S;6:                                   !Create piles
  LDS       *Q;;2:                                  !Truckloads
  DUMY      *F;/s/HTE(LDR1,LDR2);                   !Select loader
              /r/OPRS(,,0,);                        !Acquire 1 operator
                 TRKS(,,0,):                        !Acquire 1 truck
  LDR1      *F;;EX(10);/r/OPRS(0,,,3.5);*TRP:       !Return operator
  LDR2      *F;;EX(12);/r/OPRS(0,,,3.5):            !Return operator
  TRP       *A;UN(15,20)+5:                         !Travel time
            *B;TERM;/r/TRKS(,,,UN(10,15)):          !Return truck
$END:
$RUN-LENGTH=480:
$STOP:
```

Figure 17-20

The model is given in Figure 17-20. The trucks and operators are represented by two resources named TRKS and OPRS whose initial levels are 4 and 2, respectively. Queue LDS acts as an accumulator that releases one truckload for every two piles that arrive from source PILES. The sole purpose of facility DUMY (with zero service time) following queue LDS is to acquire 1 unit of each of the two resources TRKS and OPRS. This is achieved by defining the resource field as OPRS(,,0,), TRKS(,,0,), which signifies that DUMY will acquire 1 unit of each resource in zero transit time and will return none. Thus a transaction leaving DUMY has both a truck and an operator.

The selection between LDR1 and LDR2 by the transaction leaving DUMY is done based on the select condition HTE (Highest Time Empty, see Table 17-7). A transaction leaving either LDR1 or LDR2 signifies that the operator's work has been completed. The facilities thus *return* 1 unit of OPRS by using the code OPRS(0,,,3.5) in field 5. The first element of the resource is zero ($a = 0$) because LDR1 and LDR2 do not acquire the resource. Also, the fourth element of the resource is set equal to 3.5 ($d = 3.5$) to represent the delay period until the operator can start on the next load.

A transaction exiting TRP signifies that the truck has dumped its load. One unit of TRKS is thus returned by the branch from TRP to TERM. The return time is given by d = UN(10,15). Notice that fields a and b are ignored in this case and hence are defaulted. Notice also that TRKS could have been returned directly by TRP by replacing its statement with

```
TRP  *A;UN(15,20)+5;/r/TRKS(,,,UN(10,15));*TERM:
```

In this case, the branch statement must be deleted.

A comment about the use of facility DUMY is in order. We could have let LDR1 and LDR2 acquire their resources directly, by defining their resource fields as OPRS(,,,3.5), TRKS(,,0,). The difficulty with this logic is that it is conceivable that LDR1 may acquire *one* of the two resources with LDR2 acquiring the *other* resource. In this case both facilities must incorrectly await the acquisition of the remaining resource. By using DUMY, we are sure that transactions entering either loader will have *both* resources.

A partial output of the model is given in Figure 17-21. Under FACILITIES, AVERAGE BLOCKAGE generally represents the average number of servers that remain busy yet nonproductive for one or both of two reasons: (1) resources are not immediately available, and (2) the facility cannot dispose of its load because its successor finite queue or facility is full. In our example, blockage in facility DUMY (= .7886 server) is attributed solely to the unavailability of resources OPRS and/or TRKS. The AVERAGE BLKGE TIME for DUMY (= 11.47 minutes) then represents the average time a load has to wait for a truck and/or operator.

Resources statistics show that, on the average, 1.73 (out of 2) operators and 3.70 (out of 4 trucks) were in use during the simulation. Actually, the values 1.73 and 3.705 represent *gross* usage because the resources were in transit part of the time as shown by AV.TRNST UNITS. The *net* usages of the two resources is thus given by 1.73 − .262 = 1.468 operators and 3.705 − .912 = 2.793 trucks. The average transit times are given as 3.5 minutes and 12.5 minutes for OPRS and TRKS.

The AV.TIME IN USE of a resource represents the average time the resource was in actual use or transit, whereas the AV.TIME IDLE represents the average time the resource was idle at base stock. ◀

FACILITIES

	NBR SRVRS	MIN/MAX/ LAST UTILZ	AV. GROSS UTILIZ	AVERAGE BLOCKAGE	AVERAGE BLKGE TIME	AVERAGE IDLE TIME	AVERAGE BUSY TIME
DUMY	1	0/ 1/ 1	.7886	.7886	11.47	9.23	34.41
LDR1	1	0/ 1/ 1	.5097	.0000	.00	11.77	12.23
LDR2	1	0/ 1/ 1	.4843	.0000	.00	13.75	12.92

RESOURCES

	INITIAL LEVEL	MIN/MAX/ LAST LVL	AV. GROSS USAGE	AV.TRNST UNITS	AV.TRNST TIME	AV. TIME IN USE	AV. TIME IDLE
OPRS	2.000	.000 2.000 .000	1.730	.262	3.500	18.540	3.407
TRKS	4.000	.000 4.000 .000	3.705	.912	12.504	35.284	3.726

Figure 17-21

17.10.1 PRIORITY AND PREEMPTION OF RESOURCES

A resource may be assigned to facilities according to preset priority classes. In this case, a higher-priority facility may or may not have preemption priority over lower-priority facilities. SIMNET II specifies priority classes and preemption privileges directly under the definition statement $RESOURCES using the following format:

Resource name;initial level(group 1(P)/group 2(P)/.../group n):

The slashes delineate the priority classes, with group 1 facilities representing the highest priority and group n the lowest. The symbol (P) is replaced with (PR) to signify **preemption** or (NPR) to represent **nonpreemption**. The default of P is PR. As an illustration, consider the following definition:

$RESOURCES: R1;3(F1,F2/F3(NPR)/F4,F5):

The three priority classes are (F1,F2), (F3), and (F4,F5), with (F1,F2) providing the highest priority. Facilities F1 and F2 may (by default) preempt F3, F4, or F5 to satisfy their needs, if necessary. The preemption scan always starts with the lowest-priority class; that is, F1 and F2 will attempt to preeempt F4 or F5 before F3. Facility F3, on the other hand, has a higher *non*preemptive priority over F4 and F5 in acquiring R1.

The following rules govern the use of priority classes and preemption:

1. A facility that is subject to preemption can handle one resource only.
2. Under the PR option, preemption will take place only if the preempted amount at least satisfies the request of the preempting facility. Any excess amount will be left in base stock.
3. For both PR and NPR options, all multiple servers in a facility must utilize exactly the same amount of each resource. This is not the case in the absence of priority classes, as each parallel server may act completely independently of all other servers.
4. A preempting facility may preempt more than one parallel server in the preempted facility to satisfy its need. Any excess amount will be left in base stock, in the sense that a preempted server may not hold a partial amount of its resource needs.

Example 17.10-2 (Machine Repair Model). The failure of a principal part in a machine causes a breakdown after UN(400,1400) minutes of operation. When a breakdown takes place, the operator attending the machine must remove the part and replace it with a reconditioned one. It takes 10 minutes to remove the failed part and UN(10,30) minutes to install replacement. Reconditioning of failed parts is done by the same operator and takes UN(400,1200) minutes per part. A delay of 5 minutes is needed to restock a repaired part. The initial stock of spare parts includes 2 pieces.

The model is given in Figure 17-22. It uses two resources: PART and OPER. Resources OPER is used by three facilities: REMOVE where a failed part is removed, INSTALL where a new part is installed, and REPAIR where repair takes place. Both REMOVE and INSTALL have preemptive priority over REPAIR, as should be expected.

A transaction leaving MACH signals a breakdown. OPER is then called upon to REMOVE the old part. Two copy transactions are sent "simultaneously" to facility

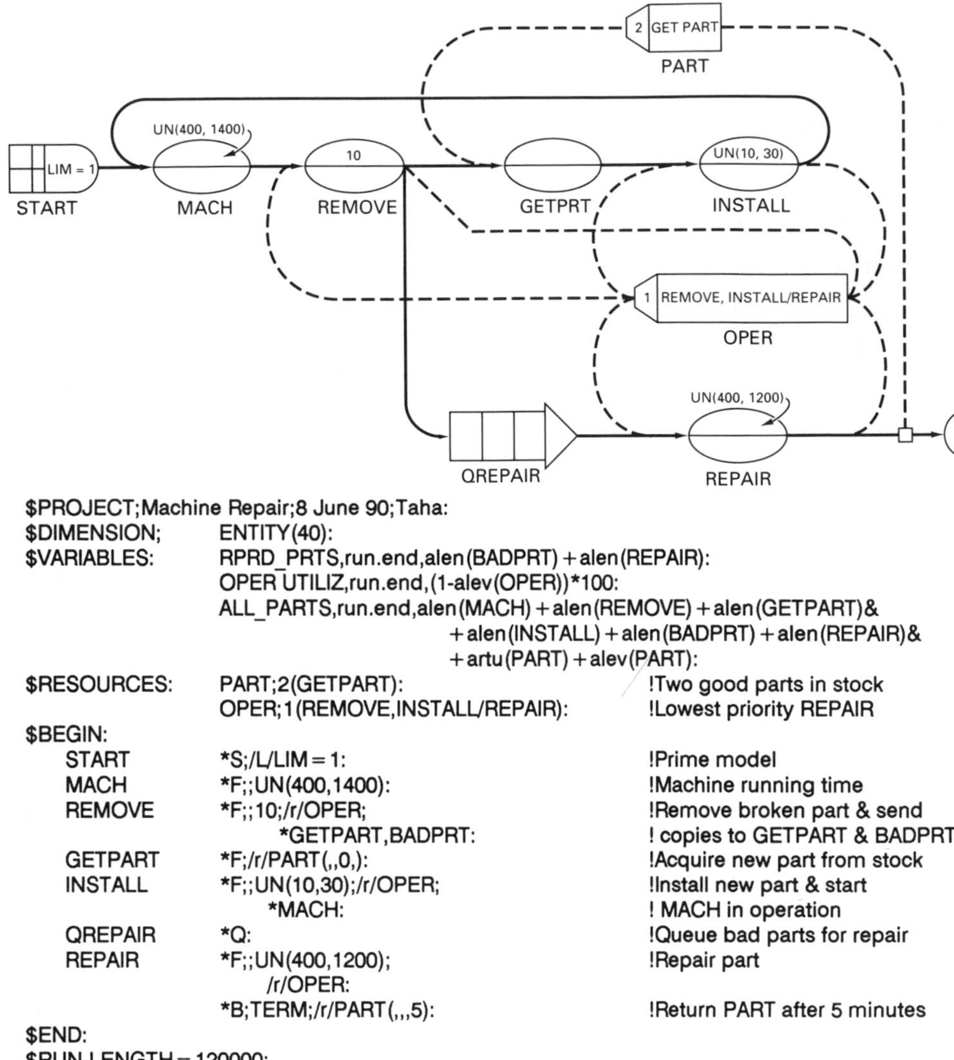


```
$PROJECT;Machine Repair;8 June 90;Taha:
$DIMENSION;      ENTITY(40):
$VARIABLES:      RPRD_PRTS,run.end,alen(BADPRT)+alen(REPAIR):
                 OPER_UTILIZ,run.end,(1-alev(OPER))*100:
                 ALL_PARTS,run.end,alen(MACH)+alen(REMOVE)+alen(GETPART)&
                                   +alen(INSTALL)+alen(BADPRT)+alen(REPAIR)&
                                   +artu(PART)+alev(PART):
$RESOURCES:      PART;2(GETPART):                    !Two good parts in stock
                 OPER;1(REMOVE,INSTALL/REPAIR):      !Lowest priority REPAIR
$BEGIN:
   START         *S;/L/LIM=1:                        !Prime model
   MACH          *F;;UN(400,1400):                   !Machine running time
   REMOVE        *F;;10;/r/OPER;                     !Remove broken part & send
                     *GETPART,BADPRT:                ! copies to GETPART & BADPRT
   GETPART       *F;/r/PART(,,0,):                   !Acquire new part from stock
   INSTALL       *F;;UN(10,30);/r/OPER;              !Install new part & start
                     *MACH:                          ! MACH in operation
   QREPAIR       *Q:                                 !Queue bad parts for repair
   REPAIR        *F;;UN(400,1200);                   !Repair part
                    /r/OPER:
                 *B;TERM;/r/PART(,,,5):              !Return PART after 5 minutes
$END:
$RUN-LENGTH=120000:
$STOP:
```

Figure 17-22

GETPART and to repair queue QREPAIR. After a good part is acquired from resource PART at dummy facility GETPART, it is INSTALLed immediately. The transaction leaving INSTALL returns OPER and enters MACH to restart the operation cycle.

There are two important observations about the model:

1. It is crucial that PART be acquired at dummy GETPART because direct requisition by INSTALL could conceivably result in acquiring OPER when no PART is available. Since INSTALL has preemptive power, OPER can be "tied up" in INSTALL incorrectly while awaiting PART.

2. Facility REPAIR cannot return PART directly because in SIMNET II a *preemptable* facility can handle *one* resource only. The restriction is overcome by returning PART via a branch emanating from REPAIR. This trick essentially does not affect the logic or the statistics of the model. ◀

17.11 ASSEMBLING AND MATCHING OF TRANSACTIONS

Transactions residing in queues can be **assembled** into a single transaction or **matched** with one another prior to leaving their respective queues. In this section we provide the details of how assembling and matching can be implemented in SIMNET II.

17.11.1 ASSEMBLE OPERATION

The assemble operation combines transactions residing in queues into a *single* exiting transaction. The operation is implemented by using a special code that defines the queues comprising the assemble (ASM) set. The code, which is placed in field 4 (select field) of *any one* of the assemble set queues, must have the following format:

ASM (queue 1, . . . ,queue m/attributes rule)

The attributes rule specifies how the attributes of the ASM transaction are computed from those of the individual transactions. Table 17-12 summarizes the permissible rules.

As an illustration, Figure 17-23 gives the graphical representation of the ASM code

ASM (Q1,Q2/LO (2))

with the assembled transaction entering facility F1. The rule LO(2) indicates that the attributes of the ASM transaction will equal those of the transaction exiting either Q1 or Q2, whichever has the smaller value of A(2).

The following rules govern the use of ASM:

1. The ASM set of queues can only feed into *exactly one* node, either by direct sequencing, direct transfer, or a branch.
2. The ASM code need only appear once in any one of the ASM queue sets, *in which case the chosen queue must define the routing of the assembled transaction into the (single) succeeding node.*

Table 17-12
Rules for Computing ASM Attributes

Rule	Description
SUM	Sum of individual attributes
PROD	Product of individual attributes
FIRST	Attributes from queue 1 (per ASM definition)
LAST	Attributes from qucuc m
SELQ(i)	Attributes of queue i, $i = 1, 2, \ldots,$ or m
HI(#)	Attributes of transaction with the HIghest A(#), where # is a positive integer constant
LO(#)	Attributes of transaction with the LOwest A(#)

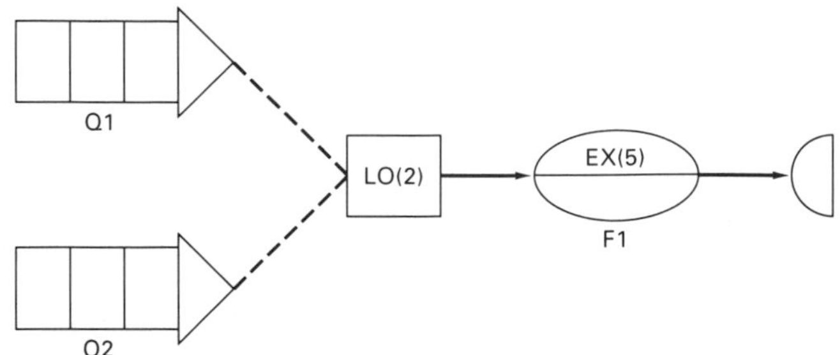

Figure 17-23

To illustrate these rules, the segment in Figure 17-23 may be translated into statements as follows:

```
Q1  *Q;/s/ASM(Q1,Q2/LO(2)):
F1  *F;;EX(5),*TERM:
 :
Q2  *Q:
```

In this case, Q1 carries the ASM code and routes the assembled transaction into F1 by direct sequencing. We can achieve the same result by letting Q2 carry the ASM code, in which case F1 must appear after Q2 instead.

We can also use direct transfer to route the assembled transaction as follows:

```
Q1  *Q;/s/ASM(Q1,Q2/LO(2));*F1:
 :
F1  *F;;EX(2);*TERM:
 :
Q2  *Q:
```

In a similar manner, a single branch may be used as follows:

```
Q1  *Q;/s/ASM(Q1,Q2/LO(2)):
    *B;F1:
 :
F1  *F;;EX(2);*TERM:
 :
Q2  *Q:
```

Observe that the queues comprising the ASM set can be "scattered" anywhere in the model as long as the queue that carries the ASM code is used to route the assembled transaction into the next node.

Example 17.11-1 (Waste Disposal Model II). The statement of this model was given in Example 17.10-1, where it was modeled using resources. ASM offers a different way for modeling the same situation. Figure 17-24 provides the details of the model. ASM is used to "combine" 1 unit of TRKS, 1 unit of LDS, and 1 unit of OPRS before allowing the transaction to enter one of the loaders. Since an ASM transaction can be routed to a single node only, dummy facility ASMBL is used to select either LDR1 or LDR2 using the HTE rule. It is important to point out that ASMBL must be a facility (an auxiliary will not work), so the node will have the capability to look back at the ASM queues and draw a new ASM transaction when

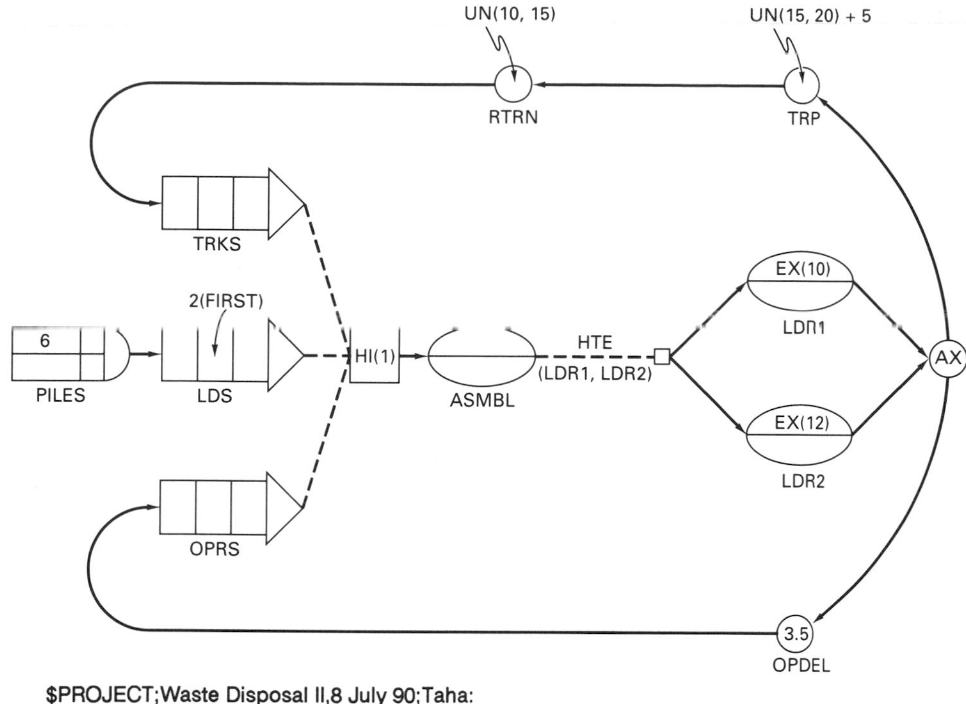


```
$PROJECT;Waste Disposal II,8 July 90;Taha:
$DIMENSION; ENTITY(40),A(1):
$VARIABLES: TRIP TIME;;TRANSIT(1):
$BEGIN:
  PILES    *S;6;;1:                              !Mark time in A(1)
  LDS      *Q;;2(FIRST):                         !Truckload
  TRKS     *Q;(4):                               !Start with 4 trucks
  OPRS     *Q;(2);                               !Start with 2 operators
             /s/ASM(TRKS,LDS,OPRS/HI(1)):        !ASM one of each
  ASMBL    *F;/s/HTE(LDR1,LDR2):                 !Select loader
  LDR1     *F;;EX(10);*AX:                       !Go to NIL auxiliary AX
  LDR2     *F;;EX(12):                           !Pass to AX
  AX       *A;NIL;*OPDEL,TRP:                    !Go to OPDEL and TRP
  OPDEL    *A;3.5;*OPRS:                         !Return operator to OPRS
  TRP      *A;UN(15,20)+5:                       !Travel time
           *B;RTRN;/v/TRIP TIME%:                !Compute TRIP TIME
  RTRN     *A;UN(10,15);*TRKS:                   !Return trip of trucks
$END:
$RUN-LENGTH=480:
$STOP:
```

Figure 17-24

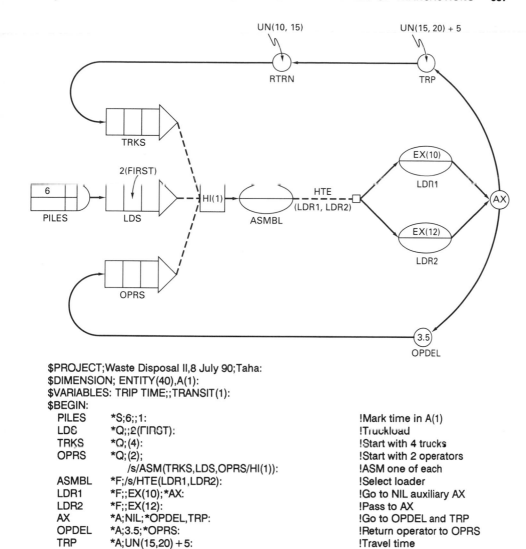

necessary. The HI(1) rule in the ASM field of OPRS guarantees that the assembled transaction will carry the highest A(1) from among all three queues. From the nature of the setup, A(1) will necessarily be that of the transaction leaving LDS. ◀

17.11.2 MATCH OPERATION

The match (MAT) operation can be applied to transactions residing in queues only. Matched transactions from the different queues must leave their respective queues concurrently. If any of the queues does not have a matching transaction, none of the remaining queues will be able to release their transactions.

The MAT code follows the following format:

MAT(queue 1, . . . ,queue m/indices of matching attributes)

As in ASM, the MAT code is placed in field 4 (the select field) of *any one* of the MAT queues. The indices of the matching attributes define the set of attributes that must have equal values in the respective queue in order for a transaction to be a member of a MAT set. These attributes may be expressed as an individual index or a range of indices. For example, MAT(Q1,Q2/1,3) indicates that the values of A(1)

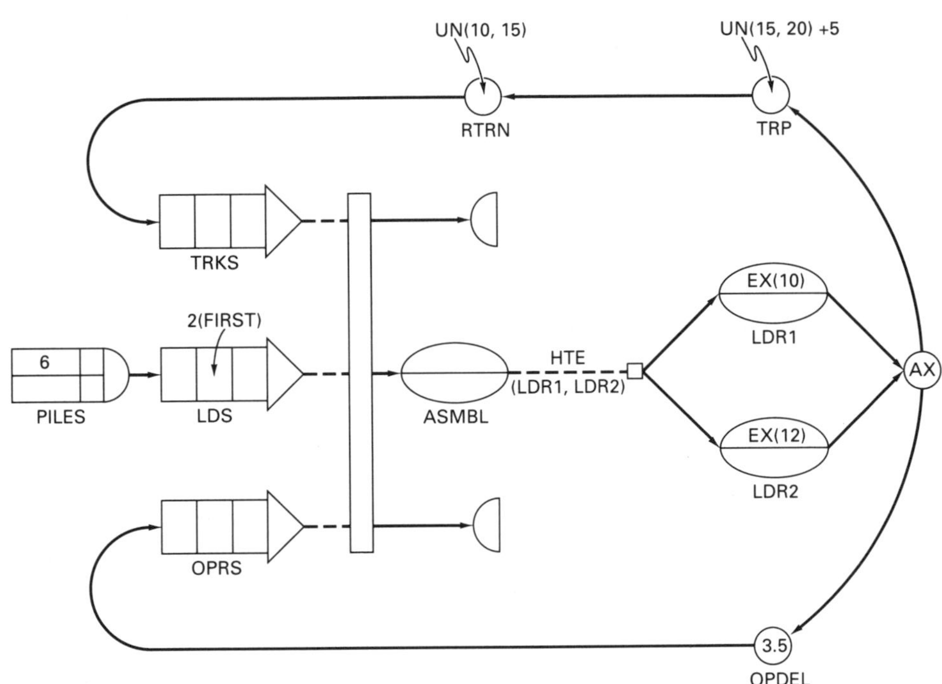


```
$PROJECT;Waste Disposal III,8 July 90;Taha:
$DIMENSION; ENTITY(40),A(1):
$VARIABLES: TRIP TIME;;TRANSIT(1):
$BEGIN:
  PILES    *S;6;;1:                              !Mark time in A(1)
  LDS      *Q;;2(FIRST);                         !A(1) of FIRST pile
              /s/MAT(TRKS,LDS,OPRS);*ASMBL:      !match queues
  TRKS     *Q;(4);*TERM:                         !Start with 4 trucks
  OPRS     *Q;(2);*TERM:                         !Start with 2 operators
  ASMBL    *F;/s/HTE(LDR1,LDR2):                 !Select loader
  LDR1     *F;;EX(10);*AX:                       !Go to NIL auxiliary AX
  LDR2     *F;;EX(12):                           !Pass to AX
  AX       *A;NIL;*OPDEL,TRP:                    !Go to OPDEL and TRP
  OPDEL    *A;3.5;*OPRS:                         !Return operator to OPRS
  TRP      *A;UN(15,20) + 5:                     !Travel time
           *B;RTRN;/v/TRIP TIME%:                !Compute TRIP TIME
  RTRN     *A;UN(10,15);*TRKS:                   !Return trip of trucks
$END:
$RUN-LENGTH=480:
$STOP:
```

Figure 17-25

and A(3) must be the same for the two transactions selected from Q1 and Q2. Again, MAT(Q1,Q2/1–3,5,6) indicates that the matching attributes are A(1), A(2), A(3), A(5), and A(6). We can also use the code ALL for the indices [e.g., MAT(Q1, Q2/ALL)] to indicate that *all* attributes must match. Finally, the indices can be defaulted altogether [e.g., MAT(Q1,Q2)] to signify that the respective transactions simply must wait for one another before departing their respective queues, which in essence means that each queue will release its *head* transaction.

Routing of transactions out of MAT queues differs from that of ASM queues in that each queue may route its respective transaction independently. As in ASM, each queue's route can lead to *exactly one* node (or TERM) by using direct sequencing, direct transfer, or a single branch. Again, the MAT code can be placed in only one of the associated queues.

Example 17.11-2 (Waste Disposal Model III). The situation in Examples 17.10-1 and 17.11-1 where resources and ASM are used will again be modeled using the MAT code. Figure 17-25 provides the details of the new model.

MAT is used to ensure that 1 unit of TRKS, 1 unit of LDS, and 1 unit of OPRS are available before the transaction leaves from ASMBL. There are no matching attributes because the transactions in the different queues simply wait for one another. The matched transactions from TRKS and OPRS are terminated. They will be replaced by two new transactions representing the truck and the operator when the transaction from LDS is split into two at auxiliary AX. ◀

17.12 SPECIAL ASSIGNMENTS

In Section 17.9 we used a **special assignment** of the type (switch name = ON or OFF) to control the status of a logic switch. One of the advantages of using the special assignment format (in place of the special node format used in other languages) is its direct amenability for use within the conditional IF-ENDIF statement, which increases its modeling power. Another advantage is that the modeling capabilities of SIMNET II can be extended without changing the four-node structure of the language, simply by adding new special assignments.

In this section we present additional SIMNET II special assignments designed to control different nodes and elements of the language. The following categorization will be used to organize the presentation:

1. Source activation/deactivation.
2. Queue parameters control.
3. File manipulations applied to:
   (a) Queues only.
   (b) Facilities only.
   (c) Queues or facilities.
4. Locating entries in files.
5. Attributes control.
6. Statistical variables collection.
7. Run length control.
8. External files READ/WRITE capability.

17.12.1 SOURCE NODE ACTIVATION AND DEACTIVATION

In the definition of the source node (Section 17.3.1), the fifth field (LIM=) is used to control the number of creations or the length of time the source node is active. However, these limits, once specified at the start of the simulation cannot be altered during execution. The source activation/deactivation assignments allow the modeler to *suspend* or *resume* source creations *instantly* at any time during the simulation. The format of these assignments is as follows:

SUSPEND=source name
RESUME=source name

Observe that the execution of these assignments will *permanently* override the time of the first creation and the limit on creations as initially defined in fields F2 and F5 of the source node.

Example 17.12-1 (Production Line with Breakdowns). An automatic production line delivers units of a product every UN(1,2) minutes for inspection. The inspection time takes 1.5 minutes per unit. The production line is known to break down every EX(120) minutes. It takes UN(5,10) minutes to complete the repair.

Figure 17-26 provides the model. P_LINE represents the production line that sends 1 unit into Q_INSPECT every UN(1,2) minutes. The breakdown of the line is simulated by a separate segment. Source S_BREAK sends its first breakdown transaction after 120 minutes from the start of the simulation [thereafter, the breakdown

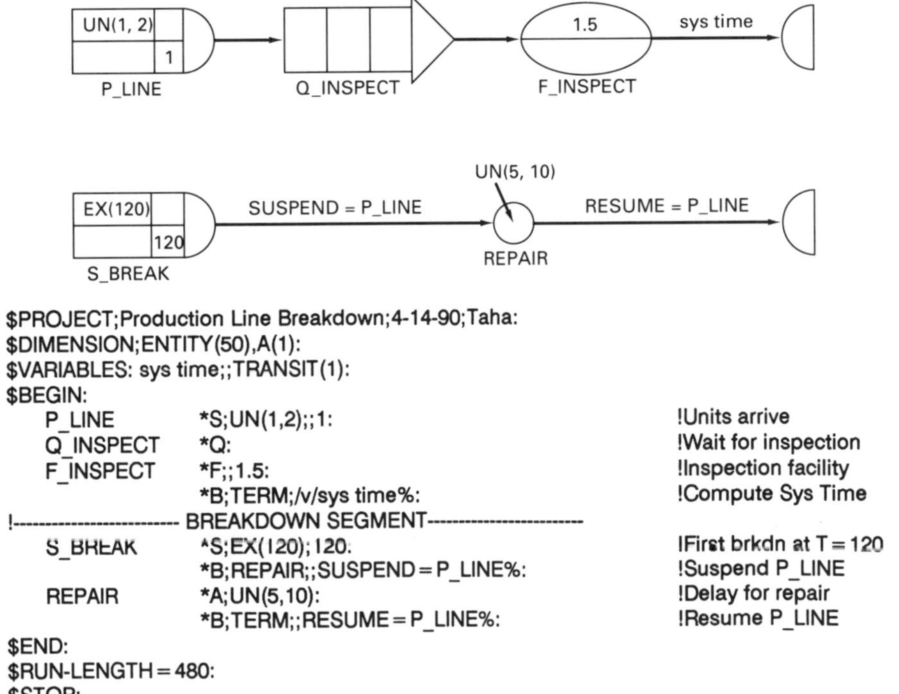


```
$PROJECT;Production Line Breakdown;4-14-90;Taha:
$DIMENSION;ENTITY(50),A(1):
$VARIABLES: sys time;;TRANSIT(1):
$BEGIN:
    P_LINE        *S;UN(1,2);;1:                          !Units arrive
    Q_INSPECT     *Q:                                     !Wait for inspection
    F_INSPECT     *F;;1.5:                                !Inspection facility
                  *B;TERM;/v/sys time%:                   !Compute Sys Time
!------------------------ BREAKDOWN SEGMENT-----------------------
    S_BREAK       *S;EX(120);120:                         !First brkdn at T=120
                  *B;REPAIR;;SUSPEND=P_LINE%:             !Suspend P_LINE
    REPAIR        *A;UN(5,10):                            !Delay for repair
                  *B;TERM;;RESUME=P_LINE%:                !Resume P_LINE
$END:
$RUN-LENGTH=480:
$STOP:
```

Figure 17-26

occurs every EX(120) minutes]. The breakdown transaction coming out of S_BREAK instantly stops P_LINE through the execution of the SUSPEND assignment. After repair takes place [a delay of UN(5,10) minutes in REPAIR], P_LINE is reactivated by executing the RESUME assignment. ◀

17.12.2 QUEUE PARAMETERS CONTROL

The queue node statement in Section 17.3.2 utilizes fields 1, 2, and 3 initially to define the queue's maximum capacity, accumulation condition, and discipline. The information content of these fields may be changed dynamically during the course of the simulation by using the following three special assignments:

```
CAP(queue name)=expression
ACCUM(queue name)=(expression)(attributes rule)
DISCIPLINE(queue name)=queue discipline
```

As the names suggest, the assignments change the CAPacity, ACCUMulate condition, and DISCIPLINE of a queue. Any SIMNET II mathematical expression may be used where indicated in the assignment. Queue discipline and attribute rules are those summarized in Tables 17-1 and 17-2 with the added convenience that the attribute number defined by HI and LO may now be any SIMNET II mathematical expression.

The following examples illustrate the use of the assignments:

```
CAP(QQ)=2*LEN(QQ)
ACCUM(QQ)=(I+J**2)(SUM)
ACCUM(QQ)=3(HI(I+A(1)))
DISCIPLINE(QQ)=LIFO
DISCIPLINE(QQ)=LO(I)
```

All expressions are evaluated at the time the assignment is executed. For example, in the third assignment above, I + A(1) defines the attribute number to be used for implementing the HI(·) rule. If I + A(1) happens to be outside the admissible range for the attributes, an error message will result.

17.12.3 FILE MANIPULATION ASSIGNMENTS

File manipulation assignments allow swapping, deleting, adding, copying, replacing, and locating transactions in queues and facilities. The use of these assignments is restricted in the sense that some of them apply to queues or facilities only.

Table 17-13 provides a summary description of the file manipulation assignments. We refer to the file on the right-hand side of the assignment as the **donor** file. The left-hand-side file will be referred to as the **recipient** file. For example, in the assignment LAST(QQ) = 1(WW), WW and QQ represent the donor and recipient queues, respectively. The assignment moves the first entry in WW to the tail (LAST) position of QQ. Actually, the quantities a and b given in Table 17-13 can be represented by any mathematical expression. For example,

```
((J+1)**2+K)(Q1)=(MAX(I+J,K-M))(Q2)
```

Table 17-13
File Manipulation Assignments

Assignment[a]	Description
Queues only	
a(Q1) = b(Q2)	Move entry b of Q2 to the ath position in Q1
a(Q1) = ALL(Q2)	Move ALL the transactions of Q2 to Q1 starting at the ath position
a(Q1) = TRANS	Place a copy of the TRANSaction currently traversing the branch in the ath position of Q1
a(Q1) = DEL	DELete (dipose of) the ath entry in Q1
ALL(Q1) = DEL	DELete all the contents of Q1 (Q1 becomes empty)
INS(Q1) = b(Q2)	INSert the bth entry of Q2 in Q1 per the queue discipline of Q1
INS(Q1) = ALL(Q2)	INSert ALL the transactions of Q2 in Q1 per the queue discipline of Q1
INS(Q1) = TRANS	INSert a copy of the current TRANSaction in Q1 per the queue discipline of Q1
Facilities only	
a(F1) = REL	RELease immediately the ath entry in facility F1
ALL(F1) = REL	RELease immediately ALL the contents of facility F1
Queues and facilities	
a(Q1 or F1) = REP	REPlace the attributes of the ath entry in Q1 or F1 with those of the current transaction
COPY = b(Q1 or F1)	Change the attributes of the current transaction traversing the branch to those of the bth entry in Q1 or F1

[a] a and b may be any SIMNET II mathematical expressions or the symbol LAST. Q1 and Q2 may represent the *same* queue if it is desired to rearrange the order of transactions in a given queue.

is perfectly valid. SIMNET II automatically truncates the expressions to integer values, if necessary.

Four general rules govern the use of the file manipulation assignments:

1. The "queues only" assignments, with the exception of those involving ALL, are *dynamic* in the sense that the recipient queue will automatically attempt to send its received transaction as far as it will go in the network. This action happens momentarily while the assignment is being executed. As for the ALL-assignments, the modeler is responsible for moving these transactions out of the recipient queue, if necessary, by using a proper switch assignment (Section 17.9).

2. Automatic movement as described in (1) above will *not* be realized if the execution of the assignment is caused by file manipulation **nesting**. By *nesting* it is meant that when an assignment of the type a(Q1) = b(Q2), a(Q1) = TRANS, or INS(Q1) = b(Q2) causes an automatic movement out of Q1, a similar assignment

on a branch leaving Q1 and involving a third queue Q3 [e.g., a(Q3) = b(Q4)] will *not* attempt to move the transaction out of Q3. The modeler must use an explicit switch assignment to effect this movement, when necessary.

3. If the donor file is empty, no action will take place.
4. If a recipient *finite-size* queue happens to be full at the time the assignment is executed, an error stop will result unless the donor and recipient queues are one and the same (i.e., reordering transactions in the same queue).

We illustrate the file manipulations by a number of examples.

Example 17.12-2 (Bank Model). We revisit Example 17.7-1 dealing with the two-lane bank with the additional stipulation that if a lane becomes shorter by at least two cars, the last car in the longer lane jockeys to the last position in the shorter lane.

Figure 17-27 gives the model. The only time we need to pay attention to jockeying cars from the longer to the shorter lane is when a car departs from either lane. The output from facilities WL and WR thus feeds into a single auxiliary AX. The branch from AX computes the user-specified variable DIFF, the difference between

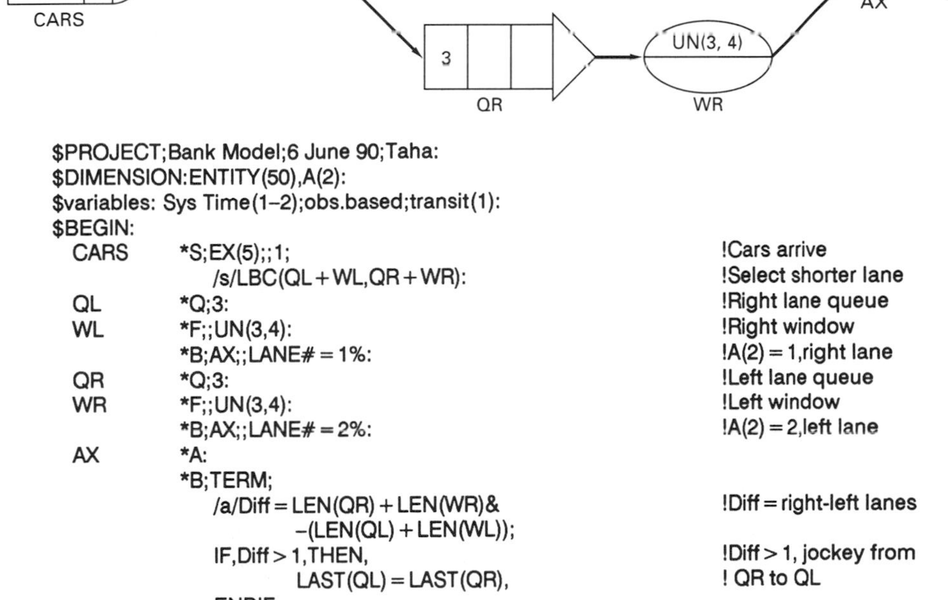


```
$PROJECT;Bank Model;6 June 90;Taha:
$DIMENSION:ENTITY(50),A(2):
$variables: Sys Time(1-2);obs.based;transit(1):
$BEGIN:
  CARS    *S;EX(5);;1;                              !Cars arrive
              /s/LBC(QL+WL,QR+WR):                  !Select shorter lane
  QL      *Q;3:                                     !Right lane queue
  WL      *F;;UN(3,4):                              !Right window
          *B;AX;;LANE#=1%:                          !A(2)=1,right lane
  QR      *Q;3:                                     !Left lane queue
  WR      *F;;UN(3,4):                              !Left window
          *B;AX;;LANE#=2%:                          !A(2)=2,left lane
  AX      *A:
          *B;TERM;
              /a/Diff=LEN(QR)+LEN(WR)&              !Diff=right-left lanes
                     -(LEN(QL)+LEN(WL));
              IF,Diff>1,THEN,                       !Diff>1, jockey from
                     LAST(QL)=LAST(QR),             ! QR to QL
              ENDIF;
              IF,Diff<-1,THEN,                      !Diff<-1, jockey from
                     LAST(QR)=LAST(QL),             ! QL to QR
              ENDIF%;
              /v/Sys Time(LANE#)%:                  !Compute Sys Time
$END:
$RUN-LENGTH=480:
$STOP:
```

Figure 17-27

the number of cars in the right and left lanes. If DIFF > 1, we jockey LAST(QR) into LAST(QL). If −DIFF > 1, the jockeying is reversed. ◀

Example 17.12-3 (Transmission Channel). Messages arrive every UN(7,8) seconds for transmission over a single channel. It takes UN(6,8) seconds to transmit a message. However, every UN(600,650) seconds, the channel malfunctions and any ongoing transmission must be started anew ahead of all waiting messages. It takes about 30 seconds to reset the channel.

Figure 17-28 summarizes the model, which consists of two disjointed segments representing the transmission channel and the failure–repair cycle. When the

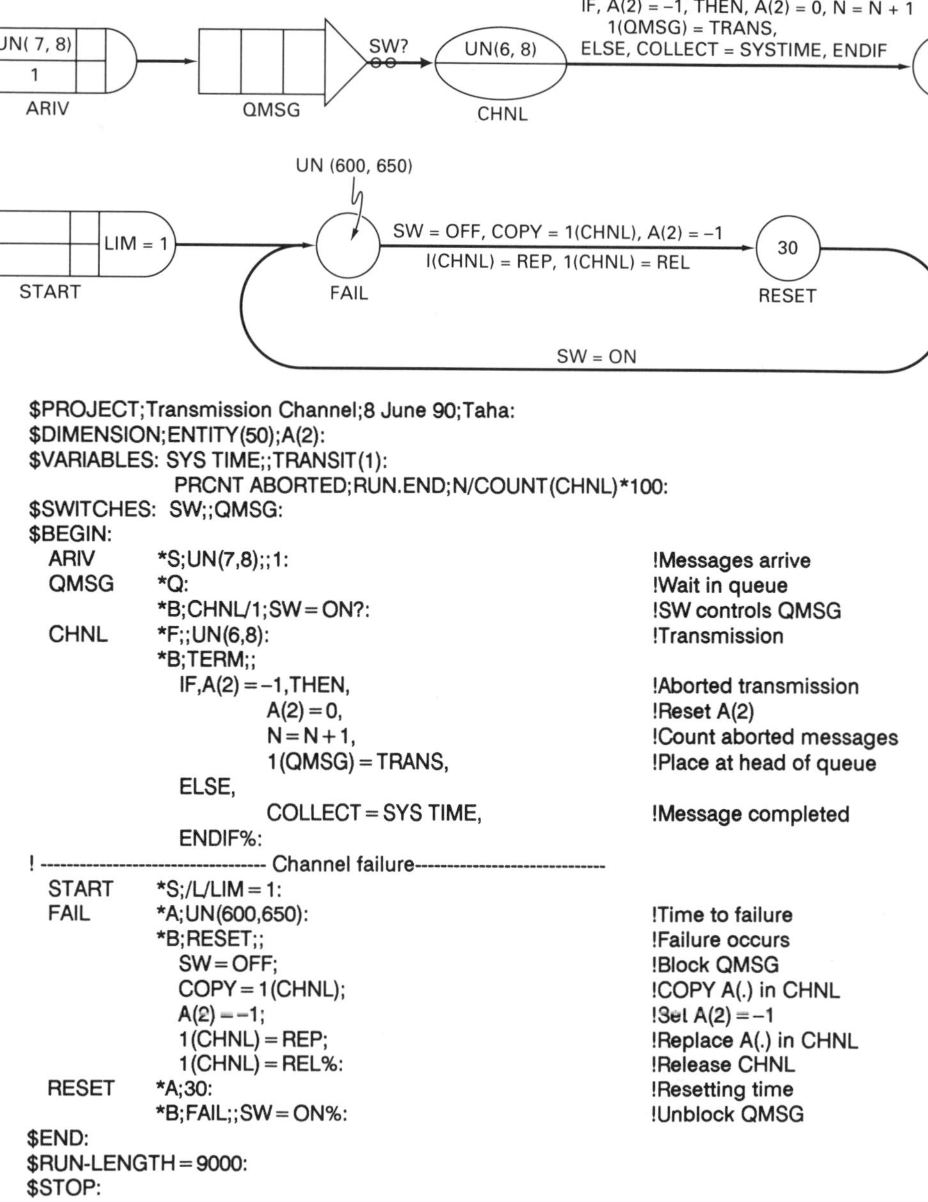


```
$PROJECT;Transmission Channel;8 June 90;Taha:
$DIMENSION;ENTITY(50);A(2):
$VARIABLES: SYS TIME;;TRANSIT(1):
                PRCNT ABORTED;RUN.END;N/COUNT(CHNL)*100:
$SWITCHES: SW;;QMSG:
$BEGIN:
  ARIV      *S;UN(7,8);;1:                          !Messages arrive
  QMSG      *Q:                                     !Wait in queue
            *B;CHNL/1;SW=ON?:                       !SW controls QMSG
  CHNL      *F;;UN(6,8):                            !Transmission
            *B;TERM;;
              IF,A(2)=-1,THEN,                      !Aborted transmission
                     A(2)=0,                        !Reset A(2)
                     N=N+1,                         !Count aborted messages
                     1(QMSG)=TRANS,                 !Place at head of queue
              ELSE,
                     COLLECT=SYS TIME,              !Message completed
              ENDIF%:
! ------------------------------- Channel failure----------------------------
  START     *S;/L/LIM=1:
  FAIL      *A;UN(600,650):                         !Time to failure
            *B;RESET;;                              !Failure occurs
              SW=OFF;                               !Block QMSG
              COPY=1(CHNL);                         !COPY A(.) in CHNL
              A(2)=-1;                              !Set A(2)=-1
              1(CHNL)=REP;                          !Replace A(.) in CHNL
              1(CHNL)=REL%:                         !Release CHNL
  RESET     *A;30:                                  !Resetting time
            *B;FAIL;;SW=ON%:                        !Unblock QMSG
$END:
$RUN-LENGTH=9000:
$STOP:
```

Figure 17-28

channel fails, the transaction leaving auxiliary FAIL immediately turns OFF switch SW to prevent messages from leaving QMSG whose exit end is controlled by the condition SW=ON?. An ongoing message in facility CHNL is then RELeased by executing the asignment 1(CHNL)=REL. However, in order for the model to recognize that an aborted message leaving CHNL must be retransmitted, we must "tag" it *before* it is released from CHNL. We achieve this result by resetting A(2)=−1 for any aborted message [otherwise A(2)=0]. The assignment COPY=1(CHNL) changes the attributes of the transaction leaving FAIL to those of 1(CHNL). Next, we set A(2)=−1 and then execute 1(CHNL)=REP, in effect changing A(2) inside CHNL to −1 while leaving A(1) unchanged. (If CHNL happens to be empty, none of the special assignments will have any effect.)

Upon leaving CHNL, a transaction having A(2)=−1 is identified as an aborted message. Thus the conditional branch from CHNL executes the assignment A(2)=0, 1(QMSG)=TRANS, which places the aborted message [with its A(2) reset to zero] back at the head of QMSG. Following the repair of the CHNL (exit from RESET), we execute SW=ON to move the transaction into CHNL for retransmission.

Notice that the special assignment COLLECT=SYS TIME allows us to compute SYS TIME conditionally in the assignments field of the branch. The general format of this assignment is COLLECT=variable name. ◀

17.12.4 LOCATING ENTRIES IN FILES

The use of the file manipulation assignments in Section 17.12.3 often necessitates identifying the location of a desired entry in a file before the assignments can be applied. The LOCate assignment is designed to account for some of these situations. Its general format is as follows:

LHS=LOC(file name/condition)

LOC will assign to LHS the rank of the *first* entry in the named file that satisfies the given condition. If no such entry can be found, LHS assumes a zero value. In this regard, LHS may be any legitimate arithmetic left-hand side of an assignment.

The condition associated with LOC follows one of the following special formats:

1. a op VAL
2. HI(a) or LO(a) op VAL
3. ALL op ALL

where op represents one of the comparison operators =, <, >, <=, >= or <>. In formats 1 and 2, a represents the *index* of an attribute of an entry in the searched file and VAL is the value to which the designated attribute is compared. Specifically, format 1 compares A(a) with VAL, and format 2 compares the HIghest or LOwest value of A(a) with VAL. Both a and VAL can be any mathematical expressions. In format 3, we compare ALL the attributes of an entry in the searched file with ALL the attributes of the transaction that is currently traversing the branch (and causing the execution of the LOC assignment).

One simple but important rule must be kept in mind when dealing with formats 1 and 2. A(a) is an attribute of an entry of the searched file. If VAL happens to be a function of A(·), then that A(·) is regarded by SIMNET II as an attribute of the transaction currently traversing the branch.

The LOC function may also be used to compare two attributes *within* the searched file. This is achieved by assigning a negative value to a.

Examples:

1. I=LOC(FILE/1=2)

The rank of the first entry in FILE whose A(1) = 2 is assigned to I. If no such entry can be found, I is assigned a zero value.

2. I=LOC(FILE/A(1)=A(2))

The rank of an entry in FILE whose A(A(1)) [where A(1) is determined from FILE] equals A(2) of the *current passing transaction* is assigned to I.

3. I=LOC(FILE/HI(I+J))

The rank of an entry in FILE having the *highest* value of A(I+J) is assigned to I.

4. I=LOC(FILE/LO(K)>J**2)

The rank of an entry in FILE having the *lowest* value of A(K) that is greater than J**2 is assigned to I.

5. I=LOC(FILE/ALL <> ALL)

The rank of an entry in FILE that has all its attributes different from the corresponding attributes of the passing transaction is assigned to I.

6. I=LOC(FILE/−1<A(2))

The rank of an entry in FILE whose A(1) is less than its A(2) [both A(1) and A(2) are from within FILE] is assigned to I.

Example 17.12-4 (Jobs with Priority I). Jobs arrive every UN(5,8) minutes for processing at a single machine. About 30% of the jobs represent rush orders that must be processed ahead of the remaining 70%. However, within each group, the job with the smallest processing time receives the highest priority. It takes UN(3,9) minutes to process a regular job and EX(6) minutes to process a rush job.

The idea of the model in Figure 17-29 is to use the code A(1) = 1 and A(1) = 2 to represent rush and regular jobs, respectively. We also use A(2) to carry the processing time of each job. Thus, as jobs are created from source JOBS, we execute the following conditional assignment to determine the respective values of A(1) and A(2):

```
IF,RND<.3,
      THEN,A(1)=1,A(2)=EX(6),
      ELSE,A(1)=2,A(2)=UN(3,9),
ENDIF
```

```
$PROJECT;Jobs with Priority I;5-12-90,Taha:
$DIMENSION;ENTITY(50),A(3):
$VARIABLES: SYS TIME;OBS.BASED;TRANSIT(3):
$BEGIN:
  COMIN    *S;UN(5,8);;3:
           *B;QJOBS;;IF,RND<.3,THEN,
                               A(1)=1,A(2)=EX(6),
                             ELSE,A(1)=2,A(2)=UN(3,9),ENDIF%:
  QJOBS    *Q,,,LO(2).
  MACH     *F;;A(2):
           *B;TERM;;K=LOC(QJOBS/1=1),
                        IF,K>1,
                          THEN,1(QJOBS)=K(QJOBS),ENDIF%;
                        SYS TIME%:
$END:
$RUN-LENGTH=480:
$STOP:
```

Figure 17-29

Queue QJOBS ranks its transactions using the discipline LO(2) thus ranking all the jobs in ascending order of their processing times regardless of whether they are rush or regular orders.

When facility MACH completes a job, the departing transaction will locate the *first* rush job in the queue by using the following LOC function:

```
K=LOC(QJOBS/1=1)
```

This assignment assigns to K the rank of the first entry in QJOBS whose $A(1) = 1$ (rush job). If $K > 1$, the located entry is not at the head of QJOBS and we must apply the file manipulation assignment 1(QJOBS) = K(QJOBS) to move it to that position. After the transaction leaving MACH has been TERMinated, MACH will then look back at QJOBS and draw the proper job for processing. ◀

17.12.5 RUN LENGTH CONTROL

Although SIMNET II specifies the length of the run by using $RUN-LENGTH, it may be necessary to control the length of the run conditionally from within the simulation during execution. SIMNET II provides the following special assignment for this purpose:

```
SIM=STOP
```

With SIM=STOP, the user may eliminate the $RUN-LENGTH control statement, thus automatically defaulting it to infinity. By executing the assignment SIM=STOP conditionally, the simulation can be stopped at any time. A typical illustration is

```
IF,COUNT(SS)=500,THEN,SIM=STOP,ENDIF.
```

This assignment says that the simulation will stop after 500 transactions have exited node SS. The branch on which this assignment is executed is purely the user's choice.

17.12.6 OTHER SPECIAL ASSIGNMENTS

SIMNET II offers other important special assignments that include the following:

1. Attributes control assignments conveniently allow the user to assign new values or retrieve old values of attributes.
2. Read and write assignments allow reading from and writing to (formatted and unformatted) external ASCII files.
3. File dump assignment that permits dumping the contents of any file for the sake of debugging.

Because of space limitations, the details of these assignments will not be presented here. The reader should consult Taha (1990) for more information.

17.13 INITIAL DATA

A model in SIMNET II may make use of six types of initial data:

1. Initial file (queues and facilities) entries.
2. Discrete probability density functions.

3. Table look-up functions.
4. Arrays values.
5. Constant variables (nonsubscripted) values.
6. Functions or mathematical expressions.

These data are presented in the model in a *run-specific* format so that several runs, each with different initial data, can be executed in a single simulation session.

17.13.1 INITIAL FILE ENTRIES

Initial entries with specific attribute values are entered using the following format:

```
$INITIAL-ENTRIES:  i-j/file 1 name/first entry attributes values;
                                            :
                                   last entry attributes values:
                                :
                         (other files repeats)
                      :
                  (i-j repeats)
```

where i and j are integer constants defining the inclusive range of run numbers for which the given entries apply. The format for each entry is

```
(d)A(1),A(2), ...,A(n)
```

where d is the number of duplicates of the list A(1),A(2), ..., A(n) to be inserted in the file (default = 1) and n is the number of attributes as defined by the $DIMENSION statement. Each entry terminates with (;) with the last entry in a file terminating with (:). Trailing *zero* attributes for any entry may be defaulted by ending the entry with (,;) or (,:).

The following example illustrates the use of $INITIAL-ENTRIES with two queues Q1 and Q2 and one facility F1. The model is assumed to have two attributes:

```
$INITIAL-ENTRIES:  1-1/Q1/(2)11,22;12,23;  !first 3 entries of Q1
                            -11,;          !fourth entry (-11,0)
                            ;              !fifth entry (0,0)
                            :              !sixth entry (0,0)
                        F1/-11,-22:        !only entry of F1
                   2-3/Q2/10,20:           !start runs 2 and 3
                        F1/110,220:
```

Note that all entries may be "strung" on the same line. The given format is more readable, however.

Example 17.13-1 at the end of Section 17.13.4 illustrates the use of $INITIAL-ENTRIES.

17.13.2 DISCRETE AND DISCRETIZED CONTINUOUS DENSITY FUNCTIONS

Empirical (discrete) distributions are defined in SIMNET II using the following format:

```
$DISCRETE-PDFS:  i-j/N1/x11,p11; ... ;xin,pin:
                        :
                      repeats
                    :
                  repeats
```

where

N = number of points (x,p) of the discrete function
x = value of the random variable
p = discrete probability value associated with x

The following example illustrates the definition of discrete functions:

```
$DISCRETE-PDFS:  1-1/3/1,.1;2,.4;3,.5:  !Function #1, run 1
                      2/0,.6;1,.4:      !Function #2, run 1
                 2-3/3/2,.3;3,.5;4,.2:  !Function #1, runs 2,3
```

SIMNET II references the discrete function by using the symbol DI(n,r), where n represents the function number within its run range and r is the random number stream (default = 1). Both n and r may be any mathematical expressions. If n is positive, sampling is made at the *discrete* points defined by $DISCRETE-PDFS. Else, if n is negative, SIMNET II will convert the discrete points into a *piecewise linear* probability density function. The DI function may be used directly in a mathematical expression.

Example 17.13-2 at the end of Section 17.13.6 illustrates the use of $DISCRETE-PDFS.

17.13.3 TABLE LOOK-UP FUNCTIONS

Table look-up functions are used to define a dependent variable y as a function of an independent variable x. The format of the function is similar to that of $DISCRETE-PDFS.

```
$TABLE-LOOKUPS:  i-j/N1/x11,y11;x12,y12; ...,x1n1,y1n1:
                     N2/x21,y21;x22,y22; ...,x2n2,y2n2:
                        :
                    :
                  repeats
```

The following example illustrates the use of the function:

```
$TABLE-LOOKUPS:  1-1/4/1,2;3,5;6,7;7,9:  !Function #1
                     3/0,0;1,4;2,11:     !Function #2
```

The symbol TL(n,x) is used to reference table look-up functions with n representing the number of the function within a given run range and x representing the value of the independent variable. If n is negative, linear interpolation is used to determine the value of y. Both n and x could be represented by mathematical expressions. In this case, n will be truncated to an integer value, if necessary, and x must assume a value in the domain in the table look-up function. The function TL may be used directly in a mathematical expression.

In the example above, TL(1,3) = 5 whereas TL(1,4) will result in an error because x = 4 is undefined for table look-up function number 1. Looking at table number 2, we see that TL(−2,1.5) = 7.5 as interpolated linearly between x = 4 and x = 11.

17.13.4 INITIALIZATION OF ARRAY ELEMENTS

Arrays defined by the $DIMENSION statement may be initialized using the following format:

```
$ARRAYS:
        array 1; i–j/list of values:
                       ⋮
                     repeats
                 ⋮
        repeats
```

There are two formats for the list of values:

1. *Explicit* in which each element is explicitly preceded by the subscript(s) defining the element.
2. *Implied* in which subscripts of the listed values are identified by their order in the list. In this case, the entire list must be preceded by the code NS/.

The following example provides an illustration of the use of the two formats given the two arrays BC(2) and YZ(3,2):

```
$ARRAYS:
  BC; 1–1/NS/11,22:        !implicit,BC(1)=11,BC(2)=22
      2–4/2,33:            !explicit,BC(2)=33
  YZ; 1–2/1,2,88;3,1,99:   !explicit,YZ(1,2)=8,YZ(3,1)=99
      3–3/NS/11,22,33:     !implicit,YZ(1,1)=11,YZ(1,2)=22,YZ(2,1)=33
```

When NS is used, the values are taken to represent respective elements of the array (read on a row-by-row basis in the case of the two-dimensional array). The explicit format is useful when it is desired to initialize selected elements of the array. Note that in the implicit case, any trailing elements that are not assigned values automatically are zero. For example, in run 3, the values of YZ(2,2), YZ(3,1), and YZ(3,2) are all zero by omission.

Example 17.13-1 (Gravel Hauling Operation). This example illustrates the use of $INITIAL-ENTRIES and $ARRAYS initialization.

A company utilizes three 20-ton and two 30-ton trucks for hauling gravel to different customers. The demand for gravel is sufficiently high to keep the operation busy on a continuous basis. It takes 10 minutes to load a 20-ton truck and 15 minutes to load a 30-ton truck. The round trip to and from customer location is

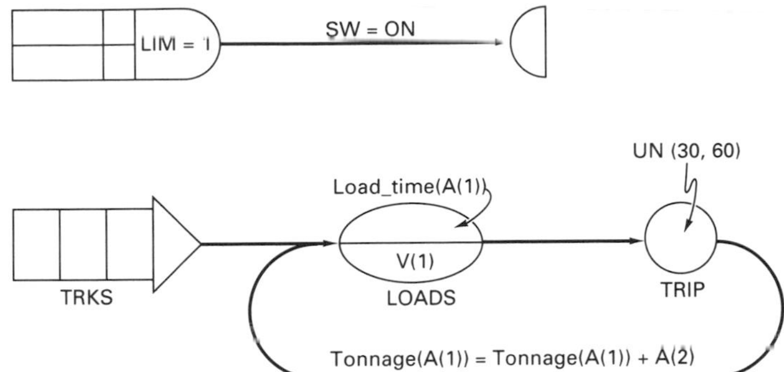


```
$PROJECT;Gravel Hauling;9 June 90;Taha:
$DIMENSION:ENTITY(50);A(2),Tonnage(2),Load_time(2):
$ATTRIBUTES: TYPE,CAPACITY:
$SWITCHES: SW;;TRKS:
$VARIABLES: Tonnage 1;RUN.END;Tonnage(1):
            Tonnage 2;RUN.END;Tonnage(2):
$BEGIN:
  ARIV    *S;/L/LIM=1:
          *B;TERM;;SW=ON%:                    !Activate TRKS
  TRKS    *Q:                                 !See $INITIAL-ENTRIES
  LOADS   *F;;Load_time(TYPE):
  TRIP    *A;UN(30,60):                       !Travel to destination
          *B;TRKS;;                           !Compute tonnage
            Tonnage(TYPE)=Tonnage(TYPE)+CAPACITY%:
$END:
$RUN-LENGTH=1440:
$INITIAL-ENTRIES: 1-3/TRKS/(3)1,20;           !3 20-ton trucks
                               (2)2,30:       !2 30-ton trucks
$ARRAYS:
  Load_time; 1-3/NS/10,15:                    !Load time for 20/30-ton
$STOP:
```

Figure 17-30

UN(30,60) minutes. The objective of the simulation is to estimate the tonnage hauled by each truck type in a 24-hour period.

Figure 17-30 gives the model. $INITIAL-ENTRIES statement places three 20-ton trucks and two 30-ton trucks in queue TRKS. Each entry has two attributes: A(1) assigns a serial number representing truck type, and A(2) specifies the tonnage of the truck. We use the names TYPE and CAPACITY to describe A(1) and A(2).

The loading time at facility LOADS is given by the initial values of the $ARRAY Load_time(1) = 10 and Load_time(2) = 15 for the 20- and 30-ton trucks. Since TYPE[A(1)] carries the type of the truck (= 1 or 2), the model uses Load_time(TYPE) to define the loading time. After loading is completed, the truck travels to the customer location before returning to TRKS. The tonnage hauled by each truck type is recorded in array Tonnage(TYPE) to be printed as a RUN.END variable.

It is the modeler's responsibility to initiate the movement of the trucks out of TRKS at the start of the simulation. The model employs the dummy source START to release one transaction which executes the assignment SW=ON that automatically activates queue TRKS. ◀

17.13.5 INITIALIZATION OF NONSUBSCRIPTED VARIABLES

In SIMNET II, a constant variable is a *non*subscripted variable. Its value is initialized by using the following format:

```
$CONSTANTS:  i-j/name 1=value,name 2=value,repeats:
```

For example, if the constant variables II and JJ must assume the values 2 and 10 at the start of run 1, we express this as

```
$CONSTANTS:  1-1/II=2,JJ=10:
```

17.13.6 MATHEMATICAL FUNCTIONS

It often happens that we would be interested in changing the *expression* representing interarrival, delay, or service times during the course of the simulation. For example, the service-time distribution may change from EX(20) to UN(15,30), depending on the job being processed. Although this result can be achieved using proper conditional statements, the use of $FUNCTIONS greatly facilitates this process. The general format of this statement is as follows:

```
$FUNCTIONS:  i-j/function 1;function 2; ... ;function n:
```

These functions are then accessed in the model by using the code FUN(m), where m is any mathematical expression whose (truncated) integer value must lie between 1 and n. For example, the statement

```
$FUNCTIONS:  1-1/SQRT(AB+EX(10));UN(10,15)**2:
```

represents two functions. When FUN(1) is encountered in the model, the SIMNET II processor will automatically evaluate SQRT(AB + EX(10)). Similarly, FUN(2) evaluates UN(10,15)**2. Observe that we can express the index m of FUN as an expression whose value can be changed as desired. For example, we can use FUN(I+J) provided that I+J = 1 or 2 to correspond to the example above. Observe also that FUN(·) may be used as part of any complex mathematical expression. However, a function may not call itself.

Function calls may also be made by using double-subscripted code FFUN(a,b), where a and b are the row and column where the desired function is located. The format $FUNCTIONS remains practically unchanged, with the exception that it must now include delimiters to indicate the end of each row. This is done simply by inserting two successive semicolons (;;) at the appropriate end of each row. As such, each row need *not* include the same number of functions. For example, in the statement

```
$FUNCTIONS:  1-1/3;WW(I)+J;;                          !row 1
                   EX(2)+10,UN(10,20),EX(3);;         !row 2
                   MAX(K,L):                          !row 3
```

FFUN(1,1) = 3, FFUN(1,2) = WW(I)+J, ..., and FFUN(3,1) = MAX(K,L).

Example 17.13-2 (Jobs with Priority II). The situation in Example 17.12-4 is remodeled using $DISCRETE-PDFS and $FUNCTIONS. Figure 17-31 gives the

```
$PROJECT;Jobs with Priority II;5-12-90,Taha:
$DIMENSION;ENTITY(50),A(3):
$ATTRIBUTES; TYPE,PROCESS_TIME:
$VARIABLES: SYS TIME;OBS.BASED;TRANSIT(3):
$BEGIN:
  COMIN   *S;UN(5,8);;3:
          *B;QJOBS;;TYPE=DI(1),                         !job type
                    PROCESS_TIME=FUN(TYPE)%:            !process time
  QJOBS   *Q;;;LO(2):
  MACH    *F;;PROCESS_TIME:
          *B;TERM;;K=LOC(QJOBS/1=1),
                  IF,K>1,
                    THEN,1(QJOBS)=K(QJOBS),ENDIF%;
                  SYS TIME%:
$END:
$RUN-LENGTH=480:
$DISCRETE-PDFS: 1-1/2/1,.3; 2,.7:                       !Job type probabilites
$FUNCTIONS:    1-1/EX(6),UN(3,9):                       !Job processing time
$STOP:
```

Figure 17-31

new model. The attributes A(1) and A(2) are given the names TYPE and PROCESS_TIME.

The type of the job is determined from the $DISCRETE-PDFS, where DI(1) assumes the random value 1 with probability .3 and 2 with probability .7. We use $FUNCTIONS to define FUN(1) = EX(6) and FUN(2) = UN(3,9). Transactions leaving source JOBS will then execute the assignments TYPE=DI(1), PROCESS_TIME=FUN(TYPE) to produce the desired values of A(1) and A(2). The remainder of the model is similar to that given in Example 17.12-4. ◀

17.14 INITIALIZING NODES AND RESOURCES WITH RUN-DEPENDENT DATA

SIMNET II allows the modeler to express certain parameters of the source, queue, facility, and resource as nonsubscripted or array variables. The values of these variables are then initialized at the start of each run using the formats presented in Sections 17.13.4 and 17.13.5 or by using READ to access external files. With such an arrangement, any number of runs, each with different initial data may be executed in a single simulation session. Again, because of space limitation, the reader is referred to Taha (1990) for details on these items.

17.15 GATHERING STATISTICAL OBSERVATIONS

Statistical observations gathering is controlled in SIMNET II by the following statements (which appear in the *control segment* of the model, see Figure 17-5):

```
$RUN-LENGTH=(simulated time period of one run):
$TRANSIENT-PERIOD=(length of the transient period):
$RUNS=(number of runs):
$OBS-RUN=(number of observations per run):
$PRINT=OBS:
```

The **transient period** is the initial warm-up period at the start of *each* simulation run during which the model output exhibits erratic variation and hence no statistical observation should be collected. SIMNET II provides graphical procedures for estimating the transient period. [See Taha (1990) for details.] The estimated period may then be entered using the $TRANSIENT-PERIOD control statement or interactively as will be explained below. The default values for $RUN-LENGTH and $TRANSIENT-PERIOD are infinity and zero, respectively. If the $RUN-LENGTH is defaulted to infinity, the user must stop the simulation conditionally using the SIM=STOP assignment (Section 17.12.5). The statement $PRINT=OBS: is used when it is desired to print the output of each observation.

The specific choices of the values of $RUNS and $OBS/RUN automatically decide the manner in which the observations are gathered and presented in the output report. SIMNET II provides three different types of output:

1. Single run.
2. Multiple runs with different initial data.
3. Global statistics based on:
   (a) Subinterval (or batch) method.
   (b) Replication method.

Table 17-14 summarizes the values of $RUNS and $OBS/RUN that *uniquely* identify each type.

Single runs have been used with all the examples so far presented in this chapter (both $RUNS and $OBS/RUN have assumed the default value 1). In the case of multiple runs, it is expected that each run will have different initial data (using the initial value formats in Section 17.13). In this case each run will have its separate output summary.

The global subinterval and replication methods are depicted graphically in Figure 17-32. In the **subinterval method**, a single run is divided into batches (after truncating the transient period, if desired) with each batch representing a statistical observation. The **replication method** involves multiple runs (each with a truncated transient period). A single observation is then represented by a single run. From the statistical standpoint, each method has its advantages and drawbacks with no clear advantage of one over the other. The global statistical summary for either method presents the mean and standard deviation together with a 95% confidence interval.

As an illustration of the use of the information in Table 17-14, the control statements below result in the application of the replication method with 10 observations ($RUN = 10 and $OBS/RUN = 1). The transient period is 90 time units and each observation (run) consumes 1000 time units (inclusive of the transient period).

```
$RUN-LENGTH=1000:  $TRANSIENT-PERIOD=90
$RUNS=10:          $OBS/RUN=1:
```

Table 17-14
Gathering Statistical Observations

	Integer Value Assigned to:	
Procedure	$RUNS	$OBS/RUN
Single run	1 (default)	1 (default)
Multiple runs	>1	0
Subinterval method	1 (default)	>1
Replication method	>1	1 (default)

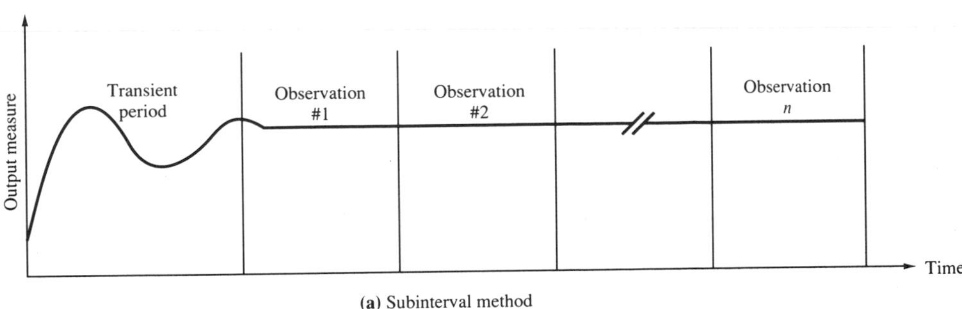

(a) Subinterval method

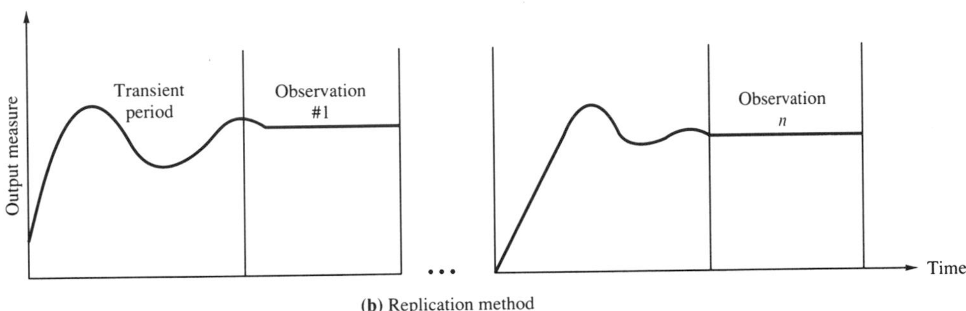

(b) Replication method

Figure 17-32

17.16 OTHER SIMNET II CAPABILITIES

Because of space limitations, we are unable to include the details of the following SIMNET II modeling capabilities:

1. Interactive debugging/execution environment.
2. Estimation of the transient period using interactive graphics.
3. Interactive implementation of the subinterval and replication method for gathering global statistics.
4. Reading from and writing to (formatted and unformatted) external files (including the keyboard and the screen) during execution.
5. Use of indexing (PROCs) to represent repetitive modeling segments.

These topics and others are detailed in Taha [1990].

17.17 SUMMARY

SIMNET II is based on the use of four nodes only, which makes it particularly easy to learn and use. In spite of its simplicity, the language is powerful enough to tackle the most complex situation. The concept of using *special assignments* within the context of the conditional IF-ENDIF provides powerful modeling capabilities.

The full SIMNET II system is totally interactive both for debugging and for obtaining the global statistical results. In particular, SIMNET II allows the estimation of the transient period and then the implementation of the subinterval or replication global statistical method, all without leaving the interactive mode of execution.

SELECTED REFERENCES

FISHMAN, G., *Principles of Discrete Event Simulation*, Wiley, New York, 1978.

GORDON, G., *System Simulation*, Prentice Hall, Englewood Cliffs, N.J., 1978.

TAHA, H. A., *Simulation Modeling and SIMNET*, Prentice Hall, Englewood Cliffs, N.J., 1988.

TAHA, H. A., *Simulation with SIMNET II*, SimTec, Inc., Fayetteville, Ark., 1990.

PROBLEMS

Section	Assigned Problems
17.3	17–1 to 17–6
17.5	17–7 to 17–9
17.7	17–10 to 17–14
17.8	17–15 to 17–20
17.9	17–21, 17–22
17.10	17–23, 17–24
17.11	17–25, 17–26
17.12	17–27 to 17–32
17.13	17–33, 17–34

☐ **17–1** In each of the following cases, what will be the values of attribute A(1) associated with the first three transactions that exit the source node?

(a) ARIV *S;5;;1:
(b) ARIV *S;5;3;1:
(c) ARIV *S;5;3;−1:

☐ **17–2** How many transactions will be generated by each of the following source statements during the first 20 time units of the simulation?

(a) ARIV *S;5;/L/LIM=3:
(b) ARIV *S;5;/m/MULT=2:

☐ **17–3** The first five transactions arriving at queue QQ have the following attributes.

Transaction	A(1)	A(2)
1	4	9
2	7	−3
3	1	10
4	3	14
5	2	6

Show how these transactions will be ordered in QQ in each of the following cases:

(a) QQ *Q:
(b) QQ *Q;/d/LIFO:
(c) QQ *Q;/d/HI(1):
(d) QQ *Q;/d/LO(2):

☐ **17–4** For the same data in Problem 17–3, identify the transactions leaving QQ and their attributes in each of the following cases assuming FIFO discipline:

(a) QQ *Q;;2(SUM):
(b) QQ *Q;;4(FIRST):
(c) QQ *Q;;3:
(d) QQ *Q;;2(LO(1)):
(e) QQ *Q;;2(HI(2)):

☐ **17–5** Consider the following model segment:

```
QQ  *Q;(3):
FF  *F;;2;(1);goto-TERM:
```

(a) How many transactions will be processed by facility FF?
(b) Determine the simulation time at which each transaction will leave FF.
(c) Repeat parts (a) and (b) assuming that the model segment is changed as follows:

Change 1:

```
QQ  *Q:
FF  *F;;2;(1);goto-TERM:
```

Change 2:

```
QQ  *Q;(3):
FF  *F;;2;goto-TERM:
```

Change 3:

```
QQ  *Q;(3):
FF  *F;;2;2(1);goto-TERM:
```

☐ **17–6** Consider the following source statement:

```
SS  *S;UN(10,15):
```

Suppose that the SIMNET II processor is using the following random numbers stream:

.1111, .2342, .6712, .8923, .4687, .3526, ...

Determine the simulation time at which the first three transactions from SS are created.

☐ **17–7** A SIMNET II model uses two arrays, ARR1 and ARR2. The respective dimensions of ARR1 and ARR2 are 2 × 6 and 10. Each transaction in the model uses four attributes with the descriptive names TYPE, STYLE, TIME_IN, and TIME_OUT. Write the SIMNET II statements for this segment of the model.

☐ **17–8** In the output in Figure 17-7, what is the relationship between the entries of the last three columns of queue LINE?

☐ **17–9** Run the post office model (Example 17.5-1) assuming that there is only one clerk and that the interarrival time is exponential with mean 3 minutes. You will get an execution error indicating that maximum size of ENTITY has been exceeded, an error that does not occur in the original model. Using the information in the error message regarding the contents of files LINE, CLRKS and E.FILE, explain why the error occurs. Can this error always be removed by increasing the $DIMENSION of ENTITY? Would this corrective action work for any length of the simulation run? (These questions are best answered by experimenting with the model.)

☐ **17–10** Write a SIMNET II model for the following situation. New customers in a bank arrive every 18 minutes on the average, exponentially distributed. A customer must consult first with a bank officer regarding the opening of the new account. It takes between 15 and 20 minutes, uniformly distributed, to complete this task. The next step is to go to one of three tellers to make the initial deposit. This activity takes 5 minutes on the average, exponentially distributed. All customers are served on a FIFO basis. Run the simulation for 480 minutes. The objectives of the simulation are to determine the following:

(a) The average length of each queue inside the bank.
(b) The average waiting time of each queue inside the bank.
(c) The percentage of customers that do not have to wait in each queue.
(d) The maximum length of each queue.
(e) The percent utilization of the bank officer and the teller.

☐ **17–11** In the output of the bank model of Figure 17-9, how many customers are denied service at the windows because the lanes are full? Suppose that these customers normally seek service inside the bank, where two tellers are available. The service time is estimated as EX(4) minutes. Modify the model in Figure 17-9 to account for this change. What is the maximum length of the queue inside the bank?

☐ **17–12** Modify the situation in Problem 17–11 so that only 75% of the customers who cannot join the window lanes will seek service inside the bank.

☐ **17–13** In the synchronized workstation model (Figure 17-11), what will happen if /E in the statement for queue WAIT is replaced with /D?

☐ **17–14** In the workstations model of Figure 17-11, show how the same modeling logic can be preserved by removing the statement for auxiliary OUT and accounting for its effect by modifying the definition of queue QEND.

[*Hint*: Use QEND as an accumulator.]

☐ **17–15** Plot the SIMNET II networks of the following two segments and show the difference between the two cases.

```
SS   *S;UN(4,5);/s/POR(Q1,Q2):      SS   *S;UN(4,5);/s/POR(Q1,Q2):
     *B;Q1/1;cur.time>100?:              *B;Q1/s;cur.time>100?:
Q1   *Q;3:                          Q1   *Q;3:
$segment:                           $segment:
Q2   *Q;3:                          Q2   *Q;3:
```

☐ **17–16** Modify the bank model of Figure 17-9 to account for the following change. A customer who cannot join the window lanes will go inside the bank for service only if no more than three customers are waiting inside. There is only one teller inside with the service time given by EX(3) minutes.

☐ **17–17** Consider the following model segment:

```
SS  *S;UN(1,2):
    *B;AX;;A(1)=II%:
AX  *A:
    *B;AY/2;A(1)<=2?:
    *B;AV/2;A(1)>=2?:
    *B;AW:
    *B;AZ/L;A(1)>2?:
```

Determine the nodes that can be reached by a transaction leaving source SS under each of the following independent conditions: II = 1, II = 2, and II = 3.

☐ **17–18** For the TV model in Figure 17-10 (Section 17.7.3), suppose that the rejection probability is increased from .2 to .45. Further assume that a TV unit can be adjusted at most once; otherwise, it must be discarded. Modify the model to account for this situation. Determine the number of discarded units during a 480-minute simulation run using a RUN.END statistical variable. Also, use an OBS.BASED variable to determine the average time a good unit spends in the system.

☐ **17–19** Regular and rush jobs arrive from two sources with the interarrival times given by EX(4) and EX(8) hours, respectively. All jobs are processed on a single machine with the processing time equal to EX(3) hours for regular jobs and EX(2) for rush jobs. The scheduling rule calls for processing jobs with the smallest processing time first. However, in any case, priority is given to rush jobs over regular jobs. Compute the average time each regular and rush job spends in the system. Model the system and run the simulation for 480 minutes.

[*Hint*: Use two separate queues for regular and rush jobs together with a POR input select rule for the machine.]

☐ **17–20** Cars arrive at a wash facility every UN(12,20) minutes. The facility includes both washing and vacuum cleaning. Customers normally prefer to wash the car before vacuuming it. The order may be reversed if the vacuum cleaning lane is shorter. After completing one activity, the car is moved to the tail end of the other activity. It takes 10 minutes to get the car washed and UN(8,9) minutes to get it vacuumed. Model the system and run the simulation for 480 minutes for the purpose of determining the average time a car spends in the entire facility.

☐ **17–21** In the machine maintenance model of Figure 17-18, it is implicitly assumed that repair will start immediately after 480 minutes have elapsed (i.e., when a transaction leaves DELAY). This assumption is correct only if MACHINE happens to be idle at that point in time. Otherwise, preventive maintenance should not start until MACHINE completes its load. Modify the model to account for this detail.

☐ **17–22** Modify the machine maintenance model in Figure 17-18 so that preventive maintenance is carried out every 50 completed jobs instead of every 8 hours.

☐ **17–23** Modify the waste disposal model in Figure 17-20 so that TRKS and OPRS are acquired directly by LDR1 and LDR2. In this case the facility DUMY is not needed. The results of the modified model will be different from those of the original model. Why?

☐ **17–24** The initial level of an inventory item is 200 units. Orders for the item arrive every EX(.7) week. The size of the order is PO(5) units. Orders are processed on a FIFO basis. Those that cannot be filled immediately are usually backlogged. Every 3 weeks the stock is reviewed. If the inventory position (on hand plus on order minus backlogged) drops below 50 units, a replenishment order that brings the inventory position back to 200 units is placed. Delivery of the stock takes place a week later. Determine the average safety stock level at the time a replenishment takes place, the average stock replenishment size, and the average inventory position during a 10-year simulation run.

☐ **17–25** Modify the model in Figure 17-24 given that queue LDS carries the ASM code.

☐ **17–26** Modify the model in Figure 17-25 so that queue TRKS carries the MAT field.

☐ **17–27** Use the SUSPEND and RESUME assignments to simulate a source that releases transactions only on demand. Specifically, consider the situation where an operator takes EX(10) minutes to complete a job. Upon completing a job, the operator will then reach for another one. For all practical purposes, we can assume that the source of new jobs is unlimited.

☐ **17–28** Solid waste is hauled to a processing facility by trucks that arrive every EX(20) minutes. The facility has two compactors that are used to reduce the solid waste into bundles for later transfer by train to a dry-fuel installation. The compactors operate in successive shifts of 8 hours each, with the third shift being used for maintenance. The capacity of the first compactor is one truck load per bundle, and that of the second is two loads per bundle. The compacting time of the first compactor is EX(12) minutes and that of the second is EX(15) minutes. Simulate the system for a period of 5 days for the purpose of determining the utilization of the two compactors.

☐ **17–29** A bank opens at 8:00 A.M. and closes at 4:30 P.M. daily. The interarrival time for customers is EX(6) minutes. It takes EX(9) minutes to serve each customer at one of the bank's two tellers. At 4:30 P.M., all customers inside the bank must be served. Estimate the maximum, minimum, and average time needed after 4:30 P.M. to serve all the remaining customers.

☐ **17–30** A precast widget is processed by two machines MACH1 and MACH2. The interarrival time of the widgets is EX(.0588) minute. The processing times at MACH1 and MACH2 are .04 and .0357 minute, respectively. The floor space available for incoming jobs to MACH1 and MACH2 are 50 and 40 widgets, respectively. The tool at MACH2 fails frequently every EX(8) minutes, at which time it must be removed and discarded. It takes UN(1,3) minutes to repair the tool. Simulate the system for 30 minutes for the purpose of determining the utilizations of all machines.

□ **17–31** Aluminum ingots are melted before being distributed in urns for later use in a manufacturing process. A complete charge of the melting furnace consists of four ingots. It takes 25 minutes to complete the melting process. The charge is then distributed among three urns. Assume that ingots arrive every 7 minutes at the furnace. Simulate the model for 480 minutes for the purpose of determining the utilization of the furnace.

[*Hint*. Use an accumulator queue to release the proper charge of the furnace. When the accumulated charge leaves the furnace, "explode" it into three urns using FOR-NEXT to place three copies of the exiting transaction into a new queue representing the urns.]

□ **17–32** Remodel Problem 17–19 using only one queue for both regular and rush jobs.

□ **17–33** Passengers arrive randomly at a bus station. The number of empty seats at the time the bus arrives at the station also varies randomly. It takes about 7 seconds for a passenger to get on the bus. A round trip that brings the bus back to the station takes about 30 minutes. At present, only one bus is in operation. A passenger is willing to wait at the station for no more than 20 minutes.

The interarrival time for the passengers at the station is determined from histogrammed empirical data as follows:

Cell Midpoint Time (minutes)	2.0	2.5	3.0	3.5	4.0
Relative Frequency	.2	.24	.28	.18	.10

The number of empty seats on the bus is 7, 8, or 9 with equal probabilities. Determine the percentage of reneging customers during a simulation run of 480 minutes.

□ **17–34** Consider a two-window drive-in bank where the interarrival time changes according to the following distributions:

Time Period	Distribution
8:00 A.M.–10:00 A.M.	EX(10) minutes
10:01 A.M.–1:00 P.M.	UN(10,15) minutes
1:01 P.M.–4:30 P.M.	GA(3,5) minutes
4:31 P.M.–7:59 A.M.	bank is closed

It takes EX(9) minutes to serve a customer in one the bank's two tellers. Simulate the bank operation for 5 days for the purpose of determining the average waiting time per customer.

[*Hint*: Use $FUNCTIONS for the interarrival-time distributions.]

Chapter 18

Markovian Decision Process

This chapter presents an application of dynamic programming to the solution of a stochastic decision process that can be described by a finite number of states. The transition probabilities between the states are described by a Markov chain. The reward structure of the process is also described by a matrix whose individual elements represent the revenue (or cost) resulting from moving from one state to another. Both the transition and revenue matrices depend on the decision alternatives available to the decision maker. The objective of the problem is to determine the optimal policy that maximizes the expected revenue of the process over a finite or infinite number of stages.

18.1 SCOPE OF THE MARKOVIAN DECISION PROBLEM: THE GARDENER EXAMPLE†

In this section we introduce a simple example that will be used as a vehicle of explanation throughout the chapter. In spite of its simplicity, the example paraphrases a number of important applications in the areas of inventory, replacement, cash flow management, and regulation of water reservoir capacity.

Every year, at the beginning of the gardening season, a gardener applies chemical tests to check the soil's condition. Depending on the outcomes of the tests, the garden's productivity for the new season is classified as good, fair, or poor.

Over the years, the gardener observed that current year's productivity can be assumed to depend only on last year's soil condition. The transition probabilities over a 1-year period from one productivity state to another can thus be represented in terms of the following Markov chain:

$$\text{State of the system this year}\left\{\begin{matrix}1\\2\\3\end{matrix}\right.\overset{\overbrace{\begin{matrix}1 & \quad 2 & \quad 3\end{matrix}}^{\text{State of the system next year}}}{\begin{bmatrix}.2 & .5 & .3\\ 0 & .5 & .5\\ 0 & 0 & 1\end{bmatrix}} = \mathbf{P}^1$$

The representation assumes the following correspondence between productivity and the states of the chain:

Productivity (Soil Condition)	State of the System
Good	1
Fair	2
Poor	3

The transition probabilities in $\mathbf{P}^1$ indicate that the productivity for a current year can be no better than last year's. For example, if the soil condition for this year is fair (state 2), next year's productivity may remain fair with probability .5 or become poor (state 3), also with probability .5.

The gardener can alter the transition probabilities $\mathbf{P}^1$ by invoking other courses of action. Typically, fertilizer is applied to boost the soil condition, which yields the following transition matrix $\mathbf{P}^2$:

$$\mathbf{P}^2 = \begin{matrix}1\\2\\3\end{matrix}\overset{\begin{matrix}1 & \quad 2 & \quad 3\end{matrix}}{\begin{bmatrix}.3 & .6 & .1\\ .1 & .6 & .3\\ .05 & .4 & .55\end{bmatrix}}$$

With the application of the fertilizer, it is possible to improve the condition of soil over last year's.

† A review of Markov chains is given in Section 18.6.

To put the decision problem in perspective, the gardener associates a return function (or a reward structure) with the transition from one state to another. The return function expresses the gain or loss during a 1-year period, depending on the states between which the transition is made. Since the gardener has the options of using or not using fertilizer, gain and losses are expected to vary depending on the decision made. The matrices $\mathbf{R}^1$ and $\mathbf{R}^2$ summarize the return functions in hundreds of dollars associated with the matrices $\mathbf{P}^1$ and $\mathbf{P}^2$, respectively. Thus $\mathbf{R}^1$ applies when no fertilizer is used; otherwise, $\mathbf{R}^2$ is utilized in the representation of the return function.

$$\mathbf{R}^1 = \|r_{ij}^1\| = \begin{matrix} & 1 & 2 & 3 \\ 1 & 7 & 6 & 3 \\ 2 & 0 & 5 & 1 \\ 3 & 0 & 0 & -1 \end{matrix}$$

$$\mathbf{R}^2 = \|r_{ij}^2\| = \begin{matrix} & 1 & 2 & 3 \\ 1 & 6 & 5 & -1 \\ 2 & 7 & 4 & 0 \\ 3 & 6 & 3 & -2 \end{matrix}$$

Notice that the elements r_{ij}^2 of $\mathbf{R}^2$ take into account the cost of applying the fertilizer. For example, if the system is in state 1 and remains in state 1 during next year, its gain will be $r_{11}^2 = 6$compared to $r_{11}^1 = 7$when no fertilizer is used.

What kind of a decision problem does the gardener have? First, we must know whether the gardening activity will continue for a limited number of years or, for all practical purposes, indefinitely. These situations are referred to as **finite-stage** and **infinite-stage** decision problems. In both cases, the gardener would need to determine the *best* course of action to be followed (fertilize or do not fertilize) given the outcome of the chemical tests (state of the system). The optimization process will be based on maximization of expected revenue.

The gardener may also be interested in evaluating the expected revenue resulting from following a prespecified course of action whenever a given state of the system occurs. For example, fertilizer may be applied whenever the soil condition is poor (state 3). The decision-making process in this case is said to be represented by a **stationary policy**.

We must note that each stationary policy will be associated with a different transition and return matrices, which, in general, can be constructed from the matrices $\mathbf{P}^1$, $\mathbf{P}^2$, $\mathbf{R}^1$, and $\mathbf{R}^2$. For example, for the stationary policy calling for applying fertilizer only when the soil condition is poor (state 3), the resulting transition and return matrices, $\mathbf{P}$ and $\mathbf{R}$, respectively, are given as

$$\mathbf{P} = \begin{bmatrix} .2 & .5 & .3 \\ 0 & .5 & .5 \\ .05 & .4 & .55 \end{bmatrix}, \qquad \mathbf{R} = \begin{bmatrix} 7 & 6 & 3 \\ 0 & 5 & 1 \\ 6 & 3 & -2 \end{bmatrix}$$

These matrices differ from $\mathbf{P}^1$ and $\mathbf{R}^1$ in the third rows only, which are taken directly from $\mathbf{P}^2$ and $\mathbf{R}^2$. The reason is that $\mathbf{P}^2$ and $\mathbf{R}^2$ are the matrices that result when fertilizer is applied in *every* state.

Exercise 18.1-1

(a) Identify the matrices $\mathbf{P}$ and $\mathbf{R}$ associated with the stationary policy calling for using fertilizer whenever the soil condition is fair or poor.

[*Ans.*

$$\mathbf{P} = \begin{bmatrix} .2 & .5 & .3 \\ .1 & .6 & .3 \\ .05 & .4 & .55 \end{bmatrix}, \quad \mathbf{R} = \begin{bmatrix} 7 & 6 & 3 \\ 7 & 4 & 0 \\ 6 & 3 & -2 \end{bmatrix}$$

(b) Identify all the stationary policies of the gardener's example.
[*Ans.* The stationary policies call for applying fertilizer whenever the system is in (1) state 1, (2) state 2, (3) state 3, (4) state 1 or 2, (5) state 1 or 3, (6) state 2 or 3, and (7) state 1, 2, or 3.]

Notice that once *all* stationary policies are enumerated, we can apply the proper analysis to select the *best* policy. This procedure, however, may be impractical even for moderate-size problems, since the number of policies may be too large. What is needed is a method that determines the best policy systematically without enumerating all the policies in advance. We develop such methods in the remainder of the chapter, for both finite- and infinite-stage problems.

18.2 FINITE-STAGE DYNAMIC PROGRAMMING MODEL

Suppose that the gardener plans to "retire" from exercising the gardening hobby in N years. We are thus interested in determining the optimal course of action for each year (to fertilize or not to fertilize) over a finite planning horizon. Optimality here is defined such that the gardener will accumulate the highest expected revenue at the end of N years.

Let $k = 1$ and 2 represent the two courses of action (alternatives) available to the gardener. The matrices $\mathbf{P}^k$ and $\mathbf{R}^k$ representing the transition probabilities and reward function for alternative k were given in Section 18.1 and are summarized here for convenience.

$$\mathbf{P}^1 = \|p_{ij}^1\| = \begin{bmatrix} .2 & .5 & .3 \\ 0 & .5 & .5 \\ 0 & 0 & 1 \end{bmatrix}, \quad \mathbf{R}^1 = \|r_{ij}^1\| = \begin{bmatrix} 7 & 6 & 3 \\ 0 & 5 & 1 \\ 0 & 0 & -1 \end{bmatrix}$$

$$\mathbf{P}^2 = \|p_{ij}^2\| = \begin{bmatrix} .3 & .6 & .1 \\ .1 & .6 & .3 \\ .05 & .4 & .55 \end{bmatrix}, \quad \mathbf{R}^2 = \|r_{ij}^2\| = \begin{bmatrix} 6 & 5 & -1 \\ 7 & 4 & 0 \\ 6 & 3 & -2 \end{bmatrix}$$

Recall that the system has three states: good (state 1), fair (state 2), and poor (state 3).

We can express the gardener's problem as a finite-stage dynamic programming (DP) model as follows. For the sake of generalization, suppose that the number of states for each stage (year) is m (= 3 in the gardener's example) and define

$f_n(i)$ = optimal *expected* revenue of stages $n, n+1, \ldots, N$, given that the state of the system (soil condition) at the beginning of year n is i

The *backward* recursive equation relating f_n and f_{n+1} can be written as (see Figure 18-1)

$$f_n(i) = \max_k \left\{ \sum_{j=1}^{m} p_{ij}^k [r_{ij}^k + f_{n+1}(j)] \right\}, \qquad n = 1, 2, \ldots, N$$

where $f_{N+1}(j) \equiv 0$ for all j.

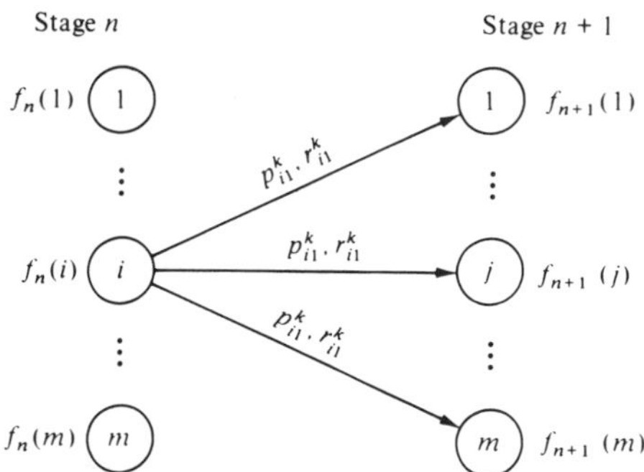

Figure 18-1

A justification for the equation is that the *cumulative* revenue, $r_{ij}^k + f_{n+1}(j)$, resulting from reaching state j at stage $n+1$ from state i at stage n occurs with probability p_{ij}^k. In fact, if v_i^k represents the expected return resulting from a single transition from state i given alternative k, then v_i^k can be expressed as

$$v_i^k = \sum_{j=1}^{m} p_{ij}^k r_{ij}^k$$

The DP recursive equation can thus be written as

$$f_N(i) = \max_k \{v_i^k\}$$

$$f_n(i) = \max_k \left\{ v_i^k + \sum_{j=1}^{m} p_{ij}^k f_{n+1}(j) \right\}, \qquad n = 1, 2, \ldots, N-1$$

Before showing how the recursive equation is used to solve the gardener's problem, we illustrate the computation of v_i^k, which is part of the recursive equation. For example, suppose that no fertilizer is used ($k = 1$); then

$$v_1^1 = .2 \times 7 + .5 \times 6 + .3 \times 3 = 5.3$$
$$v_2^1 = 0 \times 0 + .5 \times 5 + .5 \times 1 = 3$$
$$v_3^1 = 0 \times 0 + 0 \times 0 + 1 \times -1 = -1$$

These values show that if the soil condition is found good (state 1) at beginning of the year, a single transition is expected to yield 5.3 for that year. Similarly, if the soil condition is fair (poor), the expected revenue is 3 (-1).

Exercise 18.2-1

Compute the values of v_i^k for all i given that fertilizer is used only if the system is in states 2 or 3 (fair or poor); ottherwise, no fertilizer is used.
[*Ans.* $v_1^1 = 5.3$, $v_2^2 = 3.1$, $v_3^2 = .4$.]

The following example will now solve the gardener's problem. We utilize the same format of DP tabular computations introduced in Chapter 10.

Example 18.2-1. In this example, we solve the gardener's problem using the data summarized in the matrices $\mathbf{P}^1$, $\mathbf{P}^2$, $\mathbf{R}^1$, and $\mathbf{R}^2$. It is assumed that the planning horizon comprises 3 years only ($N = 3$).

Since the values of v_i^k will be used repeatedly in the computations, they are summarized here for convenience.

i	v_i^1	v_i^2
1	5.3	4.7
2	3	3.1
3	−1	.4

Stage 3

	v_i^k		Optimal Solution	
i	$k = 1$	$k = 2$	$f_3(i)$	k^*
1	5.3	4.7	5.3	1
2	3	3.1	3.1	2
3	−1	.4	.4	2

Stage 2

	$v_i^k + p_{i1}^k f_3(1) + p_{i2}^k f_3(2) + p_{i3}^k f_3(3)$		Optimal Solution	
i	$k = 1$	$k = 2$	$f_2(i)$	k^*
1	$5.3 + .2 \times 5.3 + .5 \times 3.1 + .3 \times 4 = 8.03$	$4.7 + .3 \times 5.3 + .6 \times 3.1 + .1 \times .4 = 8.19$	8.19	2
2	$3 + 0 \times 5.3 + .5 \times 3.1 + .5 \times .4 = 4.75$	$3.1 + .1 \times 5.3 + .6 \times 3.1 + .3 \times .4 = 5.61$	5.61	2
3	$-1 + 0 \times 5.3 + 0 \times 3.1 + 1 \times .4 = -.6$	$.4 + .05 \times 5.3 + .4 \times 3.1 + .55 \times .4 \cong 2.13$	2.13	2

Stage 1

	$v_i^k + p_{i1}^k f_2(1) + p_{i2}^k f_2(2) + p_{i3}^k f_2(3)$		Optimal Solution	
i	$k = 1$	$k = 2$	$f_1(i)$	k^*
1	$5.3 + .2 \times 8.19 + .5 \times 5.61 + .3 \times 2.13 \cong 10.38$	$4.7 + .3 \times 8.19 + .6 \times 5.61 + .1 \times 2.13 \cong 10.74$	10.74	2
2	$3 + 0 \times 8.19 + .5 \times 5.61 + .5 \times 2.13 = 6.87$	$3.1 + .1 \times 8.19 + .6 \times 5.61 + .3 \times 2.13 \cong 7.92$	7.92	2
3	$-1 + 0 \times 8.19 + 0 \times 5.61 + 1 \times 2.13 = 1.13$	$.4 + .05 \times 8.19 + .4 \times 5.61 + .55 \times 2.13 \cong 4.23$	4.23	2

The optimal solution shows that for years 1 and 2, the gardener should apply fertilizer ($k^* = 2$) regardless of the state of the system (soil condition as revealed by the chemical tests). In year 3, however, fertilizer should be applied only if the system is in state 2 or 3 (fair or poor soil condition). The total expected revenues for the three years are $f_1(1) = 10.74$ if the state of the system in year 1 is good, $f_1(2) = 7.92$ if it is fair, and $f_1(3) = 4.23$ if it is poor. ◀

The DP solution provided above is sometimes referred to as the **value-iteration** approach, because by the very nature of the recursive equation, the values of $f_n(i)$ are determined iteratively.

Exercise 18.2-2

Suppose that the gardener's planning horizon is 4 years; what are the optimal expected revenues and decisions? [*Hint*: You should be able to obtain the solution by adding one iteration only to the DP tableaus.]
[*Ans.* $f_1(1) = 13.097, f_1(2) = 10.195$, and $f_1(3) = 6.432$. The optimal decisions call for applying fertilizer in years 1, 2, and 3 regardless of the state of the system. In year 4, fertilizer is used when the state of the system is either fair or poor.]

The (finite horizon) gardener's problem just solved can be generalized in two ways. First, the transition probabilities and their return functions need not be the same for every year. Second, a discounting factor may be applied to the expected revenue of the successive stages so that the values of $f_1(i)$ would represent the *present value* of the expected revenues of all the stages.

The first generalization would require simply that the return values r_{ij}^k and transition probabilities p_{ij}^k be additionally functions of the stage, n. In this case the DP recursive equations appear as

$$f_N(i) = \max_k \{v_i^{k,N}\}$$

$$f_n(i) = \max_k \left\{v_k^{k,n} + \sum_{j=1}^{m} p_{ij}^{k,n} f_{n+1}(j)\right\}, \qquad n = 1, 2, \ldots, N-1$$

where

$$v_i^{k,n} = \sum_{j=1}^{m} p_{ij}^{k,n} r_{ij}^{k,n}$$

The second generalization is accomplished as follows. Let α (< 1) be the discount factor per year, which is normally computed as $\alpha = 1/(1 + t)$, where t is the annual interest rate. Thus D dollars a year from now are equivalent to αD dollars now. The introduction of the discount factor will modify the original recursive equation as follows:

$$f_N(i) = \max_k \{v_i^k\}$$

$$f_n(i) = \max_k \left\{v_i^k + \alpha \sum_{j=1}^{m} p_{ij}^k f_{n+1}(j)\right\}, \qquad n = 1, 2, \ldots, N - 1$$

The application of this recursive equation is exactly similar to that given in Example 18.2-1 except that the discount factor α is multiplied by the term that includes $f_{n+1}(j)$. In general, the use of a discount factor may result in a different optimum decision in comparison with when no discount is used.

Exercise 18.2-3
Solve Example 18.2-1 given the discount factor $\alpha = .6$
[*Ans.*

$$f_3(1) = 5.3, \quad k^* = 1; f_3(2) = 3.1, \quad k^* = 2; f_3(3) = .4, \quad k^* = 2$$
$$f_2(1) = 6.94, k^* = 1; f_2(2) = 4.61, k^* = 2; f_2(3) = 1.44, k^* = 2$$
$$f_1(1) = 7.77, k^* = 1; f_1(2) = 5.43, k^* = 2; f_1(3) = 2.19, k^* = 2$$

Note that the use of the discount factor α resulted in different optimum decisions: namely, the solution now calls for using no fertilizer in all three years if the state of the system is good.]

The DP recursive equation can be used to evaluate any *stationary policy* for the gardener's problem. If we assume that no discounting is used (i.e., $\alpha = 1$), the recursive equation for evaluating a stationary policy is

$$f_n(i) = v_i + \sum_{j=1}^{m} p_{ij} f_{n+1}(j)$$

where p_{ij} is the (i, j)th element of the transition matrix associated with the policy and v_i is the expected one-step transition revenue of the policy.

To demonstrate the use of the recursive equation above, consider the stationary policy, which calls for applying fertilizer every time the soil condition is poor (state 3). As shown in Section 18.1, we have

$$\mathbf{P} = \begin{bmatrix} .2 & .5 & .3 \\ 0 & .5 & .5 \\ .05 & .4 & .55 \end{bmatrix}, \qquad \mathbf{R} = \begin{bmatrix} 7 & 6 & 3 \\ 0 & 5 & 1 \\ 6 & 3 & -2 \end{bmatrix}$$

Thus we obtain

i	1	2	3
v_i	5.3	3	.4

and the values of $f_n(i)$ are computed as

$$f_3(1) = 5.3, \qquad f_3(2) = 3, \qquad f_3(3) = .4$$
$$f_2(1) = 5.3 + .2 \times 5.3 + .5 \times 3 + .3 \times .4 = 7.98$$
$$f_2(2) = 3 + 0 \times 5.3 + .5 \times 3 + .5 \times .4 = 4.7$$
$$f_2(3) = .4 + .05 \times 5.3 + .4 \times 3 + .55 \times .4 \cong 2.09$$
$$f_1(1) = 5.3 + .2 \times 7.98 + .5 \times 4.7 + .3 \times 2.09 \cong 9.87$$
$$f_1(2) = 3 + 0 \times 7.98 + .5 \times 4.7 + .5 \times 2.09 \cong 6.39$$
$$f_1(3) = .4 + .05 \times 7.98 + .4 \times 4.7 + .55 \times 2.09 \cong 3.83$$

The finite-stage DP model is suitable for decision problems with finite number of periods. However, many decision situations encompass either a very large number of periods or actually continue indefinitely. This makes it awkward, if not impossible, to use the finite model. The following section shows how the problem is tackled by developing an infinite-stage DP model.

18.3 INFINITE-STAGE MODEL

The long-run behavior of a Markovian process is characterized by its independence of the initial state of the system. In this case the system is said to have reached *steady state.* We are thus primarily interested in evaluating policies for which the associated Markov chains allow the existence of a steady-state solution. (Section 18.6 provides the conditions under which a Markov chain can yield steady-state probabilities.)

In this section we are interested in determining the optimum *long-run* policy of a Markovian decision problem. It is logical to base the evaluation of a policy on maximizing (minimizing) the expected revenue (cost) *per transition period.* For example, in the gardener's problem, the selection of the best (infinite-stage) policy is based on the maximum expected revenue per year.

There are two methods for solving the infinite-stage problem. The first method calls for enumerating *all* possible stationary policies of the decision problem. By evaluating each policy, the optimum solution can be determined. This is basically equivalent to an *exhaustive enumeration* process and can be used only if the total number of stationary policies is reasonably small for practical computations.

The second method, called **policy iteration**, alleviates the computational difficulties that could arise in the exhaustive enumeration procedure. The new method is generally efficient in the sense that it determines the optimum policy in a small number of iterations.

Naturally, both methods must lead to the same optimum solution. We demonstrate this point as well as the application of the two methods via the gardener example.

18.3.1 EXHAUSTIVE ENUMERATION METHOD

Suppose that the decision problem has a total of S stationary policies, and assume that $\mathbf{P}^s$ and $\mathbf{R}^s$ are the (one-step) transition and revenue matrices associated with the kth policy, $s = 1, 2, \ldots, S$. The steps of the enumeration method are as follows.

Step 1: Compute v_i^s, the *expected* one-step (one-period) revenue of policy s given state i, $i = 1, 2, \ldots, m$.

Step 2: Compute π_i^s, the long-run stationary probabilities of the transition matrix $\mathbf{P}^s$ associated with policy s. These probabilities, when they exist, are computed from the equations

$$\boldsymbol{\pi}^s \mathbf{P}^s = \boldsymbol{\pi}^s$$

$$\pi_1^s + \pi_2^s + \cdots + \pi_m^s = 1$$

where $\boldsymbol{\pi}^s = (\pi_1^s, \pi_2^s, \ldots, \pi_m^s)$.

Step 3: Determine E^s, the expected revenue of policy s per transition step (period), by using the formula

$$E^s = \sum_{i=1}^{m} \pi_i^s v_i^s$$

Step 4: The optimum policy s^* is determined such that

$$E^{s^*} = \max_s \{E^s\}$$

We illustrate the method by solving the gardener problem for an infinite-period planning horizon.

Example 18.3-1. The gardener problem has a total of eight stationary policies, as the following table shows:

Stationary Policy s	Action
1	Do not fertilize at all.
2	Fertilize regardless of the state.
3	Fertilize whenever in state 1.
4	Fertilize whenever in state 2.
5	Fertilize whenever in state 3.
6	Fertilize whenever in state 1 or 2.
7	Fertilize whenever in state 1 or 3.
8	Fertilize whenever in state 2 or 3.

As we explained in Section 18.1, the matrices $\mathbf{P}^k$ and $\mathbf{R}^k$ for policies 3 through 8 are derived from those of policies 1 and 2. We thus have

$$\mathbf{P}^1 = \begin{bmatrix} .2 & .5 & .3 \\ 0 & .5 & .5 \\ 0 & 0 & 1 \end{bmatrix}, \qquad \mathbf{R}^1 = \begin{bmatrix} 7 & 6 & 3 \\ 0 & 5 & 1 \\ 0 & 0 & -1 \end{bmatrix}$$

$$\mathbf{P}^2 = \begin{bmatrix} .3 & .6 & .1 \\ .1 & .6 & .3 \\ .05 & .4 & .55 \end{bmatrix}, \qquad \mathbf{R}^2 = \begin{bmatrix} 6 & 5 & -1 \\ 7 & 4 & 0 \\ 6 & 3 & -2 \end{bmatrix}$$

$$\mathbf{P}^3 = \begin{bmatrix} .3 & .6 & .1 \\ 0 & .5 & .5 \\ 0 & 0 & 1 \end{bmatrix}, \qquad \mathbf{R}^3 = \begin{bmatrix} 6 & 5 & -1 \\ 0 & 5 & 1 \\ 0 & 0 & -1 \end{bmatrix}$$

$$\mathbf{P}^4 = \begin{bmatrix} .2 & .5 & .3 \\ .1 & .6 & .3 \\ 0 & 0 & 1 \end{bmatrix}, \qquad \mathbf{R}^4 = \begin{bmatrix} 7 & 6 & 3 \\ 7 & 4 & 0 \\ 0 & 0 & -1 \end{bmatrix}$$

$$\mathbf{P}^5 = \begin{bmatrix} .2 & .5 & .3 \\ 0 & .5 & .5 \\ .05 & .4 & .55 \end{bmatrix}, \qquad \mathbf{R}^5 = \begin{bmatrix} 7 & 6 & 3 \\ 0 & 5 & 1 \\ 6 & 3 & -2 \end{bmatrix}$$

$$\mathbf{P}^6 = \begin{bmatrix} .3 & .6 & .1 \\ .1 & .6 & .3 \\ 0 & 0 & 1 \end{bmatrix}, \qquad \mathbf{R}^6 = \begin{bmatrix} 6 & 5 & -1 \\ 7 & 4 & 0 \\ 0 & 0 & -1 \end{bmatrix}$$

$$\mathbf{P}^7 = \begin{bmatrix} .3 & .6 & .1 \\ 0 & .5 & .5 \\ .05 & .4 & .55 \end{bmatrix}, \qquad \mathbf{R}^7 = \begin{bmatrix} 6 & 5 & -1 \\ 0 & 5 & 1 \\ 6 & 3 & -2 \end{bmatrix}$$

$$\mathbf{P}^8 = \begin{bmatrix} .2 & .5 & .3 \\ .1 & .6 & .3 \\ .05 & .4 & .55 \end{bmatrix}, \qquad \mathbf{R}^8 = \begin{bmatrix} 7 & 6 & 3 \\ 7 & 4 & 0 \\ 6 & 3 & -2 \end{bmatrix}$$

The values of v_i^k can thus be computed as given in the following table.

	v_i^s		
s	$i = 1$	$i = 2$	$i = 3$
1	5.3	3	-1
2	4.7	3.1	.4
3	4.7	3	-1
4	5.3	3.1	-1
5	5.3	3	.4
6	4.7	3.1	-1
7	4.7	3	.4
8	5.3	3.1	.4

The computations of the stationary probabilities are achieved by using the equations

$$\boldsymbol{\pi}^s\mathbf{P}^s = \boldsymbol{\pi}^s$$
$$\pi_1 + \pi_2 + \cdots + \pi_m = 1$$

As an illustration, consider $s = 2$. The associated equations are

$$.3\pi_1 + .1\pi_2 + .05\pi_3 = \pi_1$$
$$.6\pi_1 + .6\pi_2 + .4\pi_3 = \pi_2$$
$$.1\pi_1 + .3\pi_2 + .55\pi_3 = \pi_3$$
$$\pi_1 + \pi_2 + \pi_3 = 1$$

(Notice that one of the first three equations is redundant.) The solution yields

$$\pi_1^2 = 6/59, \quad \pi_2^2 = 31/59, \quad \pi_3^2 = 22/59$$

In this case, the expected yearly revenue is

$$E^2 = \sum_{i=1}^{3} \pi_i^2 v_i^2$$
$$= \frac{1}{59}(6 \times 4.7 + 31 \times 3.1 + 22 \times .4) = 2.256$$

The following table summarizes π^k and E^k for all the stationary policies. (Although this will not affect the computations in any way, note that each of policies 1, 3, 4, and 6 has an absorbing state: state 3. This is the reason $\pi_1 = \pi_2 = 0$ and $\pi_3 = 1$ for all these policies.)

s	π_1^s	π_2^s	π_3^s	E^s
1	0	0	1	$-1.$
2	6/59	31/59	22/59	**2.256**
3	0	0	1	.4
4	0	0	1	$-1.$
5	5/154	69/154	80/154	1.724
6	0	0	1	$-1.$
7	5/137	62/137	70/137	1.734
8	12/135	69/135	54/135	2.216

The last table shows that policy 2 yields the largest expected yearly revenue. Consequently, the optimum long-range policy calls for applying fertilizer regardless of the state of the system. ◀

Exercise 18-3-1
Verify the values of π^s and E^s given in the preceding table.

18.3.2 POLICY ITERATION METHOD WITHOUT DISCOUNTING

To gain an appreciation of the difficulty associated with the exhaustive enumeration method, let us assume that the gardener has four courses of action (alternatives) instead of two: do not fertilize, fertilize once during the season, fertilize twice, and fertilize three times. In this case, the gardener would have a total of $4^3 = 256$ stationary policies. Thus, by increasing the number of alternatives from 2 to 4, the number of stationary policies "soars" exponentially from 8 to 256. Not only is it difficult to enumerate all the policies explicitly, but the number of computations involved in the evaluation of these policies may also be prohibitively large.

The policy iteration method is based principally on the following development. For any specific policy, we showed in Section 18.2 that the expected total return at stage n is expressed by the recursive equation

$$f_n(i) = v_i + \sum_{j=1}^{m} p_{ij} f_{n+1}(j), \qquad i = 1, 2, \ldots, m$$

This recursive equation is the basis for the development of the policy iteration method. However, the present form must be modified slightly to allow us to study the asymptotic behavior of the process. In essence, we define η as the number of stages *remaining* for consideration. This is in contrast with n in the equation, which defines the nth stage. The recursive equation is thus written as

$$f_\eta(i) = v_i + \sum_{j=1}^{m} P_{ij} f_{\eta-1}(j), \qquad i = 1, 2, \ldots, m$$

Note that f_η is the cumulative expected revenue given that η is the number of stages *remaining* for consideration. With the new definition, the asymptotic behavior of the process can be studied by letting $\eta \to \infty$.

Given that

$$\pi = (\pi_1, \pi_2, \ldots, \pi_m)$$

is the steady-state probability vector of the transition matrix $\mathbf{P} = \|p_{ij}\|$ and

$$E = \pi_1 v_1 + \pi_2 v_2 + \cdots + \pi_m v_m$$

is the expected revenue per stage as computed in Section 18.3.1, it can be shown that for very large η,

$$f_\eta(i) = \eta E + f(i)$$

where $f(i)$ is a constant term representing the asymptotic intercept of $f_\eta(i)$ given the state i.

Since $f_\eta(i)$ is the cumulative optimum return for η stages given the state i and E is the expected revenue *per stage*, we can see intuitively why $f_\eta(i)$ equals ηE plus a correction factor $f(i)$ that accounts for the specific state i. This result, of course, assumes that η is very large.

Now, using this information, the recursive equation is written as

$$\eta E + f(i) = v_i + \sum_{j=1}^{m} p_{ij}\{(\eta - 1)E + f(j)\}, \qquad i = 1, 2, \ldots, m$$

Simplifying this equation, we get

$$E = v_i + \sum_{j=1}^{m} p_{ij} f(j) - f(i), \qquad i = 1, 2, \ldots, m$$

which results in m equations and $m + 1$ unknowns, the unknowns being $f(1)$, $f(2), \ldots, f(m)$, and E.

As in Section 18.3.1, our ultimate objective is to determine the optimum policy that yields the maximum value of E. Since there are m equations in $m + 1$ unknowns, the optimum value of E cannot be determined in one step. Instead, an iterative approach is utilized which, starting with an arbitrary policy, will then determine a new policy that yields a better value of E. The iterative process ends when two successive policies are identical.

The iterative process consists of two basic components, called the **value determination** step and the **policy improvement** step.

1. *Value determination step.* Choose an arbitrary policy s. Using its associated matrices $\mathbf{P}^s$ and $\mathbf{R}^s$ and arbitrarily assuming $f^s(m) = 0$, solve the equations

$$E^s = v_i^s + \sum_{j=1}^{m} p_{ij}^s f^s(j) - f^s(i), \qquad i = 1, 2, \ldots, m$$

in the unknowns $E^s, f^s(1), \ldots,$ and $f^s(m - 1)$. Go to the policy improvement step.

2. *Policy improvement step.* For each state i, determine the alternative k that yields

$$\max_k \left\{ v_i^k + \sum_{j=1}^{m} p_{ij}^k f^s(j) \right\}, \qquad i = 1, 2, \ldots, m$$

[The values of $f^s(j), j = 1, 2, \ldots, m$, are those determined in the value determination step.] The resulting optimum decisions k for states 1, 2, ..., m constitute the new policy t. If s and t are identical, stop; t is optimum. Otherwise, set $s = t$ and return to the value determination step.

The optimization problem of the policy improvement step needs clarification. Our objective in this step is to obtain $\max\{E\}$. As given,

$$E = v_i + \sum_{j=1}^{m} p_{ij} f(j) - f(i)$$

Since $f(i)$ does not depend on the alternatives k, it follows that the maximization of E over the alternatives k is equivalent to the maximization problem given in the policy improvement step.

Example 18.3-2. We solve the gardener example by the policy iteration method.

Let us start with the arbitrary policy that calls for not applying fertilizer. The associated matrices are

$$\mathbf{P} = \begin{bmatrix} .2 & .5 & .3 \\ 0 & .5 & .5 \\ 0 & 0 & 1 \end{bmatrix}, \qquad \mathbf{R} = \begin{bmatrix} 7 & 6 & 3 \\ 0 & 5 & 1 \\ 0 & 0 & -1 \end{bmatrix}$$

The equations of the value iteration step are

$$\begin{aligned} E + f(1) - .2f(1) - .5f(2) - .3f(3) &= 5.3 \\ E + f(2) \qquad\quad - .5f(2) - .5f(3) &= 3 \\ E + f(3) \qquad\qquad\qquad\quad - f(3) &= -1 \end{aligned}$$

If we arbitrarily let $f(3) = 0$, the equations yield the solution

$$E = -1, \quad f(1) \cong 12.88, \quad f(2) = 8, \quad f(3) = 0$$

Next, we apply the policy improvement step. The associated calculations are shown in the following tableau.

	$v_i^k + p_{i1}^k f(1) + p_{i2}^k f(2) + p_{i3}^k f(3)$		Optimal Solution	
i	$k = 1$	$k = 2$	$f(i)$	k^*
1	$5.3 + .2 \times 12.88 + .5 \times 8 + .3 \times 0$ $= 11.875$	$4.7 + .3 \times 12.88 + .6 \times 8 + .1 \times 0$ $= 13.36$	13.36	2
2	$3 + 0 \times 12.88 + .5 \times 8 + .5 \times 0$ $= 7$	$3.1 + .1 \times 12.88 + .6 \times 8 + .3 \times 0$ $= 9.19$	9.19	2
3	$-1 + 0 \times 12.88 + 0 \times 8 + 1 \times 0$ $= -1$	$.4 + .05 \times 12.88 + .4 \times 8 + .55 \times 0$ $= 4.24$	4.24	2

The new policy calls for applying fertilizer regardless of the state. Since the new policy differs from the preceding one, the value determination step is entered again. The matrices associated with the new policy are

$$\mathbf{P} = \begin{bmatrix} .3 & .6 & .1 \\ .1 & .6 & .3 \\ .05 & .4 & .55 \end{bmatrix}, \qquad \mathbf{R} = \begin{bmatrix} 6 & 5 & -1 \\ 7 & 4 & 0 \\ 6 & 3 & -2 \end{bmatrix}$$

These matrices yield the following equations:

$$\begin{aligned} E + f(1) - .3\,f(1) - .6f(2) - .1\,f(3) &= 4.7 \\ E + f(2) - .1\,f(1) - .6f(2) - .3\,f(3) &= 3.1 \\ E + f(3) - .05f(1) - .4f(2) - .55f(3) &= .4 \end{aligned}$$

Again, letting $f(3) = 0$, we get the solution

$$E = 2.26, \quad f(1) = 6.75, \quad f(2) = 3.79, \quad f(3) = 0$$

The computations of the policy imporvement step are given in the following tableau.

	$v_i^k + p_{i1}^k f(1) + p_{i2}^k f(2) + p_{i3}^k f(3)$		Optimal Solution	
i	$k = 1$	$k = 2$	$f(i)$	k^*
1	$5.3 + .2 \times 6.75 + .5 \times 3.79 + .3 \times 0$ $= 8.54$	$4.7 + .3 \times 6.75 + .6 \times 3.79 + .1 \times 0$ $= 8.99$	8.99	2
2	$3 + 0 \times 6.75 + .5 \times 3.79 + .5 \times 0$ $= 4.89$	$3.1 + .1 \times 6.75 + .6 \times 3.79 + .3 \times 0$ $= 6.05$	6.05	2
3	$-1 + 0 \times 6.75 + 0 \times 3.79 + 1 \times 0$ $= -1$	$.4 + .05 \times 6.75 + .4 \times 3.79 + .55 \times 0$ $= 2.25$	2.25	2

The new policy, which calls for applying fertilizer regardless of the state, is identical with the preceding one. Thus the last policy is optimal and the iterative process ends. Naturally, this is the same conclusion as that obtained by the exhaustive enumeration method (Section 18.3.1). Note, however, that the policy iteration method converges quickly to the optimum policy, a typical characteristic of the new method. Note that the value of E increased from -1 in the first iteration to 2.26 in the second iteration. The last value equals that obtained for the optimal policy in the exhaustive enumeration method. ◀

Exercise 18.3-2

In Example 18.3-2 we started the iterations by using the arbitrary policy of never applying fertilizer. In general, it may be better, from the viewpoint of convergence, to start with the policy whose individual decisions are those yielding $\max_k\{v_i^k\}$ for each state i. Apply these starting conditions to Example 18.3-2 and obtain the optimal policy by the policy iteration method.

[*Ans.* Starting policy consists of the decisions 1, 2, and 2 for states 1, 2, and 3. Its corresponding **P** and **R** ($\mathbf{P}^8$ and $\mathbf{R}^8$ in Example 18.3-1) used in the value determination step will yield $E = 2.216$, $f(1) = 6.207$, and $f(2) = 3.763$. The solution assumes that $f(3) = 0$. The policy improvement step will yield the decisions (2, 2, 2) with $f(1) = 8.82$, $f(2) = 5.98$, and $f(3) = 2.22$. The next iteration will be identical with that of Example 18.3-2. Notice that $E = 2.216$ in the first iteration compared with $E = -1$ in the first iteration of Example 18.3-2. This exercise demonstrates the possible influence of the starting policy on the convergence of the algorithm.]

18.3.3 POLICY ITERATION METHOD WITH DISCOUNTING

The policy iteration algorithm just described can be extended to include discounting. Specifically, given that α (< 1) is the discount factor, the finite-stage recursive equation can be written as (see Section 18.2)

$$f_\eta(i) = \max_k \left\{ v_i^k + \alpha \sum_{j=1}^{m} p_{ij}^k f_{\eta-1}(j) \right\}$$

(Note that η represents the number of stages *to go*.) It can be proved that as $\eta \to \infty$ (infinite stage model), $f_\eta(i) = f(i)$, where $f(i)$ is the expected present-worth (discounted) revenue given that the system is in state i and operating over an infinite horizon. Thus the long-run behavior of $f_\eta(i)$ as $\eta \to \infty$ is independent of the value of

η. This is in contrast with the case of no discounting, where $f_\eta(i) = \eta E + f(i)$, as stated previously. This result should be expected since in the case of discounting the effect of future revenues will asymptotically diminish to zero. Indeed, the present worth $f(i)$ should approach a constant value as $\eta \to \infty$.

Given this information, the steps of the policy iterations are modified as follows.

1. *Value determination step.* For an arbitrary policy s with its matrices $\mathbf{P}^s$ and $\mathbf{R}^s$, solve the m equations

$$f^s(i) = v_i^s + \alpha \sum_{j=1}^{m} p_{ij}^s f^s(j), \qquad i = 1, 2, \ldots, m$$

in the m unknowns $f^s(1), f^s(2), \ldots, f^s(m)$. (Note that there are m equations in exactly m unknowns.)

2. *Policy improvement step.* For each state i, determine the alternative k that yields

$$\max_k \left\{ v_i^k + \alpha \sum_{j=1}^{m} p_{ij}^k f^s(j) \right\}, \qquad i = 1, 2, \ldots, m$$

where $f^s(j)$ are those obtained from the value determination step. If the resulting policy t is the same as s, stop; t is optimum. Otherwise, set $s = t$ and return to the value determination step.

Example 18.3-3. We will solve Example 18.3-2 using a discounting factor $\alpha = .6$.

Starting with the arbitrary policy, $s = \{1, 1, 1\}$. The associated matrices $\mathbf{P}$ and $\mathbf{R}$ ($\mathbf{P}^1$ and $\mathbf{R}^1$ in Example 18.3-1) yield the equations

$$\begin{aligned}
f(1) - .6[.2f(1) + .5f(2) + .3f(3)] &= 5.3 \\
f(2) - .6[\qquad\qquad .5f(2) + .5f(3)] &= 3 \\
f(3) - .6[\qquad\qquad\qquad\qquad f(3)] &= -1
\end{aligned}$$

The solution of these equations yields

$$f_1 \cong 6.6, \quad f_2 \cong 3.21, \quad f_3 = -2.5$$

A summary of the policy improvement iteration is given in the following tableau.

	$v_i^k + .6[p_{i1}^k f(1) + p_{i2}^k f(2) + p_{i3}^k f(3)]$		Optimal Solution	
i	$k = 1$	$k = 2$	$f(i)$	k^*
1	$5.3 + .6[.2 \times 6.6 + .5 \times 3.21 + .3 \times -2.5]$ $= 6.61$	$4.7 + .6[.3 \times 6.6 + .6 \times 3.21 + .1 \times -2.5]$ $= 6.89$	6.89	2
2	$3 + .6[0 \times 6.6 + .5 \times 3.21 + .5 \times -2.5]$ $= 3.21$	$3.1 + .6[.1 \times 6.6 + .6 \times 3.21 + .3 \times -2.5]$ $= 4.2$	4.2	2
3	$-1 + .6[0 \times 6.6 + 0 \times 3.21 + 1 \times -2.5]$ $= -2.5$	$.4 + .6[.05 \times 6.6 + .4 \times 3.21 + .55 \times -2.5]$ $= .54$	.54	2

The value determination step using $\mathbf{P}^2$ and $\mathbf{R}^2$ (Example 18.3-1) yields the following equations:

$$\begin{aligned}
f(1) - .6[.3\,f(1) + .6f(2) + .1\,f(3)] &= 4.7 \\
f(2) - .6[.1\,f(1) + .6f(2) + .3\,f(3)] &= 3.1 \\
f(3) - .6[.05f(1) + .4f(2) + .55f(3)] &= .4
\end{aligned}$$

The solution of these equations yields

$$f(1) = 8.88, \quad f(2) = 6.62, \quad f(3) = 3.37$$

The policy improvement step yields the following tableau.

	$v_i^k + .6[p_{i1}^k f(1) + p_{i2}^k f(2) + p_{i3}^k f(3)]$		Optimal Solution	
i	$k = 1$	$k = 2$	$f(i)$	k^*
1	$5.3 + .6[.2 \times 8.88 + .5 \times 6.62 + .3 \times 3.37] = 8.95$	$4.7 + .6[.3 \times 8.88 + .6 \times 6.62 + .1 \times 3.37] = 8.88$	8.95	1
2	$3 + .6[0 \times 8.88 + .5 \times 6.62 + .5 \times 3.37] = 5.99$	$3.1 + .6[.1 \times 8.88 + .6 \times 6.62 + .3 \times 3.37] = 6.62$	6.62	2
3	$-1 + .6[0 \times 8.88 + 0 \times 6.62 + 1 \times 3.37] = 1.02$	$.4 + .6[.05 \times 8.88 + .4 \times 6.62 + .55 \times 3.37] = 3.37$	3.37	2

Since the new policy $\{1, 2, 2\}$ differs from the preceding one, the value determination step is entered again using $\mathbf{P}^8$ and $\mathbf{R}^8$ (Example 18.3-1). This results in the following equations:

$$f(1) - .6[.2\, f(1) + .5f(2) + .3\, f(3)] = 5.3$$
$$f(2) - .6[.1\, f(1) + .6f(2) + .3\, f(3)] = 3.1$$
$$f(3) - .6[.05f(1) + .4f(2) + .55f(3)] = \ .4$$

The solution of these equations yields

$$f(1) = 8.98, \quad f(2) = 6.63, \quad f(3) = 3.38$$

The policy improvement step yields the following tableau.

	$v_i^k + .6[p_{i1}^k f(1) + p_{i2}^k f(2) + p_{i3}^k f(3)]$		Optimal Solution	
i	$k = 1$	$k = 2$	$f(i)$	k^*
1	$5.3 + .6[.2 \times 8.98 + .5 \times 6.63 + .3 \times 3.38] = 8.98$	$4.7 + .6[.3 \times 8.98 + .6 \times 6.63 + .1 \times 3.38] = 8.91$	8.98	1
2	$3 + .6[0 \times 8.98 + .5 \times 6.63 + .5 \times 3.38] = 6.00$	$3.1 + .6[1 \times 8.98 + .6 \times 6.63 + .3 \times 3.38] = 6.63$	6.63	2
3	$-1 + .6[0 \times 8.98 + 0 \times 6.63 + 1 \times 3.38] = 1.03$	$.4 + .6[.05 \times 8.98 + .4 \times 6.63 + .55 \times 3.38] = 3.37$	3.37	2

Since the new policy $\{1, 2, 2\}$ is identical with the preceding one, it is optimal. Note that discounting has resulted in a different optimal policy (see Example 18.4-2), which calls for not applying fertilizer if the state of the system is good (state 3). ◀

Exercise 18.3-3

Solve Example 18.3-3 starting with the policy whose decision corresponds to $\max_k\{v_i^k\}$. Compare the resulting iterations with those of Example 18.3-3.

[*Ans.* The starting policy $\{1, 2, 2\}$ is optimal, as is verified after one iteration. The result indicates that it is important to select the starting policy judiciously rather than arbitrarily.]

18.4 LINEAR PROGRAMMING SOLUTION OF THE MARKOVIAN DECISION PROBLEM

The infinite-stage Markovian decision problems, both with discounting and without, can be formulated and solved as linear programs. We consider the no-discounting case first.

In Section 18.3.1 we showed that the infinite-stage Markovian problem with no discounting ultimately reduces to determining the optimal policy s^*, which corresponds to

$$\max_{s \in S}\left\{\sum_{i=1}^{m} \pi_i^s v_i^s \mid \boldsymbol{\pi}^s \mathbf{P}^s = \boldsymbol{\pi}^s, \quad \pi_1^s + \pi_2^s + \cdots + \pi_m^s = 1, \quad \pi_i^s \geq 0, \quad i = 1, 2, \ldots, m\right\}$$

where S is the collection of all possible policies of the problem. The constraints of the problem ensure that π_i^s, $i = 1, 2, \ldots, m$, represent the steady-state probabilities of the Markov chain $\mathbf{P}^s$.

We solved this problem in Section 18.3.1 by exhaustively enumerating all the elements s of S. Specifically, each policy s is specified by a fixed set of actions (as exemplified by the gardener problem in Example 18.3-1).

The problem is the basis for the development of the LP formulation of the Markovian decision problem. However, we need to modify the unknowns of the problem in such a manner that the optimal solution would *automatically* determine the optimal action (alternative) k when the system is in state i. The collection of all these optimal actions will then define s^*, the optimal policy.

This objective is achieved as follows. Let

q_i^k = conditional probability of choosing alternative k given that the system is in state i

The problem may thus be expressed as

$$\text{maximize } E = \sum_{i=1}^{m} \pi_i\left(\sum_{k=1}^{K} q_i^k v_i^k\right)$$

subject to

$$\pi_j = \sum_{i=1}^{m} \pi_i p_{ij}, \qquad j = 1, 2, \ldots, m$$

$$\pi_1 + \pi_2 + \cdots + \pi_m = 1$$

$$q_i^1 + q_i^2 + \cdots + q_i^K = 1, \qquad i = 1, 2, \ldots, m$$

$$\pi_i \geq 0, \quad q_i^k \geq 0, \quad \text{all } i \text{ and } k$$

Note that p_{ij} is a function of the policy selected and hence of the specific alternatives k of the policy.

We shall see shortly that the problem can be converted into a linear program by making proper substitutions involving q_i^k. Observe, however, that the formulation is equivalent to the original one in Section 18.3.1 only if $q_i^k = 1$ for exactly *one* k for each i, as this will reduce the sum $\sum_{k=1}^{K} q_i^k v_i^k$ to $v_i^{k^*}$, where k^* is the optimal alternative chosen. Fortunately, the linear program we develop here does account for this condition automatically.

Define

$$w_{ik} = \pi_i q_i^k, \qquad \text{for all } i \text{ and } k$$

By definition, w_{ik} represents the *joint* probability of being in state i and making decision k. From probability theory we know that

$$\pi_i = \sum_{k=1}^{K} w_{ik}$$

Hence

$$q_i^k = \frac{w_{ik}}{\sum_{k=1}^{K} w_{ik}}$$

We thus see that the restriction $\sum_{i=1}^{m} \pi_i = 1$ can be written as

$$\sum_{i=1}^{m} \sum_{k=1}^{K} w_{ik} = 1$$

Also, the restriction $\sum_{k=1}^{K} q_i^k = 1$ is automatically implied by the way we defined q_i^k in terms of w_{ik}. (Verify!) Thus the problem can be written as

$$\text{maximize } E = \sum_{i=1}^{m} \sum_{k=1}^{K} v_i^k w_{ik}$$

subject to

$$\sum_{i=1}^{m} w_{jk} - \sum_{i=1}^{m} \sum_{k=1}^{K} p_{ij}^k w_{ik} = 0, \qquad j = 1, 2, \ldots, m$$

$$\sum_{i=1}^{m} \sum_{k=1}^{K} w_{ik} = 1$$

$$w_{ik} \geq 0, \quad i = 1, 2, \ldots, m; \; k = 1, 2, \ldots, K$$

The resulting model is a linear program in w_{ik}. We show now that its optimal solution automatically guarantees that $q_i^k = 1$ for one k for each i. First, note that the linear program has m independent equations (one of the equations associated with $\boldsymbol{\pi} = \boldsymbol{\pi}\mathbf{P}$ is redundant). Hnece the problem must have m basic variables. However, it can be shown that w_{ik} must be strictly positive for at least one k for each i. From these two results, we conclude that

$$q_i^k = \frac{w_{ik}}{\sum_{k=1}^{K} w_{ik}}$$

can assume a binary value (0 or 1) only, as is desired. (As a matter of fact, the result above also shows that $\pi_i = \sum_{k=1}^{K} w_{ik} = w_{ik^*}$, where k^* is the alternative corresponding to $w_{ik} > 0$.)

Example 18.4-1. The following is an LP formulation of the gardener problem without discounting:

$$\text{maximize } E = 5.3w_{11} + 4.7w_{12} + 3w_{21} + 3.1w_{22} - w_{31} + .4w_{32}$$

subject to

$$\begin{aligned}
w_{11} + w_{12} - (.2w_{11} + .3w_{12} \qquad\qquad\quad + .1w_{22} \qquad\qquad + .05w_{32}) &= 0\\
w_{21} + w_{22} - (.5w_{11} + .6w_{12} + .5w_{21} + .6w_{22} \qquad\qquad + .4w_{32}) &= 0\\
w_{31} + w_{32} - (.3w_{11} + .1w_{12} + .5w_{21} + .3w_{22} + w_{31} + .55w_{32}) &= 0\\
w_{11} + w_{12} + w_{21} + w_{22} + w_{31} + w_{32} &= 1\\
w_{ik} \geq 0, \qquad \text{for all } i \text{ and } k
\end{aligned}$$

The optimal solution is $w_{11} = w_{12} = w_{31} = 0$ and $w_{12} = 6/59$, $w_{22} = 31/59$, and $w_{32} = 22/59$. This result means that $q_1^2 = q_2^2 = q_3^2 = 1$. Thus the optimal policy calls for selecting alternative 2 ($k = 2$) for $i = 1$, 2, and 3. The optimal value of E is $4.7(6/59) + 3.1(31/59) + .4(22/59) = 2.256$. It is interesting that the positive values of w_{ik} exactly equal the values of π_i associated with the optimal policy in the exhaustive enumeration procedure of Example 18.3-1. This observation demonstrates the direct relationship between the two solution methods. ◀

We next consider the Markovian decision problem with discounting. In Section 18.3.2 the problem is expressed by the recursive equation

$$f(i) = \max_k \left\{ v_i^k + \alpha \sum_{j=1}^{m} p_{ij}^k f(j) \right\}, \qquad i = 1, 2, \ldots, m$$

These equations are equivalent to

$$f(i) \geq \alpha \sum_{j=1}^{m} p_{ij}^k f(j) + v_i^k, \qquad \text{for all } i \text{ and } k$$

provided that $f(i)$ achieves its minimum value for each i. Now consider the objective function

$$\text{minimize } \sum_{i=1}^{m} b_i f(i)$$

where b_i (> 0 for all i) is an arbitrary constant. It can be shown that the optimization of this function subject to the inequalities given will result in the minimum value of $f(i)$, as desired. Thus the problem can be written as

$$\text{minimize } \sum_{i=1}^{m} b_i f(i)$$

subject to

$$f(i) - \alpha \sum_{i=1}^{m} p_{ij}^k f(j) \geq v_i^k, \qquad \text{for all } i \text{ and } k$$

$$f(i) \text{ unrestricted}, \quad i = 1, 2, \ldots, m$$

Now the dual of the problem is

$$\text{maximize } \sum_{i=1}^{m} \sum_{k=1}^{K} v_i^k w_{ik}$$

subject to

$$\sum_{k=1}^{K} w_{jk} - \alpha \sum_{i=1}^{m} \sum_{k=1}^{K} p_{ij}^k w_{ik} = b_j, \qquad j = 1, 2, \ldots, m$$

$$w_{ik} \geq 0, \qquad \text{for } i = 1, 2, \ldots, m;\ k = 1, 2, \ldots, K$$

Notice that the objective function has the same form as in the case of no discounting, so that w_{ik} can be interpreted similarly. The following example illustrates the application of the model.

Example 18.4-2. Consider the gardener example with the discounting factor $\alpha = .6$. If we let $b_1 = b_2 = b_3 = 1$, the dual LP problem may be written as

$$\text{maximize } 5.3w_{11} + 4.7w_{12} + 3w_{21} + 3.1w_{22} - w_{31} + .4w_{32}$$

subject to

$$
\begin{aligned}
w_{11} + w_{12} - .6[.2w_{11} + .3w_{12} \qquad\qquad + .1w_{22} \qquad\qquad + .05w_{32}] &= 1 \\
w_{21} + w_{22} - .6[.5w_{11} + .6w_{12} + .5w_{21} + .6w_{22} \qquad\qquad + \ .4w_{32}] &= 1 \\
w_{31} + w_{32} - .6[.3w_{11} + .1w_{12} + .5w_{21} + .3w_{22} + w_{31} + .55w_{32}] &= 1 \\
w_{ik} \geq 0, \qquad \text{for all } i \text{ and } k &
\end{aligned}
$$

The optimal solution is $w_{12} = w_{21} = w_{31} = 0$ and $w_{11} = 1.5678$, $w_{22} = 3.3528$, and $w_{32} = 2.8145$. The solution shows that the optimal policy is $\{1, 2, 2\}$, as was obtained in Example 18.3-3. ◀

18.5 SUMMARY

This chapter provides models for the solution of the Markovian decision problem. The models developed include the finite-stage models solved directly by the DP recursive equations. In the infinite-stage model, it is shown that exhaustive enumeration is not practical for large problems. The policy iteration algorithm, which is based on the DP recursive equation, is shown to be more efficient computationally than the exhaustive enumeration method, since it normally converges in a small number of iterations. Discounting is shown to result in a possible change of the optimal policy in comparison with the case where no discounting is used. This conclusion applies to both the finite- and infinite-stage models.

The LP formulation is quite interesting but is not as efficient computationally as the policy iteration algorithm. For problems with K decision alternatives and m states, the associated LP model would include $(m + 1)$ constraints and mK variables, which tend to be large for large values of m and K.

Although we presented the simplified gardener example to demonstrate the development of the algorithms, the Markovian decision problem has applications in such areas as inventory, maintenance, replacement, and water resources.

18.6 APPENDIX: REVIEW OF MARKOV CHAINS

Consider the discrete points in time $\{t_k\}$ for $k = 1, 2, \ldots$, and let ξ_{t_k} be the random variable that characterizes the state of the system at t_k. The family of random variables $\{\xi_{t_k}\}$ forms a **stochastic process**. The states at time t_k actually represent the (exhaustive and mutually exclusive) outcomes of the system at that time. The number of states may thus be finite or infinite. For example, the Poisson distribution

$$P_n(t) = \frac{e^{-\lambda t}(\lambda t)^n}{n!}, \qquad n = 0, 1, 2, \ldots$$

represents a stochastic process with an infinite number of states. Here the random variable n represents the number of occurrences between 0 and t (assuming that the system starts at time 0). The states of the system at any time t are thus given by $n = 0, 1, 2, \ldots$.

Another example is represented by the coin-tossing game with k trials. Each trial may be viewed as a point in time. The resulting sequence of trials forms a stochastic process. The state of the system at any trial is either a head or a tail.

This section presents a summary of an important class of stochastic systems that includes **Markov processes** and **Markov chains**. A Markov chain is actually a special case of Markov processes. It is used to study the short- and long-run behavior of certain stochastic systems.

18.6.1 MARKOV PROCESSES

A *Markov process* is a stochastic system for which the occurrence of a future state depends on the immediately preceding state and only on it. Thus if $t_0 < t_1 < \cdots t_n$ ($n = 0, 1, 2, \ldots$) represents points in time, the family of random variables $\{\xi_{t_n}\}$ is a Markov process if it possesses the following **Markovian property**:

$$P\{\xi_{t_n} = x_n \mid \xi_{t_{n-1}} = x_{n-1}, \ldots, \xi_{t0} = x_0\} = P\{\xi_{t_n} = x_n \mid \xi_{t_{n-1}} = x_{n-1}\}$$

for all possible values of $\xi_{t0}, \xi_{t1}, \ldots, \xi_{t_n}$.

The probability $p_{x_{n-1},x_n} = P\{\xi_{t_n} = x_n \mid \xi_{t_{n-1}} = x_{n-1}\}$ is called the **transition probability**. It represents the *conditional* probability of the system being in x_n at t_n, given it was in x_{n-1} at t_{n-1}. This probability is also referred to as the **one-step transition probability**, since it describes the system between t_{n-1} and t_n. An m-step transition probability is thus defined by

$$p_{x_n, x_{n+m}} = P\{\xi_{t_{n+m}} = x_{n+m} \mid \xi_{t_n} = x_n\}$$

18.6.2 MARKOV CHAINS

Let $E_1, E_2, \ldots, E_j$ ($j = 0, 1, 2, \ldots$) represent the exhaustive and mutually exclusive outcomes (states) of a system at any time. Initially, at time t_0, the system may be in any of these states. Let $a_j^{(0)}$ ($j = 0, 1, 2, \ldots$) be the absolute probability that the system is in state E_j at t_0. Assume further that the system is Markovian.

Define

$$p_{ij} = P\{\xi_{t_n} = j \mid \xi_{t_{n-1}} = i\}$$

as the one-step transition probability of going from state i at t_{n-1} to state j at t_n and assume that these probabilities are stationary (fixed) over time. Thus the transition probabilities from state E_i to state E_j can be more conveniently arranged in a matrix form as follows:

$$\mathbf{P} = \begin{pmatrix} p_{00} & p_{01} & p_{02} & p_{03} & \cdots \\ p_{10} & p_{11} & p_{12} & p_{13} & \cdots \\ p_{20} & p_{21} & p_{22} & p_{23} & \cdots \\ p_{30} & p_{31} & p_{32} & p_{33} & \cdots \\ \vdots & \vdots & \vdots & \vdots & \end{pmatrix}$$

The matrix $\mathbf{P}$ is called a **homogeneous transition** or **stochastic matrix** because all the transition probabilities p_{ij} are fixed and independent of time. The probabilities p_{ij} must satisfy the conditions

$$\sum_j p_{ij} = 1, \qquad \text{for all } i$$

$$p_{ij} \geq 0, \qquad \text{for all } i \text{ and } j$$

The definition of a **Markov chain** is now in order. *A transition matrix* $\mathbf{P}$ *together with the initial probabilities* $\{a_j^{(0)}\}$ *associated with the states* E_j *completely define a Markov chain.* One usually thinks of a Markov chain as describing the transitional behavior of a system over equally spaced intervals of time. Situations exist, however, where the time spacings are dependent on the characteristics of the system and hence may not be equal. This case is referred to as **imbedded Markov chains**.

A. Absolute and Transition Probabilities

Given $\{a_j^{(0)}\}$ and $\mathbf{P}$ of a Markov chain, the absolute probabilities of the system after a specified number of transitions are determined as follows. Let $\{a_j^{(n)}\}$ be the absolute probabilities of the system after n transitions, that is, at t_n. The general expression of $\{a_j^{(n)}\}$ in terms of $\{a_j^{(0)}\}$ and $\mathbf{P}$ can be found as follows.

$$a_j^{(1)} = a_1^{(0)}p_{1j} + a_2^{(0)}p_{2j} + a_3^{(0)}p_{3j} + \cdots = \sum_i a_i^{(0)}p_{ij}$$

Also,

$$a_j^{(2)} = \sum_i a_i^{(1)}p_{ij} = \sum_i \left(\sum_k a_k^{(0)}p_{ki}\right)p_{ij} = \sum_k a_k^{(0)}\left(\sum_i p_{ki}p_{ij}\right) = \sum_k a_k^{(0)}p_{kj}^{(2)}$$

where $p_{kj}^{(2)} = \sum_i p_{ki}p_{ij}$ is the **two-step** or **second-order transition probability**, that is, the probability of going from state k to state j in exactly two transitions.

Similarly, it can be shown by induction that

$$a_j^{(n)} = \sum_i a_i^{(0)}\left(\sum_k p_{ik}^{(n-1)}p_{kj}\right) = \sum_i a_i^{(0)}p_{ij}^{(n)}$$

where $p_{ij}^{(n)}$ is the n-step or n-order transition probability given by the recursive formula

$$p_{ij}^{(n)} = \sum_k p_{ik}^{(n-1)}p_{kj}$$

In general, for all i and j,

$$p_{ij}^{(n)} = \sum_k p_{ik}^{(n-m)}p_{kj}^{(m)}, \qquad 0 < m < n$$

These equations are known as **Chapman–Kolomogorov equations**.

The elements of a higher transition matrix $\|p_{ij}^{(n)}\|$ can be obtained directly by matrix multiplication. Thus

$$\|p_{ij}^{(2)}\| = \|p_{ij}\|\,\|p_{ij}\| = \mathbf{P}^2$$

$$\|p_{ij}^{(3)}\| = \|p_{ij}^2\|\,\|p_{ij}\| = \mathbf{P}^3$$

and, in general,

$$\|p_{ij}^{(n)}\| = \mathbf{P}^{n-1}\mathbf{P} = \mathbf{P}^n$$

Hence, if the absolute probabilities are defined in vector form as

$$\mathbf{a}^{(n)} = \{a_1^{(n)}, a_2^{(n)}, a_3^{(n)}, \ldots\}$$

then

$$\mathbf{a}^{(n)} = \mathbf{a}^{(0)}\mathbf{P}^n$$

Example 18.6-1. Consider the following Markov chain with two states,

$$\mathbf{P} = \begin{pmatrix} .2 & .8 \\ .6 & .4 \end{pmatrix}$$

with $\mathbf{a}^{(0)} = (.7 \quad .3)$. Determine $\mathbf{a}^{(1)}$, $\mathbf{a}^{(4)}$, and $\mathbf{a}^{(8)}$.

$$\mathbf{P}^2 = \begin{pmatrix} .2 & .8 \\ .6 & .4 \end{pmatrix}\begin{pmatrix} .2 & .8 \\ .6 & .4 \end{pmatrix} = \begin{pmatrix} .52 & .48 \\ .36 & .64 \end{pmatrix}$$

$$\mathbf{P}^4 = \mathbf{P}^2\mathbf{P}^2 = \begin{pmatrix} .52 & .48 \\ .36 & .64 \end{pmatrix}\begin{pmatrix} .52 & .48 \\ .36 & .64 \end{pmatrix} \cong \begin{pmatrix} .443 & .557 \\ .417 & .583 \end{pmatrix}$$

$$\mathbf{P}^8 = \mathbf{P}^4\mathbf{P}^4 = \begin{pmatrix} .443 & .557 \\ .417 & .583 \end{pmatrix}\begin{pmatrix} .443 & .557 \\ .417 & .583 \end{pmatrix} \cong \begin{pmatrix} .4281 & .5719 \\ .4274 & .5726 \end{pmatrix}$$

Thus

$$\mathbf{a}^{(1)} = (.7 \quad .3)\begin{pmatrix} .2 & .8 \\ .6 & .4 \end{pmatrix} = (.32 \quad .68)$$

$$\mathbf{a}^{(4)} = (.7 \quad .3)\begin{pmatrix} .443 & .557 \\ .417 & .583 \end{pmatrix} = (.435 \quad .565)$$

$$\mathbf{a}^{(8)} = (.7 \quad .3)\begin{pmatrix} .4281 & .5719 \\ .4274 & .5726 \end{pmatrix} = (.4279 \quad .5721)$$

The interesting result is that the rows of $\mathbf{P}^8$ tend to be identical. Also, $\mathbf{a}^{(8)}$ tends to be identical with the rows of $\mathbf{P}^{(8)}$. This result has to do with the long-run properties of Markov chains, which, as shown in this section, implies that the long-run absolute probabilities are independent of $\mathbf{a}^{(0)}$. In this case the resulting probabilities are known as the **steady-state probabilities.** ◀

B. Classification of States in Markov Chains

In using Markov chain analysis, we may be interested in studying the behavior of the system over a short period of time. In this case the absolute probabilites are computed as shown in the preceding section. A more important study, however, would involve the long-run behavior of the system, that is, when the number of transitions tends to infinity. In such a case the analysis given in the preceding section is inadequate and a systematic procedure that will predict the long-run behavior of the system becomes necessary. This section introduces definitions of the classification of states in Markov chains that will be useful in studying the long-run behavior of the system.

Irreducible Markov Chain

A Markov chain is said to be **irreducible** if every state E_j can be reached from every other state E_i after a finite number of transitions; that is, for $i \neq j$,

$$P_{ij}^{(n)} > 0, \qquad \text{for } 1 \leq n < \infty$$

In this case all the states of the chain **communicate**.

Closed Set and Absorbing States

In a Markov chain, a set C of states is said to be **closed** if the system, once in one of the states of C, will remain in C indefinitely. A special example of a closed set is a single state E_j with transition probability $p_{jj} = 1$. In this case, E_j is called an **absorbing state**. All the states of an irreducible chain must form a closed set and no other subset can be closed. The closed set C must also satisfy all the conditions of a Markov chain and hence may be studied independently.

Example 18.6-2. Consider the following Markov chain:

$$\mathbf{P} = \begin{array}{c} \\ 0 \\ 1 \\ 2 \\ 3 \end{array} \begin{array}{c} \begin{array}{cccc} 0 & 1 & 2 & 3 \end{array} \\ \begin{pmatrix} 1/2 & 1/4 & 1/4 & 0 \\ 0 & 0 & 1 & 0 \\ 1/3 & 0 & 1/3 & 1/3 \\ 0 & 0 & 0 & 1 \end{pmatrix} \end{array}$$

This chain is illustrated graphically in Figure 18-2. The figure shows that the four states do *not* constitute an irreducible chain, since states 0, 1, and 2 cannot be reached from state 3. State 3, by itself, forms a closed set and hence it is absorbing. One can also say that state 3 forms an irreducible chain. ◀

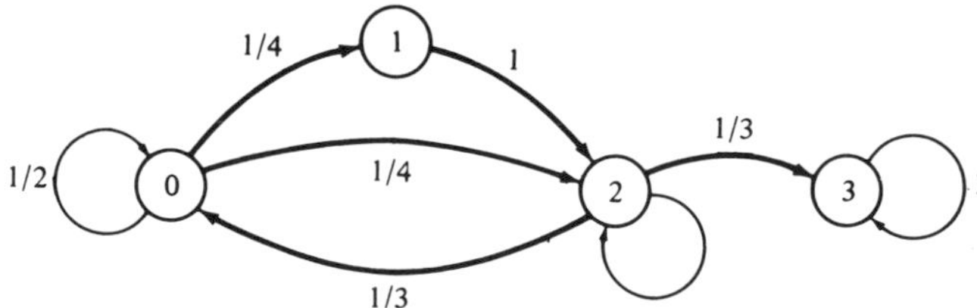

Figure 18-2

First Return Times

An important definition in Markov chains theory is the **first return time**. Given that the system is initially in state E_j, it may return to E_j *for the first time* at the nth step,

$n \geq 1$. The number of steps before the system returns to E_j is called the first return time.

Let $f_{jj}^{(n)}$ denote the probability that the first return to E_j occurs at the nth step. Then given the transition matrix

$$\mathbf{P} = \|p_{ij}\|$$

an expression for $f_{jj}^{(n)}$ can be determined as follows:

$$p_{jj} = f_{jj}^{(1)}$$
$$p_{jj}^{(2)} = f_{jj}^{(2)} + f_{jj}^{(1)} p_{jj}$$

or

$$f_{jj}^{(2)} = p_{jj}^{(2)} - f_{jj}^{(1)} p_{jj}$$

By induction it can be proved in general that

$$p_{jj}^{(n)} = f_{jj}^{(n)} + \sum_{m=1}^{n-1} f_{jj}^{(m)} p_{jj}^{(n-m)}$$

which yields the required expression as

$$f_{jj}^{(n)} = p_{jj}^{(n)} - \sum_{m=1}^{n-1} f_{jj}^{(m)} p_{jj}^{(n-m)}$$

The probability of *at least* one return to state E_j is then given by

$$f_{jj} = \sum_{n=1}^{\infty} f_{jj}^{(n)}$$

Thus the system is certain to return to j if $f_{jj} = 1$. In this case, if μ_{jj} defines the mean return (recurrence) time,

$$\mu_{jj} = \sum_{n=1}^{\infty} n f_{jj}^{(n)}$$

If $f_{jj} < 1$, it is not certain that the system will return to E_j and, consequently, $\mu_{jj} = \infty$.

The states of a Markov chain can thus be classified based on the definition of the first return times as follows:

1. A state is **transient** if $f_{jj} < 1$; that is, $\mu_{jj} = \infty$.
2. A state is **recurrent** (persistent) if $f_{jj} = 1$.
3. A recurrent state is **null** if $\mu_{jj} = \infty$ and **nonnull** if $\mu_{jj} < \infty$ (finite).
4. A state is **periodic** with period t if a return is possible only in t, $2t$, $3t$, ... steps. This means that $p_{jj}^{(n)} = 0$ whenever n is not divisible by t.
5. A recurrent state is **ergodic** if it is nonnull and aperiodic (not periodic).

Ergodic Markov Chains

An *irreducible* Markov chain is ergodic if all its states are ergodic. In this case the absolute probability distribution

$$\mathbf{a}^{(n)} = \mathbf{a}^{(0)} \mathbf{P}^n$$

always converges uniquely to a limiting distribution as $n \to \infty$, where the limiting distribution is independent of the initial probabilities $\mathbf{a}^{(0)}$.

The following theorem is now in order.

Theorem 18.6-1. *All the states in an irreducible infinite Markov chain may belong to one, and only one, of the following three classes: transient state, recurrent null state, or recurrent nonnull state. In every case all the states communicate and they have the same period. For the special case where the chain has a finite number of states, the chain cannot consist of transient states only nor can it contain any null states.*

C. Limiting Distribution of Irreducible Chains

Example 18.6-1 shows that as the number of transitions increases, the absolute probability becomes independent of the initial distribution. This was referred to as the long-run property of Markov chains. In this section determination of the limiting (long-run) distribution of an *irreducible* chain is presented. The discussion will be restricted to the aperiodic type, since this is the only type needed in this text. In addition, the analysis of the periodic case is rather involved.

The existence of a limiting distribution in an irreducible aperiodic chain depends on the class of its states. Thus, considering the three classes given in Theorem 18.6-1, the following theorem can be stated.

Theorem 18.6-2. *In an irreducible aperiodic Markov chain,*

(a) *If the states are all transient or all null, then $p_{ij}^{(n)} \to 0$ as $n \to \infty$ for all i and j and no limiting distribution exists.*

(b) *If all the states are ergodic, then*

$$\lim_{n \to \infty} a_j^{(n)} = \beta_j, \qquad j = 0, 1, 2, \ldots$$

where β_j is the limiting (steady-state) distribution. The probabilities β_j exist uniquely and are independent of $a_j^{(0)}$. In this case β_j can be determined from the set of equations†

$$\beta_j = \sum_i \beta_i p_{ij}$$

$$1 = \sum_j \beta_j$$

The mean recurrence time for state j is then given by

$$\mu_{jj} = \frac{1}{\beta_j}$$

† Notice that one of the equations $\beta_j = \sum_i \beta_i p_{ij}$ is redundant.

Example 18.6-3. Consider Example 18.6-1. To determine its steady-state probability distribution, one has

$$\beta_1 = .2\beta_1 + .6\beta_2$$
$$\beta_2 = .8\beta_1 + .4\beta_2$$
$$1 = \beta_1 + \beta_2$$

(Notice that one of the first two equations is redundant.) The solution yields $\beta_1 = 0.4286$ and $\beta_2 = 0.5714$. These results are very close to the values of $\mathbf{a}^{(8)}$ (and the rows of $\mathbf{P}^8$) in Example 18.6-1. Next we have

$$\mu_{11} = 1/\beta_1 = 2.3$$
$$\mu_{22} = 1/\beta_2 = 1.75$$

so that the mean recurrent time for the first and second states are 2.3 and 1.75 steps, respectively. ◀

Example 18.6-4. Consider the following Markov chain with three states:

$$\mathbf{P} = \begin{matrix} & \begin{matrix} 0 & 1 & 2 \end{matrix} \\ \begin{matrix} 0 \\ 1 \\ 2 \end{matrix} & \begin{pmatrix} 1/2 & 1/4 & 1/4 \\ 1/2 & 1/4 & 1/4 \\ 0 & 1/2 & 1/2 \end{pmatrix} \end{matrix}$$

This is called a **doubly stochastic matrix**, since

$$\sum_{i=1}^{s} p_{ij} = \sum_{j=1}^{s} p_{ij} = 1$$

where s is the number of states. In such cases, the steady-state probabilities are $\beta_j = 1/s$ for all j. Thus, for the matrix given,

$$\beta_0 = \beta_1 = \beta_2 = 1/3$$ ◀

SELECTED REFERENCES

DERMAN, C., *Finite State Markovian Decision Processes*, Academic Press, New York, 1970.

HOWARD, R., *Dynamic Programming and Markov Processes*, MIT Press, Cambridge, Mass., 1960.

PROBLEMS

Section	Assigned Problems
18.2	18–1 to 18–6
18.3.1	18–7 to 18–9
18.3.2	18–10 to 18–12
18.3.3	18–13
18.4	18–14, 18–15
18.6	18–16, 18–17

☐ **18–1** A company reviews the state of one of its important products on an annual basis and decides whether it is successful (state 1) or unsuccessful (state 2). The company must then decide whether or not to advertize the product to further promote the sales. The matrices $\mathbf{P}_1$ and $\mathbf{P}_2$ given here provide the transition probabilities with and without advertisement during any year. The associated returns are given by the matrices $\mathbf{R}_1$ and $\mathbf{R}_2$. Find the optimal decisions over the next 3 years.

$$\mathbf{P}_1 = \begin{bmatrix} .9 & .1 \\ .6 & .4 \end{bmatrix}, \qquad \mathbf{R}_1 = \begin{bmatrix} 2 & -1 \\ 1 & -3 \end{bmatrix}$$

$$\mathbf{P}_2 = \begin{bmatrix} .7 & .3 \\ .2 & .8 \end{bmatrix}, \qquad \mathbf{R}_2 = \begin{bmatrix} 4 & 1 \\ 2 & -1 \end{bmatrix}$$

☐ **18–2** A company can use advertisement through one of three media: radio, TV, or newspaper. The weekly costs of advertisement in the three media are estimated at $200, $900, and $300, respectively. The company can classify its sales volume during each week as (1) fair, (2) good, or (3) excellent. A summary of the transition probabilities associated with each advertisement medium follows.

$$\text{Radio} \quad \begin{array}{c} \\ 1 \\ 2 \\ 3 \end{array} \begin{array}{c} \begin{array}{ccc} 1 & 2 & 3 \end{array} \\ \begin{bmatrix} .4 & .5 & .1 \\ .1 & .7 & .2 \\ .1 & .2 & .7 \end{bmatrix} \end{array} \qquad \text{TV} \quad \begin{array}{c} \\ 1 \\ 2 \\ 3 \end{array} \begin{array}{c} \begin{array}{ccc} 1 & 2 & 3 \end{array} \\ \begin{bmatrix} .7 & .2 & .1 \\ .3 & .6 & .1 \\ .1 & .7 & .2 \end{bmatrix} \end{array} \qquad \text{Newspaper} \quad \begin{array}{c} \\ 1 \\ 2 \\ 3 \end{array} \begin{array}{c} \begin{array}{ccc} 1 & 2 & 3 \end{array} \\ \begin{bmatrix} .2 & .5 & .3 \\ 0 & .7 & .3 \\ 0 & .2 & .8 \end{bmatrix} \end{array}$$

The corresponding weekly returns (in thousands of dollars) are

$$\text{Radio} \begin{bmatrix} 400 & 520 & 600 \\ 300 & 400 & 700 \\ 200 & 250 & 500 \end{bmatrix} \qquad \text{TV} \begin{bmatrix} 1000 & 1300 & 1600 \\ 800 & 1000 & 1700 \\ 600 & 700 & 1100 \end{bmatrix} \qquad \text{Newspaper} \begin{bmatrix} 400 & 530 & 710 \\ 350 & 450 & 800 \\ 250 & 400 & 650 \end{bmatrix}$$

Find the optimal advertisement policy over the next 3 weeks.

☐ **18–3** A company is introducing a new product into the market. If the sales are high, there is a .5 probability that they will remain so next month. If they are not, the probability that they will become high next month is only .2. The company has the option of launching an advertisement campaign. If it does and the sales are high, the probability that they will remain high next month will increase to .8. On the other hand, an advertising campaign while the sales are low will raise the probability to only .4.

If no advertisement is used and the sales are high, the returns are expected to be 10 if the sales remain high next month and 4 if they do not. The corresponding returns if the product starts with high sales are 7 and -2. Using advertisement will result in returns of 7 if the product starts with high sales and continues to be so and 6 if it does not. If the sales start low, the returns are 3 and -5, depending on whether or not they remain high.

Determine the company's optimal policy over the next 3 months.

☐ **18–4** (Inventory Problem). An appliance store can place orders for refrigerators at the beginning of each month for immediate delivery. A fixed cost of $100 is incurred every time an order is placed. The storage cost per refrigerator per month is $5. The penalty for running out of stock is estimated at $150 per refrigerator per month. The monthly demand is given by the following PDF:

Demand x	0	1	2
$p(x)$	.2	.5	.3

The store's policy is that the maximum stock level should not exceed two refrigerators in any single month.

(a) Determine the transition probabilities for the different decision alternatives of the problem.
(b) Determine the expected inventory cost per month as a function of the state of the system and the decision alternative.
(c) Determine the optimal ordering policy over the next 3 months.

□ **18–5** Repeat Problem 18–4 assuming that the pdf of demand over the next quarter changes according to the following table.

Demand	Month		
x	1	2	3
0	.1	.3	.2
1	.4	.5	.4
2	.5	.2	.4

□ **18–6** The market value of a used car is estimated at $2000. The owner can get more than this amount but is willing to entertain offers from the first three prospective buyers who respond to the advertisement (which means that a decision must be made no later than the time the third offer is received). The offers are expected to be $2000, $2200, $2400, and $2600, with equal probabilities. Naturally, once an offer is accepted, all later offers are discarded. The objective is to set an acceptance limit that can be used to evaluate each offer. These limits may thus be $2000, $2200, $2400, or $2600. Develop an optimal plan for the owner.

□ **18–7** Solve Problem 18–1 for an infinite number of periods using the exhaustive enumeration method.

□ **18–8** Solve Problem 18–2 for an infinite planning horizon using the exhaustive enumeration method.

□ **18–9** Solve Problem 18–3 by the exhaustive enumeration method assuming an infinite horizon.

□ **18–10** Assume in Problem 18–1 that the planning horizon is infinite. Solve the problem by the policy iteration method.

□ **18–11** Solve Problem 18–2 by the policy iteration method, assuming an infinite planning horizon. Compare the results with those of Problem 18–8.

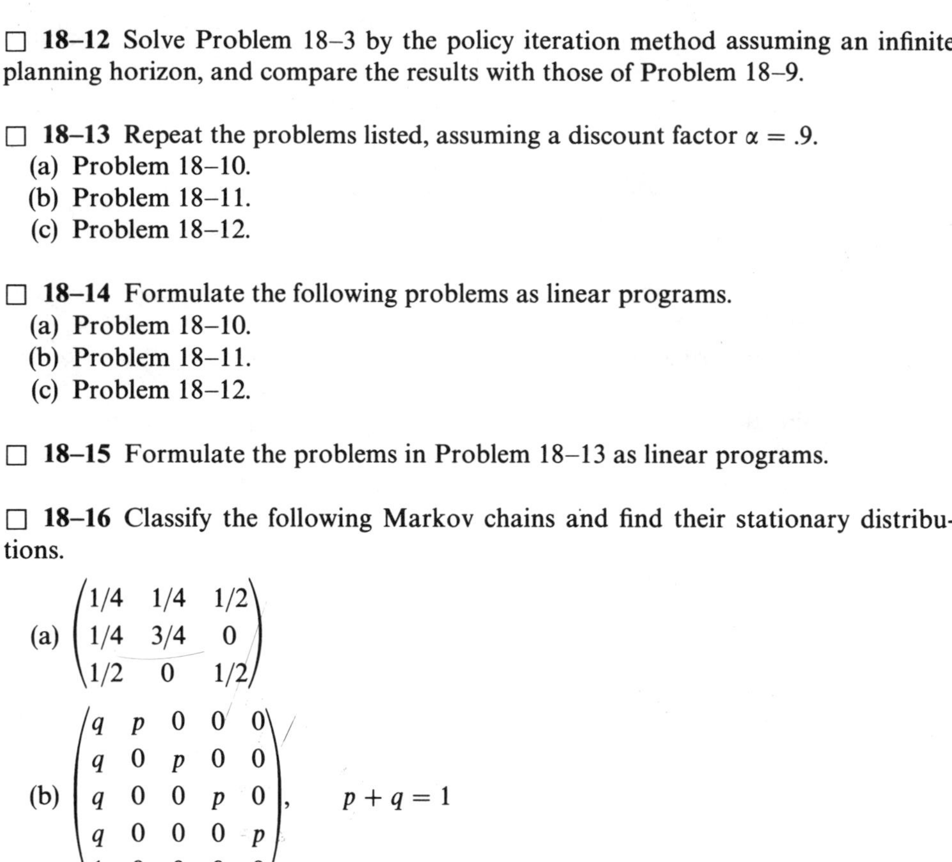

☐ **18–12** Solve Problem 18–3 by the policy iteration method assuming an infinite planning horizon, and compare the results with those of Problem 18–9.

☐ **18–13** Repeat the problems listed, assuming a discount factor $\alpha = .9$.
(a) Problem 18–10.
(b) Problem 18–11.
(c) Problem 18–12.

☐ **18–14** Formulate the following problems as linear programs.
(a) Problem 18–10.
(b) Problem 18–11.
(c) Problem 18–12.

☐ **18–15** Formulate the problems in Problem 18–13 as linear programs.

☐ **18–16** Classify the following Markov chains and find their stationary distributions.

(a) $\begin{pmatrix} 1/4 & 1/4 & 1/2 \\ 1/4 & 3/4 & 0 \\ 1/2 & 0 & 1/2 \end{pmatrix}$

(b) $\begin{pmatrix} q & p & 0 & 0 & 0 \\ q & 0 & p & 0 & 0 \\ q & 0 & 0 & p & 0 \\ q & 0 & 0 & 0 & p \\ 1 & 0 & 0 & 0 & 0 \end{pmatrix}, \qquad p + q = 1$

☐ **18–17** Find the mean recurrence time for each state of the following Markov chain:

$$\begin{pmatrix} 1/3 & 1/3 & 1/3 \\ 1/2 & 1/4 & 1/4 \\ 1/5 & 3/5 & 1/5 \end{pmatrix}$$

PART III

NONLINEAR PROGRAMMING

THIS PART INCLUDES CHAPTERS 19 AND 20. The material is designed to provide basic foundations in nonlinear programming. Further information about the subject can be found in specialized books.

Chapter 19 introduces classical optimization theory, including unconstrained optima, constrained (Jacobian and Lagrangean) methods, wherein all constraints are equations, and the Kuhn–Tucker conditions for constrained nonlinear problems. Chapter 20 concentrates on the *computational* aspects of optimizing unconstrained and constrained functions.

The material in this part assumes higher ability in mathematics than that in Parts I and II. One reason is that this type of material cannot be presented meaningfully at an elementary level. Another reason is that one of the objectives of the book is to increase your level of mathematical sophistication as you successively complete Parts I, II, and III.

The prerequisite for Part III includes completing a course in advanced calculus. Although matrix algebra is used in Part III, it is not a mandatory prerequisite and the material in Appendix A should be sufficient for this purpose.

Chapter 19

Classical Optimization Theory

Classical optimization theory develops the use of differential calculus to determine points of maxima and minima (extrema) for unconstrained and constrained functions. The methods developed may not be suitable for efficient numerical computations. However, the underlying theory provides the basis for devising most nonlinear programming algorithms (see Chapter 20).

This chapter develops necessary and sufficient conditions for determining unconstrained extrema, the *Jacobian* and *Lagrangean* methods for problems with equality constraints, and the *Kuhn–Tucker* conditions for problems with inequality constraints.

19.1 UNCONSTRAINED EXTREMAL PROBLEMS

An extreme point of a function $f(\mathbf{X})$ defines either a maximum or a minimum of the function. Mathematically, a point $\mathbf{X}_0 = (x_1, \ldots, x_j, \ldots, x_n)$ is a maximum if

$$f(\mathbf{X}_0 + \mathbf{h}) \leq f(\mathbf{X}_0)$$

for all $\mathbf{h} = (h_1, \ldots, h_j, \ldots, h_n)$ such that $|h_j|$ is sufficiently small for all j. In other words, $\mathbf{X}_0$ is a maximum if the value of f at every point in the neighborhood of $\mathbf{X}_0$ does not exceed $f(\mathbf{X}_0)$. In a similar manner, $\mathbf{X}_0$ is a minimum if for $\mathbf{h}$ as defined

$$f(\mathbf{X}_0 + \mathbf{h}) \geq f(\mathbf{X}_0)$$

Figure 19-1 illustrates the maxima and minima of a single-variable function $f(x)$ over the interval $[a, b]$. [The interval $a \leq x \leq b$ is not meant to represent restrictions on $f(x)$.] The points x_1, x_2, x_3, x_4, and x_6 are all extrema of $f(x)$. These include x_1, x_3, and x_6 as maxima and x_2 and x_4 as minima. Since

$$f(x_6) = \max\{f(x_1), f(x_3), f(x_6)\}$$

$f(x_6)$ is called **global** or **absolute** maximum, and $f(x_1)$ and $f(x_3)$ are **local** or **relative** maxima. Similarly, $f(x_4)$ is a local minimum and $f(x_2)$ is a global minimum.

Although x_1 (in Figure 19-1) is a maximum point, it differs from remaining local maxima in that the value of f corresponding to at least one point in the neighborhood of x_1 is equal to $f(x_1)$. In this respect, x_1 is called a **weak maximum** compared with x_3, for example, where $f(x_3)$ defines a **strong maximum**. A weak maximum thus implies (an infinite number of) alternative maxima. Similar results may be developed for the weak minimum at x_4. In general, $\mathbf{X}_0$ is a weak maximum if $f(\mathbf{X}_0 + \mathbf{h}) \leq f(\mathbf{X}_0)$ and a strong maximum if $f(\mathbf{X}_0 + \mathbf{h}) < f(\mathbf{X}_0)$, where $\mathbf{h}$ is as defined earlier.

An interesting observation about the extrema in Figure 19-1 is that the first derivative (slope) of f vanishes at these points. However, this property is not unique to extrema. For example, the slope of $f(x)$ at x_5 is zero.

Because a vanishing first derivative (generally, gradient) plays an important role in identifying maxima and minima (see the next section), it is essential to define points such as x_5 separately. These points are known as **inflection** (or, in special cases, **saddle**) points. If a point with zero slope (gradient) is not an extremum (maximum or minimum), then it must automatically be an inflection point.

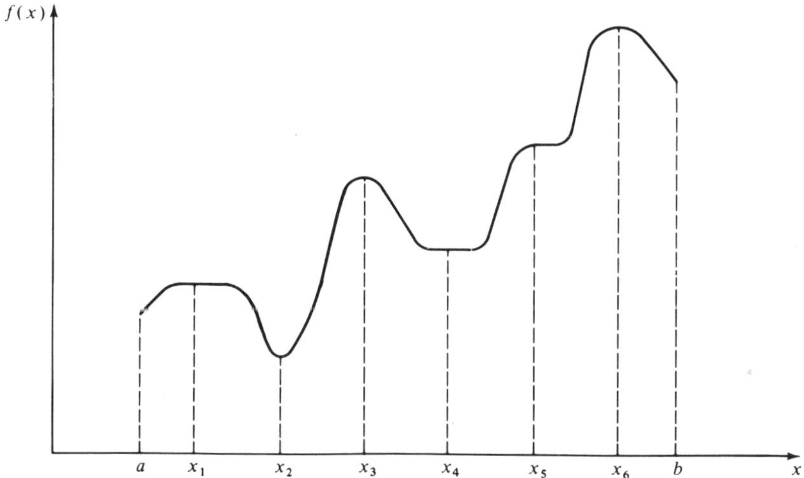

Figure 19-1

19.1.1 NECESSARY AND SUFFICIENT CONDITIONS FOR EXTREMA

This section develops theorems for establishing necessary and sufficient conditions for an n-variable function $f(\mathbf{X})$ to have extrema. It is assumed throughout that the first and second partial derivatives of $f(\mathbf{X})$ are continuous at every $\mathbf{X}$.

Theorem 19.1-1. *A necessary condition for $\mathbf{X}_0$ to be an extreme point of $f(\mathbf{X})$ is that*

$$\nabla f(\mathbf{X}_0) = \mathbf{0}$$

PROOF. By Taylor's theorem, for $0 < \theta < 1$,

$$f(\mathbf{X}_0 + \mathbf{h}) - f(\mathbf{X}_0) = \nabla f(\mathbf{X}_0)\mathbf{h} + (1/2)\mathbf{h}^T \mathrm{Hh}\Big|_{\mathbf{X}_0 + \theta\mathbf{h}}$$

where $\mathbf{h}$ is as defined.

For sufficiently small $|h_j|$, the remainder term $(1/2)$ $(\mathbf{h}^T\mathbf{Hh})$ is on the order h_j^2, and hence the expansion may be approximated as

$$f(\mathbf{X}_0 + \mathbf{h}) - f(\mathbf{X}_0) = \nabla f(\mathbf{X}_0)\mathbf{h} + O(h_j^2) \cong \nabla f(\mathbf{X}_0)\mathbf{h}$$

Suppose now that $\mathbf{X}_0$ is a minimum point; it is shown by contradiction that $\nabla f(\mathbf{X}_0)$ must vanish. Suppose it does not; then for a specific j, either

$$\frac{\partial f(\mathbf{X}_0)}{\partial x_j} < 0 \qquad \text{or} \qquad \frac{\partial f(\mathbf{X}_0)}{\partial x_j} > 0$$

By selecting h_j with appropriate sign, it is always possible to have

$$h_j \frac{\partial f(\mathbf{X}_0)}{\partial x_j} < 0$$

By setting all other h_j equal to zero, Taylor's expansion yields

$$f(\mathbf{X}_0 + \mathbf{h}) < f(\mathbf{X}_0)$$

This result contradicts the assumption that $\mathbf{X}_0$ is a minimum point. Consequently, $\nabla f(\mathbf{X}_0)$ must vanish. A similar proof can be established for the maximization case.

The conclusion from Theorem 19.1-1 is that, at any extreme point, the condition

$$\nabla f(\mathbf{X}_0) = \mathbf{0}$$

must be satisfied; that is, the gradient vector must be null.

For functions with one variable only (say, y), the condition reduces to

$$f'(y_0) = 0$$

As stated previously, the condition is also satisfied for inflection and saddle points. Consequently, these conditions are necessary but not sufficient for identifying extreme points. It is thus more appropriate to refer to the points obtained from the solution of

$$\nabla f(\mathbf{X}_0) = \mathbf{0}$$

as **stationary** points. The next theorem establishes the sufficiency conditions for $\mathbf{X}_0$ to be an extreme point.

Theorem 19.1-2. *A sufficient condition for a stationary point* $\mathbf{X}_0$ *to be extremum is that the Hessian matrix* $\mathbf{H}$ *evaluated at* $\mathbf{X}_0$ *is*

(i) *Positive definite when* $\mathbf{X}_0$ *is a minimum point.*
(ii) *Negative definite when* $\mathbf{X}_0$ *is a maximum point.*

PROOF. By Taylor's theorem, for $0 < \theta < 1$,

$$f(\mathbf{X}_0 + \mathbf{h}) - f(\mathbf{X}_0) = \nabla f(\mathbf{X}_0)\mathbf{h} + (1/2)\mathbf{h}^T\mathbf{H}\mathbf{h}\Big|_{\mathbf{X}_0+\theta\mathbf{h}}$$

Since $\mathbf{X}_0$ is a stationary point, by Theorem 19.1-1, $\nabla f(\mathbf{X}_0) = \mathbf{0}$. Thus

$$f(\mathbf{X}_0 + \mathbf{h}) - f(\mathbf{X}_0) = (1/2)\mathbf{h}^T\mathbf{H}\mathbf{h}\Big|_{\mathbf{X}_0+\theta\mathbf{h}}$$

Let $\mathbf{X}_0$ be a minimum point; then, by definition,

$$f(\mathbf{X}_0 + \mathbf{h}) > f(\mathbf{X}_0)$$

for all nonnull $\mathbf{h}$. This means that for $\mathbf{X}_0$ to be a minimum, it must be true that

$$(1/2)\mathbf{h}^T\mathbf{H}\mathbf{h}\Big|_{\mathbf{X}_0+\theta\mathbf{h}} > 0$$

However, continuity of the second partial derivative guarantees that the expression $(1/2)\mathbf{h}^T\mathbf{H}\mathbf{h}$ must yield the same sign when evaluated at both $\mathbf{X}_0$ and $\mathbf{X}_0 + \theta\mathbf{h}$. Since $\mathbf{h}^T\mathbf{H}\mathbf{h}|_{\mathbf{X}_0}$ defines a quadratic form (see Section A.3), this expression (and hence $\mathbf{h}^T\mathbf{H}\mathbf{h}|_{\mathbf{X}_0+\theta\mathbf{h}}$) is positive if and only if $\mathbf{H}|_{\mathbf{X}_0}$ is positive-definite. This means that a sufficient condition for the stationary point $\mathbf{X}_0$ to be a minimum is that the Hessian matrix evaluated at the same point is positive-definite. A similar proof can be established for the maximization case to show that the corresponding Hessian matrix is negative-definite.

Example 19.1-1. Consider the function

$$f(x_1, x_2, x_3) = x_1 + 2x_3 + x_2x_3 - x_1^2 - x_2^2 - x_3^2$$

The necessary condition

$$\nabla f(\mathbf{X}_0) = \mathbf{0}$$

gives

$$\frac{\partial f}{\partial x_1} = 1 - 2x_1 = 0$$

$$\frac{\partial f}{\partial x_2} = x_3 - 2x_2 = 0$$

$$\frac{\partial f}{\partial x_3} = 2 + x_2 - 2x_3 = 0$$

The solution of these simultaneous equations is given by

$$\mathbf{X}_0 = (1/2, 2/3, 4/3)$$

To establish sufficiency, consider

$$\mathbf{H}\Big|_{\mathbf{X}_0} = \begin{pmatrix} \dfrac{\partial^2 f}{\partial x_1^2} & \dfrac{\partial^2 f}{\partial x_1\,\partial x_2} & \dfrac{\partial^2 f}{\partial x_1\,\partial x_3} \\ \dfrac{\partial^2 f}{\partial x_2\,\partial x_1} & \dfrac{\partial^2 f}{\partial x_2^2} & \dfrac{\partial^2 f}{\partial x_2\,\partial x_3} \\ \dfrac{\partial^2 f}{\partial x_3\,\partial x_1} & \dfrac{\partial^2 f}{\partial x_3\,\partial x_2} & \dfrac{\partial^2 f}{\partial x_3^2} \end{pmatrix}_{\mathbf{X}_0} = \begin{pmatrix} -2 & 0 & 0 \\ 0 & -2 & 1 \\ 0 & 1 & -2 \end{pmatrix}$$

The principal minor determinants of $\mathbf{H}|_{\mathbf{X}_0}$ have the values -2, 4, and -6, respectively. Thus, as indicated in Section A.3, $\mathbf{H}|_{\mathbf{X}_0}$ is negative-definite and $\mathbf{X}_0 = (1/2, 2/3, 4/3)$ represents a maximum point. ◀

Exercise 19.1-1

Resolve Example 19.1-1 assuming that $f(x_1, x_2)$ is replaced by $-f(x_1, x_2)$.
[*Ans.* $\mathbf{X}_0 = (1/2, 2/3, 4/3)$ is minimum point because the associated Hessian matrix is positive-definite.]

In general, if $\mathbf{H}|_{\mathbf{X}_0}$ is indefinite, $\mathbf{X}_0$ must be a saddle point. However, for the case where it is nonconclusive, $\mathbf{X}_0$ may or may not be an extremum and the development of a sufficiency condition becomes rather involved since it would be necessary to consider higher-order terms in Taylor's expansion. (See Theorem 19.1-3 for an illustration of this point to single-variable functions.) However, in some cases such complex procedures may not be necessary since the diagonalization of $\mathbf{H}$ may lead to more conclusive information. The following example illustrates this point.

Example 19.1-2. Consider the function

$$f(x_1, x_2) = 8x_1x_2 + 3x_2^2$$

Thus

$$\nabla f(x_1, x_2) = (8x_2, 8x_1 + 6x_2) = (0, 0)$$

This gives the stationary point $\mathbf{X}_0 = (0, 0)$. The Hessian matrix at $\mathbf{X}_0$ is

$$\mathbf{H} = \begin{pmatrix} 0 & 8 \\ 8 & 6 \end{pmatrix}$$

which is nonconclusive. By using one of the diagonalization methods [see, e.g., Hadley (1961, Sec. 7–10)], the transformed Hessian matrix becomes

$$\mathbf{H}_t = \begin{pmatrix} -64/6 & 0 \\ 0 & 6 \end{pmatrix}$$

By the principal minor determinants test, $\mathbf{H}_t$ (and hence $\mathbf{H}$) is indefinite. This concludes that $\mathbf{X}_0$ is a saddle point. ◀

The sufficiency condition established by Theorem 19.1-2 applies readily to single-variable functions. Given y_0 is a stationary point, then

(i) $f''(y_0) < 0$ is a sufficient condition for y_0 to be maximum.
(ii) $f''(y_0) > 0$ is a sufficient condition for y_0 to be minimum.

These conditions are directly determined by considering the Hessian matrix with one element.

If in the single-variable case $f''(y_0)$ vanishes, higher-order derivatives must be investigated as shown by the following theorem.

Theorem 19.1-3. *If at a stationary point y_0 of $f(y)$, the first $(n-1)$ derivatives vanish and $f^{(n)}(y) \neq 0$, then at $y = y_0$, $f(y)$ has*

(i) *An inflection point if n is odd.*

(ii) *An extreme point if n is even. This extreme point will be a maximum if $f^{(n)}(y_0) < 0$ and a minimum if $f^{(n)}(y_0) > 0$.*

The proof of this theorem is left as an exercise.

Example 19.1-3. Consider the two functions

$$f(y) = y^4 \quad \text{and} \quad g(y) = y^3$$

For $f(y) = y^4$,

$$f'(y) = 4y^3 = 0$$

which yields the stationary point $y_0 = 0$. Now

$$f'(0) = f''(0) = f^{(3)}(0) = 0$$

But $f^{(4)}(0) = 24 > 0$, hence $y_0 = 0$ is a minimum point (see Figure 19-2).

For $g(y) = y^3$,

$$g'(y) = 3y^2 = 0$$

This yields $y_0 = 0$ as a stationary point. Since $g^{(n)}(0)$ is not zero at $n = 3$, $y_0 = 0$ is an inflection point. ◀

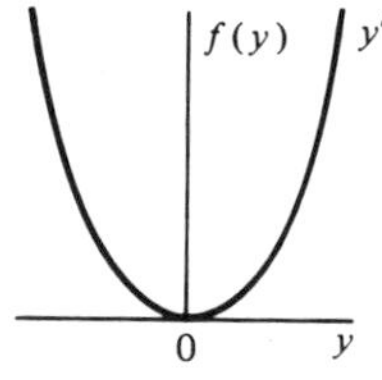

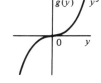

Figure 19-2

Exercise 19.1-2

Find the maxima and minima of $f(x) = x^3 + x^4$.

[*Ans.* $x_0 = 0$ is inflection point and $x_0 = -3/4$ is minimum.]

19.1.2 THE NEWTON–RAPHSON METHOD

A drawback of using the necessary condition $\nabla f(\mathbf{X}) = \mathbf{0}$ to determine stationary points is the difficulty of solving the resulting simultaneous equations numerically. The Newton–Raphson method is an iterative procedure for solving simultaneous nonlinear equations. Although the method is presented here in this context, it is actually part of the **gradient methods** for optimizing unconstrained functions numerically (see Section 20.1.2).

Consider the simultaneous equations

$$f_i(\mathbf{X}) = 0, \qquad i = 1, 2, \ldots, m$$

Let $\mathbf{X}^k$ be a given point. Then by Taylor's expansion

$$f_i(\mathbf{X}) \cong f_i(\mathbf{X}^k) + \nabla f_i(\mathbf{X}^k)(\mathbf{X} - \mathbf{X}^k), \qquad i = 1, 2, \ldots, m$$

Thus the original equations may be approximated by

$$f_i(\mathbf{X}^k) + \nabla f_i(\mathbf{X}^k)(\mathbf{X} - \mathbf{X}^k) = 0, \qquad i = 1, 2, \ldots, m$$

These equations may be written in matrix notation as

$$\mathbf{A}_k + \mathbf{B}_k(\mathbf{X} - \mathbf{X}^k) = \mathbf{0}$$

Under the assumption that all $f_i(\mathbf{X})$ are independent, $\mathbf{B}_k$ is necessarily nonsingular. Thus the preceding equation gives

$$\mathbf{X} = \mathbf{X}^k - \mathbf{B}_k^{-1}\mathbf{A}_k$$

The idea of the method is to start from an initial point $\mathbf{X}^0$. By using the foregoing equation, a new point $\mathbf{X}^{k+1}$ can always be determined from $\mathbf{X}^k$. The procedure is terminated with $\mathbf{X}^m$ as the solution when $\mathbf{X}^m \cong \mathbf{X}^{m-1}$.

Exercise 19.1-3

Given the necessary conditions $\nabla f(\mathbf{X}) = \mathbf{0}$, develop the associated Newton–Raphson equation for determining $\mathbf{X}^{k+1}$ given a current trial point X^k.

[*Ans.* $\mathbf{X}^{k+1} = \mathbf{X}^k - \mathbf{H}_k^{-1}(\nabla f(\mathbf{X}^k))^T$, where $\mathbf{H}_k$ is the Hessian matrix evaluated at $\mathbf{X}^k$.]

A geometric interpretation of the method id illustrated by a single-variable function in Figure 19-3. The relationship between x^k and x^{k+1} for a single-variable

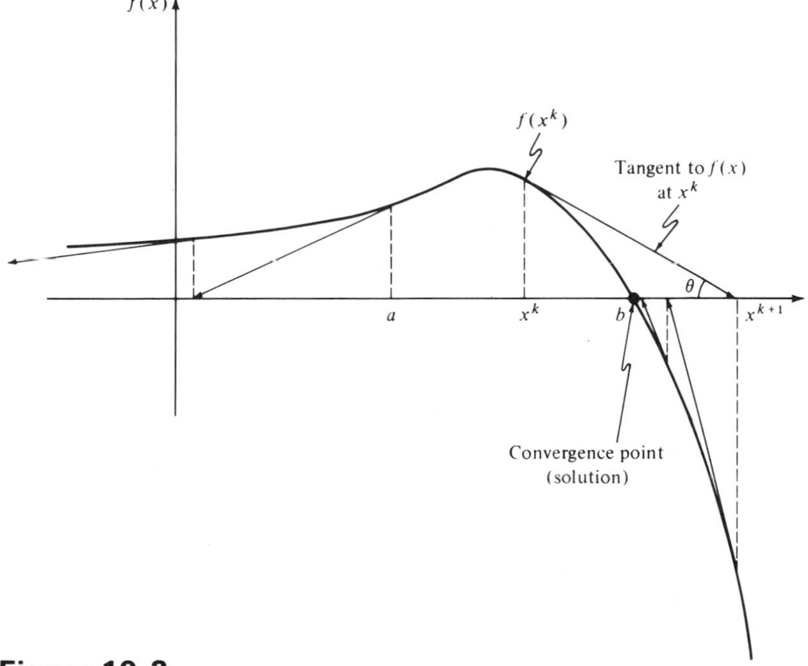

Figure 19-3

function $f(x)$ reduces to

$$x^{k+1} = x^k - \frac{f(x^k)}{f'(x^k)}$$

or

$$f'(x^k) = \frac{f(x^k)}{x^k - x^{k+1}}$$

An investigation of Figure 19-3 shows that x^{k+1} is determined from the slope of $f(x)$ at x^k, where $\tan\theta = f'(x^k)$.

One difficulty with the method is that convergence is not always guaranteed unless the function f is well behaved. In Figure 19-3, if the initial point x_0 is a, the method will diverge. There is no easy way for locating a "good" initial x_0. Perhaps a remedy to this difficulty is to use trial and error.

19.2 CONSTRAINED EXTREMAL PROBLEMS

This section deals with the optimization of continuous functions subject to side conditions or constraints. Such constraints may be in the form of equation or inequation. Section 19.2.1 introduces the case with equality constraints and Section 19.2.2 introduces the other case with inequality constraints. The presentation in Section 19.2.1 is covered for the most part in Beightler et al. (1979, pp. 45–55).

19.2.1 EQUALITY CONSTRAINTS

This section presents two methods for optimizing functions subject to equality constraints. The first is the **Jacobian** method. This method may be considered a generalization of the simplex method for linear programming. Indeed, the simplex method conditions can be derived by the Jacobian method. The second method is the **Lagrangean** procedure, which is shown to be closely related to, and indeed may be developed logically from, the Jacobian method. This relationship allows an interesting economic interpretation of the Lagrangean method.

A. Constrained Derivatives (Jacobian) Method

Consider the problem

$$\text{minimize } z = f(\mathbf{X})$$

subject to

$$\mathbf{g}(\mathbf{X}) = \mathbf{0}$$

where

$$\mathbf{X} = (x_1, x_2, \ldots, x_n)$$
$$\mathbf{g} = (g_1, g_2, \ldots, g_m)^T$$

The functions $f(\mathbf{X})$ and $g_i(\mathbf{X})$, $i = 1, 2, \ldots, m$, are assumed twice continuously differentiable.

The idea of using constrained derivatives for solving the problem is to find a closed-form expression for the first partial derivatives of $f(\mathbf{X})$ at all points that satisfy the constraints $\mathbf{g}(\mathbf{X}) = \mathbf{0}$. The corresponding stationary points are thus identified as the points at which these partial derivatives vanish. The sufficiency conditions introduced in Section 19.1 can then be used to check the identity of stationary points.

To clarify this concept, consider $f(x_1, x_2)$ illustrated in Figure 19-4. This function is to be minimized subject to the constraint

$$g_1(x_1, x_2) = x_2 - b = 0$$

where b is a constant. From Figure 19-4, the curve designated by the three points A, B, and C represents the values of $f(x_1, x_2)$ for which the given constraint is always satisfied. The constrained derivatives method then defines the gradient of $f(x_1, x_2)$ at any point on the curve ABC. The point at which the constrained derivatives vanish represents a stationary point for the constrained problem. In Figure 19-4 this is given by B. The figure also shows an example of the incremental *constrained* value $\partial_c f$ of f.

The method is now developed mathematically. By Taylor's theorem, for the points $\mathbf{X} + \Delta\mathbf{X}$ in the feasible neighborhood of $\mathbf{X}$, it follows that

$$f(\mathbf{X} + \Delta\mathbf{X}) - f(\mathbf{X}) = \nabla f(\mathbf{X})\Delta\mathbf{X} + O(\Delta x_j^2)$$

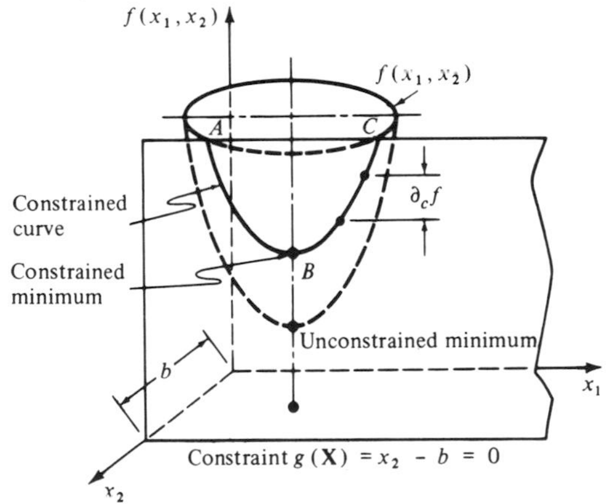

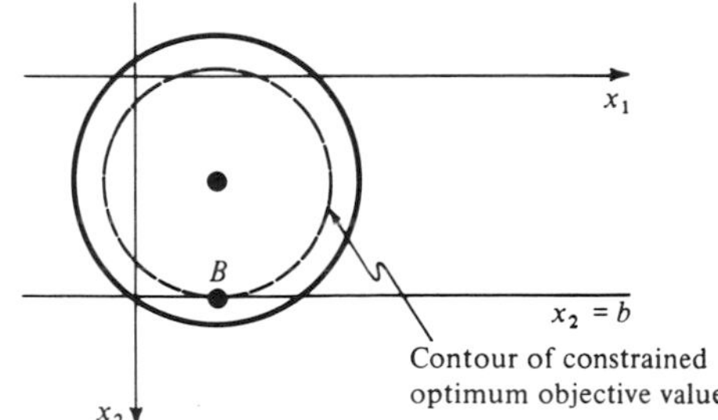

Figure 19-4

and

$$\mathbf{g}(\mathbf{X} + \Delta\mathbf{X}) - \mathbf{g}(\mathbf{X}) = \nabla\mathbf{g}(\mathbf{X})\,\Delta\mathbf{X} + O(\Delta x_j^2)$$

As $\Delta x_j \to 0$, the equations can be shown to reduce to

$$\partial f(\mathbf{X}) = \nabla f(\mathbf{X})\,\partial\mathbf{X}$$

and

$$\partial\mathbf{g}(\mathbf{X}) = \nabla\mathbf{g}(\mathbf{X})\,\partial\mathbf{X}$$

Since $\mathbf{g}(\mathbf{X}) = \mathbf{0}$, $\partial\mathbf{g}(\mathbf{X}) = \mathbf{0}$ for feasibility, and it follows that

$$\partial f(\mathbf{X}) - \nabla f(\mathbf{X})\,\partial\mathbf{X} = 0$$
$$\nabla\mathbf{g}(\mathbf{X})\,\partial\mathbf{X} = 0$$

This reduces to $(m + 1)$ equations in $(n + 1)$ unknowns, the unknowns being given by $\partial f(\mathbf{X})$ and $\partial\mathbf{X}$. The unknown $\partial f(\mathbf{X})$ is determined, however, as soon as $\partial\mathbf{X}$ is known. This means that there are, in effect, m equations in n unknowns.

If $m > n$, at least $(m - n)$ equations are redundant. After eliminating this redundancy, the system reduces to an effective number of independent equations such that $m \leq n$. For the case where $m = n$, the solution is $\partial\mathbf{X} = \mathbf{0}$. This shows that $\mathbf{X}$ has no feasible neighborhood and hence the solution space consists of one point only. Such a case is of no interest. The remaining case, where $m < n$, will be considered in detail.

Let

$$\mathbf{X} = (\mathbf{Y}, \mathbf{Z})$$

where

$$\mathbf{Y} = (y_1, y_2, \ldots, y_m) \qquad \text{and} \qquad \mathbf{Z} = (z_1, z_2, \ldots, z_{n-m})$$

are the *dependent* and *independent* variables, respectively, corresponding to the vector $\mathbf{X}$. Rewriting the gradient vectors of f and $\mathbf{g}$ in terms of $\mathbf{Y}$ and $\mathbf{Z}$, we find that

$$\nabla f(\mathbf{Y}, \mathbf{Z}) = (\nabla_{\mathbf{Y}} f, \nabla_{\mathbf{Z}} f)$$
$$\nabla\mathbf{g}(\mathbf{Y}, \mathbf{Z}) = (\nabla_{\mathbf{Y}}\mathbf{g}, \nabla_{\mathbf{Z}}\mathbf{g})$$

Define

$$\mathbf{J} = \nabla_{\mathbf{Y}}\mathbf{g} = \begin{pmatrix} \nabla_{\mathbf{Y}} g_1 \\ \vdots \\ \nabla_{\mathbf{Y}} g_m \end{pmatrix}$$

$$\mathbf{C} = \nabla_{\mathbf{Z}}\mathbf{g} = \begin{pmatrix} \nabla_{\mathbf{Z}} g_1 \\ \vdots \\ \nabla_{\mathbf{Z}} g_m \end{pmatrix}$$

$\mathbf{J}_{m \times m}$ is called the **Jacobian matrix** and $\mathbf{C}_{m \times n-m}$ the **control matrix**. The Jacobian $\mathbf{J}$ is assumed nonsingular. This is always possible, since the given m equations are independent by definition. The components of the vector $\mathbf{Y}$ can thus be selected from those of $\mathbf{X}$ such that $\mathbf{J}$ is nonsingular.

Using the definitions given, we write the original set of equations in $\partial f(\mathbf{X})$ and $\partial\mathbf{X}$ as

$$\partial f(\mathbf{Y}, \mathbf{Z}) = \nabla_{\mathbf{Y}} f\,\partial\mathbf{Y} + \nabla_{\mathbf{Z}} f\,\partial\mathbf{Z}$$

and

$$\mathbf{J}\,\partial\mathbf{Y} = -\mathbf{C}\,\partial\mathbf{Z}$$

Since **J** is nonsingular, its inverse $\mathbf{J}^{-1}$ exists. Hence

$$\partial\mathbf{Y} = -\mathbf{J}^{-1}\mathbf{C}\,\partial\mathbf{Z}$$

This set of equations relates the effect of variation in $\partial\mathbf{Z}$ (**Z** being the independent vector) on $\partial\mathbf{Y}$. Substituting for $\partial\mathbf{Y}$ in the equation for $\partial f(\mathbf{Y}, \mathbf{Z})$ gives ∂f as a function of $\partial\mathbf{Z}$. That is,

$$\partial f(\mathbf{Y}, \mathbf{Z}) = (\nabla_{\mathbf{Z}} f - \nabla_{\mathbf{Y}} f\mathbf{J}^{-1}\mathbf{C})\,\partial\mathbf{Z}$$

From this equation, the constrained derivative with respect to the independent vector **Z** is given by

$$\nabla_c f = \frac{\partial_c f(\mathbf{Y}, \mathbf{Z})}{\partial_c \mathbf{Z}} = \nabla_{\mathbf{Z}} f - \nabla_{\mathbf{Y}} f\mathbf{J}^{-1}\mathbf{C}$$

where $\nabla_c f$ represents the **constrained gradient** vector of f with respect to **Z**. Thus $\nabla_c f(\mathbf{Y}, \mathbf{Z})$ must be null at stationary points.

The sufficiency conditions are similar to those developed in Section 19.1. In this case, however, the Hessian matrix will correspond to the independent vector **Z**. In the meantime, the elements of the Hessian matrix must be the *constrained* second derivatives. To show how this is obtained, let

$$\nabla_c f = \nabla_{\mathbf{Z}} f - \mathbf{W}\mathbf{C}$$

It thus follows the ith row of the (constrained) Hessian matrix is $\partial\nabla_c f/\partial z_i$. Notice that **W** is a function of **Y** and **Y** is a function of **Z**; that is,

$$\partial\mathbf{Y} = -\mathbf{J}^{-1}\mathbf{C}\,\partial\mathbf{Z}$$

Thus, in taking the partial derivative of $\nabla_c f$ with respect to z_i, the chain rule must apply to **W**. This means that

$$\frac{\partial w_j}{\partial z_i} = \frac{\partial w_j}{\partial y_j}\frac{\partial y_j}{\partial z_i}$$

Example 19.2-1. In this example it will be shown how $\partial_c f$ can be estimated at a given point using the formulas given. Example 19.2-2 will then illustrate the application of the constrained derivative.

Consider the problem in which

$$f(\mathbf{X}) = x_1^2 + 3x_2^2 + 5x_1x_3^2$$
$$g_1(\mathbf{X}) = x_1x_3 + 2x_2 + x_2^2 - 11 = 0$$
$$g_2(\mathbf{X}) = x_1^2 + 2x_1x_2 + x_3^2 - 14 = 0$$

Given the feasible point $\mathbf{X}^0 = (1, 2, 3)$, it is required to study the variation in $f(= \partial_c f)$ in the feasible neighborhood of $\mathbf{X}^0$.

Let

$$\mathbf{Y} = (x_1, x_3) \quad \text{and} \quad \mathbf{Z} = x_2$$

Thus

$$\nabla_{\mathbf{Y}} f = \left(\frac{\partial f}{\partial x_1}, \frac{\partial f}{\partial x_3}\right) = (2x_1 + 5x_3^2, 10x_1x_3)$$

$$\nabla_{\mathbf{Z}} f = \frac{\partial f}{\partial x_2} = 6x_2$$

$$\mathbf{J} = \begin{pmatrix} \frac{\partial g_1}{\partial x_1} & \frac{\partial g_1}{\partial x_3} \\ \frac{\partial g_2}{\partial x_1} & \frac{\partial g_2}{\partial x_3} \end{pmatrix} = \begin{pmatrix} x_3 & x_1 \\ 2x_1 + 2x_2 & 2x_3 \end{pmatrix}$$

$$\mathbf{C} = \begin{pmatrix} \frac{\partial g_1}{\partial x_2} \\ \frac{\partial g_2}{\partial x_2} \end{pmatrix} = \begin{pmatrix} 2x_2 + 2 \\ 2x_1 \end{pmatrix}$$

An estimate of $\partial_c f$ in the feasible neighborhood of the feasible point $\mathbf{X}^0 = (1, 2, 3)$ resulting from a small change $\partial x_2 = .01$ is obtained as follows:

$$\mathbf{J}^{-1}\mathbf{C} = \begin{pmatrix} 3 & 1 \\ 6 & 6 \end{pmatrix}^{-1} \begin{pmatrix} 6 \\ 2 \end{pmatrix} = \begin{pmatrix} 6/12 & -1/12 \\ -6/12 & 3/12 \end{pmatrix} \begin{pmatrix} 6 \\ 2 \end{pmatrix} \cong \begin{pmatrix} 2.83 \\ -2.50 \end{pmatrix}$$

Hence

$$\partial_c f = (\nabla_{\mathbf{Z}} f - \nabla_{\mathbf{Y}} f \mathbf{J}^{-1}\mathbf{C})\, \partial\mathbf{Z} = \left(6(2) - (47, 30)\begin{bmatrix} 2.83 \\ -2.5 \end{bmatrix}\right) \partial x_2$$

$$\cong -46\ \partial x_2 = -.46$$

By specifying the value of ∂x_2 for the *independent* variable x_2, feasible values of ∂x_1 and ∂x_2 are automatically determined for the *dependent* variables x_1 and x_3 from the formula

$$\partial\mathbf{Y} = -\mathbf{J}^{-1}\mathbf{C}\ \partial\mathbf{Z}$$

This gives for $\partial x_2 = .01$,

$$\begin{pmatrix} \partial x_1 \\ \partial x_3 \end{pmatrix} = -\mathbf{J}^{-1}\mathbf{C}\ \partial x_2 = \begin{pmatrix} -.0283 \\ .0250 \end{pmatrix}$$

To check the value of $\partial_c f$ obtained, we can compute the value of f at $\mathbf{X}^0$ and $\mathbf{X}^0 + \partial\mathbf{X}$. Thus

$$\mathbf{X}^0 + \partial\mathbf{X} = (1 - .0283, 2 + .01, 3 + .025) = (.9717, 2.01, 3.025)$$

This yields

$$f(\mathbf{X}^0) = 58 \qquad \text{and} \qquad f(\mathbf{X}^0 + \partial\mathbf{X}) = 57.523$$

or

$$\partial_c f = f(\mathbf{X}^0 + \partial\mathbf{X}) - f(\mathbf{X}^0) = -.477$$

This indicates a decrease in the value of f as obtained by the formula for $\partial_c f$. The difference between the two answers ($-.477$ and $-.46$) is the result of the linear approximation at $\mathbf{X}^0$. The formula is good only for very small variations around $\mathbf{X}^0$.

◀

Exercise 19.2-1

Consider Example 19.2-1.

(a) Compute $\partial_c f$ by the two methods presented in the example, using $\partial x_2 = .001$ instead of $\partial x_2 = .01$. Does the effect of linear approximation become more negligible with the decrease in the value of ∂x_2?
[*Ans.* Yes; $\partial_c f = -.046$ and $-.04618$.]

(b) Specify a relationship among ∂x_1, ∂x_2, and ∂x_3 at the feasible point $\mathbf{X}^0 = (1, 2, 3)$ that will keep the point $(x_1^0 + \partial x_1, x_2^0 + \partial x_2, x_3^0 + \partial x_3)$ feasible.
[*Ans.* $\partial x_1 = -.283\partial x_2$, $\partial x_3 = .25\partial x_2$.]

(c) If $\mathbf{Y} = (x_2, x_3)$ and $\mathbf{Z} = x_1$, what is the value of ∂x_1 that will produce the same value of $\partial_c f$ given in the example?
[*Ans.* $\partial x_1 = -.0283$.]

(d) Verify that the result in part (c) will yield $\partial_c f = -.46$.

Example 19.2-2. This example illustrates the use of constrained derivatives. Consider the problem

$$\text{minimize } f(\mathbf{X}) = x_1^2 + x_2^2 + x_3^2$$

subject to

$$g_1(\mathbf{X}) = x_1 + x_2 + 3x_3 - 2 = 0$$
$$g_2(\mathbf{X}) = 5x_1 + 2x_2 + x_3 - 5 = 0$$

We determine the constrained extreme points as follows. Let

$$\mathbf{Y} = (x_1, x_2) \quad \text{and} \quad \mathbf{Z} = x_3$$

Thus

$$\nabla_{\mathbf{Y}} f = \left(\frac{\partial f}{\partial x_1}, \frac{\partial f}{\partial x_2}\right) = (2x_1, 2x_2), \qquad \nabla_{\mathbf{Z}} f = \frac{\partial f}{\partial x_3} = 2x_3$$

$$\mathbf{J} = \begin{pmatrix} 1 & 1 \\ 5 & 2 \end{pmatrix}, \qquad \mathbf{J}^{-1} = \begin{pmatrix} -2/3 & 1/3 \\ 5/3 & -1/3 \end{pmatrix}, \qquad \mathbf{C} = \begin{pmatrix} 3 \\ 1 \end{pmatrix}$$

Hence

$$\nabla_c f = \frac{\partial_c f}{\partial_c x_3} = 2x_3 - (2x_1, 2x_2)\begin{pmatrix} -2/3 & 1/3 \\ 5/3 & -1/3 \end{pmatrix}\begin{pmatrix} 3 \\ 1 \end{pmatrix}$$
$$= \frac{10}{3}x_1 - \frac{28}{3}x_2 + 2x_3$$

At a stationary point, $\nabla_c f = \mathbf{0}$, which together with $g_1(\mathbf{X}) = 0$ and $g_2(\mathbf{X}) = 0$ give the required stationary point(s). That is, the equations

$$\begin{pmatrix} 10 & -28 & 6 \\ 1 & 1 & 3 \\ 5 & 2 & 1 \end{pmatrix}\begin{pmatrix} x_1 \\ x_2 \\ x_3 \end{pmatrix} = \begin{pmatrix} 0 \\ 2 \\ 5 \end{pmatrix}$$

give the solution

$$\mathbf{X}^0 \cong (.81, .35, .28)$$

The identity of this stationary point is now checked by considering the sufficiency condition. Given the independent variable x_3, it follows from $\nabla_c f$ that

$$\frac{\partial_c^2 f}{\partial_c x_3^2} = \frac{10}{3}\left(\frac{dx_1}{dx_3}\right) - \frac{28}{3}\left(\frac{dx_2}{dx_3}\right) + 2 = \left(\frac{10}{3}, -\frac{28}{3}\right)\begin{pmatrix} \dfrac{dx_1}{dx_3} \\ \dfrac{dx_2}{dx_3} \end{pmatrix} + 2$$

From the development of the Jacobian method,

$$\begin{pmatrix} \dfrac{dx_1}{dx_3} \\ \dfrac{dx_2}{dx_3} \end{pmatrix} = -\mathbf{J}^{-1}\mathbf{C} = \begin{pmatrix} 5/3 \\ -14/3 \end{pmatrix}$$

Substitution gives $\partial_c^2 f/\partial_c x_3^2 = 460/9 > 0$. Hence $\mathbf{X}^0$ is the minimum point. ◀

Exercise 19.2-2

Suppose that Example 19.2-2 is solved in the following manner. First, solve the constraints expressing x_1 and x_2 in terms of x_3; then use the resulting equations to express the objective function in terms of x_3 only. By taking the derivative of the new objective function with respect to x_3, we can determine the points of maxima and minima.

(a) Would the derivative of the new objective function (expressed in terms of x_3) be different from that obtained by the Jacobian method?
[*Ans.* No, the necessary and sufficient conditions are exactly the same in both methods.]

(b) What is the prime difference between the procedure outlined and the Jacobian method?
[*Ans.* The Jacobian method computes the *constrained* gradient of the objective function directly, whereas the proposed method computes the equation of the constrained objective function from which we can compute the constrained gradient.]

The use of the Jacobian method as presented is hindered, in general, by the difficulty of obtaining $\mathbf{J}^{-1}$ for a large number of constraints. This difficulty can be overcome by applying Cramer's rule to solve for ∂f in terms of $\partial\mathbf{Z}$. Thus, if z_j represents the jth element of $\mathbf{Z}$ and y_i represents the ith element of $\mathbf{Y}$, it can be shown that

$$\frac{\partial_c f}{\partial_c z_j} = \frac{\partial(f, g_1, \ldots, g_m)/\partial(z_j, y_1, \ldots, y_m)}{\partial(g_1, \ldots, g_m)/\partial(y_1, \ldots, y_m)}$$

where

$$\frac{\partial(f, g_1, \ldots, g_m)}{\partial(z_j, y_1, \ldots, y_m)} \equiv \begin{vmatrix} \dfrac{\partial f}{\partial z_j} & \dfrac{\partial f}{\partial y_1} & \cdots & \dfrac{\partial f}{\partial y_m} \\ \dfrac{\partial g_1}{\partial z_j} & \dfrac{\partial g_1}{\partial y_1} & \cdots & \dfrac{\partial g_1}{\partial y_m} \\ \vdots & \vdots & & \vdots \\ \dfrac{\partial g_m}{\partial z_j} & \dfrac{\partial g_m}{\partial y_1} & \cdots & \dfrac{\partial g_m}{\partial y_m} \end{vmatrix}$$

and

$$\frac{\partial(g_1, \ldots, g_m)}{\partial(y_1, \ldots, y_m)} \equiv \begin{vmatrix} \dfrac{\partial g_1}{\partial y_1} & \cdots & \dfrac{\partial g_1}{\partial y_m} \\ \vdots & & \vdots \\ \dfrac{\partial g_m}{\partial y_1} & \cdots & \dfrac{\partial g_m}{\partial y_m} \end{vmatrix} = |\mathbf{J}|$$

Thus the necessary conditions become

$$\frac{\partial_c f}{\partial_c z_j} = 0, \qquad j = 1, 2, \ldots, n - m$$

Similarly, in the matrix expression

$$\frac{\partial \mathbf{Y}}{\partial \mathbf{Z}} = -\mathbf{J}^{-1}\mathbf{C}$$

the (i, j)th element is given by

$$\frac{\partial y_i}{\partial z_j} = -\frac{\partial(g_1, \ldots, g_m)/\partial(y_1, \ldots, y_{i-1}, z_j, y_{i+1}, \ldots, y_m)}{\partial(g_1, \ldots, g_m)/\partial(y_1, \ldots, y_m)}$$

which represents the rate of variation of the dependent variable y_i with respect to the independent variable z_j.

Finally, to obtain the sufficiency condition given previously, determinant expressions for the elements of $\mathbf{W} \equiv \nabla_{\mathbf{Y}} f \mathbf{J}^{-1}$ must be given. Thus the ith element of $\mathbf{W}$ is given by

$$w_i = \frac{\partial(g_1, \ldots, g_{i-1}, f, g_{i+1}, \ldots, g_m)/\partial(y_1, \ldots, y_m)}{\partial(g_1, \ldots, g_m)/\partial(y_1, \ldots, y_m)}$$

To illustrate the application of the method just described, consider the determination of the necessary condition for example 19.2-2. Thus

$$\frac{\partial_c f}{\partial_c x_3} = \frac{\begin{vmatrix} 2x_3 & 2x_1 & 2x_2 \\ 3 & 1 & 1 \\ 1 & 5 & 2 \end{vmatrix}}{\begin{vmatrix} 1 & 1 \\ 5 & 2 \end{vmatrix}} = \frac{10}{3}x_1 - \frac{28}{3}x_2 + 2x_3$$

Sensitivity Analysis in the Jacobian Method

The Jacobian method can be used to study the sensitivity of the optimal value of f due to small changes in the right-hand sides of the constraints. For example, suppose that the right-hand side of the ith constraint $g_i(\mathbf{X}) = 0$ is changed to ∂g_i instead of zero. What effect will this have on the optimum value of f? This type of investigation is called **sensitivity analysis** and, in some sense, is similar to that carried out in linear programming (see Chapter 5). However, sensitivity analysis in nonlinear programming is valid only in the small neighborhood of the extreme point due to the absence of linearity. Nevertheless, the development will be helpful in studying the Lagrangean method (see the next section).

It is shown that

$$\partial f(\mathbf{Y}, \mathbf{Z}) = \nabla_{\mathbf{Y}} f \; \partial \mathbf{Y} + \nabla_{\mathbf{Z}} f \; \partial \mathbf{Z}$$
$$\partial \mathbf{g} = \mathbf{J} \; \partial \mathbf{Y} + \mathbf{C} \; \partial \mathbf{Z}$$

Suppose that $\partial \mathbf{g} \neq \mathbf{0}$; then

$$\partial \mathbf{Y} = \mathbf{J}^{-1} \; \partial \mathbf{g} - \mathbf{J}^{-1}\mathbf{C} \; \partial \mathbf{Z}$$

Substituting in the equation for $\partial f(\mathbf{Y}, \mathbf{Z})$ gives

$$\partial f(\mathbf{Y}, \mathbf{Z}) = \nabla_{\mathbf{Y}_0} f \mathbf{J}^{-1} \; \partial \mathbf{g} + \nabla_c f \; \partial \mathbf{Z}$$

where

$$\nabla_c f = \nabla_{\mathbf{Z}} f - \nabla_{\mathbf{Y}_0} f \mathbf{J}^{-1}\mathbf{C}$$

as defined previously. The expression for $\partial f(\mathbf{Y}, \mathbf{Z})$ can be used to study variation in f in the feasible neighborhood of a feasible point $\mathbf{X}^0$ due to small changes $\partial \mathbf{g}$ and $\partial \mathbf{Z}$.

Now, at the extreme (indeed, any stationary) point $\mathbf{X}_0 = (\mathbf{Y}_0, \mathbf{Z}_0)$, the constrained gradient $\nabla_c f$ must vanish. Thus

$$\partial f(\mathbf{Y}_0, \mathbf{Z}_0) = \nabla_{\mathbf{Y}0} f \mathbf{J}^{-1} \; \partial \mathbf{g}(\mathbf{Y}_0, \mathbf{Z}_0)$$

or

$$\frac{\partial f}{\partial \mathbf{g}} = \nabla_{\mathbf{Y}0} f \mathbf{J}^{-1}$$

evaluated at $\mathbf{X}_0$. Consequently, the effect of small variations in $\mathbf{g}(= \partial \mathbf{g})$ on the *optimum* value of f can be studied by evaluating the rate of change of f with respect to $\mathbf{g}$. These rates are usually referred to as **sensitivity coefficients**.

In general, at the optimum point, $\partial f/\partial \mathbf{g}$ is independent of the specific choice of the variables in the vector $\mathbf{Y}$. This follows, since the expression for the sensitivity coefficients does not include $\mathbf{Z}$. Hence the partitioning of $\mathbf{X}$ between $\mathbf{Y}$ and $\mathbf{Z}$ is arbitrary in this case. The given coefficients are thus constant regardless of the specific choice of $\mathbf{Y}$.

Example 19.2-3. Consider the same problem of Example 19.2-2. The optimum point is given by $\mathbf{X}_0 = (x_1^0, x_2^0, x_3^0) = (.81, .35, .28)$. Since $\mathbf{Y}_0 = (x_1^0, x_2^0)$, then

$$\nabla_{\mathbf{Y}0} f = \left(\frac{\partial f}{\partial x_1}, \frac{\partial f}{\partial x_2}\right) = (2x_1^0, 2x_2^0) = (1.62, .70)$$

Consequently,

$$\left(\frac{\partial f}{\partial g_1}, \frac{\partial f}{\partial g_2}\right) = \nabla_{\mathbf{Y}0} f \mathbf{J}^{-1} = (1.62, .7)\begin{pmatrix} -2/3 & 1/3 \\ 5/3 & -1/3 \end{pmatrix} = (.0876, .3067)$$

This implies that if $\partial g_1 = 1$, f will increase *approximately* by .0867. Similarly, if $\partial g_2 = 1$, f will increase *approximately* by .3067. ◀

Example of Application of the Jacobian Method to a Linear Programming Problem

Consider the linear programming problem

$$\text{maximize } z = 2x_1 + 3x_2$$

subject to

$$\begin{aligned} x_1 + x_2 + x_3 \qquad &= 5 \\ x_1 - x_2 \qquad + x_4 &= 3 \\ x_1, x_2, x_3, x_4 &\geq 0 \end{aligned}$$

Consider the nonnegativity constraints $x_j \geq 0$. Let w_j^2 be the corresponding (nonnegative) slack variable. Thus $x_j - w_j^2 = 0$, or $x_j = w_j^2$. With this substitution, the nonnegativity conditions become implicit and the original problem becomes

$$\text{maximize } z = 2w_1^2 + 3w_2^2$$

subject to

$$\begin{aligned} w_1^2 + w_2^2 + w_3^2 &= 5 \\ w_1^2 - w_2^2 + w_4^2 &= 3 \end{aligned}$$

To apply the Jacobian method, let

$$\mathbf{Y} = (w_1, w_2) \qquad \text{and} \qquad \mathbf{Z} = (w_3, w_4)$$

(Notice that in the terminology of linear programming, **Y** and **Z** correspond to the basic and nonbasic variables, respectively.) Thus

$$\mathbf{J} = \begin{pmatrix} 2w_1 & 2w_2 \\ 2w_1 & -2w_2 \end{pmatrix}, \qquad \mathbf{J}^{-1} = \begin{pmatrix} \dfrac{1}{4w_1} & \dfrac{1}{4w_1} \\ \dfrac{1}{4w_2} & \dfrac{-1}{4w_2} \end{pmatrix}, \qquad w_1 \text{ and } w_2 \neq 0$$

$$\mathbf{C} = \begin{pmatrix} 2w_3 & 0 \\ 0 & 2w_4 \end{pmatrix}, \qquad \nabla_{\mathbf{Y}} f = (4w_1, 6w_2), \qquad \nabla_{\mathbf{Z}} f = (0, 0)$$

so that

$$\nabla_c f = (0, 0) - (4w_1, 6w_2) \begin{pmatrix} \dfrac{1}{4w_1} & \dfrac{1}{4w_1} \\ \dfrac{1}{4w_2} & \dfrac{-1}{4w_2} \end{pmatrix} \begin{pmatrix} 2w_3 & 0 \\ 0 & 2w_4 \end{pmatrix} = (-5w_3, w_4)$$

Solution of $\nabla_c f = \mathbf{0}$ together with the constraints of the problem yield the stationary point $(w_1 = 2, w_2 = 1, w_3 = 0, w_4 = 0)$. The Hessian is given by

$$\mathbf{H}_c = \begin{pmatrix} \dfrac{\partial_c^2 f}{\partial_c w_3^2} & \dfrac{\partial_c^2 f}{\partial_c w_3 \, \partial_c w_4} \\ \dfrac{\partial_c^2 f}{\partial_c w_3 \, \partial_c w_4} & \dfrac{\partial_c^2 f}{\partial_c w_4^2} \end{pmatrix} = \begin{pmatrix} -5 & 0 \\ 0 & 1 \end{pmatrix}$$

Since $\mathbf{H}_c$ is indefinite, the stationary point does not yield a maximum.

Actually, the result is not surprising, since the (nonbasic) variables w_3 and w_4 (and hence x_3 and x_4) equal zero, as contemplated by the theory of linear programming.

This means that, depending on the specific choice of **Y** and **Z**, the Jacobian method solution determines the corresponding extreme point of the solution space. This may or may not be the optimal solution. The Jacobian method has the power, however, to identify the optimum point through the use of the sufficiency conditions.

The preceding discussion suggests that one has to keep on altering the specific choices of **Y** and **Z** until the sufficiency condition is satisfied. Thus, for the above example, let $\mathbf{Y} = (w_2, w_4)$, $\mathbf{Z} = (w_1, w_3)$. Then, following the same procedure given above, the corresponding constrained gradient vector becomes

$$\nabla_c f = (4w_1, 0) - (6w_2, 0)\begin{pmatrix} \frac{1}{2w_2} & 0 \\ \frac{1}{2w_4} & \frac{1}{2w_4} \end{pmatrix}\begin{pmatrix} 2w_1 & 2w_3 \\ 2w_1 & 0 \end{pmatrix} = (-2w_1, -6w_3)$$

The corresponding stationary point is given by $w_1 = 0$, $w_2 = \sqrt{5}$, $w_3 = 0$, $w_4 = \sqrt{8}$. Now

$$\mathbf{H}_c = \begin{pmatrix} -2 & 0 \\ 0 & -6 \end{pmatrix}$$

is negative-definite. Thus the given solution corresponds to a maximum point.

The result is verified graphically in Figure 19-5. The first solution ($x_1 = 4$, $x_2 = 1$) is not optimal, whereas the second ($x_1 = 0$, $x_2 = 5$) gives the optimal solution. You can verify that the remaining two extreme points of the solution space do not yield maximum points. In fact, the extreme point ($x_1 = 0$, $x_2 = 0$) can be shown by the sufficiency condition to yield a minimum point.

It is interesting that when applied to linear programming, the sensitivity coefficients $\nabla_{\mathbf{Y}_0} f \mathbf{J}^{-1}$ introduced previously will actually yield its dual values. To illustrate this point for the given numerical example, let u_1 and u_2 be the corresponding dual variables. At the optimum point ($w_1 = 0$, $w_2 = \sqrt{5}$, $w_3 = 0$, $w_4 = \sqrt{8}$), these dual variables are given by

$$(u_1, u_2) = \nabla_{\mathbf{Y}_0} \mathbf{J}^{-1} = (6w_2, 0)\begin{pmatrix} \frac{1}{2w_2} & 0 \\ \frac{1}{2w_2} & \frac{1}{2w_4} \end{pmatrix} = (3, 0)$$

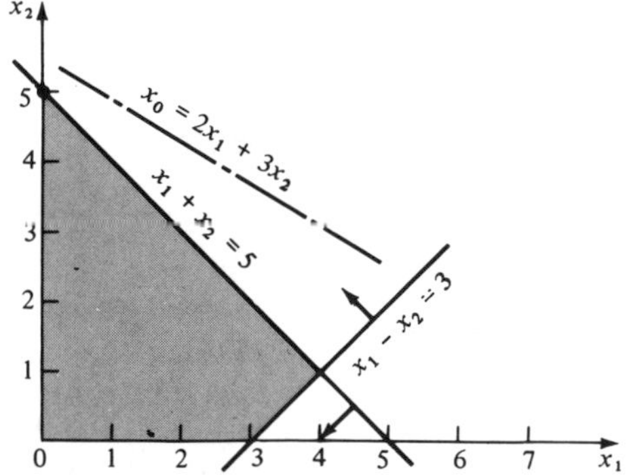

Figure 19-5

The corresponding dual objective value is equal to $5u_1 + 3u_2 = 15$, which is the same as the optimal primal objective value. The given solution also satisfies the dual constraints and hence is optimal and feasible. This shows that the sensitivity coefficients are the same as the dual variables. In fact, one notices that both have the same interpretation.

It is now possible to draw some general conclusions from the application of the Jacobian method to the linear programming problem. From the numerical example, the necessary conditions require the independent variables to equal zero. Also, the sufficiency conditions indicate that the Hessian matrix is a diagonal matrix. Thus all its diagonal elements must be positive for a minimum and negative for a maximum.

The observations suggest that the necessary condition is equivalent to specifying that only "basic" (feasible) solutions are needed to locate the optimum solution. In this case the independent variables are equivalent to the nonbasic variables in the linear programming problem. Also, the sufficiency condition suggests that there may be a strong relationship between the diagonal elements of the Hessian matrix and the optimality indicator $z_j - c_j$ (see Section 4.2.2) in the simplex method.†

B. Lagrangean Method

Section 19.2.1A shows that the sensitivity coefficients

$$\frac{\partial f}{\partial \mathbf{g}} = \nabla_{\mathbf{Y}_0} \mathbf{J}^{-1}$$

can be used to study the effect of small variations in the constraints on the *optimum* value of f. It is also indicated that these coefficients are constant. These properties can be used to solve the constrained problems with equality constraints.

Let

$$\boldsymbol{\lambda} = \nabla_{\mathbf{Y}_0} \mathbf{J}^{-1} = \frac{\partial f}{\partial \mathbf{g}}$$

Thus

$$\partial f - \boldsymbol{\lambda}\, \partial \mathbf{g} = 0$$

This equation satisfies the *necessary* conditions for stationary points since the expression for $\partial f / \partial \mathbf{g}$ is computed such that $\nabla_c f = \mathbf{0}$. A more convenient form for presenting these equations, however, is obtained by taking their partial derivatives with respect to all x_j. This yields

$$\frac{\partial}{\partial x_j}(f - \boldsymbol{\lambda}\mathbf{g}) = 0, \qquad j = 1, 2, \ldots, n$$

The resulting equations together with the constraint equations $\mathbf{g} = \mathbf{0}$ yield the feasible values of $\mathbf{X}$ and $\boldsymbol{\lambda}$ that satisfy the *necessary* conditions for stationary points.

---

† For a formal proof of the validity of these results for the general linear programming problem, see H. Taha and G. Curry, "Classical Derivation of the Necessary and Sufficient Conditions for Optimal Linear Programs," *Operations Research*, Vol. 19, 1971, pp. 1045–1049. The paper shows that all the key ideas of the simplex method can be derived by the Jacobian method.

The procedure described defines the so-called *Lagrangean method* for identifying the stationary points of optimization problems with *equality* constraints. This procedure can be developed formally as follows. Let

$$L(\mathbf{X}, \boldsymbol{\lambda}) = f(\mathbf{X}) - \boldsymbol{\lambda}\mathbf{g}(\mathbf{X})$$

The function L is called the **Lagrangean function** and the parameters $\boldsymbol{\lambda}$ the **Lagrange multipliers.** By definition, these multipliers have the same interpretation as the sensitivity coefficients introduced in Section 19.2.1A.

The equations

$$\frac{\partial L}{\partial \boldsymbol{\lambda}} = \mathbf{0} \quad \text{and} \quad \frac{\partial L}{\partial \mathbf{X}} = \mathbf{0}$$

yield the same necessary conditions given above and hence the Lagrangean function can be used directly to generate the necessary conditions. This means that optimization of $f(\mathbf{X})$ subject to $\mathbf{g}(\mathbf{X}) = \mathbf{0}$ is equivalent to optimization of the Lagrangean function $L(\mathbf{X}, \boldsymbol{\lambda})$.

The sufficiency conditions for the Lagrangean method will be stated without proof. Define

$$\mathbf{H}^B = \begin{pmatrix} \mathbf{0} \mid \mathbf{P} \\ \hline \mathbf{P}^T \mid \mathbf{Q} \end{pmatrix}_{(m+n)\times(m+n)}$$

where

$$\mathbf{P} = \begin{pmatrix} \nabla g_1(\mathbf{X}) \\ \vdots \\ \nabla g_m(\mathbf{X}) \end{pmatrix}_{m \times n} \quad \text{and} \quad \mathbf{Q} = \left\| \frac{\partial^2 L(\mathbf{X}, \boldsymbol{\lambda})}{\partial x_i \, \partial x_j} \right\|_{n \times n}, \quad \text{for all } i \text{ and } j$$

The matrix $\mathbf{H}^B$ is called the **bordered Hessian matrix.**

Given the stationary point $(\mathbf{X}_0, \boldsymbol{\lambda}_0)$ for the Lagrangean function $L(\mathbf{X}, \boldsymbol{\lambda})$ and the bordered Hessian matrix $\mathbf{H}^B$ evaluated at $(\mathbf{X}_0, \boldsymbol{\lambda}_0)$, then $\mathbf{X}_0$ is

1. A maximum point if, starting with the principal major determinant of order $(2m + 1)$, the *last* $(n - m)$ principal minor determinants of $\mathbf{H}^B$ form an alternating sign pattern starting with $(-1)^{m+1}$.
2. A minimum point if, starting with the principal minor determinant of order $(2m + 1)$, the *last* $(n - m)$ principal minor determinants of $\mathbf{H}^B$ have the sign of $(-1)^m$.

These conditions are sufficient for identifying an extreme point, but not necessary. In other words, a stationary point may be an extreme point without satisfying these conditions.

Other conditions exist that are both necessary and sufficient for identifying extreme points. The disadvantage here is that this procedure is computationally infeasible for most practical purposes. Define the matrix

$$\Delta = \begin{pmatrix} \mathbf{0} & \mathbf{P} \\ \hline \mathbf{P}^T & \mathbf{Q} - \mu\mathbf{I} \end{pmatrix}$$

evaluated at the stationary point $(\mathbf{X}_0, \boldsymbol{\lambda}_0)$, where $\mathbf{P}$ and $\mathbf{Q}$ are as defined and μ is an unknown parameter. Consider the determinant $|\Delta|$; then each of the real $(n - m)$ roots u_i of the polynomial

$$|\Delta| = 0$$

must be

1. Negative if $\mathbf{X}_0$ is a maximum point.
2. Positive if $\mathbf{X}_0$ is a minimum point.

Example 19.2-4. Consider the same problem of Example 19.2-2. The Lagrangean function is

$$L(\mathbf{X}, \boldsymbol{\lambda}) = x_1^2 + x_2^2 + x_3^2 - \lambda_1(x_1 + x_2 + 3x_3 - 2) - \lambda_2(5x_1 + 2x_2 + x_3 - 5)$$

This yields the following necessary conditions:

$$\frac{\partial L}{\partial x_1} = 2x_1 - \lambda_1 - 5\lambda_2 = 0$$

$$\frac{\partial L}{\partial x_2} = 2x_2 - \lambda_1 - 2\lambda_2 = 0$$

$$\frac{\partial L}{\partial x_3} = 2x_3 - 3\lambda_1 - \lambda_2 = 0$$

$$\frac{\partial L}{\partial \lambda_1} = -(x_1 + x_2 + 3x_3 - 2) = 0$$

$$\frac{\partial L}{\partial \lambda_2} = -(5x_1 + 2x_2 + x_3 - 5) = 0$$

The solution to these simultaneous equations yields

$$\mathbf{X}_0 = (x_1, x_2, x_3) = (.81, .35, .28)$$

$$\boldsymbol{\lambda} = (\lambda_1, \lambda_2) = (.0867, .3067)$$

This solution combines the results of Examples 19.2-2 and 19.2-3. The values of the Lagrange multipliers $\boldsymbol{\lambda}$ are the same as the sensitivity coefficients obtained in Example 19.2-3. This shows that these coefficients are independent of the choice of the dependent vector $\mathbf{Y}$ in the Jacobian method.

To show that the given point is a minimum, consider

$$\mathbf{H}^B = \left(\begin{array}{cc|ccc} 0 & 0 & 1 & 1 & 3 \\ 0 & 0 & 5 & 2 & 1 \\ \hline 1 & 5 & 2 & 0 & 0 \\ 1 & 2 & 0 & 2 & 0 \\ 3 & 1 & 0 & 0 & 2 \end{array}\right)$$

Since $n = 3$ and $m = 2$, it follows that $n - m = 1$. Thus we need to check the determinant of $\mathbf{H}^B$ only, which must have the sign of $(-1)^2$ at a minimum. Since $\det \mathbf{H}^B = 460 > 0$, $\mathbf{X}^0$ is a minimum point. ◀

A method that is sometimes convenient for solving equations resulting from the necessary conditions is to select successive numerical values of $\boldsymbol{\lambda}$ and then solve the given equations for $\mathbf{X}$. This is repeated until for some values of $\boldsymbol{\lambda}$, the resulting $\mathbf{X}$ satisfies all the active constraints in equation form. This method was illustrated in Chapter 14 as an application to the single-constraint inventory problem (see Example 14.3-4). This procedure becomes very tedious computationally, however, as the number of constraints increases. In this case one may resort to an appropriate numerical technique, such as the Newton–Raphson method (Section 19.1.2) to solve the resulting equations.

Example 19.2-5. Consider the problem

$$\text{minimize } z = x_1^2 + x_2^2 + x_3^2$$

subject to

$$4x_1 + x_2^2 + 2x_3 - 14 = 0$$

The Lagrangean function is

$$L(\mathbf{X}, \lambda) = x_1^2 + x_2^2 + x_3^2 - \lambda(4x_1 + x_2^2 + 2x_3 - 14)$$

This yields the following necessary conditions:

$$\frac{\partial L}{\partial x_1} = 2x_1 - 4\lambda = 0$$

$$\frac{\partial L}{\partial x_2} = 2x_2 - 2\lambda x_2 = 0$$

$$\frac{\partial L}{\partial x_3} = 2x_3 - 2\lambda = 0$$

$$\frac{\partial L}{\partial \lambda} = -(4x_1 + x_2^2 + 2x_3 - 14) = 0$$

whose solutions are

$$(\mathbf{X}_0, \lambda_0) = (2, 2, 1, 1)$$
$$(\mathbf{X}_0, \lambda_0)_2 = (2, -2, 1, 1)$$
$$(\mathbf{X}_0, \lambda_0)_3 = (2.8, 0, 1.4, 1.4)$$

Applying the sufficiency conditions yields

$$\mathbf{H}^B = \left(\begin{array}{c|ccc} 0 & 4 & 2x_2 & 2 \\ \hline 4 & 2 & 0 & 0 \\ 2x_2 & 0 & 2-2\lambda & 0 \\ 2 & 0 & 0 & 2 \end{array}\right)$$

Since $m = 1$ and $n = 3$, for a stationary point to be a minimum, the sign of the last $(3 - 1) = 2$ principal minor determinants must be that of $(-1)^m = -1$. Thus, for $(\mathbf{X}_0, \lambda_0)_1 = (2, 2, 1, 1)$,

$$\begin{vmatrix} 0 & 4 & 4 \\ 4 & 2 & 0 \\ 4 & 0 & 0 \end{vmatrix} = -32 < 0 \quad \text{and} \quad \begin{vmatrix} 0 & 4 & 4 & 2 \\ 4 & 2 & 0 & 0 \\ 4 & 0 & 0 & 0 \\ 2 & 0 & 0 & 2 \end{vmatrix} = -64 < 0$$

For $(\mathbf{X}_0, \lambda_0)_2 = (2, -2, 1, 1)$,

$$\begin{vmatrix} 0 & 4 & -4 \\ 4 & 2 & 0 \\ -4 & 0 & 0 \end{vmatrix} = -32 < 0 \quad \text{and} \quad \begin{vmatrix} 0 & 4 & -4 & 2 \\ 4 & 2 & 0 & 0 \\ -4 & 0 & 0 & 0 \\ 2 & 0 & 0 & 2 \end{vmatrix} = -64 < 0$$

Finally, for $(\mathbf{X}_0, \lambda_0)_3 = (2.8, 0, 1.4, 1.4)$,

$$\begin{vmatrix} 0 & 4 & 0 \\ 4 & 2 & 0 \\ 0 & 0 & -.8 \end{vmatrix} = 12.8 > 0 \quad \text{and} \quad \begin{vmatrix} 0 & 4 & 0 & 2 \\ 4 & 2 & 0 & 0 \\ 0 & 0 & -.8 & 0 \\ 2 & 0 & 0 & 2 \end{vmatrix} = 32 > 0$$

This shows that $(\mathbf{X}_0)_1$ and $(\mathbf{X}_0)_2$ are minimum points. The fact that $(\mathbf{X}_0)_3$ does not satisfy the sufficiency conditions of either a maximum or a minimum does not necessarily mean that it is not an extreme point. This, as explained earlier, follows since the given conditions, although sufficient, may not be satisfied for every extreme point. In such a case it is necessary to use the other sufficiency condition.

To illustrate the use of the other sufficiency condition that employs the roots of polynomial, consider

$$\Delta = \left(\begin{array}{c|ccc} 0 & 4 & 2x_2 & 2 \\ \hline 4 & 2-\mu & 0 & 0 \\ 2x_2 & 0 & 2-2\lambda-\mu & 0 \\ 2 & 0 & 0 & 2-\mu \end{array}\right)$$

Now, for $(\mathbf{X}_0, \lambda_0)_1 = (2, 2, 1, 1)$,

$$|\Delta| = 9\mu^2 - 26\mu + 16 = 0$$

This gives $\mu = 2$ or $8/9$. Since all $\mu > 0$, $(\mathbf{X}_0)_1 = (2, 2, 1)$ is a minimum point. Again, for $(\mathbf{X}_0, \lambda_0)_2 = (2, -2, 1, 1)$,

$$|\Delta| = 9\mu^2 - 26\mu + 16 = 0$$

which is the same as in the previous case. Hence $(\mathbf{X}_0)_2 = (2, -2, 1)$ is a minimum point. Finally, for $(\mathbf{X}_0, \lambda_0)_3 = (2.8, 0, 1.4, 1.4)$,

$$|\Delta| = 5\mu^2 - 6\mu - 8 = 0$$

This gives $\mu = 2$ and $-.8$, which means that $(\mathbf{X}_0)_3 = (2.8, 0, 1.4)$ is not an extreme point. ◀

19.2.2 INEQUALITY CONSTRAINTS

This section shows how the Lagrangean method may, in a restricted manner, be extended to handle inequality constraints. The main contribution of the section is the development of the Kuhn–Tucker conditions, which provide the basic theory for nonlinear programming.

A. Extension of the Lagrangean Method

Suppose that the problem is given by

$$\text{maximize } z = f(\mathbf{X})$$

subject to

$$g_i(\mathbf{X}) \le 0, \qquad i = 1, 2, \ldots, m$$

Nonnegativity constraints $\mathbf{X} \ge 0$, if any, are assumed included in the m constraints.

The general idea of extending the Lagrangean procedure is that if the *un*constrained optimum of $f(\mathbf{X})$ does not satisfy all constraints, the constrained optimum must occur at a boundary point of the solution space. This means that one, or more, of the m constraints must be satisfied in equation form. The procedure thus involves the following steps.

Step 1: Solve the unconstrained problem

$$\text{maximize } z = f(\mathbf{X})$$

If the resulting optimum satisfies all the constraints, there is nothing more to be done, since all constraints are redundant. Otherwise, set $k = 1$ and go to step 2.

Step 2: Activate any k constraints (i.e., convert them into equalities) and optimize $f(\mathbf{X})$ subject to the k active constraints by the Lagrangean method. If the resulting solution is feasible with respect to the remaining constraints, stop; it is a *local* optimum.† Otherwise, activate another set of k constraints and repeat the step. If *all* sets of active constraints taken k at a time are considered without encountering a feasible solution, go to step 3.

Step 3: If $k = m$, stop; no feasible solution exists. Otherwise, set $k = k + 1$ and go to step 2.

An important point often neglected in presenting the procedure described above is that, as should be expected, it does *not* guarantee global optimality even when the problem is well behaved (possesses a *unique* optimum). Another important point is the implicit misconception that, for $p < q$, the optimum of $f(\mathbf{X})$ subject to p equality constraints is always better than its optimum subject to q equality constraints. Unfortunately, this is true, in general, only if the q constraints form a subset of the p constraints. The following example is designed to illustrate these points.

Example 19.2-6

$$\text{Maximize } z = -(2x_1 - 5)^2 - (2x_2 - 1)^2$$

subject to

$$x_1 + 2x_2 \le 2$$
$$x_1, x_2 \ge 0$$

The graphical representation in Figure 19-6 should assist in understanding the analytic procedure. Observe that the problem is well behaved (concave objective function subject to a convex solution space) with the result that a reasonably well-defined algorithm would guarantee global optimality. Yet, as will be shown, the extended Lagrangean method produces a local maximum only.

† A *local* optimum is defined from among all the optima resulting from optimizing $f(\mathbf{X})$ subject to *all* combinations of k *equality* constraints, $k = 1, 2, \ldots, m$.

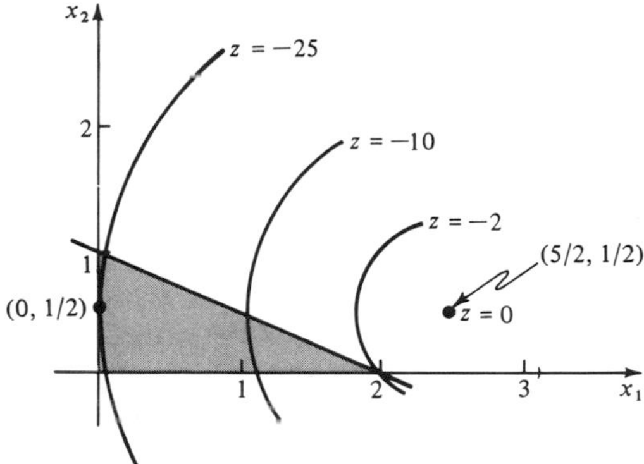

Figure 19-6

The unconstrained optimum is obtained by solving

$$\frac{\partial z}{\partial x_1} = -4(2x_1 - 5) = 0$$

$$\frac{\partial z}{\partial x_2} = -4(2x_2 - 1) = 0$$

This gives $(x_1, x_2) = (5/2, 1/2)$. Since this solution violates $x_1 + 2x_2 \leq 2$, the constraints are activated one at a time. Consider $x_1 = 0$. The Lagrangean function is

$$L(x_1, x_2, \lambda) = -(2x_1 - 5)^2 - (2x_2 - 1)^2 - \lambda x_1$$

Thus

$$\frac{\partial L}{\partial x_1} = -4(2x_1 - 5) - \lambda = 0$$

$$\frac{\partial L}{\partial x_2} = -4(2x_2 - 1) \qquad = 0$$

$$\frac{\partial L}{\partial \lambda} = -x_1 \qquad = 0$$

This gives the solution point $(x_1, x_2) = (0, 1/2)$, which can be shown by the sufficiency condition to be a maximum. Since this point satisfies all other constraints, the procedure terminates with $(x_1, x_2) = (0, 1/2)$ as a local optimal solution to the problem. (Notice that the remaining constraints $x_2 \geq 0$ and $x_1 = 2x_2 \leq 2$, activated one at a time, yield infeasible solutions.) The objective value is $z = -25$.

However, observe in Figure 19-6 that the feasible solution $(x_1, x_2) = (2, 0)$, which is the point of intersection of the *two* constraints $x_2 = 0$ and $x_1 + 2x_2 = 2$, yields the objective value $z = -2$. This value is better than the one obtained with one active constraint. ◀

The procedure just described illustrates that the best to be hoped for in using the extended Lagrangean method is a (possibly) good feasible solution to the problem. This is particularly so if the objective function is not unimodal. Of course, if the functions of the problem are well behaved (e.g., the problem possesses a unique constrained optimum as in Example 19.2-6), the procedure can be rectified to locate the global optimum. Specifically, consider the unconstrained optimum and the constrained optima subject to *all* sets of one active constraint at a time, then two active constraints at a time, and so on, until all m constraints are activated. The best of *all* such *feasible* optima would then be the global optimum.

If this procedure is followed in Example 19.2-6, it will be necessary to solve seven problems before global optimality is verified. This indicates the limited use of the method in solving problems of any practical size.

B. The Kuhn–Tucker Conditions

This section develops the Kuhn–Tucker *necessary* conditions for identifying stationary points of a nonlinear constrained problem subject to inequality constraints. The development is based on the Lagrangean method. These conditions are also sufficient under certain limitations that will be stated later.

Consider the problem

$$\text{maximize } z = f(\mathbf{X})$$

subject to

$$\mathbf{g}(\mathbf{X}) \le \mathbf{0}$$

The inequality constraints may be converted into equations by adding the appropriate *nonnegative* slack variables. Thus, to satisfy the nonnegativity conditions, let S_i^2 (≥ 0) be the slack quantity added to the ith constraint $g_i(\mathbf{X}) \le 0$. Define

$$\mathbf{S} = (S_1, S_2, \ldots, S_m)^T \quad \text{and} \quad \mathbf{S}^2 = (S_1^2, S_2^2, \ldots, S_m^2)^T$$

where m is the total number of inequality constraints. The Lagrangean function is thus given by

$$L(\mathbf{X}, \mathbf{S}, \boldsymbol{\lambda}) = f(\mathbf{X}) - \boldsymbol{\lambda}[\mathbf{g}(\mathbf{X}) + \mathbf{S}^2]$$

Given the constraints

$$\mathbf{g}(\mathbf{X}) \le \mathbf{0}$$

a necessary condition for optimality is that $\boldsymbol{\lambda}$ be nonnegative (nonpositive) for maximization (minimization) problems. This is justified as follows. Consider the maximization case. Since $\boldsymbol{\lambda}$ measures the rate of variation of f with respect to $\mathbf{g}$, that is,

$$\boldsymbol{\lambda} = \frac{\partial f}{\partial \mathbf{g}}$$

as the right-hand side of the constraint $\mathbf{g} \le \mathbf{0}$ increases above zero, the solution space becomes less constrained and hence f cannot decrease. This means that $\boldsymbol{\lambda} \ge 0$. Similarly, for minimization as a resource increases, f cannot increase, which implies that $\boldsymbol{\lambda} \le \mathbf{0}$. If the constraints are equalities, that is, $\mathbf{g}(\mathbf{X}) = \mathbf{0}$, then $\boldsymbol{\lambda}$ becomes unrestricted in sign (see Problem 19–17).

The restrictions on $\boldsymbol{\lambda}$ given must hold as part of the Kuhn–Tucker necessary conditions. The remaining conditions will now be derived.

Taking the partial derivatives of L with respect to $\mathbf{X}$, $\mathbf{S}$, and $\boldsymbol{\lambda}$, we obtain

$$\frac{\partial L}{\partial \mathbf{X}} = \nabla f(\mathbf{X}) - \boldsymbol{\lambda} \nabla \mathbf{g}(\mathbf{X}) = \mathbf{0}$$

$$\frac{\partial L}{\partial S_i} = -2\lambda_i S_i = 0, \qquad i = 1, 2, \ldots, m$$

$$\frac{\partial L}{\partial \lambda} = -(\mathbf{g}(\mathbf{X}) + \mathbf{S}^2) = \mathbf{0}$$

The second set of equations reveals the following results.

1. If λ_i is greater than zero, $S_i^2 = 0$. This means that the corresponding resource is scarce, and consequently it is exhausted completely (equality constraint).
2. If $S_i^2 > 0$, $\lambda_i = 0$. This means the ith resource is not scarce and, consequently, it does not affect the value of $f (\lambda_i = \partial f / \partial g_i = 0)$.

From the second and third sets of equations it follows that

$$\lambda_i g_i(\mathbf{X}) = 0, \qquad i = 1, 2, \ldots, m$$

This new condition essentially repeats the foregoing argument, since if $\lambda_i > 0$, $g_i(\mathbf{X}) = 0$ or $S_i^2 = 0$. Similarly, if $g_i(\mathbf{X}) < 0$, that is, $S_i^2 > 0$, then $\lambda_i = 0$.

The Kuhn–Tucker conditions necessary for $\mathbf{X}$ and $\boldsymbol{\lambda}$ to be a stationary point of the maximization problem can now be summarized as follows:

$$\boldsymbol{\lambda} \geq \mathbf{0},$$

$$\nabla f(\mathbf{X}) - \boldsymbol{\lambda} \nabla \mathbf{g}(\mathbf{X}) = \mathbf{0}$$

$$\lambda_i g_i(\mathbf{X} = 0, \qquad i = 1, 2, \ldots, m$$

$$\mathbf{g}(\mathbf{X}) \leq \mathbf{0}$$

You can verify that these conditions apply to the minimization case as well, with the exception that $\boldsymbol{\lambda}$ must be nonpositive, as shown previously. In both maximization and minimization, the Lagrange multipliers corresponding to *equality* constraints must be unrestricted in sign.

Exercise 19.2-3

Consider the problem just defined:

$$\text{maximize } f(\mathbf{X})$$

subject to

$$g(\mathbf{X}) \leq 0$$

Suppose that the Lagrangean function is formulated as

$$L(\mathbf{X}, \boldsymbol{\lambda}, \mathbf{S}) = f(\mathbf{X}) + \boldsymbol{\lambda}[g(\mathbf{X}) + \mathbf{S}^2]$$

How would this change affect the Kuhn–Tucker conditions?
[*Ans.* $\boldsymbol{\lambda}$ will be nonpositive instead of nonnegative because $\boldsymbol{\lambda}$ is defined equal to $-\partial f / \partial \mathbf{g}$ instead of $+\partial f / \partial \mathbf{g}$.]

Sufficiency of the Kuhn–Tucker Conditions

The Kuhn–Tucker necessary conditions are also sufficient if the objective function and the solution space satisfy certain conditions regarding convexity and concavity. These conditions are summarized in Table 19-1.

Table 19-1

Sense of Optimization	Required Conditions	
	Objective Function	Solution Space
Maximization	Concave	Convex set
Minimization	Convex	Convex set

It is simpler to verify that a function is convex or concave than it is to prove that a solution space is a convex set. For this reason, we provide a list of conditions that are easier to apply in practice in the sense that the convexity of the solution space can be established by checking directly the convexity or concavity of the constraint functions. To provide these conditions, we define the generalized nonlinear problems as

$$\begin{pmatrix}\text{maximize}\\ \text{or}\\ \text{minimize}\end{pmatrix} z = f(\mathbf{X})$$

subject to

$$\begin{aligned} g_i(\mathbf{X}) &\le 0, & i &= 1, 2, \ldots, r \\ g_i(\mathbf{X}) &\ge 0, & i &= r+1, \ldots, p \\ g_i(\mathbf{X}) &= 0, & i &= p+1, \ldots, m \end{aligned}$$

$$L(\mathbf{X}, \mathbf{S}, \boldsymbol{\lambda}) = f(\mathbf{X}) - \sum_{i=1}^{r} \lambda_i[g_i(\mathbf{X}) + \mathbf{S}_i^2] - \sum_{i=r+1}^{p} \lambda_i[g_i(\mathbf{X}) - \mathbf{S}_i^2] - \sum_{i=p+1}^{m} \lambda_i g_i(\mathbf{X})$$

where λ_i is the Lagrangean multiplier associated with constraint i. The conditions for establishing the sufficiency of the Kuhn–Tucker conditions can thus be summarized as shown in Table 19-2.

We must remark that the conditions in Table 19-2 represent only a subset of the conditions in Table 19-1. The reason is that a solution space may be convex without satisfying the conditions stipulated in Table 19-2 on the functions $g_i(\mathbf{X})$.

The validity of Table 19-2 rests on the fact that the given conditions yield a concave Lagrangean function $L(\mathbf{X}, \mathbf{S}, \boldsymbol{\lambda})$ in case of maximization and a convex $L(\mathbf{X}, \mathbf{S}, \boldsymbol{\lambda})$ in case of minimization. This result can be verified directly by noticing that if $g_i(x)$ is convex, then $\lambda_i g_i(x)$ is convex if $\lambda_i \ge 0$ and concave if $\lambda_i \le 0$. Similar interpretations can be established for all the remaining conditions. We must indicate,

Table 19-2

Sense of Optimization	Conditions Required			
	$f(\mathbf{X})$	$g_i(\mathbf{X})$	λ_i	
Maximization	Concave	Convex	≥ 0	$(1 \le i \le r)$
		Concave	≤ 0	$(r+1 \le i \le p)$
		Linear	Unrestricted	$(p+1 \le i \le m)$
Minimization	Convex	Convex	≤ 0	$(1 \le i \le r)$
		Concave	≥ 0	$(r+1 \le i \le p)$
		Linear	Unrestricted	$(p+1 \le i \le m)$

however, that a linear function, by definition, is both convex and concave. Notice also that if a function f is concave, then $-f$ is convex, and vice versa.

Exercise 19.2-4

Develop the conditions similar to those in Tables 19-1 and 19-2 assuming the Lagrangean function is expressed as

$$L(\mathbf{X}, \boldsymbol{\lambda}, \mathbf{S}) = f(\mathbf{X}) + \sum_{i=1}^{r} \lambda_i[g_i(\mathbf{X}) + S_i^2] + \sum_{i=r+1}^{p} \lambda_i[g_i(\mathbf{X}) - S_i^2] + \sum_{i=p+1}^{m} \lambda_i g_i(\mathbf{X})$$

[*Ans.* Table 19-1 remains unchanged. In Table 19-2 the signs of *restricted* λ_i must be reversed while the rest of the conditions remain unchanged.]

Example 19.2-7. Consider the following *minimization* problem:

$$\text{minimize } f(\mathbf{X}) = x_1^2 + x_2^2 + x_3^2$$

subject to

$$\begin{aligned} g_1(\mathbf{X}) &= 2x_1 + x_2 - 5 \le 0 \\ g_2(\mathbf{X}) &= x_1 + x_3 - 2 \le 0 \\ g_3(\mathbf{X}) &= 1 - x_1 \le 0 \\ g_4(\mathbf{X}) &= 2 - x_2 \le 0 \\ g_5(\mathbf{X}) &= -x_3 \le 0 \end{aligned}$$

Since this is a minimization problem, it follows that $\boldsymbol{\lambda} \le \mathbf{0}$. The Kuhn–Tucker conditions are thus given as follows.

$$(\lambda_1, \lambda_2, \lambda_3, \lambda_4, \lambda_5) \le \mathbf{0}$$

$$(2x_1, 2x_2, 2x_3) - (\lambda_1, \lambda_2, \lambda_3, \lambda_4, \lambda_5)\begin{pmatrix} 2 & 1 & 0 \\ 1 & 0 & 1 \\ -1 & 0 & 0 \\ 0 & -1 & 0 \\ 0 & 0 & -1 \end{pmatrix} = \mathbf{0}$$

$$\lambda_1 g_1 = \lambda_2 g_2 = \cdots = \lambda_5 g_5 = 0$$

$$\mathbf{g}(\mathbf{X}) \le \mathbf{0}$$

These conditions simplify to the following:

$$\begin{aligned} \lambda_1, \lambda_2, \lambda_3, \lambda_4, \lambda_5 &\le 0 \\ 2x_1 - 2\lambda_1 - \lambda_2 + \lambda_3 &= 0 \\ 2x_2 - \lambda_1 + \lambda_4 &= 0 \\ 2x_3 - \lambda_2 + \lambda_5 &= 0 \\ \lambda_1(2x_1 + x_2 - 5) &= 0 \\ \lambda_2(x_1 + x_3 - 2) &= 0 \\ \lambda_3(1 - x_1) &= 0 \\ \lambda_4(2 - x_2) &= 0 \\ \lambda_5 x_3 &= 0 \\ 2x_1 + x_2 &\le 5 \\ x_1 + x_3 &\le 2 \\ x_1 \ge 1, \quad x_2 \ge 2, \quad x_3 &\ge 0 \end{aligned}$$

The solution is $x_1 = 1$, $x_2 = 2$, $x_3 = 0$; $\lambda_1 = \lambda_2 = \lambda_5 = 0$, $\lambda_3 = -2$, $\lambda_4 = -4$. Since the function $f(\mathbf{X})$ is convex and the solution space $\mathbf{g}(\mathbf{X}) \leq \mathbf{0}$ is also convex, $L(\mathbf{X}, \mathbf{S}, \boldsymbol{\lambda})$ must be convex and the resulting stationary point yields a global constrained minimum. The example given shows, however, that it is difficult in general to solve the resulting conditions explicitly. Consequently, the procedure is not suitable for numerical computations. The importance of the Kuhn–Tucker conditions will be clear in developing the nonlinear programming algorithms in Chapter 20. ◀

19.3 SUMMARY

In this chapter we provided the classical theory for locating the points of maxima and minima of constrained nonlinear problems. We observe that the theory presented is generally not suitable for computational purposes. Few exceptions exist, however, where the Kuhn–Tucker theory is the basis for the development of efficient computational algorithms. *Quadratic programming*, which we present in the next chapter, is an excellent example of the use of the Kuhn–Tucker necessary conditions.

We must emphasize that no sufficiency conditions (similar to those of unconstrained problems and problems with *equality* constraints) can be established for nonlinear programs with inequality constraints. Thus, unless the conditions given in Table 19-1 or 19-2 can be established *in advance*, there is no way of verifying whether the convergence of a nonlinear programming algorithm leads to a local or a global optimum.

SELECTED REFERENCES

BAZARAA, M., and C. SHETTY, *Nonlinear Programming Theory and Algorithms*, Wiley, New York, 1979.

BEIGHTLER, C., D. PHILLIPS, and D. WILDE, *Foundations of Optimization*, 2nd ed., Prentice Hall, Englewood Cliffs, N.J., 1979.

COURANT, R., and D. HILBERT, *Methods of Mathematical Physics*, Vol. I, Interscience, New York, 1953.

HADLEY, G., *Matrix Algebra*, Addison-Wesley, Reading, Mass., 1961.

PROBLEMS

Section	Assigned Problems
19.1.1	19–1 to 19–5
19.1.2	19–6
19.2.1A	19–7 to 19–12
19.2.1B	19–13 to 19–16
19.2.2A	None
19.2.2B	19–17 to 19–20

☐ **19–1** Examine the following functions for extreme points.

(a) $f(x) = x^3 + x$

(b) $f(x) = x^4 + x^2$

(c) $f(x) = 4x^4 - x^2 + 5$
(d) $f(x) = (3x - 2)^2(2x - 3)^2$
(e) $f(x) = 6x^5 - 4x^3 + 10$

☐ **19–2** Examine the following functions for extreme points.
(a) $f(\mathbf{X}) = x_1^3 + x_2^3 - 3x_1x_2$
(b) $f(\mathbf{X}) = 2x_1^2 + x_2^2 + x_3^2 + 6(x_1 + x_2 + x_3) + 2x_1x_2x_3$

☐ **19–3** Verify that the function

$$f(x_1, x_2, x_3) = 2x_1x_2x_3 - 4x_1x_3 - 2x_2x_3 + x_1^2 + x_2^2 + x_3^2 - 2x_1 - 4x_2 + 4x_3$$

has the stationary points (0, 3, 1), (0, 1, −1), (1, 2, 0), (2, 1, 1), and (2, 3, −1). Use the sufficiency condition to find the extreme points.

☐ **19–4** Solve the following simultaneous equations by converting the system to a nonlinear objective function with no constraints.

$$x_2 - x_1^2 = 0$$
$$x_2 - x_1 = 2$$

[*Hint*: $\min f^2(x_1, x_2)$ occurs at $f(x_1, x_2) = 0$.]

☐ **19–5** Apply the Newton–Raphson method to Problem 19–1(c) and Problem 19–2(b).

☐ **19–6** Prove Theorem 19.1-3.

☐ **19–7** Apply the Jacobian method to Example 19.2-1 by selecting $\mathbf{Y} = (x_2, x_3)$ and $\mathbf{Z} = (x_1)$.

☐ **19–8** Solve by the Jacobian method:

$$\text{minimize } f(\mathbf{X}) = \sum_{i=1}^{n} x_i^2$$

subject to

$$\prod_{i=1}^{n} x_i = C$$

where C is a positive constant. Suppose that the right-hand side of the constraint is changed to $C + \delta$, where δ is a small positive quantity. Find the corresponding change in the optimal value of f.

☐ **19–9** Solve by the Jacobian method

$$\text{minimize } f(\mathbf{X}) = 5x_1^2 + x_2^2 + 2x_1x_2$$

subject to

$$g(\mathbf{X}) = x_1x_2 - 10 = 0$$

(a) Find the change in the optimal value of $f(\mathbf{X})$ if the constraint is replaced by $x_1x_2 - 9.99 = 0$.

(b) Find the change in value of $f(\mathbf{X})$ in the neighborhood of the feasible point (2, 5) given that $x_1 x_2 = 9.99$ and $\partial x_1 = .01$.

☐ **19–10** Consider the problem:

$$\text{maximize } f(\mathbf{X}) = x_1^2 + 2x_2^2 + 10x_3^2 + 5x_1 x_2$$

subject to

$$g_1(\mathbf{X}) = x_1 + x_2^2 + 3x_2 x_3 - 5 = 0$$
$$g_2(\mathbf{X}) = x_1^2 + 5x_1 x_2 + x_3^2 - 7 = 0$$

Apply the Jacobian method to find $\partial f(\mathbf{X})$ in the feasible neighborhood of the feasible point (1, 1, 1). Assume that this feasible neighborhood is specified by $\partial g_1 = -.01$, $\partial g_2 = .02$, and $\partial x_1 = .01$.

☐ **19–11** Consider the problem

$$\text{minimize } f(\mathbf{X}) = x_1^2 + x_2^2 + x_3^2 + x_4^2$$

subject to

$$g_1(\mathbf{X}) = x_1 + 2x_2 + 3x_3 + 5x_4 - 10 = 0$$
$$g_2(\mathbf{X}) = x_1 + 2x_2 + 5x_3 + 6x_4 - 15 = 0$$

Show that by selecting x_3 and x_4 as the independent variables, the Jacobian method fails to give the solution. Then solve the problem using x_1 and x_3 as the independent variables and apply the sufficiency condition to examine the resulting stationary point. Find the sensitivity coefficients of the problem.

☐ **19–12** Consider the linear programming problem.

$$\text{maximize } f(\mathbf{X}) = \sum_{j=1}^{n} c_j x_j$$

subject to

$$g_i(\mathbf{X}) = \sum_{j=1}^{n} a_{ij} x_j - b_i = 0, \qquad i = 1, 2, \ldots, m$$
$$x_j \geq 0, \qquad j = 1, 2, \ldots, n$$

Neglecting the nonnegativity constraint, show that the constrained derivatives $\nabla_c f(\mathbf{X})$ for this problem yield the same expression for $\{z_j - c_j\}$ defined by the optimality condition of the linear programming problem (Section 4.2.2). That is,

$$\{z_j - c_j\} = \{\mathbf{C}_B \mathbf{B}^{-1} \mathbf{P}_j - c_j\}, \qquad \text{for all } j$$

Can the constrained-derivative method be applied directly to the linear programming problem? Why or why not?

☐ **19–13** Solve the following linear programming problem by both the Jacobian and the Lagrangean methods:

$$\text{maximize } f(\mathbf{X}) = 5x_1 + 3x_2$$

subject to

$$g_1(\mathbf{X}) = x_1 + 2x_2 + x_3 - 6 = 0$$
$$g_2(\mathbf{X}) = 3x_1 + x_2 + x_4 - 9 = 0$$
$$x_1, x_2, x_3, x_4 \geq 0$$

☐ **19–14** Find the optimal solution to the problem

$$\text{minimize } f(\mathbf{X}) = x_1^2 + 2x_2^2 + 10x_3^2$$

subject to

$$g_1(\mathbf{X}) = x_1 + x_2^2 + x_3 - 5 = 0$$
$$g_2(\mathbf{X}) = x_1 + 5x_2 + x_3 - 7 = 0$$

Suppose that $g_1(\mathbf{X}) = .01$ and $g_2(\mathbf{X}) = .02$. Find the corresponding change in the optimal value of $f(\mathbf{X})$.

☐ **19–15** Solve Problem 19–11 by the Lagrangean method and verify that the value of the Lagrange multipliers are the same as the sensitivity coefficients obtained in Problem 19–11.

☐ **19–16** Show that the Kuhn–Tucker conditions for the problem:

$$\text{maximize } f(\mathbf{X})$$

subject to

$$\mathbf{g}(\mathbf{X}) \geq \mathbf{0}$$

are the same as in Section 19.2.2B except that the Lagrange multipliers $\boldsymbol{\lambda}$ are nonpositive.

☐ **19–17** Show that the Kuhn–Tucker conditions for the problem:

$$\text{maximize } f(\mathbf{X})$$

subject to

$$\mathbf{g}(\mathbf{X}) = \mathbf{0}$$

are

$$\boldsymbol{\lambda} \text{ unrestricted in sign}$$
$$\nabla f(\mathbf{X}) - \boldsymbol{\lambda}\nabla\mathbf{g}(\mathbf{X}) = \mathbf{0}$$
$$\mathbf{g}(\mathbf{X}) = \mathbf{0}$$

☐ **19–18** Write the Kuhn–Tucker necessary conditions for the following problems.

(a) Maximize $f(\mathbf{X}) = x_1^3 - x_2^2 + x_1x_3^2$

subject to

$$x_1 + x_2^2 + x_3 = 5$$
$$5x_1^2 - x_2^2 - x_3 \geq 0$$
$$x_1, x_2, x_3 \geq 0$$

(b) Minimize $f(\mathbf{X}) = x_1^4 + x_2^2 + 5x_1x_2x_3$

subject to

$$x_1^2 - x_2^2 + x_3^3 \leq 10$$
$$x_1^3 + x_2^2 + 4x_3^2 \geq 20$$

☐ **19–19** Consider the problem:

$$\text{maximize } f(\mathbf{X})$$

subject to

$$\mathbf{g}(\mathbf{X}) = \mathbf{0}$$

Given $f(\mathbf{X})$ is concave and $g_i(\mathbf{X})$ $(i = 1, 2, \ldots, m)$ is a *linear* function, show that the Kuhn–Tucker necessary conditions are also sufficient. Is this result true if $g_i(\mathbf{X})$ is a convex *non*linear function for all i? Why?

☐ **19–20** Consider the problem

$$\text{maximize } f(\mathbf{X})$$

subject to

$$g_1(\mathbf{X}) \geq 0, \qquad g_2(\mathbf{X}) = 0, \qquad g_3(\mathbf{X}) \leq 0$$

Develop the Kuhn–Tucker conditions for the problem; then give the stipulations under which the conditions are sufficient.

Chapter 20

Nonlinear Programming Algorithms

Chapter 19 has presented the theory for optimizing unconstrained and constrained nonlinear functions. However, the techniques developed are not suitable for computational purposes. This chapter develops working algorithms for both the unconstrained and constrained problems. Because of space limitations, the material presented here is meant to include only a selected sample of nonlinear programming algorithms.

20.1 UNCONSTRAINED NONLINEAR ALGORITHMS

This section presents two algorithms for the unconstrained problem: the *direct search* algorithm and the *gradient* algorithm. As evident from the names, the first algorithm locates the optimum by direct search over a specified region, and the second utilizes the gradient of the function to find the optimum.

20.1.1 DIRECT SEARCH METHOD

Direct search methods have been developed primarily for single-variable functions. Although this may appear trivial from the practical standpoint, it is shown in Section 20.1.2 that optimization of single-variable functions may evolve as part of the algorithms for multivariable functions.

The general idea of direct search methods is rather simple. First, an interval (called **interval of uncertainty**) that is known to include the optimum is identified. The size of the interval is then systematically reduced in a manner guaranteeing that the optimum is not missed. The procedure does not determine the exact optimum but rather minimizes the length of the interval that includes the optimum point. Theoretically, the length of the interval including the optimum can be made as small as desired.

One of the limitations of search methods is that the optimized function is assumed unimodal over the search interval. This guarantees only one local optimum. In addition, no finite intervals exist in which the slope of the function is zero. With this additional assumption, the optimized function may be referred to as *strictly unimodal.*

This section presents a method called **dichotomous search**. Suppose that the initial interval in which a local optimum occurs is defined by $a \leq x \leq b$. Suppose for convenience that the function $f(x)$ is maximized. Define the two points x_1 and x_2 symmetrically with respect to a and b such that the intervals $a \leq x \leq x_2$ and $x_1 \leq x \leq b$ overlap by a finite amount Δ (see Figure 20-1).

Now evaluate $f(x_1)$ and $f(x_2)$. Three cases will result:

1. If $f(x_1) > f(x_2)$, x^* (optimum x) must lie between a and x_2.
2. If $f(x_1) < f(x_2)$, $x_1 < x^* < b$.
3. If $f(x_1) = f(x_2)$, $x_1 < x^* < x_2$.

These results follow directly from the strict unimodality of $f(x)$. In each of these cases, the interval(s) not including x^* is discarded in future iterations.

The result of the search is that the maximum of $f(x)$ is now confined to a smaller interval. The new interval may thus be dichotomized into two (overlapping) intervals in the same manner followed for the interval $a \leq x \leq b$. Continuing in this manner, one can narrow (in the limit) the interval in which the local maximum lies to the length Δ. This means that Δ should be chosen reasonably small.

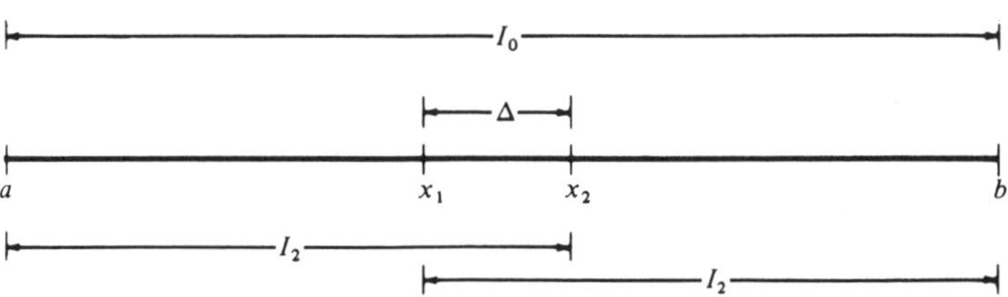

Figure 20-1

Table 20-1
Computations for Dichotomous Search Method[a]

x_L	x_R	x_1	x_2	$f(x_1)$	$f(x_2)$
0	3	1.4995^L	1.5005	4.4985	4.5015[b]
1.4995	3	2.24925	2.25025^R	5.91692[b]	5.91658
1.4995	2.25025	1.87437^L	1.87537	5.62312	5.62612[b]
1.87437	2.25025	2.06181	2.06281^R	5.97939[b]	5.97906
1.87437	2.06281	1.96809^L	1.96909	5.90427	5.90727[b]
1.96809	2.06281	2.01495	2.01595^R	5.99502[b]	5.99447
1.96809	2.01595	1.99152^L	1.99252	5.97456	5.97756[b]
1.99152	2.01595	2.00323	2.00423^R	5.99892[b]	5.99859
1.99152	2.00423	1.99737^L	1.99837	5.99213	5.99511[b]
1.99737	2.00423				

[a] $L(R)$ indicates that $x_L(x_R)$ is set equal to $x_1(x_2)$ in the next step.
[b] $\max\{f(x_1), f(x_2)\}$.

Example 20.1-1

$$\text{Maximize } f(x) = \begin{cases} 3x, & 0 \le x \le 2 \\ -\dfrac{x}{3} + \dfrac{20}{3}, & 2 \le x \le 3 \end{cases}$$

Obviously, $\max f(x)$ occurs at $x = 2$. The dichotomous search method is now used to solve the problem. Let x_L and x_R define the (left and right) boundaries of the *current* interval. Initially, $x_L = 0$ and $x_R = 3$. Define x_1 and x_2 as the points dichotomizing an interval so that the associated overlapping intervals are $x_L \le x \le x_2$ and $x_1 \le x \le x_R$, where $x_1 - x_L = x_R - x_2$ and $\Delta = x_2 - x_1$. This means that

$$x_1 = x_L + \frac{x_R - x_L - \Delta}{2}$$

$$x_2 = x_L + \frac{x_R - x_L + \Delta}{2}$$

Table 20-1 summarizes the computations given $\Delta = .001$.

The last step in Table 20-1 gives $x_L = 1.99737$ and $x_R = 2.00423$. This means that $\max f(x)$ occurs at x^*, satisfying $1.99737 \le x^* \le 2.00423$. If the midpoint is used, this will give $x = 2.0008$, which is very close to the exact optimum $x^* = 2.0$. ◀

20.1.2 GRADIENT METHOD

This section develops a method for optimizing functions that are twice continuously differentiable. The general idea is to generate successive points, starting from a given initial point, in the direction of the fastest increase (maximization) of the function. The technique is known as the *gradient method* because the gradient of the function at a point is indicative of the fastest rate of increase.

A gradient method, the Newton–Raphson method, was presented in Section 19.1.2. The method is based on solving the simultaneous equations representing the necessary condition for optimality, namely, $\nabla f(\mathbf{X}) = \mathbf{0}$. This section presents another technique, called the **steepest ascent** method.

Termination of the gradient method occurs at the point where the gradient vector becomes null. This is only a necessary condition for optimality. It is thus emphasized that optimality cannot be verified unless it is known a priori that $f(\mathbf{X})$ is concave or convex.

Suppose that $f(\mathbf{X})$ is maximized. Let $\mathbf{X}^0$ be the initial point from which the procedure starts and define $\nabla f(\mathbf{X}^k)$ as the gradient of f at the kth point $\mathbf{X}^k$. The idea of the method is to determine a particular path p along which df/dp is maximized at a given point. This result is achieved if successive points $\mathbf{X}^k$ and $\mathbf{X}^{k+1}$ are selected such that

$$\mathbf{X}^{k+1} = \mathbf{X}^k + r^k \nabla f(\mathbf{X}^k)$$

where r^k is a parameter called the optimal **step size**.

The parameter r^k is determined such that $\mathbf{X}^{k+1}$ results in the largest improvement in f. In other words, if a function $h(r)$ is defined such that

$$h(r) = f[\mathbf{X}^k + r\nabla f(\mathbf{X}^k)]$$

r^k is the value of r maximizing $h(r)$. Since $h(r)$ is a single-variable function, the search method in Section 20.1.1 may be used to find the optimum provided that $h(r)$ is strictly unimodal.

The proposed procedure terminates when two successive trial points $\mathbf{X}^k$ and $\mathbf{X}^{k+1}$ are approximately equal. This is equivalent to having

$$r^k \nabla f(\mathbf{X}^k) \cong \mathbf{0}$$

Under the assumption that $r^k \neq 0$, which will always be true unless $\mathbf{X}_0$ happens to be the optimum of $f(\mathbf{X})$, this is equivalent to the necessary condition $\nabla f(\mathbf{X}^k) = \mathbf{0}$.

Example 20.1-2. Consider maximizing the function

$$f(x_1, x_2) = 4x_1 + 6x_2 - 2x_1^2 - 2x_1x_2 - 2x_2^2$$

$f(x_1, x_2)$ is a quadratic function whose absolute optimum occurs at $(x_1^*, x_2^*) = (1/3, 4/3)$. It is shown how the problem is solved by the steepest ascent method. Figure 20-2 shows the successive points. The gradients at any two successive points are necessarily orthogonal (perpendicular).

Let the initial point be given by $\mathbf{X}^0 = (1, 1)$. Now

$$\nabla f(\mathbf{X}) = (4 - 4x_1 - 2x_2, 6 - 2x_1 - 4x_2)$$

First Iteration

$$\nabla f(\mathbf{X}^0) = (-2, 0)$$

The next point $\mathbf{X}^1$ is obtained by considering

$$\mathbf{X} = (1, 1) + r(-2, 0) = (1 - 2r, 1)$$

Thus

$$h(r) = f(1 - 2r, 1) = -2(1 - 2r)^2 + 2(1 - 2r) + 4$$

The optimal step size yielding the maximum value of $h(r)$ is $r^1 = 1/4$. This gives $\mathbf{X}^1 = (1/2, 1)$.

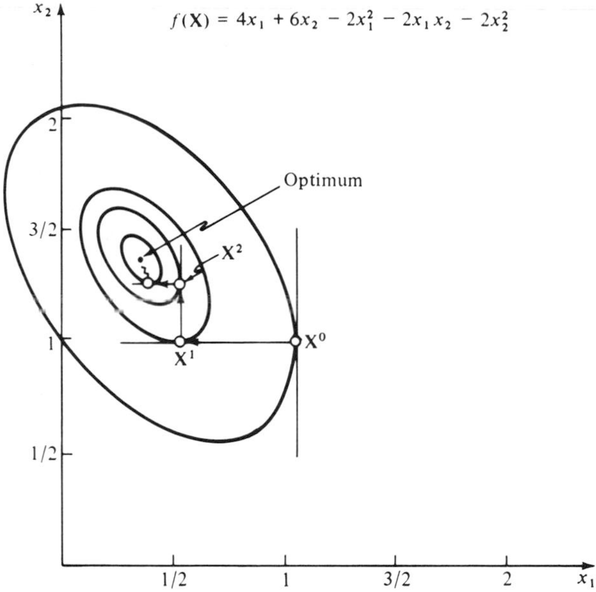

Figure 20-2

Second Iteration

$$\nabla f(\mathbf{X}^1) = (0, 1)$$

Consider

$$\mathbf{X} = (1/2, 1) + r(0, 1) = (1/2, 1 + r)$$

Thus

$$h(r) = -2(1 + r)^2 + 5(1 + r) + 3/2$$

This gives $r^2 = 1/4$ or $\mathbf{X}^2 = (1/2, 5/4)$.

Third Iteration

$$\nabla f(\mathbf{X}^2) = (-1/2, 0)$$

Consider

$$\mathbf{X} = \left(\frac{1}{2}, \frac{5}{4}\right) + r\left(-\frac{1}{2}, 0\right) = \left(\frac{1-r}{2}, \frac{5}{4}\right)$$

Thus

$$h(r) = -(1/2)(1 - r)^2 + (3/4)(1 - r) + 35/8$$

This gives $r^3 = 1/4$ or $\mathbf{X}^3 = (3/8, 5/4)$.

Fourth Iteration

$$\nabla f(\mathbf{X}^3) = (0, 1/4)$$

Consider

$$\mathbf{X} = \left(\frac{3}{8}, \frac{5}{4}\right) + r\left(0, \frac{1}{4}\right) = \left(\frac{3}{8}, \frac{5+r}{4}\right)$$

Thus

$$h(r) = -(1/8)(5+r)^2 + (21/16)(5+r) + 39/32$$

This gives $r^4 = 1/4$, or $\mathbf{X}^4 = (3/8, 21/16)$.

Fifth Iteration

$$\nabla f(\mathbf{X}^4) = (-1/8, 0)$$

Consider

$$\mathbf{X} = \left(\frac{3}{8}, \frac{21}{16}\right) + r\left(-\frac{1}{8}, 0\right) = \left(\frac{3-r}{8}, \frac{21}{16}\right)$$

Thus

$$h(r) = -\left(\frac{1}{32}\right)(3-r)^2 + \left(\frac{11}{64}\right)(3-r) + \frac{567}{128}$$

This gives $r^5 = 1/4$, or $\mathbf{X}^5 = (11/32, 21/16)$.

Sixth Iteration

$$\nabla f(\mathbf{X}^5) = (0, 1/16)$$

Since $\nabla f(\mathbf{X}^5) \cong \mathbf{0}$, the process can be terminated at this point. The *approximate* maximum point is given by $\mathbf{X}^5 = (.3437, 1.3125)$. Note that the exact optimum is $\mathbf{X}^* = (.3333, 1.3333)$. ◀

20.2 CONSTRAINED NONLINEAR ALGORITHMS

The general constrained nonlinear programming problem may be defined as

$$\text{maximize (or minimize) } z = f(\mathbf{X})$$

subject to

$$\mathbf{g}(\mathbf{X}) \le \mathbf{0}$$

The nonnegativity conditions $\mathbf{X} \ge \mathbf{0}$ are assumed to be part of the given constraints. Also, at least one of the functions $f(\mathbf{X})$ and $\mathbf{g}(\mathbf{X})$ is nonlinear. For the purpose of this presentation, these functions are continuously differentiable.

No general algorithm exists for handling nonlinear models, mainly because of the irregular behavior of the nonlinear functions. Perhaps the most general result applicable to the problem is the Kuhn–Tucker conditions. Section 19.2.2B shows that unless $f(\mathbf{X})$ and $\mathbf{g}(\mathbf{X})$ are well-behaved functions (convexity and concavity conditions), the Kuhn–Tucker theory yields only necessary conditions for optimum. This sets a big limitation on the application of the Kuhn–Tucker conditions to the general problem.

This section presents a number of algorithms, which may be classified generally as *indirect* and *direct* methods. Indirect methods basically solve the nonlinear problem by dealing with one or more *linear* problems that are extracted from the original program. Direct methods attack the nonlinear problem itself by determining successive search points. The idea is to convert constrained problems into unconstrained ones for which the gradient methods of Section 20.1.2 are applied with some modifications.

The indirect methods presented in this section include separable, quadratic, geometric, and stochastic programming. The direct methods include the method of linear combinations and a brief discussion of the sequential unconstrained maximization technique. Other important nonlinear techniques can be found in the Selected References at the end of the chapter.

20.2.1 SEPARABLE PROGRAMMING

A function $f(x_1, x_2, \ldots, x_n)$ is **separable** if it can be expressed as the sum of n single-variable functions $f_1(x_1), f_2(x_2), \ldots, f_n(x_n)$, that is,

$$f(x_1, x_2, \ldots, x_n) = f_1(x_1) + f_2(x_2) + \cdots + f_n(x_n)$$

For example, the linear function

$$h(x_1, x_2, \ldots, x_n) = a_1 x_1 + a_2 x_2 + \cdots + a_n x_n$$

(where the a's are constants) is separable. On the other hand, the function

$$h(x_1, x_2, x_3) = x_1^2 + x_1 \sin(x_2 + x_3) + x_2 e^{x3}$$

is not separable.

Some nonlinear functions are not directly separable but can be made so by appropriate substitutions. Consider, for example, the case of maximizing $z = x_1 x_2$. If we let $y = x_1 x_2$, then $\ln y = \ln x_1 + \ln x_2$ and the problem becomes

$$\text{maximize } z = y$$

subject to

$$\ln y = \ln x_1 + \ln x_2$$

which is separable. The substitution assumes that x_1 and x_2 are *positive* variables; otherwise, the logarithmic function is undefined.

The case where x_1 and x_2 assume zero values (i.e., $x_1, x_2 \geq 0$) may be handled as follows. Let δ_1 and δ_2 be positive constants and define

$$w_1 = x_1 + \delta_1$$
$$w_2 = x_2 + \delta_2$$

This means that w_1 and w_2 are strictly positive. Now

$$x_1 x_2 = w_1 w_2 - \delta_2 w_1 - \delta_1 w_2 + \delta_1 \delta_2$$

Let $y = w_1 w_2$; then the problem is equivalent to

$$\text{maximize } z = y - \delta_2 w_1 - \delta_1 w_2 + \delta_1 \delta_2$$

subject to

$$\ln y = \ln w_1 + \ln w_2$$

which is separable.

Other functions that can be made readily separable (using substitution) are exemplified by $e^{x_1+x_2}$ and $x_1^{x_2}$. A variant of the procedure just presented can be applied to such cases to effect separability.

Separable programming deals with nonlinear problems in which the objective function and the constraints are separable. This section shows how an approximate solution can be obtained for any separable problem by linear approximation and the simplex method of linear programming.

The single-variable function $f(x)$ can be approximated by a piecewise linear function using mixed integer programming (Chapter 9). Suppose that $f(x)$ is to be approximated over the interval $[a, b]$. Define a_k, $k = 1, 2, \ldots, K$, as the kth breaking point on the x-axis such that $a_1 < a_2 < \cdots < a_k$. The points a_1 and a_K coincide with the end points a and b of the interval under study. Thus $f(x)$ is approximated as follows:

$$f(x) \cong \sum_{k=1}^{K} f(a_k)t_k$$

$$x = \sum_{k=1}^{K} a_k t_k$$

where t_k is a nonnegative weight associated with the kth breaking point such that

$$\sum_{k=1}^{K} t_k = 1$$

Mixed integer programming ensures the validity of the approximation. Specifically, the approximation is valid if

1. At most two t_k are positive.
2. If t_{k^*} is a positive, then only an adjacent $t_k(t_{k^*+1}$ or $t_{k^*-1})$ is allowed to be positive.

To show how these conditions are satisfied, consider the separable problem

$$\text{maximize (or minimize) } z = \sum_{i=1}^{n} f_i(x_i)$$

subject to

$$\sum_{i=1}^{n} g_i^j(x_i) \le b_j, \qquad j = 1, 2, \ldots, m$$

This problem can be approximated as a mixed integer program as follows. Let the number of breaking points for the ith variable x_i be equal to K_i and let a_i^k be its kth breaking value. Let t_i^k be the weight associated with the kth breaking point of the ith variable. Then the equivalent mixed problem is

$$\text{maximize (or minimize) } z = \sum_{i=1}^{n} \sum_{k=1}^{K_i} f_i(a_i^k)t_i^k$$

subject to

$$\sum_{i=1}^{n} \sum_{k=1}^{K_i} g_i^j(a_i^k)t_i^k \leq b_j, \qquad j = 1, 2, \ldots, m$$

$$0 \leq t_i^1 \leq y_i^1$$

$$0 \leq t_i^k \leq y_i^{k-1} + y_i^k, \qquad k = 2, 3, \ldots, K_i - 1$$

$$0 \leq t_i^{K_i} \leq y_i^{K_i - 1}$$

$$\sum_{k=1}^{K_i - 1} y_i^k = 1$$

$$\sum_{k=1}^{K_i} t_i^k = 1$$

$$y_i^k = 0 \text{ or } 1, \qquad k = 1, 2, \ldots, K_i; \quad i = 1, 2, \ldots, n$$

The variables for the approximating problem are t_i^k and y_i^k.

This formulation shows how any separable problem can be solved, at least in principle, by mixed integer programming. The difficulty, however, is that the number of constraints increases rather rapidly with the number of breaking points. In particular, the computational feasibility of the procedure is highly questionable, since there are no efficient computer programs for handling large mixed integer programming problems.

Another method for solving the approximate model is the regular simplex method (Chapter 3) under the condition of **restricted basis**. In this case the additional constraints involving y_i^k are disregarded. The restricted basis specifies that *no more* than two *positive* t_i^k can appear in the basis. Moreover, two t_i^k can be positive only if they are adjacent. Thus the strict optimality condition of the simplex method is used to select the entering variable t_i^k *only if* it satisfies the foregoing conditions. Otherwise, the variable t_i^k having the next best optimality indicator $(z_i^k - c_i^k)$ is considered for entering the solution. The process is repeated until the optimality condition is satisfied or until it is impossible to introduce new t_i^k without violating the restricted basis condition, whichever occurs first. At this point, the last tableau gives the approximate optimal solution to the problem.

Whereas the mixed integer programming method yields global optimum to the approximate problem, the restricted basis method can only guarantee a local optimum. Also, in the two methods, the approximate solution may not be feasible for the original problem. In fact, the approximate model may give rise to additional extreme points that do not exist in the original problem. This depends mainly on the degree of refinement of the linear approximation used. These inherent risks must be taken into consideration when using separable programming.

Example 20.2-1. Consider the problem

$$\text{maximize } z = x_1 + x_2^4$$

subject to

$$3x_1 + 2x_2^2 \leq 9$$

$$x_1, x_2 \geq 0$$

This example illustrates the application of the restricted basis method.

The exact optimum solution to this problem, obtained by inspection, is $x_1^* = 0$, $x_2^* = \sqrt{9/2} = 2.12$, and $z^* = 20.25$. To show how the approximating method is used, consider the separable functions

$$f_1(x_1) = x_1$$
$$f_2(x_2) = x_2^4$$
$$g_1^1(x_1) = 3x_1$$
$$g_1^2(x_2) = 2x_2^2$$

The functions $f_1(x_1)$ and $g_1^1(x_1)$ are left in their present form, since they are already linear. In this case, x_1 is treated as one of the variables. Considering $f_2(x_2)$ and $g_1^2(x_2)$, we assume that there are four breaking points ($K_2 = 4$). Since the value of x_2 cannot exceed 3, it follows that

k	a_2^k	$f_2(a_2^k)$	$g_1^2(a_2^k)$
1	0	0	0
2	1	1	2
3	2	16	8
4	3	81	18

This yields

$$\begin{aligned} f_2(x_2) &\cong t_2^1 f_2(a_2^1) + t_2^2 f_2(a_2^2) + t_2^3 f_2(a_2^3) + t_2^4 f_2(a_2^4) \\ &\cong 0(t_2^1) + 1(t_2^2) + 16(t_2^3) + 81(t_2^4) = t_2^2 + 16t_2^3 + 81t_2^4 \end{aligned}$$

Similarly,

$$g_1^2(x_2) \cong 2t_2^2 + 8t_2^3 + 18t_2^4$$

The approximation problem thus becomes

$$\text{maximize } z = x_1 + t_2^2 + 16t_2^3 + 81t_2^4$$

subject to

$$3x_1 + 2t_2^2 + 8t_2^3 + 18t_2^4 \leq 9$$
$$t_2^1 + t_2^2 + t_2^3 + t_2^4 = 1$$
$$t_2^k \geq 0, \qquad k = 1, 2, 3, 4$$
$$x_1 \geq 0$$

together with the restricted basis condition.

The initial simplex tableau (with rearranged columns to give a starting solution) is given by

Basic	x_1	t_2^2	t_2^3	t_2^4	S_1	t_2^1	Solution
z	-1	-1	-16	-81	0	0	0
S_1	3	2	8	18	1	0	9
t_2^1	0	1	1	1	0	1	1

where S_1 (≥ 0) is a slack variable. (This problem happened to have an obvious starting solution. In general, one may have to use the artificial variables techniques, Section 3.3.1.)

From the z-row coefficients, t_2^4 is the entering variable. Since t_2^1 is basic, it must be dropped first before t_2^4 can enter the solution (restricted basis condition). By the feasibility condition, S_1 must be the leaving variable. This means that t_2^4 cannot enter the solution. Next consider t_2^3 (next best entering variable). Again t_2^1 must be dropped first. From the feasibility condition, t_2^1 is the leaving variable as desired. The new tableau thus becomes

Basic	x_1	t_2^2	t_2^3	t_2^4	S_1	t_2^1	Solution
z	-1	15	0	-65	0	16	16
S_1	3	-6	0	10	1	-8	1
t_2^3	0	1	1	1	0	1	1

Clearly, t_2^4 is the entering variable. Since t_2^3 is in the basis, t_2^4 is an admissible entering variable. The simplex method shows that S_1 will be dropped. Thus

Basic	x_1	t_2^2	t_2^3	t_2^4	S_1	t_2^1	Solution
z	37/2	-24	0	0	13/2	-36	$22\frac{1}{2}$
t_2^4	3/10	$-6/10$	0	1	1/10	$-8/10$	1/10
t_2^3	$-3/10$	16/10	1	0	$-1/10$	18/10	9/10

The tableau shows that t_2^1 and t_2^2 are candidates for the entering variable. Since t_2^1 is not an adjacent point to the basic t_2^3 and t_2^4, it cannot be admitted. Also, t_2^2 cannot be admitted, since t_2^4 cannot be dropped. The process ends at this point and the solution given is the best feasible solution for the approximate problem.

To find the solution in terms of x_1 and x_2, we consider

$$t_2^3 = 9/10 \quad \text{and} \quad t_2^4 = 1/10$$

Thus

$$x_2 \cong 2t_2^3 + 3t_2^4 = 2(9/10) + 3(1/10) = 2.1$$

and $x_1 = 0$ and $z = 22.5$. The approximate optimum value of x_2 ($= 2.1$) is very close to the true optimum value ($= 2.12$). The value of z differs by about 10% error, however. The approximation may be improved in this case by using finer breaking points. ◀

Separable Convex Programming

A special case of separable programming occurs when the functions $g_i^j(x_i)$ are convex so that the solution space of the problem is a convex set. In addition, the function $f_i(x_i)$ is convex in case of minimization and concave in case of maximization (see Table 19-2). Under such conditions, the following simplified approximation can be used.

Consider a minimization problem and let $f_i(x_i)$ be as shown in Figure 20-3. The k breaking point of the function $f_i(x_i)$ is determined by $x_i = a_{ki}$, $k = 0, 1, \ldots, K_i$. Let

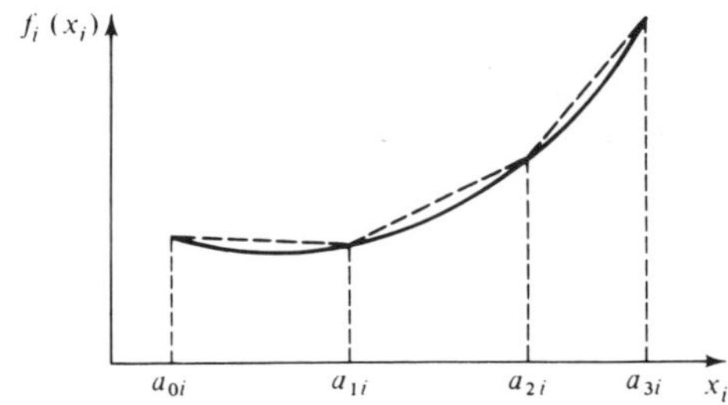

Figure 20-3

x_{ki} define the increment of the variable x_i in the range $(a_{k-1,i}, a_{ki})$, $k = 1, 2, \ldots, K_i$, and let ρ_{ki} be the corresponding slope of the line segment in the same range. Then

$$f_i(x_i) \cong \sum_{k=1}^{K_i} (\rho_{ki} x_{ki}) + f_i(a_{0i})$$

$$x_i = \sum_{k=1}^{K_i} x_{ki}$$

provided that

$$0 \le x_{ki} \le a_{ki} - a_{k-1,i}, \qquad k = 1, 2, \ldots, K_i$$

The fact that $f_i(x_i)$ is convex ensures that $\rho_{1i} < \rho_{2i} < \cdots < \rho_{K_i i}$. This means that in the minimization problem, for $p < q$, the variable x_{pi} is more attractive than x_{qi}. Consequently, x_{pi} will always enter the solution before x_{qi}. The only limitation here is that every x_{ki} must be restricted by the upper bound $(a_{ki} - a_{k-1,i})$.

The convex constraint functions $g_i^j(x_i)$ are approximated in essentially the same way. Let ρ_{ki}^j be the slope of the kth line segment corresponding to $g_i^j(x_i)$. It follows that the ith function is approximated as

$$g_i^j(x_i) \cong \sum_{k=1}^{K_i} \rho_{ki}^j x_{ki} + g_i^j(a_{0i})$$

The complete problem is thus given by

$$\text{minimize } z = \sum_{i=1}^{n} \left(\sum_{k=1}^{K_i} \rho_{ki} x_{ki} + f_i(a_{0i}) \right)$$

subject to

$$\sum_{i=1}^{n} \left(\sum_{k=1}^{K_i} \rho_{ki}^j x_{ki} + g_i^j(a_{0i}) \right) \le b_j, \qquad j = 1, 2, \ldots, m$$

$$0 \le x_{ki} \le a_{ki} - a_{k-1,i}, \qquad k = 1, 2, \ldots, K_i, \quad i = 1, 2, \ldots, n$$

where

$$\rho_{ki} = \frac{f_i(a_{ki}) - f_i(a_{k-1,i})}{a_{ki} - a_{k-1,i}}$$

$$\rho_{ki}^j = \frac{g_i^j(a_{ki}) - g_i^j(a_{k-1,i})}{a_{ki} - a_{k-1,i}}$$

The maximization problem is treated essentially the same way. In this case $\rho_{1i} > \rho_{2i} > \cdots > \rho_{K_i i}$, which shows that, for $p < q$, the variable x_{pi} will always enter the solution before x_{qi}. (See Problem 20–12 for the proof.)

The new problem can be solved by the simplex method with upper bounded variables (Section 7.1). The restricted basis concept is not necessary here because the convexity (concavity) of the functions guarantees the proper selection of variables.

Example 20.2-2. Consider the problem

$$\text{minimize } z = x_1^2 + x_2^2 + 5$$

subject to

$$3x_1^4 + x_2 \le 243$$
$$x_1 + 2x_2^2 \le 32$$
$$x_1, x_2 \ge 0$$

The separable functions of this problem are

$$f_1(x_1) = x_1^2, \qquad f_2(x_2) = x_2^2 + 5$$
$$g_1^1(x_1) = 3x_1^4 \qquad g_2^1(x_2) = x_2$$
$$g_1^2(x_1) = x_1, \qquad g_2^2(x_2) = 2x_2^2$$

These functions satisfy the convexity condition required for the minimization problems.

The range of the variables x_1 and x_2, calculated from the constraints, are given by $0 \le x_1 \le 3$ and $0 \le x_2 \le 4$. Thus x_1 and x_2 are partitioned in these ranges. Let $K_1 = 3$ and $K_2 = 4$ with $a_{01} = a_{02} = 0$. The slopes corresponding to the separable functions are as follows.

For $i = 1$,

k	a_{k1}	ρ_{k1}	ρ_{k1}^1	ρ_{k1}^2	x_{k1}
0	0	—	—	—	—
1	1	1	3	1	x_{11}
2	2	3	45	1	x_{21}
3	3	5	195	1	x_{31}

For $i = 2$,

k	a_{k2}	ρ_{k2}	ρ_{k2}^1	ρ_{k2}^2	x_{k2}
0	0	—	—	—	—
1	1	1	1	2	x_{12}
2	2	3	1	6	x_{22}
3	3	5	1	10	x_{32}
4	4	7	1	14	x_{42}

The complete problem then becomes

$$\text{minimize } z \cong x_{11} + 3x_{21} + 5x_{31} + x_{12} + 3x_{22} + 5x_{32} + 7x_{42} + 5$$

subject to

$$3x_{11} + 45x_{21} + 195x_{31} + x_{12} + x_{22} + x_{32} + x_{42} \leq 243$$
$$x_{11} + x_{21} + x_{31} + 2x_{12} + 6x_{22} + 10x_{32} + 14x_{42} \leq 32$$
$$0 \leq x_{k1} \leq 1, \qquad k = 1, 2, 3$$
$$0 \leq x_{k2} \leq 1, \qquad k = 1, 2, 3, 4$$

After solving this problem using upper bounding technique, let x_{k1}^* and x_{k2}^* be the corresponding optimal values. Optimal values of x_1 and x_2 are then given by

$$x_1^* = \sum_{k=1}^{3} x_{k1}^* \quad \text{and} \quad x_2^* = \sum_{k=1}^{4} x_{k2}^*$$ ◀

20.2.2 QUADRATIC PROGRAMMING

A quadratic programming model is defined as follows:

$$\text{maximize (or minimize) } z = \mathbf{CX} + \mathbf{X}^T\mathbf{DX}$$

subject to

$$\mathbf{AX} \leq \mathbf{b}, \qquad \mathbf{X} \geq \mathbf{0}$$

where

$$\mathbf{X} = (x_1, x_2, \ldots, x_n)^T$$
$$\mathbf{C} = (c_1, c_2, \ldots, c_n)$$
$$\mathbf{b} = (b_1, b_2, \ldots. b_m)^T$$
$$\mathbf{A} = \begin{pmatrix} a_{11} & \cdots & a_{1n} \\ \vdots & & \vdots \\ a_{m1} & \cdots & a_{mn} \end{pmatrix}$$
$$\mathbf{D} = \begin{pmatrix} d_{11} & \cdots & d_{1n} \\ \vdots & & \vdots \\ d_{n1} & \cdots & d_{nn} \end{pmatrix}$$

The function $\mathbf{X}^T\mathbf{DX}$ defines a quadratic form (Section A.3) where $\mathbf{D}$ is symmetric. The matrix $\mathbf{D}$ is assumed negative definite if the problem is maximization, and positive definite if the problem is minimization. This means that z is strictly convex in $\mathbf{X}$ for minimization and strictly concave for maximization. The constraints are assumed linear in this case, which guarantees a convex solution space.

The solution to this problem is secured by direct application of the Kuhn–Tucker necessary conditions (Section 19.2.2B). Since z is strictly convex (or concave) and the solution space is a convex set, these conditions (as proved in Section 19.2.2B) are also sufficient for a global optimum.

The quadratic programming problem will be treated for the maximization case. It is trivial to change the formulation to minimization. The problem may be written as

$$\text{maximize } z = \mathbf{CX} + \mathbf{X}^T\mathbf{DX}$$

subject to

$$\mathbf{G}(\mathbf{X}) = \begin{pmatrix} \mathbf{A} \\ -\mathbf{I} \end{pmatrix}\mathbf{X} - \begin{pmatrix} \mathbf{b} \\ \mathbf{0} \end{pmatrix} \leq \mathbf{0}$$

Let

$$\boldsymbol{\lambda} = (\lambda_1, \lambda_2, \ldots, \lambda_m)^T \qquad \text{and} \qquad \mathbf{U} = (\mu_1, \mu_2, \ldots, \mu_n)^T$$

be the Lagrange multipliers corresponding to the two sets of constraints $\mathbf{AX} - \mathbf{b} \leq \mathbf{0}$ and $-\mathbf{X} \leq \mathbf{0}$, respectively. Application of the Kuhn–Tucker conditions immediately yields

$$\boldsymbol{\lambda} \geq \mathbf{0}, \qquad \mathbf{U} \geq \mathbf{0}$$

$$\nabla z - (\boldsymbol{\lambda}^T, \mathbf{U}^T)\nabla\mathbf{G}(\mathbf{X}) = \mathbf{0}$$

$$\lambda_i\left(b_i - \sum_{j=1}^{n} a_{ij}x_j\right) = 0, \qquad i = 1, 2, \ldots, m$$

$$\mu_j x_j = 0, \qquad j = 1, 2, \ldots, n$$

$$\mathbf{AX} \leq \mathbf{b}, \qquad -\mathbf{X} \leq \mathbf{0}$$

Now

$$\nabla z = \mathbf{C} + 2\mathbf{X}^T\mathbf{D}$$

$$\nabla\mathbf{G}(\mathbf{X}) = \begin{pmatrix} \mathbf{A} \\ -\mathbf{I} \end{pmatrix}$$

Let $\mathbf{S} = \mathbf{b} - \mathbf{AX} \geq \mathbf{0}$ be the slack variables of the constraints. The conditions reduce to

$$-2\mathbf{X}^T\mathbf{D} + \boldsymbol{\lambda}^T\mathbf{A} - \mathbf{U}^T = \mathbf{C}$$

$$\mathbf{AX} + \mathbf{S} = \mathbf{b}$$

$$\mu_j x_j = 0 = \lambda_i S_i \qquad \text{for all } i \text{ and } j$$

$$\boldsymbol{\lambda}, \mathbf{U}, \mathbf{X}, \mathbf{S} \geq \mathbf{0}$$

Since $\mathbf{D}^T = \mathbf{D}$, the transpose of the first set of equations yields

$$-2\mathbf{DX} + \mathbf{A}^T\boldsymbol{\lambda} - \mathbf{U} = \mathbf{C}^T$$

Hence the necessary conditions may be combined as

$$\left(\begin{array}{c|c|c|c} -2\mathbf{D} & \mathbf{A}^T & -\mathbf{I} & \mathbf{0} \\ \hline \mathbf{A} & \mathbf{0} & \mathbf{0} & \mathbf{I} \end{array}\right)\begin{pmatrix} \mathbf{X} \\ \boldsymbol{\lambda} \\ \mathbf{U} \\ \mathbf{S} \end{pmatrix} = \begin{pmatrix} \mathbf{C}^T \\ \mathbf{b} \end{pmatrix}$$

$$\mu_j x_j = 0 = \lambda_i S_i, \qquad \text{for all } i \text{ and } j$$

$$\boldsymbol{\lambda}, \mathbf{U}, \mathbf{X}, \mathbf{S} \geq \mathbf{0}$$

Except for the conditions $\mu_j x_j = 0 = \lambda_i S_i$, the remaining equations are linear functions in $\mathbf{X}$, $\boldsymbol{\lambda}$, $\mathbf{U}$, and $\mathbf{S}$. The problem is thus equivalent to solving a set of linear equations, while satisfying the additional conditions $\mu_j x_j = 0 = \lambda_i S_i$. Because z is strictly concave and the solution space is convex, the *feasible* solution satisfying all these conditions must give the optimum solution directly. From the conditions imposed on z and the solution space (i.e., z is strictly concave and the solution space is convex), the solution (when it exists) to the set of equations above must be unique.

The solution of the system is obtained by using phase I of the two-phase method (Section 3.3.1B). The only restriction here is that the condition $\lambda_i S_i = 0 = \mu_j x_j$ should always be maintained. This means that if λ_i is in the basic solution at a *positive level*, S_i cannot become basic at positive level. Similarly, μ_j and x_j cannot be positive simultaneously. This is actually the same idea of the *restricted basis* used in Section 20.2.1. Phase I will end in the usual manner with the sum of the artificial variables equal to zero only if the problem has a feasible space. The feasibility of the solution space can be easily checked, however, by checking whether the system $\mathbf{AX} \leq \mathbf{b}, \mathbf{X} \geq \mathbf{0}$ encloses a feasible space.

Example 20.2-3. Consider the problem

$$\text{maximize } z = 4x_1 + 6x_2 - 2x_1^2 - 2x_1x_2 - 2x_2^2$$

subject to

$$x_1 + 2x_2 \leq 2$$
$$x_1, x_2 \geq 0$$

This problem can be put in matrix form as follows:

$$\text{maximize } z = (4, 6)\begin{pmatrix} x_1 \\ x_2 \end{pmatrix} + (x_1, x_2)\begin{pmatrix} -2 & -1 \\ -1 & -2 \end{pmatrix}\begin{pmatrix} x_1 \\ x_2 \end{pmatrix}$$

subject to

$$(1, 2)\begin{pmatrix} x_1 \\ x_2 \end{pmatrix} \leq 2$$
$$x_1, x_2 \geq 0$$

This automatically defines all the information required to construct the following Kuhn–Tucker conditions.

$$\left(\begin{array}{cc|c|cc|c} 4 & 2 & 1 & -1 & 0 & 0 \\ 2 & 4 & 2 & 0 & -1 & 0 \\ \hline 1 & 2 & 0 & 0 & 0 & 1 \end{array}\right)\begin{pmatrix} x_1 \\ x_2 \\ \lambda_1 \\ \mu_1 \\ \mu_2 \\ S_1 \end{pmatrix} = \begin{pmatrix} 4 \\ 6 \\ 2 \end{pmatrix}$$

The initial tableau for phase 1 is obtained by introducing the artificial variables R_1 and R_2. Thus

Basic	x_1	x_2	λ_1	μ_1	μ_2	R_1	R_2	S_1	Solution
r_0	6	6	3	-1	-1	0	0	0	10
R_1	4	2	1	-1	0	1	0	0	4
R_2	2	4	2	0	-1	0	1	0	6
S_1	1	2	0	0	0	0	0	1	2

First Iteration

Since $\mu_1 = 0$, the most promising entering variable x_1 (minimization problem) can be made basic with R_1 as the leaving variable. This yields the following tableau:

Basic	x_1	x_2	λ_1	μ_1	μ_2	R_1	R_2	S_1	Solution
r_0	0	3	3/2	1/2	−1	−3/2	0	0	4
x_1	1	1/2	1/4	−1/4	0	1/4	0	0	1
R_2	0	3	3/2	1/2	−1	−1/2	1	0	4
S_1	0	3/2	−1/4	1/4	0	−1/4	0	1	1

Second Iteration

The most promising variable x_2 can be made basic, since $\mu_2 = 0$. This gives

Basic	x_1	x_2	λ_1	μ_1	μ_2	R_1	R_2	S_1	Solution
r_0	0	0	2	0	−1	−1	0	−2	2
x_1	1	0	1/3	−1/3	0	1/3	0	−1/3	2/3
R_1	0	0	2	0	−1	0	1	−2	2
x_2	0	1	−1/6	1/6	0	−1/6	0	2/3	2/3

Third Iteration

Since $S_1 = 0$, λ_1 can be introduced into the solution. This yields

Basic	x_1	x_2	λ_1	μ_1	μ_2	R_1	R_2	S_1	Solution
r_0	0	0	0	0	0	−1	−1	0	0
x_1	1	0	0	−1/3	1/6	1/3	−1/6	0	1/3
λ_1	0	0	1	0	−1/2	0	1/2	−1	1
x_2	0	1	0	1/6	−1/12	−1/6	1/12	1/2	5/6

The last tableau gives the optimal solution for phase I. Since $r_0 = 0$, the solution given is feasible. Thus $x_1^* = 1/3$, $x_2^* = 5/6$. The optimal value of z can be computed from the original problem and is equal to 4.16. ◀

20.2.3 GEOMETRIC PROGRAMMING

A rather interesting technique for solving a special case of nonlinear problems is *geometric* programming. This technique, developed by R. Duffin and C. Zener in 1964, finds the solution by considering an associated dual problem (to be defined later). The advantage here is that it is usually much simpler computationally to work with the dual.

Geometric programming deals with problems in which the objective and the constraint functions are of the following type:

$$z = f(\mathbf{X}) = \sum_{j=1}^{N} U_j$$

where

$$U_j = c_j \prod_{i=1}^{n} x_i^{a_{ij}}, \qquad j = 1, 2, \ldots, N$$

It is assumed that all $c_j > 0$, and that N is finite. The exponents a_{ij} are unrestricted in sign. The function $f(\mathbf{X})$ takes the form of a polynomial except that the exponents a_{ij} may be negative. For this reason, and because all $c_j > 0$, Duffin and Zener give $f(\mathbf{X})$ the name **posynomial**.

This section will present the unconstrained case of geometric programming. The objective is to familiarize the reader with this type of analysis. The treatment of the constrained problem is beyond the scope of this chapter. The interested reader may refer to the excellent presentation by Beightler et al. (1979, Chap. 6) for a more detailed treatment of the subject.

Consider the *minimization* of the function $f(\mathbf{X})$ as defined in the posynomial form given. This problem will be referred to as the *primal*. The variables x_i are assumed to be *strictly positive* so that the region $x_i \leq 0$ represents an infeasible space. It will be shown later that the requirement $x_i \neq 0$ plays an essential part in the derivation of the results.

The first partial derivative of z must vanish at a minimum point. Thus,

$$\frac{\partial z}{\partial x_k} = \sum_{j=1}^{N} \frac{\partial U_j}{\partial x_k} = \sum_{j=1}^{N} c_j a_{kj} (x_k)^{a_{kj}-1} \prod_{i \neq k} (x_i)^{a_{ij}} = 0, \qquad k = 1, 2, \ldots, n$$

Since each $x_k > 0$ by assumption,

$$\frac{\partial z}{\partial x_k} = 0 = \frac{1}{x_k} \sum_{j=1}^{N} a_{kj} U_j, \qquad k = 1, 2, \ldots, n$$

Let z^* be the minimum value of z. It follows that $z^* > 0$, since z is posynomial and each $x_k^* > 0$. Define

$$y_j = \frac{U_j^*}{z^*}$$

which shows that $y_j > 0$ and $\sum_{j=1}^{N} y_j = 1$. The value of y_j thus represents the relative contribution of the jth term U_j to the optimal value of the objective function z^*.

The *necessary* conditions can now be written as

$$\sum_{j=1}^{N} a_{kj} y_j = 0, \qquad k = 1, 2, \ldots, n$$

$$\sum_{j=1}^{N} y_j = 1, \qquad y_j > 0 \quad \text{for all } j$$

These are known as the **orthogonality** and **normality conditions** and will yield a unique solution for y_j if $(n + 1) = N$ and all the equations are independent. The problem becomes more complex when $N > (n + 1)$ because the values of y_j are no longer unique. It is shown later, however, that it is possible to determine y_j uniquely for the purpose of minimizing z.

Suppose now that y_j^* are the unique values determined from the equations above. These values are used to determine z^* and x_i^*, $i = 1, 2, \ldots, n$, as follows. Consider

$$z^* = (z^*)^{\sum_{j=1}^{N} y_j^*}$$

Since $z^* = U_j^*/y_j^*$, it follows that

$$z^* = \left(\frac{U_1^*}{y_1^*}\right)^{y_1^*}\left(\frac{U_2^*}{y_2^*}\right)^{y_2^*} \cdots \left(\frac{U_N^*}{y_N^*}\right)^{y_N^*} = \left\{\prod_{j=1}^{N}\left(\frac{c_j}{y_j^*}\right)^{y_j^*}\right\}\left\{\prod_{j=1}^{N}\left(\prod_{i=1}^{N} x_i^{*a_{ij}}\right)^{y_j^*}\right\}$$

$$= \left\{\prod_{j=1}^{N}\left(\frac{c_j}{y_j^*}\right)^{y_j^*}\right\}\left\{\prod_{i=1}^{N}(x_i^*)^{\sum_{i=1}^{N} a_{ij}y_j^*}\right\} = \prod_{j=1}^{N}\left(\frac{c_j}{y_j^*}\right)^{y_j^*}$$

This step is justified, since $\sum_{j=1}^{N} a_{ij} y_j = 0$. The value of z^* is thus determined as soon as all y_j^* are determined. Now, given y_j^* and z^*, $U_j^* = y_j^* z^*$ can be determined. Since

$$U_j^* = c_j \prod_{i=1}^{N} (x_i^*)^{a_{ij}}, \qquad j = 1, 2, \ldots, n$$

simultaneous solution of these equations should yield x_i^*.

The procedure described shows that the solution to the original posynomial z can be transformed into the solution of a set of linear equations in y_j. Observe that all y_j^* are determined from the necessary conditions for a minimum. It can be shown, however, that these conditions are also sufficient. The proof (under the given restrictions on z) is given in Beightler et al. (1979, p. 333).

The variables y_j actually define the dual variables associated with the z-primal problem. To see this relationship, consider the primal problem in the form

$$z = \sum_{j=1}^{N} y_j\left(\frac{U_j}{y_j}\right)$$

Now define the function

$$w = \prod_{j=1}^{N}\left(\frac{U_j}{y_j}\right)^{y_j} = \prod_{j=1}^{N}\left(\frac{c_j}{y_j}\right)^{y_j}$$

Since $\sum_{j=1}^{N} y_j = 1$ and $y_j > 0$, by Cauchy's inequality,† we have

$$w \le z$$

The function w with its variables $y_1, y_2, \ldots, y_N$ defines the dual problem to the primal. Since w represents the lower bound on z and since z is associated with the minimization problem, it follows, by maximizing w, that

$$w^* = \max_{y_j} w = \min_{x_i} z = z^*$$

This means that the maximum value of w $(= w^*)$ over the values of y_j is equal to the minimum value of z $(= z^*)$ over the values of x_i.

Example 20.2-4. In this example a problem is considered in which $N = n + 1$ so that the solution to the orthogonality and normality conditions is unique. The next example will illustrate the other case, where $N > (n + 1)$.

† The Cauchy's inequality states that for $z_j > 0$,

$$\sum_{j=1}^{N} w_j z_j \ge \prod_{j=1}^{N} (z_j)^{w_j}, \qquad \text{where } w_j > 0 \text{ and } \sum_{j=1}^{N} w_j = 1$$

This is also called the arithmetic–geometric mean inequality.

Consider the problem

$$\text{minimize } z = 7x_1x_2^{-1} + 3x_2x_3^{-2} + 5x_1^{-3}x_2x_3 + x_1x_2x_3$$

This function may be written as

$$z = 7x_1^1x_2^{-1}x_3^0 + 3x_1^0x_2^1x_3^{-2} + 5x_1^{-3}x_2^1x_3^1 + x_1^1x_2^1x_3^1$$

so that

$$(c_1, c_2, c_3, c_4) = (7, 3, 5, 1)$$

$$\begin{pmatrix} a_{11} & a_{12} & a_{13} & a_{14} \\ a_{21} & a_{22} & a_{23} & a_{24} \\ a_{31} & a_{32} & a_{33} & a_{34} \end{pmatrix} = \begin{pmatrix} 1 & 0 & -3 & 1 \\ -1 & 1 & 1 & 1 \\ 0 & -2 & 1 & 1 \end{pmatrix}$$

The orthogonality and normality conditions are thus given by

$$\begin{pmatrix} 1 & 0 & -3 & 1 \\ -1 & 1 & 1 & 1 \\ 0 & -2 & 1 & 1 \\ 1 & 1 & 1 & 1 \end{pmatrix} \begin{pmatrix} y_1 \\ y_2 \\ y_3 \\ y_4 \end{pmatrix} = \begin{pmatrix} 0 \\ 0 \\ 0 \\ 1 \end{pmatrix}$$

This yields the unique solution

$$y_1^* = 12/24, \quad y_2^* = 4/24, \quad y_3^* = 5/24, \quad y_4^* = 3/24$$

Thus

$$z^* = \left(\frac{7}{12/24}\right)^{12/24} \left(\frac{3}{4/24}\right)^{4/24} \left(\frac{5}{5/24}\right)^{5/24} \left(\frac{1}{3/24}\right)^{3/24} = 15.22$$

From the equation $U_j^* = y_j^* z^*$ it follows that

$$\begin{aligned} 7x_1x_2^{-1} &= U_1 = (1/2)(15.22) = 7.61 \\ 3x_2x_3^{-2} &= U_2 = (1/6)(15.22) = 2.54 \\ 5x_1^{-3}x_2x_3 &= U_3 = (5/24)(15.22) = 3.17 \\ x_1x_2x_3 &= U_4 = (1/8)(15.22) = 1.90 \end{aligned}$$

The solution of these equations is given by

$$x_1^* = 1.315, \quad x_2^* = 1.21, \quad x_3^* = 1.2$$

which is the optimal solution to the primal. ◀

Example 20.2-5. Consider the problem

$$\text{minimize } z = 5x_1x_2^{-1} + 2x_1^{-1}x_2 + 5x_1 + x_2^{-1}$$

The orthogonality and normality conditions are given by

$$\begin{pmatrix} 1 & -1 & 1 & 0 \\ -1 & 1 & 0 & -1 \\ 1 & 1 & 1 & 1 \end{pmatrix} \begin{pmatrix} y_1 \\ y_2 \\ y_3 \\ y_4 \end{pmatrix} = \begin{pmatrix} 0 \\ 0 \\ 1 \end{pmatrix}$$

Since $N > n + 1$, these equations do not yield the required y_j directly. Thus solving for y_1, y_2, and y_3 in terms of y_4 gives

$$\begin{pmatrix} 1 & -1 & 1 \\ -1 & 1 & 0 \\ 1 & 1 & 1 \end{pmatrix}\begin{pmatrix} y_1 \\ y_2 \\ y_3 \end{pmatrix} = \begin{pmatrix} 0 \\ y_4 \\ 1 - y_4 \end{pmatrix}$$

or

$$y_1 = \frac{1 - 3y_4}{2}$$

$$y_2 = \frac{1 - y_4}{2}$$

$$y_3 = y_4$$

The dual problem may now be written as

$$\text{maximize } w = \left[\frac{5}{(1 - 3y_4)/2}\right]^{(1 - 3y_4)/2}\left[\frac{2}{(1 - y_4)/2}\right]^{(1 - y_4)/2}\left(\frac{5}{y_4}\right)^{y_4}\left(\frac{1}{y_4}\right)^{y_4}$$

Maximization of w is equivalent to maximization of $\ln w$. The latter is easier to manipulate, however. Thus,

$$\ln w = \frac{1 - 3y_4}{2}\{\ln 10 - \ln(1 - 3y_4)\} + \frac{1 - y_4}{2}\{\ln 4 - \ln(1 - y_4)\}$$
$$+ y_4\{\ln 5 - \ln y_4 + (\ln 1 - \ln y_4)\}$$

The value of y_4 maximizing $\ln w$ must be unique (since the primal problem has a unique minimum). Hence

$$\frac{\partial \ln w}{\partial y_4} = \left(\frac{-3}{2}\right)\ln 10 - \left\{\left(\frac{-3}{2}\right) + \left(\frac{-3}{2}\right)\ln(1 - 3y_4)\right\}$$
$$+ \left(\frac{-1}{2}\right)\ln 4 - \left\{\left(\frac{-1}{2}\right) + \left(\frac{-1}{2}\right)\ln(1 - y_4)\right\}$$
$$+ \ln 5 - \{1 + \ln y_4\} + \ln 1 - \{1 + \ln y_4\} = 0$$

This gives, after simplification,

$$-\ln\left(\frac{2 \times 10^{3/2}}{5}\right) + \ln\left[\frac{(1 - 3y_4)^{3/2}(1 - y_4)^{1/2}}{y_4^2}\right] = 0$$

or

$$\frac{\sqrt{(1 - 3y_4)^3(1 - y_4)}}{y_4^2} = 12.6$$

which yields $y_4^* \cong .16$. Hence $y_3^* = .16$, $y_2^* = .42$, and $y_1^* = .26$.

The value of z^* is obtained from

$$z^* = w^* = \left(\frac{5}{.26}\right)^{.26}\left(\frac{2}{.42}\right)^{.42}\left(\frac{5}{.16}\right)^{.16}\left(\frac{1}{.16}\right)^{.16} \cong 9.661$$

Hence

$$U_3 = .16(9.661) = 1.546 = 5x_1$$
$$U_4 = .16(9.661) = 1.546 = x_2^{-1}$$

The solution here yields $x_1^* = .309$ and $x_2^* = .647$. ◀

20.2.4 STOCHASTIC PROGRAMMING

Stochastic programming deals with situations where some or all parameters of the problem are described by random variables. Such cases seem typical of real-life problems, where it is difficult to determine the values of the parameters exactly. Chapter 5 shows that in linear programming sensitivity analysis can be used to study the effect of changes in problem's parameters on optimal solution. This, however, represents only a partial answer to the problem, especially when the parameters are actually random variables. The objective of stochastic programming is to consider these random effects explicitly in the solution of the model.

The basic idea of all stochastic programming models is to convert the probabilistic nature of the problem into an equivalent deterministic situation. Several models have been developed to handle special cases of the general problem. In this section the idea of employing deterministic equivalence is illustrated with the introduction of the interesting technique of **chance-constrained programming**.

A chance-constrained model is defined generally as

$$\text{maximize } z = \sum_{j=1}^{n} c_j x_j$$

subject to

$$P\left\{\sum_{j=1}^{n} a_{ij} x_j \le b_i\right\} \ge 1 - \alpha_i, \qquad i = 1, 2, \ldots, m; \quad x_j \ge 0, \quad \text{for all } j$$

The name "chance-constrained" follows from each constraint

$$\sum_{j=1}^{n} a_{ij} x_j \le b_i$$

being realized with a minimum probability of $1 - \alpha_i$, $0 < \alpha_i < 1$.

In the general case it is assumed that c_j, a_{ij}, and b_i are all random variables. The fact that c_j is a random variable can always be treated by replacing it by its expected value. In what follows, three cases are considered. The first two correspond to the separate considerations of a_{ij} and b_i as random variables. The third case combines the random effects of a_{ij} and b_i In all cases, it is assumed that the parameters are normally distributed with known means and variances.

Case 1: In this case, each a_{ij} is normally distributed with mean $E\{a_{ij}\}$ and variance $\text{var}\{a_{ij}\}$. Also, the covariance of a_{ij} and $a_{i'j'}$ is given by $\text{cov}\{a_{ij}, a_{i'j'}\}$.

Consider the ith constraint

$$P\left\{\sum_{j=1}^{n} a_{ij} x_j \le b_i\right\} \ge 1 - \alpha_i$$

and define

$$h_i = \sum_{j=1}^{n} a_{ij} x_j$$

Then h_i is normally distributed with

$$E\{h_i\} = \sum_{j=1}^{n} E\{a_{ij}\} x_j \qquad \text{and} \qquad \operatorname{var}\{h_i\} = \mathbf{X}^T \mathbf{D}_i \mathbf{X}$$

where $\mathbf{X} = (x_1, \ldots, x_n)^T$

$$\mathbf{D}_i = i\text{th covariance matrix} = \begin{pmatrix} \operatorname{var}\{a_{i1}\} & \cdots & \operatorname{cov}\{a_{i1}, a_{in}\} \\ \vdots & & \vdots \\ \operatorname{cov}\{a_{in}, a_{i1}\} & \cdots & \operatorname{var}\{a_{in}\} \end{pmatrix}$$

Now

$$P\{h_i \le b_i\} = P\left\{\frac{h_i - E\{h_i\}}{\sqrt{\operatorname{var}\{h_i\}}} \le \frac{b_i - E\{h_i\}}{\sqrt{\operatorname{var}\{h_i\}}}\right\} \ge 1 - \alpha_i$$

where $(h_i - E\{h_i\})/\sqrt{\operatorname{var}\{h_i\}}$ is standard normal with mean zero and variance one. This means that

$$P\{h_i \le b_i\} = \Phi\left(\frac{b_i - E\{h_i\}}{\sqrt{\operatorname{var}\{h_i\}}}\right)$$

where Φ represents the CDF of the standard normal distribution.

Let K_{α_i} be the standard normal value such that

$$\Phi(K_{\alpha_i}) = 1 - \alpha_i$$

Then the statement $P\{h_i \le b_i\} \ge 1 - \alpha_i$ is realized if and only if

$$\frac{b_i - E\{h_i\}}{\sqrt{\operatorname{var}\{h_i\}}} \ge K_{\alpha_i}$$

This yields the following nonlinear constraint:

$$\sum_{j=1}^{n} E\{a_{ij}\} x_j + K_{\alpha_i} \sqrt{\mathbf{X}^T \mathbf{D}_i \mathbf{X}} \le b_i$$

which is equivalent to the original stochastic constraint.

For the special case where the normal distributions are independent,

$$\operatorname{cov}\{a_{ij}, a_{i'j'}\} = 0$$

and the last constraint reduces to

$$\sum_{j=1}^{n} E\{a_{ij}\} x_j + K_{\alpha_i} \sqrt{\sum_{j=1}^{n} \operatorname{var}\{a_{ij}\} x_j^2} \le b_i$$

This constraint can now be put in the separable programming form (Section 20.2.1) by using the substitution

$$y_i = \sqrt{\sum_{j=1}^{n} \operatorname{var}\{a_{ij}\} x_j^2}, \qquad \text{for all } i$$

Thus the original constraint is equivalent to

$$\sum_{j=1}^{n} E\{a_{ij}\}x_j + K_{\alpha_i} y_i \leq b_i$$

and

$$\sum_{j=1}^{n} \text{var}\{a_{ij}\}x_j^2 - y_i^2 = 0$$

where $y_i \geq 0$.

Case 2: In this case only b_i is normal with mean $E\{b_i\}$ and variance $\text{var}\{b_i\}$. The analysis in this case is very similar to that of case 1. Consider the stochastic constraint

$$P\left\{b_i \geq \sum_{j=1}^{n} a_{ij}x_j\right\} \geq \alpha_i$$

As in case 1,

$$P\left\{\frac{b_i - E\{b_i\}}{\sqrt{\text{var}\{b_i\}}} \geq \frac{\sum_{j=1}^{n} a_{ij}x_j - E\{b_i\}}{\sqrt{\text{var}\{b_i\}}}\right\} \geq \alpha_i$$

This can hold only if

$$\frac{\sum_{j=1}^{n} a_{ij}x_j - E\{b_i\}}{\sqrt{\text{var}\{b_i\}}} \leq K_{\alpha_i}$$

Thus the stochastic constraint is equivalent to the deterministic linear constraint

$$\sum_{j=1}^{n} a_{ij}x_j \leq E\{b_i\} + K_{\alpha_i}\sqrt{\text{var}\{b_i\}}$$

Thus, in case 2, the chance-constrained model can be converted into an equivalent linear programming problem.

Example 20.2-6. Consider the chance-constrained problem

$$\text{maximize } z = 5x_1 + 6x_2 + 3x_3$$

subject to

$$P\{a_{11}x_1 + a_{12}x_2 + a_{13}x_3 \leq 8\} \geq .95$$
$$P\{5x_1 + x_2 + 6x_3 \leq b_2\} \geq .10$$

with all $x_j \geq 0$. Suppose that the a_{1j}'s are *independent* normally distributed random variables with the following means and variances:

$$E\{a_{11}\} = 1, \quad E\{a_{12}\} = 3, \quad E\{a_{13}\} = 9$$
$$\text{var}\{a_{11}\} = 25, \quad \text{var}\{a_{12}\} = 16, \quad \text{var}\{a_{13}\} = 4$$

The parameter b_2 is normally distributed with mean 7 and variance 9.

From standard normal tables,

$$K_{\alpha_1} = K_{.05} \cong 1.645, \qquad K_{\alpha_2} = K_{.10} \cong 1.285$$

For the first constraint, the equivalent deterministic constraint is given by

$$x_1 + 3x_2 + 9x_3 + 1.645\sqrt{25x_1^2 + 16x_2^2 + 4x_3^2} \leq 8$$

and for the second constraint

$$5x_1 + x_2 + 6x_3 \le 7 + 1.285(3) = 10.855$$

If we let

$$y^2 = 25x_1^2 + 16x_2^2 + 4x_3^2$$

the complete problem then becomes

$$\text{maximize } z = 5x_1 + 6x_1 + 3x_3$$

subject to

$$x_1 + 3x_2 + 9x_3 + 1.645y < 8$$
$$25x_1^2 + 16x_2^2 + 4x_3^2 - y^2 = 0$$
$$5x_1 + x_2 + 6x_3 \le 10.855$$
$$x_1, x_2, x_3, y \ge 0$$

which can be solved by separable programming. ◀

Case 3: In this case all a_{ij} and b_i are normal random variables. Consider the constraint

$$\sum_{j=1}^{n} a_{ij} x_j \le b_i$$

This may be written

$$\sum_{j=1}^{n} a_{ij} x_j - b_i \le 0$$

Since all a_{ij} and b_i are normal, it follows from the theory of statistics that $\sum_{j=1}^{n} a_{ij} x_j - b_i$ is also normal. This shows that the chance constraint reduces in this case to the same situation given in case 1 and is treated in a similar manner.

20.2.5 LINEAR COMBINATIONS METHOD

This method deals with a constrained problem in which all constraints are linear. Specifically, the problem is given as

$$\text{maximize } z = f(\mathbf{X})$$

subject to

$$\mathbf{AX} \le \mathbf{b}, \qquad \mathbf{X} \ge \mathbf{0}$$

where **A** is a matrix and **b** is a vector.

The procedure is based on the general idea of the steepest ascent (gradient) method (Section 20.1.2). However, the direction specified by the gradient vector may not yield a feasible solution for the constrained problem. Also, the gradient vector will not necessarily be null at the optimum (constrained) point. The steepest ascent method must be modified to handle the constrained case.

Let $\mathbf{X}^k$ be the *feasible* trial point at the kth iteration. The objective function $f(\mathbf{X})$ can be expanded in the neighborhood of $\mathbf{X}^k$ using Taylor's series. This gives

$$f(\mathbf{X}) \cong f(\mathbf{X}^k) + \nabla f(\mathbf{X}^k)(\mathbf{X} - \mathbf{X}^k) = (f(\mathbf{X}^k) - \nabla f(\mathbf{X}^k)\mathbf{X}^k) + \nabla f(\mathbf{X}^k)\mathbf{X}$$

The procedure calls for determining a feasible point $\mathbf{X} = \mathbf{X}^*$ such that $f(\mathbf{X})$ is maximized subject to the (linear) constraints of the problem. Since $(f(\mathbf{X}^k) - \nabla f(\mathbf{X}^k)\mathbf{X}^k)$ is a constant, the problem of determining $\mathbf{X}^*$ becomes

$$\text{maximize } w_k(\mathbf{X}) = \nabla f(\mathbf{X}^k)\mathbf{X}$$

subject to

$$\mathbf{AX} \leq \mathbf{b}, \qquad \mathbf{X} \geq \mathbf{0}$$

This is a linear programming problem in $\mathbf{X}$ that can now be used to determine $\mathbf{X}^*$.

Since w_k is constructed from the gradient of $f(\mathbf{X})$ at $\mathbf{X}^k$, an improved solution point can be secured if and only if $w_k(\mathbf{X}^*) > w_k(\mathbf{X}^k)$. From Taylor's expansion, this does not guarantee that $f(\mathbf{X}^*) > f(\mathbf{X}^k)$ unless $\mathbf{X}^*$ is in the neighborhood of $\mathbf{X}^k$. However, given $w_k(\mathbf{X}^*) > w_k(\mathbf{X}^k)$, there must exist a point $\mathbf{X}^{k+1}$ on the line segment $(\mathbf{X}^k; \mathbf{X}^*)$ such that $f(\mathbf{X}^{k+1}) > f(\mathbf{X}^k)$. The objective is to determine $\mathbf{X}^{k+1}$. Define

$$\mathbf{X}^{k+1} = (1 - r)\mathbf{X}^k + r\mathbf{X}^* = \mathbf{X}^k + r(\mathbf{X}^* - \mathbf{X}^k), \qquad 0 < r \leq 1$$

This means that $\mathbf{X}^{k+1}$ is a **linear combination** of $\mathbf{X}^k$ and $\mathbf{X}^*$. Since $\mathbf{X}^k$ and $\mathbf{X}^*$ are two feasible points in a *convex* solution space, $\mathbf{X}^{k+1}$ is also feasible. By comparison with the steepest ascent method (Section 20.1.2), the parameter r may be regarded as a step size.

The point $\mathbf{X}^{k+1}$ is determined such that $f(\mathbf{X})$ is maximized. Since $\mathbf{X}^{k+1}$ is a function of r only, the determination of $\mathbf{X}^{k+1}$ is secured by maximizing

$$h(r) = f[\mathbf{X}^k + r(\mathbf{X}^* - \mathbf{X}^k)]$$

in terms of r.

The procedure just described is repeated until at the kth iteration the condition $w_k(\mathbf{X}^*) \leq w_k(\mathbf{X}^k)$ is satisfied. At this point, no further improvements are possible. The process is then terminated with $\mathbf{X}^k$ as the best solution point.

The linear programming problems generated at the successive iterations differ only in the coefficients of the objective function. The sensitivity analysis procedures presented in Section 5.5 thus may be used to carry out calculations efficiently.

Example 20.2-7. Consider the quadratic programming of Example 20.2-3. This is given by

$$\text{maximize } f(\mathbf{X}) = 4x_1 + 6x_2 - 2x_1^2 - 2x_1x_2 - 2x_2^2$$

subject to

$$x_1 + 2x_2 \leq 2$$

where x_1 and x_2 are nonnegative.

Let the initial trial point be $\mathbf{X}^0 = (1/2, 1/2)$, which is feasible. Now

$$\nabla f(\mathbf{X}) = (4 - 4x_1 - 2x_2, 6 - 2x_1 - 4x_2)$$

First Iteration

$$\nabla f(\mathbf{X}^0) = (1, 3)$$

The associated linear program is to maximize $w_1 = x_1 + 3x_2$ subject to the same constraints as in the original problem. This gives the optimal solution $\mathbf{X}^* = (0, 1)$. The values of w_1 at $\mathbf{X}^0$ and $\mathbf{X}^*$ equal 2 and 3, respectively. Hence a new trial point must be determined. Thus

$$\mathbf{X}^1 = (1/2, 1/2) + r[(0, 1) - (1/2, 1/2)] = \left(\frac{1-r}{2}, \frac{1+r}{2}\right)$$

Now, maximization of

$$h(r) = f\left(\frac{1-r}{2}, \frac{1+r}{2}\right)$$

yields $r^1 = 1$. Thus $\mathbf{X}^1 = (0, 1)$ with $f(\mathbf{X}^1) = 4$.

Second Iteration

$$\nabla f(\mathbf{X}^1) = (2, 2)$$

The objective function of the new linear programming problem is $w_2 = 2x_1 + 2x_2$. The optimum solution to this problem yields $\mathbf{X}^* = (2, 0)$. Since the values of w_2 at $\mathbf{X}^1$ and $\mathbf{X}^*$ are 2 and 4 a new trial point must be determined. Thus

$$\mathbf{X}^2 = (0, 1) + r[(2, 0) - (0, 1)] = (2r, 1 - r)$$

The maximization of

$$h(r) = f(2r, 1 - r)$$

yields $r^2 = 1/6$. Thus $\mathbf{X}^2 = (1/3, 5/6)$ with $f(\mathbf{X})^2 \cong 4.16$.

Third Iteration

$$\nabla f(\mathbf{X}^2) = (1, 2)$$

The corresponding objective linear function is $w_3 = x_1 + 2x_2$. The optimum solution of this problem yields the alternative solutions $\mathbf{X}^* = (0, 1)$ and $\mathbf{X}^* = (2, 0)$. The value of w_3 for both values of $\mathbf{X}^*$ equals its value at $\mathbf{X}^2$. Consequently, no further improvements are possible. The *approximate* optimum solution is $\mathbf{X}^2 = (1/3, 5/6)$ with $f(\mathbf{X}^2) \cong 4.16$. This happens to be the exact optimum. ◀

20.2.6 SUMT ALGORITHM

In this section a more general gradient method is presented. It is assumed that the objective function $f(\mathbf{X})$ is concave and each constraint function $g_i(\mathbf{X})$ is convex. Moreover, the solution space must have an interior. This rules out both implicit and explicit use of *equality* constraints.

The SUMT (Sequential Unconstrained Maximization Technique) algorithm is based on transforming the constrained problem into an equivalent *un*constrained problem. The procedure is more or less similar to the use of the Lagrange multipliers method. The transformed problem can then be solved using the steepest ascent method (Section 20.1.2).

To clarify the concept, consider the new function

$$p(\mathbf{X}, t) = f(\mathbf{X}) + t\left(\sum_{i=1}^{m} \frac{1}{g_i(\mathbf{X})} - \sum_{j=1}^{n} \frac{1}{x_j}\right)$$

where t is a nonnegative parameter. The second summation sign is based on the nonnegativity constraints, which must be put in the form $-x_j \leq 0$ to conform with the original constraints $g_i(\mathbf{X}) \leq 0$. Since $g_i(\mathbf{X})$ is convex, $1/g_i(\mathbf{X})$ is concave. This means that $p(\mathbf{X}, t)$ is concave in $\mathbf{X}$. Consequently, $p(\mathbf{X}, t)$ possesses a unique maximum. It is now shown that optimization of the original constrained problem is equivalent to optimization of $p(\mathbf{X}, t)$.

The algorithm is initiated by arbitrarily selecting an initial *nonnegative* value for t. An initial point $\mathbf{X}^0$ is selected as the first trial solution. This point must be an interior point; that is, it must not lie on the boundaries of the solution space. Given the value of t, the steepest ascent method is used to determine the corresponding optimal solution (maximum) of $p(\mathbf{X}, t)$.

The new solution point will always be an interior point because if the solution point is close to the boundaries, at least one of the functions $1/g_i(\mathbf{X})$ or $(-1/x_i)$ will acquire a very large negative value. Since the objective is to maximize $p(\mathbf{X}, t)$, such solution points are automatically excluded. The main result is that successive solution points will always be interior points. Consequently, the problem can always be treated as an unconstrained case.

Once the optimum solution corresponding to a given value of t is reached, a new value of t is generated and the optimization process (using the steepest ascent method) is repeated. Thus, if t' is the current value of t, the next value, t'', must be selected such that $0 < t'' < t'$.

The SUMT procedure is terminated if, for two successive values of t, the corresponding *optimum* values of $\mathbf{X}$ obtained by maximizing $p(\mathbf{X}, t)$ are approximately the same. At this point further trials will produce little improvement.

Actual implementation of SUMT involves more details than have been presented here. Specifically, the selection of an initial value of t is a very important factor that affects speed of convergence. Further, determination of an initial interior point may require special techniques. These details can be found in Fiacco and McCormick (1968).

20.3 SUMMARY

The solution methods of nonlinear programming can generally be classified as either *direct* or *indirect* procedures. Examples of direct methods are the gradient algorithms, wherein the maximum (minimum) of a problem is sought by following the fastest rate of increase (decrease) of the objective function at a point. In indirect methods, the original problem is first transformed into an auxiliary one from which the optimum is determined. Examples of these situations include quadratic programming, separable programming, and stochastic programming. We note that the auxiliary problems in these cases may yield an *exact* or an *approximate* solution of the original problem. For example, the use of the Kuhn–Tucker conditions with quadratic programming yields an exact solution, whereas separable programming yields an approximate solution only.

SELECTED REFERENCES

BAZARAA, M., and C. SHETTY, *Nonlinear Programming, Theory and Algorithms*, Wiley, New York, 1979.

BEIGHTLER, C., D. PHILLIPS, and D. WILDE, *Foundations of Optimization*, 2nd ed., Prentice Hall, Englewood Cliffs, N.J., 1979.
FIACCO, A., and G. MCCORMICK, *Nonlinear Programming: Sequential Unconstrained Minimization Techniques*, Wiley, New York, 1968.
ZANGWILL, W., *Nonlinear Programming*, Prentice Hall, Englewood Cliffs, N.J., 1969.

PROBLEMS

Section	Assigned Problems
20.1.1	20–1 to 20–3
20.1.2	20–4, 20–5
20.2.1	20–6 to 20–14
20.2.2	20–15, 20–16
20.2.3	20–17 to 20–20
20.2.4	20–21, 20–22
20.2.5	20–23

☐ **20–1** Solve Example 20.1-1 assuming that $\Delta = .01$. Compare the accuracy of the results with that in Table 20-1.

☐ **20–2** Find the maximum of each of the following functions by dichotomous search. Assume that $\Delta = .05$.

(a) $f(x) = 1/|(x-3)^3|, \quad 2 \le x \le 4$
(b) $f(x) = x \cos x, \quad 0 \le x \le \pi$
(c) $f(x) = x \sin \pi x, \quad 1.5 \le x \le 2.5$
(d) $f(x) = -(x-3)^2, \quad 2 \le x \le 4$
(e) $f(x) = \begin{cases} 4x, & 0 \le x \le 2 \\ 4 - x, & 2 \le x \le 4 \end{cases}$

☐ **20–3** Develop an expression for determining the maximum number of iterations needed to terminate the dichotomous search method for a given value of Δ and an initial interval of uncertainty $I_0 = b - a$.

☐ **20–4** Show that, in general, the Newton–Raphson method (Section 19.1.2) when applied to a strictly concave quadratic function will converge in exactly one step. Apply the method to the maximization of

$$f(\mathbf{X}) = 4x_1 + 6x_2 - 2x_1^2 - 2x_1x_2 - 2x_2^2$$

☐ **20–5** Carry out at most five iterations for each of the following problems using the method of steepest descent (ascent). Assume that $\mathbf{X}^0 = \mathbf{0}$ in each case.

(a) $\min f(\mathbf{X}) = (x_2 - x_1^2)^2 + (1 - x_1)^2$
(b) $\max f(\mathbf{X}) = \mathbf{cX} + \mathbf{X}^T\mathbf{AX}$
where

$$\mathbf{c} = (1, 3, 5)$$

$$\mathbf{A} = \begin{pmatrix} -5 & -3 & -1/2 \\ -3 & -2 & 0 \\ -1/2 & 0 & -1/2 \end{pmatrix}$$

(c) $\max f(x) = 3 - x^2 - x^4$
(d) $\min f(\mathbf{X}) = x_1 - x_2 + x_1^2 - x_1 x_2$

□ **20–6** Formulate the following problem using the approximating mixed integer programming method.

$$\text{Maximize } z = e^{-x_1} + x_1 + (x_2 + 1)^2$$

subject to

$$x_1^2 + x_2 \leq 3$$
$$x_1, x_2 \geq 0$$

□ **20–7** Repeat Problem 20–6 using the restricted basis method. Then find the optimal solution.

□ **20–8** Consider the problem

$$\text{maximize } z = x_1 x_2 x_3$$

subject to

$$x_1^2 + x_2 + x_3 \leq 4$$
$$x_1, x_2, x_3 \geq 0$$

Approximate the problem as a linear programming model for use with the restricted basis method.

□ **20–9** Show how the following problem can be made separable.

$$\text{Maximize } z = x_1 x_2 + x_3 + x_1 x_3$$

subject to

$$x_1 x_2 + x_2 + x_1 x_3 \leq 10$$
$$x_1, x_2, x_3 \geq 0$$

□ **20–10** Show how the following problem can be made separable.

$$\text{Minimize } z = e^{2x_1 + x_2^2} + (x_3 - 2)^2$$

subject to

$$x_1 + x_2 + x_3 \leq 6$$
$$x_1, x_2, x_3 \geq 0$$

□ **20–11** Show how the following problem can be made separable.

$$\text{Maximize } z = e^{x_1 x_2} + x_2^2 x_3 + x_4$$

subject to

$$x_1 + x_2 x_3 + x_3 \leq 10$$
$$x_1, x_2, x_3 \leq 0$$
$$x_4 \text{ unrestricted in sign}$$

☐ **20–12** Show that in separable convex programming (Section 20.2.1), it is never optimal to have $x_{ki} > 0$ when $x_{k-1,i}$ is not at its upper nound.

☐ **20–13** Solve as a separable convex programming problem.

$$\text{Minimize } z = x_1^4 + 2x_2 + x_3^2$$

subject to

$$x_1^2 + x_2 + x_3^2 \leq 4$$
$$|x_1 + x_2| \leq 0$$
$$x_1, x_3 \geq 0$$
$$x_2 \text{ unrestricted in sign}$$

☐ **20–14** Solve the following as a separate convex programming problem.

$$\text{Minimize } z = (x_1 - 2)^2 + 4(x_2 - 6)^2$$

subject to

$$6x_1 + 3(x_2 + 1)^2 \leq 12$$
$$x_1, x_2 \geq 0$$

☐ **20–15** Consider the problem

$$\text{maximize } z = 6x_1 + 3x_2 - 4x_1x_2 - 2x_1^2 - 3x_2^2$$

subject to

$$x_1 + x_2 \leq 1$$
$$2x_1 + 3x_2 \leq 4$$
$$x_1, x_2 \leq 0$$

Show that z is strictly concave and then solve the problem using the quadratic programming algorithm.

☐ **20–16** Consider the problem:

$$\text{minimize } z = 2x_1^2 + 2x_2^2 + 3x_3^2 + 2x_1x_2 + 2x_2x_3 + x_1 - 3x_2 - 5x_3$$

subject to

$$x_1 + x_2 + x_3 \geq 1$$
$$3x_1 + 2x_2 + x_3 \leq 6$$
$$x_1, x_2, x_3 \geq 0$$

Show that z is strictly convex and then solve by the quadratic programming technique.

☐ **20–17** Solve the following problem by geometric programming.

$$\text{Minimize } z = 2x_1^{-1}x_2^2 + x_1^4x_2^{-2} + 4x_1^2$$
$$x_1, x_2 > 0$$

☐ **20–18** Solve the following problem by geometric programming.

$$\text{Minimize } z = 5x_1x_2^{-1}x_3^2 + x_1^{-2}x_3^{-1} + 10x_2^3 + 2x_1^{-1}x_2x_3^{-3}$$
$$x_1, x_2, x_3 > 0$$

☐ **20–19** Solve the following problem by geometric programming.

$$\text{Minimize } z = 2x_1^2x_2^{-3} + 8x_1^{-3}x_2 + 3x_1x_2$$

☐ **20–20** Solve the following problem by geometric programming.

$$\text{Minimize } z = 2x_1^3x_2^{-3} + 4x_1^{-2}x_2 + x_1x_2 + 8x_1x_2^{-1}$$
$$x_1, x_2 > 0$$

☐ **20–21** Convert the following stochastic problem into an equivalent deterministic model.

$$\text{Maximize } z = x_1 + 2x_2 + 5x_3$$

subject to

$$P\{a_1x_1 + 3x_2 + a_3x_3 \le 10\} \ge 0.9$$
$$P\{7x_1 + 5x_2 + x_3 \le b_2\} \ge 0.1$$
$$x_1, x_2, x_3 \ge 0$$

Assume that a_1 and a_3 are independent and normally distributed random variables with means $E\{a_1\} = 2$ and $E\{a_3\} = 5$ and variances $\text{var}\{a_1\} = 9$ and $\text{var}\{a_3\} = 16$. Assume further that b_2 is normally distributed with mean 15 and variance 25.

☐ **20–22** Consider the following stochastic programming model:

$$\text{maximize } z = x_1 + x_2^2 + x_3$$

subject to

$$P\{x_1^2 + a_2x_2^3 + a_3\sqrt{x_3} \le 10\} \ge 0.9$$
$$x_1, x_2, x_3 \ge 0$$

where a_2 and a_3 are independent and normally distributed random variables with means 5 and 2, and variance 16 and 25, respectively. Convert the problem into the (deterministic) separable programming form.

☐ **20–23** Solve the following problem by the linear combinations method.

$$\text{Minimize } f(\mathbf{X}) = x_1^3 + x_2^3 - 3x_1x_2$$

subject to

$$3x_1 + x_2 \le 3$$
$$5x_1 - 3x_2 \le 5$$
$$x_1, x_2 \ge 0$$

Appendix A

Review of Vectors and Matrices

A.1 VECTORS

A.1.1 DEFINITION OF A VECTOR

Let $p_1, p_2, \ldots, p_n$ be any n real numbers and **P** an ordered set of these real numbers, that is,

$$\mathbf{P} = (p_1, p_2, \ldots, p_n)$$

Then **P** is called an n-vector (or simply a vector). The ith component of **P** is given by p_i. For example, $\mathbf{P} = (1, 2)$ is a two-dimensional vector that joins the origin and point (1, 2).

A.1.2 ADDITION (SUBTRACTION) OF VECTORS

Let

$$\mathbf{P} = (p_1, p_2, \ldots, p_n) \qquad \text{and} \qquad \mathbf{Q} = (q_1, q_2, \ldots, q_n)$$

be two vectors in the n-dimensional space. Then the components of the vector $\mathbf{R} = (r_1, r_2, \ldots, r_n)$ such that $\mathbf{R} = \mathbf{P} \pm \mathbf{Q}$ are given by

$$r_i = p_i \pm q_i$$

In general, given the vectors **P**, **Q**, and **S**,

$$\mathbf{P} \pm \mathbf{Q} = \mathbf{Q} \pm \mathbf{P} \qquad \text{(commutative law)}$$

$$(\mathbf{P} + \mathbf{Q}) + \mathbf{S} = \mathbf{P} + (\mathbf{Q} + \mathbf{S}) \qquad \text{(associative law)}$$

$$\mathbf{P} + (-\mathbf{P}) = \mathbf{0}, \qquad \text{a zero (or null) vector}$$

A.1.3 MULTIPLICATION OF VECTORS BY SCALARS

Given a vector **P** and a scalar (constant) quantity θ, the new vector

$$\mathbf{Q} = \theta\mathbf{P} = (\theta p_1, \theta p_2, \ldots, \theta p_n)$$

is called the *scalar product* of **P** and θ.

In general, given the vectors **P** and **S** and the scalars θ and γ,

$$\theta(\mathbf{P} + \mathbf{S}) = \theta\mathbf{P} + \theta\mathbf{S} \qquad \text{(distributive law)}$$

$$\theta(\gamma\mathbf{P}) = (\theta\gamma)\mathbf{P} \qquad \text{(associative law)}$$

A.1.4 LINEARLY INDEPENDENT VECTORS

A set of vectors $\mathbf{P}_1, \mathbf{P}_2, \ldots, \mathbf{P}_n$ is said to be *linearly independent* if and only if, for all real θ_j,

$$\sum_{j=1}^{n} \theta_j \mathbf{P}_j = \mathbf{0}$$

implies that all $\theta_j = 0$, where the θ_j are scalar quantities. If

$$\sum_{j=1}^{n} \theta_j \mathbf{P}_j = \mathbf{0}$$

for some $\theta_j \neq 0$, the vectors are said to be *linearly dependent*. For example, the vectors

$$\mathbf{P}_1 = (1, 2,) \qquad \text{and} \qquad \mathbf{P}_2 = (2, 4)$$

are linearly dependent, since there exist $\theta_1 = 2$ and $\theta_2 = -1$ for which

$$\theta_1 \mathbf{P}_1 + \theta_2 \mathbf{P}_2 = \mathbf{0}$$

A.2 MATRICES

A.2.1 DEFINITION OF A MATRIX

A matrix is a rectangular array of elements. The (i, j)th element a_{ij} of the matrix **A** stands in the ith row and jth column of the array. The order (size) of a matrix is said to be $(m \times n)$ if the matrix includes m rows and n columns. For example,

$$\mathbf{A} = \begin{pmatrix} a_{11} & a_{12} & a_{13} \\ a_{21} & a_{22} & a_{23} \\ a_{31} & a_{32} & a_{33} \\ a_{41} & a_{42} & a_{43} \end{pmatrix} = \|a_{ij}\|_{4 \times 3}$$

is a (4×3)-matrix.

A.2.2 TYPES OF MATRICES

1. A *square* matrix is a matrix in which $m = n$.

2. An **identity** matrix is a square matrix in which all the diagonal elements are one and all the off-diagonal elements are zero; that is,

$$a_{ij} = 1, \qquad \text{for } i = j$$
$$a_{ij} = 0, \qquad \text{for } i \neq j$$

For example, a (3×3) identity matrix is given by

$$\mathbf{I}_3 = \begin{pmatrix} 1 & 0 & 0 \\ 0 & 1 & 0 \\ 0 & 0 & 1 \end{pmatrix}$$

3. A *row vector* is a matrix with one row and n columns.

4. A *column vector* is a matrix with m rows and one column.

5. The matrix $\mathbf{A}^T$ is called the **transpose** of $\mathbf{A}$ if the element a_{ij} in $\mathbf{A}$ is equal to element a_{ji} in $\mathbf{A}^T$ for all i and j. For example, if

$$\mathbf{A} = \begin{pmatrix} 1 & 4 \\ 2 & 5 \\ 3 & 6 \end{pmatrix}$$

then

$$\mathbf{A}^T = \begin{pmatrix} 1 & 2 & 3 \\ 4 & 5 & 6 \end{pmatrix}$$

In general, $\mathbf{A}^T$ is obtained by interchanging the rows and columns of $\mathbf{A}$. Consequently, if $\mathbf{A}$ is of the order $(m \times n)$, $\mathbf{A}^T$ is of the order $(n \times m)$.

6. A matrix $\mathbf{B} = \mathbf{0}$ is called a **zero matrix** if every element of $\mathbf{B}$ is equal to zero.

7. Two matrices $\mathbf{A} = \|a_{ij}\|$ and $\mathbf{B} = \|b_{ij}\|$ are said to be *equal matrices* if and only if they have the same order and if each element a_{ij} is equal to the corresponding b_{ij} for all i and j.

A.2.3 MATRIX ARITHMETIC OPERATIONS

In matrices only addition (subtraction) and multiplication are defined. The division, although not defined, is replaced by the concept of inversion (see Section A.2.6).

A. Addition (Subtraction) of Matrices

Two matrices $\mathbf{A} = \|a_{ij}\|$ and $\mathbf{B} = \|b_{ij}\|$ can be added together if they are of the same order $(m \times n)$. The sum $\mathbf{D} = \mathbf{A} + \mathbf{B}$ is obtained by adding the corresponding elements. Thus,

$$\|d_{ij}\|_{m \times n} = \|a_{ij} + b_{ij}\|_{m \times n}$$

If one assumes that the matrices **A**, **B**, and **C** have the same order,

$$\mathbf{A} \pm \mathbf{B} = \mathbf{B} \pm \mathbf{A} \qquad \text{(commutative law)}$$
$$\mathbf{A} \pm (\mathbf{B} \pm \mathbf{C}) = (\mathbf{A} \pm \mathbf{B}) \pm \mathbf{C} \qquad \text{(associative law)}$$
$$(\mathbf{A} \pm \mathbf{B})^T = \mathbf{A}^T \pm \mathbf{B}^T$$

B. Product of Matrices

Two matrices $\mathbf{A} = \|a_{ij}\|$ and $\mathbf{B} = \|b_{ij}\|$ can be multiplied in the order **AB** if and only if the number of columns of **A** is equal to the number of rows of **B**. That is, if **A** is of the order $(m \times r)$, then **B** is of the order $(r \times n)$, where m and n are arbitrary sizes.

Let **D** = **AB**. Then **D** is of the order $(m \times n)$, and its elements d_{ij} are given by

$$d_{ij} = \sum_{k=1}^{r} A_{ik} b_{kj}, \qquad \text{for all } i \text{ and } j$$

For example, if

$$\mathbf{A} = \begin{pmatrix} 1 & 3 \\ 2 & 4 \end{pmatrix} \qquad \text{and} \qquad \mathbf{B} = \begin{pmatrix} 5 & 7 & 9 \\ 6 & 8 & 0 \end{pmatrix}$$

then

$$\mathbf{D} = \begin{pmatrix} 1 & 3 \\ 2 & 4 \end{pmatrix}\begin{pmatrix} 5 & 7 & 9 \\ 6 & 8 & 0 \end{pmatrix} = \begin{pmatrix} (1 \times 5 + 3 \times 6) & (1 \times 7 + 3 \times 8) & (1 \times 9 + 3 \times 0) \\ (2 \times 5 + 4 \times 6) & (2 \times 7 + 4 \times 8) & (2 \times 9 + 4 \times 0) \end{pmatrix}$$
$$= \begin{pmatrix} 23 & 31 & 9 \\ 34 & 46 & 18 \end{pmatrix}$$

Notice that, in general, $\mathbf{AB} \neq \mathbf{BA}$ even if **BA** is defined.

Matrix multiplication follows these general properties:

$$\mathbf{I}_m \mathbf{A} = \mathbf{A}\mathbf{I}_n = \mathbf{A}, \qquad \text{where } \mathbf{I} \text{ is an identity matrix}$$
$$(\mathbf{AB})\mathbf{C} = \mathbf{A}(\mathbf{BC})$$
$$\mathbf{C}(\mathbf{A} + \mathbf{B}) = \mathbf{CA} + \mathbf{CB}$$
$$(\mathbf{A} + \mathbf{B})\mathbf{C} = \mathbf{AC} + \mathbf{BC}$$
$$\alpha(\mathbf{AB}) = (\alpha\mathbf{A})\mathbf{B} = \mathbf{A}(\alpha\mathbf{B}), \qquad \alpha \text{ is a scalar}$$

C. Multiplication of Partitioned Matrices

Let **A** be an $(m \times r)$-matrix and **B** an $(r \times n)$-matrix. If **A** and **B** are partitioned into the following submatrices

$$\mathbf{A} = \left(\begin{array}{c|c|c} \mathbf{A}_{11} & \mathbf{A}_{12} & \mathbf{A}_{13} \\ \hline \mathbf{A}_{21} & \mathbf{A}_{22} & \mathbf{A}_{23} \end{array}\right) \qquad \text{and} \qquad \mathbf{B} = \left(\begin{array}{c|c} \mathbf{B}_{11} & \mathbf{B}_{12} \\ \hline \mathbf{B}_{21} & \mathbf{B}_{22} \\ \hline \mathbf{B}_{31} & \mathbf{B}_{32} \end{array}\right)$$

such that the number of columns of $\mathbf{A}_{ij}$ is equal to the number of rows of $\mathbf{B}_{ji}$ and such that the number of columns of $\mathbf{A}_{ij}$ and $\mathbf{A}_{i+1,j}$ are equal, for all i and j, then

$$\mathbf{A} \times \mathbf{B} = \left(\begin{array}{c|c} \mathbf{A}_{11}\mathbf{B}_{11} + \mathbf{A}_{12}\mathbf{B}_{21} + \mathbf{A}_{13}\mathbf{B}_{31} & \mathbf{A}_{11}\mathbf{B}_{12} + \mathbf{A}_{12}\mathbf{B}_{22} + \mathbf{A}_{13}\mathbf{B}_{32} \\ \hline \mathbf{A}_{21}\mathbf{B}_{11} + \mathbf{A}_{22}\mathbf{B}_{21} + \mathbf{A}_{23}\mathbf{B}_{31} & \mathbf{A}_{21}\mathbf{B}_{12} + \mathbf{A}_{22}\mathbf{B}_{22} + \mathbf{A}_{23}\mathbf{B}_{32} \end{array}\right)$$

For example,

$$\left(\begin{array}{c|cc} 1 & 2 & 3 \\ \hline 1 & 0 & 5 \\ 2 & 5 & 6 \end{array}\right)\begin{pmatrix} 4 \\ \hline 1 \\ 8 \end{pmatrix} = \begin{pmatrix} (1)(4) + (2 \quad 3)\begin{pmatrix} 1 \\ 8 \end{pmatrix} \\ \hline \begin{pmatrix} 1 \\ 2 \end{pmatrix}(4) + \begin{pmatrix} 0 & 5 \\ 5 & 6 \end{pmatrix}\begin{pmatrix} 1 \\ 8 \end{pmatrix} \end{pmatrix} = \begin{pmatrix} 4 + 2 + 24 \\ \hline \begin{pmatrix} 4 \\ 8 \end{pmatrix} + \begin{pmatrix} 40 \\ 53 \end{pmatrix} \end{pmatrix} = \begin{pmatrix} 40 \\ 44 \\ 61 \end{pmatrix}$$

The usefulness of partitioned matrices will come later in considering the inversion of matrices.

A.2.4 THE DETERMINANT OF A SQUARE MATRIX

Given the n-square matrix

$$\mathbf{A} = \begin{pmatrix} a_{11} & a_{12} & \cdots & a_{1n} \\ a_{21} & a_{22} & \cdots & a_{2n} \\ \vdots & \vdots & & \vdots \\ a_{n1} & a_{n2} & \cdots & a_{nn} \end{pmatrix}$$

consider the product

$$P_{j_1 j_2 \cdots j_n} = a_{1j_1} a_{2j_2} \cdots a_{nj_n}$$

the elements of which are selected such that each column and each row of $\mathbf{A}$ is represented exactly once among the subscripts of $P_{j_1 j_2 \cdots j_n}$. Next define $\epsilon_{j_1 j_2 \cdots j_n}$ equal to $+1$ if $j_1 j_2 \cdots j_n$ is an even permutation and -1 if $j_1 j_2 \cdots j_n$ is an odd permutation. Thus the scalar

$$\sum_{\rho} \epsilon_{j_1 j_2 \cdots j_n} P_{j_1 j_2 \cdots j_n}$$

is called the *determinant* of $\mathbf{A}$, where ρ represents the summation over all $n!$ permutations. The notation det $\mathbf{A}$ or $|\mathbf{A}|$ is usually used to represent the determinant of $\mathbf{A}$.

To illustrate, consider

$$\mathbf{A} = \begin{pmatrix} a_{11} & a_{12} & a_{13} \\ a_{21} & a_{22} & a_{23} \\ a_{31} & a_{32} & a_{33} \end{pmatrix}$$

Then

$$|\mathbf{A}| = a_{11}(a_{22}a_{33} - a_{23}a_{32}) - a_{12}(a_{21}a_{33} - a_{31}a_{23}) + a_{13}(a_{21}a_{32} - a_{22}a_{31})$$

The major properties of determinants can be summarized as follows:

1. If every element of a column or a row is zero, then the value of the determinant is zero.
2. The value of the determinant is not changed if its rows and columns are interchanged.
3. If $\mathbf{B}$ is obtained from $\mathbf{A}$ by interchanging any two of its rows (or columns), then $|\mathbf{B}| = -|\mathbf{A}|$.
4. If two rows (or columns) of $\mathbf{A}$ are identical, then $|\mathbf{A}| = 0$.
5. The value of $|\mathbf{A}|$ remains the same if a scalar α times a column (row) vector of $\mathbf{A}$ is added to another column (row) vector of $\mathbf{A}$.

6. If every element of a column (or a row) of a determinant is multiplied by a scalar α, the value of the determinant is multiplied by α.

7. If **A** and **B** are two n-square matrices, then

$$|\mathbf{AB}| = |\mathbf{A}|\,|\mathbf{B}|$$

Definition of the Minor of a Determinant. The minor M_{ij} of the element a_{ij} in the determinant $|\mathbf{A}|$ is obtained from the matrix **A** by striking out the ith row and jth column of **A**. For example, for

$$\mathbf{A} = \begin{pmatrix} a_{11} & a_{12} & a_{13} \\ a_{21} & a_{22} & a_{23} \\ a_{31} & a_{32} & a_{33} \end{pmatrix}$$

$$M_{11} = \begin{vmatrix} a_{22} & a_{23} \\ a_{32} & a_{33} \end{vmatrix}, \quad M_{22} = \begin{vmatrix} a_{11} & a_{13} \\ a_{31} & a_{33} \end{vmatrix}, \ldots$$

Definition of the Adjoint Matrix. Let $A_{ij} = (-1)^{i+j}M_{ij}$ be defined as the **cofactor** of the element a_{ij} of the square matrix **A**. Then, by definition, the adjoint matrix of **A** is given by

$$\text{adj } \mathbf{A} = \|A_{ij}\|^T = \begin{pmatrix} A_{11} & A_{21} & \cdots & A_{n1} \\ A_{12} & A_{22} & \cdots & A_{n2} \\ \vdots & \vdots & & \\ A_{1n} & A_{2n} & \cdots & A_{nn} \end{pmatrix}$$

For example, if

$$\mathbf{A} = \begin{pmatrix} 1 & 2 & 3 \\ 2 & 3 & 2 \\ 3 & 3 & 4 \end{pmatrix}$$

then, $A_{11} = (-1)^2(3 \times 4 - 2 \times 3) = 6$, $A_{12} = (-1)^3(2 \times 4 - 2 \times 3) = -2, \ldots$, or

$$\text{adj } \mathbf{A} = \begin{pmatrix} 6 & 1 & -5 \\ -2 & -5 & 4 \\ -3 & 3 & -1 \end{pmatrix}$$

A.2.5 NONSINGULAR MATRIX

A matrix is of a rank r if the largest *square* array in the matrix with nonvanishing determinant is of order r. A *square* matrix whose determinant does not vanish is called a **full-rank** or a **nonsingular** matrix. For example,

$$\mathbf{A} = \begin{pmatrix} 1 & 2 & 3 \\ 2 & 3 & 4 \\ 3 & 5 & 7 \end{pmatrix}$$

is a **singular** matrix, since

$$|\mathbf{A}| = 1(21 - 20) - 2(14 - 12) + 3(10 - 9) = 0$$

But **A** has a rank $r = 2$, since

$$\begin{pmatrix} 1 & 2 \\ 2 & 3 \end{pmatrix} = -1 \neq 0$$

A.2.6 THE INVERSE OF A MATRIX

If **B** and **C** are two n-square matrices such that $\mathbf{BC} = \mathbf{CB} = \mathbf{I}$, then **B** is called the inverse of **C** and **C** the inverse of **B**. The common notation for the inverses is $\mathbf{B}^{-1}$ and $\mathbf{C}^{-1}$.

Theorem. *If* $\mathbf{BC} = \mathbf{I}$ *and* **B** *is* **nonsingular**, *then* $\mathbf{C} = \mathbf{B}^{-1}$, *which means that the inverse is unique.*

PROOF. By assumption,

$$\mathbf{BC} = \mathbf{I}$$

then

$$\mathbf{B}^{-1}\mathbf{BC} = \mathbf{B}^{-1}\mathbf{I}$$

or

$$\mathbf{IC} = \mathbf{B}^{-1}$$

or

$$\mathbf{C} = \mathbf{B}^{-1}$$

Two important results can be proved for nonsingular matrices:

1. If **A** and **B** are nonsingular n-square matrices, then $(\mathbf{AB})^{-1} = \mathbf{B}^{-1}\mathbf{A}^{-1}$.
2. If **A** is nonsingular, then $\mathbf{AB} = \mathbf{AC}$ implies that $\mathbf{B} = \mathbf{C}$.

The concept of matrix inversion is useful in solving n linearly independent equations. Consider

$$\begin{pmatrix} a_{11} & a_{12} & \cdots & a_{1n} \\ a_{21} & a_{22} & \cdots & a_{2n} \\ \vdots & \vdots & & \vdots \\ a_{n1} & a_{n2} & \cdots & a_{nn} \end{pmatrix} \begin{pmatrix} x_1 \\ x_2 \\ \vdots \\ x_n \end{pmatrix} = \begin{pmatrix} b_1 \\ b_2 \\ \vdots \\ b_n \end{pmatrix}$$

where x_i represent the unknowns and a_{ij} and b_i are constants. These n equations can be written in the form

$$\mathbf{AX} = \mathbf{b}$$

Since the equations are independent, it follows that **A** is nonsingular. Thus

$$\mathbf{A}^{-1}\mathbf{AX} = \mathbf{A}^{-1}\mathbf{b} \quad \text{or} \quad \mathbf{X} = \mathbf{A}^{-1}\mathbf{b}$$

gives the solution of the n unknowns.

A.2.7 METHODS OF COMPUTING THE INVERSE OF A MATRIX

A. Adjoint Matrix Method

Given $\mathbf{A}$ a nonsingular matrix of size n,

$$\mathbf{A}^{-1} = \frac{1}{|\mathbf{A}|} \text{adj } \mathbf{A} = \frac{1}{|\mathbf{A}|} \begin{pmatrix} A_{11} & A_{21} & \cdots & A_{n1} \\ A_{12} & A_{22} & \cdots & A_{n2} \\ \vdots & \vdots & & \vdots \\ A_{1n} & A_{2n} & \cdots & A_{nn} \end{pmatrix}$$

For example, for

$$\mathbf{A} = \begin{pmatrix} 1 & 2 & 3 \\ 2 & 3 & 2 \\ 3 & 3 & 4 \end{pmatrix}$$

$$\text{adj } \mathbf{A} = \begin{pmatrix} 6 & 1 & -5 \\ -2 & -5 & 4 \\ -3 & 3 & -1 \end{pmatrix} \qquad \text{and} \qquad |\mathbf{A}| = -7$$

Hence

$$\mathbf{A}^{-1} = \frac{1}{-7} \begin{pmatrix} 6 & 1 & -5 \\ -2 & -5 & 4 \\ -3 & 2 & -1 \end{pmatrix} = \begin{pmatrix} -6/7 & -1/7 & 5/7 \\ 2/7 & 5/7 & -4/7 \\ 3/7 & -3/7 & 1/7 \end{pmatrix}$$

B. Row Operations (Gauss–Jordan) Method

Consider the partitioned matrix $(\mathbf{A} | \mathbf{I})$, where $\mathbf{A}$ is nonsingular. By premultiplying this matrix by $\mathbf{A}^{-1}$, we obtain

$$(\mathbf{A}^{-1}\mathbf{A} | \mathbf{A}^{-1}\mathbf{I}) = (\mathbf{I} | \mathbf{A}^{-1})$$

Thus, by applying a sequence of row transformations only, the matrix $\mathbf{A}$ is changed to $\mathbf{I}$ and $\mathbf{I}$ is changed to $\mathbf{A}^{-1}$.

For example, consider the system of equations of the form $\mathbf{AX} = \mathbf{b}$:

$$\begin{pmatrix} 1 & 2 & 3 \\ 2 & 3 & 2 \\ 3 & 3 & 4 \end{pmatrix} \begin{pmatrix} x_1 \\ x_2 \\ x_3 \end{pmatrix} = \begin{pmatrix} 3 \\ 4 \\ 5 \end{pmatrix}$$

The solution of $\mathbf{X}$ and the inverse of basis matrix can be obtained directly by considering

$$\mathbf{A}^{-1}(\mathbf{A} | \mathbf{I} | \mathbf{b}) = (\mathbf{I} | \mathbf{A}^{-1} | \mathbf{A}^{-1}\mathbf{b})$$

Thus, by a row transformation operation, we get

$$\left(\begin{array}{ccc|ccc|c} 1 & 2 & 3 & 1 & 0 & 0 & 3 \\ 2 & 3 & 2 & 0 & 1 & 0 & 4 \\ 3 & 3 & 4 & 0 & 0 & 1 & 5 \end{array}\right)$$

Iteration 1:

$$\left(\begin{array}{ccc|ccc|c} 1 & 2 & 3 & 1 & 0 & 0 & 3 \\ 0 & -1 & -4 & -2 & 1 & 0 & -2 \\ 0 & -3 & -5 & -3 & 0 & 1 & -4 \end{array}\right)$$

Iteration 2:

$$\left(\begin{array}{ccc|ccc|c} 1 & 0 & -5 & -3 & 2 & 0 & -1 \\ 0 & 1 & 4 & 2 & -1 & 0 & 2 \\ 0 & 0 & 7 & 3 & -3 & 1 & 2 \end{array}\right)$$

Iteration 3:

$$\left(\begin{array}{ccc|ccc|c} 1 & 0 & 0 & -6/7 & -1/7 & 5/7 & 3/7 \\ 0 & 1 & 0 & 2/7 & 5/7 & -4/7 & 6/7 \\ 0 & 0 & 1 & 3/7 & -3/7 & 1/7 & 2/7 \end{array}\right)$$

This gives $x_1 = 3/7$, $x_2 = 6/7$, and $x_3 = 2/7$. The inverse of **A** is given by the right-hand-side matrix. This is the same as the inverse obtained by the method of adjoint matrix.

C. Partitioned Matrix Method

Let the two nonsingular matrices **A** and **B** of size n be partitioned as shown here such that $\mathbf{A}_{11}$ is nonsingular.

$$\mathbf{A} = \left(\begin{array}{c|c} \mathbf{A}_{11} & \mathbf{A}_{12} \\ (p \times p) & (p \times q) \\ \hline \mathbf{A}_{21} & \mathbf{A}_{22} \\ (q \times p) & (q \times q) \end{array}\right) \quad \text{and} \quad \mathbf{B} = \left(\begin{array}{c|c} \mathbf{B}_{11} & \mathbf{B}_{12} \\ (p \times p) & (p \times q) \\ \hline \mathbf{B}_{21} & \mathbf{B}_{22} \\ (q \times p) & (q \times q) \end{array}\right)$$

If **B** is the inverse of **A**, from $\mathbf{AB} = \mathbf{I}_n$,

$$\mathbf{A}_{11}\mathbf{B}_{11} + \mathbf{A}_{12}\mathbf{B}_{21} = \mathbf{I}_p$$
$$\mathbf{A}_{11}\mathbf{B}_{12} + \mathbf{A}_{12}\mathbf{B}_{22} = \mathbf{0}$$

Also, from $\mathbf{BA} = \mathbf{I}_n$,

$$\mathbf{B}_{21}\mathbf{A}_{11} + \mathbf{B}_{22}\mathbf{A}_{21} = \mathbf{0}$$
$$\mathbf{B}_{21}\mathbf{A}_{12} + \mathbf{B}_{22}\mathbf{A}_{22} = \mathbf{I}_q$$

Since $\mathbf{A}_{11}$ is nonsingular, that is, $|\mathbf{A}_{11}| \neq 0$, solving for $\mathbf{B}_{11}$, $\mathbf{B}_{12}$, $\mathbf{B}_{21}$, and $\mathbf{B}_{22}$, we get

$$\mathbf{B}_{11} = \mathbf{A}_{11}^{-1} + (\mathbf{A}_{11}^{-1}\mathbf{A}_{12})\mathbf{D}^{-1}(\mathbf{A}_{21}\mathbf{A}_{11}^{-1})$$
$$\mathbf{B}_{12} = -(\mathbf{A}_{11}^{-1}\mathbf{A}_{12})\mathbf{D}^{-1}$$
$$\mathbf{B}_{21} = -\mathbf{D}^{-1}(\mathbf{A}_{21}\mathbf{A}_{11}^{-1})$$
$$\mathbf{B}_{22} = \mathbf{D}^{-1}$$

where

$$\mathbf{D} = \mathbf{A}_{22} - \mathbf{A}_{21}(\mathbf{A}_{11}^{-1}\mathbf{A}_{12})$$

To illustrate the use of these formulas, consider the example given previously,

$$\mathbf{A} = \left(\begin{array}{c|cc} 1 & 2 & 3 \\ \hline 2 & 3 & 2 \\ 3 & 3 & 4 \end{array}\right)$$

where

$$\mathbf{A}_{11} = (1), \quad \mathbf{A}_{12} = (2, 3), \quad \mathbf{A}_{21} = \begin{pmatrix} 2 \\ 3 \end{pmatrix}, \quad \text{and} \quad \mathbf{A}_{22} = \begin{pmatrix} 3 & 2 \\ 3 & 4 \end{pmatrix}$$

It is obvious that $\mathbf{A}_{11}^{-1} = 1$ and

$$\mathbf{D} = \begin{pmatrix} 3 & 2 \\ 3 & 4 \end{pmatrix} - \begin{pmatrix} 2 \\ 3 \end{pmatrix}(1)(2, 3) = \begin{pmatrix} -1 & -4 \\ -3 & -5 \end{pmatrix}$$

$$\mathbf{D}^{-1} = -1/7\begin{pmatrix} -5 & 4 \\ 3 & -1 \end{pmatrix} = \begin{pmatrix} 5/7 & -4/7 \\ -3/7 & 1/7 \end{pmatrix}$$

Thus

$$\mathbf{B}_{11} = (-6/7) \quad \text{and} \quad \mathbf{B}_{12} = (-1/7 \quad 5/7)$$

$$\mathbf{B}_{21} = \begin{pmatrix} 2/7 \\ 3/7 \end{pmatrix} \quad \text{and} \quad \mathbf{B}_{22} = \begin{pmatrix} 5/7 & -4/7 \\ -3/7 & 1/7 \end{pmatrix}$$

which directly give $\mathbf{B} = \mathbf{A}^{-1}$.

A.3 QUADRATIC FORMS

Given

$$\mathbf{X} = (x_1, x_2, \ldots, x_n)^T$$

and

$$\mathbf{A} = \begin{pmatrix} a_{11} & a_{12} & \cdots & a_{1n} \\ a_{21} & a_{22} & \cdots & a_{2n} \\ \vdots & \vdots & & \vdots \\ a_{n1} & a_{n2} & \cdots & a_{nn} \end{pmatrix}$$

the function

$$Q(\mathbf{X}) = \mathbf{X}^T\mathbf{A}\mathbf{X} = \sum_{i=1}^{n} \sum_{j=1}^{n} a_{ij} x_i x_j$$

is called a *quadratic form*. The matrix $\mathbf{A}$ can always be assumed symmetric, since each element of every pair of coefficients a_{ij} and a_{ji} $(i \neq j)$ can be replaced by $(a_{ij} + a_{ji})/2$ without changing the value of $Q(\mathbf{X})$. This assumption has several advantages and hence is taken as a restriction.

To illustrate, the quadratic form

$$Q(\mathbf{X}) = (x_1, x_2, x_3)\begin{pmatrix} 1 & 0 & 1 \\ 2 & 7 & 6 \\ 3 & 0 & 2 \end{pmatrix}\begin{pmatrix} x_1 \\ x_2 \\ x_3 \end{pmatrix}$$

is the same as

$$Q(\mathbf{X}) = (x_1, x_2, x_3)\begin{pmatrix} 1 & 1 & 2 \\ 1 & 7 & 3 \\ 2 & 3 & 2 \end{pmatrix}\begin{pmatrix} x_1 \\ x_2 \\ x_3 \end{pmatrix}$$

Note that $\mathbf{A}$ is symmetric in the second case.

The quadratic form is said to be

1. *Positive-definite* if $Q(\mathbf{X}) > 0$ for every $\mathbf{X} \neq \mathbf{0}$.
2. *Positive-semidefinite* if $Q(\mathbf{X}) \geq \mathbf{0}$ for every $\mathbf{X}$ and there exists $\mathbf{X} \neq \mathbf{0}$ such that $Q(\mathbf{X}) = \mathbf{0}$.
3. *Negative-definite* if $-Q(\mathbf{X})$ is positive-definite.
4. *Negative-semidefinite* if $-Q(\mathbf{X})$ is positive-semidefinite.
5. *Indefinite* if it is none of these cases.

It can be proved that the necessary and sufficient conditions for the realization of the cases above are given by

1. $Q(\mathbf{X})$ is positive-definite (semidefinite) if the values of the principal minor determinants of $\mathbf{A}$ are positive (nonnegative).† In this case $\mathbf{A}$ is said to be positive-definite (semidefinite).
2. $Q(\mathbf{X})$ is negative-definite if the value of kth principal minor determinant of $\mathbf{A}$ has the sign of $(-1)^k$, $k = 1, 2, \ldots, n$. In the case, $\mathbf{A}$ is called negative-definite.
3. $Q(\mathbf{X})$ is a negative-semidefinite if the kth principal minor determinant of $\mathbf{A}$ is either zero or has the sign of $(-1)^k$, $k = 1, 2, \ldots, n$.

A.4 CONVEX AND CONCAVE FUNCTIONS

A function $f(\mathbf{X})$ is said to be strictly convex if, for any two distinct points $\mathbf{X}_1$ and $\mathbf{X}_2$,

$$f(\lambda\mathbf{X}_1 + (1-\lambda)\mathbf{X}_2) < \lambda f(\mathbf{X}_1) + (1-\lambda)f(\mathbf{X}_2)$$

where $0 < \lambda < 1$. On the other hand, a function $f(\mathbf{X})$ is strictly concave if $-f(\mathbf{X})$ is strictly convex.

An important special case of the convex (concave) function is the quadratic form (see Section A.3)

$$f(\mathbf{X}) = \mathbf{CX} + \mathbf{X}^T\mathbf{AX}$$

where $\mathbf{C}$ is a constant vector and $\mathbf{A}$ is a symmetric matrix. It can be proved that $f(\mathbf{X})$ is strictly convex if $\mathbf{A}$ is positive-definite. Similarly, $f(\mathbf{X})$ is strictly concave if $\mathbf{A}$ is negative-definite.

---

† The kth *principal minor* determinant of $\mathbf{A}_{n \times n}$ is defined by

$$\begin{vmatrix} a_{11} & a_{12} & \cdots & a_{1k} \\ a_{21} & a_{11} & \cdots & a_{2k} \\ \vdots & \vdots & & \vdots \\ a_{k1} & a_{k2} & & a_{kk} \end{vmatrix}, \qquad k = 1, 2, \ldots, n$$

SELECTED REFERENCES

Hadley, G., *Matrix Algebra*, Addison-Wesley, Reading, Mass., 1961.
Hohn, F., *Elementary Matrix Algebra*, 2nd ed., Macmillan, New York, 1964.

PROBLEMS

☐ **A–1** Show that the following vectors are linearly dependent.

(a) $\begin{pmatrix} 1 \\ -2 \\ 3 \end{pmatrix} \quad \begin{pmatrix} -2 \\ 4 \\ -2 \end{pmatrix} \quad \begin{pmatrix} 1 \\ -2 \\ -1 \end{pmatrix}$

(b) $\begin{pmatrix} 2 \\ -3 \\ 4 \\ 5 \end{pmatrix} \quad \begin{pmatrix} 4 \\ -6 \\ 8 \\ 10 \end{pmatrix}$

☐ **A–2** Given

$$\mathbf{A} = \begin{pmatrix} 1 & 4 & 9 \\ 2 & 5 & -8 \\ 3 & 7 & 2 \end{pmatrix} \quad \text{and} \quad \mathbf{B} = \begin{pmatrix} 7 & -1 & 2 \\ 9 & 4 & 8 \\ 3 & 6 & 10 \end{pmatrix}$$

find

(a) $\mathbf{A} + 7\mathbf{B}$
(b) $2\mathbf{A} - 3\mathbf{B}$
(c) $(\mathbf{A} + 7\mathbf{B})^T$

☐ **A–3** In Problem A–2, show that $\mathbf{AB} \neq \mathbf{BA}$.

☐ **A–4** Given the partitioned matrices

$$\mathbf{A} = \left(\begin{array}{c|cc} 1 & 5 & 7 \\ 2 & -6 & 9 \\ \hline 3 & 7 & 2 \\ 4 & 9 & 1 \end{array}\right) \quad \text{and} \quad \mathbf{B} = \left(\begin{array}{cccc} 2 & 3 & -4 & 5 \\ \hline 1 & 2 & 6 & 7 \\ 3 & 1 & 0 & 9 \end{array}\right)$$

find **AB** using partitioning.

☐ **A–5** In Problem A–2, find $\mathbf{A}^{-1}$ and $\mathbf{B}^{-1}$ using:

(a) The adjoint matrix method
(b) The row operations method
(c) The partitioned matrix method

☐ **A–6** Verify the formulas given in Section A.2.7C for obtaining the inverse of a partitioned matrix.

☐ **A–7** Find the inverse of

$$\mathrm{A} = \begin{pmatrix} 1 & \mathbf{G} \\ \mathbf{H} & \mathbf{B} \end{pmatrix}$$

where **B** is a nonsingular matrix.

☐ **A–8** Show that the quadratic form

$$Q(x_1, x_2) = 6x_1 + 3x_2 - 4x_1x_2 - 2x_1^2 - 3x_2^2 - 27/4$$

is negative-definite.

☐ **A–9** Show that the quadratic form

$$Q(x_1, x_2, x_3) = 2x_1^2 + 2x_2^2 + 3x_3^2 + 2x_1x_2 + 2x_2x_3$$

is positive-definite.

☐ **A–10** Show that the function $f(x) = e^x$ is strictly convex over all real values of x.

☐ **A–11** Show that the quadratic function

$$f(x_1, x_2, x_3) = 5x_1^2 + 5x_2^2 + 4x_3^2 + 4x_1x_2 + 2x_2x_3$$

is strictly convex.

☐ **A–12** In Problem A–11, show that $-f(x_1, x_2, x_3)$ is strictly concave.

Appendix B

Software (TORA and SIMNET II) Installation and Execution

In this appendix we provide instructions for the installation and execution of TORA and SIMNET II. Both systems run on the IBM PC/XT/AT and true compatible. A hard disk and MS-DOS 3.2 or later version are required. A math coprocessor is strongly recommended for the SIMNET II system. TORA and SIMNET II will each operate within 512K RAM.

B.1 TORA SYSTEM

The TORA software solves linear programming, integer programming, transportation, networks, PERT CPM, histograms/forecasting, inventory, and queueing. The system may be used in a user-guided tutorial mode or in a production mode. TORA is totally menu driven, hence requires no user's manual. The system has its tailored editor whose functions are displayed at the top of the editing screen. TORA is custom designed for the book and hence uses the same format and notation employed throughout this volume.

To install TORA, create a directory and copy TORA.EXE from the TORA diskette. Execution is initiated by typing TORA and pressing RETURN.

B.2 SIMNET II SYSTEM

An editor/execution environment named SIMEDIT can be used with SIMNET II. The SIMEDIT/SIMNET II environment is installed by copying all the contents of the SIMNET II diskettes into a single directory on the hard disk. The directory must then include the following files: simedit.bat, simnet.bat, inp.exe, sa0.exe, sca.exe, and t8.exe.

You may execute SIMNET II models without the SIMEDIT environment by entering

SIMNET filename ⟨press RETURN⟩

In this case, "filename" must be a SIMNET II ASCII file representing the model that you desire to execute. You may also include a path as part of the file name.

The SIMEDIT environment is invoked in the following manner:

1. Type SIMEDIT and press RETURN.
2. Enter ALT-F to invoke file menu, then press:
   F2 to load an old file (the same function may be realized by typing SIMEDIT followed by the filename),
   F3 to save current edited version of the file,
   F4 to edit a new file,
   F5 to provide a new name for the edited file,
   F6 to enter the DOS shell,
   ALT-X to exit SIMEDIT.
3. For the combination (ALT-F) + F2 (load an old file), or SIMEDIT followed by filename, if *.* or a partial name of a file (e.g., fn*.*) is entered, a proper directory with reverse video select mode will be displayed. The name of any of the displayed files may then be entered into the editor by moving the reverse video bar to the correct location and then pressing RETURN.
4. Use the editor commands (press F1 for editor help) to edit the file. Note in particular that ALT-P can be used to print a *blocked* segment of a file (created with ALT-L). If the file is unblocked, ALT-P will print the entire file.
5. After finishing the editing session, the file should be saved (a reminder to do so will appear on the screen at the end of the editing session).
6. To execute a SIMNET II file, you have two options:
   a. If you press ALT-R, you will enter a menu from which you can hit RETURN to start execution. This option gives you the chance to change your mind about starting the execution simply by pressing ESC.
   b. If you press CTRL-F9 from the edit screen, execution will start immediately.
7. After execution is completed, SIMEDIT will automatically display the SIMNET II output, which may now be examined by the user. If you wish to reedit the (SIMNET II) input file, simply press ALT-E. Actually, ALT-E is a toggle switch that will allow you to alternate back and forth between the input and output files.
8. At any time you may press F6 to enter the DOS shell. To return to SIMEDIT from DOS, type EXIT and press RETURN.
9. You can "cancel" any menu by pressing ESC.
10. SIMEDIT provides a complete SIMNET II help. Press CTRL-F1 to invoke help. Then by entering the first letter of the element for which you need help, SIMEDIT will "step" through all the elements that start with that letter. For example, if you press P (after CTRL-F1), you will get help for $PROJECT, PROC, $PLOT, and so on.

Answers to Selected Problems

Chapter 2

2–3 Produce 8 tables and 32 chairs; $z = \$2680$.

2–4 Mix 52.94 lb of corn and 37.06 lb of soybean meal; $z = \$32.82$.

2–5 Car loans = \$13,333 and personal loans = \$6667; $z = 2457.33$.

2–6 Allocate 12,000 lb of tomato for juice and 48,000 lb for paste; $z = \$6300$.

2–7 Produce approximately 36 units of HiFi-1 and 46 units of HiFi-2. (Exact values are 36.48 and 46.08.)

2–8 Produce 60 units of model 1 and 25 units of 2; $z = \$2300$.

2–9 Produce 54.55 units of product 1 and 10.9 units of 2; $z = \$141.8$.

2–10 Use 18.2 radio minutes and 9.1 TV minutes; $z = 245.7$.

2–11 Alternative optima at $(x_A, x_B) = (21.4, 14.3)$, or $(50, 0)$, or any point on the line segment joining the two points; $z = \$1000$.

2–12 Produce 150 hats of type 1 and 200 of type 2; $z = \$2200$.

2–13 System reduces to $4x_1 + 3x_2 \leq 12$, $-x_1 + x_2 \geq 1$, $x_1 \geq 0$.

2–14 $x_1 + x_2 \leq 5$, $x_1 - 2x_2 \leq 2$, $x_1 \geq 1$, $-x_1 + x_2 \leq 1$, $x_2 \geq 0$.

2–16 $(x_1, x_2) = (-10, -6)$; $z = -86$.

2–18 $(x_1, x_2) = (5, 5)$; $z = 35$.

2–19 $x_1 = 5$: $\{(5, 0), (5, 5)\}$; optimum at $(5, 5)$ with $z = 35$. $x_1 \leq 5$: $\{(0, 0), (5, 0), (5, 5), (0, 10)\}$; optimum at $(5, 5)$ with $z = 35$. $x_1 \geq 5$: $\{(5, 0), (5, 5), (10, 0)\}$; optimum at $(10, 0)$ with $z = 50$.

2–20 (a) Minimum at $(1, 0)$; $z = 2$. (b) Maximum at $(2, 3)$; $z = 6$. (e) Minimum at $(1, 0)$ or $(1, 2)$; $z = 1$. (f) Maximum at $(4, 1)$; $z = 4$.

2–21 (a) Dual price = 83.75, range = $(0, \infty)$. (b) Dual price = -8.125, range = $(-64, 64)$. (c) $-4 \leq C_1/C_2 \leq 4$ and use $d_1 = C_1 - 135$ and $d_2 = C_2 - 50$.

2–22 Constraint 1: dual price = .3674, range = $(0, \infty)$. Constraint 2: dual price = 0, range = $(0, 772.94)$. Constraint 3: dual price = 0, range = $(-270, 47.65)$. Constraint 4: dual price = $-.0078$, range = $(-405, 1890)$.

2–23 Dual price = \$.12286, range = $(0, \infty)$.

2–24 (a) Machine 1: dual price = 0, range = $(403.2, 495.36)$. Machine 2: dual price = 3, range = $(360, 427.2)$. Machine 3: dual price = 0, range = $(393.6, 495.36)$.

2–25 (a) Component constraint: dual price = 2.5, range = $(600, 1200)$. (b) $1.25 \leq C_1/C_2 < \infty$. (c) Line 1: dual price = 5, range = $(20, 80)$. Line 2: dual price = 0, range = $(25, \infty)$.

2–26 (a) Machine 1: dual price = .05458, range = $(514.27, 750)$. Machine 2: dual price = 0, range = $(545.456, \infty)$. Machine 3: dual price = .1818, range = $(480, 635.284)$. (b) $8/5 \leq C_1 \leq 30/5$, $1 \leq C_2 \leq 15/4$.

2–27 (a) Budget constraint: dual price = .2455, range = $(0, \infty)$. Limit constraint: dual price = $-.2273$, range = $(-20, 200)$. (b) Do not increase radio advertisement. (c) Ratio of sales of radio to TV > 1.25/25.

2–28 Maximize $z = 30x_1 + 30x_2 + 10x_3 + 15x_4$ subject to $2x_1 + 3x_2 + 4x_3 + 2x_4 \leq 500$, $3x_1 + 2x_2 + x_3 + 2x_4 \leq 380$, $x_1, x_2, x_3, x_4 \geq 0$.

2–29 Maximize $z = 30x_1 + 20x_2 + 50x_3$ subject to $2x_1 + 3x_2 + 5x_3 \leq 4000$, $4x_1 + 2x_2 + 7x_3 \leq 6000$, $x_1 + x_2/2 + x_3/3 \leq 1500$, $x_1/3 = x_2/2 = x_3/5$, $x_1 \geq 200$, $x_2 \geq 200$, $x_3 \geq 150$.

2–32 Let x_{ij} = amount invested in year i in plan j; $j = A, B$. Maximize $z = 3x_{2A} + 1.7x_{3A}$ subject to $x_{1A} + x_{1B} \leq 100{,}000$, $-1.7x_{1A} + x_{2A} + x_{2B} \leq 0$, $-3x_{1B} - 1.7x_{2A} + x_{3A} \leq 0$, all $x_{ij} \geq 0$.

2–36 Maximize $z = y$ subject to $-3x_1 + 4x_2 - 7x_3 + 15x_4 \geq y$, $5x_1 - 3x_2 + 9x_3 + 4x_4 \geq y$, $3x_1 - 9x_2 + 10x_3 - 8x_4 \geq y$, $x_1 + x_2 + x_3 + x_4 \leq 500$.

2–38 Maximize $z = 6x_1 + 4x_2 - 5(y_1'' + y_2'')$ subject to $x_1/5 + x_2/6 + y_1' - y_1'' = 8$, $x_1/4 + x_2/8 + y_2' - y_2'' = 8$, $y_1'' \leq 4$, $y_2'' \leq 4$, all variables ≥ 0.

Chapter 3

3–1 (b) Feasible extreme points: (0, 0), (2, 0), (6/7, 12/7), (0, 2). (c) Corresponding z: 0, 4, 48/7, 6. Optimum: (6/7, 12/7), $z = 48/7$.

3–2 (a) Corresponding z: 0, 12, 48/7, 2. Optimum: (2, 0), $z = 12$. (b) Corresponding z: 0, 4, 108/7, 16. Optimum: (0, 2), $z = 16$.

3–5 (a) 15. (b) (8, 0, 3, 0, 0, 0), (0, 0, 0, 0, 2, 1), (2, 0, 0, 0, 0, 3), (0, 1/2, 0, 0, 0, 0), (0, 0, 1/3, 0, 8/3, 0), (0, 0, 0, 1/4, 0/0) (c) Optimum: (8, 0, 3, 0, 0, 0), $z = 31$.

3–6 Six possible bases. Feasible extreme points: (4, 0, 0, 0), (0, 2, 0, 0). Alternative optima at either extreme point with $z = 4$.

3–7 (a) Six possible bases. Feasible extreme points: (4, 1, 0, 0), (9/2, 0, 3/2, 0), (6, 0, 0, 3). (b) Optimum: (6, 0, 0, 3), $z = 6$.

3–8 (a) (1) Yes. (2) No. (3) No. (4) No. (b) (1) Yes. (2) Yes. (3) No, C and I are not adjacent. (7) No, iterations cannot return to a previous extreme point.

3–9 A: Basic (s_1, s_2, s_3, s_4); nonbasic (x_1, x_2, x_3). E: Basic (x_1, x_2, s_3, s_4); nonbasic (s_1, s_2, x_3).

3–10 (a) $A \to B$: x_1 enters, s_2 leaves. (b) $E \to I$: x_3 enters, s_4 leaves.

3–11 (a) x_3 enters, improvement = 3. (b) x_1 enters, improvement = 5.

3–12 (a) $E = (5/2, 2)$, $z = 39/2$. (b) x_2 enters; $A \to G \to F \to E$. (c) Ratios = (2, 3, 5); x_1 enters at value 2. (d) Ratios = (1, 2, 4); x_2 enters at value 1. (e) Improvements are 8 when x_1 enters and 2 when x_2 enters.

3–13

Entering variable	x_1	x_2	x_3	x_4
Its value	3/2	1	0	0
Leaving variable	x_7	x_7	x_8	x_8

3–14

Entering variable	x_2	x_4	x_5	x_6	x_7
Its value	3	2	0	∞	2
Change in z	+15	−8	0	$+\infty$	0
Leaving variable	x_3	x_3	x_1	none	x_3

3–15 (a) (1.625, −1.114, 2.42). (b) (−3/4, 37/4, −17/4).

3–16 (a) Three iterations: (0, 1.71, 0, 4.86); $z = 26$. (b) Four iterations: (0, 2.2, 10.2, 0); $z = 43.8$. (c) Four iterations: (0, 2.2, 10.2, 0); $z = 28.4$. (d) Two iterations: (0, 3.33, 0, 0); $z = -13.33$. (e) Two iterations: (0, 0, 8, 0); $z = -16$.

3–17 $x_1 = 90$, all others = 0, $z = 450$.

3–18 (a) Four iterations. (b) Three iterations. (c) Computational experience shows that the criterion in part (a) is generally more efficient. (d) Number of iterations is the same. z-rows appear with opposite signs.

3–19 Three iterations: (0, 0, 3/2, 0, 8, 0); $z = 3$.

3–20 $32/5 \leq \max z \leq 21$.

3–21 (a) $z - (5 - 2M)x_1 - (6 + 3M)x_2 = -3M$. (b) $z - (2 + 6M)x_1 - (-7 + 16M)x_2 + Ms_2 + Ms_5 = -18M$. (c) $z - (3 - 4M)x_1 - (6 - 8M)x_2 - Ms_5 = 5M$.

3–22 (a) Three iterations: (45/7, 4/7, 0); $z = 102/7$.

3–23 Two iterations: (2, 0, 1); $z = 5$.

3–24 Three iterations: (0, 2, 2, 0); $z = 16$.

3–25 Three iterations: (0, 7/4, 0, 33/4); $z = 7/2$.

3–26 (a) Minimize R_1. (c) Minimize R_5.

3–28 (a) Two iterations: $(x_1 = 0, x_2 = 5)$; $z = 15$. (b) Three iterations: $(x_1 = 2, x_2 = 0)$; $z = 10$.

3–31 (a) No feasible solution. (b) $(x_1 = 3, x_2 = 1)$, $z = 0$, (c) Unbounded.

3–32 (a) $A \to B \to C \to D$. (b) A, B, D: one iteration; C: $C_2^4 = 6$ iterations.

3–34 Four alternative basic optima are (0, 0, 10/3, 0, 5, 1); (0, 5, 0, 0, 0, 1); (1, 4, 1/3, 0, 0, 0); (1, 0, 3, 0, 4, 0).

3–37 Solution space is unbounded in the direction of x_2 and optimum z is unbounded also because of x_2.

3–39 (a) Scarce, scarce, abundant. (b) $y_1 = 5/8$, $y_2 = 1/8$, $y_3 = 0$. (c) Resource 1. (d) $-4 \le D_1 \le 12$. (e) $-4 \le D_2 \le 2$. (f) $6 \le z \le 16$, $8 \le z \le 70/8$. (g) $-1/3 \le d_1 \le 5$. (h) $-5/4 \le d_2 \le 1/4$.

3–40 (a) Scarce, abundant. (b) $-5 \le D_1 \le 3$, $-3/2 \le D_2 < \infty$. (c) $0 \le z \le 16$, $z = 10$. (d) $d_1 \le 0$. (e) $0 \le d_2 < \infty$.

3–41 (a) (1) $D_1 = 70$: $x_6 = -120$, infeasible. (2) $D_1 = -30$: (0, 85, 230), $z = 1320$. (3) $D_2 = -10$: (0, 102.5, 225), $z = 1330$. (4) $D_3 = 20$: (0, 100, 230), $z = 1350$. (5) $D_3 = -40$: $x_6 = -20$, infeasible. (b) (1) $d_1 = -1$: solution remains optimal. (2) $d_1 = 6$: x_1 enters. (3) $d_2 = 3$: solution remains optimal. (4) $d_3 = -4$: x_1 enters.

3–42 $x_1 = 7/8$, $x_2 = 7/2$, $z = 77/8$.

3–43 $-5 \le D1 \le 3 + 2D_2$.

3–46 $\sum_{j=1}^{n} a_{ij} x_j \le b_i$ and $\sum_{j=1}^{n} a_{ij} x_j \ge -b_i$.

3–47 Minimize $z = v$ subject to $\sum_{j=1}^{n} c_{ij} x_j \le v$, $\sum_{j=1}^{n} c_{ij} x_j \ge -v$, for all i, $v \ge 0$.

Chapter 4

4–1 (a) $\mathbf{A} = \begin{pmatrix} 3 & 2 & 0 \\ 4 & -2 & -1 \end{pmatrix}$, $\mathbf{b} = \begin{pmatrix} 5 \\ 2 \end{pmatrix}$, $c = (2, 5, 0, 0, 0, M)$.

4–3 Basis: B_1 and B_2, nonbasis: B_3 and B_4.

4–4 det $B_1 = -1$, det $B_2 = -3$, det $B_3 =$ det $B_4 = 0$.

4–5 (a) Unique solution with $x_1 > 0$ and $x_2 < 0$. (b) Unique solution with x_1 and $x_2 > 0$. (c) Unique solution with $x_1 < 0$ and $x_2 = 0$. (d) Infinity of solutions. (e) No solution. (f) No solution.

4–6 (a) det $= -4$, basis. (b) det $= -8$, basis. (c) det $= 0$, nonbasis.

4–7 (a) P_1 leaves. (b) Yes, P_2 and P_4 form a feasible basis.

4–8 Five basic feasible solution corresponding to the bases (P_1, P_2), (P_1, P_4), (P_2, P_3), (P_2, P_4) and (P_3, P_4), but a total of three feasible extreme points: (0, 2, 0, 0), (3, 0, 0, 1), and (0, 0, 6, 4).

4–9

Extreme Point	Basic Variables
(4, 0, 0, 0, 0)	(x_1, x_3), (x_1, x_4), (x_1, x_5)
(0, 2, 0, 0, 0)	(x_2, x_3), (x_2, x_4), (x_2, x_5)
(0, 0, 12/5, 0, 14/5)	(x_3, x_5)
(0, 0, 0, 12, 4)	(x_4, x_5)

4–11 (a)

Basic	x_1	x_2	x_3	x_4	x_5	x_6	Solution
x_4	−1/2	2	0	1	−1/2	0	0
x_3	3/2	0	1	0	1/2	0	30
x_6	1	4	0	0	0	1	20

4–13 (a) $(x_2, x_4) = (3, 15)$; feasible. (d) $(x_1, x_4) = (21/2, -105/2)$; infeasible.

4–14 (a)

Basic	x_1	x_2	x_3	x_4	x_5	Solution
z	0	0	−2/5	−1/5	0	12/5
x_1	1	0	−3/5	1/5	0	3/5
x_2	0	1	4/5	−3/5	0	6/5
x_5	0	0	−1	1	1	0

(b) Solution is optimal and feasible.

4–15 (a) Not optimal because the z-coefficients of x_1 and x_2 are $-7/3$ and $-40/3$.

4–16 Compute the objective value from the primal and dual. $z = w = 34$.

4–17 $\mathbf{A}^{-1} = 1/26 \begin{pmatrix} -9 & -1 & 11 \\ 8 & -2 & -4 \\ 4 & 12 & -2 \end{pmatrix}$

4–23 (a) Number of extreme points = number of basic solutions. (b) Number of extreme points < number of basic solutions.

4–24 New $x_j = (1/\beta)$ old x_j.

4–25 New $x_j = (\gamma/\beta)$ old x_j.

4–27 New $(z_j - c_j) = (1/\beta)$ old $(z_j - c_j)$, which will not make x_j profitable. By making $z_j < c_j$, x_j becomes profitable.

4–29 Three iterations: $(x_1, x_2, x_3) = (4, 6, 0)$ and $z = 12$.

4–30 Three iterations: $(x_1, x_2, x_3) = (3/2, 2, 0)$ and $z = 5$.

4–31 Three iterations: $(x_1, x_2) = (3/5, 6/5)$ and $z = 12/5$.

4–32 (a) Two iterations: $(x_1, x_2) = (0, 5)$ and $z = 15$. (b) Three iterations: $(x_1, x_2) = (2, 0)$ and $z = 10$.

4–33 (a) Phase I: three iterations with (x_1, x_2, x_4) as the basic feasible solution. Phase II: two iterations with the optimum $(x_1, x_2) = (2/5, 9/5)$ and $z = 17/5$.

Chapter 5

5–1 (a) Minimize $w = 2y_1 + 5y_2$ subject to $y_1 + 2y_2 \geq -5$, $-y_1 + 3y_2 \geq 2$, $-y_1 \geq 0$, $y_2 \geq 0$. (b) Maximize $w = 2y_1 + 5y_2$ subject to $6y_1 + 3y_2 \leq 6$, $-3y_1 + 4y_2 \leq 3$, $y_1 + y_2 \leq 0$, $y_1 \geq 0$, $y_2 \geq 0$. (e) Minimize $w = 5y_1 + 6y_2$ subject to $2y_1 + 3y_2 = 1$, $y_1 - y_2 = 1$, y_1, y_2 unrestricted.

5–9 (a) Solutions feasible but not optimal. (b) Solutions infeasible. (c) Solutions feasible and optimal.

5–10 (a)

x_1	x_2	x_3	y_1	y_2	z	w
5	0	0	1	0	15	10
6	1	0	3	1	Dual infeasible	
8	2	1	2	2	Dual infeasible	
2	1	3	7/6	2/3	Primal infeasible	

(b) Both solutions are feasible, $z = w = 40/3$, hence optimal.

5–11 (b) $\mathbf{Y} - C_{\text{II}} = (5 + M, 0)$, hence $\mathbf{Y} = (5, 0)$. (c) $\mathbf{Y} = \mathbf{C_B B} - 1$ yields the same result.

5–13 (b) $z_1 - c_1 = 2$, $z_4 - c_4 = 3$, hence optimal. (c) $z_3 - c_3 = y_1 - 4 = 0$, hence $y_1 = 4$. $y_2 = 0$.

5–14 $z = 34$ computed from either the primal or the dual objective functions.

5–15 Optimal $z = 250/3$.

5–16 $x_1 = 36/13$, $x_2 = 28/13$.

5–17 Solve the dual in three iterations.The primal optimal solution is $x_1 = 0$, $x_2 = 20$, $x_3 = 0$; $z = 120$.

5–18 Use artificial variables, dual simplex, and the solution obtained from the dual problem.

5–21 Dual infeasible and primal unbounded because primal has a feasible space.

5–24 Worth per unit of leather = \$17 and of labor = \$0. Maximum unit price of leather = \$25/m_2 and of labor = \$15/hour.

5–28 $y_1 = 29/5$, $y_2 = -2/5$.

5–30 Dual slack v_j = primal $(z_j - c_j)$ of x_j, $j = 1, 2, 3$.

5–31 (a) $x_1 = 460/3$, $x_2 = 200/3$, $x_3 = 0$.

5–33 (a) Current optimum remains unchanged.

5–35 (a) x_7 will not improve solution. (b) x_7 improves solution. New solution is $(x_1, x_2, x_3) = (0, 0, 130)$.

5–36 $d_1 > 4$.

5–37 (a) x_1 remains at zero level. (b) x_1 remains at zero level.

5–38 (a) x_4 enters the solution. New solution is $(x_1, x_2, x_3, x_4) = (1, 0, 0, 1)$. (c) Solution remains unchanged and $x_4 = 0$.

5–40 x_2 remains nonbasic for $\theta \leq 23/5$.

5–41 (a) $(x_1, x_2, x_3) = (0, 95, 230)$. (b) $(x_1, x_2, x_3) = (0, 150, 200)$. (c) Apply dual simplex $(x_1, x_2, x_3) = (0, 0, 300)$. (d) Apply dual simplex $(x_1, x_2, x_3) = (0, 75/2, 200)$.

5–42 $-30 \le \theta \le 5$.

5–43 Apply dual simplex $(x_1, x_2, x_3, x_4) = (75/2, 0, 5/4, 0)$.

5–44 (a) Constraint $4x_1 + x_2 + 2x_3 \le 570$ is redundant. (b) Apply dual simplex $(x_1, x_2, x_3) = (0, 88, 230)$.

5–45 (a) Constraint redundant. (b) Apply dual simplex. No feasible solution. (c) Apply dual simplex. No feasible solution.

5–46 (a) Constraint is redundant. (b) Apply dual simplex. $(x_1, x_2, x_3) = (8/7, 12/7, 8/7)$; $z = 96/7$. (c) No feasible solution. (d) New solution is $(x_1, x_2, x_3) = (1, 7/4, 5/4)$; $z = 14$.

5–47 (a) $(x_1, x_2, x_3) = (2, 2, 0)$. (b) $(x_1, x_2, x_3) = (5, 3, 0)$. (c) x_3 enters the solution. New solution is degenerate and remains the same $(x_1, x_2, x_3) = (2, 2, 0)$.

5–50 For all $t \ge 0$, $x_1 = 2/5$, $x_2 = 9/5$, $x_5 = 0$, and $z = (17 - 29t)/5$.

5–52 For $0 \le t \le 2/13$, $x_1 = 3/5$, $x_2 = 6/5$, and $z = (12 + 27t)/5$. For $t \ge 2/13$, $x_1 = 3/2$, $x_2 = 0$, and $z = (6 + 3t)/2$.

5–53 For $0 \le t \le 1/3$, $x_1 = 0$, $x_2 = 5$, $x_3 = 30$, and $z = 160 - 180t$. For $1/3 \le t \le 5/12$, $x_1 = 5$, $x_2 = 6.25$, $x_3 = 22.5$, and $z = 140 - 120t$. For $t \ge 5/12$, $x_1 = 20$, $x_2 = 2.5$, $x_3 = 0$, and $z = 65 + 60t$.

5–54 For $0 \le t \le 1/55$, $x_1 = 0$, $x_2 = 100 + 225t$, $x_3 = 230 + 50t$, and $z = 1350 + 700t$. For $1/55 \le t \le 2.1$, $x_1 = 0$, $x_2 = 105 - 50t$, $x_3 = 230 + 50t$, and $z = 1360 + 150t$. For $t > 2.1$, no feasible solution exists.

5–55 For $0 \le t \le 3/2$, $x_1 = (2 + 7t)/5$, $x_2 = (9 - 6t)/5$, and $z = (17 + 22t)/5$. For $t > 3/2$, no feasible solution exists.

5–56 For $0 \le t \le 6/11$, $x_1 = (3 + 7t)/5$, $x_2 = (6 - 11t)/5$, and $z = (12 + 3t)/5$. For $t \ge 6/11$, $x_1 = (3 + 2t)/3$, $x_2 = 0$, and $z = (6 + 4t)/3$.

5–57 Solution remains optimal and feasible for $0 \le t \le 1/2$.

5–58 $(6\beta - 12)/(\beta - 5) \le \alpha \le 6$.

5–59 For $0 \le t \le 1/55$, $x_1 = 0$, $x_2 = 100 + 225t$, $x_3 = 230 + 50t$, and $z = 1350 - 680t - 300t^2$. For $1/55 \le t \le 5/12$, $x_1 = 0$, $x_2 = 105 - 50t$, $x_3 = 230 + 50t$, and $z = 1360 - 1230t - 300t^2$. For $5/12 \le t \le 8/7$, $x_1 = (460 + 100t)/3$, $x_2 = (200 - 175t)/3$, $x_3 = 0$, and $z = (1780 + 1330t)/3 + 100t^2$. For $8/7 \le t \le 2.1$, $x_1 = 420 - 200t$, $x_2 = x_3 = 0$, and $z = 1260 + 660t - 600t^2$. For $t > 2.1$, no feasible solution exists.

5–60 Same as Problem 5–55 except that $z = (17 - 7t + 11t^2)/5$.

5–61 For $0 \le t \le 4/5$, $x_1 = 0$, $x_2 = 2 - t/4$, $x_3 = 2 - 3t/4$, $x_4 = 0$, and $z = 16 - 10t - 7t^2/4$. For $4/5 \le t \le 1$, $x_1 = 4 - 3t/2$, $x_2 = t/2$, $x_3 = x_4 = 0$, and $z = 8 + 3t - 2t^2$. For $1 \le t \le 4/3$, $x_1 = 4 - t$, $x_2 = x_3 = 0$, $x_4 = t$, and $z = 8 - t + 2t^2$. For $4/3 \le t \le 4$, $x_1 = x_2 = 0$, $x_3 = 4 - t$, $x_4 = 8 - t$, and $z = -8 + 15t - t^2$. For $t > 4$, no feasible solution exists.

5–62 For $-\infty < t \le -5$, $x_1 = 4$, $x_2 = 0$, and $z = 16 - 40t$. For $-5 \le t \le -1$, $x_1 = -(1 + t)$, $x_2 = 5 + t$, $z = 36 - 6t + 6t^2$. For $-1 \le t \le 2$, $x_1 = 0$, $x_2 = 3 - t$, and $z = 24 - 20t + 4t^2$. For $2 \le t \le 3$, $x_1 = x_2 = 0$ and $z = 0$. For $t > 3$, no feasible solution exists.

5–63 For $0 \le t \le 1.3$, $x_1 = 0$, $x_2 = 9 - t^2$, and $z = 54 - 18t - 15t^2 + 2t^3 + t^4$. For $1.3 \le t \le 2.3$, $x_1 = 6 - 2t^2/3$, $x_2 = 0$, and $z = 18 + 6t - 8t^2 - 2(t^3 - t^4)/3$. For $2.3 \le t \le 3$, $x_1 = x_2 = 0$ and $z = 0$. For $t > 3$, no feasible solution exists.

Chapter 6

6–1

		City 1	City 2	City 3	Dummy 4	
Plant	1	600	700	400	0	**25**
Plant	2	320	300	350	0	**40**
Plant	3	500	480	450	0	**30**
Excess plant	4	1000	1000	1000	0	**18**
		36	**42**	**30**	**5**	

Optimum solution: $P1$–$C3 = 25$, $P2$–$C1 = 23$, $P2$–$C2 = 17$, $P3$–$C2 = 25$, $P3$–$C3 = 5$, $P4$–$C1 = 13$, $P4$–$C4 = 5$.

6–3 Assume that supply and demand units are expressed in millions of gallons and that the unit transportation costs are given in thousand dollars per million gallons.

	Distribution Area 1	2	3	
Refinery 1	12	18	M	**6**
2	30	10	8	**5**
3	20	25	12	**8**
	4	**8**	**7**	

Optimum solution: $R1$–$D1 = 4$, $R1$–$D2 = 2$, $R2$–$D2 = 5$, $R3$–$D2 = 1$, $R3$–$D3 = 7$, total cost = \$243,000.

6–5 Use the same units as in Problem 6–3.

	Distribution Area 1	2	3	Dummy	
Refinery 1	12	18	M	15	**6**
2	30	10	8	22	**5**
3	20	25	12	0	**8**
	4	**8**	**4**	**3**	

Optimum solution: $R1$–$D1 = 4$, $R1$–$D2 = 2$, $R2$–$D2 = 5$, $R3$–$D2 = 1$, $R3$–$D3 = 4$, $R3$–$D4 = 3$, total cost = \$207,000.

6–9

	1	2	3	4	
1	100	103	106	M	**400**
2	M	140	143	123	**300**
3	M	M	120	100	**420**
Dummy 4	M	M	M	100	**380**
5	0	0	0	0	**60**
	500	**630**	**200**	**230**	

Optimum solution: $P1$–$P1 = 400$, $P2$–$P2 = 300$, $P3$–$P2 = 220$, $P3$–$P3 = 200$, $P4$–$P1 = 100$, $P4$–$P2 = 50$, $P4$–$P4 = 230$, $P5$–$P2 = 60$. Period 2 will be 60 units short. Total cost = \$499,000.

6–13

(a)

10	**0**			**10**
	5			**5**
	0	**4**		**4**
		3	**3**	**6**
10	**5**	**7**	**3**	

(b)

					Dummy	
1						**1**
2	**4**	**5**	**2**	**3**		**16**
				5	**2**	**7**
					8	**8**
3	**4**	**5**	**2**	**8**	**10**	

6–14 (a) x_{33}: $x_{33} \to x_{23} \to x_{22} \to x_{12} \to x_{11} \to x_{31} \to x_{33}$. (b) x_{33} enters at 5 and x_{31} leaves. (c) $\bar{c}_{33} = -24$ and change in $z = +120$.

6–15 (a) $x_{13} = x_{21} = x_{22} = x_{33} = 5$, $z = 35$.

6–16 Five iterations: $x_{12} = x_{22} = x_{23} = 10$, $x_{21} = 60$, $x_{31} = 15$, and destination 3 will be 40 units short of its demand; $z = 595$.

6–18 Three iterations: $x_{13} = x_{34} = 20$, $x_{22} = x_{32} = 10$, $x_{21} = 30$; $z = 150$.

6–19 (a) $c_{11} = 0$, $c_{21} = 5$, $c_{22} = 8$, $c_{32} = 10$, $c_{33} = 15$; $z = 1475$. (b) $c_{12} \geq 3$, $c_{13} \geq 8$, $c_{23} \geq 13$, $c_{31} \geq 7$.

6–20 (a) $z = -100$. (b) $\theta = 1$ and x_{12} is the zero basic variable.

6–21 For each iteration, the z-equation coefficients for nonbasic x_{ij} will exactly equal the values of $u_i + v_j - c_{ij}$ in the corresponding transportation tableau. Also, the solutions for the corresponding iterations are exactly the same.

6–22 (a) $\Delta_{11} \leq 10$. (b) $\Delta_{21} \geq 0$. (c) $\Delta_{24} \leq 5$. (d) $\Delta_{34} = 0$.

6–23 (a) *Northwest corner*: $x_{11} = 7$, $x_{21} = 3$, $x_{22} = 9$, $x_{32} = 1$, $x_{33} = 10$, and $z = 94$. *Least cost*: $x_{13} = 7$, $x_{21} = 10$, $x_{23} = 2$, $x_{32} = 10$, $x_{33} = 1$, and $z = 61$. *VAM*: $x_{11} = 7$, $x_{21} = 2$, $x_{23} = 10$, $x_{31} = 1$, $x_{32} = 10$, and $z = 40$, which is optimum.

6–24 VAM has the best starting solution and yields the optimum in three iterations. $x_{13} = 10$, $x_{22} = 20$, $x_{31} = 30$, $x_{42} = 30$, $x_{44} = 10$, $x_{51} = 30$, $x_{52} = x_{53} = 10$, and $z = 820$.

6–25 The problem can be solved by one of three methods: (1) delete first column and reduce the supply at source 4 by 5 units; (2) assign $-M$ to c_{41}; or (3) assign $+M$ to c_{11}, c_{21}, and c_{31}. The first method is the simplest. Solution $x_{12} = 10$, $x_{12} = x_{13} = 5$, $x_{24} = 10$, $x_{34} = 15$, $x_{41} = 5$, $x_{43} = 10$, and $z = 55$.

6–27 (a) Four iterations. 1–5, 2–3, 3–2, 4–4, 5–1 with cost = 21. (b) Three iterations. 1–1, 2–2, 3–5, 4–4, 5–3 with cost = 11.

6–28 Five iterations. 1–4, 2–3, 3–2, 4–1 with cost = 14.

6–29 Machine 5 replaces machine 1.

6–30 Station one crew in A and 3 crews in B.

6–31 Optimum assignment: 1–d, 2–c, 3–a, 4–b.

6–33 (b)

	3	4	5	6	
1	1	4	M	M	**100**
2	3	2	M	M	**200**
3	0	1	6	M	**B**
4	3	0	5	8	**B**
5	M	M	0	1	**B**
	B	**B**	**150 + B**	**150**	

(c)

	5	6	
1	7	8	**100**
2	7	8	**200**
	150	**150**	

(d) 100 units: 1–3–5; 50 units: 2–4–5; 150 units: 2–4–5–6.

6–34 (a)

Hire at.	Fire at.	Number
1	2	120
1	3	10
1	6	170
5	6	30

6–36

Hire at.	Fire at.	Number
1	3	100
2	5	20
3	5	60
4	6	50

6–38 $1 \to 3 \to 6 \to 7$ and total minimum distance = 8.

6–39 Ship 50 from factory (F)1 to store (S)1, 50 from F2 to S1, 200 from F2 to S2, and 50 from F2 to S3. Alternative solution: 50 from F1 to S1, 250 from F2 to S2, 50 from F2 to S3, and 50 from S2 to S1.

6–40 Assume a buffer $B = 110$.

	2	4	5	6	7	
1	20	M	M	M	3	**50**
3	M	30	M	M	9	**60**
5	M	2	0	4	10	**110**
6	8	M	4	0	M	**110**
7	40	M	10	M	0	**110**
	90	**20**	**110**	**110**	**110**	

Chapter 7

7–2 Six iterations. $(x_1, x_2, x_3, x_4, x_5, x_6) = (0, 1, 3/4, 1, 0, 1)$, $z = 22$.

7–3 (a) Three iterations. $(x_1, x_2, x_3) = (0, 3/2, 1)$, $z = -6$.

7–4 (a) Phase I yields (x_5, x_2) as the starting basic solution. Phase II requires three iterations. $(x_1, x_2, x_3) = (3/2, 3, 2)$, $z = 13/2$.

7–6 Substitute $x_1 = 2 - x'_1$, $x_2 = 3 - x'_2$. Five iterations. Problem has no feasible solution.

7–7 Four iterations: $x_1 = 2$, $x_2 = 8$, $x_3 = 0$, $x_4 = 12$, $x_5 = 28$, $x_6 = 0$, and $z = 156$.

7–8 Five iterations: $x_1 = 0$, $x_2 = 2$, $x_3 = 9$, $x_4 = 1$, and $z = 53$.

7–9 For each subproblem, select the extreme point associated with $\max(z_j - c_j)$. Four iterations: $(x_1, x_2, x_3, x_4) = (5/3, 10/3, 0, 20)$ and $z = -245/3$.

7–10 Three iterations: $y_1 = 0$, $y_2 = 2$, $y_3 = 0$, $y_4 = 5$, $y_5 = 0$, and $z = 44$.

7–11 $\mathbf{X}_2 = (.509029, .33333, .157638)$, $z = -.157637$.

7–12 Iteration 1: $\mathbf{X}_1 = (.213917, .213916, .286084, .286084)$, $z = -.855662$. Iteration 2: $\mathbf{X}_2 = (.179304, .179304, .320696, .320696)$, $z = -.717218$. Iteration 3: $\mathbf{X}_3 = (.147407, .147407, .352593, .352593)$, $z = -.589628$.

Chapter 8

8–1 (a) Path: (1–4–5–2), loop: (1–2–4–1), circuit: (1–2–3–1), tree: (1–2, 2–3), spanning tree: (1–2, 4–2, 2–3, 3–5).

8–2 (a) (1–2), (2–5), (5–6), (4–6), [(1–3) or (3–4)]. Length = 14. (e) (1–2), (2–5), (5–3), (2–4), (4–6). Length = 13.

8–3 LA–SE–DE–DA–CH–NY–DC. Length = 5080 miles.

8–5 High pressure: (6–4), (4–3), (3–2), (2–1). Low pressure: (1–5), (5–7), (5–9), (9–8).

8–6 Let (i, j, k) represent the respective sides of each of the three slices, where i, j, and k assume the values 0, 1, or 2. Optimum sequence: (0, 0, 0), (1, 1, 0), (2, 1, 1), (2, 2, 2).

8–8 (a) Shortest distance = 8. Alternative routes: (1–3–6–8), (1–2–3–6–8), (1–3–5–6–8), (1–2–3–5–6–8).

8–10

Node	Route	Length
2	1–3–2	3
3	1–3	1
4	1–2–5–4 or 1–3–4	7
5	1–3–2–5	4
5	1–3–2–5–6 or 1–3–2–6	9
6	1–3–2–5–6–7 or 1–3–2–6–7	11

8–12 (a) Optimum route: 1–6–5. Length = 5.

8–13 Six iterations. Maximum flow = 110, pump 4 = 30, pump 5 = 50, pump 6 = 70.

8–14 Ten iterations. Maximum flow = 85.
8–16 Maximum flow = 10.
8–18 (a) Produce 210 units in period 1 and carry 110 units to period 2. Produce 220 units in period 3 and carry 125 units to period 4.
8–21 (a) Produce 100 units in period 1 and 330 units in period 3. Backorder 110 units for period 2 from period 3 and carry forward 125 units from period 3 to period 4.
8–23 Optimum: $x_{12} = 710$, $x_{13} = 750$, $x_{25} = 710$, $x_{34} = 800$, $x_{35} = 40$, $x_{57} = 750$, $x_{79} = 750$, $x_{68} = 660$, $x_{69} = 50$.
8–24 $x_{14} = 4$, $x_{16} = 4$, $x_{24} = 10$, $x_{34} = 2$, $x_{35} = 6$, $x_{36} = 10$, total cost = 90.

Chapter 9

9–1 The optimal LP solution is $x_1 = 10/3$, $x_2 = 0$, and $x_3 = 0$. The rounded solution $x_1 = 3$ and $x_2 = x_3 = 0$ satisfies the first constraint but never the second.
9–3 Minimize $z = 37x_1 + 38x_2 + 21x_3 + 20x_4 + 24x_5 + 25x_6$

$$\begin{aligned}\text{subject to } & x_1 + x_2 + x_3 \quad + x_5 + x_6 \geq 1\\ & x_1 \quad + x_3 + x_4 + x_5 \geq 1\\ & x_1 + x_2 \quad + x_4 + x_5 + x_6 \geq 1\\ & x_1 + x_2 \geq 1\\ & x_2 + x_3 + x_4 \quad + x_6 \geq 1\\ & x_j = (0, 1), j = 1, 2, \ldots, 6\end{aligned}$$

9–5 Let $x_{ij} = 1$ if the ith site is allocated and 0 otherwise. Minimize $z = 5y_1 + 6y_2 + 2x_{11} + x_{12} + 8x_{13} + 5x_{14} + 4x_{21} + 6x_{22} + 3x_{23} + x_{24}$ subject to $x_{11} + x_{21} = 1$, $x_{12} + x_{22} = 1$, $x_{13} + x_{23} = 1$, $x_{14} + x_{24} = 1$, $x_{11} + x_{12} + x_{13} + x_{14} \leq My_1$, $x_{21} + x_{22} + x_{23} + x_{24} \leq My_2$, $y_1, y_2 = (0, 1)$.
9–8 Minimize $\sum_{j=1}^{n} c_j x_j$, subject to $\sum_{j=1}^{n} a_{ij} x_j = 1$, $i = 1, 2, \ldots, m$, and $x_j = (0, 1)$, $j = 1, 2, \ldots, n$, where $a_{ij} = 1$ if the ith destination is reached on route j and zero otherwise.
9–11 (a) ($x_1 \leq 1$ and $x_2 \leq 2$) or ($x_1 + x_2 \leq 3$ and $x_1 \geq 2$), which reduces to $x_1 - My \leq 1$, $x_2 - My \leq 2$, $x_1 + x_2 - M(1 - y) \leq 3$, and $x_1 + M(1 - y) \geq 2$, where $y = (0, 1)$. The optimum solution is $(x_1, x_2) = (1, 2)$.
9–14 (a) Node 0: (2.25, 2.25), $z = 11.25$; node 1 ($x_1 \leq 2$): (2, 2.4), $z = 11.2$; node 2 ($x_1 \leq 2$, $x_2 \geq 3$): (1, 3), $z = 11$ (lower bound); node 3 ($x_1 \geq 3$): (3, 1.5), $z = 10.5$; node 4 ($x_1 \leq 2$, $x_2 \leq 2$): (2, 2), $z = 10$ (fathomed by node 2).
9–17 Alternative optima: ($x_1 = 14$, $x_4 = 19$, all others = 0), ($x_1 = 15$, $x_3 = 1$, $x_4 = 17$, all others = 0), $z = 151$.
9–20 $x_1 = 0$, $x_2 = 6$, $x_3 = 1$, $z = 12$.
9–21

Variable Solution	Rounded Solution	Integer
x_1	2 or 3	2
x_2	1	1
x_3	6	6
z	26 or 30	26

9–25 $x_1 = 5$, $x_2 = 2.75$, $x_3 = 3$, $z = 26.75$.
9–27 $x_1 = x_2 = x_3 = 1$, $z = 7$.
9–29 $x_1 = x_2 = x_3 = x_4 = 1$, $x_5 = 0$, $z = 95$.

Chapter 10

10–2 (a) Optimum projects (1, 3, 1) and optimum revenue = 13. (b) Optimum projects (3, 2, 2, 1) and optimum revenue = 14.1.
10–3 Same as in Problem 10–2.
10–5 $(m_1, m_2, m_2, m_4) = (2, 3, 4, 1)$ with total points = 250.

10–6 (a) $(k_1, k_2, k_3) = (0, 0, 3), (0, 2, 2), (0, 4, 1)$, or $(0, 6, 0)$ with value = 120. (b) $(k_1, k_2, k_3) = (0, 2, 0), (2, 1, 0)$, or $(4, 0, 0)$ with value = 120.
10–7 $x_4 = 4, 5, 6, 7$; $x_3 = 6, 7, 8, 9$; $x_2 = 9, 10, 11, 12$; $x_1 = 12, 13, 14, 15$. $(m_1, m_2, m_3, m_4) = (1, 1, 2, 2)$ with $R = .432$.
10–8 $x_1 = 0, x_2 = 2, x_3 = 0$, and $z = 6$.
10–10 (a) Successive decisions for weeks 1, 2, ..., and 5 are: hire one, fire one, fire two, hire three, and hire two. Total cost = 24.
10–11 Optimum route is $A \to 1 \to 3 \to 5 \to B$ with total distance = 12.
10–12 $x_1 = 5, x_2 = x_3 = x_4 = 0$ with $z = 74$.
10–13 $y_i = 8^{1/10}$, for all i.
10–14

Period	1	2	3	4	5
Type I investment	0	6,000	0	0	1,890
Type II investment	10,000	0	5,400	2,700	0

10–17 $(y_1, y_2, y_3) = (13/11, 7/11, 90/11)$.
10–18 Five alternative solutions: $(y_1, y_2, y_3) = (0, 0, 16), (1, 0, 12), (2, 0, 8), (3, 0, 4), (4, 0, 0)$ with total profit = 64.
10–19 $y_1 = y_2 = \cdots = y_{N-1} = 0, y_N = \alpha^N C$.
10–20 $y_i = \alpha^i C/(1 + \alpha + \cdots + \alpha^{N-1}), i = 1, 2, \ldots, N$.
10–21 Decisions: (keep, keep, replace) or (keep, replace, keep) with total return = 13.
10–25 $(x_1, x_2) = (0, 7)$ with $z = 49$.
10–27 $(x_1, x_2) = (9.6, .2)$ with $z = 707.72$.

Chapter 11

11–1 (a) Time-based. (c) Observation-based. (e) Time-based.
11–2 Mean = 3.94, standard deviation = 2.6, reject exponential.
11–3 Mean = 50.76, standard deviation = 25.28.
11–5 Mean = 2.33, variance = 1.23, histogram: (0, .0253), (1, .1315), (2, .3474), (3, .4132), (4, .0826).
11–6 Regression line: $y = 50 + .58x$, $x(25) = 64.5$. Moving average: $x(25) = 68$. Exponential smoothing: $x(25) = 59.0697$.
11–8 $x(25) = 64.8962$.
11–11 Regression line: $20.3 + .9109x$, $r = .9984$, $x(1991) = 30.31$. Exponential smoothing: $x(1991) = 26.238$.

Chapter 12

12–1 $T^* = 3$ with $EC(T^*) = 290$.
12–2 Expected costs for A, B, and C are \$190, 120, and 205. B has the highest priority.
12–3 Optimal stock = 200 loaves and the optimal expected profit is \$36.95.
12–4 $\alpha = 49$ pieces per day.
12–5 $d^* = \frac{1}{2}\left(t_L + t_u - \frac{2\sigma^2}{t_L - t_u} \ln \frac{c_2}{c_1}\right)$.
12–9 $I \geq 2, 2 \leq I \leq 4$.
12–10 $I \geq 4$.
12–11 Expected costs for A, B, and C are \$263.7, 93.3, and 168.2. B has the highest priority.
12–12 Posterior probabilities for A and B are .6097 and .3903.
12–13 (a) $E\{a_1\} = 3.2$, $E\{a_2\} = 9.8$, $E\{a_3\} = 10.6$. (b) $E\{a_1 | z_1\} = -3.7$, $E\{a_2 | z_1\} = 7.12$, $E\{a_3 | z_1\} = 13.17$.
12–15 Stock 130 loaves.
12–16 Order 130 loaves in day 1. In day 2, if demand on day 1 is 100 order 120. If it is 120, order 120. If it is 130, order 130.
12–17 Construct large plant.

12–18 Build a large plant.
12–19 (a) a_4. (b) a_2. (c) a_2. (d) a_4.
12–21 All criteria select machine 3.
12–22 (b) (1) $p \geq 5$ and $q \leq 5$. (2) $p \leq 7$ and $q \geq 7$.
12–23 (a) $2 < v < 4$. (b) $-1 < v < 0$.
12–25 The game has a saddle point at the strategy where both companies use TV, radio, and newspapers.
12–28 (a) $x_1 = x_2 = 1/2$, $y_1 = y_2 = 0$, $y_3 = 13/20$, $y_4 = 7/20$, and $v = 1/2$.
12–29 Blotto's optimal strategy is (1/5, 3/5, 1/5). His enemy's strategy is (1/3, 1/5, 0, 7/15).

Chapter 13

13–5 Critical path (*A, C, D, F, G, H, J, L, N, S, T*) with duration = 38 days.
13–7 Four critical paths with duration = 111 days: (*A, B, D, E, Q, R, S*), (*A, B, D, F, Q, R, S*), (*A, C, D, E, Q, R, S*), (*A, C, D, F, Q, R, S*).
13–8 Critical paths: (*A, C, E, F, J, L, M, P, Q, S, T, U*), (*A, C, E, F, J, L, N, P, Q, S, T, U*). Duration = 22.1.
13–10 (a) Critical path (1, 2, 3, 4, 6, 7). Duration = 35.
13–15 Minimum number of men is determined by the critical activities.
13–16 (a) Respective probabilities for events 2, 3, 4, 5, 6, and 7 are .5, .5, .5, 1., .5, and .5.
13–18 (a)

Duration	25	24	23	21	18	17	14
Cost	1150	1157	1170	1201	1276	1303	1403

Chapter 14

14–2 (a) $y = 346.6$, $t_0 = 11.55$, $\text{TCU}(y) = 17.3$.
14–3 (a) $y \cong 50$ units, $t_0 \cong 12$ days. (b) Excess annual cost = \$540.20.
14–4 Optimum number of orders per year = 129.
14–5 Let R = reorder point in number of units. (1-a) $t_0 = 11.55$, $R = 73.5$. (1-c) $t_0 = 22.36$, $R = 560$. (2-b) $t_0 = 8.16$, $R = 220.8$. (2-d) $t_0 = 15.8$, $R = 168$.
14–6 (1-a) $B \geq 8.74$. (1-c) $B \geq 23.12$. (2-a) $B \geq 12.36$. (2-d) $B \geq 17.48$.
14–8 (a) $y = 547.7$, $t_0 = 18.25$. (b) $y = 387.38$, $t_0 = 12.9$.
14–9 *Produce*: $y = 703.7$, total cost/day = \$4.05. *Buy*: $y = 326.87$, total cost/day = \$6.54.
14–11 $\dfrac{p}{p-1} \leq h \leq \dfrac{p^2}{100-p}$ and $p \geq 10$.
14–12 Let $p \to \infty$ and find the limit for y.
14–15 For $q = 300$, $y^* = 347$ and for $q = 500$, $y^* = 500$.
14–16 Order $q = 150$ units and take advantage of the discount.
14–17 There is no advantage in using the discount if it is $\leq 5.84\%$.
14–19 $y_i^* = \sqrt{(2K_i D_i - 2\lambda d_i)/h_i}$, $\lambda^* \cong -.103$.
14–26 (b) Starting from period -1, the combined requirements are (200, 0, 300, 200, 0, 300, 200, 0, 300, 200, 0, 300, 0, 0).
14–27 $z_1 = 2$, $z_2 = 0$, and $z_3 = 3$ and total cost = 65.
14–29 $(z_1, z_2, z_3, z_4) = (5, 7, 14, 0)$ or $(6, 6, 14, 0)$.
14–31 $(z_1, z_2, \ldots, z_{10}) = (100, 120, 0, 200, 0, 0, 310, 0, 190, 0)$.
14–32 $z_1 = 50$, $z_2 = 260$, $z_3 = z_4 = z_5 = 0$.
14–33 $z_1 = 150$, $z_2 = 120$, $z_4 = 110$, $z_6 = 90$, $z_7 = 310$, $z_9 = 190$, all others = 0.
14–34 Order 270 units in period 1; 110 units in period 4; 90 units in period 6; 310 units in period 7; and 190 units in period 9. Total cost = \$7410. DP cost = \$7090.
14–38 If $x = 2$, order .88; if $x = 5$, do not order.
14–40 If $x = 2$, order 6; if $x = 5$, order 3.
14–41 $19 \leq p \leq 35.7$.
14–42 If $x = 2$, order 21; if $x = 5$, order 18. Implied penalty is $p \leq 29$.

14–43 $P\{D \le y^* - 1\} \le \dfrac{r-c}{r-v} \le P\{D \le y^*\}$.

14–47 If $x < 3.78$, order $6.7 - x$; otherwise, do not order.

14–49 If $x < 1.25$, order $6.25 - x$; otherwise, do not order.

14–50 $P\{D \le y^*\} = (r + p - c - h)/(r + p - v)$.

14–53 $y^* = 4.61$.

14–56 $y^* = E\{D\} - [(1 - \alpha)c/2p]$ when $h = p$.

Chapter 15

15–5 (a) 40. (b) $p_0(2) = 0$. (c) $p_1(10/60) \simeq .0085$.

15–6 (a) $P\{n = 2 \mid t = 5 \text{ minutes}\} = .2623$. (b) $P\{t \le 2 \text{ minutes}\} = .4866$.

15–9 Jim's expected gain/8 hours = \$1.27.

15–10 Jim's expected gain/8 hours = \$1.96.

15–13 (a) $p_{70}(2) = .1251$. (b) $p_0(4) \cong .000005$. (c) $80 - \sum_{n=0}^{80} np_n(4)$.

15–14 $p_0(5) = .00008$ and $p_0(2) \cong 0$.

15–15 (a) 17.89. (b) $p_0(4) = .00069$. (c) $P\{n < 20 \mid t = 6\} = .99968$.

15–19 (a) $p_0 = .4$. (b) $L_q = .9$ customer. (c) $W_q = 2.25$ minutes. (d) $P\{n \ge 11\} = .00363$.

15–20 New device is justified based on expected number of waiting customers in old system (= 19) but not on the basis of percent idle time in new system (= 25%).

15–21 (a) $p_0 + p_1 + p_2 \cong .42$. (b) .58. (c) $W_q = .417$ hour. (d) $n \ge 2$ spaces.

15–22 $P\{\tau > W_q\} = .549$.

15–23 Expected cost/day = \$37.95.

15–24 (a) $p_0 = .40146$. (b) $L_q = .8614$ customer. (c) $W_q = 2.16$ minutes. (d) $p_{10} = 0$.

15–25 (a) $p_{50} \cong .00002$. (b) $P\{n > 47\} = .00001$.

15–26 (a) $\lambda_{\text{eff}} = 19.98$. (b) $p_0 = .00076$. (c) $W_s = .652$ hour.

15–28

c	4	5	6	7
p_0	.0042	.01662	.02013	.0212
W_q	1.05	.081	.022	.0068

15–29 (a) .15. (b) .85. (c) .52.

15–30 (a) .70225. (b) $W_s = 1.202$ hours. (c) $L_q = 3.5$ programs. (d) .5. (e) $p_0 = .04494$. (f) 16.7%.

15–31 (a) Three counters. (b) Three counters. (c) At most five counters.

15–32 (a) Two tellers. (b) Two tellers.

15–33 (a) 8.33 vacant lots. (b) $p_{10} \cong 0$. (c) $\lambda_{\text{eff}} \cong 10$.

15–36 (a) $L_s = 4.17$. (b) $p_0 = .0155$.

15–37 (a) .081%. (b) $L_q \cong 6$.

15–38 (a) $p_0 = .04305$, $p_1 = .16144$. (b) $L_q = .911$.

15–39 Pooling reduces waiting time.

15–40 (a) $W_s = .618$ hour, $W_q = .451$ hour. (b) $W_s = .368$ hour, $W_q = .236$ hour.

15–41 $L_q = 7.04$ items.

15–42 $L_q = .333$ customer.

15–43 (a) $W_q^1 = 1.16$ hours, $W_q^2 = 7.27$ hours, $W_q^3 = 65.1$ hours. (b) $W_q = 17.4$ hours. (c) $L_q^1 = .194$ job, $L_q^2 = .909$ job, $L_q^3 = 5.42$ jobs. (d) $L_q = 6.5$ jobs.

Chapter 16

16–4 $\mu = 14.47$ units per day.

16–7 Daily cost of model A = \$1441.33, of model B = \$420.60.

16–9 $c = 6$ servers.

16–10 Expected cost per unit time for first repairperson is \$146 and for the second repairperson \$138.

16–12 Expected monthly costs are no WATS = \$15,000, one WATS = \$9090, and two WATS = \$6200.

16–13 (b) $c = 5$ servers. (c) $c = 6$ servers.

Chapter 17

17–1 (a) $A(1) = 0, 5, 10.$

17–2 (b) Six transactions: two at each of $t = 0$, 5, and 10.

17–3 (c)

A(1)	A(2)
7	−3
4	9
3	14
2	6
1	10

17–6 Creation times are 0, 10.5555, and 21.726.

17–8 All customers = 96, those with positive wait = 40.

17–10
```
$PROJECT;Problem 17-10;2-22-91;Taha:
$DIMENSION;ENTITY(30):
$BEGIN:
    ARVL     *S;EX(18):                  !arrivals
    QOFCR    *Q:                         !wait in QOFCR
    OFCR     *F;;UN(15,20):              !served by bank officer
    QTLRS    *Q:                         !wait in QTLRS
    TLRS     *F;;EX(5);3;goto-TERM:      !served by one of 3 clerks
$END:
$RUN-LENGTH=480:                         !run model for 480 minutes
$RUNS=1:                                 !for one run only
$STOP:
```

17–14
```
$PROJECT;Problem 17-14;2-22-1991;Taha:
$DIMENSION;ENTITY(90):
$BEGIN:
    FEED     *S;UN(20,30):
    WAIT     *Q;goto-RST,LST/F:          !enter both stations
    RST      *F;;UN(20,30);goto-QEND:    !RST finished
    LST      *F;;UN(18,20):              !LST finished
    QEND     *Q;;2:                      !receiving area
$END:
$RUN-LENGTH=480:
$RUNS=1:
$STOP:
```

17–18
```
$PROJECT;Problem 17-18;4-3-1990;Sloan:
$DIMENSION;ENTITY(50),A(2):
$VARIABLES: nbr_discarded;RUN.END;NTERM(CHK):
            sys_time;OBS.BASED;TRANSIT(1):
$BEGIN:
    TVS      *S;12;;1:                   !TV arrives
    QINSP    *Q:                         !wait for FINSP
    FINSP    *F;;UN(10,15):              !inspect
             *B;CHK/.45:                 !ADJ with prob = .45
             *B;TERM/.55;/v/sys_time%:   !else, finish
    CHK      *A:
             *B;QADJ/1; A(2)=0?;         !check nbr of cycles
                        A(2)=1%:         !set nbr cycles = 1
             *B;TERM/L:                  !else, discard
    QADJ     *Q:                         !wait for FADJ
    FADJ     *F;;UN(6,8);*QINSP:         !adjust & return to QINSP
$END:
$RUN-LENGTH=480:
$STOP:
```

17–21

```
$PROJECT;Problem 17-21;2-27-91;Taha:
$DIMENSION;ENTITY(30):
$SWITCHES:  SW;on;QJOBS:
            SIDLE;;QDELAY:
$BEGIN:
   SS       *S;/L/LIM = 1:                      !maintenance segment
   DELAY    *A;480:
            *B;QDELAY;;SW = off%:               !SW = off blocks QJOBS
   QDELAY   *Q:                                 !wait for MACH to be idle
            *B;MAINT/1;SIDLE = on?:
   MAINT    *A;UN(15,20):
            *B;DELAY;;SW = on%:
   ARIV     *S;EX(11):                          !machine segment
   QJOBS    *Q:
            *B;MACH/1; SW = on?;
                       SIDLE = off%:            !block Qdelay
   MACH     *F;;EX(12):
            *B;TERM;;SIDLE = on%:               !until MACH is idle
$END:
$RUN-LENGTH = 1000:
$STOP:
```

17–23

```
$PROJECT;Problem 17-23;11/5/90;Taha:
$DIMENSION; ENTITY(50):
$RESOURCES: OPRS;2(LDR1,LDR2):                  !2 operators
            TRKS;4(LDR1,LDR2):                  !4 trucks
$BEGIN:
   PILES    *S;6:                               !Create piles
   LDS      *Q;;2;                              !Truckloads
              /4/HTE(LDR1,LDR2):                !Select loader
   LDR1     *F;;EX(10);/r/OPRS(1,,,3.5),        !acquire/return OPRS
                       TRKS(,,0,);              !Acquire 1 truck
                       goto-TRP:
   LDR2     *F;;EX(12);/r/OPRS(1,,,3.5),        !acquire/return OPRS
                       TRKS(,,0,):              !Acquire 1 truck
   TRP      *A;UN(15,20) + 5:                   !Travel time
            *B;TERM;/5/TRKS(,,,UN(10,15)):      !Return truck
$END:
$RUN-LENGTH = 480:
$STOP:
```

17–26

```
$PROJECT;Problem 17-26,8 July 90;Taha:
$DIMENSION; ENTITY(40),A(1):
$VARIABLES: TRIP TIME;;TRANSIT(1):
$BEGIN:
   PILES    *S;6;;1:                            !Mark time in A(1)
   LDS      *Q;;2(FIRST);goto-ASMBL:            !A(1) of FIRST pile
   TRKS     *Q;(4);                             !Start with 4 trucks
              /s/MAT(TRKS,LDS,OPRS);*TERM:      !match queues
   OPRS     *Q;(2);*TERM:                       !Start with 2 operators
   ASMBL    *F;/s/HTE(LDR1,LDR2):               !Select loader
   LDR1     *F;;EX(10);*AX:                     !Go to NIL auxiliary AX
   LDR2     *F;;EX(12):                         !Pass to AX
   AX       *A;NIL;*OPDEL,TRP:                  !Go to OPDEL and TRP
   OPDEL    *A;3.5;*OPRS:                       !Return operator to OPRS
   TRP      *A;UN(15,20) + 5:                   !Travel time
            *B;RTRN;/v/TRIP TIME%:              !Compute TRIP TIME
   RTRN     *A;UN(10,15);*TRKS:                 !Return trip of trucks
$END:
$RUN-LENGTH = 480: $TRACE = 0-50:
$STOP:
```

17–27
```
$PROJECT;Problem 17-27;3-1-91;Taha:
$DIMENSION; ENTITY(40):
$BEGIN:
    JOBS       *s:                                   !create a job
               *b;PROCESS;;suspend=JOBS%:            !suspend JOBS
    PROCESS    *f;;ex(12):
               *b;TERM;;resume=JOBS%:                !resume JOBS
$END:
$RUN-LENGTH=3600: $TRACE=0-200:
$STOP:
```

17–31
```
$project;Problem 17-31;3-1-91;Taha:
$dimension; ENTITY(200):
$begin:
    SINGOT     *s;7:                                 !ingots arrive
    QINGOT     *q;;4:                                !4 ingots per charge
    FURNACE    *f;;25:
               *b;TERM;;for,i=1,to,3,do,             !3 urns
                            last(QURN)=trans,
                         next%:
    QURN       *q:
$end:
$run-length=200:
$stop:
```

Chapter 18

18–1 Years 1 and 2: advertise only if product is unsuccessful. Year 3: do not advertise.

18–2 Use radio advertisement if sales volume is poor; otherwise, use newspaper advertisement.

18–4 If beginning of month stock is zero, order two refrigerators; otherwise, order none.

18–5 Order 2 in state 0; otherwise, order none.

18–7 Advertise whenever in state 1.

Chapter 19

19–1 (a) None. (b) Minimum at $x = 0$. (e) Inflection at $x = 0$, minimum at $x = .63$, and maximum at $x = -.63$.

19–2 (a) Minimum at (1, 1).

19–3 Minimum occurs at (1, 2, 0) only.

19–5 One root of $4x^4 - x^2 + 5 = 0$ occurs at $x \cong .353$ if starting point is $x = 1$.

19–8 $\partial f = 2\delta C^{(2-n)/n}$.

19–9 For $\partial g = -.01$, (a) $\partial f = -.0647$, (b) $\partial f = -.12$.

19–11 Minimum point, $(x_1, x_2, x_3, x_4) = (-5/74, -10/74, 155/74, 60/74)$. Sensitivity coefficients are $(-90/37, 85/37)$.

19–20 $\lambda_1 \le 0$, λ_2 unrestricted, $\lambda_3 \ge 0$. The necessary conditions are sufficient if f is concave, g_1 concave, g_2 linear, and g_3 convex.

Chapter 20

20–3 Maximum number of iterations $= 1.44 \ln\{(b-a)/\Delta - 1\}$.

20–7 $x_1 = 0, x_2 = 3, z = 17$.

20–11 Let $w_j = x_j + 1, j = 1, 2, 3$ and substitute for x_j in terms of w_j.

20–15 $x_1 = 1, x_2 = 0, z = 4$.

20–16 $x_1 = 0, x_2 = .4, x_3 = .7$.

20–17 Necessary conditions are not satisfied for $x_j > 0$. The problem has an infimum at $x_j = 0$; that is, $z \to 0$ as $x_j \to 0$ for all j.

20–18 $x_1 = 1.26, x_2 = .41, x_3 = .59, z = 10.28$.

20–20 $x_1 = 1.26, x_2 = 1.887, z = 13.07$.

Index

C

D

K

L

M

N

O

P

T